Lecture Notes in Artificial Intelligence 3720
Edited by J. G. Carbonell and J. Siekmann

Subseries of Lecture Notes in Computer Science

João Gama   Rui Camacho
Pavel Brazdil   Alípio Jorge
Luís Torgo (Eds.)

Machine Learning: ECML 2005

16th European Conference on Machine Learning
Porto, Portugal, October 3-7, 2005
Proceedings

Series Editors

Jaime G. Carbonell, Carnegie Mellon University, Pittsburgh, PA, USA
Jörg Siekmann, University of Saarland, Saarbrücken, Germany

Volume Editors

João Gama
Pavel Brazdil
Alípio Jorge
Luís Torgo
LIACC/FEP, University of Porto
Rua de Ceuta, 118, 6°, 4050-190 Porto, Portugal
E-mail: {jgama,pbrazdil,amjorge,ltorgo}@liacc.up.pt

Rui Camacho
LIACC/FEUP, University of Porto
Rua de Ceuta, 118, 6°, 4050-190 Porto, Portugal
E-mail: rcamacho@fe.up.pt

Library of Congress Control Number: 2005933045

CR Subject Classification (1998): I.2, F.2.2, F.4.1, H.2.8

ISSN   0302-9743
ISBN-10   3-540-29243-8 Springer Berlin Heidelberg New York
ISBN-13   978-3-540-29243-2 Springer Berlin Heidelberg New York

This work is subject to copyright. All rights are reserved, whether the whole or part of the material is concerned, specifically the rights of translation, reprinting, re-use of illustrations, recitation, broadcasting, reproduction on microfilms or in any other way, and storage in data banks. Duplication of this publication or parts thereof is permitted only under the provisions of the German Copyright Law of September 9, 1965, in its current version, and permission for use must always be obtained from Springer. Violations are liable to prosecution under the German Copyright Law.

Springer is a part of Springer Science+Business Media

springeronline.com

© Springer-Verlag Berlin Heidelberg 2005
Printed in Germany

Typesetting: Camera-ready by author, data conversion by Scientific Publishing Services, Chennai, India
Printed on acid-free paper   SPIN: 11564096   06/3142   5 4 3 2 1 0

Preface

The European Conference on Machine Learning (ECML) and the European Conference on Principles and Practice of Knowledge Discovery in Databases (PKDD) were jointly organized this year for the fifth time in a row, after some years of mutual independence before. After Freiburg (2001), Helsinki (2002), Cavtat (2003) and Pisa (2004), Porto received the 16th edition of ECML and the 9th PKDD in October 3–7.

Having the two conferences together seems to be working well: 585 different paper submissions were received for both events, which maintains the high submission standard of last year. Of these, 335 were submitted to ECML only, 220 to PKDD only and 30 to both. Such a high volume of scientific work required a tremendous effort from Area Chairs, Program Committee members and some additional reviewers. On average, PC members had 10 papers to evaluate, and Area Chairs had 25 papers to decide upon. We managed to have 3 highly qualified independent reviews per paper (with very few exceptions) and one additional overall input from one of the Area Chairs. After the authors' responses and the online discussions for many of the papers, we arrived at the final selection of 40 regular papers for ECML and 35 for PKDD. Besides these, 32 others were accepted as short papers for ECML and 35 for PKDD. This represents a joint acceptance rate of around 13% for regular papers and 25% overall. We thank all involved for all the effort with reviewing and selection of papers.

Besides the core technical program, ECML and PKDD had 6 invited speakers, 10 workshops, 8 tutorials and a Knowledge Discovery Challenge. Our special thanks to the organizers of the individual workshops and tutorials and to the workshop and tutorial chairs Floriana Esposito and Dunja Mladenić and to the challenge organizer Petr Berka. A very special word to Richard van de Stadt for all his competence and professionalism in the management of CyberChairPRO. Our thanks also to everyone from the Organization Committee mentioned further on who helped us with the organization. Our acknowledgement also to Rodolfo Matos and Assunção Costa Lima for providing logistic support.

Our acknowledgements to all the sponsors, Fundação para a Ciência e Tecnologia (FCT), LIACC-NIAAD, Faculdade de Engenharia do Porto, Faculdade de Economia do Porto, KDubiq –Knowledge Discovery in Ubiquitous Environments — Coordinated Action of FP6, Salford Systems, Pascal Network of Excellence, PSE/SPSS, ECCAI and Comissão de Viticultura da Região dos Vinhos Verdes. We also wish to express our gratitude to all other individuals and institutions not explicitly mentioned in this text who somehow contributed to the success of these events.

Finally, our word of appreciation to all the authors who submitted papers to the main conferences and their workshops, without whom none of this would have been possible.

July 2005   João Gama, Rui Camacho, Pavel Brazdil,
Alípio Jorge and Luís Torgo

Organization

ECML/PKDD 2005 Organization

Executive Committee

General Chair

Pavel Brazdil (LIACC/FEP, Portugal)

Program Chairs

ECML
Rui Camacho (LIACC/FEUP, Portugal)
João Gama (LIACC/FEP, Portugal)

PKDD
Alípio Jorge (LIACC/FEP, Portugal)
Luís Torgo (LIACC/FEP, Portugal)

Workshop Chair

Floriana Esposito (University of Bari, Italy)

Tutorial Chair

Dunja Mladenić (Jozef Stefan Institute, Slovenia)

Challenge Chairs

Petr Berka (University of Economics, Czech Republic)
Bruno Crémilleux (Université de Caen, France)

Local Organization Committee

Pavel Brazdil, Alípio Jorge, Rui Camacho, Luís Torgo and João Gama, with the help of people from LIACC-NIAAD, University of Porto, Portugal, Rodolfo Matos, Pedro Quelhas Brito, Fabrice Colas, Carlos Soares, Pedro Campos, Rui Leite, Mário Amado Alves, Pedro Rodrigues; and from IST, Lisbon, Portugal, Cláudia Antunes.

Steering Committee

Nada Lavrač, Jozef Stefan Institute, Slovenia
Dragan Gamberger, Rudjer Boskovic Institute, Croatia
Ljupčo Todorovski, Jozef Stefan Institute, Slovenia
Hendrik Blockeel, Katholieke Universiteit Leuven, Belgium
Tapio Elomaa, Tampere University of Technology, Finland
Heikki Mannila, Helsinki Institute for Information Technology, Finland
Hannu T.T. Toivonen, University of Helsinki, Finland
Jean-François Boulicaut, INSA-Lyon, France
Floriana Esposito, University of Bari, Italy
Fosca Giannotti, ISTI-CNR, Pisa, Italy
Dino Pedreschi, University of Pisa, Italy

Area Chairs

Michael R. Berthold, Germany
Elisa Bertino, Italy
Ivan Bratko, Slovenia
Pavel Brazdil, Portugal
Carla E. Brodley, USA
Rui Camacho, Portugal
Luc Dehaspe, Belgium
Peter Flach, UK
Johannes Fürnkranz, Germany
João Gama, Portugal
Howard J. Hamilton, Canada
Thorsten Joachims, USA

Alípio Jorge, Portugal
Hillol Kargupta, USA
Pedro Larranaga, Spain
Ramon López de Mántaras, Spain
Dunja Mladenić, Slovenia
Hiroshi Motoda, Japan
José Carlos Príncipe, USA
Tobias Scheffer, Germany
Michele Sebag, France
Peter Stone, USA
Luís Torgo, Portugal
Gerhard Widmer, Austria

Program Committee

Agnar Aamodt, Norway
Jesus Aguilar, Spain
Michael Bain, Australia
Antonio Bahamonde, Spain
José Luis Balcázar, Spain
Ho Tu Bao, Japan
Michael R. Berthold, Germany
Fernando Berzal, Spain
Concha Bielza, Spain
Hendrik Blockeel, Belgium
Daniel Borrajo, Spain
Henrik Boström, Sweden
Marco Botta, Italy
Jean-François Boulicaut, France
Ivan Bratko, Slovenia
Pavel Brazdil, Portugal
Carla E. Brodley, USA
Wray Buntine, Finland
Rui Camacho, Portugal
Amilcar Cardoso, Portugal
David Cheung, Hong Kong, China
Nguyen Phu Chien, Japan
Ian Cloete, Germany
Joaquim Costa, Portugal
Rémi Coulom, France
James Cussens, UK
Luc Dehaspe, Belgium
Sašo Džeroski, Slovenia

Tapio Elomaa, Finland
Floriana Esposito, Italy
Ad Feelders, The Netherlands
Cèsar Ferri, Spain
Peter Flach, UK
Eibe Frank, New Zealand
Alex Freitas, UK
Johannes Fürnkranz, Germany
João Gama, Portugal
Dragan Gamberger, Croatia
Jean-Gabriel Ganascia, France
Minos N. Garofalakis, USA
Fosca Giannotti, Italy
Attilio Giordana, Italy
Christophe Giraud-Carrier, USA
Marko Grobelnik, Slovenia
Howard J. Hamilton, Canada
Colin de la Higuera, France
Melanie Hilario, Switzerland
Robert J. Hilderman, Canada
Haym Hirsh, USA
Huan Liu, USA
Frank Höppner, Germany
Thomas Hofmann, Germany
Se June Hong, USA
Nitin Indurkhya, Australia
Inaki Inza, Spain
Jean-Christophe Janodet, France

Thorsten Joachims, USA
Alípio Jorge, Portugal
Alexandros Kaloussis, Switzerland
Hillol Kargupta, USA
Dimitar Kazakov, UK
Eamonn Keogh, USA
Roni Khardon, USA
Ross D. King, UK
Igor Kononenko, Slovenia
Stefan Kramer, Germany
Miroslav Kubat, USA
Gregory Kuhlmann, USA
Stephen Kwek, USA
Pedro Larranaga, Spain
Nada Lavrač, Slovenia
Jinyan Li, Singapore
Charles Ling, Canada
Huan Liu, USA
Jose A. Lozano, Spain
Rich Maclin, USA
Donato Malerba, Italy
Ramon López de Mántaras, Spain
Stan Matwin, Canada
Michael May, Germany
Thorsten Meinl, Germany
Prem Melville, USA
Rosa Meo, Italy
José del R. Millán, Switzerland
Dunja Mladenić, Slovenia
Maria Carolina Monard, Brazil
Katharina Morik, Germany
Shinichi Morishita, Japan
Hiroshi Motoda, Japan
Claire Nédellec, France
Richard Nock, France
Masayuki Numao, Japan
Arlindo Oliveira, Portugal
Johann Petrak, Austria
Bernhard Pfahringer, New Zealand
Enric Plaza, Spain
André Ponce Leon, Brazil
José M. Peña, Sweden
José Carlos Príncipe, USA

Jan Rauch, Czech Republic
Solange Rezende, Brazil
José Riquelme, Spain
Josep Roure, Spain
Juho Rousu, UK
Céline Rouveirol, France
Stefan Rüping, Germany
Salvatore Ruggieri, Italy
Marques de Sá, Portugal
Lorenza Saitta, Italy
Tobias Scheffer, Germany
Bruno Scherrer, France
Michele Sebag, France
Giovanni Semeraro, Italy
Jude Shavlik, USA
Arno Siebes, The Netherlands
Robert H. Sloan, USA
Maarten van Someren,
  The Netherlands
Ashwin Srinivasan, India
Olga Stepankova, Czech Republic
Peter Stone, USA
Einoshin Suzuki, Japan
Washio Takashi, Japan
Takao Terano, Japan
Kai Ming Ting, Australia
Ljupčo Todorovski, Slovenia
Luís Torgo, Portugal
Peter Turney, Canada
Ricardo Vilalta, USA
Paul Vitanyi, The Netherlands
Ke Wang, Canada
Louis Wehenkel, Belgium
Gary Weiss, USA
Shimon Whiteson, USA
Gerhard Widmer, Austria
Marco Wiering, The Netherlands
Graham Williams, Australia
Ying Yang, Australia
Gerson Zaverucha, Brazil
Thomas Zeugmann, Japan
Zhi-Hua Zhou, China
Blaž Zupan, Slovenia

Additional Reviewers

Erick Alphonse
Annalisa Appice
Eva Armengol
Maurizio Atzori
Vincent Auvray
Miriam Baglioni
Jose Baranauskas
Valmir Carneiro Barbosa
Cristina Baroglio
Teresa Basile
Gustavo Batista
Margherita Berardi
Flavia Bernardini
Guillaume Beslon
Matjaž Bevk
Andraž Bežek
Steffen Bickel
Janneke H. Bolt
Marco Botta
Eva Bou
Janez Brank
Ulf Brefeld
Klaus Brinker
Paula Brito
Michael Brückner
Lijuan Cai
Rossella Cancelliere
Nguyen Canh Hao
Giuliana Carello
Maria Fernanda Caropreso
Costantina Caruso
Michelangelo Ceci
Nicolo Cesa-Bianchi
Jie Chen
Antonio Cisternino
E.S. Correa
Tomaž Curk
Marco Degemmis
Alexandre Delbem
Janez Demšar
Nicola Di Mauro
Norberto Diaz-Diaz
Kurt Driessens

Isabel Drost
Nguyen Duc Dung
Tomaž Erjavec
Damien Ernst
Roberto Esposito
Vicent Estruch
Timm Euler
Rémi Eyraud
Stefano Ferilli
Fernando Fernandez
Francisco Ferrer
Daan Fierens
Ingrid Fischer
Blaž Fortuna
Alexandre Francisco
Jorge Garcia-Gutierrez
Vincenzo Gervasi
Pierre Geurts
Rémi Gilleron
Robby Goetschalckx
Paulo Gomes
Warwick Graco
Andrea Grosso
Amaury Habrard
Mark Hall
Ahlem Ben Hassine
Hongxing He
Luís Henriques
José Hernández-Orallo
Phan Xuan Hieu
Le Minh Hoang
Vera Hollink
Jin Huang
Ignazio Infantino
Aleks Jakulin
Huidong Jin
Warren Jin
Peter Juvan
Matti Kääriäinen
Gour Karmakar
Rohit Kate
Svetlana Kiritchenko
Matevž Kovačič

Jussi Kujala
Matjaž Kukar
Satoshi Kurihara
Wacław Kuśnierczyk
Marina Langlois
Helge Langseth
Christine Largeron
Gregor Leban
Huei Diana Lee
Alessandro Lenci
Jure Leskovec
Zhao Liang
Oriana Licchelli
Weiqiang Lin
Fei Tony Liu
Carlos Linares López
Alneu de Andrade Lopes
Pasquale Lops
Ana Carolina Lorena
Ule von Luxburg
Alain-Pierre Manine
Raphael Maree
Daniel Mateos
Edson Takashi Matsubara
Rosa Meo
Ingo Mierswa
Joseph Modayil
Torulf Mollestad
Lukas Molzberger
Koichi Moriyama
Martin Možina
David Nadeau
Tran Tuan Nam
Mirco Nanni
Cholwich Nattee
Blaž Novak
Aline Marins Paes
Rui Pedro Paiva
Pavel Petrovic
Aloisio Carlos de Pina
Jan Poland
Ronaldo C. Prati
Jaqueline Pugliesi
Le Si Quang

Stefan Raeymaekers
Alessandra Raffaetà
Enda Ridge
Carsten Riggelsen
Salvatore Rinzivillo
Céline Robardet
Pedro Rodrigues
Roseli Romero
Ulrich Rückert
Roberto Ruiz
Aleksander Sadikov
Jaime dos Santos
    Cardoso
Craig Saunders
Robert Schapire
Martin Scholz
Tatiana Semenova
Marko Robnik-Šikonja
Alexandre Silva
Fernanda Sousa
Alexander L. Strehl
Alexandre Termier
Vu Tat Thang
Franck Thollard
Ivan Titov
Fabien Torre
Alicia Troncoso
György Turán
Werner Uwents
Pascal Vaillant
Anneleen Van Assche
Antonio Varlaro
Santi Ontañón Villar
Daniel Vladušič
Van-Thinh Vu
Yuk Wah Wong
Adam Woznica
Michael Wurst
Sule Yildirim
Kihoon Yoon
Jure Žabkar
Jilian Zhang
Xingquan Zhu

ECML/PKDD 2005 Tutorials

Ontology Learning from Text
Paul Buitelaar, Philipp Cimiano, Marko Grobelnik, Michael Sintek

Learning Automata as a Basis for Multi-agent Reinforcement Learning
Ann Nowe, Katja Verbeeck, Karl Tuyls

Web Mining for Web Personalization
Magdalini Eirinaki, Michalis Vazirgiannis

A Practical Time-Series Tutorial with MATLAB
Michalis Vlachos

Mining the Volatile Web
Myra Spiliopoulou, Yannis Theodoridis

Spectral Clustering
Chris Ding

Bioinspired Machine Learning Techniques
André Carlos Ponce de Leon Ferreira de Carvalho

Probabilistic Inductive Logic Programming
Luc De Raedt, Kristian Kersting

ECML/PKDD 2005 Workshops

Sub-symbolic Paradigms for Learning in Structured Domains
Marco Gori, Paolo Avesani

European Web Mining Forum 2005 (EWMF 2005)
Bettina Berendt, Andreas Hotho, Dunja Mladenić, Giovanni Semeraro, Myra Spiliopoulou, Gerd Stumme, Maarten van Someren

Knowledge Discovery in Inductive Databases (KDID 2005)
Francesco Bonchi, Jean-François Boulicaut

Mining Spatio-temporal Data
Gennady Andrienko, Donato Malerba, Michael May, Maguelonne Teisseire

Cooperative Multiagent Learning
Maarten van Someren, Nikos Vlassis

Data Mining for Business
Carlos Soares, Luís Moniz, Catarina Duarte

Mining Graphs, Trees and Sequences (MGTS 2005)
Siegfied Nijssen, Thorsten Meinl, George Karypis

Knowledge Discovery and Ontologies (KDO 2005)
Markus Ackermann, Bettina Berendt, Marko Grobelnik, Vojtech Svátek

Knowledge Discovery from Data Streams
Jesús Aguilar, João Gama

Reinforcement Learning in Non-stationary Environments
Ann Nowé, Timo Honkela, Ville Könönen, Katja Verbeeck

Discovery Challenge
Petr Berka, Bruno Cremilleux

Table of Contents

Invited Talks

Data Analysis in the Life Sciences — Sparking Ideas
  Michael R. Berthold 1

Machine Learning for Natural Language Processing (and Vice Versa?)
  Claire Cardie 2

Statistical Relational Learning: An Inductive Logic Programming Perspective
  Luc De Raedt 3

Recent Advances in Mining Time Series Data
  Eamonn Keogh 6

Focus the Mining Beacon: Lessons and Challenges from the World of E-Commerce
  Ron Kohavi 7

Data Streams and Data Synopses for Massive Data Sets (Invited Talk)
  Yossi Matias 8

Long Papers

Clustering and Metaclustering with Nonnegative Matrix Decompositions
  Liviu Badea 10

A SAT-Based Version Space Algorithm for Acquiring Constraint Satisfaction Problems
  Christian Bessiere, Remi Coletta, Frédéric Koriche, Barry O'Sullivan 23

Estimation of Mixture Models Using Co-EM
  Steffen Bickel, Tobias Scheffer 35

Nonrigid Embeddings for Dimensionality Reduction
  Matthew Brand 47

Multi-view Discriminative Sequential Learning
  Ulf Brefeld, Christoph Büscher, Tobias Scheffer 60

Robust Bayesian Linear Classifier Ensembles
Jesús Cerquides, Ramon López de Màntaras 72

An Integrated Approach to Learning Bayesian Networks of Rules
*Jesse Davis, Elizabeth Burnside, Inês de Castro Dutra, David Page,
Vítor Santos Costa* 84

Thwarting the Nigritude Ultramarine: Learning to Identify Link Spam
Isabel Drost, Tobias Scheffer 96

Rotational Prior Knowledge for SVMs
Arkady Epshteyn, Gerald DeJong 108

On the LearnAbility of Abstraction Theories from Observations for
Relational Learning
*Stefano Ferilli, Teresa M.A. Basile, Nicola Di Mauro,
Floriana Esposito* 120

Beware the Null Hypothesis: Critical Value Tables for Evaluating
Classifiers
George Forman, Ira Cohen 133

Kernel Basis Pursuit
Vincent Guigue, Alain Rakotomamonjy, Stéphane Canu 146

Hybrid Algorithms with Instance-Based Classification
Iris Hendrickx, Antal van den Bosch 158

Learning and Classifying Under Hard Budgets
Aloak Kapoor, Russell Greiner 170

Training Support Vector Machines with Multiple Equality Constraints
Wolf Kienzle, Bernhard Schölkopf 182

A Model Based Method for Automatic Facial Expression Recognition
Hans van Kuilenburg, Marco Wiering, Marten den Uyl 194

Margin-Sparsity Trade-Off for the Set Covering Machine
François Laviolette, Mario Marchand, Mohak Shah 206

Learning from Positive and Unlabeled Examples with Different Data
Distributions
Xiao-Li Li, Bing Liu 218

Towards Finite-Sample Convergence of Direct Reinforcement Learning
Shiau Hong Lim, Gerald DeJong 230

Infinite Ensemble Learning with Support Vector Machines
  Hsuan-Tien Lin, Ling Li 242

A Kernel Between Unordered Sets of Data: The Gaussian Mixture Approach
  Siwei Lyu 255

Active Learning for Probability Estimation Using Jensen-Shannon Divergence
  *Prem Melville, Stewart M. Yang, Maytal Saar-Tsechansky,
  Raymond Mooney* 268

Natural Actor-Critic
  Jan Peters, Sethu Vijayakumar, Stefan Schaal 280

Inducing Head-Driven PCFGs with Latent Heads: Refining a Tree-Bank Grammar for Parsing
  Detlef Prescher 292

Learning (k,l)-Contextual Tree Languages for Information Extraction
  *Stefan Raeymaekers, Maurice Bruynooghe,
  Jan Van den Bussche* 305

Neural Fitted Q Iteration - First Experiences with a Data Efficient Neural Reinforcement Learning Method
  Martin Riedmiller 317

MCMC Learning of Bayesian Network Models by Markov Blanket Decomposition
  Carsten Riggelsen 329

On Discriminative Joint Density Modeling
  Jarkko Salojärvi, Kai Puolamäki, Samuel Kaski 341

Model-Based Online Learning of POMDPs
  Guy Shani, Ronen I. Brafman, Solomon E. Shimony 353

Simple Test Strategies for Cost-Sensitive Decision Trees
  Shengli Sheng, Charles X. Ling, Qiang Yang 365

$\mathcal{U}$-Likelihood and $\mathcal{U}$-Updating Algorithms: Statistical Inference in Latent Variable Models
  *Jaemo Sung, Sung-Yang Bang, Seungjin Choi,
  Zoubin Ghahramani* 377

An Optimal Best-First Search Algorithm for Solving Infinite Horizon
DEC-POMDPs
    Daniel Szer, François Charpillet 389

Ensemble Learning with Supervised Kernels
    Kari Torkkola, Eugene Tuv 400

Using Advice to Transfer Knowledge Acquired in One Reinforcement
Learning Task to Another
    Lisa Torrey, Trevor Walker, Jude Shavlik, Richard Maclin 412

A Distance-Based Approach for Action Recommendation
    *Ronan Trepos, Ansaf Salleb, Marie-Odile Cordier,
    Véronique Masson, Chantal Gascuel* 425

Multi-armed Bandit Algorithms and Empirical Evaluation
    Joannès Vermorel, Mehryar Mohri 437

Annealed Discriminant Analysis
    Gang Wang, Zhihua Zhang, Frederick H. Lochovsky 449

Network Game and Boosting
    Shijun Wang, Changshui Zhang 461

Model Selection in Omnivariate Decision Trees
    Olcay Taner Yıldız, Ethem Alpaydın 473

Bayesian Network Learning with Abstraction Hierarchies and
Context-Specific Independence
    Marie desJardins, Priyang Rathod, Lise Getoor 485

Short Papers

Learning to Complete Sentences
    Steffen Bickel, Peter Haider, Tobias Scheffer 497

The Huller: A Simple and Efficient Online SVM
    Antoine Bordes, Léon Bottou 505

Inducing Hidden Markov Models to Model Long-Term Dependencies
    Jérôme Callut, Pierre Dupont 513

A Similar Fragments Merging Approach to Learn Automata on Proteins
    François Coste, Goulven Kerbellec 522

Nonnegative Lagrangian Relaxation of K-Means and Spectral Clustering
  Chris Ding, Xiaofeng He, Horst D. Simon 530

Severe Class Imbalance: Why Better Algorithms Aren't the Answer
  Chris Drummond, Robert C. Holte 539

Approximation Algorithms for Minimizing Empirical Error by Axis-Parallel Hyperplanes
  Tapio Elomaa, Jussi Kujala, Juho Rousu 547

A Comparison of Approaches for Learning Probability Trees
  *Daan Fierens, Jan Ramon, Hendrik Blockeel,
  Maurice Bruynooghe* 556

Counting Positives Accurately Despite Inaccurate Classification
  George Forman 564

Optimal Stopping and Constraints for Diffusion Models of Signals with Discontinuities
  Ramūnas Girdziušas, Jorma Laaksonen 576

An Evolutionary Function Approximation Approach to Compute Prediction in XCSF
  Ali Hamzeh, Adel Rahmani 584

Using Rewards for Belief State Updates in Partially Observable Markov Decision Processes
  Masoumeh T. Izadi, Doina Precup 593

Active Learning in Partially Observable Markov Decision Processes
  Robin Jaulmes, Joelle Pineau, Doina Precup 601

Machine Learning of Plan Robustness Knowledge About Instances
  Sergio Jiménez, Fernando Fernández, Daniel Borrajo 609

Two Contributions of Constraint Programming to Machine Learning
  Arnaud Lallouet, Andreï Legtchenko 617

A Clustering Model Based on Matrix Approximation with Applications to Cluster System Log Files
  Tao Li, Wei Peng 625

Detecting Fraud in Health Insurance Data: Learning to Model Incomplete Benford's Law Distributions
  Fletcher Lu, J. Efrim Boritz 633

Efficient Case Based Feature Construction
  Ingo Mierswa, Michael Wurst 641

Fitting the Smallest Enclosing Bregman Ball
  Richard Nock, Frank Nielsen 649

Similarity-Based Alignment and Generalization
  *Daniel Oblinger, Vittorio Castelli, Tessa Lau,
  Lawrence D. Bergman* 657

Fast Non-negative Dimensionality Reduction for Protein Fold
Recognition
  Oleg Okun, Helen Priisalu, Alexessander Alves 665

Mode Directed Path Finding
  *Irene M. Ong, Inês de Castro Dutra, David Page,
  Vítor Santos Costa* 673

Classification with Maximum Entropy Modeling of Predictive
Association Rules
  *Hieu X. Phan, Minh L. Nguyen, S. Horiguchi,
  Bao T. Ho, Y. Inoguchi* 682

Classification of Ordinal Data Using Neural Networks
  Joaquim Pinto da Costa, Jaime S. Cardoso 690

Independent Subspace Analysis on Innovations
  Barnabás Póczos, Bálint Takács, András Lőrincz 698

On Applying Tabling to Inductive Logic Programming
  Ricardo Rocha, Nuno Fonseca, Vítor Santos Costa 707

Learning Models of Relational Stochastic Processes
  Sumit Sanghai, Pedro Domingos, Daniel Weld 715

Error-Sensitive Grading for Model Combination
  Surendra K. Singhi, Huan Liu 724

Strategy Learning for Reasoning Agents
  Hendrik Skubch, Michael Thielscher 733

Combining Bias and Variance Reduction Techniques for Regression
Trees
  Yuk Lai Suen, Prem Melville, Raymond J. Mooney 741

Analysis of Generic Perceptron-Like Large Margin Classifiers
  Petroula Tsampouka, John Shawe-Taylor 750

Multimodal Function Optimizing by a New Hybrid Nonlinear Simplex
Search and Particle Swarm Algorithm
  Fang Wang, Yuhui Qiu 759

Author Index 767

Data Analysis in the Life Sciences
— Sparking Ideas —

Michael R. Berthold

ALTANA-Chair for Bioinformatics and Information Mining,
Dept. of Computer and Information Science, Konstanz University, Germany
`Michael.Berthold@uni-konstanz.de`

Data from various areas of Life Sciences have increasingly caught the attention of data mining and machine learning researchers. Not only is the amount of data available mind-boggling but the diverse and heterogenous nature of the information is far beyond any other data analysis problem so far. In sharp contrast to classical data analysis scenarios, the life science area poses challenges of a rather different nature for mainly two reasons. Firstly, the available data stems from heterogenous information sources of varying degrees of reliability and quality and is, without the interactive, constant interpretation of a domain expert, not useful. Furthermore, predictive models are of only marginal interest to those users – instead they hope for new insights into a complex, biological system that is only partially represented within that data anyway. In this scenario, the data serves mainly to create new insights and generate new ideas that can be tested. Secondly, the notion of feature space and the accompanying measures of similarity cannot be taken for granted. Similarity measures become context dependent and it is often the case that within one analysis task several different ways of describing the objects of interest or measuring similarity between them matter.

Some more recently published work in the data analysis area has started to address some of these issues. For example, data analysis in parallel universes [1], that is, the detection of patterns of interest in various different descriptor spaces at the same time, and mining of frequent, discriminative fragments in large, molecular data bases [2]. In both cases, sheer numerical performance is not the focus; it is rather the discovery of interpretable pieces of evidence that lights up new ideas in the users mind. Future work in data analysis in the life sciences needs to keep this in mind: the goal is to trigger new ideas and stimulate interesting associations.

References

1. Berthold, M.R., Wiswedel, B., Patterson, D.E.: Interactive exploration of fuzzy clusters using neighborgrams. Fuzzy Sets and Systems 149 (2005) 21-37
2. Hofer, H., Borgelt, C., Berthold, M.R.: Large scale mining of molecular fragments with wildcards. Intelligent Data Analysis 8 (2004) 376-385

Machine Learning for Natural Language Processing (and Vice Versa?)

Claire Cardie

Department of Computer Science, Cornell University, USA
cardie@cs.cornell.edu
http://www.cs.cornell.edu/home/cardie/

Over the past 10-15 years, the influence of methods from machine learning has transformed the way that research is done in the field of natural language processing. This talk will begin by covering the history of this transformation. In particular, learning methods have proved successful in producing stand-alone text-processing components to handle a number of linguistic tasks. Moreover, these components can be combined to produce systems that exhibit shallow text-understanding capabilities: they can, for example, extract key facts from unrestricted documents in limited domains or find answers to general-purpose questions from open-domain document collections. I will briefly describe the state of the art for these practical text-processing applications, focusing on the important role that machine learning methods have played in their development.

The second part of the talk will explore the role that natural language processing might play in machine learning research. Here, I will explain the kinds of text-based features that are relatively easy to incorporate into machine learning data sets. In addition, I'll outline some problems from natural language processing that require, or could at least benefit from, new machine learning algorithms.

Statistical Relational Learning: An Inductive Logic Programming Perspective

Luc De Raedt

Institute for Computer Science, Machine Learning Lab,
Albert-Ludwigs-University, Georges-Köhler-Allee, Gebäude 079,
D-79110, Freiburg i. Brg., Germany
deraedt@informatik.uni-freiburg.de

In the past few years there has been a lot of work lying at the intersection of probability theory, logic programming and machine learning [14,18,13,9,6,1,11]. This work is known under the names of statistical relational learning [7,5], probabilistic logic learning [4], or probabilistic inductive logic programming. Whereas most of the existing works have started from a probabilistic learning perspective and extended probabilistic formalisms with relational aspects, I shall take a different perspective, in which I shall start from inductive logic programming and study how inductive logic programming formalisms, settings and techniques can be extended to deal with probabilistic issues. This tradition has already contributed a rich variety of valuable formalisms and techniques, including probabilistic Horn abduction by David Poole, PRISMs by Sato, stochastic logic programs by Muggleton [13] and Cussens [2], Bayesian logic programs [10,8] by Kersting and De Raedt, and Logical Hidden Markov Models [11].

The main contribution of this talk is the introduction of three probabilistic inductive logic programming settings which are derived from the learning from entailment, from interpretations and from proofs settings of the field of inductive logic programming [3]. Each of these settings contributes different notions of probabilistic logic representations, examples and probability distributions. The first setting, probabilistic learning from entailment, is incorporated in the well-known PRISM system [19] and Cussens's Failure Adjusted Maximisation approach to parameter estimation in stochastic logic programs [2]. A novel system that was recently developed and that fits this paradigm is the nFOIL system [12]. It combines key principles of the well-known inductive logic programming system FOIL [15] with the naïve Bayes' appraoch. In probabilistic learning from entailment, examples are ground facts that should be probabilistically entailed by the target logic program. The second setting, probabilistic learning from interpretations, is incorporated in Bayesian logic programs [10,8], which integrate Bayesian networks with logic programs. This setting is also adopted by [6]. Examples in this setting are Herbrand interpretations that should be a probabilistic model for the target theory. The third setting, learning from proofs [17], is novel. It is motivated by the learning of stochastic context free grammars from tree banks. In this setting, examples are proof trees that should be probabilistically provable from the unknown stochastic logic programs. The sketched settings (and their instances presented) are by no means the only possible settings for probabilistic inductive logic programming, but still – I hope – provide useful insights into the state-of-the-art of this exciting field.

For a full survey of statistical relational learning or probabilistic inductive logic programming, the author would like to refer to [4], and for more details on the probabilistic inductive logic programming settings to [16], where a longer and earlier version of this contribution can be found.

Acknowledgements

This is joint work with Kristian Kersting. The author would also like to thank Niels Landwehr and Sunna Torge for interesting collaborations on nFOIL and the learning of SLPs, respectively. This work is part of the EU IST FET project APRIL II (Application of Probabilistic Inductive Logic Programming II).

References

1. C. R. Anderson, P. Domingos, and D. S. Weld. Relational Markov Models and their Application to Adaptive Web Navigation. In D. Hand, D. Keim, O. R. Zaïne, and R. Goebel, editors, *Proceedings of the Eighth International Conference on Knowledge Discovery and Data Mining (KDD-02)*, pages 143–152, Edmonton, Canada, 2002. ACM Press.
2. J. Cussens. Loglinear models for first-order probabilistic reasoning. In K. B. Laskey and H. Prade, editors, *Proceedings of the Fifteenth Annual Conference on Uncertainty in Artificial Intelligence (UAI-99)*, pages 126–133, Stockholm, Sweden, 1999. Morgan Kaufmann.
3. L. De Raedt. Logical settings for concept-learning. *Artificial Intelligence*, 95(1):197–201, 1997.
4. L. De Raedt and K. Kersting. Probabilistic Logic Learning. *ACM-SIGKDD Explorations: Special issue on Multi-Relational Data Mining*, 5(1):31–48, 2003.
5. T. Dietterich, L. Getoor, and K. Murphy, editors. *Working Notes of the ICML-2004 Workshop on Statistical Relational Learning and its Connections to Other Fields (SRL-04)*, 2004.
6. N. Friedman, L. Getoor, D. Koller, and A. Pfeffer. Learning probabilistic relational models. In T. Dean, editor, *Proceedings of the Sixteenth International Joint Conferences on Artificial Intelligence (IJCAI-99)*, pages 1300–1309, Stockholm, Sweden, 1999. Morgan Kaufmann.
7. L. Getoor and D. Jensen, editors. *Working Notes of the IJCAI-2003 Workshop on Learning Statistical Models from Relational Data (SRL-03)*, 2003.
8. K. Kersting and L. De Raedt. Adaptive Bayesian Logic Programs. In C. Rouveirol and M. Sebag, editors, *Proceedings of the Eleventh Conference on Inductive Logic Programming (ILP-01)*, volume 2157 of *LNCS*, Strasbourg, France, 2001. Springer.
9. K. Kersting and L. De Raedt. Bayesian logic programs. Technical Report 151, University of Freiburg, Institute for Computer Science, April 2001.
10. K. Kersting and L. De Raedt. Towards Combining Inductive Logic Programming and Bayesian Networks. In C. Rouveirol and M. Sebag, editors, *Proceedings of the Eleventh Conference on Inductive Logic Programming (ILP-01)*, volume 2157 of *LNCS*, Strasbourg, France, 2001. Springer.

11. K. Kersting, T. Raiko, S. Kramer, and L. De Raedt. Towards discovering structural signatures of protein folds based on logical hidden markov models. In R. B. Altman, A. K. Dunker, L. Hunter, T. A. Jung, and T. E. Klein, editors, *Proceedings of the Pacific Symposium on Biocomputing*, pages 192 – 203, Kauai, Hawaii, USA, 2003. World Scientific.
12. N. Landwehr, K. Kersting, and L. De Raedt. nfoil: Integrating naive bayes and foil. In *Proceedings of the 20th National Conference on Artificial Intelligence*. AAAI Press, 2005.
13. S. H Muggleton. Stochastic logic programs. In L. De Raedt, editor, *Advances in Inductive Logic Programming*. IOS Press, 1996.
14. D. Poole. Probabilistic Horn abduction and Bayesian networks. *Artificial Intelligence*, 64:81–129, 1993.
15. J. R. Quinlan and R. M. Cameron-Jones. Induction of logic programs:FOIL and related systems. *New Generation Computing*, pages 287–312, 1995.
16. L. De Raedt and K. Kersting. Probabilistic inductive logic programming. In *Proceedings of the 15th International Conference on Algorithmic Learning Theory*. Springer, 2004.
17. L. De Raedt, K. Kersting, and S. Torge. Towards learning stochastic logic programs from proof-banks. In *Proceedings of the 20th National Conference on Artificial Intelligence*. AAAI Press, 2005.
18. T. Sato. A Statistical Learning Method for Logic Programs with Distribution Semantics. In L. Sterling, editor, *Proceedings of the Twelfth International Conference on Logic Programming (ICLP-1995)*, pages 715 – 729, Tokyo, Japan, 1995. MIT Press.
19. T. Sato and Y. Kameya. Parameter learning of logic programs for symbolic-statistical modeling. *Journal of Artificial Intelligence Research*, 15:391–454, 2001.

Recent Advances in Mining Time Series Data

Eamonn Keogh

Department of Computer Science & Engineering,
University of California, Riverside, USA
eamonn@cs.ucr.edu
http://www.cs.ucr.edu/~eamonn

Much of the world's supply of data is in the form of time series. Furthermore, as we shall see, many types of data can be meaningfully converted into "time series", including text, DNA, video, images etc. The last decade has seen an explosion of interest in mining time series data from the academic community. There has been significant work on algorithms to classify, cluster, segment, index, discover rules, visualize, and detect anomalies/novelties in time series.

In this talk I will summarize the latest advances in mining time series data, including:

- New representations of time series data.
- New algorithms/definitions.
- The migration from static problems to online problems.
- New areas and applications of time series data mining.

I will end the talk with a discussion of "what's left to do" in time series data mining.

References

1. E. Keogh. Exact indexing of dynamic time warping. In *Proceedings of the 8th International Conference on Very Large Data Bases*, pages 406–417, 2002.
2. E. Keogh and S. Kasetty. On the need for time series data mining benchmarks: A survey and empirical demonstration. In *Proceedings of the 8th ACM SIGKDD International Conference on Knowledge Discovery and Data Mining*, pages 102–111, 2002.
3. E. Keogh, J. Lin, and W. Truppel. Clustering of time series subsequences is meaningless: Implications for past and future research. In *Proceedings of the 3rd IEEE International Conference on Data Mining*, pages 115–122, 2003.
4. E. Keogh, S. Lonardi, and C. Ratanamahatana. Towards parameter-free data mining. In *Proceedings of the tenth ACM SIGKDD International Conference on Knowledge Discovery and Data Mining*, 2004.
5. C.A. Ratanamahatana and E. Keogh. Everything you know about dynamic time warping is wrong. In *Proceedings of the Third Workshop on Mining Temporal and Sequential Data, in conjunction with the Tenth ACM SIGKDD International Conference on Knowledge Discovery and Data Mining (KDD-2004)*, 2004.

Focus the Mining Beacon: Lessons and Challenges from the World of E-Commerce

Ron Kohavi

Microsoft Corporation, USA
ronnyk@cs.stanford.edu
http://www.kohavi.com

Electronic Commerce is now entering its second decade, with Amazon.com and eBay now in existence for ten years. With massive amounts of data, an actionable domain, and measurable ROI, multiple companies use data mining and knowledge discovery to understand their customers and improve interactions. We present important lessons and challenges using e-commerce examples across two dimensions: (i) business-level to technical, and (ii) the mining lifecycle from data collection, data warehouse construction, to discovery and deployment. Many of the lessons and challenges are applicable to domains outside e-commerce.

Data Streams and Data Synopses for Massive Data Sets
(Invited Talk)

Yossi Matias

Tel Aviv University,
HyperRoll Inc., Stanford University
matias@tau.ac.il

Abstract. With the proliferation of data intensive applications, it has become necessary to develop new techniques to handle massive data sets. Traditional algorithmic techniques and data structures are not always suitable to handle the amount of data that is required and the fact that the data often streams by and cannot be accessed again. A field of research established over the past decade is that of handling massive data sets using data synopses, and developing algorithmic techniques for data stream models. We will discuss some of the research work that has been done in the field, and provide a decades' perspective to data synopses and data streams.

1 Summary

In recent years, we have witnessed an explosion in data used in various applications. In general, the growth rate in data is known to exceed the increase rate in the size of RAM, and of the available computation power (a.k.a. Moore's Law). As a result, traditional algorithms and data structures are often no longer adequate to handle the massive data sets required by these applications.

One approach to handle massive data sets is to use *external memory algorithms*, designed to make an effective utilization of I/O. In such algorithms the data structures are often implemented in external storage devices, and the objective is in general to minimize the number of I/Os. For a survey of works on external memory algorithms see [6]. Such algorithms assume that the entire input data is available for further processing. There are, however, many applications where the data is only seen once, as it "streams by". This may be the case in, e.g., financial applications, network monitoring, security, telecommunications data management, web applications, manufacturing, and sensor networks. Even in data warehouse applications, where the data may in general be available for additional querying, there are many situations where data analysis needs to be done as the data is loaded into the data warehouse, since the cost of accessing the data in a fully loaded production system may be significantly larger than just the basic cost of I/O. Additionally, even in the largest data warehouses, consisting of hundreds of terabytes, data is only maintained for a limited time, so access to historical data may often be infeasible.

It had thus become necessary to address situations in which massive data sets are required to be handled as they "stream by", and using only limited memory. Motivated by this need, the research field of data streams and data synopses has emerged and established over the last few years. We will discuss some of the research work that has been done in the field, and provide a decades' perspective to data streams and data synopses. A longer version of this abstract will be available at [4].

The data stream model is quite simple: it is assumed that the input data set is given as a sequence of data items. Each data item is seen only once, and any computation can be done utilizing the data structures maintained in main memory. These memory resident data structures are substantially smaller than the input data. As such, they cannot fully represent the data as is the case for traditional data structures, but can only provide a synopsis of the input data; hence they are denoted as *synopsis data structures*, or *data synopses* [3].

The use of data synopses implies that data analysis that is dependent on the entire streaming data will often be approximated. Furthermore, ad hoc queries that are dependent on the entire input data could only be served by the data synopses, and as a result only approximate answers to queries will be available. A primary objective in the design of data synopses is to have the smallest data synopses that would guarantee small, and if possible bounded, error on the approximated computation.

As we have shown in [1], some essential statistical data analysis, the so-called *frequency moments*, can be approximated using synopses that are as small as polynomial or even logarithmic in the input size. Over the last few years there has been a proliferation of additional works on data streams and data synopses. See, e.g., the surveys [2] and [5]. These works include theoretical results, as well as applications in databases, network traffic analysis, security, sensor networks, and program profiling; synopses include samples, random projections, histograms, wavelets, and XML synopses, among others. There remain a plethora of interesting open problems, both theoretical as well as applied.

References

1. Alon, N., Matias, Y., Szegedy, M.: The space complexity of approximating the frequency moments. J. of Computer and System Sciences 58 (1999), 137-147. STOC'96 Special Issue
2. Babcock, B., Babu, S., Datar, M., Motwani, R. Widom, J.: Models and issues in data stream systems. In Proc. Symposium on Principles of Database Systems (2002), 1-16
3. Gibbons, P.B., Matias, Y.: Synopses data structures for massive data sets. In: External memory algorithms, DIMACS Series Discrete Math. & TCS, AMS, 50 (1999). Also SODA'99
4. Matias, Y.: Data streams and data synopses for massive data sets.
http://www.cs.tau.ac.il/~matias/streams/
5. Muthukrishnan, S.: Data streams: Algorithms and applications.
http://www.cs.rutgers.edu/~muthu/stream-1-1.ps
6. Vitter, J.S.: External memory algorithms and data structures. ACM Comput Surv. 33(2): 209-271 (2001)

Clustering and Metaclustering with Nonnegative Matrix Decompositions

Liviu Badea

AI Lab, National Institute for Research and Development in Informatics,
8-10 Averescu Blvd., Bucharest, Romania
badea@ici.ro

Abstract. Although very widely used in unsupervised data mining, most clustering methods are affected by the instability of the resulting clusters w.r.t. the initialization of the algorithm (as e.g. in k-means). Here we show that this problem can be elegantly and efficiently tackled by *meta-clustering* the clusters produced in several different runs of the algorithm, especially if *"soft"* clustering algorithms (such as Nonnegative Matrix Factorization) are used both at the object- and the meta-level. The essential difference w.r.t. other meta-clustering approaches consists in the fact that our algorithm detects frequently occurring *sub*-clusters (rather than *complete* clusters) in the various runs, which allows it to outperform existing algorithms. Additionally, we show how to perform *two-way meta*-clustering, i.e. take both object and sample dimensions of clusters simultaneously into account, a feature which is essential e.g. for *bi*clustering gene expression data, but has not been considered before.

1 Introduction and Motivation

Clustering is one of the most widely used unsupervised learning methods and the number of different clustering approaches is overwhelming. However, despite their wide variety, most clustering methods are affected by a common problem: the *instability* of the resulting clusters w.r.t. the initialization of the algorithm (as in the case of k-means) and w.r.t. slight differences in the input dataset as a result of resampling the initial data (e.g. in the case of hierarchical clustering). This is not surprising if we adopt a unifying view of clustering as a constrained optimization problem, since the fitness landscape of such a complex problem may involve many different local minima into which the algorithm may get caught when started off from different initial states.

Although such an instability seems hard to avoid, we may be interested in the clusters that keep reappearing in the majority of the runs of the algorithm. This is related to the problem of *combining multiple clustering systems*, which is the unsupervised analog of the classifier combination problem [8], a comparatively simpler problem that has attracted a lot of research in the past decade. Combining clustering results is more complicated than combining classifiers, as it involves solving an additional so-called *cluster correspondence* problem, which amounts to finding the best matches between clusters generated in different runs.

The cluster correspondence problem can also be cast as an unsupervised optimization problem, which can be solved by a (meta-) clustering algorithm. Choosing an appropriate meta-clustering algorithm for dealing with this problem crucially depends on the precise notion of cluster correspondence.

A very strict notion of *one-to-one correspondence* between the clusters of each pair of clustering runs may be too tough to be realized in most practical cases. For example, due to the above-mentioned *instability*, different runs of k-means clustering with different initializations may easily produce different sets of clusters, e.g. $run_1 = \{\{1,2,3\},\{4,5\}\}$, $run_2 = \{\{1,2\}, \{3,4,5\}\}$, ...

A more lenient notion of cluster correspondence would look for clusters that keep reappearing in all runs (while ignoring the rest), but only very few (if any) such clusters may exist for a large enough number of runs.

An even less restrictive notion could be envisioned by looking for clusters that are most similar (although not necessarily identical) across all runs. This is closest to performing something like single-linkage hierarchical clustering on the sets of clusters produced in the various clustering runs, with the additional constraint of allowing in each meta-cluster no more than a single cluster from each individual run. Unfortunately, this constraint will render the meta-clustering algorithm highly unstable. Thus, while trying to address the instability of (object-level) clustering using meta-level clustering, we end up with instability in the meta-clustering algorithm itself. Therefore, a "softer" notion of cluster correspondence is needed.

The main motivation for this work comes from genomics, more precisely from clustering *gene expression data* [2]. (Therefore, in the following we will frequently refer to clusters of genes rather than clusters of more abstract objects.) Most currently used clustering algorithms produce *non-overlapping* clusters, which represents a serious limitation in this domain, since a gene is typically involved in several biological processes. Here we adopt a biologically plausible simplifying assumption that the overlap of influences (biological processes) is *additive*

$$X_{sg} = \sum_c X(s, g \mid c) \qquad (1)$$

where X_{sg} is the expression level of gene g in data sample s, while $X(s,g \mid c)$ is the expression level of g in s due to biological process c. We also assume that $X(s,g \mid c)$ is multiplicatively decomposable into the expression level A_{sc} of the biological process (cluster) c in sample s and the membership degree S_{cg} of gene g in c: $X(s, g \mid c) = A_{sc} \cdot S_{cg}$ \qquad (2)

2 Nonnegative Matrix Factorization as a Soft Clustering Method

Combining (1) and (2) leads to the reformulation of our clustering problem as a *Nonnegative Matrix Factorization* (of the $n_s \times n_g$ matrix X as a product of an $n_s \times n_c$ matrix A and an $n_c \times n_g$ matrix S):

$$X_{sg} \approx \sum_c A_{sc} \cdot S_{cg} \qquad (3)$$

with the additional nonnegativity constraints: $A_{sc} \geq 0$, $S_{cg} \geq 0$ (4)
(Expression levels and membership degrees cannot be negative.)

Such a problem can be cast as a constrained optimization problem:

$$\text{minimize } C(A,S) = \frac{1}{2} \| X - A \cdot S \|_F^2 = \frac{1}{2} \sum_{s,g} (X - A \cdot S)_{sg}^2 \quad (5)$$

subject to the nonnegativity constraints (4), and could be solved using Lee and Seung's *Nonnegative Matrix Factorization (NMF)* algorithm [4,5].

As explained above, such a factorization can be viewed as a "soft" clustering algorithm allowing for overlapping clusters, since we may have several significant S_{cg} entries on a given column g of S (so a gene g may "belong" to several clusters c).

Allowing for cluster overlap alleviates but does not completely eliminate the instability of clustering, since the optimization problem (5), (4) is non-convex.

In particular, the NMF algorithm produces different factorizations (biclusters) $(A^{(i)}, S^{(i)})$ for different initializations and meta-clustering the resulting "soft" clusters $S^{(i)}$ could be used to obtain a more stable set of clusters.

However, using a "hard" *meta*-clustering algorithm would once again entail an unwanted instability. Therefore, we propose using Nonnegative Matrix Factorization as a "soft" meta-clustering approach.

This not only alleviates the instability of a "hard" meta-clustering algorithm, but also produces a "base" set of "*cluster prototypes*", out of which all clusters of all individual runs can be recomposed, despite the fact that they may not correspond to identically reoccurring clusters in all individual runs (see Figure 1).

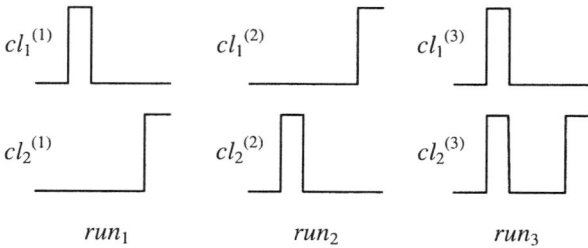

Fig. 1. Clusters obtained in different runs are typically combinations of a "base" set of "cluster prototypes" (rather than identical across all runs)

3 Metaclustering with NMF

We propose using NMF both for object-level clustering *and* meta-clustering. This unified approach solves in an elegant manner both the clustering and the cluster correspondence problem. More precisely, we first run NMF as object-level clustering r times:

$$X \approx A^{(i)} \cdot S^{(i)} \qquad i = 1, \ldots, r \quad (6)$$

where X is the data matrix to be factorized (samples × objects to be factorized), $A^{(i)}$ (samples × clusters) and $S^{(i)}$ (clusters × objects).

To allow the comparison of membership degrees S_{cg} for different clusters c, we scale the rows of $S^{(i)}$ to unit norm by taking advantage of the scaling invariance of the above factorization (6). More precisely:

Proposition. The NMF objective function (5) is invariant under the transformation $A \leftarrow A \cdot D$, $S \leftarrow D^{-1} \cdot S$, where $D = diag(d_1,...,d_{nc})$ is a positive diagonal matrix.

Since a diagonal matrix D operates on the rows of S and on the columns of A, we can scale the rows of S to unit norm by using a diagonal scaling with $d_c = \sqrt{\sum_g S_{cg}^2}$.

Next, we build a global S-matrix of size $r \cdot n_c \times n_g$:

$$S^G = \begin{pmatrix} S^{(1)} \\ \vdots \\ S^{(r)} \end{pmatrix} \quad (7)$$

by collecting all clusters (i.e. rows of $S^{(i)}$) from all runs and then use NMF once more to meta-cluster these clusters (i.e. the *rows* of S^G):

$$S^G \approx \alpha \cdot \gamma \quad (8)$$

where α and γ are of sizes $r \cdot n_c \times n_c$ and $n_c \times n_g$ respectively. Note that whereas object level NMF clusters *columns* of X (e.g. genes in our genomics application), meta-clustering clusters *rows* of S^G.

Note that α encodes the *cluster – metacluster correspondence*. On the other hand, the rows of γ make up a base set of *cluster prototypes*, out of which all clusters of all individual runs can be recomposed:

$$S_c^{(i)} = \sum_m \alpha_{c+(i-1)n_c, m} \cdot \gamma_m \quad (9)$$

where $S_c^{(i)}$ is the row c of $S^{(i)}$, while γ_m is the row m of γ.

Using the notation $\alpha_{cm}^{(i)}$ for $\alpha_{c+(i-1)n_c, m}$, we can rewrite (9) as

$$S_c^{(i)} = \sum_m \alpha_{cm}^{(i)} \cdot \gamma_m \quad (9')$$

Ideally (in case of a perfect one-to-one correspondence of clusters across runs), we would expect the rows of α to contain a single significant entry $\alpha_{c,m(i,c)}^{(i)}$, so that each cluster $S_c^{(i)}$ corresponds to a single cluster prototype $\gamma_{m(i,c)}$ (where $m(i,c)$ is a function of i and c): $S_c^{(i)} = \alpha_{c,m(i,c)}^{(i)} \cdot \gamma_{m(i,c)} \quad (10)$

Additionally, each meta-cluster m should contain no more than a single cluster from each individual run, i.e. there should be no significant entries $\alpha_{c'm}^{(i)}$ and $\alpha_{c''m}^{(i)}$ with $c' \neq c''$. Although it could be easily solved by a hard meta-clustering algorithm, such an ideal cluster correspondence is only very seldom encountered in practice, mainly due to the *instability* of most clustering algorithms.

Thus, instead of such a perfect correspondence (10), we settle for a weaker one (9) in which the rows of α can contain several significant entries, so that all clusters (rows of S^G) are recovered as *combinations* of cluster prototypes (rows of γ).

The nonnegativity constraints of NMF meta-clustering are essential both for allowing the interpretation of γ as cluster prototypes as well as for obtaining sparse factorizations (α, γ). (Experimentally, the rows of α tend to contain typically one or only very few significant entries.)

In order to make the prototype clusters (rows of γ) directly comparable to the clusters (rows) from S^G, we use the diagonal scaling

$$\alpha \leftarrow \alpha \cdot D^{-1}, \quad \gamma \leftarrow D \cdot \gamma \quad \text{with} \quad D = diag\left(\frac{1}{r}\sum_j \alpha_{jm}\right).$$

The cluster prototypes matrix γ produced by meta-clustering (8) is subsequently used as seed for a final NMF run aiming at producing the final factorization. More precisely, the seed for the final NMF run is (A_0, γ), where A_0 is the *nonnegative least squares* solution to $X \approx A_0 \cdot \gamma$.

We thus obtain a final factorization (3), which can be interpreted as a stable clustering of X allowing for overlapping clusters. The algorithm is summarized below.

Clustering with Metaclustering (X) → (A, S)

for $i = 1, \ldots, r$
  run NMF($X, A^{(0i)}, S^{(0i)}$) with random initial matrices $A^{(0i)}, S^{(0i)}$ to produce a factorization with n_c clusters: $X \approx A^{(i)} \cdot S^{(i)}$
  scale the rows of $S^{(i)}$ to unit norm:
  $A^{(i)} \leftarrow A^{(i)} \cdot D, \quad S^{(i)} \leftarrow D^{-1} \cdot S^{(i)}$ with $D = diag\left(\sqrt{\sum_g S_{cg}^2}\right)$
end

Construct $S^G = \begin{pmatrix} S^{(1)} \\ \vdots \\ S^{(r)} \end{pmatrix}$ and use NMF($S^G, \alpha^{(0)}, \gamma^{(0)}$) (with random $\alpha^{(0)}, \gamma^{(0)}$) to

produce a factorization ("meta-clustering") with internal dimensionality n_c: $S^G \approx \alpha \cdot \gamma$
scale the columns of α: $\alpha \leftarrow \alpha \cdot D^{-1}, \quad \gamma \leftarrow D \cdot \gamma$ with $D = diag\left(\sum_j \alpha_{jm}/r\right)$
Let A_0 be the *nonnegative least squares* solution to $X \approx A_0 \cdot \gamma$
Run NMF(X, A_0, γ) to produce the final factorization $X \approx A \cdot S$

NMF(X, A_0, S_0) → (A,S)
$A \leftarrow A_0, \quad S \leftarrow S_0$
loop $\quad S_{cg} \leftarrow S_{cg} \dfrac{(A^T \cdot X)_{cg}}{(A^T \cdot A \cdot S)_{cg}}$

$$A_{sc} \leftarrow A_{sc} \frac{(X \cdot S^T)_{sc}}{(A \cdot S \cdot S^T)_{sc}}$$

until convergence.

4 Sparser Decompositions

Although NMF tends to produce sparse factorizations that are quite immune to moderate levels of noise [4], even sparser decompositions may be desired to cope with higher noise levels. An ad-hoc approach to obtaining such sparser factorizations would fix to zero all the elements below a given threshold of an NMF factorization and then apply several re-optimization rounds until a fixpoint is attained. Hoyer's *Nonnegative Sparse Coding (NNSC)* algorithm [3] is a more elegant approach that factorizes $X \approx A \cdot S$ by optimizing an objective function that combines the *fit* of the factorization to the original data with a *size term* penalizing the non-zero entries of S:

$$\text{minimize} \quad C(A, S) = \frac{1}{2}\|X - AS\|_F^2 + \lambda \sum_{c,g} S_{cg} \quad (11)$$

subject to the nonnegativity constraints $A_{sc} \geq 0$, $S_{cg} \geq 0$.
(NMF is recovered by setting the size parameter λ to zero, while a non-zero λ would lead to sparser factorizations.) Unfortunately however, the scaling invariance of the fitness term $\frac{1}{2}\|X - AS\|_F^2$ makes the size term ineffective, since the latter can be forced as small as needed by using a diagonal scaling D with small enough entries. Additional constraints are therefore needed to render the size term operational. Since a diagonal matrix D operates on the rows of S and on the columns of A, we could impose unit norms either for the rows of S, or for the columns of A.

Unfortunately, the objective function (11) used in [3] produces decompositions that depend on the scale of the original matrix X (i.e. the decompositions of X and ηX are essentially different), regardless of the normalization scheme employed. For example, if we constrain the rows of S to unit norm, then we cannot have decompositions of the form $X \approx A \cdot S$ and $\eta X \approx \eta A \cdot S$, since at least one of these is in general non-optimal due to the dimensional inhomogeneity of the objective function w.r.t. A and X: $C_{\eta X}(\eta A, S) = \eta^2 \frac{1}{2}\|X - AS\|_F^2 + \lambda \sum_{c,g} S_{cg}$. On the other hand, if we constrain the columns of A to unit norm, the decompositions $X \approx A \cdot S$ and $\eta X \approx A \cdot \eta S$ cannot be both optimal, again due to the dimensional inhomogeneity of C, now w.r.t. S and X: $C_{\eta X}(A, \eta S) = \eta^2 \frac{1}{2}\|X - AS\|_F^2 + \eta \lambda \sum_{c,g} S_{cg}$.

Therefore, as long as the size term depends only on S, we are forced to constrain the columns of A to unit norm, while employing an objective function that is *dimensionally homogeneous* in S and X. One such dimensionally homogeneous objective function is:

$$C(A,S) = \frac{1}{2}\|X - AS\|_F^2 + \lambda\|S\|_F^2 \tag{12}$$

which will be minimized subject to the nonnegativity constraints and the constraints on the norm of the columns of A: $\|A_c\| = 1$ (i.e. $\sum_s A_{sc}^2 = 1$).

It can be easily verified that this produces *scale independent decompositions*, i.e. if $X \approx A \cdot S$ is an optimal decomposition of X, then $\eta X \approx A \cdot \eta S$ is an optimal decomposition of ηX.

The constrained optimization problem could be solved with a gradient-based method. However, in the case of NMF, faster so-called "multiplicative update rules" exist [5,3], which we have modified for the NNSC problem as follows.

Modified NNSC algorithm

Start with random initial matrices A and S

loop $S_{cg} \leftarrow S_{cg} \dfrac{(A^T \cdot X)_{cg}}{(A^T \cdot A \cdot S + \lambda S)_{cg}}$

$A \leftarrow A + \mu(X - A \cdot S) \cdot S^T$

normalize the columns of A to unit norm: $A \leftarrow A \cdot D^{-1}$, $D = diag\left(\sqrt{\sum_s A_{sc}^2}\right)$

until convergence.

Note that we factorize X rather than X^T since the sparsity constraint should affect the clusters of genes (i.e. S) rather than the clusters of samples A. (This is unlike NMF, for which the factorizations of X and X^T are symmetrical.)

4.1 Sparser Factorizations and Noise

To demonstrate that sparser factorizations are better at coping with noise than simple NMF, we generated a synthetic dataset with highly overlapping clusters and very large additive noise (the standard deviation of the noise was 0.75 of the standard deviation of the original data).

We ran our modified NNSC algorithm with increasingly larger λ (ranging from 0 to 0.75) and observed that the gene clusters were recovered almost perfectly despite the very large noise, especially for small values of λ.

Figure 2 shows the original data without and with noise respectively (upper row), as well as the reconstructed data ($A \cdot S$) for $\lambda=0.05$ and $\lambda=0.75$ (lower row). Note that the reconstructed data is closer to the original noise-free data than to the noisy original. The following Table shows the relative error computed w.r.t. the noisy data X_{noisy} (i.e. $\varepsilon_{noisy} = \|X_{noisy} - AS\|_F / \|X_{noisy}\|_F$) as well as the relative error w.r.t. the original data X_{orig} (before adding noise, i.e. $\varepsilon_{orig} = \|X_{orig} - AS\|_F / \|X_{orig}\|_F$) for several values of λ ranging from 0 to 0.75.

λ	0	0.02	0.05	0.1	0.2	0.4	0.5	0.75
ε_{noisy}	0.2001	0.2017	0.2053	0.2161	0.2295	0.2452	0.2983	0.3228
ε_{orig}	0.1403	0.1375	**0.1364**	0.1419	0.1544	0.1719	0.2323	0.2604

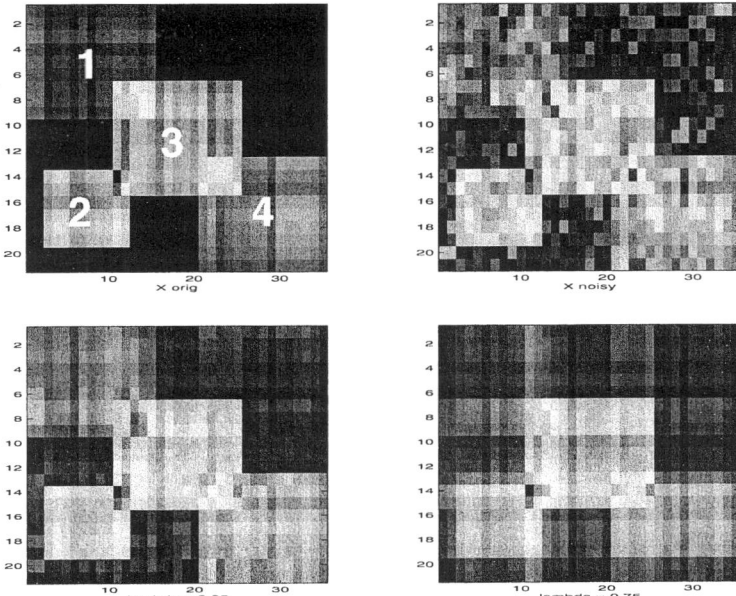

Fig. 2. A synthetic dataset

Note that ε_{orig} is always lower than ε_{noisy}. Also, whereas ε_{noisy} increases as expected with λ, ε_{orig} attains a minimum at $\lambda=0.05$ showing that small values of λ tend to improve not only the clusters, but also the error w.r.t. the *original* data.

5 Two-Way Meta-clustering

The meta-clustering approach based on (8) takes only the gene clusters (rows of $S^{(i)}$) into account. Although this works very well in many cases, it will fail whenever two clusters correspond to very similar sets of genes, while differing along the sample dimension. For example, clusters 1 and 2 from Figure 2 are quite similar along the gene dimension, so a meta-clustering method looking just at genes would be incapable of discriminating between the two clusters, unless it also looks at the "sample clusters" $A^{(i)}$. In the following, we show that a slight generalization of NMF, namely *Positive Tensor Factorization* (*PTF*) [6] can be successfully used to perform *two-way* meta-clustering, which takes both the gene and the sample dimensions into account. (As far as we know, this elegant view of metaclustering as a PTF problem has not been considered before.)

Naively, one would be tempted to try clustering the biclusters[1] $A_c^{(i)} \cdot S_c^{(i)}$ instead of the gene clusters $S_c^{(i)}$, but this is practically infeasible in most real-life datasets because it involves factorizing a matrix of size $r \cdot n_c \times n_s \cdot n_g$. On closer inspection,

---

[1] $A_c^{(i)}$ is the column c of $A^{(i)}$, while $S_c^{(i)}$ is the row c of $S^{(i)}$.

however, it turns out that it is not necessary to construct this full-blown matrix – actually we are searching for a *Positive Tensor Factorization* of this matrix [2]

$$A_{sc}^{(i)} \cdot S_{cg}^{(i)} \approx \sum_{k=1}^{n_c} \alpha_{ck}^{(i)} \cdot \beta_{sk} \cdot \gamma_{kg} \tag{14}$$

The indices in (14) have the following domains: s – samples, g – genes, c – clusters, k – metaclusters. To simplify the notation, we could merge the indices i and c into a single index (ic), so that the factorization becomes:

$$A_{s(ic)} \cdot S_{(ic)g} \approx \sum_{k=1}^{n_c} \alpha_{(ic)k} \cdot \beta_{sk} \cdot \gamma_{kg} \tag{14'}$$

Note that β and γ are the "unified" versions of $A^{(i)}$ and $S^{(i)}$ respectively, while α encodes the *cluster-metacluster correspondence*.

The factorization (14') can be computed using the following multiplicative update rules (the proofs are straightforward generalizations of those for NMF and can also be found e.g. in [6]):

$$\alpha \leftarrow \alpha * \frac{(A^T \cdot \beta) * (S \cdot \gamma^T)}{\alpha \cdot [(\beta^T \cdot \beta) * (\gamma \cdot \gamma^T)]}$$

$$\beta \leftarrow \beta * \frac{A \cdot [\alpha * (S \cdot \gamma^T)]}{\beta \cdot [(\alpha^T \cdot \alpha) * (\gamma \cdot \gamma^T)]} \tag{15}$$

$$\gamma \leftarrow \gamma * \frac{[\alpha * (A^T \cdot \beta)]^T \cdot S}{[(\alpha^T \cdot \alpha) * (\beta^T \cdot \beta)]^T \cdot \gamma}$$

where '$*$' and '—' denote element-wise multiplication and division of matrices, while '$\cdot$' is ordinary matrix multiplication.

The PTF factorization (14') should be contrasted with our previous metaclustering approach (8) based on NMF:

$$S_{cg}^{(i)} \approx \sum_{k=1}^{n_c} \alpha_{ck}^{(i)} \cdot \gamma_{kg} \tag{8'}$$

It can be easily seen that whereas (14) groups biclusters by taking both the gene and the sample dimension into account, (8') may confuse two biclusters that have similar gene components (even if they have different sample supports). For example, (8') confuses biclusters 1 and 2 from Figure 2, while (14) is able to perfectly discriminate between the two despite the noise and the difference in intensity between the two biclusters.

After convergence of the PTF update rule, we normalize the rows of γ to unit norm ($\|\gamma_k\| = 1$), as well as the columns of α such that $\sum_{i,c} \alpha_{ck}^{(i)} = r$ (r being the number of runs): [3]

---

[2] More precisely, we are dealing with the constrained optimization problem
$$\min C(\alpha, \beta, \gamma) = \frac{1}{2} \sum_{i,c,s,g} \left(A_{sc}^{(i)} S_{cg}^{(i)} - \sum_{k=1}^{n_c} \alpha_{ck}^{(i)} \beta_{sk} \gamma_{kg} \right)^2 \text{ subject to } \alpha, \beta, \gamma \geq 0.$$

[3] In order to be able to interpret β and γ as "unified" $A^{(i)}$ and $S^{(i)}$ respectively, we need to have $\sum_c \alpha_{ck}^{(i)} \approx 1$, i.e. $\sum_{i,c} \alpha_{ck}^{(i)} \approx r$, since $X \approx \sum_c A_{sc}^{(i)} \cdot S_{cg}^{(i)} \approx \sum_{k=1}^{n_c} \left(\sum_c \alpha_{ck}^{(i)} \right) \cdot \beta_{sk} \cdot \gamma_{kg}$.

$$\gamma_{kg} \mapsto \frac{1}{\|\gamma_k\|} \cdot \gamma_{kg}$$

$$\alpha_{(ic)k} \mapsto \frac{r}{\sum_{i',c'} \alpha_{(i'c')k}} \cdot \alpha_{(ic)k}$$

$$\beta_{sk} \mapsto \frac{\|\gamma_k\|}{r} \cdot \sum_{i,c} \alpha_{(ic)k} \cdot \beta_{sk}$$

and then run NMF initialized with (β, γ) to produce the final factorization $X \approx A \cdot S$.

6 Experimental Evaluation

We evaluated our algorithm on synthetic datasets[4] generated by continuous latent variable graphical models as in Figure 3. (The clusters corresponding to the latent variables L_k *overlap* in the variables X_i influenced by *several* L_k.) To generate *nonnegative bi*clusters as in Figure 2, we set L_k to nonzero values (drawn from the absolute of a normal distribution) only in certain subsets of samples. The observable variables X_i were affected by additive normal noise with a standard deviation $\sigma(\varepsilon_i) = v \cdot \sigma(X_i^{(0)})$ equal to a fraction v of the standard deviation of the noise-free "signal" $X_i^{(0)}$. (It can be easily seen that this model is equivalent to $X = A^{(0)} \cdot S^{(0)} + \varepsilon$, where $X = (X_1 \ldots X_{ng})$ and $S^{(0)}{}_{kj}$ are the coefficients associated to the $L_k \to X_j$ edges.)

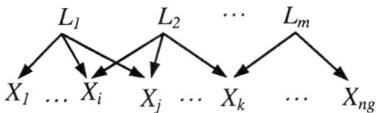

Fig. 3. Latent variable model for overlapping clusters

The Table below presents a comparison of various combinations of clustering and meta-clustering algorithms – columns of the Table correspond to clustering algorithms (k-means, fuzzy k-means [7] and NMF), while the rows are associated to meta-clustering algorithms (k-means, fuzzy k-means, NMF and PTF) with or without a final NMF step, as well as to the best individual clustering run (resampling). The figures in the Table represent average *matches* of the reconstructed clusters with the original ones, together with the associated *relative errors* (we display both averages and standard deviations for 10 runs of each metaclustering method with different input data X).

---

[4] The small dataset from Figure 2 with 21 samples and 35 genes allows a human analysis of the results.

Defining the *match* between two sets of possibly *overlapping* clusters is nontrivial. For each cluster C_1 from clustering 1, we determine the single cluster C_2 from clustering 2 into which it is best included, i.e. the one with the largest $|C_1 \cap C_2|/|C_1|$. We proceed analogously for the clusters C_2 from clustering 2. Then, for each cluster C_1 (from clustering 1), we determine its match $|C_1 \cap C_2|/|C_1 \cup C_2|$ with the *union* C_2 of clusters from clustering 2, for which C_1 is the best including cluster (as determined in the previous step). Similarly, we determine matches for clusters C_2 from clustering 2. The average match of the two clusterings is then the mean of all these matches (for all C_1 and all C_2).

The Table clearly demonstrates the necessity of using nonnegative decompositions like NMF (either as individual runs or as the final step) for obtaining reasonable results. Indeed, the best match *without* any nonnegative decompositions is 55% and the lowest relative error 0.2, whereas *with* nonnegative decompositions, we obtain a nearly perfect match (98%) with a relative error of 10^{-3}.

match (std match) relative error (std error)	Kmeans	fcm	NMF
kmeans(meta)	0.53 (0.021) 0.306 (0.032)	0.55 (0.058) 0.2 (0.018)	0.81 (0.123) 0.052 (0.033)
kmeans(meta) + NMF(final)	0.62 (0.056) 0.153 (0.059)	0.63 (0.181) 0.094 (0.046)	0.9 (0.148) 0.002 (0.001)
fcm(meta)	0.51 (0.041) 0.315 (0.054)	0.53 (0.011) 0.202 (0.019)	0.92 (0.126) 0.014 (0.004)
fcm(meta) + NMF(final)	0.65 (0.178) 0.092 (0.044)	0.56 (0.024) 0.112 (0.008)	0.92 (0.126) 0.002 (0)
NMF(meta)	0.5 (0.032) 0.313 (0.042)	0.53 (0.009) 0.194 (0.018)	0.69 (0.008) 0.027 (0.043)
NMF(meta) + NMF(final)	0.59 (0.049) 0.132 (0.016)	0.55 (0.008) 0.119 (0.012)	0.74 (0.111) 0.012 (0.025)
PTF(meta)	0.49 (0.044) 0.287 (0.023)	0.53 (0.01) 0.212 (0.019)	0.98 (0.037) 0.023 (0.006)
PTF(meta) + NMF(final)	0.58 (0.04) 0.122 (0.015)	0.55 (0.011) 0.116 (0.014)	0.98 (0.043) 0.001 (0)
Best clustering run (out of 10)	0.49 (0.017) 0.307 (0.011)	0.53 (0.008) 0.208 (0.018)	0.76 (0.089) 0.001 (0)

Note that *clustering* runs based on NMF are far superior to other methods. On the other hand, all tested *meta-clustering* algorithms perform reasonably well (with PTF faring best), especially in terms of relative error. However, as already discussed in Section 5, meta-clustering with NMF does not recover the clusters very well (average matches are around 74% versus virtually perfect matches for PTF (98%), 92% for fuzzy k-means and about 90% for k-means+NMF). NMF and PTF on NMF runs are also quite stable (the std of the match is 0.8% and 4% respectively).

Also note that although meta-clustering does not always outperform the best individual run in terms of *relative error*, it *does* outperform it in terms of the *match* with the original clusters (98% versus 76%).

We also considered larger problems in which the overlapping clusters can be discriminated by looking at the gene dimension only. As expected, in such cases the best results are obtained by a combination which uses NMF for meta-clustering: (NMF, NMF, NMF).

We also observed that k-means and fuzzy k-means are far inferior to NMF (as meta-clustering algorithms) in problems with a larger number of clusters. This is because, as the number of clusters increases, the fraction of perfectly reconstructed clusters *in a limited number of runs* decreases sharply. This makes meta-clustering algorithms like k-means or fuzzy k-means less effective, since these algorithms search for clusters that reoccur in a large fraction of runs. On the other hand, our approach using nonnegative decompositions looks for cluster prototypes out of which the clusters of all individual runs can be recomposed (recall Fig. 1) and therefore may behave well *even with a limited number of runs* (such as 10-20 in our experiments).

7 Related Work and Conclusions

Bradley and Fayyad [1] use *k-means* for meta-clustering a number of *k-means* runs on subsamples of the data for initializing a final k-means run. However, the use of a "hard" clustering approach like k-means in domains featuring *overlapping bi*clusters produces dramatically less accurate results than our approach using NMF or PTF for meta-clustering NMF runs (53% match and 30.6% error vs. 98% match and 0.1% error for our algorithm).[5]

The main technical contribution of this paper consists in showing how NMF and PTF can be used to solve the cluster correspondence problem for "*soft*" *bi*clustering algorithms such as NMF (which is significantly more involved than the cluster correspondence problem for "hard" algorithms and, as far as we know, has not been addressed before). The present approach is significantly different from other biclustering approaches – for example Cheng's biclustering [9] is based on a simpler additive model that is not scale invariant (problematic in the case of gene expression data). Our algorithm not only significantly outperforms all existing approaches (especially in terms of recovering the original clusters), but – more importantly – provides a conceptually elegant solution to the cluster correspondence problem. Furthermore, an initial application of the method to a large lung cancer dataset [10] proved computationally tractable and was able to perfectly recover the known histological classification of the various lung cancer types in the dataset. (For lack of space, we refer to the supplementary information at http://www.ai.ici.ro/ecml05/meyerson.pdf). The genomics applications will be the subject of future research.

Acknowledgements. I am grateful to Doina Tilivea who helped in the experimental evaluation of the algorithms.

References

1. Bradley P.S., Fayyad U.M. Refining Initial Points for K-Means Clustering, Proc. ICML-98, pp. 91-99.
2. Eisen M.B., P.T. Spellman, P.O. Brown, D. Botstein. Cluster analysis and display of genome-wide expression patterns, PNAS Vol.95, 14863-8, Dec. 1998.

---

[5] However, it is fair to say that [1] did not aim at improving the stability of clustering as we do, but at handling large datasets.

3. Hoyer P.O. Non-negative sparse coding. Neural Networks for Signal Processing XII, 557-565, Martigny, 2002.
4. Lee D.D., H.S. Seung. Learning the parts of objects by non-negative matrix factorization. Nature, vol. 401, no. 6755, pp. 788-791, 1999.
5. Lee D.D., H.S. Seung. Algorithms for non-negative matrix factorization. Proc. NIPS*2000, MIT Press, 2001.
6. Welling M., Weber M. Positive tensor factorization. Pattern Recognition Letters 22(12): 1255-1261 (2001).
7. Bezdek J.C. Pattern Recognition with Fuzzy Objective Function Algorithms. Plenum Press, 1981.
8. Bauer E. Kohavi R. An empirical comparison of voting classification algorithms: bagging, boosting, and variants. Machine Learning 36 (1999) 105-139.
9. Cheng Y. Church G. Biclustering of expression data. Proc. ISMB-2000, 93-103.
10. Bhattacharjee et al. Classification of human lung carcinomas by mRNA expression profiling reveals distinct adenocarcinoma subclasses. Proc. Natl. Acad. Sci. USA. 2001 Nov. 20;98(24):13790-5.

A SAT-Based Version Space Algorithm for Acquiring Constraint Satisfaction Problems

Christian Bessiere[1], Remi Coletta[1], Frédéric Koriche[1], and Barry O'Sullivan[2]

[1] LIRMM, CNRS / U. Montpellier, Montpellier, France
[2] Cork Constraint Computation Centre, University College Cork, Ireland
{bessiere, coletta, koriche}@lirmm.fr, b.osullivan@4c.ucc.ie

Abstract. Constraint programming is rapidly becoming the technology of choice for modelling and solving complex combinatorial problems. However, users of this technology need significant expertise in order to model their problems appropriately. The lack of availability of such expertise is a significant bottleneck to the broader uptake of constraint technology in the real world. We present a new SAT-based version space algorithm for acquiring constraint satisfaction problems from examples of solutions and non-solutions of a target problem. An important advantage is the ease with which domain-specific knowledge can be exploited using the new algorithm. Finally, we empirically demonstrate the algorithm and the effect of exploiting domain-specific knowledge on improving the quality of the acquired constraint network.

1 Introduction

Over the last thirty years, considerable progress has been made in the field of Constraint Programming (CP), providing a powerful paradigm for solving combinatorial problems. Applications in many areas, such as resource allocation, scheduling, planning and design have been reported in the literature [16]. Informally, the basic idea underlying constraint programming is to model a combinatorial problem as a constraint network, i.e., using a set of variables, a set of domain values and a collection of constraints. Each constraint specifies a restriction on some set of variables. For example, a constraint such as $x_1 \leq x_2$ states that the value assigned to x_1 must be less or equal than the value assigned to x_2. A solution of the constraint network is an assignment of domain values to variables that satisfies every constraint in the network. The Constraint Satisfaction Problem (CSP) is the problem of finding a solution for a given network.

However, the specification of constraint networks still remains limited to specialists in the field. Actually, modelling a combinatorial problem in the constraints formalism requires significant expertise in constraint programming. One of the reasons for this bottleneck stems from the fact that, for any problem at hand, different models of this problem are possible, and two distinct constraint networks that represent the same problem can critically differ on performance. An expert in constraint programming typically knows how to decompose the problem into a set of constraints for which very efficient propagation algorithms have been developed. Such a level of background knowledge precludes novices from being able to use constraint networks on complex problems without the help of an expert. Consequently, this has a negative effect on the uptake of constraint technology in the real world by non-experts.

To alleviate this issue, this paper envisions the possibility of *acquiring* a constraint network from a set of examples and a library of constraints. The constraint acquisition process is regarded as an interaction between a user and a learner. The user has a combinatorial problem in mind, but does not know how this problem can be modelled as an efficient constraint network. Yet, the user has at her disposal a set of solutions (positive examples) and non-solutions (negative examples) for this problem. For its part, the learner has at its disposal a library of constraints for which efficient propagation algorithms are known. The goal for the learner is to induce a constraint network that uses combinations of constraints defined from the library and that is consistent with the solutions and non-solutions provided by the user.

The main contribution of this paper is a SAT-based algorithm, named CONACQ (for CONstraint ACQuisition), that is capable of learning a constraint network from a set of examples and a library of constraints. The algorithm is based on the paradigm of version space learning [11]. In the context of constraint acquisition, a version space can be regarded as the set of all constraint networks defined from the given library that are consistent with the received examples. The key idea underlying the CONACQ algorithm is to consider version-space learning as a satisfiability problem. Namely, any example is encoded as a set of clauses using as atoms the constraint vocabulary defined from the library, and any model of the resulting satisfiability problem captures an admissible constraint network for the corresponding acquisition problem.

This approach has a number of distinct advantages. Firstly and most importantly, the formulation is generic, so we can use any SAT solver as a basis for version space learning. Secondly, we can exploit powerful SAT concepts such as unit propagation and backbone detection [12] to improve learning rate. Thirdly, and finally, we can easily incorporate domain-specific knowledge in constraint programming to improve the quality of the acquired network. Specifically, we develop two generic techniques for handling redundant constraints in constraint acquisition. The first is based on the notion of *redundancy rules*, which can deal with some, but not all, forms of redundancy. The second technique, based on *backbone detection*, is far more powerful.

2 Preliminaries

A constraint network consists of a set of variables, a set of domain values and a set of constraints. We assume that the set of variables and the set of domain values are finite, pre-fixed and known to the learner. This vocabulary is, thus, part of the common knowledge shared between the learner and the user. Furthermore, the learner has at its disposal a constraint library from which it can build and compose constraints. The problem is to find an appropriate combination of constraints that is consistent with the examples provided by the user. Finally, for sake of clarity, we shall assume that every constraint defined from the library is binary. This assumption greatly simplifies the notation used in the paper. Yet, we claim that the results presented here can be easily extended to constraints of higher arity.

More formally, the constraint vocabulary consists of a finite set of variables X and a finite set of domain values D. We implicitly assume that every variable in X uses the same set D of domain values, but this condition can be relaxed in a straightforward way. The cardinalities of X and D are denoted n and d, respectively.

A *binary constraint* is a tuple $c = (var(c), rel(c))$ where $var(c)$ is a pair of variables in X and $rel(c)$ is a binary relation defined on D. The sequence $var(c)$ is called the *scope* of c and the set $rel(c)$ is called the *relation* of c. With a slight abuse of notation, we shall often use c_{ij} to refer to the constraint with relation c defined on the scope (x_i, x_j). For example, $\leq_{12}$ denotes the constraint specified on (x_1, x_2) with relation "less than or equal to". A *binary constraint network* is a set C of binary constraints.

A *constraint library* is a collection B of binary constraints. From a constraint programming point of view, any library B is a set of constraints for which (efficient) propagation algorithms are known. A constraint network C is said to be *admissible* for a library B if for each constraint c_{ij} in C there exists a set of constraints $\{b_{ij}^1, \cdots, b_{ij}^k\}$ in B such that $c_{ij} = b_{ij}^1 \cap \cdots \cap b_{ij}^k$. In other words, a constraint network is admissible for some library if each constraint in the network is defined as the intersection of a set of allowed constraints from the library.

An *example* is a map e that assigns to each variable x in X a domain value $e(x)$ in D. Equivalently, an example e can be regarded as a tuple in D^n. An example e *satisfies* a binary constraint c_{ij} if the pair $(e(x_i), e(x_j))$ is an element of c_{ij}. An example e *satisfies* a constraint network C if e satisfies every constraint in C. If e satisfies C then e is called a *solution* of C; otherwise, e is called a *non-solution* of C. In the following, $sol(C)$ denotes the set of solutions of C.

Finally, a *training set* consists of a pair (E^+, E^-) of sets of examples. Elements of E^+ are called *positive* examples and elements of E^- are called *negative* examples. A constraint network C is said to be *consistent* with a training set (E^+, E^-) if every example in E^+ is a solution of C and every example in E^- is a non-solution of C.

Definition 1 (Constraint Acquisition Problem). *Given a constraint library* B *and a training set* (E^+, E^-), *the* Constraint Acquisition Problem *is to find a constraint network* C *admissible for the library* B *and consistent with the training set* (E^+, E^-).

Example 1. Consider the vocabulary defined by the set $X = \{x_1, x_2, x_3\}$ and the set $D = \{1, 2, 3, 4, 5\}$. In the following, the symbols $\top$ and $\bot$ refer to the total relation and the empty relation over D, respectively. Let B be the constraint library defined as follows: B = $\{\top_{12}, \leq_{12}, \neq_{12}, \geq_{12}, \top_{23}, \leq_{23}, \neq_{23}, \geq_{23}\}$.

Note that the constraints $=_{12}, <_{12}, >_{12}, \bot_{12}$ and $=_{23}, <_{23}, >_{23}, \bot_{23}$ can be derived from the intersection closure of B. Now, consider the two following networks $C_1 = \{\leq_{12} \cap \geq_{12}, \top_{23} \cap \leq_{23} \cap \neq_{23}\}$ and $C_2 = \{\leq_{12} \cap \geq_{12}, \leq_{23} \cap \geq_{23}\}$. Each network is admissible for B. Finally, consider the training set E formed by the three examples $e_1^+ = ((x_1, 2), (x_2, 2), (x_3, 5))$, $e_2^- = ((x_1, 1), (x_2, 3), (x_3, 3))$, and $e_3^-((x_1, 1), (x_2, 1), (x_3, 1))$. The first example is positive and the last two are negative. We can easily observe that C_1 is consistent with E, while C_2 is inconsistent with E.

The following lemma captures an important semantic property of constraint networks. It will be frequently used in the remaining sections.

Lemma 1. *Let* B *be a constraint library,* C *be a constraint network admissible for* B *and e be an example. Then e is a non-solution of* C *iff there exists a pair of constraints* b_{ij} *and* c_{ij} *such that in* $b_{ij} \in$ B, $c_{ij} \in$ C, $c_{ij} \subseteq b_{ij}$ *and e does not satisfy* b_{ij}.

Proof. ($\Rightarrow$) Let us consider that e is a non-solution of C. By definition, there exists a constraint $c_{ij} \in$ C such that e does not satisfy c_{ij}. It follows that the pair $(e(x_i), e(x_j))$ is not an element of c_{ij}. Furthermore, since C is admissible for B, there exists a set $\{b_{ij}^1, \cdots, b_{ij}^k\}$ of constraints in B such that $c_{ij} = b_{ij}^1 \cap \cdots \cap b_{ij}^k$. Consequently, the pair $(e(x_i), e(x_j))$ is not an element of $b_{ij}^1 \cap \cdots \cap b_{ij}^k$. It follows that $(e(x_i), e(x_j))$ is not an element of b_{ij}, for some constraint b_{ij} in the set $\{b_{ij}^1, \cdots, b_{ij}^k\}$. By construction, $c_{ij} \subseteq b_{ij}$. Since e does not satisfy b_{ij}, the result follows.

($\Leftarrow$) Now, let us assume that there exists a pair of constraints b_{ij} and c_{ij} such that in $b_{ij} \in$ B, $c_{ij} \in$ C, $c_{ij} \subseteq b_{ij}$ and e does not satisfy b_{ij}. Obviously, the pair $(e(x_i), e(x_j))$ is not an element of b_{ij}. Since $c_{ij} \subseteq b_{ij}$, it follows that $(e(x_i), e(x_j))$ is not an element of c_{ij}. Therefore, e does not satisfy c_{ij} and hence, e is a non-solution of C. □

3 The CONACQ Algorithm

In this section we present a SAT-based algorithm for acquiring constraint satisfaction problems based on version spaces. Informally, the version space of a constraint acquisition problem is the set of all constraint networks that are admissible for the given library and that are consistent with the given training set. In the SAT-based framework this version space is encoded in a clausal theory, and each model of the theory is a candidate constraint network.

Let B be a constraint library. An *interpretation* over B is a map I that assigns to each constraint atom b_{ij} in B a value $I(b_{ij})$ in $\{0, 1\}$. A *transformation* is a map ϕ that assigns to each interpretation I over B the corresponding constraint network $\phi(I)$ defined according to the following condition:

$$c_{ij} \in \phi(I) \text{ iff } c_{ij} = \bigcap \{b_{i'j'} \in B : i = i', j = j' \text{ and } I(b_{i'j'}) = 1\}.$$

The transformation is not necessarily injective. However, it is surjective: for every network C admissible for B there exists a corresponding interpretation I such that $\phi(I) =$ C. Indeed, for each constraint c_{ij} in C, consider the set of all constraints $\{b_{ij}^1, \cdots, b_{ij}^k\}$ in B such that $c_{ij} = b_{ij}^1 \cap \cdots \cap b_{ij}^k$. Set $I(b_{ij}^1) = \cdots = I(b_{ij}^k) = 1$. Then $\phi(I) =$ C.

A literal is either an atom b_{ij} in B, or its negation $\neg b_{ij}$. Notice that $\neg b_{ij}$ is *not* necessarily a constraint: it merely captures the absence of b_{ij} in the learned network. A clause is a disjunction of literals, and a clausal theory is a conjunction of clauses. An interpretation I is a *model* of a clausal theory K if K is true in I according to the standard propositional semantics. The set of all models of K is denoted $Models(K)$.

The SAT-based formulation of constraint acquisition is presented as Algorithm 1. The algorithm starts from the empty theory (line 1) and iteratively builds a set of clauses for each received example (lines 2-6). The resulting theory encodes all candidate networks for the constraint acquisition problem.

This result is formalised in the next theorem. Let B be a constraint library and (E^+, E^-) be a training set. Then the *version space* of (E^+, E^-) with respect to B, denoted $V_B(E^+, E^-)$, is the set of all constraint networks that are admissible for B and that are consistent with (E^+, E^-).

Algorithm 1. The CONACQ Algorithm

    input   : a training set (E^+, E^-) and a constraint library B
    output : a set of clauses K
1 K ← ∅
2 **foreach** *training example e* **do**
3       $\kappa_e \leftarrow \{b_{ij} \in B : e \text{ does not satisfy } b_{ij}\}$
4   **if** $e \in E^-$ **then** K ← K $\wedge$ ($\bigvee_{b_{ij} \in \kappa_e} b_{ij}$)
5   **if** $e \in E^+$ **then** K ← K $\wedge \bigwedge_{b_{ij} \in \kappa_e} \neg b_{ij}$
6   **if** *UnitPropagation*(K) *detects* ⊥ **then** Return(*"collapsing"*)

Theorem 1 (Correctness). *Let* (E^+, E^-) *be a training set and* B *be a library. Let* K *be the clausal theory returned by* CONACQ *with* B *and* (E^+, E^-) *as input. Then*

$$V_B(E^+, E^-) = \{\phi(I) : I \in Models(K)\}.$$

Proof. (⇒) Let C be a candidate network in $V_B(E^+, E^-)$. Since ϕ is surjective, there exists an interpretation I such that $\phi(I) = C$. Suppose that I is not a model of K. We show that this leads to a contradiction. If I is not a model of K then there is at least one example e in the training set such that I falsifies the set of clauses generated from e. Since e is either positive or negative, two cases must be considered. First, suppose that $e \in E^+$. In this case, $I(b_{ij}) = 1$ for at least one atom b_{ij} in κ_e, the set of literals encoding e. By construction of $\phi(I)$, there must exist a constraint c_{ij} in C such that c_{ij} is contained in b_{ij}. By Lemma 1, e is a non-solution of C and hence, C cannot be a member of $V_B(E^+, E^-)$. Now, suppose that $e \in E^-$. By construction, $I(b_{ij}) = 0$ for each $b_{ij} \in \kappa_e$. Therefore, there is no constraint $c_{ij} \in C$ contained in some b_{ij} such that b_{ij} rejects e. By contraposition of Lemma 1, e is a solution of C and hence, C cannot be a member of $V_B(E^+, E^-)$.

(⇐) Let I be a model of K and C be $\phi(I)$. Assume that C is not in $V_B(E^+, E^-)$. We show that this leads to a contradiction. Obviously, C must be inconsistent with at least one example e in the training set. Again, two cases must be considered. Suppose that $e \in E^+$. Since e is a non-solution of C then, by Lemma 1, there exists a pair of constraints $b_{ij} \in B$ and $c_{ij} \in C$ such that $c_{ij} \subseteq b_{ij}$ and e does not satisfy b_{ij}. By construction, $I(b_{ij}) = 1$. It follows that, I is not a model of $\bigwedge_{b_{ij} \in \kappa_e} \neg b_{ij}$. Therefore, I cannot be a model of K. Now, suppose that $e \in E^-$. Since e is a solution of C then, by contraposition of Lemma 1, there is no pair of constraints $b_{ij} \in B$ and $c_{ij} \in C$ such that $c_{ij} \subseteq b_{ij}$ and e does not satisfy b_{ij}. Therefore, $I(b_{ij}) = 0$ for each b_{ij} in B that rejects e. It follows that I is not a model of $\bigvee_{b_{ij} \in \kappa_e} b_{ij}$. Hence, I cannot be a model of C. □

The CONACQ algorithm provides an implicit representation of the version space of the constraint acquisition problem. This representation allows the learner to perform several useful operations in polynomial time. We conclude this section by examining the complexity of these operations. In the following, we consider a library B containing b constraints and a training set (E^+, E^-) containing m examples.

A version space has *collapsed* if it is empty. In other words, there is no constraint network C admissible for B such that C is consistent with the training set (E^+, E^-).

Proposition 1 (Collapse). *The* collapsing *test takes* $\mathcal{O}(bm)$ *time.*

Proof. Based on Theorem 1, we know that $V_B(E^+, E^-)$ is empty iff K is unsatisfiable. The size of κ_e is upper bounded by b. Then, the size of K is bounded by mb. By construction, K is a *dual Horn formula* where each clause contains at most one negative literal. In this setting, unit propagation, which requires $\mathcal{O}(K)$ time, is enough to determine whether K is satisfiable or not [3]. Therefore, the collapsing test can be done in $\mathcal{O}(bm)$ time. □

The *membership* test involves checking whether or not a constraint network belongs to the version space of the problem.

Proposition 2 (Membership). *The* membership *test takes* $\mathcal{O}(bm)$ *time.*

Proof. Let C be a constraint network and I an interpretation such that $C = \phi(I)$. Based on Theorem 1, determining whether C belongs to $V_B(E^+, E^-)$ is equivalent to determining whether I is a model of K. Since the size of K is bounded by mb, the membership test takes $\mathcal{O}(bm)$ time. □

The *update* operation involves computing a new version space once a new example e has been added to the training set.

Proposition 3 (Update). *The* update *operation takes* $\mathcal{O}(b)$ *time.*

Proof. Checking whether a binary constraint is satisfied or violated by an example e is $\mathcal{O}(1)$. The number of such checks is bounded by b (line 3 of Algorithm 1). □

Consider a pair of training sets (E_1^+, E_1^-) and (E_2^+, E_2^-), and their corresponding version spaces $V_B(E_1^+, E_1^-)$ and $V_B(E_2^+, E_2^-)$. The *intersection* operation requires computing the version space $V_B(E_1^+, E_1^-) \cap V_B(E_2^+, E_2^-)$. In the following, we assume that (E_1^+, E_1^-) and (E_2^+, E_2^-) contain m_1 and m_2 examples, respectively.

Proposition 4 (Intersection). *The* intersection *operation takes* $\mathcal{O}(b(m_1 + m_2))$ *time.*

Proof. Let K_1 and K_2 be the representations of the version spaces $V_B(E_1^+, E_1^-)$ and $V_B(E_2^+, E_2^-)$, respectively. In the SAT-based framework, the representation of the version space $V_B(E_1^+, E_1^-) \cap V_B(E_2^+, E_2^-)$ is simply obtained by $K_1 \wedge K_2$. □

Finally, given a pair of training sets (E_1^+, E_1^-) and (E_2^+, E_2^-), and their corresponding version spaces $V_B(E_1^+, E_1^-)$ and $V_B(E_2^+, E_2^-)$, we may wish to determine whether $V_B(E_1^+, E_1^-)$ is a *subset* of (resp. *equal* to) $V_B(E_2^+, E_2^-)$.

Proposition 5 (Subset and Equality). *The* subset *and* equality *tests take* $\mathcal{O}(b^2 m_1 m_2)$ *time.*

Proof. Let K_1 and K_2 be the representations of the version spaces $V_\mathsf{B}(E_1^+, E_1^-)$ and $V_\mathsf{B}(E_2^+, E_2^-)$, respectively. Based on Theorem 1, we know that determining whether $V_\mathsf{B}(E_1^+, E_1^-)$ is a subset of $V_\mathsf{B}(E_2^+, E_2^-)$ is equivalent to deciding whether $Models(\mathsf{K}_1)$ is a subset of $Models(\mathsf{K}_2)$. This is equivalent to deciding whether K_1 entails K_2. By application of Lemma 5.6.1 from [9], the entailment problem of two Horn or dual Horn formulas K_1 and K_2 can be decided in $\mathcal{O}(|\mathsf{K}_1||\mathsf{K}_2|)$ time. It follows that the subset operation takes $\mathcal{O}(b^2 m_1 m_2)$ time. For the equality operation, we simply need to check whether K_1 entails K_2 and K_2 entails K_1. □

4 Exploiting Domain-Specific Knowledge

In constraint programming, constraints can be interdependent. For example, two constraints such as $\geq_{12}$ and $\geq_{23}$ impose a restriction on the relation of any constraint defined on the scope (x_1, x_3). This is a crucial difference with propositional logic where atomic variables are pairwise independent. As a consequence of such interdependency, some constraints in a network can be *redundant*. For example, the constraint $\geq_{13}$ is redundant with $\geq_{12}$ and $\geq_{23}$. An important difficulty for the learner is its ability to "detect" redundant constraints. This problem is detailed in the following example.

Example 2. Consider a vocabulary formed by a set of variables $\{x_1, x_2, x_3\}$ and a set of domain values $D = \{1, 2, 3, 4\}$. The learner has at its disposal the constraint library $\mathsf{B} = \{\top_{12}, \leq_{12}, \neq_{12}, \geq_{12}, \top_{23}, \leq_{23}, \neq_{23}, \geq_{23}, \top_{13}, \leq_{13}, \neq_{13}, \geq_{13}\}$. We suppose that the target network is given by $\{\geq_{12}, \geq_{13}, \geq_{23}\}$. The training set is given in Table 1. In the third column of the table, we present the growing clausal theory K obtained after processing each example and after performing unit propagation.

After processing each example in the training set, the constraints $\geq_{12}$ and $\geq_{23}$ have been found. Yet, the redundant constraint $\geq_{13}$ has not. For the scope (x_1, x_3) the version space contains four possible networks where c_{13} can alternatively be $>_{13}, \geq_{13}, \neq_{13}$ or $\top_{13}$. In fact, the version space cannot converge to the target concept since it is impossible to find a set of negative examples which would force the learner to reduce its version space. Indeed, in order to converge we would need a negative example e where $e(x_1) < e(x_3)$, $e(x_1) \geq e(x_2)$ and $e(x_2) \geq e(x_3)$. Due to the semantics of inequality constraints, no such example exists. Consequently, the inability for the learner to detect redundancy may hinder the converge process and hence, can overestimate the number of candidate models in the version space.

As illustrated in the previous example, redundancy is a crucial notion that must be carefully handled if we need to allow version space convergence, or at least if we want to

Table 1. A set of examples and the corresponding set of clauses K (unit propagated), illustrating the effect of redundancy

	x_1	x_2	x_3	K
e_1^+	4	3	1	$(\neg \leq_{12}) \wedge (\neg \leq_{13}) \wedge (\neg \leq_{23})$
e_2^-	2	3	1	$(\neg \leq_{12}) \wedge (\neg \leq_{13}) \wedge (\neg \leq_{23}) \wedge (\geq_{12})$
e_3^-	3	1	2	$(\neg \leq_{12}) \wedge (\neg \leq_{13}) \wedge (\neg \leq_{23}) \wedge (\geq_{12}) \wedge (\geq_{23})$

have a more accurate idea of which parts of the target network are not precisely learned. The notion of redundancy is formalised as follows. Let C be a constraint network and c_{ij} a constraint in C. We say that c_{ij} is *redundant* in C if $sol(C \setminus \{c_{ij}\}) = sol(C)$. In other words, c_{ij} is redundant if the constraint network obtained by deleting c_{ij} from C is equivalent to C.

4.1 Redundancy Rules

Any binary constraint b_{ij} can be seen as a first-order atom $b(x_i, x_j)$, where b is a predicate symbol and x_i, x_j are variables that take values in the domain D. For example, the constraint $\leq_{12}$ can be regarded as a first-order atom $x_1 \leq x_2$. From this perspective, a constraint network can be viewed as a conjunction of first-order binary atoms. In order to tackle redundancy, we may introduce first-order rules that convey some knowledge about dependencies between constraints. A *redundancy rule* is a Horn clause:

$$\forall x_1, x_2, x_3, b(x_1, x_2) \wedge b'(x_2, x_3) \rightarrow b''(x_1, x_3).$$

such that for any constraint network C for which a substitution θ maps $b(x_1, x_2)$, $b'(x_2, x_3)$ and $b''(x_1, x_3)$ into in C, the constraint $b''_{\theta(x_1)\theta(x_3)}$ is redundant in C.

As a form of background knowledge, the learner can use redundancy rules in its acquisition process. Given a library of constraints B and a set R of redundancy rules, the learner can start building each possible substitution on R. Namely, for each rule $b(x_1, x_2) \wedge b'(x_2, x_3) \rightarrow b''(x_1, x_3)$ and each substitution θ that maps $b(x_1, x_2)$, $b'(x_2, x_3)$, and $b''(x_1, x_3)$ to constraints b_{ij}, b'_{jk} and b''_{ik} in the library, a clause $\neg b_{ij} \vee \neg b'_{jk} \vee b''_{ik}$ can be added to the clausal theory K.

Example 3. The Horn clause $\forall x, y, z, (x \geq y) \wedge (y \geq z) \rightarrow (x \geq z)$ is a redundancy rule since any constraint network in which we have two constraints '$\geq$' such that the second argument of the first constraint is equal to the first argument of the second constraint implies the '$\geq$' constraint between the first argument of the first constraint and the second argument of the second constraint.

We can apply the redundancy rule technique to Example 2. After performing unit propagation on the clausal theory K obtained after processing the examples $\{e_1^+, e_2^-, e_3^-\}$, we know that $\geq_{12}$ and $\geq_{23}$ have to be set to 1. When instantiated on this constraint network, the redundancy rule from Example 3 becomes $\geq_{12} \wedge \geq_{23} \rightarrow \geq_{13}$. Since all literals of the left part of the rule are forced by K to be true, we can fix literal $\geq_{13}$ to 1.

The tractability of CONACQ depends on the fact that the clausal theory K is a dual Horn formula. While we are no longer left with such a formula once K is combined with the set of redundancy rules R, it is nonetheless the case that satisfiability testing for $K \wedge R$ remains tractable: $K \wedge R$ is satisfiable iff K is. The only effect that redundancy rules have is to give an equivalent, but potentially smaller version space for the target network.

4.2 Backbone Detection

While redundancy rules can handle a particular type of redundancy, there are cases where applying these rules on the version space is not sufficient to find all redundancies.

Specifically, redundancy rules are only able to discover implications of "conjunctions" of constraints. However, more complex forms of redundancies can arise due to combinations of "conjunctions" and "disjunctions" of constraints. This higher-order form of redundancy is illustrated in the following example.

Example 4. Consider the example in Table 2 where the target network comprises the set of constraints $\{=_{12}, =_{13}, =_{23}\}$ and all negative examples differ from the single positive example by *at least* two constraints. The version space in this example contains 4 possible constraints for each scope, due to the disjunction of possible reasons that would classify the negative examples correctly. Without any further information, particularly negative examples which differ from the positive example by one constraint, redundancy rules cannot restrict the version space any further.

Table 2. A set of examples and the corresponding set of clauses K (unit propagated), illustrating the effect of higher-order redundancy

	x_1 x_2 x_3	K
e_1^+	2 2 2	$(\neg \neq_{12}) \wedge (\neg \neq_{13}) \wedge (\neg \neq_{23})$
e_2^-	3 3 4	$(\neg \neq_{12}) \wedge (\neg \neq_{13}) \wedge (\neg \neq_{23}) \wedge (\geq_{13} \vee \geq_{23})$
e_3^-	1 3 3	$(\neg \neq_{12}) \wedge (\neg \neq_{13}) \wedge (\neg \neq_{23}) \wedge (\geq_{13} \vee \geq_{23}) \wedge (\geq_{12} \vee \geq_{13})$

In Example 4, there is a constraint that is implied by the set of negative examples but redundancy rules are not able to detect it. However, all the information necessary to deduce this constraint is contained in the set of redundancy rules and K. The reason for their inability to detect it is that the redundancy rules are in the form of Horn clauses that are applied only when *all* literals in the left-hand side are true (i.e., unit propagation is performed on these clauses). However, the powerful concept of *backbone* of a propositional formula can be used here. Informally, a literal belongs to the backbone of a formula if it belongs to all models of the formula [12]. Once the literals in the backbone are detected, they can be exploited to update the version space.

If an atom b_{ij} appears positively in all models of K ∧ R, then it belongs to its backbone and we can deduce that $c_{ij} \subseteq b_{ij}$. Indeed, by construction of K ∧ R, the constraint c_{ij} cannot reject all negative examples in E^- and, at the same time, be more general than b_{ij}. Thus, given a new negative example e in E^-, we simply need to build the corresponding clause κ_e, add it to K, and test if the addition of κ_e causes some literal to enter the backbone of K ∧ R. The process above guarantees that all the possible redundancies will be detected.

Example 5. We now apply this method to Example 4. To test if the literal $\geq_{13}$ belongs to the backbone, we solve R ∪ K ∪ $\{\neg \geq_{13}\}$. If the redundancy rule $\geq_{12} \wedge \geq_{23} \rightarrow \geq_{13}$ belongs to R, we detect inconsistency. Therefore, $\geq_{13}$ belongs to the backbone. The version space can now be refined, by setting the literal $\geq_{13}$ to 1, effectively removing from the version space the constraint networks containing $\leq_{13}$ or $\top_{13}$.

5 Experiments

We have performed several experiments in order to validate the effectiveness of the CONACQ algorithm and the various approaches to exploiting domain-specific knowledge presented in Section 4. We implemented CONACQ using SAT4J.[1] For each experiment, the vocabulary contains 12 variables and 12 domain values per variable. The target constraint networks are sets of binary constraints defined from the set of relations $\{\leq, \neq, \geq\}$. The learner is not informed about the scope of the constraints, so the available library involves all 66 possible binary constraint scopes. The level of dependency between constraints is controlled by introducing constraint "patterns" of various lengths and type. Patterns are paths of the same constraint selected either from the set $\{\leq, \geq\}$ (looser constraints) or $\{<, =, >\}$ (tighter constraints). For example, a pattern of length k based on $\{<, =, >\}$ could be $x_1 > x_2 > \ldots > x_k$. Based on the parameter k and the type of constraint, we examined 7 types of target networks. In the first, the variables were connected arbitrarily. In the others, we introduce a single pattern of length $n/3, n/2$ or n, with constraints taken from either $\{\leq, \geq\}$ or $\{<, =, >\}$. The remaining constraints in the problem were selected randomly.

We ran 100 experiments of each type and report average results in Table 3. The first column specifies the length and type of allowed patterns. The three next columns report the results obtained by the basic algorithm (CONACQ), the algorithm with redundancy rules (CONACQ + $rules$), and the algorithm with redundancy rules and backbone detection (CONACQ +$rules$ + $backbone$). Each column is divided in two parts. The left part is the number of models of the formula K. This number is obtained using the binary decision diagram compilation tool CLab[2] when $|V_B|$ is smaller than 10^4. An estimate, exponential in the number of free literals in K, is presented otherwise. From Theorem 1, this corresponds to the number of candidate networks encoded in the version space for the acquired problem. The right part measures the average time needed to process an example in seconds on a Pentium IV 1.8 GHz processor. Finally, the last column reports the number of examples needed to obtain convergence of at least one of the algorithms. The threshold on the number of possible examples is fixed to 1000. The training set contains 10% of positive examples and 90% of negative examples. We chose such an unbalanced proportion because positive examples are usually much less frequent than negative ones in a constraint network. Negative examples were *partial* non-solutions to the problem involving a subset of variables. The cardinality of this subset was selected from a uniform distribution over the interval $[2, 5]$.

Based on these results, we can make several important observations. Firstly, we note that the rate of convergence improves if we exploit domain-specific knowledge. In particular, the variant of CONACQ using redundancy rules and backbone detection is able to eliminate all redundant networks in all experiments with patterns. In contrast, the performance of the first two algorithms decreases as the length of redundant patterns increases. This is clearly noticeable, in the case of the basic algorithm, if one compares the top-line of the table, where no redundant pattern was enforced, with the last line in the table, where a pattern of length n was present, keeping the number of

---

[1] Available from http://www.sat4j.org.
[2] Available from http://www-2.cs.cmu.edu/~runej/systems/clab10.html.

Table 3. Comparison of the CONACQ variants (CSPs have 12 variables, 12 values, 18 constraints)

Redundant Pattern		CONACQ	CONACQ +rules	CONACQ +rules +backbone	
Length {constraints}		$\|V_B\|(secs)$	$\|V_B\|(secs)$	$\|V_B\|(secs)$	#Exs
none		4.29×10^9 (0.11)	6.71×10^7 (0.32)	1.68×10^7 (2.67)	1000
n/3	$\{\leq, \geq\}$	4.10×10^3 (0.11)	64 (0.31)	1 (2.61)	360
n/2	$\{\leq, \geq\}$	1.72×10^{10} (0.11)	4.10×10^3 (0.32)	1 (2.57)	190
n	$\{\leq, \geq\}$	1.44×10^{17} (0.11)	2.62×10^5 (0.32)	1 (2.54)	90
n/3	$\{<, =, >\}$	2.68×10^8 (0.11)	1.02×10^3 (0.32)	1 (2.60)	280
n/2	$\{<, =, >\}$	7.38×10^{19} (0.11)	4.19×10^7 (0.32)	1 (2.58)	170
n	$\{<, =, >\}$	2.08×10^{34} (0.11)	6.87×10^{10} (0.32)	1 (2.54)	70
n	$\{<, =, >\}$	9.01×10^{15} (0.11)	2.04×10^4 (0.32)	1 (0.24)	1000

examples constant in both cases. When no redundant pattern was enforced, simply combining redundancy rules with CONACQ is sufficient to detect much of the redundancy that is completely discovered by backbone detection. Secondly, we observe that for patterns involving tighter constraints ($<$, $=$, or $>$), significantly better improvements are obtained as we employ increasingly powerful techniques for exploiting redundancy. Thirdly, we observe that the learning time progressively increases with the sophistication of the method used. The basic CONACQ algorithm is about 3 times faster than CONACQ+ $rules$ and 25 times faster than CONACQ+$rules + backbone$. Clearly, there is a tradeoff to be considered between learning rate and learning time.

6 Related Work

Recently, researchers have become interested in techniques that can be used to acquire constraint networks in situations where a precise statement of the constraints of the problem is not available [4, 10, 14, 15]. The use of version space learning as a basis for constraint acquisition has received most attention from the constraints community [1, 2, 13]. Version space learning [11] is a standard approach to concept learning. A variety of representations for version spaces have been proposed in an effort to overcome the worst-case exponential complexity of version space learning [5–8].

The approach we propose is quite novel with respect to the existing literature on both constraint acquisition and version space learning. We formalise version space learning as a satisfiability problem, which has the advantage of being able to exploit advances in SAT solvers, backbone detection, and unit propagation, to dramatically enhance learning rate. However, it is incorporating domain-specific knowledge into the acquisition process that gives the approach considerable power.

7 Conclusions

Users of constraint programming technology need significant expertise in order to model their problems appropriately. In this paper we have proposed a SAT-based version space algorithm that is capable of learning a constraint network from a set of examples and a library of constraints. This approach has a number of distinct advantages. Firstly, the formulation is generic, so we can use any SAT solver as a basis for version space learning. Secondly, we can exploit efficient SAT techniques such as unit propagation and backbone detection to improve learning rate. Finally, we can easily incorporate domain-specific knowledge into constraint programming to improve the quality of the acquired network. Our empirical evaluation convincingly demonstrated the power of exploiting domain-specific knowledge as part of the acquisition process.

Acknowledgments. This work was supported by a Ulysses Travel Grant from Enterprise Ireland, the Royal Irish Academy and CNRS (Grant Number FR/2003/022). This work also received support from Science Foundation Ireland under Grant 00/PI.1/C075.

References

1. C. Bessiere, R. Coletta, E.C. Freuder, and B. O'Sullivan. Leveraging the learning power of examples in automated constraint acquisition. In *Proceedings of CP-2004*, LNCS 3258, pages 123–137. Springer, 2004.
2. R. Coletta, C. Bessiere, B. O'Sullivan, E.C. Freuder, S. O'Connell, and J. Quinqueton. Constraint acquisition as semi-automatic modeling. In *Proc. of AI'03*, pages 111–124, 2003.
3. W. F. Dowling and J. H. Gallier. Linear-time algorithms for testing the satisfiability of propositional horn formulae. *Journal of Logic Programming*, 1(3):267–284, 1984.
4. E.C. Freuder and R.J. Wallace. Suggestion strategies for constraint-based matchmaker agents. In *Proceedings of CP-1998*, LNCS 1520, pages 192–204, October 1998.
5. D. Haussler. Quantifying inductive bias: AI learning algorithms and Valiant's learning framework. *Artificial Intelligence*, 36(2):177–221, 1988.
6. H. Hirsh. Polynomial-time learning with version spaces. In *Proceedings of AAAI-92*, pages 117–122, 1992.
7. H. Hirsh, N. Mishra, and L. Pitt. Version spaces without boundary sets. In *Proceedings AAAI-97*, pages 491–496, 1997.
8. H. Hirsh, N. Mishra, and L. Pitt. Version spaces and the consistency problem. *Artificial Intelligence*, 156(2):115–138, 2004.
9. H. Kleine Büning and T. Lettmann. *Propositional Logic: Deduction and Algorithms*. Cambridge University Press, 1999.
10. A. Lallouet, A. Legtchenko, E. Monfroy, and A. Ed-Dbali. Solver learning for predicting changes in dynamic constraint satisfaction problems. In *Changes'04*, 2004.
11. T. Mitchell. Generalization as search. *Artificial Intelligence*, 18(2):203–226, 1982.
12. R. Monasson, R. Zecchina, S. Kirkpatrick, B. Selman, and L. Ttroyansky. Determining computational complexity from characteristic 'phase transition'. *Nature*, 400:133–137, 1999.
13. B. O'Sullivan, E.C. Freuder, and S. O'Connell. Interactive constraint acquisition – position paper. In *Workshop on User-Interaction in Constraint Satisfaction*, pages 73–81, 2001.
14. S. Padmanabhuni, J.-H. You, and A. Ghose. A framework for learning constraints. In *Proceedings of the PRICAI Workshop on Induction of Complex Representations*, August 1996.
15. F. Rossi and A. Sperduti. Acquiring both constraint and solution preferences in interactive constraint systems. *Constraints*, 9(4):311–332, 2004.
16. M. Wallace. Practical applications of constraint programming. *Constraints*, 1(1–2):139–168, 1996.

Estimation of Mixture Models Using Co-EM

Steffen Bickel and Tobias Scheffer

Humboldt-Universität zu Berlin, School of Computer Science,
Unter den Linden 6, 10099 Berlin, Germany
{bickel, scheffer}@informatik.hu-berlin.de

Abstract. We study estimation of mixture models for problems in which multiple views of the instances are available. Examples of this setting include clustering web pages or research papers that have intrinsic (text) and extrinsic (references) attributes. Our optimization criterion quantifies the likelihood and the consensus among models in the individual views; maximizing this consensus minimizes a bound on the risk of assigning an instance to an incorrect mixture component. We derive an algorithm that maximizes this criterion. Empirically, we observe that the resulting clustering method incurs a lower cluster entropy than regular EM for web pages, research papers, and many text collections.

1 Introduction

In many application domains, instances can be represented in two or more distinct, redundant views. For instance, web pages can be represented by their text, or by the anchor text of inbound hyperlinks ("miserable failure"), and research papers can be represented by their references from and to other papers, in addition to their content. In this case, multi-view methods such as co-training [7] can learn two initially independent hypotheses. These hypotheses bootstrap by providing each other with conjectured class labels for unlabeled data. Multi-view learning has often proven to utilize unlabeled data effectively, increase the accuracy of classifiers (*e.g.,* [20, 7]) and improve the quality of clusterings [4].

Nigam and Ghani [17] propose the co-EM procedure that resembles semi-supervised learning with EM [15], using two views that alternate after each iteration. The EM algorithm [12] is very well understood. In each iteration, it maximizes the expected joint log-likelihood of visible and invisible parameters given the parameter estimates of the previous iteration—the Q function. This procedure is known to greedily maximize the likelihood of the data. By contrast, the primary justification of the co-EM algorithm is that it often works very well; it is not known which criterion the method maximizes.

We take a top down approach on the problem of mixture model estimation in a multi-view setting. Dasgupta et al. [10] motivate our work by showing that a high consensus of independent hypotheses implies a low error rate. We construct a criterion that quantifies likelihood and consensus and derive a procedure that maximizes it. We contribute to an understanding of mixture model estimation for multiple views by showing that the co-EM algorithm is a special case of the resulting procedure. Our solution naturally generalizes co-EM because it operates on more than two views. We show that a variant of the method in which the consensus term is annealed over time is guaranteed to converge.

The rest of this paper is organized as follows. Section 2 discusses related work. In Section 3, we define the problem setting. Section 4 motivates our approach, discusses the new Q function, the unsupervised co-EM algorithm, and its instantiation for mixture of multinomials. We conduct experiments in Section 5 and conclude with Section 6.

2 Related Work

Most studies on multi-view learning address semi-supervised classification problems. de Sa [11] observes a relationship between consensus of multiple hypotheses and their error rate and devised a semi-supervised learning method by cascading multi-view vector quantization and linear classification. A multi-view approach to word sense disambiguation combines a classifier that refers to the local context of a word with a second classifier that utilizes the document in which words co-occur [20]. Blum and Mitchell [7] introduce the co-training algorithm for semi-supervised learning that greedily augments the training set of two classifiers. A version of the AdaBoost algorithm boosts the agreement between two views on unlabeled data [9]. Co-training for regression is proposed by Zhou and Li [22].

Dasgupta et al. [10] and Abney [1] give PAC bounds on the error of co-training in terms of the disagreement rate of hypotheses on unlabeled data in two independent views. This justifies the direct minimization of the disagreement. The co-EM algorithm for semi-supervised learning probabilistically labels all unlabeled examples and iteratively exchanges those labels between two views [17,13]. Muslea et al. [16] extend co-EM for active learning. Brefeld and Scheffer [8] study a co-EM wrapper for the Support Vector Machine.

For unsupervised learning, several methods combine models that are learned using distinct attribute subsets in a way that encourages agreement. Becker and Hinton [3] maximize mutual information between the output of neural network modules that perceive distinct views of the data. Models of images and their textual annotations have been combined [2,6]. Bickel and Scheffer [4] use the co-EM algorithm for clustering of data with two views. Clustering by maximizing the dependency between views is studied by Sinkkonen et al. [18]. Also, the density-based DBSCAN clustering algorithm has a multi-view counterpart [14].

3 Problem Setting

The *multi-view* setting is characterized by available attributes X which are decomposed into views $X^{(1)}, \ldots, X^{(s)}$. An instance $x = (x^{(1)}, \ldots, x^{(s)})$ has representations $x^{(v)}$ that are vectors over $X^{(v)}$. We focus on the problem of estimating parameters of a generative mixture model in which data are generated as follows.

The *data generation process* selects a mixture component j with probability α_j. Mixture component j is the value of a random variable Z. Once j is fixed, the generation process draws the s independent vectors $x^{(v)}$ according to the likelihoods $P(x^{(v)}|j)$. The likelihoods $P(x^{(v)}|j)$ are assumed to follow a parametric model $P(x^{(v)}|j, \Theta)$ (distinct views may of course be governed by distinct distributional models).

The *learning task* involved is to estimate the parameters $\Theta = (\Theta^{(1)}, \ldots, \Theta^{(s)})$ from data. The *sample* consists of n observations that usually contain only the visible attributes $x_i^{(v)}$ in all views v of the instances x_i. The vector Θ contains priors $\alpha_j^{(v)}$ and parameters of the likelihood $P(x_i^{(v)}|j, \Theta^{(v)})$, where $1 \leq j \leq m$ and m is the number of mixture components assumed by the model (clusters). Given Θ, we will be able to calculate a posterior $P(j|x^{(1)}, \ldots, x^{(s)}, \Theta)$. This posterior will allow us to assign a cluster membership to any instance $x = (x^{(1)}, \ldots, x^{(s)})$. The *evaluation metric* is the impurity of the resulting clusters as measured by the entropy; the elements of each identified cluster should originate from the same true mixture component.

4 Derivation of the Algorithm

Dasgupta et al. [10] have studied the relation between the consensus among two independent hypotheses and their error rate. Let us review a very simple result that motivates our approach, it can easily be derived from their general treatment of the topic. Let $h^{(v)}(x) = \text{argmax}_j P(j|x^{(v)}, \Theta^{(v)})$ be two independent clustering hypotheses in views $v = 1, 2$. For clarity of the presentation, let there be two true mixture components. Let x be a randomly drawn instance that, without loss of generality belongs to mixture component 1, and let both hypotheses $h^{(1)}$ and $h^{(2)}$ have a probability of at least 50% of assigning x to the correct cluster 1. We observe that

$$P(h^{(1)}(x) \neq h^{(2)}(x)) \geq \max_v P(h^{(v)}(x) \neq 1).$$

That is, the probability of a disagreement $h^{(1)}(x) \neq h^{(2)}(x)$ is an upper bound on the risk of an error $P(h^{(v)}(x) \neq 1)$ of either hypothesis $h^{(v)}$.

We give a brief *proof* of this observation. In Equation 1 we distinguish between the two possible cases of disagreement; we utilize the independence assumption and order the summands such that the greater one comes first. In Equation 2, we exploit that the error rate be at most 50%: both hypotheses are less likely to be wrong than just one of them. This leads to Equation 3.

$$\begin{aligned}
&P(h^{(1)}(x) \neq h^{(2)}(x)) \\
&= P(h^{(v)}(x) = 1, h^{(\bar{v})}(x) = 2) + P(h^{(v)}(x) = 2, h^{(\bar{v})}(x) = 1) \quad (1)\\
&\quad \text{where } v = \text{argmax}_u P(h^{(u)}(x) = 1, h^{(\bar{u})}(x) = 2) \\
&\geq P(h^{(v)}(x) = 2, h^{(\bar{v})}(x) = 2) + P(h^{(v)}(x) = 2, h^{(\bar{v})}(x) = 1) \quad (2)\\
&= \max_v P(h^{(v)}(x) \neq 1) \quad (3)
\end{aligned}$$

In unsupervised learning, the risk of assigning instances to wrong mixture components cannot be minimized directly, but this argument shows that we can minimize an upper bound on this risk by minimmizing the disagreement of multiple hypotheses.

The Q function is the core of the EM algorithm. We will now review the usual definition, include a consensus term, and find a maximization procedure.

4.1 Single-View Criterion

Even though the goal is to maximize $P(X|\Theta)$, EM iteratively maximizes an auxiliary (single-view) criterion $Q^{SV}(\Theta, \Theta_t)$. The criterion refers to the visible variables X, the invisibles Z (the mixture component), the optimization parameter Θ and the parameter estimates Θ_t of the last iteration. Equation 4 defines $Q^{SV}(\Theta, \Theta_t)$ to be the expected log-likelihood of $P(X, Z|\Theta)$, given X and given that the hidden mixture component Z be distributed according to $P(j|x, \Theta_t)$.

The criterion $Q^{SV}(\Theta, \Theta_t)$ can be determined as in Equation 5 for mixture models. It requires calculation of the posterior $P(j|x_i, \Theta_t)$ as in Equation 6; this is referred to as the E step of the EM algorithm. In the M step, it finds the new parameters $\Theta_{t+1} = \text{argmax}_\Theta Q^{SV}(\Theta, \Theta_t)$ that maximize Q^{SV} over Θ. The parameters Θ occur in Equation 5 only in the prior probabilities α_j and likelihood terms $P(x_i|j, \Theta)$.

$$Q^{SV}(\Theta, \Theta_t) = E[\log P(X, Z|\Theta)|X, \Theta_t] \qquad (4)$$

$$= \sum_{i=1}^{n} \sum_{j=1}^{m} P(j|x_i, \Theta_t) \log(\alpha_j P(x_i|j, \Theta)) \qquad (5)$$

$$P(j|x_i, \Theta_t) = \frac{\alpha_j P(x_i|j, \Theta_t)}{\sum_k \alpha_k P(x_i|k, \Theta_t)} \qquad (6)$$

The EM algorithm starts with some initial guess at the parameters Θ_0 and alternates E and M steps until convergence. Dempster et al. [12] prove that, in each iteration, $P(X|\Theta_{t+1}) - P(X|\Theta_t) \geq 0$. Wu [19] furthermore proves conditions for the convergence of the sequence of parameters $(\Theta)_t$.

4.2 Multi-view Criterion

We want to maximize the likelihood in the individual views and the consensus of the models because we know that the disagreement bounds the risk of assigning an instance to an incorrect mixture component. Equations 7 and 8 define our *multi-view Q function* as the sum over s single-view Q functions minus a penalty term $\Delta(\cdot)$ that quantifies the disagreement of the models $\Theta^{(v)}$, regularized by η.

$$Q^{MV}(\Theta^{(1)}, \ldots, \Theta^{(s)}, \Theta_t^{(1)}, \ldots, \Theta_t^{(s)})$$

$$= \sum_{v=1}^{s} Q^{SV}(\Theta^{(v)}, \Theta_t^{(v)}) - \eta \Delta(\Theta^{(1)}, \ldots, \Theta^{(s)}, \Theta_t^{(1)}, \ldots, \Theta_t^{(s)}) \qquad (7)$$

$$= \sum_{v=1}^{s} E\left[\log P(X^{(v)}, Z^{(v)}|\Theta^{(v)})|X^{(v)}, \Theta_t^{(v)}\right] \qquad (8)$$

$$- \eta \Delta(\Theta^{(1)}, \ldots, \Theta^{(s)}, \Theta_t^{(1)}, \ldots, \Theta_t^{(s)})$$

When the regularization parameter η is zero, then $Q^{MV} = \sum_v Q^{SV}$. In each step, co-EM then maximizes the s terms Q^{SV} independently. It follows immediately from Dempster et al. [12] that each $P(X^{(v)}|\Theta^{(v)})$ increases in each step and therefore $\sum_v P(X^{(v)}|\Theta^{(v)})$ is maximized.

The disagreement term Δ should satisfy a number of desiderata. Firstly, since we want to minimize Δ, it should be convex. Secondly, for the same reason, it should be differentiable. Given Θ_t, we would like to find the maximum of $Q^{MV}(\Theta, \Theta_t)$ in one single step. We would, thirdly, appreciate if Δ was zero when the views totally agree.

We construct Δ to fulfill these desiderata in Equation 9. It contains the pairwise cross entropy $H(P(j|x_i^{(v)}, \Theta_t^{(v)}), P(j|x_i^{(u)}, \Theta^{(u)}))$ of the posteriors of any pair of views u and v. The second cross entropy term $H(P(j|x_i^{(v)}, \Theta_t^{(v)}), P(j|x_i^{(v)}, \Theta^{(v)}))$ scales Δ down to zero when the views totally agree. Equation 10 expands all cross-entropy terms. At an abstract level, Δ can be thought of as all pairwise Kullback-Leibler divergences of the posteriors between all views. Since the cross entropy is convex, Δ is convex, too.

$$\Delta(\Theta^{(1)}, \ldots, \Theta^{(s)}, \Theta_t^{(1)}, \ldots, \Theta_t^{(s)})$$
$$= \frac{1}{s-1} \sum_{v \neq u} \sum_{i=1}^{n} \Big(H(P(j|x_i^{(v)}, \Theta_t^{(v)}), P(j|x_i^{(u)}, \Theta^{(u)}))$$
$$- H(P(j|x_i^{(v)}, \Theta_t^{(v)}), P(j|x_i^{(v)}, \Theta^{(v)})) \Big) \quad (9)$$
$$= \frac{1}{s-1} \sum_{v \neq u} \sum_{i=1}^{n} \sum_{j=1}^{m} P(j|x_i^{(v)}, \Theta_t^{(v)}) \log \frac{P(j|x_i^{(v)}, \Theta^{(v)})}{P(j|x_i^{(u)}, \Theta^{(u)})} \quad (10)$$

In order to implement the M step, we have to maximize $Q^{MV}(\Theta, \Theta_t)$ given Θ_t. We have to set the derivative to zero. Parameter Θ occurs in the logarithmized posteriors, so we have to differentiate a sum of likelihoods within a logarithm. Theorem 1 solves this problem and rewrites Q^{MV} analogously to Equation 5.

Equation 12 paves the way to an algorithm that maximizes Q^{MV}. The parameters Θ occur only in the log-likelihood terms $\log P(x_i^{(v)}|j, \Theta^{(v)})$ and $\log \alpha_j^{(v)}$ terms, and Q^{MV} can be rewritten as a sum over local functions Q_v^{MV} for the views v. It now becomes clear that the M step can be executed by finding parameter estimates of $P(x_i^{(v)}|j, \Theta^{(v)})$ and $\alpha_j^{(v)}$ independently in each view v. The E step can be carried out by calculating and averaging the posteriors $P^{(v)}(j|x_i, \Theta_t, \eta)$ according to Equation 13; this equation specifies how the views interact.

Theorem 1. *The multi-view criterion Q can be expressed as a sum of local functions Q_v^{MV} (Equation 11) that can be maximized independently in each view v. The criterion can be calculated as in Equation 12, where $P^{(v)}(j|x_i, \Theta_t, \eta)$ is the averaged posterior as detailed in Equation 13 and $P(j|x_i^{(v)}, \Theta_t^{(v)})$ is the local posterior of view v, detailed in Equation 14.*

$$Q^{MV}(\Theta^{(1)},\ldots,\Theta^{(s)},\Theta_t^{(1)},\ldots,\Theta_t^{(s)})$$

$$= \sum_{v=1}^{s} Q_v^{MV}(\Theta^{(v)},\Theta_t^{(1)},\ldots,\Theta_t^{(s)}) \qquad (11)$$

$$= \sum_{v=1}^{s}\left(\sum_{i=1}^{n}\sum_{j=1}^{m} P^{(v)}(j|x_i,\Theta_t,\eta)\log\alpha_j^{(v)}\right. \qquad (12)$$

$$\left. + \sum_{i=1}^{n}\sum_{j=1}^{m} P^{(v)}(j|x_i,\Theta_t,\eta)\log P(x_i^{(v)}|j,\Theta^{(v)})\right)$$

$$P^{(v)}(j|x_i,\Theta_t^{(1)},\ldots,\Theta_t^{(s)},\eta) \qquad (13)$$
$$= (1-\eta)P(j|x_i^{(v)},\Theta_t^{(v)}) + \frac{\eta}{s-1}\sum_{\bar{v}\neq v} P(j|x_i^{(\bar{v})},\Theta_t^{(\bar{v})})$$

$$P(j|x_i^{(v)},\Theta_t^{(v)}) = \frac{\alpha_j^{(v)} P(x_i^{(v)}|j,\Theta_t^{(v)})}{\sum_k \alpha_k^{(v)} P(x_i^{(v)}|k,\Theta_t^{(v)})} \qquad (14)$$

The proof of Theorem 1 can be found in [5].

4.3 Generalized Co-EM Algorithm

Theorem 1 describes the unsupervised co-EM algorithm with arbitrarily many views mathematically. The M steps can be executed independently in the views but Theorem 1 leaves open how the E and M steps should be interleaved. Co-EM can be implemented such that a global E step is followed by M steps in all views or, alternatively, we can iterate over the views in an outer loop and execute an E step and an M step in the current view in each iteration of this loop.

Our implementation of co-EM uses the latter strategy because consecutive M steps in multiple views impose the following risk. Cases can arise in which Q_1^{MV} can be maximized by changing $\Theta_{t+1}^{(1)}$ such that it agrees with $\Theta_t^{(2)}$. A consecutive M step in view 2 can then maximize Q_2^{MV} by changing $\Theta_{t+1}^{(2)}$ such that it agrees with $\Theta_t^{(1)}$. As a result, the two models flip their dissenting opinions. We observe empirically that this effect slows down the convergence; if the Q function consisted of only the Δ term, then this could even lead to alternation.

The unsupervised co-EM algorithm with multiple views is shown in Table 1. When the execution has reached time step t and view v, the parameters $\Theta_{t+1}^{(1)},\ldots,$ $\Theta_{t+1}^{(v-1)}$ and $\Theta_t^{(v)},\ldots,\Theta_t^{(s)}$ have already been estimated. In the E step, we can therefore determine the posterior $P^{(v)}(j|x_i,\Theta_{t+1}^{(1)},\ldots,\Theta_{t+1}^{(v-1)},\Theta_t^{(v)},\ldots,\Theta_t^{(s)},\eta)$ using the most recent parameter estimates. In the succeeding M step, the local Q_v^{MV} function is maximized over the parameters $\Theta^{(v)}$. Note that the co-EM algorithm of Nigam and Ghani [17] is a special case of Table 1 for two views, $\eta = 1$, and semi-supervised instead of unsupervised learning.

In every step 2(a)ii, the local function Q_v^{MV} increases. Since all other $Q_{\bar{v}}^{MV}$ are constant in $\Theta^{(v)}$, this implies that also Q^{MV} increases. In each iteration of the single-view EM algorithm, $P(X|\Theta_{t+1}) - P(X|\Theta_t) \geq 0$. For co-EM, this is clearly

Table 1. Unsupervised Co-EM Algorithm with Multiple Views

Input: Unlabeled data $\{(x_i^{(1)}, \ldots, x_i^{(s)})_{1 \leq i \leq n}\}$. Regularization parameter η (default 1).

1. Initialize $\Theta_0^{(1)}, \ldots, \Theta_0^{(s)}$ at random; let $t = 1$.
2. Do until convergence of Q^{MV}:
   (a) For $v = 1 \ldots s$:
      i. E step in view v: For all i, compute the posterior $P^{(v)}(j | x_i, \Theta_{t+1}^{(1)}, \ldots, \Theta_{t+1}^{(v-1)}, \Theta_t^{(v)}, \ldots, \Theta_t^{(s)}, \eta)$ in v using Eq. 13.
      ii. M step in view v: maximize Q^{MV};
      $\Theta_{t+1}^{(v)} = \arg\max_{\Theta^{(v)}} Q_v^{MV}(\Theta^{(v)}, \Theta_{t+1}^{(1)}, \ldots, \Theta_{t+1}^{(v-1)}, \Theta_t^{(v)}, \ldots, \Theta_t^{(s)})$.
   (c) Increment t.
3. Return $\Theta = (\Theta_t^{(1)}, \ldots, \Theta_t^{(s)})$.

not the case since the Q function has been augmented by a dissent penalization term. Wu [19] proves conditions for the convergence of the sequence $(\Theta)_t$ for regular EM. Sadly, the proof does not transfer to co-EM.

We study a variant of the algorithm for which convergence can be proven. In an additional step 2(b), η is decremented towards zero according to some annealing scheme. This method can be guaranteed to converge; the proof is easily derived from the convergence guarantees of regular EM [12,19]. We can furthermore show that co-EM with annealing of η maximizes $\sum_v P(X^{(v)} | \Theta)$. In the beginning of the optimization process, Δ contributes strongly to the criterion Q^{MV}; the dissent Δ is convex and we know that it upper-bounds the error. Therefore, Δ guides the search to a parameter region of low error. The contribution of Δ vanishes later; $\sum_v P(X^{(v)} | \Theta)$ usually has many local maxima and having added Δ earlier now serves as a heuristic that may lead to a good local maximum.

4.4 Global Prior Probabilities

According to our generative model we have one global prior for each mixture component, but in step 2(a)ii the co-EM algorithm so far estimates priors in each view v from the data. We will now focus on maximization of Q subject to the constraint that the estimated priors of all views be equal.

We introduce two sets of Lagrange multipliers and get Lagrangian $L(\alpha, \lambda, \gamma)$ in Equation 15. Multiplier $\lambda^{(v)}$ guarantees that $\sum_j \alpha_j^{(v)} = 1$ in view v and $\gamma^{(j,v)}$ enforces the constraint $\alpha_j^{(1)} = \alpha_j^{(v)}$ for component j.

$$L(\alpha, \lambda, \gamma) = \sum_{v=1}^{s} \sum_{i=1}^{n} \sum_{j=1}^{m} P^{(v)}(j|x_i, \Theta_t, \eta) \log \alpha_j^{(v)}$$
$$+ \sum_{v=1}^{s} \lambda^{(v)} \left(\sum_{j=1}^{m} \alpha_j^{(v)} - 1 \right) + \sum_{v=2}^{s} \sum_{j=1}^{m} \gamma^{(j,v)} (\alpha_j^{(1)} - \alpha_j^{(v)}) \quad (15)$$

Setting the partial derivatives of $L(\alpha, \lambda, \gamma)$ to zero and solving the resulting system of equations leads to Equation 16. Expanding $P^{(v)}(j|x_i, \Theta_t, \eta)$, the regularization parameter η cancels out and we reach the final M step for $\alpha_j^{(v)}$ in Equation 17. We can see that the estimated prior is an average over all views and is therefore equal for all views.

$$\alpha_j^{(v)} = \frac{1}{sn}\sum_{v=1}^{s}\sum_{i=1}^{n}P^{(v)}(j|x_i,\Theta_t,\eta) \tag{16}$$

$$= \frac{1}{sn}\sum_{v=1}^{s}\sum_{i=1}^{n}P(j|x_i^{(v)},\Theta_t^{(v)}) = \alpha_j \tag{17}$$

4.5 Cluster Assignment

For cluster analysis, an assignment of instances to clusters has to be derived from the model parameters. The risk of deciding for an incorrect cluster is minimized by choosing the *maximum a posteriori* hypothesis as in Equation 18. Bayes' rule and the conditional independence assumption lead to Equation 19.

$$h(x_i) = \operatorname{argmax}_j P(j|x_i,\Theta) \tag{18}$$

$$= \operatorname*{argmax}_j \frac{\alpha_j \prod_{v=1}^{s} P(x_i^{(v)}|j,\Theta^{(v)})}{\sum_k^m \alpha_k \prod_{v=1}^{s} P(x_i^{(v)}|k,\Theta^{(v)})} \tag{19}$$

4.6 Mixture of Multinomials

In step 2(a)ii the co-EM algorithm estimates parameters in view v from the data. This step is instantiated for the specific distributional model used in a given application. We will detail the maximization steps for multinomial models which we use in our experimentation because they model both text and link data appropriately.

A multinomial model j is parameterized by the probabilities $\theta_{lj}^{(v)}$ of word w_l in view v and mixture component j. The likelihood of document $x_i^{(v)}$ is given by Equation 20. Parameters $n_{il}^{(v)}$ count the occurrences of word w_l in document $x_i^{(v)}$. $P(|x_i^{(v)}|)$ is the prior on the document length; since they are constant in the mixture component j, they cancel out in the posterior. The factorials account for all possible sequences that result in the set of words $x_i^{(v)}$, they also cancel out in the posterior.

$$P(x_i^{(v)}|j,\Theta^{(v)}) = P(|x_i^{(v)}|)|x_i^{(v)}|!\prod_l \frac{(\theta_{lj}^{(v)})^{n_{il}^{(v)}}}{n_{il}^{(v)}!} \tag{20}$$

We will now focus on maximization of Q^{MV} over the parameters $\theta_{lj}^{(v)}$. Lagrangian $L(\theta,\lambda)$ in Equation 21 guarantees that the word probabilities sum to one.

$$L(\theta,\lambda) = \sum_{v=1}^{s}\sum_{i=1}^{n}\sum_{j=1}^{m} P^{(v)}(j|x_i,\Theta_t,\eta)\left(\log P(|x_i^{(v)}|)|x_i^{(v)}|! + \sum_l n_{il}^{(v)} \log \frac{\theta_{lj}^{(v)}}{n_{il}^{(v)}!}\right) \tag{21}$$
$$+ \sum_{v=1}^{s}\sum_{j=1}^{m}\lambda_j^{(v)}\left(\sum_l \theta_{lj}^{(v)} - 1\right)$$

Setting the partial derivatives to zero and solving the resulting system of equations yields Equation 22.

$$\theta_{lj}^{(v)} = \frac{\sum_i P^{(v)}(j|x_i, \Theta_t, \eta) n_{il}^{(v)}}{\sum_k \sum_i P^{(v)}(j|x_i, \Theta_t, \eta) n_{ik}^{(v)}} \qquad (22)$$

5 Empirical Studies

We want to find out (1) whether generalized co-EM with multiple views finds better clusters in sets of linked documents with mixture of multinomials than regular single-view EM; (2) whether co-EM is still beneficial when there is no natural feature split in the data; (3) whether there are problems for which the optimal number of views lies above 2; and (4) whether the consensus regularization parameter η should be annealed or fixed to some value. To answer these questions, we experiment on archives of linked documents and plain text collections.

All data sets that we use contain labeled instances; the labels are not visible to the learning method but we use them to measure the impurity of the returned clusters. Our quality measure is the average entropy over all clusters (Equation 23). This measure corresponds to the average number of bits needed to code the real class labels given the clustering result. The frequency $\hat{p}_{i|j}$ counts the number of elements of class i in cluster j, and n_j is the size of cluster j.

$$H = \sum_{j=1}^{m} \frac{n_j}{n} \left(-\sum_i \hat{p}_{i|j} \log \hat{p}_{i|j} \right) \qquad (23)$$

The mixture of multinomials model for text assumes that a document is generated by first choosing a component j, and then drawing a number of words with replacement according to a component-specific likelihood. The multinomial link model analogously assumes that, for a document x, a number of references *from* or *to* other documents are drawn according to a component-specific likelihood. We first use three sets of linked documents for our experimentation. The *Citeseer* data set contains 3,312 entries that belong to six classes. The text view consists of title and abstract of a paper; the two link views are inbound and outbound references. The *Cora* data set contains 9,947 computer science papers categorized into eight classes. In addition to the three views of the Citeseer data set we extract an anchor text view that contains three sentences centered at the occurrence of the reference in the text. The *WebKB* data set is a collection of 4,502 academic web pages manually grouped into six classes. Two views contain the text on the page and the anchor text of all inbound links, respectively. The total number of views are 2 (WebKB), 3 (Citeseer), and 4 (Cora).

Note that web pages or publications do not necessarily have inbound or outbound links. We require only the title/abstract and web page text views to contain attributes. The other views are empty in many cases; the inbound link view of 45% of the Cora instances is empty. In order to account for this application-specific property, we include only non-empty views in the averaged posterior $P^{(v)}(j|x_i, \Theta_t, \eta)$.

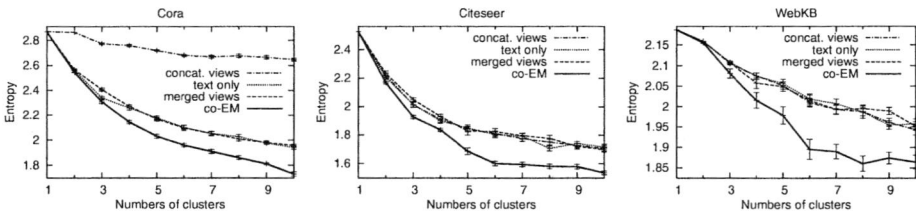

Fig. 1. Average cluster impurity over varying numbers of clusters

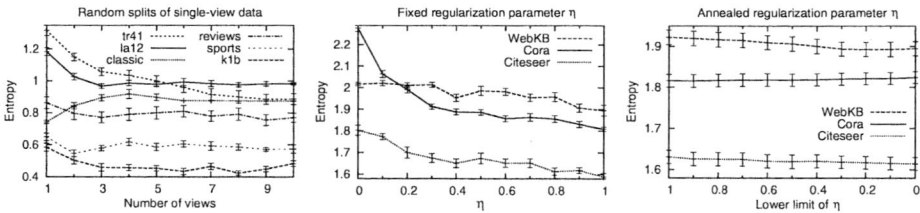

Fig. 2. Six single-view data sets with random feature splits into views (left); tuning the regularization parameter η to a fixed value (center); annealing η during the optimization process (right).

We use two single-view baselines. The first baseline applies single-view EM to a concatenation of all views (caption "concat. views"). The second baseline merges all text views (anchor text and intrinsic text are merged into one bag) and separately merges all link views (corresponding to an undirected graphical model). Single-view EM is then applied to the concatenation of these views ("merged views"). All results are averaged over 20 runs and error bars indicate standard error. Figure 1 details the clustering performance of the algorithm and baselines for various numbers of clusters (mixture components assumed by the model). Generalized co-EM outperforms the baselines for all problems and any number of clusters.

In order to find out how multi-view co-EM performs when there is no natural feature split in the data, we randomly draw six single-view document data sets that come with the cluto clustering toolkit [21]. We randomly split the available attributes into s subsets (as proposed in [17]) and average the performance over 20 distinct attribute splits. We set the number of clusters to the respective number of true mixture components. Figure 2 (left) shows the results for several numbers of views. We can see that in all but one case the best number of views is greater than one. In four of six cases we can reject the null hypothesis that one view incurs a lower entropy than two views at a significance level of $\alpha = 0.01$. Additionally, in 2 out of six cases, three views lead to significantly better clusters than two views; in four out of six cases, the entropy has its empirical minimum for more than two views.

In all experiments so far, we have fixed $\eta = 1$. Let us study whether tuning or annealing η can improve the cluster quality. Figure 2 (center) shows the entropy for various fixed values of η; we see that 1 is always the best setting ($\eta > 1$ would imply negative word probabilities $\theta_{lj}^{(v)}$).

Let us finally study whether a fixed value of η or annealing η results in a better cluster quality. In the following experiments, η is initialized at 1 and slowly annealed towards 0. Figure 2 (right) shows the development of the cluster entropy as η approaches towards 0. We see that fixing and annealing η empirically works equally well; annealing η causes a slight improvement in two cases and a slight deterioration of the quality in one case. The distinction between co-EM with and without annealing of η lies in the fact that convergence can only be proven when η is annealed; empirically, these variants are almost indistinguishable.

6 Conclusion

The Q^{MV} function defined in Equation 7 augments the single-view optimization criterion Q^{SV} by penalizing disagreement among distinct views. This is motivated by the result that the consensus among independent hypotheses upperbounds the error rate of either hypothesis. Theorem 1 rewrites the criterion $Q^{MV}(\Theta, \Theta_t)$ such that it can easily be maximized over Θ when Θ_t is fixed: an M step is executed locally in each view. Maximizing Q^{MV} naturally leads to generalized co-EM algorithm for arbitrarily many views and unlabeled data. Our derivation thus explains, motivates, and generalizes the co-EM algorithm.

While the original co-EM algorithm cannot be shown to converge, a variant of the method that anneals η over time can be guaranteed to converge and to (locally) maximize $\sum_v P(X^{(v)}|\Theta)$. Initially amplifying the convex error bound Δ in the criterion Q^{MV} serves as a heuristic that guides the search towards a better local optimum.

Our experiments show that co-EM is a better clustering procedure than single-view EM for actual multi-view problems such as clustering linked documents. Surprisingly, we also found that in most cases the impurity of text clusters can be reduced by splitting the attributes at random and applying multi-view clustering. This indicates that the consensus maximization principle may contribute to methods for a broader range of machine learning problems.

Acknowledgment

This work has been supported by the German Science Foundation DFG under grant SCHE540/10-1.

References

1. S. Abney. Bootstrapping. In *Proceedings of the 40th Annual Meeting of the Association for Computational Linguistics*, 2002.
2. K. Barnard, P. Duygulu, D. Forsyth, N. de Freitas, D. Blei, and M. Jordan. Matching words and pictures. *Journal of Machine Learning Research*, 3:1107–1135, 2002.

3. S. Becker and G. Hinton. A self-organizing neural network that discovers surfaces in random-dot stereograms. *Nature*, 355:161–163, 1992.
4. S. Bickel and T. Scheffer. Multi-view clustering. In *Proceedings of the IEEE International Conference on Data Mining*, 2004.
5. S. Bickel and T. Scheffer. Estimation of mixture models using Co-EM. In *Proceedings of the ICML Workshop on Learning with Multiple Views*, 2005.
6. D. Blei and M. Jordan. Modeling annotated data. In *Proceedings of the ACM SIGIR Conference on Information Retrieval*, 2003.
7. A. Blum and T. Mitchell. Combining labeled and unlabeled data with co-training. In *Proceedings of the Conference on Computational Learning Theory*, 1998.
8. U. Brefeld and T. Scheffer. Co-EM support vector learning. In *Proceedings of the International Conference on Machine Learning*, 2004.
9. M. Collins and Y. Singer. Unsupervised models for named entity classification. In *Proc. of the Conf. on Empirical Methods in Natural Language Processing*, 1999.
10. S. Dasgupta, M. Littman, and D. McAllester. PAC generalization bounds for co-training. In *Proceedings of Neural Information Processing Systems*, 2001.
11. V. de Sa. Learning classification with unlabeled data. In *Proceedings of Neural Information Processing Systems*, 1994.
12. A. Dempster, N. Laird, and D. Rubin. Maximum likelihood from incomplete data via the EM algorithm. *Journal of the Royal Statistical Society, Series B*, 39, 1977.
13. R. Ghani. Combining labeled and unlabeled data for multiclass text categorization. In *Proceedings of the International Conference on Machine Learning*, 2002.
14. K. Kailing, H. Kriegel, A. Pryakhin, and M. Schubert. Clustering multi-represented objects with noise. In *Proceedings of the Pacific-Asia Conference on Knowledge Discovery and Data Mining*, 2004.
15. A. McCallum and K. Nigam. Employing EM in pool-based active learning for text classification. In *Proc. of the International Conference on Machine Learning*, 1998.
16. I. Muslea, C. Kloblock, and S. Minton. Active + semi-supervised learning = robust multi-view learning. In *Proc. of the International Conf. on Machine Learning*, 2002.
17. K. Nigam and R. Ghani. Analyzing the effectiveness and applicability of co-training. In *Proceedings of the Workshop on Information and Knowledge Management*, 2000.
18. J. Sinkkonen, J. Nikkilä, L. Lahti, and S. Kaski. Associative clustering. In *Proceedings of the European Conference on Machine Learning*, 2004.
19. J. Wu. On the convergence properties of the EM algorithm. *The Annals of Statistics*, 11:95–103, 1983.
20. D. Yarowsky. Unsupervised word sense disambiguation rivaling supervised methods. In *Proc. of the Annual Meeting of the Association for Comp. Ling.*, 1995.
21. Y. Zhao and G. Karypis. Criterion functions for document clustering: Experiments and analysis. Technical Report TR 01-40, Department of Computer Science, University of Minnesota, Minneapolis, MN, 2001, 2001.
22. Z. Zhou and M. Li. Semi-supervised regression with co-training. In *Proceedings of the International Joint Conference on Artificial Intelligence*, 2005.

Nonrigid Embeddings for Dimensionality Reduction

Matthew Brand

Mitsubishi Electric Research Labs,
Cambridge, MA, USA

Abstract. Spectral methods for embedding graphs and immersing data manifolds in low-dimensional spaces are notoriously unstable due to insufficient and/or numerically ill-conditioned constraint sets. Why show why this is endemic to spectral methods, and develop low-complexity solutions for stiffening ill-conditioned problems and regularizing ill-posed problems, with proofs of correctness. The regularization exploits sparse but complementary constraints on affine rigidity and edge lengths to obtain isometric embeddings. An implemented algorithm is fast, accurate, and industrial-strength: Experiments with problem sizes spanning four orders of magnitude show $O(N)$ scaling. We demonstrate with speech data.

1 Introduction

Embedding a graph under metric constraints is a central operation in nonlinear dimensionality reduction (NLDR), ad-hoc wireless network mapping, and visualization of relational data. Despite a recent wave of advances in spectral embeddings, it has not yet become a practical, reliable tool. At root is the difficulty of automatically generating embedding constraints that make the problem well-posed, well-conditioned, and solvable on practical time-scales. Well-posed constraints guarantee a unique solution. Well-conditioned constraints make the solution numerically separable from poor solutions. Spectral embeddings from local constraints are frequently ill-posed and almost always ill-conditioned. Both problems manifest as a tiny or zero eigengap in the spectrum of the embedding constraints, indicating that the graph is effectively *nonrigid* and there is an eigen-space of solutions whose optimality is numerically indistinguishable.

Section 2 shows why small eigengaps are endemic to spectral methods for combining local constraints, making it numerically infeasible to separate a solution from its modes of deformation. To remedy this, section 3 presents a linear-time method for stiffening an ill-conditioned problem at all scales, and prove that it inflates the eigengap between the space of optimal solutions and the space of suboptimal deformations.

If a problem is ill-posed, the graph is qualitatively nonrigid and the space of optimal solutions spans all of its degrees of freedom. Section 4 shows how to choose the most dispersed embedding from this space in a semidefinite programming problem (SDP) with a small number of variables and constraints, and proves feasability. Although SDP for graphs has $O(N^6)$ complexity, our methods give a problem reduction that yields embeddings of very large graphs in a matter of seconds or minutes, making million-point problems practical on a ordinary consumer PC.

2 Setting

This paper considers the family of Laplacian-like *local-to-global* graph embeddings, where the embedding of each graph vertex is constrained by the embeddings of its immediate neighbors (in graph terminology, its 1-ring). For dimensionality reduction, the vertices are datapoints that are viewed as samples from a manifold that is somehow curled up in the ambient sample space, and the graph embedding constraints are designed to reproduce local affine structure of that manifold while unfurling it in a lower dimensional target space. Examples include Tutte's method [Tut63], Laplacian eigenmaps [BN02], locally linear embeddings (LLE) [RS00], Hessian LLE [DG03], charting [Bra03], linear tangent-space alignment (LTSA) [ZZ03], and geodesic nullspace analysis (GNA) [Bra04]. The last three methods construct local affine constraints of maximal possible rank, leading to the stablest solutions. Due to their simplicity, our analysis will be couched in terms of LTSA and GNA. All other methods employ an subset of their affine constraints, so our results will be applicable to the entire family of embeddings.

LTSA and GNA take an N-vertex graph already embedded in an ambient space $\mathbb{R}^D$ with vertex positions $\mathbf{X} = [\mathbf{x}_1, \cdots, \mathbf{x}_N] \in \mathbb{R}^{D \times N}$, and re-embed it in a lower-dimensional space $\mathbb{R}^d$ with new vertex positions $\mathbf{Y} = [\mathbf{y}_1, \cdots, \mathbf{y}_N] \in \mathbb{R}^{d \times N}$, preserving local affine structure. Typically the graph is constructed from point data by some heuristic such as k-nearest neighbors. The embedding works as follows: Take one such neighborhood of k points and construct a local d-dimensional coordinate system $\mathbf{X}_m \doteq [\mathbf{x}_i, \mathbf{x}_j, \cdots] \in \mathbb{R}^{d \times k}$, perhaps by local principal components analysis. Now consider the nullspace matrix $\mathbf{Q}_m \in \mathbb{R}^{k \times (k-d-1)}$, whose orthonormal columns are orthogonal to the rows of $\mathbf{X}_m$ and to the constant vector $\mathbf{1}$. This nullspace is also orthogonal to any affine transform $A(\mathbf{X}_m)$ of the local coordinate system, such that any translation, rotation, or stretch that preserves parallel lines in the local coordinate system will satisfy $A(\mathbf{X}_m)\mathbf{Q}_m = \mathbf{0}$. Any other transform $T(\mathbf{X}_m)$ can then be separated into an affine component $A(\mathbf{X}_m)$ plus a nonlinear distortion, $N(\mathbf{X}_m) = T(\mathbf{X}_m)\mathbf{Q}_m\mathbf{Q}_m^\top$. The algorithm LTSA (resp. GNA) assembles these *nullspace projectors* $\mathbf{Q}_m\mathbf{Q}_m^\top$, $m = 1, 2, \cdots$ into a sparse matrix $\mathbf{K} \in \mathbb{R}^{N \times N}$ that sums (resp. averages with weights) nonlinear distortions over all neighborhoods in the graph. Now let $\mathbf{V} \in \mathbb{R}^{d \times N}$ have row vectors that are orthonormal and that span the the column nullspace of $[\mathbf{K}, \mathbf{1}]$; i.e., $\mathbf{V}\mathbf{V}^\top = \mathbf{I}$ and $\mathbf{V}[\mathbf{K}, \mathbf{1}] = \mathbf{0}$. It follows immediately that if $\mathbf{V}$ exists and we use it as a basis for embedding the graph in $\mathbb{R}^d$, each neighborhood in that embedding will have *zero nonlinear distortion* with respect to its original local coordinate systems [ZZ03]. Furthermore, if the neighborhoods are sufficiently overlapped to make the graph affinely rigid in $\mathbb{R}^d$, the transform from the original data $\mathbf{X}$ to the embedding basis $\mathbf{V}$ must stretch every neighborhood *the same way* [Bra04]. Then we can estimate a linear transform $\mathbf{T} \in \mathbb{R}^{d \times d}$ that removes this stretch giving $\mathbf{Y} = \mathbf{TV}$, such that the transform from $\mathbf{X}$ to $\mathbf{Y}$ involves only rigid transforms of local neighborhoods [Bra04]. I.e., the embedding $\mathbf{Y}$ is isometric.

When there is any kind of noise or measurement error in this process, a least-squares optimal approximate basis $\mathbf{V}$ can be obtained via thin SVD of $\mathbf{K} \in \mathbb{R}^{N \times N}$ or thin EVD of $\mathbf{KK}^\top$. Because $\mathbf{K}$ is very sparse with $O(N)$ nonzero values, iterative subspace estimators typically exhibit $O(N)$ time scaling. When $\mathbf{K}$ is built with GNA, the corresponding singular values $\sigma_{N-1}, \sigma_{N-2}, \cdots$ measure the pointwise average distortion per dimension.

One of the central problems of this paper is that the eigenvalues of $\mathbf{KK}^\top$—and indeed of *any* constraint matrix in local NLDR—grow quadratically near $\lambda_0 = 0$, which is the end of the spectrum that furnishes the embedding basis **V**. (A proof is given in the first two propositions in the appendix.) Quadratic growth means that the eigenvalue curve is almost flat at the low end of the spectrum ($\lambda_{i+1} - \lambda_i \approx 0$) such that the eigengap that separates the embedding basis from other eigenvectors is negligible. A similar phenomenon is observed in the spectra of simple *graph* Laplacians[1] which are also sigmoidal with quadratic growth near zero.

3 Stiffening Ill-Conditioned Problems with Multiscale Constraints

In graph embeddings the constraint matrix plays a role akin to the stiffness matrix in finite-element methods, and in both cases the eigenvectors associated with the near-zero eigenvalues specify an optimal parameterization and its modes of vibration. The problem facing the eigensolver (or any other estimator of the nullspace) is that convergence rate is a linear function of the relative eigengap $\frac{|\lambda_c - \lambda_{c+1}|}{\lambda_{max} - \lambda_{min}}$ or eigenratio $\frac{\lambda_{c+1}}{\lambda_c}$ between the desired and remaining principle eigenvalues [Kny01]. The numerical stability of the eigenvectors similarly depends on the eigengap [SS90]. As just noted, in local-to-global NLDR the eigengap and eigenratio are both very small, making it hard to separate the solution from its distorting modes of vibration. Intuitively, low-frequency vibrations make very smooth bends in the graph, which incur very small deformation penalties at the local constraint level. Since the eigenvalues sum these penalties, the eigenvalues associated with low-frequency modes of deformation have very small values, leading to poor numerical conditioning and slow convergence of eigensolvers. The problem gets much worse for large problems where fine neighborhood structure makes for closely spaced eigenvalues, making it impossible for iterative eigensolvers to accurately compute the smallest eigenvalues and vectors.

We propose to solve this problem by stiffening the mesh with longer-range constraints that damp out lower-frequency vibrations. This can be done without looking at the point data. Indeed, it must, because long-range distances in the ambient space are presumed to be untrustworthy. Instead we combine short-range constraints from overlapping rings in the graph, as follows:

ALGORITHM: Neighborhood expansion
1. Select a subgraph consisting of a small set of overlapped neighborhoods and compute an basis $\mathbf{V}_{subgraph}$ for embedding its points in $\mathbb{R}^d$.
2. Form a new neighborhood with at least d+1 points taken from the embedding basis and add (LTSA) or average (GNA) its nullspace projector into **K**.

Because the **K** matrix penalizes distortions in proportion to the distances between the points, these larger-scale constraints can significantly drive up the eigenvalues outside the nullspace, enlarging the eigengap. It can be shown that

Proposition 1. *The nullspace of* **K** *is invariant to neighborhood expansions.*

See the appendix for all proofs. Neighborhood expansion is physically analogous to adding short ribs to a 2D plate to stiffen it against small-radius bends in 3D. However, in

---
[1] E.g., see http://www.cs.berkeley.edu/~demmel/ cs267/lecture20/lecture20.html

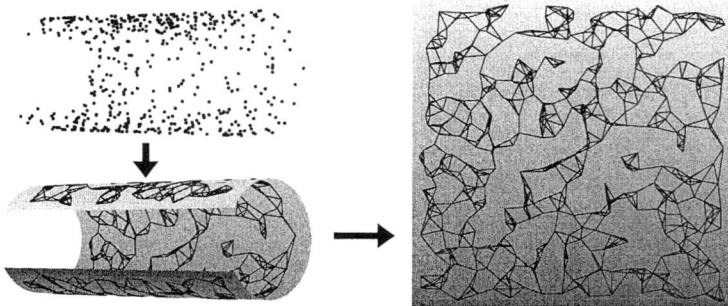

Fig. 1. $N = 500$ points are randomly sampled from a square patch of a cylindrical surface in $\mathbb{R}^{D=3}$, and connected in a $k = 4$ nearest neighbors graph which is then isometrically embedded in $\mathbb{R}^{d=2}$. Spectral embedding methods preserve affine structure of local star-shaped neighborhoods; convex optimization methods preserve edge lengths. Neither is sufficient for sparse graphs, while more densely connected graphs present exploding compute costs and/or may not embed without distortion and folds. Sparse graphs also yield numerically ill-conditioned problems. This paper shows how to obtain well-conditioned problems from very sparse neighborhood graphs and combine them with distance constraints to obtain high quality solutions in linear time.

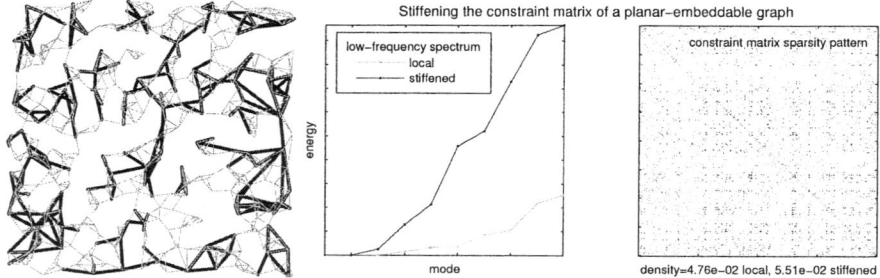

Fig. 2. Stiffening the embedding constraint matrix drives up the eigenvalues associated with low-frequency bending modes. In this example, the constraint matrix is derived from $N = 500$ points forming a 2D manifold embedded in $\mathbb{R}^{256}$. The original graph (green) is shown in green superimposed on a random multiscale stiffening (blue). The low-frequency tail of the eigenspectrum is plotted at center, before (green) and after (blue) stiffening. (The eigenvalue associated with the constant eigenvector $\mathbf{v}_0 = N^{-1/2} \cdot \mathbf{1}$ is suppressed.) The eigengap between the true 2D nullspace and the remaining approximate nullspace is improved by almost 2 orders of magnitude, whereas the original spectrum appears to have a 3D nullspace. The price is a modest 15% increase in constraint matrix density, shown at right as dark blue dots superimposed on the original sparsity pattern. However, the subspace computation is better conditioned and converges four times faster.

order to usefully improve the eigengap, one must brace against large-radius bends. Fortunately, stiffening lends itself very naturally to a multiscale scheme: We construct a set of neighborhood expansions that approximately covers the graph but adds constraints on just a small subset of all vertices. Note that this subset of vertices plus their parameterizations in the new neighborhoods constitutes a new embedding problem. Thus we may recursively stiffen this problem in the same manner, and so on until the original problem is stiffened at all scales:

ALGORITHM: Multiscale stiffening
1. Choose a constant fraction of vertices to be anchors.
2. Cover or partially cover the data with neighborhood expansions, adding constraints on any anchors that fall in an expansion.
3. Recurse only on the anchors, using their parameterizations in the neighborhood expansions.

Proposition 2. *If the number of neighborhoods and points is halved at each recursion, multiscale stiffening can be performed in $O(N)$ time with no more than a doubling of the number of nonzeros in the $\mathbf{K}$ matrix.*

For modern iterative nullspace estimators (e.g., LOBPCG [Kny01]), compute time of each iteration is typically linear in the number of nonzeros in $\mathbf{K}$ while convergence rate is supra-linear in the eigengap. Consequently, stiffening is a winning proposition. Figure 2 shows a simple example where stiffening the graph in figure 1 makes the spectrum rank-revealing and cuts the EVD time by 3/4. However, due to the difficulty of implementing the appropriate data structures efficiently in Matlab, there was no reduction in overall "wall time".

4 Regularizing Ill-Posed Problems with Edge Length Constraints

Even if the eigenvector problem is numerically well-conditioned, it may be the case that the graph is intrinsically nonrigid. This commonly happens when the graph is generated by a heuristic such as k-nearest neighbors. In such cases the embedding basis $\mathbf{V} \in \mathbb{R}^{c \times N}$ has greater dimension c than desired ($c > d$). For example, the initial constraints might allow for a variety of folds in $\mathbb{R}^d$, then $\mathbf{V}$ must span all possible folded configurations. The embedding is thus ill-posed, and some regularization is needed to choose from the space of possible embeddings. We will presume that in the most unfolded configuration, some subset of vertices are maximally dispersed. For example, we might maximize the distance between each vertex and all of its 4-hop neighbors. In order to prevent the trivial solution of an infinitely large embedding, we must fix the scale in each dimension by fixing some distances, i.e., edge lengths. Thus we seek an embedding that satisfies the affine constraints encoded in the $\mathbf{K}$ matrix, maximizes distances between a mutually repelling subset of vertices, and satisfies exact distance constraints on some subset of edges. For this we adapt the semidefinite graph embedding of [LLR95].

Formally, let mixing matrix $\mathbf{U} \in \mathbb{R}^{c \times d}$ have orthogonal columns of arbitrary nonzero norm. Let error vector $\sigma = [\sigma_1, \cdots, \sigma_c]^\top$ contain the singular values of distortion matrix $\mathbf{K}$ associated with its left singular vectors, the rows of $\mathbf{V}$. The matrix $\mathbf{U}$ will select a metrically correct embedding from the space of possible solutions spanned by the rows of $\mathbf{V}$. The target embedding, $\mathbf{Y} = [\mathbf{y}_1, \cdots, \mathbf{y}_N] \doteq \mathbf{U}^\top \mathbf{V} \in \mathbb{R}^{d \times N}$, will have overall distortion $\|\mathbf{U}^\top \sigma\|$ and distance $\|\mathbf{y}_i - \mathbf{y}_j\| = \|\mathbf{U}^\top (\mathbf{v}_i - \mathbf{v}_j)\|$ between any two points ($\mathbf{v}_i$

being the ith column of $\mathbf{V}$). The optimization problem is to minimize the distortion while maximizing the dispersion

$$\mathbf{U}^* = \max_{\mathbf{U}} -\|\mathbf{U}^\top \boldsymbol{\sigma}\|^2 + \sum_{pq} r_{pq}^2 \|\mathbf{y}_p - \mathbf{y}_q\|^2 \tag{1}$$

for some choice of weights $r_{pq} \geq 0$, preserving distances

$$\forall_{ij \in \text{EdgeSubset}} \|\mathbf{y}_i - \mathbf{y}_j\| \leq D_{ij} \tag{2}$$

on at least d edges forming a simplex of nonzero volume in $\mathbb{R}^d$ (otherwise the embedding can collapse in some dimensions). We use inequality instead of equality because the D_{ij}, measured as straight-line distances, are chordal in the ambient space $\mathbb{R}^D$ rather than geodesic in the manifold, and thus may be inconsistent with a low dimensional embedding (or infeasible). The inequality allows some edges to be slightly shortened in favor of more dispersed and thus flatter, lower-dimensional embeddings. In general, we will enforce distance constraints corresponding to all or a random sample of the edges in the graph. Unlike [LLR95] (and [WSS04], discussed below), *the distance constraints do not have to form a connected graph.*

Using the identity $\|\mathbf{Y}\|_F^2 = \|\mathbf{U}^\top \mathbf{V}\|_F^2 = \text{trace}(\mathbf{U}^\top \mathbf{V}\mathbf{V}^\top \mathbf{U}) = \text{trace}(\mathbf{V}\mathbf{V}^\top \mathbf{U}\mathbf{U}^\top)$, we massage eqns. 1-2 into a small semidefinite program (SDP) on objective $\mathbf{G} \doteq \mathbf{U}\mathbf{U}^\top \succ \mathbf{0}$:

$$\max_{\mathbf{G}} \text{trace}((\mathbf{C} - \text{diag}(\boldsymbol{\sigma})^2)\mathbf{G}) \tag{3}$$

$$\text{with } \mathbf{C} \doteq \sum_{pq} r_{pq}^2 (\mathbf{v}_p - \mathbf{v}_q)(\mathbf{v}_p - \mathbf{v}_q)^\top \tag{4}$$

$$\text{subject to } \forall_{i,j \in \text{EdgeSubset}} \text{trace}((\mathbf{v}_i - \mathbf{v}_j)(\mathbf{v}_i - \mathbf{v}_j)^\top \mathbf{G}) \leq D_{ij}^2. \tag{5}$$

In particular, when all points repel equally ($\forall_{pq} r_{pq} = 1$), then $\mathbf{C} = \mathbf{V}\mathbf{V}^\top = \mathbf{I}$, and $\text{trace}(\mathbf{CG}) = \sum_{pq} \|\mathbf{y}_p - \mathbf{y}_q\|^2 = \|\mathbf{Y}\|_F^2$. Because $\mathbf{V} \perp \mathbf{1}$, the embedding is centered.

At the extreme of $c = d$, we recover pure LTSA/GNA, where $\mathbf{U} = \mathbf{T}$ is the upgrade to isometry (the SDP is unnecessary). At $c = D - 1$ we have an alternate formulation of the semidefinite graph embedding [LLR95], where $\text{range}(\mathbf{V}) = \text{span}(\mathbb{R}^N \perp \mathbf{1})$ replaces the centering constraints (the LTSA/GNA is unnecessary). In between we have a blend that we will call Nonrigid Alignment (NA). With iterative eigensolving, LTSA/GNA takes $O(N)$ time, but requires a globally rigid set of constraints. The semidefinite graph embedding does not require rigid constraints, but has $O(N^6)$ time scaling. Nonrigid Alignment combines the best of these methods by using LTSA/GNA to construct a basis that drastically reduces the semidefinite program. In addition, we have the option of combining an incomplete set of neighborhoods with an incomplete set of edge length constraints, further reducing both problems. (A forthcoming paper will detail which subsets of constraints guarantee affine rigidity.)

Although this method does require an estimate of the local dimension for the initial LTSA/GNA, it inherits from semidefinite graph embeddings the property that the spectrum of $\mathbf{X}$ gives a sharp estimate of the global embedding dimension, because the embedding is spanned by $\mathbf{V}$. In fact, one can safely over-estimate the local dimension—this reduces the local nullspace dimension and thus the global rigidity, but the additional degrees of freedom are then fixed in the SDP problem.

4.1 Reducing the SDP Constraints

The SDP equality constraints can be rewritten in matrix-vector form as $\mathbf{A}^\top \text{svec}(\mathbf{G}) = \mathbf{b}$, where $\text{svec}(\mathbf{G})$ forms a column vector from the upper triangle of $\mathbf{X}$ with the off-diagonal elements multiplied by $\sqrt{2}$. Here each column of $\mathbf{A}$ contains a vectorized edge length constraint (e.g., $\text{svec}((\mathbf{v}_i - \mathbf{v}_j)(\mathbf{v}_i - \mathbf{v}_j)^\top)$ for an equality constraint) for some edge $i \leftrightarrow j$; the corresponding element of vector $\mathbf{b}$ contains the value D_{ij}^2. A major cost of the SDP solver lies in operations on the matrix $\mathbf{A} \in \mathbb{R}^{c^2 \times e}$, which may have a large number of linearly redundant columns. Note that c^2 is relatively small due to the choice of basis, but e, the number of edges whose distance constraints are used in the SDP, might be very large. When the problem has an exact solution (equation 5 is feasible as an equality), this cost can be reduced by projection: Let $\mathbf{F} \in \mathbb{R}^{e \times f}$, $f \ll e$ be a column-orthogonal basis for the principal row-subspace of $\mathbf{A}$, which can be estimated in $O(ef^2 c^2)$ time via thin SVD. From the Mirsky-Eckart theorem it trivially follows that the f equality constraints,

$$\mathbf{F}^\top \mathbf{A}^\top \text{vec}(\mathbf{G}) = \mathbf{F}^\top \mathbf{b} \qquad (6)$$

are either equivalent to or a least-squares optimal approximation of the original equality constraints. In our experience, for large, exactly solvable problems, it is not unusual to reduce the cardinality of constraint set by 97% without loss of information.

Proposition 3. *The resulting* SDP *problem is feasible.*

When the problem does not have an exact solution (equation 5 is only feasible as an inequality), one can solve the SDP problem with a small subset of randomly chosen edge length inequality constraints. In conjunction with the affine constraints imposed by the subspace $\mathbf{V}$, this suffices to satisfy most of the remaining unenforced length constraints. Those that are violated can be added to the active set and the SDP re-solved, possibly repeating until all are satisfied.

These reductions yield a practical algorithm for very large problems:

ALGORITHM: Nonrigid LTSA/GNA
1. Obtain basis: Compute extended approximate nullspace $\mathbf{V}$ and residuals σ_i of (stiffened) $\mathbf{K}$ matrix.
2. SDP: Find $\mathbf{G}$ maximizing eq. 3 subject to eq. 6 or eq. 5 with a constraint subset.
2a. Repeat 2 with violated constraints, if any.
3. Upgrade to isometry: Factor $\mathbf{G} \rightarrow \mathbf{U} \text{diag}(\lambda)^2 \mathbf{U}^\top$ and set embedding $\mathbf{Y} = \text{diag}(\lambda) \mathbf{U}^\top \mathbf{V}$.

4.2 Related Work

Recently [WSS04] introduced an algorithm that applies the LLR embedding to densely triangulated graphs, and [WPS05] introduced a related scheme called ℓSDE which uses a landmark basis derived from LLE to reduce the semidefinite program. We can highlight some substantial differences between our approach and ℓSDE: 1) Because LLE is quasi-conformal and has no isometry properties, one would expect that a much higher-dimensional LLE basis will be necessary to span the correct isometric embedding (this we have verified numerically), either substantially increasing the SDP time

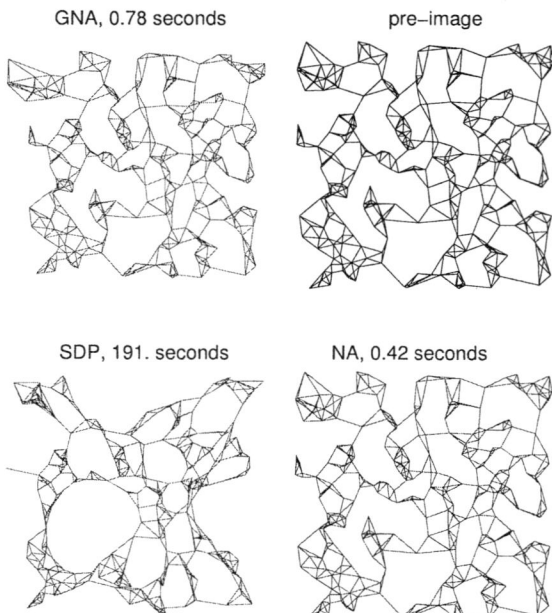

Fig. 3. A 2D NA embedding of a 4-neighbors graph on 300 points in $\mathbb{R}^{256}$ perfectly recovers the pre-image. The LTSA/GNA solution has five affine degrees of freedom associated with the distorted subgraphs on the bottom boundary. The SDP solution "foams" around large cycles where the graph is nonrigid.

or decreasing solution quality if a lower-dimensional basis is used. 2) If the manifold has nonzero genus or concave boundary, the number of randomly selected landmarks—and thus basis dimensions—needed to span the isometric embedding can grow exponentially; not so for the LTSA/GNA basis, which depends only on local properties of the manifold. 3) graph triangulation increases the number of graph edges by a factor of k^2 and the complexity of the SDP problem by k^6—a major issue because k itself should grow quadratically with the intrinsic dimension of the manifold. Thus we can solve problems 2 orders of magnitude larger in considerably less time, and report *exact* solutions.

4.3 Example

In this example, the source manifold is a square planar patch, which is embedding isometrically in $\mathbb{R}^4$ through the toric map that takes each ordinate $(x) \to (\sin x, \cos x)$. $\mathbb{R}^4$ is in turn embedded in $\mathbb{R}^8$ by the same map, and so on until the ambient space has $D = 256$ dimensions. The patch is randomly sampled in $\mathbb{R}^D$ and each point connected to its four nearest neighbors. The graph is too sparsely connected to determine a rigid embedding for either LTSA/GNA or the LLR SDP (see figure 3). Nonrigid GNA yields near-perfect embeddings. For example, figure 3 depicts the pre-image and three embeddings of a small $N = 300$ point, $K = 4$ neighbors graph. Ordinary LTSA/GNA has a 7-dimensional nullspace, indicating that some subgraphs have unwanted affine degrees of freedom. This can be resolved by increasing K, but that risks bringing untrusted edge lengths into the constraint set. SDE can fix most (but not necessarily all) of these DOFs by fully triangulating each neighborhood, but that increases the number of edges by a factor of K^2 and the SDP time complexity by a factor of K^6. Even for this small problem NA is almost three orders of magnitude faster than untriangulated SDE; that gap widens rapidly as problem size grows.

Empirically, NA exhibits the predicted linear scaling over a wide range of problem sizes. Working in MatLab on a 3GHz P4 with 1Gbyte memory, 10^2 points took roughly 0.3 seconds; 10^3 points took roughly 2 seconds; 10^4 points took 21 seconds; 10^5 points took roughly 232 seconds; we see linear scaling in between. The dominant computation is the EVD, not the SDP.

5 Application to Speech Data

The TIMIT speech database is a widely available collection of audio waveforms and phonetic transcriptions for 2000+ sentences uttered by 600+ speakers. We sought to model the space of acoustic variations in vowel sounds. Starting with a standard representation, we computed a vector of $D = 13$ mel-cepstral features for each 10 millisecond frame that was labelled as a vowel in the transcriptions. To reduce the impact of transcription errors and co-articulatory phenomena, we narrowed the data to the middle half of each vowel segment, yielding roughly $N = 240,000$ samples in $\mathbb{R}^{13}$. Multiple applications of PCA to random data neighborhoods suggested that the data is locally 5-dimensional. An NA embedding of the 7 approximately-nearest neighbors graph with 5-dimensional neighborhoods and a 25-dimensional basis took slightly less than 11 minutes to compute. The spectrum is sharp, with ¿99% of the variance in 7 dimensions, ¿95% in 5 dimensions, and ¿75% in 2 dimensions. A PCA rotation of the raw data matches these percentages at 13, 9, and 4 dimensions respectively. Noting the discrepancy between the estimated local dimensionality and global embedding dimension, we introduced slack variables with low penalties to explore the possibility that the graph was not completely unfolding. Since this left the spectrum substantially unchanged, we conjecture that there may be topological loops or unnoticed 7-dimensional clusters, and indeed some projections of the embedding showed holes.

Figure 4 shows how the phonemes are organized in the two principal dimensions of the NA and PCA representations. The NA axes are clearly correlated with the physical degrees of freedom of the speech apparatus: Roughly speaking, as one moves to the right the mouth narrows horizontally, from iy (beet) and ey (bait) to ao (bought) and aw (bout); as one moves up the mouth narrows vertically with the lower lip moving forward and upward, from ah (but) and eh (bet) to ow (boat) and uh (book). The third dimension (not shown) appears to be correlated with the size of the resonant chamber at the back of the mouth, i.e. tongue position. After considerable study, it is still not clear how to interpret the raw PCA axes.

A low-dimensional representation is advantageous for speech recognition because it makes it practical to model phoneme classes with full covariance Gaussians. A longstanding rule-of-thumb in speech recognition is that a full-covariance Gaussian is competitive with a mixture of 3 or 4 diagonal-covariance Gaussians [LRS83]. The important empirical question is whether the NA representation offers a better separation of the classes than the PCA. This can be quantified (independently of any down-

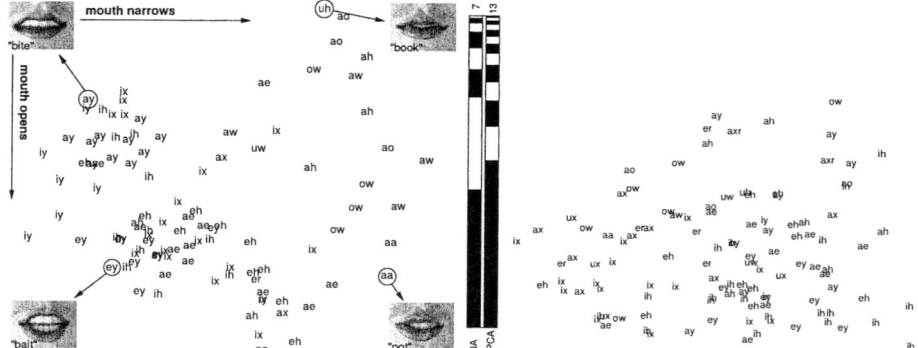

Fig. 4. LEFT: A thin slice along the two principal axes of an NA embedding of 2.5×10^5 vowel feature vectors. TIMIT phoneme labels are scatter-plotted according to their embedding coordinates. The distribution of phonemes is well correlated with mouth shape (see discussion in section 5). MIDDLE: Normalized spectra of the NA and PCA representations, showing the fraction of total variance captured in each dimension. RIGHT: An equivalent slice through the PCA representation slice scatter-plot is far less interpretable. Some sounds (e.g., ix in deb<u>i</u>t) depend little on lip shape and are thus distributed freely through both plots.

stream speech processing) by fitting a Gaussian to each phoneme class and calculating the symmetrized KL-divergence between classes. Higher divergence means that one will need fewer bits to describe classification errors made by a (Gaussian) quadratic classifier. We found that the *divergence between classes in the $d = 5$ NA representation was on average approximately 2.2 times the divergence between classes in the $d = 5$ PCA representation, with no instances where the NA representation was inferior.* Similar advantages were observed for other values of d, even, surprisingly, $d = 1$ and $d = D$.

Even though both representations are unsupervised, we may conclude that preserving short-range metric structure (NA) is more conducive to class separation than preserving long-range distances (PCA). We are now working on a larger embedding of all phonemes which, when combined with the GNA out-of-sample extension, will be incorporated into a speech recognition engine.

6 Discussion

We have demonstrated that rigidity is a key obstacle for viable nonlinear dimensionality reduction, but by stiffening the constraint set and recasting the upgrade to isometry as a small SDP problem, problems that are severely ill-posed and ill-conditioned can be solved—in linear time. At time of submission, we have successfully embedded problems of up to 10^6 points, and it appears that the principal challenge in using these methods will be the most advantageous choice of basis dimension. The is a matter of finding the eigengap of ill-posed problems, and we hope to make connections with an existing literature on large-scale physical eigenproblems. Another issue is the initial problem of graph building—at 10^5 points, the approximate nearest-neighbor algorithms that make graph-building tractable begin to make substantial errors. For NLDR to be practical above 10^7 points—the size of bioinformatic and econometric problems—the problem of reliable graph-building will have to be solved.

References

[BN02] Mikhail Belkin and Partha Niyogi. Laplacian eigenmaps for dimensionality reduction and data representation. volume 14 of *Advances in Neural Information Processing Systems*, 2002.

[Bra03] Matthew Brand. Charting a manifold. In *Advances in Neural Information Processing Systems*, volume 15, 2003.

[Bra04] Matthew Brand. From subspaces to submanifolds. In *Proceedings, British Machine Vision Conference*, 2004.

[DG03] David L. Donoho and Carrie Grimes. Hessian eigenmaps. *Proceedings, National Academy of Sciences*, 2003.

[Kny01] A. V. Knyazev. Toward the optimal preconditioned eigensolver. *SIAM Journal on Scientific Computing*, 23(2):517–541, 2001.

[LLR95] N. Linial, E. London, and Y. Rabinovich. The geometry of graphs and some of its algorithmic applications. *Combinatorica*, 15(2):215–245, 1995.

[LRS83] S. Levinson, L. Rabiner, and M. Sondhi. An introduction to the application of the theory of probabilistic functions of a markov process to automatic speech recognition. *Bell System Technical Journal*, 62(4):1035–1074, 1983.

[RS00] Sam T. Roweis and Lawrence K. Saul. Nonlinear dimensionality reduction by locally linear embedding. *Science*, 290:2323–2326, December 22 2000.

[SS90] G.W. Stewart and Ji-Guang Sun. *Matrix perturbation theory*. Academic Press, 1990.

[Tut63] W.T. Tutte. How to draw a graph. *Proc. London Mathematical Society*, 13:743–768, 1963.

[WPS05] K.Q. Weinberger, B.D. Packer, and L.K. Saul. Nonlinear dimensionality reduction by semidefinite programming and kernel matrix factorization. In *Proc. AI & Statistics*, 2005.

[WSS04] K. Q. Weinberger, F. Sha, and L. K. Saul. Learning a kernel matrix for nonlinear dimensionality reduction. In *Proc. 21st ICML*, 2004.

[ZZ03] Z. Zhang and H. Zha. Nonlinear dimension reduction via local tangent space alignment. In *Proc., Conf. on Intelligent Data Engineering and Automated Learning*, number 2690 in Lecture Notes on Computer Science, pages 477–481. Springer-Verlag, 2003.

A Analysis of Local-to-Global Spectral Models and Misc. Proofs

We can view the constraint matrix $\mathbf{K}$ as a discrete approximation to a convolution of a candidate embedding $\mathbf{Z}$ with a filter If we plot columns of $\mathbf{K}$, this filter resembles an inverted Laplacian. Analysis shows that this is indeed the case:

Proposition 4. *Let* $\mathbf{Z} \doteq [\mathbf{z}_1, \cdots, \mathbf{z}_N] \in \mathbb{R}^{d \times N}$ *with* $\mathbf{z}_i = z(\mathbf{y}_i)$ *be a data parameterization given by some C^2 multivalued map* $z : \mathcal{M} \to \mathbb{R}^d$ *on the intrinsic coordinates* $\mathbf{y}_i$. *Let*

$$\mathbf{K} \doteq \left(\sum_m \mathbf{S}_m \mathbf{Q}_m \mathbf{Q}_m^\top diag(\mathbf{w}_m) \mathbf{S}_m^\top \right) diag(\sum_m \mathbf{S}_m \mathbf{w}_m)^{-1} \qquad (7)$$

where binary indexing matrix $\mathbf{S}_m \in \{0,1\}^{N \times k}$ *select k points forming the mth neighborhood and neighborhood weight vector* $\mathbf{w}_m \in \mathbb{R}^k$ *assigns points weights according to their distance from the neighborhood center:* $(\{\mathbf{w}_m\}_i \propto \exp(-\|\{\mathbf{X}_m\}_i -$

$\overline{\mathbf{X}_m}\|^2/2\sigma^2)/\sigma)$. Then each column of $\mathbf{K}$ is a discrete difference of Gaussians operator with the parameterization error $\|\mathbf{ZK}\|_F^2$ approximating $\|z - G*z - \nabla^2 G*z\|^2$, the difference between z and a smoothed version of itself, minus its convolution with a Laplacian-of-Gaussian operator.

Proof. (prop. 4) For simplicity, we will first consider the case of a 1D manifold sampled at regular intervals. Recall that $\mathbf{K}$ is an average of neighborhood nullspace projectors, each of the form $\mathbf{N}_m = \mathbf{Q}_m \mathbf{Q}_m^\top = \mathbf{I} - \frac{1}{k}\mathbf{1}\mathbf{1}^\top - \mathbf{P}_m \mathbf{P}_m^\top$, where $\mathbf{P}_k \in \mathbb{R}^{k \times d}$ is an orthogonal basis of centered local coordinates $\mathbf{X}_m - \overline{\mathbf{X}_m}\mathbf{1}^\top$. Because orthogonalization is a linear operation, $\frac{1}{k} - \{\mathbf{N}_m\}_{i \neq j}$ is proportional to $\|\{\mathbf{X}_m\}_i - \overline{\mathbf{X}_m}\| \cdot \|\{\mathbf{X}_m\}_j - \overline{\mathbf{X}_m}\|$, the product of the distances of points i and j from the clique centroid. Viewing the elements of the matrix $\mathbf{P}_m \mathbf{P}_m^\top$ as surface heights, we have a quadratic saddle surface, maximally positive in the upper left and lower right corners, and maximally negative in the upper right and lower left corners. In our simplified case, $\mathbf{P}_m = k^{-1/2} \cdot [-j, 1-j, \cdots, j-1, j]^\top$ where $k = 2j + 1$ is the size of each neighborhood, and elements in each column of $\mathbf{K}$ are Gaussian-weighted sums along the diagonals of $\mathbf{N}_m$. Precisely, for the pth non-boundary neighborhood, the nth nonzero subdiagonal element in a column of $\mathbf{K}$ is

$$K_{p+n,p} = -\frac{1}{k}\sum_{i=n}^{i=2j}(1 + (i-j)(i-j-n)\frac{3}{j(j+1)})e^{-(i-j)^2}$$

$$= -\frac{1}{k}\frac{3}{j(j+1)}\sum_{i=n}^{i=2j}\{(1-(i-j)^2)e^{-(i-j)^2}$$

$$-(1-n(i-j))e^{-(i-j)^2} + \frac{j(j+1)}{3}e^{-(i-j)^2}\}.$$

Note that $(1-(i-j)^2)e^{-(i-j)^2}$ is a Laplacian-of-Gaussian, and that if we hold $i = n$ and iterate over n (the elements of a column in $\mathbf{K}$), we obtain a difference of Gaussians and LoG's, each with finite support; summing over i gives a superposition of these curves, each with a different support. To generalize to non-regular sampling, simply increment i by the difference between neighboring points. To generalize to multidimensional manifolds, note that the above arguments apply to any subset of points forming a geodesic line on $\mathcal{M}$, and by the linearity of $\mathbf{K}$ and the Laplacian operator, to any linear combination of different subsets of points forming different geodesics.

Proposition 5. *The near-zero eigenvalues of $I - G - \nabla^2 G$ grow quadratically.*

Proof. (prop. 5) Consider the harmonic equation, which describes how the graph vibrates in the space normal to its embedding: $-(I - G - \nabla^2 G)Y(x,t) = d^2Y(x,t)/d^2t$, with $Y(x,t)$ being the displacement at time t and position x (in manifold-intrinsic coordinates). For periodic motion, set $Y(x,t) = \sin(\omega t) \cdot Y(x)$, with $Y(x)$ being a vibrational mode. After substitution and cancellation, the harmonic equation simplifies to $(I - G - \nabla^2 G)Y(x) = \omega^2 \cdot Y(x)$, confirming that the mode $Y(x)$ is an eigenfunction of the operator $I - G - \nabla^2 G$. One can verify by substitution that $Y(x) = \sin(ax+b)$ for $a \in \{1, 2, \cdots, N\}, b \in \mathbb{R}$ is an orthogonal basis for solutions (eigenvectors) with eigenvalues on the sigmoid curve $\omega^2 = 1 - (1 + a^2/\sqrt{2\pi})e^{-a^2}$. A series expansion around $a = 0$ reveals that the leading term is quadratic.

Proof. (prop. 1) Expansion generates a new neighborhood whose parameterization is affine to those of its constituent neighborhoods, thus its nullspace is orthogonal to $\mathbf{K}$.

Proof. (prop. 2) Because of halving, at any scale the number of vertices in each neighborhood expansion is, on average, a constant $v \ll N$ that is determined only by the intrinsic dimensionality and the average size of the original local neighborhoods. Halving also guarantees that the total number of neighborhood expansions is $\sum_i (\frac{1}{2})^i N < N$. Together these establish $O(N)$ time. In each of the fewer than N neighborhood expansions, a point receives on average d constraints from new neighbors—the same or less than it receives in each of the N original neighborhoods.

Proof. (prop. 3) Since $\mathbf{F}$ is a variance-preserving rotation of the constraints, one can always rotate the f-dimensional row-space of $\mathbf{F} = [\mathbf{f}_1, \cdots, \mathbf{f}_f]$ so that $\forall_i \mathbf{f}_i^\top \mathbf{b} > 0$. Then any infeasible solution $\tilde{\mathbf{G}}$ can be scaled by $z > 0$ such that $\forall_i \mathbf{f}_i^\top \mathbf{A}^\top \operatorname{svec}(z\tilde{\mathbf{G}}) \leq \mathbf{f}_i^\top \mathbf{b}$, with any differences made up by nonnegative slack variables.

Multi-view Discriminative Sequential Learning

Ulf Brefeld, Christoph Büscher, and Tobias Scheffer

Humboldt-Universität zu Berlin, Department of Computer Science,
Unter den Linden 6, 10099 Berlin, Germany
{brefeld, buescher, scheffer}@informatik.hu-berlin.de

Abstract. Discriminative learning techniques for sequential data have proven to be more effective than generative models for named entity recognition, information extraction, and other tasks of discrimination. However, semi-supervised learning mechanisms that utilize inexpensive unlabeled sequences in addition to few labeled sequences – such as the Baum-Welch algorithm – are available only for generative models. The multi-view approach is based on the principle of maximizing the consensus among multiple independent hypotheses; we develop this principle into a semi-supervised hidden Markov perceptron, and a semi-supervised hidden Markov support vector learning algorithm. Experiments reveal that the resulting procedures utilize unlabeled data effectively and discriminate more accurately than their purely supervised counterparts.

1 Introduction

The problem of labeling observation sequences has applications that range from language processing tasks such as named entity recognition, part-of-speech tagging, and information extraction to biological tasks in which the instances are often DNA strings. Traditionally, sequence models such as the hidden Markov model and variants thereof have been applied to the label sequence learning problem. Learning procedures for generative models adjust the parameters such that the joint likelihood of training observations and label sequences is maximized. By contrast, from the application point of view the true benefit of a label sequence predictor corresponds to its ability to find the correct label sequence given an observation sequence.

In the last years, conditional random fields [14, 15], hidden Markov support vector machines [4] and their variants have become popular; their discriminative learning procedures minimize criteria that are directly linked to their accuracy of retrieving the correct label sequence. In addition, kernel conditional random fields and hidden Markov support vector machines utilize kernel functions which enables them to learn in very high dimensional feature spaces. These features may also encode long-distance dependencies which cannot adequately be handled by first-order Markov models. Experiments uniformly show that discriminative models have advanced the accuracy that can be obtained for sequence labeling tasks; for instance, some of the top scoring systems in the BioCreative named entity recognition challenge used conditional random fields [18].

In the training process of generative sequence models, additional inexpensive and readily available unlabeled sequences can easily be utilized by employing Baum-Welch, a variant of the EM algorithm. But since EM uses generative models, it cannot directly be applied to discriminative learning. Text sequences are often described by high-dimensional attribute vectors that include, for instance, word features, letter n-grams, orthographical and many other features. These vectors can be split into two distinct, redundant views and thus the multi-view approach can be followed. Multi-view algorithms such as co-training [5] learn two initially independent hypotheses, and then minimize the disagreement of these hypotheses regarding the correct labels of the unlabeled data [11]. Thereby, they minimize an upper bound on the error rate [10].

The rest of our paper is structured as follows. Section 2 reports on related work and Section 3 reviews input output spaces and provides some background on multi-view learning. In Section 4 and 5 we present the dual multi-view hidden Markov kernel perceptron, and then leverage this algorithm to the multi-view hidden Markov support vector machine. We report on experimental results in Section 6. Section 7 concludes.

2 Related Work

In a rapidly developing line of research, many variants of discriminative sequence models are being explored. Recently studied variants include maximum entropy Markov models [17], conditional random fields [14], perceptron re-ranking [7], hidden Markov support vector machines [4], label sequence boosting [3], max-margin Markov models [21], case-factor diagrams [16], sequential Gaussian process models [2], kernel conditional random fields [15] and support vector machines for structured output spaces [22].

De Sa [11] observes a relationship between consensus of multiple hypotheses and their error rate and devises a semi-supervised learning method by cascading multi-view vector quantization and linear classification. A multi-view approach to word sense disambiguation combines a classifier that refers to the local context of a word with a second classifier that utilizes the document in which words co-occur [23]. Blum and Mitchell [5] introduce the co-training algorithm for semi-supervised learning that greedily augments the training set of two classifiers. A version of the AdaBoost algorithm boosts the agreement between two views on unlabeled data [9].

Dasgupta et al. [10] and Abney [1] give PAC bounds on the error of co-training in terms of the disagreement rate of hypotheses on unlabeled data in two independent views. This justifies the direct minimization of the disagreement. The co-EM algorithm for semi-supervised learning probabilistically labels all unlabeled examples and iteratively exchanges those labels between two views [20, 12]. Muslea et al. [19] extend co-EM for active learning and Brefeld and Scheffer [6] study a co-EM wrapper for the support vector machine.

3 Background

In this section we review "input output spaces" [2] and the consensus maximization principle that underlies multi-view algorithms for the reader's convenience. In the remainder of our paper we adopt the clear notation proposed by [4].

3.1 Learning in Input Output Space

The setting of the *label sequence learning problem* is as follows. The labeled sample consists of n pairs $(\mathbf{x}_1, \mathbf{y}_1), \ldots, (\mathbf{x}_n, \mathbf{y}_n)$, where $\mathbf{x}_i \in \mathcal{X}$ denotes the i-th input or observation sequence of length T_i; i.e., $\mathbf{x}_i = \langle x_{i,1}, x_{i,2}, \ldots, x_{i,T_i}\rangle$, and $\mathbf{y}_i \in \mathcal{Y}$ the corresponding label sequence with $\mathbf{y}_i = \langle y_{i,1}, \ldots, y_{i,T_i}\rangle$. We denote the set of all labels by Σ; i.e., $y_{i,t} \in \Sigma$.

In label sequence learning, joint features of the input and the label sequence play a crucial role (*e.g.*, "is the previous token labeled a named entity and both the previous and current token start with a capital letter"?). Such joint features of input and output cannot appropriately be modeled when the hypothesis is assumed to be a function from input to output sequences. The intuition of the input output space is that the decision function $f : \mathcal{X} \times \mathcal{Y} \to \mathbb{R}$ operates on a joint feature representation $\Phi(\mathbf{x}_i, \mathbf{y}_i)$ of input sequence $\mathbf{x}_i$ and output sequence $\mathbf{y}_i$. Given an input, the classifier retrieves the output sequence

$$\hat{\mathbf{y}} = \underset{\bar{\mathbf{y}}}{\operatorname{argmax}} f(\mathbf{x}_i, \bar{\mathbf{y}}). \tag{1}$$

This step is referred to as decoding. Given the sample, the learning problem is to find a discriminator f that correctly decodes the examples. We utilize the **w**-parameterized linear model $f(\mathbf{x}, \mathbf{y}) = \langle \mathbf{w}, \Phi(\mathbf{x}, \mathbf{y})\rangle$. The joint feature representation $\Phi(\mathbf{x}, \mathbf{y})$ allows capturing non-trivial interactions of *label-label* pairs

$$\phi_{\sigma,\tau}(\mathbf{y}_i|t) = [[y_{i,t-s} = \sigma \wedge y_{i,t} = \tau]], \qquad \sigma, \tau \in \Sigma, \tag{2}$$

($[[cond]]$ returns 1 if *cond* is true and 0 otherwise) and *label-observation* pairs

$$\bar{\phi}_{\sigma,j}(\mathbf{x}_i, \mathbf{y}_i|t) = [[y_{i,t} = \sigma]]\psi_j(x_{i,t-s}), \tag{3}$$

where many features $\psi_j(x_{i,t-s})$ extract characteristics of token $x_{i,t-s}$; *e.g.*, $\psi_{234}(x_{i,t-s})$ may be 1 if token $x_{i,t-s}$ starts with a capital letter and 0 otherwise. We will refer to the vector $\psi(x) = (\ldots, \psi_j(x), \ldots)^\mathsf{T}$ and denote the dot product by means of $k(x, \bar{x}) = \langle \psi(x), \psi(\bar{x})\rangle$.

The feature representation $\Phi(\mathbf{x}_i, \mathbf{y}_i)$ of the i-th sequence is defined as the sum of all feature vectors $\Phi(\mathbf{x}_i, \mathbf{y}_i|t) = (\ldots, \phi_{\sigma,\tau}(\mathbf{y}_i|t), \ldots, \bar{\phi}_{\sigma,j}(\mathbf{x}_i, \mathbf{y}_i|t), \ldots)^\mathsf{T}$ extracted at time t

$$\Phi(\mathbf{x}_i, \mathbf{y}_i) = \sum_{t=1}^{T_i} \Phi(\mathbf{x}_i, \mathbf{y}_i|t). \tag{4}$$

Restricting the possible features to consecutive label-label (Equation 2 with $s = 1$) and label-observation (Equation 3 with $s = 0$) dependencies is essentially

In general, we have to allow pointwise relaxations of the hard margin constraint by slack variables leading us to a soft-margin optimization problem for each view,

$$\min \tfrac{1}{2}\|\mathbf{w}\|^2 + \tfrac{C}{r}\left(\sum_{i=1}^{n}\xi_i^r + C_u\sum_{i=n+1}^{n+m}(\min\{\gamma_i^{\bar{v}},1\})\xi_i^r\right)$$
$$\text{s.t.} \quad \forall_{i=1}^{n}, \forall_{\bar{\mathbf{y}}\neq \mathbf{y}_i} \quad \langle \mathbf{w}, \Phi(\mathbf{x}_i,\mathbf{y}_i) - \Phi(\mathbf{x}_i,\bar{\mathbf{y}})\rangle \geq 1-\xi_i \quad (25)$$
$$\forall_{i=n+1}^{n+m}, \forall_{\bar{\mathbf{y}}\neq \mathbf{y}^{\bar{v}}} \quad \langle \mathbf{w}, \Phi(\mathbf{x}_i,\mathbf{y}^{\bar{v}}) - \Phi(\mathbf{x}_i,\bar{\mathbf{y}})\rangle \geq 1-\xi_i$$
$$\forall_{i=1}^{n+m} \quad \xi_i \geq 0,$$

where $r = 1, 2$ denotes a linear or quadratic penalization of the error, respectively, $C > 0$ determines the trade-off between margin maximization and error minimization, and C_u is a balancing factor that regularizes the influence of the unlabeled data. Weights of $\min\{\gamma_i^{\bar{v}},1\}$ to the slacks $\xi_{n+1},\ldots,\xi_{n+m}$ relate errors on unlabeled examples to the confidence of the peer view's prediction.

In case of a linear loss – i.e., $r = 1$ – the inclusion of slack variables, costs, and balancing factor resolves into $n + m$ additional constraints of optimization problem 21 that upper bound the sum of the α_i.

$$\forall_{i=1}^{n}: \sum_{\bar{\mathbf{y}}\neq \mathbf{y}_i}\alpha_i(\bar{\mathbf{y}}) \leq C; \quad \forall_{i=n+1}^{n+m}: \sum_{\bar{\mathbf{y}}\neq \mathbf{y}_i^{\bar{v}}}\alpha_i(\bar{\mathbf{y}}) \leq (\min\{\gamma_i^{\bar{v}},1\})C_u\,C. \quad (26)$$

The necessary changes to optimization problem 21 in case of a quadratic penalty ($r = 2$) can be incorporated into the kernel by $K''_{i\bar{\mathbf{y}},j\bar{\mathbf{y}}'} = K'_{i\bar{\mathbf{y}},j\bar{\mathbf{y}}'} + \Delta_{i\bar{\mathbf{y}},j\bar{\mathbf{y}}'}$ where

$$\Delta_{i\bar{\mathbf{y}},j\bar{\mathbf{y}}'} = \begin{cases} \frac{1}{C} & i = j, \bar{\mathbf{y}} = \bar{\mathbf{y}}', 1 \leq i,j \leq n \\ \frac{1}{(\min\{\gamma_j^{\bar{v}},1\})C_u\,C} & i = j, \bar{\mathbf{y}} = \bar{\mathbf{y}}', n+1 \leq i,j \leq n+m \\ 0 & \text{otherwise.} \end{cases} \quad (27)$$

Table 3. Working set optimization for unlabeled examples

Input: i-th unlabeled sequence $(\mathbf{x}_i^1, \mathbf{x}_i^2)$, $C, C_u > 0$, repetitions r_{max}.

1. $S^1 = S^2 = \emptyset$, $\alpha_i^1 = \alpha_i^2 = 0$.
2. **Loop**
3.   compute $\hat{\mathbf{y}}^1 = \text{argmax}_\mathbf{y}\, f^1(\mathbf{x}_i^1, \mathbf{y})$ and $\hat{\mathbf{y}}^2 = \text{argmax}_\mathbf{y}\, f^2(\mathbf{x}_i^2, \mathbf{y})$
4.   **If** $\hat{\mathbf{y}}^1 = \hat{\mathbf{y}}^2$ **then** return α_i^1 and α_i^2.
5.   **Else For** $v = 1, 2$:
6.   Substitute former target: $\hat{\mathbf{y}}_i = \hat{\mathbf{y}}^{\bar{v}}$.
7.   Add pseudo sequence: $S^v = S^v \bigcup\{\hat{\mathbf{y}}^v\}$
8.   Optimize $\alpha_i^v(\bar{\mathbf{y}})$ over $\Phi(\mathbf{x}_i^v, \hat{\mathbf{y}}_i) - \Phi(\mathbf{x}_i^v, \bar{\mathbf{y}})$, $\forall \bar{\mathbf{y}} \in S^v$
9. $\forall \bar{\mathbf{y}} \in S^v$ with $\alpha_i^v(\bar{\mathbf{y}}) = 0$: $S^v = S^v \backslash \{\bar{\mathbf{y}}\}$
10.   **End for** v. **End if.**
11. **Until** consensus or r_{max} repetitions without consensus.

Output: Optimized α_i^1 and α_i^2.

Since the dual variables $\alpha_i(\bar{\mathbf{y}})$ are tied to observation sequences $\mathbf{x}_i$, the optimization problem (Equation 21) splits into $n+m$ disjoint subspaces spanned by $\alpha_i(\cdot)$ with fixed values for the $\alpha_{j\neq i}(\cdot)$; the optimization iterates over these subspaces.

In an outer loop, the Hidden Markov SVM iterates over the examples and consecutively optimizes the example's parameters $\alpha_i(\cdot)$, using distinct working set approaches for labeled (Table 2) and unlabeled (Table 3) data. Difference vectors $\bar{\mathbf{y}}$ with $\alpha_i(\bar{\mathbf{y}}) = 0$ are removed in order to speed up computation. When the loop reaches an unlabeled sequence, all pseudo sequences $\alpha_i(\cdot)$ of that example are removed since the disagreements that they used to correct in earlier iterations of the main loop may have been resolved.

Since the cost factors upper-bound the growth of the α_i for the 1-norm machine, consensus might not be established and we therefore integrate a user defined constant r_{max} that bounds the number of iterations. Linear Viterbi decoding can be performed similarly to Equation 5 and Equation 6.

6 Empirical Results

We concentrate on named entity recognition (NER) problems. We use the data set provided for task 1A of the BioCreative challenge and the Spanish news wire article corpus of the shared task of CoNLL 2002.

The BioCreative data contains 7500 sentences from biomedical papers; gene and protein names are to be recognized. View 1 consists of the token itself together with letter 2, 3 and 4-grams; view 2 contains surface clues like capitalization, inclusion of Greek symbols, numbers, and others as documented in [13]. The CoNLL2002 data contains 9 label types which distinguish person, organization, location, and other names. We use 3100 sentences of between 10 and 40 tokens which we represent by a token view and a view of surface clues.

In each experiment we draw a specified number of (labeled and unlabeled) training and holdout sentences without replacement at random in each iteration. We assure that each label occurs at least once in the labeled training data; otherwise, we discard and draw again. Each holdout set consists of 500 (BioCreative) and 300 (Spanish news wire) sentences, respectively. We first optimize parameter C_u using resampling; we then fix C_u and present curves that show the average token-based error over 100 randomly drawn training and holdout sets. The baseline methods (single-view HM perceptron and HM SVM) are trained on concatenated views; errorbars indicate standard error.

We use Alex Smola's Loqo implementation as QP solver and initialize $r_{max} = 10$, $C = 1$. We employ a constant C_u for multi-view perceptron and use an exponential scheme to increase C_u to its maximal value in the 30th iteration. We want to answer the following questions.

Is the inclusion of unlabeled data beneficial for sequential learning?
Figure 1 shows learning curves for single-view and multi-view HM perceptron and HM SVM for both problems. With the exception of one point, the multi-view methods always outperform their single-view, purely supervised

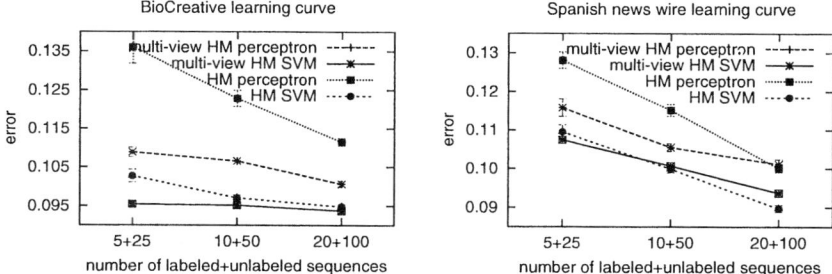

Fig. 1. Learning curves for BioCreative and Spanish news wire

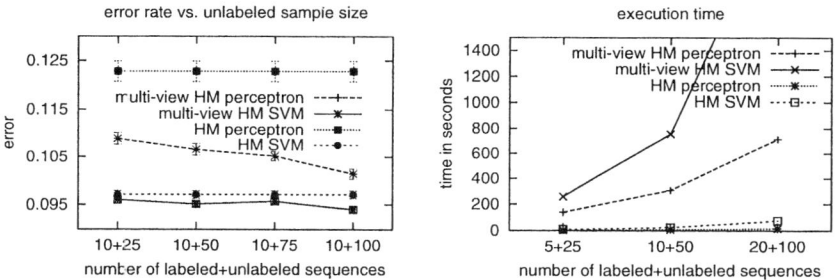

Fig. 2. Left: Error depending on the unlabeled sample size for BioCreative. Right: Execution time.

counterparts significantly; the multi-view HM SVM is the most accurate sequence learning method. We use a regular HMM as an additional baseline; its error rates of 23.59%, 20.04%, and 15.31% for 5, 10, and 20 training sequences for the news wire and 17.98%, 14.31%, and 12.31% (5, 10, 20 training sequences) for the BioCreative data lie above the plotted range of Figure 1. In Figure 2 (left) we vary the number of unlabeled sequences for the BioCreative data set. As the number of unlabeled data increases, the advantage of multi-view over single-view sequence learning increases further.

How costly is the training process?

Figure 2 (right) plots execution time against training set size. The performance benefits are at the cost of significantly longer training processes. The multi-view HM perceptron scales linearly and the multi-view HM SVM quadratically in the number of unlabeled sequences.

Are there better ways of splitting the features into views?

We compare the feature split into the token itself and letter n-grams versus surface clues to the average of 100 random splits. Surprisingly, Figure 3 shows that random splits work even (significantly) better. We also construct a feature split in which view 1 contains all odd, and view 2 all even features. Hence, each view contains half of the Boolean token features as well as half of the surface

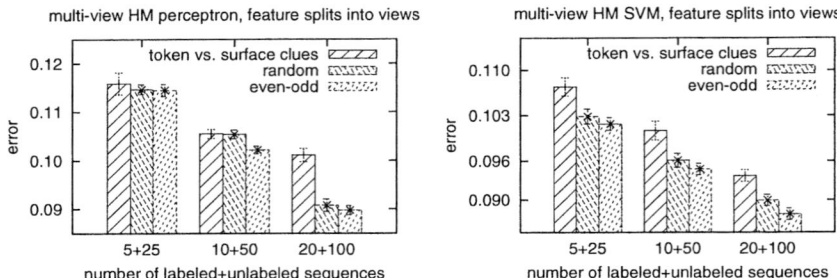

Fig. 3. Error for several splits of features into views for Spanish news wire

clues. Figure 3 shows that this split performs slightly but significantly better than the random split. Hence, our experiments show that even though multi-view learning using the split of token and n-grams versus surface clues leads to a substantial improvement over single-view learning, a random or odd-even split lead to an even better performance.

7 Conclusion

Starting from two discriminative sequence learning algorithms – the Hidden Markov perceptron and SVM – we constructed semi-supervised learning methods by utilizing the principle of consensus maximization between hypotheses. We derived the multi-view HM perceptron as well as multi-view 1-norm and 2-norm HM SVMs. Our experiments show that, on average, these methods utilize unlabeled data effectively and outperform their purely supervised counterparts significantly; the multi-view HM SVM achieves the highest performance.

We observed that random feature splits perform better than splitting the features into a token view and a view of surface clues. Nevertheless, the multi-view algorithms outperform their supervised counterparts even for the initial weak split. Our future work will address the construction of good feature splits.

Acknowledgment

This work has been funded by the German Science Foundation DFG under grant SCHE540/10-1.

References

1. S. Abney. Bootstrapping. In *Proceedings of the Annual Meeting of the Association for Computational Linguistics*, 2002.
2. Y. Altun, T. Hofmann, and A. J. Smola. Gaussian process classification for segmenting and annotating sequences. In *Proceedings of the International Conference on Machine Learning*, 2004.

3. Y. Altun, M. Johnson, and T. Hofmann. Discriminative learning for label sequences via boosting. In *Advances in Neural Information Processing Systems*, 2003.
4. Y. Altun, I. Tsochantaridis, and T. Hofmann. Hidden Markov support vector machines. In *Proc. of the International Conference on Machine Learning*, 2003.
5. A. Blum and T. Mitchell. Combining labeled and unlabeled data with co-training. In *Proc. of the Conference on Computational Learning Theory*, 1998.
6. U. Brefeld and T. Scheffer. Co-em support vector learning. In *Proceedings of the International Conference on Machine Learning*, 2004.
7. M. Collins. Ranking algorithms for named-entity extraction: Boosting and the voted perceptron. In *Proceedings of the Annual Meeting of the Association for Computational Linguistics*, 2002.
8. M. Collins and N. Duffy. Convolution kernels for natural language. In *Advances in Neural Information Processing Systems*, 2002.
9. M. Collins and Y. Singer. Unsupervised models for named entity classification. In *Proceedings of the Joint SIGDAT Conference on Empirical Methods in Natural Language Processing and Very Large Corpora*, 1999.
10. S. Dasgupta, M. Littman, and D. McAllester. PAC generalization bounds for co-training. In *Proceedings of Neural Information Processing Systems*, 2001.
11. V. de Sa. Learning classification with unlabeled data. In *Proceedings of Neural Information Processing Systems*, 1994.
12. R. Ghani. Combining labeled and unlabeled data for multiclass text categorization. In *Proceedings of the International Conference on Machine Learning*, 2002.
13. J. Hakenberg, S. Bickel, C. Plake, U. Brefeld, H. Zahn, L. Faulstich, U. Leser, and T. Scheffer. Systematic feature evaluation for gene name recognition. *BMC Bioinformatics*, 6(1):S9, 2005.
14. J. Lafferty, A. McCallum, and F. Pereira. Conditional random fields: probabilistic modesl for segmenting and labeling sequence data. In *Proceedings of the International Conference on Machine Learning*, 2001.
15. J. Lafferty, X. Zhu, and Y. Liu. Kernel conditional random fields: representation and clique selection. In *Proc. of the Int. Conference on Machine Learning*, 2004.
16. D. McAllester, M. Collins, and F. Pereira. Case-factor diagrams for structured probabilistic modeling. In *Proceedings of the Conference on Uncertainty in Artificial Intelligence*, 2004.
17. A. McCallum, D. Freitag, and F. Pereira. Maximum entropy markov models for information extraction and segmentation. In *Proceedings of the International Conference on Machine Learning*, 2000.
18. R. McDonald and F. Pereira. Identifying gene and protein mentions in text using conditional random fields. In *Proceedings of the BioCreative Workshop*, 2004.
19. I. Muslea, C. Kloblock, and S. Minton. Active + semi-supervised learning = robust multi-view learning. In *Proc. of the International Conf. on Machine Learning*, 2002.
20. K. Nigam and R. Ghani. Analyzing the effectiveness and applicability of co-training. In *Proceedings of Information and Knowledge Management*, 2000.
21. B. Taskar, C. Guestrin, and D. Koller. Max-margin Markov networks. In *Advances in Neural Information Processing Systems*, 2003.
22. I. Tsochantaridis, T. Hofmann, T. Joachims, and Y. Altun. Support vector machine learning for interdependent and structured output spaces. In *Proceedings of the International Conference on Machine Learning*, 2004.
23. D. Yarowsky. Unsupervised word sense disambiguation rivaling supervised methods. In *Proc. of the Annual Meeting of the Association for Comp. Ling.*, 1995.

Robust Bayesian Linear Classifier Ensembles

Jesús Cerquides[1] and Ramon López de Màntaras[2]

[1] Dept. de Matemàtica Aplicada i Anàlisi, Universitat de Barcelona
cerquide@maia.ub.es
[2] Artificial Intelligence Research Institute - IIIA,
Spanish Council for Scientific Research - CSIC
mantaras@iiia.csic.es

Abstract. Ensemble classifiers combine the classification results of several classifiers. Simple ensemble methods such as uniform averaging over a set of models usually provide an improvement over selecting the single best model. Usually probabilistic classifiers restrict the set of possible models that can be learnt in order to lower computational complexity costs. In these restricted spaces, where incorrect modeling assumptions are possibly made, uniform averaging sometimes performs even better than bayesian model averaging. Linear mixtures over sets of models provide an space that includes uniform averaging as a particular case. We develop two algorithms for learning maximum a posteriori weights for linear mixtures, based on expectation maximization and on constrained optimizition. We provide a nontrivial example of the utility of these two algorithms by applying them for one dependence estimators. We develop the conjugate distribution for one dependence estimators and empirically show that uniform averaging is clearly superior to Bayesian model averaging for this family of models. After that we empirically show that the maximum a posteriori linear mixture weights improve accuracy significantly over uniform aggregation.

1 Introduction

An ensemble of classifiers is a set of classifiers whose individual decisions are combined in some way (typically by weighted or unweighted voting) to classify new examples. Uniform averaging and other improper linear models have been demonstrated to be better than selecting a single best model [5].

Bayesian model averaging (BMA) [19,20] provides a coherent, theoretically optimal mechanism for accounting with model uncertainty. BMA, under the name Bayesian voting, is commonly understood as a method for learning ensembles [6]. With some exceptions [4,2], the application of BMA in machine learning has not proven as successful as expected [7]. A reasonable explanation of this mismatch between expected and real performance of BMA has been given in a short note by Minka [27], where it is clearly pointed out that BMA is not a model combination technique, and that it should be thought of as a method for 'soft model selection'. This understanding has led to the proposal of techniques for the bayesian combination of classifiers [13]. In spite of that, BMA is still being considered by many scientists as an ensemble learning technique and as such it is compared with other ensemble learning techniques such as stacking, bagging or boosting [3,9].

Accepting BMA as 'soft model selection', it can happen that uniform averaging improves over BMA when modeling assumptions are incorrect. Many times this is the case when classifiers are applied "out-of-the-box". However, an ensemble classifier should be able to recognize which models are right and which are incorrect. In order to do that, we propose two algorithms for adjusting the weights for a linear mixture of classifiers and are robust to incorrect modeling assumptions of the base classifiers.

The issue of generative versus discriminative classifiers has raised a lot of attention in the community in the last years [28,1,30,16,15,31]. It is widely believed that, provided enough data, discriminative classifiers outperform their generative pairs. Since both generative and discriminative classifiers are in use nowadays, two different initial settings are assumed in order to construct a linear ensemble of classifiers. In the first one, we are given a set of base classifiers that after receiving an unclassified observation, output the conditional probability distribution for each class. On the second setting, our base classifiers are assumed to output the joint probability for each class and the observation (instead of contioned to the observation). We could name the first setting linear averaging of discriminative classifiers and the second linear averaging of generative classifiers. We propose the usage of an expectation maximization algorithm for the first setting. The second setting is tougher and we propose the usage of augmented lagrangian techniques [14,29] for constrained nonlinear optimization.

In the last years there have been several attempts to improve the naive Bayes classifier by relaxing its restrictive independence assumption [10,22,38,2]. Averaged One Dependence Estimators (AODE) classifiers have been proposed [36] as an efficient and effective alternative to naive Bayes. They are based on k-dependence estimators [32], which are classifiers where the probability of each attribute value is conditioned by the class and at most k other attributes. AODE classifiers estimate the class probabilities by performing an equally weighted linear combination of the estimates of all possible 1-dependence estimators. Since AODE is a classifier based on uniform aggregation of simple classifiers that make very hard assumptions that are likely not to be fulfilled, it can act as a good test case for our algorithms. We describe AODE in section 4. In section 5 we find a conjugate distribution for the problem and we prove that it is possible to perform exact BMA over the set of 1-dependence estimators in polynomial time. After that, in section 6 we adapt our weight adjustment algorithms for ODEs and finally in section 7 we empirically compare the results of BMA with uniform averaging and our two linear mixtures, obtaining results that clearly confirm the previously exposed ideas.

In [33,34] a Bayesian technique for finding maximum likelihood ensembles of Bayesian networks is described. In [26,25] an EM algorithm for finding linear mixtures of trees is proposed. Those works were stated in the setting of density estimation (mixtures were learned with a generative approach in mind) and our explicitly deals with the problem of classification or conditional density estimation (discriminative approach). Ghahramani et al. [13] presented Bayesian methods for averaging classifiers. They assume the predicted class to be the only information available as output from the classifiers to be averaged. We assume a bit more and ask classifiers to output a probability distribution. This setting was already proposed by them as a rellevant line of future work.

To summarize, the main contribution of the paper is the proposal of two maximum a posteriori algorithms for averaging probability distributions in a supervised setting.

As side results, we provide the conjugate distribution for ODEs and empirically confirm the limitations of BMA when understood as an ensemble learning technique in a nontrivial case. A more detailed study of the two algorithms proposed and a comparison with other general ensemble learning methods will be the subject of future work.

2 Formalization and Notation

A *discrete attribute* is a finite set, for example we can define attribute $Pressure$ as $Pressure = \{Low, Medium, High\}$. A *discrete domain* is a finite set of discrete attributes. We denote $\Omega_C = \{A_1, \ldots, A_n, C\}$ for a classified discrete domain where A_u are attributes other than the class and C is the class attribute. We will use i and j as values of an attribute and u and v as indexes over attributes in a domain. We denote $X_{-C} = \{A_1, \ldots, A_n\}$ the set that contains all the attributes in a classified discrete domain except the class attribute.

Given an attribute X, we denote $\#X$ as the number of different values of X. An *observation* x in Ω_C is an ordered tuple $x = (x_1, \ldots, x_n, x_C) \in A_1 \times \ldots \times A_n \times C$. An *unclassified observation* x_{-C} in Ω_C is an ordered tuple $x_{-C} = (x_1, \ldots, x_n) \in A_1 \times \ldots \times A_n$. To be homogeneous we will abuse this notation a bit noting x_C for a possible value of the class for x_{-C}. A *dataset* $\mathcal{D}$ in Ω_C is a multiset of classified observations in Ω_C.

We will denote N for the number of observations in the dataset. We will also denote $N_u(i)$ for the number of observations in $\mathcal{D}$ where the value for A_u is i, $N_{u,v}(i,j)$ the number of observations in $\mathcal{D}$ where the value for A_u is i and the value for A_v is j and similarly for $N_{u,v,w}(i,j,k)$ and so on.

3 Learning Mixtures of Probability Distributions

In order to aggregate the predictions of a set of different models, we can use a linear mixture assigning a weigth to each model. If modeling assumptions are correct, BMA provides the best linear mixture. Otherwise, uniform averaging has been demonstrated to improve over single model selection and many times also over BMA. We would like to develop an algorithm for assigning weigths to models in a linear mixture that improves over uniform averaging while being robust to incorrect modeling assumptions of the base classifiers.

3.1 Formalization of the Problem

On a classified discrete domain Ω_C, we define two different types of probability distributionss. A generative probability distribution (GPD) is a probability distribution over Ω_C. A discriminative probability distribution (DPD) is a probability distribution over C given X_{-C}. Obviously, from every GPD, we can construct a DPD, but not *vice versa*.

A linear mixture of n DPDs (LMD in the following) is defined by the equation:

$$P_{LMD}(x_C|x_{-C}) = \sum_{u=1}^{n} \alpha_u P_{DPD_u}(x_C|x_{-C}). \tag{1}$$

The model is more widely known as the *linear opinion pool* [12,11].

A linear mixture of n GPDs (LMG in the following) is defined by the equation:

$$P_{LMG}(x_C, x_{-C}) = \sum_{u=1}^{n} \alpha_u P_{GPD_u}(x_C, x_{-C}), \qquad (2)$$

in both cases $\sum_{u=1}^{n} \alpha_u = 1$ and $\forall u \; \alpha_u > 0$.

Supervised Posteriors. From a frequentistic point of view, in order to learn conditional probability distributions we need to maximize conditional likelihood. In [17] the concept of *supervised posterior* is introduced as a Bayesian response to this frequentistic idea. The proposal in [17] is that from a Bayesian point of view, in order to learn conditional probability distributions, given a family of models $\mathcal{M}$, we need to compute the BMA over models using the supervised posterior $P^s(M|\mathcal{D})$:

$$P(x_C|x_{-C}, \mathcal{D}, \xi) = \int_{M \in \mathcal{M}} P(x_C|x_{-C}, M, \xi) P^s(M|\mathcal{D}, \xi), \qquad (3)$$

where

$$P^s(M|\mathcal{D}, \xi) = P^s(\mathcal{D}|M, \xi) P(M|\xi) \qquad (4)$$

and

$$P^s(\mathcal{D}|M, \xi) = \prod_{x \in \mathcal{D}} P(x_C|x_{-C}, M, \xi). \qquad (5)$$

Supervised posterior for LMD. In order to perform Bayesian learning over LMD and LMG we define a prior distribution over $\boldsymbol{\alpha}$. A natural choice in this case is to use a Dirichlet distribution. For conciseness we fix the Dirichlet hyperparameters to 1, that is $P(\boldsymbol{\alpha}|\xi) \propto \prod_{u=1}^{n} \alpha_u$, although the development can be easily generalized to any Dirichlet prior. The supervised posterior after an i.i.d. dataset $\mathcal{D}$ for a LMD is:

$$P_{LMD}(\boldsymbol{\alpha}|\mathcal{D}, \xi) = \frac{P(\mathcal{D}|\boldsymbol{\alpha},\xi) P(\boldsymbol{\alpha}|\xi)}{P(\mathcal{D}|\xi)} = \frac{\prod_{x \in \mathcal{D}} P(x_C|x_{-C}, \boldsymbol{\alpha},\xi) P(x_{-C}|\boldsymbol{\alpha},\xi) P(\boldsymbol{\alpha}|\xi)}{P(\mathcal{D}|\xi)} =$$

$$= \prod_{x \in \mathcal{D}} P(x_C|x_{-C}, \boldsymbol{\alpha},\xi) P(\boldsymbol{\alpha}|\xi) \frac{\prod_{x \in \mathcal{D}} P(x_{-C}|\boldsymbol{\alpha},\xi)}{P(\mathcal{D}|\xi)}. \qquad (6)$$

Assuming that $P(x_{-C}|\boldsymbol{\alpha}, \xi)$ does not depend on $\boldsymbol{\alpha}$ we can conclude that

$$P_{LMD}(\boldsymbol{\alpha}|\mathcal{D}, \xi) \propto \prod_{x \in \mathcal{D}} \sum_{u=1}^{n} \alpha_u P_{DPD_u}(x_C|x_{-C}) \prod_{u=1}^{n} \alpha_u. \qquad (7)$$

The exact BMA prediction in this setting will be given by:

$$P_{LMD}(x_C|x_{-C}, \mathcal{D}, \xi) = \int_{\boldsymbol{\alpha}} P_{LMD}(\boldsymbol{\alpha}|\mathcal{D}, \xi) \sum_{u=1}^{n} \alpha_u P_{DPD_u}(x_C|x_{-C}) d\boldsymbol{\alpha}. \qquad (8)$$

Supervised Posterior for LMG. The supervised posterior after an i.i.d. dataset $\mathcal{D}$ for LMG is

$$P_{LMG}(\boldsymbol{\alpha}|\mathcal{D},\xi) = \prod_{x \in \mathcal{D}} \frac{\sum_{u=1}^{n} \alpha_u P_{GPD_u}(x_C, x_{-C})}{\sum_{c \in C} \sum_{u=1}^{n} \alpha_u P_{GPD_u}(c, x_{-C})} \prod_{u=1}^{n} \alpha_u, \qquad (9)$$

and the exact BMA prediction in this setting

$$P_{LMG}(x_C|x_{-C},\mathcal{D},\xi) = \int_{\boldsymbol{\alpha}} P_{LMG}(\boldsymbol{\alpha}|\mathcal{D},\xi) \frac{\sum_{u=1}^{n} \alpha_u P_{GPD_u}(x_C, x_{-C})}{\sum_{c \in C} \sum_{u=1}^{n} \alpha_u P_{GPD_u}(c, x_{-C})} d\boldsymbol{\alpha}. \qquad (10)$$

3.2 Proposed Solutions

MAPLMD. To the best of our knowledge there is no closed form solution for computing the result of equation 8. Hence, we will have to approximate its value. A first possibility would be to directly approximate it using Markov Chain Monte Carlo (MCMC). However, each iteration of the model will require the computation of the product in equation 8 that ranges over all the observations in the dataset, resulting in a heavy use of computational resources. A second possibility is approximating the expression using only the maximum a posteriori (MAP) value for $\boldsymbol{\alpha}$ (which we denote $\boldsymbol{\alpha}_{LMD}^{MAP}$) as

$$P(x_C|x_{-C},\mathcal{D},\xi) \approx \sum_{u=1}^{n} \alpha_{u\,LMD}^{MAP} P_{DPD_u}(x_C|x_{-C}). \qquad (11)$$

It is known [24,23] that, since we are dealing with a finite mixture model, we can determine $\boldsymbol{\alpha}_{LMD}^{MAP}$ by means of the Expectation-Maximization (EM) algorithm by posing the problem into an incomplete-data one introducing an additional unobservable variable for each observation corresponding to the mixture component that generated the data. This gives us a reasonably efficient procedure for determining $\boldsymbol{\alpha}_{LMD}^{MAP}$. The aggregation method resulting from finding $\boldsymbol{\alpha}_{LMD}^{MAP}$ and then applying it in equation 1 is MAPLMD.

MAPLMG. The case of LMG is not so simple. As we did for LMD, we can approximate the exact BMA prediction using only the MAP value for $\boldsymbol{\alpha}$ (that we denote $\boldsymbol{\alpha}_{LMG}^{MAP}$). However, in this case, there is no straightforward way to use the EM algorithm. From an optimization point of view, we have to find $\boldsymbol{\alpha}_{LMG}^{MAP}$, under the inequality constraints that each component of the vector $\boldsymbol{\alpha}_{LMG}^{MAP}$ should be greater that 0 and the equality constraint that the components of $\boldsymbol{\alpha}_{LMG}^{MAP}$ should add up to 1. This is a constrained nonlinear optimization problem that can be solved by using the augmented (or penalized) lagrangian method [14,29] for constrained nonlinear optimization. This method transforms a constrained nonlinear optimization problem into a sequence of unconstrained optimization problems, progresively adjusting the penalization provided by not fulfilling the constraints. For solving each of the resulting unconstrained optimization problems several efficient methods are available. In our case we have used the well known Broyden-Fletcher-Goldfarb-Shanno (BFGS) algorithm. It is a quasi-Newton method which builds up an approximation to the second derivatives of the function using the difference between successive gradient vectors. By combining the first and second derivatives the algorithm is able to take Newton-type steps towards the function minimum, assuming quadratic behavior in that region. This technique requires the computation of the partial derivative of the function to be optimized with respect to each of the α_i. Fortunately this can be done efficiently if we calculate it together with the function. By simple algebraic manipulations it can be seen that the derivative of equation 9 is:

$$\frac{\partial P(\boldsymbol{\alpha}|\mathcal{D},\xi)}{\partial \alpha_u} = P(\boldsymbol{\alpha}|\mathcal{D},\xi) \left(\sum_{x \in \mathcal{D}} \frac{p_{u,x_C} \sum_{u=1}^{n} \alpha_u p_u - p_u \sum_{u=1}^{n} \alpha_u p_{u,x_C}}{\sum_{u=1}^{n} \alpha_u p_u \sum_{u=1}^{n} \alpha_u p_{u,x_C}} + \frac{1}{\alpha_u} \right), \quad (12)$$

where $p_{u,c} = P_{GPD_u}(c, x_{-C})$ and $p_u = \sum_{c \in C} P_{GPD_u}(c, x_{-C})$. In order to complete the Lagrangian, we also need to compute the derivatives of the constraints, $\sum u = 1^n \alpha_u = 1$ and $\forall u \; \alpha_u > 0$, with respect to each α_u, that are very simple. The aggregation method resulting from finding α_{LMG}^{MAP} and then predicting using equation 2 is named MAPLMG.

4 AODE

In this section we review the AODE classifier as presented in [36]. Given a classified domain, AODE learns a set of 1-dependence probability distribution estimators (ODE) containing those where the class attribute and another single attribute are the parents of all other attributes. Obviously there are n ODEs satisfying our condition, one for each choice of root attribute. The probablity estimates for an ODE are:

$$P_u(x) = P_u(x_C, x_{-C}) = P_u(x_C, x_u) \prod_{\substack{v=1 \\ v \neq u}}^{n} P_u(x_v | x_C, x_u), \quad (13)$$

where $P_u(x_C, x_u) = \frac{N_{C,u}(x_C, x_u)+1}{N+\#C\#A_u}$ and $P_u(x_v | x_C, x_u) = \frac{N_{C,u,v}(x_C, x_u, x_v)+1}{N_{C,u}(x_C, x_u)+\#A_v}$ (these equations are slightly different to the ones presented in [36] and correspond to the AODE classifier implemented in Weka[37] version 3.4.3). After learning these models, AODE uniformly combines the probabilities for each of them:

$$P_{AODE}(x_C, x_{-C}) = \sum_{\substack{u=1 \\ N_u(x_u) > t}}^{n} P_u(x_C, x_{-C}). \quad (14)$$

In equation 14, the condition $N_u(x_u) > t$ is used as a threshold in order to avoid making predictions from attributes having few observations. If no attribute fulfills the condition, AODE returns the results of predicting using naive Bayes.

5 Exact Bayesian Model Averaging of ODEs

In this section we provide a conjugate distribution for ODEs and show how it can be used to efficiently perform BMA over ODEs.

5.1 Conjugate Distribution for One Dependence Estimators

In order to define a probability distribution over ODEs, we define how we compute the probability that an ODE is the generating model. After that, we define the probability distribution over the parameters of that ODE. Probability distribution over the parameters of two different ODEs u and v (denoted $^u\Theta$ and $^v\Theta$) are assumed independent.

Definition 1 (Decomposable distribution over ODEs). *The probability of an ODE with concrete structure and parameters under a decomposable distribution over ODEs with hyperparameters $\alpha, \mathbf{N}' = \bigcup_{u=1}^{n} {}^u\mathbf{N}'$ is the product of the probability that its root is the selected root ($P(\rho_B|\xi)$) times the probability that its parameters are the right parameters ($P(^{\rho_B}\Theta|\xi)$):*

$$P(B|\xi) = P(\rho_B|\xi)P(^{\rho_B}\Theta|\xi). \quad (15)$$

The probability distribution for the root is a multinomial with hyperparameter α. The probability for the parameter set, $^u\Theta$, for each possible root u factorizes following the ODE structure:

$$P(^u\Theta|\xi) = P(^u\theta_{u,C}|\xi) \prod_{\substack{v=1 \\ v \neq u}}^{m} P(^u\theta_{v|u,C}|\xi) \quad (16)$$

and the distribution over each conditional probability table follows a Dirichlet distribution (where the needed hyperparameters are given by $^u\mathbf{N}'$):

$$P(^u\theta_{u,C}|\xi) = D(^u\theta_{u,C}(.,.); {}^u N'_{u,C}(.,.)) \quad (17)$$

$$P(^v\theta_{v|u,C}|\xi) = D(^u\theta_{v|u,C}(.,i,c); {}^u N'_{v,u,C}(.,i,c)) \quad (18)$$

5.2 Learning Under Decomposable Distributions over ODEs

If a decomposable distribution over ODEs is accepted as prior, we can efficiently calculate the posterior after a complete i.i.d. dataset:

Theorem 1. *If $P(B|\xi)$ follows a decomposable distribution over ODEs with hyperparameters $\alpha, \mathbf{N}'$, the posterior distribution given an i.i.d. dataset D is a decomposable distribution over ODEs with hyperparameters $\alpha^*, \mathbf{N}'^*$ given by:*

$$\alpha_u^* = \alpha_u W_u \quad (19)$$

$$^u N'^*_{u,C}(i,c) = {}^u N'_{u,C}(i,c) + N_{u,C}(i,c) \quad (20)$$

$$^u N'^*_{v,u,C}(j,i,c) = {}^u N'_{v,u,C}(j,i,c) + N_{v,u,C}(j,i,c) \quad (21)$$

where

$$W_u = \frac{\Gamma(N')}{\Gamma(N'^*)} \prod_{c \in C} \prod_{i \in A_u} \left[\frac{\Gamma(^u N'^*_{u,C}(i,c))}{\Gamma(^u N'_{u,C}(i,c))} \prod_{\substack{v=1 \\ v \neq u}}^{m} \left(\frac{\Gamma(^{u,s(v)} N'_{u,C}(i,c))}{\Gamma(^{u,s(v)} N'^*_{u,C}(i,c))} \prod_{j \in A_v} \frac{\Gamma(^u N'^*_{v,u,C}(j,i,c))}{\Gamma(^u N'_{v,u,C}(j,i,c))} \right) \right],$$
(22)

and

$$^u N' = \sum_{c \in C} \sum_{i \in A_u} {^u N'_{u,C}(i,c)} \tag{23}$$

$$^{u,s(v)} N'_{u,C}(i,c)) = \sum_{j \in A_v} {^u N'_{v,u,C}(j,i,c)}, \tag{24}$$

and the equivalent of equations 23 and 24 hold for N'^*.

5.3 Classifying Under Decomposable Distributions over ODEs

Under a decomposable distribution over ODEs, we can efficiently calculate the probability of an observation by averaging over both structure and parameters:

Theorem 2. *If $P(B|\xi)$ follows a decomposable distribution over ODEs with hyperparameters $\alpha, \mathbf{N}'$, the probability of an observation given ξ is*

$$P(\mathcal{X} = x|\xi) = \sum_{u=1}^{m} \alpha_u P(\mathcal{X} = x|\rho_B = u, \xi)$$

where $P(\mathcal{X} = x|\rho_B = u, \xi) = \frac{^u N'_{u,C}(x_u, x_C)}{^u N'} \prod_{\substack{v=1 \\ v \neq u}}^{m} \frac{^u N'_{v,u,C}(x_v, x_u, x_C)}{^{u,s(v)} N'_{u,C}(x_u, x_C)}.$

Theorems 1 and 2 demonstrate that exact learning can be performed in polynomial time under the assumption of decomposable distributions over ODEs. Furthermore, the overhead with respect to the standard AODE algorithm in terms of computational complexity can be considered very small. Proofs are omitted due to space limitations. For domains where we do not have prior information we will assign a value of 1 to each of the hyperparameters in α and $\mathbf{N}'$. We name the resulting classifier BMAAODE.

6 Learning Mixtures of ODEs

It is worth noting that the development in section 3 was done under the assumption that the dataset $\mathcal{D}$ used for determining α^{MAP} is assumed to be independent of the dataset used to learn the individual classifiers. To allow the successful application of this results to ODEs, instead of using $P_u(c, x_{-C})$ as the probability distribution being averaged, we will use $P_u^{LOO}(c, x_{-C})$ (from Leave-One-Out), where the observation being classified (x) is excluded from the training set. After computing the counts $N_{C,u,v}(c,i,j), N_{C,u}(c,x_u)$, and N, P_u^{LOO} is simply:

$$P_u^{LOO}(c, x_{-C}) = P_u^{LOO}(c, x_u) \prod_{\substack{v=1 \\ v \neq u}}^{n} P_u^{LOO}(x_v|c, x_u) \tag{25}$$

$$P_u^{LOO}(c, x_u) = \frac{N_{C,u}(c, x_u) + 1 - \delta(c = x_C)}{N + \#C \#A_u - 1} \tag{26}$$

$$P_u^{LOO}(x_v|c, x_u) = \frac{N_{C,u,v}(c, x_u, x_v) + 1 - \delta(c = x_C)}{N_{C,u}(c, x_u) + \#A_v - \delta(c = x_C)} \tag{27}$$

so almost no computational burden is introduced by this strategy. This can be understood as performing the best possible stacking [35] strategy with the data at hand, with an ODE for each attribute as the set of *level-0 models* and MAPLMD or MAPLMG as the *level-1 generalizer*. This particularization of MAPLMD and MAPLMG for ODE are named MAPLMDODE and MAPLMGODE respectively.

7 Empirical Results

In this section we compare AODE with BMAAODE, MAPLMGODE and MAPLMDODE on two different scenarios. On the first one we compare performance over Irvine datasets and on the secondone over randomly generated Bayesian networks with different sets of parameters. In the following sections, we explain the experimental setup and then show the results and draw some conclusions.

7.1 Experimental Setup

We used three different measures to compare the performance of the algorithms: the error rate, the conditional log-likelihood and the area under the ROC curve [8] which we will refer to as AUC. For this last measure, when the class is multivalued, we use the formula provided in [18].

Irvine Setup. We ran each algorithm on 38 datasets from the Irvine repository repeating 10 runs of 10 fold cross validation. Continuous attributes were discretized into 5 equal frequency intervals.

Random Bayesian Networks Setup. We compared the algorithms over random Bayesian networks varying the number of attributes in {5, 10, 20, 40}, the number of maximum values of an attribute in {2, 5, 10} and the maximum induced width in {2, 3, 4}. For each configuration of parameters we generated randomly 100 Bayesian networks using BNGenerator [21]. For each Bayesian network we obtained 5 learning samples of sizes {25, 100, 400, 1600, 6400} and a testing sample of size of 500.

7.2 Results and Conclusions

A summary of the results can be seen in tables 1 and 2. The tables describe the number of Wins/Draws/Loses at a 95% statistical t-test confidence level for each measure. AODE0 and AODE30 are two versions of AODE, with different thresholds $t = 0$ and $t = 30$ respectively. The results show that the condition $N_u(x_u) > t$ proposed in [36] although intuitively appealing, does not improve performance on none of both settings and can safely be simplified.

Table 1. Empirical results over Irvine datasets

Algorithms	AUC	ER	LogP
AODE0-AODE30	7/24/7	10/22/6	13/18/7
AODE0-BMAAODE	26/11/1	25/8/5	29/4/5
MAPLMGODE-AODE0	12/20/6	18/18/2	29/5/4
MAPLMDODE-AODE0	14/9/15	17/11/10	26/6/6

Table 2. Empirical results over random Bayesian networks

Algorithms	AUC	ER	LogP
AODE0-AODE30	38/124/18	45/128/7	85/92/3
AODE0-BMAAODE	101/77/2	90/83/7	143/26/11
MAPLMGODE-AODE0	155/24/1	138/41/1	151/17/12
MAPLMDODE-AODE0	176/4/0	145/27/8	177/2/1

It can be seen that BMAAODE performance is significantly worse than uniform aggregation in both settings. In order to understand the reason why, we note that in our Bayesian formalization of the problem an additional assumption has been introduced 'unnoticed': the assumption that one of the ODEs is the right model generating the data. This assumption has the effect that the posterior after a small number of observations concentrates most of its weight in a single model. AODE also makes a strong assumption: that the right model generating the data is a uniform aggregation of ODEs. This assumption turns out to be less restrictive that the one made by BMAAODE. Obviously, neither AODE nor BMAAODE assumptions are fulfilled by the datasets nor by the Bayesian networks used for the experimentation, but AODE is able to provide a better approximation than BMAAODE to their probability distributions most of the times. This result obviously does not change the fact that the assumption of a single generating model, as a generic assumption underlying Bayesian learning, is completely reasonable. However, it points out that we should be careful and understand that BMA provides the optimal linear ensemble only when the assumption is fulfilled.

Comparing AODE0 with MAPLMDODE and MAPLMGODE we can see that, with the only exception of MAPLMDODE over Irvine datasets and the AUC measure, both algorithms consistently improve AODE0 in a statistically significant way. Hence, we have shown that the general scheme for determining weights of linear mixtures developed in section 3, when particularized for ODEs, improves uniform aggregation significantly, even when the models make incorrect modeling assumptions.

8 Conclusions

We have argued that under incorrect modeling assumptions BMA can be worse than uniform aggregation. We have provided two maximum a posteriori algorithms to improve over uniform aggregation even in the case that the classifiers make incorrect modeling assumptions. We have shown by means of a nontrivial example that the algorithms can be applied with significant accuracy gains. A more detailed study of these algorithms and a comparison with other general ensemble learning methods will be the subject of future work.

References

1. G. Bouchard and B. Triggs. The tradeoff between generative and discriminative classifiers. In *IASC International Symposium on Computational Statistics (COMPSTAT)*, pages 721–728, Prague, August 2004.
2. J. Cerquides and R. López de Màntaras. Tan classifiers based on decomposable distributions. *Machine Learning- Special Issue on Graphical Models for Classification*, 59(3):323–354, 2005.
3. B. Clarke. Comparing bayes model averaging and stacking when model approximation error cannot be ignored. *Journal of Machine Learning Research*, 4:683–712, 2003.
4. D. Dash and G. F. Cooper. Model averaging for prediction with discrete bayesian networks. *Journal of Machine Learning Research*, 5:1177–1203, 2004.
5. R. Dawes. The robust beauty of improper linear models. *American Psychologist*, 34:571–582, 1979.
6. T. G. Dietterich. Ensemble methods in machine learning. In *MCS '00: Proceedings of the First International Workshop on Multiple Classifier Systems*, pages 1–15. Springer-Verlag, 2000.
7. P. Domingos. Bayesian averaging of classifiers and the overfitting problem. In *Proceedings of the Seventeenth International Conference on Machine Learning*, pages 223–230, 2000.
8. T. Fawcett. Roc graphs: Notes and practical considerations for data mining researchers. Technical Report HPL-2003-4, HP Laboratories Palo Alto, 2003.
9. J. Friedman. Importance sampling: An alternative view of ensemble learning. Workshop on Data Mining Methodology and Applications, October 2004.
10. N. Friedman, D. Geiger, and M. Goldszmidt. Bayesian network classifiers. *Machine Learning*, 29:131–163, 1997.
11. C. Genest and K. McConway. Allocating the weights in the linear opinion pool. *Journal of Forecasting*, 9:53–73, 1990.
12. C. Genest and J. Zidek. Combining probability distributions: A critique and an annotated bibliography. *Statistical Science*, 1(1):114–148, 1986.
13. Z. Ghahramani and H.-C. Kim. Bayesian classifier combination. Gatsby Technical report, 2003.
14. P. Gill, W. Murray, M. Saunders, and M. Wright. Constrained nonlinear programming. In G. Nemhauser, A. Rinnooy Kan, and M. Todd, editors, *Optimization*, Handbooks in Operations Research and Management Science. North-Holland, 1989.
15. R. Greiner, X. Su, B. Shen, and W. Zhou. Structural extension to logistic regression: Discriminant parameter learning of belief net classifiers. *Machine Learning - Special Issue on Graphical Models for Classification*, 59(3):297–322, 2005.
16. D. Grossman and P. Domingos. Learning bayesian network classifiers by maximizing conditional likelihood. In C. E. Brodley, editor, *ICML*. ACM, 2004.
17. P. Gruenwald, P. Kontkanen, P. Myllymäki, T. Roos, H. Tirri, and H. Wettig. Supervised posterior distributions. presented at the Seventh Valencia International Meeting on Bayesian Statistics, Tenerife, Spain, 2002.
18. D. Hand and R. Till. A simple generalization of the area under the roc curve to multiple class classification problems. *Machine Learning*, 45(2):171–186, 2001.

19. J. Hoeting, D. Madigan, A. Raftery, and C. Volinsky. Bayesian model averaging: A tutorial (with discussion). *Statistical science*, 14:382–401, 1999.
20. J. Hoeting, D. Madigan, A. Raftery, and C. Volinsky. Bayesian model averaging: A tutorial (with discussion) - correction. *Statistical science*, 15:193–195, 1999.
21. J. Ide and F. Cozman. Generation of random bayesian networks with constraints on induced width, with applications to the average analysis od d-connectivity, quasi-random sampling, and loopy propagation. Technical report, University of Sao Paulo, June 2003.
22. E. Keogh and M. Pazzani. Learning augmented bayesian classifiers: A comparison of distribution-based and classification-based approaches. In *Uncertainty 99: The Seventh International Workshop on Artificial Intelligence and Statistics*, Ft. Lauderdale, FL, 1999.
23. G. McLachlan and T. Krishnan. *The EM Algorithm and Extensions*. Wiley, 1997.
24. G. J. McLachlan and K. E. Basford. *Mixture Models*. Marcel Dekker, 1988.
25. M. Meila and M. I. Jordan. Learning with mixtures of trees. *Journal of Machine Learning Research*, 1:1–48, 2000.
26. M. Meila-Predoviciu. *Learning with mixtures of trees*. PhD thesis, Department of Electrical Engineering and Computer Science, MIT, 1999.
27. T. Minka. Bayesian model averaging is not model combination. MIT Media Lab note, December 2002.
28. A. Y. Ng and M. I. Jordan. On discriminative vs. generative classifiers: A comparison of logistic regression and naive bayes. In T. G. Dietterich, S. Becker, and Z. Ghahramani, editors, *Advances in Neural Information Processing Systems 14*, pages 841–848, Cambridge, MA, 2002. MIT Press.
29. P. Pedregal. *Introduction to Optimization*. Number 46 in Texts in Applied Mathematics. Springer, 2004.
30. R. Raina, Y. Shen, A. Y. Ng, and A. McCallum. Classification with hybrid generative/discriminative models. In S. Thrun, L. Saul, and B. Schölkopf, editors, *Advances in Neural Information Processing Systems 16*. MIT Press, Cambridge, MA, 2004.
31. T. Roos, H. Wettig, P. Grünwald, P. Myllymäki, and H. Tirri. On discriminative bayesian network classifiers and logistic regression. *Machine Learning - Special Issue on Graphical Models for Classification*, 59(3):267–296, 2005.
32. M. Sahami. Learning limited dependence Bayesian classifiers. In *Second International Conference on Knowledge Discovery in Databases*, pages 335–338, 1996.
33. B. Thiesson, C. Meek, D. Chickering, and D. Heckerman. Learning mixtures of bayesian networks, 1997.
34. B. Thiesson, C. Meek, D. Chickering, and D. Heckerman. Learning mixtures of dag models. In *Proceedings of the 14th Conference on Uncertainty in Artificial Intelligence (UAI-98)*, pages 504–513, 1998.
35. K. Ting and I. Witten. Issues in stacked generalization. *Journal of Artificial Intelligence Research*, 10:271–289, 1999.
36. G. I. Webb, J. Boughton, and Z. Wang. Not so naive bayes: Aggregating one-dependence estimators. *Machine Learning*, 58(1):5–24, 2005.
37. I. H. Witten and E. Frank. *Data Mining: practical machine learning tools and techniques with java implementations*. Morgan Kaufmann, 2000.
38. Z. Zheng and G. I. Webb. Lazy learning of bayesian rules. *Machine Learning*, 41(1):53–84, 2000.

An Integrated Approach to Learning Bayesian Networks of Rules

Jesse Davis[1], Elizabeth Burnside[1], Inês de Castro Dutra[2],
David Page[1], and Vítor Santos Costa[2]

[1] Department of Biostatistics and Medical Informatics,
University of Wisconsin-Madison, USA
[2] COPPE/Sistemas, UFRJ, Centro de Tecnologia, Bloco H-319,
Cx. Postal 68511 Rio de Janeiro, Brasil

Abstract. Inductive Logic Programming (ILP) is a popular approach for learning rules for classification tasks. An important question is how to combine the individual rules to obtain a useful classifier. In some instances, converting each learned rule into a binary feature for a Bayes net learner improves the accuracy compared to the standard decision list approach [3,4,14]. This results in a two-step process, where rules are generated in the first phase, and the classifier is learned in the second phase. We propose an algorithm that interleaves the two steps, by incrementally building a Bayes net during rule learning. Each candidate rule is introduced into the network, and scored by whether it improves the performance of the classifier. We call the algorithm SAYU for Score As You Use. We evaluate two structure learning algorithms Naïve Bayes and Tree Augmented Naïve Bayes. We test SAYU on four different datasets and see a significant improvement in two out of the four applications. Furthermore, the theories that SAYU learns tend to consist of far fewer rules than the theories in the two-step approach.

1 Introduction

Inductive Logic Programming (ILP) is a popular approach for learning in a relational environment. Given a set of positive and negative examples, an ILP system finds a logical description of the underlying data model that differentiates between the positive and negative examples. Usually this description is a set of *rules* or clauses, forming a logic program. In this case, unseen examples are applied to each clause in succession, forming a *decision list*. If the example matches one of the rules, it receives a positive label. If the example does not match any rule, it receives the negative classification. In an ideal world, where the rules would perfectly discriminate between the two classes, the decision list would represent an optimal combination scheme. In practice, it is difficult to find rules that do not cover any negative examples. As the precision of the individual rules declines, so does the accuracy of the decision list, as it maximizes the number of false positives.

The key question becomes how to combine a set of rules to obtain a useful classifier. Previous work has shown that an effective approach is to treat each learned rule as an attribute in a propositional learner, and to use the classifier to determine the final label of the example [3,4,14]. This methodology defines a two-step process. In the first step, an ILP algorithm learns a set of rules. In the second step, a classifier combines the learned rules. One weakness of this approach is that the rules learned in the first step are being evaluated by a different metric than how they are ultimately scored in the second step. ILP traditionally scores clauses through a coverage score or compression metric. Thus we have no guarantee that the rule learning process will select the rules that best contribute to the final classifier.

We propose an alternative approach, based on the idea of *constructing the classifier as we learn the rules*. In our approach, rules are scored by how much they improve the classifier, providing a tight coupling between rule generation and rule usage. We call this methodology *Score As You Use* or *SAYU*. Recently Landwehr, Kersting and De Raedt[10] have also provided a tight coupling between rule generation and rule usage, by integrating FOIL and Naïve Bayes, although their scoring function for rules is not exactly the improvement in performance of the Naïve Bayes classifier that the rule provides. The relationship to this important work is discussed in Section 5.

In order to implement SAYU, we first defined an interface that allows an ILP algorithm to control a propositional learner. Second, we developed a greedy algorithm that uses the interface to decide whether to retain a candidate clause. We implemented this interface using Aleph to learn ILP rules, and Bayesian networks as the combining mechanism. Previous experience has shown good results in using Bayes nets as a combining mechanism [3,4,14]. We used two different Bayes net structure learning algorithms, Naïve Bayes and Tree Augmented Naïve Bayes (TAN) [6] as propositional learners. Our results show that, given the same amount of CPU time, SAYU clearly outperforms the original two-step approach. Furthermore, SAYU learns smaller theories. These results were obtained even though SAYU considers far fewer rules than standard ILP.

2 Implementing SAYU

SAYU requires an interface to propose rules to the propositional learner. Additionally, SAYU needs to know the score of each clause in order to help guide rule search. The interface consists of the following three methods.

The $Init()$ function initializes the propositional learner with a table containing only the class attribute. The $NewAttribute(NewFeature)$ function introduces $NewFeature$ into the training set and learns a new classifier incorporating this attribute. It returns a score for the new network on a set of examples. The $Commit()$ function permanently incorporates the most recently evaluated feature into the classifier.

We use the interface to design a greedy learning algorithm, where the ILP system proposes a rule and converts it into a new attribute. The rule is then incorporated into the learner. If the rule improves the score, it is retained by the classifier. Otherwise, we discard the rule and revert back to the old classifier.

```
Input: Stop Criteria, Scoring Function
Output: Propositional Classifier
CurrentScore = Init();
while Stop criteria not met do
    Choose a positive example as a seed and saturate the example;
    repeat
        NewFeature = Generate new clause according to saturated example;
        NewScore = NewAttribute(NewFeature);
        if NewScore exceeds CurrentScore then
            | Commit();
        end
    until NewScore exceeds CurrentScore;
end
```
Algorithm 1: Implementing SAYU

Our implementation depends on the ILP system and on the propositional learner. Following previous work, we used saturation based learning ILP systems, in the style of the MDIE algorithm used in Progol [12] and Aleph [19]. In MDIE, the ILP search proceeds by randomly choosing an unexplained seed, and saturating that seed to obtain its most specific, or *saturated* clause. It then searches the space of clauses that generalize the saturated clause until finding the *best* clause.

The algorithm we used for this work follows the same principles, with one major difference: we search for the first *good* clause for each seed, instead of continuing search until finding the best clause. The main reason for picking the first good clause is that the best clause may be hard to find, thus exhaustively searching for the best clause may end up wasting our time on a single seed. Our implementation is shown in Algorithm 1.

Next, we present our propositional learning algorithms. Bayesian learning algorithms have several important advantages for our purposes. First, they allow us to give examples a probability. Second, Naïve Bayes is a well known approach that often performs well, and is particularly suitable for incremental learning. The drawback of Naïve Bayes is that it assumes that all of the rules are independent, given the class value. We evaluate Naïve Bayes against Tree Augmented Naïve Bayes (TAN) [6]. TAN networks can be learned efficiently, and can represent a limited set of dependencies between the attributes.

Finally, we need to define a scoring function. The main goal is to use the scoring function for both learning and evaluation. Furthermore, we wish to be able to handle datasets that have a highly skewed class distribution. In the presence of skew, precision and recall are often used to evaluate classifier quality. In order to characterize how the algorithm performs over the whole precision recall space, we follow Goadrich et.al. [7], and adopt the area under the precision-recall curve as our score metric. When calculating the area under the precision-recall curve, we integrate from recall levels of 0.2 or greater. Precision-recall curves can be misleading at low levels of recall as they have high variation in that region.

3 Methodology

We evaluated our algorithm with four very different datasets, corresponding to different applications of ILP. Two of the applications are relatively novel, the *Mammography* and *Yeast Proteins* datasets. The other application, *Carcinogenesis*, is well-known in the Inductive Logic Programming Community. Finally, we used the Univeristy of Washington *Advised By* dataset that is becoming a popular benchmark in Statistical Relational Learning [9,17].

Mammography. The *Mammography* dataset was the original motivation of this work. The National Mammography Database (NMD) standard established by the American College of Radiology. The NMD was designed to standardize data collection for mammography practices in the United States and is widely used for quality assurance. The database consisted of 47,669 mammography examinations on 18,270 patients. The dataset contains 435 malignant abnormalities and 65,365 benign abnormalities. It is important to note that the data consists of a radiologist's interpretation of a mammogram and not the raw image data. A mammogram can contain multiple abnormalities. The target predicate we are trying to predict is whether a given abnormality is benign or malignant. We randomly divided the abnormalities into ten roughly equal-sized sets, each with approximately one-tenth of the malignant abnormalities and one-tenth of the benign abnormalities. We ensured that all abnormalities belonging to a given patient appeared in the same fold [2].

Yeast Protein. Our second task consists of learning whether a yeast gene codes for a protein involved in the general function category of *metabolism*. We used for this task the MIPS (Munich Information Center for Protein Sequence) Comprehensive Yeast Genome Database, as of February 2005 [11]. Positive and negative examples were obtained from the MIPS function category catalog. The positives are all proteins/genes that code for metabolism, according to the MIPS functional categorization. The negatives are all genes that have known functions in the MIPS function categorization and do not code for metabolism. Notice that the same gene may code for several different functions, or may code for different sub-functions. We used information on gene location, phenotype, protein class, and enzymes. We also used gene-to-gene interaction and protein complex data. The dataset contains 1,299 positive examples and 5,456 negative examples. We randomly divided the data into ten folds. Each fold contained approximately the same number of positive and negative examples.

Carcinogenesis. Our third dataset concerns the well-known problem of predicting carcinogenicity test outcomes on rodents [18]. This dataset has a number of attractive features: it is an important practical problem; the background knowledge consists of a number of non-determinate predicate definitions; experience suggests that a fairly large search space needs to be examined to obtain a good clause. The dataset contains 182 positive carcinogenicity tests and 148 negative tests. We randomly divided the data into ten folds. Each fold contained approximately the same number of positive and negative examples.

Table 1. Mammography. All metrics given are averages over all ten folds.

Algorithm	Clauses in Theory	Number Predicates per Clause	Clauses Scored
Aleph	99.6	2.8213	620000.0
SAYU-NB	39.1	1.4655	85342.9
SAYU-TAN	32.8	1.4207	20944.4

Advised By. Our last dataset concerns learning whether one entity is advised by other entity, and it is based on real data obtained by Richardson and Domingos from the University of Washington CS Department [17]. The example distribution are skewed, we have 113 positive examples versus 2,711 negative examples. Following the original authors, we divide the data in 5 folds, each one corresponding to a different group in the CS Department.

4 Experimental Setup and Results

On the first three datasets we perform stratified, ten-fold cross validation in order to obtain significance results. On each round of cross validation, we use five folds as a training set, four folds as a tuning set and one fold as a test set. We only saturate examples from the training set. Since the Advised By dataset only has five folds, we used two folds for a training set and two folds as a tuning set. The communication between the Bayes net learner and the ILP algorithm is computationally expensive. The Bayes net algorithm might have to learn a new network topology and new parameters. Furthermore, inference must be performed to compute the score after incorporating a new feature. The SAYU algorithm is strictly more expensive than standard ILP as SAYU also has to prove whether a rule covers each example in order to create the new feature. To reflect the added cost, we use a time-based stop criteria for the new algorithm. In effect, we test whether, given an equal amount of CPU time, the two-step approach or SAYU performs better.

To obtain a performance baseline we first ran a set of experiments that use the original two-step process. In all experiments we use Srinivasan's Aleph ILP System [19] as the rule learning algorithm. First, we used Aleph running under induce_cover to learn a set of rules for each fold. Induce_cover implements a a variant of Progol's MDIE greedy covering algorithm, where we do not discard previously covered examples when we score a new clause. Second, we selected the rules using a greedy algorithm, where we pick the rule with the highest m-estimate such that it covers an unexplained training example. Subsequently, we converted each rule into a binary feature for a Naïve Bayes and TAN classifier. In the baseline experiments, we used both the training and tuning data to construct the classifier and learn its parameters. Furthermore, we recorded the CPU time that it took for each fold to run to completion. This time was used as the stop criteria for the corresponding fold when evaluating the integrated approach. To offset potential differences in computer speeds, all of the experiments for a given dataset were run on the same machine.

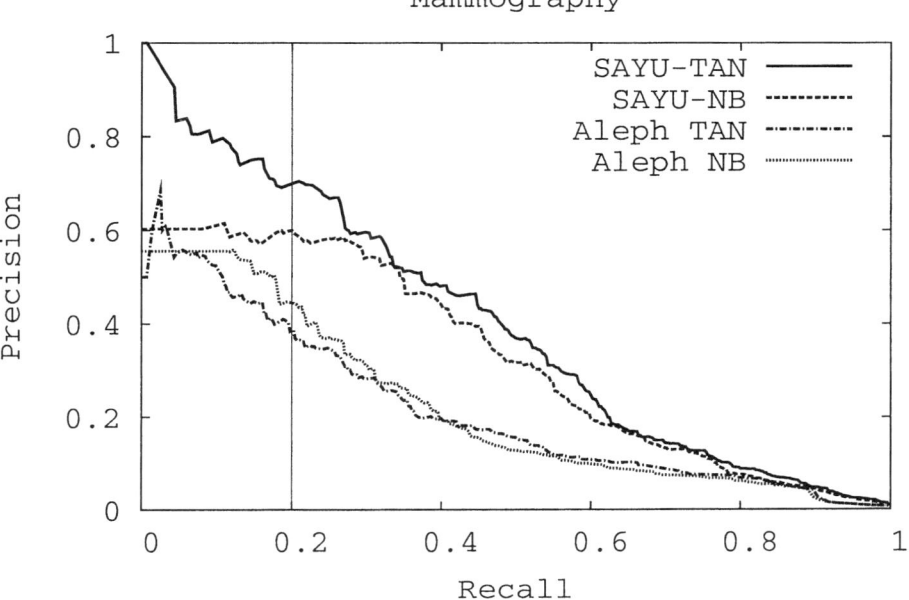

Fig. 1. Mammography Precision-Recall Curves

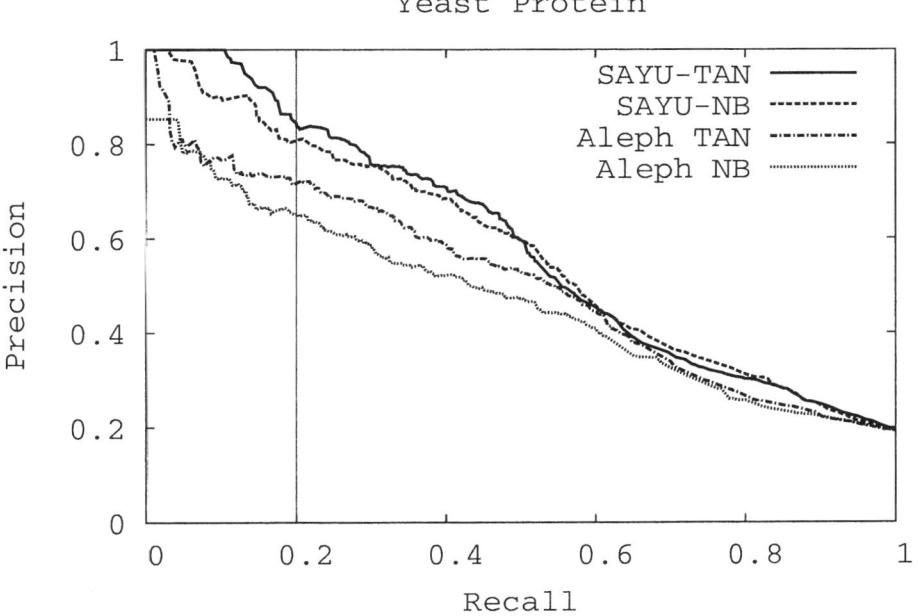

Fig. 2. Yeast Protein Function Precision-Recall Curves

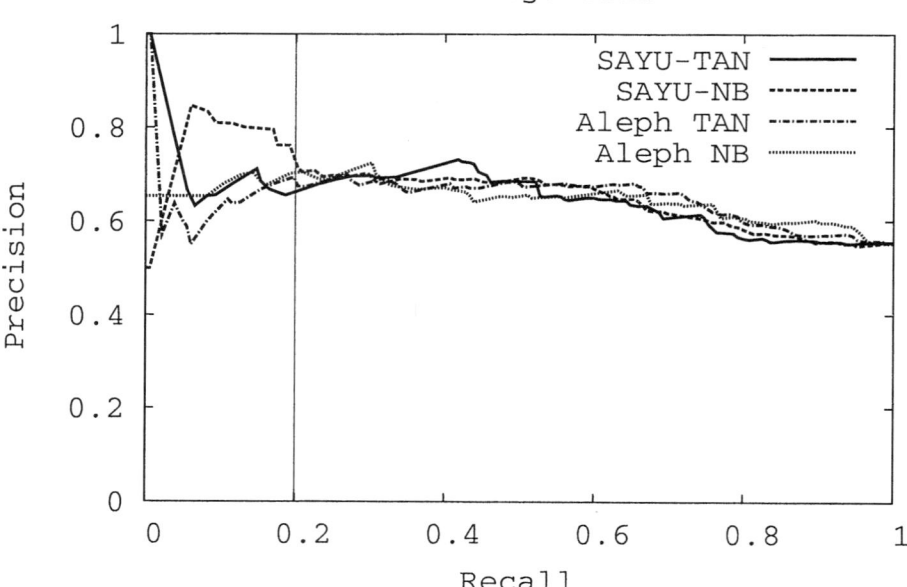

Fig. 3. Carcinogenesis Precision-Recall Curves

Table 2. Yeast Protein. All metrics given are averages over all ten folds.

Algorithm	Clauses in Theory	Number Predicates per Clause	Clauses Scored
Aleph	169.5	2.9345	915654.3
SAYU-NB	13.9	1.1367	190320.4
SAYU-TAN	12.5	1.152	131719.8

Table 3. Carcinogenesis. All metrics given are averages over all ten folds.

Algorithm	Clauses in Theory	Number Predicates per Clause	Clauses Scored
Aleph	185.6	3.5889	3533521.1
SAYU-NB	8.7	1.6897	874587.7
SAYU-TAN	12.1	1.9504	679274.6

For SAYU, we use only the training set to learn the rules. We use the training set to learn the structure and parameters of the Bayes net, and we use the tuning set to calculate the score of a network structure. Again, we use Aleph to perform the clause saturation and propose candidate clauses to include in the Bayes Net. In order to retain a clause in the network, the area under the precision-recall curve of the Bayes net incorporating the rule must achieve at least a two percent improvement over the area of the precision-recall curve of the best Bayes net.

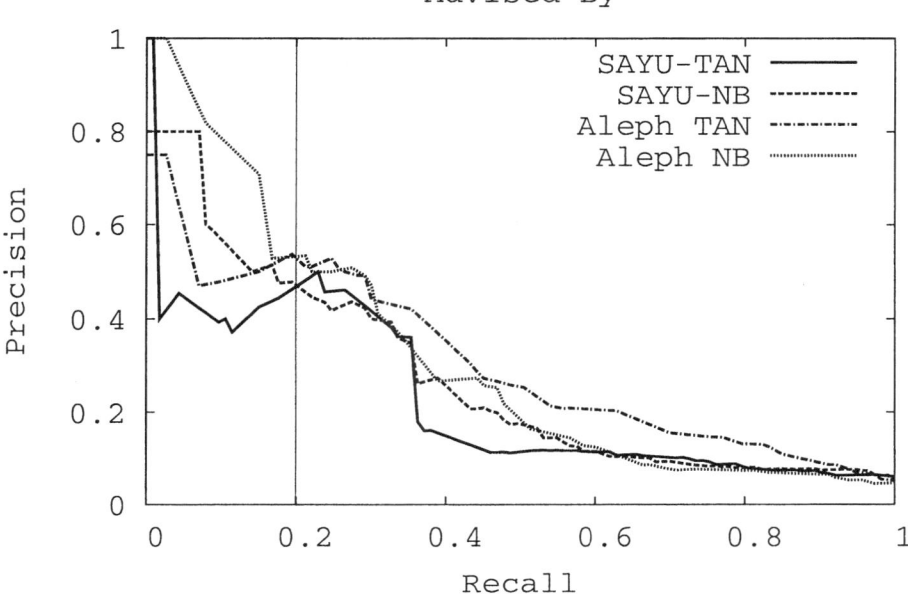

Fig. 4. Advised By Precision-Recall Curves

Figures 1 through 4 show precision-recall curves for all four datasets. In all graphs, curves were generated by pooling results over all ten folds. SAYU-NB refers to the integrated approach of incrementally learning a Naïve Bayes net. SAYU-TAN refers to the integrated approach of incrementally learning a TAN network. Aleph-NB refers to the two-step approach consisting of rule learning with Aleph and rule combination with Naïve Bayes. We use Aleph-TAN to represent learning rules with Aleph and then layering a TAN network over them.

The Mammography dataset (Figure 1) shows a clear win for SAYU over the original two-step methodology. We used the paired *t-test* to compare the areas under the curve for every fold, and we found the difference to be statistically significant at the 99% level of confidence. The difference between using SAYU-TAN and SAYU-NB is not significant. The difference between using TAN and Naïve Bayes to combine the Aleph learned rules is also not significant. Moreover, the results using SAYU match our best results on this dataset [2], which had required more computational effort.

The Yeast Protein dataset (Figure 2) also shows a win for SAYU over the original two-step methodology. The difference is not as striking as in the Mammography dataset, mostly because Aleph TAN learning did very well on one of the folds. In this case Aleph TAN is significantly better than Aleph NB with 98% confidence. SAYU-TAN learning is significantly better than Aleph NB with 99% confidence, and Aleph TAN with 95% confidence. SAYU-NB is better than

Aleph NB with 99% confidence. However, it is not significantly better than Aleph TAN (only at 90% confidence), despite the fact that SAYU-NB beats two-step TAN on nine out of ten folds.

The results for Carcinogenesis (Figure 3) are ambiguous: no method is significantly better than the other. One possible explanation is that precision-recall might not be an appropriate evaluation metric for this dataset. Unlike the other datasets, this one only has a small skew in the class distribution and there are more positive examples than negative examples. A more appropriate scoring function for this dataset might be the area under the ROC curve. We ran SAYU using this metric and again found no difference between the integrated approach and the two-step method. We believe an essential piece of future work is to run a simulation study to try better discern the conditions under which the SAYU algorithm provides an advantage over the two-step approach.

As we had discussed before, implementing SAYU is costly, as we now need to build a new propositional classifier when evaluating each rule. Moreover, the differences in scoring methods may lead to learning very different sets of clauses. Tables 1 through 3 display several statistics for the first three datasets. We have omitted the statistics for the Advised By dataset in interest of space. First, we look at the average number of clauses in a theory in the two-step approach, and compare it with SAYU-NB and SAYU-TAN. Second, we compare average clause length, measured by the number of literals per clause body. Finally, we show the average number of clauses scored in each fold. Table 1 shows that SAYU's theories contain far fewer clauses than the two-step algorithm in Mammography. Moreover, if finds shorter clauses, some even with a single attribute. The two columns are very similar for SAYU-NB and SAYU-TAN. The last column shows that the cost of using SAYU is very high on this dataset: we only generate a tenth of the number of clauses when using Naïve Bayes. Results for SAYU-TAN are even worse as it only generates 3% as many clauses as the original Aleph run. Even so, the SAYU-based algorithms perform better.

The Yeast dataset (Table 2) tells a similar story. Again, the SAYU-based approaches require fewer clauses to obtain a better result. Again, SAYU generates smaller clauses with the average clause length lower than for Mammography. The cost of implementing SAYU was less in this case. We believe this is because of the cost of transporting the bitmaps (representing the new feature) through the Java-Prolog interface is smaller, since the dataset is not as large. Finally, Carcinogenesis (Table 3) again shows SAYU-based approaches learning smaller theories with shorter clauses, and paying a heavy price for interfacing with the propositional learning. Carcinogenesis is the smallest benchmark, so its cost is smaller than Mammography or Yeast Protein.

In all datasets, the theory found by SAYU consists of significantly fewer and shorter clauses. Even with the simpler classifier, SAYU does at least as well as the two-step approach. Furthermore, SAYU achieves these benefits despite evaluating significantly fewer rules than Aleph.

Subsequent to these experiments, we have more recently run a further experiment on the "Advised-By" task of Domingos, used to test learning in Markov

Logic Networks (MLN) [9]. The task is to predict students' advisors from web pages. Using the same folds for 5-fold cross-validation used in [9], SAYU with either TAN or Naïve Bayes achieves higher area under the PR curve than MLN; specifically, SAYU-TAN achieves 0.414, SAYU-NB achieves 0.394, and MLN achieves 0.295 (taken from [9]). We do not know whether the comparison with MLN is significant, because we do not have the per-fold numbers of MLN. SAYU-TAN, SAYU-NB, Aleph-TAN and Aleph-NB all achieve roughly the same areas, and the differences among them are not significant.

All our results show no significant benefit from using SAYU-TAN over SAYU-NB. We believe there are two reasons for that. First, the SAYU algorithm itself might be searching for independent attributes for the classifier, especially when we are using SAYU-NB. Second, Naïve Bayes is computationally more efficient, as the network topology is fixed. In fact, only the conditional probability table corresponding to the newly introduced rule must be built in order to evaluate the new rule. Thus, SAYU-NB benefits from considering more rules.

5 Related Work

The present work builds upon previous work on using ILP for feature construction. Such work treats ILP-constructed rules as Boolean features, re-represents each example as a feature vector, and then uses a feature-vector learner to produce a final classifier. To our knowledge, Pompe and Kononenko [14] were the first to apply Naïve Bayes to combine clauses. Other work in this category was by Srinivasan and King [18], who use rules as extra features for the task of predicting biological activities of molecules from their atom-and-bond structures. More generally, research on propositionalization of First Order Logic [1] is similar in that it converts the training sets to propositions and then applies feature vector techniques in the learning phase.

There also has been significant research on alternatives to the standard decision list approach. One can use formalisms such as relational trees [13] to change the structure of rules themselves. A popular alternative to decision lists is *voting*. Voting has been used in ensemble-based approaches, such as bagging [5] and boosting [8,16]. Boosting relies on the insight that one should focus on misclassified examples. Search is directed by having a sequence of steps, such that at each consecutive step misclassified examples become more and more valuable. We do not change example weights at each step. Instead, we rely on the classifier itself and trust the tuning data to give us approximate performance of the global system. On the other hand, we do try to focus search on examples where we perform worse, by skewing seed selection.

ROCCER is a more recent example of a two-step algorithm that starts from a set of rules and tries to maximize classifier performance [15]. ROCCER takes a set of rules, and returns a subset that corresponds to a convex hull in ROC space. ROCCER relies on the Apriori algorithm to obtain the set of rules.

To our knowledge, the first work to replace a two-step approach with a tight coupling between rule learning and rule usage is the work appearing earlier this year (done in parallel with ours) by Landwehr, Kersting and De Raedt [10]. That work presented a new system called nFOIL. The significant differences in the two pieces of work appear to be the following. First, nFOIL scores clauses by conditional log likelihood rather than improvement in classifier accuracy or classifier AUC (area under ROC or PR curve). Second, nFOIL can handle multiple-class classification tasks, which SAYU cannot. Third, the present paper reports experiments on data sets with significant class skew, to which probabilistic classifiers are often sensitive. Finally, both papers cite work last year showing that TAN outperformed Naïve Bayes for rule combination [4]; the present paper shows that once clauses are scored as they are actually used, the advantage of TAN seems to disappear. More specifically, TAN no longer significantly outperforms Naïve Bayes. Hence the present paper may be seen as providing some justification for the decision of Landwehr et al. to focus on Naïve Bayes.

6 Conclusions and Future Work

Prior work has shown that combining ILP-induced rules by a learned Bayesian network can improve classification performance over an ordinary union of the rules [3,4]. Nevertheless, in that earlier work, rules were scored using a standard ILP scoring function (compression), and the Bayesian network was constructed afterward. The present paper proposes an approach that integrates rule learning and Bayesian network learning. Each candidate rule is temporarily added to the current set of rules, and a Bayesian network is learned over these rules. The score of the rule is the improvement in performance of the new Bayesian network over the previous best network. Performance is measured as area under the precision-recall curve, omitting recalls between 0 and 0.2. (Precision-recall curves have high variation in that region.)

This paper shows that the new integrated approach results in significantly improved performance over the prior, two-step approach on two of three datasets, and no significant change on a third dataset. In addition, on all three datasets, the integrated approach results in a simpler classifier—and hence potentially improved comprehensibility—as measured by the average number and length of learned clauses.

Acknowledgments. Support for this research was partially provided by U.S. Air Force grant F30602-01-2-0571. Inês Dutra and Vítor Santos Costa were visiting UW-Madison. Vítor Santos Costa was partially supported by the Fundação para a Ciência e Tecnologia. We would like to thank Mark Goadrich and Rich Maclin for reading over drafts of this paper.

References

1. E. Alphonse and C. Rouveirol. Lazy propositionalisation for relational learning. In Horn W., editor, *ECAI'00, Berlin, Allemagne*, pages 256–260. IOS Press, 2000.
2. J. Davis, E. Burnside, I. C. Dutra, D. Page, R. Ramakrishnan, V. Santos Costa, and J. Shavlik. View learning for statistical relational learning: With an application to mammography. In *IJCAI05*, Edinburgh, Scotland, 2005.

3. J. Davis, I. C. Dutra, D. Page, and V. Santos Costa. Establishing Entity Equivalence in Multi-Relation Domains. In *International Conference on Intelligence Analysis*, Vienna, Va, May 2005.
4. J. Davis, V. Santos Costa, I. M. Ong, D. Page, and I. C. Dutra. Using Bayesian Classifiers to Combine Rules. In *3rd MRDM*, Seattle, USA, August 2004.
5. I. C. Dutra, D. Page, and J. Shavlik V. Santos Costa. An empirical evaluation of bagging in inductive logic programming. pages 48–65, September 2002.
6. N. Friedman, D. Geiger, and M. Goldszmidt. Bayesian networks classifiers. *Machine Learning*, 29:131–163, 1997.
7. M. Goadrich, L. Oliphant, and J. Shavlik. Learning Ensembles of First-Order Clauses for Recall-Precision Curves: A Case Study in Biomedical Information Extraction. In *Proceedings of the 14th ILP*, Porto, Portugal, 2004.
8. S. Hoche and S. Wrobel. Relational learning using constrained confidence-rated boosting. In *ILP01*, volume 2157, pages 51–64, September 2001.
9. S. Kok and P. Domingos. Learning the structure of Markov Logic Networks. In *National Conference on Artificial Intelligene (AAAI)*, 2005.
10. N. Landwehr, K. Kersting, and L. De Raedt. nFOIL: Integrating Naive Bayes and FOIL. In *National Conference on Artificial Intelligene (AAAI)*, 2005.
11. H. W. Mewes, D. Frishman, C. Gruber, B. Geier, D. Haase, A. Kaps, K. Lemcke, G. Mannhaupt, F. Pfeiffer, C. Schüller, S. Stocker, and B. Weil. Mips: a database for genomes and protein sequences. *Nucleic Acids Research*, 28(1):37–40, Jan 2000.
12. S. Muggleton. Inverse entailment and Progol. *New Generation Computing*, 13:245–286, 1995.
13. J. Neville, D. Jensen, L. Friedland, and M. Hay. Learning relational probability trees. In *KDD '03*, pages 625–630. ACM Press, 2003.
14. U. Pompe and I. Kononenko. Naive Bayesian classifier within ILP-R. In L. De Raedt, editor, *ILP95*, pages 417–436, 1995.
15. R. Prati and P. Flach. Roccer: an algorithm for rule learning based on roc analysis. In *IJCAI05*, Edinburgh, Scotland, 2005.
16. J. R. Quinlan. Boosting first-order learning. *Algorithmic Learning Theory, 7th International Workshop, Lecture Notes in Computer Science*, 1160:143–155, 1996.
17. M. Richardson and P. Domingos. Markov logic networks, 2004.
18. A. Srinivasan and R. King. Feature construction with inductive logic programming: A study of quantitative predictions of biological activity aided by structural attributes. In *ILP97*, pages 89–104, 1997.
19. Ashwin Srinivasan. *The Aleph Manual*, 2001.

Thwarting the Nigritude Ultramarine: Learning to Identify Link Spam

Isabel Drost and Tobias Scheffer

Humboldt-Universität zu Berlin, Department of Computer Science,
Unter den Linden, 6, 10099 Berlin, Germany
{drost, scheffer}@informatik.hu-berlin.de

Abstract. The page rank of a commercial web site has an enormous economic impact because it directly influences the number of potential customers that find the site as a highly ranked search engine result. *Link spamming* – inflating the page rank of a target page by artificially creating many referring pages – has therefore become a common practice. In order to maintain the quality of their search results, search engine providers try to oppose efforts that decorrelate page rank and relevance and maintain blacklists of spamming pages while spammers, at the same time, try to camouflage their spam pages. We formulate the problem of identifying link spam and discuss a methodology for generating training data. Experiments reveal the effectiveness of classes of intrinsic and relational attributes and shed light on the robustness of classifiers against obfuscation of attributes by an adversarial spammer. We identify open research problems related to web spam.

1 Introduction

Search engines combine the similarity between query and page content with the page rank [18] of candidate pages to rank their results. Intuitively, every web page "creates" a small quantity of page rank, collects additional rank via inbound hyperlinks, and propagates its total rank via its outbound links. A web page that is referred to by many highly ranked pages thus becomes more likely to be returned in response to a search engine query.

The success of commercial web sites crucially depends on the number of visitors that find the site while searching for a particular product. Because of the enormous commercial impact of a high page rank, an entire new business sector – *search engine optimization* – is rapidly developing. Search engine optimizers offer a service that is referred to as *link spamming*: they create *link farms*, arrays of densely linked web pages that refer to the target page, thus inflating its page rank. In 2004, the search engine optimization industry tournamented in the "DarkBlue SEO Challenge". The goal of this competition was to be ranked first on Google for the query "nigritude ultramarine", a nonsense term that used to produce zero hits prior to the challenge and produced over 500,000 hits by the competition deadline. Industry insiders believe that as many as 75 million out of the 150 million web servers that are online today may be operated with the sole purpose of increasing the page rank of their target sites.

As the page rank becomes subject to manipulation, it loses its correlation to the true relevance of a web page. This deteriorates the quality of search engine results. Search engine companies maintain blacklists of link spamming pages, but they fight an uneven battle in which humans identify and penalize spamming pages and software tools automatically create new spamming domains, and camouflage them, for instance by filling in inconspicuous content.

We formulate and analyze the problem of link spam identification, present a method for generation of labeled examples, and discuss intrinsic and relational features. Experiments with recursive feature elimination shed light on the relevance of several classes of attributes and their contribution to the classifier's robustness against adversarial obfuscation of discriminating properties.

The rest of the paper is organized as follows. We discuss related work in Section 2 and introduce our problem setting in Section 3. Section 4 introduces the features and employed methods. Section 5 details our experimental results. We discuss open research problems in Section 6 and conclude in Section 7.

2 Related Work

Henzinger [15] refers to automatic identification of link spam as one of the most important challenges for search engines. Davison [8] studies the problem of recognizing "nepotistic" links. A decision tree experiment using features that refer to URL, IP, content, and some linkage properties indicates a number of relevant features. Classifying links imposes the effort of labeling individual links, not just entire pages, on the user. Lempel et al. [17] use similar features to classify web pages into business, university, and other general classes.

Fetterly et al. [11] analyze the distribution of many web page features over 429 million pages. They find that many outliers in several features are link spam. Pages that change frequently and clusters of near-identical pages are also more likely to be spam [12,10]. They conclude that experiments should be conducted to reveal whether these features can be used by a machine learning method.

Similarly, Broder et al. [5] and Bharat et al. [3] analyze large amounts of web pages and observe that the in-degree and out-degree of web pages that *should be* governed by Zipf's law, empirically deviates from this distribution. They find that "artificially" generated link farms distort the distribution.

The TrustRank approach [14] propagates trust weights along the hyperlinks. But while page rank is generated by every web page (including link farms), trust rank is generated only by manually selected trusted web pages. The manual selection of trusted pages, however, creates a perceptive bias as unknown and remote websites become less visible. Wu and Davison [19] study a simple heutistic that discovers some link farms: pages which have many inlinks and outlinks whose domains match are collected as candidate pages. They use a paopagation strategy, and remove edges between likely link farms to compute a page rank that is less prone to manipulation.

3 Problem Description

The correlation between page rank and relevance of a web page is based on the assumption that each hyperlink expresses a vote for the relevance of a site. The PageRank algorithm [18] calculates the rank (Equation 1) of a page y that consists of a small constant amount (d corresponds to the probability that a surfer follows a link rather than restarting at a random site, N is the number of web pages), plus the accumulated rank of all referring pages x.

$$R(y) = \frac{1-d}{N} + d \sum_{x \to y} \frac{R(x)}{outlinks(x)} \qquad (1)$$

Link spamming is referred to as any intentional manipulation of the page rank of a web page. Pages created for this purpose are called *link spam*. Artificially generated arrays of web pages violate the assumption that links are independent votes of confidence, and therefore decorrelate page rank and relevance.

Several common techniques inflate the page rank of a target site. They are often combined. We will describe these techniques briefly. A more detailed taxonomy of web spam techniques is presented by Gyöngyi [13].

Link farms are densely connected arrays of pages. A target page "harvests" the constant amount of page rank that each page creates and propagates through its links. Each page within the link farm has to be connected to the central, strongly connected component of the web. The farming pages have to propagate their page rank to the target. This can for instance be achieved by a linear or funnel-shaped architecture in which the majority of links points directly or indirectly towards the target page. In order to camouflage link farms, tools fill in inconspicuous content, for instance, by copying news bulletins.

Link exchange services create listings of (often unrelated) hyperlinks. In order to be listed, businesses have to provide a back link that enhances the page rank of the exchange service and, in most cases, pay a fee.

Guestbooks, discussion boards, and weblogs ("blogs") allow readers to create HTML comments via a web interface. Automatic tools post large amounts of messages to many such boards, each message contains a hyperlink to the target website.

In order to maintain a tight coupling between page rank and relevance, it is necessary to eliminate the influence that link spam has on the page rank. Search engines maintain a blacklist of spamming pages. It is believed that Google employs the *BadRank* algorithm. The "bad rank" (Equation 2) is initialized to a high value $E(x)$ for blacklisted pages. It propagates bad rank to all *referring* pages (with a damping factor) thus penalizing pages that refer to spam.

$$BR(x) = E(x)(1-d) + d \sum_{x \to y} \frac{BR(y)}{inlinks(y)} \qquad (2)$$

This method, however, is not suited to automatically detect newly created link farms that do not include links to an older, already blacklisted site. Search engines therefore rely on manual detection of new link spam. We focus on the problem of automatically identifying link spam. We seek to construct a classifier that receives a URL as input and decides whether the encoded page is created for the sole purpose of manipulating the page rank of some page ("spam"), or whether it is a regular web page created for a different purpose ("ham").

The typical application scenario of a link spam identification method would be as follows. Search engines interleave crawling and page rank updating. After crawling a web page, the page's impact on the page rank of referenced pages is updated – the BadRank and blacklist status of the page are considered at this point. In addition, the output of a spam classifier for the crawled page can now be taken into account. Depending on the output, the page's impact on the page rank can be reduced, or the page can be disregarded entirely.

Since the class distribution of spam versus ham is not known, we use the area under the ROC curve (AUC) as evaluation metric. The AUC equals the probability that a randomly drawn spam page receives a higher decision function value than a random ham page; the AUC is invariant of the class prior.

Link spam identification is an *adversarial classification problem* [7]. Spammers will probe any filter that is in effect and manipulate the properties of their generated pages in order to dodge the classifier. Therefore, a high classification accuracy is not sufficient to imply its practical usefulness. The practical benefit of a classifier is furthermore dependent of its robustness against purposeful obfuscation of attributes by an adversary. We study how the performance of classifiers deteriorates as an increasing number of attributes becomes obfuscated as the corresponding properties of spam pages are adapted to those of ham pages.

4 Representing and Obtaining Examples

In this section, we address the issues of representing instances and obtaining training examples. We describe our publicly available link spam data set.

Table 1 provides an overview on the features that we use in our experiments to represent an instance x_0. Many of these features are reimplementations of, or have been inspired by, features suggested by [8] and [11]. Notably, however, the tfidf representation of the page, and also other features including the MD5 hash features, have not been studied for web spam problems before.

Figure 1 illustrates the neighborhood of the pivotal page x_0 represented by intrinsic and relational properties. Most elementarily, the tfidf (term frequency, inverse document frequency) representation of the page content provides an intrinsic representation. It creates one dimension in the feature vector for each word in the corpus. It gives large weights to terms that are frequent in the document but infrequent in the whole document corpus.

The next block of attributes is determined for the page x_0 itself as well as for its predecessors $pred(x_0)$ and successors $succ(x_0)$. The features are determined for every element $x \in pred(x_0)$ (or $x \in succ(x_0)$, respectively) and

Table 1. Attributes of web page x_0

Textual content of the page x_0; tfidf vector.

The following features for x_0 are computed (1) for the pivotal page itself ($X = \{x_0\}$). Here, no aggregation is necessary. (2) For the predecessors $X = pred(x_0)$. The attributes are aggregated over the elements of X using aggregation functions sum and average. (3) For the successors ($X = succ(x_0)$). Aggregation functions sum and average. Boolean features are aggregated by treating "true" as 1, and "false" as 0.
 Number of tokens in keyword meta-tag, aggregated over all pages $x \in X$.
 Number of tokens in title, aggregated over all pages $x \in X$.
 Number of tokens in description meta-tag, aggregated over all pages $x \in X$.
 Is the page a redirection? Aggregated over all pages $x \in X$.
 Number of inlinks of x, aggregated over all pages $x \in X$.
 Number of outlinks of x, aggregated over all pages $x \in X$.
 Number of characters in the URL of x, aggregated over all pages $x \in X$.
 Number of characters in the domain name of x, aggregated over all pages $x \in X$.
 Number of subdomains in the URL of x, aggregated over all pages $x \in X$.
 Page length of x, aggregated over all pages $x \in X$.
 Domain ending ".edu" or ".org"? Aggregated over all pages $x \in X$
 Domain ending ".com" or ".biz"? Aggregated over all pages $x \in X$.
 URL contains tilde? Aggregated over all pages $x \in X$.

The following block of context similarity features are calculated (1) for predecessors ($X = pred(x_0)$) and (2) for the successors ($X = succ(x_0)$); sum and ratio are used to aggregate the features over all elements of X.
 Clustering coefficient of X; sum and ratio of elements of X with links between them.
 Elements of X with the same IP address as some other element of X; sum and ratio.
 Elements of X that have the same length as some other element of X; sum and ratio.
 Pages that are referred to in x_0 and also in an elements of X, sum and ratio.
 Pages referred to from an element of X that are also referred to from another element of X; sum and ratio.
 Pages in X that have the same MD5 hash code as some other element of X. This value is high if X contains many identical pages; sum and ratio.
 Elements of X that have the same IP as x_0.
 Elements of X that have the same length as x_0.
 Pages in X that have the same MD5 hash code as x_0.

---

aggregated over all elements x. Both, summation and averaging are used as aggregation functions. The third block quantifies collective features of x_0 and its predecessors, and x_0 and its successors. Some of them require further elaboration.

Following [9], we define the clustering coefficient of a set X of web pages as the number of linked pairs divided by the number of all possible pairs, $|X|(|X|-1)$. The clustering coefficient is 1 if all elements in X are mutually linked and 0 if no links between elements of X exist. The MD5 hash is frequently used as a mechanism for digital signatures. It maps a text to a code word of 128 bit such

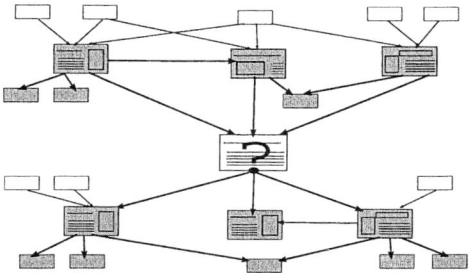

Fig. 1. Neighborhood of page x_0 to classify. The tfidf vector is calculated for x_0; intrinsic features (second block of Table 1) are calculated for x_0, $pred(x_0)$, and $succ(x_0)$; context similarity features (third block of Table 1) for $pred(x_0)$ and $succ(x_0)$.

that collisions are "unlikely". That is, when two documents have the same MD5 hash code, then it is unlikely that they differ. The MD5 features quantify the number and ratio of predecessors and successors of x_0 that are textually equal.

In total, each page is represented by 89 features plus its tfidf vector. Web pages explicitly contain outbound links but, of course, not their inbound links. To be able to determine the feature vector of a given page x_0, it is necessary to crawl its direct successors with standard web crawling tools (we use nutch [6] for our experiments). Crawling backwards (moving from a page to its references) can be achieved by specific search engine query tokens (*e.g.*, "link:" in Google).

4.1 Crawling Examples

Training a classifier requires labeled samples. Deciding whether an example web page is link spam requires human judgment, but we can exploit efforts already exercised by other persons. The Dmoz open directory project is a taxonomy of web pages that covers virtually all topics on the web. All entries have been reviewed by volunteers. While the Dmoz entries do contain pages whose rank is being inflated by link farms (*e.g.*, online casinos) the listed pages themselves contain valid content and there are no instances of spam. We create examples of "ham" (non-link-spam) by drawing 854 Dmoz entries at random.

Search engine operators maintain blacklists of spamming pages. They could, if public, provide a rich supply of examples of spam. In order to investigate their distinct characteristics, we differentiate between guestbook spam and a second class of spam that includes link farms and link exchange sites, and generate distinct samples for these sets. We obtain 251 examples of guestbook spam by drawing URLs from a publicly available manually edited blacklist that aims at helping guestbook and weblog operators to identify and remove spam entries.

Link farms are never returned as a highly ranked search result – this is not their goal – but they promote the ranking of their *target site*. After posting 36 search queries (e.g. 'gift links", "shopping links", "dvd links", "wedding links", "seo links", "pharmacy links", "viagra", and "casino links"), we draw some of the top-rated search results. We manually identify 180 link farm and link exchange pages. In order to correctly decide which pages are link spam, we review each page's content and context (referring and linked pages). This careful manual labeling consumed the largest part of the effort of assembling the data set. We do not distinguish between link exchange and link farm pages because this distinction cannot easily be made for many of the examples.

5 Experimental Evaluation

In our experiments, we want to explore how well guestbook spam and link farms can be discriminated against regular web pages, and which features contribute the most to a discrimination. In addition we are interested in the robustness of classifiers against obfuscation of attributes by an adversarial spammer who purposefully adapts properties of spam pages to those of ham pages. We use the Support Vector Machine SVM^{light} [16] with standard parameters. We would also like to find out which kernel is appropriate.

5.1 Finding Discriminative Features

In the following experiments we discriminate ham versus spam, where spam is the union of all categories discussed in Section 3. In order to investigate possible differences between guestbook spam and link farms, we furthermore discriminate

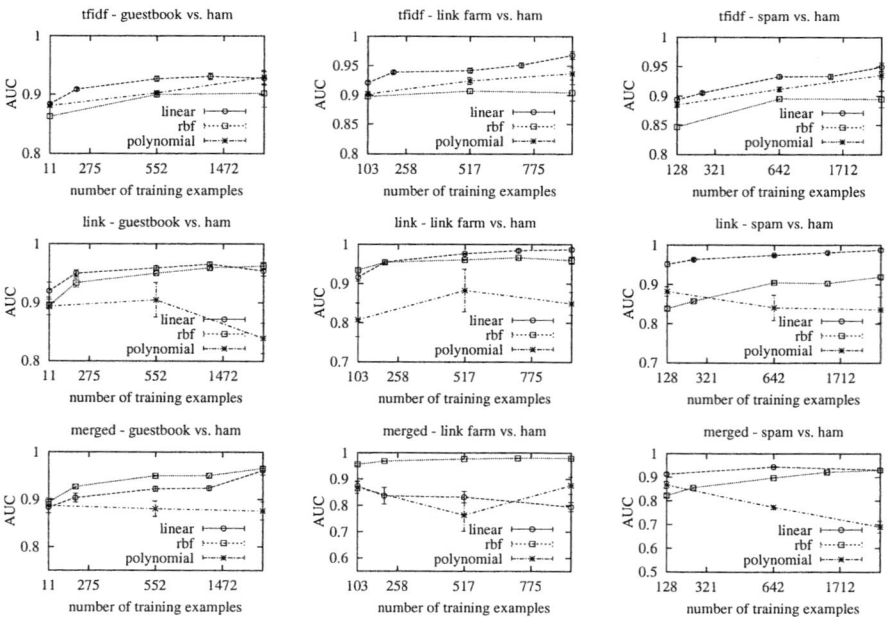

Fig. 2. Comparison of kernels

guestbook spam against ham, and link farm plus link exchange pages versus ham. In order to obtain learning curves, we randomly draw a training subset of specified size from the sample, use the remaining examples for testing, and average the results over 10 randomly resampled iterations.

We first study the suitability of several kernels for three instance representations: we consider the tfidf representation, a representation based only on link based features (Table 1), and the joint attribute vectors of concatenated tfidf and link features. We tune the degree (for polynomial kernels), the kernel width for RBF kernels (on a separate tuning set) and use default parameters otherwise. Figure 2 shows that, on average, linear kernels perform best for the tfidf vectors and link features. Both, RBF and linear kernels work for the combined representation; polynomial kernels perform poorly for the link and combined representation.

Next, we study learning curves for the tfidf representation, the attributes of Table 1, and the joint features. Figure 3 shows that link and merged representations work equally well for guestbook spam, the merged representation performs best for link farms. For the mixed spam dataset, tfidf is the most discriminative feature set, but the offset to the combined representation is small. Using the combined represantation is always better than using only the link based features.

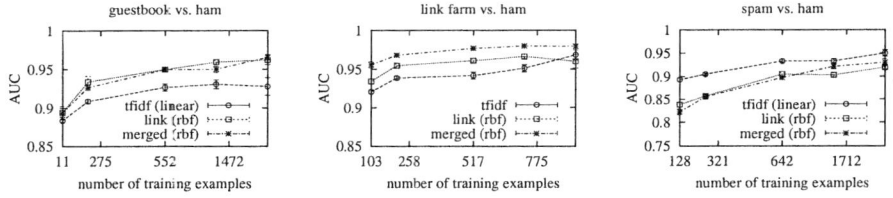

Fig. 3. Comparison of feature representations

Which features are discriminative? We use 10 resampled iterations of recursive feature elimination and determine the average rank of all features. The recursive feature elimination procedure initialy uses an active feature set containing all features. It then trains a Support Vector Machine, eliminates the feature with the least weight from the active set, and recurs. The best (highest ranked) features are those that remain in the active set longest.

Table 2 presents the 20 highest ranked link features for the "spam vs. ham" discrimination. We do not rank tfidf features for individual words. Treated as a whole, the entire block of tfidf features has the highest rank. Among the most discriminative link features are the number of inbound and outbound links of $pred(x_0)$, the title length of $succ(x_0)$; also, clustering coefficient and the MD5 feature are relevant.

5.2 Robustness Against Adversarial Obfuscation

The previous experiments show that *today* the tfidf representation is the most discriminative feature set. Once a spam filter is in effect, spammers can be ex-

Table 2. RFE ranking for spam vs. ham

Sign	Rank	Attribute
-	1	Average number of inlinks of pages in $pred(x_0)$.
+	2	Average number of tokens in title of pages in $succ(x_0)$.
+	3	Number of elements of $pred(x_0)$ that have the same length as some other element of $pred(x_0)$.
-	4	Average number of in- and outlinks of pages in $pred(x_0)$.
+	5	Average number of outlinks of pages in $pred(x_0)$.
+	6	Number of tokens in title of x_0.
-	7	Summed number of outlinks of pages in $succ(x_0)$.
-	8	Summed number of inlinks of pages in $pred(x_0)$.
+	9	Clustering coefficient of pages in $pred(x_0)$.
+	10	Summed number of tokens in title of pages in $succ(x_0)$.
+	11	Number of outlinks of pages in $succ(x_0)$.
+	12	Average number of characters of URLs of pages in $pred(x_0)$.
-	13	Number of pages in $pred(x_0)$ and $succ(x_0)$ with same MD5 hash as x_0.
-	14	Number of characters in domain name of (x_0).
-	15	Number of pages in $pred(x_0)$ with same IP as x_0.
+	16	Average number of characters in domain name of pages in $succ(x_0)$.
-	17	Average Number of in- and outlinks of pages in $succ(x_0)$.
+	18	Number of elements of $succ(x_0)$ that have the same length as some other element of $succ(x_0)$.
+	19	Average number of in- and outlinks of elements in $succ(x_0)$.
+	20	Number of pages in $succ(x_0)$ with same IP as x_0.

pected to probe the filter and to modify properties of their link farms in order to deceive the filter. Any single feature of a set of web pages can, at some cost, be adapted to the distribution which governs that attribute in ham pages. For instance, the tfidf feature can be obfuscated by copying the content of a randomly drawn ham page from the Dmoz directory, the number of inbound or outbound links can be decreased by splitting pages or increased by merging pages.

We consider the following classifiers and study their robustness against such obfuscations of discriminative attributes.

1. A *purely text-based* classifier which refers to only the tfidf features.
2. A *simple contextual* classifier uses the set of intrinsic features of the pivotal page x_0 with aggregation function identity.
3. The *complex contextual classifier* utilizes all features.

We use the following experimental protocol to assess the three classifiers' robustness. We first train the classifiers using their respective attribute sets. Now we simulate the adversary's attempts to deceive the classifiers. The adversary obfuscates an increasing number of attributes, starting with the entire block of tfidf features (this can be achieved by pasting the textual content of a "ham" page into the spam page), and subsequently obfuscating additional attributes in the order of their discriminatory power (Table 2). The obfuscation of attributes is simulated as follows. For each instance, the value of the obfuscated attributes is replaced by the attribute value of a randomly drawn ham page. This simulates that the adversary has adapted the generation program to match some property of the link farm pages to that of natural web pages. We evaluate the performance of the four classifiers on the obfuscated test sets.

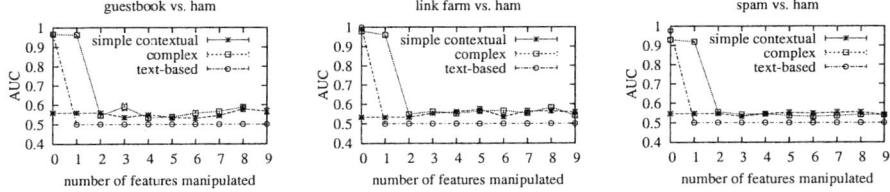

Fig. 4. Influence of attribute obfuscation

Figure 4 shows that the purely text-based classifier is immediately rendered useless when the content of the spam pages is replaced by the content of a randomly drawn page from the Dmoz directory. The combined classifier that utilizes multiple features deteriorates slightly slower. However, Figure 4 emphasizes the need to re-train a classifier quickly when the underlying distribution changes.

6 Open Problems

The problem area of link spam contains a plentitude of open research questions. We summarize some of them.

Collective Classification. Rather than classifying individual web pages, search engine operators will have to classify all pages on the web. Hence, the problem intrinsically is a collective classification problem. A benchmark collective classification data set has to include a network of example instances with a reasonable degree of context. Because of the small world property of the web, such a dataset quickly becomes very large.

Game Theory. Link spam identification is an adversarial classification problem [7]. Rather than being stationary, the distribution of instances is changed by an adversary over time. The adversary probes any link spam filter that is being used by a search engine, and modifies properties of the generated link spam such as to dodge the filtering algorithm. Possible modifications include, for instance, changing the link topology, generating pages with differing content and experimenting with various sub-domain names. The topic of learning the ranking function of a search engine from rankings and page features is adressed by Bifet et al. [4]. Yet, identifying conditions under which a filtering strategy can be shown to be an equilibrium of the "spam filtering game" is a great challenge.

Identifying "Google Bombers". Search engines associate the anchor text that is used to refer to a page with that page. By referring to target pages with anchor terms that have a negative connotation, malicious sites cause these targets to become search results for negative query terms. This form of web spam is often referred to as "Google bombing". For instance the query "miserable failure" usually returns the CVs of George W. Bush or Michael Moore as the first result, depending on whose supporters are currently heading this particular Google bombing arms race. Adali et. al [1] study the layout of an optimal link bomb. The influence of more general collusion topologies on page rank is examined by Baeza-Yates et al. [2]. But the development of methods that decide whether a reference is unbiased or malicious is still an open research goal.

Other Forms of Web Spam. *Click spamming* is a particularly vicious form of web spam. Companies allocate a fixed budged to the sponsored links program of, for instance, Google. The sponsored link is returned along with results of related search queries until the budget is used up. Rivaling companies now employ "click bots" that post a search query, and then automatically click on their competitor's sponsored link until the budged is exceeded and the link disappears. This practice undermines the benefit of the sponsored link program, and search engine operators therefore have to identify whether a reference to a sponsored link has been made by a human, or by a "rogue bot". This classification task is extremely challenging because the state-less HTTP protocol provides hardly any information about the client.

7 Conclusion

We motivated and introduced the problem of link farm discovery. We discussed intrinsic and contextual features of web pages, and presented a methodology for collecting training examples. Our experiments show that today the tfidf representation of the page provides the most discriminatory attribute set. Many additional contextual attributes contribute to a more accurate discrimination. We identify the most discriminatory relational attributes.

Our experiments also show that a purely text-based classifier is brittle and can easily be deceived; the contextual classifiers have the potential to be more robust because deceiving them requires to adapt a larger number of properties to the distribution of values observed in ham pages. In order to be able to react to purposeful obfuscation of characteristic properties of link farms, a repository of discriminatory features is required.

Web spam is a major challenge for search engines. We sketched open research challenges; research in this direction has the potential to substantially improve search engine technology and make it more robust to manipulations.

Acknowledgment

This work has been supported by the German Science Foundation DFG under grant SCHE 540/10-1.

References

1. S. Adali, T. Liu, and M. Magdon-Ismail. Optimal link bombs are uncoordinated. In *Proc. of the Workshop on Adversarial IR on the Web*, 2005.
2. R. Baeza-Yates, C. Castillo, and V. López. Pagerank increase under different collusion topologies. In *Proc. of the Workshop on Adversarial IR on the Web*, 2005.
3. K. Bharat, B. Chang, M. Henzinger, and M. Ruhl. Who links to whom: Mining linkage between web sites. In *Proc. of the IEEE International Conference on Data Mining*, 2001.
4. A. Bifet, C. Castillo, P.-A. Chirita, and I. Weber. An analysis of factors used in search engine ranking. In *Proc. of the Workshop on Adversarial IR on the Web*, 2005.
5. A. Broder, R. Kumar, F. Maghoul, P. Raghavan, S. Rajagopalan, R. Stata, A. Tomkins, and J. Wiener. Graph structure in the web. In *Proc. of the International WWW Conference*, 2000.
6. M. Cafarella and D. Cutting. Building Nutch: Open source search. *ACM Queue*, 2(2), 2004.
7. N. Dalvi, P. Domingos, Mausam, S. Sanghai, and D. Verma. Adversarial classification. In *Proc. of the ACM International Conference on Knowledge Discovery and Data Mining*, 2004.
8. B. Davison. Recognizing nepotistic links on the web, 2000. In Proceedings of the AAAI-2000 Workshop on Artificial Intelligence for Web Search.
9. Holger Ebel, Lutz-Ingo Mielsch, and Stefan Bornholdt. Scale free topology of e-mail networks. *Physical Review E*, 2002.
10. D. Fetterly, M. Manasse, and M. Najork. On the evolution of clusters of near-duplicate web pages. In *Proc. of the Latin American Web Congress*, 2003.
11. D. Fetterly, M. Manasse, and M. Najork. Spam, damn spam, and statistics: Using statistical analysis to locate spam web pages. In *Proc. of the International Workshop on the Web and Databases*, 2004.
12. D. Fetterly, M. Manasse, M. Najork, and J. Wiener. A large-scale study of the evolution of web pages. In *Proc. of the International WWW Conference*, 2003.
13. Zoltn Gyngyi and Hector Garcia. Web spam taxonomy. In *Proc. of the Workshop on Adversarial IR on the Web*, 2005.
14. Z. Gyongyi, H. Garcia-Molina, and J. Pedersen. Combating web spam with TrustRank. In *Proc. of the International Conf. on Very Large Data Bases*, 2004.
15. M. Henzinger, R. Motwani, and C. Silverstein. Challenges in web search engines. In *Proc. of the International Joint Conference on Artificial Intelligence*, 2003.
16. T. Joachims. Making large-scale SVM learning practical. In *Advances in Kernel Methods – Support Vector Learning*. MIT Press, 1998.
17. R. Lempel, E. Amitay, D. Carmel, A. Darlow, and A. Soffer. The connectivity sonar: Detecting site functionality by structural patterns. *Journal of Digital Information*, 4(3), 2003.
18. L. Page and S. Brin. The anatomy of a large-scale hypertextual web search engine. In *Proc. of the Seventh International World-Wide Web Conference*, 1998.
19. Baoning Wu and Brian D. Davison. Identifying link farm spam pages. In *Proc. of the 14th International WWW Conference*, 2005.

Rotational Prior Knowledge for SVMs

Arkady Epshteyn and Gerald DeJong

University of Illinois at Urbana-Champaign, Urbana, IL 61801, USA
{aepshtey, dejong}@uiuc.edu

Abstract. Incorporation of prior knowledge into the learning process can significantly improve low-sample classification accuracy. We show how to introduce prior knowledge into linear support vector machines in form of constraints on the rotation of the normal to the separating hyperplane. Such knowledge frequently arises naturally, e.g., as inhibitory and excitatory influences of input variables. We demonstrate that the generalization ability of rotationally-constrained classifiers is improved by analyzing their VC and fat-shattering dimensions. Interestingly, the analysis shows that large-margin classification framework justifies the use of stronger prior knowledge than the traditional VC framework. Empirical experiments with text categorization and political party affiliation prediction confirm the usefulness of rotational prior knowledge.

1 Introduction

Support vector machines (SVMs) have outperformed competing classifiers on many classification tasks [1,2,3]. However, the amount of labeled data needed for SVM training can be prohibitively large for some domains. Intelligent user interfaces, for example, must adopt to the behavior of an individual user after a limited amount of interaction in order to be useful. Medical systems diagnosing rare diseases have to generalize well after seeing very few examples. Natural language processing systems learning to identify infrequent social events (e.g., revolutions, wars, etc.) from news articles have access to very few training examples. Moreover, they rely on manually labeled data for training, and such data is often expensive to obtain. Various techniques have been proposed specifically to deal with the problem of learning from very small datasets. These include active learning [4], hybrid generative-discriminative classification [5], learning-to-learn by extracting common information from related learning tasks [6], and using prior knowledge.

In this work, we focus on the problem of using prior knowledge to increase the accuracy of a large margin classifier at low sample sizes. Several studies have shown the efficacy of this method. Scholkopf et. al. [7] demonstrate how to integrate prior knowledge about invariance under transformations and importance of local structure into the kernel function. Fung et. al. [8] use domain knowledge in form of labeled polyhedral sets to augment the training data. Wu and Srihari [9] allow human users to specify their confidence in the example's label, varying the effect of each example on the separating hyperplane proportionately to its confidence. Mangasarian et. al. [10] introduce prior knowledge into the large-margin regression framework.

While the ability of prior knowledge to improve any classifier's generalization performance is well-known, the properties of large margin classifiers with prior knowledge are not well understood. In order to study this problem, we introduce a new form of prior knowledge for SVMs (rotational constraints) and prove that it is possible to obtain stronger guarantees for the generalization ability of constrained classifiers in the large-margin framework than in the classical VC framework. Specifically, we show that the VC dimension of our classifier remains large even when its hypothesis space is severely constrained by prior knowledge. The fat-shattering dimension, however, continues to decrease with decreasing hypothesis space, justifying the use of stronger domain knowledge. We conduct experiments to demonstrate improvements in performance due to rotational prior knowledge and compare them with improvements achievable by active learning.

2 Preliminaries

The SVM classifier with a linear kernel learns a function of the form

$$sign(f(x;\omega,\theta)) = \omega^T x + \theta = \sum_{i=1}^{n} \omega_i x_i + \theta)^1 \quad (1)$$

that maps $(x;\omega,\theta) \in \mathbb{R}^n \text{x} W, \Theta$ to one of the two possible output labels $\{1, -1\}$. Given a training sample of m points $(x_1, y_1)...(x_m, y_m)$, SVM seeks to maximize the margin between the separating hyperplane and the points closest to it [1]. For canonical hyperplanes (i.e., hyperplanes with unit margins), the maximum-margin hyperplane minimizes the regularized risk functional

$$R_{reg}[f,l] = \frac{1}{m} \sum_{i=1}^{m} l(y_i, f(x_i;\omega,\theta)) + \frac{C_1}{2} \|\omega\|_2^2 \quad (2)$$

with hard margin 0-1 loss given by $l(y_i, f(x_i;\omega,\theta)) = I_{\{-y_i f(x_i;\omega,\theta) > 0\}}$.

The soft margin formulation allows for deviation from the objective of maximizing the margin in order to better fit the data. This is done by substituting the hinge loss function $l(y_i, f(x_i;\omega,\theta)) = max(1 - y_i f(x_i;\omega,\theta), 0)$ into (2).

Minimizing the regularized risk (2) in the soft margin case is equivalent to solving the following (primal) optimization problem:

$$\underset{\omega,\theta,\xi}{minimize} \ \tfrac{1}{2}\|\omega\|_2^2 + \tfrac{1}{C_1 m} \sum_{i=1}^{m} \xi_i \ subj. \ to \ y_i(\omega^T x + \theta) \geq 1 - \xi_i, \ i = 1...m \quad (3)$$

---

[1] $sign(y) = 1$ if $y \geq 0$, -1 otherwise

Calculating the Wolfe dual from (3) and solving the resulting maximization problem:

$$\underset{\alpha}{maximize} \sum_{i=1}^{m} \alpha_i - \tfrac{1}{2} \sum_{i,j=1}^{m} \alpha_i \alpha_j y_i y_j (x_i^T x_j) \quad (4)$$

$$subject\ to \quad \tfrac{1}{Cm} \geq \alpha_i \geq 0,\ i=1...m \quad and \quad \sum_{i=1}^{m} \alpha_i y_i = 0$$

yields the solution $\omega = \sum_{i=1}^{m} \alpha_i y_i x_i$ \quad (5)

Setting $\xi_i = 0$, $i = 1...m$, (3), (4), and (5) can be used to define and solve the original hard margin optimization problem.

The generalization error of a classifier is governed by its VC dimension [1]:

Definition 1. *A set of points $S = \{x^1...x^m\}$ is shattered by a set of functions F mapping from a domain X to $\{-1,1\}$ if, for each $b \in \{-1,1\}^m$, there is a function f_b in F with $bf_b(x^i) = 1$, $i = 1..m$. The VC-dimension of F is the cardinality of the largest shattered set S.*

Alternatively, the fat-shattering dimension can be used to bound the generalization error of a large margin classifier[11]:

Definition 2. *A set of points $S = \{x^1...x^m\}$ is γ-shattered by a set of functions F mapping from a domain X to $\mathbb{R}$ if there are real numbers $r^1,...,r^m$ such that, for each $b \in \{-1,1\}^m$, there is a function f_b in F with $b(f_b(x^i) - r^i) \geq \gamma$, $i = 1..m$. We say that $r^1,...,r^m$ witness the shattering. Then the fat-shattering dimension of F is a function $fat_F(\gamma)$ that maps γ to the cardinality of the largest γ-shattered set S.*

3 Problem Formulation and Generalization Error

In this work, we introduce prior knowledge which has not been previously applied in the SVM framework. This prior is specified in terms of explicit constraints placed on the normal vector of the separating hyperplane. For example, consider the task of determining whether a posting came from the newsgroup alt.atheism or talk.politics.guns, based on the presence of the words "gun" and "atheism" in the posting. Consider the unthresholded perceptron $f(posting; \omega_{atheism}, \omega_{gun}, \theta) = \omega_{atheism} * I_{\{atheism\ present\}} + \omega_{gun} * I_{\{gun\ present\}} + \theta$ ($I_{\{x\ present\}}$ is the indicator function that is 1 when the word x is present in the *posting* and 0 otherwise). A positive value of $\omega_{atheism}$ captures excitatory influence of the word "atheism" on the outcome of classification by ensuring that the value of $f(posting; \omega_{atheism}, \omega_{gun}, \theta)$ increases when the word "atheism" is encountered in the posting, all other things being equal. Similarly, constraining ω_{gun} to be negative captures an inhibitory influence. Note that such constraints restrict the rotation of the hyperplane, but not its translation offset θ. Thus, prior knowledge by itself does not determine the decision boundary. However, it does restrict the hypothesis space.

We are interested in imposing constraints on the parameters of the family F of functions $sign(f(x;\omega,\theta))$ defined by (1). Constraints of the form $\omega^T c > 0$ generalize excitatory and inhibitory sign constraints[2] (e.g., $\omega_i > 0$ is given by $c = [c_1 = 0, ..., c_i = 1, ..., c_n = 0]^T$). In addition, sometimes it is possible to determine the approximate orientation of the hyperplane a-priori. Normalizing all the coefficients ω_i in the range $[-1, 1]$ enables the domain expert to specify the strength of the contribution of ω_{gun} and $\omega_{atheism}$ in addition to to the signs of their influence. When prior knowledge is specified in terms of an orientation vector v, the conic constraint $\frac{\omega^T v}{\|\omega\| \|v\|} > \rho$ ($\rho \in [-1, 1)$) prevents the normal ω from deviating too far from v.

It is well-known that the VC-dimension of F in $\mathbb{R}^n$ is $n + 1$ (see, e.g., [12]). Interestingly, the VC-dimension of *constrained* F is at least n with any number of constraints imposed on $\omega \in W$ as long as there is an open subset of W that satisfies the constraints (this result follows from [13]). This means that any value of ρ in the conic constraint cannot result in significant improvement in the classifier's generalization ability as measured by its VC-dimension. Similarly, sign constraints placed on all the input variables cannot decrease the classifier's VC-dimension by more than 1. The following theorem shows that the VC-dimension of a relatively weakly constrained classifier achieves this lower bound of n:

Theorem 1. *For the class* $F_C = \{x \to sign(\sum_{i=1}^{n} \omega_i x_i + \theta) : \omega_1 > 0\}$, *VC-dimension of* $F_C = n$.

Proof. The proof uses techniques from [12]. Let $F_C = \{x \to sign(\omega_1 x_1 + \overline{\omega}^T \overline{x} + \theta) : \omega_1 > 0\}$, where $\overline{x} = [x_2, ..., x_n]^T$ is the projection of x into the hyperplane $\{\omega_1 = 0\}$ and $\overline{\omega} = [\omega_2, ... \omega_n]^T$.

First, observe that $\{\omega_1 > 0\}$ defines an open subset of W. Hence, the VC-dimension of F_C is at least n. Now, we show by contradiction that a set of $n + 1$ points cannot be shattered by F_C. Assume that some set of points $x^1, ..., x^{n+1} \in \mathbb{R}^n$ can be shattered. Let $\overline{x^1}, ..., \overline{x^{n+1}} \in \mathbb{R}^{n-1}$ be their projections into the hyperplane $\{\omega_1 = 0\}$. There are two cases: Case 1: $\overline{x^1}, ..., \overline{x^{n+1}}$ are distinct. Since these are $n + 1$ points in an $(n - 1)$-dimensional hyperplane, by Radon's Theorem [14] they can be divided into two sets S_1 and S_2 whose convex hulls intersect. Thus, $\exists \lambda_i, \lambda_j (0 \leq \lambda_i, \lambda_j \leq 1)$

---

[2] In the rest of the paper, we refer to excitatory and inhibitory constraints of the form $\omega_i > 0$ ($\omega_i < 0$) as sign constraints because they constrain the sign of w_i.

such that
$$\sum_{i:\overline{x^i}\in S_1} \lambda_i \overline{x^i} = \sum_{j:\overline{x^j}\in S_2} \lambda_j \overline{x^j} \quad (6)$$

and
$$\sum_{i:\overline{x^i}\in S_1} \lambda_i = \sum_{j:\overline{x^j}\in S_2} \lambda_j = 1 \quad (7)$$

Since $x^1, ..., x^{n+1}$ are shattered in $\mathbb{R}^n$, $\exists \omega_1, \overline{\omega}, \theta$ such that $\omega_1 x_1^i + \overline{\omega}^T \overline{x^i} \geq \theta$ for all $\overline{x^i} \in S_1$. Multiplying by λ_i and summing over i, we get (after applying (7))

$$\overline{\omega}^T \sum_{i:\overline{x^i}\in S_1} \lambda_i \overline{x^i} \geq \theta - \omega_1 \sum_{i:\overline{x^i}\in S_1} \lambda_i x_1^i \quad (8)$$

Similarly, for all $\overline{x^j} \in S_2$, $\omega_1 x_1^j + \overline{\omega}^T \overline{x^j} < \theta \Rightarrow$

$$\overline{\omega}^T \sum_{j:\overline{x^j}\in S_2} \lambda_j \overline{x^j} < \theta - \omega_1 \sum_{j:\overline{x^j}\in S_2} \lambda_j x_1^j \quad (9)$$

Combining (8), (9), and (6) yields $\omega_1(\sum_{j:\overline{x^j}\in S_2} \lambda_j x_1^j - \sum_{i:\overline{x^i}\in S_1} \lambda_i x_1^i) < 0$

$$(10)$$

Since $\omega_1 > 0$, $(\sum_{j:\overline{x^j}\in S_2} \lambda_j x_1^j - \sum_{i:\overline{x^i}\in S_1} \lambda_i x_1^i) < 0 \quad (11)$

Now, shattering the same set of points, but reversing the labels of S_1 and S_2 implies that $\exists \omega_1', \overline{\omega}', \theta'$ such that $\omega_1' x_1^i + \overline{\omega}'^T \overline{x^i} < \theta'$ for all $\overline{x^i} \in S_1$ and $\omega_1' x_1^j + \overline{\omega}'^T \overline{x^j} \geq \theta'$ for all $\overline{x^j} \in S_2$. An argument identical to the one above shows that

$$\omega_1'(\sum_{j:\overline{x^j}\in S_2} \lambda_j x_1^j - \sum_{i:\overline{x^i}\in S_1} \lambda_i x_1^i) > 0 \quad (12)$$

Since $\omega_1' > 0$, $(\sum_{j:\overline{x^j}\in S_2} \lambda_j x_1^j - \sum_{i:\overline{x^i}\in S_1} \lambda_i x_1^i) > 0$, which contradicts (11)

Case 2: Two distinct points x^1 and x^2 project to the same point $\overline{x^1} = \overline{x^2}$ (13) on the hyperplane $\{\omega_1 = 0\}$. Assume, wlog, that $x_1^1 < x_1^2$ (14). Since x^1 and x^2 are shattered, $\exists \omega_1, \overline{\omega}, \theta$ such that $\omega_1 x_1^1 + \overline{\omega}^T \overline{x^1} \geq \theta > \omega_1 x_1^2 + \overline{\omega}^T \overline{x^2}$, which, together with (13) and (14), implies that $\omega_1 < 0$, a contradiction. □

This result means that imposing a sign constraint on a single input variable or using $\rho = 0$ in the conic constraint is sufficient to achieve the maximum theoretical improvement within the VC framework[3]. However, it is unsatisfactory in a sense that it contradicts our intuition (and empirical results) which suggests that stronger prior knowledge should help the classifier reduce its generalization error faster. The following theorem shows that the fat-shattering dimension decreases continuously with increasing ρ in the conic constraint, giving us the desired guarantee. Technically, the fat-shattering dimension is a function of the margin γ, so we use the following definition of function domination to specify what we mean by decreasing fat-shattering dimension:

Definition 3. *A function $f_1(x)$ is dominated by a function $f_2(x)$ if, for all x, $f_1(x) \leq f_2(x)$ and, at least for one a, $f_1(a) < f_2(a)$. When we say that $f_\rho(x)$ decreases with increasing ρ, we mean that $\rho_1 < \rho_2$ implies that $f_{\rho_2}(x)$ is dominated by $f_{\rho_1}(x)$.*

Theorem 2. *For the class $F_{v,\rho} = \{x \to \omega^T x + \theta : \|\omega\|_2 = 1, \|v\|_2 = 1, \|x\|_2 \leq R, \omega^T v > \rho \geq 0\}$, $fat_{F_{v,\rho}}(\gamma)$ decreases with increasing ρ.* [4]

Proof. The fat-shattering dimension obviously cannot increase with increasing ρ, so we only need to find a value of γ where it decreases. We show that this happens at $\gamma' = R\sqrt{1 - \rho_2^2}$. First, we upper bound $fat_{F_{v,\rho_2}}(\gamma')$ by showing that, in order to γ'-shatter two points, the separating hyperplane must be able to rotate through a larger angle than that allowed by the constraint $\omega^{1^T} v > \rho_2$. Assume that two points x^1, x^2 can be γ'-shattered by F_{v,ρ_2}. Then $\exists \omega^1, \omega^2, \theta^1, \theta^2, r^1, r^2$ such that $\omega^{1^T} x^1 + \theta^1 - r^1 \geq \gamma'$, $\omega^{1^T} x^2 + \theta^1 - r^2 \leq -\gamma'$, $\omega^{2^T} x^1 + \theta^2 - r^1 \leq -\gamma'$, $\omega^{2^T} x^2 + \theta^2 - r^2 \geq \gamma'$. Combining the terms and applying the Cauchy-Schwartz inequality, we get $\|\omega^1 - \omega^2\| \geq \frac{2\gamma'}{R}$. Squaring both sides, expanding $\|\omega^1 - \omega^2\|^2$ as $\|\omega^1\|^2 + \|\omega^2\|^2 - 2\omega^{1^T}\omega^2$, and using the fact that $\|\omega^1\| = \|\omega^2\| = 1$ yields

$$\omega^{1^T}\omega^2 \leq 1 - \frac{2\gamma'^2}{R^2} = 2\rho_2^2 - 1 \quad (15)$$

Since the angle between ω^1 and ω^2 cannot exceed the sum of the angle between ω^1 and the prior v and the angle between v and ω^2, both of which are bounded above by $\arccos(\rho_2)$, we get (after some algebra) $\omega^{1^T}\omega^2 > 2\rho_2^2 - 1$, which contradicts (15).

$$\text{Thus, } fat_{F_{v,\rho_2}}(R\sqrt{1 - \rho_2^2}) < 2 \quad (16)$$

---

[3] The constraint $\{w_1 > 0\}$ is weak since it only cuts the volume of the hypothesis space by $\frac{1}{2}$.

[4] Note that the statement of this theorem deals with hyperplanes with unit normals, not canonical hyperplanes. The margin of a unit-normal hyperplane is given by $min_{i=1..m}|\omega x^i + \theta|$.

Now, we lower bound $fat_{F_{v,\rho_1}}(\gamma')$ by exhibiting two points γ'-shattered by F_{v,ρ_1}. Wlog, let $v = [0, 1, 0, ..0]^T$. It is easy to verify that $x^1 = [R, 0, ..0]^T$ and $x^2 = [-R, 0, ..0]^T$ can be $R\sqrt{1-\rho_2^2}$-shattered by F_{v,ρ_1}, witnessed by $r^1 = r^2 = 0$.

$$\text{Hence, } fat_{F_{v,\rho_1}}(R\sqrt{1-\rho_2^2}) \geq 2 \tag{17}$$

which, combined with (16), completes the argument. □

The result of Theorem 1 is important because it shows that even weak prior knowledge improves the classifier's generalization performance in the VC framework which makes less assumptions about the data than the fat-shattering framework. However, it is the result of Theorem 2 within the fat-shattering framework which justifies the use of stronger prior knowledge.

4 Implementation

The quadratic optimization problem for finding the maximum margin separating hyperplane (2) can be easily modified to take into account linear rotational constraints of the form $\omega^T c_j > 0$, $j = 1...l$. The soft margin/soft constraint formulation that allows for possibility of violating both the margin maximization objective and the rotational constraints minimizes the following regularization functional:

$$R_{reg}[f, l, l'] = \frac{1}{m} \sum_{i=1}^{m} l(y_i, f(x_i; \omega, \theta)) + \frac{C_1}{C_2 l} \sum_{j=1}^{l} l'(\omega, c_j) + \frac{C_1}{2} \|\omega\|_2^2 \tag{18}$$

with 0-1 losses for the data and the prior: $l(y_i, f(x_i; \omega, \theta)) = I_{\{-y_i f(x_i; \omega, \theta) > 0\}}$ and $l'(\omega, c_j) = I_{\{-\omega^T c_j > 0\}}$ in the hard margin/hard rotational constraints case and hinge losses: $l(y_i, f(x_i; \omega, \theta)) = max(1 - y_i f(x_i; \omega, \theta), 0), l'(\omega, c_j) = max(-\omega^T c_j, 0)$ in the soft margin/soft rotational constraints case. The regularization functional above is the same as in (2) with an additional loss function which penalizes the hyperplanes that violate the prior. Minimizing (18) with hinge loss functions is equivalent to solving:

$$\underset{\omega, \theta, \xi, \nu}{minimize} \tfrac{1}{2}\|\omega\|_2^2 + \tfrac{1}{C_1 m} \sum_{i=1}^{m} \xi_i + \tfrac{1}{C_2 l} \sum_{j=1}^{l} \nu_j \tag{19}$$

$subject\ to\ y_i(\omega^T x + \theta) \geq 1 - \xi_i, \xi_i \geq 0,\ i = 1...m,$
$\qquad\qquad \omega^T c_j \geq 0 - \nu_j, \nu_j \geq 0,\ j = 1...l.$

Constructing the Lagrangian from (19) and calculating the Wolfe dual results in the following maximization problem:

$$\underset{\alpha, \beta}{maximize} \sum_{i=1}^{m} \alpha_i - \tfrac{1}{2} \sum_{i,j=1}^{m} \alpha_i \alpha_j y_i y_j (x_i^T x_j) -$$

$$\sum_{i=1}^{m} \sum_{j=1}^{l} \alpha_i \beta_j y_i (x_i^T c_j) - \tfrac{1}{2} \sum_{i,j=1}^{l} \beta_i \beta_j (x_i^T c_j) \tag{20}$$

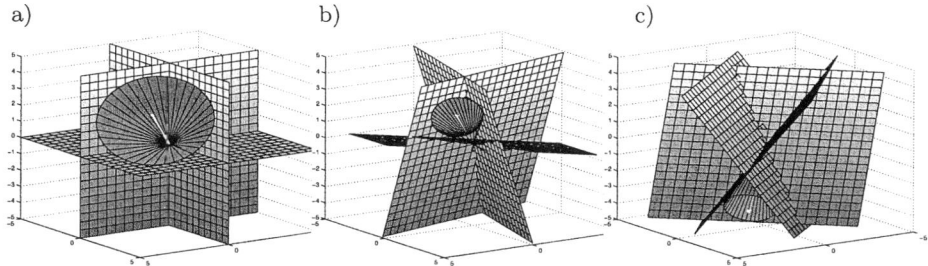

Fig. 1. Approximating a conic constraint:

a) Start with the known constraints $\omega_1 \geq 0$, $\omega_2 \geq 0$, and $\omega_3 \geq 0$ around $v^1 = [\frac{1}{\sqrt{3}}, \frac{1}{\sqrt{3}}, \frac{1}{\sqrt{3}}]^T$. The figure shows linear constraints around v^1 (white vector) and the cone $\frac{\omega^T v^1}{\|\omega\|} > \frac{1}{\sqrt{3}}$ approximated by these constraints.
b) Rotate the bounding hyperplanes $\{\omega_1 = 0\}$, $\{\omega_2 = 0\}$, $\{\omega_3 = 0\}$ into v^1, approximating a cone with the required angle ρ' around v^1
c) Rotate the whole boundary from v^1 (white vector in (a),(b)) to the required orientation v' (white vector in (c)).

$$subj.\,to\;\tfrac{1}{C_1 m} \geq \alpha_i \geq 0,\, i=1...m,\;\tfrac{1}{C_2 l} \geq \beta_j \geq 0,\, i=1...l,\; and\; \sum_{i=1}^{m} \alpha_i y_i = 0$$

The solution to (20) is given by $\omega = \sum_{i=1}^{m} \alpha_i y_i x_i + \sum_{j=1}^{l} \beta_j c_j.$ \hfill (21)

As before, setting $\xi_i = 0$, $\nu_j = 0$, $i = 1...m$, $j = 1...l$, (19), (20), and (21) can be used to solve the hard margin/hard rotational constraints optimization problem. Note that in the soft-margin formulation, constants C_1 and C_2 define a trade-off between fitting the data, maximizing the margin, and respecting the rotational constraints.

The above calculation can impose linear constraints on the orientation of the large margin separating hyperplane when such constraints are given. This is the case with sign-constrained prior knowledge. However, domain knowledge in form of a cone centered around an arbitrary rotational vector v' cannot be represented as a linear constraint in the quadratic optimization problem given by (19). The approach taken in this work is to approximate an n-dimensional cone with n hyperplanes. For example, sign constraints $\omega_1 \geq 0$, $\omega_2 \geq 0$, and $\omega_3 \geq 0$ approximate a cone of angle $\rho^1 = \frac{1}{\sqrt{3}}$ around $v^1 = [\frac{1}{\sqrt{3}}, \frac{1}{\sqrt{3}}, \frac{1}{\sqrt{3}}]^T$ (see Figure 1-(a)). To approximate a cone of arbitrary angle ρ' around an arbitrary orientation vector v', 1) the normal ω'_i of each bounding hyperplane $\{\omega_i = 0\}$ (as defined by the sign constraints above) is rotated in the plane spanned by $\{\omega'_i, v^1\}$ by an angle $acos(\omega'^T_i v^1) - \rho'$, and 2) a solid body rotation that transforms v^1 into v' is subsequently applied to all the bounding hyperplanes, as illustrated in Figure 1. This construction generalizes in a straightforward way from $\mathbb{R}^3$ to $\mathbb{R}^n$.

5 Experiments

Experiments were performed on two distinct real-world domains:

Voting Records. This is a UCI database [15] of congressional voting records. The vote of each representative is recorded on the 16 key issues. The task is to predict the representative's political party (Democrat or Republican) based on his/her votes. The domain theory was specified in form of inhibitory/excitatory sign constraints. An excitatory constraint means that the vote of "yea" correlates with the Democratic position on the issue, an inhibitory constraint means that Republicans favor the proposal. The complete domain theory is specified in Figure 2-(a). Note that sign constraints are imposed on relatively few features (7 out of 16). Since this type of domain knowledge is weak, a hard rotational constraint SVM was used. Only representatives whose positions are known on all the 16 issues were used in this experiment. The results shown in Figure 2-(b) demonstrate that sign constraints decrease the generalization error of the classifier. As expected, prior knowledge helps more when the data is scarce.

Text classification. The task is to determine the newsgroup that a posting was taken from based on the posting's content. We used the 20-newsgroups dataset [16]. Each posting was treated as a bag-of-words, with each binary feature encoding whether or not the word is present in the posting. Stemming was used in the preprocessing stage to reduce the number of features. Feature selection based on mutual information between each individual feature and the label was employed (300 maximally informative features were chosen). Since SVMs are best suited for binary classification tasks, all of our experiments involve pairwise newsgroup classification. The problem of applying SVMs to multicategory classification has been researched extensively([2,3]), and is orthogonal to our work.

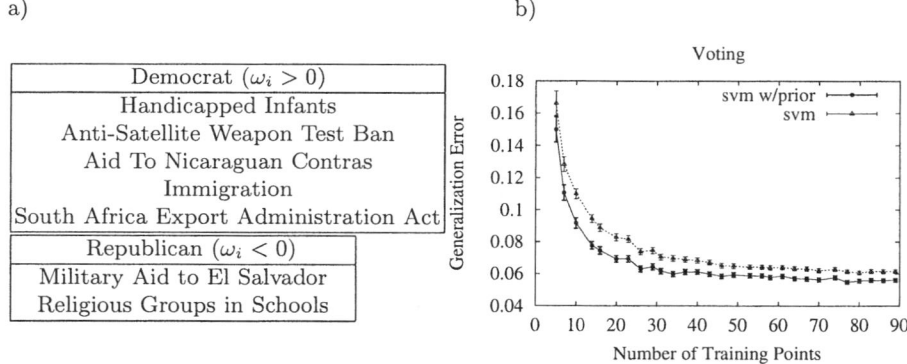

Fig. 2. a) Prior Knowledge for voting b)Generalization error as a percentage versus number of training points for voting classification. For each classification task, the data set is split randomly into training and test sets in 1000 different ways. SVM classifier is trained on the training set with and without prior knowledge, and its average error on the test set is plotted, along with error bars showing 95% confidence intervals.

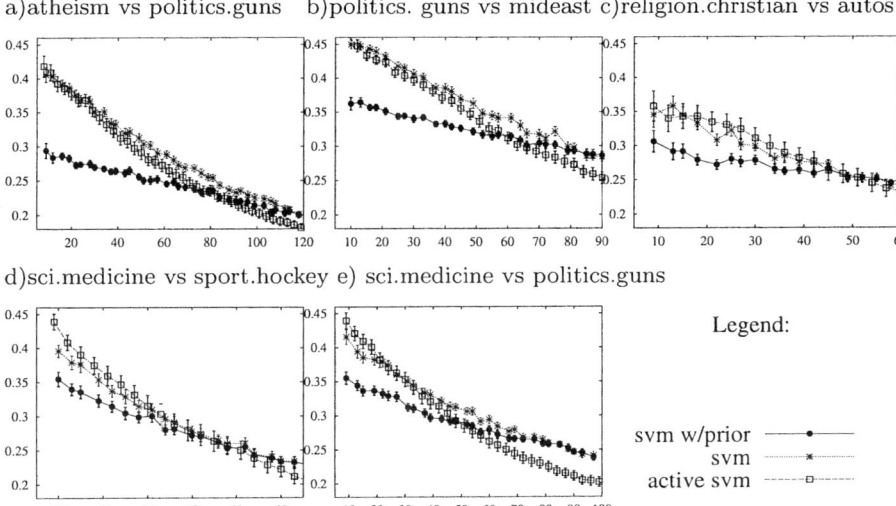

Fig. 3. Generalization error as a percentage versus number of training points for 5 different classification experiments. For each random sample selection, the data set is split randomly into training and test sets in 100 different ways. For active learning experiments, the data set is split randomly into two equal-sized sets in 100 different ways, with one set used as the unlabeled pool for query selection, and the other set - for testing. All error bars are based on 95% confidence intervals.

Prior knowledge in this experiment is represented by a conic constraint around a specific orientation vector v'. While it may be hard for human experts to supply such a prior, there are readily available sources of domain knowledge that were not developed specifically for the classification task at hand. In order to be able to utilize them, it is essential to decode the information into a form usable by the learning algorithm. This is the virtue of rotational constraints: they are directly usable by SVMs and they can approximate more sophisticated pre-existing forms of information. In our experiments, domain knwoledge from Wordnet, a lexical system which encodes semantic relations between words [17], is automatically converted into v'. The coefficient v'_x of each word x is calculated from the relative proximity of x to each category label in the hypernym (is-a) hierarchy of Wordnet (measured in hops). A natural approximation of v'_x is given by $\frac{hops(x, label_+)}{hops(x, label_-) + hops(x, label_+)}$, normalized by a linear mapping to the required range $[-1, 1]$, where $label_+$ and $label_-$ are the names of the two newsgroups. Performance of the following three classifiers on this task was evaluated:

1. A soft rotational constraint SVM ($C_1 = C_2 = 10^{-5}$) with Wordnet prior ($\rho = 0.99$) (reasonable values of constants were picked based on the alt.atheism vs. politics.guns classification task, with no attempt to optimize them for other tasks).

2. An SVM which actively selects the points to be labeled out of a pool of unlabeled newsgroup postings. We implemented a strategy suggested in [4] which always queries the point closest to the separating hyperplane.
3. Traditional SVM ($C_1 = 10^{-5}$) trained on a randomly selected sample.

Typical results of this experiment for a few different pairwise classification tasks appear in Figure 3. For small data samples, the prior consistently decreases generalization error by up to 25%, showing that even a very approximate prior orientation vector v' can result in significant performance improvement. Since prior knowledge is imposed with soft constraints, the data overwhelms the prior with increasing sample size. Figure 3 also compares the effect of introducing rotational constraints with the effect of active learning. It has been shown theoretically that active learning can improve the convergence rate of the classification error under a favorable distribution of the input data [18], although no such guarantees exist for general distributions. In our experiments, active learning begins to improve performance only after enough data is collected. Active learning does not help when the sample size is very small, probably due to the fact that the separating hyperplane of the classifier cannot be approximated well, resulting in uninformative choices of query points. Rotational prior knowledge, on the other hand, is more helpful for lowest sample sizes and ceases to be useful in the region where active learning helps. Thus, the strengths of prior knowledge and active learning are complementary. Combining them is a direction for future research.

6 Conclusions

We presented a simple framework for incorporating rotational prior knowledge into support vector machines. This framework has proven not only practically useful, but also useful for gaining insight into generalization ability of a-priori constrained large-margin classifiers.

Related work includes using Wordnet for feature creation for text categorization ([19]) and introducing sign constraints into the perceptron learning algorithm [20,21]. These studies do not provide generalization error guarantees for classification.

Acknowledgement. We thank Ilya Shpitser and anonymous reviewers for helpful suggestions on improving this paper. This material is based upon work supported in part by the National Science Foundation under Award NSF CCR 01-21401 ITR and in part by the Information Processing Technology Office of the Defense Advanced Research Projects Agency under award HR0011-05-1-0040. Any opinions, findings, and conclusions or recommendations expressed in this publication are those of the authors and do not necessarily reflect the views of the National Science Foundation or the Defense Advanced Research Projects Agency.

References

1. Vapnik, V.: The Nature of Statistical Learning Theory. Springer-Verlag (1995)
2. Joachims, T.: Text categorization with support vector machines: learning with many relevant features. In: Proceedings of the Tenth European Conference on Machine Learning. Number 1398 (1998)
3. Dumas, S., Platt, J., Heckerman, D., Sahami, M.: Inductive learning algorithms and representations for text categorization. Proceedings of the Seventh International Conference on Information and Knowledge Management (1998)
4. Campbell, C., Cristianini, N., Smola, A.: Query learning with large margin classifiers. Proceedings of The Seventeenth International Conference on Machine Learning (2000) 111–118
5. Raina, R., Shen, Y., Ng, A., McCallum, A.: Classification with hybrid generative/discriminative models. Proceedings of the Seventeenth Annual Conference on Neural Information Processing Systems (2003)
6. Fink, M.: Object classification from a single example utilizing class relevance metrics. Proceedings of the Eighteenth Annual Conference on Neural Information Processing Systems (2004)
7. Scholkopf, B., Simard, P., Vapnik, V., Smola, A.: Prior knowledge in support vector kernels. Advances in kernel methods - support vector learning (2002)
8. Fung, G., Mangasarian, O., Shavlik, J.: Knowledge-based support vector machine classifiers. Proceedings of the Sixteenth Annual Conference on Neural Information Processing Systems (2002)
9. Wu, X., Srihari, R.: Incorporating prior knowledge with weighted margin support vector machines. Proceedings of the Tenth ACM SIGKDD International Conference on Knowledge Discovery and Data Mining (2004)
10. Mangasarian, O., Shavlik, J., Wild, E.: Knowledge-based kernel approximation. Journal of Machine Learning Research (2004)
11. Shawe-Taylor, J., Bartlett, P.L., Williamson, R.C., Anthony, M.: Structural risk minimization over data-dependent hierarchies. IEEE Transactions on Information Theory **44** (1998)
12. Anthony, M., Biggs, N.: PAC learning and artificial neural networks. Technical report (2000)
13. Erlich, Y., Chazan, D., Petrack, S., Levy, A.: Lower bound on VC-dimension by local shattering. Neural Computation **9** (1997)
14. Grunbaum, B.: Convex Polytopes. John Wiley (1967)
15. Blake, C., Merz, C.: UCI repository of machine learning databases, http://www.ics.uci.edu/~mlearn/mlrepository.html (1998)
16. Blake, C., Merz, C.: 20 newsgroups database, http://people.csail.mit.edu/people/jrennie/ 20newsgroups/ (1998)
17. Miller, G.: WordNet: an online lexical database. International Journal of Lexicography **3** (1990)
18. Dasgupta, S., Kalai, A.T., Monteleoni, C.: Analysis of perceptron-based active learning. Eighteenth Annual Conference on Learning Theory (2005)
19. Gabrilovich, E., Markovitch, S.: Text categorization with many redundant features: Using aggressive feature selection to make svms competitive with c4.5. Proceedings of The Twenty-First International Conference on Machine Learning (2004)
20. Amit, D., Campbell, C., Wong, K.: The interaction space of neural networks with sign-constrained weights. Journal of Physics (1989)
21. Barber, D., Saad, D.: Does extra knowledge necessarily improve generalization? Neural Computation **8** (1996)

On the LearnAbility of Abstraction Theories from Observations for Relational Learning

Stefano Ferilli, Teresa M.A. Basile,
Nicola Di Mauro, and Floriana Esposito

Department of Computer Science,
University of Bari, Italy
{ferilli, basile, ndm, esposito}@di.uniba.it

Abstract. The most common methodology in symbolic learning consists in inducing, given a set of observations, a general concept definition. It is widely known that the choice of the proper description language for a learning problem can affect the efficacy and effectiveness of the learning task. Furthermore, most real-world domains are affected by various kinds of imperfections in data, such as inappropriateness of the description language which does not contain/facilitate an exact representation of the target concept. To deal with such kind of situations, Machine Learning approaches moved from a framework exploiting a single inference mechanism, such as induction, towards one integrating multiple inference strategies such as abstraction. The literature so far assumed that the information needed to the learning systems to apply additional inference strategies is provided by a domain expert. The goal of this work is the automatic inference of such information.

The effectiveness of the proposed method was tested by providing the generated abstraction theories to the learning system INTHELEX as a background knowledge to exploit its abstraction capabilities. Various experiments were carried out on the real-world application domain of scientific paper documents, showing the validity of the approach.

1 Introduction

Although the efficacy of induction algorithms has been demonstrated on a wide variety of benchmark domains, current Machine Learning techniques are inadequate for more difficult real-world domains. The nature of the problem can be of different types, such as noise in the descriptions and lack of data but also the low level representation of the examples of the target concept. It is well known that the inappropriateness of a description language that does not contain/facilitate an exact representation of the target concept can affect the efficacy/effectiveness of the learning task. Hence, the choice of the proper representation for a learning problem has a significant impact on the performance, of Machine Learning systems in general, and of ILP systems [10] in particular. Generally, a low level representation provides all the information necessary to the learning task, but its individual parts are only remotely related to the target concept, making patterns hard to identify. Low level representations are common in real-world domains, where examples are naturally described by many small measurements, in which there is not enough knowledge to represent the data with few highly relevant features.

Among various strategies proposed to overcome this limitation, there are different ways to exploit the *abstraction* framework proposed in [14]. For example, [16] addresses the problem of potentially many mappings that can hold between descriptions in a first-order representation language by selecting one particular type of mapping at a time and using it as a basis to define a new hypothesis space, thus performing a *representation change*. [15] used it to overcome the knowledge acquisition bottleneck that limits the learning task in particular application domains such as the automation of cartographic generalization. More generally, abstraction is used to model *a priori* the hypothesis space before the learning process starts introducing it as a multi-strategy capability that could shift to a higher language bias when the current one does not allow to capture the target predicate definition [3, 6, 8]. From an operational viewpoint, it should deal with cases in which learning can be more effective if it takes place at multiple (different) levels of complexity, which can be compared to the language bias shift considered in [2]; a useful perspective for the integration of this inference operator in an inductive learning framework was given in [14]. According to such a framework, the abstraction operator was endowed in the learning system INTHELEX [4] making it able to perform the shift.

In the current practice, it is in charge of the human expert to specify all the information needed by such a strategy for being applicable. It goes without saying that quality, correctness and completeness in the formalization of such information is a critical issue, that can determine the very feasibility of the learning process. Providing it is a very difficult task because it requires a deep knowledge of the application domain, and is in any case an error-prone activity, since omissions and errors may take place. For instance, the domain and/or the language used to represent it might be unknown to the experimenter, because he is just in charge of properly setting and running the learning system on a dataset provided by third parties and/or generated by other people. In any case, it is often not easy for non-experts to single out and formally express such knowledge in the form needed by the automatic systems, just because they are not familiar with the representation language and the related technical issues.

These considerations would make it highly desirable to develop procedures that automatically generate such information. This work aims at proposing solutions to automatically infer the information required by the abstraction framework from the same observations that are input to the inductive process, assuming that they are sufficiently significant, and at assessing the validity and performance of the corresponding procedures. In the following, after an introduction to the general framework for abstraction, the method for the automatic definition of appropriate rules to fire the operator will be presented along with an experimental session on a real-world domain.

2 Abstraction Inference Strategy: The General Framework

Abstraction is defined as a mapping between representations that are related to the same reference set but contain less detail (typically, only the information that is relevant to the achievement of the goal is maintained). It is useful in inductive learning when the current language bias proves not to be expressive enough for representing concept descriptions that can explain the examples, as discussed in [2].

Definition 1. *Given two clausal theories T (ground theory) and T' (abstract theory) built upon different languages $\mathcal{L}$ and $\mathcal{L}'$ (and derivation rules), an abstraction is a triple (T, T', f), where f is a computable total mapping between clauses in $\mathcal{L}$ and those in $\mathcal{L}'$.*

An Abstraction Theory (an operational representation of f) is used to perform such a *shift of language bias* [13, 2] to a higher level representation:

Definition 2. *An abstraction theory from $\mathcal{L}$ to $\mathcal{L}'$ is a consistent set of clauses $c : -d_1, \ldots, d_m$ where c is a literal built on predicates in $\mathcal{L}'$, and d_j, $j = 1, \ldots, m$ are literals built on predicates of $\mathcal{L}$. In other words, it is a collection of intermediate concepts represented as a disjunction of alternative definitions.*

Inverse resolution operators [10], by tracking back resolution steps, can suggest new salient properties and relations of the learning domain. Thus, they can be a valuable mechanism to build abstraction theories, as introduced in [7]. To this purpose, the absorption, inter-construction and intra-construction operators can be exploited, also in the case of first-order clauses. In this work we are interested in the case of a Datalog program [1, 9] as ground space of the abstraction, as in [11], where clauses are *flattened*, hence function-free.

Definition 3 (Absorption & Inter-construction).

absorption: *let C and D be Datalog clauses. If $\exists \theta$ unifier such that $\exists S \subset body(C)$, $S = body(D)\theta$, then applying the absorption operator yields the new clause C' such that:*
- $head(C') = head(C)$
- $body(C') = (body(C) \setminus S) \cup \{head(D)\theta\}$,

i.e., if all conditions in D are verified in the body of C, the corresponding literals are eliminated and replaced by $head(D)$.

Example 1. Let be C and D the following clauses:
C = bicycle(bb) ← has_pedals(bb,p), has_saddle(bb,s), has_frame(bb,f),
    part_of(bb,w1), circular(w1), has_rim(w1), has_tire(w1),
    part_of(bb,w2), circular(w2), has_rim(w2), has_tire(w2).
D = wheel(X) ← circular(X), has_rim(X), has_tire(X).
For such two clauses there exists $\theta_1 = X\backslash w1$ and $\theta_2 = X\backslash w2$, thus, applying absorption operator twice we obtain the following clause:
C' = bicycle(bb) ← has_pedals(bb,p), has_saddle(bb,s), has_frame(bb,f),
    part_of(bb,w1), wheel(w1), part_of(bb,w2), wheel(w2).

inter-construction: *let $C = \{C_i | i = 1, \ldots, n\}$ be a set of Datalog clauses. If there exists a set of literals R and a unifier θ_i for each clause C_i, such that $\exists S_i \subset body(C_i)$, $S_i = R\theta_i$, then we define:*
- *a new predicate $L \leftarrow R$*
- *for all $i = 1, \ldots, n$ $body(C_i)$ can be rewritten as $(body(C_i) \setminus S_i) \cup \{L\theta_i\}$. i.e., if all conditions in R are verified in the body of each $C_i \in C$, the corresponding literals are eliminated and replaced by L that is a new predicate, with a definition in the theory, never present in the description language.*

Example 2. Let C be the following set of clauses:
C_1 = monocycle(m) ← has_small_pedals(m,sp), has_small_saddle(m,ss),
            part_of(m,w1), circular(w1), has_rim(w1), has_tire(w1).
C_2 = bicycle(bi) ← has_pedals(bi,p), has_saddle(bi,s), has_frame(bi,f),
            part_of(bi,wbi1),circular(wbi1),has_rim(wbi1),has_tire(wbi1),
            part_of(bi,wbi2), circular(wbi2), has_rim(wbi2), has_tire(wbi2).
C_3 = car(c) ← has_motor_engine(c,me), has_steering_wheel(c,sw),
            part_of(c,wc1),circular(wc1),has_rim(wc1),has_tire(wc1),
            part_of(c,wc2),circular(wc2),has_rim(wc2),has_tire(wc2),
            part_of(c,wc3),circular(wc3),has_rim(wc3),has_tire(wc3),
            part_of(c,wc4),circular(wc4),has_rim(wc4),has_tire(wc4).
As we can note, the set $R = part\_of(A,B), circular(B), has\_rim(B), has\_tire(B)$ is present in all the clauses and there exists an unifier between R and each of the clauses C_1, C_2, C_3, then it is possible to define a new predicate, let be it $l(A,B)$, and the clause $l(A,B) : -part\_of(A,B), circular(B), has\_rim(B), has\_tire(B)$. By this definition the set C can be rewritten as:
C_1 = monocycle(m) ← has_small_pedals(m,sp), has_small_saddle(m,ss), l(m,w1).
C_2 = bicycle(bi) ← has_pedals(bi,p), has_saddle(bi,s), has_frame(bi,f),
            l(bi,wbi1), l(bi,wbi2).
C_3 = car(c) ← has_motor_engine(c,me), has_steering_wheel(c,sw),
            l(c,wc1), l(c,wc2), l(c,wc3), l(c,wc4).

In the framework for integrating abstraction and inductive learning given in [14], concept representation deals with entities belonging to three different levels, that together form a *reasoning context*. Underlying any source of experience is the *world*, where *concrete* objects (the 'real things') reside, that is not directly known, since any observer's access to it is mediated by his *perception* of it $P(W)$ (consisting of the 'physical' stimuli produced on the observer). To be available over time, these stimuli must be memorized in an organized *structure* S, i.e. an *extensional* representation of the perceived world, in which stimuli related to each other are stored together. Finally, to reason about the perceived world and communicate with other agents, a *language* L is needed, that describes it *intensionally*. Generally these sets contain operators for performing operations such as: grouping indistinguishable objects into equivalence classes; grouping a set of ground objects to form a new compound object that replaces them in the abstract world; ignoring terms, that disappear in the abstract world; merging a subset of values that are considered indistinguishable; dropping predicate arguments, thus reducing the arity of a relation (even to zero, thus moving to a propositional logic setting). Corresponding instances of these operators are present at each level of the reasoning context, so that it is possible to reason at any of the given levels.

3 Learning Abstraction Theories

The abstraction procedure reported in Section 2 aims at discarding or hiding the information that is insignificant to the achievement of the goal. According to Definitions 1 and 2, abstraction is based on a computable mapping f whose operational representation is an Abstraction Theory that encodes the abstraction operators by means of a consistent set of clauses, i.e. domain rules. Thus, in order to perform abstraction, an inductive concept learning system must be provided with an abstraction theory for the specific application domain at hand. As already pointed out, a common assumption is that such a knowledge is provided by an expert of the application domain. Here, we propose a general approach to automatically learn such a knowledge (domain rules) by looking for correspondences that often or seldom hold among a significant set of observations. These correspondences are generated according to the *inter-construction* operator (Definition 3) and are then exploited to simplify the description language in two different ways: by generating *shifting rules* that replace significant (characteristic or discriminant) groups of literals by one single literal representing their conjunction, or by generating *neglecting rules* that eliminate groups of literals that are not significant. Both kinds of rules will be applied in order to perform the shift of language bias according to the absorption operator presented in Definition 3 in this way reducing the description length and thus improving the induction performance.

Algorithm 1 sketches the overall procedure conceived to discover common paths in the application domain that potentially could make up the Abstraction Theory. It firstly generates domain rules involving unary predicates only, that represent the characteristics of an object in the description, and then the rules made up of predicates whose arity is greater than 1, that represent the relationships between two or more objects contained in the descriptions. The algorithm is based on the choice of an observation (referred to in the following as the *seed*) that will act as the representative of the concepts to be abstracted (currently it is the first encountered positive observation).

For each constant c_i in the seed description, the algorithm collects the unary predicates it is argument of, and computes all their subsets (excluding those having cardinality equal to 0, that do not give information about the object, or 1, that represent only properties of the objects). Each subset identified in this way is a candidate to compose the body of a rule, in the Abstraction Theory, made up of unary predicates. The selection among these subsets is done considering the ones that are the best representative for the class of the concept to be abstracted according to the seed e. Thus, each subset is assigned a score based on the number of times that it occurs in the positive and negative descriptions. This value represents the *coverage rate* of the subset with respect to the observations

Algorithm 1. Identification of domain rules for Abstraction Operators

Require: $\mathcal{E}^+$: set of positive observations; $\mathcal{E}^-$: set of negative observations; e: seed;
Provide: AT: set of domain rules that make up an abstraction theory;
if $\exists$ unary predicates in e then
  $S := \emptyset$, $UnaryPreds :=$ set of unary predicates in e
  $C := \{c_1, c_2, \ldots, c_n\}$ set of constants in the description of e
  for all $c_i \in C$ do
    $S_i := \{l_i \in UnaryPreds$ s.t. c_i is argument of $l_i\}$
    if $(|S_i| \neq 0$ and $|S_i| \neq 1)$ then $S := S \bigcup S_i$
  for i=1..n do
    for all $S_j \in S$ do
      find all the subsets s_{jm} of S_j s.t.
        $(0 - \alpha \leq Score(s_{jm}) \leq 0 + \alpha)$ OR $(Max - \alpha \leq Score(s_{jm}) \leq Max + \alpha)$
      create the rule: $rule_{s_{jm}}(c_i) \leftarrow s_{jm}$
      replace in $\mathcal{E}^+$, in $\mathcal{E}^-$ and in e, s_{jm} with $rule_{s_{jm}}(c_i)$
while F (:= set of all leaf predicates of e) $\neq \emptyset$ do
  for all $l_i \in F$ do
    if l_i has only one parent (let $g_i(a_i, \ldots, a_n)$ be the l_i's parent) then
      create the rule: $rule_{l_i}(a_i, \ldots a_n) \leftarrow g_i, l_i$; H := true
      replace in $\mathcal{E}^+$, in $\mathcal{E}^-$ and in e, g_i, l_i with $rule_{l_i}(a_i, \ldots a_n))$
  for all $rule_i \leftarrow l_{i_1}, \ldots, l_{i_n}$ generated do
    if $\{l_{i_1}, \ldots, l_{i_n}\}$ occurs in some rule $rule_j$ then
      replace $l_{i_1}, \ldots, l_{i_n}$ in $rule_j$ by $rule_i$
      eliminate $rule_i$ form the set of rules generated
Evaluate the set of generated rules

and indicates the quality of the subset. This kind of selection allows to choose the subsets that are neither too specific, because they are present in few observations, nor too general, because they are encountered in almost all the observations. Once the subsets S_j are selected, the rules to make the Abstraction Theory are formulated in the following way:

$$abstract\_predicate(c_i) \leftarrow S_j \quad \text{iff} \quad score(S_j) \geq P \quad \text{(shifting rule)}$$
$$\leftarrow S_j \quad \text{iff} \quad score(S_j) \leq P \quad \text{(neglecting rule)}$$

where P is a threshold depending on the application domain at hand (in order to make P independent on the specific domain, the score can be normalized as a percentage of the maximum score actually computed in the given dataset). In the case of shifting rules, the rule's body S_j, that is a conjunction of literals, is very characterizing of either the positive or the negative observations, thus it is fundamental for the learning process and deserves to be identified by a specific predicate. In the case of neglecting rules, S_j could indicate a detail in the description that is not very significant for the learning process and thus it can be dropped. In both cases, replacing the rule's body with its head in the observations reduces the length of observations, this way making the learning process more efficient.

The algorithm continues with the identification of rules made up of predicates whose arity is greater than 1. Thus, once the previously identified abstraction rules are replaced in all the observations, they don't contain any unary predicates belonging to the original representation language. At this point, an iteration that groups together the n-ary predicates is performed until one of the following conditions succeeds: 1) the description of the seed e does not contain *leaf predicates* (predicates that share arguments with at least another predicate, excluding the head's predicate); 2) all the rules generated at step n have already been generated at step $n-1$. The search for leaf predicates is particularly complex due to the large number of relationships that could hold between the objects in the descriptions. The identification of such predicates is done by representing the observation with a tree (see Figure 1 for an example) in which each level is determined by the propagation of the variables/constants (no relation has to be imposed between two or more predicates at the same level even if they share some variable/constant): the root is the head of the observation and its direct descendants are all the predicates that share with it at least one argument. This procedure is iterated until all the predicates in the description have been inserted in the tree (a considered predicate does not participate anymore to the tree construction). Note that this procedure allows to represent any observation as a tree even when it does not naturally have a tree structure. After the tree is built, the leaf nodes that have only one parent are selected. Let $L = l_1, l_2, \ldots, l_n$ be the set of such leaf predicates: for each element $l_i \in L$ its parent (say $g(a_1, \ldots, a_m)$) is extracted from the tree, and the following rule is generated:

$$rule(a_1, \ldots, a_m) \leftarrow g(a_1, \ldots, a_m), l_i$$

Finally, for each generated rule $R_i = rule_i \leftarrow l_{i_1}, \ldots, l_{i_n}$, if the body $l_{i_1}, \ldots, l_{i_n}$, appears in some rule R_j then $l_{i_1}, \ldots, l_{i_n}$ is replaced in R_j by the predicate $rule_i$ and R_i is eliminated by the set of rules that are being generated. At the end of this step the evaluation phase of the potential rules to make up the Abstraction Theory is performed again according to the procedure above mentioned.

Associating a score to each subset requires a statistical model able to take into account the significance of the subset for the descriptions, i.e. its frequency in them. Specifically, a good subset should have a great discriminating power, i.e. it should be able to discriminate better than any other subset a description from the others. To this aim we exploit the distribution of the subset in the whole set of observations: an high discriminating power means that the subset is fundamental for the concept description since it helps to distinguish a concept from another, while a low discriminating power is interpreted as a hint that the subset is superfluous for the learning process and thus it could be eliminated from the description of the observations. The statistical model that reflects such considerations is the *Term Frequency - Inverse Document Frequency (TF-IDF)* [12], adapted to our work context facing positive and negative observations as follows. For each subset S_i a vector $V_i = (V_{i1}, V_{i2}, \ldots, V_{iN})$ is created, where N is the number of available observations and V_{ij} is the weight of the i-th subset in the j-th observation, computed as:

$$V_{ij} = FREQ_{ij} * (\lg \frac{N}{IFREQ_i} + 1)$$

The term ($\lg \frac{N}{IFREQ_i} + 1$) represents the inverse of the frequency of S_i in the whole set of observations. The result of this computation will be positive if the j-th observation is positive, negative otherwise, thus the resulting vector will be of the form $V_i = (+, -, +, +, -, +, ...)$. This allows to distinguish the significance of the subset according to its presence in the positive and negative observations. Now, for each subset we have the vector of its weights in each observation. To select the best subset the following value is computed for each subset:

$$score(S_i) = \sum_{j=1,...,N} V_{ij}$$

It is worth noting that this score will be around zero if the subset equally occurs in both positive and negative observations, in which case it is considered insignificant and could be exploited as a neglecting rule in the abstraction phase. Conversely, an high absolute value indicates a strong correlation of the subset with the positive or the negative observations. Specifically, highly positive (resp., negative) scores indicate that the subset is very frequent in the positive (resp., negative) observations. In both cases, it is considered significant and hence it could be exploited to build shifting rules for the abstraction phase.

Example 3. Let $h(1) : -p(1,2), p(1,4), p(1,5), c(2,3), f(5,6), d(4), s(6)$ the seed chosen in the set of the observations.

- **Step 1**:
  - *Grouping unary predicates:* $S = \emptyset$, no groups of unary predicates with cardinality strictly greater than 1 can be recognized;
- **Step 2**:
  - *Recognize Leaf Nodes:*
    $F = \{c(2,3), d(4), s(6)\}$, indeed $c(2,3)$ has only one parent $p(1,2)$; $d(4)$ has only one parent $p(1,4)$; $s(6)$ has only one parent $f(5,6)$.
  - *Create the rules - $rule_{l_i}(a_i, ...a_n) \leftarrow g_i, l_i$:*
    $c(2,3)$ with parent $p(1,2) \rightarrow rule1(X,Y) : -p(X,Y), c(Y,Z)$.
    $d(4)$ with parent $p(1,4) \rightarrow rule2(X,Y) : -p(X,Y), d(Y)$.
    $s(6)$ with parent $f(5,6) \rightarrow rule3(X,Y) : -f(X,Y), s(Y)$.
  - *Replace the rule in the set of the observations, for example:*
    $h(1) : -p(1,2), p(1,4), p(1,5), c(2,3), f(5,6), d(4), s(6). \rightarrow$
    $h(1) : -rule1(1,2), rule2(1,4), p(1,5), rule3(5,6)$.
- **Step 3**:
  - *Recognize Leaf Nodes:*
    $F = \{rule3(5,6)\}$, indeed $rule3(5,6)$ has only one parent $p(1,5)$.
  - *Create the rules - $rule_{l_i}(a_i, ...a_n) \leftarrow g_i, l_i$:*
    $rule3(5,6)$ with parent $p(1,5) \rightarrow rule4(X,Y) : -p(X,Y), rule3(Y,Z)$.
  - *Replace the rule in the set of the observations:*
    $h(1) : -rule1(1,2), rule2(1,4), p(1,5), rule3(5,6). \rightarrow$
    $h(1) : -rule1(1,2), rule2(1,4), rule4(5,6)$.
- **Step 4**: END - No more Leaf Nodes can be recognized

Figure 1 reports steps 2 and 3 of the tree and rule construction. The procedure continues with the evaluation step of the generated rules, that are:

$rule1(X,Y) : -p(X,Y), c(Y,Z)$. $rule2(X,Y) : -p(X,Y), d(Y)$.
$rule3(X,Y) : -f(X,Y), s(Y)$. $rule4(X,Y) : -p(X,Y), rule3(Y,Z)$.

Now, suppose that P, the percentage empirically computed on the domain at handle, is equal to 95% and that the Score Percentage of each rule is: $score(1) = 95\%$; $score(2) = 99\%$; $score(3) = 75\%$; $score(4) = 86\%$. Then, $rule1$ and $rule2$ will be shifting rules while $rule3$ and $rule4$ neglecting rules:

$rule1(X,Y) : -p(X,Y), c(Y,Z).$ $rule2(X,Y) : -p(X,Y), d(Y).$
$: -f(X,Y), s(Y).$ $: -p(X,Y), rule3(Y,Z).$

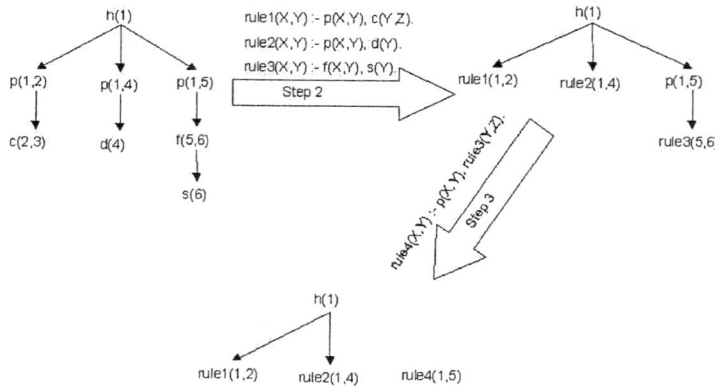

Fig. 1. Tree construction of an observation

4 Experimental Results

The proposed method was implemented in SICStus Prolog and tested providing the resulting abstraction theories to the incremental ILP system INTHELEX [4] allowing it to exploit its abstraction capabilities. Various experiments were carried out on a real world application domain of scientific paper documents [5].

The learning tasks to which the learning system was applied, involved the induction of classification rules for 3 classes of scientific papers (96 documents of which 28 formatted according to the International Conference on Machine Learning proceedings (ICML), 32 according to the Springer-Verlag Lecture Notes style (SVLN) and 36 formatted according to the IEEET style), and of rules for identifying the logical components *Author* [36+, 332-], *Page Number* [27+, 341-] and *Title* [28+, 340-] in ICML papers (square brackets report the number of positive and negative instances for each label). Figure 2 shows an example of document and its *simplified* description in first order language. 33 repetitions of each learning task were carried out, in each of which the dataset was randomly split into a training set (including 70% of the observations), exploited also to induce the rules for the abstraction operators, and a test set (made up of the remaining 30%).

To build neglecting rules, the threshold for considering low discriminating power (i.e. the score near to zero) was empirically set to ±5% of the minimum positive value and of the maximum of the negative ones in the vector associated

Fig. 2. Sample ICML document and an extract of its whole description

to the rule. To build shifting rules that have an high discriminating power (i.e. very frequent either in positive or in negative observations only) the threshold was empirically set to the score less then 95% of the minimum positive value and of the maximum of the negative ones in the vector associated to the rule for the classification task and less then 75% of the minimum positive value and of the maximum of the negative ones in the vector associated to the rule for the understanding task.

The average results along with the number of refinements and of clauses learned, the predictive accuracy of the learned theories and the runtime (sec), including both the time for the abstraction step and the learning task, are reported in Table 1. According to a paired t-test, there is no statistical difference between the results with and without abstraction, except for runtime. Having the same performance (predictive accuracy) and behavior (no. of clauses and refinements) both with and without abstraction means that the proposed technique was actually able to eliminate superfluous details only, leaving all the information that was necessary for the learning task, which was a fundamental requirement for abstraction. Conversely, runtime was dramatically reduced when using abstraction thanks to the shorter descriptions obtained by eliminating the details, which was exactly the objective of using abstraction. Note that the abstraction theory for a domain is learned once at the beginning of the learning process and is reused every time the learning system is applied on the same domain.

Table 1. System performance exploiting the discovered abstraction theories

	ICML		SVLN		IEEET	
	With Abs	No Abs	With Abs	No Abs	With Abs	No Abs
Lgg	5.81	5.54	7.36	8.12	8.03	8.30
Cl	1.21	1.27	2.75	2.69	2.03	2.27
Accuracy	96.93%	96.75%	86.54%	87.36%	90.69%	90.57%
Runtime	2.00	3.16	11.34	19.46	7.64	27.55

ICML	Author		Page Number		Title	
	With Abs	No Abs	With Abs	No Abs	With Abs	No Abs
Lgg	8.9	8.96	8.15	8.12	8.81	9.09
Cl	2.33	2.06	2.39	2.45	2.42	2.54
Accuracy	97.18%	97.12%	97.81%	97.54%	98.12%	97.87%
Runtime	14.44	29.07	34.06	76.22	27.70	51.67

An example of neglecting rule identified with the proposed strategy is:

`:- type_graphic(A), pos_upper(A).`

meaning that a graphics being placed in upper position is not discriminant between positive and negative examples. An example of shifting rule learned is:

`pos_upper_type_text(A) :- type_text(A), pos_upper(A).`

As expected, exploiting the abstraction operators the system learns shorter clauses. For instance, the theory learned for *author* contains two clauses made up of 18 and 15 literals (against the 19 and 37 without using abstraction):

```
logic_type_author(A) :- height_medium_small(A), pos_upper_type_text(A),
   part_of(B, A), part_of(B, C), height_very_small_type_text(C),
   pos_upper_type_text(C), part_of(B, D), width_very_large(D),
   height_smallest(D), type_hor_line(D), pos_center_pos_upper(D),
   alignment_left_col(D, E), on_top(F, E), part_of(B, E), part_of(B, F),
   part_of(B, G), type_text_width_medium_large(G), pos_left_type_text(G).
logic_type_author(A) :- part_of(B, A), part_of(B, C),
   pos_upper_type_text(A), pos_center_pos_upper(A),
   pos_upper_type_text(C), pos_left_type_text(C),
   height_very_very_small_type_text(C), on_top(C, D),
   part_of(B, D), on_top(E, A), width_very_large(E), height_smallest(E),
   pos_center_pos_upper(E), on_top(F, E), alignment_center_col(F, E).
```

where the presence of several abstract predicates confirms that the automatically generated abstraction theory was able to identify discriminative intermediate concepts.

5 Conclusion and Future Works

The integration of inference strategies supporting pure induction in a relational learning setting, such as *abstraction* to reason at multiple levels, can be very advantageous both in effectiveness and efficiency for the learning process. In inductive learning, the shift to a higher level representation can be performed directly when the abstraction theory is given and usually an expert domain has to built such a theory. This paper presented a technique for automatically inferring the information needed to apply abstraction operators in an inductive learning framework, exploiting the same observations that are input to the inductive algorithm. Application of the proposed technique in a real learning system proved its viability for significantly improving learning time in complex real-world domains. Future work will concern the analysis of heuristics to choose the seed, to improve the generation of abstraction theories and the design of techniques that can provide information for further abstraction operators.

References

[1] S. Ceri, G. Gottlöb, and L. Tanca. *Logic Programming and Databases*. Springer-Verlag, Heidelberg, Germany, 1990.

[2] L. De Raedt. *Interactive Theory Revision - An Inductive Logic Programming Approach*. Academic Press, 1992.

[3] G. Drastah, G. Czako, and S. Raatz. Induction in an abstraction space: A form of constructive induction. In *Proceedings of the International Joint Conference on Artificial Intelligence*, pages 708–712, 1989.

[4] F. Esposito, S. Ferilli, N. Fanizzi, T.M.A. Basile, and N. Di Mauro. Incremental multistrategy learning for document processing. *Applied Artificial Intelligence: An Internationa Journal*, 17(8/9):859–883, 2003.

[5] S. Ferilli, N. Di Mauro, T.M.A. Basile, and F. Esposito. Incremental induction of rules for document image understanding. In A. Cappelli and F. Turini, editors, *AI*IA 2003*, volume 2829 of *LNCS*, pages 176–188. Springer, 2003.

[6] N. S. Flann and T. G. Dietterich. Selecting appropriate representations for learning from examples. In *AAAI*, pages 460–466, 1986.

[7] A. Giordana, D. Roverso, and L. Saitta. Abstracting concepts with inverse resolution. In *Proceedings of the 8th International Workshop on Machine Learning*, pages 142–146, Evanston, IL, 1991. Morgan Kaufmann.

[8] A. Giordana and L. Saitta. Abstraction: A general framework for learning. In *Working Notes of the Workshop on Automated Generation of Approximations and Abstractions*, pages 245–256, Boston, MA, 1990.

[9] P.C. Kanellakis. Elements of relational database theory. In J. Van Leeuwen, editor, *Handbook of Theoretical Computer Science*, volume B of *Formal Models and Semantics*, pages 1073–1156. Elsevier Science Publishers, 1990.

[10] S.H. Muggleton and L. De Raedt. Inductive logic programming. *Journal of Logic Programming: Theory and Methods*, 19:629–679, 1994.

[11] C. Rouveirol and J. Puget. Beyond inversion of resolution. In *Proceedings of ICML97*, pages 122–130, Austin, TX, 1990. Morgan Kaufmann.

[12] G. Salton and C. Buckley. Term-weighting approaches in automatic text retrieval. *Information Processing and Management*, 24(5):513–523, 1988.

[13] P.E. Utgoff. Shift of bias for inductive concept learning. In R.S. Michalski, J.G. Carbonell, and T.M. Mitchell, editors, *Machine Learning: an artificial intelligence approach*, volume II, pages 107–148. Morgan Kaufmann, Los Altos, CA, 1986.

[14] J.-D. Zucker. Semantic abstraction for concept representation and learning. In R. S. Michalski and L. Saitta, editors, *Proceedings of the 4th International Workshop on Multistrategy Learning*, pages 157–164, 1998.

[15] J.-D. Zucker. A grounded theory of abstraction in artificial intelligence. *Philosophical Transactions: Biological Sciences*, 358(1435):1293–1309, 2003.

[16] J.-D. Zucker and J.-G. Ganascia. Representation changes for efficient learning in structural domains. In L. Saitta, editor, *Proceedings of the 13th International Conference on Machine Learning*, pages 543–551. Morgan Kaufmann, 1996.

Beware the Null Hypothesis: Critical Value Tables for Evaluating Classifiers

George Forman and Ira Cohen

Hewlett-Packard Labs,1501 Page Mill Rd,
Palo Alto, CA 94304, USA
`ghforman, icohen@hpl.hp.com`

Abstract. Scientists regularly decide the statistical significance of their findings by determining whether they can, with sufficient confidence, rule out the possibility that their findings could be attributed to random variation—the 'null hypothesis.' For this, they rely on tables with *critical values* pre-computed for the normal distribution, the t-distribution, etc. This paper provides such tables (and methods for generating them) for the performance metrics of binary classification: accuracy, F-measure, area under the ROC curve (AUC), and true positives in the top ten. Given a test set of a certain size, the tables provide the critical value for accepting or rejecting the null hypothesis that the score of the best classifier would be consistent with taking the best of a set of random classifiers. The tables are appropriate to consult when a researcher, practitioner or contest manager selects the best of many classifiers measured against a common test set. The risk of the null hypothesis is especially high when there is a shortage of positives or negatives in the testing set (irrespective of the training set size), as is the case for many medical and industrial classification tasks with highly skewed class distributions.

1 Introduction

Much practice and research work in the field of data mining amounts to trying a number of models or parameterizations, and selecting or recommending the best based on the performance scores on a test set. Sometimes the difference in performance of the top two scoring methods is not statistically significant according to standard statistical tests, in which case one is usually satisfied that either is a good choice. Unfortunately, even this conclusion may be suspect if the test set is too small, and it may not be obvious how small is 'too small.' Often it is difficult or expensive to obtain additional validated test data, as in many medical or industrial classification tasks. Furthermore, even a large test set can yield insignificant conclusions if the number of positives or negatives is unsuited for the particular performance metric.

As the number of competing models grows, the performance level required for statistical significance may be surprisingly large. For example, the organizers of the 2001 KDD Cup provided an interesting real-world biology classification challenge with a respectably large test set (150 positives and 484 negatives). However, the winning score of the 114 contestants was later found to be no greater than one should expect from 114 randomly generated trivial classifiers [4]. Consider also well-known datasets, such as the Wisconsin Breast cancer dataset (241 positive/malignant and 458 negative/benign), to which many researchers have applied a variety of learning models and published the best of these [7]. Other examples abound. Examining the datasets contributed to the UCI machine learning repository [2], 45 out of the 69 datasets contain less than 2000 samples for both training and testing. Of these 45 datasets, many were collected in real world medical experiments, which further raises the importance of determining the statistical significance of the results. Medical researchers regularly attempt to evaluate classifiers with fewer than 100 patients [1].

Table 1. Summary of conditions

α	= 0.01	significance level: 1% chance of failing to reject the null hypothesis
C	= 10;100;1000	number of competing classifiers
P	= 2..1000	positives in test set
N	= 2..1000	negatives in test set
Performance metrics:		
AUC		area under the ROC curve (true- vs. false-positives)
TP10		true positives in top 10
Accuracy		percent correct (= 1 − error rate)
F-measure		2 × Precision × Recall ÷ (Precision + Recall) (harmonic average of precision and recall)

Practitioners and researchers need a convenient method or statistical reference table in order to determine whether the selection of the best classifier based on its winning score on their limited test set is statistically significant—that is, ruling out with sufficient probability that the best score found could have been obtained without substantial learning. (Note this differs from common pair-wise testing to determine whether the scores of one method are significantly better than the scores of another method—which is blind to the possibility that both are excellent or both terrible.) This paper lays out explicit significance tests for binary classification performance metrics based on the standard statistical method of rejecting the null hypothesis with high probability. We also provide reference charts showing the critical value for various test set sizes, to evaluate the significance of one's 'best' classifier.

The critical value depends on the number of positives and negatives in the test set, irrespective of the size of the training set, and applies to both cross-validation studies and held-out test sets. We develop the method and tables for each of the following four performance metrics: accuracy, F-measure, area under the ROC curve (AUC), and number of positives identified in the top ten cases predicted to be positive (TP10). Table 1 summarizes the range of conditions for which we offer pre-computed results.

Furthermore, with a qualitative understanding of these results, one can more intelligently select the distribution of positives and negatives in future test sets and/or select the performance metrics appropriate to a given test set.

Sections 2 and 3 lay out the statistical foundation and define the null hypothesis for four different performance metrics, one of which is computed analytically. Section 4 presents the critical value charts, with additional detail provided in tables in the appendix, which is only available in the online version of this paper [5].

2 Statistics Background

Generally, to determine whether an apparent measured difference in performance is *statistically significant*, one must consider the probability that the same measured result would occur under the *null hypothesis*—the hypothesis that the difference is simply due to natural random variation and not due to true differences in the methods. To decide this, one must establish an acceptable level of risk that one will mistakenly *fail to reject the null hypothesis*. This is characterized as the level of significance α, and is usually chosen to be 0.01. That is, a result is reported to be statistically significant if its probability of occurring by chance under the null hypothesis is less than 1%. Given α, one can determine the region of values of the test statistic where one can safely reject the null hypothesis. The statistical test in our case has the form 'reject the null hypothesis if m > m*,' where m is the maximum test score of the classifiers. The value m* here is called the *critical value* and is defined as $F(m^*) = (1-\alpha)$, where $F(x)$ is the *cumulative distribution function* (*CDF*) of the test statistic under the null hypothesis, i.e. $F(x)$ equals the probability that a random sample drawn from the distribution under the null hypothesis is less than or equal to x.

Table 2. Significance test for competing classifiers

Input:	C:	number of competing classifiers
	m:	maximum score by the winner
	P,N:	positives and negatives in test set
	α:	significance level, conventionally 0.01

For $R = 1000 \div (1 - (1 - \alpha)^{1/C})$ repetitions:
   | Randomly shuffle P 1's and N 0's in an array
   | Score this ordering by the desired performance metric
   | Keep track of the top 1000 scores in a priority queue/heap
m^* = the 1000th best score retained, i.e. $F^{-1}((1-\alpha)^{1/C})$.
Decide statistically significant iff m > m*

Given a competition among C=10 competitors where the winner achieves a maximum score m under some performance measure, one determines whether this result is statistically significant as follows: Consider the null hypothesis that each competitor performs its task in a trivial and random fashion. Determine the distribution of scores one competitor would expect to achieve under the null hypothesis. This establishes a CDF $F(x)$ for a single competitor. We assume under the null hypothesis that the scores of the C competitors are drawn independently and identically distributed (iid) from this distribution. Given that the maximum score is m in the true competition, the probability under the null hypothesis that all of the C independent competitors would score $\le$ m is $F(m)^C$. Given this joint CDF, we solve the equation given in the previous paragraph to determine the critical value m*:

$F(m^*)^C = (1 - \alpha)$
$F(m^*) = (1-\alpha)^{1/C} = (1-0.01)^{1/10} = 0.99^{0.1}$ = 99.8995th percentile

If the maximum score m exceeds this critical value m*, then we can safely reject the null hypothesis. (Alternately, one may report the p-value for the maximum m.) All that remains is to determine the inverse CDF value $F^{-1}(0.998995)$ for the given performance measure for a single competitor under the null hypothesis. We instantiate this for four binary classification performance measures in the next section.

3 Null Hypothesis for Classifiers

A classifier under the null hypothesis learns nothing whatsoever from the training set. Its ranking of the test set amounts to random shuffling of the positives and negatives.

Given the arbitrary ranking of the test cases by the classifier under the null hypothesis, the AUC score and the TP10 score are computed just as if a well-trained classifier generated the ranking. TP10 performance simply measures the number of true positives identified in the first ten positions of the ranking—a precision measure commonly used in information retrieval benchmarks. The AUC score measures the area under the ROC curve (x-axis = false positive rate, y-axis = true positive rate). We walk the array incrementally, counting the number of true positives and false positives collected as we adjust a hypothetical threshold to encompass a growing prefix of the array. See [3] for explicit AUC subroutines and useful guidelines on ROC curves.

In order to determine accuracy, a specific threshold is required on the ROC curve, indicating that all cases above this threshold are predicted positive, and the rest negative. One choice is to also select the threshold randomly, but this would rarely perform as well as majority voting. Instead, we take a conservative approach and select the threshold along the randomly generated ROC curve having the greatest accuracy. We call this measure the *best accuracy* under the null hypothesis. This choice of definition is conservative in that if a given competition exceeds the critical value for *best* accuracy, it surely exceeds the critical value for a less optimally chosen threshold. While some may suggest this might be too conservative for their liking, we would be uncomfortable promoting a classifier that does not exceed this null hypothesis. (Naturally, the popular *error rate* metric is equal to (1-accuracy), thus our definition provides a natural equivalent for *best error rate*.)

The same applies for F-measure: to measure the 'best F-measure' achieved by the random ranking, we walk along the ROC curve, counting true-positives and false-positives to determine the precision and recall at each point, and record the maximum F-measure achieved over the entire curve. F-measure is a popular metric in information retrieval settings, where the class of interest is in such a minority as to give majority voting a very high accuracy. For example, to select 30 relevant (positive) articles out of a database of 1030, majority voting achieves an accuracy of 97% by predicting the negative class for all test cases. This trivial strategy gives zero recall to the positive class, and so achieves zero F-measure. A high F-measure is achievable only by balancing high precision with high recall.

Given the statistical machinery described in the previous section, the definition of the null hypothesis and the description of how to score each of the four performance metrics, we give in Table 2 an explicit procedure for determining the statistical significance that the winner of a competition of C binary classifiers achieves score m on a test set comprising P positives and N negatives. The loop determines the required inverse CDF value empirically. We note that the empirical method presented in Table 2 is general for any performance metric and can be used without a need for analytical knowledge of the statistics behind a particular metric.

Figure 1 shows the entire CDF for three of the performance metrics over a test set with P=10 positives and N=1000 negatives. (TP10 is not shown because its x-axis spans 0 to 10.) The horizontal line near the top indicates the 99th percentile, above which each of the CDFs extend to the right substantially. Despite the large size of the test set, the highest percentiles of the CDF can yield surprisingly good scores.

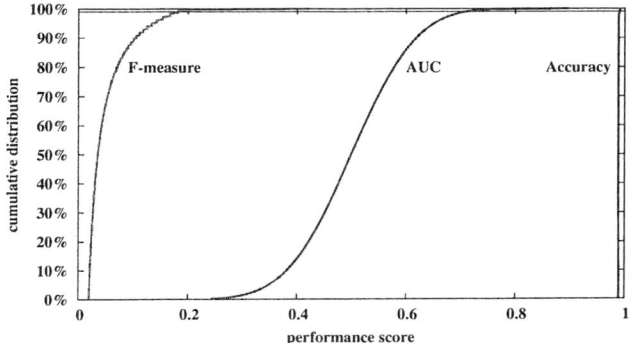

Fig. 1. CDF of scores for AUC, accuracy and F-measure for P=10, N=1000.

Computational Efficiency: All of the computations are simple to implement, yet its cost is in CPU cycles to accurately estimate the tail of the distribution. For C=100, it requires R=9,950,416 repetitions, which takes 5.5 hours for our implementation to compute for P=N=100 on a 1.8GHz HP Evo laptop. For C=1000, nearly 100M repetitions are called for, though fewer may be performed at some loss of precision in the estimation of the critical value. By keeping only the top scores, the memory required is minor; but to record the entire CDF would consume R floating point numbers, e.g. 380MB for C=1000.

Generating the critical value charts in the following section consumed more than a year of CPU time, run on over a hundred CPUs provided by the HP Labs Utility Data Center. Calling the procedure outlined in Table 2 for each performance metric and test condition would have required nearly 12 years of CPU time. To make this reference work feasible, a more efficient computation was performed, which computes the critical value for all performance measures and all values of C during a single run of R repetitions. This procedure is given in Table 3. We use R=10M, being sufficient for the level of accuracy displayable in the charts following. The number of top scores to keep track of is established at initialization by the smallest C value. Because such high scores are rare in the top tail of the distribution, a great deal of priority heap management can be avoided by not inserting values smaller than the smallest value in the heap once it reaches the maximum size required. Otherwise, the value is inserted, and the smallest value is deleted if the heap is full.

Table 3. Procedure for computing critical value charts

For P = 2..1000:
  For N = 2..1000:
    Declare an empty scores array for each performance metric
    For R=10,000,000 repetitions:
      Randomly order P positives and N negatives
      Score the ordering by each performance metric
      Keep only the top scores for each in the associated array
    For each C = 10; 100; 1000:
      Output the $(R * (1 - 0.99^{1/C}))^{th}$ best score

Analytical Solution for TP10: We derive the solution for TP10 analytically rather than by simulation. The formula is valid for TP<n>, where n is any positive integer.

For a random classifier, the TP10 score represents the number of positives drawn *without replacement* in ten trials from an 'urn' containing P positives and N negatives. Therefore, the TP10 score is represented by the hypergeometric distribution, with parameters P, N+P and ten trials. The CDF of the hyper-geometric distribution for any number of trials n is given by:

$$p = F(x \mid N+P, P, n) = \sum_{i=1}^{x} \frac{\binom{P}{i}\binom{N}{n-i}}{\binom{N+P}{n}}$$

The result, p, is the probability of drawing up to x of the P positives in n drawings without replacement from a group of $N+P$ positives and negatives.

Given the desired α value, we can compute the inverse of the CDF above at the point $(1-\alpha)$ and get the smallest TP10 score (that is, x) for which the CDF is at least $(1-\alpha)$. Using this analytical knowledge, we compute the entire set of significance tables for TP10 shown in the following section, varying N and P as discussed earlier. The computations were performed in MATLAB, and take under a minute for all the points presented in the tables. The results also allowed us to corroborate the correctness of the simulation software.

4 Critical Value Charts

In this section we provide the critical value charts for each of the four performance metrics: AUC, accuracy, F-measure and TP10. From these charts, researchers and practitioners can read an estimate of the critical value for their experiment for up to 1000 positives and 1000 negatives in their test set.

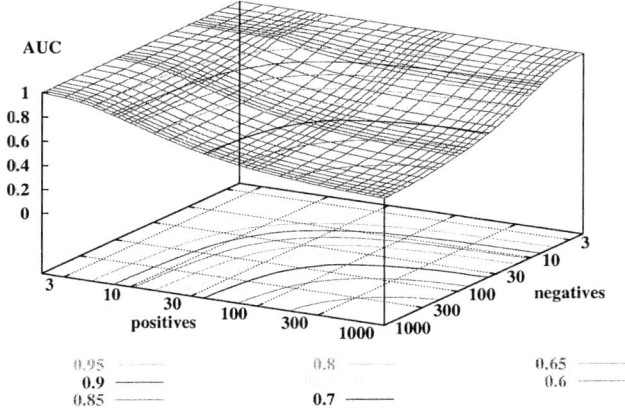

Fig. 2. Critical values for the AUC performance metric, significance level $\alpha=1\%$ for C=1000 competing classifiers

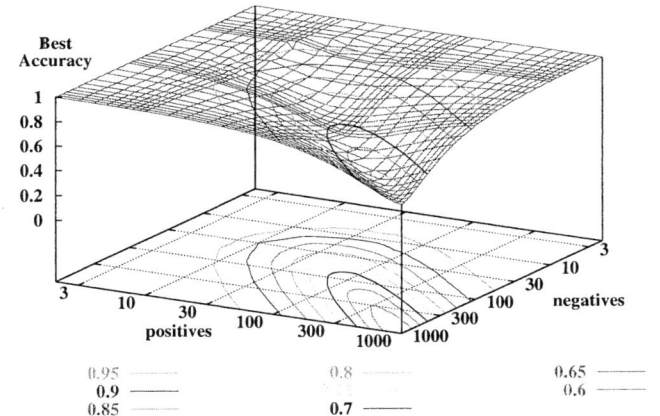

Fig. 3. Critical values for Accuracy, $\alpha=1\%$, C=1000

Figures 2—5 show 3D perspectives of the critical values for C=1000 competing classifiers as we vary N and P along the x-axis and y-axis, respectively. These charts demark the surface of critical values with colored isoclines overlaid and also projected onto the plane below the surface to aid in reading the absolute z-value. For example, given a test set of 100 positives and 300 negatives, the critical value for AUC with 1000 competitors is about 0.65. If the best classifier achieved an AUC greater than this value, the null hypothesis is rejected, deeming the result significant.

The surfaces of the different measures reveal information on what mix of positives and negatives provides low critical values (easier to obtain significance), and what test sets are more demanding for obtaining significant results. Both the accuracy and

AUC surfaces are symmetric with respect to the number of positives and negatives. The critical value for AUC is nearly 1.0 with very few positives *or* very few negatives, but as the test set becomes large, the critical value approaches 0.5—the expected area under the ROC curve of a single random classifier. AUC has a relatively large region with low values, indicating it is relatively insensitive to the mix of positives and negatives, as long as the neither is especially small.

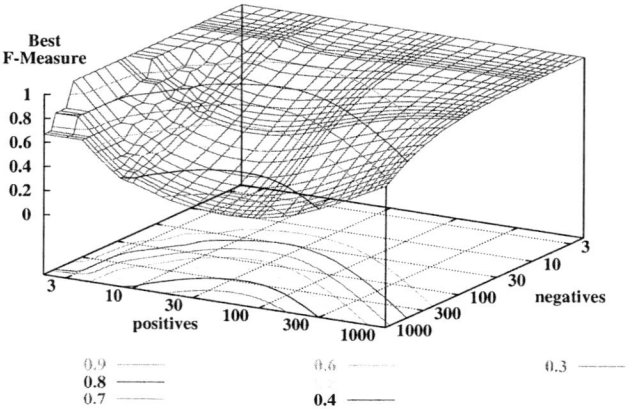

Fig. 4. Critical values for F-measure. $\alpha=1\%$, $C=1000$

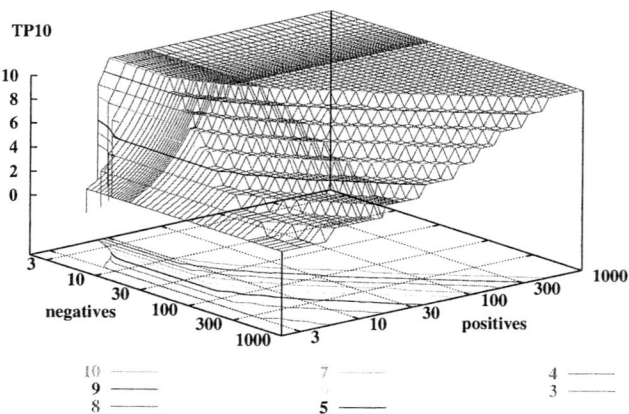

Fig. 5. Critical values for TP10. $\alpha=1\%$, $C=1000$
Note: The x and y axes are rotated differently than Fig. 4

Accuracy, on the other hand, has a much smaller valley of low critical values, concentrated around the line N=P (having ~50% accuracy). This is due to the fact that the expected value under the null hypothesis depends on the ratio of P and N; with highly skewed class distributions, the critical value can approach 100% accuracy, just

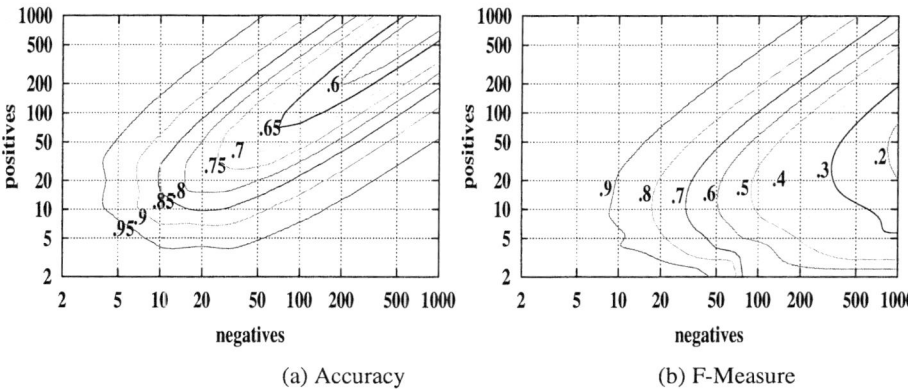

(a) Accuracy (b) F-Measure

Fig. 6. Contours of critical values for $\alpha=1\%$, C=10 competitors

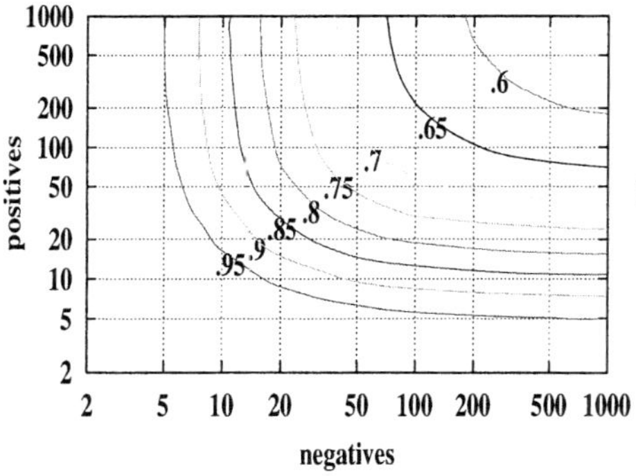

(a) AUC 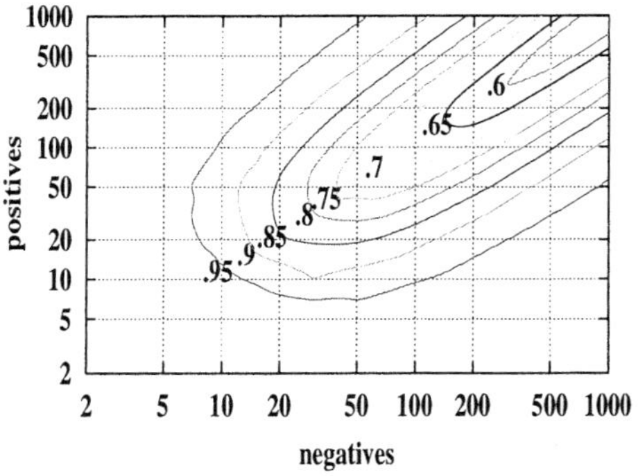 (b) Accuracy

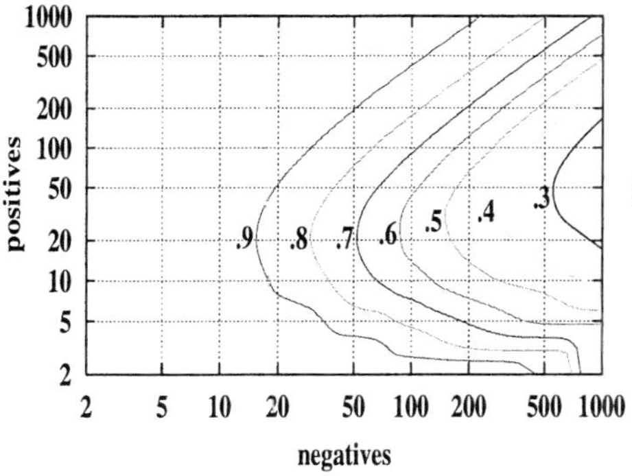

(c) F-Measure 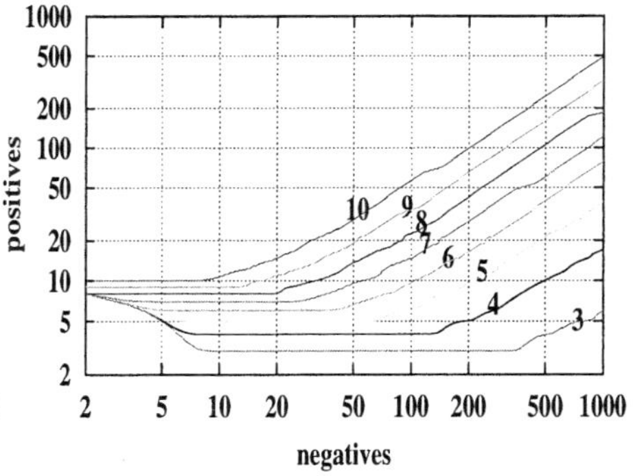 (d) TP10

Fig. 7. Contours of critical values for $\alpha=1\%$, C=1000 competitors

as with majority voting. Majority voting, however, maintains 50% accuracy for P=N=10, whereas with C=1000 competitors, the critical value for best accuracy climbs to 95%, as witnessed at the back of the valley. (For comparison, at P=N=100, the critical value is 67% accuracy for C=1000 competitors, and 65% for C=100 competitors.)

F-measure and TP10 are not symmetric with respect to N and P, and depend more on varying P. With TP10, a small number of positives and large number of negatives yields lower critical values, and higher values as the number of positives increases. When P=N, TP10 is useless for discriminating good performance. For F-measure, a test set with large number of negatives and smaller number of positives, yields the lowest critical value. Note that F-measure has a larger valley than accuracy, making it preferable over a wider range of P and N values, albeit over a somewhat different region than accuracy.

To make the charts easier to read, we show in Figures 6-7 only the projections of the isoclines onto the plane below the surfaces, for C=10 and 1000 for each performance measure. The isoclines are labeled with their critical value, making it easy to find the critical value for a given P and N in a test set. For visual clarity, the density of the isoclines is low; to obtain precise critical values, refer to the tables in the appendix provided in the online version of this paper [5]. It also contains a complete set of color charts for C=10, C=100 and C=1000 competitors, for each of the four performance metrics.

5 Discussion

Consider the realistic scenario of a data-mining practitioner at a pharmaceutical company who is given a difficult biomedical classification task with a limited dataset that was expensive and slow to obtain. If the best of a dozen learning methods obtains only a mediocre AUC score, the method and critical value charts in this paper provide the practitioner with a simple way to determine whether the finding of the 'best' classifier is statistically significant. If not, the company can make an informed decision either to accept greater risk of failing to reject the null hypothesis, or to collect additional testing data.

As researchers and practitioners, we want to perform effective experiments that are statistically significant. Towards this end, we desire to select our test metrics and/or test set class distributions such that we operate in a region with generally low critical values. When selecting test metrics, accuracy may be appropriate when P≈N, but AUC may be preferred for its larger valley, or F-measure when P<N.

In some situations the choice of metric is fixed by the application, e.g. TP10 is most appropriate for many information retrieval applications. Suppose we are given P=N=1000 test examples. For proper testing, it would be most effective to omit a large fraction of the positives, so that the critical value for TP10 is small. A similar scenario can be painted for F-measure when too great a ratio of positives to negatives is available for testing. Of course, if the class distribution of the target population is known, it may be the most appropriate for comparison. Commonly, however, the number of positives and negatives available is due to irrelevant historical reasons.

The independence assumption used in this work is between the competitors, and so it holds equally for cross-validation testing as for held-out validation testing. However, if the many competitors amount to a single learning algorithm with hundreds of different parameterizations, then the independence assumption is in question. One might choose to reduce C below the number of parameterizations attempted, but there is no sanctioned method for doing this.

Finally, we note that by averaging performance scores across many independent test sets, one increases the effective size of the test set, but this also changes the distribution under the null hypothesis. Separate critical value calculations may be required in this case.

6 Related Work

The most common form of significance testing in machine learning papers or anywhere is in determining whether one method is statistically significantly better than another method on average. For this, one computes the mean and standard deviation of the differences over a sample of n test problems, and refers to reference tables of the critical values for the standard Normal(0,1) distribution, or the Student t-distribution if the sample size is small (less than 30). This significance test only compares a single pair of methods, so if there are 100 methods, there are ~100 x 100 comparisons to make, and at $\alpha=0.01$, there could easily be ~100 cases where we fail to reject the null hypothesis and mistakenly claim significance. This is known as the problem of *multiple comparisons* [6]. The problem also occurs for the common practice of counting wins/ties/losses for each pair of competing classifiers.

The *Bonferroni correction* is a well-known method for adjusting α when there are multiple comparisons. For example, with 100 competitors and performing each of the (100 choose 2) pair-wise comparisons, there would be ~50 'statistically significant differences' found by chance alone if we use the uncorrected α of 0.01. With the Bonferroni correction, one would have to lower α for each test to 0.00000203 to bring the overall α risk back to 0.01. This correction has several problems [8]. It requires evaluating the inverse CDF much further down the tail of the distribution, resulting in 50× as much computation for C=100. Moreover, by being so extremely conservative for the type II error of failing to reject the null hypothesis, it greatly increases the type I risk of failing to accept a significant difference when one is present. The root problem stems from the quadratic number of pair-wise comparisons, which are not actually the desired result for most purposes.

Ultimately, what people want to know is which model is best, with confidence in the significance of the finding—our focus. The *randomization method* [6] addresses this issue by training the chosen best learning model repeatedly on the training set, but randomly overwriting the labels of the training set, to produce a distribution of scores under this null hypothesis. For large training sets and/or computation-intense learning models such as neural networks, this approach can be computationally intractable. Also, this approach is infeasible in some situations, such as in a data mining competition or a proprietary model generated for evaluation by a business. The *randomized distribution analysis method* [4] resolves these issues by generating many trivial classifier models that are quick to train and evaluate, such as Naïve Bayes based on one or a few randomly chosen features. Note that the training labels are not randomly overwritten, so this null hypothesis is a stronger condition—stating that the result could be achieved by trivial classifiers. Assuming some of the features are predictive individually, this null hypothesis is likely to achieve higher scores, and thus reject the statistical significance of comparisons more often. However, it is a good baseline to use when deciding, for example, whether some complicated, expensive method is worthwhile to deploy over simple methods. This null hypothesis helps determine whether the winning learning model has a competitive advantage over simple methods available to all. One disadvantage of the method as reported is that it is not founded on the principles of statistical significance, but on expected value: If the maximum score achieved by the best classifier is a small amount greater than the expected value, it gives one no guidance on how rare this event is. The method could be recast in terms of statistical significance if sufficiently many features are available to generate enough random samples.

One advantage our method has over both of these randomized methods is that it does not depend on the training data or the features of the dataset whatsoever. In this way, we can pre-compute critical value tables for quick reference by all researchers.

7 Conclusion

This paper applied statistical foundations to develop the critical value charts and procedure for determining when the best classifier performance found from among C independent competitors on a test set containing P positives and N negatives is a statistically significant finding. When not, there is a $\alpha \geq 1\%$ chance that the finding could have been generated by random processes under the null hypothesis. We developed the method for four commonly used performance metrics for binary classification tasks.

The charts presented in this paper, and in the online appendix [5], serve as a quick reference guide for practitioners seeking to reject the null hypothesis. The charts can easily be extended to cover other situations, using the procedures described.

To conclude, in addition to providing the critical values for significance testing of binary classifiers, this paper tries to emphasize the importance of the null hypothesis test in machine learning and data mining research and to remind ourselves to beware of the null hypothesis, so we know that our results are really significant. Nonetheless, passing these statistical tests cannot guarantee that a given classifier is genuinely useful, as always.

Acknowledgments

We wish to thank the volunteers who arrange interesting challenges for each year's KDD Cup—valuable lessons are regularly brought to light through them. We are grateful to Hsiu-Khuern Tang for his valuable statistics consulting, and the Hewlett-Packard Utility Data Center for computing cycles.

References

1. Abroise, C. & McLachlan, G.: Selection bias in gene extraction on the basis of microarray gene-expression data. *Proc. Natl. Acad. Sci. USA,* 99, 10 (2002), 6562-6566.
2. Blake, C.L. & Merz, C.J.: UCI Repository of machine learning databases. University of California, Dept. of Information and Computer Science, Irvine, CA. (1998).
3. Fawcett, T.: *ROC Graphs: Notes and Practical Considerations for Data Mining Researchers.* Tech. Report HPL-2003-4, Hewlett-Packard, (2003).
4. Forman, G.: *A Method for Discovering the Insignificance of One's Best Classifier and the Unlearnability of a Classification Task.* Data Mining Lessons Learned Workshop, 19th International Conference on Machine Learning (ICML), Sydney, Australia, (2002).
5. Forman, G. & Cohen, I.: Beware the Null Hypothesis: Critical Value Tables for Evaluating Classifiers. Tech. Report HPL-2005-70, Hewlett-Packard, (2005). http://www.hpl.hp.com/techreports/2005/HPL-2005-70.html
6. Jensen, D. & Cohen, P.: Multiple Comparisons in Induction Algorithms. *Machine Learning,* 38, 3 (2000), 309-338.
7. Mangasarian, O. L. & Wolberg, W. H.: Cancer diagnosis via linear programming. *SIAM News,* 23, 5 (Sept. 1990), 1-18.
8. Perneger, T. V.: What is wrong with Bonferroni adjustments. *British Medical Journal, 136* (1998), 1236-1238.

Kernel Basis Pursuit[*]

Vincent Guigue, Alain Rakotomamonjy, and Stéphane Canu

Lab. Perception, Systèmes, Information, CNRS, FRE 2645
Avenue de l'Université, 76801, St Étienne du Rouvray
Vincent.Guigue@insa-rouen.fr

Abstract. Estimating a non-uniformly sampled function from a set of learning points is a classical regression problem. Kernel methods have been widely used in this context, but every problem leads to two major tasks: optimizing the kernel and setting the fitness-regularization compromise.

This article presents a new method to estimate a function from noisy learning points in the context of RKHS (Reproducing Kernel Hilbert Space). We introduce the Kernel Basis Pursuit algorithm, which enables us to build a ℓ_1-regularized-multiple-kernel estimator. The general idea is to decompose the function to learn on a sparse-optimal set of spanning functions. Our implementation relies on the Least Absolute Shrinkage and Selection Operator (LASSO) formulation and on the Least Angle Regression (LARS) solver. The computation of the full regularization path, through the LARS, will enable us to propose new adaptive criteria to find an optimal fitness-regularization compromise. Finally, we aim at proposing a fast parameter-free method to estimate non-uniform-sampled functions.

Keywords: Regression, Multiple Kernels, LASSO, Parameter Free.

1 Introduction

The context of our work is the following: we wish to estimate the functional dependency between an input x and an output y of a system given a set of examples $\{(x_i, y_i), x_i \in \mathbb{R}^d, y_i \in \mathbb{R}, i = 1\ldots n\}$ which have been drawn i.i.d from an unknown probability distribution $P(X, Y)$. Thus, our aim is to recover the function $\hat{f}$ belonging to a hypothesis space $\mathcal{H}$ which minimizes the following risk:

$$R[f] = \mathbb{E}\{(f(X) - Y)^2\} \qquad (1)$$

but as $P(X, Y)$ is unknown, we have to look for the function $\hat{f}$ which minimizes the empirical risk:

$$R_{emp}[f] = \frac{1}{n}\sum_{i=1}^{n}(f(x_i) - y_i)^2 \qquad (2)$$

---

[*] This work was supported in part by the IST Program of the European Community, under the PASCAL Network of Excellence, IST-2002-506778. This publication only reflects the authors' views.

Depending on $\mathcal{H}$, this problem can be ill-posed and a classical way to turn it into a well-posed one is to use regularization theory [1, 2]. In this framework, the solution of the problem is the function $\hat{f} \in \mathcal{H}$ that minimizes the regularized empirical risk:

$$R_{reg}[f] = \frac{1}{n}\sum_{i=1}^{n}(y_i - f(x_i))^2 + \lambda \Omega(f) \tag{3}$$

where Ω is a functional which measures the smoothness of $\hat{f}$ and λ a regularization parameter [3]. Under general conditions on $\mathcal{H}$ (Reproducing Kernel Hilbert Space) [4], the solution of this minimization problem is of the form:

$$\hat{f}(x) = \sum_{i=1}^{n}\beta_i K(x_i, x) \tag{4}$$

where K is the reproducing kernel of $\mathcal{H}$.

The objective of the Kernel Basis Pursuit (KBP) is two-fold: to propose a method to build a sparse multi-kernel-based solution for this regression problem and to introduce new solutions for the bias-variance compromise problem. The multiple kernel has two advantages: it allows us to build adapted solutions for multiscale problems and it leads to an easier setting of the kernel hyperparameters. The multiple kernel can be seen as a dictionary of spanning functions $\mathcal{D}$ and the KBP solution will be a sparse decomposition of the function to be estimated based on this family of functions. The question of sparsity is addressed by using the Least Absolute Shrinkage and Selection Operator (LASSO) formulation [5], namely using $\Omega = \|\beta\|_1$ as a regularization term in equation (3). Using the Stepwise Least Angle Regression (LARS)[6] as a solver of optimization problem (3) enables us to compute the full set of regression solutions with varying λ in equation (3). This set of optimal solution is the so-called regularization path [7]. We use this property to introduce some heuristics which set the bias-variance compromise dynamically. Combining a forward-iterative solver (LARS) with efficient early-stopping heuristics make the KBP both sparse and fast.

The paper is organized as follows: in section 2, we will compare two common strategies to face the problem of building a sparse regression function $\hat{f}$: the Matching Pursuit and the Basis Pursuit. We will explain the building and the use of the multiple kernels, combined with the LARS in section 3. Section 4 deals with the setting of the bias-variance compromise and the kernel parameters. Our results on synthetic and real data are presented in section 5. Section 6 gives our conclusions and perspectives on this work.

2 Basis vs Matching Pursuit

The question of the sparsity of the solution $\hat{f}$ can be addressed in two different ways. The first approach is based on stepwise method consisting in adding functions from a dictionary whereas the second one is to use a regularization term in equation (3) that imposes sparsity of β.

Mallat and Zhang introduced the Matching Pursuit algorithm [8]: they proposed to construct a regression function $\hat{f}$ as a linear combination of elementary functions g_i picked from a finite redundant dictionary $\mathcal{D} = \{g_k\}$. This algorithm is iterative and one new function g_i is introduced at each step, associated with a weight β_i. At step k, we get the following approximation of f: $\hat{f}^{(k)} = \sum_{i=1}^{k} \beta_i g_i$. Given $R^{(k)}$, the residue generated by $\hat{f}^{(k)}$, the function g_{k+1} and its associated weight $\beta^{(k+1)}$ are selected according to:

$$(g_{k+1}, \beta^{(k+1)}) = \mathrm{argmin}_{g_i \in \mathcal{D}, \beta \in \mathbb{R}} \| R^{(k)} - \sum_{i=1}^{k} \beta_i g_i \|^2 \tag{5}$$

The improvements described by Pati et al. (Orthogonal Matching Pursuit algorithm) [9] keep the same framework, but optimize all the weights β_i at each step. A third algorithm called pre-fitting [10] enables us to choose $(g_{k+1}, \beta^{(k+1)})$ according to $R^{(k+1)}$. All those methods are iterative and greedy. The different variations improve the weights or the choice of the function g_{k+1} but the main characteristic remains unchanged. Matching Pursuit does not allow to get rid of a previously selected function g_k, which means that its solution is sub-optimal.

The Basis Pursuit approach proposed by Chen et al. [11] is different: they consider the whole dictionary of functions and look for the best linear solution to estimate f, namely, the solution which minimizes the regularized empirical risk. Using $\Omega = \|\beta\|_1$ leads to the LASSO formulation. Such a formulation requires costly and complex linear programming [12] or modified EM implementation [13] to be solved. Finally it enables them to find an exact solution to the regularized learning problem.

The Stepwise Least Angle Regression (LARS) offers new opportunities, by combining an iterative and efficient approach with the exact solution of the LASSO. The fact that the LARS begins with an empty set of variables, combined with the sparsity of the solution explains the efficiency of such method. The ability of deleting dynamically useless variables enables the method to converge to the exact solution of the LASSO problem.

3 Learning with Multiple Kernels

3.1 LARS

We note the matrix of the learning points: $X = \begin{pmatrix} x_1^T \\ \ldots \\ x_n^T \end{pmatrix} \in \mathbb{R}^{n \times d}$. Each column i of the matrix X is a variable denoted by X_i and each of them can be considered as a single source of information. The LARS [6] is a stepwise iterative algorithm which provides an exact solution to the LASSO (equation (3) with $\Omega = \|\beta\|_1$). LASSO can also be written as:

$$\begin{array}{c} \min_\beta \sum_{j=1}^{n}(y_i - x_i^T \beta)^2 \\ \sum_{i=1}^{d} |\beta_i| \leq t \end{array} \tag{6}$$

where t is the regularization parameter.

When the variables X_i are normalized, LARS turns this learning problem into a variable selection problem. We note $\mathcal{A}$ the set of indexes of the active variables and $X_\mathcal{A}$ the learning set reduced to the variables that are in $\mathcal{A}$. At each step k, given the residue $R^{(k)} = y - \hat{f}^{(k)}$, the LARS selects the variable which is most correlated with $R^{(k)}$ and add its index to $\mathcal{A}$. The ability of dynamically suppressing a source of information which becomes useless enables the algorithm to fit the LASSO solution. $\hat{f}^{(k)}$ belongs to the space spanned by $X_\mathcal{A}$, the $\beta^{(k)}$ are computed to minimize $R^{(k+1)}$ under the constraints that each variable of $X_\mathcal{A}$ is equi-correlated with $R^{(k+1)}$. This leads to the property that each $\hat{f}^{(k)}$ corresponds to an optimal solution of (6) for a given value of t: LARS computes the whole regularization path.

Solving the LASSO is really fast with this method, due to the fact that it is both forward and sparse. The first steps are not expensive, because of the small size of $\mathcal{A}$, then it becomes more and more time-consuming with iterations. But the sparsity of ℓ_1 regularization limits the number of required iterations. LARS begins with an empty active set whereas other backward methods [13, 12] begin with all β being non-zero and require to solve high dimensional linear system to set irrelevant coefficients to zero. Given the fact that only one point is added (or removed) during an iteration, it is possible to update the solution at each step instead of fully computing it. This leads to a simple-LARS algorithm, similar to the simple-SVM formulation [14], which also increases the speed of the method.

3.2 Building a Multiple Kernel Regression Function

Vincent and Bengio [10] proposed to treat the kernel K exactly in the same way as the matrix of the learning points X. Each column of K is then considered as a source of information that can be added to the active set to build a linear estimation of f: $\hat{f}(x) = \sum_{i=1}^{n} \beta_i K(x_i, x)$. This function $\hat{f}$ is β-linear in the Reproducing Kernel Hilbert Space (RKHS) $\mathcal{H}$ spanned by K, and non-linear in the original data space.

We propose here a simple extension of this framework to the multiple kernel setting: it consists in building a set of kernel $\{K_i\}_{i=1,...,N}$, which respectively spans the spaces $\mathcal{H}_i$. Each source of information $K_i(x_j, \cdot)$ is characterized by a point x_j of the learning set and a kernel parameter i. Hence, the multiple kernel K can be written as:

$$K = \begin{bmatrix} K_1 \ldots K_i \ldots K_N \end{bmatrix} \quad K \in \mathbb{R}^{n \times s}, \text{ with } s = nN. \quad (7)$$

Assuming that each column of K is normalized, the LARS will pick automatically the most relevant $K_i(x_j, \cdot)$ among the whole set of sources of information. The solution $\hat{f}$ is a weighted sum of $K_i(x_j, \cdot)$:

$$\hat{f}(x) = \sum_{i=1}^{N} \sum_{j=1}^{n} \beta_{ij} K_i(x_j, x) \quad , \hat{f} \in \mathcal{H}_1 + \ldots + \mathcal{H}_N \quad (8)$$

The Kernel Basis Pursuit algorithm consists in solving the following problem:

$$\min_\beta \|y - K\beta\|^2$$
$$\sum_{i,j} |\beta_{ij}| \leq t \qquad (9)$$

It is important to note that no assumption is made on the kernels K_i which can be non-positive. K can associate kernels of the same type (e.g. Gaussian) with different parameter values as well as different types of kernels (e.g. Gaussian and polynomial). The resulting matrix K is neither positive definite nor square.

4 Setting of Regularization and Kernel Parameters

The optimization problem (9) requires the setting of several hyperparameters: the bias-variance compromise t as well as the N kernel hyperparameters. Considering that each kernel has a single parameter, this would lead to $N+1$ parameters to select. Thus, the model selection problem is difficult. It can be solved by cross-validation but it is very expensive in time-computation. In the following section, we propose some strategies to tackle this problem.

4.1 Optimization of Regularization Parameter

Finding a good setting for t in equation (9) is very important: when t becomes too large, the LARS becomes equivalent to Ordinary Least Square (OLS) and it requires the resolution of linear system of size $s \times s$. Early stopping enable us to decrease the time computation (which is linked to the sparsity of the solution) as well as to improve the generalization of the learning (by regularizing).

One of the most interesting property of the LARS is the fact that it computes the whole regularization path (section 3.1). The LARS enables us to compute a set of optimal solutions corresponding to different values of t, with only one learning stage. We are going to take advantage of this property to dynamically select the optimal t.

Different compromise parameters. We look for different expressions of the regularization parameter t. The aim is to find the most meaningful one, namely the easiest way to set this parameter.

- The original formulation of the LARS relies on the compromise parameter t which is a bound on the sum of the absolute values of the β coefficients. t is difficult to set because it is somewhat meaningless.
- It is possible to apply Ljung criterion [15] on the autocorrelation of the residue. The parameter is then a threshold which decides when the residue can be considered as white noise.
- Another solution consists in the study of the evolution of a loss function $\ell(y_i, \hat{f}(x_i))$ with regards to the step j. The criterion is a bound on the variation of this cost.

- ν-KBP. It is possible to define a criterion on the size of $\mathcal{A}$, namely on the number of support vectors or on the rate of support vectors among the learning set. It is important to note that ν is then a threshold, whereas in the ν-SVM method where ν can be seen as an upper bound on the rate of support vectors [16].

However, all these methods require the *a priori* setting of a parameter which is usually estimated by cross-validation.

Trap source. We propose a novel method for dynamically selecting the regularization parameter based on a trap parameter. The idea is to introduce one or many sources of information that we do not want to use. When the most correlated source with the residue belongs to the trap set, the learning procedure is stopped. We use two heuristics to build the trap sources:

- KBP-σ_s: we build a Gaussian kernel $K_{\sigma_s}(x_i, x_j) = \exp\left(-\frac{\|x_i - x_j\|^2}{2\sigma_s^2}\right)$ and we add it to the information sources. σ_s is a very small bandwidth.
- KBP-RV: we add iid Gaussian random variables among the sources of information. This heuristic has already been used for variable selection [17].

The use of a trap scale is closely linked to the way that LARS selects the sources of information (section 3.1). We illustrate the behavior of the trap scale during the learning of a toy function: $\cos(\exp(\omega x))$ (figure 1(c)). The correlation with the residue is an energetic criterion, that is why the first selected variables explain the low frequency regions of the $\cos(\exp(\omega x))$ function. The selected sources of information belong to higher and higher scales with iterations (figure 1(d)). If we further assume that y contains white noise, then there is no correlation between noises occurring at two different instants: the noise is a local phenomenon. As a consequence, the sources of information that explain the noise will belong to narrow bandwidth Gaussian kernel K_{σ_s} and will be selected at the end of the learning procedure. Moreover, the selection of a source from K_{σ_s} means that there are no more correlated sources of information in other K_i, namely the residue is only composed of components correlated with noise.

The use of Gaussian random variables as a trap scale is more intuitive: it supposes that when a random variable is selected as the most correlated source with the residue, it remains no more interesting information in the residue. Figure 1(b) illustrates the evolution of the residue with iterations, the 3rd picture shows the residue when a random variable is selected.

4.2 Optimizing Kernel Parameters

In this section, we propose a new method to set the kernel parameters of the KBP in the Gaussian case, without using cross-validation. We aim at finding a key parameter σ_k representing the smallest bandwidth which can be useful for a given problem. In this case: $K_{\sigma_k} \approx I_n$ and $\hat{f}$ will interpolate y and overfit. Then, we propose to build a series of larger and larger Gaussian parameters from this key scale to improve the generalization of the learning.

σ_k is obtained according to the following steps: a one nearest neighbor is performed on the training data. Then, we focus on the shortest distances between neighbors. The key distance D_k is the distance between x_i and x_j, the two nearest points in the input space. The corresponding key Gaussian parameter σ_k is defined so that:

$$K_{\sigma_k}(x_i, x_j) = \exp\left(-\frac{D_k^2}{2\sigma_k^2}\right) = 0.1 \qquad (10)$$

that is to say, the bandwidth σ_k is designed so that a learning point in high density regions has little influence on its neighbors. For more robustness, it is recommended to use an improved definition of D_k. Given $\mathcal{S}$ the set of the one-nearest-neighbor distances. We define D_k as the mean distance of the 0.01 quantile of $\mathcal{S}$.

Then, a series of bandwidth is build as follow (figure 1(a)):

$$\sigma = \{\sigma_k, \sigma_k p, \sigma_k p^2, \sigma_k p^3, \sigma_k p^4, \sigma_k p^5, \sigma_k p^6\} \quad \text{with: } p > 1 \qquad (11)$$

A small value of p provides more accuracy for the design of the sources of information, when p becomes close to 1, the family becomes exhaustive. However,

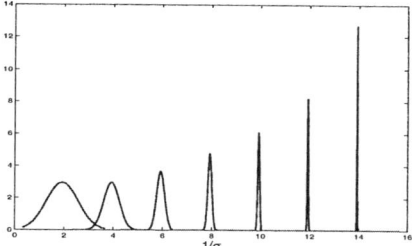

(a) Examples of sources of information from different Gaussian kernels K_{σ_i}.

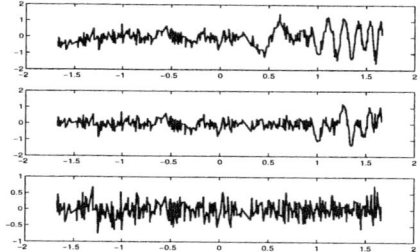

(b) Residues at iteration 10, 20 and 30.

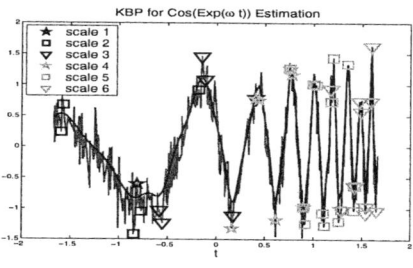

(c) Learning of the $\cos(\exp(\omega x))$ function.

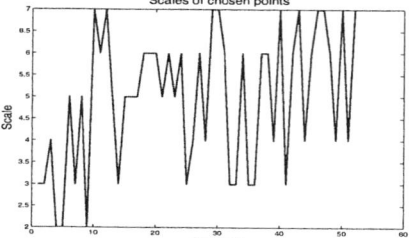

(d) Scale of the variable selected at each step of the LARS.

Fig. 1.

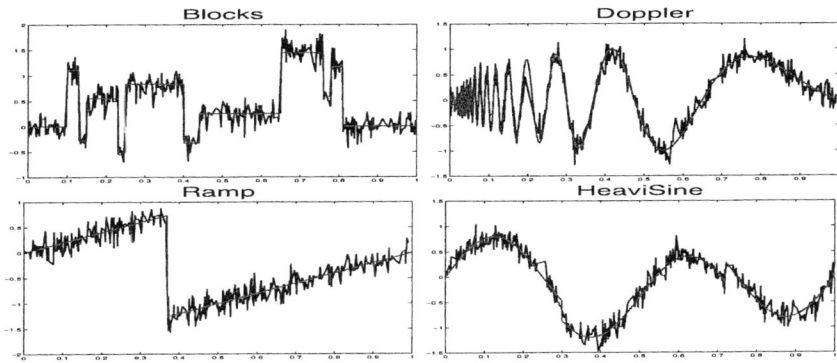

Fig. 2. Toy signals and learning data

a small value of p leads to a more redundant family of functions, which penalizes the sparsity of the solution. In fact, when two sources of information are correlated, they are both almost equi-correlated to the residue and the LARS often selects both sources of information in two successive iterations. The 2nd line of table 1 shows that the number of support vectors first decreases with p due to this phenomenon. On the contrary, when p is too large, the accuracy of the sources of information decreases and the LARS requires many sources of information to describe a single region of the signal. That is why in our example the size of the optimal active set $\mathcal{A}$ increases with p when $p > 2$.

Table 1. Estimation of the function $\cos(\exp(\omega x))$ (10 runs). Evolution of the best solution in terms of sparsity (number of support vector) and Mean Square Error (MSE) in function of parameter p.

p	1.2	1.5	2	2.5	3	4	5	6
MSE	0.02255	0.02225	0.02234	0.02198	0.02090	**0.02050**	0.02487	0.02543
$|\mathcal{A}|$	45.33	44.66	**39.0**	40.25	44.5	48.33	48.66	48.33

Cross-validations over synthetic and real data lead to set $p = 3$. We choose to set the cardinality of σ to 7, given the fact that experimental results are not improved beyond this value.

KBP results presented in the next section rely on this parameter-free Gaussian strategy (equation (11)), but it is also possible to build multiple kernels with different degrees of polynomial kernels or to mix different kernels.

5 Experiments

We illustrate the efficiency of the methodology on synthetic and real data. Tables 2 and 3 present the results with two different algorithms: the SVM and the LARS. We use four strategies to stop the learning stage of the KBP.

Table 2. Results of SVM and LARS for the cos(exp(x)) and Donoho's classical functions estimation. Mean and standard deviation of MSE on the test set (30 runs), number of support vectors used for each solution, number of best performances. The total of best performances sometimes exceeds 30 due to the fact the 2 different KBP can lead to the same solution.

Nb kernel	1				
Algorithm	ϵ - SVM	KBP- $\sum_i \|\beta_i\|$	ν-KBP	KBP-RV	KBP-σ_s
cos(exp(t))	0.032 ± 0.0086 105.4 0	0.028 ± 0.0051 87.3 0	0.028 ± 0.0052 85 0	0.026 ± 0.0047 95.3 0	0.029 ± 0.0062 95.3 0
Doppler	0.023 ± 0.0071 59.3 0	0.019 ± 0.0068 47.1 0	0.019 ± 0.0060 47 0	0.020 ± 0.0053 48.8 0	0.019 ± 0.0056 51.3 0
Blocks	0.039 ± 0.0020 75.3 0	0.025 ± 0.0013 65.1 0	0.026 ± 0.0015 65 0	0.024 ± 0.0012 69.4 0	0.024 ± 0.0012 65.2 0
Ramp	**0.0072 ± 0.0034** 54.2 **16**	0.0114 ± 0.0013 45.6 0	0.0112 ± 0.0022 48 0	0.0107 ± 0.0020 45.9 0	0.0108 ± 0.0015 49.7 0
HeaviSine	**0.0028 ± 0.0002** 51.4 11	**0.0028 ± 0.0002** 17.2 **15**	0.0030 ± 0.0002 20 5	0.0029 ± 0.0002 21.1 8	0.0028 ± 0.0002 19.5 11

Nb kernel	6 (Multiple Kernels)			
Algorithm	KBP- $\sum_i \|\beta_i\|$	ν-KBP	KBP-RV	KBP-σ_s
cos(exp(t))	**0.020 ± 0.0039** 47.4 14	0.023 ± 0.0059 46 5	**0.020 ± 0.0039** 48.4 **15**	0.021 ± 0.0035 47.8 10
Doppler	0.011 ± 0.0052 46.1 13	0.013 ± 0.0060 46 3	**0.010 ± 0.0059** 52.70 **17**	0.013 ± 0.0055 49.80 5
Blocks	0.020 ± 0.0011 64.6 13	0.020 ± 0.0012 65 10	0.020 ± 0.0012 67.5 9	**0.019 ± 0.0011** 66.3 **17**
Ramp	**0.0072 ± 0.0033** 20.1 12	0.0073 ± 0.0035 18 11	0.0080 ± 0.0030 22.5 5	0.0077 ± 0.0029 20.3 4
HeaviSine	0.0035 ± 0.0003 44.30 0	0.0036 ± 0.0003 45 0	0.0032 ± 0.0003 48.2 0	0.0032 ± 0.0003 49.0 0

- KBP-$\sum_i |\beta_i|$ is the classical method where a bound is defined on the sum of the regression coefficient. This bound is estimated by cross-validation.
- ν-KBP is based on the fraction of support vectors. ν is also estimated by cross-validation.
- KBP-RV relies on the introduction of Gaussian random variables as sources of information.[1]
- KBP-σ_s relies on a Gaussian trap scale with very small bandwidth. We use $\sigma_s = \sigma_k$ of equation (10).[1]

To validate this approach, we compare the results with classical Gaussian ϵ-SVM regression. Parameters ϵ, C and σ are optimized by cross validation. In order to

---

[1] To make KBP-σ_s and KBP-RV methods more robust, we wait until 3 information sources from the trap-scale are selected to stop the learning stage.

Table 3. Results of SVM and KBP for the different regression database. Mean and standard deviation of MSE on the test set (30 runs), number of support vectors used for each solution, number of best performances. The total of best performances sometimes exceeds 30 due to the fact the 2 different KBP can lead to the same solution.

Nb kernel	1				
Algo	SVM		KBP		
	[19]	ϵ-SVM	$\sum_i |\beta_i|$	RV	σ_s
pyrim	0.007 ± 0.007 – –	0.008 ± 0.010 47.1 0	0.010 ± 0.011 29.7 0	0.011 ± 0.009 31.2 0	0.010 ± 0.011 33.6 0
triazines	0.021 ± 0.005 – –	0.022 ± 0.006 60.8 0	0.021 ± 0.006 27.0 0	0.021 ± 0.005 32.4 0	0.021 ± 0.006 29.0 0
housing	**9.19 ± 2.73** – –	17.54 ± 4.18 405.4 0	12.83 ± 3.31 289.0 0	14.12 ± 3.17 295.2 0	12.33 ± 3.04 304.2 0
abalone	**5.071 ± 0.678** – –	12.871 ± 0.461 652.2 0	9.293 ± 0.518 491.9 0	9.181 ± 0.421 502.3 0	10.311 ± 0.513 546.2 0

Nb kernel	6 (Multiple Kernels)		
Algo	KBP		
	$\sum_i |\beta_i|$	RV	σ_s
pyrim	0.006 ± 0.006 47.0 13	0.006 ± 0.006 48.1 17	**0.005 ± 0.006** 49.3 **18**
triazines	**0.019 ± 0.006** 23.0 **22**	0.020 ± 0.005 27.1 8	0.020 ± 0.008 27.8 9
housing	10.52 ± 3.56 305.4 12	11.03 ± 3.31 317.3 9	10.13 ± 3.23 315.2 **17**
abalone	7.189 ± 0.568 607.4 **17**	8.363 ± 0.616 512.8 7	8.127 ± 0.620 548.3 10

distinguish the benefit of the early stopping methods from the benefits of the multiple kernel learning, we also give the results of KBP algorithm when using a single kernel. In this case, the kernel is chosen by cross-validation. Even with a single kernel, the KBP relies on a multiple kernel architecture to be add the trap scales. KBP-RV and KBP-σ_s are fully parameter-free. We use the method describe in the previous section 4.2 to build our multiple kernels, with $p = 3$.

5.1 Synthetic Data

We test our method for the learning of $\cos(\exp(\omega x))$ regression function. We try to learn:

$$f(x) = \cos(\exp(\omega x)) + b(x) \tag{12}$$

where $b(x)$ is a Gaussian white noise of variance $\sigma_b^2 = 0.15$. We also tested the method over classical synthetic data described by Donoho and Johnstone [18].

For all signals, we use $x \in [0,1]$, drawn according to a uniform distribution. We use 400 points for the learning set and 1000 points for the testing set. The noise is added only on the learning set. Parameters $(\nu, \sum_i |\beta_i|...)$ are computed by cross validation on the learning set. Table 2 presents the results over 30 runs for each dataset.

These results point out the sparsity and the efficiency of KBP solutions. Figure 1(c) illustrates how multiple kernel learning enables the regression function to fit the local frequency of the model. The results with different Donoho's synthetic signals enable us to distinguish the benefits of the KBP method from the benefits of the multiple kernels. The KBP improves the sparsity of the solution, whereas the multiple kernels improve the results on signals that require a multi-scale approach.

ϵ-SVM achieves the best results for Ramp and HeaviSine signals. This can be explained by the fact that the Ramp and HeaviSine signals are almost uniform in term of frequency. The ϵ tube algorithm of the SVM regression is especially efficient on this kind of problem.

The results from the different KBP are very close (and often similar), that is why the total of best performances sometimes exceeds 30 (the number of run). Then, KBP-RV and KBP-σ_s become very attractive, due to the fact that they are parameter-free methods. KBP obtains the best results for 4 experiments, and parameter-free-KBP for 3 experiments on a total of 5 experiments.

5.2 Real Data

Experiments are carried out over regression data bases available in the UCI repository [20]. We compare our results with [19].

The experimental procedure for real data is the following one: Thirty training/testing set are randomly produced. Respectively 80% and 20% of the points are used for training and testing. Hyperparameters $(\nu, \sum_i |\beta_i|...)$ are computed by cross-validation on the learning set. Table 3 presents mean and standard deviation of MSE (mean square error) on the test set.

ϵ-SVM solution is not really competitive but it gives an interesting information on the number of support vectors required for each solution. KBP-RV and KBP-σ_s results are very interesting: they are parameter free using the heuristic describe in section 4.2, moreover the KBP-RV achieves the best results for pyrim.

6 Conclusion

The Kernel Basis Pursuit algorithm enables us to meet two objectives: proposing a sparse multi-kernel-based solution for the regression problem and introducing new solutions for the bias-variance compromise problem and the kernel setting.

The sparsity is due to ℓ_1 regularization, and the interpretation of the $K_i(x_j, \cdot)$ as simple source of information enables the KBP to deal with multiple kernels. The heuristics proposed to set the different parameters or compromises of the KBP rely both on the LARS properties and the multiple kernel: multiple kernels allow easy and efficient setting for the kernel parameters and the fact that LARS computes the whole regularization path enables us to implement powerful early-stopping strategies. The KBP gives good results on synthetic and real data. In the meantime, the required time computation is reduced compared with SVM, due to the sparsity of the obtained solutions. Moreover, the KBP becomes fully parameter-free in the KBP-RV and KBP-σ_k cases and though they achieve very competitive results.

The perspectives of this work are the following ones: we now plan to use this description of the data for signal classification purpose. Then, the idea would be to optimize the representation of the data for the classification task.

References

1. Tikhonov, A., Arsénin, V.: Solutions of ill-posed problems. W.H. Winston (1977)
2. Girosi, F., Jones, M., Poggio, T.: Regularization theory and neural networks architectures. Neural Computation **7** (1995) 219–269
3. Wahba, G.: Spline Models for Observational Data. Series in Applied Mathematics, Vol. 59, SIAM (1990)
4. Kimeldorf, G., Wahba, G.: Some results on Tchebycheffian spline functions. J. Math. Anal. Applic. **33** (1971) 82–95
5. Tibshirani, R.: Regression shrinkage and selection via the lasso. J. Royal. Statist. **58** (1996) 267–288
6. Efron, B., Hastie, T., Johnstone, I., Tibshirani, R.: Least angle regression. Annals of statistics **32** (2004) 407–499
7. Bach, F., Thibaux, R., Jordan, M.: Computing regularization paths for learning multiple kernels. In: Neural Information Processing Systems. Volume 17. (2004)
8. Mallat, S., Zhang, Z.: Matching pursuits with time-frequency dictionaries. IEEE Transactions on Signal Processing **41** (1993) 3397–3415
9. Pati, Y.C., Rezaiifar, R., Krishnaprasad, P.S.: Orthogonal matching pursuits : recursive function approximation with applications to wavelet decomposition. In: 27th Asilomar Conference in Signals, Systems, and Computers. (1993)
10. Vincent, P., Bengio, Y.: Kernel matching pursuit. Machine Learning Journal **48** (2002) 165–187
11. Chen, S., Donoho, D., Saunders, M.: Atomic decomposition by basis pursuit. SIAM Journal on Scientific Computing **20** (1998) 33–61
12. Chen, S.: Basis Pursuit. PhD thesis, Department of Statistics, Stanford University (1995)
13. Grandvalet, Y.: Least absolute shrinkage is equivalent to quadratic penalization. In: ICANN. (1998) 201–206
14. Loosli, G., Canu, S., Vishwanathan, S., Smola, A.J., Chattopadhyay, M.: Une boîte à outils rapide et simple pour les svm. In: CAp. (2004)
15. Ljung, L.: System Identification - Theory for the User. (1987)
16. Schölkopf, B., Smola, A.: Learning with kernels. (2002)
17. Bi, J., Bennett, K., Embrechts, M., Breneman, C., Song, M.: Dimensionality reduction via sparse support vector machines. Journal of Machine Learning Research **3** (2003) 1229–1243
18. Donoho, D., Johnstone, I.: Ideal spatial adaptation by wavelet shrinkage. Biometrika **81** (1994) 425–455
19. Chang, M., Lin, C.: Leave-one-out bounds for support vector regression model selection. Neural Computation (2005)
20. Blake, C., Merz, C.: UCI rep. of machine learning databases (1998)

Hybrid Algorithms with Instance-Based Classification

Iris Hendrickx and Antal van den Bosch

ILK / Computational Linguistics and AI, Tilburg University,
P.O.Box 90153, NL-5000 LE Tilburg, The Netherlands
{i.h.e.hendrickx, antalb}@uvt.nl

Abstract. In this paper we aim to show that instance-based classification can replace the classifier component of a rule learner and of maximum-entropy modeling, thereby improving the generalization accuracy of both algorithms. We describe hybrid algorithms that combine rule learning models and maximum-entropy modeling with instance-based classification. Experimental results show that both hybrids are able to outperform the parent algorithm. We analyze and compare the overlap in errors and the statistical bias and variance of the hybrids, their parent algorithms, and a plain instance-based learner. We observe that the successful hybrid algorithms have a lower statistical bias component in the error than their parent algorithms; the fewer errors they make are also less systematic.

1 Introduction

A distinguishing characteristic of instance-based learning [1, 2] is that it is non-abstracting local learning method. It does not abstract from the training instances to form a model, but stores them as such in memory. All effort is diverted to the classification phase. To classify a new instance the instance-based learning algorithm searches through memory to find the most similar instances in the local neighborhood of the new instance, and assigns the majority class label of the neighborhood.

Instance-based learning is also referred to as *lazy* learning as opposed to *eager* learning. Eager learning algorithms put significant effort in abstracting from the training instances by creating condensed representations (decision trees, rule sets, probability matrices, hyperplanes, etc.) during the learning phase. The classification phase of an eager learner reduces to a relatively effortless application of the abstracted representation to new instances.

This contrast between instance-based learning (which puts effort in classification) and eager learning (which invests its effort in the learning phase) forms the motivation for constructing the hybrids described in this paper. Earlier work has shown that combining lazy and eager learning techniques can be beneficial to generalization performance [3, 5]. In this paper we describe hybrid algorithms in which we combine effort-intensive eager learning in rule learning and maximum-entropy models with effort-intensive instance-based classification. We take the system as constructed by the eager learner and replace its standard classification component by instance-based classification through the k-nearest neighbor (k-NN) classifier. From the eager learner perspective we hope that replacing their simple classification method with the more sensitive local k-NN classification method could improve generalization performance. Put alternatively, we take the eager learner's model and transplant it into the distance metric of the instance-based learner. The hybrid algorithms use the model as produced by the eager learner to modify the distance calculations central in k-NN.

We construct three hybrid algorithms. The first combines maximum-entropy modeling with k-NN, the second and third hybrids both combine rule learning with k-NN, in two different ways. We investigate the performance of the hybrid algorithms and compare them to the performance of their parent algorithms. We also analyze to which extent the hybrid deviates functionally from its two parent algorithms. To get a deeper insight in the differences and commonalities of the parent algorithms and the hybrids, we analyze their overlap in errors and the statistical bias and variance.

In Section 2 we discuss the different learning algorithms and the construction of the hybrid algorithms. Section 3 and 4 provide a description of the experimental setup and the results, respectively. Section 5 describes the error analysis and bias-variance analysis. We discuss our findings in Section 6.

2 Algorithms

We first describe the three machine learning algorithms involved in this study briefly: instance-based learning, maximum-entropy modeling and rule learning. With instance-based learning we focus on two aspects: the MVDM distance metric and feature weighting, because these play a role in the hybrid algorithms. In the next two subsections we describe the construction of each of the hybrid algorithms and our motivations.

The k-nearest neighbor classification rule [1] is the classifier engine of the instance-based learning algorithm. The rule classifies new instances by searching for the k nearest neighbors to the new instance and extrapolating the majority class label found among the k nearest neighbors to the new instance. The distance between instances can be estimated with different distance metrics. A simple metric for nominal features is the overlap metric (or Manhattan distance, or L1-norm distance) which counts the number of mismatching feature values between two instances. A more sophisticated metric that estimates real-valued distances between pairs of nominal values is the Modified Value Difference Metric (MVDM) introduced in [6].

MVDM estimates, from training data, the distance between two symbolic feature values v_1 and v_2 as a vector distance between their two class distributions:

$$\delta(v_1, v_2) = \sum_{i=1}^{j} |P(C_i|v_1) - P(C_i|v_2)| \qquad (1)$$

where the vector length is determined by j, the number of classes, and $P(C_i|v_1)$ represents the conditional probability of class i co-occurring with value 1.

Other possible metrics include alternative distance metrics for vector distances, such as the Jeffrey divergence metric (a symmetrical version of Kullback-Leibler distance), and the dot product metric or the cosine distance metric for numerical features. In addition, the k-NN algorithm can have several other algorithmic parameters such as the k parameter, feature weighting metrics, individual instance weighting metrics, and distance-weighted class voting among nearest neighbors. Feature weighting is an important parameter as its purpose is to assign higher weights to more important features [7]. A mismatch on a feature with a high weight will enlarge the distance between two instances more than a mismatch on a low weighted feature will. Some examples of feature weighting methods are Information Gain, Gain Ratio and Chi-square. In our experiments we employ the TiMBL software [8][1], which implements all of the mentioned optional distance metrics and weighting metrics.

Maximum-entropy modeling [9] is a statistical learning approach that learns a probability distribution from labeled training data. Maximum-entropy models (MAXENT) only represent what is known from the labeled training instances and assume as little as possible about what is unknown; MAXENT converges to a distribution with maximal entropy. Finding the distribution matrix between values and classes with the maximal entropy is done in an iterative way with algorithms such as L-BFGS [10]. In our experiments we use the maximum-entropy modeling software package *maxent* by Zhang Le [2].

Rule learning produces a set of classification rules based on a labeled training set. The condition part of the rules is, depending on the learner's rule grammar, a test on the presence of certain values in the input, combined with for example boolean operators. Many variants of rule learning exist, varying in the way the rules are induced or in the way the rules are applied. A prominent class of rule learners is those using *sequential covering*. In an iterative process they learn one rule at the time (prioritized by some maximized weighted function that considers coverage, accuracy, and byte length), and remove all examples from the data that are covered by this rule. We adopt RIPPER (Repeated Incremental Pruning to Produce Error Reduction) [11] as the rule learning algorithm in our experiments[3]. Ripper can produce ordered and unordered rule sets. In classification, the first matching rule in a ordered rule set determines the class. For an unordered rule set, the matching rule with the lowest error on the training set determines the class.

2.1 k-NN and Maximum-Entropy Modeling

In this section we describe the construction and motivation of the hybrid algorithm that combines k-NN with maximum-entropy modeling.

---

[1] We ran experiments with TiMBL version 5.1.
[2] URL: http://homepages.inf.ed.ac.uk/s0450736/maxent_toolkit.html. We ran experiments with maxent version 20041229.
[3] In our experiments we used RIPPER version 2.5 (patch 1).

The distribution matrix structure of MAXENT is identical to the class distribution matrix structure between feature values and classes used by the MVDM metric of k-NN. We exploit this structural equivalence to construct the hybrid algorithm we will henceforth refer to as MAXENT-H. We employ the method proposed by [12]. After training MAXENT, we replace the class distribution matrix of the MVDM metric with the matrix produced by the maximum-entropy learning algorithm. We refer to this new metric as the MAXENT–MVDM distance metric.

By constructing this hybrid we hypothetically repair a known weakness of the MVDM metric of k-NN: its sensitivity to data sparseness. As the normal MVDM metric uses raw conditional probabilities calculated from frequency counts, two low-frequent feature values that accidently occur with the same class will be regarded as identical by MVDM; when they occur with different classes their distance is estimated as maximal. A re-estimation of probabilities such as produced by the maximum-entropy algorithm may smooth the MVDM metric.

Seen from the perspective of MAXENT, the major difference between MAXENT and the hybrid MAXENT-H is that the latter does not use the maximum-entropy matrix and the exponential maximum-entropy probability function to produce class likelihood estimates, but instead uses the MAXENT–MVDM distance metric to find the k nearest neighbors in the data, and extrapolates the neighbors' majority output class.

Relevant related work is reported in [4]. They compare instance-based learning (with MVDM metric) with Naive Bayes, and construct a range of intermediate hybrid variants, each more or less similar to Naive Bayes or the instance-based learner with MVDM. One of these variants has a close resemblance to our hybrid MAXENT-H, namely the variant that stores all training instances in memory, and uses the Naive Bayes metric to calculate distances between instances. The results of the reported experiments are quite diverse and inconclusive.

2.2 k-NN and Rule Learning

In this section we describe and motivate the construction of two different hybrid algorithms that combine rule learning with k-NN.

We use the rule set as induced by RIPPER to construct the hybrid algorithm, analogous to [13]. Per instance, whether it is in the training data or in the test data, we convert the rules into binary features that represent whether or not the rule fires on the instance. We generate two versions of the hybrid algorithm. In the first version the binary rule-features replace the original features in the instances. In other words, this operation transforms the original feature space into a new one [5]. We convert all training and test instances into this binary format and feed them to the instance-based learner. The hybrid subsequently uses the k-NN classification method to classify new examples. We refer to this hybrid as RULES-R-H, where the middle R denotes *replace*.

From the k-NN perspective, replacing the original features of the instances by rule-features can be considered as a compression and filtering step in which the rule learning algorithm has removed noise and irrelevant information, and grouped interacting feature values together of which k-NN is incapable. From the perspective of the rule learning algorithm, we do not have the simple classification strategy of taking the class of the rule that fires first, but the local classification method of k-NN.

In the hybrids, rules are presented as active-inactive binary features, and more than one rule can be active for a particular instance. As k-NN can be used with $k > 1$, the nearest neighbors can also contain different active rules that are applied to the new instance. Several rules, instead of only one, may be involved in the classification.

In the second version of the hybrid, RULES-A-H, where A stands for *adding*, the rule-features are added to the original instance features. Thus, this hybrid is a k-NN classifier with extra added features that represent the per-instance firing patterns of the induced rule set. In this case the rule features cannot be considered as a compression and filtering step, but adding these rule-features modifies the distance calculations in k-NN. As explained above feature weighting in k-NN gives a higher weight to more important features. As many of the created rule-features will have a strong predictive power, they are likely to receive high feature weights, making them able to influence the distance calculation.

[3] also proposes a hybrid algorithm that combines rule learning with k-NN called 'RISE'. RISE applies creates a rule set by carefully generalizing instances. It searches for an optimal rule set by repeatedly finding the nearest instances, and generalizing over them. The most important difference between RISE and our approach is that RISE considers rules as generalized instances, while our approach differentiates between rules and instances as we transform rules to create features that are added to the instances or replace the original features in the instances.

3 Experimental Setup

We apply the three parent algorithms and the three hybrid algorithms on 29 data sets from the UCI repository of machine learning databases [14]. We perform 10-fold cross validation (CV) experiments and measure the mean accuracy and standard deviation on the ten folds. We conduct paired t-tests between outcomes of pairs of algorithms to determine the significance of the difference in performance.

k-NN and RULES offer several algorithmic parameters that, individually and in combination, can affect the functioning of the algorithms in unpredictable ways. We use a wrapped-based method to set them automatically for all k-NN and RULES modules involved in our study, including the hybrids. For small datasets it is feasible to run pseudo-exhaustively a large amount of wrapped validation experiments [15], covering all possible combinations of nominal parameter values and sequences of selected values of real-valued parameters. We do this for data sets below 1,000 instances: we perform wrapped internal 10-fold CV experiments nested within the main 10-fold CV experiments. We measure accuracy and select the average-best combination of settings over the internal ten folds.

For larger data sets a complete recombination of algorithmic parameter settings tested on the entire training set becomes infeasible. Rather than running the algorithms with their default settings, we adopt *wrapped progressive sampling*, or WPS [16], a heuristic automatic procedure that, on the basis of validation experiments internal to the training material, searches among algorithmic parameter combinations for a combination likely to yield optimal generalization performance on unseen data.

We test five algorithmic parameters of k-NN with a total of 925 parameter combinations, default settings are marked in bold:

- number of nearest neighbors: **1**, 3, 5, 7, 9, 11, 13, 15, 19, 25, 35;
- feature weighting: none, **gain ratio**, information gain, shared variance, chi-square;
- distance metric: **overlap**, MVDM, Jeffrey divergence;
- neighbor weighting: **normal majority voting**, inversed linear weighting, inversed distance weighting (only when $k > 1$)
- frequency threshold for switching from MVDM distance metric to overlap metric: **1**, 2;

For the rule learning algorithm RIPPER we test seven algorithmic parameters which leads to a total of 972 parameter combinations to be tested:

- number of extra optimization rounds: 0, 1, **2**;
- order of the classes: starts by making rules for **the most frequent classes**, start with least frequent classes, unordered.
- rule simplification: **0.5**, 1.0, 2.0;
- misclassification cost: 0.5, **1.0**, 2.0;
- minimum number of instances covered by rule: **1**, 2, 5, 10, 20, 50;
- negative tests for nominal valued features: yes, **no**;

We did not optimize the parameters of MAXENT as it was shown in [16] that neither exhaustive wrapping nor WPS increased the generalization accuracy of this algorithm. We train MAXENT with L-BFGS parameter estimation, 100 iterations and a Gaussian prior with mean zero and σ^2 of 1.0.

Different machine learning algorithms have different methods to deal with continuous feature values. In order to rule out differences between algorithms we discretize the continuous features in some of the UCI benchmark tasks in a preprocessing step, using the entropy-based discretization method of [17].

4 Results

In this section we describe the results of all algorithms discussed in Section 2. Table 1 lists the names and number of instances of the 29 data sets, along with the mean accuracies and standard deviations of 10-fold CV experiments with all algorithms. (Note: *cl-h-disease* stands for 'cleveland-heart-disease', and *soybean-l* stands for 'soybean large'.)

We first look at the performance of the three parent machine learning algorithms. Table 2 shows the results of significance tests on the 29 UCI benchmarks

Table 1. Mean accuracy and standard deviation of the 10-fold CV experiments on the 29 UCI tasks for all algorithms. Best performances per task are printed in boldface.

task	# inst.	k-NN	MAXENT	RULES	MAXENT-H	RULES-R-H	RULES-A-H
abalone	4177	24.6 ± 2.8	23.6 ± 1.7	18.1 ± 1.7	22.8 ± 2.2	18.0 ± 1.7	**25.0 ± 2.5**
audiology	226	80.5 ± 6.3	80.9 ± 5.0	76.5 ± 7.7	81.3 ± 5.8	61.0 ± 9.4	**81.8 ± 5.2**
bridges	104	54.7 ± 10.6	**61.6 ± 9.1**	53.8 ± 14.3	55.7 ± 13.1	52.9 ± 17.2	55.7 ± 13.1
car	1728	96.5 ± 1.3	90.9 ± 2.2	97.6 ± 1.1	96.5 ± 1.5	94.0 ± 4.0	**98.4 ± 0.9**
cl-h-disease	303	55.7 ± 5.4	55.1 ± 5.0	**58.4 ± 5.9**	54.8 ± 5.8	**58.4 ± 5.9**	**58.4 ± 5.2**
connect4	67557	77.7 ± 1.8	75.7 ± 0.5	76.3 ± 1.7	78.1 ± 1.9	75.2 ± 1.3	**78.6 ± 2.5**
ecoli	336	**79.5 ± 4.9**	76.5 ± 7.8	69.7 ± 10.9	78.6 ± 2.8	72.6 ± 12.1	78.0 ± 6.3
flag	194	66.9 ± 11.4	**69.8 ± 13.4**	61.8 ± 8.8	68.9 ± 14.9	61.8 ± 7.8	65.8 ± 10.9
glass	214	67.7 ± 8.4	**70.1 ± 11.6**	60.7 ± 6.5	61.5 ± 9.9	60.8 ± 8.0	66.9 ± 10.1
kr-vs-kp	3196	96.8 ± 1.2	96.8 ± 0.6	**99.2 ± 0.5**	99.1 ± 0.4	**99.2 ± 0.5**	**99.2 ± 0.5**
letter	20000	**95.6 ± 0.5**	85.0 ± 0.7	73.8 ± 1.5	95.9 ± 0.7	74.6 ± 1.4	95.6 ± 0.4
lung-cancer	32	33.3 ± 12.9	39.2 ± 24.7	31.7 ± 24.1	**43.3 ± 13.3**	25.0 ± 12.9	34.2 ± 16.0
monks1	432	**100.0 ± 0.0**	75.0 ± 4.0	99.3 ± 2.0	93.7 ± 10.5	**100.0 ± 0.0**	**100.0 ± 0.0**
monks2	432	94.0 ± 11.8	65.1 ± 5.5	72.0 ± 8.1	96.3 ± 8.3	89.9 ± 1.0	**97.0 ± 4.2**
monks3	432	**97.2 ± 2.5**	**97.2 ± 2.5**	**97.2 ± 2.5**	**97.2 ± 2.5**	96.5 ± 2.6	**97.2 ± 2.5**
mushroom	8124	**100.0 ± 0.0**	**100.0 ± 0.0**	**100.0 ± 0.0**	**100.0 ± 0.0**	98.7 ± 2.6	**100.0 ± 0.0**
nursery	12960	**99.4 ± 0.5**	92.4 ± 0.4	97.7 ± 0.8	97.9 ± 1.1	97.9 ± 0.7	99.2 ± 0.4
optdigits	5620	**98.0 ± 0.7**	95.8 ± 0.6	89.3 ± 1.0	97.3 ± 0.6	89.9 ± 1.0	97.9 ± 0.6
pendigits	10992	**93.4 ± 0.9**	86.0 ± 1.2	82.6 ± 1.7	92.0 ± 1.4	81.7 ± 3.5	92.5 ± 1.5
promoters	106	87.0 ± 7.1	92.5 ± 9.0	79.4 ± 7.9	**93.5 ± 8.2**	80.3 ± 8.7	83.5 ± 11.2
segment	2310	95.7 ± 0.9	92.1 ± 2.8	90.5 ± 3.6	95.9 ± 1.1	90.6 ± 3.6	**95.8 ± 1.3**
solar-flare	1389	94.2 ± 2.2	**94.7 ± 1.8**	94.6 ± 1.5	94.2 ± 1.8	94.6 ± 1.5	94.2 ± 1.9
soybean-l	683	92.8 ± 4.2	92.2 ± 2.8	91.1 ± 3.0	**93.1 ± 3.2**	91.8 ± 3.2	92.8 ± 3.5
splice	3190	95.3 ± 1.0	94.6 ± 0.8	94.1 ± 1.6	94.8 ± 1.5	94.2 ± 1.1	**95.8 ± 0.7**
tictactoe	958	95.8 ± 3.8	98.3 ± 0.7	99.7 ± 0.7	**100.0 ± 0.0**	**100.0 ± 0.0**	**100.0 ± 0.0**
vehicle	846	**67.6 ± 4.5**	63.5 ± 5.2	55.7 ± 5.0	66.3 ± 5.4	56.0 ± 5.2	64.2 ± 5.7
votes	435	95.2 ± 2.4	**96.5 ± 2.1**	94.2 ± 1.6	95.4 ± 2.3	94.2 ± 1.6	94.9 ± 1.3
wine	178	96.1 ± 2.6	94.9 ± 5.3	93.2 ± 6.5	**96.6 ± 2.7**	92.7 ± 7.0	95.5 ± 4.9
yeast	1484	53.3 ± 2.9	49.3 ± 3.9	42.2 ± 3.2	**55.4 ± 3.0**	40.2 ± 2.1	52.0 ± 4.7

Table 2. Comparison of the three parent algorithms through summary counts of won/tied/lost outcomes of paired t-tests on the mean accuracy and standard deviation of the 10-fold CV experiments on the 29 UCI tasks.

	k-NN	MAXENT	RULES
k-NN		10/17/2	14/12/3
MAXENT	2/17/10		10/13/6
RULES	3/12/14	6/13/10	

tasks of each of the algorithms compared to the other. Each cell shows the number of times the algorithm in the row won/tied/lost as compared to the algorithm in the column. The counts in the table are based on paired t-tests at $p < 0.05$ on the pairwise accuracies obtained in 10-fold CV experiments. Overall, the results indicate that k-NN performs better than the other two parent algorithms. MAXENT tends to perform better than RULES on 10 data sets, and RULES outperforms MAXENT on 6 data sets.

Comparisons (again in won/tied/lost counts) between the hybrid algorithms and their three parent algorithms are displayed in Table 3. We observe that MAXENT-H performs quite equally to k-NN, while outperforming MAXENT on 12

Table 3. Comparison of the three hybrids with their parent algorithms, through summary counts of won/tied/lost outcomes of paired t-tests on the mean accuracy and standard deviation of the 10-fold CV experiments on 29 UCI tasks.

	k-NN	MAXENT
MAXENT-H	4/21/4	12/17/0

	k-NN	RULES
RULES-R-H	2/14/13	3/23/3
RULES-A-H	4/24/1	16/13/0

data sets. RULES-R-H performs worse than k-NN: it wins only on two data sets and has a significantly lower accuracy in 13 cases. RULES-R-H performs very similarly to RULES. The second rule learning hybrid RULES-A-H has a significantly higher accuracy than k-NN on 4 data sets, and on 16 tasks compared to RULES.

5 Analysis

We are not solely interested in whether each hybrid has a better overall generalization performance than one or both of the parent algorithms. We also investigate to which extent the hybrid deviates functionally from its two parent algorithms. In this section we take a closer look at the degree of overlap in the errors made by the hybrids compared to their parents. Additionally, we measure the statistical bias and variance of the algorithms.

5.1 Complementary Error Rate Analysis

The complementary error rate between two algorithms A and B, $Comp(A, B)$, measures the percentage of mistakes that A makes which are not made by algorithm B [18]:

$$Comp(A, B) = \left(1 - \frac{\# \text{ of common errors}}{\# \text{ of errors of A only}}\right) * 100 \qquad (2)$$

The relative magnitude of the complementary error rate between two algorithms can be seen as an indication of their functional similarity with respect to classification behavior. The lower the complimentary error rate between a pair of algorithms is, the more they are functionally similar.

We calculate the complementary rates between each hybrid compared to its two parent algorithms where the hybrid is A in $Comp(A, B)$. Table 4 (second column) lists macro averages over the 29 data sets. Almost all pairs of algorithms have complementary rates of more than 30%, meaning that at least one-third of the misclassified instances by the hybrid is classified correctly by the parent

Table 4. Complementary rates and overlapping errors between hybrids and their parent algorithms, macro-averaged over the 29 data sets

Two algorithms	Complementary rate	Error overlap
MAXENT-H – k-NN	32.9	60.0
MAXENT-H – MAXENT	34.9	54.2
RULES-A-H – k-NN	32.3	60.9
RULES-A-H – RULES	28.7	56.2
RULES-R-H – k-NN	54.8	32.0
RULES-R-H – RULES	21.3	74.3

classifier. The exception to this observation is the pair RULES-R-H – RULES which produces the low rate of 21.3%, indicating that their functional classification behavior is relatively similar.

Besides calculating whether the classifiers misclassify the same instances, we also count whether they make the same errors. We investigate the errors that are made by the hybrid algorithms and we calculate the percentage of times that the parent algorithms assign the same incorrect label. Table 4 (third column) displays the macro average of overlap in error labels on the 29 data sets. We see that the hybrids MAXENT-H and RULES-A-H have approximately 5% more overlap in error with k-NN than with the eager parent algorithm. The hybrid RULES-R-H makes the same errors as RULES to a very high extent (74%), while having little overlap (32%) with k-NN.

5.2 Bias–Variance Analysis

The expected average error of a classifier can be decomposed in three components: *statistical bias, variance* and *noise*. The statistical bias of an algorithm reflects the systematic error of the algorithms whereas the term variance expresses the variability in error over a set of different training sets. Noise presents the errors in the data.

In this section we analyze whether the hybrid algorithms have a different statistical bias and variance than their two parent algorithms. We employ the method of [19]: we perform sampling experiments, measure the average error rate and calculate the decomposition into bias and variance components.[4] We select 16 data sets from our original set of 29 that have more than 500 instances.

[19] use the following formula to decompose the expected zero-one loss $E(C)$ of discrete classifiers into bias and variance, given a fixed target and averaged over a sampling of training sets:

---

[4] We did not optimize the algorithmic parameters, as small training samples do not allow any reliable cross-validated wrapping.

$$E(C) = \sum_x p(x)(\sigma_x^2 + \text{bias}_x^2 + \text{variance}_x) \qquad (3)$$

$$\text{bias}_x^2 \equiv 1/2 \sum_{y \epsilon Y} [p(Y_T = y|x) - p(Y_H = y|x)]^2 \qquad (4)$$

$$\text{variance}_x \equiv 1/2(1 - \sum_{y \epsilon Y} P(Y_H = y|x)^2) \qquad (5)$$

where x represents test example x, and σ_x^2 represents the noise in the data set ([19] argue to estimate noise to be zero as it is hard to calculate in practice); bias^2 (4) is estimated as the squared difference between the true target class and the predicted class, averaged over the training samples. (We refer to bias^2 as 'bias'.) Variance (5) is estimated as the variability over the different training sets. $p(Y_T = y|x)$ is the estimation that test example x is classified as y by the learning algorithm, averaged over the training set samples. $p(Y_F = y|x)$ is the probability that test example x has the true target label y, averaged over the training set samples. Both components are summed over all classes $y \epsilon Y$.

The purpose of these analyses is to investigate whether the proportion between bias and variance differs for the hybrids and their parent algorithms. In order to get a better view on the balance between bias and variance we scaled all error rates to 100%. Table 5 shows the macro averaged bias over the 16 data sets (the variance always being 100 − bias^2%). MAXENT has the highest bias; RULES-R-H has the lowest. When we compare each hybrid algorithm to its two parent algorithms, we see that all hybrids have a lower bias than k-NN, and also lower than the other parent algorithm. The three hybrids make less systematic errors than both of their parent algorithms.

Table 5. The scaled bias component in the error of all algorithms, macro averaged over the 16 data sets

Algorithm	Bias	Algorithm	Bias
k-NN	57.29	MAXENT-H	56.92
MAXENT	65.56	RULES-R-H	51.63
RULES	55.50	RULES-A-H	54.99

6 Discussion

Our experiments have brought forward evidence in two cases that instance-based classification can replace other classification procedures successfully. We constructed hybrids in which the learning component consisted either of rule learning or of maximum-entropy modeling, and in which the classification was performed with the k-NN classification rule. When comparing the hybrid algorithms to their parent algorithms, we observed that MAXENT-H and RULES-A-H both outperform the eager parent algorithm often, and are never significantly outperformed by them. At the same time these two hybrids perform almost identically to k-NN. When investigating more deeply to which extent the functional behavior of the hybrid algorithms differs from their parent algorithms by error analysis, we see that the hybrids MAXENT-H and RULES-A-H both misclassify different instances than both their parent algorithms in at least 30% of the cases, while RULES-R-H functions quite similarly to RULES. The two successful hybrids, MAXENT-H and RULES-A-H, have a slight higher overlap with k-NN of approximately 5% compared to the error overlap with either RULES or MAXENT.

An intriguing observation is that the bias of the three hybrids is lower than that of their parent algorithms. Combining the observed performance differences (Table 3) and the bias components of all algorithms (Table 5), we can assume that the performance gains of MAXENT-H and RULES-A-H over MAXENT and RULES, respectively, are due to a decrease in the number of systematic errors the hybrids generate. Given that the relative bias components of the two hybrids are also lower than that of k-NN, at virtually no loss of performance, we conclude that these two hybrids, MAXENT-H and RULES-A-H, represent a "best of both worlds" situation, since their different-source components cause them to avoid systematic errors their parent algorithms make.

The hybrid RULES-R-H shows a different behavior than the other two hybrids. RULES-R-H performs worse than k-NN and equals the performance of the rule learning algorithm. Also, complementary rates and overlap in error show that RULES-R-H has a quite similar functional classification behavior to that of the rule learning algorithm. Our expectation was that the hybrid would differ from RULES in classification behavior, as more than one binary rule-feature can be active in the feature representation of the hybrid and larger k values allow several nearest instances with different active bits to be involved. In our experiments on the 29 data sets, the average number of active binary rule-features in the training folds was 1.3 bits on average 67.5 rule-features per instance. However, in 70% of the experiments with RULES-R-H the automatic algorithmic parameter selection has chosen the k value to be 1, meaning that the potential benefit of k-NN classification is not fully explored. The hybrid RULES-A-H uses $k = 1$ in only 23% of the experiments, thereby profiting from the k-NN classification method.

In future work we plan to compare the hybrids to external classifier combination schemes. As our hybrids, classifier combination schemes benefit from combining partly complementary classifier biases; our method has the intrinsic advantage that the resulting classifier is one integrated model rather than two.

Acknowledgments

This research is funded by the Netherlands Organization for Scientific Research (NWO). The authors wish to thank Zhang Le for sharing information on the internals of his MAXENT implementation.

References

1. Cover, T.M., Hart, P.E.: Nearest neighbor pattern classification. Institute of Electrical and Electronics Engineers Transactions on Information Theory **13** (1967) 21–27
2. Aha, D.W., Kibler, D., Albert, M.: Instance-based learning algorithms. Machine Learning **6** (1991) 37–66
3. Domingos, P.: Unifying instance-based and rule-based induction. Machine Learning **24** (1996) 141–168
4. Ting, K., Cameron-Jones, R.: Exploring a framework for instance based learning and naive bayesian classifiers. In: Proceedings of the Seventh Australian Joint Conference on Artificial Intelligence. (1994) 100–107
5. Sebag, M., Schoenauer, M.: A rule-based similarity measure. In: Topics in case-based reasoning. Springer Verlag (1994) 119–130
6. Cost, S., Salzberg, S.: A weighted nearest neighbour algorithm for learning with symbolic features. Machine Learning **10** (1993) 57–78
7. Wettschereck, D., Aha, D.W., Mohri, T.: A review and comparative evaluation of feature-weighting methods for a class of lazy learning algorithms. Artificial Intelligence Review, special issue on Lazy Learning **11** (1997) 273–314
8. Daelemans, W., Zavrel, J., Van der Sloot, K., Van den Bosch, A.: TiMBL: Tilburg Memory Based Learner, version 5.1, reference manual. Technical Report ILK-0402, ILK, Tilburg University (2004)
9. Guiasu, S., Shenitzer, A.: The principle of maximum entropy. The Mathematical Intelligencer **7** (1985)
10. Nocedal, J.: Updating quasi-Newton matrices with limited storage. Mathematics of Computation **35** (1980) 773–782
11. Cohen, W.: Fast effective rule induction. In: Proceedings 12th International Conference on Machine Learning. (1995) 115–123
12. Hendrickx, I., Van den Bosch, A.: Maximum-entropy parameter estimation for the k-nn modified value-difference kernel. In: Proceedings of the 16th Belgian-Dutch Conference on Artificial Intelligence. (2004) 19–26
13. Van den Bosch, A.: Feature transformation through rule induction, a case study with the k-nn classifier. In: Proceedings on the workshop on advances in Inductive rule learning at the ECML/PKDD 2004. (2004) 1–15
14. Blake, C., Merz, C.: UCI repository of machine learning databases (1998) http://www.ics.uci.edu/ mlearn/MLRepository.html.
15. Kohavi, R., John, G.: Wrappers for feature subset selection. Artificial Intelligence Journal **97** (1997) 273–324
16. Van den Bosch, A.: Wrapped progressive sampling search for optimizing learning algorithm parameters. In: Proceedings of the 16th Belgian-Dutch Conference on Artificial Intelligence. (2004) 219–226
17. Fayyad, U., Irani, K.: Multi-interval discretization of continuous-valued attributes for classification learning. In: Proceedings of the 13th International Joint Conference on Artificial Intelligence. (1993) 1022–1027
18. Brill, E., Wu, J.: Classifier combination for improved lexical disambiguation. In: Proceedings of the COLING-ACL'1998. (1998) 191–195
19. Kohavi, R., Wolpert, D.: Bias plus variance decomposition for zero-one loss functions. In: Proceedings of the thirteenth International Conference on Machine Learning. (1996) 275–283

Learning and Classifying Under Hard Budgets

Aloak Kapoor and Russell Greiner*

Department of Computing Science,
University of Alberta, Edmonton, AB T6J 2E8
{aloak, greiner}@cs.ualberta.ca

Abstract. Since resources for data acquisition are seldom infinite, both learners and classifiers must act intelligently under hard budgets. In this paper, we consider problems in which feature values are unknown to both the learner and classifier, but can be acquired at a cost. Our goal is a learner that spends its fixed learning budget b_L acquiring training data, to produce the most accurate "active classifier" that spends at most b_C per instance. To produce this fixed-budget classifier, the fixed-budget learner must sequentially decide which feature values to collect to learn the relevant information about the distribution. We explore several approaches the learner can take, including the standard "round robin" policy (purchasing every feature of every instance until the b_L budget is exhausted). We demonstrate empirically that round robin is problematic (especially for small b_L), and provide alternate learning strategies that achieve superior performance on a variety of datasets.

1 Introduction

While a doctor may have the option of using a wide variety of medical tests (including MRIs, blood work, etc.) to diagnose a patient, many medical plans involve capitation payments that restrict the per-patient cost of medical diagnosis and treatment. These physicians can only consider diagnostic strategies that spend at most a specified amount; they would clearly want to use the most accurate such strategy. In general, these strategies can operate sequentially: e.g. first performing test $Blood_7$ (at cost $C(Blood_7)$), then using this information to decide on the next action; perhaps performing $Liver_3$ if $Blood_7$ was positive, but performing $Urine_2$ if $Blood_7$ was negative, and so forth. Once the total cost of the tests performed reaches the capitation amount b_C (i.e. if $C(Blood_7) + C(Urine_2) + \cdots = b_C$), the strategy must stop collecting information and render a decision — e.g. "Cancer = true". We call such a strategy a "bounded active classifier" [1].

Earlier results [1] have shown that one can PAC-learn the decision-theoretic optimal "bounded active classifier" $BAC^* = \arg\min_b\{\text{error}(b) | b \in \text{cost-}b_C\text{-active classifiers}\}$, assuming the *learner* has no *a priori* resource bound — i.e.

---

* Both authors wish to thank NSERC and iCORE for their generous support. We also thank Dan Lizotte and Omid Madani for insights on various related problems, and the anonymous reviewers for their comments. Russell Greiner also thanks the Alberta Ingenuity Centre for Machine Learning.

it can purchase every feature of as many instances as necessary. Of course, if we are charging the classifier (read "physician") for each feature, it seems strange to provide this information for free to the learner (think "experimental designer"). This paper extends those earlier results by investigating the challenge of learning this BAC* when the *learner* has a fixed budget to spend acquiring the relevant training data — i.e., when the learner can spend only a total of b_L to produce the best classifier that can spend only b_C per instance. Thus, we investigate the problem of budgeted learning a bounded active classifier.

In Sect. 2, we introduce the formal framework for budgeted learning a bounded active classifier, highlight the simplifying assumptions we make, and derive complexity results that show our task is NP-hard in general. Section 3 demonstrates how to improve the running time of the (intractable) optimal algorithm, while Sect. 4 discusses a variety of tractable algorithms that attempt to find good approximate solutions to the problem. Section 5 describes the loss functions that are required by some of our approaches, and Sect. 6 gives empirical results that compare the proposed algorithms. Finally, Sect. 7 reviews related literature and Sect. 8 summarizes our contributions. The proofs, and other information about these studies, all appear in the website [5].

2 Formal Description

The "budgeted bounded-active-classifier learner", BBACL, is given the (non-negative) cost $C(X_i) \in \mathbb{R}^+$ of acquiring each individual feature X_i of any single specified instance[1] and the loss matrix $L = [\ell_{i,j}]$ whose (i, j) element specifies the penalty for returning the class c_i when the true class is c_j; by convention we assume $\ell_{i,i} = 0$ and $\ell_{i,j} > 0$ for $i \neq j$. BBACL also knows the total amount the learner can spend $b_L \in \mathbb{R}^+$, and how much the resulting active classifier can spend per instance $b_C \in \mathbb{R}^+$.

At any time, the BBACL can see the current $m \times (r+1)$ "tableau", whose rows each correspond to an instance $i \in \{1, \ldots, m\}$ and whose first r columns each correspond to a feature, and whose $r+1$st column is the class label. Initially, only the class label is specified; the other $m \times r$ entries are all unknown. In general, we will let $x_i^{(j)}$ refer to the initially unknown value of the ith feature of the jth instance. At any point, BBACL can perform the (i, j) "probe" to determine the value of $x_i^{(j)}$, at cost $C(X_i)$. This also reduces BBACL's remaining budget from b_L to $b_L - C(X_i)$. Once this budget reaches zero, BBACL stops collecting information and returns a bounded active classifier BAC, which corresponds to a decision tree of bounded depth [2].

The score of any BAC B is its expected misclassification error:

$$Q(B) = \sum_{\mathbf{x},y} P(\mathbf{x},y)\, L(B(\mathbf{x}), y) \ . \qquad (1)$$

---

[1] We assume that these costs are independent of each other, both within and across instances. Moreover, if any test costs $C(X_i) = 0$, we can simply gather that information for each instance and then consider the resulting reduced problem where $C(X_i) > 0$ for all remaining X_is.

Letting $All(b_C)$ be the set of all such active classifiers that spend at most b_C per instance, our goal is the BAC from this set that minimizes this error:

$$\text{BAC}^* = \underset{B \in All(b_C)}{\arg\min} \ Q(B) \ . \tag{2}$$

2.1 Simplifying Assumptions

For our work we will assume a constant misclassification cost $\ell_{ij} = 1$ for $i \neq j$ and $\ell_{ii} = 0$. Our algorithms will need to estimate the probabilities over the values of the features of an instance $P(x_i^{(j)})$ to decide which probe to perform. We will take a Bayesian stance by assuming there is a prior distribution over labeled instances, before seeing any data.[2] As a simplification, we will make the Naïve Bayes assumption, which means the distribution of $x_i^{(j)}$ is independent of $x_k^{(j)}$ (for $k \neq i$) as we know the value of the class y_j.[3] Hence, if instance j is labeled with class $+$, we will model the distribution of its ith feature $x_i^{(j)} \sim \text{Dir}(\alpha_{1,+}^{(i)}, \ldots, \alpha_{w,+}^{(i)})$ as a Dirichlet distribution with parameters $\alpha_{j,+}^{(i)} > 0$, assuming X_i has $|X_i| = w$ values [3]. These parameters are unrelated to the ones for negatively labeled instances $\alpha_{j,-}^{(i)}$ and also unrelated to the parameter values for other features X_h, for $h \neq i$. Initially, we will assume that each such distribution is uniform $\text{Dir}(1, \ldots, 1)$. If we later see a sample S with 29 $Y = +$ instances with $X_i = +$ and 14 $Y = +$ instances with $X_i = -$, the posterior distribution for $x_i^{(j)}$ for a new $Y = +$ instance would be $\text{Dir}(1 + 29, 1 + 14)$. The mean probability for $X_i = +$ here would be $P(X_i = +|S) = 30/(30 + 15) = 2/3$.

In general, if a variable X's prior distribution is $X \sim \text{Dir}(\alpha_1, \ldots, \alpha_w)$, then

$$P(X = i) \ = \ \frac{\alpha_i}{\sum_k \alpha_k} \tag{3}$$

If we then observe a sample S that includes a_i instances of $X = i$, then X's posterior distribution remains a Dirichlet, with new parameters

$$X|S \ \sim \ \text{Dir}(\alpha_1 + a_1, \ldots, \alpha_w + a_w) \ . \tag{4}$$

In the formal description above, a probe of the form $x_i^{(j)}$ specifies the feature to probe (X_i) and the specific instance in the tableau (instance j) on which to perform the probe. However, because of our Naïve Bayes assumption, we can treat all instances with the same class label identically. Thus, rather than querying specific instances, we only consider probes of the form (i, y) that request the ith feature of a randomly chosen instance in the tableau whose class label is y. (By convention, this process selects the value of an (i, y) feature-value that has not been seen before.)

---

[2] The sparsity of the data means the obvious frequentist approach of using simple frequencies is problematic.

[3] Note that Naïve Bayes models often produce good classifiers even for datasets that violate this assumption.

2.2 Complexity Results

Madani et al. [4] proves the following much simpler task is NP-hard: Given a set of coins with known prior distributions and a fixed total number of flips, decide when to flip which coin to decide which coin has the highest head probability. Our framework inherits that negative result. (Identify each coin f_i with a binary feature, whose head probability corresponds to the probability the class is true, given f_i is true, $P(c = +|f_i = +)$; we also let $P(c = +|f_i = -) = 0$ for all features.) In addition, [1] shows that computing the best active classifier is NP-hard in general, even if we know the entire distribution. Our framework inherits that negative result as well.

3 The Optimal Policy

As our problem is a finite Markov Decision Process, there exists a deterministic optimal policy for spending the learning budget such that the expected$_1$ total (expected$_2$) misclassification error[4] of the final bounded active classifier is minimized. Mathematically, the optimal learning policy is the one that minimizes:

$$\sum_{i \in Outcomes} P(i) \sum_{\mathbf{x},y} P(\mathbf{x},y|i) \ L(BAC^*(\mathbf{x}),y) \tag{5}$$

where each "outcome" corresponds to a state in which our learning budget has been fully exhausted and has resulted in posterior Dirichlet distributions over the feature values.

Such a policy can be computed via a bottom-up dynamic program. Unfortunately, the number of outcomes (and hence the computational complexity) has a prohibitive lower bound:

Proposition 1. [5] *Let $|X_i|$ denote the domain size of feature X_i, $|S|$ denote the number of classes, $t = |S| \sum_i |X_i| - 1$, and each feature has unit cost. Then the bottom-up dynamic program must compute the value of*

$\Omega \left(\left(\frac{b_L + t}{b_L} \right)^{b_L} \left(\frac{b_L + t}{t} \right)^t \frac{1}{\sqrt{t}} \right)$ *outcomes.*

We have considered improving upon this naïve dynamic program by reducing the number of subproblems that must be solved. Below we show an interesting way to achieve this reduction by exploiting the equivalence of two "permuted" states under the conditional independence assumption.

Definition 1. *A proper permutation for a feature X_i with w domain values is a bijective function $f : [1, w] \to [1, w]$ that applies the same reordering of the w parameters for every Dirichlet distribution on X_i.*

---

[4] The first expectation$_1$ is over the set of possible Dirichlet distributions produced by the learner's purchases, and the second expectation$_2$ is over the possible labelled instances $(\mathbf{x}, y)$ that can occur *given* the resulting Dirichlets.

Example 1. Let
$$(X_i|Y=0) \sim \text{Dir}(4,2,7), \quad (X_i|Y=1) \sim \text{Dir}(3,8,5)$$
Then a proper permutation for feature X_i is:
$$(X_i|Y=0) \sim \text{Dir}(7,2,4), \quad (X_i|Y=1) \sim \text{Dir}(5,8,3).$$

Proposition 2. [5] *Assume the Naïve Bayes assumption holds, and identify a "state" of our problem by the value of b_L and the set of Dirichlets over the feature-class pairs. Consider any two states A and B, that have equal values of b_L and are such that the Dirichlets of A can be made equal to the Dirichlets of B by specifying a set of r proper permutations, one for each feature X_i. Under these conditions, the expected value of state A is equal to the expected value of state B when following an optimal policy, and the optimal action to take from state A is the optimal action to take from state B.*

This proposition allows us to improve the naïve dynamic program by reusing the computed value of a state A for properly permuted versions of A. The realtime improvement using Proposition 2 is shown in Table 1. In the last case, the naïve dynamic program ran out of memory after more than two hours, while our improved version finished properly in under an hour. Unfortunately such improvements are not sufficient to remove the exponential complexity of the dynamic program (recall that this task is NP-complete); therefore, we consider the following more tractable, suboptimal approaches.

Table 1. Reduction in computation time using Proposition 2

b_L	b_C	Features	Domain Size	Naïve	Improved
2	4	6	4	161 sec	65 sec
3	2	4	3	888 sec	432 sec
4	3	4	3	8280 sec	3360 sec

4 Algorithms

This section summarizes a number of "budgeted bounded-active-classifier learners". We focus on only the data collection part of the algorithms; after collecting $\$b_L$ worth of feature-values, each of the algorithms then passes its learned (posterior) Dirichlet distributions to a dynamic program that produces the BAC* in (2).

4.1 Round Robin (RR)

This obvious algorithm simply purchases *complete* instances until its budget b_L is exhausted. It draws examples randomly, and so expects to have collected data about members of each class y in proportion to $P(Y=y)$. If there are r unit-cost features, we expect to know everything about roughly b_L/r instances. Notice RR implicitly assumes all features are equally valuable in learning the target concept.

4.2 Biased Robin (BR)

A more selective approach than Round Robin is to purchase a single feature and test whether or not its observed value has increased some measure of quality. The Biased Robin algorithm is more selective than RR, continually purchasing feature X_i as long as it improves quality, and otherwise moving to feature X_{i+1} (and of course looping back to X_1 after X_r). There are several choices for how to measure quality or loss; see Sect. 5. Of course, BR must also specify a class y from which to purchase its desired feature, and it does this by drawing from the class distribution $P(Y = y)$ on each purchase. As further motivation for this algorithm, [6] found it to be one of the best approaches for budgeted learning of a passive Naïve Bayes classifier, albeit with a different loss function. This method also corresponds to the "Play the Winner" approach discussed in [7].

4.3 Single Feature Lookahead (SFL)

One would always like to avoid wasting purchases on poor features, especially when faced with a limited learning budget. This motivates a prediction-based approach, which uses a loss function to estimate the expected loss incurred after making a sequence of purchases of a single, specified feature.

SFL uses this prediction based approach, and controls the level of myopia or "greediness" involved by providing an additional parameter, d = the lookahead depth. With a lookahead depth of d, SFL calculates the expected loss of spending its next $\$d$ sequentially purchasing feature i of instances of class j. That is, if S denotes our current set of Dirichlets and S' denotes the Dirichlets after spending $\min(\$d, \$b_L)$ purchasing feature X_i of $Y = j$ instances, then the expected loss for (i, j) is:

$$SFL(i,j) = \sum_{S'} P(S'|S)\, Loss(S') \ . \qquad (6)$$

SFL determines the feature-class pair (i, j) with lowest expected loss, then purchases the value of this best (i, j) feature for *one* instance, and updates the Dirichlets based on the observed outcome of that purchase (and reduces the available remaining budget). It then recurs, using (6) to compute the score for all feature-class pairs in this new situation — with its updated Dirichlets and a smaller budget. This process repeats until the learning budget is exhausted. The lookahead depth d can be set based on the computational resources available. If only the next one purchase is considered, then this reduces to the (1-step) greedy algorithm. SFL was originally used in two previously investigated variants of the budgeted learning problem [6,8].

4.4 Randomized SFL (RSFL)

Our experiments show that the SFL algorithm often spends the majority of its probes purchasing a single discriminative feature-class pair and neglects to explore other potentially good features. This property can be problematic, particularly when a dataset contains several discriminative features that can jointly yield a more accurate BAC than any single feature by itself. The Randomized Single Feature Lookahead algorithm (RSFL) alleviates this problem by increasing exploration among the best looking feature-class pairs. The RSFL algorithm is very similar to SFL, as it too calculates the expected loss in (6) for each feature-class pair. However, rather than deterministically purchasing the pair with the best SFL score, RSFL considers the best K feature-class pairs and for each feature-class pair (i, j) in this set, it chooses to purchase feature i of class j with probability:

$$\frac{\exp \frac{-SFL(i,j)}{\tau}}{\sum_{i,j} \exp \frac{-SFL(i,j)}{\tau}} \tag{7}$$

Here, τ is a temperature controlling exploration versus exploitation. Although we set τ to one throughout this paper, we include it in (7) to show the relationship to the Gibbs distribution. After experimenting with various values for the number of feature-class pairs, K, we found that $K =$ (number of classes) $\times b_c$ seemed to perform well, particularly when the learning budget was not much greater than the number of features.

5 Loss Functions

As mentioned earlier, several of our algorithms rely on a loss function

$$Loss : \{\text{Dirichlet distributions over features}\} \to \mathbb{R} \tag{8}$$

that attempts to measure the quality of a given probability distribution. After experimenting with several different choices of loss functions, we found Conditional Entropy Loss and Depth 1 BAC Loss to be effective.[5]

Conditional Entropy measures the uncertainty of the class label Y given the value of a feature X_i:

$$-\sum_{x} P(X_i = x) \sum_{y} P(Y = y | X_i = x) \log_2 P(Y = y | X_i = x) \ . \tag{9}$$

The Biased Robin algorithm uses (9) before and after the purchase of feature X_i to determine whether the purchase improved the ability of X_i to predict the class Y.

On the other hand, other algorithms (SFL, RSFL, and greedy) use

$$\min_{i} \sum_{x} P(X_i = x) \min_{y} (1 - P(Y = y | X_i = x)) \tag{10}$$

which calculates the expected misclassification error of the best Depth 1 BAC. Since BR needs to detect small changes in a distribution, it tends to perform better with the more sensitive conditional entropy calculation in (9).

---

[5] The obvious loss function is just to use (2) to compute the expected error of the optimal BAC. However, since loss functions can be called several times on a single purchase, the computational expense of computing (2) is prohibitive.

6 Experimental Results

To compare the algorithms, we tested their performance on several datasets from the UCI Machine Learning Repository [9]. We used supervised entropy discretization [10] to discretize datasets with continuous values. Each dataset was then randomly partitioned into five folds. The algorithms were run five times, and on each run a single fold was set aside for testing, while the remaining four were available for purchasing. For each algorithm, we used the average value of these five runs as the algorithm's misclassification error on the whole dataset. We repeated this process 50 times to reduce the variance and get a measure of the average misclassification error. Thus, each point in the graphs that follow represents 50 repetitions of five-fold cross validation.

In the first set of experiments, all features have unit cost and the datasets contain some irrelevant features. We set the classifier's budget to $b_c = 3$, as this is large enough to allow several features to be used, but small enough to keep computations tractable. All Dirichlets parameters are uniformly initialized to 1. For reference, each graph also includes a gold standard "All Data" algorithm, which is allowed to see the *entire* dataset, and thus represents the best that one can do using the Naïve Bayes assumption on the data.

Figure 1 shows the performance of the algorithms on the Glass Identification dataset: a binary class problem with nine features whose domain sizes vary between one and three. The four features that have a domain size of one represent irrelevant information that any learning algorithm (especially one under a constraining budget) should avoid. Both RSFL and BR learn better than the obvious RR algorithm for all learning budgets considered. In fact, we found the optimal $b_C = 3$ BAC produced by the "All Data" algorithm involves four different features, and these four features are precisely the ones that RSFL and BR purchase heavily during learning. This is in contrast to the RR purchasing behaviour that spends equally on all features, despite their unequal predictive power. Finally, SFL and Greedy spend their entire budget on only one or two features during learning, which accounts for their low accuracy BACs.

The Breast Cancer dataset contains ten features, only one of which is irrelevant to the concept. This dataset is particularly interesting because nearly all its features are good predictors, but three features have markedly lower conditional entropy than the rest. To produce the lowest error BAC, the learning algorithms must discover the superiority of these three features. We find RSFL does exactly this, spending 20%, 21%, and 32% of its budget respectively on the three strong features. In comparison, RR spends 10% of its budget on every feature which makes it much more difficult for it to separate the top features from the rest. BR also performs better than RR for all learning budgets considered.

The next set of experiments, shown in Fig. 2, considers datasets without any irrelevant features. The Iris dataset has only four features and is a three class problem. Given that all four features are relevant, and that $b_C = 3$ in this experiment, the optimal BAC requests every feature at some point in its tree. With only four features to consider, RSFL is able to test them all effectively and

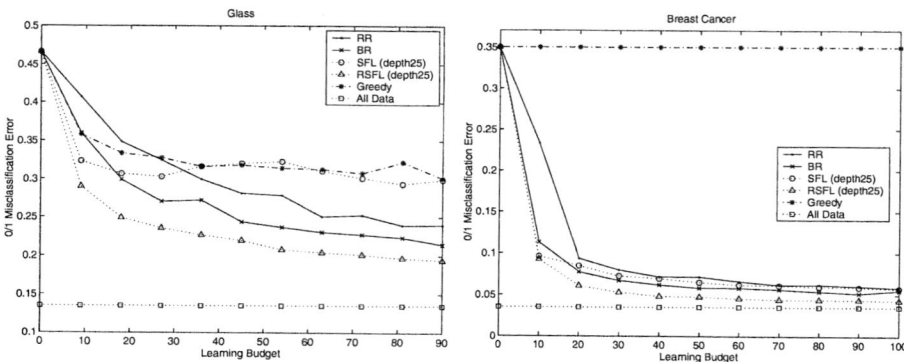

Fig. 1. Identical costs and some irrelevant features — RSFL and BR outperform RR

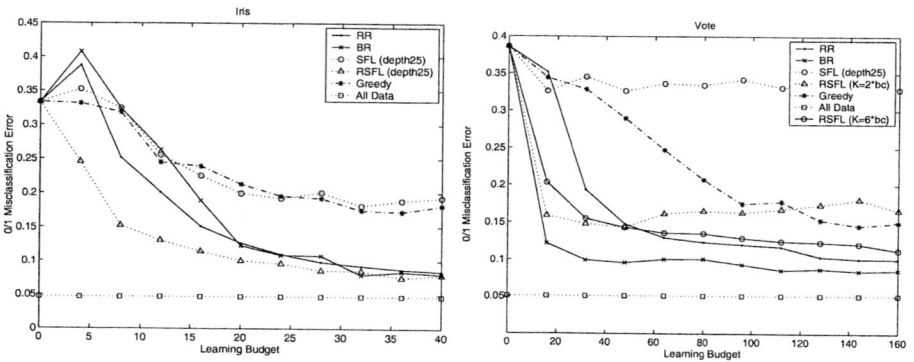

Fig. 2. Identical costs, no irrelevant features — RR still suboptimal

produce better BACs than RR for all budgets considered. BR is also competitive with RR, except at some of the very low budgets where BR's exploration model prevents it from ever investigating some of the features.

Figure 2 (right) shows another binary class problem, the Vote dataset, that contains 16 features. Many of these features have similar (high) predictive power. Once again we see that both RSFL and BR beat RR when the learning budget is small. RSFL asymptotes after about 50 purchases — it spends its budget finding a few strong features quickly and outputs a fairly low error BAC. As expected, at larger budgets RR collects enough information on every feature to find many more suitable candidates for its BAC than RSFL can. The graph shows that one can improve the performance of RSFL by increasing the number of top feature-class pairs that RSFL considers on this dataset. We also observe that BR's exploration model is particularly well suited to this task because it is able to collect information on every feature at larger budgets, which is crucial on a dataset such as Vote with a large number of predictive features.

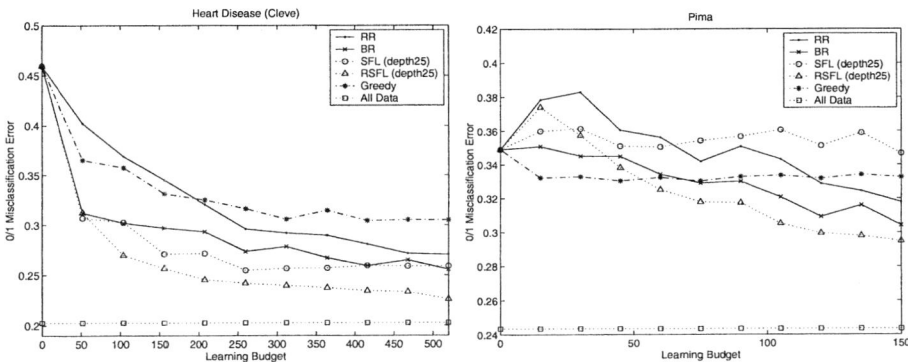

Fig. 3. Different feature costs — RSFL and BR dominate RR

Our final set of experiments involved datasets where the features differed in cost. Both the Heart Disease dataset and the Pima Indians dataset have known cost data [9], which we used in our tests. The scaled Heart Disease costs range from \$1 to \$7, and our tests are run with $b_c = \$7$. This dataset represents the worst case for RR, because the irrelevant features happen to be the most expensive ones. In fact, RSFL achieves the same error rate after \$100 that RR takes \$500 to reach. In the Pima dataset, feature costs are between \$1 and \$5, and we set $b_c = \$5$. The two irrelevant features have cost \$1, and the single best feature is \$4. Once again, BR and RSFL dominate RR for all budgets considered.

7 Related Work

There are a number of different senses of "costs" in the context of learning [11]. Our research considers two of these: the costs paid by the learner to acquire the relevant information at training time to produce an effective classifier and also the costs paid by the classifier, at performance time, to acquire relevant information about the current instance. We impose hard constraints on the total cost of tests that can be performed per instance, and on the expenses paid by the learner.

Many existing (sub)fields, such as active learning [12] and experimental design [13] (as well as earlier results such as [6]) focus on only the first of these costs – e.g., bounding how much the learner can spend to produce an accurate *passive* classifier. In addition, many of these systems request the *class label* for an otherwise *completely specified instance*. Thus they require only a single quantity per instance. Our problem is the complement of this: class labels are known but feature information must be purchased. Unlike most of the other models, this means our work may need to consider the correlations amongst the many unknown properties of an instance. Other results seeking to reduce the sample complexity for learning include decision theoretic subsampling [14], on-line stopping rules [15], progressive sampling [16], and active feature value acquisition [17]. We note that these techniques differ from our approach because we place a firm prior budget on the learner's ability to acquire information, while these approaches typically allow the learner to purchase until some external stopping criteria (for instance, accuracy) is satisfied.

Weiss and Provost [18] recently explored a problem related to one that we encounter in our overall framework: how to represent the class distribution when only a firm budget of n training examples can be used. As discussed in Sect. 4, our algorithms select which class to probe in different ways (e.g. performing lookahead (SFL, Greedy), drawing from the true class distribution (RR and BR), or combining lookahead with a Gibbs distribution (RSFL)).

As for the costs paid by the classifier at performance time, both [19] and [1] attempt to produce a decision tree that minimizes expected total cost. However, neither work assumes an a priori resource bound on the learner, thereby allowing for unconstrained amounts of training data with which to build these classifiers. Again, our work makes the more realistic assumption that if data costs money at performance time, it very likely costs money at learning time as well.

Finally, we can view our model as a (fixed horizon, partially observable) Markov Decision Process (MDP) [20]. We note that although the MDP formulation is theoretically clear, it has not yielded strong results in our experiments due to the dimensionality and lack of suitable features for function approximation; see [21]. A simpler version of our problem also exists in the MDP framework [8], and the results of that work motivate several of the policies that we adapt for budgeted learning of bounded active classifiers.

8 Conclusions

Many standard learning algorithms implicitly assume the features are always available for free, to both the learner at "training time" and later the classifier, at "performance time". This paper extends those systems by explicitly considering these costs, at both training and performance time. It introduces the formal framework for budgeted learning a bounded active classifier, and presents some complexity results. We also propose a more efficient way to implement the optimal algorithm, which we prove works effectively. Moreover, this paper motivates and defines a variety of tractable learning strategies and shows they work effectively on various types of data — both with identical and with different feature costs. In particular, we demonstrated that our proposed strategies can often do much better than the obvious algorithm – "Round Robin" – especially when training data is limited.

References

1. Greiner, R., Grove, A.J., Roth, D.: Learning cost sensitive active classifiers. Artificial Intelligence (2002)
2. Dobkin, D., Gunopoulos, D., Kasif, S.: Computing optimal shallow decision trees. In: International Workshop on Mathematics in Artificial Intelligence. (1996)

3. Heckerman, D.: A tutorial on learning in bayesian networks. In: Learning in Graphical Models. The MIT Press (1999)
4. Madani, O., Lizotte, D.J., Greiner, R.: Active model selection. Technical report, University of Alberta (2004)
5. Website: http://www.cs.ualberta.ca/~greiner/RESEARCH/blweb.html (2005)
6. Lizotte, D.J., Madani, O., Greiner, R.: Budgeted learning of naive-bayes classifiers. In: Proceedings of Uncertainty In Artificial Intelligence. (2003)
7. Robbins, H.: Some aspects of the sequential design of experiments. Bulletin of the American Mathematical Society (1952)
8. Madani, O., Lizotte, D.J., Greiner, R.: Active model selection. In: Proceedings of Uncertainty in Artificial Intelligence. (2004)
9. S. Hettich, C.B., Merz, C.: UCI repository of machine learning databases (1998)
10. Fayyad, U., Irani, K.: Multi-interval discretization of continuous-valued attributes for classification learning. In: IJCAI. (1993)
11. Turney, P.: Types of cost in inductive concept learning. In: Workshop on cost sensitive learning (ICML). (2000)
12. Cohn, D.A., Ghahramani, Z., Jordan, M.I.: Active learning with statistical models. In: Advances in Neural Information Processing Systems. (1995)
13. Chaloner, K., Verdinelli, I.: Bayesian experimental design: A review. Statistical Science (1995)
14. Musick, R., Catlett, J., Russell, S.: Decision theoretic subsampling for induction on large databases. In: International Conference on Machine Learning. (1993)
15. Schuurmans, D., Greiner, R.: Sequential pac learning. In: COLT. (1995)
16. Provost, F., Jensen, D., Oates, T.: Efficient progressive sampling. In: International Knowledge Discovery and Data Mining Conference. (1999)
17. Melville, P., Saar-Tsechansky, M., Provost, F., Mooney, R.: Active feature-value acquisition for classifier induction. In: ICDM. (2004)
18. Weiss, G.M., Provost, F.: Learning when training data are costly: the effect of class distribution on tree induction. Journal of Artificial Intelligence Research (2003)
19. Turney, P.: Cost-sensitive classification: empirical evaluation of a hybrid genetic decision tree induction algorithm. Journal of Artificial Intelligence Research (1995)
20. Russell, S., Norvig, P.: Artificial Intelligence: A Modern Approach. Prentice Hall (2002)
21. Kapoor, A., Greiner, R.: Reinforcement learning for active model selection. In: Utility Based Data Mining Workshop (KDD). (2005)

Training Support Vector Machines with Multiple Equality Constraints

Wolf Kienzle and Bernhard Schölkopf

Max-Planck-Institute for Biological Cybernetics,
Empirical Inference Department, Spemannstr. 38,
72076 Tübingen, Germany
{kienzle, bs}@tuebingen.mpg.de

Abstract. In this paper we present a primal-dual decomposition algorithm for support vector machine training. As with existing methods that use very small working sets (such as *Sequential Minimal Optimization* (SMO), *Successive Over-Relaxation* (SOR) or the *Kernel Adatron* (KA)), our method scales well, is straightforward to implement, and does not require an external QP solver. Unlike SMO, SOR and KA, the method is applicable to a large number of SVM formulations regardless of the number of equality constraints involved. The effectiveness of our algorithm is demonstrated on a more difficult SVM variant in this respect, namely semi-parametric support vector regression.

1 Introduction

Support Vector Machines (SVM) rank among the most widely used techniques in machine learning today. Besides their good generalization ability, a major benefit is that the training phase in SVMs is a convex optimization problem and hence, unlike that of many competing methods does not suffer from local minima. However, the nature of this training problem is such that a naïve implementation will require $\mathcal{O}(m^2)$ memory, where m is the number of training points.

This dilemma has motivated the development of algorithms with more efficient memory usage. Most approaches that have been studied in this respect exploit the fact that the SVM problem can be solved incrementally, i.e. it can be decomposed into a series of smaller problems that can be solved independently. In fact, such *decomposition methods* [10] not only solve larger problems for a given amount of memory, but have turned out to to give significant speed improvements. As a result, essentially all of the popular SVM solvers today are based on this idea, e.g. *SVMlight* [8], *LIBSVM* [3], *SVMTorch* [5] or *HeroSVM* [6]. These implementations differ in mainly two respects, namely in the size of the subproblems and in how the corresponding training subsets (i.e. the working sets) are chosen. A common choice for the working set size is *two*, in which case the subproblems can be solved analytically. Also, choosing a good working set is simpler when fewer points have to be selected. This was first proposed in [11] as *Sequential Minimal Optimization* (SMO), which forms the basis for three of the four packages listed above (the fourth one includes SMO as a special case).

It seems natural to ask whether *one* point working sets can further improve on the results of SMO. In fact, this has been studied in various forms, e.g. under the name of *Kernel Adatron* (KA) [7] or *Successive Over-Relaxation* (SOR) [9], and indeed, all these methods yielded performances that were comparable, if not superior to SMO. However, this comes at the price of solving a modified problem, since equality constraints (there is one in C-SVMs and two in ν-SVMs) cannot be treated using single point updates. To remedy this, the authors changed the SVM formulation such that the equality constraints vanished. A similar problem was faced by Chang and Lin [2] during the implementation of a ν-SVM solver for *LIBSVM*: the second equality constraint in ν-SVMs is cumbersome for an SMO based optimizer, since the latter can only deal with one such constraint naturally. The bottom line is that the number of equality constraints, which varies among different SVM formulations, determines if we can use the efficient two (or even one) point variant of the decomposition method.

In this paper we propose an algorithm that naturally handles any (small and constant) number of equality constraints, and at the same time allows for arbitrary working sets sizes, in particular, down to a single point. This is achieved through a primal-dual scheme that does not require feasibility in terms of the equality constraints, except at the solution. We demonstrate the benefits of our method by means of a generalized SVM formulation known as semi-parametric SVMs [13]. Here, the number of equality constraints corresponds to the number of

Table 1. Parameter settings for (1), for various support vector problems with no more than $k = 2$ equality constraints. Top two rows: C and ν soft margin SV classification, respectively. 3rd row: one-class SVM. Bottom two rows: ε and ν SV regression. Here, m is the number of data points $\mathbf{x}_i \in \mathbf{X}$. Note that in (1), the domain of $\boldsymbol{\alpha}$ is $\mathbb{R}^n$, and that $n = m$ in all cases except SVR, where we have $n = 2m$. $\mathbf{y} = (y_1, \ldots, y_m)^\top$ contains the target values ($y_i \in \{-1, 1\}$ for classification, $y_i = 1$ for single class problems, $y_i \in \mathbb{R}$ for regression). Furthermore, $\mathbf{0} = (0, \ldots, 0)^\top \in \mathbb{R}^m$, $\mathbf{1} = (1, \ldots, 1)^\top \in \mathbb{R}^m$, and $e_1 = 0$ in all cases. Finally, $\mathbf{K} \in \mathbb{R}^{m \times m}$, where $\mathbf{K}_{ij} = K(\mathbf{x}_i, \mathbf{x}_j)$ for regression and $\mathbf{K}_{ij} = y_i y_j K(\mathbf{x}_i, \mathbf{x}_j)$ otherwise, and $K(\cdot, \cdot) : \mathbf{X} \times \mathbf{X} \to \mathbb{R}$ denotes the kernel function.

	$\mathbf{H}$	d	$\mathbf{f}_0$	$\mathbf{f}_1$	e_1	$\mathbf{f}_2$	e_2
C-SVC	$\mathbf{K}$	$\frac{C}{m}$	-1	$\mathbf{y}$	0	-	-
ν-SVC	$\mathbf{K}$	$\frac{1}{\nu m}$	0	$\mathbf{y}$	0	$\mathbf{1}$	1
1-SVM	$\mathbf{K}$	$\frac{1}{\nu m}$	0	$\mathbf{1}$	1	-	-
ε-SVR	$\begin{bmatrix} \mathbf{K} & -\mathbf{K} \\ -\mathbf{K} & \mathbf{K} \end{bmatrix}$	$\frac{C}{m}$	$\begin{bmatrix} -\mathbf{y} \\ \mathbf{y} \end{bmatrix} + \varepsilon$	$\begin{bmatrix} \mathbf{1} \\ -\mathbf{1} \end{bmatrix}$	0	-	-
ν-SVR	$\begin{bmatrix} \mathbf{K} & -\mathbf{K} \\ -\mathbf{K} & \mathbf{K} \end{bmatrix}$	$\frac{C}{m}$	$\begin{bmatrix} -\mathbf{y} \\ \mathbf{y} \end{bmatrix}$	$\begin{bmatrix} \mathbf{1} \\ -\mathbf{1} \end{bmatrix}$	0	$\frac{1}{C\nu}\begin{bmatrix} \mathbf{1} \\ \mathbf{1} \end{bmatrix}$	1

free parameters and is therefore arbitrary. As a result, nontrivial semi-parametric SVMs cannot be trained with SMO, but are well suited for our algorithm.

2 Problem Formulation

In the following, we consider the class of optimization problems

$$\begin{aligned}
&\min \tfrac{1}{2}\boldsymbol{\alpha}^\top \mathbf{H}\boldsymbol{\alpha} + \mathbf{f}_0^\top \boldsymbol{\alpha} \\
&\text{s.t.}\ \ 0 \leq \alpha_i \leq d, \quad i = 1\ldots n \\
&\quad\ \ \mathbf{f}_i^\top \boldsymbol{\alpha} = e_i \quad i = 1\ldots k
\end{aligned} \quad (1)$$

w.r.t. $\boldsymbol{\alpha} = (\alpha_1, \ldots, \alpha_n)^\top \in \mathbb{R}^n$, i.e. SVM problems with k equality constraints. The particular type of SVM that is implemented depends on the following parameters: the matrix $\mathbf{H} \succeq \mathbf{0} \in \mathbb{R}^{n \times n}$, symmetric and positive definite, $k+1$ column vectors $\mathbf{f}_0, \ldots, \mathbf{f}_k \in \mathbb{R}^n$ and $k+1$ scalars $d \in \mathbb{R}$, $d > 0$ and $e_i \in \mathbb{R}$, $i = 1\ldots k$. Table 1 shows the parameter settings for (1) for several standard SVM problems [12]. Any of the SVMs in Table 1 can be made semi-parametric [13], which introduces one additional equality constraint per parameter (this will be discussed in more detail in Section 6). Please note that we will refer to (1) as the primal problem, for reasons that will become clear below.

3 Optimality Conditions

If the kernel $K(\cdot,\cdot)$ is positive definite, then so is the matrix $\mathbf{H}$ (see Table 1). This renders the primal objective convex. Since in addition, all constraints in (1) are affine, strong duality holds and the Karush-Kuhn-Tucker (KKT) conditions

$$\begin{aligned}
\forall\, i = 1\ldots k \quad &\text{(i)}\ \ \mathbf{f}_i^\top \boldsymbol{\alpha} = e_i \\[4pt]
\forall\, i = 1\ldots n \quad &\text{(ii)}\ \ 0 \leq \alpha_i \leq d \\
&\text{(iii)}\ \ \alpha_i = 0 \ \ \Rightarrow s_i \geq 0 \\
&\text{(iv)}\ \ 0 < \alpha_i < d \Rightarrow s_i = 0 \\
&\text{(v)}\ \ \alpha_i = d \ \ \Rightarrow s_i \leq 0
\end{aligned} \quad (2)$$

where $\mathbf{s} = \mathbf{H}\boldsymbol{\alpha} + \mathbf{f}_0 + \mathbf{F}\boldsymbol{\eta}$, $\mathbf{F} = [\mathbf{f}_1, \ldots, \mathbf{f}_k]$, and $\boldsymbol{\eta} \in \mathbb{R}^k$. are sufficient for optimality, i.e. any tuple $(\boldsymbol{\eta}, \boldsymbol{\alpha})$ that satisfies (2) is primal and dual optimal and has zero duality gap. Note that the dual variable(s) $\boldsymbol{\eta} = (\eta_1, \ldots, \eta_k)^\top$ correspond to the k equality constraints in the primal problem (1). The n dual variables associated with the box constraints have been eliminated via a fusion with the complementary slackness conditions, resulting in the three implications (iii–v).

4 Decomposition Methods

The need for customized SVM solvers arises from the fact that briefly, learning works better the more training data is used; but then, as mentioned earlier, storing **H**, which holds the information about the training data, requires a quadratically increasing amount of memory. The use of generic QP solvers is often not possible, especially when they require **H** to reside in memory throughout the optimization process. To remedy this, various so-called decomposition methods have been proposed (originally by Osuna et al. [10]). In a decomposition method, at each step, all α_i except a working set of size q are fixed. Then, after solving the respective subproblem (w.r.t. the q variable α_i), a new working set is selected, and the new subproblem is solved. This procedure is repeated until the global optimality criterion (i.e. regarding all n α_i) is met. Note that this requires only q columns of **H** to reside in memory at a time, so we can solve very large problems by using small working sets, i.e. small q. The following two subsections give a short review of two extreme versions of the decomposition method, namely the cases $q = 2$ and $q = 1$.

4.1 SMO (q=2)

The *Sequential Minimal Optimization* (SMO) method, introduced in [11], was originally proposed for C-SVC. As opposed to decomposition methods that use larger working sets $q > 2$, SMO has the striking property that its subproblems can be solved analytically, which makes the algorithm very simple to implement. A slightly modified, very efficient implementation of this algorithm is at the core of the widely used *LIBSVM* package [3]. Further implementations can be found in *SVMTorch* [5] and *HeroSVM* [6].

In SMO, subproblems are of size $q = 2$. For C-SVC, where we have only one equality constraint $\mathbf{y}^\top \boldsymbol{\alpha} = 0$ (see Table 1), the algorithm is as follows: first, we initialize $\boldsymbol{\alpha} = \mathbf{0}$, which is a feasible point for (1), since we have $0 \leq \alpha_i \leq \frac{C}{m}$ and $\mathbf{y}^\top \boldsymbol{\alpha} = 0$. At each iteration, a working set $\{\alpha_i, \alpha_j\}$ is selected and the quadratic objective function is minimized along the line $\mathbf{y}^\top \boldsymbol{\alpha} = 0$. Then, the new values for α_i and α_j are clipped to the interval $[0; \frac{C}{m}]$ in order to meet the inequality constraints as well. Note that this ensures that $\boldsymbol{\alpha}$ is always primal feasible, i.e. ((2), (i–ii)) are always fulfilled. Since the KKT conditions (2) are sufficient for optimality (see Section 3), $\boldsymbol{\alpha}$ is optimal as soon as the remaining conditions ((2), (iii–v)) are satisfied. In practice, one usually tests whether the largest KKT violation falls below some predefined threshold. If so, the method stops; otherwise, the next iteration starts.

In general, SMO cannot be applied to problems of type (1) when there are multiple equality constraints. For instance, if we have $k = 2$, the two equality constraints and the $q = 2$ working set form a 2×2 linear system. If it has full rank (which we have to assume), it already restricts the feasible set to a single point, which leaves us with *zero* degrees of freedom for updating α_i and α_j.

4.2 GS, KA and SOR (q=1)

The term "minimal" in SMO stems from the fact that if $\boldsymbol{\alpha}$ is required to be primal feasible ((2), (i–ii)) at any time, and if we have one equality constraint (as in C-SVC), the working set size must be at least $q = 2$. To see this, consider the C-SVC equality constraint $\mathbf{y}^\top \boldsymbol{\alpha} = 0$: clearly, if $\boldsymbol{\alpha}$ is feasible, then changing the value of a single α_i leads to $\mathbf{y}^\top \boldsymbol{\alpha} \neq 0$ and thus to infeasibility. To overcome this problem, several modified SVM formulations have been proposed, based on the following idea: In C-SVC for instance, the equality constraint $\mathbf{y}^\top \boldsymbol{\alpha} = 0$ in (1) originates from the bias term in the decision function (usually referred to as b). Therefore, changing the role of the bias will also change the structure of the optimization problem (1). This boils down to two possible modifications. The bias term may be either penalized, as in *Successive Over-Relaxation* (SOR) by [9] or simply left out, as in *Kernel Adatron* (KA) [7]. In both cases, the primal problem (1) is left with the box constraints only and can be solved with $q = 1$ methods. KA and SOR are equivalent in the sense that they essentially implement *Gauss-Seidel* (GS) iterations (or the closely related SOR iterations) to solve the linear system

$$\mathbf{H}\boldsymbol{\alpha} = -\mathbf{f}_0 \tag{3}$$

subject to the box constraints $0 \leq \alpha_i \leq d$. An actual implementation can be very similar to SMO: first, we chose $\boldsymbol{\alpha} = \mathbf{0}$ as a feasible starting point. At each iteration, a working set $\{\alpha_i\}$ is selected and the objective is minimized — in contrast to SMO, without any constraints: $\Delta \alpha_i = -(\mathbf{H}\boldsymbol{\alpha} + \mathbf{f}_0)_i / \mathbf{H}_{ii}$, which is a GS step. Then, the new value for α_i is clipped to the interval $[0; \frac{C}{m}]$ which ensures primal feasibility. As with SMO, if ((2), (iii–v)) are met, the method stops. It can be shown that such box-constrained GS methods converge from any starting point $\boldsymbol{\alpha}$, given that $\mathbf{H} \succeq \mathbf{0}$.

4.3 Platt vs. Gauss

To summarize,

- SVMs with *one* equality constraint (e.g. those listed in Table 1, except ν-SVC and ν-SVR) can be solved in a straightforward manner using SMO. In contrast, GS methods cannot deal with any equality constraint and are thus not applicable to any SVM problem in Table 1, unless the problem is modified accordingly.
- SVMs with *two* equality constraints (e.g. ν-SVC and ν-SVR) cannot be solved in general with either SMO or GS.
- SVMs with *three or more* equality constraints (e.g. semi-parametric SVMs) cannot be solved at all with either SMO or GS.

As an aside, the *LIBSVM* implementation [3] *does* solve ν-SVC and ν-SVR via SMO. In the initial version [2], this was accomplished through a bias penalty that eliminates one of the equality constraints (as in SOR). In its current version, *LIBSVM* uses a special working set selection heuristic which makes this modification obsolete [3, 4].

5 A Minimal Primal-Dual Method

This section develops the minimal primal-dual (MPD) algorithm for SVM training. It should be mentioned that other primal-dual methods have been proposed for this purpose [12]. However, to our knowledge, these approaches neither exploit the fact that the dual function is approximately quadratic, nor do they scale well. In the spirit of [11], we call our method "minimal", since the working sets have minimum possible size $q = 1$.

5.1 Motivation

Recall that SOR and KA (Section 4.2) exploit the fact that the equality constraint $\mathbf{y}^\top \boldsymbol{\alpha} = 0$ in C-SVC is closely connected to the bias term b in the decision function. In particular, if we *remove* the bias term from our problem (KA), or if we *penalize* it via $\frac{1}{2}b^2$ (SOR), the constraint $\mathbf{y}^\top \boldsymbol{\alpha} = 0$ vanishes. In fact, the equality constraint also vanishes if we *fix* the bias to *any* value. It is easy to show (see e.g. [3]) that the dual variable η_1 associated with the equality constraint $\mathbf{y}^\top \boldsymbol{\alpha} = 0$ actually *is* the bias b. As a result, we may remove equality constraints by fixing their associated dual variables η_i. In the following, we show how this motivates the MPD method. To begin, consider the Lagrangian of (1), for the moment without the box constraints, i.e.

$$L(\boldsymbol{\alpha}, \eta_1) = \frac{1}{2}\boldsymbol{\alpha}^\top \mathbf{H}\boldsymbol{\alpha} + \mathbf{f}_0^\top \boldsymbol{\alpha} + \boldsymbol{\eta}^\top (\mathbf{F}^\top \boldsymbol{\alpha} - \mathbf{e}) \quad (4)$$

which is quadratic in the primal variables $\boldsymbol{\alpha}$ and linear in the dual variables $\boldsymbol{\eta}$. Since we required $\mathbf{H} \succeq \mathbf{0}$, it is convex and bounded from below and therefore the infimum exists for any $\boldsymbol{\eta}$. Now we put the box constraints back in as a (non-relaxed) domain restriction on $\boldsymbol{\alpha}$. This yields the dual function

$$g(\boldsymbol{\eta}) = \inf_{0 \leq \alpha_i \leq d} L(\boldsymbol{\alpha}, \boldsymbol{\eta}), \quad (5)$$

whose maximization w.r.t $\boldsymbol{\eta}$ constitutes the dual problem of (1). Notice that unlike the equality constraints, which have been relaxed via the Lagrange multipliers $\boldsymbol{\eta}$, the inequalities are still present. In practice, the latter are met by clipping the unconstrained minimizer of (4) to the polytope described by the box-constraints. This operation has combinatoric complexity, but is well tractable for small working sets (see SMO etc.).

By construction, $g(\boldsymbol{\eta})$ is concave in $\boldsymbol{\eta}$, i.e. we are left with a k-dimensional, unconstrained, concave maximization problem. Now assume that we know the optimal dual variable $\boldsymbol{\eta}^*$. As mentioned earlier, since all constraints are affine and since the Lagrangian is convex in $\boldsymbol{\alpha}$, we have strong duality. Thus, finding the saddlepoint in $(\boldsymbol{\alpha}, \boldsymbol{\eta})$ is sufficient for the optimum. Since we know $\boldsymbol{\eta}^*$, we merely need to compute the corresponding $\boldsymbol{\alpha}$ via the new primal problem

$$\begin{aligned} \min\ & L(\boldsymbol{\alpha}, \boldsymbol{\eta}^*) \\ \text{s.t.}\ & 0 \leq \alpha_i \leq d,\ i = 1 \ldots n \end{aligned} \quad (6)$$

w.r.t. $\boldsymbol{\alpha}$. As opposed to the initial primal (1), (6) has no equality constraints. Thus, the feasibility of particular working set sizes is not affected, but we still obtain the optimal solution of the unaltered problem.

Needless to say, we cannot know $\boldsymbol{\eta}^*$ in advance. The basic idea of our MPD method is to fix some $\boldsymbol{\eta}$, solve (6) via GS — pretending that $\boldsymbol{\eta}$ is optimal — use the resulting $\boldsymbol{\alpha}$ to compute a new estimate for $\boldsymbol{\eta}$, and go back to solving (6). This is repeated until convergence, i.e. until $\boldsymbol{\eta} = \boldsymbol{\eta}^*$. The $\boldsymbol{\eta}$ estimates are updated via approximate Newton steps: since the dual function (5) is concave, we find its global optimum by merely following the direction of steepest ascent. While the derivatives of $g(\boldsymbol{\eta})$ cannot be written in closed form, the following approximation turns out to be sufficient in practice: neglecting the box constraints, we find that the minimizer of (4) reads $\boldsymbol{\alpha}^*(\boldsymbol{\eta}) = -\mathbf{H}^{-1}(\mathbf{f}_0 - \mathbf{F}\boldsymbol{\eta})$. Plugging this into (4), we get an approximation to the dual function (5), whose gradient w.r.t. $\boldsymbol{\eta}$ is given by $\mathbf{F}^\top \mathbf{H}^{-1}(\mathbf{f}_0 - \mathbf{F}\boldsymbol{\eta})$, or simply

$$\frac{\partial g}{\partial \eta_i} = \mathbf{f}_i^\top \boldsymbol{\alpha} - e_i. \qquad (7)$$

if $\boldsymbol{\alpha} = \boldsymbol{\alpha}^*(\boldsymbol{\eta})$. For the second derivatives, we assume further that the Hessian is diagonal, which yields

$$\frac{\partial^2 g}{\partial \eta_i \eta_j} = \begin{cases} -\mathbf{f}_i \mathbf{H}^{-1} \mathbf{f}_i & \text{if } i = j \\ 0 & \text{otherwise} \end{cases} \qquad (8)$$

Note that the gradient depends on $\boldsymbol{\eta}$, but is readily computed by virtue of equation (7). In contrast, the Hessian is constant, but costly to compute (8). In order to avoid a direct computation of $\mathbf{H}^{-1}$, we solve the k linear systems $\mathbf{H}\boldsymbol{\gamma}_i = -\mathbf{f}_i$ for $\boldsymbol{\gamma}_i$ via GS. After this, the diagonal elements of the Hessian (8) reduce to $\mathbf{f}_i^\top \boldsymbol{\gamma}_i$. We will see that effectively, our method trades the k equality constraints for k additional GS steps per iteration.

As an aside, a less crude approximation is to *clamp* active box constraints, i.e. assume that for all $\boldsymbol{\eta}$, the set of α_i that are at bound, is constant. In (7) and (8), this amounts to setting the components of $\mathbf{f}_i$ for which the box constraint is active, to zero. In our experiments, we could not detect a significant difference between this and the above approximation (besides a slight computational disadvantage of the former), so we decided to not use the clamping heuristic.

5.2 The Algorithm

The following paragraphs describe the minimal primal-dual algorithm in detail. An outline of the method is given as Algorithm 1, we will refer to particular line numbers in the text.

Variables and Initialization. During the whole optimization process, we keep the following variables: the current primal and dual variable $\boldsymbol{\alpha}$ and $\boldsymbol{\eta}$, the primal and dual gradient of the Lagrangian $g_{\boldsymbol{\alpha}} = \nabla_{\boldsymbol{\alpha}} L(\boldsymbol{\alpha}, \boldsymbol{\eta}) = \mathbf{H}\boldsymbol{\alpha} + \mathbf{f}_0 + \mathbf{F}\boldsymbol{\eta}$ and $g_{\boldsymbol{\eta}} = \nabla_{\boldsymbol{\eta}} L(\boldsymbol{\alpha}, \boldsymbol{\eta}) = \mathbf{F}^\top \boldsymbol{\alpha} - \mathbf{e}$. Furthermore we keep estimates of the the k Hessian diagonal elements $h_i = -\mathbf{f}_i \mathbf{H}^{-1} \mathbf{f}_i$, as well as the residuals $\mathbf{r}_i = \mathbf{H}\boldsymbol{\gamma}_i + \mathbf{f}_i$ of the corresponding linear systems. The initial value of the primal variable $\boldsymbol{\alpha}$ can be

Algorithm 1. Minimal Primal-Dual SVM Training

1: initialize primal/dual variables
2: initialize gradients
3: initialize variables for the Hessian estimation
4: **loop**
5:   update dual Hessian estimate
6:   update primal variables
7:   **if** (primal optimal) **then**
8:     **if** (dual gradient is small) **then**
9:       converged
10:    **else**
11:      update dual variables
12:    **end if**
13: **end if**
14: **end loop**

chosen arbitrarily up to the box constraints $0 \leq \alpha_i \leq d$ (see the discussion on feasibility below). For the sake of simplicity we set $\boldsymbol{\alpha} = \mathbf{0}$ (Line 2). The dual variables η_i are completely unconstrained and we set them to zero as well. This implies to $g_\alpha = \mathbf{f}_0$ and $g_\eta = -\mathbf{e}$ (Line 3). Finally, we initialize $\boldsymbol{\gamma}_i = \mathbf{0}$ and thus $h_i = 0$, $\mathbf{r}_i = \mathbf{f}_i$, $i = 1 \ldots k$ (Line 4).

Hessian and Primal Updates At the beginning of each iteration, we update the Hessian estimates h_i (Line 7). To this end, we do the following for all $i = 1 \ldots k$: we pick the largest component of the residual $\mathbf{r}_i$, $\mathbf{r}_{ij}$ say, and perform a GS step $\Delta\gamma_{ij} = -\mathbf{r}_{ij}/\mathbf{H}_{jj}$ in that direction. Note that we never actually compute the γ_i, instead, we update h_i and r_i via $\Delta h_i = -\Delta\gamma_{ij}\mathbf{f}_{ij}$ and $\Delta\mathbf{r}_i = \Delta\gamma_{ij}\mathbf{H}_j$. The next step is the primal update (Line 8) via box-constrained GS. The working set is chosen to be the α_i corresponding to the largest KKT violation ((2), (iii-v)), which is in fact a $q = 1$ version of the heuristic used by [8] and [3]. Note that this is an $\mathcal{O}(n)$ operation since we keep $\nabla_\alpha L(\boldsymbol{\alpha}, \boldsymbol{\eta})$, which is in fact the quantity $\mathbf{s}$ in (2). The GS update amounts to $\Delta\alpha_i = -s_i/\mathbf{H}_{ii}$ and the subsequent clipping of the new value to $[0; d]$. A change in α_i also affects the gradients, so we update them as well via $\Delta g_\alpha = \delta \mathbf{H}_i$ and $\Delta g_\eta = \delta \mathbf{F}_i$, where δ is the actual change in α_i after clipping.

Primal Stopping The primal updates ensured that the box constraints (and thus ((2), (ii)) are always met. Therefore, the condition in Line 9 evaluates to true as soon as ((2), (iii-v)) hold. To this end, we check if the largest (in magnitude) violation of ((2), (iii-v)) falls below a predefined primal threshold ϵ_p. Note that this can be done efficiently since the variable $\mathbf{s}$ in (2) is simply the primal gradient $\nabla_\alpha L(\boldsymbol{\alpha}, \boldsymbol{\eta})$.

Dual Stopping In Line 10, we check the current solution $\boldsymbol{\alpha}, \boldsymbol{\eta}$ for optimality. At this point we already have ((2), (ii-v)) satisfied, so what remains to be checked are the violations ((2), (i)), which coincide with the components of the dual gradient $\nabla_\eta L(\alpha, \eta)$. We therefore say that the algorithm has converged if the largest (in magnitude) component of $\nabla_\eta L(\alpha, \eta)$ is smaller than the dual stopping threshold ε_d.

Dual Updates. If the optimality check in Line 10 fails, we update the dual variables via Newton steps (Line 13) $\Delta \eta_i = -(\mathbf{f}_i^\top \alpha - \mathbf{e})/h_i$. As with the primal updates, a change in η results in a change in g_α, so we update the latter via $\Delta g_\alpha = \mathbf{F} \Delta \eta$.

5.3 Implementation

The minimal primal-dual method is designed to solve various SVM problems of the form (1) in a consistent manner. Thus, it seems natural to implement it in a two-layered fashion: a core function that implements Algorithm 1, and a wrapper function that implements the mappings in Table 1. The user may then call the wrapper function with the data and the type of SVM as arguments. The wrapper functions translates this into values for $\mathbf{H}$, $\mathbf{f}_i$, etc. and calls the core function. When the core function returns, the wrapper computes the values of the so-called free variables (such as the bias term b). This is extremely simple, since the free variables not only correspond to the equality constraints, but actually coincide with the respective dual variables η_i. This is sometimes referred to as the "dual-dual trick" [12]. It can be seen as an advantage of our algorithm (or primal-dual methods in general) over the methods described in Section 4, since the latter require a manual recovery of these values. The latter becomes difficult if the solution is degenerate, e.g. if the solution of a C-SVC lacks unbounded support vectors (see [3]). Algorithm 1 (the core) and Table 1 (the wrapper) are readily implemented in a few lines of *Matlab*, which is the version we used in our experiments. It can be downloaded from www.kyb.mpg.de/~kienzle.

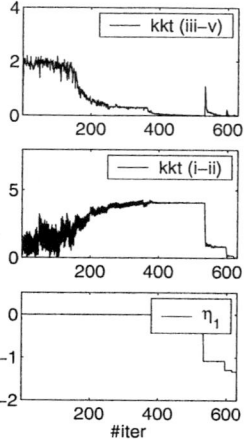

Fig. 1. Typical values for the KKT violations and the dual variable η_1 during MPD training of a C-SVC, plotted against the number of iterations. The data were two 2D Gaussians with 20 points each, standard deviation $\sigma = 1$, and their means $\sqrt{2}$ apart. We trained a C-SVC with $C = 1000$ and a Gaussian kernel with $\sigma = 1$, the stopping thresholds were set to $\varepsilon_p = \varepsilon_d = .01$. The method performed four dual updates (at iteration 532, 595, 616 and 627) among a total of 630 iterations. Notice the complementary nature of the top two plots: the primal/dual updates reduce the (iii-v)/(i) KKT violations, while sacrificing the fulfillment of the "competing" conditions (i)/(iii-v), respectively.

5.4 Complexity and Convergence

The MPD method can be seen as solving $k+1$ linear systems in parallel, where every time the primal (box constrained) system has converged, its parameters are updated using the current values from the k Hessian (unconstrained) systems. All updates are $\mathcal{O}(n)$, so each loop has time complexity $\mathcal{O}(kn)$. The total number of required operations is therefore $\mathcal{O}(tkn)$, where t is problem-dependent, as it is common to iterative methods. The memory usage is $\mathcal{O}(n)$.

It has been shown that box-constrained GS iterations (i.e. those that solve our primal problem) converge for any starting point, given that $\mathbf{H} \succeq \mathbf{0}$ (see e.g. [7] and references). The natural question arises whether the dual variables converge to their optimum $\boldsymbol{\eta}^*$. A sketch of the proof that we are currently working on is based on an idea from [1] (the actual proof will be included in a longer version of this paper): training with MPD is equivalent to solving a slightly modified problem whose solution is equivalent to that of (1), using an *Augmented Lagrangian Method*. In this setting, the method can be shown to converge if the dual stepsize is bounded from above by some threshold. Interestingly, the approximations (7) and (8) aim at satisfying this very condition. It should be mentioned that due to the approximative nature of the derivatives or because of numerical effects, the stepsizes may yet turn out too large, although we have not experienced this in our experiments. Figure 1 illustrates the typical behavior of MPD on a toy problem.

6 Experiments

In this experiment, we have tested our method on a multiple equality constraint problem called semi-parametric SV regression. To introduce this concept, recall that SVM decision (or regression) functions are linear in the reproducing kernel Hilbert space (RKHS) induced by the kernel function $K(\cdot, \cdot)$. In [13], the class of admissible (linear) functions is augmented by a parametric term. As an example, for ε-SVR we have

$$f(\mathbf{x}) = \langle \mathbf{w}, K(\mathbf{x}, \cdot) \rangle + \sum_{i=1}^{k} \beta_i \varphi_i(\mathbf{x}) \qquad (9)$$

instead of the usual $f(\mathbf{x}) = \langle \mathbf{w}, K(\mathbf{x}, \cdot) \rangle + b$. The $\varphi_i(\mathbf{x})$ allow us to incorporate domain knowledge about the target function (e.g. the presence of a sinusoidal component in f). It has been shown that each parameter β_i introduces one equality constraint $\mathbf{f}_i, e_i$ to (1), where $e_i = 0$ and $\mathbf{f}_i$ contains the values of $\varphi_i(\mathbf{x})$ on the training points $\mathbf{x}_i$. Moreover, as with all free variables, at the solution we have $\beta_i = \eta_i$ [13]. In particular, the bias term b in standard SVMs can be seen as a special case of such a β_i, namely for $\varphi_i(\mathbf{x}) = 1$.

Let us now consider the problem studied by [13], namely a semi-parametric ε-SVR on $y_i = f(\mathbf{x}_i) + \xi_i$, with $\mathbf{x}_i$ uniformly sampled from the interval $[0; 10]$ and $f(\mathbf{x}) = \sin(\mathbf{x}) + \text{sinc}(2\pi(\mathbf{x} - 5)) + \xi_i$. The noise ξ_i is zero-mean and uniform with standard deviation 0.2 and the parameter of the ε-insensitive loss function

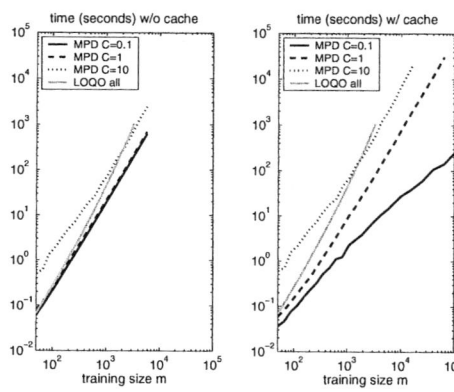

Fig. 2. Training a large-scale semi-parametric SVR with MPD vs. LOQO. The plots show cpu times against training sizes (between $m = 50$ to $m = 100000$) on a loglog scale. For the left plot, we explicitly computed the matrix $\mathbf{H}$ for both methods. Here, we increased m, until *Matlab* ran out of memory ($m \approx 3300$ for LOQO, $m \approx 5700$ for MPD). For the right plot, we used a 2Gbyte least-recently-used (LRU) kernel cache (as it is common practice, e.g. in [3]) for MPD, the LOQO plot is the same as on the left.

$\|\cdot\|_\varepsilon$ is $\varepsilon = 0.05$. The latter is not to be confused with the stopping thresholds $\varepsilon_p, \varepsilon_d$, which we set to 0.01. As in [13], our model for $f(\mathbf{x})$ has two parameters β_1, β_2 that are associated with the functions $\varphi_1(\mathbf{x}) = \sin(\mathbf{x})$, $\varphi_2(\mathbf{x}) = \mathrm{sinc}(2\pi(\mathbf{x} - 5))$. In the original experiment, the authors computed cross-validation errors for the above problem of size $m = 50$ and various values of C, which yielded an optimum at $C = 1$. Here, we test our method for three values around the optimal C, i.e. 0.1, 1 and 10, and for various training sizes $m = 50 \ldots 100000$.

Figure 2 illustrates the scaling properties of MPD training compared to that of the LOQO method [14] used in [13]; both methods are implemented in *Matlab*. We tested two versions of MPD, with and without using a cache for $\mathbf{H}$. The left plot shows the former case for $m < 3300$, which is where Matlab runs out of memory. Here, both methods yielded the same accuracy, and comparable time complexity (note that slopes on the loglog scale correspond to exponents on a linear scale). The right plot shows the performance of MPD with kernel caching (see caption). This experiment supports that MPD can deal with large training sets, e.g. up to $m = 10^5$ or more while it has a similar (in fact, slightly lower) time complexity than the LOQO method. Note that in [13], LOQO was chosen due to the lack of a more appropriate method. We suspect that it is the training size limit which prevented semi-parametric SVMs from gaining more attention in the past. MPD does not have this limitation and thus allows for further exploration of not only this but other equally interesting paradigms.

7 Discussion and Future Work

We have presented a large scale primal-dual method for SVM training. The main contributions are the following: First, the MPD method combines all standard SVM formulations into a unifying framework. Second, as with SMO or GS methods, it is straightforward to implement, scales well, and does not require external QP packages. Third, MPD is able to implement more general SVM paradigms, e.g. semi-parametric SVMs, that cannot be solved with SMO based packages, and for which generic solvers run out of memory.

What remains to be explored is whether the convergence of the Hessian estimates should be enforced *before* any dual updates are performed, since this is required for the Newton step approximations to be reliable. In the current version, we merely rely on the fact that the estimate will *eventually* have converged. Finally, in order to compare MPD to existing methods, note that for $k = 0$, MPD is equivalent to KA/SOR. A comparison of SOR and SMO can be found in [9].

Acknowledgments

The authors would like to thank Oliver Chapelle, Alexander Zien and Kristin Bennett for useful comments. This work was supported in part by the IST Programme of the European Community, under the PASCAL Network of Excellence, IST-2002-506778. This publication only reflects the authors' views.

References

1. D. P. Bertsekas. *Nonlinear Programming*. Athena Scientific, 1999.
2. C.-C. Chang and C.-J. Lin. Training ν-support vector classifiers: Theory and algorithms. *Neural Computation*, 13(9):2119–2147, 2001.
3. C.-C. Chang and C.-J. Lin. LIBSVM – a library for support vector machines, version 2.71, http://www.csie.ntu.edu.tw/~cjlin/libsvm/, August 2004.
4. P.-H. Chen, C.-J. Lin, and B. Schölkopf. A tutorial on ν-support vector machines. *Applied Stochastic Models in Business and Industry (to appear)*, 2005.
5. R. Collobert and S. Bengio. SVMTorch: Support vector machines for large-scale regression problems. *Journal of Machine Learning Research*, 1:143–160, 2001.
6. J. Dong, A. Krzyzak, and C. Y. Suen. Fast svm training algorithm with decomposition on very large data sets. *IEEE Transactions on Pattern Analysis and Machine Intelligence*, 27(4):603–618, April 2005.
7. T. Friess, N. Cristianini, and C. Campbell. The kernel adatron algorithm: a fast and simple learning procedure for support vector machine. In *International Conference on Machine Learning*, pages 188–196, 1998.
8. T. Joachims. Making large-scale SVM learning practical. In B. Schlkopf, C. Burges, and A. Smola, editors, *Advances in Kernel Methods*, pages 42–56. MIT Press, 1999.
9. O. L. Mangasarian and D. R. Musicant. Successive overrelaxation for support vector machines. *IEEE Transactions on Neural Networks*, 10:1032–1037, 1999.
10. E. Osuna, R. Freund, and F. Girosi. Support vector machines: Training and applications. Technical Report AIM-1602, 1997.
11. J. Platt. Fast training of support vector machines using sequential minimal optimization. In B. Schlkopf, C. Burges, and A. Smola, editors, *Advances in Kernel Methods*, pages 185–208. MIT Press, 1998.
12. B. Schölkopf and A. J. Smola. *Learning with Kernels*. MIT Press, Cambridge, MA, 2002.
13. A. J. Smola, T. Friess, and B. Schölkopf. Semiparametric support vector and linear programming machines. In *Advances in Neural Information Processing Systems 11*, pages 585–591, 1998.
14. R. J Vanderbei. LOQO: An interior point code for quadratic programming. Technical Report SOR 94-15, Princeton University, NJ, 1994.

A Model Based Method for Automatic Facial Expression Recognition

Hans van Kuilenburg[1], Marco Wiering[2], and Marten den Uyl[3]

[1] VicarVision, Amsterdam, The Netherlands
van.kuilenburg@wanadoo.nl
http://home.wanadoo.nl/van.kuilenburg/
[2] Utrecht University, Utrecht, The Netherlands
marco@cs.uu.nl
[3] VicarVision, Amsterdam, The Netherlands
denuyl@vicarvision.nl

Abstract. Automatic facial expression recognition is a research topic with interesting applications in the field of human-computer interaction, psychology and product marketing. The classification accuracy for an automatic system which uses static images as input is however largely limited by the image quality, lighting conditions and the orientation of the depicted face. These problems can be partially overcome by using a holistic model based approach called the Active Appearance Model. A system will be described that can classify expressions from one of the emotional categories joy, anger, sadness, surprise, fear and disgust with remarkable accuracy. It is also able to detect smaller, local facial features based on minimal muscular movements described by the Facial Action Coding System (FACS). Finally, we show how the system can be used for expression analysis and synthesis.

1 Introduction

Facial expressions can contain a great deal of information and the desire to automatically extract this information has been continuously increasing. Several applications for automatic facial expression recognition can be found in the field of human-computer interaction. In every day human-to-human interaction, information is exchanged in a highly multi-modal way in which speech only plays a modest role. An effective automatic expression recognition system could take human-computer interaction to the next level.

Automatic expression analysis can be of particular relevance for a number of expression monitoring applications where it would be undesirable or even infeasible to manually annotate the available data. E.g., the reaction of people in test-panels could be automatically monitored and forensic investigation could benefit from a method to automatically detect signs of extreme emotions, fear or aggression as an early warning system.

Decades of research have already led to the development of systems that achieve a reasonable expression classification performance. A detailed account of all the advances on the field of automatic expression analysis can be found in [17] or [10]. Unfortunately, most of the developed systems have severe limitations on the settings of their use, making them unsuitable for real-life applications.

The limitations in automatic expression classification performance are to a large extend the result of the high variability that can be found in images containing a face. If we do not want to be limited to a specific setting and if we do not want to require active participation of the individuals depicted on the images, we will see an extremely large variety in lighting conditions, resolution, pose and orientation. In order to be able to analyze all these images correctly, an approach seems to be desirable that can compactly detect and describe these sources of variation and thus separate them from the actual information we are looking for.

The Active Appearance Model (AAM) first described by Cootes and Taylor [4] enables us to (fully) automatically create a model of a face depicted in an image. The created models are realistic looking faces, closely resembling the original. Previous research projects have indicated that the AAM provides a good generalization to varying lighting / pose conditions as it is able to compactly represent these sources of variations.

Many leading researchers in the field of expression classification have chosen very different, local methods for classification. Local methods have the advantage of potentiality achieving a very high resolution in a small area of the face. However, as they lack global facial information, it will be very hard for a local method to separate changes caused by differences in lighting or pose from changes caused by expressions. Consequently, the local method will have rather poor generalization properties. We do not want to limit ourself to situations where we have high-resolution video material available either, but instead want a single facial image to be sufficient. We have therefore chosen to use the holistic, model based Active Appearance Model as our core technique. To make this system fully automatic, a deformable template face framing method, very similar to the one described in [20] is used preliminary to the AAM modeling phase.

The next section will describe the AAM implementation that was used for this project (based on previous work by [16]). In section 3 we will show how appearance models can be used to classify facial expressions based on two different categorization systems. Section 4 describes how we can further analyze or synthesize facial expressions. Finally, we will come to a conclusion in section 5.

2 The Active Appearance Model

To train the AAM [4], we require the presence of a (manually) annotated set X of facial images. The shape of a face is defined by a *shape vector* S containing the coordinates of M *landmark points* in a face image I.

$$S = ((x_1, y_1), (x_2, y_2), ..., (x_M, y_M))^T$$

Landmark points are points in the 2D plane of a face image at easily distinguishable reference points, points which can be identified reliably in any face image we might want to analyze. Considering the invariability of shapes under Euclidian transformations, we can remove the effect of misplacement, size and rotation by aligning each shape vector in the set of all shape vectors X^s to the mean shape vector $\bar{s}$, which can be implemented as an iterative procedure.

We then apply Principle Component Analysis (PCA) [13], which transforms the shapes to a new low dimensional shape subspace in R^D where $D < 2M$. An element S from the original set of shapes can now be approximated by some b^s of length D where:

$$S \approx \Phi^s \cdot b^s + \bar{s} \qquad (1)$$

Where Φ^s is the covariance matrix consisting of the D principal orthogonal modes of variation in X^s:

$$\Phi^s = (e_1^s|e_2^s|...|e_D^s)$$

The eigenvalues λ_j^s of the covariance matrix define the variance of the data in the direction of the corresponding eigenvector e_j^s. Thus, when generating new shapes, we can bound the elements in b^s as shown below, to allow variation within 99% of a normally distributed function:

$$-3\sqrt{\lambda_j^s} \leq b_j^s \leq 3\sqrt{\lambda_j^s}$$

A *texture vector* of a face image is defined as the vector of intensity values of N pixels that lie within the outer bounds of the corresponding shape vector:

$$T = [g_1, g_2, ..., g_N]^T$$

Delauny triangulation [19] is performed on the texture maps to transform them to a reference shape (the mean shape can be used for this). This results in so called *shape-free patches* of pixel intensities, which should then be *photometrically aligned* to remove the effect of general lightning differences. This can again be done using an iterative approach.

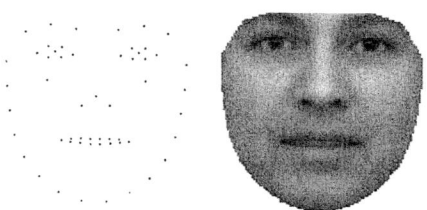

Fig. 1. The mean face shape and the mean face texture aligned to the mean shape

PCA is then applied on the texture vectors, after which a texture vector T from the original data set can be represented by a vector b^t.

$$T \approx \Phi^t \cdot b^t + \bar{t} \qquad (2)$$

The elements in b^t are again bounded by:

$$-3\sqrt{\lambda_k^t} \leq b_k^t \leq 3\sqrt{\lambda_k^t}$$

Where λ_k^t represents the eigenvalue of the corresponding eigenvector across the data set X^t.

The appearance model combines the two vectors b^s and b^t into a single parameter vector b^a. First, the shape and texture vector are concatenated. Because these two are of a different nature and thus of a different relevance, one of the terms will be weighted:

$$b^{st} = \begin{pmatrix} w^s b^s \\ b^t \end{pmatrix}$$

Estimating the correct value for w^s can be done by systematically displacing the elements of the shape vector over the examples in the training set and calculating the corresponding difference in pixel intensity. As an alternative, we can set w^s as the ratio of the total pixel intensity variation to the total shape variation. PCA is then applied one last time to remove possible correlation between shape and texture parameters and create an even more compact representation:

$$b^{st} = \Phi^a b^a \tag{3}$$

We will refer to b^a as the *appearance vector* from now on as it compactly describes both the shape and the texture of an object.

The online task of the Active Appearance Model is to find a model instance which optimally models the face in a previously unseen image (a model-fit). Given a face image I, the AAM attempt to find the optimal model parameters b^a and the optimal pose parameters $u = [t^x, t^y, s, \Theta]^T$ where t^x and t^y are translations in the x and y directions, s is the scaling factor and Θ is the rotation.

The difference vector $\delta t = t^{image} - t^{model}$ defines the difference in pixel intensity between input image and the model instance. By minimizing $E = ||\delta t||^2$ we thus minimize the difference in pixel intensities. The method used by the AAM for doing this assumes that the optimal parameter update can be estimated from δt. Moreover, this relationship is assumed to be nearly linear.

A prediction matrix is used to update the model parameters b^a and u in an iterative way until no significant change occurs anymore. Usually, separate prediction matrices are used for b^a and u, so we have:

$$\delta b^a = R^{b^a} \delta t \quad \text{and} \quad \delta u = R^u \delta t$$

The prediction matrices R^{b^a} and R^u are learned from the training data by linear regression using examples which are systematically displaced over one of the model or pose parameters.

After obtaining the prediction matrices, parameters are updated in an iterative way ($b^a \leftarrow b^a + \alpha \delta b^a$ and $u \leftarrow u + \alpha \delta u$) where α is a stepsize parameter, until no significant change in error occurs anymore. Under this iterative approach, the linearity assumption seems to hold well enough when the initial model placement does not deviate too much from the actual position of the face in the image.

3 Expressions and Classification

In order to create a system that can automatically derive meaningful expression information from a face, it might prove important to have a clear and formalized method of describing the expression on a face, for which several methods have been proposed. We describe two commonly used classification systems for facial expressions and then present our results.

3.1 Facial Action Coding System (FACS)

The Facial Action Coding System (FACS) presented by Ekman & Friesen in 1978 [7] is by far the most used system. It codes the various possible facial movements based on an analysis of the facial anatomy. FACS contains a list of approximately (depending on the specific revision) 46 minimal facial movements called 'Action Units' and their underlying muscular basis. Over the years, this system has become a standard for coding facial expressions. The original system has undergone a major revision in 2002 [9] and extended to include gradations of activation for the Action Units (AUs).

Using FACS, practically all facial cues can be accurately described in terms of Action Units, which appear to be the smallest possible changing units in a face. This makes it a very powerful system to accurately annotate facial expressions.

The only major downside to this approach is the fact that no or little meaning can be attached to the activation of one of the Action Units. E.g., to know that the Levator palpebrae superioris is contracted is information that might only be relevant for a very select number of applications. Instead, a categorization based on the meaning expressions convey may be more useful for most applications.

3.2 Emotional Expressions

Many expressions carry an emotional content with them. The exact relationship between expressions and emotions has been studied extensively, which has resulted in several theories. For a detailed discussion see [11, 8, 18, 6].

Already in 1970, P. Ekman reported the existence of 6 universal facial expressions related to the emotional states: anger, disgust, fear, joy, sadness and surprise [5]. A constant debate on whether these expressions are really universal, or vary by culture, has been going on ever since.

Obviously it is not the case that any expression can be classified into one of Ekman's 6 emotional expression categories [12]. Facial movements can be of varying intensity and there are blends of emotional expressions and variations within a category. Also, there are facial movements which are meant only for conversational purposes or are considered idiosyncratic. However, if we do want to make a categorization of expressions based on emotions, Ekman's universal emotional expressions might be an obvious choice, for the system is already widely used and categories that are made represent clear concepts, making them intuitively easy to deal with.

3.3 Automatic Emotion Expression Classification

In the previous section, we described how the AAM can be used to derive a realistic model of a depicted face. There are several ways to extract a compact representation of the facial features using this model. After a model fit has been created, the accurate position of a face is clear and so are the locations of all the key points in the face (the landmark points). This introduces two promising options. First, accurate image slices can be made of selected regions of the face to be used directly by a classifier or after applying a 'smart' compression. However, an easier option seems to exist. The face model which has been constructed is represented entirely by a very compact vector (the appearance vector). This appearance vector could be perfectly suitable for use as input for a classification method, if it contains all relevant information needed to distinguish between the different expression classes. Previous experiments [21, 14] have shown that this latter option gives far better results.

Our goal is to come to a classification of all the 6 universal emotional expressions, plus the neutral expression. In principle, we can achieve this by creating and training 7 independent classifiers. We used neural networks trained with backpropagation since these have been proven their abilities for pattern recognition tasks [1]. The final expression judgement of a face image could then be based on the network with the highest output. Experiments have shown, however, that the networks resulting from this procedure miss what you might call 'mutual responsiveness'. When observing a series of images, where one emotional expression is shown with increased intensity, one would expect the output of one network to increase and the outputs of the other networks to automatically decrease or level out to zero. However, this behavior does not appear in all situations and not seldom are there several or no networks at all with a high output, even though this situation does not appear in the training data.

We can create more favorable behavior by training one classification network with 7 outputs for the different emotional categories. This also boosts overall performance significantly. We used a 3-layer feed-forward neural network, with 94 input neurons (=the length of the appearance vector), 15 hidden neurons and 7 output neurons (=the number of expression categories). We used the backpropagation algorithm to train the network and leave-one-out cross-validation to determine the true test performance. The optimal number of training epochs (which was around 1500) was estimated by iteratively searching around the optimum found using a small stop-set. The training material consisted of 1512 appearance vectors that were automatically extracted and had an accurate AAM fit.

Table 1 shows the results in the form of a confusion matrix when we force the network to make a choice (by picking the highest output value) on the 'Karolinska Directed Emotional Faces' set [15] containing 980 high quality facial images showing one of the universal emotional expressions or a neutral expression. 89% of all faces presented to the classifier is classified correctly, which is a very promising result as it is among the highest reported results on emotional expression classification from static images.

Table 1. Performance of the 7-fold classifier on the Karolinska data set using leave-one-out cross-validation

predicted \ actual	happy	angry	sad	surprise	scared	disgust	neutral	recall
happy	138	1	3	0	0	1	0	0.97
angry	0	116	4	1	8	5	11	0.80
sad	1	2	109	6	5	3	2	0.85
surprise	0	1	19	128	2	0	1	0.85
scared	0	3	2	0	115	3	1	0.93
disgust	0	11	1	0	5	125	0	0.88
neutral	1	0	1	0	3	0	125	0.96
precision	0.99	0.87	0.78	0.95	0.83	0.91	0.89	0.89

3.4 FACS Classification

Although we have mainly focussed on the automatic classification of facial expressions in one of Ekman's 6 universal emotional expression categories, we have as a side-study, trained the system to give the FACS scoring of a face (using the 2002 revision including gradations). If this classifier performs well, this would suggest that even local features can be modeled correctly by the AAM, without requiring a training set specifically selected for this.

Action Units (AUs) described by the FACS do not necessarily have to be independent. In practice, there are many constraints on the co-occurrence of AUs. This is reason to take a similar approach as we did for the emotional classifier concerning the choice between building separate classifiers and building one large classifier for all AUs at once. If there are constraints, these can be modeled in the large network and outputs could be better adjusted to one another.

For some AUs, far too little training data was available to perform a meaningful training. Only the 15 AUs present most frequently in the training set (AUs 1, 2, 4, 5, 6, 7, 9, 12, 15, 17, 20, 23, 24, 25 and 27) were therefore selected for training. This limits the functionality of the system, but retraining the classifier with more annotated faces will always remain an option for real applications. Again, we used a 3-layer feedforward neural network, with 94 input neurons, 20 hidden neurons and 15 output neurons (=the number of selected AUs) and use backpropagation with leave-one-out cross-validation. The training material consisted of 858 appearance vectors of images from the Cohn-Kanade AU-Coded Facial Expression Database [3] with an accurate AAM fit.

Table 2 shows the performance of the FACS classifier after training, where a classification is considered correct if it does not deviate more than one point on the five-point scale of intensity by which the training data is annotated. The AUs are detected with an average accuracy of 86%, but it should be mentioned

Table 2. FACS classifier performance on 15 Action Units

Action Unit:	01	02	04	05	06	07	09	12	15	17	20	23	24	25	27	Average
Accuracy:	.86	.88	.81	.86	.81	.89	.93	.83	.89	.86	.84	.83	.83	.90	.89	**.86**

that this still means that most classified faces will have one or more AUs scored incorrectly. If we are only interested in the activation of one or two AUs, these results are promising, but if we are looking for an accurate automatic FACS scoring device, significant improvements are still needed.

4 Expression Analysis and Synthesis

The previous experiments have shown that the appearance vector contains expression information that can be used to classify a face model. Alternatively, it is also possible to extract and isolate the information that is related to expressions, which enables us to visualize the distinguishing features for a certain expression and also allows expression synthesis.

4.1 Visualization of Features Relevant for Emotional Expression Classification

Blanz and Vetter (1999) have shown that the information concerning expressions can be extracted from appearance vectors in a straightforward way. Consider two images of the same individual with similar lighting and pose, one image showing some expression and the other showing a neutral face. We can calculate the difference between the two corresponding appearance vectors, which would give us information about the expression shown for this person. By averaging over a set of image-pairs, we can derive 'prototypical vectors' for a certain expression.

Besides some concerns about the reliability of this approach, since features might be averaged out, another downside is the fact that although the derived 'prototypical vectors' can give some cues to what expressions look like, where they are formed and what influence they have on shape and texture of a face, they can not be used directly to analyze those features which are important to *distinguish* one expression from another, even though this would be very useful information to have for anyone working in the field of expression classification.

There is an alternative possibility however. Consider a feedforward neural network, which is calculated as [1]:

$$y_k = g(\sum_{j=0}^{M_2} w_{kj} f(\sum_{i=0}^{M_1} w_{ji} x_i)) \qquad (4)$$

Where y_k is the output of the k-th output neuron; g and f are the activation functions of the output layer and hidden layer respectively, w_{kj} is the weight between the k-th output neuron and the j-th hidden neuron, w_{ji} is the weight between the j-th hidden neuron and the i-th input neuron and x_i is the activation of the i-th input neuron.

We train a network using face images showing a certain expression as positive examples and using images of all other expressions as negative examples. This network turns out to have an optimal (or nearly optimal) performance when it has only one hidden neuron. In this case formula 4 can be greatly simplified to:

$$y_1 = g(w_1 f(\sum_{i=0}^{M_1} w_{1i} x_i)) \tag{5}$$

Since all our input neurons are connected to all hidden neurons, we can also write: $y_1 = g(w_1 f(w^T x))$ where x is the input vector and w is a vector containing the weights between input neurons and hidden neuron.

By iteratively propagating an error over the network we can find an instance of x which gives the output $y_1 = 1$. This is not necessary however, as we can already see in the formula above that w determines exactly the relative magnitude of the influence the input neurons will have on the output of the network, since functions g and h are monotonously increasing and w_1 only determines the sign of this influence. w thus denotes the relevance of elements in the appearance vector for the classifier output.

In order to visualize what w represents, we can create a new model instance where we take w directly as the appearance vector ($b^a = w$) with the bias value left out of w. As explained in section 2, we can extract the uncompressed texture and shape vectors from this new appearance vector using formulas 1 and 2, but for visualization purposes we do not add the mean shape and texture. These vectors are indicators of the relevance of either the positioning of landmark points or the pixel intensity in a shape-free patch. The relevance of pixel intensities can be visualized straightforwardly as shown in figure 2. All elements have been converted to absolute values, and a global scaling and offset operator has been used to create black pixels for the most significant indicators and white pixels for what is considered not significant at all by the classifier.

Some of the features we can distinguish are according to what we might have expected beforehand, just to name a few, we can see the changes in the mouth corners when a person smiles, the drawn together eyebrows for an angry face, eyes being slightly closed and opened wide for the sad and surprised expression respectively, the 'lip puckerer' in the sad expression and the widened nose in the disgusted expression. Another indicator that the method is working successfully is that the irises are considered irrelevant for all expressions since their appearance remains fairly constant for all expressions. Other features that are considered very significant by the classifier are less obvious to explain and might be interesting material for experts to look at and further analyze.

The vector containing the relevance of shape information does not consist of coordinates, but rather of directed velocity vectors starting at the landmark points we have defined. This can be visualized by drawing the velocity vectors using the mean shape as a reference frame [21].

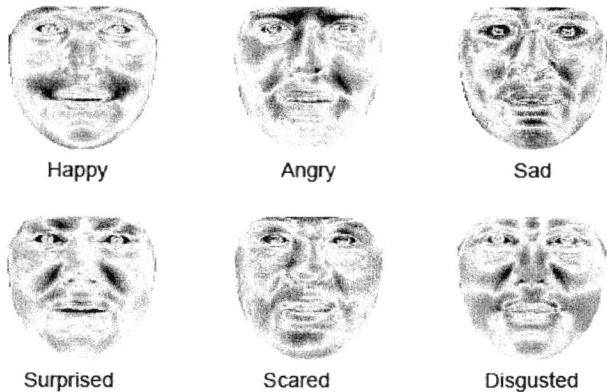

Fig. 2. Relevance of texture information for the 6 emotional expression classifier

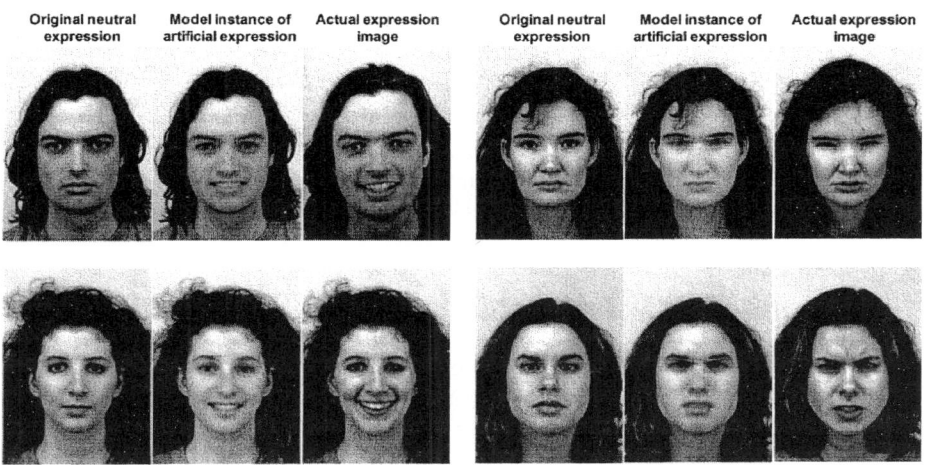

Fig. 3. Artificially created expressions; original images from [15]

4.2 Expression Synthesis Through Network Analysis

In the previous experiment, we have modeled the information considered relevant by an emotional expression classifier. If we on the other hand purely want to synthesize an expression, the discriminating features between one emotional expression and all the other different expression categories are of little use. Therefore, we trained new neural networks using only neutral images and images of one emotional expression category at a time. Thus, the discriminating features the classifier is supposed to model are those features which discriminate between a neutral face and a face showing some expression. Extracting the weight vector from these networks and adding a multiple of them to an appearance vector might proof to be a successful way for expression synthesis. Since the elements of the appearance vector are orthogonal, this is a valid operation.

Figure 3 gives some examples of neutral faces which have been changed into faces displaying a certain expression using the method above. As a reference, a real picture of the person displaying this expression has been added.

The artificially created expressions look natural and convincing and only little identity information appears to be lost. As we only have one fixed difference vector for each expression, one might expect that the synthesized expressions contain no personal traits. However, the two series on the right in figure 3 show that variations in expressions can occur for different initial model instances.

5 Conclusions

By using the Active Appearance Model and directly using the appearance vectors as classifier input, we have managed to achieve very promising classification performance. Since we are using a model based method, lighting and orientation differences have little, if any, effect on the classifier's performance. Background variation is no significant problem for the system and the system requires only static images of reasonable quality; laboratory conditions are not required.

An emotional expression classifier was trained which has an accuracy of 89%. The emotional expressions that were investigated must thus have been represented quite accurately in the appearance vectors. Using a similar approach, a classifier has been trained to detect very local facial movements which can be coded using the Facial Action Coding System. This classifier has been trained on 15 different facial movements (Action Units) and classifies each Action Unit with an average performance of 86%.

Using trained classification networks, it is possible to visualize exactly what the classifiers consider relevant/discriminating information for a certain expression. This provides us with accurate information concerning the areas of the face which provide information that is important for a good classifier performance. Further analysis of these results is needed in order to come to a more detailed conclusion.

Again using information obtained from trained classifiers, a difference vector can be extracted which characterizes a certain emotional expression. By adding this difference vector to the appearance vector of a face model, we have shown how expressions can be generated. This method seems to work rather well, as only little personal information appears to be lost, while the generated expressions are clearly identifiable and convincing to a human observer.

References

1. C. M. Bishop. *Neural Networks for Pattern Recognition.* Clarendon Press, Oxford, 1995.
2. V. Blanz and T. Vetter. A morphable model for the synthesis of 3D faces. In *Proceedings of the 26th annual conference on Computer graphics and interactive techniques*, pages 187–194. ACM Press/Addison-Wesley Publishing Co., 1999.

3. J.F. Cohn and T. Kanade. Cohn-Kanade AU-Coded Facial Expression Database. Pittsburgh University, 1999.
4. T. Cootes and C. Taylor. Statistical models of appearance for computer vision. Technical report, University of Manchester, Wolfson Image Analysis Unit, Imaging Science and Biomedical Engineering, 2000.
5. P. Ekman. Universal facial expressions of emotion. *California Mental Health Research Digest*, 8:151–158, 1970.
6. P. Ekman and R.J. Davidson. *The Nature of Emotion - Fundamental Questions*. Oxford University Press, New York, 1994.
7. P. Ekman and W. Friesen. *Facial Action Coding System: A Technique for the Measurement of Facial Movement*. Consulting Psychologists Press, Palo Alto, CA, 1978.
8. P. Ekman, W.V. Friesen, and P. Ellsworth. *Emotion in the Human Face*. Pergamon Press, 1972.
9. P. Ekman, W.V. Friesen, and J.C. Hager. *The Facial Action Coding System*. Weidenfeld & Nicolson, London, 2002.
10. B. Fasel and J. Luettin. Automatic facial expression analysis: A survey. *Pattern Recognition*, 36(1):259–275, 2003.
11. N. Frijda. *The Emotions*. Cambridge University Press & Editions de la Maison des Sciences de l'Homme, Cambridge, Paris, 1986.
12. J. Hager and P. Ekman. The essential behavioral science of the face and gesture that computer scientists need to know. In *Proceedings of the International Workshop on Automatic Face and Gesture Recognition*, pages 7–11, 1995.
13. J.E. Jackson. *A User's Guide to Principal Components*. John Wiley and Sons, Inc., 1991.
14. E. Lebert. Facial expression classification. Experiment report, Sentient Machine Research, Amsterdam, the Netherlands, 1997.
15. D. Lundqvist, A. Flykt, and A. Öhman. The Karolinska Directed Emotional Faces - KDEF. CD ROM from Department of Clinical Neuroscience, Psychology section, Karolinska Institutet, 1998.
16. M. Nieber. Global structure of the ActiveModelLib. Software architecture description, Vicar Vision BV, Amsterdam, the Netherlands, 2003.
17. M. Pantic. Automatic analysis of facial expressions: The state of the art. *IEEE Transactions on Pattern Analysis and Machine Intelligence*, 22(12):1424–1445, 2000.
18. J.A. Russell and J.M. Fernandez-Dols, editors. *The Psychology of Facial Expression*. Cambridge University Press, 1997.
19. J.R. Shewchuk. Triangle: engineering a 2D quality mesh generator and Delaunay triangulator. *Applied Computational Geometry, FCRC96 Workshop*, pages 203–222, 1996.
20. K.K. Sung and T. Poggio. Example-based learning for view-based human face detection. *IEEE Transactions on Pattern Analysis and Machine Intelligence*, 20(1):39–51, 1998.
21. H. Van Kuilenburg. Expressions exposed: Model based methods for expression analysis. Master's thesis, Department of Philosophy, Utrecht University, The Netherlands, 2005.

Margin-Sparsity Trade-Off for the Set Covering Machine

François Laviolette[1], Mario Marchand[1], and Mohak Shah[2]

[1] IFT-GLO, Université Laval,
Sainte-Foy (QC) Canada, G1K-7P4
{Francois.Laviolette, Mario.Marchand}@ift.ulaval.ca
[2] SITE, University of Ottawa,
Ottawa, Ont. Canada, K1N-6N5
mshah@site.uottawa.ca

Abstract. We propose a new learning algorithm for the set covering machine and a tight data-compression risk bound that the learner can use for choosing the appropriate tradeoff between the sparsity of a classifier and the magnitude of its separating margin.

1 Introduction

There exists a wide spectrum of different leaning strategies currently used by learning algorithms to produce classifiers having good generalization. At one end of the spectrum, we have the set covering machine (SCM), proposed by Marchand and Shawe-Taylor (2002), that tries to find the sparsest classifier having few training errors. At the other end of the spectrum, we have the support vector machine (SVM), proposed by Boser et. al. (1992), that tries to find the maximum soft-margin separating hyperplane on the training data. Since both of these learning machines can produce classifiers having good generalization, it is worthwhile to investigate if classifiers with improved generalization could be found by learning algorithms that try to optimize a nontrivial function that depends on both the sparsity of a classifier and the magnitude of its separating margin.

There seems to be a widespread belief that learning algorithms should somehow try to find such a non-trivial margin-sparsity trade-off. For example, to find a sparser SVM (but with a smaller margin), Bennett (1999) and Bi et. al. (2003) have proposed to minimize an ℓ_1-norm functional (instead of the traditional ℓ_2-norm) and have found that, indeed, the sparser SVM sometimes had better generalization. Therefore, from this SVM perspective, we should consider algorithms that minimizes an ℓ_β-norm functional for any $\beta \in [0, 2]$. In the $\beta = 2$ limit, we obtain the SVM with the largest possible separating margin (without considering its sparsity). In the $\beta = 0$ limit, we would obtain the sparsest SVM (without considering the magnitude of its separating margin). This parameter β would then control the margin-sparsity trade-off of the final classifier. Unfortunately, this optimization problem is currently efficiently solvable only for $\beta = 2$ and 1.

This computational difficulty does not arise (so abruptly) if, instead, we consider margin-sparsity trade-off learning algorithms from the SCM perspective. Indeed, the learning algorithm for the SCM proposed by Marchand and Shawe-Taylor (2002) consists of a set covering greedy heuristic that, at each greedy step, appends, to a conjunction, the Boolean-valued feature that covers the largest number of negative examples without making too many errors on the positive examples. If, in addition, we force the algorithm to use only features having the property that all the (remaining) training examples are at least a distance γ from its decision surface, we are assured that a conjunction of such features will give a classifier having no training examples within a distance γ of its decision surface. In the $\gamma = 0$ limit, the goal of the learner is to produce the sparsest SCM without considering the magnitude of its separating margin (as in the original SCM algorithm). For finite γ, we will achieve a separating margin of at least γ at the expense of having more features in the SCM. Hence, γ is a parameter that controls the margin-sparsity trade-off of the final classifier without introducing any substantial computational difficulty. We therefore propose, in Section 3, a margin-sparsity trade-off learning algorithm for the SCM which was inspired by this simple idea.

The widespread belief that learning algorithms should try to find a non-trivial margin-sparsity trade-off is, to our knowledge, not currently supported by a generalization error bound (also called risk bound) that explicitly depends on *both* the sparsity of a classifier *and* the magnitude of its separating margin. However, both sparsity and margin can be considered as different forms of data-compression. Indeed, sparsity is a form of data compression known as sample-compression (Littlestone and Warmuth, 1986) since it means that a classifier can be reconstructed from a small subset of the training data. Less obviously, the magnitude of the separating margin of a classifier can also be considered as a form of data compression since it means that there exists a small code that can specify a "good" location for the classifier's decision surface. For the SCM of Marchand and Shawe-Taylor (2002), each *data-dependent ball* feature is identified by two training points: a *center* and a *border* (to define the radius of the ball). In section 3, we propose instead to code the radius of each ball by a *message string*. Hence, the existence of a large margin of "equally good radius values" for a ball will imply the existence of a short code for its radius. With this new version of the SCM, we therefore identify each classifier by two distinct information sources: a *compression set* which consists of the center of each ball in the classifier and a *message string* which encodes the radius value of each ball.

In section 2 of this paper, we therefore propose a tight data-compression risk bound that depends explicitly on these two information sources. This bound therefore exhibits a non trivial trade-off between sparsity (the inverse of the compression set size) and the margin (the inverse of the message length) that classifiers should attempt to optimize on the training data. In contrast with other sample-compression bounds, the proposed bound is valid for any compression set-dependent distribution of messages and, as we argue, permits the usage of smaller message strings which, in turn, can help reduce significantly the size of the risk bound. We then show, in section 3, how we can apply this risk bound to the SCM by providing an appropriate compression set-dependent distribution of messages. Finally, we show, on natural data sets, that the new SCM algorithm compares favorably to the SCM algorithm of Marchand and Shawe-Taylor (2002) and we also show that the data-compression risk bound is an effective guide for choosing the proper margin-sparsity trade-off of a classifier.

2 A Data-Compression Risk Bound

We consider binary classification problems where the input space $\mathcal{X}$ consists of an arbitrary subset of $\mathbb{R}^n$ and the output space $\mathcal{Y} = \{-1, +1\}$. An example $\mathbf{z} \stackrel{\text{def}}{=} (\mathbf{x}, y)$ is an input-output pair where $\mathbf{x} \in \mathcal{X}$ and $y \in \mathcal{Y}$. We are interested in learning algorithms that have the following property. Given a training set $S = \{\mathbf{z}_1, \ldots, \mathbf{z}_m\}$ of m examples, the classifier $A(S)$ returned by algorithm A is described entirely by two *complementary sources of information*: a subset $\mathbf{z_i}$ of S, called the *compression set*, and a *message string* σ which represents the additional information needed to obtain a classifier from the compression set $\mathbf{z_i}$.

Given a training set S, the compression set $\mathbf{z_i}$ is defined by a vector $\mathbf{i}$ of indices $\mathbf{i} \stackrel{\text{def}}{=} (i_1, i_2, \ldots, i_{|\mathbf{i}|})$ with $i_j \in \{1, \ldots, m\}$ $\forall j$ and $i_1 < i_2 < \ldots < i_{|\mathbf{i}|}$ and where $|\mathbf{i}|$ denotes the number of indices present in $\mathbf{i}$. Hence, $\mathbf{z}_i$ denotes the ith example of S whereas $\mathbf{z_i}$ denotes the subset of examples of S that are pointed by the vector of indices $\mathbf{i}$ defined above. We will use $\bar{\mathbf{i}}$ to denote the set of indices not present in $\mathbf{i}$. Hence, we have $S = \mathbf{z_i} \cup \mathbf{z_{\bar{i}}}$ for any vector $\mathbf{i} \in \mathcal{I}$ where $\mathcal{I}$ denotes the set of the 2^m possible realizations of $\mathbf{i}$.

The fact that any classifier returned by algorithm A is described by a compression set and a message string implies that there exists a *reconstruction function* $\mathcal{R}$, associated with A, that outputs a classifier $\mathcal{R}(\sigma, \mathbf{z_i})$ when given an arbitrary compression set $\mathbf{z_i} \subseteq S$ and message string σ chosen from the set $\mathcal{M}(\mathbf{z_i})$ of all distinct messages that can be supplied to $\mathcal{R}$ with the compression set $\mathbf{z_i}$. It is only when such a $\mathcal{R}$ exists that the classifier returned by $A(S)$ is *always* identified by a compression set $\mathbf{z_i}$ and a message string σ.

The perceptron learning rule and the SVM are examples of learning algorithms where the final classifier can be reconstructed solely from a compression set (Graepel. et. al.,2000, 2001). In contrast, the reconstruction function for SCMs needs both a compression set and a message string. Later, we will see how the learner can trade-off the compression set size with the length of the message string to obtain a classifier with a smaller risk bound and, hopefully, a smaller true risk.

We seek a tight risk bound for arbitrary reconstruction functions that holds uniformly for all compression sets and message strings. For this, we adopt the PAC setting where each example $\mathbf{z}$ is drawn according to a fixed, but unknown, probability distribution D on $\mathcal{X} \times \mathcal{Y}$. The risk $R(f)$ of any classifier f is defined as the probability that it misclassifies an example drawn according to D:

$$R(f) \stackrel{\text{def}}{=} \Pr_{(\mathbf{x},y) \sim D} (f(\mathbf{x}) \neq y) = \mathbf{E}_{(\mathbf{x},y) \sim D} I(f(\mathbf{x}) \neq y)$$

where $I(a) = 1$ if predicate a is true and 0 otherwise. Given a training set $S = \{\mathbf{z}_1, \ldots, \mathbf{z}_m\}$ of m examples, the *empirical risk* $R_S(f)$ on S, of any classifier f, is defined according to:

$$R_S(f) \stackrel{\text{def}}{=} \frac{1}{m} \sum_{i=1}^{m} I(f(\mathbf{x}_i) \neq y_i) \stackrel{\text{def}}{=} \mathbf{E}_{(\mathbf{x},y) \sim S} I(f(\mathbf{x}) \neq y)$$

Let $\mathbf{Z}^m$ denote the collection of m random variables whose instantiation gives a training sample $S = \mathbf{z}^m = \{\mathbf{z}_1, \ldots, \mathbf{z}_m\}$. Let us denote $\Pr_{\mathbf{Z}^m \sim D^m}(\cdot)$ by $\mathbf{P}_{\mathbf{Z}^m}(\cdot)$. To obtain the tightest possible risk bound, we fully exploit the fact that the distribution of classification errors is a binomial. The binomial tail distribution $\text{Bin}(\frac{k}{m}, r)$ associated with a classifier of (true) risk r is defined as the probability that this classifier makes at most k errors on a test set of m examples: $\text{Bin}\left(\frac{k}{m}, r\right) \stackrel{\text{def}}{=} \sum_{i=0}^{k} \binom{m}{i} r^i (1-r)^{m-i}$.

Following Langford (2005) and Blum and Langford (2003), we now define the *binomial tail inversion* $\overline{\text{Bin}}\left(\frac{k}{m}, \delta\right)$ as the largest risk value that a classifier can have while still having a probability of at least δ of observing at most k errors out of m examples:

$$\overline{\text{Bin}}\left(\frac{k}{m}, \delta\right) \stackrel{\text{def}}{=} \sup\left\{r : \text{Bin}\left(\frac{k}{m}, r\right) \geq \delta\right\}$$

From this definition, it follows that $\overline{\text{Bin}}(R_S(f), \delta)$ is the *smallest* upper bound, which holds with probability at least $1 - \delta$, on the true risk of any classifier f with an observed empirical risk $R_S(f)$ on a test set of m examples:

$$\mathbf{P}_{\mathbf{Z}^m}\left\{R(f) \leq \overline{\text{Bin}}\left(R_{\mathbf{Z}^m}(f), \delta\right)\right\} \geq 1 - \delta \quad \forall f \tag{1}$$

Note that the quantifier $\forall f$ appears *outside* the probability $\mathbf{P}_{\mathbf{Z}^m}\{\cdot\}$ because the bound $\overline{\text{Bin}}(R_S(f), \delta)$ does not hold *simultaneously* (and uniformly) for all classifiers f member of some predefined class $\mathcal{F}$. In contrast, the proposed risk bound of Theorem 1 holds uniformly for all compression sets and message strings.

The proposed risk bound is a generalization of the sample-compression risk bound of Langford (2005) to the case where part of the data-compression information is given by a message string. It also has the property to reduce to the Occam's razor bound when the compression set $\mathbf{z_i}$ vanishes. The idea of using a message string as an additional source of information was also used by Littlestone and Warmuth (1986) and Ben-David and Litman (1998) to obtain a sample-compression bound looser than the bound presented here. Moreover, in contrast with these bounds, Theorem 1 applies to any compression set-dependent distribution of messages $P_{\mathcal{M}(\mathbf{z_i})}$ satisfying:

$$\sum_{\sigma \in \mathcal{M}(\mathbf{z_i})} P_{\mathcal{M}(\mathbf{z_i})}(\sigma) \leq 1 \quad \forall \mathbf{z_i} \tag{2}$$

and any prior distribution $P_\mathcal{I}$ of vectors of indices satisfying:

$$\sum_{\mathbf{i} \in \mathcal{I}} P_\mathcal{I}(\mathbf{i}) \leq 1 \tag{3}$$

Theorem 1. *For any reconstruction function $\mathcal{R}$ that maps arbitrary subsets of a training set and message strings to classifiers, for any prior distribution $P_\mathcal{I}$ of vectors of indices, for any compression set-dependent distribution of messages $P_{\mathcal{M}(\mathbf{z_i})}$, and for any $\delta \in (0, 1]$, we have:*

$$\mathbf{P}_{\mathbf{Z}^m}\Big\{\forall \mathbf{i} \in \mathcal{I}, \forall \sigma \in \mathcal{M}(\mathbf{Z_i}): R(\mathcal{R}(\sigma, \mathbf{Z_i})) \leq$$
$$\overline{\text{Bin}}\Big(R_{\mathbf{Z}_{\bar{\mathbf{i}}}}(\mathcal{R}(\sigma, \mathbf{Z_i})), P_\mathcal{I}(\mathbf{i}) P_{\mathcal{M}(\mathbf{z_i})}(\sigma)\delta\Big)\Big\} \geq 1 - \delta$$

where, for any training set $\mathbf{z}^m$, $R_{\mathbf{z}_{\bar{\mathbf{i}}}}(f)$ denotes the empirical risk of classifier f on the examples of $\mathbf{z}^m$ that do not belong to the compression set $\mathbf{z}_{\mathbf{i}}$.

Proof. Consider:

$$P' \stackrel{\text{def}}{=} \mathbf{P}_{\mathbf{Z}^m} \left\{ \exists \mathbf{i} \in \mathcal{I} \colon \exists \sigma \in \mathcal{M}(\mathbf{Z_i}) \colon R(\mathcal{R}(\sigma, \mathbf{Z_i})) > \overline{\text{Bin}}\left(R_{\mathbf{Z}_{\bar{\mathbf{i}}}}(\mathcal{R}(\sigma, \mathbf{Z_i})), P_{\mathcal{I}}(\mathbf{i}) P_{\mathcal{M}(\mathbf{z_i})}(\sigma) \delta \right) \right\}$$

To prove the theorem, we show that $P' \leq \delta$. Since $\mathbf{P}_{\mathbf{Z}^m}(\cdot) = \mathbf{E}_{\mathbf{Z_i}} \mathbf{P}_{\mathbf{Z}_{\bar{\mathbf{i}}}|\mathbf{Z_i}}(\cdot)$, the union bound and Equations 1, 2, and 3 imply that we have:

$$P' \leq \sum_{\mathbf{i} \in \mathcal{I}} \mathbf{E}_{\mathbf{Z_i}} \sum_{\sigma \in \mathcal{M}(\mathbf{Z_i})} \mathbf{P}_{\mathbf{Z}_{\bar{\mathbf{i}}}|\mathbf{Z_i}} \left\{ R(\mathcal{R}(\sigma, \mathbf{Z_i})) > \overline{\text{Bin}}\left(R_{\mathbf{Z}_{\bar{\mathbf{i}}}}(\mathcal{R}(\sigma, \mathbf{Z_i})), P_{\mathcal{I}}(\mathbf{i}) P_{\mathcal{M}(\mathbf{z_i})}(\sigma) \delta \right) \right\}$$

$$\leq \sum_{\mathbf{i} \in \mathcal{I}} \mathbf{E}_{\mathbf{Z_i}} \sum_{\sigma \in \mathcal{M}(\mathbf{Z_i})} P_{\mathcal{I}}(\mathbf{i}) P_{\mathcal{M}(\mathbf{z_i})}(\sigma) \delta \leq \delta \qquad \blacksquare$$

The risk bound of Theorem 1 appears to be as tight as it possibly can. Indeed, the proof of Theorem 1 contains three inequalities. The last two inequalities come from Equations 1, 2, and 3 and cannot be improved. The first inequality comes from the application of the union bound for all the possible choices of a compression subset of the training set and is unavoidable for statistically independent training examples.

It is important to note that, once $P_{\mathcal{I}}$ and $P_{\mathcal{M}(\mathbf{z_i})}$ are specified, the risk bound of Theorem 1 for classifier $\mathcal{R}(\mathbf{z_i}, \sigma)$ depends on its empirical risk *and* on the product $P_{\mathcal{I}}(\mathbf{i}) P_{\mathcal{M}(\mathbf{z_i})}(\sigma)$. However, $\ln\left(\frac{1}{P_{\mathcal{I}}(\mathbf{i}) P_{\mathcal{M}(\mathbf{z_i})}(\sigma)}\right)$ is just the amount of information needed to specify a classifier $\mathcal{R}(\mathbf{z_i}, \sigma)$ once we are given a training set and the priors $P_{\mathcal{I}}$ and $P_{\mathcal{M}(\mathbf{z_i})}$. The $\ln(1/P_{\mathcal{I}}(\mathbf{i}))$ term is the information content of the vector of indices $\mathbf{i}$ that specifies the compression set and the $\ln(1/P_{\mathcal{M}(\mathbf{z_i})}(\sigma))$ term is the information content of the message string σ. Consequently the bound of Theorem 1 specifies quantitatively how much training errors learning algorithms should trade-off with the amount of information needed to specify a classifier by $\mathbf{i}$ and σ.

Any bound expressed in terms of the binomial tail inversion can be turned into a more conventional and looser bound by inverting a standard approximation of the binomial tail such as those obtained from the inequalities of Chernoff and Hoeffding. In this paper, we make use of the following approximations (provided here without proof) for the binomial tail inversion:

Lemma 1. *For any integer $m \geq 1$ and $k \in \{0, \ldots, m\}$, we have:*

$$\overline{\text{Bin}}\left(\frac{k}{m}, \delta\right) \leq 1 - \exp\left(\frac{-1}{m-k}\left[\ln\binom{m}{k} + \ln\left(\frac{1}{\delta}\right)\right]\right) \qquad (4)$$

$$\leq \frac{1}{m-k}\left[\ln\binom{m}{k} + \ln\left(\frac{1}{\delta}\right)\right] \qquad (5)$$

Therefore, these approximations enable us to rewrite the bound of Theorem 1 into the following looser (but somewhat clearer and more conventional) form:

Corollary 1. *For any reconstruction function $\mathcal{R}$ that maps arbitrary subsets of a training set and message strings to classifiers, for any prior distribution $P_\mathcal{I}$ of vectors of indices, for any compression set-dependent distribution of messages $P_{\mathcal{M}(\mathbf{z_i})}$, and for any $\delta \in (0, 1]$, we have:*

$$\mathbf{P}_{\mathbf{Z}^m}\left\{\forall \mathbf{i} \in \mathcal{I}, \forall \sigma \in \mathcal{M}(\mathbf{Z_i}) \colon R(\mathcal{R}(\sigma, \mathbf{Z_i})) \leq \right.$$
$$\left. 1 - \exp\left(\frac{-1}{m-d-k}\left[\ln\binom{m-d}{k} + \ln\left(\frac{1}{P_\mathcal{I}(\mathbf{i})P_{\mathcal{M}(\mathbf{z_i})}(\sigma)\delta}\right)\right]\right)\right\} \geq 1 - \delta \quad (6)$$

and, consequently:

$$\mathbf{P}_{\mathbf{Z}^m}\left\{\forall \mathbf{i} \in \mathcal{I}, \forall \sigma \in \mathcal{M}(\mathbf{Z_i}) \colon R(\mathcal{R}(\sigma, \mathbf{Z_i})) \leq \right.$$
$$\left. \frac{1}{m-d-k}\left[\ln\binom{m-d}{k} + \ln\left(\frac{1}{P_\mathcal{I}(\mathbf{i})P_{\mathcal{M}(\mathbf{z_i})}(\sigma)\delta}\right)\right]\right\} \geq 1 - \delta \quad (7)$$

where $d \stackrel{\text{def}}{=} |\mathbf{i}|$ is the sample compression set size of classifier $\mathcal{R}(\sigma, \mathbf{Z_i})$ and $k \stackrel{\text{def}}{=} |\overline{\mathbf{i}}|R_{\mathbf{Z_{\bar{i}}}}(\mathcal{R}(\sigma, \mathbf{Z_i}))$ is the number of training errors that this classifier makes on the examples that are not in the compression set.

It is now quite clear from Corollary 1 that the risk bound of classifier $\mathcal{R}(\sigma, \mathbf{Z_i})$ is small when its compression set size d and its number k of training errors are both much smaller than the number m of training examples. These are uniform bounds over a set of data-dependent classifiers defined by the reconstruction function $\mathcal{R}$. In contrast, VC bounds (Vapnik 1998) and Rademacher bounds (Mendelson, 2002) are uniform bounds over a set of functions defined *without reference to the training data*. Hence, these latter bounds do not apply to our case.

The bound of Equation 6 is very similar to (and slightly tighter than) the recent bound of Marchand and Sokolova (2005).

The looser bound of Equation 7 is similar to the bounds of Littlestone and Warmuth (1986) and Floyd and Warmuth (1995) when the set $\mathcal{M}$ of all possible messages is independent of the compression set $\mathbf{z_i}$ and when we choose:

$$P_{\mathcal{M}(\mathbf{z_i})}(\sigma) = 1/|\mathcal{M}| \quad \forall \sigma \in \mathcal{M} \quad (8)$$

$$P_\mathcal{I}(\mathbf{i}) = \binom{m}{|\mathbf{i}|}^{-1}(m+1)^{-1} \quad \forall \mathbf{i} \in \mathcal{I} \quad (9)$$

But other choices that give better bounds are clearly possible. For example, in the following sections we will use:

$$P_\mathcal{I}(\mathbf{i}) = \binom{m}{|\mathbf{i}|}^{-1}\zeta(|\mathbf{i}|) \quad \text{with} \quad \zeta(a) \stackrel{\text{def}}{=} \frac{6}{\pi^2}(a+1)^{-2} \quad \forall a \in \mathbb{N} \quad (10)$$

which satisfies the constraint of Equation 3 since $\sum_{i=1}^{\infty} i^{-2} = \pi^2/6$. This choice for $P_{\mathcal{I}}$ has the advantage that the risk bounds do not deteriorate too rapidly when $|\mathbf{i}|$ increases.

In the next section, we show how we can apply the risk bounds of Theorem 1 and Corollary 1 to the SCM. For this task, we will provide choices for the distribution of messages $P_{\mathcal{M}(\mathbf{z_i})}$ which are more appropriate than the simplest choice given by Equation 8. Indeed, we feel that it is important to allow the set of messages to depend on the sample compression $\mathbf{z_i}$ since it is conceivable that for some $\mathbf{z_i}$, very little extra information may be needed to identify the classifier whereas for some other $\mathbf{z_i}$, more information may be needed. Without such a dependency on $\mathbf{z_i}$, the set of possible messages $\mathcal{M}$ would be unnecessarily large and would loosen the risk bound. But, more importantly, the risk bound would not depend on the particular message σ used. However, we feel that it is important for learning algorithms to be able to trade-off the complexity (or information content) of $\mathbf{i}$ with the complexity of σ. Hence, a good risk bound should somehow indicate what the proper trade-off should be.

3 Application to the Set Covering Machine

Recall that the task of the SCM (Marchand and Shawe-Taylor 2002) is to construct the smallest possible conjunction of (Boolean-valued) features. We discuss here only the conjunction case. The disjunction case is treated similarly just by exchanging the role of the positive with the negative examples.

For the case of *data-dependent balls*, each feature is identified by a training example, called a *center* $(\mathbf{x}_c, y_c)$, and a radius ρ. Given any metric d, the output $h(\mathbf{x})$ on any input example $\mathbf{x}$ of such a feature is given by:

$$h(\mathbf{x}) = \begin{cases} y_c & \text{if } d(\mathbf{x}, \mathbf{x}_c) \leq \rho \\ -y_c & \text{otherwise} \end{cases}$$

3.1 Coding Each Radius with a Training Example

Marchand and Shawe-Taylor (2002) have proposed to use another training example $\mathbf{x}_b$, called a *border point*, to code for the radius so that $\rho = d(\mathbf{x}_c, \mathbf{x}_b)$. In this case, given a compression set $\mathbf{z_i}$, we need to specify the examples in $\mathbf{z_i}$ that are used for a border point without being used as a center. As explained by Marchand and Shawe-Taylor (2002), no additional amount of information is required to pair each center with its border point whenever the reconstruction function $\mathcal{R}$ is constrained to produce a classifier that always correctly classifies the compression set. Furthermore, as argued by Marchand and Shawe-Taylor (2002), we can limit ourselves to the case where each border point is a positive example. In that case, each message $\sigma \in \mathcal{M}(\mathbf{z_i})$ just needs to specify the positive examples that are a border point without being a center. Let $n(\mathbf{z_i})$ and $p(\mathbf{z_i})$ be, respectively, the number of negative and the number of positive examples in compression set $\mathbf{z_i}$. Let $b(\sigma)$ be the number of border point examples specified in message σ and let $\zeta(a)$ be the same as defined in Equation 10. We can then use:

$$P_{\mathcal{M}(\mathbf{z_i})}(\sigma) = \zeta(b(\sigma)) \cdot \binom{p(\mathbf{z_i})}{b(\sigma)}^{-1} \quad (11)$$

since, in that case, we have for any compression set $\mathbf{z_i}$:

$$\sum_{\sigma \in \mathcal{M}(\mathbf{z_i})} P_{\mathcal{M}(\mathbf{z_i})}(\sigma) = \sum_{b=0}^{p(\mathbf{z_i})} \zeta(b) \sum_{\sigma: b(\sigma)=b} \binom{p(\mathbf{z_i})}{b(\sigma)}^{-1} \leq 1$$

With this distribution $P_{\mathcal{M}(\mathbf{z_i})}$, the risk bound of Theorem 1 is tighter than the one provided by Marchand and Shawe-Taylor (2002) because of the more efficient treatment of the training errors made by using the binomial tail inversion.

3.2 Coding Each Radius with a Small Message String

Another alternative, not considered by Marchand and Shawe-Taylor (2002), is to code each radius value by a message string having the fewest number of bits. In this case, no border points are used and the compression set only consists of ball centers. Consequently, the risk bounds of Theorem 1 and Corollary 1 will be smaller for classifiers described by this method provided that we do not use to many bits to code each radius. We expect that this will be the case whenever there exists a large interval $[r_1, r_2]$ (*i.e.*, a margin) of radius values such that no training examples are present between the two concentric spheres, centered on $\mathbf{x}_c$, with radius r_1 and r_2. The best radius value in that case will be the one that has the shortest code. A similar idea was applied by von Luxburg et. al. (2004) for coding the maximum-margin hyperplane solution for support vector machines.

Hence, consider the problem of coding a radius value $r \in [r_1, r_2] \subset [0, R]$ where R is some predefined value that cannot be exceeded and where $[r_1, r_2]$ is an interval of "equally good" radius values[1]. We propose the following diadic coding scheme for the identification of a radius value that belongs to that interval. Let l be the number of bits that we use for the code. We adopt the convention that a code of $l = 0$ bits specifies the radius value $R/2$. A code of $l = 1$ bit either specifies the value $R/4$ (when the bit is 0) or the value $3R/4$ (when the bit is 1). A code of $l = 2$ specifies one of the following values: $R/8, 3R/8, 5R/8, 7R/8$. Hence, a code of l bits specifies one value among the set Λ_l of radius values:

$$\Lambda_l \overset{\text{def}}{=} \left\{ \frac{2j-1}{2^{l+1}} R \right\}_{j=1}^{2^l}$$

Given an interval $[r_1, r_2] \subset [0, R]$ of radius values, we take the smallest number l of bits such that there exists a radius value in Λ_l that falls in the interval $[r_1, r_2]$. In this way, we will need at most $\lfloor \log_2(R/(r_2 - r_1)) \rfloor$ bits to obtain a radius value that falls in $[r_1, r_2]$.

Hence, to specify the radius for each center of a compression set, we need to specify the number l of bits and a l-bit string s that identifies one of the radius values in Λ_l. Therefore, the message string σ sent to the reconstruction function $\mathcal{R}$, for a compression set $\mathbf{z_i}$, consists of the set of pairs (l_i, s_i) of numbers needed to identify the radius of each center $i \in \mathbf{i}$. The risk bound does not depend on how we actually code σ

---

[1] By a "good" radius value, we mean a radius value for a ball that would cover many negative examples and very few positive examples (see the learning algorithm).

(for some receiver). It only depends on the a priori probabilities assigned to each possible realization of σ. We choose the following distribution:

$$P_{\mathcal{M}(\mathbf{z_i})}(\sigma) \stackrel{\text{def}}{=} P_{\mathcal{M}(\mathbf{z_i})}(l_1, s_1, \ldots, l_{|\mathbf{i}|}, s_{|\mathbf{i}|}) = \prod_{i \in \mathbf{i}} \zeta(l_i) \cdot 2^{-l_i} \tag{12}$$

where $\zeta(l_i)$ is the same as given in Equation 10.

Note that by giving equal a priori probability to each of the 2^{l_i} strings s_i of length l_i, we give no preference to any radius value in Λ_{l_i} once we have chosen a scale R that we believe is appropriate. The distribution ζ that we have chosen for each string length l_i has the advantage of decreasing slowly so that the risk bound does not deteriorate to rapidly as l_i increases. Other choices are clearly possible.

By comparing the risk bounds of Corollary 1 for the two possible choices we have for coding each radius (either with an example or with a message string), we notice that it should be preferable to code explicitly a radius value with a string whenever we use a number l of bits less than $\log_2 m$ (roughly). Hence, this will be the case whenever there exists an interval $[r_1, r_2]$ of "good" radius values such that $(r_2 - r_1)/R \gtrsim 1/m$.

Finally, we emphasize that the risk bounds of Theorem 1 and Corollary 1, used in conjunction with the distribution of messages given by Equation 12, provides a guide for choosing the appropriate trade-off between sparsity (the inverse of the size of the compression set) and margin (the inverse of the length of the message string). Indeed, the risk bound for an SCM with a decision surface having a large margin of separation (small l_is) may be smaller than the risk bound of a sparser SCM having a smaller margin (large l_is).

4 The Learning Algorithm

Ideally, we would like to find a conjunction of balls that minimizes the risk bound of Theorem 1 with the distribution given by Equation 12. Unfortunately, this cannot be done efficiently in all cases since this problem is at least as hard as the (NP-complete) minimum set cover problem (Marchand and Shawe-Taylor 2002). However, the simple *set covering greedy heuristic* will construct a conjunction of at most $r \ln(m)$ balls whenever there exists a conjunction of r balls that makes no errors with a training set of m examples (Marchand and Shawe-Taylor 2002).

We say that a ball *covers* an example iff it assigns -1 to that example. The set covering greedy heuristic simply consists of using a ball that covers the largest number of negative examples (without making any errors on the positives), remove these negative covered examples and repeat until all the negative examples are covered. Marchand and Shawe-Taylor (2002) have modified this heuristic by incorporating the possibility of making training errors if the final classifier is much smaller. It can be described as follows. Let N be the set of negative examples and P be the set of positive examples. We start with $N' = N$ and $P' = P$. Let Q_i be the subset of N' covered by ball i and let R_i be the subset of P' covered by ball i. We choose the ball i that maximizes the *utility* U_i defined as:

$$U_i \stackrel{\text{def}}{=} |Q_i| - p \cdot |R_i| \tag{13}$$

where p is the *penalty* suffered by covering (and hence, misclassifying) a positive example. Once we have found a ball maximizing U_i, we update $N' = N' - Q_i$ and $P' = P' - R_i$ and repeat to find the next ball until either $N' = \emptyset$ or the maximum number v of balls has been reached (early stopping the greedy).

Here we first modify the heuristic of Marchand and Shawe-Taylor (2002) by allowing a maximum number of bits l^* that can be used for coding the radius of each ball. Classifiers obtained with a small value of l^* will, on average, have a large separating margin. Moreover, for this new learning algorithm, the distribution of messages given by Equation 12 is defined for a fixed value of R (the "predefined radius value that cannot be exceeded"). Hence, in this case, R should be chosen from the *definition* of each input attribute *without observing the data*. Consequently, this will generally force *each ball* of the classifier to use a large number of bits for its radius value; otherwise the final classifier is likely to make numerous training errors. We have therefore used the following scheme to choose R *from the training data*. We first choose a value R^* from the definition of each input attribute (without observing the data). This could be $R^* = \sqrt{n}$ for the case of n $\{0,1\}$-valued attributes. Then, we consider t equally-spaced values for R in the interval $]0, R^*]$. The message string σ described in Section 3.2 is then just preceded by the index to one of these t possible values. The value of R referred to by this index will then be used for *every ball* of the classifier. For this extra part of the message, we have assigned equal probability to each of the t possible values for R. With this scheme, we only need to multiply $P_{\mathcal{M}(\mathbf{z}_i)}(\sigma)$ of Equation 12 by $1/t$. Nevertheless, this introduces one more adjustable parameter in the learning algorithm: the value of R.[2] Therefore, p, v, l^*, and R are the "learning parameters" that our heuristic uses to generate a set of classifiers. At the end, we can use the bound of Theorem 1 to select the best classifier. Another alternative is to determine the best parameter values by cross-validation.

5 Empirical Results on Natural Data

We have compared the new learning algorithm (called here SCM2), that codes each ball radius with a message string, with the old algorithm (called here SCM1), that codes each radius with a training example. Both of these algorithms were also compared with the support vector machine (SVM) equipped with a RBF kernel of variance $1/2\gamma$ and a soft margin parameter C. Each SCM algorithm used the L_2 metric since this is the metric present in the argument of the RBF kernel.

Each algorithm was tested on the UCI data sets of Table 1. Each data set was randomly split in two parts. About half of the examples was used for training and the remaining set of examples was used for testing. The corresponding values for these numbers of examples are given in the "train" and "test" columns of Table 1. The learning parameters of all algorithms were determined from the training set *only*. The parameters C and γ for the SVM were determined by the 5-fold cross validation (CV) method performed on the training set. The parameters that gave the smallest 5-fold CV error were then used to train the SVM on the whole training set and the resulting classifier was then run on the testing set. Exactly the same method (with the same 5-fold

---

[2] We have used $t \approx 30$ different values of R in our experiments.

Table 1. SVM and SCM results on UCI data sets

Data Set			SVM results				SCM1-cv		SCM1-b		SCM2-cv			SCM2-b		
Name	train	test	C	γ	SVs	errs	b	errs	b	errs	b	l^*	errs	b	l^*	errs
breastw	343	340	1	0.1	38	15	2	11	1	12	1	3	12	1	1	12
bupa	170	175	2	3.0	169	66	2	71	2	70	2	7	69	11	7	67
credit	353	300	100	0.25	282	51	12	65	1	57	11	6	49	8	5	46
haberman	144	150	2	0.5	81	39	2	41	1	39	8	2	36	2	2	37
pima	400	368	0.5	0.02	241	96	1	108	1	105	4	1	107	13	5	103
USvotes	235	200	1	0.02	53	13	8	26	3	19	7	3	19	4	2	15
Hart	150	147	1	3.0	64	26	1	28	1	23	1	2	24	1	2	23
Glass	107	107	10	3.0	51	29	4	20	4	19	7	6	19	3	5	18

split) was used to determine the learning parameters of both SCM1 and SCM2. These results are referred to (in Table 1) as SCM1-cv and SCM2-cv. In addition to this, we have compared this 5-fold CV model selection method with a model selection method that uses the risk bound 6 of Corollary 1 to select the best SCM classifier obtained from the *same* possible choices of the learning parameters that we have used for the 5-fold CV method. The SCM that minimizes the risk bound (computed from the training set) was then run on the testing set. These results are referred to (in Table 1) as SCM1-b and SCM2-b. For SCM1, the risk bound was used in conjunction with the distribution of messages given by Equation 11. For SCM2, the risk bound was used in conjunction with the distribution of messages given by Equation 12.

The SVM results are reported in Table 1 where the "SVs" column refers to the number of support vectors present in the final classifier and the "errs" column refers to the number of classification errors obtained on the testing set. This last notation is used also for all the SCM results reported in Table 1. In addition to this, the "b" and "l^*" columns refer, respectively, to the number of balls and the maximum number of bits used by the final classifier.

We observe that SCMs are always much sparser than SVMs with roughly the same generalization error. Moreover, the risk bound is often better than 5-fold CV for choosing the classifier with the smallest generalization error. (We have observed that the risk bound was almost always within a factor of three of the test error.) We also observe that SCM2 is generally as good as, and sometimes clearly better than, SCM1 for producing classifiers with a small generalization error. Finally, it is interesting to note the strong tendency of SCM2 to produce classifiers with more balls than those produced by SCM1. This is especially true for SCM2-b versus SCM1-b. Hence SCM2 generally sacrifices sparsity to obtain a larger margin.

6 Conclusion

We have proposed a new representation for the SCM that uses two distinct sources of information to represent a conjunction of data-dependent balls: a *compression set* to specify the center of each ball and a *message string* to encode the radius value of each ball. Moreover, we have proposed a general data-compression risk bound that depends explicitly on these two information sources. This bound therefore exhibits a non trivial trade-off between sparsity (the inverse of the compression set size) and the margin (the inverse of the message length) that classifiers should attempt to optimize on the training data. We have also proposed a new learning algorithm for the SCM where the learner can control the amount of trade-off between the sparsity of the classifier and the magnitude of its separating margin. Compared to the algorithm of Marchand and Shawe-Taylor (2002), our experiments on natural data sets indicate that this new learning algorithm generally produces classifiers having a larger separating margin at the expenses of having more balls. The generalization error of classifiers produced by the new algorithm was generally slightly better. Finally, the proposed data-compression risk bound seems to be an effective guide for choosing the proper margin-sparsity trade-off of a classifier.

References

Shai Ben-David and A. Litman. Combinatorial variability of Vapnik-Chervonenkis classes. *Discrete Applied Mathematics*, 86 (1998) 3–25

Kristin P. Bennett. Combining support vector and mathematical programming methods for classifications. In B. Schölkopf, C. J. C. Burges, and A. J. Smola, editors, *Advances in Kernel Methods—Support Vector Learning*, MIT Press, Cambridge MA, (1999) 307–326.

Jinbo Bi, Kristin P. Bennett, Mark Embrechts, Kurt M. Breneman, and Minghu Song. Dimensionality reduction via sparse support vector machines. *Journal of Machine Learning Reasearch*, 3 (2003) 1229–1245

Avrim Blum and John Langford. PAC-MDL bounds. In *Proceedings of 16th Annual Conference on Learning Theory, COLT 2003,* Washington, DC, August 2003, volume 2777 of *Lecture Notes in Artificial Intelligence*, Springer, Berlin (2003) 344–357

B. E. Boser, I. M. Guyon, and V. N. Vapnik. A training algorithm for optimal margin classifiers. In *Proceedings of the 5th Annual ACM Workshop on Computational Learning Theory*, ACM Press, (1992) 144–152

Sally Floyd and Manfred Warmuth. Sample compression, learnability, and the Vapnik-Chervonenkis dimension. *Machine Learning*, 21**3** (1995) 269–304

Thore Graepel, Ralf Herbrich, and John Shawe-Taylor. Generalisation error bounds for sparse linear classifiers. In *Proceedings of the Thirteenth Annual Conference on Computational Learning Theory* (2000) 298–303

Thore Graepel, Ralf Herbrich, and Robert C. Williamson. From margin to sparsity. In *Advances in neural information processing systems 13*, (2001) 210–216

John Langford. Tutorial on practical prediction theory for classification. *Journal of Machine Learning Reasearch*, 3 (2005) 273–306.

N. Littlestone and M. Warmuth. Relating data compression and learnability. Technical report, University of California Santa Cruz, Santa Cruz, CA, (1986)

Mario Marchand and John Shawe-Taylor. The set covering machine. *Journal of Machine Learning Reasearch*, 3 (2002) 723–746.

Mario Marchand and Marina Sokolova. Learning with decision lists of data-dependent Features. *Journal of Machine Learning Reasearch*, 6 (2005) 427-451.

S. Mendelson. Rademacher averages and phase transitions in Glivenko-Cantelli class. *IEEE Transactions on Information Theory*, 48 (2002) 251–263

Vladimir N. Vapnik. *Statistical Learning Theory*. Wiley, New York, NY (1998)

Ulrike von Luxburg, Olivier Bousquet, and Bernhard Schölkopf. A compression approach to support vector model selection. *Journal of Machine Learning Research*, 5(2004) 293–323

Learning from Positive and Unlabeled Examples with Different Data Distributions

Xiao-Li Li[1] and Bing Liu[2]

[1] Institute for Infocomm Research, Heng Mui Keng Terrace, 119613, Singapore
xlli@i2r.a-star.edu.sg
[2] Department of Computer Science, University of Illinois at Chicago,
851 S. Morgan Street, Chicago, IL 60607-7053
liub@cs.uic.edu

Abstract. We study the problem of learning from positive and unlabeled examples. Although several techniques exist for dealing with this problem, they all assume that positive examples in the positive set P and the positive examples in the unlabeled set U are generated from the same distribution. This assumption may be violated in practice. For example, one wants to collect all printer pages from the Web. One can use the printer pages from one site as the set P of positive pages and use product pages from another site as U. One wants to classify the pages in U into printer pages and non-printer pages. Although printer pages from the two sites have many similarities, they can also be quite different because different sites often present similar products in different styles and have different focuses. In such cases, existing methods perform poorly. This paper proposes a novel technique A-EM to deal with the problem. Experiment results with product page classification demonstrate the effectiveness of the proposed technique.

1 Introduction

Learning from positive and unlabeled examples (or PU learning) can be regarded as a two-class (positive and negative) classification problem, where there are only labeled positive training data, but no labeled negative training data. Since traditional classification techniques require both labeled positive and negative examples to build a classifier, they are thus not suitable for this problem. Although it is possible to manually label some negative examples, it is labor-intensive and time consuming. In the past three years, several techniques [12][13][23][11][9] were proposed to solve the problem. These techniques mainly use a two-step strategy. The first step tries to identify a set of reliable negative documents from the unlabeled set. The second step builds a classifier by iteratively applying a classification algorithm, i.e. EM [5] or SVM [20].

All the existing techniques assume that positive examples in the positive set P and positive examples (which are not known) in the unlabeled set U are generated from the same distribution. In the context of the Web or text documents, this means that the word features of positive documents in both P and U are similar and with similar frequencies. This assumption may be violated in practice. For example, one wants to collect all printer pages from Web. One can use the printer pages from one site as the set P of positive pages and use product pages from each of the other Web sites as U.

One wants to classify all the pages in U into printer pages and non-printer pages. Although printer pages from the two sites have many similarities, they may also be quite different. The reason is that different Web sites present similar products in different styles and have different focuses. In such cases, directly applying the existing methods gives poor results. The reason is that the first step of these methods is unable to find reliable negative pages. Consequently, the second step builds poor classifiers.

This paper proposes a novel technique to deal with the problem. The proposed method (called A-EM for Augmented EM) is in the framework of EM [5]. The proposed technique has two novelties:

- We add a large set of irrelevant documents O (which contains almost no positive document) to U. This reduces the level of noise in U (here we regard positive documents in U as noise), which enables us to compute the parameters of the classifier more accurately.
- The EM algorithm generates a sequence of classifiers. However, the performances of this sequence of classifiers may not be necessarily improving. This is a well-known phenomenon due to the mismatch of mixture components and document classes [16][12][11]. We propose a classifier selection (or catch) criterion to select a good classifier from the set of classifiers produced by EM. Although there exist classifier selection methods given in [12] and [9], they perform poorly also due to the different data distributions identified above.

Note that although a classifier can be built using positive documents P (positive class) and irrelevant documents O (negative class), our experiments show that classifiers built with P and O are very poor since irrelevant documents in O can be totally different from the negative documents in U. For example, irrelevant documents in O are about sports, finance, and politics, while the negative documents in U are about computers, TV and digital cameras. In PU learning, the unlabeled set U is usually also the test set. Since irrelevant documents in O are not representative of the negative documents in U, O thus cannot be used as the negative set to build an accurate classifier to classify U.

We have performed a large number of experiments using Web product pages. Classifying such data is critical for many e-commerce applications, which also provides an ideal test case for our technique. Our results show that the new method outperforms existing methods dramatically.

2 Related Work

In [6], a theoretical study of PAC learning from positive and unlabeled examples is reported. [15] studies the problem in a Bayesian framework where the distribution of functions and examples are assumed known. [12] reports sample complexity results and shows from a theoretical point of view how the problem may be solved.

A few practical algorithms were also proposed in [9][11][12][13][23]. They conform to the theory given in [12], and follow a two-step strategy: (1) automatically identifying a set of reliable negative examples from the unlabeled set; and (2) building a classifier using EM or SVM iteratively. The differences among these methods are in the details of the two steps.

In [12], Liu et al. proposed a method (called S-EM) to solve the problem. It is based on naïve Bayesian classification (NB) and the EM algorithm. The main idea of the method is to first use a spy technique to identify some reliable negative documents from the unlabeled set. It then runs EM to build the final classifier. In [23], a SVM based technique (called PEBL) is proposed to classify Web pages given positive and unlabeled pages. It reports a different method for identifying reliable negative examples and then uses SVM iteratively for classifier building. [24] estimates SVM boundary of positive class for small positive data. [11] reports a technique called Roc-SVM. In this technique, reliable negative documents are extracted by using the information retrieval technique Rocchio [17]. Again, SVM is used in the second step. A classifier selection criterion is also proposed to catch a good classifier from iterations of SVM. In [13], a more principled approach based on a biased formulation of SVM is proposed. The method does not have the first step. Lee and Liu propose a logistic regression based method with a classifier selection method [9].

In [19], one-class SVM is proposed. This technique uses only positive data to build a SVM classifier. However, [11] shows that the results are poor. Unlabeled data does help classification. One-class SVM is also studied in [8] and [4].

Other related works include semi-supervised learning (from a small labeled set and a large unlabeled set), co-training and cross-training [1][2][3][7][16][18][25][21]. They are different from our work as we use no labeled negative data.

In this paper, we only focus on texts in Web pages. It is known that structures and hyperlink information in Web pages also help classification.

3 The Proposed Technique

We now introduce algorithm A-EM to deal with the problem that positive examples in P and hidden positive examples in U may be generated from different distributions.

3.1 NB Classification and EM Algorithm

As mentioned in the introduction section, this work employs the EM framework as in [14][16][12]. Our EM algorithm here is based on naïve Bayesian classification (NB). Before presenting the proposed method, we give an overview of both NB and EM.

The Naive Bayesian method is an effective technique for text classification [10][16]. Given a set of training documents D, each document is considered an ordered list of words. We use $w_{d_i,k}$ to denote the word in position k of document d_i, where each word is from the vocabulary $V = <w_1, w_2, \ldots, w_{|V|}>$. The vocabulary is the set of all words we consider for classification. We also have a set of predefined classes, $C = \{c_1, c_2, \ldots, c_{|C|}\}$ (in this paper we only consider two class classification, so, $C=\{c_1, c_2\}$). In order to perform classification, we need to compute the posterior probability, $Pr(c_j|d_i)$, where c_j is a class and d_i is a document. Based on the Bayesian probability and the multinomial model, we have

$$\Pr(c_j) = \frac{\sum_{i=1}^{|D|} \Pr(c_j \mid d_i)}{|D|} \tag{1}$$

and with Laplacian smoothing,

$$\Pr(w_t \mid c_j) = \frac{1 + \sum_{i=1}^{|D|} N(w_t, d_i) \Pr(c_j \mid d_i)}{|V| + \sum_{s=1}^{|V|} \sum_{i=1}^{|D|} N(w_s, d_i) \Pr(c_j \mid d_i)} \tag{2}$$

where $N(w_t, d_i)$ is the count of the number of times that the word w_t occurs in document d_i and $Pr(c_j|d_i) \in \{0,1\}$ depending on the class label of the document.

Finally, assuming that the probabilities of the words are independent given the class, we obtain the NB classifier:

$$Pr(c_j | d_i) = \frac{Pr(c_j) \prod_{k=1}^{|d_i|} Pr(w_{d_i,k} | c_j)}{\sum_{r=1}^{|C|} Pr(c_r) \prod_{k=1}^{|d_i|} Pr(w_{d_i,k} | c_r)} \qquad (3)$$

In the naive Bayesian classifier, the class with the highest $Pr(c_j|d_i)$ is assigned as the class of the document.

The Expectation-Maximization (EM) algorithm [5] is a popular class of iterative algorithms for maximum likelihood estimation in problems with incomplete data. It is often used to fill the missing values in the data using existing values by computing the expected value. The EM algorithm consists of two steps, the *Expectation* step, and the *Maximization* step. The *Expectation step* basically fills in the missing data. The parameters are estimated in the *Maximization step* after the missing data are filled. This leads to the next iteration. For the naive Bayesian classifier, the steps used by EM are identical to that used to build the classifier (equations (3) for the *Expectation step*, and equations (1) and (2) for the *Maximization step*). In EM, the probability of the class given a document takes the value in [0, 1] instead of {0, 1}.

3.2 The General Algorithm: A-EM

We now present the general algorithm A-EM in this work. The proposed technique consists of three steps: (1) initialization by introducing irrelevant documents, (2) running EM, and (3) selecting the final classifier.

Algorithm A-EM(P, U, O)
1. Let $N = U \cup O$;
2. **For** each $d_i \in N$, let $Pr(+|d_i) = 0$, $Pr(-|d_i) = 1$;
3. **For** each $d_i \in P$, let $Pr(+|d_i) = 1$, $Pr(-|d_i) = 0$;
4. Build the initial naïve Bayesian classifier NB-C using equations (1) and (2);
5. **Loop while** classifier parameters change
6.   **For** each document $d_i \in N$
7.   Compute $Pr(+|d_i)$ and $Pr(-|d_i)$ using NB-C;
8.   Update $Pr(c_j)$ and $Pr(w_t|c_j)$ by replacing equations (1) and (2) with the new probabilities in step 7 (a new NB-C is being built in the process)
9. Select a good classifier from the series of classifiers produced by EM.

Fig. 1. The A-EM algorithm with the NB classifier

Initially, each positive document d_i in P is assigned the class label "+" (positive). As we have no labeled negative documents, each document d_j in unlabeled set U is assigned the class label "-" (negative). Our problem is turned into a one-side error problem, i.e., there is a large error in the negative set (which is U here). Using this initial labeling a NB classifier can be built, which is applied to classify documents in U to obtain the posterior probabilities ($Pr(+|d_j)$ and $Pr(-|d_j)$) for each document in U. We then iteratively employ the revised posterior probabilities to build a new NB classifier.

The process goes on until the parameters converge. This is the EM algorithm with U as negative N. Figure 1 shows the A-EM algorithm. O (line 1) can be ignored for now. We assume N is U (Section 3.4 will explain why we need to use O).

We now discuss in what situation this algorithm will work well. In our problem, the difficulty in building an accurate classifier lies in the fact that we do not have labeled negative data (but a noisy unlabeled set U). As a result, initially we use all documents in U as negative documents. After learning, the NB classifier $NB\text{-}C$ (line 4) will use the values of $Pr(c_j)$ and $Pr(w_t|c_j)$ to classify the documents in the unlabeled set U. Equivalently, we can say that we use the classifier to compute the posterior probabilities for each document d_i in U, i.e., $Pr(+|d_i)$ and $Pr(-|d_i)$. If the $NB\text{-}C$ classifier is good, it will assign most positive documents in U small probabilities of $Pr(-|d_i)$ while high probabilities of $Pr(+|d_i)$. When the EM algorithm is applied to estimate $Pr(c_j)$ and $Pr(w_t|c_j)$ again in the next iteration, it will be more accurate than the first $NB\text{-}C$ classifier because the EM algorithm does not regard U as negative. Instead, for each document in U, it uses the revised posterior probabilities. So the key issue of this problem is whether the original $NB\text{-}C$ classifier is able to assign positive documents in U high probabilities. If this is possible, EM will be able to improve the first $NB\text{-}C$ classifier. However, in practice this may not be the case.

3.3 Problems and Solutions

As discussed previously, in practice positive examples in P and hidden positive examples in U may be generated from different distributions. Thus, they may not be sufficiently similar. As a result, positive examples in U may not be assigned right probabilities by the algorithm in Figure 1. Then EM will produce poor classifiers. We experimented with the above algorithm using the Web page data. The results were quite poor. We also tried the classifier selection methods in [12] and [9], but they do not work either. We believe that the reasons are:

1) Positive documents in P are not sufficiently representative of positive documents in U, although these documents are still similar to a large extend.
2) Due to the problem above, it is difficult to estimate the behavior of positive documents in U using positive documents in P. This makes the existing classifier selection methods ineffective because they all estimate the information about positive documents in U using P.

To deal with these two problems, we propose the following strategies: For the first problem, we amplify or boost the similarity of positive documents in U and P (their similarities are small initially) while reducing the similarity of positive and negative documents in U. We do this by introducing a large number of irrelevant documents (they are definitely negative documents). This can be easily done because irrelevant documents are easy to find. For example, we are interested in product page classification. We can add a large number of news articles from newspapers.

To deal with the second problem, we need to design a classifier selection method that does not depend on positive documents in P, but only on U. Thus, the distribution difference will not cause problem.

3.4 Introducing Irrelevant Documents: Initialization of A-EM

Recall that the key piece of information needed for classification is $Pr(w_t|c_j)$, where w_t is a word and c_j is a class. If there are a large number of positive examples in U or there are many keywords that are indicative of positive documents also occurring in U very often, then the NB classifier will not be able to separate positive and negative class well.

To deal with this problem, we introduce additional irrelevant documents O (negative) into the original unlabeled set U (line 1 in Fig 1), which reduces the error in U. Basically, adding O will change the probability $Pr(w_t|-)$. Obviously, the proportion of positive documents in $O+U$ is reduced and consequently $Pr(w_t|-)$ is reduced for a positive keyword w_t. Note that $Pr(w_t|+)$ does not change because we do not add anything in the positive set P. In effect, we amplify the positive features in P. In classifying documents in U, those positive documents are likely to get much higher values of $Pr(+|d_i)$, and lower values of $Pr(-|d_i)$. This means that we have boosted the similarity of positive documents in P and U, which allows us to build more accurate classifiers.

3.5 Selecting a Good Classifier

EM works well when the local maximum that the classifier is approaching to separate positive and negative documents. In practice, the behavior of EM can be quite unpredictable due to mismatch of mixture components and document classes [16][9][11] (due to model misfit). Thus, each iteration of EM gives a classifier that may potentially be a better classifier than the classifier produced at convergence. If we run EM n iterations, we have n classifiers from which we need to select a good classifier (to choose the best is difficult).

There are two existing techniques for selecting a classifier in EM. S-EM [12] estimates the change in the probability of error in order to decide which iteration of EM is the final classifier. More specifically, in the selection formula, it estimates the probability that positives in U are classified as negative through checking how many positives in P are classified as negative, i.e., using $Pr_P(f(x)=-|Y=+)$ as an approximation of $Pr_U(f(x)=-|Y=+)$. Lee and Liu proposes another performance criterion in [9], $Pr(f(x)=+|Y=+)^2 / Pr(f(x)=+)$, which also use positive documents from P in a validation set in computation. Note that $f()$ is the classifier, x is a document vector and Y is the class attribute.

As we discussed in Section 3.3, since the positive documents in P are not sufficiently similar to the positive documents in U, the two techniques do not work because they both depend on P. We now propose a new technique that depends primarily on the unlabeled set U. Since it does not use P in evaluation, it is thus independent of positive set P.

Since our task here is to identify positive documents from the unlabeled set U, therefore it is appropriate to use information retrieval measures for our purpose. Here we use the F value to evaluate the performance of the classifier. F value is commonly used in text classification: $F = 2pr/(p+r)$, where p is the precision and r is the recall. We try to select a classifier from EM iterations with the maximal F value.

We now use the confusion matrix to introduce our method (Table 1). A confusion matrix contains information about actual and predicted results given by a classifier.

Table 1. Confusion Matrix of a classifier

	Classified Positive	Classified Negative
Actual Positive	TP	FN
Actual Negative	FP	TN

Here *TP* is the number of correct predictions of positive documents (true positive); *FN* is the number of incorrect predictions of positive documents (false negative); *FP* is the number of incorrect predictions of negative documents (false positive); and *TN* is the number of correct predictions of negative documents (true negative). Based on the matrix, the precision and recall of positive class can be written as:

$$p = \frac{TP}{TP + FP} \qquad r = \frac{TP}{TP + FN} \qquad (4)$$

F value can be written as

$$F = 2 * \frac{TP}{TP + FP} * \frac{TP}{TP + FN} / (\frac{TP}{TP + FP} + \frac{TP}{TP + FN})$$
$$= \frac{2TP}{(TP + FP) + (TP + FN)} \qquad (5)$$

Note that *TP+FP* is the number of documents that are classified as positive (we denote the document set as *CP*) and *TP+FN* is the actual number of positive documents in *U* (we denote it as *PD*, and it is a constant).

So *F* value can then be expressed as:

$$F = \frac{2TP}{|CP| + PD} \qquad (6)$$

We use an estimate of change in *F* value to decide which iteration of EM to select as the final classifier. The change in *F* value from iteration *i*-1 to *i* (*F* value in *i*th iteration divided the *F* value in (*i*-1)th iteration) is

$$\Delta_i = \frac{F_i}{F_{i-1}} = \frac{TP_i}{TP_{i-1}} * \frac{|CP_{i-1}| + PD}{|CP_i| + PD} \qquad (7)$$

In the EM algorithm, we select iteration *i* as our final classifier if Δ_i is the last iteration with value greater than 1. $|CP_{i-1}|$ and $|CP_i|$ are the number of documents classified as positive in iteration *i* and *i*+1 respectively. We estimate *PD* by using the number of documents classified as positive when EM converges. Next, we estimate TP_i/TP_{i-1} since it is impossible to directly estimate either TP_i or TP_{i-1}.

Our idea here is that first we get a set *K* of representative keywords for the positive class. This is done as follows: first we compute $Pr(w_i|+)$ for each word in the positive set *P*. We then rank the probabilities from large to small and fetch the top |*K*| keywords. We observe that although the distributions of positive documents in *U* and *P* are different, we can still find good keywords from the positive class. For example, in category *printer* of our data, we obtain representative keywords "printer", "inkjet", "Hewlett", "Packard", "ppm" etc.

For a document, the more positive keywords it contains, the more likely it belongs to the positive class. So, we use

$$\frac{\sum_{t}^{|K|} N(w_t, d_i), d_i \in CP_i}{\sum_{t}^{|K|} N(w_t, d_i), d_i \in CP_{i-1}} \tag{8}$$

to estimate TP_i/TP_{i-1}, where $\sum_{t}^{|K|} N(w_t, d_i), d_i \in CP_i$ is the total number of keywords in the document set CP_i. Intuitively, for a set CP_i (documents classified as positive) in an EM iteration, the larger the total number of positive keywords are in CP_i, the more true positive documents it contains. For instance, if CP_i contains more printer keywords, then it is likely that CP_i contains more true printer pages. It is thus reasonable to use equation (8) to estimate TP_i/TP_{i-1}.

4 Empirical Evaluation

This section evaluates the proposed technique. We compare it with existing methods, i.e., Roc [17], Roc-SVM [11], and PEBL [23]. Roc-SVM is available on the Web as a part of the LPU system (http://www.cs.uic.edu/~liub/LPU/LPU-download.html). We implemented PEBL and Roc as they are not publicly available. We do not include the results of S-EM [12] as it does not perform well due to its spy technique which heavily depends on the similarity of positive pages in U and in P.

4.1 Datasets

Our empirical evaluation is done using Web pages from 5 commercial Web sites, Amazon, CNet, PCMag, J&R and ZDnet. These sites contain many description pages of different kinds of products. We use Web pages that focus on the following categories of products: Notebook, Digital Camera, Mobile Phone, Printer and TV. Table 2 lists the number of documents downloaded from each Web site, and their corresponding classes.

The construction of positive set P and unlabeled set U is done as follows: we use web pages of a particular type of product from a single site ($Site_i$) as positive pages P, e.g., camera pages from Amazon. The unlabeled set U is the set of all product pages from another site ($Site_j$) ($i \neq j$), e.g., CNet. We also use U as the test set in our experiments because our objective is to extract or to recover those hidden positive pages in U, e.g., camera pages in CNet. In preprocessing, we removed stopwords but did not perform stemming.

Note that traditional text classification corpora, e.g., 20-Newsgroups and Reuters, are not used as the primary datasets in our experiments because these datasets do not have the different distribution problem discussed in this paper.

The irrelevant document set O is from the corpora: 20-Newsgroups and Reuters-21578. In each experiment, we randomly select $a\%$ of documents from the Reuters or 20-Newsgroups collection and add them to U. In our experiments, we use 6 a values to create different settings, i.e., 0%, 20%, 40%, 60%, 80%, and 100%.

Table 2. Number of Web pages and their classes

Web sites	Amazon	CNet	J&R	PCMag	ZDnet
Notebook	434	480	51	144	143
Camera	402	219	80	137	151
Mobile	45	109	9	43	97
Printer	767	500	104	107	80
TV	719	449	199	0	0

4.2 Results

We performed a comprehensive set of experiments using all 86 P and U combinations. For each combination dataset, we randomly add irrelevant documents from Reuters and 20-Newsgroups respectively with different a values. In other words, we select every entry (one type of product from each Web site) in Table 2 as the positive set P and use each of the other 4 Web sites as the unlabeled set U. As we discussed in Section 3.5, we use F value to evaluate the performance of our classifiers. F value only measures retrieval results of the positive class. This is suitable for us as we want to see if we can identify positive pages from the unlabeled set.

Table 3 shows the results when P is the set of camera pages from Amazon and U is the set of all product pages from CNet. We added Reuters data to U. Column 1 gives the percentage of Reuters documents added to U ($a=0\%$ means that no Reuters document is added). Column 2 to Column 10 show the results of NB, 1EM, ..., 8EM (EM usually converges within 8 iterations). From Table 3, we observe that for this dataset when $a = 0\%$, the results of NB and all EM iterations are zero. For other values of a, EM improves NB's results tremendously if we are able to select a good EM classifier. Note that we can see that the converged EM may not give the best classifier.

Table 3. A-EM results (F values in %) for P (camera pages from Amazon) and U (pages from Cnet) with different a settings

Add%	NB	1EM	2EM	3EM	4EM	5EM	6EM	7EM	8EM
$a=0$	0.00	0.00	0.00	0.00	0.00	0.00	0.00	0.00	0.00
$a=20$	2.70	4.50	12.0	30.9	83.8	**100**	100	100	100
$a=40$	19.0	93.7	**100**	100	100	100	100	100	100
$a=60$	44.7	**100**	98.9	98.0	96.5	95.6	95.0	93.6	89.2
$a=80$	70.4	**98.9**	96.1	92.8	82.8	75.1	72.9	69.5	60.5
$a=100$	80.2	**96.3**	87.8	74.9	70.1	59.2	41.8	40.9	37.0

In our experiments, we use $|K| = 10$ (10 keywords) in equation (8). We found that different values of $|K|$ give similar results as long as $|K|$ is not too small.

For this dataset, our technique in Section 3.5 is able to catch the best classifier for each a value. That is, for $a=20\%$, $a=40\%$, $a=60\%$, $a=80\%$ and $a=100\%$, the selected classifiers are from 5EM ($F = 100\%$), 2EM ($F = 100\%$), 1EM ($F = 100\%$), 1EM ($F = 98.9\%$), 1EM ($F = 96.3\%$) respectively. These results and those in Table 3 show that the amount of irrelevant data added to the unlabeled set also has an effect on the final classifier. Thus we also need to decide which classifier to use from the series of classifiers produced using different a values. We select the final classifier with the following formula:

$$\max_{a} \left(\frac{\sum_{t}^{|K|} N(w_t, d_i), d_i \in CP_{a,i}}{|CP_{a,i}|} \right), \qquad (9)$$

where $CP_{a,i}$ is the set of documents in U classified as positive using the selected classifier i for a particular a. This formula shows that we choose the classifier of the a value that has the highest average keyword count per page in $CP_{a,i}$.

Table 3 gives a good sample of the type of results that we get using EM with or without adding irrelevant documents to the unlabeled set. We observe that adding irrelevant data helps tremendously (see NB and 1EM).

Since we have conducted a large number of experiments (all 86 combinations) and compared A-EM with existing methods, to avoid gory details we summarize all the results here. Table 4 shows the summarized results when Reuters data and 20-Newsgroups data (as the irrelevant data set O) are added to U. Columns 2, 3 and 4 give the average F values of Roc, Roc-SVM and PEBL respectively. Column 5 shows the corresponding results of A-EM. For techniques Roc-SVM and PEBL, we use the same classifier selection methods as for A-EM.

Table 4. Results (F values in %) of adding Reuters and 20 Newsgroups data

Dataset added	Roc	Roc-SVM	PEBL	A-EM
Reuters	64.5	73.4	72.3	87.2
20 Newsgroups	66.7	72.6	72.1	89.1

Clearly, we can see that A-EM outperforms the other techniques dramatically. For adding Reuters data, the average F value for A-EM is 87.2%, much higher than other methods. The results of adding 20-Newsgroups are similar and A-EM's average F value is 89.1%, which is also much higher than other methods. This shows that the type of irrelevant data is not important. Another important observation is that A-EM's results are consistent, while the results of the other methods vary a great deal.

Next, we show the effectiveness of adding irrelevant documents. Table 3 already gives a good indication. However, it only shows a single data set. Table 5 summaries the average all 86 experiments of adding 20-Newsgroups documents with different a values using A-EM. From the table we can see that after adding irrelevant documents to the unlabeled sets, the results of both NB and EM (1EM-4EM) improve as compared to adding nothing ($a=0\%$). The situation is similar for adding Reuters data. From these results, we conclude that adding irrelevant data to unlabeled sets can improve the results dramatically with almost no negative effect. Comparing the results of A-EM in Tables 4 and results of EM in Table 5, it is also clear that fixing any particular iteration of EM (Table 5) as the final classifier is not a good solution. Classifier selection is an essential step in A-EM.

Table 6 further illustrates the effectiveness of our classifier selection method, which lists another set of summarized results. It compares the optimal results (manually selected best results after checking the test results from all EM iterations) and our selection results. We observe that the selection results are very close to the optimal results for both adding 20-Newsgroups data and Reuters data to the unlabeled sets, which means our classifier selection method is very effective.

Table 5. Average results (F values) of adding 20 Newsgroup documents with different a values

Add%	NB	1EM	2EM	3EM	4EM	5EM	6EM	7EM	8EM
a=0	20.0	28.4	36.3	40.9	43.4	45.9	47.0	47.6	48.5
a=20	54.9	76.1	77.8	75.5	73.9	71.2	68.9	67.5	66.1
a=40	65.2	78.2	71.9	64.4	59.7	56.8	54.3	53.3	52.4
a=60	69.5	78.4	67.4	59.1	53.8	51.6	50.0	49.0	48.6
a=80	71.9	76.2	62.6	53.9	49.5	46.9	45.0	44.2	44.2
a=100	73.4	75.7	60.4	51.8	47.2	44.6	43.7	43.4	43.4

Table 6. Best results and results of A-EM selected classifiers

Dataset Added	Best results	Selection results
20 Newsgroups	92.0	89.1
Reuters	89.8	87.2

Finally, we also tried to use O as the negative set (instead of U) to build a classifier (SVM or NB) with P, the results were very poor. On average, the NB classifier learned based on P and O only gets 12.1% F value because most negative pages in U are very different from those in O.

5 Conclusion

This paper studied the PU learning problem with different distributions of positive examples in P and positive examples in U. We showed that existing techniques performed poorly in this setting. This paper proposed an effective technique called A-EM to deal with the problem. The algorithm first boosts the similarity of the positive documents in U and P by introducing a large number of irrelevant documents into U. It then runs EM to construct a series of classifiers. A novel method for selecting a good classifier from the set of classifiers was also presented. Experimental results with product page classification show that the proposed technique is more effective than existing techniques.

Acknowledgments. The work of Bing Liu is supported by the National Science Foundation (NSF) under the NSF grant IIS-0307239. Xiaoli Li would like to thank Dr See-Kiong Ng for his help.

References

1. Basu S., Banerjee A., and Mooney R. 2002. Semi-supervised clustering by seeding. ICML-2002.
2. Blum A. and Mitchell T. 1998. Combining labeled and unlabeled data with co-training. COLT-98.
3. Bockhorst J. and Craven M. 2002. Exploiting relations among concepts to acquire weakly labeled training data. ICML-2002.
4. Crammer K., Chechik G. 2004. A needle in a haystack: local one-class optimization, ICML-2004.
5. Dempster A., Laird N. and Rubin D. 1977. Maximum likelihood from incomplete data via the EM algorithm. Journal of the Royal Statistical Society, 1977.
6. Denis F. 1998. PAC learning from positive statistical queries. ALT-98, pages 112-126. 1998.
7. Goldman S., Zhou Y. 2000. Enhancing supervised learning with unlabeled data. ICML-2000.
8. Koppel M. and Schler J. 2004. Authorship Verification as a one-class classification problem, ICML-2004.
9. Lee W., Liu B. 2003. "Learning with positive and unlabeled examples using weighted logistic regression. ICML-2003.
10. Lewis D. and Gale W. 1994. A sequential algorithm for training text classifiers. SIGIR-1994.
11. Li X., Liu B. 2003. Learning to classify text using positive and unlabeled data. IJCAI-2003.
12. Liu B., Lee W., Yu P., and Li X. 2002. Partially supervised classification of text documents. ICML-2002.
13. Liu B., Dai Y., Li X., Lee W., and Yu P. 2003. Building text classifiers using positive and unlabeled examples. ICDM-2003.
14. McCallum A. 1999. Multi-label text classification with a mixture model trained by EM. In AAAI 99 Workshop on Text Learning.
15. Muggleton S. 2001. Learning from the positive data. Machine Learning, 2001.
16. Nigam K., McCallum A., Thrun S., Mitchell T. 2000. Text classification from labeled and unlabeled documents using EM. Ma-chine Learning, 2000.
17. Rocchio J. 1971. Relevant feedback in information retrieval. In Salton G. eds. The smart retrieval system: experiments in auto-matic document processing. Englewood Cliffs, 1971.
18. Sarawagi S., Chakrabarti S. and Godbole S. 2003. Cross-training: learning probabilistic mappings between topics. KDD-2003.
19. Scholkopf B., Platt J., Shawe J., Smola A. and Williamson R. 1999. Estimating the support of a high-dimensional distribution. Technical Report MSR-TR-99-87, Microsoft Research, 1999.
20. Vapnik V. 1995. The nature of statistical learning theory.
21. Wu P., Dietterich T., G. 2004. Improving SVM accuracy by training on auxiliary data sources, ICML-2004.
22. Yang Y. and Liu X. 1999. A re-examination of text categorization methods. SIGIR-1999.
23. Yu H., Han J., and Chang K. 2002. PEBL: Positive example based learning for Web page classification using SVM. KDD-2002.
24. Yu H. 2003. General MC: Estimating boundary of positive class from small positive data. ICDM-2003.
25. Zelikovitz S. and Hirsh H. 2000. Improving short text classification using unlabeled background knowledge to assess document similarity. ICML-2000.

Towards Finite-Sample Convergence of Direct Reinforcement Learning

Shiau Hong Lim and Gerald DeJong

Dept. of Computer Science, University of Illinois, Urbana-Champaign
{shonglim, dejong}@cs.uiuc.edu

Abstract. While direct, model-free reinforcement learning often performs better than model-based approaches in practice, only the latter have yet supported theoretical guarantees for finite-sample convergence. A major difficulty in analyzing the direct approach in an online setting is the absence of a definitive exploration strategy. We extend the notion of admissibility to direct reinforcement learning and show that standard Q-learning with optimistic initial values and constant learning rate is admissible. The notion justifies the use of a greedy strategy that we believe performs very well in practice and holds theoretical significance in deriving finite-sample convergence for direct reinforcement learning. We present empirical evidence that supports our idea.

1 Introduction

Indirect (or model-based) reinforcement learning (RL) derives a policy from an estimation of state utilities and transition probabilities. It has been shown that indirect RL can provide near-optimal performance in polynomial time, e.g. E^3 (Kearns and Singh, 1998), R-max (Brahman and Tennenholtz, 2002). That is, given a Markov decision problem (MDP), a good solution can be found efficiently.

Direct (or model-free) reinforcement learners, on the other hand, estimate the utility of performing an action in a state. Thus, they learn a policy directly. But there is no corresponding formal guarantee that direct RL can produce near-optimal solutions to MDPs. However, direct methods, such as Q (Watkins, 1989) or SARSA (Rummery and Niranjan, 1994) often outperform their indirect counterparts.

While the theoretical analyses provide an important formal assurance, they appear to contribute little in the way of insights as to how to improve actual reinforcement learning algorithms. Furthermore, the particular algorithms that possess the formal guarantees (E^3 and R-max), can perform quite poorly in practice. Figure 1 shows the number of learning examples needed for convergence to a good policy as a function of problem difficulty. Here we employ a simple family of Markov decision problems we call Task 1. It will be described in section 4.

Note that the ordinate axis is logarithmic, indicating that the performance of E^3 is many orders of magnitude worse than Q. Furthermore, this Q explores purely randomly. Since Q is an off-policy learner, it acquires the optimal policy even though every action is chosen with equal probability during learning.

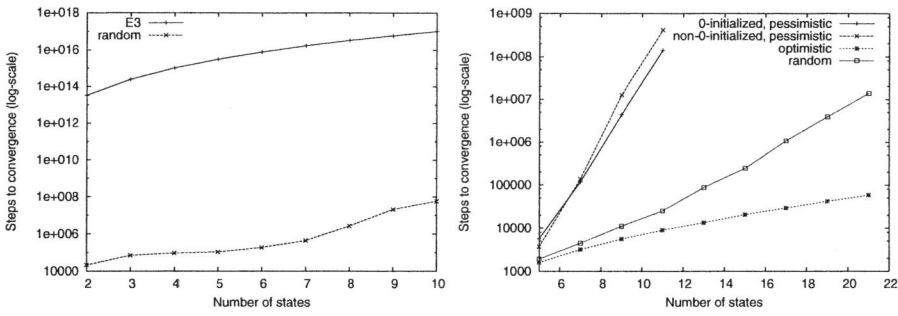

Fig. 1. Task 1   **Fig. 2.** Task 2 - Different initial Q-values

Clearly, Task 1 represents only a narrow family of MDPs but the results suggest that a theoretical analysis of direct RL may shed light on this discrepancy and may point toward even more efficient learning algorithms.

Experience suggests that there is an interesting structure differentiating direct reinforcement learners. Figure 2 shows the behavior of three Q learners that differ only in initialization. Following the principle of optimism under uncertainty (Brahman and Tennenholtz, 2002, Sutton and Barto, 1998, Koenig and Summons, 1996) one learner is initialized to optimistic random Q values, one to pessimistic random Q values, and one to all zeros. Since all the rewards are positive, this is also a pessimistic initialization. All 3 cases employ a constant learning rate ($\alpha = 0.05$) with ϵ-greedy exploration ($\epsilon = 0.1$). For comparison we also include as a fourth condition, the purely random Q learner of Fig. 1. All are exercised on a simple but more challenging problem, Task 2, which is also described in section 4. Figure 2 illustrates that optimistic initial Q-values can result in an exponential improvement in learning rate, suggesting that any attempt to derive a polynomial convergence bound without accounting for this distinction will likely be futile.

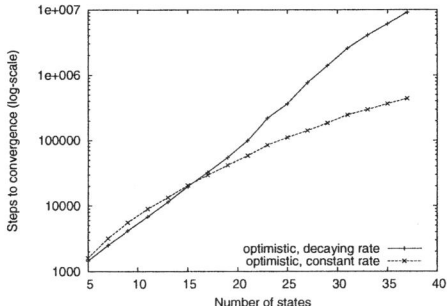

Fig. 3. Task 2 - Different learning rates

Another tension between practical and theoretical understanding concerns the learning rate, α. Asymptotic convergence of reinforcement learning dictates that $\sum \frac{1}{\alpha_i}$ must diverge but $\sum (\frac{1}{\alpha_i})^2$ must converge uniformly (Bertsekas and Tsitsiklis, 1996). But Sutton and Barto (1998) note that often a constant learning rate performs much better than a decaying one. Figure 3 compares two versions of the successful optimistic Q learner of Fig. 2. One employs the constant rate of 0.05 while the other employs a decaying rate of $\frac{1}{i^p}$ for the ith update of a state-action pair. The results shown are based on $p = 0.5001$, which is nearly the slowest possible decay that fulfills the stochastic approximation requirement for asymptotic convergence. A larger p will result in slower convergence. The results clearly favor the constant rate, at least on Task 2.

We believe there is a theoretical justification for the observed good behavior of direct reinforcement learning under optimistic initial Q-values and a small constant learning rate. The motivation of this paper is to share our theoretical findings and empirically-guided intuitions concerning such a tight polynomial convergence bound. Central is an adaptation to stochastic domains of Koenig and Simmons (1996) notion of "admissible" Q-values and Q-updates. We discuss the implications of this notion and explain the empirical observations above, as well as the results from more challenging problems.

2 Previous Work

Koenig and Simmons (1996) have shown that online Q-learning acquires an optimal policy in polynomial time if the initial Q-values are optimistic, but only for deterministic environments. The notion of "admissible" Q-values and Q-updates (similar to admissibility in A* search) plays a major role in their results. As in A*, admissibility ensures that a greedy algorithm does not miss the true optimal solution. The notion unfortunately does not directly extend to the stochastic domains. Since Q-values are defined as expected values and are estimated through sampling, any action may (temporarily) result in a Q-value that is lower than its true average and therefore risks being permanently missed by an algorithm that chooses actions greedily. This problem is called "sticking" by Kaelbling (1990) due to the fact that the algorithm may not be able to abandon a sub-optimal solution. The workaround for the problem is usually to allow some randomness in selecting actions instead of being purely greedy. It is, however, unclear how to correctly balance the tradeoff between exploration and greedy exploitation. Clearly, a purely random action selection is not desirable; a random walk may require an exponential number of steps, on average, to reach a particular state.

Even when following the optimal policy in the stochastic case, the expected number of steps to reach a particular state (e.g. the goal state) may be exponential in the size of the state space. This makes it impossible to solve a problem in polynomial time (with respect to the number of states) unless some form of relaxation is introduced. It has been shown for the model-based reinforcement learning algorithm, that a PAC learning setting allows polynomial time convergence to a near-optimal solution with high probability. In E^3 for example, this problem is addressed by defining the "ϵ-return mixing time" for a policy (with respect to the average return), and limiting attention to the class of policies with bounded mixing times. Alternatively, when discounted return is used with bounded rewards, one only needs to consider the states that are close (given the discount rate) to the initial state and reachable with significant probability. Other states simply cannot sufficiently influence the expected utility of decisions. These suggest that a similar setting should be applicable to the direct algorithms.

A critical advantage in analyzing a model-based algorithm is that the exploration can be separated from the actual learning updates. Due to strong statistical guarantees for independent samples, an accurate model can be built with a reasonable amount of sampling, and an appropriate exploration strategy that either exploits or explores (Kearns and Singh, 1998) can be derived from any partial model. In the direct, online case, such as the standard Q-learning algorithm, the coupling between noise from sampling and the policy improvement itself, frustrate assessing the benefit of exploration based upon Q-values alone. This also suggests that if certain properties of the estimated Q-values (such as admissibility) can be preserved, one might have a more easily analyzed strategy for exploration.

In (Kearns and Singh, 1999), a parallel sampling model is employed, and a direct algorithm (phased Q-learning) based on this model can achieve polynomial-time convergence, in terms of number of calls to the parallel sampling procedure. This procedure can in turn be simulated by a stationary (possibly stochastic) policy π that defines an ergodic Markov process in the MDP. The overall complexity depends on the mixing time of π to reach its stationary distribution. In practice, however, such policy might not exist, and even if it does, its mixing time might be prohibitively large with exponential dependency on the number of states and actions (the policy could simply be a random walk). We encounter this in our Task 2.

Even-Dar and Mansour (2003) analyzed the convergence rate for Q-learning with respect to different choice of the learning rate, α. They show that a linearly decaying rate ($\alpha = 1/k$ for the kth update) has an exponential dependence on $\frac{1}{1-\gamma}$. This eliminates the possibility of polynomial-time convergence for direct Q-learning based on linearly decaying α. For a polynomial learning rate ($\alpha = 1/k^w$ where $0.5 < w < 1$), the convergence rate depends largely on what was called the "covering time", which is a bound on the number of learning steps within which every state will be visited. Again, the "covering time" depends on the exploration strategy, and may not be polynomially bounded.

3 Admissibility of Q-Learning

We have seen that the major difficulty in analyzing direct, online reinforcement learning comes mostly from the fact that different exploration strategy may result in very different performance. Analysis that decouples the exploration strategy from the learning algorithm, while useful theoretically, hides the problem that we face in practice. We have also seen that "optimism under uncertainty", which is a useful notion in AI, plays significant roles in the design and verification of many algorithms. It can be realized, in the case of reinforcement learning, by using optimistic initial values and exploring greedily, as long as the probability of getting stuck is low. This motivates the definition of a slightly relaxed notion of admissibility and we show that Q-learning with optimistic initial Q-values and a constant learning rate is admissible.

We consider standard Q-learning on an MDP with a finite set of states S and a finite set of actions A. We define the optimal policy π^* with respect to a discounted return with discount factor $0 \leq \gamma < 1$ where the optimal action for a state s is given by $\pi^*(s)$. The Q-value of a state-action pair (s, a) at an unspecified point during learning is denoted by $Q(s, a)$. The Q-value of a state-action pair (s, a) after k updates (of that particular pair) is denoted by $Q_k(s, a)$. The optimal Q-value of a state-action pair (i.e. with respect to the optimal policy) is denoted by $Q^*(s, a)$, and the optimal value (utility) of a state s is given by $V^*(s) = \max_a Q^*(s, a)$. We assume discrete time step $t \in \{0, 1, 2, ...\}$, where at each time step, exactly one state-action pair will be executed and updated with Q-update:

$$Q^{t+1}(s, a) = (1 - \alpha_t)Q^t(s, a) + \alpha_t(r_t + \gamma V^t(s'))$$

where $Q^t(s, a)$ denotes the Q-value of (s, a) at time t, α_t denotes the learning rate used at time t, r_t denotes the reward received after executing the action at time t, s' denotes the next state visited, and $V^t(s') = \max_{a'} Q^t(s', a')$. We assume that the magnitude of any reward is bounded by $R_{max} > 0$, and therefore the magnitude of any discounted return is bounded by $V_{max} = \frac{R_{max}}{1-\gamma}$.

We define the notion of admissibility for direct, online Q-learning as follows:

Definition 1. *A Q-learning algorithm is admissible if after every Q-update, with probability at least $1 - \delta$,*

$$Q(s, a) \geq Q^*(s, a) - \epsilon, \quad \forall s \in S, \forall a \in A \ .$$

We would like to establish the fact that Q-learning with optimistic initial Q-values and a constant learning rate is admissible. The following lemma will help.

Lemma 1. *For any state-action pair (s, a), after k updates with constant learning rate α, with probability at least $1 - \delta$,*

$$Q_k(s, a) - Q^*(s, a) \geq -\beta + (1-\alpha)^k \Delta_0(s, a) + \gamma\alpha \sum_{i=1}^{k}(1-\alpha)^{k-i} \Delta^{t(i)}(s_i')$$

and

$$|Q_k(s, a) - Q^*(s, a)| \leq \beta + (1-\alpha)^k |\Delta_0(s, a)| + \gamma\alpha \sum_{i=1}^{k}(1-\alpha)^{k-i} |\Delta^{t(i)}(s_i')|$$

where $\Delta_0(s,a) = Q_0(s,a) - Q^*(s,a)$, s'_i is the next state visited after the ith update, $t(i)$ is the time step during the ith update, $\Delta^{t(i)}(s'_i) = V^{t(i)}(s'_i) - V^*(s'_i)$, and

$$\beta = V_{max}\sqrt{\frac{\alpha}{2(2-\alpha)}\ln\frac{2}{\delta}}.$$

Proof. For a particular state s and action a, the Q-value after the kth update is given by

$$Q_k(s,a) = (1-\alpha)^k Q_0(s,a) + \alpha\sum_{i=1}^{k}(1-\alpha)^{k-i}\Big(r_{t(i)} + \gamma V^{t(i)}(s'_i)\Big)$$

and therefore

$$Q_k(s,a) = (1-\alpha)^k\Big(Q^*(s,a) + \Delta_0(s,a)\Big) +$$

$$\alpha\sum_{i=1}^{k}(1-\alpha)^{k-i}\Big(r_{t(i)} + \gamma V^*(s'_i) + \gamma\Delta^{t(i)}(s'_i)\Big)$$

$$= (1-\alpha)^k Q^*(s,a) + \alpha\sum_{i=1}^{k}(1-\alpha)^{k-i}\hat{Q}_i(s,a)$$

$$+(1-\alpha)^k\Delta_0(s,a) + \gamma\alpha\sum_{i=1}^{k}(1-\alpha)^{k-i}\Delta^{t(i)}(s'_i)$$

where $\hat{Q}_i(s,a)$ is an unbiased sample of $Q^*(s,a)$. Since $|\hat{Q}_i(s,a)| \leq V_{max}$ and each sample is weighted by $\alpha(1-\alpha)^{k-i}$, we define

$$\bar{Q}_k(s,a) = \alpha\sum_{i=1}^{k}(1-\alpha)^{k-i}\hat{Q}_i(s,a)$$

as sum of k random variables with bounded values. Then

$$E(\bar{Q}_k(s,a)) = \alpha\sum_{i=1}^{k}(1-\alpha)^{k-i}Q^*(s,a) = \Big(1 - (1-\alpha)^k\Big)Q^*(s,a).$$

By Hoeffding's inquality,

$$Pr(|\bar{Q}_k(s,a) - E(\bar{Q}_k(s,a))| \geq \beta) \leq 2e^{-2\beta^2/\sum_{i=1}^{k}\alpha^2(1-\alpha)^{2(k-i)}V_{max}^2} \leq 2e^{-\frac{2\beta^2(2-\alpha)}{V_{max}^2\alpha}}.$$

Then, with probability at least $1-\delta$, $|\bar{Q}_k(s,a) - E(\bar{Q}_k(s,a))| \leq \beta$. Since

$$Q_k(s,a) - Q^*(s,a) = \bar{Q}_k(s,a) - E(\bar{Q}_k(s,a))$$

$$+(1-\alpha)^k\Delta_0(s,a) + \gamma\alpha\sum_{i=1}^{k}(1-\alpha)^{k-i}\Delta^{t(i)}(s'_i)$$

the Lemma follows. □

Due to the constant learning rate, we cannot expect the error in any estimated Q-value to become arbitrarily small since there is always a "window" of the most recent updates with significant weight that potentially increase the error in the Q-value. Given any rate α, there is always potential error with the magnitude of β introduced with each update. In fact, if all Q-values are initialized to the true optimal Q-values of the optimal policy and a greedy exploration is used, errors will be introduced within each Q-value in the order of β due to the inherent stochasticity of the problem. Lemma 1 suggests that we can bound this error by choosing a small enough α. This leads to the following result.

Proposition 1. *If the Q-value for every state-action pair is initialized such that*

$$\Delta_0(s,a) = Q_0(s,a) - Q^*(s,a) \geq 0, \quad \forall s \in S \forall a \in A$$

and with a constant learning rate

$$\alpha \leq 2(\frac{\epsilon^2(1-\gamma)^2}{V_{max}^2 \ln \frac{2}{\delta}})$$

then the standard Q-learning algorithm is admissible.

Proof. We will show that for all $t \geq 0$, s and a,

$$Q^t(s,a) \geq Q^*(s,a) - \epsilon$$

by strong induction on t. The statement holds trivially when $t = 0$ (before any updates) since all Q-values are initialized optimistically. Assume that it holds for $0 \leq t \leq T$. Let the update at time step T be at state s and for action a. Assume that this is the kth update for (s,a). By Lemma 1, with probability at least $1 - \delta$,

$$Q_k(s,a) - Q^*(s,a) \geq -\beta + (1-\alpha)^k \Delta_0(s,a) + \gamma\alpha \sum_{i=1}^{k}(1-\alpha)^{k-i}\Delta^{t(i)}(s_i') .$$

By the definition of β (in Lemma 1), $\alpha \leq 2(\frac{\epsilon^2(1-\gamma)^2}{V_{max}^2 \ln \frac{2}{\delta}})$ implies that $\frac{\beta}{1-\gamma} < \epsilon$. Let $b_i = \text{argmax}_{a'} Q^{t(i)}(s_i', a')$. By the induction hypothesis,

$$\Delta^{t(i)}(s_i') = Q^{t(i)}(s_i', b_i) - V^*(s_i') \geq Q^{t(i)}(s_i', b) - Q^*(s_i', b) \geq -\epsilon$$

and therefore

$$Q_k(s,a) - Q^*(s,a) \geq -\epsilon(1-\gamma) - \gamma\alpha \sum_{i=1}^{k}(1-\alpha)^{k-i}\epsilon \geq -\epsilon .\qquad\square$$

Proposition 1 essentially provides a guideline to select a learning rate small enough such that the (estimated) Q-values are never too far below the true optimal Q-value:

$$\alpha = 2(\frac{\epsilon^2(1-\gamma)^2}{V_{max}^2 \ln \frac{2}{\delta}})$$

Note that the definition of admissibility only requires that the probability of error after each update is bounded by δ. This means that the probability of error increases with the number of updates. This is partially due to the fact that we use a constant learning rate. However, note that the cost of having higher confidence (logarithmic dependency) is much lower than having higher accuracy (quadratic dependency). This means that as long as the total number of updates needed is a polynomial (in terms of all other parameters), the effect on α is relatively small.

4 Experiments

We have established the admissibility of Q-learning with optimistic initial values and a constant learning rate. The natural consequence is that a greedy exploration strategy would seem to be the most efficient, since it always focuses on the most promising region of the state space. We support this by first analyzing the experiment results for both Task 1 and Task 2.

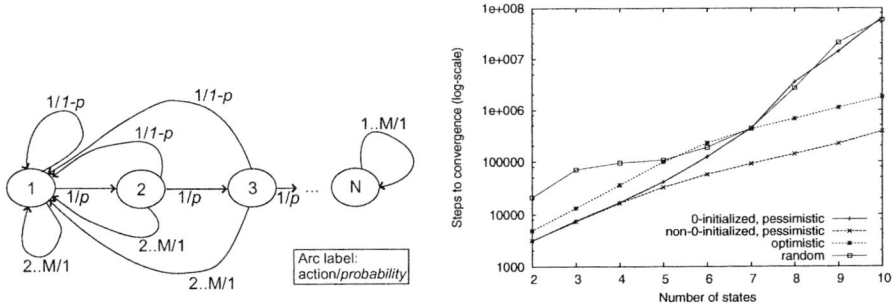

Fig. 4. Task 1 **Fig. 5.** Task 1 Results

Figure 4 shows task 1, which is an MDP with N states ($N \geq 2$) and M actions. State 1 is a fixed, initial state, and state N is an absorbing, goal state. Executing action 1 in any non-goal state s results in state $s+1$ with probability p and in state 1 with probability $1-p$. Executing actions $2 \leq a \leq M$ in any non-goal state results in state 1 with probability 1. All transitions give zero rewards except the transition to the goal state, where a reward $R = 10$ will be received.

The learning results for direct Q-learning with various setups are shown in Fig. 5. Note that the y-axis uses logarithmic scale. Each graph is the average of 10 independent learning instances. For each instance, we evaluate the resulting policy after every episode (of 200 steps each) and stop when more than 95% of the last 500 episodes end with the optimal policy. We omit error bars in all the results for both Task 1 and Task 2 since the observed variances are barely visible under the logarithmic scale.

Task 1 is a problem where the average number of steps to reach the goal is exponential in the number of states (in the order of $(\frac{1}{p})^{N-1}$), even with the optimal policy. As mentioned in section 2, under the PAC model, we allow a small amount of error, and the cost (in terms of learning time) to reduce the error will be considered reasonable as long as it is a polynomial in $\frac{1}{\epsilon}$. This is best illustrated by an example. Consider task 1, where the optimal Q-value for the initial state is given by:

$$Q^*(1,1) = \frac{Rp(1-p\gamma)(p\gamma)^{N-2}}{1-\gamma+\gamma(1-p)(\gamma p)^{N-1}}.$$

The optimal policy for task 1 requires that action 1 be chosen in every non-goal state. Any deviation from the optimal policy will result in a policy π with expected return $Q^\pi(1,\pi(1)) = 0$. This also implies that if $Q^\pi(1,\pi(1)) - Q^*(1,1) < \epsilon$, then every policy satisfies the requirement and therefore no learning is needed. We therefore assume that $Q^\pi(1,\pi(1)) - Q^*(1,1) < \epsilon$, which implies:

$$\frac{Rp(1-p\gamma)(p\gamma)^{N-2}}{1-\gamma+\gamma(1-p)(\gamma p)^{N-1}} \geq \epsilon \quad \Rightarrow \quad (\frac{R}{1-\gamma})\frac{1}{\epsilon} \geq (\frac{1}{p})^{N-1}.$$

Regardless of the value of p, whenever ϵ is small enough such that finding the optimal policy is necessary, the average number of steps to reach the goal state is in the order of $\mathcal{O}\{(\frac{R}{1-\gamma})\frac{1}{\epsilon}\}$. This renders the problem tractable in terms of the amount of learning needed with respect to the acceptable error.

We see that in task 1, the pessimistic case with non-zero initial Q-values actually performs better than the optimistic case, but they both have roughly the same rate of growth in learning time as the size of the problem grows. The difference in performance can be accounted by the fact that the optimistic case starts with a much higher Q-value estimate for most of the states and needs more learning updates to approach the true Q-values. On the other hand, the pessimistic case with zero-initialized values has a significantly higher rate of growth, and actually performs no better than the purely random strategy (especially when N is large). Since task 1 naturally requires an exponential number of learning steps (with respect to N), one might ask whether the error that we discussed above applies. It only applies whenever the optimal policy is executed. Since in the case of zero-initialized Q-values, the initial phase of learning is essentially a random walk (the Q-values remain unchanged) and in Task 1, it takes an exponential number of trials (in M) to realize a sequence of actions that corresponds to the optimal policy, this cost is in addition to the fact that the average number of steps to reach the goal through the optimal policy is exponential in N.

Task 1 does not reveal the problem with using pessimistic (but non-zero) initial Q-values since there is only one goal state and one optimal policy. Figure 6 shows Task 2, whose learning results are shown in Fig. 2 (Section 1). In this MDP, there are two absorbing states (N and -N). The states that lead to state N behaves exactly like those in Task 1, that is, progress is made only when action 1 is executed. On the other hand, progress is made toward state -N when any action except action 1 is executed. In our actual experiment, we use $p = 0.8$

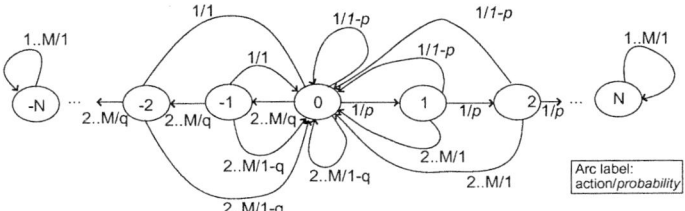

Fig. 6. Task 2

and $q = 0.99$. The reward for reaching state N is 10 while the reward for reaching state $-N$ is 1. This makes state N harder to reach, but more desirable in terms of the actual return (for small N). We use ϵ-greedy exploration with $\epsilon = 0.1$ for both pessimistic cases. Both cases converge to the wrong goal very quickly, and get "stuck" on this policy. It takes an extremely large number of trials to escape from this situation, relying on the randomness (ϵ) in the exploration strategy. Figure 2 shows that a purely random exploration actually performs better in this case since sticking cannot happen. Task 2 shows a clear performance advantage for the strategy with optimistic initial values.

4.1 More Challenging Problems

We further illustrate the advantage of greedy exploration with optimistic initial Q-values with more realistic problems. We use the acrobot swing-up problem as described in Sutton and Barto, (1998). We first run the acrobot using the original configuration, then we add friction and noise to the system to increase its difficulty. We run 10 independent instances of both optimistic and pessimistic strategies on both experiments. The results are shown in Figs. 7 and 8. We observe that when the difficulty of the problem increases (in the sense that less random action sequences can reach the goal) the difference in performance becomes more significant as well.

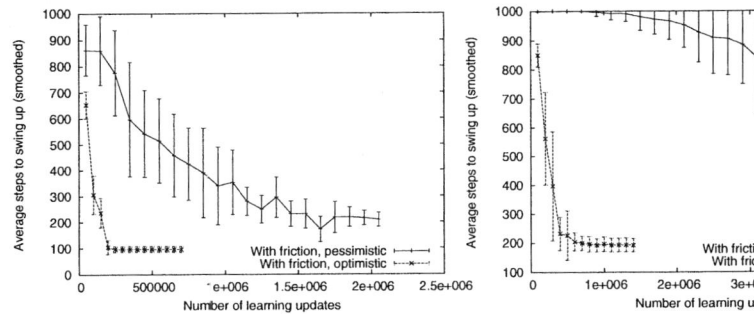

Fig. 7. Acrobot (No friction)   **Fig. 8.** Acrobot (With friction)

We repeat the experiment on a 2-dimensional mountain-car problem, which is similar to the mountain-car problem described in (Sutton, 1996), but extended to 2 dimensions (for the navigation). We use a steepness factor to control the difficulty of the problem. The results are shown in Figs. 9 and 10. We observe the same performance pattern as in the acrobot problem when we increase the steepness of the mountain. It is conceivable that good action sequences become rarer as problems become harder. We believe that greedy exploration with optimistic initial Q-values results in a rather "uniform" but efficient search in the policy space. This explains the relatively minor increase in learning time as the problem becomes more difficult.

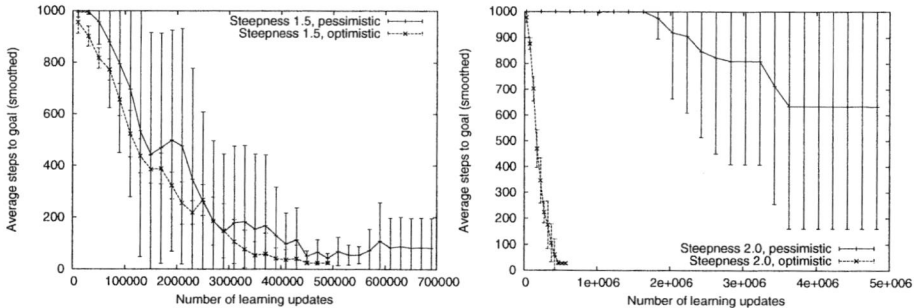

Fig. 9. 2D Mountain Car (steepness 1.5)   **Fig. 10.** 2D Mountain Car (steepness 2.0)

5 Conclusion

The admissibility of Q-learning justifies the use of a greedy policy with constant learning rate. We have observed empirically that this strategy outperforms the others in simple and challenging problems. We believe that the empirical evidence of the effectiveness of this strategy makes it worthy of further attention in search of a more theoretical understanding of direct reinforcement learning. We believe that the same strategy also applies to more general learning algorithms that require exploration. We speculate that the final piece of puzzle needed to obtain a polynomial convergence bound for direct reinforcement learning is to establish the fact that the errors introduced in the initial Q values vanish at a reasonably high rate. We argue but cannot yet prove that this is achievable (at least with a constant learning rate) due to the contraction property of value iteration, which underlies the Q-learning algorithm.

Acknowledgements

This material is based upon work supported in part by the Information Processing Technology Office of the Defense Advanced Research Projects Agency under award HR0011-05-1-0040 and in part by the National Science Foundation under Award NSF IIS 04-13161. Any opinions, findings, and conclusions or recommendations expressed in this publication are those of the authors and do not necessarily reflect the views of the Defense Advanced Research Projects Agency or the National Science Foundation.

References

Bertsekas, D.P., Tsitsiklis, J.N. (1996): Neuro-Dynamic Programming. Athena Scientific, Belmont, MA.

Brafman, R.I., Tennenholtz, M. (2002): R-max, A General Polynomial Time Algorithm for Near-Optimal Reinforcement Learning. Journal of Machine Learning Research, 3, pp. 213–231.

Even-Dar, E., Mansour, Y. (2003): Learning rates for Q-Learning. Journal of Machine Learning Research, 5, pp. 1–25.

Kaelbling, L. (1990): Learning in Embedded Systems. PhD thesis, Computer Science Department, Stanford University.

Kearns, M., Singh, S. (1998): Near-Optimal Reinforcement Learning in Polynomial Time. Proc. of 15th ICML, pp. 260–268, Morgan Kaufman.

Kearns, M., Singh, S. (1999): Finite-Sample Rates of Convergence for Q-Learning and Indirect Methods. Advances in Neural Information Processing Systems 11, The MIT Press, pp. 996–1002.

Koenig, S., Simmons, R.G. (1996): The Effect of Representation and Knowledge on Goal-Directed Exploration with Reinforcement Learning Algorithms. Machine Learning, 22 (1/3), pp. 227–250.

Rummery, G. A., Niranjan, M. (1994): On-line Q-learning using connectionist systems. Tech. Report CUED/F-INFENG/TR 166, Cambridge University Engineering Dept.

Sutton, R. (1996): Generalization in Reinforcement Learning: Successful Examples Using Sparse Coarse Coding. Advances in Neural Information Processing Systems 8 pp. 1038–1044, MIT Press.

Sutton, R., Barto, A. (1998): Reinforcement Learning. MIT Press, Cambridge, MA.

Watkins, C.J.C.H. (1989): Learning from Delayed Rewards. PhD thesis, Cambridge, England.

Infinite Ensemble Learning with Support Vector Machines

Hsuan-Tien Lin and Ling Li

Learning Systems Group, California Institute of Technology, USA
htlin@caltech.edu, ling@caltech.edu

Abstract. Ensemble learning algorithms such as boosting can achieve better performance by averaging over the predictions of base hypotheses. However, existing algorithms are limited to combining only a finite number of hypotheses, and the generated ensemble is usually sparse. It is not clear whether we should construct an ensemble classifier with a larger or even infinite number of hypotheses. In addition, constructing an infinite ensemble itself is a challenging task. In this paper, we formulate an infinite ensemble learning framework based on SVM. The framework can output an infinite and nonsparse ensemble, and can be used to construct new kernels for SVM as well as to interpret some existing ones. We demonstrate the framework with a concrete application, the stump kernel, which embodies infinitely many decision stumps. The stump kernel is simple, yet powerful. Experimental results show that SVM with the stump kernel is usually superior than boosting, even with noisy data.

1 Introduction

Ensemble learning algorithms, such as boosting [1], are successful in practice. They construct a classifier that averages over some base hypotheses in a set $\mathcal{H}$. While the size of $\mathcal{H}$ can be infinite in theory, existing algorithms can utilize only a small finite subset of $\mathcal{H}$, and the classifier is effectively a finite ensemble of hypotheses. On the one hand, the classifier is a regularized approximation to the optimal one (see Subsection 2.2), and hence may be less vulnerable to overfitting [2]. On the other hand, it is limited in capacity [3], and may not be powerful enough. Thus, it is unclear whether an infinite ensemble would be superior for learning. In addition, it is a challenging task to construct an infinite ensemble of hypotheses [4].

The goal of this paper is to conquer the task of infinite ensemble learning in order to see if an infinite ensemble could achieve better performance. We formulate a framework for infinite ensemble learning based on the support vector machine (SVM) [4]. The key is to embed an infinite number of hypotheses into an SVM kernel. Such a framework can be applied both to construct new kernels for SVM, and to interpret some existing ones [5]. Furthermore, the framework allows a fair comparison between SVM and ensemble learning algorithms.

As a concrete application of the framework, we introduce the stump kernel, which embodies an infinite number of decision stumps. The stump kernel is novel and is simpler than most existing kernels for SVM. Somehow it is powerful both in theory and in practice. Experimental results show that with the stump kernel, our framework usually achieves better performance than popular ensemble learning algorithms. Our results also bring in some important insights for both SVM and ensemble learning.

The paper is organized as follows. In Section 2, we show the connections between SVM and the ensemble learning. Next in Section 3, we propose the framework for embedding an infinite number of hypotheses into the kernel. We then present the stump kernel in Section 4. Finally, we show the experimental results in Section 5, and conclude in Section 6.

2   SVM and Ensemble Learning

2.1   Support Vector Machine

Given a training set $\{(x_i, y_i)\}_{i=1}^{N}$, which contains input vectors $x_i \in \mathcal{X} \subseteq \mathbb{R}^D$ and their corresponding labels $y_i \in \{-1, +1\}$, the soft-margin SVM [4] constructs a classifier $g(x) = \text{sign}(\langle w, \phi_x \rangle + b)$ from the optimal solution to the following problem:[1]

$$(P_1) \quad \min_{w \in \mathcal{F}, b \in \mathbb{R}, \xi \in \mathbb{R}^N} \frac{1}{2} \langle w, w \rangle + C \sum_{i=1}^{N} \xi_i$$

$$\text{s.t.} \quad y_i(\langle w, \phi_{x_i} \rangle + b) \geq 1 - \xi_i, \quad \xi_i \geq 0.$$

Here $C > 0$ is the regularization parameter, and $\phi_x = \Phi(x)$ is obtained from the feature mapping $\Phi \colon \mathcal{X} \to \mathcal{F}$. We assume the feature space $\mathcal{F}$ to be a Hilbert space equipped with the inner product $\langle \cdot, \cdot \rangle$ [6]. Because $\mathcal{F}$ can be of an infinite number of dimensions, SVM solvers usually work on the dual problem:

$$(P_2) \quad \min_{\lambda \in \mathbb{R}^N} \frac{1}{2} \sum_{i=1}^{N} \sum_{j=1}^{N} \lambda_i \lambda_j y_i y_j \mathcal{K}(x_i, x_j) - \sum_{i=1}^{N} \lambda_i$$

$$\text{s.t.} \quad \sum_{i=1}^{N} y_i \lambda_i = 0, \quad 0 \leq \lambda_i \leq C.$$

Here $\mathcal{K}$ is the kernel function defined as $\mathcal{K}(x, x') = \langle \phi_x, \phi_{x'} \rangle$. Then, the optimal classifier becomes

$$g(x) = \text{sign}\left(\sum_{i=1}^{N} y_i \lambda_i \mathcal{K}(x_i, x) + b \right), \tag{1}$$

where b can be computed through the primal-dual relationship [4, 6].

The use of a kernel function $\mathcal{K}$ instead of computing the inner product directly in $\mathcal{F}$ is called the kernel trick, which works when $\mathcal{K}(\cdot, \cdot)$ can be computed

---
[1] $\text{sign}(\theta)$ is 1 when θ is nonnegative, -1 otherwise.

efficiently. Alternatively, we can begin with an arbitrary $\mathcal{K}$, and check whether there exist a space $\mathcal{F}$ and a mapping Φ such that $\mathcal{K}(\cdot,\cdot)$ is a valid inner product in $\mathcal{F}$. A key tool here is the Mercer's condition, which states that a symmetric $\mathcal{K}(\cdot,\cdot)$ is a valid inner product if and only if its Gram matrix K, defined by $K_{\{i,\,j\}} = \mathcal{K}(x_i, x_j)$, is always positive semi-definite (PSD) [4,6].

The soft-margin SVM originates from the hard-margin SVM, where the margin violations ξ_i are forced to be zero. This can be achieved by setting the regularization parameter $C \to \infty$ in (P_1) and (P_2).

2.2 Adaptive Boosting

Adaptive boosting (AdaBoost) [1] is perhaps the most popular and successful algorithm for ensemble learning. For a given integer T and a hypothesis set $\mathcal{H}$, AdaBoost iteratively selects T hypotheses $h_t \in \mathcal{H}$ and weights $w_t \geq 0$ to construct an ensemble classifier

$$g(x) = \text{sign}\left(\sum_{t=1}^{T} w_t h_t(x)\right).$$

Under some assumptions, it is shown that when $T \to \infty$, AdaBoost asymptotically approximates an infinite ensemble classifier $\text{sign}(\sum_{t=1}^{\infty} w_t h_t(x))$ [7], such that (w, h) is an optimal solution to

$$(P_3) \quad \min_{w_t \in \mathbb{R}, h_t \in \mathcal{H}} \|w\|_1$$

$$\text{s.t.} \quad y_i \left(\sum_{t=1}^{\infty} w_t h_t(x_i)\right) \geq 1, \quad w_t \geq 0.$$

The problem (P_3) has infinitely many variables. In order to approximate the optimal solution well with a fixed T, AdaBoost has to resort to two related properties of the optimal solutions for (P_3). First, when two hypotheses have the same prediction patterns on the training vectors, they can be used interchangeably in constructing an ensemble, and are thus called "ambiguous". Since there are at most 2^N prediction patterns on N input vectors, we can partition $\mathcal{H}$ into at most 2^N groups, each containing mutually ambiguous hypotheses. Some optimal solutions of (P_3) only assign one or a few nonzero weights within each group [8]. Thus, it is possible to work on a finite subset of $\mathcal{H}$ instead of $\mathcal{H}$ itself without losing optimality.

Second, minimizing the ℓ_1-norm $\|w\|_1$ often leads to sparse solutions [2,9]. That is, for hypotheses in the finite (but possibly still large) subset of $\mathcal{H}$, only a small number of weights needs to be nonzero. Many ensemble learning algorithms, including AdaBoost, try to find or approximate such a finite and sparse ensemble. However, it is not clear whether the performance could further be improved if either or both the finiteness and the sparsity restrictions are removed.[2]

---

[2] Qualitatively, sparsity is algorithm-dependent and more restricted than finiteness.

2.3 Connecting SVM to Ensemble Learning

SVM and AdaBoost are related. Consider the feature transform

$$\Phi(x) = (h_1(x), h_2(x), \ldots). \tag{2}$$

We can clearly see that the problem (P_1) with this feature transform is similar to (P_3). The elements of ϕ_x in SVM and the hypotheses $h_t(x)$ in AdaBoost play similar roles. They both work on linear combinations of these elements, though SVM has an additional intercept term b. SVM minimizes the ℓ_2-norm of the weights while AdaBoost approximately minimizes the ℓ_1-norm. Note that AdaBoost requires $w_t \geq 0$ for ensemble learning.

Another difference is that for regularization, SVM introduces slack variables ξ_i, while AdaBoost relies on the choice of a finite T [2]. Note that we can also introduce proper slack variables to (P_3) and solve it by the linear programming boosting method [8]. In the scope of this paper, however, we shall focus only on AdaBoost.

The connection between SVM and AdaBoost is well known in literature [10]. Several researchers have developed interesting results based on the connection [2,7]. However, as limited as AdaBoost, previous results could utilize only a finite subset of $\mathcal{H}$ when constructing the feature mapping (2). One reason is that the infinite number of variables w_t and constraints $w_t \geq 0$ are difficult to handle. We will further illustrate these difficulties and our remedies in the next section.

3 SVM-Based Framework for Infinite Ensemble Learning

Vapnik [4] proposed a challenging task of designing an algorithm that actually generates an infinite ensemble classifier. Traditional algorithms like AdaBoost cannot be directly generalized to solve this problem, because they select the hypotheses in an iterative manner, and only run for finite number of iterations.

The connection between SVM and ensemble learning shows another possible approach. We can formulate a kernel that embodies all the hypotheses in $\mathcal{H}$. Then, the classifier (1) obtained from SVM with this kernel is a linear combination of those hypotheses (with an intercept term). However, there are still two main obstacles. One is to actually derive the kernel, and the other is to handle the constraints $w_t \geq 0$ to make (1) an ensemble classifier. In this section, we integrate several ideas to deal with these obstacles, and propose a framework of infinite ensemble learning based on SVM.

3.1 Embedding Hypotheses into the Kernel

We start by embedding the infinite number of hypotheses in $\mathcal{H}$ into an SVM kernel. We have shown in (2) that we could construct a feature mapping from $\mathcal{H}$. In Definition 1, we extend this idea to a more general form, and define a kernel based on the feature mapping.

Definition 1. *Assume that $\mathcal{H} = \{h_\alpha : \alpha \in \mathcal{C}\}$, where $\mathcal{C}$ is a measure space. The kernel that embodies $\mathcal{H}$ is defined as*

$$\mathcal{K}_{\mathcal{H},r}(x, x') = \int_{\mathcal{C}} \phi_x(\alpha) \phi_{x'}(\alpha) \, d\alpha, \tag{3}$$

where $\phi_x(\alpha) = r(\alpha) h_\alpha(x)$, and $r \colon \mathcal{C} \to \mathbb{R}^+$ is chosen such that the integral exists for all $x, x' \in \mathcal{X}$.

Here, α is the parameter of the hypothesis h_α. Although two hypotheses with different α values may have the same input-output relation, we would treat them as different objects in our framework. We shall denote $\mathcal{K}_{\mathcal{H},r}$ by $\mathcal{K}_{\mathcal{H}}$ when r is clear from the context.

If $\mathcal{C}$ is a closed interval $[L, R]$, the right-hand-side of (3) is obviously an inner product [6], and hence Definition 1 constructs a valid kernel. In the following theorem, the validity is formalized for a general $\mathcal{C}$.

Theorem 1. *Consider the kernel $\mathcal{K}_{\mathcal{H}} = \mathcal{K}_{\mathcal{H},r}$ in Definition 1.*

1. *The kernel is an inner product for ϕ_x and $\phi_{x'}$ in the Hilbert space $\mathcal{F} = \mathcal{L}_2(\mathcal{C})$, which contains functions $\varphi(\cdot) \colon \mathcal{C} \to \mathbb{R}$ that are square integrable.*
2. *For a set of input vectors $\{x_i\}_{i=1}^N \in \mathcal{X}^N$, the Gram matrix of $\mathcal{K}$ is PSD.*

Proof. The first part is in function analysis [11], and the second part follows Mercer's condition. □

The technique of constructing kernels from an integral inner product is known in literature [6]. Our framework utilizes this technique for embedding the hypotheses, and thus could handle the situation even when $\mathcal{H}$ is uncountable.

When we use $\mathcal{K}_{\mathcal{H}}$ in (P_2), the primal problem (P_1) becomes

$$(P_4) \quad \min_{w \in \mathcal{L}_2(\mathcal{C}), b \in \mathbb{R}, \xi \in \mathbb{R}^N} \frac{1}{2} \int_{\mathcal{C}} w^2(\alpha) \, d\alpha + C \sum_{i=1}^N \xi_i$$

$$\text{s.t.} \quad y_i \left(\int_{\mathcal{C}} w(\alpha) r(\alpha) h_\alpha(x_i) \, d\alpha + b \right) \geq 1 - \xi_i, \quad \xi_i \geq 0.$$

In particular, the classifier obtained after solving (P_2) with $\mathcal{K}_{\mathcal{H}}$ is the same as the classifier obtained after solving (P_4):

$$g(x) = \text{sign}\left(\int_{\mathcal{C}} w(\alpha) r(\alpha) h_\alpha(x) \, d\alpha + b \right). \tag{4}$$

When $\mathcal{C}$ is uncountable, it is possible that each hypothesis h_α only takes an infinitesimal weight $w(\alpha) r(\alpha) \, d\alpha$ in the ensemble. This is very different from the situation in traditional ensemble learning, and will be discussed further in Subsection 4.3.

3.2 Negation Completeness and Constant Hypotheses

Note that (4) is not an ensemble classifier yet, because we do not have the constraints $w(\alpha) \geq 0$, and we have an additional term b. Next, we would explain that (4) is equivalent to an ensemble classifier under some reasonable assumptions.

We start from the constraints $w(\alpha) \geq 0$, which cannot be directly considered in (P_1). It has been shown that even if we add a countably infinite number of constraints to (P_1), we introduce infinitely many variables and constraints in (P_2), which makes the later problem difficult to solve [4].

One remedy is to assume that $\mathcal{H}$ is negation complete, that is, $h \in \mathcal{H}$ if and only if $(-h) \in \mathcal{H}$.[3] Then, every linear combination over $\mathcal{H}$ has an equivalent linear combination with only nonnegative weights. Negation completeness is usually a mild assumption for a reasonable $\mathcal{H}$. Following this assumption, the classifier (4) can be interpreted as an ensemble classifier over $\mathcal{H}$ with an intercept term b. Somehow b can be viewed as the weight on a constant hypothesis c.[4] We shall further add a mild assumption that $\mathcal{H}$ contains both c and $(-c)$, which makes $g(\cdot)$ in (4) or (1) indeed equivalent to an ensemble classifier.

We summarize our framework in Fig. 1. The framework shall generally inherit the profound performance of SVM. Most of the steps in the framework could be done by existing SVM algorithms, and the hard part is mostly in obtaining the kernel $\mathcal{K}_{\mathcal{H}}$. We have derived several useful kernels with the framework [5]. In the next section, we demonstrate one concrete instance of those kernels.

---

1. Consider a training set $\{(x_i, y_i)\}_{i=1}^{N}$ and the hypothesis set $\mathcal{H}$, which is assumed to be negation complete and to contain a constant hypothesis.
2. Construct a kernel $\mathcal{K}_{\mathcal{H}}$ according to Definition 1 with a proper r.
3. Choose proper parameters, such as the soft-margin parameter C.
4. Solve (P_2) with $\mathcal{K}_{\mathcal{H}}$ and obtain Lagrange multipliers λ_i and the intercept term b.
5. Output the classifier $g(x) = \text{sign}\left(\sum_{i=1}^{N} y_i \lambda_i \mathcal{K}_{\mathcal{H}}(x_i, x) + b\right)$, which is equivalent to some ensemble classifier over $\mathcal{H}$.

Fig. 1. Steps of the SVM-based framework for infinite ensemble learning

4 Stump Kernel

In this section, we present the stump kernel, which embodies infinitely many decision stumps, as a concrete application of our framework. The decision stump $s_{q,d,\alpha}(x) = q \cdot \text{sign}((x)_d - \alpha)$ works on the d-th element of x, and classifies x according to $q \in \{-1, +1\}$ and the threshold α [12]. It is widely used for ensemble learning because of its simplicity [1].

---

[3] We use $(-h)$ to denote the function $(-h)(\cdot) = -(h(\cdot))$.
[4] A constant hypothesis $c(\cdot)$ predicts $c(x) = 1$ for all $x \in \mathcal{X}$.

4.1 Formulation

To construct the stump kernel, we consider the following set of decision stumps

$$\mathcal{S} = \{s_{q,d,\alpha_d} : q \in \{-1, +1\}, d \in \{1, \ldots, D\}, \alpha_d \in [L_d, R_d]\}.$$

In addition, we assume that $\mathcal{X} \subseteq [L_1, R_1] \times [L_2, R_2] \times \cdots \times [L_D, R_D]$. Then, $\mathcal{S}$ is negation complete, and contains $s_{+1,1,L_1}(\cdot)$ as a constant hypothesis. Thus, the stump kernel $\mathcal{K}_\mathcal{S}$ defined below can be used in our framework (Fig. 1) to obtain an infinite ensemble of decision stumps.

Definition 2. *The stump kernel $\mathcal{K}_\mathcal{S}$ is defined as in Definition 1 for the set $\mathcal{S}$ with $r(q, d, \alpha_d) = \frac{1}{2}$,*

$$\mathcal{K}_\mathcal{S}(x, x') = \Delta_\mathcal{S} - \sum_{d=1}^{D} \left|(x)_d - (x')_d\right| = \Delta_\mathcal{S} - \|x - x'\|_1,$$

where $\Delta_\mathcal{S} = \frac{1}{2} \sum_{d=1}^{D} (R_d - L_d)$ is a constant.

To obtain the stump kernel in Definition 2, we separate the integral (3) into two parts: stumps having the same outputs on x and x', and stumps having different outputs on x and x'. Both parts exist and are easy to compute when we simply assign a constant r to all $r(q, d, \alpha_d)$. Note that scaling r is equivalent to scaling the parameter C in SVM. Thus, without loss of generality, we choose $r = \frac{1}{2}$ to obtain a cosmetically cleaner kernel function.

Following Theorem 1, the stump kernel produces a PSD Gram matrix for $x_i \in \mathcal{X}$. Given the ranges $[L_d, R_d]$, the stump kernel is very simple to compute. In fact, the ranges are even not necessary in general, because dropping the constant $\Delta_\mathcal{S}$ does not affect the classifier obtained from SVM:

Theorem 2. *Solving (P_2) with $\mathcal{K}_\mathcal{S}$ is the same as solving (P_2) with the simplified stump kernel $\tilde{\mathcal{K}}_\mathcal{S}(x, x') = -\|x - x'\|_1$. That is, they obtain equivalent classifiers in (1).*

Proof. We extend from [13] to show that $\tilde{\mathcal{K}}_\mathcal{S}(x, x')$ is conditionally PSD (CPSD). In addition, a CPSD kernel $\tilde{\mathcal{K}}(x, x')$ works exactly the same for (P_2) as any PSD kernel of the form $\tilde{\mathcal{K}}(x, x') + \Delta$, where Δ is a constant, because of the linear constraint $\sum_{i=1}^{N} y_i \lambda_i = 0$ [6,14]. The proof follows with $\Delta = \Delta_\mathcal{S}$. □

Although the simplified stump kernel is simple to compute, it provides comparable classification ability for SVM, as shown below.

4.2 Power of the Stump Kernel

The classification ability of the stump kernel comes from the following positive definite (PD) property under some mild assumptions:

Theorem 3. *Consider input vectors $\{x_i\}_{i=1}^{N} \in \mathcal{X}^N$. If there exists a dimension d such that $(x_i)_d \in (L_d, R_d)$ and $(x_i)_d \neq (x_j)_d$ for all $i \neq j$, the Gram matrix of $\mathcal{K}_\mathcal{S}$ is PD.*

Proof. See [5] for details. □

The PD-ness of the Gram matrix is directly connected to the classification power of the SVM classifiers. Chang and Lin [15] show that when the Gram matrix of the kernel is PD, a hard-margin SVM with such kernel can always dichotomize the training vectors. Thus, Theorem 3 implies:

Theorem 4. *The class of SVM classifiers with $\mathcal{K}_\mathcal{S}$, or equivalently, the class of infinite ensemble classifiers over $\mathcal{S}$, has an infinite V-C dimension.*

Theorem 4 indicates the power of the stump kernel. A famous kernel that also provides infinite power to SVM is the Gaussian kernel [16]. The theorem shows that the stump kernel has theoretically almost the same power as the Gaussian kernel. Note that such power needs to be controlled with care because the power of fitting any data can also be abused to fit noise. For the Gaussian kernel, it has been observed that soft-margin SVM with suitable parameter selection can regularize the power and achieve good generalization performance even in the presence of noise [16, 17]. The stump kernel, which is similar to the Gaussian kernel, also has such property when used in soft-margin SVM. We shall further demonstrate this property experimentally in Section 5.

4.3 Averaging Ambiguous Stumps

We have shown in Subsection 2.2 that the set of hypotheses can be partitioned into groups and traditional ensemble learning algorithms can only pick a few representatives within each group. Our framework acts in a different way: the ℓ_2-norm objective function of SVM leads to an optimal solution that combines the average predictions of each group. In other words, the consensus output of each group is the average prediction of all hypotheses in the group rather than the predictions of a few selected ones. The averaging process constructs a smooth representative for each group. In the following theorem, we shall demonstrate this with our stump kernel, and show how the decision stumps group together in the final ensemble classifier.

Theorem 5. *Define $(\tilde{x})_{d,a}$ as the a-th smallest value in $\{(x_i)_d\}_{i=1}^{N}$, and A_d as the number of different $(\tilde{x})_{d,a}$. Let $(\tilde{x})_{d,0} = L_d$, $(\tilde{x})_{d,(A_d+1)} = R_d$, and*

$$\hat{s}_{q,d,a}(x) = q \cdot \begin{cases} 1, & \text{when } (x)_d \geq (\tilde{x})_{d,t+1}; \\ -1, & \text{when } (x)_d \leq (\tilde{x})_{d,t}; \\ \frac{2(x)_d - (\tilde{x})_{d,a} - (\tilde{x})_{d,a+1}}{(\tilde{x})_{d,a+1} - (\tilde{x})_{d,a}}, & \text{otherwise.} \end{cases}$$

Then, for $r(q,d,a) = \frac{1}{2}\sqrt{(\tilde{x})_{d,a+1} - (\tilde{x})_{d,a}}$,

$$K_\mathcal{S}(x,x') = \sum_{q \in \{-1,+1\}} \sum_{d=1}^{D} \sum_{a=0}^{A_d} r^2(q,d,a)\hat{s}_{q,d,a}(x)\hat{s}_{q,d,a}(x').$$

We can prove Theorem 5 by carefully writing down the equations. Note that the function $\hat{s}_{q,d,t}(\cdot)$ is a smoother variant of the decision stump. Each $\hat{s}_{q,d,t}(\cdot)$ represents the group of ambiguous decision stumps with $\alpha_d \in ((\tilde{x})_{d,t}, (\tilde{x})_{d,t+1})$. When the group is larger, $\hat{s}_{q,d,t}(\cdot)$ is smoother because it is the average over more decision stumps. Traditional ensemble learning algorithms like AdaBoost usually consider the middle stump $m_{q,d,t}(\cdot)$, which has threshold at the mean of $(\tilde{x})_{d,t}$ and $(\tilde{x})_{d,t+1}$, as the only representative of the group. Our framework, on the other hand, enjoys a smoother decision by averaging over more decision stumps. Even though each decision stump only has an infinitesimal hypothesis weight, the averaged stump $\hat{s}_{q,d,t}(\cdot)$ could have a concrete weight in the ensemble, which explains how the infinitesimal weights work.

5 Experiments

We test and compare several ensemble learning algorithms, including our framework with the stump kernel, on various datasets.

The first algorithm we test is our framework with the simplified stump kernel, denoted as SVM-Stump. It is compared with AdaBoost-Stump, AdaBoost with decision stumps as base hypotheses. A common implementation of AdaBoost-Stump only chooses the middle stumps (see Subsection 4.3). For further comparison, we take the set of middle stumps $\mathcal{M}$, and construct a kernel $\mathcal{K}_{\mathcal{M}}$ with $r = \frac{1}{2}$ according to Definition 1. Because $\mathcal{M}$ is a finite set, the integral in (3) becomes a summation when computed with the counting measure. We test our framework with this kernel, and call it SVM-Mid. We also compare SVM-Stump with SVM-Gauss, which is SVM with the Gaussian kernel. For AdaBoost-Stump, we demonstrate the results using $T = 100$ and $T = 1000$. For SVM algorithms, we use LIBSVM [18] with the general procedure of soft-margin SVM [17], which selects a suitable parameter with cross validation before actual training.

The three artificial datasets from Breiman [19] (twonorm, threenorm, and ringnorm) are used with training set size 300 and test set size 3000. We create three more datasets (twonorm-n, threenorm-n, ringnorm-n), which contain mislabeling noise on 10% of the training examples, to test the performance of the algorithms on noisy data. We also use eight real-world datasets from the UCI repository [20]: australian, breast, german, heart, ionosphere, pima, sonar, and votes84. Their feature elements are normalized to $[-1, 1]$. We randomly pick 60% of the examples for training, and the rest for testing. All the results are averaged over 100 runs, presented with standard error bar.

5.1 Comparison of Ensemble Learning Algorithms

Table 1 shows the test performance of our framework and traditional ensemble learning algorithms. We can see that SVM-Stump is usually the best of the four algorithms, and also has superior performance even in the presence of noise. That is, SVM-Stump performs significantly better than AdaBoost-Stump. Not surprisingly, SVM-Stump also performs better than SVM-Mid. These results demonstrate that it is beneficial to go from a finite ensemble to an infinite one.

Table 1. Test error (%) of several ensemble learning algorithms

dataset	SVM-Stump	SVM-Mid	AdaBoost-Stump $T=100$	AdaBoost-Stump $T=1000$
twonorm	**2.86 ± 0.04**	3.10 ± 0.04	5.06 ± 0.06	4.97 ± 0.06
twonorm-n	**3.08 ± 0.06**	3.29 ± 0.05	12.6 ± 0.14	15.5 ± 0.17
threenorm	**17.7 ± 0.10**	18.6 ± 0.12	21.8 ± 0.09	22.9 ± 0.12
threenorm-n	**19.0 ± 0.14**	19.6 ± 0.13	25.9 ± 0.13	28.2 ± 0.14
ringnorm	**3.97 ± 0.07**	5.30 ± 0.07	12.2 ± 0.13	9.95 ± 0.14
ringnorm-n	**5.56 ± 0.11**	7.03 ± 0.14	19.4 ± 0.20	20.3 ± 0.19
australian	**14.5 ± 0.21**	15.9 ± 0.18	**14.7 ± 0.18**	16.9 ± 0.18
breast	3.11 ± 0.08	**2.77 ± 0.08**	4.27 ± 0.11	4.51 ± 0.11
german	**24.7 ± 0.18**	**24.9 ± 0.17**	**25.0 ± 0.18**	26.9 ± 0.18
heart	**16.4 ± 0.27**	19.1 ± 0.35	19.9 ± 0.36	22.6 ± 0.39
ionosphere	**8.13 ± 0.17**	**8.37 ± 0.20**	11.0 ± 0.23	11.0 ± 0.25
pima	**24.2 ± 0.23**	**24.4 ± 0.23**	24.8 ± 0.22	27.0 ± 0.25
sonar	**16.6 ± 0.42**	18.0 ± 0.37	19.0 ± 0.37	19.0 ± 0.35
votes84	4.76 ± 0.14	4.76 ± 0.14	**4.07 ± 0.14**	5.29 ± 0.15

(results that are as significant as the best ones are marked in bold)

The three algorithms, AdaBoost-Stump, SVM-Mid, and SVM-Stump, generate three different kinds of ensembles. AdaBoost-Stump produces finite and sparse ensembles, SVM-Mid produces finite but nonsparse ensembles, and SVM-Stump produces infinite and nonsparse ensembles. Interestingly, SVM-Mid often performs better than AdaBoost-Stump, too. This indicates that a nonsparse ensemble, introduced by the ℓ_2-norm objective function, may be better than a sparse one. We further illustrate this by a simplified experiment. In Fig. 2 we show the decision boundaries generated by the three algorithms on 300 training examples from the 2-D version of the twonorm dataset. AdaBoost-Stump performs similarly with $T=100$ or $T=1000$. Hence only the former is shown. The Bayes optimal decision boundary is the line $(x)_1 + (x)_2 = 0$. We can see that SVM-Stump produces a decision boundary close to the optimal, SVM-Mid is slightly worse, and AdaBoost-Stump fails to generate a decent boundary. SVM-Stump obtains the smooth boundary by averaging over infinitely many decision stumps. SVM-Mid, although using finite number of decision stumps, can still have a smooth boundary in the center area by constructing a nonsparse ensemble. However, AdaBoost-Stump, which produces a finite and sparse ensemble, does not have the ability to approximate the Bayes optimal boundary well.

Although sparsity is often considered beneficial in learning paradigms like Occam's razor, a sparse classifier is not always good. In our case, because the decision stumps are very simple, a general dataset would require many of them to describe a suitable decision boundary. Thus, AdaBoost would suffer from the finite choice of middle stumps, the sparsity introduced by the ℓ_1-norm, and the approximation by T iterations. The comparison between AdaBoost-Stump and SVM-Mid indicates that the second restriction could be crucial. On the other hand, our framework (SVM-Stump), which does not have all those restrictions, has an advantage by averaging over an infinite number of hypotheses.

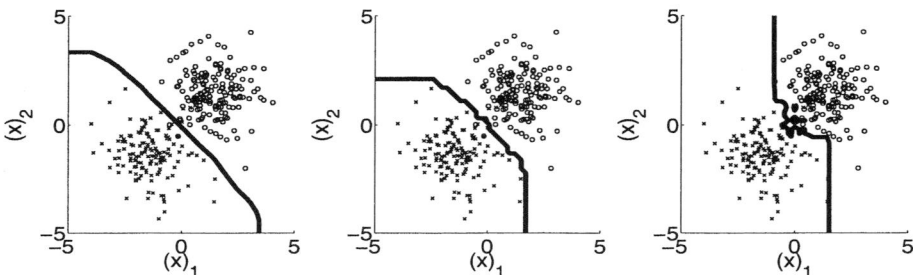

Fig. 2. Decision boundaries of SVM-Stump (left), SVM-Mid (middle), and AdaBoost-Stump with $T = 100$ (right) on a 2-D twonorm dataset

Table 2. Test error (%) of SVM with different kernels

dataset	SVM-Stump	SVM-Gauss	dataset	SVM-Stump	SVM-Gauss
twonorm	2.86 ± 0.04	$\mathbf{2.64 \pm 0.05}$	twonorm-n	3.08 ± 0.06	$\mathbf{2.86 \pm 0.07}$
threenorm	17.7 ± 0.10	$\mathbf{14.6 \pm 0.11}$	threenorm-n	19.0 ± 0.14	$\mathbf{15.6 \pm 0.15}$
ringnorm	3.97 ± 0.07	$\mathbf{1.78 \pm 0.04}$	ringnorm-n	5.56 ± 0.11	$\mathbf{2.05 \pm 0.07}$
australian	$\mathbf{14.5 \pm 0.21}$	$\mathbf{14.7 \pm 0.18}$	breast	$\mathbf{3.11 \pm 0.08}$	3.53 ± 0.09
german	$\mathbf{24.7 \pm 0.18}$	$\mathbf{24.5 \pm 0.21}$	heart	$\mathbf{16.4 \pm 0.27}$	17.5 ± 0.31
ionosphere	8.13 ± 0.17	$\mathbf{6.54 \pm 0.19}$	pima	24.2 ± 0.23	$\mathbf{23.5 \pm 0.19}$
sonar	16.6 ± 0.42	$\mathbf{15.5 \pm 0.50}$	votes84	$\mathbf{4.76 \pm 0.14}$	$\mathbf{4.62 \pm 0.14}$

(results that are as significant as the best one are marked in bold)

5.2 Comparison to Gaussian Kernel

To further test the performance of the stump kernel in practice, we compare SVM-Stump with a popular and powerful setting, SVM-Gauss. Table 2 shows the test errors of them. From the table, SVM-Stump could have comparable yet slightly worse performance. However, the stump kernel has the advantage of faster parameter selection because scaling the stump kernel is equivalent to scaling the soft-margin parameter C. Thus, only a simple parameter search on C is necessary. For example, in our experiments, SVM-Gauss involves solving 550 optimization problems using different parameters, but we only need to deal with 55 problems for SVM-Stump. None of the commonly-used nonlinear SVM kernel can do fast parameter selection like the stump kernel. With the comparable performance, when time is a big concern, SVM-Stump could be a first-hand choice.

6 Conclusion

We proposed a framework to construct ensemble classifiers that average over an infinite number of base hypotheses. This is achieved with SVM by embedding infinitely many hypotheses in an SVM kernel. In contrast to ensemble learning algorithms like AdaBoost, our framework inherits the profound generalization performance from the soft-margin SVM, and would generate infinite and non-sparse ensembles, which are usually more robust than sparse ones.

We demonstrated our framework with decision stumps and obtained the stump kernel, which is novel and useful. Experimental comparisons with AdaBoost showed that SVM with the stump kernel usually performs much better than AdaBoost with stumps. Therefore, existing applications that use AdaBoost with stumps may be improved by switching to SVM with the stump kernel. In addition, we can benefit from the property of fast parameter selection when using the stump kernel. The property makes the kernel favorable to the Gaussian kernel in the case of large datasets.

Acknowledgment

We thank Yaser Abu-Mostafa, Amrit Pratap, Kai-Min Chung, and the anonymous reviewers for valuable suggestions. This work has been mainly supported by the Caltech Center for Neuromorphic Systems Engineering under the US NSF Cooperative Agreement EEC-9402726. Ling Li is currently sponsored by the Caltech SISL graduate Fellowship.

References

1. Freund, Y., Schapire, R.E.: Experiments with a new boosting algorithm. In: Machine Learning: Proceedings of the Thirteenth International Conference. (1996) 148–156
2. Rosset, S., Zhu, J., Hastie, T.: Boosting as a regularized path to a maximum margin classifier. Journal of Machine Learning Research **5** (2004) 941–973
3. Freund, Y., Schapire, R.E.: A decision-theoretic generalization of on-line learning and an application to boosting. Journal of Computer and System Sciences **55** (1997) 119–139
4. Vapnik, V.N.: Statistical Learning Theory. John Wiley & Sons, New York (1998)
5. Lin, H.T.: Infinite ensemble learning with support vector machines. Master's thesis, California Institute of Technology (2005)
6. Schölkopf, B., Smola, A.: Learning with Kernels. MIT Press, Cambridge, MA (2002)
7. Rätsch, G., Onoda, T., Müller, K.: Soft margins for AdaBoost. Machine Learning **42** (2001) 287–320
8. Demiriz, A., Bennett, K.P., Shawe-Taylor, J.: Linear programming boosting via column generation. Machine Learning **46** (2002) 225–254
9. Meir, R., Rätsch, G.: An introduction to boosting and leveraging. In Mendelson, S., Smola, A.J., eds.: Advanced Lectures on Machine Learning. Springer-Verlag, Berlin (2003) 118–183
10. Freund, Y., Schapire, R.E.: A short introduction to boosting. Journal of Japanese Society for Artificial Intelligence **14** (1999) 771–780
11. Reed, M., Simon, B.: Functional Analysis. Revised and enlarged edn. Methods of Modern Mathematical Physics. Academic Press (1980)
12. Holte, R.C.: Very simple classification rules perform well on most commonly used datasets. Machine Learning **11** (1993) 63–91
13. Berg, C., Christensen, J.P.R., Ressel, P.: Harmonic Analysis on Semigroups: Theory of Positive Definite and Related Functions. Springer-Verlag, New York (1984)

14. Lin, H.T., Lin, C.J.: A study on sigmoid kernels for SVM and the training of non-PSD kernels by SMO-type methods. Technical report, National Taiwan University (2003)
15. Chang, C.C., Lin, C.J.: Training ν-support vector classifiers: Theory and algorithms. Neural Computation **13** (2001) 2119–2147
16. Keerthi, S.S., Lin, C.J.: Asymptotic behaviors of support vector machines with Gaussian kernel. Neural Computation **15** (2003) 1667–1689
17. Hsu, C.W., Chang, C.C., Lin, C.J.: A practical guide to support vector classification. Technical report, National Taiwan University (2003)
18. Chang, C.C., Lin, C.J.: LIBSVM: A library for support vector machines. (2001) Software available at http://www.csie.ntu.edu.tw/~cjlin/libsvm.
19. Breiman, L.: Prediction games and arcing algorithms. Neural Computation (1999) **11** 1493–1517
20. Hettich, S., Blake, C.L., Merz, C.J.: UCI repository of machine learning databases (1998) Downloadable at http://www.ics.uci.edu/~mlearn/MLRepository.html.

A Kernel Between Unordered Sets of Data: The Gaussian Mixture Approach

Siwei Lyu

Department of Computer Science,
Dartmouth College, Hanover, NH 03755, USA

Abstract. In this paper, we present a new kernel for unordered sets of data of the same type. It works by first fitting a set with a Gaussian mixture, then evaluate an efficient kernel on the two fitted Gaussian mixtures. Furthermore, we show that this kernel can be extended to sets embedded in a feature space implicitly defined by another kernel, where Gaussian mixtures are fitted with the kernelized EM algorithm [6], and the kernel for Gaussian mixtures are modified to use the outputs from the kernelized EM. All computation depends on data only through their inner products as evaluations of the base kernel. The kernel is computable in closed form, and being able to work in a feature space improves its flexibility and applicability. Its performance is evaluated in experiments on both synthesized and real data.

1 Introduction

Kernel methods received attention originally as a "trick" to introduce non-linearity into the support vector machines (SVM) [20]. Evaluating a kernel function between two data is equivalent to computing the inner product of their images in a non-linearly mapped Hilbert space (the feature space). It is realized later that kernel methods are more general: similar to SVMs, many other linear algorithms also depend on data through their inner products. By substituting the inner products with kernel evaluations, these linear algorithms assume power to discover non-linear patterns in data [18]. Recent years have seen significant development in "kernelizing" existing algorithms, examples include kernel PCA [15], kernel FLD [14] and kernel k-means [1]. The kernelized algorithms inherit the innate stability of their linear ancestors, thus largely reduce the possibility of over-fitting the training data.

One important advantage of the kernel methods [18] is that they enable algorithms originally designed for vectors of finite dimensions (e.g., PCA, FLD or SVM) to work with discrete, structured or infinite dimensional data types, such as strings [21], statistical manifolds [7] and graphs [11]. With properly designed kernels, these data types are implicitly embedded into a vector space and lend themselves to kernel-based algorithms.

In this paper, we present a kernel for unordered sets of data of the same type, which are useful data models in many applications. For instance, in document categorization, documents are usually represented as "bag-of-words", which are unordered set of key words. Images can also be treated as "bag-of-tuples", where the element is the tuple of the position and intensity of a pixel in an image[8]. Instead of directly defining a kernel between two sets, we take the methodology of first modeling each set probabilistically, and then constructing a kernel between the two probabilistic models. More specifically, each set is treated as a collection of i.i.d. samples from an unknown probability distribution, whose probability density function (pdf) is taken from a parametric family. The kernel between two sets is thus computed as evaluating a kernel between the two pdfs. In this paper, we employ Gaussian mixtures to model the generating pdf of a vector set. On the two estimated Gaussian mixtures, the (normalized) expected likelihood kernel is evaluated, which affords an efficient computation without integration. Furthermore, the Gaussian mixture fitting and kernel evaluation are extended to a feature space implicitly defined by another kernel. The proposed method is evaluated on both synthesized and real data sets.

2 Kernel Function and Kernel-Induced Feature Space

Given an input space $\mathcal{X}$, a kernel K is a function $K(x, z) = \langle \phi(x), \phi(z) \rangle_{\mathcal{H}}$ for any $x, z \in \mathcal{X}$, where ϕ is a mapping from $\mathcal{X}$ to a Hilbert space $\mathcal{H}$ (the feature space), and $\langle \cdot, \cdot \rangle_{\mathcal{H}}$ is the inner product operator in $\mathcal{H}$ [18]. Admissible kernel can be specified without implicit reference to $\mathcal{H}$ or ϕ with the finite positive definite property: any real-valued symmetric binary function on $\mathcal{X}$ is a kernel if it satisfies the finite positive definite property:

$$\sum_{i,j=1}^{m} c_i c_j K(x_i, x_j) \geq 0$$

for any $m \in \mathbb{N}$, any subset $\{x_1, \cdots, x_m\}$ of $\mathcal{X}$ and any choice of real numbers $c_1, \cdots, c_m$. Equivalently, the finite positive definite property can be expressed as that the matrix formed by restricting the kernel function on any finite subset of $\mathcal{X}$ is positive semi-definite. There is an equivalence between a kernel function $K(\cdot, \cdot)$ and a corresponding kernel-induced feature space $\mathcal{H}$: any admissible kernel function also ensures the existence of a feature space and vice versa.

3 The Gaussian Mixture Model

We consider unordered sets of d-dimensional vectors, $\chi = \{x_1, \cdots, x_N\}$. One can model the data in χ as i.i.d samples from a multivariate Gaussian distribution $G(x; \mu, C) = \frac{1}{(2\pi)^{\frac{d}{2}} |C|^{\frac{1}{2}}} \exp(-\frac{1}{2}(x-\mu)^T C^{-1}(x-\mu))$, parameterized by the mean μ and the covariance matrix, C. Parameters μ and C are estimated from data with the sample mean $\bar{\mu} = \frac{1}{N} \sum_{i=1}^{N} x_i$ and the empirical covariance matrix $\bar{C} = \frac{1}{N-1} \sum_{i=1}^{N} (x_i - \bar{\mu})(x_i - \bar{\mu})^T$, respectively. Major advantages of Gaussian is simplicity. However, a Gaussian cannot model a multi-modal distribution, which usually is the case in practice. In this aspect, a Gaussian mixture has much more modeling flexibility. A finite Gaussian mixture is defined as:

$$p(x) = \sum_{k=1}^{M} \alpha_k G(x; \mu_k, C_k), \tag{1}$$

where $M \in \mathbb{N}$ is the number of components, $\alpha_1, \cdots, \alpha_M$ are the mixing coefficients satisfying $\sum_{k=1}^{M} \alpha_k = 1$ and $\alpha_i \geq 0$ for $i = 1, \cdots M$. Parameters μ_k and C_k are the mean and covariance of each Gaussian in the mixture. It can be shown that [16] with a sufficient number of components, any probability density can be approximated to any degree by a Gaussian mixture.

The parameters in a Gaussian mixture, the mixing coefficients, $\alpha_1, \cdots, \alpha_M$, the mean and covariance of each component, $\mu_1, \cdots, \mu_M$ and $C_1, \cdots, C_M$, can be estimated from set χ with the expectation-maximization (EM) algorithm [2], given that the number of components M is known. Starting from initial values of these parameters, the EM algorithm proceeds by executing the following steps until convergence,

$$p_k(i) = \frac{\alpha_k G(x_i; \mu_k, C_k)}{\sum_{j=1}^{M} \alpha_j G(x_i; \mu_j, C_j)} \text{ for } i = 1, \cdots, N, k = 1, \cdots, M \tag{2}$$

$$\alpha_k = \frac{1}{N} \sum_{i=1}^{N} p_k(i), \text{ for } k = 1, \cdots, M \tag{3}$$

$$\mu_k = \frac{\sum_{i=1}^{N} x_i p_k(i)}{\sum_{i=1}^{N} p_k(i)}, \text{ for } k = 1, \cdots, M \tag{4}$$

$$C_k = \frac{\sum_{i=1}^{N} (x_i - \mu_k)(x_i - \mu_k)^T p_k(i)}{\sum_{i=1}^{N} p_k(i)}, \text{ for } k = 1, \cdots, M. \tag{5}$$

The EM algorithm guarantees to converge within finite steps to a local maximum of the log-likelihood function of the parameters given data χ. More details of the EM estimation for Gaussian mixtures can be found in [2].

4 Kernels Between Sets of Vectors

A kernel function for unordered sets of d-dimensional vectors, $\chi = \{x_1, \cdots, x_N\}$, can be built from the probabilistic modeling of the set. Specifically, each set can be treated as a collection of i.i.d. samples from a probability distribution, whose density function (pdf) is approximated with a parametric family $\mathcal{P}$. A kernel between the estimated two pdfs can be defined and used as the kernel between the two sets. With the estimated pdfs, generally, any similarity measures between two pdfs, such as the Jensen-Shannon divergence, Kullback-Leibler divergence or the χ^2 distance, can be used to construct kernels between two pdfs [5]. The problem is that such measures may not be efficiently computable, especially in high-dimensional data spaces. In a related work [10], $\mathcal{P}$ was chosen as the multivariate Gaussian distributions. Then the Bhattacharyya kernel,

$K_B(p,q) = \int_\mathcal{X} \sqrt{p(x)}\sqrt{q(x)}dx$, was computed between the two Gaussian distributions. This kernel is a special case of the more general class of probability product kernels [9], which is defined as $K_{PP}(p,q) = \int_\mathcal{X} p(x)^\rho q(x)^\rho dx$, with $\rho = 1/2$. For pdfs in the exponential family (multivariate Gaussian as a special case), the probability product kernels can be computed efficiently without integration. However, when the two distributions are Gaussian mixtures, the general probability product kernels do not give rise to efficient evaluation, as numerical integration can not be avoided.

5 Expected Likelihood Kernel Between Gaussian Mixtures

In this work, we employ the expected likelihood kernel between the two estimated Gaussian mixtures, as the results of running the EM algorithm on the two unordered sets of d-dimensional vectors. The expected likelihood kernel is defined as:

$$K_{EL}(p,q) = \int_\mathcal{X} p(x)q(x)dx, \qquad (6)$$

which is seen to be a special case of the probability product kernel with $\rho = 1$. As formally stated in the following theorem, the expected likelihood kernel affords an efficient computation for Gaussian mixtures.

Theorem 1. *For two Gaussian mixtures of d dimensional real random vectors,*

$$p(x) = \sum_{k=1}^{M_1} \alpha_k^{(1)} G(x; \mu_k^{(1)}, C_k^{(1)}) \quad \text{and} \quad q(x) = \sum_{k=1}^{M_2} \alpha_k^{(2)} G(x; \mu_k^{(2)}, C_k^{(2)}),$$

the expected likelihood kernel, Eq.(6), is computed as

$$K_{EL}(p,q) = (2\pi)^{-\frac{d}{2}} \alpha^T \Gamma \beta,$$

for $\alpha = (\alpha_1^{(1)}, \cdots, \alpha_{M_1}^{(1)})^T$ and $\beta = (\alpha_1^{(2)}, \cdots, \alpha_{M_2}^{(2)})^T$. The $M_1 \times M_2$ matrix Γ is formed as $(\Gamma)_{ij} = g(\mu_i^{(1)}, C_i^{(1)}, \mu_j^{(2)}, C_j^{(2)})$, where function g is defined as:

$$g(\mu_1, C_1, \mu_2, C_2) = \frac{|C|^{\frac{1}{2}} \exp(\frac{1}{2}\mu^T C \mu)}{\prod_{i=1}^{2} |C_i|^{\frac{1}{2}} \exp(\frac{1}{2}\mu_i^T C_i^{-1} \mu_i)}, \qquad (7)$$

with $\mu = C_1^{-1}\mu_1 + C_2^{-1}\mu_2$ and $C = \left(C_1^{-1} + C_2^{-1}\right)^{-1}$.

Proof. First, the integration of the product of two Gaussians, $G(x; \mu_1, C_1)$ and $G(x; \mu_2, C_2)$, is computed as [17]:

$$\int_{\mathbb{R}^d} G(x;\mu_1,C_1) \times G(x;\mu_2,C_2)dx = (2\pi)^{-\frac{d}{2}} g(\mu_1, C_1, \mu_2, C_2). \qquad (8)$$

Substituting Eq.(8) into Eq.(6) and interchange the order of addition and multiplication (using Fubini's theorem) yields

$$\int_{\mathbb{R}^d} p(x)q(x)dx = \int_{\mathbb{R}^d} \sum_{i=1}^{M_1} \alpha_i^{(1)} G(x; \mu_i^{(1)}, C_i^{(1)}) \times \sum_{j=1}^{M_2} \alpha_j^{(2)} G(x; \mu_j^{(2)}, C_j^{(2)}) dx$$

$$= \sum_{i=1}^{M_1} \sum_{j=1}^{M_2} \alpha_i^{(1)} \alpha_j^{(2)} \int_{\mathbb{R}^d} G(x; \mu_i^{(1)}, C_i^{(1)}) \times G(x; \mu_j^{(2)}, C_j^{(2)}) dx$$

$$= \sum_{i=1}^{M_1} \sum_{j=1}^{M_2} \alpha_i^{(1)} \alpha_j^{(2)} (2\pi)^{-\frac{d}{2}} g\left(\mu_i^{(1)}, C_i^{(1)}, \mu_j^{(2)}, C_j^{(2)}\right) = (2\pi)^{-\frac{d}{2}} \alpha^T \Gamma \beta. \qquad \square$$

Theorem 1 shows that one can evaluate the expected likelihood kernel on two Gaussian mixtures in closed-form without integration. The kernel can further be made independent of the dimensionality of data, if we use its normalization: $K_{NEL}(p,q) = \frac{K_{EL}(p,q)}{\sqrt{K_{EL}(p,p)}\sqrt{K_{EL}(q,q)}}$, which can be shown to be an admissible kernel function. This property is essential when we extend to Gaussian mixtures estimated in a kernel-induced feature space, where the dimensionality of the data is usually not known.

6 Kernels Between Sets in Feature Space

The expected likelihood kernel evaluation for unordered sets can be extended to data in a feature space implicitly defined by another base kernel κ. This is the case when the sets contain non-vectorial data, the base kernel is used to implicitly map them into a vector space. For vectors, such implicit nonlinear mapping is also desirable when nonlinear data patterns are sought. Our basic methodology stays the same: Gaussian mixtures are first fitted to data sets and the (normalized) expected likelihood kernel is evaluated between the two fitted Gaussian mixtures. What differs is that all steps are implicitly performed in a feature space.

Working in a feature space poses two fundamental difficulties for the kernel evaluation described in Section 5. First, we may not fully recover a Gaussian in a feature space from a finite set. This is especially true when the dimension of the feature space is larger than the number of data in the set - only the partial covariance of each Gaussian restricted in the subspace spanned by the data (with a rank up to the size of the set) can be recovered. Another difficulty is that we usually do not have direct access to individual data except their inner products, computed with the evaluation of the base kernel. This renders the EM algorithm and the evaluation of the expected likelihood kernel not directly applicable: the estimation of the mean and covariance of each Gaussian (Eq.(4) and (5)) depend on individual data.

In face of these problems, the kernel evaluation is modified in the following aspects. First, in both the EM algorithm and the kernel evaluation, in lieu of the determinants and inverses of the full covariance matrices, the pseudo-determinants and pseudo-inverse [3] of the partial rank-deficient covariance matrix are used to avoid recovering the full covariance matrices. The pseudo-determinant of a matrix is the product of all its non-zero singular values[1] and its pseudo-inverse is obtained by inverting all nonzero singular values in its singular value decomposition. A property of the pseudo-determinant and pseudo-inverse important for the computation hereafter is Lemma 1. Due to limit of space, its is not presented here and can be found in the longer version of this paper [13].

Lemma 1. *If $C = XRR^TX^T$, and R and X^TX are invertible, then we have*

$$d(C) = |\tilde{R}^TX^TX\tilde{R}| \quad \text{and} \quad C^\dagger = X\tilde{R}\tilde{R}^TX^T,$$

where $\tilde{R} = (R^TX^TX)^{-1}$ and † is the pseudo-inverse operator.

Another change is that both the EM algorithm and the (normalized) expected likelihood kernel are reformulated to depends only on base kernel evaluation. Specifically, the Gaussian mixtures are fitted with a variant of the kernelized EM [6] and the evaluation of the (normalized) expected likelihood kernel is modified to use the outputs of the kernelized EM.

To avoid clumsiness in notation, hereafter in this section we still describe the reformulated algorithms in a vector space, bearing in mind that the inner products of these vectors will be replaced with evaluations of the base kernel in the feather space. Specifically, each datum is represented as a column vector, and a data set $\chi = \{x_1, \cdots, x_N\}$ is a matrix $X = [x_1, \cdots, x_N] \in \mathcal{R}^{d \times N}$. For two different data sets, X_1 and X_2, their inner product matrix $X_1^TX_2$ contains inner products between all pairs of data from the two sets.

6.1 Kernelized EM

To make the EM algorithm, Eq.(2)-(5), depend on inner products of data while being independent of individual data, we view it from an alternative perspective. Rewriting Eq.(4) and (5), the updating steps of the mean and covariance of each Gaussian in the mixture become

$$\mu_k = \sum_{i=1}^{N} x_i w_k(i), \quad (9)$$

$$C_k = \sum_{i=1}^{N} (x_i - \mu_k)(x_i - \mu_k)^T w_k(i), \quad (10)$$

for $k = 1, \cdots, M$, where $w_k(i) = \frac{p_k(i)}{\sum_{i=1}^{N} p_k(i)}$ is the weight associated with each Gaussian component and each datum in the set. Denote $w_k = [w_k(1), \cdots, w_k(N)]^T$. Eq.(9) and (10) can be rewritten more compactly as:

$$\mu_k = Xw_k, \quad (11)$$

$$C_k = X(I_N - w_k \mathbf{1}_N^T)\text{diag}(w_k)(I_N - \mathbf{1}_N w_k^T)X^T. \quad (12)$$

---

[1] More formally, $d(C) = \prod_{i=1}^{n}(\lambda_i + 1 - \text{sign}(\lambda_i)^2)$ where λ_i is the singular value of matrix C and $\text{sign}(x) = 1$ for positive x, and 0 for $x = 0$ and -1 for negative x.

where I_N is the $N \times N$ identity matrix and $\mathbf{1}_N$ is the N-dimensional column vector with all 1s. Operator diag($\cdot$) outputs a diagonal matrix whose diagonal is set to the input vector. Modulo to the data matrix X, the estimated mean and covariance of each Gaussian in the mixture are fully determined by weights w_k. EM can then be viewed as iteratively updating these weights in a bootstrapping fashion.

To update weights w_k, it is sufficient to compute $p_k(i)$ with Eq.(2). In a feature space, as suggested previously, the updating step is modified to use the pseudo-determinant and pseudo-inverse of the partial covariance matrices as:

$$p_k(i) = \frac{\alpha_k d(C_k)^{-\frac{1}{2}} \exp\left(-\frac{1}{2}(x_i - \mu_k)^T C_k^\dagger (x_i - \mu_k)\right)}{\sum_{j=1}^m \alpha_j d(C_j)^{-\frac{1}{2}} \exp\left(-\frac{1}{2}(x_i - \mu_j)^T C_j^\dagger (x_i - \mu_j)\right)}. \tag{13}$$

The key step in updating $p_k(i)$ and hence w_k is to compute $d(C_k)$ and $(x_i - \mu_k)^T C_k^\dagger (x_i - \mu_k)$ for each data in the set and each Gaussian component. According to Lemma 1, the pseudo-determinant and pseudo-inverse of the partial covariance matrix C_k can be computed as:

$$d(C_k) = |R_k^T X^T X R_k| \tag{14}$$
$$C_k^\dagger = X R_k R_k^T X^T \tag{15}$$

where the $N \times N$ matrix R_k is

$$R_k = \left[(I_N - w_k \mathbf{1}_N^T)\sqrt{\text{diag}(w_k)} X^T X\right]^{-1}, \tag{16}$$

with the square root computed component-wisely. Accordingly, $d(C_k)$ is computed from Eq.(14) and (16). With Eq.(15), term $(x_i - \mu_k)^T C_k^\dagger (x_i - \mu_k)$ is evaluated as

$$(x_i - \mu_k)^T C_k^\dagger (x_i - \mu_k) = (x_i - X w_k)^T X R_k R_k^T X^T (x_i - X w_k)$$
$$= \|R_k X^T X (\delta_i - w_k)\|^2, \tag{17}$$

where δ_i is the N-dimensional column vector of all zeros except the i-th component being 1. $\|\cdot\|$ is the 2-norm of a vector. Note that no direct dependence on individual data or the data matrix appears in these computations. Matrix $X^T X$ is formed by inner products between each pair of data in X and is computed from evaluating the kernel matrix of κ on the input data set in the feature space.

In summarizing words, with initial values, the kernelized EM algorithm[2] proceeds by running the following steps until convergence

---

[2] The algorithm described here is in the same spirit as the original kernelized EM algorithm [6], differing in notations and the relaxed requirement of only recovering partial covariances.

- **step 1:** compute p_k with Eq.(17), (14) and (13);
- **step 2:** update weights w_k as $w_k(i) = \frac{p_k(i)}{\sum_{i=1}^N p_k(i)}$;
- **step 3:** update mixing coefficients α_k with Eq.(3);
- **step 4:** compute R_k with Eq.(16);

At the completion of the kernelized EM algorithm, the mixing coefficients α_k, vector w_k and matrix $R_k{}^3$ are output for each Gaussian in the mixture. It is from these outputs that the (normalized) expected likelihood kernel is evaluated in the feature space.

6.2 Kernel Evaluation

In the feature space, the expected likelihood kernel (and its normalization) is computed as in Theorem 1 with slight changes. First, the constant factor in the expected likelihood kernel is dropped, to yield $\widetilde{K_{EL}}(p,q) = \alpha^T \tilde{M} \beta$ on two Gaussian mixtures p and q. Denote X_1 and X_2 as the data matrices for the two mixtures. Vector α and β contains the mixing coefficients for p and q respectively. Matrix $\tilde{M}$ is formed as $(\tilde{M})_{ij} = \tilde{g}(\mu_i^{(1)}, C_i^{(1)}, \mu_j^{(2)}, C_j^{(2)})$ for each pair of Gaussians from the two mixtures. Function $\tilde{g}$ is defined as:

$$\tilde{g}(\mu_1, C_1, \mu_2, C_2) = \frac{d(C)^{\frac{1}{2}} \exp(\frac{1}{2}\mu^T C \mu)}{\prod_{i=1}^2 d(C_k)^{\frac{1}{2}} \exp(\frac{1}{2}\mu_k^T C_k{}^\dagger \mu_k)}, \tag{18}$$

with $\mu = C_1{}^\dagger \mu_1 + C_2{}^\dagger \mu_2$ and $C = \left(C_1{}^\dagger + C_2{}^\dagger\right)^\dagger$, which is computed in four steps.

Compute $d(C_k)$: From the outputs of the kernelized EM algorithm, $d(C_k)$ is computed with R_k and Eq.(14) as $d(C_k) = |R_k^T X^T X R_k|$, for $k = 1, 2$.

Compute $\mu_k^T C_k{}^\dagger \mu_k$: With R_k, Eq.(9) and (14), term $\mu_k^T C_k{}^\dagger \mu_k$ is computed as:

$$\mu_k^T C_k{}^\dagger \mu_k = w_k^T X_k^T X_k R_k R_k^T X_k^T X_k w_k = \|R_k^T X_k^T X_k w_k\|^2 \tag{19}$$

for $k = 1, 2$.

Compute $d(C)$: With $C_k^\dagger = X_k R_k R_k^T X_k^T$ for $k = 1, 2$, we then have

$$C_1^\dagger + C_2^\dagger = X_1 R_1 R_1^T X_1^T + X_2 R_2 R_2^T X_2^T = [X_1 \; X_2] \begin{bmatrix} R_1 & 0 \\ 0 & R_2 \end{bmatrix} \begin{bmatrix} R_1^T & 0 \\ 0 & R_2^T \end{bmatrix} \begin{bmatrix} X_1^T \\ X_2^T \end{bmatrix}.$$

Now denote

$$R = \left(\begin{bmatrix} R_1^T & 0 \\ 0 & R_2^T \end{bmatrix} \begin{bmatrix} X_1^T X_1 & X_1^T X_2 \\ X_2^T X_1 & X_2^T X_2 \end{bmatrix} \right)^{-1} = \begin{bmatrix} R_1^T X_1^T X_1 & R_1^T X_1^T X_2 \\ R_2^T X_2^T X_1 & R_2^T X_2^T X_2 \end{bmatrix}^{-1} \tag{20}$$

and with Lemma 1, it holds that

---
[3] Note it is not necessary to output R_k as it can be computed from w_k with Eq.(16). However, it facilitates the evaluation of the kernel in next section.

$$C = \left(C_1^\dagger + C_2^\dagger\right)^\dagger = [X_1 \ X_2]RR^T \begin{bmatrix} X_1^T \\ X_2^T \end{bmatrix}, \tag{21}$$

from which $d(C)$ is computed as

$$d(C) = \left| R^T \begin{bmatrix} X_1^T X_1 & X_1^T X_2 \\ X_2^T X_1 & X_2^T X_2 \end{bmatrix} R \right| \tag{22}$$

Compute $\mu^T C \mu$: Since we have $\mu = C_1^\dagger \mu_1 + C_2^\dagger \mu_2$, expanding $\mu^T C \mu$ yields

$$\mu^T C \mu = (C_1^\dagger \mu_1 + C_2^\dagger \mu_2)^T C (C_1^\dagger \mu_1 + C_2^\dagger \mu_2) = \sum_{i,j \in \{1,2\}} \mu_i^T C_i^{\dagger^T} C C_j^\dagger \mu_j. \tag{23}$$

Each term in the sum can be further expanded with $\mu_k = X_k w_k$ and $C_k^\dagger = X_k R_k R_k^T X_k^T$ for $k = 1, 2$, as:

$$\mu_i^T C_i^{\dagger^T} C C_j^\dagger \mu_j = w_i^T X_i^T X_i R_i R_i^T X_i^T [X_1 \ X_2] R R^T \begin{bmatrix} X_1^T \\ X_2^T \end{bmatrix} X_j R_j R_j^T X_j^T X_j w_j$$

$$= w_i^T X_i^T X_i R_i R_i^T [X_i^T X_1 \ X_i^T X_2] R R^T \begin{bmatrix} X_1^T X_j \\ X_2^T X_j \end{bmatrix} R_j R_j^T X_j^T X_j w_j. \tag{24}$$

All the above steps depend on data only through their inner products. Thus replacing these inner products with base kernel evaluations lead to computing function $\tilde{g}$ in the feature space with base kernel evaluations. Subsequently, the modified (normalized) expected likelihood kernel can also be computed based on kernel κ. Combining with the kernelized EM algorithm, this yields a kernel for unordered sets in the feature space.

7 Experiments

In this section, experimental results empirically evaluating the proposed kernel with other works are presented. The experiments were conducted on both synthesized and real data sets. In all experiments, the proposed kernel was coupled with SVM classifiers. Our SVM classifiers were implemented based on package LIBSVM [4] and were enhanced to work with kernels between sets. A simple multi-class classification protocol, a one-versus-the-rest scheme in training and a winner-takes-all strategy in testing was employed in classification.

7.1 Synthesized Data

Our synthesized data were $1,000$ sets of 5-D vectors of sizes ranging from 80 to 250, each of which were random samples of one of the four different 5-D Gaussian mixtures with five components. All data sets were categorized into four different classes based on the Gaussian mixtures they were generated from. 700 out of the $1,000$ samples were used for training and the rest for testing. For a base of comparison, an SVM classifier with an RBF kernel $K_{RBF}(x, z) = \exp(-\frac{\|x-z\|^2}{\sigma^2})$ on 5-D vectors was trained. Each vector inherited class label of the set to which it belongs. The classification of a set was the result of a majority vote with the projected class labels of all its members. As no consideration is given to the correlation within a set, this plain RBF kernel did not perform well, as evident from Figure 7(a).

Another SVM classifier with a kernel between unordered sets as described in [10] was also compared, where a Gaussian was fitted to each set and the Bhattacharyya kernel $K_B(p,q) = \int_\mathcal{X} \sqrt{p(x)}\sqrt{q(x)}dx$ was evaluated on the two fitted Gaussians. For pdfs in the exponential family (Gaussian as a special case) it has been shown that the Bhattacharyya kernel afford a close-form evaluation [10]. However, for Gaussian mixtures with more than one components, the Bhattacharyya kernel loses that advantage, as the integration is not able to be removed. As shown in Figure 7(a), the Bhattacharyya kernel achieved a better performance than the simple RBF kernel. The improvement is most probably due to the better data modeling with a Gaussian fitting.

However, it is the normalized expected likelihood kernel with a proper number of components in the estimated Gaussian mixture (M = 5) that achieved the best overall performance, due to the more precise data modeling with Gaussian mixtures. For the other choices of component number M, with single component Gaussian mixture fitting, the normalized expected likelihood kernel is similar to the Bhattacharyya kernel (without the square root in the definition), which is reflected in their similar performance. For Gaussian mixtures with fewer components than the ground truth (as in the case of M = 3), the performance is not uniformly better than the base line case with M = 1. On the other hand, using more mixture components (e.g., M = 7) did not achieve significant improvement in performance yet the computational effort was increased. This bears the question of how to know the number of components in advance, as the EM can not be used to find it. Empirically, The number of components can be found by cross-validation. A more systematic approach is to use techniques that can automatically determine the number of components need on a data

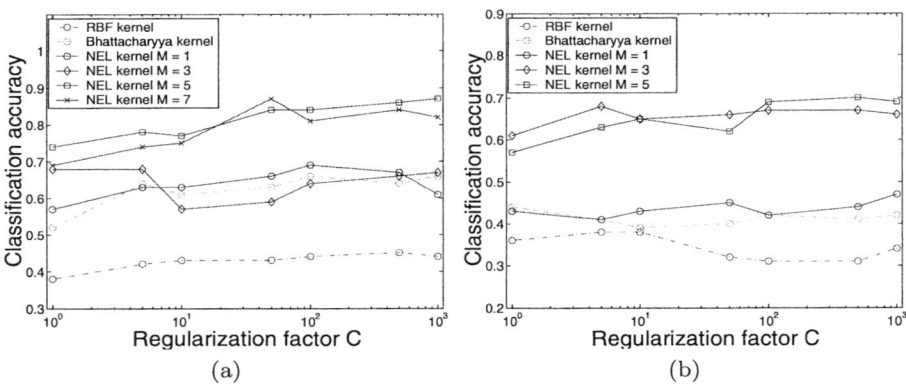

Fig. 1. Performance of the normalized expected likelihood kernel on the testing set for (a) synthesized data and (b) MNIST handwritten digit image dataset. Solid lines are for the Gaussian mixture with normalized expected likelihood kernel. Dashed lines are for the Bhattacharyya kernel.

set (e.g., [19]) and is left for future study. Also, in this experiment, for simplicity we fitted the same number of Gaussians to all sets. It is straightforward to extend to fitting Gaussian mixtures with different number of components to different sets.

7.2 Handwritten Digits Recognition

Our real data were a small subset of handwritten digit images. Specifically, we randomly chose 100 images for each of the 10 handwritten digit from the MNIST database [12], with 700 for training and the rest for testing. Similar to [10], each image was transformed to a set by sampling pixels with intensity greater than 191 on a 0 to 255 scale. The coordinates of these sampled pixel along with their intensities were presented to the algorithm. From each image, a set of size ranging from 50 to 108 with an average of 72 was obtained. Using a small subset of pixels is to avoid inverting a large inner product matrix, which is the most time consuming step in the kernel evaluation. Anticipating nonlinearity in data modeling, we chose an RBF kernel as the base kernel to nonlinearly map the 3-D tuples in each set into a feature space. To simplify the training process, we avoided extensive tuning of the parameter in the base kernel and in all cases the RBF kernel was set to have a width of $\sigma = 0.1$. The results were the average over 100 random splits of the training/testing splits of all the images chosen.

We trained again different SVM classifiers and their performances are shown in Figure 7(b). As in the case of the synthesized data, a simple RBF kernel led to the most inferior performance. However, the Bhattacharyya kernel with a RBF base kernel and the normalized expected likelihood kernel with a one-component Gaussian mixture modeling did not introduce much improvement, as a single Gaussian is not sufficient to model the generating probability distributions of these data sets. We then tested the normalized expected likelihood kernel with different number of mixture components ($M = 3$ and 5). Compared to other kernels, they achieved a substantial improvement in performance. Contrary to the previous case, it seems that the specific number of mixture components is somehow irrelevant in this case, as using 3 and 5 components did not result in significant difference in performance. We also observed that classification was relatively stable with regards to the regularization factor in the SVM classification.

8 Discussion

In this paper, we present a kernel between two unordered sets of data of the same type. Each set is first fitted with a Gaussian mixture. Then the expected likelihood kernel is evaluated between the two estimated Gaussian mixtures. Furthermore, this kernel function can be extended to cases when the data are in an implicitly defined feature space. The performance of this kernel is evaluated on both synthesized and real data sets. One drawback of the proposed algorithm, however, is running efficiency. Evaluating the kernel is quadratic in running time, which can be prohibitive in case of large data sets. We are working on approximation algorithms that achieve fast running time. Also, we are working on incorporating techniques that can automatically determine the number of components in a Gaussian mixture estimation.

References

1. A. Ben-Hur, D. Horn, H. T. Siegelmann, and V. Vapnik. Support vector clustering. Journal of Machine Learning Research, 2(2):125-137, 2002.
2. J. Bilmes. A gentle tutorial on the EM algorithm and its application to parameter estimation for gaussian mixture and hidden Markov models. Technical Report ICSI-TR-97-021, UC Berkeley, 1997.
3. S.L. Campbell and C.D. Meyer Jr. Generalized Inverses of Linear Transformations. Dover, New York, 1991.
4. C. Chang and C. Lin. LIBSVM: a library for support vector machines, 2001. Software available at http://www.csie.ntu.edu.tw/ cjlin/libsvm.
5. M. Hein and O. Bousquet. Hilbertian metrics and positive definite kernels on probability measures. Technical report, MPI for Biological Cybernetics, 2004.
6. J. Lee J. Wang and C. Zhang. Kernel trick embedded gaussian mixture model. In Lecture Notes in Artificial Intelligence, volume 2842, pages 159-174, 2003.
7. T. Jaakkola and D. Haussler. Exploiting generative models in discriminative classifiers. In Advances in Neural Information Processing Systems (NIPS), 1999.
8. T. Jebara. Image as bag of pixels. In International Conference on Computer Vision (ICCV), 2003.
9. T. Jebara, R. Kondor, and A. Howard. Probability product kernels. Journal of Machine Learning Research, 5, 2004.
10. R. Kondor and T. Jebara. A kernel between sets of vectors. In International Conference on Machine Learning (ICML), 2003.
11. R. Kondor and J. Lafferty. Diffusion kernels on graphs and other discrete input spaces. In International Conference on Machine Learning (ICML), 2002.
12. Y. LeCun, L. Bottou, Y. Bengio, and P. Haffner. Gradient-based learning applied to document recognition. Proceedings of the IEEE, 86(11):2278-2324, November 1998.
13. S. Lyu. Kernel between sets: the gaussian mixture approach. Technical Report TR2005-214, Computer Science Department, Dartmouth College, 2005.
14. S. Mika, G. Rütsch, J. Weston, B. Schölkopf, and K.-R. Müller. Fisher discriminant analysis with kernels. In IEEE Conference on Neural Networks for Signal Processing, 1999.
15. S. Mika, B. Schölkopf, A. Smola, K.-R. Müller, M. Scholz, and G. Rütsch. Kernel PCA and de-noising in feature spaces. In Advances in Neural Information Processing Systems 11, pages 536-542, Cambridge, MA, 1999.
16. E. Parzen. On estimation of a probability density function and mode. Ann. Math. Statistics, 33:1,065-1,076, 1962.
17. S. Roweis. Gaussian Identities. Department of Computer Science, U. Toronto, Manuscript available at http://www.cs.toronto.edu/roweis/notes.html, 2001.
18. J. Shawe-Taylor and N. Cristianini. Kernel Methods for Pattern Analysis. Cambridge, 2004.

19. C.A. Sugar and G.M. James. Finding the number of clusters in a dataset: An information-theoretic approach. Journal of American Statistical Association, 98(463):750-763, 2003.
20. V. Vapnik. Statistical Learning Theory. Wiley, New York, NY,1998.
21. S. Vishwanathan and A. Smola. Fast kernels for string and tree matching. In Advances in Neural Information Processing Systems (NIPS), 2003.

Active Learning for Probability Estimation Using Jensen-Shannon Divergence

Prem Melville[1], Stewart M. Yang[2], Maytal Saar-Tsechansky[4], and Raymond Mooney[3]

[1] Dept. of Computer Sciences, Univ. of Texas at Austin
melville@cs.utexas.edu
[2] windtown@cs.utexas.edu
[3] mooney@cs.utexas.edu
[4] Red McCombs School of Business, Univ. of Texas at Austin
maytal.saar-tsechansky@mccombs.utexas.edu

Abstract. Active selection of good training examples is an important approach to reducing data-collection costs in machine learning; however, most existing methods focus on maximizing classification accuracy. In many applications, such as those with unequal misclassification costs, producing good class probability estimates (CPEs) is more important than optimizing classification accuracy. We introduce novel approaches to active learning based on the algorithms Bootstrap-LV and ACTIVEDECORATE, by using Jensen-Shannon divergence (a similarity measure for probability distributions) to improve sample selection for optimizing CPEs. Comprehensive experimental results demonstrate the benefits of our approaches.

1 Introduction

Many supervised learning applications require more than a simple classification of instances. Often, also having accurate Class Probability Estimates (CPEs) is critical for the task. Class probability estimation is a fundamental concept used in a variety of applications including marketing, fraud detection and credit ranking. For example, in direct marketing the probability that each customer would purchase an item is employed in order to optimize marketing budget expenditure. Similarly, in credit scoring, class probabilities are used to estimate the utility of various courses of actions, such as the profitability of denying or approving a credit application. While prediction accuracy of CPE improves with the availability of more labeled examples, acquiring labeled data is sometimes costly. For example, customers' preferences may be induced from customers' responses to offerings; but solicitations made to acquire customer responses (labels) may be costly, because unwanted solicitations can result in negative customer attitudes. It is therefore critical to reduce the number of label acquisitions necessary to obtain a desired prediction accuracy.

The *active learning* literature [1] offers several algorithms for cost-effective label acquisitions. Active learners acquire training data incrementally, using the model induced from the available labeled examples to identify helpful additional training examples for labeling. Different active learning approaches employ different utility scores to estimate how informative each unlabeled example is, if it is labeled and added to the training data. When successful, active learning methods reduce the number of instances that must be labeled to achieve a particular level of accuracy. Almost all work in active learning has focused on acquisition policies for inducing accurate *classification* models and thus are aimed at improving classification accuracy. Although active learning algorithms for classification can be applied for learning accurate CPEs, they may not be optimal. Active learning algorithms for classification may (and indeed should) avoid acquisitions that can improve CPEs but are not likely to impact classification. Accurate classification only requires that the model accurately assigns the highest CPE to the correct class, even if the CPEs across classes may be inaccurate. Therefore, to perform well, active learning methods for classification ought to acquire labels of examples that are likely to change the rank-order of the most likely class. To improve CPEs, however, it is necessary to identify potential acquisitions that would improve the CPE accuracy, regardless of the implications for classification accuracy. Bootstrap-LV [2] is an active learning approach designed specifically to improve CPEs for binary class problems. The method acquires labels for examples for which the current model exhibits high variance for its CPEs. BOOTSTRAP-LV was shown to significantly reduce the number of label acquisitions required to achieve a given CPE accuracy compared to random acquisitions and existing active learning approaches for classification.

In this paper, we propose two new active learning approaches. In contrast to BOOTSTRAP-LV, the methods we propose can be applied to acquire labels to improve the CPEs of an arbitrary number of classes. The two methods differ by the measures each employs to identify informative examples: the first approach, BOOTSTRAP-JS, employs the Jensen-Shannon divergence measure (JSD) [3]. The second approach, BOOTSTRAP-LV-EXT, uses a measure of variance inspired by the local variance proposed in BOOTSTRAP-LV. We demonstrate that for binary class problems, BOOTSTRAP-JS is at least comparable and often superior to BOOTSTRAP-LV. In addition, we establish that for multi-class problems, BOOTSTRAP-JS and BOOTSTRAP-LV-EXT identify particularly informative examples that significantly improve the CPEs compared to a strategy in which a representative set of examples are acquired uniformly at random. This paper also extends the work of Melville and Mooney [4], which introduced a method, ACTIVEDECORATE, for active learning for classification. They compared two measures for evaluating the utility of examples - label margins and JSD. The results showed that both measures are effective for improving classification accuracy, though JSD is less effective than margins. It was conjectured that JSD would be a particularly useful measure when the objective is improving CPEs. We demonstrate here that, for the task of active learning for CPE, ACTIVEDECORATE using JSD indeed performs significantly better than using margins.

2 Jensen-Shannon Divergence

Jensen-Shannon divergence (JSD) is a measure of the "distance" between two probability distributions [3] which can also be generalized to measure the distance (similarity) between a finite number of distributions [5]. JSD is a natural extension of the Kullback-Leibler divergence (KLD) to a set of distributions. KLD is defined between two distributions, and the JSD of a set of distributions is the average KLD of each distribution to the mean of the set. Unlike KLD, JSD is a true metric and is bounded. If a classifier can provide a distribution of class membership probabilities for a given example, then we can use JSD to compute a measure of similarity between the distributions produced by a set (ensemble) of such classifiers. If $P_i(x)$ is the class probability distribution given by the i-th classifier for the example x (which we will abbreviate as P_i) we can then compute the JSD of a set of size n as $JS(P_1, P_2, ..., P_n) = H(\sum_{i=1}^{n} w_i P_i) - \sum_{i=1}^{n} w_i H(P_i)$; where w_i is the vote weight of the i-th classifier in the set;[1] and $H(P)$ is the Shannon entropy of the distribution $P = \{p_j : j = 1, ..., K\}$, defined as $H(P) = -\sum_{j=1}^{K} p_j \log p_j$. Higher values for JSD indicate a greater spread in the CPE distributions, and it is zero if and only if the distributions are identical. JSD has been successfully used to measure the utility of examples in active learning for improving classification accuracy [4]. A similar measure was also used for active learning for text classification by McCallum and Nigam [6].

3 Bootstrap-LV and JSD

To the best of our knowledge, Bootstrap-LV [2] is the only active learning algorithm designed for learning CPEs. It was shown to require significantly fewer training examples to achieve a given CPE accuracy compared to random sampling and *uncertainty sampling*, which is an active learning method focused on classification accuracy [7]. Bootstrap-LV reduces CPE error by acquiring examples for which the current model exhibits relatively high local variance (LV), i.e., the variance in CPE for a particular example. A high LV for an unlabeled example indicates that the model's estimation of its class membership probabilities is likely to be erroneous, and the example is therefore more desirable to be selected for learning.

Bootstrap-LV, as defined in [2] is only applicable to binary class problems. We first provide the details of this method, and then describe how we extended it to solve multi-class problems. Bootstrap-LV is an iterative algorithm that can be applied to any base learner. At each iteration, we generate a set of n bootstrap samples [8] from the training set, and apply the given learner $\mathcal{L}$ to each sample to generate n classifiers $C_i : i = 1, ..., n$. For each example in the unlabeled set U, we compute a score which determines its probability of being selected, and which is proportional to the variance of the CPEs. More specifically, the score for example x_j is computed as $(\sum_{i=1}^{n} (p_i(x_j) - \bar{p}_j)^2)/\bar{p}_{j,min}$; where $p_i(x_j)$ denotes the estimated probability the classifier C_i assigns to the event that example x_j belongs to class 0 (the choice of performing the calculation for class 0 is arbitrary, since the variance for both classes is identical), $\bar{p}_j$ is the average estimate for class 0 across classifiers C_i, and $\bar{p}_{j,min}$ is the average probability estimate assigned to the minority class by the different classifiers. Saar-Tsechansky and Provost [2] attempt to compensate for the under-representation of the minority class by introducing the term $\bar{p}_{j,min}$ in the utility score. The scores produced for the set of unlabeled examples are normalized to produce a distribution, and then a subset of unlabeled examples are selected based on this distribution. The labels for these examples are acquired and the process is repeated.

---
[1] Our experiments use uniform vote weights, normalized to sum to one.

The model's CPE variance allows the identification of examples that can improve CPE accuracy. However as noted above, the local variance estimated by Bootstrap-LV captures the CPE variance of a single class and thus is not applicable to multi class problems. Since we have a set of probability distributions for each example, we can instead, use an information theoretic measure, such as JSD to measure the utility of an example. The advantage to using JSD is that it is a theoretically well-motivated distance measure for probability distributions [3] that can be therefore used to capture the uncertainty of the class distribution estimation; and furthermore, it naturally extends to distributions over multiple classes. We propose a variation of BOOTSTRAP-LV, where the utility score for each example is computed as the JSD of the CPEs produced by the set of classifiers C_i. This approach, BOOTSTRAP-JS, is presented in Algorithm 1.

Our second approach, BOOTSTRAP-LV-EXT, is inspired by the Local Variance concept proposed in BOOTSTRAP-LV. For each example and for each class, the variance in the prediction of the class probability across classifiers $C_i, i = 1, ..., n$ is computed, capturing the uncertainty of the CPE for this class. Subsequently, the utility score for each potential acquisition is calculated as the mean variance across classes, reflecting the average uncertainty in the estimations of all classes. Unlike BOOTSTRAP-LV, BOOTSTRAP-LV-EXT does not incorporate the factor of $\bar{p}_{j,min}$ in the score for multi-class problems, as this is inappropriate in this scenario.

Algorithm 1. Bootstrap-JS

Given: set of training examples T, set of unlabeled training examples U, base learning algorithm $\mathcal{L}$, number of bootstrap samples n, size of each sample m

1. Repeat until stopping criterion is met
2.   Generate n bootstrap samples $B_i, i = 1, ..., n$ from T
3.   Apply learner $\mathcal{L}$ to each sample B_i to produce classifier C_i
4.   For each $x_j \in U$
5. $\forall C_i$ generate CPE distribution $P_i(x_j)$
6. $score_j = JS(P_1, P_2, ..., P_n)$
7. $\forall x_j \in U, D(x_j) = score_j / \sum_j score_j$
8.   Sample a subset S of m examples from U based on the distribution D
9.   Remove examples in S from U and add to T
10. Return $C = \mathcal{L}(T)$

---

4 ActiveDecorate and JSD

ACTIVEDECORATE is an active learning method that selects examples to be labeled so as to improve classification accuracy [4]. It is built on the *Query by Committee* (QBC) framework for selective sampling [9]; and has been shown to outperform other QBC approaches, Query by Bagging and Query by Boosting. ACTIVEDECORATE is based on DECORATE [10,11], which is a recently introduced ensemble meta-learner that directly constructs diverse committees of classifiers by employing specially-constructed artificial training examples.

Given a pool of unlabeled examples, ACTIVEDECORATE iteratively selects examples to be labeled for training. In each iteration, it generates a committee of classifiers by applying DECORATE to the currently labeled examples. Then it evaluates the potential utility of each example in the unlabeled set, and selects a subset of examples with the highest expected utility. The labels for these examples are acquired and they are transfered to the training set. The utility of an example is determined by some measure of *disagreement* in the committee about its predicted label. Melville and Mooney [4] compare two measures of utility for ACTIVEDECORATE— *margins* and JSD. Given the CPEs predicted by the committee for an example,[2] the margin is defined as the difference between the highest and second highest predicted probabilities. It was shown that ACTIVEDECORATE using either measure of utility produces substantial error reductions in classification compared to random sampling. However, in general, using margins produces greater improvements. Using JSD tends to select examples that reduce the uncertainty in CPE, which indirectly helps to improve classification accuracy. On the other hand, ACTIVEDECORATE using margins focuses more directly on determining the decision boundary. This may account for its better classification performance. It was conjectured that if the objective is improving CPEs, then JSD may be a better measure.

In this paper, we validate this conjecture. In addition to using JSD, we made two more changes to the original algorithm, each of which independently improved its performance. First, each example in the unlabeled set is assigned a probability of being sampled, which is proportional to the measure of utility for the example. Instead of selecting the examples with the m highest utilities, we sample the unlabeled set based on the assigned probabilities (as in BOOTSTRAP-LV). This sampling has been shown to improve the selection mechanism as it reduces the probability of adding outliers to the training data and avoids selecting many similar or identical examples [12].

The second change we made is in the DECORATE algorithm. DECORATE ensembles are created iteratively; where in each iteration a new classifier is trained. If adding this new classifier to the current ensemble increases the ensemble training error, then this classifier is rejected, else it is added to the current ensemble. In previous work, training error was evaluated using the 0/1 loss function; however, DECORATE can use any loss (error) function. Since we are interested in improving CPE we experimented with two alternate error functions — Mean Squared Error (MSE) and Area Under the Lift Chart (AULC) (defined in the next section). Using MSE performed better on the two metrics used, so we present these results in the rest of the paper. Our approach, ACTIVEDECORATE-JS, is shown in Algorithm 2.

5 Experimental Evaluation

5.1 Methodology

To evaluate the performance of the different active CPE methods, we ran experiments on 24 representative data sets from the UCI repository [13]. 12 of these datasets were

---

[2] The CPEs for a committee are computed as the simple average of the CPEs produced by its constituent classifiers.

Algorithm 2. ActiveDecorate-JS

Given: set of training examples T, set of unlabeled training examples U, base learning algorithm $\mathcal{L}$, number of bootstrap samples n, size of each sample m

1. Repeat until stopping criterion is met
2.   Generate an ensemble of classifiers, $C^* = Decorate(\mathcal{L}, T, n)$
3.   For each $x_j \in U$
4. $\forall C_i \in C^*$ generate CPE distribution $P_i(x_j)$
5. $score_j = JS(P_1, P_2, ..., P_n)$
6. $\forall x_j \in U, D(x_j) = score_j / \sum_j score_j$
7.   Sample a subset S of m examples from U based on the distribution D
8.   Remove examples in S from U and add to T
9. Return $Decorate(\mathcal{L}, T, n)$

two-class problems, the rest being multi-class. For three datasets (*kr-vs-kp*, *sick*, and *optdigits*), we used a random sample of 1000 instances to reduce experimentation time.

All the active learning methods we discuss in this paper are meta-learners, i.e., they can be applied to any base learner. For our experiments, as a base classifier we use a Probability Estimation Tree (PET) [14], which is an unpruned J48[3] decision tree for which Laplace correction is applied at the leaves. Saar-Tsechansky and Provost [2] showed that using Bagged-PETs for prediction produced better probability estimates than single PETs for BOOTSTRAP-LV; so we used Bagged-PETs for both BOOTSTRAP-LV and BOOTSTRAP-JS. The number of bootstrap samples and the size of ensembles in ACTIVEDECORATE was set to 15.

The performance of each algorithm was averaged over 10 runs of 10-fold cross-validation. In each fold of cross-validation, we generated learning curves as follows. The set of available training examples was treated as an unlabeled pool of examples, and at each iteration the active learner selected a sample of points to be labeled and added to the training set. Each method was allowed to select a total of 33 batches of training examples, measuring performance after each batch in order to generate a learning curve. To reduce computation costs, and because of diminishing variance in performance for different selected examples along the learning curve, we incrementally selected larger batches at each acquisition phase. The resulting curves evaluate how well an active learner orders the set of available examples in terms of utility for learning CPEs. As a baseline, we used random sampling, where the examples in each iteration were selected randomly.

To the best of our knowledge, there are no publicly-available datasets that provide true class probabilities for instances; hence there is no direct measure for the accuracy of CPEs. Instead, we use two indirect metrics proposed in other studies for CPEs [16]. The first metric is squared error, which is defined for an instance x_j, as $\sum_y (P_{true}(y|x_j) - P(y|x_j))^2$; where $P(y|x_j)$ is the predicted probability that x_j belongs to class y, and $P_{true}(y|x_j)$ is the true probability that x_j belongs to y. We compute the Mean Squared Error (MSE) as the mean of this squared error for each example in the test set. Since we only know the true class labels and not the probabilities, we define $P_{true}(y|x_j)$ to be 1 when the class of x_j is y and 0 otherwise. Given that we are comparing with

---
[3] J48 is the Weka [15] implementation of C4.5

this extreme distribution, squared error tends to favor classifiers that produce accurate classification, but with extreme probability estimates. Hence, we do not recommend using this metric by itself.

The second measure we employ is the area under the lift chart (AULC) [17], which is computed as follows. First, for each class k, we take the $\alpha\%$ of instances with the highest probability estimates for class k. r_α is defined to be the proportion of these instances actually belonging to class k; and r_{100} is the proportion of all test instances that are from class k. The lift $l(\alpha)$, is then computed as $\frac{r_\alpha}{r_{100}}$. The AULC$_k$ is calculated by numeric integration of $l(\alpha)$ from 0 to 100 with a step-size of 5. The overall AULC is computed as the weighted-average of AULC$_k$ for each k; where AULC$_k$ is weighted by the prior class probability of k according to the training set. AULC is a measure of how good the probability estimates are for ranking examples correctly, but not how accurate the estimates are. However, in the absence of a direct measure, an examination of MSE and AULC in tandem provides a good indication of CPE accuracy. We also measured log-loss or cross-entropy, but these results were highly correlated with MSE, so we do not report them here.

To effectively summarize the comparison of two algorithms, we compute the percentage reduction in MSE of one over the other, averaged along the points of the learning curve. We consider the reduction in error to be *significant* if the difference in the errors of the two systems, averaged across the points on the learning curve, is determined to be statistically significant according to paired t-tests ($p < 0.05$). Similarly, we report the percentage *increase* in AULC.[4]

5.2 Results

The results of all our comparisons are presented in Tables 1-3. In each table we present two active learning methods compared to random sampling as well as to each other. We present the statistics *% MSE reduction* and *% AULC increase* averaged across the learning curves. All statistically significant results are presented in bold font. The bottom of each table presents the win/draw/loss (w/d/l) record; where a win or loss is only counted if the improved performance is determined to be significant as defined above.

5.3 Bootstrap-JS, Bootstrap-LV and Bootstrap-LV-EXT

We first examine the performance of BOOTSTRAP-JS for binary-class problems and compared it with that of BOOTSTRAP-LV and of random sampling. As shown in Table 1, BOOTSTRAP-JS often exhibits significant improvements over BOOTSTRAP-LV, or is otherwise comparable to BOOTSTRAP-LV. For all data sets, BOOTSTRAP-JS shows substantial improvements with respect to examples selected uniformly at random on both MSE and AULC. The effectiveness of BOOTSTRAP-JS can be clearly seen in Figure 1. (The plot shows the part of learning curve where the two active learners diverge in performance.)

In the absence of an active class probability estimation approach that can be applied to multi-class problems, we compare BOOTSTRAP-JS and BOOTSTRAP-LV-EXT with

---

[4] A larger AULC usually implies better probability estimates.

Table 1. BOOTSTRAP-JS versus BOOTSTRAP-LV on binary datasets

Data set	%MSE Reduction			%AULC Increase		
	LV vs. Random	JS vs. Random	JS vs. LV	LV vs. Random	JS vs. Random	JS vs. LV
breast-w	14.92	14.81	-0.12	0.55	0.52	-0.02
colic	-1.45	-0.04	1.39	-0.95	-0.56	0.41
credit-a	2.1	3.98	1.92	-0.49	-0.01	0.48
credit-g	-0.16	0.77	0.93	-0.01	0.3	0.32
diabetes	1.01	1.75	0.75	0.18	0.58	0.4
heart-c	1.68	0.29	-1.43	0.57	-0.08	-0.64
hepatitis	0.19	2.64	2.43	0.19	1.03	0.84
ion	10.65	12.26	1.82	1.13	0.96	-0.16
kr-vs-kp	38.97	43	8.07	1.64	1.79	0.15
sick	19.97	20.84	1.03	0.62	0.41	-0.21
sonar	2.44	1.32	-1.17	0.58	0.74	0.16
vote	6.3	9.14	3.08	0.28	0.46	0.18
w/d/l	9/2/1	10/2/0	9/1/2	7/3/2	9/2/1	8/2/2

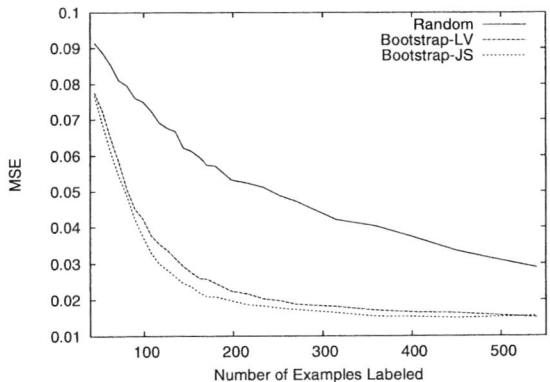

Fig. 1. Comparing different algorithms on *kr-vs-kp*

acquisitions of a representative set of examples selected uniformly at random. Table 2 presents results on multi-class datasets for BOOTSTRAP-JS and BOOTSTRAP-LV-EXT. Both active methods acquire particularly informative examples, such that for a given number of acquisitions, both methods produce significant reductions in error over random sampling. The two active methods perform comparably to each other for most data sets, and JSD performs slightly better in some domains. Because JSD successfully measures the uncertainty of the distribution estimation over all classes, we would recommend using BOOTSTRAP-JS for actively learning CPE models in multi-class domains.

5.4 ActiveDecorate: JSD Versus Margins

Table 3 shows the results of using JSD versus margins for ACTIVEDECORATE. In previous work, it was shown that ACTIVEDECORATE, with both these measures, performs very well on the task of active learning for classification. Our results here confirm that

Table 2. BOOTSTRAP-JS versus BOOTSTRAP-LV-EXT on multi-class datasets

Data set	% MSE Reduction			% AULC Increase		
	LV-Ext vs. Rand.	JS vs. Rand.	JS vs. LV-Ext	LV-Ext vs. Rand.	JS vs. Rand.	JS vs. LV-Ext
anneal	12.27	13.06	0.89	0.05	0.5	0.45
autos	0.96	0.38	-0.58	1.51	0.83	-0.66
balance-s	1.39	0.92	-0.48	0.72	0.58	-0.14
car	7.21	6.93	-0.31	1.53	1.41	-0.12
glass	-0.55	-0.19	0.36	0.61	0.48	-0.11
hypo	46.62	46.41	-0.9	0.49	0.47	-0.02
iris	6.64	10.79	4.58	0.46	0.83	0.39
nursery	14.37	14.25	-0.20	0.44	0.42	-0.01
optdigits	0.35	0.71	0.35	0.9	1.13	0.23
segment	11.08	11.19	0.08	0.83	0.79	-0.04
soybean	1.5	0.78	-0.74	-0.46	0.4	0.87
wine	13.13	13.34	0.36	1.11	1.08	-0.02
w/d/l	10/1/1	11/1/0	4/5/3	10/1/1	12/0/0	4/6/2

both measures are also effective for active learning for CPE. ACTIVEDECORATE using margins focuses on picking examples that reduce the uncertainty of the classification boundary. Since having better probability estimates usually improves accuracy, it is not surprising that a method focused on improving classification accuracy selects examples that may also improve CPE. However, using JSD directly focuses on reducing the uncertainty in probability estimates and hence performs much better on this task than margins. On the AULC metric both measures seem to perform comparably; however, on MSE, JSD shows clear and significant advantages over using margins. As noted above, one needs to analyze a combination of these metrics to effectively evaluate any active CPE method. Figure 2 presents the comparison of ACTIVEDECORATE with JSD versus margins on the AULC metric on *glass*. The two methods appear to be comparable, with JSD performing better earlier in the curve and margins performing better later. However, when the two methods are compared on the same dataset, using the MSE metric (Figure 3), we note that JSD outperforms margins throughout the learning curve. Based on the combination of these results, we may conclude that using JSD is more likely to produce accurate CPEs for this dataset. This example reinforces the need for examining multiple metrics.

5.5 ActiveDecorate-JS vs Bootstrap-JS

In addition to demonstrating the effectiveness of JSD, we also compare the two active CPE methods that use JSD. The comparison is made in two scenarios. In the *full dataset* scenario, the setting is the same as in previous experiments. In the *early stages* scenario, each algorithm is allowed to select 1 example at each iteration starting from 5 examples and going up to 20 examples. This characterizes the performance at the beginning of the learning curve. In the interest of space, we only present the win/draw/loss statistics (Table 4). For the *full dataset*, on the AULC metric, the methods perform comparably, but BOOTSTRAP-JS outperforms ACTIVEDECORATE-JS on MSE. However, for most datasets, ACTIVEDECORATE-JS shows significant advantages over BOOTSTRAP-JS in

Table 3. ACTIVEDECORATE-JS versus Margins

Data set	% MSE Reduction			% AULC Increase		
	Margin vs. Rand.	JS vs. Rand.	JS vs. Margin	Margin vs. Rand.	JS vs. Rand.	JS vs. Margin
breast-w	9.32	23.91	12.73	0.29	-0.50	-0.79
colic	8.65	17.99	10.17	4	2.44	-1.47
credit-a	15.83	21.97	7.08	2.85	2.98	0.07
credit-g	7.06	8.91	2.02	6.98	7.79	0.75
diabetes	-3.11	0.07	2.9	4.98	0.84	-3.94
heart-c	4.66	6.3	1.72	1.54	0.53	-0.99
hepatitis	4.49	7.34	2.99	1.93	0.14	-1.95
ion	29.23	36.51	10.01	5.73	5.53	-0.2
kr-vs-kp	34	65.27	50.77	6.46	2.19	-3.99
sick	39.18	64.38	42.24	10.49	9.11	-1.24
sonar	9.3	9.31	0.15	5.84	5.37	-0.41
vote	12.15	45.79	38.12	0.81	-0.51	-1.31
anneal	45.51	63.8	32.1	7.62	11.14	3.27
autos	8.32	11.38	3.57	15.34	11.52	-3.34
balance-s	14.1	24.63	12.05	5.24	6.14	0.86
car	2.9	53.32	52.27	5.56	16.23	10.3
glass	7.62	12.31	5.02	8.62	10.51	1.82
hypo	31.37	89.87	86.34	4.03	4.7	0.65
iris	-1.32	34.32	32.7	-1.56	1.52	3.16
nursery	2.62	69.99	69.52	0.56	6.43	5.9
optdigits	32.56	39.8	10.67	19.38	17.79	-1.4
segment	56.95	71.12	27.27	6.11	6.85	0.71
soybean	15.82	21.84	7.42	21.1	34.35	10.89
wine	17.09	28.85	13.81	1.66	1.17	-0.5
w/d/l	22/0/2	23/1/0	23/1/0	23/0/1	22/2/0	10/3/11

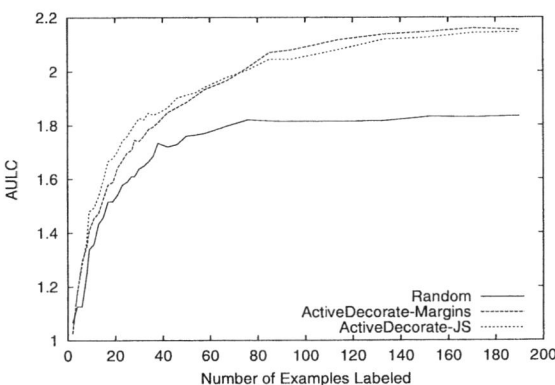

Fig. 2. Comparing AULC of different algorithms on *glass*

the *early stages*. These results could be explained by the fact that DECORATE (used by ACTIVEDECORATE-JS) has a clear advantage over Bagging (used by BOOTSTRAP-JS) when training sets are small, as explained in [11].

Table 4. BOOTSTRAP-JS vs. ACTIVEDECORATE-JS: Win/Draw/Loss records

	% MSE Reduction	% AULC Increase
Full dataset	18/0/6	13/0/11
Early stages	8/2/14	2/5/17

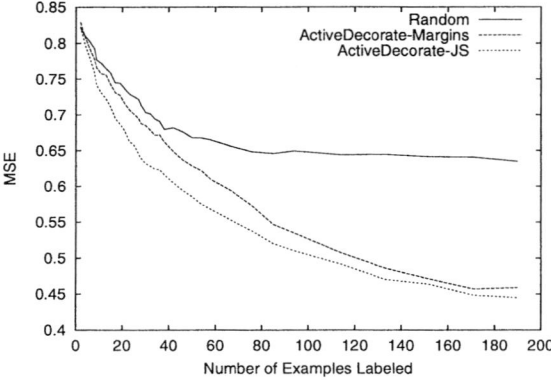

Fig. 3. Comparing MSE of different algorithms on *glass*

For DECORATE, we only specify the desired ensemble size; the ensembles formed could be smaller depending on the maximum number of classifiers it is permitted to explore. In our experiments, the desired size was set to 15 and a maximum of 50 classifiers were explored. On average DECORATE ensembles formed by ACTIVEDECORATE-JS are much smaller than those formed by Bagging in BOOTSTRAP-JS. Having larger ensembles generally increases classification accuracy [10] and may improve CPE. This may account for the weaker overall performance of ACTIVEDECORATE-JS to BOOTSTRAP-JS; and may be significantly improved by increasing the ensemble size.

6 Conclusions and Future Work

In this paper, we propose the use of Jensen-Shannon divergence as a measure of the utility of acquiring labeled examples for learning accurate class probability estimates. Extensive experiments have demonstrated that JSD effectively captures the uncertainty of class probability estimation and allows us to identify particularly informative examples that significantly improve the model's class distribution estimation. In particular, we show that, for binary-class problems, BOOTSTRAP-JS which employs JSD to acquire training examples is either comparable or significantly superior to BOOTSTRAP-LV, an existing active CPE learner for binary class problems. BOOTSTRAP-JS maintains its effectiveness for multi-class domains as well: it acquires informative examples which result in significantly more accurate models as compared to models induced from examples selected uniformly at random. We have also demonstrated that when JSD is used with ACTIVEDECORATE, an active learner for classification, it produces substantial improvements over using margins, which focuses on classification accuracy. Furthermore, our results indicate that, in general, BOOTSTRAP-JS with Bagged-PETs is a preferable method for active CPE compared to ACTIVEDECORATE-JS. However, if one is concerned primarily with the early stages of learning, then ACTIVEDECORATE-JS has a significant advantage.

Our study uses standard metrics for evaluating CPE employed in existing research. However, we have shown that JSD is a good measure for selecting examples for improving CPE; and therefore it should also be a good measure for evaluating CPE. When the true class probabilities are known, we propose to also evaluate CPEs by computing the JSD between the estimated and the true class distributions.

Acknowledgments

This research was supported by DARPA grant HR0011-04-1-007.

References

1. Cohn, D., Atlas, L., Ladner, R.: Improving generalization with active learning. Machine Learning **15** (1994) 201–221
2. Saar-Tsechansky, M., Provost, F.J.: Active learning for class probability estimation and ranking. In: Proc. of 17th Intl. Joint Conf. on Artificial Intelligence. (2001) 911–920
3. Cover, T.M., Thomas, J.A.: Elements of Information Theory. Wiley, New York, NY (1991)
4. Melville, P., Mooney, R.J.: Diverse ensembles for active learning. In: Proc. of 21st Intl. Conf. on Machine Learning (ICML-2004), Banff, Canada (2004) 584–591
5. Dhillon, I., Mallela, S., Kumar, R.: Enhanced word clustering for hierarchical classification. In: Proc. of 8th ACM Intl. Conf. on Knowledge Discovery and Data Mining (2002)
6. McCallum, A., Nigam, K.: Employing EM and pool-based active learning for text classification. In: Proc. of 15th Intl. Conf. on Machine Learning (1998)
7. Lewis, D.D., Catlett, J.: Heterogeneous uncertainty sampling for supervised learning. In: Proc. of 11th Intl. Conf. on Machine Learning, (1994) 148–156
8. Efron, B., Tibshirani, R.J.: An Introduction to the Bootstrap. Chapman and Hall, New York, NY (1993)
9. Seung, H.S., Opper, M., Sompolinsky, H.: Query by committee. In: Proc. of the ACM Workshop on Computational Learning Theory, Pittsburgh, PA (1992)
10. Melville, P., Mooney, R.J.: Constructing diverse classifier ensembles using artificial training examples. In: Proc. of 18th Intl. Joint Conf. on Artificial Intelligence (IJCAI-2003), Acapulco, Mexico (2003) 505–510
11. Melville, P., Mooney, R.J.: Creating diversity in ensembles using artificial data. Journal of Information Fusion: Special Issue on Diversity in Multi Classifier Systems **6** (2004) 99–111
12. Saar-Tsechansky, M., Provost, F.: Active sampling for class probability estimation and ranking. Machine Learning **54** (2004) 153–178
13. Blake, C.L., Merz, C.J.: UCI repository of machine learning databases. http://www.ics.uci.edu/~mlearn/MLRepository.html (1998)
14. Provost, F., Domingos, P.: Tree induction for probability-based rankings. Machine Learning **52** (2003) 199–215
15. Witten, I.H., Frank, E.: Data Mining: Practical Machine Learning Tools and Techniques with Java Implementations. Morgan Kaufmann, San Francisco (1999)
16. Zadrozny, B., Elkan, C.: Obtaining calibrated probability estimates from decision trees and naive Bayesian classifiers. In: Proc. of 18th Intl. Conf. on Machine Learning (2001)
17. Nielsen, R.D.: MOB-ESP and other improvements in probability estimation. In: Proc. of 20th Conf. on Uncertainty in Artificial Intelligence, (2004) 418–425

Natural Actor-Critic

Jan Peters[1], Sethu Vijayakumar[2], and Stefan Schaal[1]

[1] University of Southern California, Los Angeles CA 90089, USA
[2] University of Edinburgh, Edinburgh EH9 3JZ, United Kingdom

Abstract. This paper investigates a novel model-free reinforcement learning architecture, the Natural Actor-Critic. The actor updates are based on stochastic policy gradients employing Amari's natural gradient approach, while the critic obtains both the natural policy gradient and additional parameters of a value function simultaneously by linear regression. We show that actor improvements with natural policy gradients are particularly appealing as these are independent of coordinate frame of the chosen policy representation, and can be estimated more efficiently than regular policy gradients. The critic makes use of a special basis function parameterization motivated by the policy-gradient compatible function approximation. We show that several well-known reinforcement learning methods such as the original Actor-Critic and Bradtke's Linear Quadratic Q-Learning are in fact Natural Actor-Critic algorithms. Empirical evaluations illustrate the effectiveness of our techniques in comparison to previous methods, and also demonstrate their applicability for learning control on an anthropomorphic robot arm.

1 Introduction

Reinforcement learning algorithms based on value function approximation have been highly successful with discrete lookup table parameterization. However, when applied with continuous function approximation, many of these algorithms failed to generalize, and few convergence guarantees could be obtained [14]. The reason for this problem can largely be traced back to the greedy or ϵ-greedy policy updates of most techniques, as it does not ensure a policy improvement when applied with an approximate value function [6]. During a greedy update, small errors in the value function can cause large changes in the policy which in return can cause large changes in the value function. This process, when applied repeatedly, can result in oscillations or divergence of the algorithms. Even in simple toy systems, such unfortunate behavior can be found in many well-known greedy reinforcement learning algorithms [4,6].

As an alternative to greedy reinforcement learning, policy gradient methods have been suggested. Policy gradients have rather strong convergence guarantees, even when used in conjunction with approximate value functions, and recent results created a theoretically solid framework for policy gradient estimation from sampled data [15,11]. However, even when applied to simple examples with rather few states, policy gradient methods often turn out to be quite inefficient

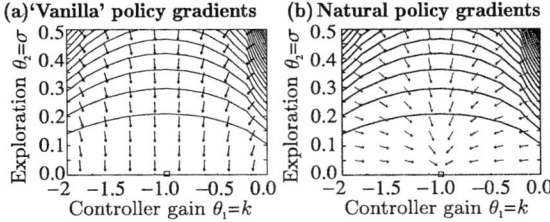

Fig. 1. When plotting the expected return landscape for simple problem as 1d linear quadratic regulation, the differences between 'vanilla' and natural policy gradients becomes apparent [13]

[10], partially caused by the large plateaus in the expected return landscape where the gradients are small and often do not point directly towards the optimal solution. A simple example that demonstrates this behavior is given in Fig. 1.

Similar as in supervised learning, the steepest ascent with respect to the Fisher information metric [1], called the 'natural' policy gradient, turns out to be significantly more efficient than normal gradients. Such an approach was first suggested for reinforcement learning as the 'average natural policy gradient' in [10], and subsequently shown in preliminary work to be the true natural policy gradient [13,2]. In this paper, we take this line of reasoning one step further in Section 2.2 by introducing the "Natural Actor-Critic" which inherits the convergence guarantees from gradient methods. Furthermore, in Section 3, we show that several successful previous reinforcement learning methods can be seen as special cases of this more general architecture. The paper concludes with empirical evaluations that demonstrate the effectiveness of the suggested methods in Section 4.

2 Natural Actor-Critic

2.1 Markov Decision Process Notation and Assumptions

For this paper, we assume that the underlying control problem is a *Markov Decision Process* (MDP) in discrete time with continuous state set $\mathbb{X} = \mathbb{R}^n$, and a continuous action set $\mathbb{U} = \mathbb{R}^m$ [6]. The system is at an initial state $\boldsymbol{x}_0 \in \mathbb{X}$ at time $t = 0$ drawn from the start-state distribution $p(\boldsymbol{x}_0)$. At any state $\boldsymbol{x}_t \in \mathbb{X}$ at time t, the actor will choose an action $\boldsymbol{u}_t \in \mathbb{U}$ by drawing it from a stochastic, parameterized policy $\pi(\boldsymbol{u}_t|\boldsymbol{x}_t) = p(\boldsymbol{u}_t|\boldsymbol{x}_t, \boldsymbol{\theta})$ with parameters $\boldsymbol{\theta} \in \mathbb{R}^N$, and the system transfers to a new state $\boldsymbol{x}_{t+1}$ drawn from the state transfer distribution $p(\boldsymbol{x}_{t+1}|\boldsymbol{x}_t, \boldsymbol{u}_t)$. The system yields a scalar reward $r_t = r(\boldsymbol{x}_t, \boldsymbol{u}_t) \in \mathbb{R}$ after each action. We assume that the policy $\pi_{\boldsymbol{\theta}}$ is continuously differentiable with respect to its parameters $\boldsymbol{\theta}$, and for each considered policy $\pi_{\boldsymbol{\theta}}$, a state-value function $V^\pi(\boldsymbol{x})$, and the state-action value function $Q^\pi(\boldsymbol{x}, \boldsymbol{u})$ exist and are given by

$$V^\pi(\boldsymbol{x}) = E_\tau\left\{\sum_{t=0}^\infty \gamma^t r_t \big| \boldsymbol{x}_0 = \boldsymbol{x}\right\}, Q^\pi(\boldsymbol{x}, \boldsymbol{u}) = E_\tau\left\{\sum_{t=0}^\infty \gamma^t r_t \big| \boldsymbol{x}_0 = \boldsymbol{x}, \boldsymbol{u}_0 = \boldsymbol{u}\right\},$$

where $\gamma \in [0,1[$ denotes the discount factor, and τ a trajectory. It is assumed that some basis functions $\phi(x)$ are given so that the state-value function can be approximated with linear function approximation $V^\pi(x) = \phi(x)^T v$. The general goal is to optimize the normalized expected return

$$J(\theta) = E_\tau \left\{ (1-\gamma)\sum_{t=0}^\infty \gamma^t r_t \mid \theta \right\} = \int_X d^\pi(x) \int_U \pi(u|x) r(x,u) dx du$$

where $d^\pi(x) = (1-\gamma)\sum_{t=0}^\infty \gamma^t p(x_t = x)$ is the discounted state distribution.

2.2 Actor Improvements with Natural Policy Gradients

Actor-Critic and many other policy iteration architectures consist of two steps, a policy evaluation step and a policy improvement step. The main requirements for the policy evaluation step are that it makes efficient usage of experienced data. The policy improvement step is required to improve the policy on every step until convergence while being efficient.

The requirements on the policy improvement step rule out greedy methods as, at the current state of knowledge, a policy improvement for approximated value functions cannot be guaranteed, even on average. 'Vanilla' policy gradient improvements (see e.g., [15,11]) which follow the gradient $\nabla_\theta J(\theta)$ of the expected return function $J(\theta)$ often get stuck in plateaus as demonstrated in [10]. Natural gradients $\widetilde{\nabla}_\theta J(\theta)$ avoid this pitfall as demonstrated for supervised learning problems [1], and suggested for reinforcement learning in [10]. These methods do not follow the steepest direction in parameter space but the steepest direction with respect to the Fisher metric given by

$$\widetilde{\nabla}_\theta J(\theta) = G^{-1}(\theta) \nabla_\theta J(\theta), \tag{1}$$

where $G(\theta)$ denotes the Fisher information matrix. It is guaranteed that the angle between natural and ordinary gradient is never larger than ninety degrees, i.e., convergence to the next local optimum can be assured. The 'vanilla' gradient is given by the policy gradient theorem (see e.g., [15,11]),

$$\nabla_\theta J(\theta) = \int_X d^\pi(x) \int_U \nabla_\theta \pi(u|x) (Q^\pi(x,u) - b^\pi(x)) du dx, \tag{2}$$

where $b^\pi(x)$ denotes a baseline. [15] and [11] demonstrated that in Eq. (2), the term $Q^\pi(x,u) - b^\pi(x)$ can be replaced by a compatible function approximation

$$f_w^\pi(x,u) = (\nabla_\theta \log \pi(u|x))^T w \equiv Q^\pi(x,u) - b^\pi(x), \tag{3}$$

parameterized by the vector w, *without* affecting the unbiasedness of the gradient estimate and irrespective of the choice of the baseline $b^\pi(x)$. However, as mentioned in [15], the baseline may still be useful in order to reduce the variance of the gradient estimate when Eq.(2) is approximated from samples. Based on Eqs.(2, 3), we derive an estimate of the policy gradient as

$$\nabla_\theta J(\theta) = \int_X d^\pi(x) \int_U \pi(u|x) \nabla_\theta \log \pi(u|x) \nabla_\theta \log \pi(u|x)^T du dx\ w = F_\theta w. \tag{4}$$

as $\nabla_\theta \pi(u|x) = \pi(u|x) \nabla_\theta \log \pi(u|x)$. Since $\pi(u|x)$ is chosen by the user, even in sampled data, the integral $F(\theta, x) = \int_U \pi(u|x) \nabla_\theta \log \pi(u|x) \nabla_\theta \log \pi(u|x)^T du$ can be evaluated analytically or empirically without actually executing all actions. It is also noteworthy that the baseline does not appear in Eq. (4) as it integrates out, thus eliminating the need to find an optimal selection of this open parameter. Nevertheless, the estimation of $F_\theta = \int_X d^\pi(x) F(\theta, x) dx$ is still expensive since $d^\pi(x)$ ist not known. However, Equation (4) has more surprising implications for policy gradients, when examining the meaning of the matrix F_θ in Eq.(4). Kakade [10] argued that $F(\theta, x)$ is the point Fisher information matrix for state x, and that $F(\theta) = \int_X d^\pi(x) F(\theta, x) dx$, therefore, denotes a weighted 'average Fisher information matrix'[10]. However, going one step further, we demonstrate in Appendix A that F_θ is indeed the true Fisher information matrix and does not have to be interpreted as the 'average' of the point Fisher information matrices. Eqs.(4) and (1) combined imply that the natural gradient can be computed as

$$\widetilde{\nabla}_\theta J(\theta) = G^{-1}(\theta) F_\theta w = w, \qquad (5)$$

since $F_\theta = G(\theta)$ (c.f. Appendix A). Therefore we only need estimate w and not $G(\theta)$. The resulting policy improvement step is thus $\theta_{i+1} = \theta_i + \alpha w$ where α denotes a learning rate. Several properties of the natural policy gradient are worthwhile highlighting:

- Convergence to a local minimum guaranteed as for 'vanilla gradients'. [1]
- By choosing a more direct path to the optimal solution in parameter space, the natural gradient has, from empirical observations, faster convergence and avoids premature convergence of 'vanilla gradients' (cf. Figure 1).
- The natural policy gradient can be shown to be **covariant**, i.e., independent of the coordinate frame chosen for expressing the policy parameters (cf. Section 3.1).
- As the natural gradient analytically averages out the influence of the stochastic policy (including the baseline of the function approximator), it requires fewer data point for a good gradient estimate than 'vanilla gradients'.

2.3 Critic Estimation with Compatible Policy Evaluation

The critic evaluates the current policy π in order to provide the basis for an actor improvement, i.e., the change $\Delta\theta$ of the policy parameters. As we are interested in natural policy gradient updates $\Delta\theta = \alpha w$, we wish to employ the compatible function approximation $f_w^\pi(x, u)$ from Eq.(3) in this context. At this point, a most important observation is that the compatible function approximation $f_w^\pi(x, u)$ is mean-zero w.r.t. the action distribution, i.e.,

$$\int_U \pi(u|x) f_w^\pi(x, u) du = w^T \int_U \nabla_\theta \pi(u|x) du = 0, \qquad (6)$$

since from $\int_U \pi(u|x) du = 1$, differention w.r.t. to θ results in $\int_U \nabla_\theta \pi(u|x) du = 0$. Thus, $f_w^\pi(x, u)$ represents an *advantage function* $A^\pi(x, u) = Q^\pi(x, u) - V^\pi(x)$ in general. The advantage function *cannot* be learned with TD-like bootstrapping without knowledge of the value function as the essence of TD is to compare the value $V^\pi(x)$ of the two adjacent states – but this value has been subtracted out in $A^\pi(x, u)$. Hence, a TD-like bootstrapping using exclusively the compatible function approximator is impossible.

As an alternative, [15,11] suggested to approximate $f_w^\pi(x, u)$ from unbiased estimates $\hat{Q}^\pi(x, u)$ of the action value function, e.g., obtained from roll-outs and using least-squares minimization between f_w and $\hat{Q}^\pi$. While possible in theory, one needs to realize that this approach implies a function approximation problem where the parameterization of the function approximator only spans a much smaller subspace of the training data – e.g., imagine approximating a quadratic function with a line. In practice, the results of such an approximation depends crucially on the training data distribution and has thus unacceptably high variance – e.g., fit a line to only data from the right branch of a parabola, the left branch, or data from both branches.

To remedy this situation, we observe that we can write the Bellman equations (e.g., see [3]) in terms of the advantage function and the state-value function

$$Q^\pi(x, u) = A^\pi(x, u) + V^\pi(x) = r(x, u) + \gamma \int_X p(x'|x, u) V^\pi(x') dx'. \quad (7)$$

Inserting $A^\pi(x, u) = f_w^\pi(x, u)$ and an appropriate basis functions representation of the value function as $V^\pi(x) = \phi(x)^T v$, we can rewrite the Bellman Equation, Eq., (7), as a set of linear equations

$$\nabla_\theta \log \pi(u_t|x_t)^T w + \phi(x_t)^T v = r(x_t, u_t) + \gamma \phi(x_{t+1})^T v + \epsilon(x_t, u_t, x_{t+1}) \quad (8)$$

where $\epsilon(x_t, u_t, x_{t+1})$ denotes an error term which mean-zero as can be observed from Eq.(7). These equations enable us to formulate some novel algorithms in the next sections.

Critic Evaluation with LSTD-Q(λ). Using Eq.(8), a solution to Equation (7) can be obtained by adapting the LSTD(λ) policy evaluation algorithm [7].

Table 1. Natural Actor-Critic Algorithm with LSTD-Q(λ)

Input: Parameterized policy $\pi(u|x) = p(u|x, \theta)$ with initial parameters $\theta = \theta_0$, its derivative $\nabla_\theta \log \pi(u|x)$ and basis functions $\phi(x)$ for the value function $V^\pi(x)$.
1: Draw initial state $x_0 \sim p(x_0)$, and select parameters $A_{t+1} = 0$, $b_{t+1} = z_{t+1} = 0$.
2: **For** $t = 0, 1, 2, \ldots$ **do**
3:   **Execute:** Draw action $u_t \sim \pi(u_t|x_t)$, observe next state $x_{t+1} \sim p(x_{t+1}|x_t, u_t)$, and reward $r_t = r(x_t, u_t)$.
4:   **Critic Evaluation (LSTD-Q(λ)):** Update
4.1:   basis functions: $\tilde{\phi}_t = [\phi(x_{t+1})^T, 0^T]^T$, $\hat{\phi}_t = [\phi(x_t)^T, \nabla_\theta \log \pi(u_t|x_t)^T]^T$,
4.2:   statistics: $z_{t+1} = \lambda z_t + \hat{\phi}_t$; $A_{t+1} = A_t + z_{t+1}(\hat{\phi}_t - \gamma\tilde{\phi}_t)^T$; $b_{t+1} = b_t + z_{t+1} r_t$,
4.3:   critic parameters: $[w_{t+1}^T, v_{t+1}^T]^T = A_{t+1}^{-1} b_{t+1}$.
5:   **Actor:** When the natural gradient is converged, $\angle(w_{t+1}, w_{t-\tau}) \leq \epsilon$, update
5.1:   policy parameters: $\theta_{t+1} = \theta_t + \alpha w_{t+1}$,
5.2:   forget statistics: $z_{t+1} \leftarrow \beta z_{t+1}, A_{t+1} \leftarrow \beta A_{t+1}, b_{t+1} \leftarrow \beta b_{t+1}$.
6: **end.**

For this purpose, we define

$$\widehat{\phi}_t = [\phi(x_t)^T, \nabla_\theta \log \pi(u_t|x_t)^T]^T, \quad \widetilde{\phi}_t = [\phi(x_{t+1})^T, \mathbf{0}^T]^T, \qquad (9)$$

as new basis functions, where $\mathbf{0}$ is the zero vector. This definition of basis function reduces bias and variance of the learning process in comparison to SARSA and previous LSTD(λ) algorithms for state-action value functions [7] as the basis functions $\widetilde{\phi}_t$ do not depend on stochastic future actions u_{t+1}, i.e., the input variables to the LSTD regression are not noisy due to u_{t+1} (e.g., as in [8]) – such input noise would violate the standard regression model that only takes noise in the regression targets into account. LSTD(λ) with the basis functions in Eq.(9), called LSTD-Q(λ) from now on, is thus currently the theoretically cleanest way of applying LSTD to state-value function estimation. It is exact for deterministic or weekly noisy state transitions and arbitrary stochastic policies. As all previous LSTD suggestions, it loses accuracy with increasing noise in the state transitions since $\widetilde{\phi}_t$ becomes a random variable. The complete LSTD-Q(λ) algorithm is given in the *Critic Evaluation* (lines 4.1-4.3) of Table 1.

Once LSTD-Q(λ) converges to an approximation of $A^\pi(x_t, u_t) + V^\pi(x_t)$, we obtain two results: the value function parameters v, and the natural gradient w. The natural gradient w serves in updating the policy parameters $\Delta\theta_t = \alpha w_t$. After this update, the critic has to forget at least parts of its accumulated sufficient statistics using a forgetting factor $\beta \in [0, 1]$ (cf. Table 1). For $\beta = 0$, i.e., complete resetting, and appropriate basis functions $\phi(x)$, convergence to the true natural gradient can be guaranteed. The complete Natural Actor Critic (NAC) algorithm is shown in Table 1.

However, it becomes fairly obvious that the basis functions can have an influence on our gradient estimate. When using the counterexample in [5] with a typical Gibbs policy, we will realize that the gradient is affected for $\lambda < 1$; for $\lambda = 0$ the gradient is flipped and would always worsen the policy. However, unlike in [5], we at least could guarantee that we are not affected for $\lambda = 1$.

Episodic Natural Actor-Critic. Given the problem that the additional basis functions $\phi(x)$ determine the quality of the gradient, we need methods which guarantee the unbiasedness of the natural gradient estimate. Such method can be determined by summing up Equation (8) along a sample path, we obtain

$$\sum_{t=0}^{N-1} \gamma^t A^\pi(x_t, u_t) = V^\pi(x_0) + \sum_{t=0}^{N-1} \gamma^t r(x_t, u_t) - \gamma^N V^\pi(x_N) \qquad (10)$$

It is fairly obvious that the last term disappears for $N \to \infty$ or episodic tasks (where $r(x_{N-1}, u_{N-1})$ is the final reward); therefore each roll-out would yield one equation. If we furthermore assume a single start-state, an additional scalar value function of $\phi(x) = 1$ suffices. We therefore get a straightforward regression problem:

$$\sum_{t=0}^{N-1} \gamma^t \nabla \log \pi(u_t, x_t)^T w + J = \sum_{t=0}^{N-1} \gamma^t r(x_t, u_t) \qquad (11)$$

with exactly $\dim \theta + 1$ unknowns. This means that for non-stochastic tasks we can obtain a gradient after $\dim \theta + 1$ rollouts. The complete algorithm is shown in Table 2.

Table 2. Episodic Natural Actor-Critic Algorithm (eNAC)

Input: Parameterized policy $\pi(u|x) = p(u|x, \boldsymbol{\theta})$ with initial parameters $\boldsymbol{\theta} = \boldsymbol{\theta}_0$, its derivative $\nabla_{\boldsymbol{\theta}}\log\pi(u|x)$.
For $u = 1, 2, 3, \ldots$ **do**
  For $e = 1, 2, 3, \ldots$ **do**
    Execute Rollout: Draw initial state $x_0 \sim p(x_0)$.
    For $t = 1, 2, 3, \ldots, N$ **do**
      Draw action $u_t \sim \pi(u_t|x_t)$, observe next state $x_{t+1} \sim p(x_{t+1}|x_t, u_t)$, and reward $r_t = r(x_t, u_t)$.
    end.
  end.
  Critic Evaluation (Episodic): Determine value function
  $J = V^\pi(x_0)$, compatible function approximation $f_w^\pi(x_t, u_t)$.
  Update: Determine basis functions: $\phi_t = \left[\sum_{t=0}^{N}\gamma^t\nabla_{\boldsymbol{\theta}}\log\pi(u_t|x_t)^T, 1\right]^T$;
  reward statistics: $R_t = \sum_{t=0}^{N}\gamma^t r$;
  Actor-Update: When the natural gradient is converged,
  $\angle(w_{t+1}, w_{t-\tau}) \leq \epsilon$, update the policy parameters: $\boldsymbol{\theta}_{t+1} = \boldsymbol{\theta}_t + \alpha w_{t+1}$.
6: **end.**

---

3 Properties of Natural Actor-Critic

In this section, we will emphasize certain properties of the natural actor-critic. In particular, we want to give a simple proof of covariance of the natural policy gradient, and discuss [10] observation that in his experimental settings the natural policy gradient was non-covariant. Furthermore, we will discuss another surprising aspect about the Natural Actor-Critic (NAC) which is its relation to previous algorithms. We briefly demonstrate that established algorithms like the classic Actor-Critic [14], and Bradtke's Q-Learning [8] can be seen as special cases of NAC.

3.1 On the Covariance of Natural Policy Gradients

When [10] originally suggested natural policy gradients, he came to the disappointing conclusion that they were not covariant. As counterexample, he suggested that for two different linear Gaussian policies, (one in the normal form, and the other in the information form) the probability distributions represented by the natural policy gradient would be affected differently, i.e., the natural policy gradient would be non-covariant. We intend to give a proof at this point showing that the natural policy gradient is in fact covariant under certain conditions, and clarify why [10] experienced these difficulties.

Theorem 1. *Natural policy gradients updates are covariant for two policies $\pi_{\boldsymbol{\theta}}$ parameterized by $\boldsymbol{\theta}$ and π_h parameterized by h if (i) for all parameters θ_i there exists a function $\theta_i = f_i(h_1, \ldots, h_k)$, (ii) the derivative $\nabla_h\boldsymbol{\theta}$ and its inverse $\nabla_h\boldsymbol{\theta}^{-1}$.*

For the proof see Appendix B. Practical experiments show that the problems occurred for Gaussian policies in [10] are in fact due to the selection the stepsize α which determines the length of $\boldsymbol{\Delta\theta}$. As the linearization $\boldsymbol{\Delta\theta} = \nabla_h \boldsymbol{\theta}^T \boldsymbol{\Delta h}$ does not hold for large $\boldsymbol{\Delta\theta}$, this can cause divergence between the algorithms even for analytically determined natural policy gradients which can partially explain the difficulties occurred by Kakade [10].

3.2 NAC's Relation to Previous Algorithms

Original Actor-Critic. Surprisingly, the original Actor-Critic algorithm [14] is a form of the Natural Actor-Critic. By choosing a Gibbs policy $\pi(u_t|x_t) = \exp(\theta_{xu})/\sum_b \exp(\theta_{xb})$, with all parameters θ_{xu} lumped in the vector $\boldsymbol{\theta}$, (denoted as $\boldsymbol{\theta} = [\theta_{xu}]$) in a discrete setup with tabular representations of transition probabilities and rewards. A linear function approximation $V^\pi(x) = \boldsymbol{\phi}(x)^T \boldsymbol{v}$ with $\boldsymbol{v} = [v_x]$ and unit basis functions $\boldsymbol{\phi}(x) = \boldsymbol{u}_x$ was employed. Sutton et al. online update rule is given by

$$\theta_{xu}^{t+1} = \theta_{xu}^t + \alpha_1 \left(r(x,u) + \gamma v_{x'} - v_x \right), v_x^{t+1} = v_x^t + \alpha_2 \left(r(x,u) + \gamma v_{x'} - v_x \right),$$

where α_1, α_2 denote learning rates. The update of the critic parameters v_x^t equals the one of the Natural Actor-Critic in expectation as TD(0) critics converges to the same values as LSTD(0) and LSTD-Q(0) for discrete problems [7]. Since for the Gibbs policy we have $\partial \log \pi(b|a)/\partial \theta_{xu} = 1 - \pi(b|a)$ if $a = x$ and $b = u$, $\partial \log \pi(b|a)/\partial \theta_{xu} = -\pi(b|a)$ if $a = x$ and $b \neq u$, and $\partial \log \pi(b|a)/\partial \theta_{xu} = 0$ otherwise, and as $\sum_b \pi(b|x) A(x,b) = 0$, we can evaluate the advantage function and derive

$$A(x,u) = A(x,u) - \sum_b \pi(b|x) A(x,b) = \sum_b \frac{\partial \log \pi(b|x)}{\partial \theta_{xu}} A(x,b).$$

Since the compatible function approximation represents the advantage function, i.e., $f_w^\pi(\boldsymbol{x},\boldsymbol{u}) = A(x,u)$, we realize that the advantages equal the natural gradient, i.e., $\boldsymbol{w} = [A(x,u)]$. Furthermore, the TD(0) error of a state-action pair (x,u) equals the advantage function in expectation, and therefore the natural gradient update $w_{xu} = A(x,u) = E_{x'}\{r(x,u) + \gamma V(x') - V(x)|x,u\}$, corresponds to the average online updates of Actor-Critic. As both update rules of the Actor-Critic correspond to the ones of NAC, we can see both algorithms as equivalent.

Bradtke's Q-Learning. Bradtke [8] proposed an algorithm with policy $\pi(u_t|x_t) = \mathcal{N}(u_t|\boldsymbol{k}_i^T \boldsymbol{x}_t, \sigma_i^2)$ and parameters $\boldsymbol{\theta}_i = [\boldsymbol{k}_i^T, \sigma_i]^T$ (where σ_i denotes the exploration, and i the policy update time step) in a linear control task with linear state transitions $\boldsymbol{x}_{t+1} = \boldsymbol{A}\boldsymbol{x}_t + \boldsymbol{b}u_t$, and quadratic rewards $r(\boldsymbol{x}_t, \boldsymbol{u}_t) = \boldsymbol{x}_t^T \boldsymbol{H} \boldsymbol{x}_t + R u_t^2$. They evaluated $Q^\pi(\boldsymbol{x}_t, \boldsymbol{u}_t)$ with LSTD(0) using a quadratic polynomial expansion as basis functions, and applied greedy updates:

$$\boldsymbol{k}_{i+1}^{\text{Bradtke}} = \operatorname{argmax}_{\boldsymbol{k}_{i+1}} Q^\pi(\boldsymbol{x}_t, \boldsymbol{u}_t = \boldsymbol{k}_{i+1}^T \boldsymbol{x}_t) = -(R + \gamma \boldsymbol{b}^T \boldsymbol{P}_i \boldsymbol{b})^{-1} \gamma \boldsymbol{b} \boldsymbol{P}_i \boldsymbol{A}, \quad (12)$$

where $\boldsymbol{P}_i$ denotes policy-specific value function parameters related to the gain $\boldsymbol{k}_i$; no update the exploration σ_i was included. Similarly, we can obtain the natural policy gradient $\boldsymbol{w} = [\boldsymbol{w_k}, w_\sigma]^T$, as yielded by LSTD-Q($\lambda$) analytically using the compatible function approximation and the same quadratic basis functions. As discussed in detail in [13], this gives us

$$\boldsymbol{w_k} = (\gamma \boldsymbol{A}^T \boldsymbol{P}_i \boldsymbol{b} + (R + \gamma \boldsymbol{b}^T \boldsymbol{P}_i \boldsymbol{b})\boldsymbol{k})^T \sigma_i^2, w_\sigma = 0.5(R + \gamma \boldsymbol{b}^T \boldsymbol{P}_i \boldsymbol{b}) \sigma_i^3. \quad (13)$$

Similarly, it can be derived that the expected return is $J(\boldsymbol{\theta}_i) = -(R + \gamma \boldsymbol{b}^T \boldsymbol{P}_i \boldsymbol{b}) \sigma_i^2$ for this type of problems, see [13]. For a learning rate $\alpha_i = 1/\|J(\boldsymbol{\theta}_i)\|$, we see

$$\boldsymbol{k}_{i+1} = \boldsymbol{k}_i + \alpha_t \boldsymbol{w_k} = \boldsymbol{k}_i - (\boldsymbol{k}_i + (R + \gamma \boldsymbol{b}^T \boldsymbol{P}_i \boldsymbol{b})^{-1} \gamma \boldsymbol{A}^T \boldsymbol{P}_i \boldsymbol{b}) = \boldsymbol{k}_{i+1}^{\text{Bradtke}},$$

which demonstrates that *Bradtke's Actor Update is a special case of the Natural Actor-Critic*. NAC extends Bradtke's result as it gives an update rule for the exploration – which was not possible in Bradtke's greedy framework.

4 Evaluations and Applications

In this section, we present several evaluations comparing the episodic Natural Actor-Critic architectures with previous algorithms. We compare them in optimization tasks such as cart-pole balancing and simple motor primitive evaluations and compare them only with episodic NAC. Furthermore, we apply the combination of episodic NAC and the motor primitive framework to a robotic task on a real robot, i.e., 'hitting a T-ball with a baseball bat'.

4.1 Cart-Pole Balancing

Cartpole balancing is a well-known benchmark for reinforcement learning. We assume the cart as shown in Figure 2 (1.a) can be described by

$$ml\ddot{x}\cos\theta + ml^2\ddot{\theta} - mgl\sin\theta = 0, (m + m_c)\ddot{x} + ml\ddot{\theta}\cos\theta - ml\dot{\theta}^2\sin\theta = F,$$

with $l = 0.75$m, $m = 0.15$kg, $g = 9.81$m/s^2 and $m_c = 1.0$kg. The resulting state is given by $\boldsymbol{x} = [x, \dot{x}, \theta, \dot{\theta}]^T$, and the action $\boldsymbol{u} = F$. The system is treated as

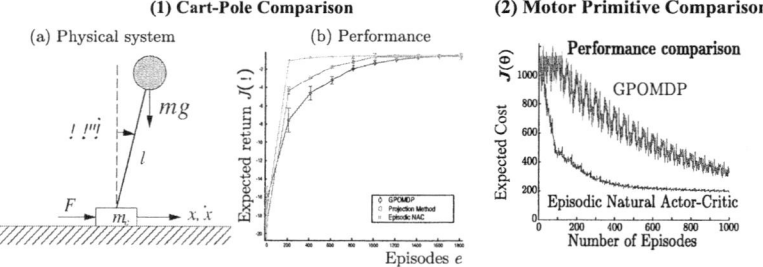

Fig. 2. This figure shows two comparisons, (1) cart-pole and (2) motor primitive learning. The physical set-up of a cart-pole balancing is shown in (1.a), and in (1.b) the performance of GPOMDP, the projection natural gradient, and the Episodic Natural Actor-Critic in comparison. The latter clearly outperforms the first two.

if it was sampled at a rate of $h = 60$Hz, and the reward is given by $r(\boldsymbol{x}, \boldsymbol{u}) = \boldsymbol{x}^T \boldsymbol{Q} \boldsymbol{x} + \boldsymbol{u}^T \boldsymbol{R} \boldsymbol{u}$ with $\boldsymbol{Q} = \text{diag}(1.25, 1, 12, 0.25)$, $\boldsymbol{R} = 0.01$. We chose a linear Gaussian policy given by $\pi(\boldsymbol{u}|\boldsymbol{x}) = \mathcal{N}(\boldsymbol{u}|\boldsymbol{k}^T\boldsymbol{x}, 1/(1+\exp(-\xi)))$, with parameters $\boldsymbol{\theta}^T = [\boldsymbol{k}^T, \xi]$. While this can also be treated with LSTD-Q(λ), see [13], we will focus on comparing it with GPOMDP and the projection suggested in [11], and in [10]. The results can be seen in Figure 2 (1.b) which makes clear that episodic natural actor-critic clearly outperforms both other methods.

4.2 Motor Primitive Learning for Baseball

This section will turn towards optimizing nonlinear dynamic motor primitives for robotics. In [9], a novel form of representing movement plans $(\boldsymbol{q}_d, \dot{\boldsymbol{q}}_d)$ for the degrees of freedom (DOF) robot systems was suggested in terms of the time evolution of the nonlinear dynamical systems

$$\dot{q}_{d,k} = h(q_{d,k}, z_k, g_k, \tau, \theta_k) \tag{14}$$

where $(q_{d,k}, \dot{q}_{d,k})$ denote the desired position and velocity of a joint, z_k the internal state of the dynamic system, g_k the goal (or point attractor) state of each DOF, τ the movement duration shared by all DOFs, and θ_k the open parameters of the function h. The original work in[9] demonstrated how the parameters θ_k can be learned to match a template trajectory by means of supervised learning – this scenario is, for instance, useful as the first step of an imitation learning system. Here we will add the ability of self-improvement of the movement primitives in Eq.(14) by means of reinforcement learning, which is the crucial second step in imitation learning. The system in Eq.(14) is a point-to-point movement, i.e., this task is rather well suited for episodic Natural Actor-Critic. In Figure 2 (2), we show a comparison with GPOMDP for simple, single DOF task with a reward of $r_k(x_{0:N}, u_{0:N}) = \sum_{i=0}^{N} c_1 \dot{q}_{d,k,i}^2 + c_2 (q_{d;k;N} - g_k)^2$; where $c_1 = 1$, $c_2 = 1000$, and g_k is chose appropriately. We also evaluated the same setup in a challenging robot task, i.e., the planning of these motor primitives for a seven DOF robot task. The task of the robot is to hit the ball properly so that it flies as far as possible. Initially, it is taught in by supervised learning as can be seen in Figure 3 (b); however, it fails to reproduce the behavior as shown in (c); subsequently, we improve the performance using the episodic Natural Actor-Critic which yields the performance shown in (a) and the behavior in (d).

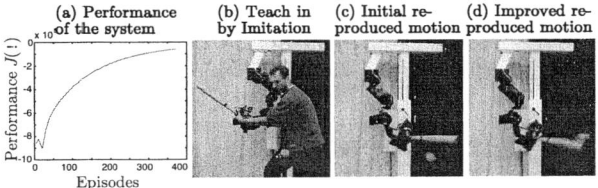

Fig. 3. This figure shows(a) the performance of a baseball swing task when using the motor primitives for learning. In (b), the learning system is initialized by imitation learning, in (c) it is initially failing at reproducing the motor behavior, and (d) after several hundred episodes exhibiting a nicely learned batting.

5 Conclusion

In this paper, we have summarized novel developments in policy-gradient reinforcement learning, and based on these, we have designed a novel reinforcement learning architecture, the Natural Actor-Critic algorithm. This algorithm comes in (at least) two forms, i.e., the LSTD-Q(λ) form which depends on sufficiently rich basis functions, and the Episodic form which only requires a constant as additional basis function. We compare both algorithms and apply the latter on several evaluative benchmarks as well as on a baseball swing robot example.

References

1. S. Amari. Natural gradient works efficiently in learning. *Neural Computation*, 10:251–276, 1998.
2. J. Bagnell and J. Schneider. Covariant policy search. In *International Joint Conference on Artificial Intelligence*, 2003.
3. L.C. Baird. *Advantage Updating*. Wright Lab. Tech. Rep. WL-TR-93-1146, 1993.
4. L.C. Baird and A.W. Moore. Gradient descent for general reinforcement learning. In *Advances in Neural Information Processing Systems 11*, 1999.
5. P. Bartlett. An introduction to reinforcement learning theory: Value function methods. In *Machine Learning Summer School*, pages 184–202, 2002.
6. D.P. Bertsekas and J.N. Tsitsiklis. *Neuro-Dynamic Programming*. Athena Scientific, Belmont, MA, 1996.
7. J. Boyan. Least-squares temporal difference learning. In *Machine Learning: Proceedings of the Sixteenth International Conference*, pages 49–56, 1999.
8. S. Bradtke, E. Ydstie, and A.G. Barto. *Adaptive Linear Quadratic Control Using Policy Iteration*. University of Massachusetts, Amherst, MA, 1994.
9. A. Ijspeert, J. Nakanishi, and S. Schaal. Learning rhythmic movements by demonstration using nonlinear oscillators. In *IEEE International Conference on Intelligent Robots and Systems (IROS 2002)*, pages 958–963, 2002.
10. S. A. Kakade. Natural policy gradient. In *Advances in Neural Information Processing Systems 14*, 2002.
11. V. Konda and J. Tsitsiklis. Actor-critic algorithms. In *Advances in Neural Information Processing Systems 12*, 2000.
12. T. Moon and W. Stirling. *Mathematical Methods and Algorithms for Signal Processing*. Prentice Hall, 2000.
13. J. Peters, S. Vijaykumar, and S. Schaal. Reinforcement learning for humanoid robotics. In *IEEE International Conference on Humandoid Robots*, 2003.
14. R.S. Sutton and A.G. Barto. *Reinforcement Learning*. MIT Press, 1998.
15. R.S. Sutton, D. McAllester, S. Singh, and Y. Mansour. Policy gradient methods for reinforcement learning with function approximation. In *Advances in Neural Information Processing Systems 12*, 2000.

A Fisher Information Property

In Section 5, we explained that the all-action matrix F_θ equals in general the Fisher information matrix $G(\theta)$. In [12], we can find the well-known lemma that by differentiating $\int_{\mathbb{R}^n} p(x)dx = 1$ twice with respect to the parameters θ, we can obtain

$$\int_{\mathbb{R}^n} p(x)\nabla_\theta^2 \log p(x)dx = -\int_{\mathbb{R}^n} p(x)\nabla_\theta \log p(x)\nabla_\theta \log p(x)^T dx \qquad (15)$$

for any probability density function $p(x)$. Furthermore, we can rewrite the probability $p(\tau_{0:n})$ of a rollout or trajectory $\tau_{0:n} = [x_0, u_0, r_0, x_1, u_1, r_1, \ldots, x_n, u_n, r_n, x_{n+1}]^T$ as $p(\tau_{0:n}) = p(x_0) \prod_{t=0}^{n} p(x_{t+1}|x_t, u_t) \pi(u_t|x_t)$ which implies that

$$\nabla_\theta^2 \log p(\tau_{0:n}) = \sum_{t=0}^{n} \nabla_\theta^2 \log \pi(u_t|x_t).$$

Using Equations (15, A), and the definition of the Fisher information matrix [1], we can determine Fisher information matrix for the average reward case by

$$G(\theta) = \lim_{n\to\infty} n^{-1} E_\tau \{\nabla_\theta \log p(\tau) \nabla_\theta \log p(\tau_{0:n})^T\} = -\lim_{n\to\infty} n^{-1} E_\tau \{\nabla_\theta^2 \log p(\tau)\},$$

$$= -\lim_{n\to\infty} n^{-1} E_\tau \{\sum_{t=0}^{n} \nabla_\theta^2 \log \pi(u_t|x_t)\} = -\int_X d^\pi(x) \int_U \pi(u|x) \nabla_\theta^2 \log \pi(u|x)$$

$$du dx = \int_X d^\pi(x) \int_U \pi(u|x) \nabla_\theta \log \pi(u|x) \nabla_\theta \log \pi(u|x)^T du dx = F_\theta \quad (16)$$

This proves that the all-action matrix is indeed the Fisher information matrix for the average reward case. For the discounted case, with a discount factor γ we realize that we can rewrite the problem where the probability of rollout is given by $p_\gamma(\tau_{0:n}) = p(\tau_{0:n})(\sum_{i=0}^{n} \gamma^i \mathbb{I}_{x_i, u_i})$, and derive that the all-action matrix equals the Fisher information matrix by the same kind of reasoning as in Eq.(16). Therefore, we can conclude that in general, i.e., $G(\theta) = F_\theta$.

B Proof of the Covariance Theorem

For small parameter changes Δh and $\Delta \theta$, we have $\Delta \theta = \nabla_h \theta^T \Delta h$. If the natural policy gradient is a covariant update rule, a change Δh along the gradient $\nabla_h J(h)$ would result in the same change $\Delta \theta$ along the gradient $\nabla_\theta J(\theta)$ for the same scalar step-size α. By differentiation, we can obtain $\nabla_h J(h) = \nabla_h \theta \nabla_\theta J(\theta)$. It is straightforward to show that the Fisher information matrix includes the Jacobian $\nabla_h \theta$ twice as factor,

$$F(h) = \int_X d^\pi(x) \int_U \pi(u|x) \nabla_h \log \pi(u|x) \nabla_h \log \pi(u|x)^T du dx,$$
$$= \nabla_h \theta \int_X d^\pi(x) \int_U \pi(u|x) \nabla_\theta \log \pi(u|x) \nabla_\theta \log \pi(u|x)^T du dx \nabla_h \theta^T,$$
$$= \nabla_h \theta F(\theta) \nabla_h \theta^T.$$

This shows that natural gradient in the h parameterization is given by

$$\widetilde{\nabla}_h J(h) = F^{-1}(h) \nabla_h J(h) = \left(\nabla_h \theta F(\theta) \nabla_h \theta^T\right)^{-1} \nabla_h \theta \nabla_\theta J(\theta).$$

This has a surprising implication as it makes it straightforward to see that the natural policy is covariant since

$$\Delta \theta = \alpha \nabla_h \theta^T \Delta h = \alpha \nabla_h \theta^T \widetilde{\nabla}_h J(h), = \alpha \nabla_h \theta^T \left(\nabla_h \theta F(\theta) \nabla_h \theta^T\right)^{-1} \nabla_h \theta \nabla_\theta J(\theta),$$
$$= \alpha F^{-1}(\theta) \nabla_\theta J(\theta) = \alpha \widetilde{\nabla}_\theta J(\theta),$$

assuming that $\nabla_h \theta$ is invertible. This concludes that the natural policy gradient is in fact a **covariant** gradient update rule.

Inducing Head-Driven PCFGs with Latent Heads: Refining a Tree-Bank Grammar for Parsing

Detlef Prescher

Institute for Logic, Language and Computation,
University of Amsterdam
prescher@science.uva.nl

Abstract. Although *state-of-the-art* parsers for natural language are lexicalized, it was recently shown that an *accurate* unlexicalized parser for the Penn tree-bank can be simply read off a manually refined tree-bank. While *lexicalized* parsers often suffer from sparse data, *manual mark-up* is costly and largely based on individual linguistic intuition. Thus, across domains, languages, and tree-bank annotations, a fundamental question arises: Is it possible to *automatically* induce an *accurate* parser from a tree-bank without resorting to full lexicalization? In this paper, we show how to induce a probabilistic parser with latent head information from simple linguistic principles. Our parser has a performance of 85.1% (LP/LR F_1), which is as good as that of early *lexicalized* ones. This is remarkable since the induction of probabilistic grammars is in general a hard task.

1 Introduction

State-of-the-art statistical parsers for natural language are based on probabilistic grammars acquired from tree-banks. The method of acquiring a probabilistic grammar from the tree-bank is of major influence on the accuracy and coverage of the statistical parser. It turns out that directly acquiring the probabilistic grammar from the tree-bank results in a suboptimal statistical parser [1]. Thus, various linguistically motivated transformation techniques have been applied to the tree-bank trees, all of them gathering important local information at the context-free production level. Two major transforms are currently used in the literature: *Parent encoding* and *lexicalization* ([2], [3], [4], [5], [6], etc.). Parent encoding appends the parent label to the tree nodes. Lexicalization labels every node with the head word. These transforms have been specifically developed for English based on the linguistic intuition that the original tree-bank annotations are not refined enough to capture the various lexical and contextual influences that could improve parser performance. It turns out, however, that these transforms do not carry over across different tree-banks for other languages, annotations or domains ([7], [8]), and even parsing English relies on some sophisticated further refinements [9]. Finally, all lexicalized models we are aware of have to incorporate smoothing and pruning techniques to solve a serious sparse-data problem (cp. Section 2).

Recently, [10] showed that a carefully performed *linguistic mark-up* leads to almost the same performance results as lexicalization (both combined with parent encoding). This result is attractive since unlexicalized grammars are easy to estimate, easy to parse with, and time- and space-efficient. Furthermore, linguistic annotations orthogonal to lexicalization could presumably be used to benefit lexicalized parsers as well. A drawback of [10]'s method is, however, that their manual linguistic mark-up is not based on abstract rules but rather on individual linguistic intuition, which makes it difficult to repeat their experiment and to generalize their findings for languages other than English.

In this context, it is thus important to answer the following question: Is it possible to *automatically induce* a more refined probabilistic grammar from a given tree-bank with improved performance? Our answer is yes, and the resulting parser is located in the middle of two extremes: a fully-lexicalized parser on one side *versus* an accurate unlexicalized parser based on a manually refined tree-bank on the other side. In greater detail, our induction method uses the same linguistic principles of headedness as other methods: We do believe that lexical information represents an important knowledge source. Simply percolating lexical information including the words, however, leads to data sparseness. Various advanced linguistic theories (e.g. Lexical-Functional Grammar [11]) suggest that more abstract categories based on feature combinations could represent the lexical effect. Our main assumption is based on these theories but complemented by a learning paradigm: Lexical entries carry *latent* extra information, and the *combinations of POS tags and extra-information* serve as partly hidden head elements of a probabilistic grammar to be induced from the tree-bank. It is important to emphasize that our task is to *automatically induce* a more refined probabilistic grammar based on a few linguistic principles. With *automatic refinement* it is harder to guarantee improved performance than with manually tailored refinements [10] or with refinements based on direct lexicalization [6]. However, if the induced refinement provides improved performance then it has a clear advantage: it is automatically induced, which gives the hope that it will be applicable across different domains, languages and tree-bank annotations.

In this paper we study the utility of a well-known statistical learning algorithm, the Expectation-Maximization (EM) algorithm [12] for the refinement of probabilistic grammars. Because we work with Probabilistic Context-Free Grammars (PCFGs), we specifically employ the Inside-Outside version of the EM. Applying our method to the benchmark Penn tree-bank Wall-Street Journal (WSJ), we obtain a refined probabilistic grammar that significantly improves over the original tree-bank grammar and that shows performance that is on par with early work with lexicalized probabilistic grammars that were obtained using a direct transform. This is a remarkable result given the hard task of automatic induction of improved probabilistic grammars.

2 Head Lexicalization

As previously shown ([2], [3], [4], etc.), Context-Free Grammars (CFGs) can be transformed to lexicalized CFGs provided that a head-marking scheme for rules is given. The basic idea is that the head marking on the rules is used to project lexical items up a chain of nodes. One of the simplest approaches to lexicalization is the one of [13]. It is characterized by the following transformation of the original tree-bank CFG.

Definition. The set T of terminal symbols of the original CFG and of its transform are identical. The non-terminal symbols of the transform have the form $X[v]$ or $\langle Y \langle X[v] \rangle\rangle$.

Here, X and Y are two arbitrary non-terminal symbols of the original CFG, and v is an arbitrary head chosen from a finite set $\mathcal{H}$ of head symbols. The set of rules of the transformed CFG consists of the following types:

Lexicalized starting rules: For all heads $v \in \mathcal{H}$ (where ROOT is a new start symbol and S is the original one):
$$\text{ROOT} \rightarrow S[v]$$

Lexicalized rules: For all heads $v \in \mathcal{H}$ and for all rules $X \rightarrow \ldots X_{i-1}\, X_i\, X_{i+1} \ldots$ of the original CFG (with a head marker on the child X_i):
$$X[v] \rightarrow \ldots \langle X_{i-1} \langle X[v] \rangle\!\rangle\, X_i[v]\, \langle X_{i+1} \langle X[v] \rangle\!\rangle \ldots$$

Lexicalized grammatical relations: For all new non-terminal symbols $\langle Y \langle X[v] \rangle\!\rangle$ and for all heads $w \in \mathcal{H}$:
$$\langle Y \langle X[v] \rangle\!\rangle \rightarrow Y[w]$$

Lexical rules: For all lexical rules $X \rightarrow w$ of the original CFG:
$$X[h(w)] \rightarrow w$$

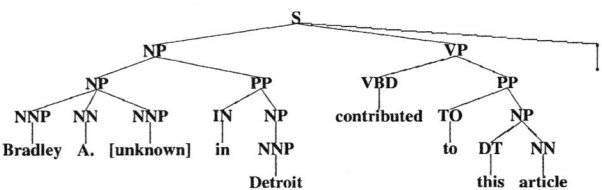

Fig. 1. Original context-free tree (Note: One word was replaced earlier by the unknown-word symbol '[unknown]').

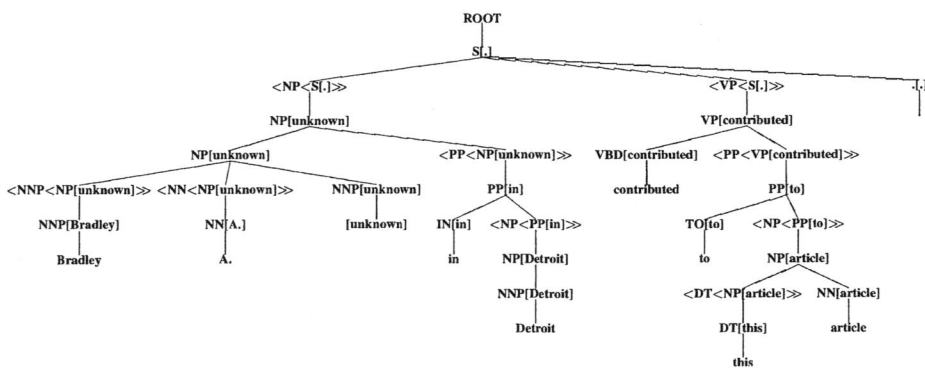

Fig. 2. Transformed tree: Lexicalization with leaf nodes of the original tree. The nodes $\langle cat_1 \langle cat_2[head] \rangle\!\rangle$ are auxiliary nodes which have been introduced to model the lexicalization of rules independently from the lexicalization of grammatical relations [13]. Additionally, auxiliary nodes reduce the sparse-data problem.

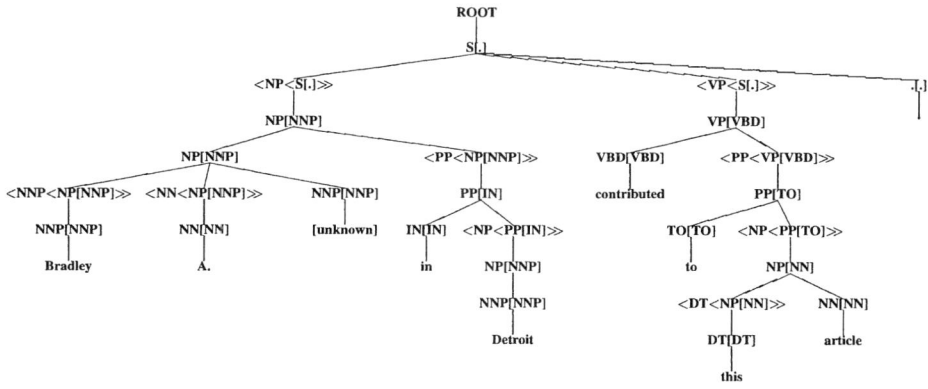

Fig. 3. Transformed tree: The same model but with lexicalization performed with POS tags

Here, $h : V \rightarrow \mathcal{H}$ is a many-to-one function mapping a non-terminal $w \in V$ to its head symbol $h(w) \in \mathcal{H}$ (e.g. to the word itself or to the lemma of the word). Figure 2 displays the result of this transformation for one of the trees of the training section of the Penn tree-bank. Compared to the original tree in Figure 1, it is note worthy that the lexicalized tree has more nodes than the original tree: for each non-head daughter cat_1 of a mother node cat_2 in the original tree, a new node <cat_1<cat_2[$head$]≫ is introduced in the lexicalized tree. We call these extra nodes **auxiliary nodes**. The main reason for introducing them is simply that one does not want to lexicalize rules with more than one head (otherwise, it would be difficult to overcome the arising sparse-data problem). Note also that standard-probabilistic conditioning of the lexicalized rules results simply in conditioning the *un*lexicalized rules on a lexical head, such as in:

$$p(\text{NP[article]} \rightarrow \text{<DT<NP[article]≫ NN[article] | NP[article]})$$
$$=$$
$$p(\text{NP} \rightarrow \text{DT NN | NP, article})$$

One problem of head-lexicalization techniques is that they lead to serious sparse data problems. For the standard case $h(w) = w$, for example, the large number $|T|$ of full word forms makes it difficult to reliably estimate the probability weights of the $O(|T|^2)$ lexicalized grammatical relations and $O(|T|)$ lexicalized rules of the model of [13]. An obvious approach to the problem is to use lemmas instead of full word forms to decrease the number of heads. From a computational perspective (but of course not from the linguistic one) the sparse data problem can be solved if part-of-speech tags are used as heads since the number of POS tags is tiny compared to $|T|$. Figure 3 displays the result of this type of transformation. Although we will demonstrate that parsing results benefit from this naive lexicalization routine, we expect that (computationally and linguistically) optimal head-lexicalized models are arranged around a number $|\mathcal{H}|$ of head symbols such that $|POS| \leq |\mathcal{H}| \ll |T|$, where POS is the set of POS tags and T is the full-word-form lexicon.

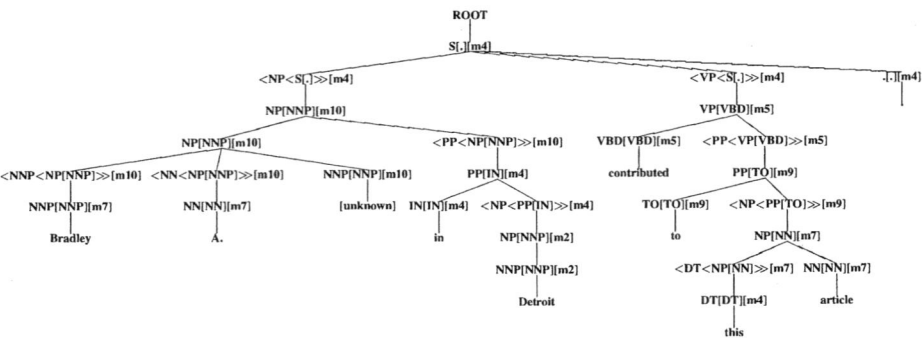

Fig. 4. Head-lexicalized tree with hidden information mark-up: In addition to the part-of-speech information, the terminal nodes carry extra-information (like m7, m10, m4, etc.). This satisfies principle (iii). The possible combinations of part-of-speech tags and extra-information (e.g., [NNP][m7], [NNP][m10], [IN][m4], etc.) serve as the new head elements of a head-lexicalized CFG, because the combined information is projected up a chain of categories. This satisfies principles (i) and (ii). The extra-information of the lexical items is hidden since it is not annotated in the Penn tree-bank. Therefore, the information mark-up is highly ambiguous, and there are many more (differently marked-up) trees beside the displayed tree.

3 Modeling Hidden Head-Information

This section defines probability models over the trees licensed by a lexicalized CFG with hidden head-information, thereby exploiting three simple linguistic principles:

(i) all rules have head markers,
(ii) information is projected up a chain of categories marked as heads,
(iii) lexical entries carry hidden extra-information which can be revealed.

Principles (i) and (ii) are satisfied by all head lexicalization routines which we know of. We base our model on the relatively simple head-lexicalized model presented in Section 2 because we do not want to explore **how** hidden extra-information flows in a tree-bank. Rather we would like to induce **which** extra-information flows in single trees and in tree-banks. Figure 4 displays a simple example of the type of extra-information mark-up we are interested in. Compared to the tree in Figure 3, all nodes carry some abstract extra-information type of the form $m_1, m_2, m_3, \ldots$. These information types are introduced at the part-of-speech level, and the combination of POS tag and extra-information flows bottom-up along a chain of categories marked as heads. In other words, the combination of POS tags and extra-information forms new but more complex heads of the head-lexicalized CFG. Moreover, we explicitly allow for ambiguous heads in the lexical rules. Formally, the mark-up of extra-information and the flow of the combination of original heads and extra-information can be done via the following transformation of the head-lexicalized CFG introduced in Section 2.

Definition. The set T of terminal symbols and the set $\mathcal{H}$ of head symbols remain unchanged. The non-terminal symbols of the transform have the form $X[v][m]$ or

⟨Y⟨X[v]⟩⟩[m]. Here, $X[v]$ and ⟨Y⟨X[v]⟩⟩ are non-terminals of the original head-lexicalized CFG, while m is an extra-information type chosen from a finite set $\mathcal{I}$. (Throughout this paper, we use $\mathcal{I} = \{m_1 \ldots m_n\}$.) The set of rules of the transform consists of the following types:

Lexicalized starting rules with info mark-up: For all extra-information types $m \in \mathcal{I}$ and for all heads $v \in \mathcal{H}$ (where TOP is a new start symbol):

$$\text{TOP} \to S[v][m]$$

Lexicalized rules with info mark-up: For all extra-information types $m \in \mathcal{I}$ and for all rules $X[v] \to \ldots \langle X_{i-1} \langle X[v] \rangle\!\rangle \, X_i[v] \, \langle X_{i+1} \langle X[v] \rangle\!\rangle \ldots$ of the head-lexicalized CFG:

$$X[v][m] \to \ldots \langle X_{i-1} \langle X[v] \rangle\!\rangle [m] \; X_i[v][m] \; \langle X_{i+1} \langle X[v] \rangle\!\rangle [m] \ldots$$

Lexicalized grammatical relations with info mark-up: For all pairs of extra-information types $i, j \in \mathcal{I}$ and for all rules ⟨Y⟨X[v]⟩⟩ $\to Y[w]$ of the head-lexicalized CFG:

$$\langle Y \langle X[v] \rangle\!\rangle [i] \to Y[w][j]$$

Lexical rules with info mark-up: For all extra-information types $m \in \mathcal{I}$ and for all lexical rules $X[h(w)] \to w$ of the head-lexicalized CFG:

$$X[h(w)][m] \to w$$

Thus, a head-lexicalized CFG with unambiguous extra-information mark-up contains exactly the same information as the original head-lexicalized CFG. In the rest of the paper, we show, however, that it is possible to learn hidden, richer, and more accurate head information from tree-banks.

4 Estimating Hidden Head-Information

Given a head-lexicalized CFG, the inductive problem is to estimate a head-lexicalized CFG with extra-information mark-up. The difficulty is that the rules of the marked-up CFG can not be directly estimated from the Penn tree-bank (by counting rules) because the extra-information mark-up is not annotated in the tree-bank. Therefore, we work with the standard method for unsupervised estimation of PCFGs, the inside-outside algorithm [14]. This algorithm induces probabilities for the grammar rules from a corpus of sentences. To exploit all linguistic information provided by the given tree-bank, we have to use *trees* as *input sentences* for the IO algorithm.

We thus create a context-free grammar which takes a whole head-lexicalized tree as input (see Figure 3) and which outputs the same tree marked-up with extra-information (see Figure 4). We call this grammar a **tree-transformation grammar**, as both its input and its output are trees. The tree-transformation grammar is characterized by the following transformation of the head-lexicalized CFG introduced in Section 2.

Definition. The set of terminal symbols of the transform comprises all symbols occurring in the bracket notations of the input trees, i.e., it consists of both terminal and non-terminal symbols of the head-lexicalized CFG, as well as of two bracket-symbols '(' and ')'. The non-terminal symbols of the transform have the form $X[v][m]$ or $\langle Y\langle X[v]\rangle\rangle[m]$. Here, $X[v]$ and $\langle Y\langle X[v]\rangle\rangle$ are non-terminals of the original head-lexicalized CFG, and m is an extra-information type chosen from a finite set $\mathcal{I}$. The set of rules of the transform consists of the following types:

Lexicalized starting rules with info mark-up: For all extra-information types $m \in \mathcal{I}$ and for all heads $v \in \mathcal{H}$ (where TOP is a new start symbol):

$$\text{TOP} \to (\text{ ROOT } S[v][m] \text{ })$$

Lexicalized rules with info mark-up: For all extra-information types $m \in \mathcal{I}$ and for all rules $X[v] \to \ldots \langle X_{i-1}\langle X[v]\rangle\rangle\ X_i[v]\ \langle X_{i+1}\langle X[v]\rangle\rangle \ldots$ of the head-lexicalized CFG:

$$X[v][m] \to (\ X[v]\ \ldots\ \langle X_{i-1}\langle X[v]\rangle\rangle[m]\ X_i[v][m]\ \langle X_{i+1}\langle X[v]\rangle\rangle[m]\ \ldots)$$

Lexicalized grammatical relations with info mark-up: For all pairs of extra-information types $i, j \in \mathcal{I}$ and for all rules $\langle Y\langle X[v]\rangle\rangle \to Y[w]$ of the head-lexicalized CFG:

$$\langle Y\langle X[v]\rangle\rangle[i] \to (\ \langle Y\langle X[v]\rangle\rangle\ Y[w][j]\ )$$

Lexical rules with info mark-up: For all extra-information types $m \in \mathcal{I}$ and for all lexical rules $X[h(w)] \to w$ of the head-lexicalized CFG:

$$X[h(w)][m] \to (\ X[h(w)]\ w\ )$$

For example, the bracket notation of the tree in Figure 3 is as follows:

```
( ROOT ( S[.] ( <NP<S[.]>> ( NP[NNP] ( NP[NNP] ( <NNP<NP[NNP]>> ( NNP[NNP]
Bradley ) ) ( <NN<NP[NNP]>> ( NN[NN] A. ) ) ( NNP[NNP] [unknown] ) )
( <PP<NP[NNP]>> ( PP[IN] ( IN[IN] in ) ( <NP<PP[IN]>> ( NP[NNP] ( NNP[NNP]
Detroit ) ) ) ) ) ) ( <VP<S[.]>> ( VP[VBD] ( VBD[VBD] contributed ) (
<PP<VP[VBD]>> ( PP[TO] ( TO[TO] to ) ( <NP<PP[TO]>> ( NP[NN] ( <DT<NP[NN]>>
( DT[DT] this ) ) ( NN[NN] article ) ) ) ) ) ) ( .[.] . ) ) )
```

It is easy to check that the tree-transformation grammar is able to parse this term. Moreover, the output for this input tree is a parse forest containing (amongst others) the marked-up tree displayed in Figure 4.

Estimation via de-transformation of the tree-transformation grammar: Comparing the definition in this section with the one in the previous section, it is obvious that there is a one-to-one mapping from the rules of the tree-transformation grammar to the rules of the mark-up grammar. For instance, a rule of the tree-transformation grammar having the form

$$marked\_up\_cat \to (\ cat\ marked\_up\_child_1 \ldots marked\_up\_child_n\ )$$

can be simply de-transformed to the following rule of the mark-up grammar

$$marked\_up\_cat \to marked\_up\_child_1 \ldots marked\_up\_child_n$$

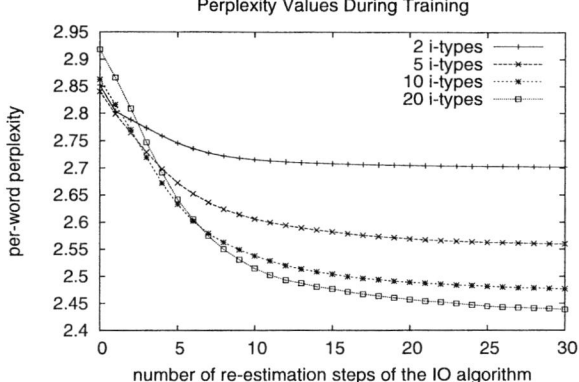

Fig. 5. The plot displays the perplexity of the training corpus for different models at each re-estimation step of the inside-outside algorithm. The displayed perplexity values are per-word-perplexity values as defined in the implementation of [15]. Just as in the standard case, a lower perplexity value corresponds to a higher corpus probability. The models differ in the number of extra-information types for the lexical items. After about 10 iterations, a model with more extra-information types always has a lower perplexity on the training corpus.

In fact, the significant difference between the tree-transformation grammar and the mark-up grammar is that the tree-transformation grammar acts on input trees, whereas the mark-up grammar operates on the yields of these trees. In more detail, the mark-up grammar produces for an *input sentence* the trees of the POS-lexicalized grammar marked-up with all the possible extra-information, whereas the tree-transformation grammar produces the mark-up only for one single *input tree*.

To summarize, the transformation of the mark-up grammar to the tree-transformation grammar enables estimation on the basis of a corpus of trees, whereas the de-transformation of the tree-transformation grammar results in a trained mark-up grammar. Inside-outside estimation of a probabilistic version of the tree-transformation grammar on the tree-bank results thus in a probabilistic version of the mark-up grammar introduced in Section 3. This solves our induction problem.

Implementation (for efficiency improvement): Instead of a single left-bracket symbol '(', we use multiple left-bracket symbols '$(_{id}$' to represent the tree-transformation grammar and its training corpus. The numbers id are identifiers for the rules of the underlying POS-lexicalized CFG. As a consequence, the information mark-up is not estimated in cubic but rather in linear time (in the tree size).

5 Experiments

Using the grammar described in Section 3 and the estimation method described in Section 4, we estimated our models for parts of the Penn tree-bank [16]. To facilitate comparison with previous work, we trained our models on sections 2-21 of the WSJ section

Table 1. Features of the final models: The first column lists the number of extra-information types for the different models. Note that the model with 1 extra-information type is equivalent to lexicalization with POS tags as heads. This model is unambiguous and was not trained with the IO algorithm. The second column lists the total number of rules of the tree-transformation grammars (being used to train our models), thereby only counting the rules with a final non-zero probability. The third column displays the rough number of inside-outside iterations for training, whereas the fourth column lists the rough total training time (resulting from a training time of $2\frac{1}{2} - 4$ hours per iteration step). Finally, the fifth column displays the perplexity of the training corpus for the final models.

i-types	rules	iter	training time	perp
1	53 437	0	0 days	2.821
2	101 385	35	4 days	2.701
5	226 748	35	5 days	2.559
10	396 618	50	7 days	2.467
20	760 894	50	8 days	**2.426**

of the Penn tree-bank. All trees were modified such that: node labels consisted solely of syntactic category information, empty nodes (i.e. nodes dominating the empty string) were deleted, and finally, words in rules occurring less than 3 times in the tree-bank were replaced by an unknown-word symbol '[unknown]'. No other changes were made.

We trained our models with the standard IO algorithm for *un*lexicalized context-free grammars as implemented in [15], thereby activating the built-in (absolute discounting) smoothing routine for grammar rules. We also performed some preliminary experiments *without* smoothing but after observing that about 3000 trees of our training corpus were allocated a zero-probability under IO estimation (resulting from the fact that too many grammar rules got a zero-probability), we decided to smooth all rule probabilities.

Figure 5 displays the training behavior of our models, and Table 1 displays some characteristic features of the final models. After observing that a uniform initialization of the models had no training effect at all, we started the inside-outside algorithm with randomly initialized models. So far, we have not tried to find optimal starting parameters (by repeating the whole training process multiple times), because the current experiment took already months. We also have not tried to find optimal iteration numbers (by evaluating our models after each iteration step on a held-out corpus) because also our evaluation routine is relatively time costly. We therefore simply trained the models until the perplexity values converged. Although our training regime may be sub-optimal (with respect to its fixed starting parameters and the chosen number of iterations), it allows us to systematically investigate models with hundreds of thousands of rules.

6 Evaluation on a Parsing Task

In this section, we evaluate our automatically induced probabilistic grammars on a parsing task. Although parsers developed on the Penn tree-bank are usually evaluated on Section 23 of the WSJ section of the Penn tree-bank, we decided to use Section 22 as evaluation set (sentences with a length ≤ 40 only). The reasons for doing this are

Table 2. PARSEVAL scores on our evaluation corpus (Section 22 of the WSJ section of the Penn tree-bank). The columns labeled with LB, LR, F_1, Exact, and CB display values for labeled precision and recall, the harmonic mean, the exact-match rate and the average number of crossing brackets respectively. The table at the top displays the parsing results of our baseline grammar, the original grammar read off slightly modified trees in the training corpus (cp. Figure 1). The larger table displays parsing results for the different models. The first column lists the number of extra-information types for the different models. The model with 1 extra-information type is equivalent to lexicalization with POS tags as heads. It can be regarded as a second baseline. To facilitate comparisons of the PARSEVAL scores with other model features, the second column displays the training-corpus perplexity for the different models. There is a strong correlation with the parsing results: The lower the perplexity the better the parsing result.

Original grammar	LP	LR	F_1	Exact	CB
	75.7	70.1	72.8	10.5	2.14

i-types	perp	LP	LR	F_1	Exact	CB
1	2.821	79.3	77.2	78.2	17.1	1.81
2	2.701	81.6	79.9	80.7	20.1	1.64
5	2.559	84.0	83.2	83.6	25.4	1.44
10	2.467	**85.2**	**85.0**	**85.1**	**27.9**	**1.27**

two-fold. First, most performance figures of [10] refer to parsing results on Section 22 (serving as their development set). Using the same section will facilitate comparison. Second, we envision many extensions and improvements of the present model, and therefore would like to leave Section 23 for future evaluations.

For parsing the sentences of our evaluation corpus, we mapped all unknown words to the unknown word symbol '[unknown]', and applied the Viterbi algorithm as implemented in [17], exploiting its ability to deal with highly-ambiguous grammars. That is, we did not use any pruning or smoothing routines for parsing sentences. We then de-transformed the resulting maximum-probability parses to the format described in Section 5. That is, we deleted the extra-information types, the auxiliary nodes, and the POS tags which served as heads. All grammars presented in this section were able to exhaustively parse the evaluation corpus. Table 2 displays our results in terms of the commonly used PARSEVAL scores [18]. The average parsing time in 2GB of memory was 10 seconds per sentence, which is comparable to what is reported in [10].

7 Discussion

In this section, we briefly discuss the experimental results of our final models and compare it to other models. First of all, the size of our models increases almost linear in the number of extra-information types (see Table 1). For instance, the mark-up grammar with 10 extra-information types contains about 400 000 rules, whereas the POS-lexicalized grammar has only about 50 000 rules (i-types=1). The explanation is that the *combinations* of POS tags and extra-information types serve as new abstract head elements in our models, and therefore, a grammar with x extra-information types contains roughly x-times the number of rules of the POS-lexicalized grammar. However, compared to fully lexicalized grammars, our biggest models are still smaller. Second, the parsing results improve in the number of extra-information types (see Table 2). For instance, modeling with 10 extra-information types results in a F_1 gain of about **12%** compared to the original grammar, and of about **7%** compared to the POS-lexicalized grammar. The only plausible explanation for these significant improvements is that abstract head classes have been learned by our method which are very useful for parsing. Third, it is striking that the difference between the LP and LR scores is almost 6% for the original grammar, about 2% for the POS-lexicalized grammar, and almost 0% for the grammar with 10 extra-information types. In other words, the difference in precision and recall vanishes in the number of extra-information types. We argue that this effect is also related to the fact that useful *classes* of heads have been learned by our models.

In the rest of this section, we compare our method to related methods. To start with performance values, the following table displays previous results on parsing Section 23 of the WSJ section of the Penn tree-bank (sentences of length ≤ 40):

Previous Work	LP	LR	F_1	Exact	CB
Johnson'98			79.7*		
Magerman'95	84.9	84.6			1.26
Collins'96	86.3	85.8			1.14
Klein&Manning'03	86.9	85.7	86.3	30.9	1.10
Charniak'97	87.4	87.5			1.00
Collins'99	88.7	88.6			0.90

Comparison indicates that our best model outperforms parent encoding [5] (*best score of several variants investigated in [10]). It is already as good as the early lexicalized model of [3], a bit worse than the unlexicalized parsing model of [10], and of course also worse than state-of-the-art lexicalized parsers. (Experience shows that evaluation results on sections 22 and 23 do not differ much.) Beyond performance values, we believe our formalism and methodology have the following attractive features:

1. The models incorporate context and lexical information collected from the whole tree-bank. Information is bundled into abstract heads of higher-order information. This is in sharp contrast to the fixed-word statistics used in most lexicalized parsing models ([2], [3], [4], [6], etc.) 2. The models have a drastically reduced parameter space compared to lexicalized parsing. Thus they do not suffer from sparse-data problems. 3. The method is based on the original tree-bank and it is not dependent on the success of transformations applied beforehand (like parent-encoding in [6], [10], etc.) 4. The method results in an *automatic* linguistic mark-up of tree-bank grammars. In contrast, manual linguistic mark-up of the tree-bank like in [10] is based on individual linguistic intuition and might be cost and time intensive. 5. The method, we introduced in this paper, can be thought of a new lexicalization scheme of CFG based on the notion of hidden head-information. 6. The method can also be thought of a successful attempt to incorporate lexical classes into parsers, combined with a new word clustering method

based on the context represented in tree structure. 7. It thus complements and extends the approach of [19], which aims at discovering latent head *markers* in tree-banks to improve manually written head-percolation rules. 8. The method is also an extension of *factorial HMMs* [20] to PCFGs: The node labels on trees are enriched with a hidden state and the hidden states are learned with the EM algorithm.

Some of the benefits come at a cost: Clear linguistic interpretation of the induced extra information is currently lacking. It is also possible that extensive manual linguistic mark-up is partly orthogonal to the one we induced. These compromises were made in this paper to answer the important question whether it is possible to *induce* an *accurate* parser from the Penn tree-bank which is not based on full lexicalization.

To conclude, we automatically induced a head-driven PCFG with latent-head statistics from the Penn tree-bank. The resulting parser is as good as early lexicalized parsers. This is a promising result and suggests that our method can be successfully applied across domains, languages, and tree-bank annotations.

Acknowledgment

This work was supported by the Netherlands Organization for Scientific Research, project no. 612.000.312, 'Learning Stochastic Tree-Grammars from Treebanks'. I also would like to thank Karin Müller, Yoav Seginer, Jelle Zuidema, and the anonymous reviewers. A special thanks goes to Helmut Schmid, Khalil Sima'an, and Tylman Ule.

References

1. Charniak, E.: Tree-bank grammars. Technical Report CS-96-02, Brown University (1996)
2. Charniak, E.: Parsing with context-free grammars and word statistics. Technical Report CS-95-28, Department of Computer Science, Brown University (1995)
3. Magerman, D.M.: Statistical decision-tree models for parsing. In: Proc. of ACL'95. (1995)
4. Collins, M.: A new statistical parser based on bigram lexical dependencies. In: Proc. of the ACL'96. (1996)
5. Johnson, M.: PCFG models of linguistic tree representations. Comp. Linguistics **24** (1998)
6. Collins, M.: Head-Driven Statistical Models for Natural Language Parsing. PhD thesis, U of Pennsylvania (1999)
7. Dubey, A., Keller, F.: Probabilistic parsing for German using sister-head dependencies. In: Proc. of ACL'03. (2003)
8. Fissaha, S., Olejnik, D., Kornberger, R., Müller, K., Prescher, D.: Experiments in German treebank parsing. In: Proc. of TSD-03. (2003)
9. Bikel, D.: Intricacies of Collins' parsing model. Computational Linguistics (to appear)
10. Klein, D., Manning, C.D.: Accurate unlexicalized parsing. In: Proc. of ACL-03. (2003)
11. Bresnan, J., Kaplan, R.M.: Lexical functional grammar: A formal system for grammatical representation. In: The Mental Representation of Grammatical Relations. MIT Press (1982)
12. Dempster, A.P., Laird, N.M., Rubin, D.B.: Maximum likelihood from incomplete data via the *EM* algorithm. J. Royal Statist. Soc. **39** (1977)
13. Carroll, G., Rooth, M.: Valence induction with a head-lexicalized PCFG. In: Proc. of EMNLP-3. (1998)
14. Lari, K., Young, S.J.: The estimation of stochastic context-free grammars using the inside-outside algorithm. Computer Speech and Language **4** (1990)

15. Schmid, H.: LoPar. Design and Implementation. Technical report, IMS, U Stuttgart (1999)
16. Marcus, M., Santorini, B., Marcinkiewicz, M.: Building a large annotated corpus of english: The Penn treebank. Computational Linguistics **19** (1993)
17. Schmid, H.: Efficient parsing of highly ambiguous context-free grammars with bit vectors. In: Proc. of COLING-04. (2004)
18. Black, E., etal.: A procedure for quantitatively comparing the syntactic coverage of English grammars. In: Proc. of DARPA-91. (1991)
19. Chiang, D., Bikel, D.: Recovering latent information in treebanks. In: Proc. of COLING'02. (2002)
20. Ghahramani, Z., Jordan, M.: Factorial Hidden Markov Models. Technical report, MIT (1995)

Learning (k,l)-Contextual Tree Languages for Information Extraction

Stefan Raeymaekers[1], Maurice Bruynooghe[1], and Jan Van den Bussche[2]

[1] K.U.Leuven, Dept. of Computer Science, Celestijnenlaan 200A, B-3001 Leuven
{stefanr, maurice}@cs.kuleuven.ac.be
[2] Universiteit Hasselt, Dept. Theoretical Computer Science,
Agoralaan D, B-3590 Diepenbeek
jan.vandenbussche@uhasselt.be

Abstract. This paper introduces a novel method for learning a wrapper for extraction of text nodes from web pages based upon (k, l)-contextual tree languages. It also introduces a method to learn good values of k and l based on a few positive and negative examples. Finally, it describes how the algorithm can be integrated in a tool for information extraction.

1 Introduction

The World Wide Web is an indispensable source of information. Extracting its content for further processing however, is difficult because it is formatted in HTML, which is primarily focussed on presentation. A wrapper is a general name for a procedure that extracts data (often from machine generated HTML-pages) based on the structure of the documents, commonly without the use of linguistic knowledge. Various tools are designed to facilitate wrapper building, but the process remains tedious. Hence the efforts [5, 12, 13, 14, 17, 21] to create algorithms that learn wrappers from examples.

Several approaches [6, 7, 17] process documents in a string representation. Flattening the tree structure of the document to a string representation though can project sibling nodes arbitrarily far from one another, and increases the complexity of the wrapper to express relations between these nodes. In [13], documents are represented as (ranked) binary trees; this improves locality and gives better results. An unranked tree representation is for the first time used in [12]. Combined with a number of ad-hoc design decisions, it leads to superior results.

Note that most string-based approaches can extract a substring of a text node, while most tree-based approaches aim to extract tree nodes (either a whole text node or a subtree of the document). If a task needs sub-node extraction though, it is very natural to learn first a wrapper to retrieve the containing text node, and focus then on learning a (string based) wrapper that extracts the required information from this text.

The contributions of this paper are:

- The introduction of the notion of a (k,l)-contextual tree language for unranked trees and an algorithm to infer such a language from positive examples (trees) only. A major virtue is that this algorithm needs very few examples to learn. This algorithm is then applied on marked trees to induce wrappers. We obtain better results than [12] while avoiding its ad-hoc design decisions. All this is described in Section 2.

- Whereas [12] needed cross validation to learn the parameters (i.e., a fully annotated data set), we introduce a method to learn the parameters with only a few negative examples (Section 3).
- In Section 4, we integrate our results into an interactive system that guides the user in building a wrapper by posing equivalence queries. For example, if a user wants to extract book prices from www.amazon.com, he clicks on an example page (in the browser of the GUI-front end) on one or more prices. The algorithm then learns a wrapper from these (positive only) examples and highlights all elements that are extracted by this wrapper. When the current hypothesis is erroneous, the user can either click on a highlighted item to indicate it as a false positive or click on an item that is not yet highlighted to indicate that it is a false negative. The application then adjusts the wrapper. This interaction continues (possibly with other example pages), until the user is satisfied.

In Section 5 we round up with a discussion and a summary.

2 Induction from Positive Examples Only

In the language learning approach to information extraction setting, it is important that we can start learning from positive examples only, because that is typically all we have to begin with. Only after the learner has inferred a hypothesis, false positives give us sensible negative examples, which we can then exploit to refine the hypothesis. Unfortunately, the whole class of regular languages cannot be learned from positive examples only [10]. Intuitively the reason is that there is no boundary to end the generalization, and therefore the resulting language will accept everything. A common solution for this negative result is to define a learnable subclass of the regular languages. Examples of learnable subclasses of string languages are k-reversible languages [2], k-contextual languages [16] and k-testable languages [9]. The latter two are often referred to as k-local languages as they are equivalent [1]. Similar developments occurred for tree languages. Algorithms for induction of string automata have been upgraded for tree automata. Several works exist for ranked trees, e.g., [8, 11] (k-testable tree languages) and [20] (probabilistic extensions). In ranked trees, the number of children of a node is fixed in advance (determined by its label). HTML or XML documents are clearly *not* ranked; hence an awkward encoding is needed in order to apply k-testable tree language learning to Web information extraction [13].

Therefore, in this section, we introduce (k, l)-contextual tree languages, which are unranked, and therefore directly applicable. But first some background is introduced.

2.1 Preliminary Definitions

We define the alphabet Σ as a finite set of symbols. The set of all finite trees with nodes labeled by elements of Σ can be recursively defined as $T(\Sigma) = \{f(s) \mid f \in \Sigma, s \in T(\Sigma)^*\}$. We usually denote $f(\epsilon)$, where ϵ is the empty sequence, by f. A *tree language* is any subset of $T(\Sigma)$. The set of (k,l)-roots of a tree $t = f(t_1, \ldots, t_n)$ is the singleton $\{f\}$ if $l=1$; otherwise, it is the set of trees obtained by extending the root f with $(k, l-1)$-roots of k successive children of t (all children if $k > n$). Formally, we can define inductively[1]:

---
[1] f(S) denotes $\{f(s) \mid s \in S\}$.

$R_{(k,l)}(f(t_1 \ldots t_n)) =$
$$\begin{cases} \{f\} & \text{if } l=1 \\ f(R_{(k,l-1)}(t_1) \ldots R_{(k,l-1)}(t_n)) & \text{if } l>1 \text{ and } k>n \\ \bigcup_{p=1}^{n-k+1} f(R_{(k,l-1)}(t_p) \ldots R_{(k,l-1)}(t_{p+k-1})) & \text{otherwise} \end{cases}$$

Finally, a (k,l)-*fork* of a tree t is a (k,l)-root of any subtree of t. The set of (k,l)-forks of t is denoted by $F_{(k,l)}(t)$.

Example 1. Below we show graphically the $(2,3)$-forks of a tree t. The first 6 of these forks, are the $(2,3)$-roots of t.

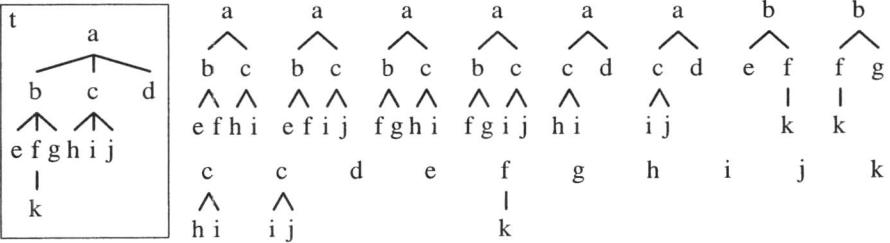

2.2 (k,l)-Contextual Tree Languages

Let G be a set of trees over Σ, such that every tree in G has height at most l, and every node of each tree in G has at most k children. The (k,l)-*contextual tree language based on G* is defined as $L_{k,l}(G) = \{t \in T(\Sigma) \mid F_{(k,l)}(t) \subseteq G\}$; i.e., a tree is part of the language defined by a set of forks, if each of its (k,l)-forks is an element of that set. Obviously, $L_{k,l}(G_1) \subseteq L_{k,l}(G_2)$ iff $G_1 \subseteq G_2$. Let G be the set of forks of a given set of examples. The (k,l)-contextual languages that accept these examples are those based on a superset of G. $L_{k,l}(G)$ is the least (most specific) language accepting the examples.

Our inference algorithm avoids overgeneralisation by learning for a given k and l, the most specific (k,l)-contextual language that accepts all the examples. It does so by collecting all the (k,l)-forks of the examples. Checking for membership of a tree t in $L_{k,l}(G)$ is done by checking whether all (k,l)-forks of t are among the forks of G.

As is the case for local languages such as k-contextual languages [16, 1], k-testable languages [9], and k-testable tree languages [8, 11], (k,l)-contextual tree languages learned from a given training set are anti-monotone in the parameters; i.e., increasing either k or l decreases the set of trees accepted by the learned language.

Our definition generalizes to unranked trees the notion of k-testable string language "in the strict sense". If we had wanted to generalize the more expressive notion of k-testable, studied by McNaughton [15], we would have taken a set of sets of forks for G (one for each example), and would have then accepted a tree if its forks are a subset of those from one example. Our experiments (Section 2.5) indicate that k-testable languages in the strict sense are sufficiently expressive, hence we explore only the strict notion.

The local unranked tree automata of [12] correspond to the special case $l = 2$ in our approach. The lack of expressiveness in vertical direction was remedied with some extra preprocessing (see Section 2.4).

2.3 Wrapper Induction

We follow [12, 13] for defining wrappers. A wrapper is a language that accepts only trees that are correctly marked. Marking a node s consists of replacing it by a marked equivalent s_x. To decide whether to extract a node, the candidate node is marked. When the wrapper accepts the resulting tree, the original text of the marked node is extracted. The wrapper is learned from examples, as described above, where each example is a HTML page with one target node marked. However, simply collecting all forks from a few examples typically results in a too specific wrapper.

A first problem is that text nodes are from an (almost) infinite alphabet and cannot be learned from a small number of examples. To solve this, we follow [12, 13]: More generalization is obtained by replacing all text nodes by a special symbol (@)[2]. Sometimes this leads to overgeneralisation as a text node close to the target is needed to disambiguate between a positive and a negative example. A preprocessor finds such a distinguishing context and text nodes containing it are not replaced.

looseness 2 A second problem is that a small number of examples does not cover all the variance of possible forks in areas far away from the targets. One can argue that the forks containing the marker provide the local context needed to decide whether a node should be extracted or not, while the other forks describe the general structure of the document. The latter merely serve to decide whether the document is in the class of documents that contains relevant information. Learning that class typically requires substantially more examples than learning the local context. However, in our setting, we assume all documents are from the right class; hence there is no need to learn the document class and we can ignore all forks that do not contain the marker during learning and extraction.

Combining the preprocessing of text nodes with the filtering of forks, one obtains a lot more generalization and wrappers can be learned from a small set of examples.

2.4 Expressiveness

To compare the expressiveness of our languages with that of [12], we first explain the latter briefly. As already mentioned above, after preprocessing, each text node is either a marker (x), a distinguished context (c) or a generalized text node (@). The method basically infers a $(k, 2)$-contextual language. However, the tree representing an example is subject to two other preprocessing steps.

The first transformation replaces every node f into a node $f.x$, if its subtree contains the x-node. If the subtree does not contain the x-node but a c-node then it is replaced by $f.c$. Hence, limited information is passed infinitely upwards, making the method not purely local. However, the subclass remains inferable and the expressiveness is enhanced.

The second transformation in [12], although part of the inference algorithm, can also be explained as a preprocessing step. The automaton accepts everything below a node that is not of the form $f.x$, i.e., all subtrees below such nodes can be removed and only the path from the root to the x-node is left, together with the siblings of the nodes

---

[2] When the node is extracted, the original test is returned.

on that path; parts farther away from the marked node are ignored. This enhances the generalizing power of the resulting language (and reduces the expressiveness).

Example 2. The left tree below shows a tree after the first transformation, while the tree on the right shows the result of applying the second transformation to that same tree.

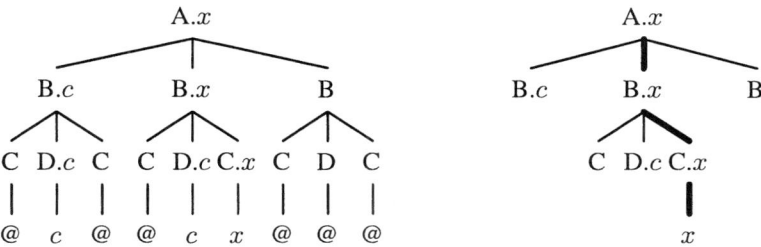

Thanks to the first transformation, the algorithm of [12] (K) can express some global vertical relations. While added to retain information in the vertical direction, it can also describe the relation between a node and an ancestor that is an arbitrary number of levels higher. Our algorithm (KL) is purely local and does not have this expressiveness. Our experiments showed that local information in the vertical direction (the l parameter) was sufficient for all data sets.

The second transformation in K makes it less expressive than KL as all information about the siblings of the target node is removed while KL retains the neighborhood. We encountered several data sets where that information was needed to disambiguate positive and negative examples[3].

2.5 Experiments

We evaluate our approach on the WIEN[4] data sets. We use the F1 score as a fitness criterium. Given E, the number of text nodes extracted from the test set, C, the number of correctly extracted text nodes, and T, the total number of text nodes to be extracted from the test set. Precision(P) is defined as P=C/E, recall(R) as R=C/T. The F1 score is defined as the harmonic mean: F1=2PR/(P+R).

Our algorithm as well as the K algorithm [12] are expressive enough to handle all tasks of the WIEN data sets, i.e., given enough examples, they reach a 100% F1 score. In those tasks where sub-node extraction is required, both algorithms return the text node containing the substring to be extracted. In comparison, in [17] it is stated that neither STALKER nor WIEN [14] are expressive enough to handle all tasks. Also STALKER with Aggressive Co-testing still fails on some tasks according to [18]. Note that on the tasks where the other algorithms did not reach the maximal score, this was not due to the fact that the sub-node extraction posed extra difficulties. [12] compares the K algorithm also with HMM [7] and BWI [6]. They report an experiment where the K algorithm reaches a 100% F1 score whereas the other ones have a significantly lower score on some (difficult) WIEN data sets (the number of examples was limited in this

---

[3] E.g., a table with bargains. The aim is to extract those with a picture of the item. The picture, when present, occupies the first cell of the row, (a sibling of the cell containing the target).
[4] These are available at the RISE repository: http://www.isi.edu/info-agents/RISE/index.html.

Table 1. Results for data sets with 5 examples

Data set	ctx	K	KL	Data set	ctx	K	KL	Data set	ctx	K	KL
s1-1		89.1	**100.0**	s11-2	✔	100.0	100.0	s23-1		97.6	**100.0**
s1-3		90.4	**98.7**	s12-2		98.4	**98.5**	s23-3		94.4	**100.0**
s1-4		78.8	**100.0**	s13-2		100.0	100.0	s25-2		97.2	**100.0**
s3-2		97.6	**100.0**	s13-4		100.0	100.0	s29-1		96.6	96.6
s3-3		98.2	**100.0**	s14-3		99.5	**100.0**	s29-2		**100.0**	87.8
s4-1		91.6	**100.0**	s15-2		97.1	**100.0**	s30-2		96.0	**100.0**
s5-2		93.8	**98.9**	s19-4		100.0	100.0	bigbook-2		94.3	**100.0**
s8-2		100.0	100.0	s20-3	✔	98.5	**100.0**	bigbook-3		88.0	**100.0**
s8-3		100.0	100.0	s20-4	✔	97.5	**100.0**	okra-1	✔	100.0	100.0
s10-2		100.0	100.0	s20-5	✔	97.5	**100.0**	okra-2	✔	99.3	**100.0**
s10-4		100.0	100.0	s20-6	✔	98.5	**100.0**	okra-3	✔	99.1	**100.0**
s11-1	✔	100.0	100.0	s22-2		93.3	**100.0**	okra-4	✔	99.1	**100.0**

experiment). This is a strong indication that our method is more expressive than previous methods. Only the K algorithm has a comparable expressivity, however it contains a number of ad-hoc design decisions.

A second experiment compares these both algorithms in their ability to learn from a small set of positive examples. Each experiment randomly selects 5 examples (each one target in a document) in a data set and compares the F1 score of both algorithms (for optimal parameter setting) with the whole data set as test set. This experiment is not intended to measure the number of examples needed by each algorithm but to measure which one learns best from a given sample of (incomplete) data. We use a well-defined subset of 36 extraction tasks from the available WIEN data tasks, namely those that extract a complete text node and for which the information on the nodes to be extracted is available in the WIEN data. Tasks aiming at the extraction of a n-tuple are split in n extraction tasks. We refer to them with the name of the original data set and the index of the field in the tuple. Table 1 shows for each data set the mean over 5 experiments. The variance over the different experiments was low. In most cases when a mean does not reach 100%, all the experiments do not reach 100%. The column *ctx* indicates whether both algorithms used a (same) distinguishing context. One can observe that our KL algorithm gives a better F1 score for 24 tasks out of 36 and a worse one for only 1 data set. This is evidence that it learns better from a small set of positive examples.

3 Learning the Parameters

As shown in Section 2.5, our (k, l)-contextual tree language improves upon the local unranked tree automata of [12] by being able to learn from fewer examples. However, a problem shared with [12] is that the method needs **parameter tuning** for each task. Selecting the optimal parameters requires to run the program on a set of completely annotated documents to obtain precision and recall. Hence parameter selection is in fact based on a large set of positive and negative examples.

Here, we describe how to learn parameters based on a small set of negative examples. In addition, it is indicated when (k, l)-contextual tree languages are not expressive enough to reach a 100% F1-score for the extraction task at hand.

3.1 Algorithm

Order relations. We can distinguish two order relations on languages. Firstly, a partial order $\geq$ defined as $L_1 \geq L_2 \Leftrightarrow L_2 \subseteq L_1$ which is anti-monotonic in the parameters. Secondly, let S be a finite set of trees and $\#acc(S, L)$ the number of trees from S that is accepted by the language L (the *count*). Then we define the total order $\geq_S^\#$ as $L_1 \geq_S^\# L_2 \Leftrightarrow \#acc(S, L_1) \geq \#acc(S, L_2)$ [5]. Note that $\forall S \mid L_1 \geq L_2 \Rightarrow L_1 \geq_S^\# L_2$, hence $\geq_S^\#$ is also anti-monotonic in the parameters, i.e., the count decreases with increasing parameter values.

Solutions. A solution is a (k, l)-contextual language that is consistent with the examples. We define a solution L_1 to be better than L_2 when it extracts more solutions from the documents used to learn the wrapper; more formally, when $\#acc(S, L_1) \geq \#acc(S, L_2)$ where S has a tree for each candidate node (with the candidate marked cnfr. Section 2.3). Hence the best solution is the solution that is maximal in the order $\geq_S^\#$.

Heuristic. In what follows, we denote with $[k, l]$ the (k, l)-contextual language learned from the given examples. Due to the anti-monotonicity, we have that $\#acc(S, [k, l]) \leq \#acc(S, [k-1, l])$ and $\#acc(S, [k, l]) \leq \#acc(S, [k, l-1])$, hence $\#acc(S, [k-1, l])$ and $\#acc(S, [k-1, l])$ are upper bounds on the value of $\#acc(S, [k, l])$. The algorithm uses them to estimate the value of $\#acc(S, [k, l])$ and, at each step, computes the count of the language with the best estimate. The search stops when the best estimate cannot improve upon the best current solution.

Initialisation. All $(k, 1)$-contextual languages extract all single node forks from the examples, hence are overly general and of no interest. Therefore, the search starts from the $(1, 2)$-contextual language as it has the largest count.

Algorithm. To reduce the space requirements, our algorithm maintains for a given l-value the count of at most one (k, l)-contextual language. If the (k, l)-contextual language is a solution, then the $(k+1, l)$-contextual language is of no interest as it has a lower count; if it is inconsistent, then its count is discarded as soon as the count of the $(k+1, l)$-contextual language is computed. These counts are maintained in a *front* (of the search). For each l-value, the front maintains the k-value ($F.k[l]$), the count ($F.c[l]$) and whether it is a solution ($F.sol[l]$) (see the right of Figure 1). In each step, the algorithm selects the minimal value l such that the language $[F.k[l], l])$ is most promising for exploration (the function BestRefinement): $[F.k[l], l]$ is not a solution and the estimation of its refinement has the highest bounds on its count. For $k > 1$, the refinement is the language $[F.k[l] + 1, l]$, however for $k = 1$, also $[1, l+1]$ is a refinement.

Example 3. Given the data in Figure 1, the languages $[1, 5]$, $[4, 3]$ and $[2, 5]$ are candidates for refinement. Although $[4, 3]$ has the highest count, its refinement $[5, 3]$ has a count bounded by 33 while both refinements of $[1, 5]$ have a count bounded by 48, hence the latter is selected for refinement.

---
[5] A total order over equivalence classes with the same count.

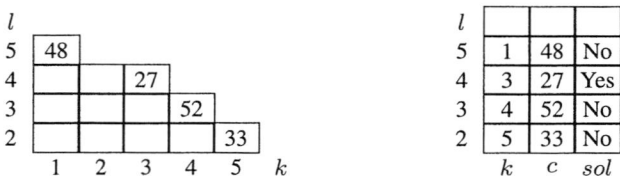

Fig. 1. Parameter Space and Data Representation

A final point to remark is that it is useless to consider a language $[k, l]$ with k larger than $MaxK(P, N, l)$, the maximum branching factor for the forks of a given depth l (it depends on l because only the forks containing the target are considered). Indeed, an increase of k will not affect the number of extractions. The algorithm below achieves this by setting the k-value at level l to ∞ and the count to 0 when refining it. When this happens for all l values, then it means that no wrapper based on (k, l)-contextual tree languages is expressive enough to reach a 100% F1-score. Note that there is always a solution when all examples come from a single document. The final set of forks then becomes ultimately the set of marked versions of the whole document.

Algorithm 1. Learning the Parameters

Input: P and N, The sets of positive and negative examples.
Output: The parameters k and l of the wrapper.
1: calc(P,N, 1, 2) // initialisation
2: $bestL = 2$
3: **while** not $F.sol[bestL]$ **do**
4:   **if** $F.k[bestL]=1$ **then**
5:     calc(P,N, 1, $bestL$+1)
6:   **end if**
7:   calc(P,N, $F.k[bestL]$+1, $bestL$)
8:   $bestL$ = BestRefinement(F);
9: **end while**
10: return $F.k[bestL]$ and $bestL$

Function: calc(P,N, k, l)
1: **if** $k > $ maxK(P,N, l) **then**
2:   $F.k[l]=\infty$
3:   $F.c[l]=0$
4: **else**
5:   $F.k[l]=k$;
6:   W = learnWrapper(P, k, l)
7:   $F.sol[l]=W$ rejects all N
8:   $F.c$ = cnt(extractions(W,P,N))
9: **end if**

The algorithm is sketched in Algorithm 1. F is the array representing the front as shown in Fig. 1. For a given l value, the values $F.k[l]$, $F.c[l]$, and $F.sol[l]$ give respectively the k-value, the count and whether $[k, l]$ is a solution. It is initialized for

$l = 2$ with k-value 1. The function $BestRefinement(F)$ returns the l-value of the best candidate for refinement (as described above) if it exists, otherwise it either returns the l-value of the solution or reports failure. The function $calc(P, N, k, l)$ updates $F[l]$ with the appropriate values. Note that two refinements are computed when the selected best candidate has a k-value of 1.

3.2 Learning with Context

We define a new preprocessing step to identify a distinguishing context, to replace the ad hoc procedure in [12, 13] that returns zero or one context string. For each positive example we collect the set of text nodes that occur in the marked (k, l)-forks for that example. We define the *context* as the set of text nodes that is the common subset of all these sets. This way text nodes are only generalized when there is a positive example for which they do not occur in its parameterized neighborhood. This procedure guarantees that (given sufficient examples) all the strings in the resulting set are context for the target node. It is possible though that some discriminative context string is not found (for example the target is a node with as context either c1 or c2). We haven't yet encountered the need for a more elaborate procedure. Note that the count of a wrapper decreases with increasing context and that, given this procedure, the context increases with an increase in k or l, hence the anti-monotonicity property is still valid and our algorithm can easily be extended to learn a wrapper with context.

Not all data sets need a context. In principle, one could learn the wrapper with context and the wrapper without context independently of each other. However, one can easily integrate both in one algorithm that maintains two fronts and selects the most promising point of both for refinement. Note that, for a given point (k, l), the count of the wrapper with context is bounded by the count of the wrapper without context; i.e., the latter value can be used as an extra bound on the count of the former (hence selection is such that the former will only be evaluated when that bound is already known).

4 Induction with Equivalence Queries

Arbitrary sets of positive and negative examples contain often redundant information. It is more efficient to use queries. The system will ask itself the information that it needs to improve its hypothesis. In this section we present a system based on the algorithms from previous section, that uses equivalence queries[3]. The system allows the user to inspect its hypothesis by checking the extraction results (possibly for different pages). When detecting an error, the user signals it to the system as a counterexample (a false positive or a false negative), so that it can update its hypothesis.

In Section 4.1 we indicate how to adapt the algorithm of previous section for an efficient interactive use. In Section 4.2 we discuss some details of the implementation of our system and finally in Section 4.3 we give an evaluation of its usability.

4.1 Interactive Algorithm

After each interaction the system updates its hypothesis. This is done by finding the $\geq_S^\#$-most general language that is consistent with the current set of examples. For this update step we can use the algorithm from Section 3. However, an incremental algorithm is feasible. This would certainly improve the timings in Table 2 (see Section 4.3).

Adding a positive example (a false negative) to the set of examples increases the set of forks, hence the counts of all wrappers. However, a (k, l)-wrapper that covers negative examples still does so and cannot become a solution. It means that the search of a solution can start from the current front. The initialization of the new search for parameters consists of updating the count fields ($F.c$) in the front.

Adding a negative example (a false positive) does not affect the set of forks. However the solution is invalid as it covers the new negative example. After updating the (true) solution fields ($F.sol$)[6], the search can resume from the current front.

In short, the algorithm from Section 3 can be used. When a new example is received, the values in the front are updated and the search resumes.

4.2 Implementation

Representing the wrappers as sets of forks is straightforward, and works fine most of the time. For some tasks (requiring large k and l-values, and with pages with a large branching factor), the time for learning and extraction becomes noticeable and becomes an annoyance in an interactive application. We developed an implementation that represents the wrappers by unranked tree automata based on a technique described in [19]. This substantially reduces the memory consumption and the execution time without affecting the language accepted by the wrapper.

We added a graphical user interface to our application, which is basically a HTML-compliant browser, that allows the user to right-click on an element of the page to add an extra example. The system colors the background of all elements that are extracted by its hypothesis. A click on a colored element is interpreted as a false positive, a click on a plain element is interpreted as a false negative. This way the user is restricted to give only counterexamples to the equivalence query posed by the system.

Table 2. Number of interactions needed to learn the wrappers

Data set	P/N	ms	Data set	P/N	ms	Data set	P/N	ms	Data set	P/N	ms
s1-1	1/1	87	s10-2	1/1	33	s19-4	1/1	53	s29-1	3/2	2446
s1-3	4/1	915	s10-4	1/1	555	s20-3	1/0	35	s29-2	4/2	5628
s1-4	1/0	27	s11-1	1/2	885	s20-4	1/1	1364	s30-2	2/1	46
s3-2	1/1	56	s11-2	1/2	766	s20-5	1/1	1568	bigbook-2	1/2	2013
s3-3	1/1	127	s12-2	1/2	108	s20-6	1/1	1472	bigbook-3	1/1	723
s4-1	1/0	10	s13-2	1/2	45	s22-2	2/1	200	okra-1	1/2	123
s5-2	2/1	230	s13-4	1/1	584	s23-1	1/2	242	okra-2	1/1	684
s8-2	1/1	38	s14-3	1/0	26	s23-3	1/1	38	okra-3	1/2	235
s8-3	1/2	181	s15-2	1/0	18	s25-2	1/1	25	okra-4	1/1	536

---

[6] When the example is from a new document, also the counts are updated.

4.3 Evaluation

To evaluate our system, we use the same tasks as in the second experiment of Section 2.5. Each task is learned until a 100% F1-score is obtained. In Table 2 we show the number of interactions that are needed to learn the wrapper. The first column contains the data set, the second indicates the numbers of positive and negative examples[7] needed, and the last column indicates the total time needed by all the learning steps in Algorithm 1. The number of examples needed (P+N) is in the same range as those reported in [18] for Aggressive Co-Testing for tasks where the latter reaches 100% F1-score. The system is highly responsive and suited for interactive use.

5 Conclusion

We have introduced a new subclass of the regular unranked tree languages, called (k, l)-contextual tree languages, that is learnable from positive examples only. We applied this class of languages to the problem of wrapper induction by representing a wrapper as a language of marked trees. Experiments on generally used data sets show the expressiveness of this wrapper representation to be superior over other approaches. We made an in-depth comparison with a wrapper inference algorithm based on Local Unranked Tree automata [12], which corresponds to $(k, 2)$-contextual tree languages; they lack expressivity and their authors tweak the representation of the documents by annotating the path from the root to the target node. An experiment learning wrappers from a small set of positive examples shows that our pure local languages usually yield a better wrapper than theirs.

Both our new algorithm as [12] need to tune parameters for each task. In [12] this is solved by evaluating wrappers on a sufficiently large set of completely annotated documents (representing positive and negative examples) to find the optimal parameter setting for a given extraction task. We developed a technique that learns a good parameter setting from a small set of positive and negative examples.

Another limitation of [12] was the need for an ad-hoc preprocessing step to identify a so called distinguishing context that in some applications is needed to disambiguate positive from negative examples. We developed a technique that preserves text nodes close to the target node when they occur in all examples.

We integrated the algorithm in an interactive system that allows a user to build a wrapper by selecting an initial positive example, and possibly a small number of false positives or false negatives, in sample documents. Experiments show that the resulting system is indeed able to learn a wrapper from a few positive and negative examples for a large number of extraction tasks. Interestingly, the system indicates failure when the extraction task is not expressible as a (k, l)-contextual tree language. In this case, one could switch to more expressive languages, e.g., the tRPNI algorithm [4] that needs a set of completely annotated documents (so far we have not met an existing data set requiring this).

---

[7] P/N = 1/0 means that the initial (1,2)-wrapper given one positive example is a solution.

References

1. H. Ahonen. *Generating grammars for structured documents using grammatical inference methods*. PhD thesis, University of Helsinki, Department of Computer Science, 1996.
2. D. Angluin. Inference of reversible languages. *Journal of the ACM (JACM)*, 29(3):741–765, 1982.
3. D. Angluin. Queries and concept-learning. *Machine Learning*, 2:319–342, 1988.
4. J. Carme, A. Lemay, and J. Niehren. Learning node selecting tree transducer from completely annotated examples. In *International Colloquium on Grammatical Inference*, volume 3264 of *Lecture Notes in Artificial Intelligence*, pages 91–102. Springer Verlag, Oct. 2004.
5. B. Chidlovskii, J. Ragetli, and M. de Rijke. Wrapper generation via grammar induction. In *Proc. 11th European Conference on Machine Learning (ECML)*, volume 1810, pages 96–108. Springer, Berlin, 2000.
6. D. Freitag and N. Kushmerick. Boosted wrapper induction. In *Proceedings of the Seventeenth National Conference on Artificial Intelligence and Twelfth Innovative Applications of AI Conference*, pages 577–583. AAAI Press, 2000.
7. D. Freitag and A. McCallum. Information extraction with HMMs and shrinkage. In *AAAI-99 Workshop on Machine Learning for Information Extraction*, 1999.
8. P. García. Learning k-testable tree sets from positive data. Technical report, Technical Report DSIC-ii-1993-46, DSIC, Universidad Politecnica de Valencia, 1993.
9. P. García and E. Vidal. Inference of k-testable languages in the strict sense and application to syntactic pattern recognition. *IEEE Trans. Pattern Anal. Mach. Intell.*, 12(9):920–925, 1990.
10. E. M. Gold. Language identification in the limit. *Information and Control*, 10(5):447–474, 1967.
11. T. Knuutila. Inference of k-testable tree languages. In H. Bunke, editor, *Advances in Structural and Syntactic Pattern Recognition: Proc. of the Intl. Workshop*, pages 109–120, Singapore, 1993. World Scientific.
12. R. Kosala, M. Bruynooghe, H. Blockeel, and J. V. den Bussche. Information extraction from web documents based on local unranked tree automaton inference. In *Intl. Joint Conference on Artificial Intelligence (IJCAI)*, pages 403–408, 2003.
13. R. Kosala, J. Van den Bussche, M. Bruynooghe, and H. Blockeel. Information extraction in structured documents using tree automata induction. In *PKDD*, volume 2431 of *Lecture Notes in Computer Science*, pages 299–310. Springer, 2002.
14. N. Kushmerick, D. S. Weld, and R. B. Doorenbos. Wrapper induction for information extraction. In *Intl. Joint Conference on Artificial Intelligence (IJCAI)*, pages 729–737, 1997.
15. R. McNaughton. Algebraic decision procedures for local testability. *Math. Systems Theory*, 8(1):60–76, 1974.
16. S. Muggleton. *Inductive Acquisition of Expert Knowledge*. Addison-Wesley, 1990.
17. I. Muslea, S. Minton, and C. Knoblock. Hierarchical wrapper induction for semistructured information sources. *Journal of Autonomous Agents and Multi-Agent Systems*, 4:93–114, 2001.
18. I. Muslea, S. Minton, and C. Knoblock. Active learning with strong and weak views: A case study on wrapper induction. In *Intl. Joint Conference on Artificial Intelligence (IJCAI)*, 2003.
19. S. Raeymaekers and M. Bruynooghe. Extracting information from structured documents with automata in a single run. In *Proc. 2nd Int. Workshop on Mining Graphs, Trees and Sequences (MGTS 2004, Pisa, Italy)*, pages 71–82, Pisa, Italy, 2004. University of Pisa.
20. J. R. Rico-Juan, J. Calera-Rubio, and R. C. Carrasco. Probabilistic k-testable tree languages. In A. Oliveira, editor, *Proceedings of 5th International Colloquium, ICGI*, pages 221–228, 2000.
21. S. Soderland. Learning information extraction rules for semi-structured and free text. *Machine Learning*, 34(1-3):233–272, 1999.

Neural Fitted Q Iteration - First Experiences with a Data Efficient Neural Reinforcement Learning Method

Martin Riedmiller

Neuroinformatics Group,
University of Onsabrück, 49078 Osnabrück

Abstract. This paper introduces NFQ, an algorithm for efficient and effective training of a Q-value function represented by a multi-layer perceptron. Based on the principle of storing and reusing transition experiences, a model-free, neural network based Reinforcement Learning algorithm is proposed. The method is evaluated on three benchmark problems. It is shown empirically, that reasonably few interactions with the plant are needed to generate control policies of high quality.

1 Introduction

When addressing interesting Reinforcement Learning (RL) problems in real world applications, one sooner or later faces the problem of an appropriate method to represent the value function. Neural networks, in particular multi-layer perceptrons, offer an interesting perspective due to their ability to approximate nonlinear functions. Although a lot of successful applications exist [Tes92, Lin92, Rie00], also a lot of problems have been reported [BM95]. Many of these problems arise, since the representation mechanism in a multi-layer perceptron is not local, but global: A weight change induced by an update in a certain part of the state space might influence the values in arbitrary other regions - and therefore destroy the effort done so far in other regions. This leads to typically very long learning times or even to the final failure of learning at all. On the other hand, a global representation scheme can in principle have a very positive effect: by assigning similar values to related areas, it can exploit generalisation effects and therefore accelerate learning considerably.

Therefore the question is: how can we exploit the positive properties of a global approximation realized in a multi-layer perceptron while avoiding the negative ones? One key access to this question is that we need to constrain the malificious influence of a new update of the value function in a multi-layer perceptron. The principle idea that underlies our approach is simple: we have to make sure, that at the same time we make an update at a new datapoint, we also offer previous knowledge explicitly. Here, we implement this idea by storing all previous experiences in terms of state-action transitions in memory. This data is then reused every time the neural Q-function is updated.

The algorithm proposed belongs to the family of fitted value iteration algorithms [Gor95]. They can be seen as a special form of the 'experience replay' technique [Lin92], where value iteration is performed on all transition experiences seen so far. Recently, several algorithms have been introduced in this spirit of batch or off-line Reinforcement Learning, e.g. LSPI [LP03]. Our method is a special realisation of the 'Fitted Q Iteration', recently proposed by Ernst et.al [EPG05]. Whereas Ernst et.al examined tree based regression methods, we propose the use of multilayer-perceptrons with an enhanced weight update method. Our method is therfore called 'Neural Fitted Q Iteration' (NFQ). In particular, we want to stress the following important properties of NFQ:

- the method is model-free. The only information required from the plant are transition triples of the form (state, action, successor state).
- learning of successful policies is possible with relatively few training examples (data efficiency). This enables the learning algorithm to directly learn from real world interactions.
- although requiring much less knowledge about the plant than analytical controllers, the method is able to find control policies, that are able to compare well to analytically designed controllers (see cart-pole regulator benchmark).

2 Main Idea

2.1 Markovian Decision Processes

The control problems considered in this paper can be described as Markovian Decision Processes (MDPs). An MDP is described by a set S of states, a set A of actions, a stochastic transition function $p(s, a, s')$ describing the (stochastic) system behavior and an immediate reward or cost function $c : S \times A \to \mathbf{R}$. The goal is to find an optimal policy $\pi^* : S \to A$, that minimizes the expected cumulated costs for each state. In particular, we allow S to be continuous, assume A to be finite for our learning system, and p to be unknown to our learning system (model-free approach). Decisions are taken in regular time steps with a constant cycle time.

2.2 Classical Q-Learning

In classical Q-learning, the update rule is given by

$$Q_{k+1}(s,a) := (1-\alpha)Q(s,a) + \alpha(c(s,a) + \gamma \min_b Q_k(s',b))$$

where s denotes the state where the transition starts, a is the action that is applied, and s' is the resulting state. α is a learning rate that has to be decreased in the course of learning in order to fulfill the conditions of stochastic approximation and γ is a discounting factor (see e.g. [SB98]). It can be shown, that under mild assumptions Q-learning converges for finite state and action spaces, as long as every state action pair is updated infinitely often. Then, in the limit, the optimal Q-function is reached.

Typically, the update is performed on-line in a sample-by-sample manner, that is, every time a new transition is made, the value function is updated.

2.3 Q-Learning for Neural Networks

In principle, the above Q-learning rule can be directly implemented in a neural network. Since no direct assignment of Q-values like in a table based representation can be made, instead, an error function is introduced, that aims to measure the difference between the current Q-value and the new value that should be assigned. For example, a squared-error measure like the following can be used: $error = (Q(s,a) - (c(s,a) + \gamma \min_b Q(s',b)))^2$. At this point, common gradient descent techniques (like the 'backpropagation' learning rule) can be applied to adjust the weights of a neural network in order to minimize the error. Like above, this update rule is typically applied after each new sample.

The problem with this on-line update rule is that, typically, several ten thousands of episodes have to be done until an optimal or near optimal policy has been found [Rie00]. One reason for this is, that if weights are adjusted for one certain state action pair, then unpredictable changes also occur at other places in the state-action space. Although in principle this could also have a positive effect (generalisation) in many cases, in our experiences this seems to be the main reason for unreliable and slow learning.

3 Neural Fitted Q Iteration (NFQ)

3.1 Basic Idea

The basic idea underlying NFQ is the following: Instead of updating the neural value function on-line (which leads to the problems described in the previous section), the update is performed off-line considering an entire set of transition experiences. Experiences are collected in triples of the form (s, a, s') by interacting with the (real or simulated) system[1]. Here, s is the original state, a is the chosen action and s' is the resulting state. The set of experiences is called the sample set $\mathcal{D}$.

The consideration of the entire training information instead of on-line samples, has an important further consequence: It allows the application of advanced supervised learning methods, that converge faster and more reliably than online gradient descent methods. Here we use Rprop [RB93], a supervised learning method for batch learning, which is known to be very fast and very insensitive with respect to the choice of its learning parameters. The latter fact has the advantage, that we do not have to care about tuning the parameters for the supervised learning part of the overall (RL) learning problem.

---

[1] Note that often experiences are collected in four-tuples with the additional entry denoting the immediate costs or reward from the environment. Since we take an engineering view of the learning problem, we think of the immediate costs as something being specified by the designer of the learning system rather than something that occurs naturally in the environment and can only be observed. Therefore, costs come in at a later point and also potentially can be changed without collecting further experiences. However, the basic working of the algorithm is not touched by this.

3.2 The NFQ -Algorithm

NFQ is an instance of the Fitted Q Iteration family of algorithms [EPG05], where the regression algorithm is realized by a multi-layer perceptron. The algorithm is displayed in figure 1. It consists of two major steps: The generation of the training set P and the training of these patterns within a multi-layer perceptron. The input part of each training pattern consists of the state s^l and action a^l of training experience l. The target value is computed by the sum of the transition costs $c(s^l, a^l, s^{l+1})$ and the expected minimal path costs for the successor state s'^l, computed on the basis of the current estimate of the Q-function, Q_k.

NFQ_main() {
input: a set of transition samples D; output: Q-value function Q_N
    k=0
    init_MLP() $\to Q_0$;
    Do {
        generate_pattern_set $P = \{(input^l, target^l), l = 1, \ldots, \#D\}$ where:
          $input^l = s^l, u^l,$
          $target^l = c(s^l, u^l, s'^l) + \gamma \, min_b Q_k(s'^l, b)$
        Rprop_training(P) $\to Q_{k+1}$
        k:= k+1
    } WHILE $(k < N)$

Fig. 1. Main loop of NFQ

Since at this point, training the Q-function can be done as batch learning of a fixed pattern set, we can use more advanced supervised learning techniques, that converge more quickly and more reliably than ordinary gradient descent techniques. In our implementation, we use the Rprop algorithm for fast supervised learning [RB93]. The training of the pattern set is repeated for several epochs (=complete sweeps through the pattern set), until the pattern set is learned succesfully.

3.3 Sample Setting of Costs

Here, we will give an example setting of the immediate cost structure, which can be used in many typical reinforcement learning settings. We find it useful to use a more or less standardized procedure to setup the learning problem, but we want to stress that NFQ is by no means tailored this type of cost function, but works with arbitrary cost structures.

In the following, we denote the set of goal states $\mathcal{S}^+$, the set of forbidden states are denoted by $\mathcal{S}^-$. $\mathcal{S}^+$ therefore denotes the region, where the system should finally be controlled to (and in case of a regulator problem, should be kept in), and $\mathcal{S}^-$ denotes regions in state space, that must be avoided by a correct control policy.

Within this setting, the generation of training patterns is modified as follows:

$$target^l = \begin{cases} c(s^l, u^l, s'^l) &, \text{ if } s'^l \in \mathcal{S}^+ \\ C^- &, \text{ if } s'^l \in \mathcal{S}^- \\ c(s^l, u^l, s'^l) + \gamma \min_b Q_k(s'^l, b) &, \text{ else (standard case)} \end{cases} \quad (1)$$

Setting $c(s^l, u^l, s'^l)$ to a positive constant value c_{trans} means to aim for a minimum-time controller. In technical process control, this is often desirable, and therefore we choose this setting in the following. C^- is set to 1.0, since this is the maximum output value of the multi-layer perceptron that we use. In regulator problems (see section 4), reaching a goal state does not terminate the episode. Therefore, the first line in the above equation must not be applied. Instead, only line 2 and 3 are executed and $c(s^l, u^l, s'^l) = 0$, if $s'^l \in \mathcal{S}^+$ and $c(s^l, u^l, s'^l) = c_{trans}$, otherwise.

Note that due to its purity, this setting is widely applicable and no prior knowledge about the environment (like for example the distance to the goal) is incorporated.

3.4 Variants

Several variants can be applied to the basic algorithm. In particular, for the experiments in section 5.2 and 5.3 we used a version, where we incrementally add transitions to the experience set. This is especially useful in situations, where a reasonable set of experiences can not be collected by controlling the system with purely random actions. Instead, training samples are collected by greedily exploiting the current Q_k function and added to the sample set D.

Another heuristic that we found helpful, is to add 'artificial' training patterns from the goal region, which have a known target value of 0. This technique 'clamps' the neural value function to zero in the goal region, and we therefore call it the *hint-to-goal*-heuristic. Note that no additional prior knowledge is required to generate the patterns, since the goal region is already known in the task specification.

4 Benchmarking

The following gives a short overview of the intention of the benchmarks done in the empirical section.

4.1 Types of Tasks

In control problems, three basic types of task specification might be distinguished (there might be more, but for our purposes, this categorisation is sufficient):

- avoidance control task - keep the system somewhere within the 'valid' region of state space. Pole balancing is typically defined as such a problem, where the task is to avoid that the pole crashes or the cart hits the boundary of the track.
- reaching a goal - the system has to reach a certain area in state space. As soon as it gets there, the task is immediately finished. Mountaincar is typically defined as getting the cart to a certain position up the hill.
- regulator problem - the system has to reach a certain region in state space and has to be actively kept there by the controller. This corresponds to the problems typically tackled with methods of classical control theory.

The problem types show different levels of difficulty, even when the underlying plant to be controlled is the same. In the following, we consider three benchmark problems, where each belongs to one of the above categories.

4.2 Evaluating Learning Performance

Each learning experiment consists of a number of episodes. An episode is a sequence of control cycles, that starts with an initial state and ends if the current state fulfills some termination condition (e.g. the system reached its goal state or a failure occured) or some maximum number of cycles has been reached.

Learning time in principle can be measured in many different ways: number of episodes needed, number of cycles needed, number of updates performed, absolute computation time, etc.

Since we are interested in methods that can directly learn on real systems, our preferred measure of learning effort is the number of cycles needed to achieve a certain performance. This number is directly related to the amount of interaction with the plant to be controlled. By multiplying the number of cycles with the length of the control interval, we get the absolute real time that we would have to spend on a real system to achieve a certain performance.

We also give the number of episodes that is needed to learn a task. Although this is not as expressive as the number of cycles (since this figure drastically depends on the maximum allowed length of a training episode), it is a commonly used measure and gives at least a rough intuition about the learning effort.

4.3 Evaluating Controller Performance

Controller performance is evaluated with respect to some cost-measure, that evaluates the average performance over a certain amount of control episodes. In principle this cost measure can be chosen arbitrary. Due to its practical relevance, we use the average time to the goal as a performance measure for the controller. In the regulator problem case, we measure the overall time outside the target region. This takes the fact into account, that a controlled system might leave the target region again. Note that the learning controller might have an internal goal formulation that differs from the performance measure (i.e. by using discounting or shaping rewards).

Another important aspect when evaluating controller performance is to specify the 'working region' of the controller, that means the set of starting states, for which the controller should work. We distinguish between the following types of working regions:

- always start from a single starting state
- start from one of a finite set of starting states
- start from an arbitrary random state within a starting region

In the following experiments, we use the third case, which is the most general and (typically) the most challenging one.

5 Empirical Results

All experiments are done using CLS^2 (Closed Loop System Simulator)[2], a software system designed to benchmark (not only) RL controllers on a wide variety of plants.

5.1 The Pole Balancing Task

The task is to balance a pole at the upright position by applying appropriate forces to the system. System equations and parameters are the same as in [LP03]. Three actions are available, left force (-50 N), right force (+50 N) and no force. Uniform noise in $[-10, 10]$ is added to the system. Cycle length is 0.1 s. The state space is continuous and consists of the angle and the angular velocity. An episode was counted as a failure, if the angle of the pole exceeded $\pm\pi/2$ respectively.

Learning System Setup. For comparison, we choose the same cost structure as in [LP03]: Immediate costs of 0 arise, if the angle remains within $[-\pi/2, \pi/2]$ ('$\mathcal{S}^+$'), if the angle gets outside this region, the episode is stopped and costs of $+1$ are given. A discount factor of $\gamma = 0.95$ is used. Transition samples were generated by starting the pole in an upright position and then applying random control signals until failure. The average length of a training episode was about 6 cycles.

NFQ uses a multilayer-perceptron with 3 inputs (2 for the state, 1 for the action), two hidden layers with 5 neurons each and 1 output. For all neurons, sigmoidal activation functions with outputs between 0 and 1 were used.

Results. Lagoudakis and Parr reported very good results both for their LSPI approach and Q-learning with experience replay using a linear function approximator with reasonably selected basis functions [LP03]. The learned controllers were tested on 1000 test episodes with a maximum length of 300 seconds each. LSPI reached an average balancing time of 285 seconds after 1000 training episodes. This means, that most but not all of the training trials generated totally successful policies. For Q-learning with experience replay they report a balancing time of 'about 300' seconds after 750 episodes of training [LP03].

---

[2] available at clss.sf.net

Table 1. Results of NFQ on the pole balancing benchmark. Left column reports the number of random episodes that were used for training. The length of each episode was about 6 cycles. Altogether, 50 repetitions of the experiment were done. For each experiment, a new set of random episodes was produced. Using 200 or more training episodes (about 1200 cycles, corresponding to 2 minutes real time), all experiments generated successful policies, i.e. the controller balanced the pole for all the test cases for the maximum time 300 s.

# random episodes	successful learning trials
50	23/50 (46%)
100	44/50 (88 %)
150	48/50 (96 %)
200	50/50 (100 %)
300	50/50 (100 %)
400	50/50 (100 %)

Results of the NFQ method are shown in table 1. The experiments were repeated for 50 times. Each experiment had a different set of training samples and a different initialisation of the neural network weights. With only 50 training episodes (corresponding to about 300 transition samples), NFQ was able to find totally successful policies (policies that balanced the pole for the full 300 seconds for all the test episodes) in 23 out of 50 experiments. Using more training episodes, the result improves. Using only 200 training episodes, a successful policy could be found reliably in all of the 50 experiments. This is a remarkable result with respect to training data efficiency and gives some hint to the benefit of generalisation ability of a multilayer-perceptron.

5.2 The Mountain Car Benchmark

The mountain car benchmark is about accelerating a car up to the top of the hill, where for many situations the acceleration of the car is too weak to directly go to the top, but instead the car has to move to the other direction to get enough energy [SB98]. The control interval is $\Delta_t = 0.05s$. Actions are restricted within the interval $[-4, 4]$. The road ends at -1m, i.e. the position must fulfill the constraint $position > -1m$. The task is to reach the top, which means that then, the position must be larger or equal to $0.7m$. For testing performance, 1000 starting states are drawn randomly from the interval $(-1, 0.7)$. The initial velocity of the cart is set to 0. Performance is measured by the average number of cycles to the goal.

Learning System Setup. Two actions are provided to the learning controller, -4 and +4. For training, initial starting positions are drawn randomly from $(-1, 0.7)$, the initial velocity of the car was always set to zero. Training trajectories had a maximum length of 50 cycles. An episode was stopped, if the system entered $\mathcal{S}^-$ (failure by constraint violation) or entered $\mathcal{S}^+$ (success). Each training trajectory was generated by a controller, that greedily exploited the current

Q-value function. The Q-value function was represented by a multi-layer perceptron with 3 input neurons (2 state variables and 1 action), 2 layers of 5 hidden neurons each and 1 output neuron, all equiped with sigmoidal activation functions. The weights of the network were randomly initialized within $[-0.5, 0.5]$. After each episode, one iteration of the inner NFQ loop was performed. The hint-to-goal heuristic was used with a factor of 100. For each transition, costs of $c_{trans} = 0.01$ were given.

Results. Results of the NFQ approach on the mountain car benchmark are shown in table 2. The results are averaged over 20 experiments. Experiments differ in the randomly drawn starting states for training and the randomly initialized neural Q-function. Each trial was stopped after 500 training episodes. All 20 experiments produced a successful policy, i.e. a policy that was able to reach the goal state for all of the 1000 randomly drawn starting positions.

To generate a successful policy, only about 71 episodes or 2777 cycles were needed in average over all experiments. This corresponds to less than 2 and a half minutes of training in real time. In the best case, a successful policy could be found in only 356 cycles, but even in worst case, only 10054 cycles were needed, which corresponds to about 8 and a half minutes in real time and therefore still is a very realistic number for an assumed interaction with a real system. Finding a fast policy to the goal can be done in about 296 episodes or about 11000 cycles respectively, corresponding to about 9 minutes in real time. Again, this is a very reasonable number for direct interaction with a real system.

Table 2. Results of NFQ on the mountain car benchmark. The upper part reports on the training effort to reach a succesful policy. A policy is successful, if all test situations are controlled to the goal state. The table shows the figures for the average (best/ worst) number of episodes, the average (best/ worst) number of cycles and the corresponding time for interacting with a real system. The lower part reports on the learning effort to reach an optimized policy. In average over all training trials, the average best costs are 28.7. This value is slightly better than the performance achieved with a fine granulated Q-table (29.0).

	Mountain Car			
	First successful policy			
	episodes	cycles	interaction time	costs
average	70.95	2777.0	2m19s	41.05
best	10	356		
worst	243	10054		
	Best policy found (within 500 episodes)			
	episodes	cycles	interaction time	costs
average	296.6	10922.8	9m06s	28.7
best	101	3660		
worst	444	16081		

The best policies found needed only an average of 28.7 cycles to reach the goal. This figure compares well to a table-based Q-learning approach, which yielded an average of 29.0 cycles to reach the goal. This means that we can expect the NFQ controllers to be pretty close to the optimum. As a side remark (not meant as a true comparison): to get to this result, table based Q-learning required 300,000 episodes (with a maximum length of 300 cycles), and the Q-table had a resolution of 250 × 250 × 2 entries.

5.3 The Cartpole Regulator Benchmark

System dynamics of the cartpole system are described in [SB98]. The control interval is $\triangle_t = 0.02s$. Actions are restricted within the interval $[-10, 10]$. The position is restricted by the constraint $-2.4 \leq pos \leq 2.4$. For testing performance, 1000 starting states are drawn randomly. Results on the cartpole system are typically reported with respect to maximum balancing time. Here, we report results on a more difficult task that comprises balancing, namely cartpole regulation. The task is to move the cart to a certain position *and keep it there* while preventing the pole from falling. The target position of the cart is the middle of the track, with a tolerance of $\pm 0.05m$. As a further complication, we allow initial starting states deviating a lot from the 'all-zero' position: for testing performance, initial pole angles are randomly drawn from $[-0.3, 0.3]$ (in rad), positions are drawn from $[-1., 1.]$ (in m), initial velocities are set to 0.

This more complicated formulation of the cartpole benchmark is closer to realistic control tasks and the resulting controllers can be compared to control policies derived by classical controller design methods.

Learning System Setup. Two actions are available to the learning controller, -10N and +10N. For training, initial starting positions for the cart are drawn randomly from $[-2.3, 2.3]$, initial pole angles are drawn from $[-0.3, 0.3]$ (in rad), cart velocity and angular velocity are initially set to zero. Training episodes had a maximum length of 100 cycles. Each training episode was generated by a controller, that greedily exploited the current Q-value function. The Q-value function was represented by a multi-layer perceptron with 5 inputs, 2 hidden layers with 5 neurons each, and one output neuron, all equiped with sigmoidal activation functions. The weights of the network were randomly initialized within $[-0.5, 0.5]$. After each episode, one loop of the NFQ algorithm was performed. The hint-to-goal heuristic was used with a factor of 100. For each transition, costs of $c_{trans} = 0.01$ were given.

Results. Results for the cart-pole benchmark are shown in table 3. Performance is tested on 1000 testing episodes starting from randomly drawn initial states and having a maximum length of 3000 cycles. In the cartpole regulator benchmark, a controller is successful, if at the end of the episode, the pole is still upright and the cart is at its target position 0 within $\pm 0.05m$ tolerance. Note that all the controllers that solve the regulator problem also solve the balancing problem. Typically, the balancing problem is solved much earlier than the regulator problem (figures not shown here).

Table 3. Results of NFQ on the cart-pole regulator benchmark. Training time was restricted to 500 episodes per trial. For an interpretation of the figures, see explanation at table for the mountain car benchmark.

Cart Pole Regulator				
First successful policy				
	episodes	cycles	interaction time	costs
average	197.3	14439.8	4m49s	319.1
best	75	4016		
worst	309	24132		
Best policy found (within 500 episodes)				
	episodes	cycles	interaction time	costs
average	354.0	28821.1	9m 36s	132.9
best	119	8044		
worst	489	43234		

Again, training is done very efficiently. Although the control problem is challenging, a moderate amount of sample transitions - an average of 14439.8 cycles to find a successful policy and an average of 28821.1 cycles to find the best controller - are sufficient. This corresponds to an average real time of 5 minutes (or 10 minutes respectively for the best controller) that would be needed to do the collection of transition samples on a corresponding real system.

To have a better feeling for the control performance of the learned controller, we analytically designed a linear controller for the cartpole regulator benchmark. We used a pole assignment method where we placed the poles of the closed loop system such that it was stable. Additionally, we tried to find parameters that produced control actions within the interval $[-10, +10]$ according to the above specification. The control law used was $u = -Rx$, where $R = (30.61, 7.77, 0.45, 1.72)$ and x is the state vector. For the linear controller, the average number of cycles outside the goal region was 402.1 over the 1000 test starting positions. The neural controllers that were learned had an average cost of 132.9, which means that they are about 3 times as fast as the linear controller. This is an even more remarkable result, if one considers, that no prior knowledge about plant behaviour was available to develop the neural policy.

6 Conclusion

The paper proposes NFQ, a memory based method to train Q-value functions based on multi-layer perceptrons. By storing and reusing all transition experiences, the neural learning process can be made very data efficient and reliable. Additionally, by allowing for batch supervised learning in the core of adaptation, advanced supervised learning techniques can be applied that provide reliable and quick convergence of the supervised learning part of the problem. NFQ allows to exploit the positive effects of generalisation in multi-layer perceptrons while avoiding their negative effects of disturbing previously learned experiences.

The exploitation of generalisation leads to highly data efficient learning. This is shown in the three benchmarks performed. The amount of training experience required for learning successful policies is considerably low. The corresponding time for acquisition of the training data on a hypothetic real plant lies in the range of a few minutes for all three benchmarks performed.

For all three benchmarks, the same neural network structure was successfully used. Of course, this does not mean, that we have found the one neural network that solves all control problems, but it is a positive hint with respect to the robustness of NFQ with respect to the choice of the underlying neural network. Robustness against the parametrisation of a method is of special importance for practical applications, since the search for sensitive parameters can be a resource consuming issue.

References

[BM95]   Boyan and Moore. Generalization in reinforcement learning: Safely approximating the value function. In *Advances in Neural Information Processing Systems 7*. Morgan Kaufmann, 1995.

[EPG05] D. Ernst and and L. Wehenkel P. Geurts. Tree-based batch mode reinforcement learning. *Journal of Machine Learning Research*, 6:503–556, 2005.

[Gor95] G. J. Gordon. Stable function approximation in dynamic programming. In A. Prieditis and S. Russell, editors, *Proceedings of the ICML*, San Francisco, CA, 1995.

[Lin92] L.-J. Lin. Self-improving reactive agents based on reinforcement learning, planning and teaching. *Machine Learning*, 8:293–321, 1992.

[LP03]   M. Lagoudakis and R. Parr. Least-squares policy iteration. *Journal of Machine Learning Research*, 4:1107–1149, 2003.

[RB93]   M. Riedmiller and H. Braun. A direct adaptive method for faster backpropagation learning: The RPROP algorithm. In H. Ruspini, editor, *Proceedings of the IEEE International Conference on Neural Networks (ICNN)*, pages 586 – 591, San Francisco, 1993.

[Rie00] M. Riedmiller. Concepts and facilities of a neural reinforcement learning control architecture for technical process control. *Journal of Neural Computing and Application*, 8:323–338, 2000.

[SB98]   R. S. Sutton and A. G. Barto. *Reinforcement Learning*. MIT Press, Cambridge, MA, 1998.

[Tes92] G. Tesauro. Practical issues in temporal difference learning. *Machine Learning*, (8):257–277, 1992.

MCMC Learning of Bayesian Network Models by Markov Blanket Decomposition

Carsten Riggelsen

Institute of Information & Computing Sciences,
Utrecht University, P.O. Box 80.098, 3508TB, Utrecht, The Netherlands
carsten@cs.uu.nl

Abstract. We propose a Bayesian method for learning Bayesian network models using Markov chain Monte Carlo (MCMC). In contrast to most existing MCMC approaches that define components in term of single edges, our approach is to decompose a Bayesian network model in larger *dependence* components defined by Markov blankets. The idea is based on the fact that MCMC performs significantly better when choosing the right decomposition, and that edges in the Markov blanket of the vertices form a natural dependence relationship. Using the ALARM and Insurance networks, we show that this decomposition allows MCMC to mix more rapidly, and is less prone to getting stuck in local maxima compared to the single edge approach.

1 Introduction

Bayesian networks is a convenient framework for reasoning and manipulating beliefs about the real world. It occupies a prominent position in decision support environments where it is used for diagnostic and prediction purposes. Also, in the context of data mining especially the graphical structure (model) of a Bayesian network is an appealing formalism for visualising the relationships between domain variables. This paper is concerned with the latter of the two.

We approach model learning from a Bayesian point of view, and apply a method that is based on the marginal likelihood scoring criterion. The reason for being Bayesian is first of all related to the relatively small amount of data that we often have at our disposal in practice. When data is scarce, there may be several models that are structurally quite different from each other, yet are almost equally likely given the data. In other words, the data supports several models that differ widely, yet from a scoring perspective are very close. Model selection methods on the other hand will return "the best" model, but give no clue as to how and in what respect models differ that score almost equally well.

For large data sets—where "large" of course is related to the number of variables of our domain—the best model is much more likely than any other model, and model selection may be adequate.

The usual obstacle with the Bayesian statistical approach is the analytically intractable integrals, normalising constants and large mixtures encountered when performing the required computations. With MCMC, Bayesian computations are performed using stochastic simulation.

When learning Bayesian network models the Bayesian way, MCMC is usually done over the model space of DAGs [11] or (simulated) essential graphs [5]. Usually the models are incrementally built by adding, removing or reversing arcs selected at random, thereby "moving" around in the state space. Unfortunately, by exploring the search space using moves defined solely in terms of single edges selected in a uniform fashion, we may easily get stuck in local maxima.

In this paper we suggest to traverse the model space in a more intelligent fashion by considering larger blocks. Rather than selecting edges uniformly, we select a set of vertices that are related to each other and propose a change of *how* these vertices are related by considering different edge assignments. We show that in doing so, MCMC is less prone to get stuck in local maxima compared to uniform edge proposals.

We proceed as follows: Section two introduces the basic theory for learning Bayesian networks based on the marginal likelihood criterion. In section three we discuss a Gibbs and a Metropolis-Hastings sampler for obtaining models from the posterior model distribution. Our new MCMC method is presented in section four, and in section five the pseudocode is given and some implementation issues are discussed. In section six we evaluate our method, and compare experimental results to those of a single edge MCMC approach. We draw conclusions in section seven.

2 Learning Models

A Bayesian network (BN) for the discrete random variables $\boldsymbol{X} = (X^1, \ldots, X^p)$ represents a joint probability distribution. It consists of a directed acyclic graph (DAG) M, called the model, where every vertex corresponds to a variable X^i, and a vector of conditional probabilities $\boldsymbol{\Theta}$, called the parameter, corresponding to that model. The joint distribution factors recursively according to M as $\Pr(\boldsymbol{X}|M, \boldsymbol{\Theta}) = \prod_{i=1}^{p} \Pr(X^i|\boldsymbol{\Pi}_i, \boldsymbol{\Theta}) = \prod_{i=1}^{p} \Theta_{X^i|\boldsymbol{\Pi}_i}$, where $\boldsymbol{\Pi}_i$ is the parent set of X^i in M. We consider $\boldsymbol{\Theta}$ a random (stochastic) vector with the following (prior) product Dirichlet distribution:

$$\Pr(\boldsymbol{\Theta}|M) = \prod_{i=1}^{p} \prod_{\boldsymbol{\pi}_i} \mathrm{Dir}(\Theta_{X^i|\boldsymbol{\pi}_i}|\boldsymbol{\alpha}) = \prod_{i=1}^{p} \prod_{\boldsymbol{\pi}_i} C(i, \boldsymbol{\pi}_i, \boldsymbol{\alpha}) \prod_{x^i} \Theta_{x^i|\boldsymbol{\pi}_i}^{\alpha(x^i, \boldsymbol{\pi}_i) - 1},$$

with $C(i, \boldsymbol{\pi}_i, \boldsymbol{\alpha})$ the normalising factor:

$$C(i, \boldsymbol{\pi}_i, \boldsymbol{\alpha}) = \frac{\Gamma\big(\alpha(\boldsymbol{\pi}_i)\big)}{\prod_{x^i} \Gamma\big(\alpha(x^i, \boldsymbol{\pi}_i)\big)},$$

where $\boldsymbol{\alpha}$ is the vector of hyper parameters, $\alpha(\cdot)$ the function returning the prior *counts* for a particular configuration and $\Gamma(\cdot)$ the gamma function. The product Dirichlet captures the assumption of *parameter independence* [13], i.e. all parameters of the BN are distributed independently, each according to a Dirichlet distribution. We are given a multinomial data sample $\mathcal{D} = (\boldsymbol{d}_1, \ldots, \boldsymbol{d}_c)$ with c i.i.d. cases, $\boldsymbol{d}_i = (x_i^1, \ldots, x_i^p)$, for which the product Dirichlet is conjugate. This means that Bayesian updating is easy because the posterior once $\mathcal{D}$ has been taken into consideration is again product Dirichlet:

$$\Pr(\Theta|\mathcal{D},M) = \prod_{i=1}^{p}\prod_{\pi_i} \mathrm{Dir}(\Theta_{X^i|\pi_i}|\alpha+s) = \frac{\Pr(\mathcal{D}|\Theta,M)\cdot \Pr(\Theta|M)}{\Pr(\mathcal{D}|M)}$$

$$= \frac{\prod_{i=1}^{p}\prod_{x^i}\prod_{\pi_i}\Theta_{x^i|\pi_i}^{s(x^i,\pi_i)}\cdot \Pr(\Theta|M)}{\Pr(\mathcal{D}|M)},$$

where s is the vector of sufficient statistics from $\mathcal{D}$ and $s(\cdot)$ returns the counts for a particular configuration. We can now easily isolate the marginal likelihood $\Pr(\mathcal{D}|M)$:

$$\frac{\prod_{i=1}^{p}\prod_{x^i}\prod_{\pi_i}\Theta_{x^i|\pi_i}^{s(x^i,\pi_i)}\cdot \Pr(\Theta|M)}{\Pr(\Theta|\mathcal{D},M)} = \frac{\prod_{i=1}^{p}\prod_{\pi_i}C(i,\pi_i,\alpha)\prod_{x^i}\Theta_{x^i|\pi_i}^{\alpha(x^i,\pi_i)+s(x^i,\pi_i)-1}}{\prod_{i=1}^{p}\prod_{\pi_i}C(i,\pi_i,\alpha+s)\prod_{x^i}\Theta_{x^i|\pi_i}^{\alpha(x^i,\pi_i)+s(x^i,\pi_i)-1}},$$

where everything except the normalising factors cancels out. By filling in the normalising factors we arrive at the marginal likelihood score, being a product of p terms, one term per variable, each term a function of the parent set of the variable in question:

$$\Pr(\mathcal{D}|M) = \prod_{i=1}^{p}\prod_{\pi_i}\frac{\Gamma\big(\alpha(\pi_i)\big)}{\Gamma\big(\alpha(\pi_i)+s(\pi_i)\big)}\prod_{x^i}\frac{\Gamma\big(\alpha(x^i,\pi_i)+s(x^i,\pi_i)\big)}{\Gamma\big(\alpha(x^i,\pi_i)\big)}.$$

In [8] the marginal likelihood is derived from a Bayesian prediction (*prequential*) point of view using the chain rule $\Pr(\mathcal{D}|M) = \Pr(d_1|M)\cdots\Pr(d_c|d_1,\ldots,d_{c-1},M)$.

The posterior model distribution is computed by applying Bayes' law:

$$\Pr(M|\mathcal{D}) = \frac{\Pr(\mathcal{D}|M)\cdot \Pr(M)}{\sum_{m}\Pr(\mathcal{D}|m)\cdot \Pr(m)},$$

and then, if we are interested in some feature over models quantified by Δ, we can average:

$$\mathrm{E}[\Delta(M)|\mathcal{D}] = \sum_{m}\Delta(m)\cdot \Pr(m|\mathcal{D}).$$

The problem is however that we can't calculate the normalising factor $\Pr(\mathcal{D})$ due to the large number of models. A way of dealing with that problem is to apply MCMC over models; an alternative is described in [10].

3 MCMC for Model Learning

In this section we discuss two methods for learning models via MCMC; other MCMC approaches for learning BN models exist, see for instance [4]. An MCMC approach for model learning which does not employ the marginal likelihood criterion is given in [7].

Define for all $r = 1, \ldots, \frac{p \cdot (p-1)}{2}$ edges of M the random variables E_r with state space $\Omega_{E_r} = \{\leftarrow, \rightarrow, \not\leftrightarrow\}$, i.e. every edge of the graph can take on a direction, or can be absent. If the configuration of all edges forms a DAG, we can calculate the posterior joint distribution $\Pr(E_1, \ldots, E_{\frac{p \cdot (p-1)}{2}} | \mathcal{D})$.

3.1 Gibbs Sampling

The problem with the normalising factor mentioned in the previous section is solved by applying Gibbs sampling. Draw edges at iteration t from the full conditional given the data:

$$e_1^t \sim \Pr(E_1 | e_2^{t-1}, \ldots, e_{\frac{p \cdot (p-1)}{2}}^{t-1}, \mathcal{D})$$

$$\vdots$$

$$e_{\frac{p \cdot (p-1)}{2}}^t \sim \Pr(E_{\frac{p \cdot (p-1)}{2}} | e_1^t, \ldots, e_{\frac{p \cdot (p-1)}{2} - 1}^t, \mathcal{D})$$

$$e_1^{t+1} \sim \Pr(E_1 | e_2^t, \ldots, e_{\frac{p \cdot (p-1)}{2}}^t, \mathcal{D})$$

$$\vdots$$

where each draw is subject to the constraint that all edges together must form an acyclic graph. In order to draw edge E_l from the full conditional given the data we calculate:

$$\Pr(E_l | \{e_{r \neq l}\}, \mathcal{D}) = \frac{\Pr(e_1, \ldots, E_l, \ldots, e_{\frac{p \cdot (p-1)}{2}} | \mathcal{D})}{\sum_{e_l} \Pr(e_1, \ldots, e_l, \ldots, e_{\frac{p \cdot (p-1)}{2}} | \mathcal{D})}$$

$$= \frac{\Pr(\mathcal{D} | e_1, \ldots, E_l, \ldots, e_{\frac{p \cdot (p-1)}{2}})}{\sum_{e_l} \Pr(\mathcal{D} | e_1, \ldots, e_l, \ldots, e_{\frac{p \cdot (p-1)}{2}})},$$

where a uniform model prior $\Pr(M)$ on the model space, and the denominator $\Pr(\mathcal{D})$ both cancel out. It is easy to simplify the ratio even more because of the marginal likelihood decomposition. When drawing an edge from the Gibbs sampler, say E_l, at most two terms are affected, namely the terms pertaining to the vertices of edge E_l. All remaining factors stay the same and cancel out in the ratio given above.

The Markov chain defined here is irreducible, because at every draw the state $\not\leftrightarrow$ is a possibility and this state never induces a cycle. Hence there is a non-zero probability of removing arcs that obstruct the addition of other edges in any direction in the graph (obstruct in the sense that the graph becomes cyclic). Also, since there is a non-zero probability of remaining in the current state the chain is aperiodic, and we conclude that the Markov chain is ergodic. Thus for $t \to \infty$ we have $(e_1, \ldots, e_{\frac{p \cdot (p-1)}{2}}) \sim$

$\Pr(E_1, \ldots, E_{\frac{p \cdot (p-1)}{2}} | \mathcal{D})$, i.e. the chain converges to the joint distribution over collections of edges that form models.

To approximate the expected value of model features, we use the empirical average (also called the Monte Carlo approximation):

$$\mathrm{E}[\Delta(M)|\mathcal{D}] \approx \frac{1}{N} \sum_{t=1}^{N} \Delta(m^t),$$

where N denotes the total number of samples from the Markov chain. Often this kind of averaging is done over features one can read directly off a model, e.g. Markov blanket features of vertices, but theoretically any statement that the model entails can be averaged.

3.2 Metropolis-Hastings Sampling

To our knowledge the model Gibbs sampler has not been proposed before in the form discussed in the previous section. However, an alternative set-up of MCMC sampling over models is to use MCMC Metropolis-Hastings sampling which is discussed in [11,9]. Here a *proposal distribution*, $q(\cdot)$, guides the incremental changes of the models by proposing which components to change. This proposal is produced by drawing $m^{t+1} \sim q(M|m^t)$. With probability:

$$\delta(m^{t+1}, m^t) = \min \left\{ 1, \frac{q(m^t|m^{t+1}) \Pr(m^{t+1}|\mathcal{D})}{q(m^{t+1}|m^t) \Pr(m^t|\mathcal{D})} \right\},$$

the proposal is accepted, otherwise $m^{t+1} = m^t$. For $t \to \infty$ models from the invariant distribution are obtained. Note that a uniform model prior, and $\Pr(\mathcal{D})$ cancel out in the acceptance ratio.

In all existing implementations we are aware of [5,11], the proposals pertain to components that correspond to single edges that are chosen in a uniform fashion. This is more or less similar to the Gibbs sampler presented above with the slight difference that the Gibbs sampler draws edges $E_1, \ldots, E_{\frac{p \cdot (p-1)}{2}}$ systematically. However, changing the visitation scheme does not invalidate the Gibbs sampler. The invariant distribution is reached no matter which visitation scheme is used, as long as all edges are sampled "infinitely often". With a random visitation scheme, both MCMC samplers behave very much the same way.

4 Markov Blanket Approach

The fundamental issue with a single edge approach is that from a MCMC perspective it is not the preferred way of decomposing the joint distribution. If we compare to a deterministic procedure where each single edge component is maximised on an individual basis, it would be quite obvious that this does not produce the best global solution per se. Although the MCMC samplers mentioned in the previous section, don't *maximise* individual edge components, the analogy holds because there is nevertheless a pressure toward "good" or "maximum" solutions when drawing edges. A bad decomposition can make the sampler almost reducible, and we might easily get trapped in a local maximum. For the Gibbs sampler this means that the individual conditionals are very narrow (low variance), and although it is guaranteed that in the limit one will eventually escape from the local maximum, for all practical purposes this isn't useful.

In general for MCMC to perform well, the components should be as "self-contained" as possible in the sense that a component should be considered a unit that can't be split (see for instance Robert, Casella [12]). So, although the overall score of a model is a function of single edges, one should not necessarily reduce the sampling problem to one in terms of single edges. Instead we should try to discern (not necessarily disjoint) *blocks* or *sets* of edges that form a dependency relationship. These dependent edge variables of a DAG require special treatment because they inherently belong together.

The dependency between edges is expressed through the current parent sets of the vertices. By adding or removing a parent from a vertex through the addition, reversal or removal of an edge, the score of the vertex changes, and this change in score depends on the parent set: The probability of adding or removing an arc from, say X^1 to X^2, depends directly on all edges from the parents of X^2 to X^2 because the score of X^2 is a function of all its parents. Similarly, the probability of adding or removing an arc in the other direction depends directly on the edges from the parents of X^1 to X^1 because the score of X^1 is a function of its parents.

The dependency goes even further: the edge between X^1 and X^2 *indirectly* depends on the current edges to the vertices in the parent set and the child set of X^1 and X^2, etc. When the number of intermediate steps (arcs) is large between two edges connected through a series of arcs, the two edges are less dependent than when the number of intermediate steps is small; edges far apart are only *indirectly* relevant to each other. In this way different levels of dependency can be discerned depending on the distance between edges.

One way of defining component i is to group together currently dependent edges in the neighbourhood of vertex X^i. The strength of this edge dependency depends on how far from vertex X^i the edges are collected. We suggest to disregard edges that lie beyond the vertices of the Markov blanket of X^i. However, this set of edges only defines the *current* dependency relationship but not necessarily *the right* one which is exactly what is subject to learning. Therefore we suggest to also include in component i all edge variables *between* the vertices of the Markov blanket of X^i. Edges in the component are now perturbed by drawing (new) edge values, and because the edges were "close" to each other prior to the perturbation, the new value assignments may substantially change the edge dependencies within the component. This way, after several iterations, the component settles on a very likely assignment of all the edges.

Notice that the components overlap: many edge variables are part of several Markov blankets. Edge variables that are shared by many Markov blankets are crucial for determining the probability of the states of several other edge variables, i.e. for several edges they strongly influence the probability of adding, removing or reversing an arc.

Another form of edge dependency which is unrelated to the form of dependency we investigated here, is the dependency between variables (X^i) which stems from the domain the variables belong to. The *vertices* in the Markov blanket form a relatively strong relationship, so proposing assignments ← or → to edge variables in the Markov blanket is from a domain perspective a good heuristic; edges distant to each other are less likely to be associated.

The idea is as follows: Either shrink or grow the Markov blanket of a vertex by adding or removing vertices, *or* change the internal relationships between the vertices of the Markov blanket. The probability of doing the latter should be higher than the probability of doing the former; we want to try several Markov blanket configurations.

4.1 MCMC by Relevant Edges

We use a "Metropolis-within-Gibbs" MCMC, where Gibbs sampling and Metropolis-Hastings sampling are combined in order to sample models from the invariant model posterior. We define the set of *relevant edges*, $\mathcal{E}_i$, of vertex X^i as $\mathcal{E}_i = \mathcal{E}'_i \cup \mathcal{E}''_i$, where $\mathcal{E}'_i$ is the set of all edge variables between vertices of the Markov blanket of X^i including X^i itself, i.e.:

$$\mathcal{E}'_i = \{E = (X^s, X^t) | X^s, X^t \in \mathrm{MB}(X^i) \cup \{X^i\}\},$$

and $\mathcal{E}''_i$ is the set of all edge variables between X^i and any other vertex of X, i.e.:

$$\mathcal{E}''_i = \{E = (X^i, X^t) | X^t \in X\} \setminus \mathcal{E}'_i.$$

We refer to $\mathcal{E}'_i$ as the set of *currently relevant edges*, because it consists of all edges between all the relevant vertices given the Markov blanket as it is now. Observe that $\mathcal{E}'_i$ actually captures the notion of a sub-graph. $\mathcal{E}''_i$ is referred to as the set of *potentially relevant edges* because it consists of edges between a vertex that is currently relevant and vertices that may become relevant. In figure 1 the two relevance sets are illustrated.

Using block Gibbs sampling we now draw an instantiation of the edges in the set of relevant edges per vertex:

$$\varepsilon^t_1 \sim \Pr(\mathcal{E}_1 | \bar{\varepsilon}_1, \mathcal{D}) \quad \cdots \quad \varepsilon^t_p \sim \Pr(\mathcal{E}_p | \bar{\varepsilon}_p, \mathcal{D}) \quad \varepsilon^{t+1}_1 \sim \Pr(\mathcal{E}_1 | \bar{\varepsilon}_1, \mathcal{D}) \quad \cdots$$

where $\bar{\varepsilon}_j$ is the *current* configuration of the edges in the complement of the set $\mathcal{E}_j$.

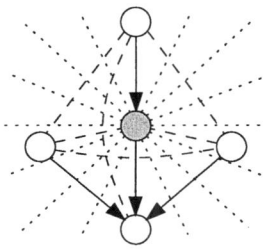

Fig. 1. The set of relevant edges of the shaded vertex. The solid lines (arcs) connect the *vertices* belonging to the Markov blanket. Dashed *and* solid lines indicate the set of currently relevant edges, and dotted lines indicate the set of potentially relevant edges.

The Gibbs sampler visits every vertex, thus every edge will eventually be part of a *potentially relevant edge set*; we can't guarantee that it will be part a *currently relevant edge set* however, but as long as all edges *are* considered, we have that $(e_1, \ldots, e_{\frac{p \cdot (p-1)}{2}}) \sim \Pr(E_1, \ldots, E_{\frac{p \cdot (p-1)}{2}} | \mathcal{D})$ for $t \to \infty$.

Each draw from the above Gibbs sampler is performed by a Metropolis-Hastings sampler. The proposal distribution is a mixture distribution, where one component, $f(\cdot)$, deals with the edges in the currently relevant edge set, and the other component, $g(\cdot)$, deals with the edges in the potentially relevant edge set, that is:

$$q(\mathcal{E}^{t+1}|\mathcal{E}^t) = w \cdot f(\mathcal{E}^{t+1}|\mathcal{E}'^t) + (1-w) \cdot g(\mathcal{E}^{t+1}|\mathcal{E}''^t),$$

where $0 < w < 1$ determines the mixture weights. When $f(\cdot)$ is applied, values for the edges in the currently relevant set are drawn, i.e. MCMC is run in order to obtain the posterior distribution of those edges. The cardinality of the set of relevant edges is kept fixed once the Metropolis-Hasting sampler is applied—we merely assign (new) values to the edge variables. Hence, the set of relevant edges is determined before entering the Metropolis-Hastings sampler, and does not change until control is given back to the overall Gibbs sampler. For $g(\cdot)$ the same holds, but here assignments are considered to the variables in the potentially relevant set. The distribution $f(\cdot)$ produces uniform proposals by selecting an edge $E_r \in \mathcal{E}'$ with probability $1/|\mathcal{E}'|$. Depending on the current value of e_r, a state change is proposed to one of the (at most) two alternatives with probability 0.5. E.g. if $E_r^t = \nleftrightarrow$ then either $E_r^{t+1} = \to$ or $E_r^{t+1} = \leftarrow$ is proposed. For the distribution $g(\cdot)$ the same holds, but here we have $E_r \in \mathcal{E}''$ with probability $1/|\mathcal{E}''|$. Notice that edges not in either of these two sets remain unchanged.

For Metropolis-Hastings, the acceptance probability depends on the proposal fraction $q(\mathcal{E}^t|\mathcal{E}^{t+1})/q(\mathcal{E}^{t+1}|\mathcal{E}^t)$, which is required to ensure detailed balance and hence invariance. For both the mixture in the numerator and in the denominator, the weights are the same, the conditional distributions select edges with equal probability and there is always the same number of alternative edge assignments, i.e. the distributions are uniform, hence, the ratio cancels out.

The proposal distribution of the sampler will with a non-zero probability propose a state change to any edge in the relevant edge set, which guarantees irreducibility. With a non-zero probability it will remain in the current state for any edge implying aperiodicity. We may thus conclude that the Metropolis-Hastings sampler will in the limit return realisations from the invariant distribution $\Pr(\mathcal{E}_l|\bar{\mathcal{E}}_l, \mathcal{D})$, i.e. realisations for the edges in $\mathcal{E}_l$ given all other edges.

By introducing the *currently relevant edge* set, which is dealt with by $f(\cdot)$, we can through the weight w vary how much "attention to pay" to the configuration of the edge variables in the Markov blanket of the current vertex. Note that because edges in the currently relevant edge set are proposed uniformly, edge variables that are part of several Markov blankets are sampled relatively often. This entails that edges in dense regions of the graph are sampled more often than edges in less dense regions. Edge variables in dense regions are more dependent on each other, hence we sample more in that region because it is easy to get "stuck" there since the edges constrain each other strongly. Sampling more often in dense regions corresponds to putting more effort into avoiding getting trapped in sub-optimal assignments to the edge variables.

4.2 Covered Arcs

In recent years so-called *inclusion-driven* learning approaches [3] for model selection have emerged, in which the essential graph space is traversed by respecting the *inclusion order*. Unfortunately, it is inefficient to score essential graphs directly while traversing the search space. As an alternative, one can *simulate* the essential graph space by repeatedly reversing arcs that have the same parent set—the covered edges. Although our MCMC method is not really an inclusion driven approach, we may still profit from the essential graph simulation idea. By doing covered arc reversal often enough all DAGs representing the same set of independences are reached. All these DAGs have the same marginal likelihood score, yet the individual score of the vertices (recall that the marginal likelihood score decomposes) is different for equivalent DAGs. By reversing covered arcs we may increase the probability of assigning alternative values to dependent edge variables that prior to reversal perhaps obstruct each other. We employ the Repeated Covered Arc Reversal (RCAR) algorithm [3] to perform the covered arc reversals. RCAR takes an argument, that determines the maximum number of times covered arcs will be reversed. A value between 4 and 10 should suffice, and in particular 10 seems to work well.

5 Implementation Issues

In figure 2 the pseudocode of the Markov blanket MCMC (MB-MCMC) algorithm is given. Line 2 determines the component to pay attention to, here a systematic sweep is shown, but a random choice is also possible. Line 3 calls the algorithm for reversing covered arcs. Lines 4–5 determines the edges to consider, and in lines 7–9 the edges are drawn from the sets of relevant edges. The proposals are accepted or rejected in line 11–12. In line 13 the configuration of all edges is recorded, i.e. here the actual models from the posterior are saved. One may decide to sub-sample the Markov chain of models by only recording the draws once in a while.

Algorithm MB-MCMC(k, w)

```
1   for r ← 0 to ∞
2       i ← (r mod p) + 1
3       RCAR(10)
4       E'_i ← {E = (X^s, X^l) | X^s, X^l ∈ MB(X^i) ∪ {X^i}}
5       E''_i ← {E = (X^i, X^l) | X^l ∈ X} \ E'_i
6       for t ← 0 to k
7           draw u ~ U[0, 1]
8           if u < w and E'_i ≠ ∅ then draw ε_i^{t+1} ~ f(E_i | ε_i'^t)
9           else draw ε_i^{t+1} ~ g(E_i | ε_i''^t)
10          δ ← Pr(D | ε_i^{t+1}) / Pr(D | ε_i^t)
11          draw u ~ U[0, 1]
12          if u ≥ min{1, δ} then ε_i^{t+1} ← ε_i^t
13      RECORD(e_1, ..., e_{p·(p-1)/2})
```

Fig. 2. Pseudocode of the Markov blanket MCMC

The algorithm takes two arguments: k determines the number of times the Metropolis-Hastings sampler is run, and w determines the probability of changing the internal configuration of a component vs. adding or removing new vertices. Parameter k need not be large for the overall invariant model distribution to be reached, i.e. the Metropolis-Hastings sampler need not converge at every call. In fact we have found it to be beneficial for the convergence rate to assign k a small value; too large a value may lead to premature convergence. In our experiments we have set $k = 5$, and $w = 0.95$.

When every vertex is assigned a cache that keeps the sufficient statistics indexed by the parent set, we may drastically improve the speed of MCMC by querying the cache before querying the data. We have implemented the Markov blanket sampler in C++ using STL, and for the experiments in the next section we were able to reach what we believe are the invariant distributions in less than 10 minutes on a 2 GHz machine.

6 Evaluation

We considered two BNs for the experiments: the ALARM BN with 37 vertices and 46 arcs [1], and the Insurance BN with 27 vertices and 52 arcs [2]. We used the BDeu metric for the counts α with an equivalent sample size of 1. All experiments were run for 1,000,000 iterations. As convergence diagnostic we monitored the number of edges as suggested in for instance [6]. We compared the Markov blanket MCMC with eMC^3, a single edge MCMC sampler that also employs the RCAR algorithm.

In figure 3a the results of the ALARM network are illustrated. With 1000 samples, we see that two independent runs of the MB-MCMC both converge towards models with about 50–53 edges. There is no significant difference in the convergence behaviour. For eMC^3 two runs produce different behaviour and result in models with 68–77 edges. For 5000 records similar observations hold, but overall the number of edges is lower: 45–51 for MB-MCMC and 57–70 for eMC^3. We notice that eMC^3 seems sensitive to the starting point of the chain. To show this more clearly, we ran both samplers starting from the empty graph, and from the actual ALARM graph for 7000 samples. For the 7000 records we would expect that the number of edges on average should converge to 46, i.e. there is enough data to support the data generating model. For MB-MCMC, both chains converge towards models with 44–50 edges. The most frequently sampled model is similar to the ALARM network ± 2 arcs. For eMC^3 there is a big difference. The chain started from the actual network stays at around 50–55 edges, but the chain started from the empty graph gets stuck at 63–70. The most frequently sampled model is in both situations less similar to the actual ALARM network than in the MB-MCMC case (excess of ± 10 and ± 25 arcs).

Next we consider results of the Insurance network in figure 3b. We would like to note that the association between several parent-child variables in the Insurance network is rather weak and that even for large data sets these associations will be deemed absent by the marginal likelihood score. For 500 records the MB-MCMC converges to an invariant distribution where models are sampled with 36–40 edges. The two runs meet at around 150,000 iterations. For eMC^3 however, the two chains don't quite agree in the number of edges: somewhere between 37–46. We also ran both samplers beginning from the empty and the actual Insurance graph. For MB-MCMC both starting points produce models with 45–47 edges. Also here we see that eMC^3 is sensitive to

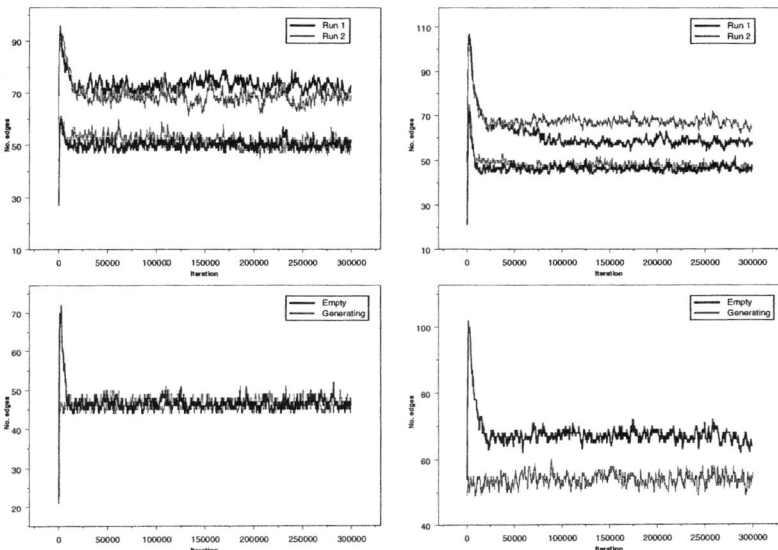

Fig. 3a. ALARM network. *Top:* Convergence behaviour given 1000 (*left*) and 5000 (*right*) records for two independent runs. The lower lines are from the Markov blanket MCMC, and the upper lines from eMC^3. *Bottom:* Convergence behaviour of the Markov blanket MCMC (*left*) and eMC^3 (*right*) given 7000 records starting from the empty and the data generating model.

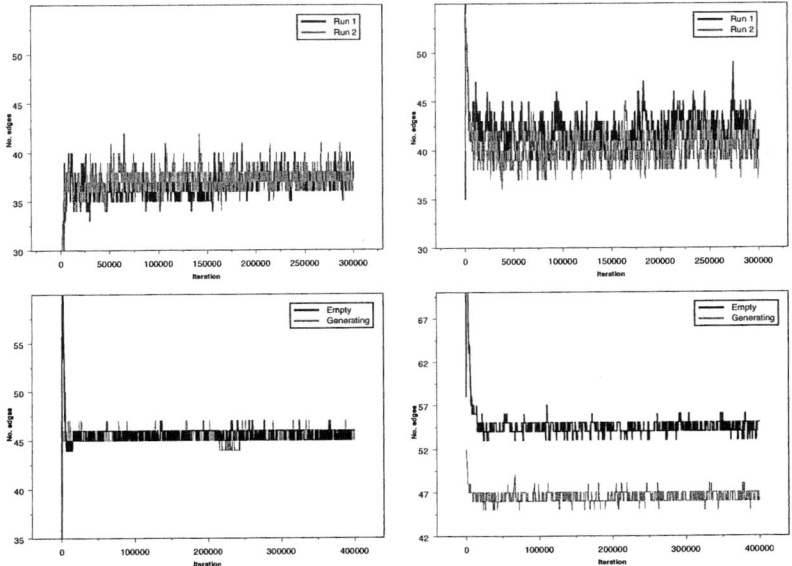

Fig. 3b. Insurance network. *Top:* Convergence behaviour given 500 records for two independent runs (common y-axis) of the Markov blanket MCMC (*left*) and eMC^3 (*right*). *Bottom:* Convergence behaviour of the Markov blanket MCMC (*left*) and eMC^3 (*right*) given 10,000 records starting from the empty and the data generating model.

the initial model. Starting from the data generating model, the sampler converges to an invariant distribution where models with 45–47 edges are sampled. Starting from the empty graph, models with 54–56 edges are sampled. We see that even with 10,000 records, there is not enough information in the data sample to support the 52 arcs in the data generating Insurance network. Also notice that the variability of the plots for 500 records is larger than for 10,000 records. This is to be expected because there is no pronounced "best" model with merely 500 records.

7 Conclusion

We have proposed a new MCMC method for learning Bayesian network models. By defining components of MCMC in terms of all edges in the Markov blankets of the vertices, we group relatively strongly dependent edges together. This effectively means that edges in dense regions of a model are sampled more often than in less dense regions.

Our experiments on the ALARM and the Insurance networks show that this Markov blanket decomposition performs better than the naive MCMC approach, where all edges are sampled equally often. The chain mixes faster, and it is less sensitive to the departure model. This indicates that MB-MCMC is less prone to getting stuck in local maxima.

References

1. I.A. Beinlich, H.J. Suermondt, R.M. Chavez, and G.F. Cooper. The ALARM monitoring system: A case study with two probabilistic inference techniques for belief networks. In *Proc. of the European Conf. on AI in Medicine*, 1989.
2. J. Binder, D. Koller, S. J. Russell, and K. Kanazawa. Adaptive probabilistic networks with hidden variables. *Machine Learning*, 29:213–244, 1997.
3. R. Castelo and T. Kocka. On inclusion-driven learning of Bayesian networks. *J. of Machine Learning Research*, 4:527–574, 2003.
4. N. Friedman and D. Koller. Being Bayesian about network structure. A Bayesian approach to structure discovery in Bayesian networks. *Machine Learning*, 50(1–2):95–125, 2003.
5. P. Giudici and R. Castelo. Improving Markov chain Monte Carlo model search for data mining. *Machine Learning*, 50(1):127–158, 2003.
6. P. Giudici and P. Green. Decomposable graphical gaussian model determination. *Biometrika*, 86(4):785–801, 1999.
7. P. Green. Reversible jump Markov chain Monte Carlo computation and Bayesian model determination. *Biometrika*, 82:711–732, 1998.
8. D. Heckerman, D. Geiger, and D.M. Chickering. Learning Bayesian networks: The combination of knowledge and statistical data. *Machine Learning*, 20:197–243, 1995.
9. T. Kocka and R. Castelo. Improved learning of Bayesian networks. In D. Koller and J. Breese, editors, *Proc. of the Conf. on Uncertainty in AI*, pages 269–276, 2001.
10. D. Madigan and A. Raftery. Model selection and accounting for model uncertainty in graphical models using Occam's window. *J. of the Am. Stat. Assoc.*, 89:1535–1546, 1994.
11. D. Madigan and J. York. Bayesian graphical models for discrete data. *Intl. Statistical Review*, 63:215–232, 1995.
12. C. P. Robert and G. Casella. *Monte Carlo statistical methods*. Springer-Verlag, 3rd edition, 2002.
13. D. J. Spiegelhalter and S. L. Lauritzen. Sequential updating of conditional probabilities on directed graphical structures. *Networks*, 20:579–605, 1990.

On Discriminative Joint Density Modeling

Jarkko Salojärvi[1], Kai Puolamäki[1], and Samuel Kaski[1,2]

[1] Laboratory of Computer and Information Science,
Helsinki University of Technology,
P.O. Box 5400, FI-02015 HUT, Finland
{forename.surname}@hut.fi
[2] Department of Computer Science, University of Helsinki,
P.O. Box 68, FI-00014 University of Helsinki, Finland

Abstract. We study discriminative joint density models, that is, generative models for the joint density $p(c, \mathbf{x})$ learned by maximizing a discriminative cost function, the conditional likelihood. We use the framework to derive generative models for generalized linear models, including logistic regression, linear discriminant analysis, and discriminative mixture of unigrams. The benefits of deriving the discriminative models from joint density models are that it is easy to extend the models and interpret the results, and missing data can be treated using justified standard methods.

1 Introduction

We study a classification task where a learning set, consisting of paired data $(\mathbf{x}, c)$, is given. The c is the value of a categorical variable, associated with observations $\mathbf{x}$. The observations may be collected from several different kinds of data sources; some may be real-valued measurements from sensors, whereas some may be probabilistic predictions. What all the values $\mathbf{x}$ have in common is that the c are assumed to depend on them. The task is to predict c for a test set where only the values of $\mathbf{x}$ are known. The c are often referred to as the (values of the) dependent variable, and the $\mathbf{x}$ the values of the independent variable or covariate.

There are two traditional modeling approaches for predicting c, discriminative and generative. Discriminative models optimize the conditional probability $p(c|\mathbf{x})$ (or some other discriminative criterion) directly. The models are good classifiers, since they do not waste resources on modeling those properties of the data that do not affect the value of c, that is, the distribution of $\mathbf{x}$. A classic example of a discriminative model is logistic regression, which is a special case of Generalized Linear Models (GLMs) [1]. In GLMs, functions of linear combinations $\beta^T \mathbf{x}$ of the independent variables are sought in order to predict $p(c|\mathbf{x}, \beta)$.

The other traditional approach is generative modeling of the joint distribution $p(c, \mathbf{x})$. The benefit of generative models is that compared to purely discriminative models, they add prior knowledge of the distribution of $\mathbf{x}$ into the task. This facilitates for example inferring missing values, since the model is assumed to generate also the covariates **x**. The models are often additionally simpler to construct, and their parameters offer simple explanations in terms of expected sufficient statistics. A classic example of generative models is the linear discriminant analysis (LDA).

Several publications have been devoted to comparing the discriminative and generative approaches [2,3,4]. A common model pair in the comparisons has been Linear Discriminant Analysis (or Naive Bayes) vs. logistic regression. With infinite amount of data, generative modeling by maximizing the joint likelihood produces optimal parameters for classification, assuming that the true data distribution is contained in the model family. However, with real-world data this is unlikely [5], and better predictions for c can be achieved by maximizing the conditional likelihood.[1] In practice, with large amounts of data, generative models are inferior to discriminative models, since the assumed model is always incorrect, but with small sample sizes generative models may show better performance [4].

The two modeling approaches are related. A discriminative classifier can be obtained by simply changing the objective function from the joint likelihood $p(c, \mathbf{x}|\theta)$ to the conditional likelihood $p(c|\mathbf{x}, \theta)$ by use of the Bayes formula, and then optimizing the model parameters. The method has been put to extensive use in speech processing applications, where good results have been obtained using discriminative hidden Markov models [6]. What is often neglected is that even after converting a joint density model to a discriminative model, the model still constructs a density estimate for **x**. In this paper we show that this information may be useful, even if the model is inaccurate, for example in predicting missing values of **x**. We also show that the discriminative joint density models are very close to so-called generalized linear models with random effects. The models operate in the same parameter space, but the generative formulation restricts the space.

Discriminative joint density models allow straightforward generalization to combining different types of measured data: continuous, categorical, or probabilities. In this paper we introduce, as an example, a discriminative joint density model for multinomial data, a discriminative version of the mixture of unigrams model.

---

[1] Joint density modeling minimizes the Kullback-Leibler divergence between the model $p(c, \mathbf{x}|\theta)$ and the "true" model $p(c, x)$,

$$\mathcal{D}_{KL} = \sum p(c, \mathbf{x}) \log \frac{p(c, \mathbf{x})}{p(c, \mathbf{x}|\theta)} = \sum p(c, x) \log \frac{p(c|x)}{p(c|x, \theta)} + \sum p(x) \log \frac{p(x)}{p(x|\theta)} ,$$

where the first term is the conditional likelihood. If the true model is included in the model family, the latter term can be made to vanish, but otherwise, in the case of an incorrect model, it is always nonzero for joint likelihood models. When the true model is not within the model family, the joint likelihood model is thus asymptotically always worse than the conditional likelihood model.

2 Background

2.1 Exponential Family Distributions

An exponential family distribution can always be written in the canonical form

$$p(\mathbf{x}|\theta) = \exp\left(T(\mathbf{x})^T \theta - \log Z(\theta) - \log Y(\mathbf{x})\right) \quad , \tag{1}$$

where the $T(\mathbf{x})$ are the (observed) sufficient statistics, θ the natural parameters, and $\log Z(\theta)$ is the convex normalization term (partition function).

The key definition [7] needed here is the dual parameter μ, [2]

$$\mu = \langle T(\mathbf{x}) \rangle_{p(\mathbf{x}|\theta)} = \frac{\partial \log Z}{\partial \theta} \quad . \tag{2}$$

The natural parameters do not in general (with Gaussian being the exception) lie within the same space as the sufficient statistics [8], which complicates their use and interpretation. This is why exponential distributions are usually expressed in terms of dual parameters μ which lie in the same space as the mean of the sufficient statistics (and sometimes they are referred to as expected sufficient statistics, for obvious reasons). The mapping Eq. (2) constrains the allowed values of dual parameters to a plane tangential to the partition function $\log Z(\theta)$. This means that it is always possible to find a θ^* corresponding to the sufficient statistics $T(x)$ (see [7, 8] for more details).

2.2 Generalized Linear Models

In GLMs [1] the dependent variable c is modelled with an exponential family distribution of the form

$$p(c|\mathbf{x}, \mathbf{B}) = \exp\{T(c)^T(\mathbf{B}^T\mathbf{x}) - F(\mathbf{B}^T\mathbf{x}) - \log Y(c)\} \quad . \tag{3}$$

The GLM thus assumes a mapping $\theta = \mathbf{B}^T\mathbf{x}$ to natural parameters. The function $\mu = f(\theta) = \frac{\partial}{\partial \theta} F(\theta)$ then provides a mapping to dual parameters. Here $f(\theta)$ is the inverse of a *link function*. The most often used is the *canonical link* function which is obtained if we select the partition function $f(\theta) = \frac{\partial}{\partial \theta} \log Z(\theta)$.

Generalized Linear Model with Random Effects. It is realistic to assume that there is uncertainty associated with the measured values of $\mathbf{x}$, that is, they contain noise. In statistical modeling the most common assumption is additive noise, $\theta = \mathbf{B}^T\mathbf{x} + \mathbf{Z}\mathbf{u}$, where $\mathbf{Z}$ is assumed to be known and $\mathbf{u}$ is an exponential family noise term [9]. The approach thus makes a probabilistic mapping to natural parameters. Here $\mathbf{B}^T\mathbf{x}$ provides the sufficient statistics for θ. Notice that the approach is still fully discriminative; the distribution of $\mathbf{x}$ is not modelled.

In GLMs with random effects the log-likelihood $\log p(c|\mathbf{x}, \mathbf{B}, \mathbf{u}) + \log p(\mathbf{u}|\mathbf{A})$ is then optimized with respect to β and $\mathbf{u}$ [9], with known values of the noise variance $\mathbf{A}$ (it is determined by $\mathbf{Z}$). See [1, 9] for more detailed descriptions.

---

[2] For compactness of our formulas, we will denote $\langle T(x) \rangle_{p(x|\theta)} = E_{p(x|\theta)}\{T(x)\}$.

3 Discriminative Joint Density Modeling

In a *discriminative joint density model* the set of variables Y is divided into two classes, $Y = C \cup X$, where the C are the dependent variables over which we want to discriminate and the X are the independent variables. The log-likelihood of the discriminative model is $\log p(C|X, \theta) = \log p(Y|\theta) - \log p(X|\theta)$. Optimization of discriminative generative mixture models is usually done using gradient ascent-based methods (as in this paper). Various EM-type algorithms have also been proposed (see [10] and references therein).

We concentrate here on mixture models, where the identity of the mixture component is a hidden variable. The theory is more general, however. Each value of the hidden variable is associated with a deterministic mapping to a value of the dependent variable c. We will next illustrate the differences between discriminative and ordinary joint density modeling with Linear Discriminant Analysis (LDA).

3.1 Linear Discriminant Analysis

As usually expressed in terms of dual parameters, the a posteriori decision rule of LDA is [11]

$$p(C = j|\mathbf{x}_i) = \frac{\pi(j)p(\mathbf{x}_i|\bar{\mathbf{m}}_j, \mathbf{S})}{\sum_{j'} \pi(j')p(\mathbf{x}_i|\bar{\mathbf{m}}_{j'}, \mathbf{S})} \quad , \tag{4}$$

where $\pi(j)$ is the prior class probability, and $\bar{\mathbf{m}}_j$ denotes the mean of the distribution of $\mathbf{x}$ for the class j. Index i runs over data items, $i \in [1 \ldots N]$. LDA assumes that data from each class is generated from a Gaussian distribution, all of the classes having the same within-class covariance S.

The decision rule (4) is a direct formulation of a discriminative joint density model cost function, with each class being modeled by one Gaussian. Usually, the above equation is not optimized directly. Instead, an asymptotically optimal classifier that models the joint likelihood is obtained by estimating μ_i by class centroids, and $\mathbf{S}$ by the within-class covariance. The joint likelihood solution and the discriminative solution obtained by optimizing Eq. (4) are asymptotically the same if the "true" data distribution follows the assumptions of the LDA model. Otherwise the solutions differ (see Fig.1 for a toy example).

3.2 Log-Linear Regression

As illustrated in the toy example of Figure 1, the best model for classification optimizes $p(c|\mathbf{x}, \beta)$, which in the case of LDA is the a posteriori decision rule. A classic example of a case where $p(c|\mathbf{x}, \beta)$ is optimized directly is the log-linear regression.

In log-linear regression the probability of a class j for a data item $\mathbf{x}_i$ is computed by

$$p(C = j|\mathbf{x}_i, \mathbf{B}) \equiv p_{ji} = \frac{e^{\beta_j^T \mathbf{x}_i}}{\sum_{j'} e^{\beta_{j'}^T \mathbf{x}_i}} \quad , \tag{5}$$

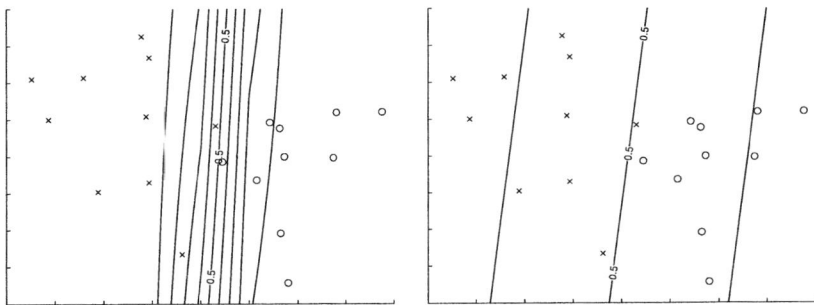

Fig. 1. Difference of class distributions of discriminative and joint density models. Discriminative modeling is optimal for predicting c (Left). In a joint likelihood model the class difference is optimized only implicitly, resulting in softer class borders (Right). In this toy example both models have the same covariance matrix, the within-class covariance, and only the cluster centroids are optimized. The contour plot shows the probability $p(c|x)$ in 0.1 intervals. "X" and "O" denote samples from different classes.

where $\mathbf{x}$ is the vector of independent variables and β_j the vector of coefficients for a given class j. The β_j is constructed to incorporate also a constant term β_{j0} by having one component of $\mathbf{x}$ to be always 1. The β_j form the columns of matrix $\mathbf{B}$. Each observation i can be considered as a draw from a multinomial, and hence the log-likelihood will be

$$\mathcal{L} = \sum_{i=1}^{N} \sum_{j=1}^{C} \delta(c_i, j) \log p_{ji} \quad , \tag{6}$$

where $\delta(c_i, j)$ picks the class index j corresponding to the class of sample i.

We will next show the relationship between LDA and loglinear models. By inserting Eq. (5) into the log-likelihood (6), we get

$$\mathcal{L} = \sum_{i=1}^{N} \sum_{j=1}^{C} \delta(c_i, j) \beta_j^T \mathbf{x}_i - \log \left(\sum_{j'} e^{\beta_{j'}^T \mathbf{x}_i} \right) \quad . \tag{7}$$

We may take the constant term β_{j0} out from $\beta_j = [\beta_{j0} \ \beta_{j,1...d}]$,

$$\mathcal{L} = \sum_{i=1}^{N} \sum_{j=1}^{C} \delta(c_i, j) \left(\beta_{j0} + \beta_{j,1...d}^T \mathbf{x}_i \right) - \log \left(\sum_{j'} e^{\beta_{j'0}} e^{\beta_{j',1...d}^T \mathbf{x}_i} \right) \quad . \tag{8}$$

At this point we insert prior information into the model family: we require that the β_{j0} and $\mathbf{x}$ come from exponential family distributions. We first require that β_{j0} comes from a multinomial distribution by reparameterizing $\beta_{j0} \to \log \pi(j) - \log \sum_j \pi(j)$ (here we in effect add a constraint that $\sum_j \pi(j) = 1$). The term $\beta_{j,1...d}^T \mathbf{x}_i$ can be interpreted to be $\log p(\mathbf{x}_i | \beta_{j,1...d})$ without the normalization term. We can restrict $\mathbf{x}$ to an exponential family model by reparameterizing $\beta_{j,1...d}^T \mathbf{x}_i \rightarrow \beta_{j,1...d}^T \mathbf{x}_i - \log Z(\beta_{j,1...d}) - \log Y(\mathbf{x}_i)$. The $\beta_{j,1...d}$ then form the natural parameters and $\mathbf{x}_i$ the sufficient statistics of the model.

Using Equation (1), we get

$$\mathcal{L} = \sum_{i=1}^{N} \sum_{j=1}^{C} \delta(c_i,j) \left(\log \pi(j) + \log p(\mathbf{x}_i|\beta_{j,1...d})\right) - \log \left(\sum_{j'} \pi(j') p(\mathbf{x}_i|\beta_{j',1...d}) \right)$$

$$= \sum_{i=1}^{N} \log \frac{\prod_j \left(\pi(j) p(\mathbf{x}_i|\beta_{j,1...d})\right)^{\delta(c_i,j)}}{\sum_{j'} \pi(j') p(\mathbf{x}_i|\beta_{j',1...d})} .$$

This is the same as LDA in Eq. (4) if the $p(\mathbf{x}_i|\beta_{j,1...d})$ are Gaussian.

Notice that the constraint that $\mathbf{x}$ can be modelled by an exponential family distribution restricts the parameter space of $\beta_{j,1...d}$ through $\log Z(\beta_{j,1...d})$.[3] As an example, for multinomial distributions this effectively removes one degree of freedom, since $\sum \mu = 1$. Note additionally that the discriminative joint density model prefers values of β which are close to the θ^* corresponding to the mean of the observed sufficient statistics of $\mathbf{x}$.

4 General Description of Discriminative Joint Density Models

We will now formalize a general description of the discriminative joint density model. We define a model that generates the observed (categorical) values c and the associated measurements $\mathbf{x}$. Each measurement $\mathbf{x}_i$ consists of S different kinds of data sources indexed by s, each modelled with an appropriate exponential family distribution. Our goal is to optimize $P(c|X,\theta)$, where $\theta = \{\pi, \beta\}$ denote all parameters of the model. We assume that X can be modelled using an exponential family distribution, given a mixture component l. The information $\mathbf{x}$ carries about c is therefore visible also in the sufficient statistics of X, and thus the parameters of the generative distributions. The model can be optimized for discriminating the classes by maximizing the conditional likelihood

$$p(c_i|\mathbf{x}_i,\theta) = \frac{\prod_k \left(\sum_{l \in \mathcal{C}_k} p(l,\mathbf{x}_i|\beta_l,\pi(l))\right)^{\delta(c_i,k)}}{\sum_{l'} p(l',\mathbf{x}_i|\beta_{l'},\pi(l'))} , \qquad (9)$$

where l indexes the mixture component, and $\mathcal{C}_k$ is the set of components associated with class k. $\pi(l)$ is the probability that the data was generated from mixture component l, and β_l are the parameters of the component l. See also Figure 2.

The observed variables of our model are the classification C and the associated independent variables X_s. The parameters of the model are given by

---

[3] Logistic regression, on the other hand, assumes that the β are independent with values allowed to vary over the whole real-valued space.

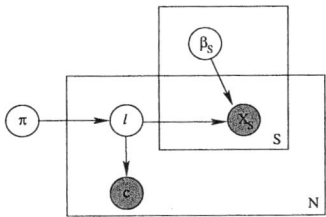

Fig. 2. A graphical model of the discriminative joint density model. Here l is the index of the distribution that is used to predict class c. The grey circles indicate observed values. S is the number of data sources, and N the number of data items.

$\theta = \{\pi, \beta_{1...S}^{1...L}\}$. Notice that the generative models are the same for the discriminative and joint likelihood models. The difference is in the optimization.

A benefit of the discriminative joint density formulation, compared to alternative discriminative models, is that the model (and thus logistic regression) is easy to extend into cases where $\mathbf{x}$ is better modelled by a mixture of exponential family models. The generative formulation also makes it simple to model several independent variables and different forms of data, such as multinomial or probability distributions [12]. Besides giving class predictions, the parameters of the discriminative joint density models are directly interpretable in terms of sufficient statistics for $\mathbf{x}$.

4.1 Generative Model for Generalized Linear Models

The generative formulation can be easily extended to the GLM model class, of which the log-linear model (see Section 3.2) is a special case. For simplicity, we will assume that exactly one mixture component j corresponds to each class label c. For convenience we will drop out the index i from $\mathbf{x}_i, c_i$ in the following.

We begin with the objective function of discriminative joint density models, Eq. (9), which can also be written as

$$p(c|\mathbf{x}, \beta) = \exp\{\delta(c,j) \log p(\mathbf{x}, j|\beta_j, \pi(j)) - \log \sum_{j'} p(\mathbf{x}, j'|\beta_{j'}, \pi(j'))\} \ . \quad (10)$$

By comparing this form with (1), we notice that the form corresponds to a multinomial distribution with natural parameters $\theta_j = \log p(\mathbf{x}, j|\beta_j, \pi(j))$, sufficient statistics $T(c) = \delta(c, j)$, and with $\log Z(\theta) = \log \sum_{j'} p(\mathbf{x}, j'|\beta_{j'}, \pi(j'))\} = \log Z(p(\mathbf{x}|\beta, \pi))$. Since we pick one class for each $\mathbf{x}$, the $\log Y(c)$ is zero.

By writing θ in an exponential family notation, we get

$$\theta_j = \log p(\mathbf{x}, j|\beta_j, \pi(j)) = T(\mathbf{x})^T \beta_j - \log Z(\beta_j) - \log Y(\mathbf{x}) + \log \pi(j) - \log Z(\pi) \ . \quad (11)$$

The $\log Y(\mathbf{x})$-term can be left out, since it is the same for all components j. By inserting Eq. (11) into Eq. (10), we get

$$p(c|\mathbf{x}, \beta) = \exp\{T(c)^T \left(\mathbf{B}^T T(\mathbf{x}) - \log Z(\beta) + \log \pi - \log Z(\pi)\right) - \log Z(p(\mathbf{x}|\beta))\}. \quad (12)$$

The π and $\log Z(\pi)$ can be incorporated into the matrix $\mathbf{B}$, similarly to the log-linear case. The vector $\log Z(\beta)$ consists of components $\log Z(\beta_j)$.

Now, when the generative model and the GLM have been expressed in the exponential family notation in Equations (12) and (3), respectively, we will point out their difference. In case of multinomials considered in this paper, the $Y(c)$ in (3) is zero because of the form of the sufficient statistics. Of the remaining terms within the exponent, the last one in both models is the normalization term. The essential difference then is the term $\log Z(\beta_j)$ in (12). In case of multinomial distribution it removes one degree of freedom in the model. This can be shown by adding a displacement λ to each component of β_j, which does not change the predictions of the model (12). GLM, in contrast, does not have such a restriction.

The generative model in effect introduces prior information into GLMs: assuming that the generative model for $\mathbf{x}$ is (nearly) correct, we can restrict the (effective) parameter space of β. The restriction provides an additional benefit, since by mapping the parameters to their dual parameters (through $\log Z(\beta)$), the values of β can be interpreted in terms of sufficient statistics of $\mathbf{x}$.

The model is very similar to GLMs (with random effects), since both models define a probabilistic mapping to θ. However, in discriminative joint density models the uncertainty is defined for values of $\mathbf{x}$, whereas in GLMs with random effects the uncertainty is defined for θ. The discriminative joint density models, however, have an additional benefit: By expressing the noise terms for individual $\mathbf{x}$, we form a generative distribution for $\mathbf{x}$.

4.2 Connection to Maximum Entropy Discrimination

In maximum entropy discrimination (MED) [13], *discriminative functions* of the form $\mathcal{L}(X|\theta) = \log \frac{p_+}{p_-}$ are optimized. The p_+, p_- denote probabilistic models for the class $+$ and $-$, respectively. In contrast, the discriminative joint density modeling cost function can be expressed by

$$\frac{p_+}{p_+ + p_-} = \frac{1}{1 + \exp\{-\log \frac{p_+}{p_-}\}} = \frac{1}{1 + \exp\{-\mathcal{L}(X|\theta)\}} \quad . \quad (13)$$

The cost function thus is a monotonic (sigmoid) transformation of the MED objective function.

The main advantage of the discriminative joint density modeling cost function over MED is that the output is the probability of the corresponding class, thus expressing directly the level of uncertainty in class prediction. Generalization to the case of several classes is also simpler and more straightforward to implement.

4.3 Missing Data

It is of interest to know whether the estimate $p(c|\mathbf{x}, \theta)$ can benefit from data where the $\mathbf{x}$ is incomplete for some data items. Let us denote vectors with missing values by $\mathbf{x} = [\mathbf{y}\ \mathbf{z}]$, where $\mathbf{y}$ is the missing data and $\mathbf{z}$ the known components.

The conditional log-likelihood with missing data can then be written as

$$\mathcal{L} = \sum_{i \in D_{full}} \log p(c_i|\mathbf{x}_i, \theta) + \sum_{i \in D_{miss}} \int p(\mathbf{y}|c_i, \mathbf{z}_i, \theta) \log p(c_i|\mathbf{y}, \mathbf{z}_i, \theta) d\mathbf{y} \quad , \quad (14)$$

where we denote by D_{full} the data set with all entries known, and by D_{miss} the data with missing entries. In order to infer the value for missing data, we need to make a distributional assumption for $\mathbf{y}$. A feasible one is $p(\mathbf{y}|c_i, \theta)$ used in the generative model. If the data really has been generated from the model family this is the correct assumption, but in the real world the performance depends on how close the model family is to the "true" generative distribution.

Practical Implementation. There are several possibilities to optimize Eq. (14). We now present a simple approach that makes computations tractable by constructing a lower bound for $\mathcal{L}_{miss}$, the cost function for the missing part of the data. For discriminative joint density models it can be written as

$$\mathcal{L}_{miss} = \sum_{i \in D_{miss}} \langle \log p(c_i, \mathbf{y}, \mathbf{z}_i|\theta) \rangle_{p(\mathbf{y}|c_i, \mathbf{z}_i, \theta)} - \langle \log \sum_j p(j, \mathbf{y}, \mathbf{z}_i|\theta) \rangle_{p(\mathbf{y}|c_i, \mathbf{z}_i, \theta)} \cdot \quad (15)$$

The latter term can be upper bounded (and thus we obtain a lower bound for $\mathcal{L}_{miss}$) by applying Jensen inequality

$$\langle \log \sum_j p(j, \mathbf{y}, \mathbf{z}_i|\theta) \rangle_{p(\mathbf{y}|c_i, \mathbf{z}_i, \theta)} \leq \log \sum_j \langle p(j, \mathbf{y}, \mathbf{z}_i|\theta) \rangle_{p(\mathbf{y}|c_i, \mathbf{z}_i, \theta)} \leq \log \sum_j p(j, \mathbf{z}_i|\theta),$$

where the last expression follows from $\langle p(\mathbf{y}|j, \mathbf{z}_i, \theta) \rangle_{p(\mathbf{y}|c_i, \mathbf{z}_i, \theta)} \leq 1$. A simple lower bound of the cost function for missing data then follows

$$\mathcal{L}_{miss} \geq \sum_i \langle \log p(c_i, \mathbf{y}, \mathbf{z}_i|\theta) \rangle_{p(\mathbf{y}|c_i, \mathbf{z}_i, \theta)} - \sum_j \log p(j, \mathbf{z}_i|\theta) \quad , \quad (16)$$

where the missing values $\mathbf{y}$ are replaced by their expectation under $p(\mathbf{y}|c_i, z_i, \theta)$ in the first term, and omitted in the second term.

4.4 Discriminative Document Modeling

The mixture of unigrams model [14] is a hidden variable model that generates word counts for documents. The model assumes that each document is generated from a mixture of M hidden "topics", $\sum_{j=1}^{M} \pi_j p(\mathbf{x}_i|\beta_j)$, where j is the index of the topic, and β_j the multinomial parameters that generate words from the topic. The vector $\mathbf{x}_i$ is the observed word counts for document i, and π_j the probability of generating the words from the topic j. In its simplest form with one topic per class the model is a naive Bayes classifier.

In a discriminative mixture of unigrams the document vector is generated from a mixture of topics (multinomials), where each class is assigned a subset of topics. In this paper we will illustrate the functionality of the discriminative mixture of unigrams in two cases: either with one or five topic vectors per class.

5 Experiments

We used the Reuters data set [15]. A subset of 4000 documents from four categories was selected, 1000 from each category. The categories were: Corporate-Industrial (CCAT), Economics and Economic Indicators (ECAT), Government and Social (GCAT), and Securities and Commodities Trading and Markets (MCAT). Each of the selected documents was classified to only one of the four classes. The words that occurred less than 200 times in the whole subset were left out, thus leaving 1952 words. The data set was then split into equal-sized training and test sets.

The second data set was the MNIST data[4]. The data consists of gray level images of handwritten digits. The data was thresholded to ones and zeros with a threshold gray level value of 128 (with a maximum of 255) before evaluating the models. The training and test data sets each consisted of 10000 samples, each sample being a binary image of 784 pixels.

A discriminative mixture of unigrams model (d-MUM) with one and five components was applied. Reference methods included the naive Bayes classifier, loglinear regression, k-means algorithm (where each class was modelled by its centroid), and k-nearest neighbor search (k-NN), where the size of the neighborhood was chosen by dividing the full training set to training and validation sets.[5] The k-means and k-NN algorithms were computed using dot product and Hellinger distances. The classification accuracies for the test data set are reported in Table 1. With the Reuters data the performances of the loglinear model and

Table 1. Classification accuracies for the test sets. Comparisons [(1),(2),(3)]: significant ($p < 0.01$) difference (McNemar's test).

Method	Accuracy (%)	
	Reuters	MNIST
k-means	79.9	64.1
k-means (Hellinger)	81.9	76.0
k-NN	(5-nn) 74.6	(9-nn) 84.8
k-NN (Hellinger)	(5-nn) 86.9 [(1)]	(5-nn) 94.9
naive Bayes	59.0	68.9
loglinear	92.2	90.9 [(2)(3)]
d-MUM 1 component	92.5 [(1)]	90.5 [(2)]
d-MUM 5 components	92.3	93.2 [(3)]

d-MUM are roughly equal. With MNIST data, the loglinear model is better than 1-component d-MUM, but loses to 5-component d-MUM. Both models clearly outperform the joint likelihood (naive Bayes) model.

---

[4] Available at http://yann.lecun.com/exdb/mnist/
[5] The computational complexity of k-NN is not comparable to the other methods, since the method computes pairwise distances between every data point pair, whereas in the other methods only C "prototypes" are used.

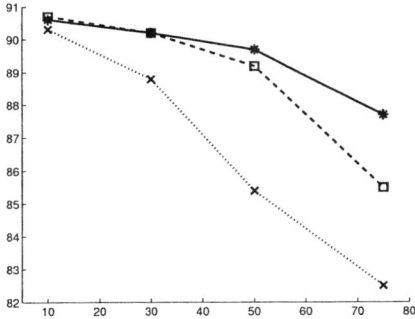

Fig. 3. Performance with missing data. The performance of discriminative MUM (solid line) compared to logistic regression with k-NN imputation (dashed line) and imputation by the mean of the class (dotted line). Horizontal axis: Percentage of missing data. Vertical axis: Classification accuracy (%). The difference between k-NN imputation and d-MUM is significant with 75 %, and mildly significant (p=0.033) with 50% missing data.

In a second experiment the MNIST teaching data was corrupted by randomly replacing pixels with missing values. The experiment was run for 10, 30, 50, and 75 % missing data. A baseline comparison method was logistic regression where missing values were imputed by the mean of the known pixel values for the given pixel and class. We also compared to the current state-of-the-art, k-NN imputation which has been reported to outperform several other methods [16].

The discriminative MUM compares favourably to the k-NN imputation with missing values computed based on the 10 nearest neighbors. Besides being more accurate, our method is considerably faster, since k-NN imputation is $\mathcal{O}(N^2)$, where N is the amount of samples[6]. This is an additional cost, since the optimization durations for the loglinear model and discriminative MUM (with missing value imputation) are roughly equal.

6 Discussion

The aim of this paper has been to set the stage for further contributions on discriminative joint density models. Several theoretical connections were explored. We have also shown that the paradigm can be easily applied to discriminative document modeling with a simple case of mixture of unigrams model introduced in this paper, and that the generative mechanism for **x** in discriminative joint density models still contains useful information for example in predicting missing values.

---

[6] For computational reasons, we divided the data set to blocks of 1000 samples and then imputed the missing values. This took more than 12 hours for each data set.

Acknowledgements. This work was supported in part by Academy of Finland, decision 79017, and the IST Programme of the European Community, under the PASCAL Network of Excellence, IST-2002-506778. This publication only reflects the authors' views. All rights are reserved because of other commitments.

References

1. McCullagh, P., Nelder, J.A.: Generalized Linear Models. 2nd edn. CRC Press (1990)
2. Rubinstein, Y.D., Hastie, T.: Discriminative vs informative learning. In Heckerman, D., Mannila, H., Pregibon, D., Uthurusamy, R., eds.: Proc. ACM KDD. AAAI Press (1997) 49–53
3. Kontkanen, P., Myllymäki, P., Tirri, H.: Classifier learning with supervised marginal likelihood. In Breese, J., Koller, D., eds.: Proc. UAI'01, Morgan Kaufmann Publishers (2001) 277–284
4. Ng, A.Y., Jordan, M.I.: On discriminative vs. generative classifiers: A comparison of logistic regression and naive Bayes. In Dietterich, T.G., Becker, S., Ghahramani, Z., eds.: Advances in NIPS 14. MIT Press, Cambridge, MA (2002) 841–848
5. Nádas, A., Nahamoo, D., Picheny, M.A.: On a model-robust training method for speech recognition. IEEE Tr. on Acoustics, Speech, and Signal Processing **39** (1988) 1432–1436
6. Povey, D., Woodland, P., Gales, M.: Discriminative MAP for acoustic model adaptation. In: Proc. IEEE ICASSP'03. Volume 1. (2003) 312–315
7. Buntine, W.: Variational extensions to EM and multinomial PCA. In Elomaa, T., Mannila, H., Toivonen, H., eds.: Proc. ECML-2002. Springer-Verlag (2002) 23–34
8. Efron, B.: The geometry of exponential families. The Annals of Statistics **6** (1978) 362–376
9. Schall, R.: Estimation in generalized linear models with random effects. Biometrika **78** (1991) 719–727
10. Salojärvi, J., Puolamäki, K., Kaski, S.: Expectation maximization algorithms for conditional likelihoods. In: Proc. ICML-2005. (2005) in press.
11. Sharma, S.: Applied Multivariate Techniques. John Wiley & Sons, Inc. (1996)
12. Puolamäki, K., Salojärvi, J., Savia, E., Simola, J., Kaski, S.: Combining eye movements and collaborative filtering for proactive information retrieval. In: Proc. SIGIR 2005. (2005) in press.
13. Jaakkola, T.S., Meila, M., Jebara, T.: Maximum entropy discrimination. In Solla, S.A., Leen, T.K., Müller, K.R., eds.: Advances in NIPS 12. MIT Press, Cambridge, MA (2000) 470–476
14. Nigam, K., McCallum, A.K., Thrun, S., Mitchell, T.M.: Text classification from labeled and unlabeled documents using EM. Machine Learning **39** (2000) 103–134
15. Lewis, D.D., Yang, Y., Rose, T., Li, F.: Rcv1: A new benchmark collection for text categorization research. Journal of Machine Learning Research **5** (2004) 361–397
16. Troyanskaya, O., Cantor, M., Sherlock, G., Brown, P., Hastie, T., Tibshirani, R., Botstein, D., Altman, R.B.: Missing value estimation methods for DNA microarrays. Bioinformatics **17** (2001) 520–525

Model-Based Online Learning of POMDPs

Guy Shani, Ronen I. Brafman, and Solomon E. Shimony

Ben-Gurion University, Beer-Sheva, Israel

Abstract. Learning to act in an unknown partially observable domain is a difficult variant of the reinforcement learning paradigm. Research in the area has focused on model-free methods — methods that learn a policy without learning a model of the world. When sensor noise increases, model-free methods provide less accurate policies. The model-based approach — learning a POMDP model of the world, and computing an optimal policy for the learned model — may generate superior results in the presence of sensor noise, but learning and solving a model of the environment is a difficult problem. We have previously shown how such a model can be obtained from the learned policy of model-free methods, but this approach implies a distinction between a learning phase and an acting phase that is undesirable. In this paper we present a novel method for learning a POMDP model online, based on McCallums' Utile Suffix Memory (USM), in conjunction with an approximate policy obtained using an incremental POMDP solver. We show that the incrementally improving policy provides superior results to the original USM algorithm, especially in the presence of increasing sensor and action noise.

1 Introduction

Consider an agent situated in a partially observable domain: It executes an action that may change the state of the world; this change is reflected, in turn, by the agent's sensors; the action may have some associated cost, and the new state may have some associated reward or penalty. Thus, the agent's interaction with this environment is characterized by a sequence of action-observation-reward steps, known as *instances*. In this paper we focus our attention on agents with imperfect and noisy sensors that learn to act in such environments without any prior information about the underlying set of world-states and the world's dynamics, except for information about their sensors' capabilities (namely, a predefined sensor model). This is a known variant of reinforcement learning (RL) in partially observable domains (see, e.g. [3]).

Learning in partially observable domains can take one of two forms; the agent can either learn a policy directly [8, 7], or it can use methods such as the Baum-Welch algorithm for learning HMMs (see, e.g. [2]) to learn a model of the environment, usually represented as a Partially Observable Markov Decision Process (POMDP)[1] , and solve it [4, 9]. This approach has not been favored by researchers, as learning a model appears to be a difficult task, and computing an optimal solution is also difficult.

Moreover, model-free methods naturally support online learning and adapt to changing environments, whereas this is not always the case with model-based methods. In this paper, we return to the model-based approach motivated by a number of recent

---
[1] See Section 2.1 for an overview of MDPs and POMDPs.

developments: (1) Our recent work on learning POMDP models is able to leverage policies of model-free methods for constructing a POMDP and scales much better than the Baum-Welch algorithm (2) Improvements in approximate POMDP solution methods no longer make it a bottle-neck for this approach. The main contribution of this paper is to show how we can adapt the above ideas to provide online model-based learning of POMDPs, thereby providing a well-rounded approach for model-based learning in partially observable domains. Our algorithm still suffers from the problem that plagues model-free and model-based algorithms for this difficult problem: it works in relatively small domains. However, given the relatively small number of algorithms in this area, it offers a new entry that is both faster, much more robust to sensor noise, and adaptive.

Some research in RL has focused on the problem of *perceptual aliasing* [4], where different actions should be executed in two states where sensors provide the same output. For example, in Figure 1 the left and right corridors are perceptually aliased if sensors can only sense adjacent walls. Model-free methods[2] - such as using variant-length history windows [7] - can be used to disambiguate the perceptually aliased states. When the agent's sensors provide deterministic output, learning to properly identify the underlying world states reduces the problem to a fully observable MDP, making it possible for methods such as Q-learning to compute an optimal policy.

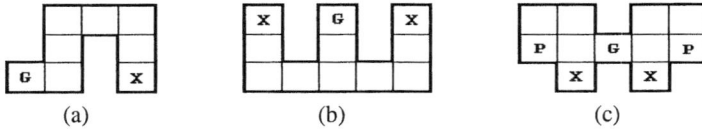

Fig. 1. Three maze domains. The agent receives a reward of 9 upon reaching the goal state (marked with 'G'). Immediately afterwards (in the same transition) the agent is transferred to one of the states marked 'X'. Arrival at a state marked 'P' results in a negative reward of 9.

When sensors provide output that is only slightly noisy, model-free methods produce near-optimal results. However, as noise in the sensors increases, their performance rapidly decreases [10]. This is because disambiguating the perceptually aliased states under noisy sensors does not result in an MDP, but rather in a POMDP. POMDP models are harder to solve, but their solution handles noisy observations optimally.

We have previously shown [11] how well-known model-free methods such as internal memory and McCallum's USM algorithm can be adapted to create after convergence a POMDP model. A solution to such a model provides superior results to the original policy computed by the model-free methods, especially in the presence of noise. This approach, much like earlier methods that rely on the Baum-Welch algorithm, has its disadvantages, as it separates the process into a learning stage and an acting stage. Such separation is undesirable because it is unclear when we should switch from learning to acting, and it also does not handle even slowly changing environments very well.

In this paper we present an algorithm for learning a POMDP model together with its policy online. We adapt the USM algorithm, originally designed for learning a simpler MDP model, for learning the more complicated POMDP model. USM has two

---

[2] As the discussed problems are properly defined as a POMDP, we call methods that do not learn all the POMDP parameters "model-free", though they may learn state representations.

parts — clustering histories to form a state representation and a planning algorithm based on the learned states. We suggest augmenting the first part to learn a POMDP model using a predefined sensor model, and replacing the original MDP planner with an approximate POMDP planner. The algorithm hence updates the POMDP parameters and continuously computes an approximate policy, using an online version of the Perseus algorithm [12]. Executing policies in a POMDP requires the maintenance of a belief state. The computational cost of our incremental learning algorithm is no greater than the time it takes for the required computation of the belief state. Belief states can also be used to improve the insertion of instances into the POMDP construction algorithm.

Our algorithm makes one important assumption — the existence of a pre-defined sensor model. For instance, in the maze domain, it knows the probability by which a wall is observed given that a wall exists. In general we require a sensor model that provides a distribution over observations given features of a state (rather than given the actual state). While not universally applicable, we believe that such sensor models are quite natural for many domains, robotics in particular.

This paper is structured as follows: we begin (Section 2) with an overview of MDPs, POMDPs and the USM algorithm. We then explain how the USM algorithm can be adapted to incrementally maintain a POMDP in Section 3 and how to compute an approximate policy online in Section 4. We provide an experimental evaluation of our work in Section 5 and conclude in Section 6.

2 Background

2.1 MDPs and POMDPs

A Markov Decision Process (MDP) [5] is a model for sequential stochastic decision problems. An MDP is a four-tuple: $\langle S, A, R, tr \rangle$, where S is the set of the states of the world, A is a set of actions an agent can use, R is a reward function, and tr is the stochastic state-transition function. A solution to an MDP is a policy $\pi : S \to A$ that defines which action should be executed in each state.

Various exact and approximate algorithms exist for computing an optimal policy, and the best known are policy-iteration [5] and value-iteration [1]. A value function assigns for each state a value $V(s)$ — the expected utility from acting optimally beginning in s and on to infinity. Value iteration computes an optimal value function by iteratively solving the equation:

$$V_{n+1}(s) = \max_a R(s,a) + \gamma \sum_{s'} tr(s,a,s') V_n(s') \qquad (1)$$

A standard extension to the MDP model is the Partially Observable Markov Decision Process (POMDP) model [3]. A POMDP is a tuple $\langle S, A, R, tr, \Omega, O \rangle$, where S, A, R, tr define an MDP, Ω is a set of possible observations and $O(a, s, o)$ is the probability of executing action a, reaching state s and observing o. The agent is unable to identify the current state and is therefore forced to estimate it given the current observations (e.g. output of the robot sensors) and the agents' history. In many application domains POMDPs are a more precise and natural formalization than an MDP, but using POMDPs increases the difficulty of computing an optimal solution.

History may be represented by a belief state $b(s) = p(s|h)$ — the probability of being in state s after executing and observing history h. The next belief state b_a^o resulting by executing action a and observing o in belief state a can be computed using:

$$b_a^o(s) = \frac{O(a,s,o)\sum_{s'} b(s')tr(s',a,s)}{pr(o|b,a)} \quad (2)$$

2.2 Approximate Solutions to POMDPs

Solving a POMDP is an extremely difficult computational problem, and various attempts have been made to compute approximate solutions that work reasonably well in practice.

Early research [6] suggested the use of an optimal policy for the underlying MDP in conjunction with the belief state to provide a number of approximations that define a policy over belief states. We can select the action that:

- Most Likely State (MLS): corresponds to the maximal Q-value of the state that is most likely given the current belief state.

$$\pi_{MLS}(b) = \mathrm{argmax}_a\, Q(\mathrm{argmax}_s\, b(s), a) \quad (3)$$

- Voting: recommended by most states, weighted by the state probability.

$$\pi_{Voting}(b) = \mathrm{argmax}_a \sum_s b(s)\delta(s,a) \quad (4)$$

where $\delta(s,a) = 1 \Leftrightarrow a = \mathrm{argmax}_{a'}\, Q(s,a)$ and 0 otherwise.
- Q_{MDP}: has the highest Q-value weighted by the state probabilities.

$$\pi_{QMDP}(b) = \mathrm{argmax}_a \sum_s b(s)Q(s,a) \quad (5)$$

An exact solution to a POMDP can be computed using the belief state MDP — an MDP over the belief space of the POMDP. A value function for a POMDP can be described using a set of $|S|$ dimensional vectors defining the expected utility, where each vector $\alpha_a \in V$ corresponds to an action a. We can compute the value function over the belief state MDP iteratively:

$$V_{n+1}(b) = \max_a [b \cdot r_a + \gamma \sum_o pr(o|a,b) V_n(b_a^o)] \quad (6)$$

where $r_a(s) = R(s,a)$ and $\alpha \cdot \beta = \sum_i \alpha(i)\beta(i)$. The computation of the next value function $V_{n+1}(b)$ out of the current one V_n (Equation 6) is known as a *backup* step. Using such a value function V we can define a policy π_V over the belief state:

$$\pi_V(b) = \mathrm{argmax}_{a:\alpha_a \in V}\, \alpha_a \cdot b \quad (7)$$

A point-based algorithm is an algorithm that computes a value function over a finite set of belief points (belief states). Point based algorithms compute an approximate solution as they do not iterate over the entire (infinite) belief space.

Spaan *et al.* explore randomly the world to gather a set B of belief points and then execute the Perseus algorithm (Algorithm 1). Spaan *et al.* also explain how backups can be computed efficiently. Perseus appears to provide good approximations with small sized value functions rapidly.

Algorithm 1. Perseus

Input: B — a set of belief points
1: **repeat**
2:     $\tilde{B} \leftarrow B$
3:     $V' \leftarrow \phi$
4:     **while** $\tilde{B}$ not empty **do**
5:         Sample $b \in \tilde{B}$
6:         $\alpha \leftarrow backup(b)$
7:         **if** $\alpha \cdot b > V(b)$ **then**
8:             $V' \leftarrow V' \cup \{\alpha\}$
9:         **else**
10:            $V' \leftarrow V' \cup \{\max_{\beta \in V} \beta \cdot b\}$
11:        $\tilde{B} \leftarrow \{b \in \tilde{B} : V'(b) < V(b)\}$
12:    $V \leftarrow V'$
13: **until** V has converged

2.3 Model Based Approaches

The idea of learning a POMDP model of the environment was examined by early researchers [4, 7] who used a variant of the Baum-Welch algorithm for learning hidden Markov models, refining the state space when it was observed to be inadequate. These methods were slow to converge and could not outperform the rapid convergence and reasonable results generated by model-free methods.

Weirstra and Weiring [13] recently proposed an improvement to McCallums' UDM algorithm allowing it to look farther into the past and speeding its convergence. They however compute an approximate policy using Q-values for the underlying MDP and not by any modern policy computation mechanism. We note that their algorithm is not truly online as it is split into as exploration stage and then a model update stage in order to avoid the long update time of the Baum-Welch algorithm.

Nikovski [9] used McCallum's earlier model-free method, Nearest Sequence Memory (NSM) [7], to identify the states of the world and learn the transition, reward, and observation functions. He showed that the learned models produced superior results to the models obtained by using the Baum-Welch algorithm. His models, however, were tested on domains with little noise, and are much less adequate when sensors are noisy. This is to be expected, as NSM handles noisy environments poorly, where USM can still produce reasonable results, though in no way optimal. Nikovski also did not maintain an incremental model, splitting the learning into a learning phase, followed by model construction and then used the resulting model.

2.4 Utile Suffix Memory

Instance-based state identification [7] resolves perceptual aliasing with variable length short term memory. An instance is a tuple $T_t = \langle T_{t-1}, a_{t-1}, o_t, r_t \rangle$ — the individual observed raw experience. Algorithms of this family keep all the observed raw data (sequences of instances), and use it to identify matching subsequences. It is assumed that two sequences with similar suffixes were likely generated in the same world state.

Utile Suffix Memory creates a tree structure, based on suffix trees for string operations. This tree maintains the raw experiences and identifies matching suffixes. The root of the tree is an unlabeled node, holding all available instances. Each immediate child of the root is labeled with one of the observations encountered during the test. A node holds all the instances $T_t = \langle T_{t-1}, a_{t-1}, o_t, r_t \rangle$ whose final observation o_t matches the node's observation. At the next level, instances are split based on the last action of the instance a_t. We split again based on (the next to last) observation o_{t-1}, etc. All nodes act as buckets, grouping together instances that have matching history suffixes of a certain length. Leaves act as states, holding Q-values and updating them. The deeper a leaf is in the tree, the more history the instances in this leaf share.

The tree is built on-line during the test run. To add a new instance to the tree, we examine its percept, and follow the path to the child node labeled by that percept. We then look at the action before this percept and move to the node labeled by that action, then branch on the percept prior to that action and so forth, until a leaf is reached.

When sensors provide noisy outputs, it is possible that an instance corresponding to a certain location in the world will be inserted into a leaf that represents a different location, due to a noisy observation[10]. Such noisy observations can be reduced by maintaining a belief state. Instead of refereing to a single (possibly noisy) observation, we can consider all possible observations weighted by their probability $p(o|b)$ where b is the current belief state. In USM, $p(o|b)$ is easy to compute as each state (leaf) corresponds to a specific assignment to world features (for example, a specific wall configuration), and therefore $p(o|b) = \sum_{s \in S_o} b(s)$ where S_o is the set of all states that correspond to world configuration o.

We can hence insert a new instance T_t into all states, weighted by $p(o|b_t)$, or replace the noisy observation o_t with the observation with maximal probability $\operatorname{argmax}_o p(o|b_t)$. In the experiments reported below we take the second approach.

Leaves should be split if their descendants show a statistical difference in expected future discounted reward associated with the same action. We split a node if knowing where the agent came from helps predict future discounted rewards. Thus, the tree must keep what McCallum calls fringes, i.e., subtrees below the "official" leaves. Figure 2.4 presents an example of a possible USM tree, without fringe nodes.

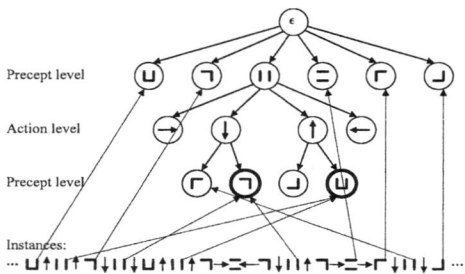

Fig. 2. A possible USM suffix tree generated by the maze in Figure 1. Below is a sequence of instances demonstrating how some instances are clustered into the tree leaves. The two bolded leaves correspond to the same state — the right perceptually aliased corridor. During most executions under deterministic sensor output the above tree structure was generated.

After inserting new instances into the tree, we update Q-values in the leaves using:

$$R(s,a) = \frac{\sum_{T_i \in T(s,a)} r_i}{|T(s,a)|} \tag{8}$$

$$Pr(s'|s,a) = \frac{|\forall T_i \in T(s,a), L(T_{i+1}) = s'|}{|T(s,a)|} \tag{9}$$

$$Q(s,a) = R(s,a) + \gamma \sum_{s'} Pr(s'|s,a) U(s') \tag{10}$$

where $L(T_i)$ is the leaf associated with instance T_i and $U(s) = max_a(Q(s,a))$. We use s and s' to denote the leaves of the tree, as in an optimal tree configuration for a problem the leaves of the tree define the states of the underlying MDP. The above equations correspond to a single step of the value iteration algorithm (see Section 2.1).

Now that the Q-values have been updated, the agent chooses the next action to perform based on the Q-values in the leaf corresponding to the current instance T_t:

$$a_{t+1} = argmax_a Q(L(T_t), a) \tag{11}$$

McCallum uses the fringes of the tree for a smart exploration strategy. In our implementation we use a simple ϵ-greedy technique for exploration.

We note that if a perceptually aliased state can be reached from two different locations, it may have two different leaves that represent it. For example, consider the two leaves in thick line-style in Figure 2.4, corresponding to arriving at the right corridor from above or from below. This phenomenon gives rise to two problems: relevant information is split between leaves, thus requiring a longer learning process, and more seriously, this can lead to a non-compact state space. This is a fundamental problem with USM, and future research should focus on better structures that avoid this duplication, such as using a DAG instead of a tree structure. We note that given any such improvement to USM our algorithms can be modified accordingly.

3 Constructing a POMDP Model over Utile Suffix Memory

Obtaining the POMDP parameters from the USM tree structure is straightforward. The state space (S) is defined as the set of (constantly expanding) tree leaves computed by USM. The actions (A) and observations (Ω) are known to the agent prior to learning the model. The transition function (tr) is defined by Equation 9 and the reward function (R) by Equation 8, as in the original USM. These functions are refined throughout the learning process.

Learning the observation function is harder, as in USM a state always corresponds to a single "true" observation, and all instances mapped to the state hence observe the same sensor output. This "true" state observation is defined by the topmost node below the root, on the path to the state leaf, corresponding to the latest observation in every instance that was added to the leaf. It is therefore unclear how to learn $pr(o|a,s)$ — the probability of observing o **after** reaching state s with action a. We are able to learn a different probability function — the probability of observing o after executing action a **from** state s, but in most of the domains modelled by POMDPs the observation depends on the target state, not on the source state, making the latter definition improper.

It is, however, possible to measure the accuracy of sensors offline, prior to the learning process. For example, we can place a robot in front of an obstacle and measure how likely are its sensors to identify the obstacle. Similarly, it is possible to measure the temperature of a patient multiple times to obtain an error model of the thermometer.

We therefore adopt the approach taken by Shani et al. [10, 11], where an observation model is assumed, and define the observation function based on the observation model. We assume that the agent has some sensor model defining $pr(o|w)$ — the probability that the agent will observe o in world state w. Note that the requirement of a sensor model (which is sufficient for us) is often weaker than the requirement for an observation function. For instance, in maze domains, different rooms with identical wall configurations correspond to different states. However, we only require the ability to assess the likelihood of a certain wall configuration given the sensor's signals, not of the actual state. Thus, in general, it is possible to define a good observation function based on the state's features (which are uniquely determined by the state: the walls are the features in our experiment), but without knowledge of the actual state space (i.e., which rooms actually exist and where).

4 Online POMDP Policy Computation

The Perseus algorithm (Algorithm 1) is executed using a POMDP and a set of belief points. However, since convergence of the algorithm still takes considerable time, we would like to incrementally improve a value function (and hence, a policy) as we learn and act, without requiring the complete execution of Perseus after each step. Our method is an online version of the Perseus algorithm — an algorithm that receives a single belief point and adjusts the computed value function accordingly.

Algorithm 2 is an adaptation of the original algorithm, using two value functions - the current function V and the next function V'. V' is updated until no change has been noted for a period of time, upon which V' becomes the active function V.

Algorithm 2. Iterative Perseus

Input: b — a single belief point
1: **if** $V'(b) < V(b)$ **then**
2:    $\alpha \leftarrow backup(b)$
3: **if** $\alpha \cdot b > V(b)$ **then**
4:    $V' \leftarrow V' \cup \{\alpha\}$
5: **else**
6:    $V' \leftarrow V' \cup \{\max_{\beta \in V} \beta \cdot b\}$
7: **if** V' has not been updated in a long while **then**
8:    $V \leftarrow V'$
9:    $V' \leftarrow \phi$

In the original, offline version of Perseus, belief points for updating are selected randomly. The iterative version we suggest selects the points we update not randomly, but following some track through the environment. If this track is chosen wisely (i.e. using a good exploration policy) we can hope that the points that are updated are ones that improve the solution faster.

Using Perseus in conjunction with a model learning algorithm can be problematic, due to the greedy nature of the algorithm. As the value of the next value function over all (tested) belief points always increases, wrong over-estimates, originating from some unlearned world feature, can be persisted in the value function even though they can not be achieved. Such maxima can be escaped using some randomization technique, such as occasionally removing vectors, or by slowly decaying older vectors. We note this problem, even though it does not manifest in our experiments.

5 Experimental Results

In our experiments we ran the USM-based POMDP on the toy mazes in Figure 1. While these environments are uncomplicated compared to real world problems, they demonstrate important problem features such as multiple perceptual aliasing (Figure 1(b)) and the need for an information gain action (Figure 1(c)). While USM is limited in scaling up to real-world problems, its successor, U-Tree, handles larger domains, and we note that all our methods can be implemented on U-Tree much the same way as for USM.

During execution the model maintains a belief state and states were updated as explained in Section 2.4. The system also ran the iterative Perseus algorithm (Algorithm 2) for each observed belief state. During the learning phase, the next action was selected using the MLS (most likely state) technique (Section 2.1). Once the average reward collected by the algorithms passed a certain threshold, exploration was stopped (as the POMDP policy does not explore).

From this point onwards, learning was halted and runs were continued for 5000 iterations for each approximation technique to calculate the average reward gained — MLS, Voting, Q_{MDP} and the policy computed by the iterative Perseus algorithm. In order to provide a gold standard, we manually defined a POMDP model for each of the mazes above, solved it using Perseus and ran the resulting policy for 5000 iterations.

Execution time in our tests was around 6 milliseconds for an iteration of USM, compared to about 234 milliseconds for an iteration of the POMDP learning (including parameter and policy updates), on the maze in Figure 1(b) with sensor accuracy 0.9, on a Pentium 4 with 2.4 GHz CPU and 512 MB memory. The performance of the POMDP learning algorithm is much slower (about n^3) but still feasible for online robotic application, where an action execution is usually measured in seconds. Moreover, much of that time is required for simply updating the belief state, an operation required even for only executing a POMDP policy. For example, the executed policy of the manually defined model (without any learning), takes about 42 milliseconds per iteration.

The agent in our experiments has four sensors allowing it to sense an immediate wall above, below, to the left, and to the right of its current location. Sensors have a boolean output with probability p of being correct. The probability of all sensors providing the correct output is therefore p^4. We assume that the agent knows in advance the probability of sensing a wall if a wall exists, and compute the observation function from this information. In the maze there is a single location that grants the agent a reward of 9. In the maze in Figure 1(c) there are two locations where the agent receives a negative reward (punishment) of 9. Upon receiving a reward or punishment, the agent is transformed to any of the states marked by X. If the agent bumps into a wall it pays a cost (a negative reward) of 1. For every move the agent pays a cost of 0.1.

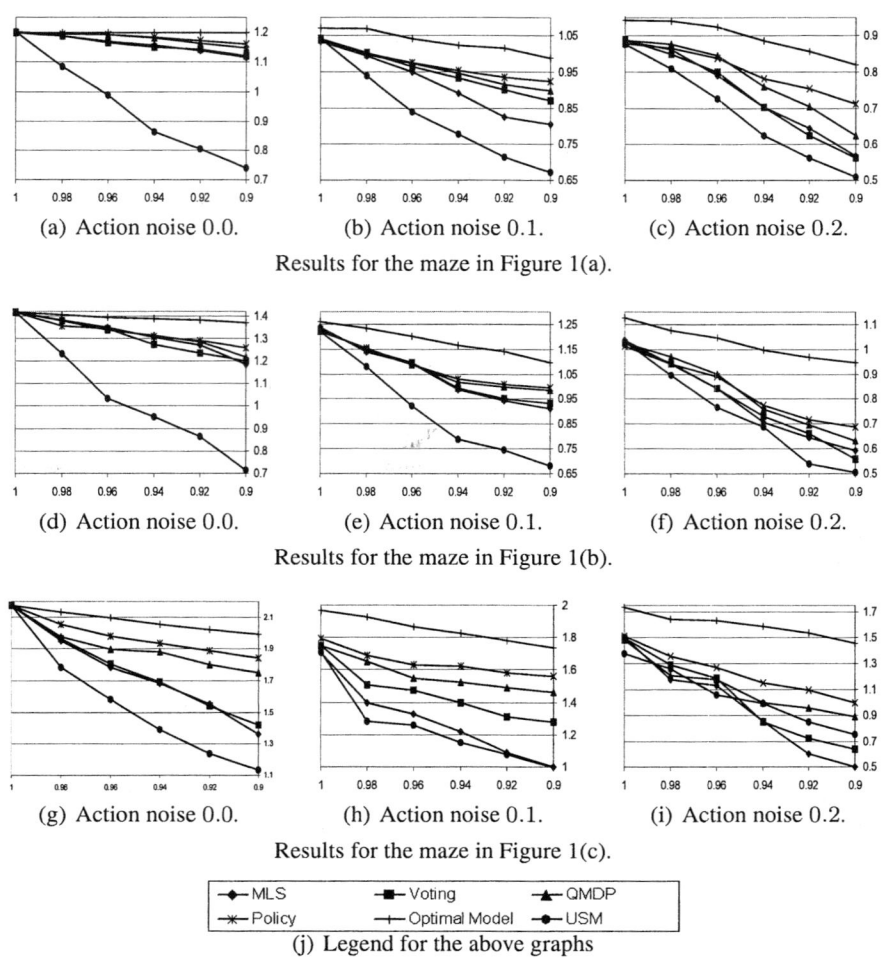

Fig. 3. Results for the mazes in Figure 1. In all the above graphs, the X axis contains the diminishing sensor accuracy p, and the Y axis marks average reward per agent action. The above results are averaged over 5 different executions for each observation accuracy and method. All variances were below 0.01 and in most cases below 0.005.

Figure 5 presents our experimental results. The graphs compare the performance of the original USM algorithm and our various enhancements: the belief state approximations (MLS, Voting and Q_{MDP}) and the policy computed by the Online Perseus algorithm (Algorithm2), denoted "Policy". We also show the results of the policy for manually defined model, denoted "Optimal Model" as an upper bound.

Observe that the performance of USM decreases sharply as observation noise increases, but the performance of the POMDP based methods remains reasonably high. The improvement is due to the fact that all the POMDP methods model the noise using the belief state, whereas pure USM ignores it. The differences between the POMDP solution methods are not too significant for the first two mazes, and are more noticeable in the last model. Incremental Perseus provides better solutions than the approximations in all the experiments. The third model exhibits more uncertainty in the belief states, and a more pronounced reward variability due to error (this maze is less forgiving w.r.t. deviations from the optimal, especially in the states where the agent observes no walls, where the same action causes a large reward in one state, and a large penalty in the other), making the difference in performance significant. Here, the MDP based methods (MLS, Voting and Q_{MDP}) do not perform nearly as well as the computed policy on that model.

The performance of the policy generated from the USM-based model is not as good as the policy of the manually defined model. This is because the USM-based model has many redundant states, as explained in Section 2.4. The lower performance is not due to the use of the incremental Perseus instead of the offline version. In experiments unreported here, we executed a simulation on a predefined POMDP model, using incremental Perseus to compute a policy. The resulting policy was no worse than the one computed by the offline Perseus on an identical model.

6 Conclusions and Future Work

Model-based algorithms for partially observable environments are widely disfavored due to their slow convergence and the difficulty of computing an optimal policy even when the model is known. This paper presents a model-based algorithm that learns a POMDP model and its solution in conjunction, avoiding the slow computation of the Baum-Welch algorithm. The learned POMDP policy presents superior performance to McCallums' USM in the presence of noisy actions and sensors. The main contribution of this paper is in providing an incremental approach for constructing and solving a POMDP model created online by the agent and demonstrating its effectiveness.

The online Perseus we have presented can also be useful for obtaining policies on standard, predefined, POMDPs and we intend to continue experimenting with it on such domains. Efficient exploration using the online Perseus remains an open question as currently, the policy resulting from it performs very poorly before collecting enough data — much worse than the MDP based approximations.

Improving the construction of the model is probably the main challenge to future work. Currently, the main bottleneck is the size of the learned models. It is possible that USM will create different leaves that correspond to the same state. This leads to large models which require more work to solve and provide lower quality policies. In the future, we plan to examine ways of more aggressively joining states that look similar.

We also believe that model-based methods offer significant advantages in using the current model to guide exploration that is targeted at reaching unknown states and generating instances that improve the model. Indeed, more advanced model-based algorithm may consider issues such as the robustness of the learned model and may attempt to directly model uncertainty about the model parameters, using these to direct additional exploration. Finally, McCallums' USM algorithm provides just one way of constructing a POMDP model, and there may be other methods from which it is easier to induce more accurate models.

Acknowledgments

Partially supported by the Israeli Ministry of Science Infrastructure grant No. 3-942, by the Lynn and William Frankel Center for Computer Sciences, and by the Paul Ivanier Center for Robotics and Production Management at BGU. Guy Shani is partially supported by the Friedman Fund.

References

1. R. E. Bellman. *Dynamic Programming*. Princeton University Press, 1962.
2. J. Bilmes. A gentle tutorial on the em algorithm and its application to parameter estimation for gaussian mixture and hidden markov models. Technical Report ICSI-TR-97-021, 1997.
3. A. R. Cassandra, L. P. Kaelbling, and M. L. Littman. Acting optimally in partially observable stochastic domains. In *AAAI'94*, pages 1023–1028, 1994.
4. L. Chrisman. Reinforcement learning with perceptual aliasing: The perceptual distinctions approach. In *AAAI'02*, pages 183–188, 1992.
5. R. A. Howard. *Dynamic Programming and Markov Processes*. MIT Press, 1960.
6. M. L. Littman, A. R. Cassandra, and L. P. Kaelbling. Learning policies for partially observable environments: Scaling up. In *ICML'95*.
7. A. K. McCallum. *Reinforcement Learning with Selective Perception and Hidden State*. PhD thesis, University of Rochester, 1996.
8. N. Meuleau, L. Peshkin, K. Kim, and L. P. Kaelbling. Learning finite-state controllers for partially observable environments. In *UAI'99*, pages 427–436, 1999.
9. D. Nikovski. *State-Aggregation Algorithms for Learning Probabilistic Models for Robot Control*. PhD thesis, Carnegie Mellon University, 2002.
10. G. Shani and R. I. Brafman. Resolving perceptual aliasing in the presence of noisy sensors. In *NIPS'17*, 2004.
11. G. Shani, R. I. Brafman, and S. E. Shimony. Partial observability under noisy sensors — from model-free to model-based. In *ICML RRfRL Workshop*, 2005.
12. M. T. J. Spaan and N. Vlassis. Perseus: Randomized point-based value iteration for POMDPs. Technical Report IAS-UVA-04-02, University of Amsterdam, 2004.
13. D. Wierstra and M. Wiering. Utile distinction hidden markov models. In *ICML*, July 2004.

Simple Test Strategies for Cost-Sensitive Decision Trees

Shengli Sheng[1], Charles X. Ling[1], and Qiang Yang[2]

[1] Department of Computer Science, The University of Western Ontario
London, Ontario N6A 5B7, Canada
{cling, ssheng}@csd.uwo.ca
[2] Department of Computer Science, Hong Kong UST, Hong Kong
qyang@cs.ust.hk

Abstract. We study cost-sensitive learning of decision trees that incorporate both test costs and misclassification costs. In particular, we first propose a lazy decision tree learning that minimizes the total cost of tests and misclassifications. Then assuming test examples may contain unknown attributes whose values can be obtained at a cost (the test cost), we design several novel test strategies which attempt to minimize the total cost of tests and misclassifications for each test example. We empirically evaluate our tree-building and various test strategies, and show that they are very effective. Our results can be readily applied to real-world diagnosis tasks, such as medical diagnosis where doctors must try to determine what tests (e.g., blood tests) should be ordered for a patient to minimize the total cost of tests and misclassifications (misdiagnosis). A case study on heart disease is given throughout the paper.

1 Introduction

In many real-world machine learning applications, minimizing misclassification error is often not the ultimate goal, as "errors" can cost differently. This type of learning is called cost-sensitive learning. Turney [13] surveys a wide range of costs in cost-sensitive learning, among which two types of costs are singled out as most important: misclassification costs and test costs. For example, in a binary classification task, the costs of false positive (FP) and false negative (FN) are often very different. In addition, attributes may have costs (test costs) when acquiring values. The goal of learning is to minimize the total cost of misclassifications and tests.

Tasks involving both misclassification and test costs are abundant in real-world applications. For example, when building a model for medical diagnosis from the training data, we must consider the cost of tests (such as blood tests, X-ray, etc.) and the cost of misclassifications (errors in the diagnosis). Further, when a doctor sees a new patient (a test example), tests are normally ordered, at a cost to the patient or the insurance company, to better diagnose or predict the disease of the patient (i.e., reducing the misclassification cost). Doctors must balance the trade-off between potential misclassification costs and test costs to determinate which tests should be ordered, and at what order, to reduce the expected total cost. A case study on heart disease is given in the paper.

In this paper, we propose a lazy-tree learning that improves on a previous decision tree algorithm that minimizes the total cost of misclassifications and tests. We then describe several novel "test strategies" to determine what tests should be performed, and at what order, for attributes with unknown values in test examples such that the total expected cost is minimum. Extensive experiments have been conducted to show the effectiveness of our tree building and test strategies compared to previous methods.

2 Review of Previous Work

Cost-sensitive learning has received an extensive attention in recent years. Much work has been done in considering non-uniform misclassification costs (alone), such as [4, 5, 7]. Those works can often used to solve the problem of learning with very imbalanced datasets [3]. Some previous work, such as [11], considers the test cost alone without incorporating misclassification cost. As pointed out by [13] it is obviously an oversight. A few previous works consider both misclassification and test costs, and they are reviewed below.

In [14], the cost-sensitive learning problem is cast as a Markov Decision Process (MDP). They adopt an optimal search strategy, which may incur a high computational cost. In contrast, we adopt the local search similar to C4.5 [10], which is very efficient. Lizotte et al. [9] study the theoretical aspects of active learning with test costs using naïve Bayes classifiers. Turney [12] presents a system called ICET, which uses a genetic algorithm to build a decision tree to minimize the cost of tests and misclassifications. Our algorithm again is expected to be more efficient than Turney's genetic algorithm.

Ling et al. [8] propose a new decision tree learning algorithm that uses minimum total cost of tests and misclassifications as the attribute split criterion. However, a single tree is built for all test examples. The information of some known attributes in a test example is ignored if they do not appear in the path through which the test example goes down the tree to a leaf, and their test strategies are very simple. In this paper, we propose a lazy-tree learning to minimize the total cost of misclassifications and tests. But it can make use of the known attributes in each test example to reduce the total cost. We also propose an improved attribute selection criterion to split the training data. In addition, we propose several novel and sophisticated test strategies for obtaining missing attribute values when classifying new test examples that, as far as we know, have not been published previously.

Chai et al. [1] propose a naïve Bayes based algorithm, called CSNB, which searches for minimal total cost of tests and misclassifications. Our test strategies utilize the tree structure while naïve Bayes does not. Experiments show that our tree-based test strategies outperform CSNB in most situations (see experimental comparisons later in the paper).

3 Lazy Decision Trees for Minimum Total Cost

We assume that we are given a set of training data (with possible missing attribute values), the misclassification costs (FP and FN), and test costs for each attribute.

Instead of building a single decision tree for all test examples [8], we propose a lazy-tree approach to utilize as much information in the known attributes as possible. More specifically, given a test example with known and unknown attributes, we first reassign the test cost of the known attributes to be 0 while the cost of the unknown attributes remains unchanged. For example, suppose that there are 3 attributes and their costs are $30, $40, and $60 respectively. If in a test example, the second attribute value is unknown (obtain by testing), then the new test costs would be reset to $0, $40, and $0 respectively. Then a tree is built using the split criterion that minimizes the total cost of tests and misclassifications. Clearly our method builds different trees for test examples with different sets of unknown attributes. As our lazy-tree learning approach utilizes as much information in the known attributes as possible, we expect it will reduce the total cost in testing significantly. The rationale is that attributes with the zero test cost are more likely to be chosen early during the tree building process. When a test example is classified by this specific tree, it is less likely to be stopped by unknown attributes near the top of the decision tree. This tends to reduce the total test cost, and thus the total cost, as shown later in the experiments.

Another improvement we made over [8] is that we use the *expected* total misclassification cost when selecting an attribute for splitting. This gives a more accurate choice for attribute selection. That is, an attribute may be selected as a root node of a decision tree if the sum of the test cost and the expected misclassification costs of all branches is minimum among other attributes, and is less than that of the root. For a subset of examples with *tp* positive examples and *tn* negative examples, if $C_P = tp \times TP + tn \times FP$ is the total misclassification cost of being a positive leaf, and $C_N = tn \times TN + tp \times FN$ is the total misclassification cost of being a negative leaf, then the probability of being positive is estimated by the relative cost of C_P and C_N; the smaller the cost, the larger the probability (as minimum cost is sought). Thus, the probability of being positive is: $1 - \frac{C_P}{C_P + C_N} = \frac{C_N}{C_P + C_N}$. The expected misclassification cost of being positive is: $E_P = \frac{C_N}{C_P + C_N} \times C_P$. Similarly, the probability of being a negative leaf is $\frac{C_P}{C_P + C_N}$; and the expected misclassification cost of being negative is: $E_N = \frac{C_P}{C_P + C_N} \times C_N$. Therefore, without splitting, the expected total misclassification cost of a given set of examples is: $E = E_P + E_N = \frac{2 \times C_P \times C_N}{C_P + C_N}$. If an attribute A has *l* branches, then the expected total misclassification cost after splitting on A is: $E_A = 2 \times \sum_{i=1}^{l} \frac{C_{P_i} \times C_{N_i}}{C_{P_i} + C_{N_i}}$. Thus, $(E - E_A - T_c)$ is the expected cost reduction splitting on A, where T_c is the total test cost for all examples on A. it is easy to find out which attribute has the smallest expected total cost (the sum of the test cost and the expected misclassification cost), and if it is smaller than the one without split (if so, it is worth to split). With the expected total misclassification cost described above as the splitting criterion, the lazy-tree learning algorithm is shown as follows.

LazyTree(Examples, Attributes, TestCosts, testExample)
1. For each attribute
   a. If its value is known in *testExample*, its test cost is assigned as *0*
2. call *CSDT(Examples, Attributes, TestCostsUpdated)* to build a cost-sensitive decision tree

CSDT(Examples, Attributes, TestCosts)
1. Create a *root* node for the tree
2. If all examples are positive, return the single-node tree, with *label* = +
3. If all examples are negative, return the single-node tree, with *label* = -
4. If attributes is empty, return the single-node tree, with label assigned according to min (E_P, E_N)
5. Otherwise Begin
   a. If *maximum cost reduction* < *0* return the single-node tree, with label assigned according to min (E_P, E_N)
   b. *A* is an attribute which produces maximum cost reduction among all the remaining attributes
   c. Assign the attribute *A* as the tree *root*
   d. For each possible value vi of the attribute *A*
      i. Add a new branch below root, corresponding to the test $A=v_i$
      ii. Segment the training examples into each branch *Example_v_i*
      iii. If no examples in a branch, add a leaf node in this branch, with label assigned according to min (E_P, E_N)
      iv. Else add a subtree below this branch, CSDT(*examples_v_i, Attributes-A, TestCosts*)
6. End
7. Return *root*

One weakness of our method is higher computational cost associated with lazy learning. However, our tree-building process has the same time complexity as C4.5, so it is quite efficient. In addition, lazy trees for the same set of unknown attributes are the same. Trees frequently used can be stored in memory for the speed trade-off.

4 A Case Study on Heart Disease

We apply our lazy decision tree learning on a real dataset, the Heart Disease, with known test costs. The dataset was used in the cost-sensitive genetic algorithm by [12]. The learning problem is to predict the coronary artery disease from the 13 non-invasive tests on patients. The class label 0 or negative class indicates a less than 50% of artery narrowing, and 1 indicates more than 50%. The costs of the 13 non-invasive tests are in Canadian dollars, and were obtained from the Ontario Health Insurance Program's fee schedule [12]. These individual tests and their costs are: age ($1), sex ($1), cp (chest pain type, $1), trestbps (resting blood pressure, $1), chol (serum cholesterol in mg/dl, $7.27), fbs (fasting blood sugar, $5.20), restecg (resting electrocardiography results, $15.50), thalach (maximum heart rate achieved, $102.90), exang (exercise induced angina, $87.30), oldpeak (ST depression induced by exercise, $87.30), slope (slope of the peak exercise ST segment, $87.30), ca (number of major vessels colored by fluoroscopy, $100.90), and thal ($102.90). Tests such as thalach, exang, oldpeak, and slope are electrocardiography results when the patient runs on a treadmill, and are usually performed as a group. Tests done in a group may be discounted in costs, but this is not considered in this paper (see future work). However, no information about misclassification costs was given. After consulting a researcher in the Heart-Failure Research Group in the local medical school, a positive prediction normally entails a more expensive and invasive test, the angiographic test, to be performed, which accurately measures the percentage of artery narrowing. A negative prediction may prompt doctors to prescribe medicines, but the angiographic test may still be ordered if other diseases (such as diabetes) exist. An angiographic test costs about $600. Thus, it seems reasonable to assign false positive and false negative to be $600 and $1000 respectively.

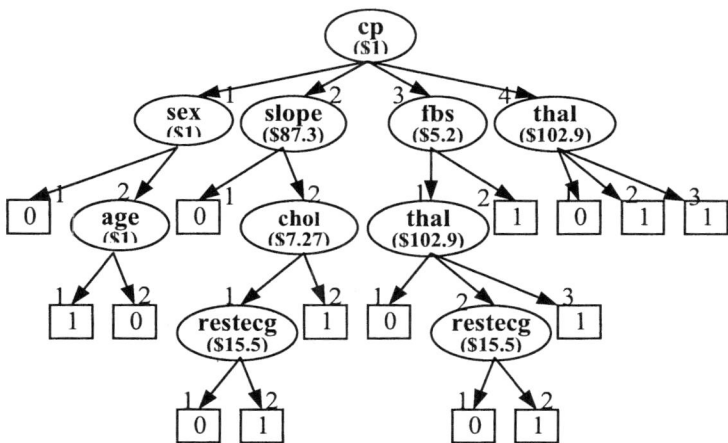

Fig. 1. Lazy tree for the test case with missing values for all attributes

Assuming in a new test example all attribute values are missing (as seeing a completely new patient), the original test costs given above are used directly for the tree building. The numerical attributes in datasets are discretized into integers (1, 2, ...) using the minimal entropy method of [6]. We apply our lazy decision tree learning for this test case, and obtain a decision tree shown in Figure 1.

We can see that often less expensive tests are used in the top part of the tree. For example, cp is selected as the root of the tree, sex and fbs are in the second level of the tree. But slope and thal, expensive tests, are also selected in the second level, since they have higher merit to reduce the total cost. That is, the splitting criterion selects tests according to their relative merit of reducing the total cost. When this tree is presented to the Heart-Failure researcher, he thinks that the tree is reasonable in predicting artery narrowing. Note that it is not feasible for us to compare our results on this dataset with [12] and other previous work using the same dataset, as they have very different settings. Here we present this case to show intuitively how our lazy-tree building algorithm and test strategies (to be discussed next) work.

5 Two Categories of Test Strategies

We define two categories of test strategies: Sequential Test and Single Batch Test. For a given test example with unknown attributes, the Sequential Test can request only one test at a time, and wait for the test result to decide which attribute to be tested next, or if a final prediction is made. The Single Batch Test, on the other hand, can request one set (batch) of one or many tests to be done simultaneously before a final prediction is made.

The related test strategies have many corresponding applications in the real world. In medical diagnoses, for example, doctors normally order one set of tests (at a cost) to be done at once. This is the case of the Single Batch Test. If doctors only order one test at a time (this can happen if tests are very expensive and/or risky), this is the case of the Sequential Test. In the next two subsections the two types of test strategies will be discussed in great details.

5.1 Lazy-Trees Optimal Sequential Test (LazyOST)

Recall that Sequential Test allows one test to be performed (at a cost) each time before the next test is determined, until a final prediction is made. Ling et al. [8] described a simple strategy called Optimal Sequential Test (or OST in short) that directly utilizes the decision tree built to guide the sequence of tests to be performed in the following way: when the test example is classified by the tree, and is stopped by an attribute whose value is unknown, a test of that attribute is made at a cost. This process continues until the test case reaches a leaf of the tree. According to the leaf reached, a prediction is made, which may incur a misclassification cost if the prediction is wrong. Clearly the time complexity of OST is only linear to the depth of the tree.

One weakness with this approach is that it uses the same tree for all testing examples. In this work, we have proposed a lazy decision-tree learning algorithm (Section 3) that builds a different tree for each test example. We apply the same test process above in the lazy tree, and call it Lazy-tree Optimal Sequential Test (LazyOST). Note that this approach is "optimal" by the nature of the decision tree built to minimize the total cost; that is, subtrees are built because there is a cost reduction in the training data. Therefore, the tree's suggestions for tests will also result in minimum total cost. (Note the terms such as "optimal" and "minimum" used in this paper do not mean in the absolute and global sense. As in C4.5, the tree building algorithm and test strategies use heuristics which are only locally optimal).

Note that it is not obvious that this lazy-tree Optimal Sequential (LazyOST) Test should always produce a small total cost compared to the single-tree OST. This is because in both approaches, the test costs of the known attributes do not count during the classifying of a test example. However, when we build decision tree specifically for a test example, the tree minimizes the total cost without counting the known attributes in the training data. This would produce a smaller total cost for that test example. In contrast, in the single tree approach, only one tree is built for all test examples, and specific information about known and unknown attributes in each test example is not utilized. In Section 4.1.2 we will compare LazyOST and OST on ten real-world datasets to see which one is better in terms of having a smaller total cost.

Case Study on Heart Disease Continued. Continuing on the heart-disease example, we next choose a test example with most attribute values known from the dataset, as the known values serve as the test results. The discretized attribute values for this test case are: age=1, sex=2, cp=3, trestbps=1, chol=1, fbs=1, restecg=1, thalach=1, exang=2, oldpeak=2, slope=1, ca=?, thal=2, and class=0 (a negative case). We apply LazyOST on the tree in Figure 1. Again assuming all values are unknown, LazyOST requests the sequence of tests as: cp (=3), fbs (=1), thal (=2), and restecg (=1), with a total test cost of $124.60. The prediction of the tree is 0 (correct), thus the misclassification cost is 0. Therefore, the total cost for this test case is $124.60.

Comparing Sequential Test Strategies. To compare various sequential test strategies, we choose 10 real-world datasets, listed in Table 1, from the UCI Machine Learning Repository [1]. These datasets are chosen because they are binary class, have at least some discrete attributes, and have a good number of examples. Each dataset is split into two parts: the training set (60%) and the test set (40%). Unlike the case study of heart disease, the detailed test costs of these datasets are unknown. To make the comparison possible, we simply choose randomly the test costs of all attributes to be some values between 0 and 100. This is reasonable because we compare the relative performance of all test strategies under the same chosen costs. The misclassification cost is set to 200/600 (200 for false positive and 600 for false negative). For test examples, a certain ratio of attributes (0.2, 0.4, 0.6, 0.8, and 1) are randomly selected and marked as unknown to simulate test cases with various degrees of missing values. Three Sequential Test strategies, OST [8], LazyOST (our work), and CSNB [2] are compared. We repeat this process 25 times, and the average total costs for the 10 datasets are plotted in Figure 2.

Table 1. Datasets used in the experiments

	No. of Attributes	No. of Examples	Class dist. (N/P)
Ecoli	6	332	230/102
Breast	9	683	444/239
Heart	8	161	98/163
Thyroid	24	2000	1762/238
Australia	15	653	296/357
Tic-tac-toe	9	958	332/626
Mushroom	21	8124	4208/3916
Kr-vs-kp	36	3196	1527/1669
Voting	16	232	108/124
Cars	6	446	328/118

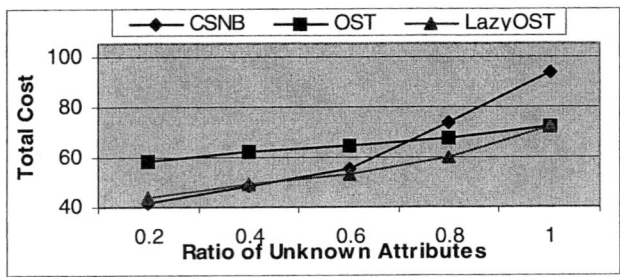

Fig. 2. Comparing our new Sequential Test strategy LazyOST with CSNB and OST

We can make several interesting conclusions. First, we can see clearly that LazyOST outperforms OST on all 10 datasets under every unknown attribute ratio, except 1. When all attributes are unknown, the eager and lazy tree learners produce the same tree. Second, the difference between OST and LazyOST is larger at a lower ratio of unknown attributes compared to a higher ratio. This is because when the ratio is low, most attributes are known, and LazyOST takes advantages of these known attributes for individual test examples while OST does not. This confirms our early expectation that our new lazy trees learning algorithm produces a tree with smaller total costs compared to the previous single tree approach. Last, we also see that the CSNB [2] performs better than OST when the ratio of unknown attributes is less than 0.7 (confirming results in [2]), since CSNB has a lower misclassification cost than OST with lower ratios of unknown attributes. However, LazyOST performs best among the three strategies when the ratio of unknown attributes is greater than 0.3.

5.2 Single Batch Tests

The Sequential Test Strategies discussed in the previous section have to wait for the result of each test to determine which test will be the next one. Waiting not only agonizes the patient in medical diagnosis, it may also be life threatening if the disease is not diagnosed and treated promptly. Thus doctors normally order one set (batch) of tests to be done at once. This is the case of the Single Batch Test. Note that results of the tests in the batch can only be obtained simultaneously after the batch is determined.

In [8] a very simple heuristic is described. The basic idea is that when a test example is classified by a minimum-cost tree and is stopped by the first attribute whose value is unknown in the test case, all unknown attributes under and including this first attribute would be tested, as a single batch. Clearly, this strategy would have exactly the same misclassification cost as the Optimal Sequential Test, but the total test cost is higher as extra tests are performed. We call this strategy Naïve Single Batch (NSB).

We propose two new and more sophisticated Single Batch Test strategies, and discuss their strengths and weaknesses. We will show experimentally that they are better than the Naïve Single Batch and the single batch based on naïve Bayes [2].

Greedy Single Batch (GSB). The rationale behind GSB is to find the most likely leaf (the most typical case) that the test example may fall into, and collect the tests on the path to this leaf for the batch test (to "confirm" the case). More specifically, it first locates all "reachable" leaves under the first unknown attribute (let us call it u) when the test example is classified by the tree. Reachable leaves are the leaves that can be possibly reached from u given the values of known attributes and all possible values of the unknown attributes under u. Then a reachable leaf with the maximum number of training examples is located, and the unknown attributes on the path from u to this leaf are collected as the batch of tests to be performed.

Intuitively this strategy reduces the total test cost than the Naïve Single Batch as only a subset of the tests is performed. However, it may increase the misclassification costs compared to the Optimal Sequential Test, as the greedy "guesses" may not be correct, in which case the test example will not reach a leaf, and must be classified by an internal node in the decision tree, which is usually less accurate than a leaf node. This will incur a higher misclassification cost.

Optimal Single Batch (OSB). The Optimal Single Batch (OSB) seeks a set of tests to be performed such that the sum of the test costs and expected misclassification cost after those tests are done is optimal (minimal). Intuitively, it finds the expected cost reduction for each unknown attribute (test), and adds a test to the batch if the cost reduction is positive and maximum (among other tests). More specifically, when a test example is classified by the tree, and is stopped by the first unknown attribute u in the tree, the total expected cost $misc(u)$ can be calculated. At this point, $misc(u)$ is simply the expected misclassification cost of u, and there is no test cost. If u is tested at a cost C, then the test example is split according to the percentage of training examples that belong to different attribute values, and is duplicated and distributed into different branches of the tree (as we do not know u's value since this is a batch test), until it reaches some leaves, or is stopped by other unknown attributes. For each such reachable leaf or unknown attribute, the expected cost can be calculated again, and the weighted misclassification cost can be obtained (let us call it S). The sum of C and S is then the expected cost if u is tested, and the difference between $misc(u)$ and $C+S$ is the cost reduction $E(u)$ if u is tested. If such a cost reduction is positive, then u is put into the batch of tests. Then from the current set of reachable unknown attributes, a node with the maximum positive cost reduction is chosen, and it is added into the current batch of tests. This process is continued until the maximum cost reduction is no longer greater than 0, or there is no reachable unknown attributes (all unknown attributes under u are in the batch, reducing to Naïve Single Batch). The batch of tests is then discovered. The pseudo-code of OSB is shown here.

In the pseudo-code, $misc(.)$ is the expected misclassification cost of a node, $c(.)$ is the test cost of an attribute, $R(.)$ is all reachable unknown nodes and leaves under a node, and $p(.)$ is the probability (estimated by ratios in the training data) that a node is reached. Therefore, the formula $E(i)$ in the pseudo-code calculates the cost difference between no test at i (so only misclassification cost at i) and after testing i (the test cost plus the weighted sum of misclassification costs of reachable nodes under i). That is, $E(i)$ is the expected cost reduction if i is tested. Then the node t with the maximum cost reduction is found, and if such reduction is positive, t should be tested in the batch. Thus, t is removed from L and added into the batch list B, and all reachable unknown nodes or leaves of t, represented by the function $r(t)$, is added into L for further consideration. This process continues until there is no positive cost reduction or there is no unknown nodes to be considered (i.e., L is empty). The time complexity is linear to the size of the tree, as each node is considered only once.

> L = empty /* list of reachable and unknown attributes */
> B = empty /* the batch of tests */
> u = the first unknown attribute when classifying a test case
> Add u into L
> Loop
>   For each $i \in L$, calculate $E(i)$:
>
> $$E(i) = misc(i) - [c(i) + \sum p(R(i)) \times misc(R(i)) \;]$$
>
> $E(t) = max\ E(i)$ /* t has the maximum cost reduction */
>   If $E(t) > 0$ then add t into B, delete t from L, add $r(t)$ into L
>   else exit Loop /* No positive cost reduction */
>   Until L is empty
> Output B as the batch of tests

Comparing the two new single batch strategies, Greedy Single Batch (GSB) is simple and intuitive; it finds the most likely situation (leaf) and requests tests to "confirm" it. The time complexity is linear to the depth of the tree. It works well if there is a reachable leaf with a large number of training examples. The time complexity of the Optimal Single Batch (OSB) is linear to the size of the tree, but it is expected to have a smaller total cost than GSB. Both GSB and OSB may suggest tests that may be wasted, and test examples may not fall into a leaf.

Case Study on Heart Disease Continued. We apply GSB and OSB on the same test case as in Section 4.1.1 with the decision tree in Figure 1. The GSB suggests the (single) batch of (cp, and thal), while the OSB suggests the single batch of (cp, sex, slope, fbs, thal, age, chol, and restecg) to be tested. With both GSB and OSB, the test case does not go into a leaf, and some tests are wasted. The test cost is $103.9 for GSB and $221.17 for OSB, while the misclassification costs are 0 for both GSB and OSB. Thus, the total cost for the test case is $103.9 and $221.17 for GSB and OSB respectively. Note that we cannot conclude here GSB is better than OSB as this is only for a test case.

Comparing Single Batch Test Strategies. We use the same experiment procedure on the same 10 datasets to compare various Single Batch Test strategies including CSNB-SB [2]. The misclassification costs are set to 2000/6000. These costs are set to larger values so the trees will be larger to show more clearly the effect of batch tests. The total costs for the 10 datasets are compared and the average total costs for the 10 datasets are plotted in Figure 3.

From Figure 3 we can clearly see that Optimal Single Batch (OSB) performs the best among other single batch test strategies. When the ratio of missing attributes is relatively small (0.2), the three tree-based single batch test strategies are similar, as very few attributes would need to be tested. When the ratio of missing attributes increases, the differences become more evident, especially between Naïve Single Batch and Greedy Single Batch. All the tree-based single batch strategies perform better than the single batch with naïve Bayes. The reason is that the structure of the decision tree is utilized when deciding the single batch, while naïve Bayes has no such structure to rely on.

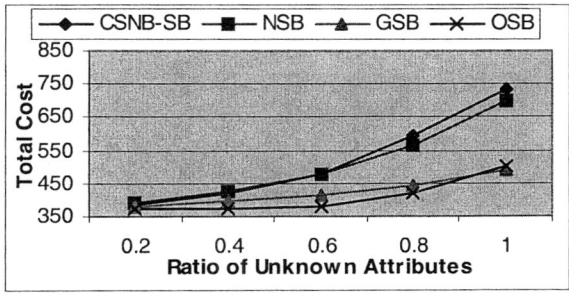

Fig. 3. Comparing our new Single Batch Test strategies GSB and OSB CSNB-SB and NSB

6 Conclusions and Future Work

In this paper, we present a lazy decision tree learning algorithm to minimize the total cost of misclassifications and tests. We then design two categories of test strategies: Sequential Test and Single Batch Test, to determine which unknown attributes should be tested, and in what order, to minimize the total cost of tests and misclassifications. We evaluate the performance (in terms of the total cost) empirically, compared to previous methods using a single decision tree and naïve Bayes. The results show that the new test strategies, Lazy-tree Optimal Sequential Test, and Optimal Single Batch, work best in the corresponding categories. The time complexity of these new test strategies is linear to the tree depth or the tree size, making them efficient for testing a large number of test cases. These strategies can be readily applied to large datasets in the real world. A detailed case study on heart disease is given in the paper.

In our future work we plan to continue to work with medical doctors to apply our algorithms to medical data with real costs. We also plan to consider discounts when groups of tests are ordered at the same time, and to incorporate other types of costs in our decision tree learning and test strategies.

References

1. Blake, C.L., and Merz, C.J. 1998. *UCI Repository of machine learning databases (website)*. Irvine, CA: University of California.
2. Chai, X., Deng, L., Yang, Q., and Ling,C.X.. 2004. Test-Cost Sensitive Naïve Bayesian Classification. *In Proceedings of the Fourth IEEE International Conference on Data Mining.* Brighton, UK : IEEE Computer Society Press.
3. Chawla,N.V., Japkowicz, N., and Kolcz, A. eds. 2004. *Special Issue on Learning from Imbalanced Datasets. SIGKDD*, 6(1): ACM Press.

4. Domingos, P. 1999. MetaCost: A General Method for Making Classifiers Cost-Sensitive. *In Proceedings of the Fifth International Conference on Knowledge Discovery and Data Mining*, 155-164. San Diego, CA: ACM Press.
5. Elkan, C. 2001. The Foundations of Cost-Sensitive Learning. *In Proceedings of the Seventeenth International Joint Conference of Artificial Intelligence*, 973-978. Seattle, Washington: Morgan Kaufmann.
6. Fayyad, U.M., and Irani, K.B. 1993. Multi-interval discretization of continuous-valued attributes for classification learning. *In Proceedings of the 13th International Joint Conference on Artificial Intelligence*, 1022-1027. France: Morgan Kaufmann.
7. Ting, K.M. 1998. Inducing Cost-Sensitive Trees via Instance Weighting. *In Proceedings of the Second European Symposium on Principles of Data Mining and Knowledge Discovery,* 23-26. Springer-Verlag.
8. Ling, C.X., Yang, Q., Wang, J., and Zhang, S. 2004. Decision Trees with Minimal Costs. *In Proceedings of the Twenty-First International Conference on Machine Learning,* Banff, Alberta: Morgan Kaufmann.
9. Lizotte, D., Madani, O., and Greiner R. 2003. Budgeted Learning of Naïve-Bayes Classifiers. *In Proceedings of the Nineteenth Conference on Uncertainty in Artificial Intelligence*. Acapulco, Mexico: Morgan Kaufmann.
10. Quinlan, J.R. eds. 1993. *C4.5: Programs for Machine Learning.* Morgan Kaufmann.
11. Tan, M. 1993. Cost-sensitive learning of classification knowledge and its applications in robotics. *Machine Learning Journal,* 13:7-33.
12. Turney, P.D. 1995. Cost-Sensitive Classification: Empirical Evaluation of a Hybrid Genetic Decision Tree Induction Algorithm. *Journal of Artificial Intelligence Research* 2:369-409.
13. Turney, P.D. 2000. Types of cost in inductive concept learning. *In Proceedings of the Workshop on Cost-Sensitive Learning at the Seventeenth International Conference on Machine Learning,* Stanford University, California.
14. Zubek, V.B., and Dietterich, T. 2002. Pruning improves heuristic search for cost-sensitive learning. *In Proceedings of the Nineteenth International Conference of Machine Learning,* 27-35, Sydney, Australia: Morgan Kaufmann.

$\mathcal{U}$-Likelihood and $\mathcal{U}$-Updating Algorithms: Statistical Inference in Latent Variable Models

Jaemo Sung[1], Sung-Yang Bang[1], Seungjin Choi[1], and Zoubin Ghahramani[2]

[1] Department of Computer Science,
POSTECH, Republic of Korea
{emtidi, sybang, seungjin}@postech.ac.kr
[2] Gatsby Computational Neuroscience Unit,
University College London, 17 Queen Square,
London WC1N 3AR, England
zoubin@gatsby.ucl.ac.uk

Abstract. In this paper we consider latent variable models and introduce a new $\mathcal{U}$-*likelihood* concept for estimating the distribution over hidden variables. One can derive an estimate of parameters from this distribution. Our approach differs from the Bayesian and Maximum Likelihood (ML) approaches. It gives an alternative to Bayesian inference when we don't want to define a prior over parameters and gives an alternative to the ML method when we want a better estimate of the distribution over hidden variables. As a practical implementation, we present a $\mathcal{U}$-*updating algorithm* based on the mean field theory to approximate the distribution over hidden variables from the $\mathcal{U}$-likelihood. This algorithm captures some of the correlations among hidden variables by estimating reaction terms. Those reaction terms are found to penalize the likelihood. We show that the $\mathcal{U}$-updating algorithm becomes the EM algorithm as a special case in the large sample limit. The useful behavior of our method is confirmed for the case of mixture of Gaussians by comparing to the EM algorithm.

1 Introduction

Latent variable models are important tools for probabilistic methods and have wide applications in machine learning, computer vision, pattern recognition, and speech processing, to name a few. The Bayesian and the Maximum Likelihood (ML) approaches have been extensively studied for learning such models in the past decades.

In Bayesian Inference [1], we define a prior over parameters $P(\boldsymbol{\theta})$ and from this all inference is automatically performed. In particular, using this prior we can compute the *marginal probability* of data set $Y = \{\boldsymbol{y}_1, \ldots, \boldsymbol{y}_n\}$ and hidden variable set $X = \{\boldsymbol{x}_1, \ldots, \boldsymbol{x}_n\}$:

$$P(Y, X) = \int P(Y, X|\boldsymbol{\theta})P(\boldsymbol{\theta})d\boldsymbol{\theta}. \qquad (1)$$

We can further marginalize out hidden variables to get the marginal probability of just data set Y:

$$P(Y) = \sum_X P(Y, X), \qquad (2)$$

assuming all hidden variables are discrete. The Bayesian approach basically provides a way of solving the overfitting problem by eliminating model parameters by integrating over them.

In certain settings it may be undesirable to define a prior over parameters. For example, many statisticians don't like the subjective nature of Bayesian inference even though all modelling contains an element of subjectivity. Moreover, in some cases it is very difficult to define one's prior belief about the model parameters. This motivates the use of ML method for parameter estimation.

Starting from the likelihood of the parameters, which is the probability of data set Y given the parameters, in the ML approach one can find the parameters which maximize the likelihood function given by

$$\mathcal{L}(\boldsymbol{\theta}) = \sum_X P(Y, X|\boldsymbol{\theta}). \qquad (3)$$

We wish to find the parameters that maximize the likelihood: $\boldsymbol{\theta}^* = \arg\max_{\boldsymbol{\theta}} \mathcal{L}(\boldsymbol{\theta})$. From this estimate of parameters, we can find the distribution over hidden variables $P(X|Y, \boldsymbol{\theta}^*)$, regarding $\boldsymbol{\theta}^*$ as true parameters. The fundamental problem of the ML approach is overfitting since it considers only a single estimate of ML parameters, whereas the Bayesian approach solves this problem by integrating over parameters.

If we don't want a Bayesian approach, we can still eliminate the parameters, not by marginalizing over them as in (1), but by maximizing over them. This is the key of our work. By doing so, we obtain a method somewhat analogous to the Bayesian approach without specifying the parameter prior.

In this paper, we introduce a new concept, $\mathcal{U}$-*likelihood*, to infer the distribution over hidden variables, which differs from the Bayesian and the ML approaches. We obtain the $\mathcal{U}$-likelihood, which is an analogous quantity to the marginal probability of data set in (2), by marginalizing the maximum of the complete-data likelihood over hidden variables. We show that the $\mathcal{U}$-likelihood can be bounded using variational method [2] and this gives the joint distribution over hidden variables $Q(X)$ (Sec. 3). Like the Bayesian and the ML approaches, the exact $Q(X)$ is intractable to compute for large data sets. As a practical implementation, we introduce a $\mathcal{U}$-*updating algorithm*, which iteratively solves mean field equations for hidden variables under $Q(X)$. We show that the $\mathcal{U}$-updating algorithm estimates the reaction of all the other hidden variables and it penalizes the likelihood term to alleviate the overfitting problem. The EM algorithm appears as a special case of $\mathcal{U}$-updating algorithm in the large sample limit. (Sec. 4). We demonstrate the useful behavior of our $\mathcal{U}$-updating algorithm, compared to the EM algorithm, through the example of mixtures of Gaussians on synthetic and real data sets (Sec. 5).

2 General Framework

Throughout this paper, we assume that data set $Y = \{y_1, \ldots, y_n\}$ of n data points is always given. Let $X = (x_1, \ldots, x_n)$ denote hidden variable set. Allowing y_i and x_i, to be multidimensional, we assume that a complete data point (y_i, x_i) is IID from a sampling distribution which is parameterized by parameter vector θ such as $P(y_i, x_i|\theta)$. For simplicity, we here focus on the discrete type hidden variable x_i, but the understanding of the case of continuous hidden variables is straightforward by exchanging sums into integrals.

For Bayesian inference, we can form a lower bound of $\log P(Y)$ in (2) for any $Q(X)$ using Jensen's inequality:

$$\log P(Y) \geq \sum_X Q(X) \log \frac{P(Y, X)}{Q(X)} \equiv \mathcal{F}_\mathcal{B}(Q(X)), \tag{4}$$

and then we can find $Q(X)$ by maximizing $\mathcal{F}_\mathcal{B}$. The maximization of $\mathcal{F}_\mathcal{B}$ is equivalent to the minimization of the Kullback-Leibler divergence between $Q(X)$ and $P(X|Y) = P(Y, X)/P(Y)$. Therefore, at maxima of $\mathcal{F}_\mathcal{B}$, $Q(X)$ gives the exact $P(X|Y)$. However, for most models of interest this is intractable to compute. For example, for a mixture model with m components, the sum $\sum_X$ of $P(Y)$ in (2) contains m^n terms. As practical implementations, MCMC [3] methods, the Expectation-Propagation (EP) [4] and the variational Bayes (VB) [5] methods were introduced but we will not tackle them in this paper.

For the ML approach, we can form the lower bound of log likelihood in a similar way to (4):

$$\log \mathcal{L}(\theta) \geq \sum_X Q(X) \log \frac{P(Y, X|\theta)}{Q(X)} \equiv \mathcal{F}_\mathcal{L}(Q(X), \theta). \tag{5}$$

The maximization of $\mathcal{F}_\mathcal{L}$ is equivalent to the maximization of $\mathcal{L}$ since if (Q^*, θ^*) occurs at maxima of $\mathcal{F}_\mathcal{L}$, then θ^* occurs at maxima of $\mathcal{L}(\theta)$ and $Q^*(X)$ becomes $P(X|Y, \theta^*)$. Since the global maximization of $\mathcal{F}_\mathcal{L}$ is intractable in most cases like in the Bayesian approach, the well-known EM algorithm [6] independently maximizes $\mathcal{F}_\mathcal{L}$ w.r.t. Q or θ by fixing the other as a practical implementation. Refer [6, 7] for more details on the EM algorithm.

3 $\mathcal{U}$-Likelihood

If we don't want a Bayesian approach, we can still eliminate the parameters, not by marginalizing over them as in (1), but by maximizing over them. We start by defining the $\mathcal{U}$-function which is the maximum of the complete-data likelihood:

$$\mathcal{U}(Y, X) \equiv \max_\theta P(Y, X|\theta) = P(Y, X|\widehat{\theta}(Y, X)) > 0, \tag{6}$$

where $\widehat{\theta}(Y, X)$ denotes the ML parameter estimator, a function of the complete-data set, defined by

$$\widehat{\theta}(Y, X) \equiv \arg\max_\theta P(Y, X|\theta). \tag{7}$$

The $\mathcal{U}$-function is analogous to the marginal probability in (1) except that it maximizes over parameters rather than integrating over parameters. Another way to think about it is that instead of a parameter prior, we substitute in (1) a delta function of the ML parameter estimate on the complete-data set, e.g. $P(\boldsymbol{\theta}) = \delta(\boldsymbol{\theta} - \widehat{\boldsymbol{\theta}}(Y, X))$. This is certainly not coherent from the point of view of Bayesian inference since the prior cannot depend on the data, but we will see some of the interesting properties of this approach.

We can take the $\mathcal{U}$-function and marginalize out the hidden variable set X:

$$\mathcal{U}(Y) \equiv \sum_X \mathcal{U}(Y, X). \qquad (8)$$

We call this quantity $\mathcal{U}$-*likelihood* and it is analogous to $P(Y)$ in (2). Another view of it is that it forms an upper bound of the likelihood function: $\mathcal{U} \geq \mathcal{L}^* \geq \mathcal{L}(\boldsymbol{\theta})$, where $\mathcal{L}^* = \max_{\boldsymbol{\theta}} \mathcal{L}(\boldsymbol{\theta})$ denotes the maximum likelihood value. Analogous to (4), we can lower bound it for any distribution $Q(X)$ over hidden variables:

$$\log \mathcal{U}(Y) \geq \sum_X Q(X) \log \frac{\mathcal{U}(Y, X)}{Q(X)} \equiv \mathcal{F}_\mathcal{U}(Q(X)). \qquad (9)$$

We can use the optimal $Q(X)$ maximizing $\mathcal{F}_\mathcal{U}$ as a joint conditional distribution over hidden variables given data set: $P(X|Y)$. The next theorem shows the form of $Q(X)$ at the maxima of $\mathcal{F}_\mathcal{U}$.

Theorem 1. *The optimal joint distribution $Q(X)$ maximizing the lower bound $\mathcal{F}_\mathcal{U}(Q(X))$ is of the form*

$$Q(X) = \frac{\mathcal{U}(Y, X)}{\mathcal{U}(Y)}. \qquad (10)$$

Proof: Let $Q'(X) = \frac{\mathcal{U}(Y,X)}{\mathcal{U}(Y)}$. Then, the Kullback-Leibler divergence between $Q(X)$ and $Q'(X)$ is given by $KL[Q\|Q'] = \log \mathcal{U}(Y) - \mathcal{F}_\mathcal{U}(Q)$. It follows from Gibbs inequality that $KL[Q\|Q'] = 0$ when $Q(X) = Q'(X)$, implying that $\mathcal{F}_\mathcal{U}(Q)$ is maximized at $Q(X) = Q'(X)$. ∎

We illustrate the joint distribution $Q(X)$ in (10) when data set Y consists of 12 data points generated from the mixture of two Gaussians. The true X^* is a binary vector with 12 components. Figure 1 plots $\log Q(X)$ as a function of Manhattan distance from the true X^*. This demonstrates that $Q(X)$ tends to give higher probability to hidden states that are similar to the true states.

We have seen the relationship of $\mathcal{U}$-likelihood to Bayesian inference. We can also see a simple relationship to maximum likelihood methods:

$$\text{Maximum likelihood} \quad : \quad \mathcal{L}^* = \max_{\boldsymbol{\theta}} \sum_X P(Y, X|\boldsymbol{\theta}), \qquad (11)$$

$$\mathcal{U}\text{-likelihood} \quad : \quad \mathcal{U} = \sum_X \max_{\boldsymbol{\theta}} P(Y, X|\boldsymbol{\theta}), \qquad (12)$$

where we here dropped the data dependency. The former gives a single value of the model parameters $\boldsymbol{\theta}^*$, from which a distribution over hidden variables can

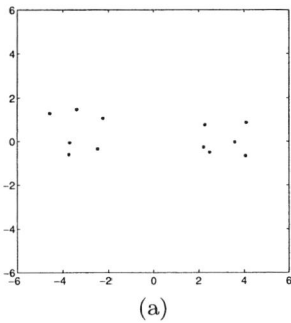 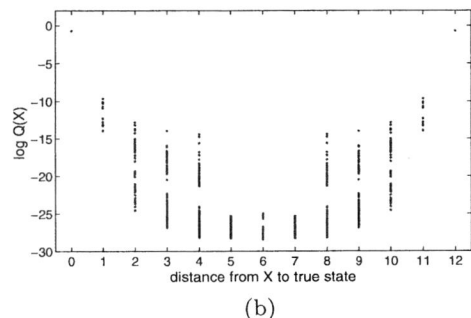

Fig. 1. Demonstration of $Q(X)$ in Theorem 1 given data set Y of 12 data points generated from the mixture of two Gaussians, i.e. $\mathcal{N}([-3,0],\mathbf{I})$ and $\mathcal{N}([3,0],\mathbf{I})$. (a) data set Y. (b) $\log Q(X)$ as a function of Manhattan distance from the true state, $\sum_{i=1}^{12} |x_i - x_i^*|$. Each dot indicates a state of 2^{12} possible configurations of X. The symmetrical phenomenon stems from the identifiability of the mixture of Gaussians.

be derived: $P(X|Y, \boldsymbol{\theta}^*)$. The latter no longer gives a single value of parameters. However, it may give a better estimate of the distribution over hidden variables, $Q(X)$, which captures some of correlations among hidden variables. From this distribution $Q(X)$ one can derive an estimate of parameters.

We outline some of the possible advantages of $\mathcal{U}$-likelihood approach over the Bayesian and the ML approaches:

1. High dimensional integrals like (1) required for Bayesian inference can be intractable. For many models, the optimum of $\boldsymbol{\theta}$ given the complete-data set (Y, X) is a simple function of the sufficient statistics. So no explicit optimization is necessary to compute (6).
2. Many researchers may not wish to define a prior over parameters. The $\mathcal{U}$-likelihood method provides an alternative.
3. Optimizing over parameters in the ML method is often fraught with local optima. By optimizing out parameters, the $\mathcal{U}$-likelihood method is sometimes found to have better convergence properties than the ML method. That is, it can find good solutions without falling into local optima as often. We show this empirically.

The distribution $Q(X)$ in (10) may be intractable to compute, excepting for small n, since it requires all possible configurations of X. As a practical implementation, we will use a mean field approximation and present the $\mathcal{U}$-updating algorithm as an alternative to the EM algorithm in the next section.

4 $\mathcal{U}$-Updating Algorithm

We start by considering a case where the sampling distribution of the complete-data $(\boldsymbol{y}_i, \boldsymbol{x}_i)$ is in the exponential family with the following form

$$P(\boldsymbol{y}_i, \boldsymbol{x}_i|\boldsymbol{\theta}) = f(\boldsymbol{s}_i(\boldsymbol{y}_i, \boldsymbol{x}_i))g(\boldsymbol{\theta}) \exp\left\{\boldsymbol{\phi}(\boldsymbol{\theta})^{\mathrm{T}} \boldsymbol{s}_i(\boldsymbol{y}_i, \boldsymbol{x}_i)\right\}, \tag{13}$$

where $\boldsymbol{\phi}(\boldsymbol{\theta})$ is a vector of natural parameters and $\boldsymbol{s}_i(\boldsymbol{y}_i, \boldsymbol{x}_i)$ is a vector of sufficient statistics. The normalizing constant is denoted by $g(\boldsymbol{\theta})$. Probability distributions of the exponential family have been widely used in latent variable models such as mixture of Gaussians, factor analysis, hidden Markov models, state-space models, and so on. For the case of the exponential family, the complete-data likelihood depends on the complete-data set only through sufficient statistics:

$$P(Y, X|\boldsymbol{\theta}) = \left[\prod_{i=1}^{n} f(\boldsymbol{s}_i(\boldsymbol{y}_i, \boldsymbol{x}_i))\right] g(\boldsymbol{\theta})^n \exp\left\{\boldsymbol{\phi}(\boldsymbol{\theta})^{\mathrm{T}} \boldsymbol{s}(Y, X)\right\}, \tag{14}$$

where $\boldsymbol{s}(Y, X) = \sum_{i=1}^{n} \boldsymbol{s}_i(\boldsymbol{y}_i, \boldsymbol{x}_i)$. Moreover, a closed-form solution of $\widehat{\boldsymbol{\theta}}$ and $\mathcal{U}$-function always exists as a function of sufficient statistics: $\widehat{\boldsymbol{\theta}}(Y, X) = \widehat{\boldsymbol{\theta}}(\boldsymbol{s}(Y, X))$ and $\mathcal{U}(Y, X) = \mathcal{U}(\boldsymbol{s}(Y, X))$.

The mean field theory [8], originally from statistical physics, has been widely used in the machine learning community to approximate joint distributions in graphical models when exact inference is intractable because of highly-coupled interactions among variables. Consider the marginal distribution over $\boldsymbol{x}_i$:

$$Q(\boldsymbol{x}_i) = \sum_{X_{\backslash i}} Q(X) = \frac{1}{\mathcal{U}(Y)} \sum_{X_{\backslash i}} \mathcal{U}(\boldsymbol{s}(Y, X)), \tag{15}$$

where $X_{\backslash i}$ denotes a subset of hidden variables where $\boldsymbol{x}_i$ is excluded: $X_{\backslash i} = X \setminus \boldsymbol{x}_i$. In general, the exact calculation of $Q(\boldsymbol{x}_i)$ is intractable since it requires all possible realizations of $X_{\backslash i}$. Assuming weak dependencies among hidden variables, the mean field theory suggests that the influence of the other hidden variables $\boldsymbol{s}_j(\boldsymbol{y}_j, \boldsymbol{x}_j)$ in the marginal distribution $Q(\boldsymbol{x}_i)$ can be approximated by the expected values $\langle \boldsymbol{s}_j(\boldsymbol{y}_j, \boldsymbol{x}_j) \rangle$. This leads to the mean field distributions $Q_i(\boldsymbol{x}_i)$:

$$Q_i(\boldsymbol{x}_i) \equiv \frac{1}{\mathcal{U}_i} \mathcal{U}(\bar{\boldsymbol{s}}_i(\boldsymbol{x}_i)) \approx Q(\boldsymbol{x}_i), \tag{16}$$

where $\bar{\boldsymbol{s}}_i(\boldsymbol{x}_i) = \boldsymbol{s}_i(\boldsymbol{y}_i, \boldsymbol{x}_i) + \sum_{j=1, j\neq i}^{n} \langle \boldsymbol{s}_j(\boldsymbol{y}_j, \boldsymbol{x}_j) \rangle$ and $\mathcal{U}_i = \sum_{\boldsymbol{x}_i} \mathcal{U}(\bar{\boldsymbol{s}}_i(\boldsymbol{x}_i))$ is the normalizing constant. The joint distribution $Q(X)$ is approximated by the factored form with all mean field distributions $Q_i(\boldsymbol{x}_i)$: $Q(X) \approx \prod_{i=1}^{n} Q_i(\boldsymbol{x}_i)$. Moreover, the expected sufficient statistics $\langle \boldsymbol{s}(Y, X) \rangle$ can be obtained by solving self-consistent equations called mean field equations, which are stationary conditions:

$$\langle \boldsymbol{s}_i(\boldsymbol{y}_i, \boldsymbol{x}_i) \rangle = \sum_{\boldsymbol{x}_i} \boldsymbol{s}_i(\boldsymbol{y}_i, \boldsymbol{x}_i) Q_i(\boldsymbol{x}_i). \tag{17}$$

Table 1. $\mathcal{U}$-updating algorithm and EM algorithm

$\mathcal{U}$-updating algorithm	EM algorithm

Initialize $\langle s \rangle^{(0)} = \sum_{i=1}^{n} \langle s_i(y_i, x_i) \rangle^{(0)}$.
 Set $\langle s \rangle^{(1)} = \langle s \rangle^{(0)}$.
 Repeat $t = 1, 2, \ldots$ until convergence .
    Repeat $i = 1, \ldots, n$.
      Update $Q_i^{(t)}(x_i) \propto \mathcal{U}(\bar{s}_i^{(t)}(x_i))$,
      $\bar{s}_i^{(t)}(x_i) =$
      $\langle s \rangle^{(t)} + s_i(y_i, x_i) - \langle s_i(y_i, x_i) \rangle^{(t-1)}$.
      Refine
      $\langle s \rangle^{(t)} \leftarrow$
      $\langle s \rangle^{(t)} + \langle s_i(y_i, x_i) \rangle^{(t)} - \langle s_i(y_i, x_i) \rangle^{(t-1)}$
      with $\langle s_i(y_i, x_i) \rangle^{(t)}$ under new $Q_i^{(t)}(x_i)$.
    End (Repeat)
    Set $\langle s \rangle^{(t+1)} = \langle s \rangle^{(t)}$.
 End (Repeat)
	Initialize $\theta^{(0)}$.
	 Repeat $t = 1, 2, \ldots$ until convergence.
	    E-Step :
	      Update $Q_i^{(t)}(x_i) = P(x_i \vert y_i, \theta^{(t)})$
	      for all $i = 1, \ldots, n$.
	    M-Step :
	      Estimate $\theta^{(t+1)} = \widehat{\theta}(\langle s \rangle^{(t)})$
	      with $\langle s \rangle^{(t)} = \sum_{i=1}^{n} \langle s_i(y_i, x_i) \rangle^{(t)}$
	      under new $\{Q_i^{(t)}(x_i)\}$.
	 End (Repeat)

Therefore, the distribution $Q_i(x_i)$ in (16) can be computed by iterative procedure solving the mean field equations in (17). This iterative procedure is referred to as the $\mathcal{U}$-*updating algorithm* and gives an alternative to the EM algorithm.

The Table 1 summarizes the $\mathcal{U}$-updating algorithm in comparison with the EM algorithm. In order to estimate ML parameter $\theta^{(t+1)}$ in M-Step, the EM algorithm requires distributions $P(x_i \vert y_i, \theta^{(t)})$ in E-Step built on the ML parameter $\theta^{(t)}$ which may be overfitted to the data set at the previous iteration. Therefore, the overfitting effects may accumulate throughout iterations in the EM algorithm. However, the $\mathcal{U}$-updating algorithm alleviates this overfitting-accumulation problem by estimating the reaction of all the other hidden variables, which penalizes the likelihood. Therefore, it can give better distribution $Q_i(x_i)$ than the EM algorithm. We can simply use all $Q_i(x_i)$ resulted from the $\mathcal{U}$-updating algorithm to estimate parameters like the M-Step of the EM algorithm.

In order to see how the $\mathcal{U}$-updating algorithm penalizes the likelihood, decompose the $\mathcal{U}$-function:

$$\mathcal{U}(\bar{s}_i(x_i)) = \alpha_i(x_i)\,\beta_i(x_i), \tag{18}$$

where $\alpha_i(x_i) = P(s_i(y_i, x_i) \vert \widehat{\theta}(\bar{s}_i(x_i)))$ and $\beta_i(x_i) = \prod_{j=1, \neq i}^{n} \rho(\langle s_j(y_j, x_j) \rangle \vert \widehat{\theta}(\bar{s}_i(x_i)))$, given by

$$\rho(\langle s_j(y_j, x_j) \rangle \vert \widehat{\theta}(\bar{s}_i(x_i))) = f(\langle s_j \rangle) g(\widehat{\theta}(\bar{s}_i(x_i))) \exp\left\{ \phi(\widehat{\theta}(\bar{s}_i(x_i)))^{\mathrm{T}} \langle s_j \rangle \right\}.$$

The term $\alpha_i(x_i)$ is the likelihood on the complete data point i. The term $\beta_i(x_i)$ can be interpreted as a reaction of all the other hidden variables via the expected values $\langle s_j(y_j, x_j) \rangle$. When computing $Q_i(x_i)$, the $\mathcal{U}$-updating algorithm therefore penalizes the likelihood $\alpha_i(x_i)$ by estimating the reaction $\beta_i(x_i)$ of the other hidden variables, which captures some correlations among hidden variables.

The $\mathcal{U}$-updating algorithm generalizes the EM algorithm since if we ignore the reaction term $\beta_i(\boldsymbol{x}_i)$ in (18), it will be same to the EM algorithm. The following theorem states the behavior of $\mathcal{U}$-updating algorithm in the large sample limit.

Theorem 2. *For the case of the exponential family, the $\mathcal{U}$-updating algorithm is equivalent to the EM algorithm in the limit of large samples.*

Proof: In the large sample limit, the sufficient statistic $s(Y, X)$ will be insensitive to one hidden variable: $s_i(\boldsymbol{y}_i, \boldsymbol{x}_i) + \sum_{j=1, \neq i}^{n} \langle s_j(\boldsymbol{y}_j, \boldsymbol{x}_j) \rangle \approx \langle s(Y, X) \rangle$ as $n \to \infty$. Therefore, in the large sample limit, the reaction term $\beta_i(\boldsymbol{x}_i)$ becomes a constant and $Q_i(\boldsymbol{x}_i)$ of the $\mathcal{U}$-updating algorithm becomes the distribution resulted from the E-step of the EM algorithm:

$$Q_i(\boldsymbol{x}_i) = \frac{P(\boldsymbol{y}_i, \boldsymbol{x}_i \mid \widehat{\boldsymbol{\theta}}(\langle s \rangle))}{\sum_{\boldsymbol{x}'_i} P(\boldsymbol{y}_i, \boldsymbol{x}'_i \mid \widehat{\boldsymbol{\theta}}(\langle s \rangle))} = P(\boldsymbol{x}_i \mid \boldsymbol{y}_i, \widehat{\boldsymbol{\theta}}(\langle s \rangle)). \tag{19}$$

From the fact that $\widehat{\boldsymbol{\theta}}(\langle s \rangle)$ gives the ML parameter in the M-step of the EM algorithm, the $\mathcal{U}$-updating algorithm is equivalent to the EM algorithm in the large sample limit. ∎

5 Numerical Experiments

5.1 Mixture of Gaussians

For the p-dimensional observational vector $\boldsymbol{y}_i \in \mathbb{R}^p$, the mixture model [9, 10] of m components with parameter $\boldsymbol{\theta}$ is generally defined as $P(\boldsymbol{y}_i|\boldsymbol{\theta}) = \sum_{k=1}^{m} P(\boldsymbol{y}_i|x_i = k, \boldsymbol{\theta})P(x_i = k|\boldsymbol{\theta})$, where $x_i \in \{k = 1, \ldots, m\}$ denotes the hidden variable indicating which mixture component is in charge of generating $\boldsymbol{y}_i$. The components are labelled by k. Although our method can be applied to an arbitrary mixture model, for simplicity, we consider the case of Gaussian components. In this case, the mixture model parameterized by $\boldsymbol{\theta} = (\{\boldsymbol{\mu}_k\}, \{\boldsymbol{\Sigma}_k\}, \{w_k\})$ is given by $P(\boldsymbol{y}_i|\boldsymbol{\theta}) = \sum_{k=1}^{m} \mathcal{N}(\boldsymbol{y}_i; \boldsymbol{\mu}_k, \boldsymbol{\Sigma}_k) w_k$, where $w_k = P(x_i = k|\boldsymbol{\theta})$ is the mixing proportion satisfying $\sum_{k=1}^{m} w_k = 1$ and $\mathcal{N}(\boldsymbol{y}_i; \boldsymbol{\mu}_k, \boldsymbol{\Sigma}_k) = P(\boldsymbol{y}_i|x_i = k, \boldsymbol{\theta})$ denotes the kth Gaussian component distribution with the mean vector $\boldsymbol{\mu}_k$ and covariance matrix $\boldsymbol{\Sigma}_k$. The sampling distribution of the mixture of Gaussians is given by

$$P(\boldsymbol{y}_i, x_i|\boldsymbol{\theta}) = \prod_{k=1}^{m} \left[\mathcal{N}(\boldsymbol{y}_i; \boldsymbol{\mu}_k, \boldsymbol{\Sigma}_k) w_k\right]^{\delta_k(x_i)}, \tag{20}$$

where $\delta_k(x_i)$ denotes the Kronecker delta function given by $\delta_k(x_i) = 1$ for $x_i = k$ and $\delta_k(x_i) = 0$ for $x_i \neq k$.

Let (Y, X) denote the complete data set of n IID observations, where $Y = \{\boldsymbol{y}_1, \ldots, \boldsymbol{y}_n\}$ and $X = \{x_1, \ldots, x_n\}$. Since the sampling distribution $P(\boldsymbol{y}_i, x_i|\boldsymbol{\theta})$ is in the exponential family, the complete data likelihood $P(Y, X|\boldsymbol{\theta})$ and the ML parameter estimator $\widehat{\boldsymbol{\theta}}(Y, X)$ become the function of the sufficient statistics.

Table 2. $\mathcal{U}$-updating Algorithm : Mixture of Gaussians

---

Initialize $\langle\gamma_k\rangle^{(0)} = \sum_{i=1}^{n}\langle\delta_k(x_i)\rangle^{(0)}$,
$\quad\langle\boldsymbol{\xi}_k\rangle^{(0)} = \sum_{i=1}^{n}\langle\delta_k(x_i)\rangle^{(0)}\,\boldsymbol{y}_i$,
$\quad\langle\boldsymbol{\lambda}_k\rangle^{(0)} = \sum_{i=1}^{n}\langle\delta_k(x_i)\rangle^{(0)}\,\boldsymbol{y}_i\boldsymbol{y}_i^{\mathrm{T}}$,
$\quad$ where $\langle\delta_k(x_i)\rangle^{(0)} = Q_i^{(0)}(x_i = k)$.
Set $\langle\gamma_k\rangle^{(1)} = \langle\gamma_k\rangle^{(0)}$, $\langle\boldsymbol{\xi}_k\rangle^{(1)} = \langle\boldsymbol{\xi}_k\rangle^{(0)}$ and $\langle\boldsymbol{\lambda}_k\rangle^{(1)} = \langle\boldsymbol{\lambda}_k\rangle^{(0)}$.
Repeat $t = 1, 2, 3, \ldots$ until convergence.
$\quad$ Repeat $i = 1, \ldots, n$.
$\quad\quad$ 1) Update $Q_i^t(x_i) \propto \prod_{k=1}^{m}\left(\bar{\gamma}_k^{(t)}(x_i)^{1+\frac{p}{2}}|\bar{C}_k^{(t)}(x_i)|^{-\frac{1}{2}}\right)^{\bar{\gamma}_k^{(t)}(x_i)}$,
$\quad\quad\quad$ where $\bar{\gamma}_k^{(t)}(x_i) = \langle\gamma_k\rangle^{(t)} + [\delta_k(x_i) - \langle\delta_k(x_i)\rangle^{(t-1)}]$,
$\quad\quad\quad\quad\bar{\boldsymbol{\xi}}_k^{(t)}(x_i) = \langle\boldsymbol{\xi}_k\rangle^{(t)} + [\delta_k(x_i) - \langle\delta_k(x_i)\rangle^{(t-1)}]\,\boldsymbol{y}_i$,
$\quad\quad\quad\quad\bar{\boldsymbol{\lambda}}_k^{(t)}(x_i) = \langle\boldsymbol{\lambda}_k\rangle^{(t)} + [\delta_k(x_i) - \langle\delta_k(x_i)\rangle^{(t-1)}]\,\boldsymbol{y}_i\boldsymbol{y}_i^{\mathrm{T}}$,
$\quad\quad\quad\quad\bar{C}_k^{(t)}(x_i) = \bar{\boldsymbol{\lambda}}_k^{(t)}(x_i) - \bar{\gamma}_k^{(t)}(x_i)^{-1}\bar{\boldsymbol{\xi}}_k^{(t)}(x_i)\bar{\boldsymbol{\xi}}_k^{(t)}(x_i)^{\mathrm{T}}$.
$\quad\quad$ 2) Refine sufficient statistics
$\quad\quad\quad\langle\gamma_k\rangle^{(t)} \leftarrow \langle\gamma_k\rangle^{(t)} + [\langle\delta_k(x_i)\rangle^{(t)} - \langle\delta_k(x_i)\rangle^{(t-1)}]$,
$\quad\quad\quad\langle\boldsymbol{\xi}_k\rangle^{(t)} \leftarrow \langle\boldsymbol{\xi}_k\rangle^{(t)} + [\langle\delta_k(x_i)\rangle^{(t)} - \langle\delta_k(x_i)\rangle^{(t-1)}]\,\boldsymbol{y}_i$,
$\quad\quad\quad\langle\boldsymbol{\lambda}_k\rangle^{(t)} \leftarrow \langle\boldsymbol{\lambda}_k\rangle^{(t)} + [\langle\delta_k(x_i)\rangle^{(t)} - \langle\delta_k(x_i)\rangle^{(t-1)}]\,\boldsymbol{y}_i\boldsymbol{y}_i^{\mathrm{T}}$
$\quad\quad$ with $\langle\delta_k(x_i)\rangle^{(t)} = Q_i^{(t)}(x_i)$.
$\quad$ End (Repeat)
$\quad$ Set $\langle\gamma_k\rangle^{(t+1)} = \langle\gamma_k\rangle^{(t)}$, $\langle\boldsymbol{\xi}_k\rangle^{(t+1)} = \langle\boldsymbol{\xi}_k\rangle^{(t)}$ and $\langle\boldsymbol{\lambda}_k\rangle^{(t+1)} = \langle\boldsymbol{\lambda}_k\rangle^{(t)}$.
End (Repeat)

Therefore, the $\mathcal{U}$-function is also a function of the sufficient statistics $s(Y, X) = (\{\gamma_k, \boldsymbol{\xi}_k, \boldsymbol{\lambda}_k\})$:

$$\mathcal{U}(\{\gamma_k, \boldsymbol{\xi}_k, \boldsymbol{\lambda}_k\}) = c\prod_{k=1}^{m}\left(\gamma_k^{1+\frac{p}{2}}|C_k|^{-\frac{1}{2}}\right)^{\gamma_k}, \qquad (21)$$

where $C_k = \boldsymbol{\lambda}_k - \gamma_k^{-1}\boldsymbol{\xi}_k\boldsymbol{\xi}_k^{\mathrm{T}}$ and

$$\gamma_k = \sum_{i=1}^{n}\delta_k(x_i), \quad \boldsymbol{\xi}_k = \sum_{i=1}^{n}\delta_k(x_i)\,\boldsymbol{y}_i, \quad \boldsymbol{\lambda}_k = \sum_{i=1}^{n}\delta_k(x_i)\,\boldsymbol{y}_i\boldsymbol{y}_i^{\mathrm{T}}, \qquad (22)$$

and c is a constant. Using $\langle\delta_k(x_i)\rangle = Q_i(x_i = k)$, we present the $\mathcal{U}$-updating algorithm for the mixture of Gaussians in Table 2. We can simply obtain the estimate of the parameters by $\boldsymbol{\theta}^* = \widehat{\boldsymbol{\theta}}(\{\langle\gamma_k\rangle, \langle\boldsymbol{\xi}_k\rangle, \langle\boldsymbol{\lambda}_k\rangle\})$ under all $Q_i(\boldsymbol{x}_i)$ resulted from the $\mathcal{U}$-updating algorithm like as the M-Step of the EM algorithm, where the ML parameter estimator is given by

$$\widehat{\boldsymbol{\theta}}(\{\gamma_k, \boldsymbol{\xi}_k, \boldsymbol{\lambda}_k\}) = \left(\left\{\widehat{w}_k = \frac{\gamma_k}{n}, \widehat{\boldsymbol{\mu}}_k = \frac{\boldsymbol{\xi}_k}{\gamma_k}, \widehat{\boldsymbol{\Sigma}}_k = \frac{C_k}{\gamma_k}\right\}\right). \qquad (23)$$

5.2 Numerical Results

In order to demonstrate $\mathcal{U}$-updating algorithm in comparison with the EM algorithm, we first used the data set of 800 data points generated from the mixture

386   J. Sung et al.

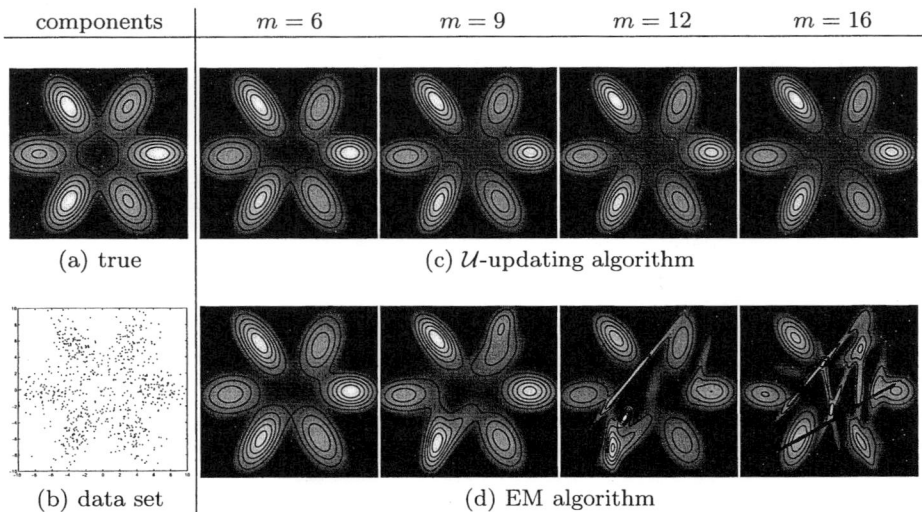

Fig. 2. Results on a mixture of 6 well-clustered Gaussian components: (a) true Gaussian-mixture distribution, where the more bright, the higher probability is there. (b) 800 data points generated from the true distribution. (c) and (d) learned distributions by $\mathcal{U}$-updating and EM algorithms when the models have the components $m = 6, 9, 12, 16$.

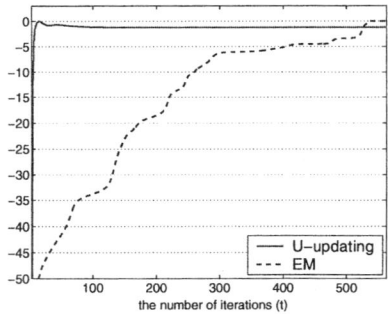

Fig. 3. Intermediate log likelihood values, subtracted from the maximum value, of the $\mathcal{U}$-updating and the EM algorithms in the case of $m = 16$ on data set shown in Figure 2

of 6 well-clustered Gaussian components having equal mixing proportion w_k but having different volume. Both algorithms started by the same initial guess from k-means algorithm. Figure 2 shows that the $\mathcal{U}$-updating algorithm alleviates the overfitting in comparison with the EM algorithm. Although models were more complicated than the true model ($m = 6$), the $\mathcal{U}$-updating algorithm demonstrated that all of the learned distributions ($m = 6, 9, 12, 16$) were very similar

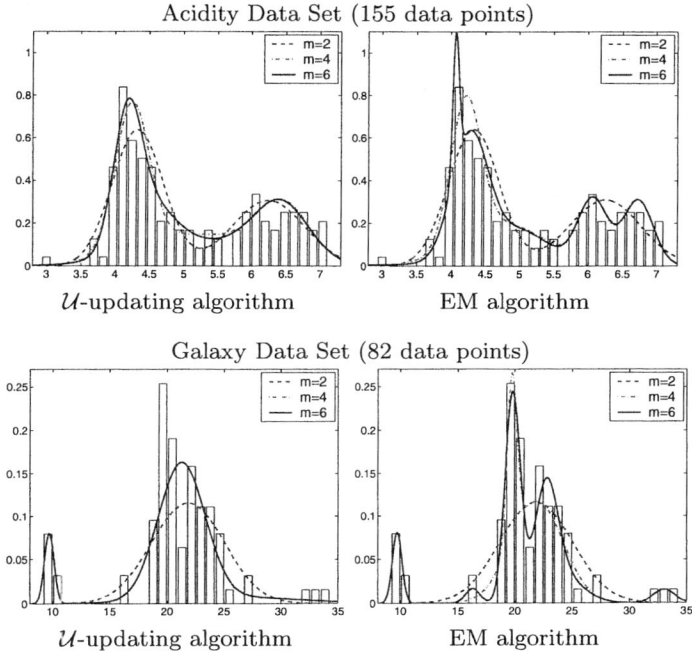

Fig. 4. Learned distributions by $\mathcal{U}$-updating and EM algorithms when the models have the components $m = 2, 4, 6$

to the true distribution. However, for the EM algorithm, the more complicated the model we considered, the more overfitted the distribution that resulted.

As a practical issue, overfitting leads to slow convergence. Figure 3 shows the convergence curves in term of log likelihood subtracted from the maximum value in the case of $m = 16$. By penalizing the likelihood term α_i by the reaction term β_i, the $\mathcal{U}$-updating algorithm achieved much faster convergence, approximately more than three times, than the EM algorithm. The $\mathcal{U}$-updating algorithm met the convergence threshold, that was $\sqrt{\sum_{k=1}^{m} |w_k^{(t)} - w_k^{(t-1)}|^2} < 10^{-4}$, after 153 iterations, whereas the EM algorithm met the same threshold after 563 iterations.

Next, we used real data sets, acidity and galaxy data sets shown in [10]. Figure 4 shows the learned distributions when the models have 2, 4, and 6 components and the Table 3 shows that the optimized mixing proportions $\hat{w}_k$ when the model has 6 components.

6 Conclusions

In this paper, we introduced the $\mathcal{U}$-likelihood approach for learning latent variable models, which differs from the Bayesian and the ML approaches. We presented some advantages of our approach over them in section 3. Our $\mathcal{U}$-likelihood method gives an alternative to Bayesian inference and the ML method when we

Table 3. Optimized mixing proportions ($\hat{w}_k$) of learned model having 6 components

Component	1	2	3	4	5	6
Acidity Data Set						
$\mathcal{U}$-updating algorithm	0.295	0.259	0.187	0.086	0.086	0.086
EM algorithm	0.386	0.188	0.171	0.169	0.073	0.013
Galaxy Data Set						
$\mathcal{U}$-updating algorithm	0.267	0.267	0.267	0.083	0.058	0.058
EM algorithm	0.403	0.277	0.171	0.085	0.037	0.026

don't want to use these. As a practical implementation, we presented the $\mathcal{U}$-updating algorithm to compute the distribution over hidden variables, which was found to penalize the likelihood by estimating the reaction of the other hidden variables and to alleviate the overfitting-accmulation problem of the EM algorithm.

We leave some of issues for the future work: 1) How can we more accurately approximate $Q(X)$ in (10) than the $\mathcal{U}$-updating algorithm. 2) How can we perform the model selection in the framework of the $\mathcal{U}$-likelihood. 3) Comparison with the Bayesian approach, e.g. EP and VB.

References

1. A. Gelman, J. B. Carlin, H. S. Stern, D. B. Rubin, and A. Gelman. *Bayesian Data Analysis*. Chapman & Hall/CRC, 1995.
2. M. Jordan, Z. Ghahramani, T. Jaakkola, and L. Saul. An introduction to variational methods for graphical models. *Machine Learning*, 72(2):183–233, 1999.
3. R. M. Neal. Probabilistic Inference Using Markov Chain Monte Carlo Methods. Technical Report CRG-TR-93-1, Dept. of Computer Science, University of Toronto, 1993.
4. T. Minka. Expectation Propagation for approximate Bayesian inference. In *Proc. Uncertainty in Artificial Intelligence*, 2001.
5. Z. Ghahramani and M. J. Beal. Propagation algorithms for variational bayesian learning. In *Advances in Neural Information Processing Systems*, volume 13. MIT Press, 2001.
6. A. P. Dempster, N. M. Laird, and D. B. Rubin. Maximum likelihood from incomplete data via the EM algorithm. *Journal of the Royal Statistical Society B*, 39:1–38, 1977.
7. R. M. Neal and G. E. Hinton. A view of the EM algorithm that justifies incremental, sparse, and other variants. In M. I. Jordan, editor, *Learning in Graphical Models*, pages 355–368. Kluwer Academic Publishers, 1988.
8. M. Opper and D. Saad, editors. *Advanced Mean Field Methods : Theory and Practice*. MIT Press, 2001.
9. G. McLachlan and D. Peel. *Finite Mixture Models*. Wiley-Interscience, 2000.
10. S. Richardson and P. J. Green. On Bayesian analysis of mixtures with an unknown number of components. *Journal of the Royal Statistical Society B*, 59:731–792, 1997.

An Optimal Best-First Search Algorithm for Solving Infinite Horizon DEC-POMDPs

Daniel Szer and François Charpillet

INRIA Lorraine - LORIA, MAIA Group,
54506 Vandœuvre-lès-Nancy, France
{szer, charp}@loria.fr
http://maia.loria.fr

Abstract. In the domain of decentralized Markov decision processes, we develop the first complete and optimal algorithm that is able to extract deterministic policy vectors based on finite state controllers for a cooperative team of agents. Our algorithm applies to the discounted infinite horizon case and extends best-first search methods to the domain of decentralized control theory. We prove the optimality of our approach and give some first experimental results for two small test problems. We believe this to be an important step forward in learning and planning in stochastic multi-agent systems.

1 Introduction

Efficient learning and planning algorithms for problems within distributed and only partially observable stochastic environments can be particularly useful in a large number of todays research areas, such as network traffic routing [1], decentralized supply chains [7], or the control of a robot team for space exploration [12] or humanitarian missions [11]. Formalizing the problem of optimal control in a rigorous way is an important part of the solution, and the theory of Markov Decision Processes (MDPs) has been shown to be particularly powerful in that context [16]. It is only recently however, that the Markov framework has been extended to problems of decentralized control [5], [3]. The major additional complexity in multi-agent decision making lies in the fact that agents may have different partial information about both the underlying system state and the local information held by the remaining agents. Reasoning about the potential private information of a teammate may in fact lead into an infinite loop of "*I believe that you believe*"-like assumptions. This is the reason why solving decentralized partially observable MDPs optimally is significantly harder, namely NEXP-complete [3], than solving their centralized counterparts.

While some important progress has been made in solving single-agent MDPs, we still lack in efficient algorithms for the multi-agent case. Depending on the problem constraints, different solution concepts are required, and for some of them, optimal non-trivial algorithms have not yet been established. Characterizing the optimal solution of a general decentralized MDP however constitutes a crucial step toward both efficient approximation techniques and learning algorithms. We will focus in this paper on infinite horizon problems that can be solved using deterministic finite memory controllers, and we are able to present the first complete algorithm to solve this class of problems optimally. Our approach is an extension of best-first search techniques to decentralized control theory and shows to be very effective compared to existing solutions.

In the remainder of the paper, we will introduce the DEC-POMDP framework for decentralized decision making under uncertainty and expose some existing approaches within this problem family, before describing our search method and related experimental results.

2 Decentralized Markov Decision Processes

The family of Markov decision processes describes discrete stochastic systems that evolve under the influence of one or multiple controllers. With each transition of the system is associated a reward value, and the objective of the controller is to select precisely that sequence of actions that maximizes the collection of rewards in the long run. For the case of several distributed but cooperative controllers, their objective is to act selfishly as to maximize the reward collected by the team.

2.1 The DEC-POMDP Model

We base our work on the DEC-POMDP formalism introduced by [3], although alternative definitions are equally allowed.

Definition 1 (DEC-POMDP). *An n-agent DEC-POMDP is given as a tuple $\langle S, \{A_i\}, P, R, \{\Omega_i\}, O, p_0 \rangle$, where*

- *S is a finite set of states*
- *A_i is a finite set of actions, available to agent i*
- *$P(s, a_1, \ldots a_n, s')$ is a function of transition probabilities*
- *$R(s, a_1, \ldots a_n, s')$ is a reward function*
- *Ω_i is a finite set of observations for agent i*
- *$O(s, a_1, \ldots a_n, o_1, \ldots o_n, s')$ is a function of observation probabilities*
- *p_0 is the initial state distribution of the system*

Solving a DEC-POMDP can be seen as finding a set of n *policies*, one for each controller, that yield maximum reward when being executed synchronously. The optimization problem can therefore be stated as maximizing the following expectation value

$$E\left[\sum_{t=0}^{\infty} \gamma^t R(s_t, (a_1, \ldots a_n)_t, s_{t+1}) \,\Big|\, p_0\right] \quad \text{with} \quad 0 \leq \gamma < 1 \tag{1}$$

where γ is a discount factor to avoid infinite sums. We will denote q_i the policy associated with agent i. In order to be optimal, the Markov assumption requires a policy to depend on the whole information available to the agent at time t, namely its complete history of past observations and actions: $(q_i)_t = q_i((a_i)_0, \ldots (a_i)_{t-1}, (o_i)_0, \ldots (o_i)_t \mid p_0)$. For infinite horizon problems however, this would require a controller to have infinite memory, which is not always possible. We will therefore specify the nature of the controller in more detail.

2.2 Policies for DEC-POMDPs

A widely accepted class of policies for single-agent POMDPs can be represented as *policy graphs*. A policy graph can be described by a set of nodes, which contain the actions to be executed, and a set of arcs, which are parametrized by the observations the agent gets. A step in policy execution consists of executing the action given by the current node, and transitioning to the next node, based on the observation signal that occurred. For finite horizon problems, an optimal policy graph can always be represented as a tree [10], whereas for the infinite horizon case, loops have to be allowed. A policy graph with loops is called a *finite state controller*:

Definition 2 (FSC). *A finite state controller (FSC) is a policy graph, defined as* $q = \langle N, \alpha, \eta, n_0 \rangle$, *where*

- N *denotes a set of nodes*
- $\alpha = \alpha(n)$ *is the action selected in node* n
- $\eta = \eta(n, o)$ *is the successor node when observation* o *is perceived in node* n
- n_0 *is the starting node*

An example of a 3-node FSC is given in Figure 1. For the case of decentralized problems with multiple controllers, the goal is it to find a set of FSCs, one for each agent, such that their concurrent execution maximizes the expectation value given in (1). We will call such a set a *policy vector*:

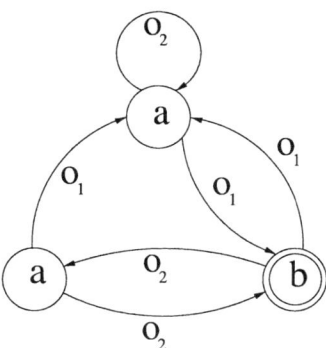

Fig. 1. A deterministic finite state controller with 3 nodes for a problem with 2 actions (a and b) and 2 observations (o_1 and o_2)

Definition 3 (Policy Vector). *A policy vector δ is defined as $\delta = (q_1, \ldots q_n)$, such that q_i constitutes a policy, in our case a FSC, assigned to agent i.*

As stated earlier, finite memory controllers are naturally limited in treating infinite horizon problems, and increasing the controller size will in general lead to higher rewards. We therefore state our optimization criterion as finding the best policy vector *for a given controller size*.

2.3 Related Work

Solving cooperative but decentralized Markov decision processes has only been recently addressed by the research community. After the establishment of the formal DEC-POMDP model by [3], and the alternative MTDP model by [17], the first optimal algorithm for finite horizon problems, based on dynamic programming, has been suggested in [9]. We recently proposed an alternative approach, based on heuristic search [19]. Furthermore, there exist several suboptimal solutions that adopt concepts from game theory, such as described in [6], [14], or that use local optimization techniques as described in [15]. Although these algorithms are often much easier to apply, the quality of their solution can be more or less unsatisfactory depending on the problem. A first attempt to solve general DEC-POMDPs with infinite horizon has been made by Bernstein et al. in [4]. Their algorithm is based on policy iteration for stochastic finite state controllers, and is therefore related to our approach, although it is not guaranteed to produce optimal controllers. We will indeed be able to show that, while we restrict ourselves to deterministic automata only, our algorithm outperforms their approach on the test problems we studied. There exist several algorithms that treat special subclasses of decentralized MDPs, such as transition independent DEC-MDPs, where agents do not interfere directly while execution [2].

3 Best-First Search for Infinite Horizon DEC-POMDPs

Solving Markov decision problems usually involves maximizing an evaluation function in either state space or policy space, with our approach being an example for the latter.

3.1 Searching in the Space of Policy Vectors

Forward search in the space of policy vectors can be considered as an incremental construction of an optimal policy based on evaluations of only partially completed policy stubs. In each step, the most promising stub is selected and further developed, hence the best-first approach. A section of such a search tree is shown in Figure 2. We recall that $\delta = (q_1, \ldots q_n)$ denotes a policy vector of FSCs. For a completely defined policy vector, we set $V_\delta(p_0)$ as the *value* of executing δ in p_0, which is nothing more than the expectation introduced in (1). We then state our maximization problem as follows:

$$\delta^* = \arg\max_\delta V_\delta(p_0) \qquad (2)$$

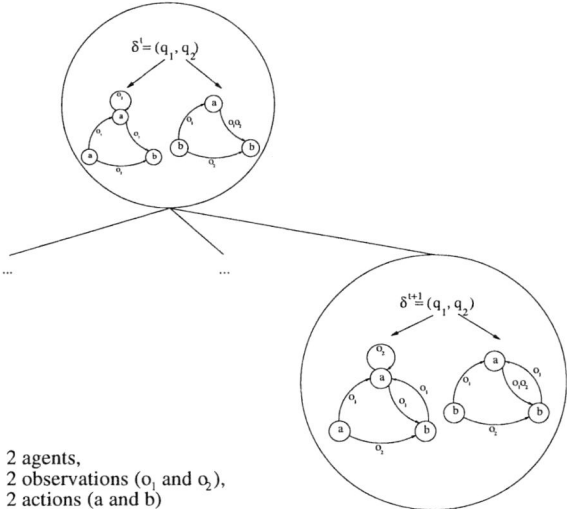

Fig. 2. A section of the multi-agent best-first search tree, showing a partially defined policy vector for 2 agents, and one of its stronger constrained child vectors

Evaluating policy vectors can be done using the model parameters P, R, and O of the DEC-POMDP. We will describe this in more detail in the following subsections.

3.2 Evaluating Partially Defined Policy Vectors

Because of the incremental nature of the search process, we will have to emphasize on what we understand by a policy stub. We recall that each FSC is defined by its number of nodes N, and its two functions $\alpha : N \to A$ and $\eta : N \times O \to N$. A policy stub is a FSC where either α or η or both are only *partially defined*. Obviously, any partially defined FSC can be completed easily at random by assigning actions and successor nodes at those points where α and η are not constrained. The crucial step however consists in estimating efficiently *all* possible completions of a policy stub, in order to determine whether or not to expand the corresponding leaf node of the search tree. Heuristic search methods such as A* have been shown to be very efficient in those cases where an *upper bound* estimate for the set of possible completions can be established. In order to show that a similar upper bound can indeed be defined in our case, we will introduce two mappings that specify the current constrainment of the FSCs:

$$\Lambda_i(n) = \begin{cases} \{\alpha_i(n)\}, & \text{if } \alpha_i \text{ is defined in } n \\ A, & \text{otherwise} \end{cases}$$

$$\Pi_i(n,o) = \begin{cases} \{\eta_i(n,o)\}, & \text{if } \eta_i \text{ is defined for } n \text{ and } o \\ N, & \text{otherwise} \end{cases}$$

Similarly, we define the multi-controller extensions $\Lambda(\mathbf{n}) = (\Lambda_1(n), \ldots \Lambda_n(n))$ and $\Pi(\mathbf{n}, \mathbf{o}) = (\Pi_1(n, o), \ldots \Pi_n(n, o))$.

It has been pointed out by Sondik and later by Hansen [8] that evaluating a policy represented as a FSC consists in solving a system of linear equations. In fact, the cross-product between a FSC and a POMDP constitutes itself a finite MDP [13]. We extend this result to the multi-agent case:

Definition 4 (Multi-agent cross-product MDP). *Given a DEC-POMDP $\langle S, \{A_i\}, P, R, \{\Omega_i\}, O, p_0 \rangle$ and a policy vector $\delta = \langle \{N_i\}, \{\alpha_i\}, \{\eta_i\} \rangle$, we define a cross-product MDP $\langle \overline{S}, \overline{A}, \overline{P}, \overline{R} \rangle$, with*

- $\overline{S} = (\times_i N_i) \times S$
- $\overline{A} = \times_i (A_i \times N_i^{\Omega_i})$
- $\overline{P}((\mathbf{n}, s), (\mathbf{a}, \eta^\mathbf{n}), (\mathbf{n}', s')) = P(s, \mathbf{a}, s') \sum_{\substack{\mathbf{o} \in \times \Omega \\ \text{s.t. } \eta^\mathbf{n}(\mathbf{o}) = \mathbf{n}'}} O(s, \mathbf{a}, \mathbf{o}, s')$
- $\overline{R}((\mathbf{n}, s), (\mathbf{a}, \eta^\mathbf{n}), (\mathbf{n}', s')) = R(s, \mathbf{a}, s')$

and where $\eta^\mathbf{n}$ is a mapping that - given a vector of nodes $\mathbf{n}$ - determines a vector of successor nodes $\mathbf{n}'$ for each vector of observations $\mathbf{o}$, $\eta^\mathbf{n} : \Omega \to \mathbf{N}$.

Solving the cross-product MDP can be done through common dynamic programming techniques, leading to a value function over the augmented state space $\overline{S}$ and the following fixed point:

$$\overline{V}_\delta(\mathbf{n}, s) = \max_{\mathbf{a} \in \Lambda(\mathbf{n})} \left\{ \sum_{s', \mathbf{o}} P(s', \mathbf{o}|s, \mathbf{a}) \left[R(s, \mathbf{a}, s') + \gamma \max_{\mathbf{n}' \in \Pi(\mathbf{n}, \mathbf{o})} \overline{V}_\delta(\mathbf{n}', s') \right] \right\} \quad (3)$$

This value function is the multi-agent extension of the one given in [13].

Lemma 1. *For any policy vector δ' that can be obtained from δ by adding further constraints on Λ or Π, $\overline{V}_\delta \geq \overline{V}_{\delta'}$.*

Proof. The lemma states that $\overline{V}_\delta$ is indeed an upper bound for all policy vectors that might result from δ by further constraining it. This is true since constraining Λ or Π will simply result in reducing the set of options under the max-operators $\max_{\mathbf{a} \in \Lambda(\mathbf{n})}$ and $\max_{\mathbf{n}' \in \Pi(\mathbf{n}, \mathbf{o})}$ in (3), and the value function can therefore never increase.

If the vector of FSCs is completely defined, the cross-product MDP degenerates to a simple Markov chain, and the upper bound coincides with the true value of the policy vector. We can evaluate an upper bound for the value of any partially defined policy vector and start state distribution p_0:

$$\overline{V}_\delta(p_0) = \max_\mathbf{n} \sum_{s_i} p_0(s_i) \overline{V}_\delta(\mathbf{n}, s_i) \quad (4)$$

3.3 An Optimal Heuristic Search Algorithm for Decentralized POMDPs

Theorem 1. *The heuristic best-first search algorithm in [Algorithm 1] is complete and returns the optimal solution for the given controller size.*

Proof. The search process will eventually terminate in the worst case after enumerating all possible policy vectors, which means after constructing the complete search tree. The leaf node with the highest value then contains an optimal solution to the problem. If the search terminates earlier and returns a policy vector δ, we can guarantee by the "best-first" property that no other active leaf node presents a higher evaluation. Since the evaluation function itself constitutes an upper bound for the value of any further constrained policy vector, we know that all unvisited child nodes will present values that fall below this bounded. This excludes the existence of any policy vector with a higher value, and thus guarantees the optimality of the solution.

Algorithm 1. Best-first search for infinite horizon DEC-POMDPs

---
Require: D_0 initialized with the skeleton of an unconstrained policy vector
1: **repeat**
2:     Select $\delta^* \in D_i$ such that $\forall \delta \in D_i$: $\overline{V}_\delta(p_0) \leq \overline{V}_{\delta^*}(p_0)$
3:     Construct $\delta^{*'}$, the next child of δ^*
4:     **if** $\delta^{*'}$ is an improved suboptimal solution **then**
5:         Report $\delta^{*'}$
6:         **for all** $\delta \in D_i$ **do**
7:             **if** $\overline{V}_\delta(p_0) \leq \overline{V}_{\delta^{*'}}(p_0)$ **then**
8:                 $D_i \leftarrow D_i \setminus \delta$
9:             **end if**
10:        **end for**
11:    **end if**
12:    $D_i \leftarrow D_i \cup \delta^{*'}$
13:    **if** δ^* is fully expanded **then**
14:        $D_i \leftarrow D_i \setminus \delta^*$
15:    **end if**
16: **until** $\exists \delta^* \in D_i$ s.t. δ^* is *complete* and $\forall \delta \in D_i$: $\overline{V}_\delta(p_0) \leq \overline{V}_{\delta^*}(p_0) = V_{\delta^*}(p_0)$

---

4 Experimental Results

We tested the heuristic search approach on two problems that have already been studied before in [4], namely a broadcast channel problem, and a 2-robot navigation task. The discount rate for all problems is $\gamma = 0.9$.

4.1 A Broadcast Channel Problem

The first setting simulates a simplified multi-access broadcast channel, where agents are situated at the nodes of the system. Each agent has to decide whether or not to send one of the messages from its message buffer. Sending is exclusive, which means that only one message can go through a channel at each time. If both agents try to send a message at the same time over the same channel, a collision occurs, and messages will remain in the buffer. The problem is partially observable and hence decentralized, since agents can only observe the state of their own message buffers but do not know whether or not any other agent has something to send as well. The common goal of all participating agents is to maximize the throughput of the system, with a reward of 1.0 given for any message that has been transmitted. In the experiments we conducted, there are 2 agents and 2 possible actions for each one of them (send, not send). The buffer size is 1, and the number of global states thus is 4, namely the cross-product of the local buffer states. There are 6 possible observations, characterized by the local buffer state (empty, full) and a status flag of the channel from the previous time step (idle, active, collision). New messages arrive with a rate of $p_1 = 0.9$ for agent 1, and $p_2 = 0.1$ for agent 2.

The highest possible discounted sum of rewards that can be attained for this problem assuming full global observability is $\sum_t \gamma^t(1.0) = 9.0$, which would mean that a message could be transmitted at each time step. Surprisingly, we can see in Figure 5 that this value is almost attained in our case with just a deterministic single-node FSC, although the problem is now decentralized and only partially observable. The bounded policy iteration approach for stochastic controllers produces less competitive policies.

4.2 A Robot Navigation Task

In the second problem, two agents navigate on a two by two grid-world, without interfering with each other. Their goal is to stay both on the same grid cell - which produces a reward of 1.0 - but their observation capabilities are limited so they don't see each other, and they also have limited sensing capabilities concerning the environment: There are only 4 observations, indicating whether there is a wall to their left and/or to their right. Each agent has 5 actions to move in any direction or stay on its current cell, but transitions are stochastic as given by Figure 4: The agent only moves with probability 0.6 to its intended direction. The problem has 16 states. Figure 5 shows that

Buffer$_t$	Action	Buffer$_{t+1}$	Prob
empty	(any)	empty	$1.0 - p_i$
		full	p_i
full	send	empty	$1.0 - p_i$
		full	p_i
	not send	empty	0.0
		full	1.0

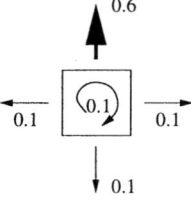

Fig. 3. Channel problem: Transition probabilities for each one of the buffers

Fig. 4. Navigation task: Transition probabilities for action North

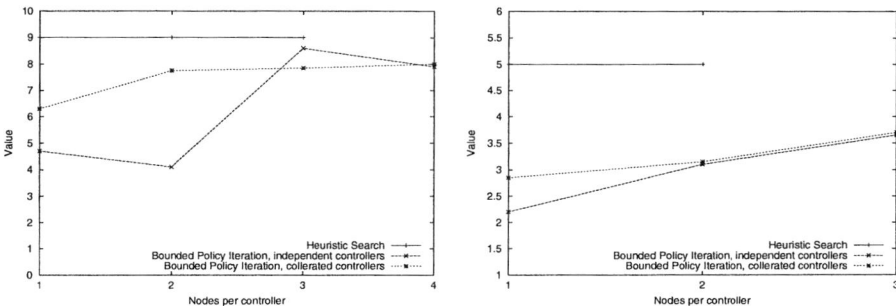

Fig. 5. Value of optimal deterministic policy vector for the heuristic approach, and average value per trial run for two versions of bounded policy iteration on stochastic controllers. Left: Channel problem - Right: Robot problem.

the search algorithm is again more competitive than the policy iteration approach. However, it takes more time to converge and may in the end run out of memory.

The experimental results show that the advantage of using stochastic controllers, which have the theoretical ability to produce higher average rewards than deterministic ones [18], might be more than consumed by the local optimality of the algorithms that compute them. In addition, the deterministic controllers with more than one node are degenerated versions of the one controller case: In the given example problems, having a larger memory does not necessary help, which is why the value of the deterministic controllers do not increase with increasing size.

5 Discussion

We have presented a new optimal algorithm to solve a particular class of decentralized POMDPs with infinite horizon. It is able to compute better controllers than a very recent policy iteration algorithm on two test problems, although it still suffers from the proved complexity of this class of problems. It should be a valuable step forward in establishing more efficient algorithms and approximation techniques. There are other possible ways of tackling problems of decentralized control: Instead of constraining the controller size, one could for example impose a bound on the solution quality. It remains an open problem, whether decentralized policy vectors can also be learned in an efficient way when the environment is only partially observable.

Acknowledgments

We thank Shlomo Zilberstein and the anonymous reviewers for their helpful comments.

References

1. Eitan Altman. Applications of Markov Decision Processes in Communication Networks: A Survey. Technical Report RR-3984, INRIA Sophia-Antipolis, 2000.
2. Raphen Becker, Shlomo Zilberstein, Victor Lesser, and Claudia V. Goldman. Solving Transition Independent Decentralized Markov Decision Processes. *Journal of Artificial Intelligence Research*, 22:423–455, 2004.
3. Daniel S. Bernstein, Robert Givan, Neil Immerman, and Shlomo Zilberstein. The Complexity of Decentralized Control of Markov Decision Processes. *Mathematics of Operations Research*, 27(4):819–840, 2002.
4. Daniel S. Bernstein, Eric A. Hansen, and Shlomo Zilberstein. Bounded Policy Iteration for Decentralized POMDPs. In *Proceedings of the 24th International Joint Conference on Artificial Intelligence*, 2005.
5. Craig Boutilier. Sequential Optimality and Coordination in Multiagent Systems. In *Proceedings of the Eighteenth International Joint Conference on Artificial Intelligence*, pages 478–485, 1999.
6. Iadine Chadès, Bruno Scherrer, and François Charpillet. A Heuristic Approach for Solving Decentralized-POMDP: Assessment on the Pursuit Problem. In *Proceedings of the 2002 ACM Symposium on Applied Computing*, 2002.
7. Fangruo Chen. Decentralized supply chains subject to information delays. *Management Science*, 45:1076–1090, 1999.
8. Eric A. Hansen. An Improved Policy Iteration Algorithm for Partially Observable MDPs. In *Proceedings of the 10th Conference on Neural Information Processing Systems*, 1997.
9. Eric A. Hansen, Daniel S. Bernstein, and Shlomo Zilberstein. Dynamic Programming for Partially Observable Stochastic Games. In *Proceedings of the 19th National Conference on Artificial Intelligence*, 2004.
10. Leslie Pack Kaelbling, Michael L. Littman, and Anthony Cassandra. Planning and Acting in Partially Observable Stochastic Domains. *Artificial Intelligence*, 101:99–134, 1998.
11. Hiroaki Kitano and Satoshi Tadoroko. Robocup-rescue: A Grand Challenge for Multiagent and Intelligent Systems. *AI Magazine*, 22(1):39–51, 2001.
12. Maja J. Mataric and Gaurav S. Sukhatme. Task-allocation and Coordination of Multiple Robots for Planetary Exploration. In *Proceedings of the 10th International Conference on Advanced Robotics*, 2001.
13. Nicolas Meuleau, Kee-Eung Kim, Leslie Pack Kaelbling, and Anthony Cassandra. Solving POMDPs by Searching the Space of Finite Policies. In *Proceedings of the 15th Annual Conference on Uncertainty in Artificial Intelligence*, 1999.
14. R. Nair, M. Tambe, M. Yokoo, D. Pynadath, and S. Marsella. Taming Decentralized POMDPs: Towards Efficient Policy Computation for Multiagent Settings. In *Proceedings of the 18th International Joint Conference on Artificial Intelligence*, 2003.
15. Leonid Peshkin, Kee-Eung Kim, Nicolas Meuleau, and Leslie Kaelbling. Learning to Cooperate via Policy Search. In *Proceedings of the 16th Conference on Uncertainty in Artificial Intelligence*, 2000.
16. Martin L. Puterman. *Markov Decision Processes – Discrete Stochastic Dynamic Programming*. John Wiley & Sons, 1994.

17. David V. Pynadath and Milind Tambe. The Communicative Multiagent Team Decision Problem: Analyzing Teamwork Theories and Models. *Journal of Artificial Intelligence Research*, pages 389–423, 2002.
18. Satinder P. Singh, Tommi Jaakkola, and Michael I. Jordan. Learning Without State-Estimation in Partially Observable Markovian Decision Processes. In *Proceedings of the 11th International Conference on Machine Learning*, 1994.
19. Daniel Szer, François Charpillet, and Shlomo Zilberstein. MAA*: A heuristic search algorithm for solving decentralized POMDPs. In *Proceedings of the 21th Conference on Uncertainty in Artificial Intelligence*, 2005.

Ensemble Learning with Supervised Kernels

Kari Torkkola[1] and Eugene Tuv[2]

[1] Motorola, Intelligent Systems Lab, Tempe, AZ, USA
Kari.Torkkola@motorola.com
[2] Intel, Analysis and Control Technology, Chandler, AZ, USA
eugene.tuv@intel.com

Abstract. Kernel-based methods have outstanding performance on many machine learning and pattern recognition tasks. However, they are sensitive to kernel selection, they may have low tolerance to noise, and they can not deal with mixed-type or missing data. We propose to derive a novel kernel from an ensemble of decision trees. This leads to kernel methods that naturally handle noisy and heterogeneous data with potentially non-randomly missing values. We demonstrate excellent performance of regularized least square learners based on such kernels.

1 Introduction

Kernel-based learners, such as Support Vector Machines (SVM) or Regularized Least Squares (RLS) learners have shown excellent performance compared to any other methods in numerous current classification and regression applications [23]. A key issue in the successful application of a kernel-based learner is the proper choice of the kernel and its parameters since this determines the capability of the kernel to capture and to represent the structure of the input space. Typical kernel choices for continuous data are Gaussian and polynomial, for example.

However, if the data has variables of mixed type, both continuous and discrete, kernel construction becomes a difficult problem. Furthermore, if the data contains many irrelevant variables, especially if the number of available observations is small, standard kernel methods require variable selection to perform well [13]. This paper suggests a solution to both problems by deriving a kernel from an ensemble of trees.

Tree-based ensemble methods partition the input space using decision trees and then combine the partitioning, or response in case of regression, over a stochastic ensemble of trees. Random Forest (RF) is an example of such an ensemble [4]. Trees provide the capability to handle mixed-type variables and missing data. Stochastic selection of input variables for each tree of the forest provides tolerance to irrelevant variables. These properties of trees can be extended to kernel-based methods by taking advantage of the supervised engine of the Random Forest. We show how the kernel can be derived from the structure of the forest.

The structure of this paper is as follows. We describe first generic kernel-based learners concentrating on Regularized Least Squares learners. We then show how a "supervised kernel" can be derived from a tree-based ensemble that has been trained either for a classification or a regression task. Ensembles of kernel-based learners are described next, followed by illustrations and experimentation with the supervised kernel. We use both synthetic and real data sets to demonstrate both the insights from supervised kernels as well as their relevance to real problems. A summary concludes the paper.

2 Regularized Least Squares Learners

In supervised learning the training data $(x_i, y_i)_{i=1}^m$ is used to construct a function $f : X \to Y$ that predicts or generalizes well.

To measure goodness of the learned function $f(x)$ a loss function $L(f(x), y_{true})$ is needed, for example the square loss, L_2: $L(f(x), y) = (f(x) - y)^2$.

Given a loss function, the goal of learning is to find an approximation function $f(x)$ that minimizes the expected risk, or the generalization error

$$E_{P(x,y)} L(f(x), y) \qquad (1)$$

where P(x,y) is the unknown joint distribution of future observations (x,y).

Given a finite sample from the (X,Y) domain this problem is ill-posed.

The regularization approach rooted in Tikhonov regularization theory [24] restores well-posedness (existence, uniqueness, and stability) by restricting the hypothesis space, the functional space of possible solutions:

$$\hat{f} = \operatorname*{argmin}_{f \in H} \frac{1}{m} \sum_{i=1}^m L(f(x_i), y_i) + \gamma \|f\|_K {}^2 \qquad (2)$$

The hypothesis space H here is a Reproducing Kernel Hilbert Space (RKHS) defined by kernel K, and γ is a positive regularization parameter.

The mathematical foundations for this framework as well as a key algorithm to solve (2) are derived elegantly in [21] for the quadratic loss function. The algorithm can be summarized as follows:

1. Start with the data $(x_i, y_i)_{i=1}^m$.
2. Choose a symmetric, positive definite kernel, such as

$$K(x, x') = e^{-\frac{\|x-x'\|^2}{2\sigma^2}}. \qquad (3)$$

3. Set

$$f(x) = \sum_{i=1}^m c_i K(x_i, x), \qquad (4)$$

where **c** is a solution to

$$(m\gamma \mathbf{I} + \mathbf{K})\mathbf{c} = \mathbf{y}, \qquad (5)$$

which represents well-posed linear system.

The generalization ability of this solution, as well choosing the regularization parameter γ were studied by [7, 8].

It is important to note that the same result can be obtained from the classical linear ridge regression proposed by [16, 15] to deal with potential singularity of $\mathbf{X}'\mathbf{X}$ in linear regression.

$$f(x) = \mathbf{X}(\mathbf{X}'\mathbf{X} + \gamma \mathbf{I})^{-1}\mathbf{X}'y \tag{6}$$

It is easy to see that we could use the *kernel trick* if we rewrite equation (6) in terms of matrix of inner products

$$f(x) = (\mathbf{K} + \gamma \mathbf{I})^{-1}\mathbf{K}y \tag{7}$$

where $\mathbf{K} = \mathbf{X}\mathbf{X}'$.

Thus, the regularized least-squares (RLS) algorithm defined above solves a simple well defined linear problem. The solution is a linear kernel expansion of the same form as the one given by support vector machines (SVM). Note also that SVM formulation naturally fits in the regularization framework (2). Inserting the SVM hinge loss function $L(f(x), y) = (1 - yf(x))_+$ in (2) leads to solving a quadratic optimization problem instead of a linear solution.

The regularized least-squares classifier (RLSC) with quadratic loss function, that is more common for regression, has also proven to be very effective in binary classification problems [22]. In a recent feature selection and classification competition organized at NIPS2003, stochastic ensembles of RLSCs with Gaussian kernels were the second best entry [13].

The success of kernel-based methods stems partly from the capability of the kernel to capture the structure of the (expanded) input space. However, while some of that structure is relevant to the task at hand, much of it may not be. Selection of an appropriate kernel is the key issue. Furthermore, crafting kernels for mixed type noisy data with potential missing values is a form of art at its best.

Recently, a series of papers were dedicated to a problem how to learn the kernel itself. Cristianini et al. introduced notion of kernel target alignment [6]. The goal is to construct a kernel $K(x, x')$ that is similar to (aligned with) the target kernel defined as outer product of y, $\mathbf{K}^* = yy^T$. While this framework could construct powerful kernels, there is still an overfitting issue since there is no guarantee that the learned kernel is aligned on the data other than the given training data set. It is not clear also how to use this framework in regression or multiclass classification. Lanckriet et al. proposed semidefinite programming approach to optimize target alignment (or bound, margin) over the set of kernel matrices on the data [17]. Overfitting is still an issue here as well as a computational complexity ($O(n^6)$). None of these methods deal with mixed type data.

The following section discusses how ensembles of trees can be used for deriving the kernel in a supervised fashion.

3 Extracting Kernels from Tree-Based Ensembles

A decision tree such as CART explicitly partitions the input space into a set of disjoint regions, and assigns a response value to each corresponding region [5]. This is the key property that we will use in the derivation of a similarity matrix (that is, a kernel) from a tree.

As a new observation x is run through the tree, the search ends at a terminal node $t(x)$. Let us denote the depth of a node in the tree by $d(n)$, and the deepest common parent of two nodes by $p(n_1, n_2)$.

Breiman defined a similarity measure between two observations x_1 and x_2 as follows [4]:
$$s_B(x_1, x_2) = \begin{cases} 1 & \text{if } t(x_1) = t(x_2) \\ 0 & \text{otherwise} \end{cases} \tag{8}$$

This a very coarse measure by which two observations are similar only if they end up in the same terminal node. In order to express with finer granularity how far in the tree two observations lie, we define a new similarity measure as the depth of the lowest common parent node normalized by the level of the deeper observation in the tree:
$$s(x_1, x_2) = \frac{d(p(t(x_1), t(x_2)))}{\max[\,d(t(x_1)), d(t(x_2))\,]} \tag{9}$$

It is easy to show that the similarity matrix defined this way is symmetric and positive-definite. Two observations with large $s(x_1, x_2)$ would indicate both geometric closeness and similarity in terms of the target. This kind of partitioning (and thus similarity) can be constructed for practically any kind of data since CART is fast, works with mixed-type data, handles missing values elegantly, and is invariant to monotone transformations of the input variables, and therefore is resistant to outliers in input space. However, such a supervised partitioning of the input space induced by a single tree is unstable (in the sense of [2]), and it would be sensible to measure the derived similarity over an ensemble of trees by averaging.

We discuss two of the most recent advances in tree ensembles, MART (gradient tree boosting) [11, 12] and Random Forest [4]. MART is a serial ensemble where every new expert that is constructed relies on previously built experts. At every iteration of MART a new tree is fitted to the generalized residuals from the previous iteration.

Random Forest (RF) is an improved bagging method that extends the "random subspace" method [14]. It is a parallel ensemble that grows a forest of independent random trees on bagged samples. RF does not overfit, and can be summarized as follows:

1. A number m is specified much smaller than the total number of variables M (typically $m \sim \sqrt{M}$).
2. Each tree of maximum depth is grown on a bootstrap sample of the training set.
3. At each node, m out of the M variables are selected at random.
4. The split used is the best split on these m variables.

We will be using RF throughout our experimentation because of it simplicity and excellent performance. In general, RF is resistant to irrelevant variables, it can handle mixed-type data and missing data, and it can handle massive numbers of variables and observations. These properties now carry over to the kernel constructed from a RF. Similarity matrices according to Eq. (9) will now be averaged over all the trees in the forest.

We illustrate now some properties of this kernel using two simple data sets.

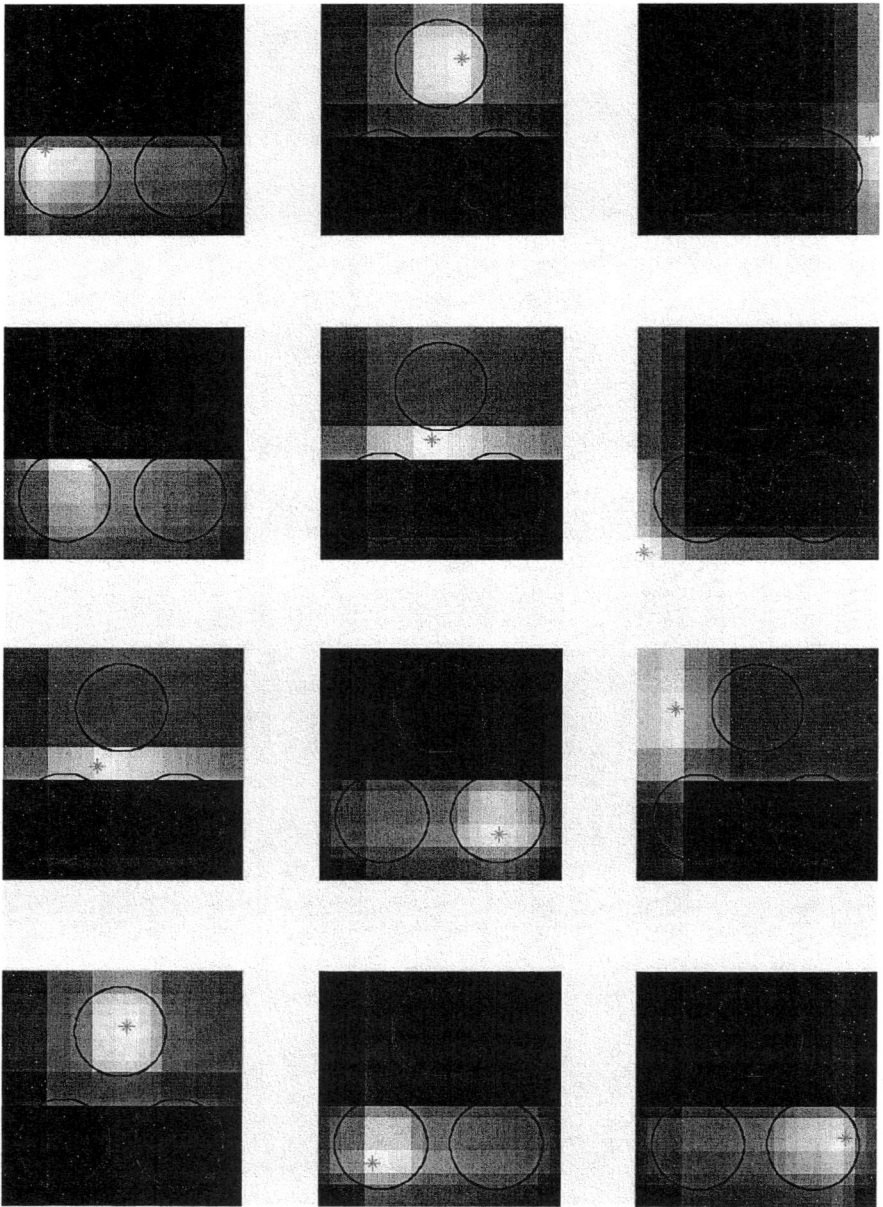

Fig. 1. Illustration of the similarity measure between samples of two different classes. Class one is the inside of the three circles and class two is the outside of the circles. Each panel displays one randomly chosen data point within a square as a grey asterisk, and the similarity between the point and every other point is illustrated by shades of grey. Light shade denotes similarity between the data points. See text for discussion.

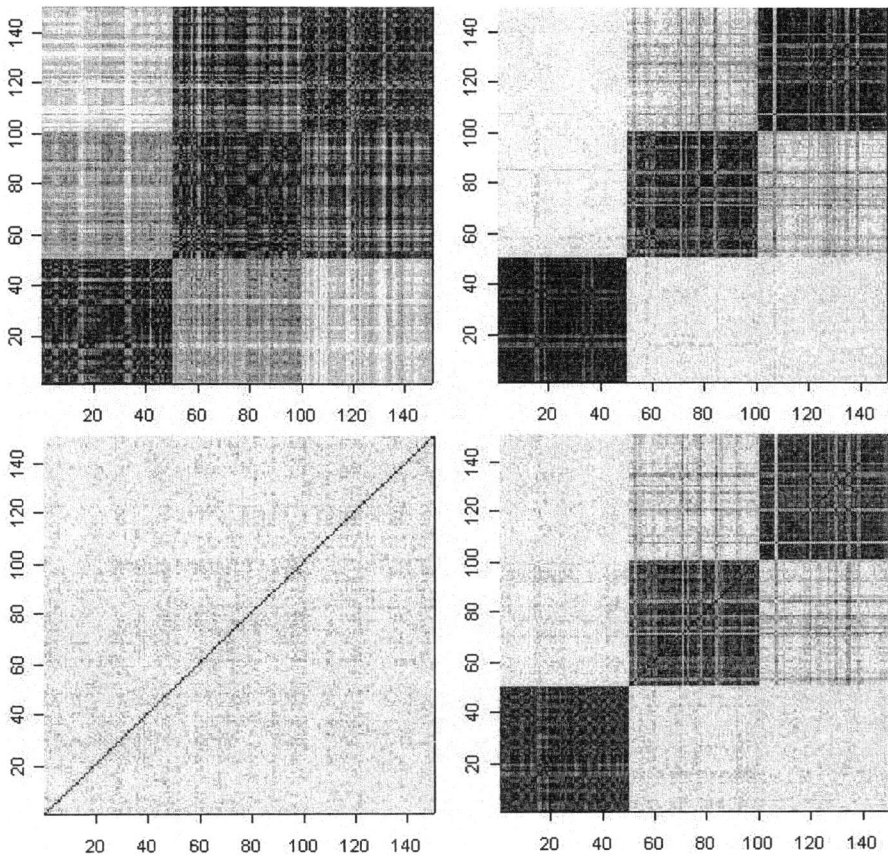

Fig. 2. Similarity matrices (kernels) derived from the Iris data set with three classes. Dark color represents high similarity, light represents low. The left panels depict Euclidean similarity metric (a linear kernel), and the right panels show the similarity derived from a Random Forest. The top panels represent the original four variables, and the bottom panels show the same data but with 40 additional noise variables. This is a demonstration of the tolerance of the supervised kernel to irrelevant input variables.

Figure 1 depicts the similarity measure in the case of two-dimensional data with two classes. The region consisting of the union of the three circles is considered class one and the region outside the circles represents class two. Similarity between a randomly chosen point and every other point in the square is encoded by shade of grey, the lighter the more similar. We can see how the kernel captures the local structure and at the same time enhances separation of the classes. We can also see the limitations of trees as the rectangular partitioning.

Figure 2 uses the well-known Iris data set (3 classes) to demonstrate how class discrimination is enhanced (top panels) as compared to a linear kernel, and how the derived kernel matrix is tolerant to irrelevant input variables (bottom panels).

4 Stochastic Ensembles of RLS Learners

The derived kernel matrix can now be used with any kernel-based learner, such as a Support Vector Machine. This section describes how we use it with stochastic ensembles of RLS learners. We begin by briefly recalling the motivation for using ensemble methods in the first place.

Generalization ability of a learned function is closely related to its stability. Stability of the solution could be loosely defined as continuous dependence on the data. A stable solution changes very little for small changes in data. Recently, a series of theoretical developments also confirmed the fundamental role of stability for generalization of any learning engine [2, 20, 18, 19].

Supervised ensemble methods construct a set of base learners, or experts, and use their weighted outcome to predict new data. Numerous empirical studies confirm that ensemble methods often outperform any single base learner [10, 1, 9]. Due to increased stability, the improvement is intuitively clear when a base algorithm is unstable (such as for decision tree, neural network, etc). However, it has even been shown that ensembles of low-bias support vector machines (SVM) often outperform a single, best-tuned, canonical SVM [25].

It is well known that bagging (bootstrap aggregation) can dramatically reduce variance of unstable learners providing some regularization effect [3]. Bagged ensembles do not overfit. Low bias of the base learner and low correlation between base learners are crucial to good ensemble performance.

It is thus advantageous to implement diverse low biased experts. For RLSC, bias can be lowered by decreasing the regularization parameter, and narrowing the σ in case of Gaussian kernel. Instead of bootstrap sampling from training data which imposes fixed sampling strategy, we found that often much smaller sample sizes improve performance.

Typically, in the following experiments, once a kernel is derived, we construct 100-250 experts, each using a random sample of 50-90% of the training data. This is fast since we are actually just sampling a pre-computed kernel matrix, and solving a linear equation for each expert. The regularization parameter was fixed to a very small value only to ensure that a solution exists.

Combining the outputs of the experts in an ensemble can be done in several ways. In classification tasks, we performed majority voting over the outputs of the experts. In binary classification this is equivalent to averaging the discretized (+1,-1) predictions of the experts. In regression tasks simple averaging was used.

5 Experiments with Synthetic Data

We describe now experiments for the purpose of highlighting the differences between RF and a stochastic ensemble of RLSCs using the new RF kernel. This

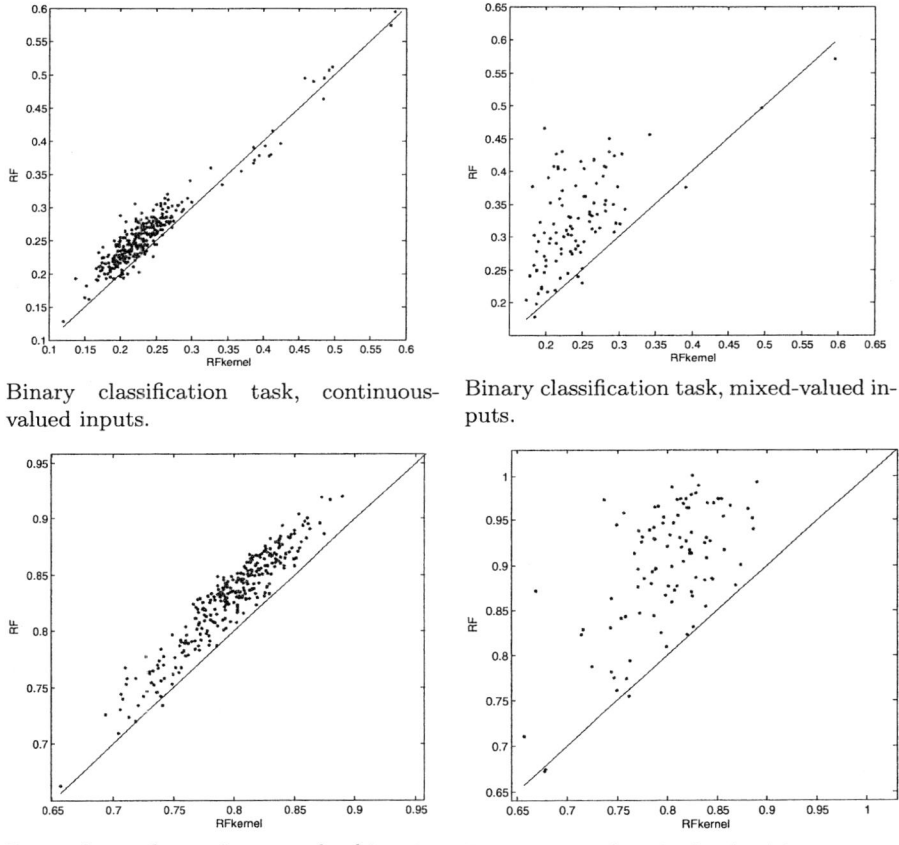

Fig. 3. RMS error and classification error rate comparison of Random Forest to an ensemble of RLSCs using a random forest kernel. See text for discussion.

is an important comparison because if the kernel does not improve over the plain RF, it obviously is not worth using at all.

A very useful data generator for this purpose is described by [11]. This generator produces data sets with multiple non-linear interactions between input variables.

We present results using 100 generated data sets, 500 observations each. For each data set, twenty $N(0,1)$ distributed input variables were generated. The target is a multivariate function of ten of those, thus ten are pure noise. The target function is generated as a weighted sum of L multidimensional Gaussians, each Gaussian at a time involving about four input variables randomly drawn from the "important" ten variables. Thus all of the "important" ten input variables are involved in the target, to a varying degree. The Gaussian functions also have a random mean vector and a random covariance matrix as described in [11]. In this experiment, we used $L = 20$. Weights for the Gaussians are randomly drawn from $U[-1, 1]$.

The data generator produces continuous valued variables. Thus the data sets can be used as such for regression problems. In order to generate a classification problems, the target variable was discretized to two levels. Furthermore, to create data sets with mixed type variables, randomly selected 50% of the input variables were discretized. The number of discretization levels was itself a random variable drawn from a uniform distribution between 2 and 10.

Figure 3 depicts the performance of the RF kernel (horizontal axis) against RF (vertical axis) in four different tasks:

1. Classification, continuous inputs, top left,
2. Regression, continuous inputs, bottom left,
3. Classification, mixed type inputs, top right,
4. Regression, mixed type inputs, bottom right.

Each point in the figures depicts one generated data set, 500 observations for training, and 500 observations for testing. The y-coordinate of a point represents either the error rate (classification problem) or the RMS error (regression) evaluated by a random forest. The x-coordinate of a point represents the same for a stochastic ensemble of RLSCs using supervised kernel derived from the random forest. Thus every point above the diagonal line is a data set with which the supervised kernel was better than the RF. The difference is clear for continuous data, both for classification and regression (left panels), and dramatic for mixed type data (right panels).

This difference could be explained by the difference between the base learners of the ensembles. Both are parallel ensembles, but the base learner in RF is less capable than the base learner in an ensemble of RLSCs.

6 High-Dimensional Noisy Problems

In order to assess the performance of the proposed supervised kernel method in real high dimensional noisy problems, we ran tests using the data sets from the NIPS 2003 feature selection competition. The purpose of the challenge in feature selection was to find feature selection algorithms that significantly outperform methods using all features, on all five benchmark data sets [13]. These are significantly harder problems than, for example, typical problems in the UCI machine learning database. The diverse characteristics of these five data sets are listed in Table 1.

As seen in Table 1, these problems are high-dimensional, have a small amount of training data relative to the dimension, and a large proportion of variables are noise. Of these data sets, only Dorothea was highly unbalanced with approximately 12% of samples in one class, and 88% in the other. The rest of the sets had an approximately balanced class distribution. All tasks are two-class classification problems.

Table 1. NIPS2003 Feature Selection Challenge Data. Probes refer to artificially inserted random noise variables.

Data Set	Domain	Size	Type	# of Variables	Training Examples	Validation Examples	% of Probes
Arcene	Mass Spectrometry	8.7 MB	Dense	10000	100	100	30
Gisette	Digit Recogn.	22.5 MB	Dense	5000	6000	1000	30
Dexter	Text Classific.	0.9 MB	Sparse	20000	300	300	50
Dorothea	Drug Discovery	4.7 MB	Sparse bin.	100000	800	350	50
Madelon	Artificial	2.9 MB	Dense	500	2000	600	96

Table 2. Classification error rates on NIPS 2003 feature selection competition data sets. Error rates with validation data sets are reported. The Gaussian kernel was used without feature selection with the Arcene data set.

Data Set	Random Forest	Gaussian Kernel RLSC Ensemble	Gaussian Kernel RLSC Ensemble with Feature Selection	Supervised Kernel RLSC Ensemble
Arcene	23.0	13.31	13.31	19.0
Dexter	9.0	32.4	6.67	6.0
Dorothea	11.94	-	11.83	11.78
Gisette	3.4	-	2.2	1.9
Madelon	9.5	25.4	7.0	11.83

Table 2 compares the classification error rates of a RF to a stochastic RLSC ensemble that uses a Gaussian kernel and to a stochastic RLSC ensemble that uses the proposed supervised kernel. The latter pair is a relevant comparison because we use the supervised RF kernel here exactly in the same fashion as the Gaussian kernel is used in training an ensemble of RLSCs. Note that none of these are mixed-type problems. Thus the Gaussian kernel is near-ideal for these data sets once irrelevant variables are removed. Our baseline is thus the column "Gaussian Kernel RLSC Ensemble with Feature Selection".

Comparison to RF is also very relevant because the supervised kernel is derived from a random forest. This naturally begs the question "Why not use just a RF?". Error rates for the RF and the "Gaussian kernel RLSC Ensemble with Feature Selection" entries were taken from the original December 1st entries in the challenge website[1].

These results show that a stochastic ensemble of RLSCs using a supervised kernel derived from a RF significantly outperforms plain RF on four of the five data sets. Comparing to using a Gaussian kernel with feature selection, the supervised kernel has a comparable performance except for the two cases that were near ideal for the Gaussian kernel once feature selection was used [13] (The data in the Madelon and Arcene sets consisted of Gaussian-like clusters).

Although the purpose of the NIPS 2003 competition was feature selection, we do not perform here feature selection for the supervised kernel prior to classification in order to demonstrate that supervised kernels are tolerant to noise variables due to the properties of tree-based ensembles. Thus the "Supervised Kernel" column does not include feature selection. For comparison, we also eval-

---
[1] http://www.nipsfsc.ecs.soton.ac.uk

uated the Gaussian kernel without feature selection on some of the data sets. These results clearly indicate that removing irrelevant variables is a crucial step in using the Gaussian kernel, whereas the supervised RF kernel does not require this at all.

The results here are thus the best we could hope for: Even when the problem does not fit our specific motivation for the kernel choice, the supervised kernel has about equal performance with the (near) optimal method for those problems.

7 Conclusion

This paper shows how the power of kernel-based methods can be extended to heterogeneous and more complex data domains.

We demonstrated how to derive kernels from Random Forests. This brings the nice properties of tree-based learners, such as natural handling of mixed-type data, tolerance to missing data, tolerance to noise, and to irrelevant inputs to all kernel-based learners.

Using the derived kernels, we train ensembles of simple regularized least squares learners and show that such ensembles outperform Random Forest itself on practically any task. The improvement with mixed-type inputs was especially dramatic. Furthermore, the performance on continuous-valued data is comparable to the best methods for such domains.

References

1. E. Bauer and R. Kohavi. An empirical comparison of voting classification algorithms: Bagging, boosting and variants. *Machine Learning*, 36:525–536, 1999.
2. O. Bousquet and A. Elisseeff. Algorithmic stability and generalization performance. In *NIPS*, pages 196–202, 2000.
3. L. Breiman. Bagging predictors. *Machine Learning*, 24(2):123–140, 1996.
4. L. Breiman. Random forests. *Machine Learning*, 45(1):5–32, 2001.
5. L. Breiman, J.H. Friedman, R.A. Olshen, and C.J. Stone. *Classification and Regression Trees*. CRC Press, 1984.
6. Nello Cristianini, John Shawe-Taylor, André Elisseeff, and Jaz S. Kandola. On kernel-target alignment. In *Proc. NIPS*, pages 367–373, 2001.
7. F. Cucker and S. Smale. On the mathematial foundations of learning. *Bulletin of the American Mathematical Society*, 89(1):1–49, 2001.
8. F. Cucker and S. Smale. Best choices for regularization parameters in learning theory: on the bias-variance problem. *Foundations of Computational Mathematics*, 2(4):413–428, 2003.
9. T. G. Dietterich. An experimental comparison of three methods for constructing ensembles of decision trees: Bagging, boosting, and randomization. *Machine Learning*, 40:139–157, 2000.
10. Y. Freund and R. E. Schapire. Experiments with a new boosting algorithm. In *Proc. 13th ICML*, 1996.
11. J.H. Friedman. Greedy function approximation: a gradient boosting machine. Technical report, Dept. of Statistics, Stanford University, 1999.
12. J.H. Friedman. Stochastic gradient boosting. Technical report, Dept. of Statistics, Stanford University, 1999.

13. Isabelle Guyon, Steve Gunn, Asa Ben-Hur, and Gideon Dror. Result analysis of the nips 2003 feature selection challenge. In Lawrence K. Saul, Yair Weiss, and Léon Bottou, editors, *Advances in Neural Information Processing Systems 17*. MIT Press, Cambridge, MA, 2005.
14. T. K. Ho. The random subspace method for constructing decision forests. *IEEE Transactions on Pattern Analysis and Machine Intelligence*, 20(8):832–844, 1998.
15. A. Hoerl and R. Kennard. Ridge regression: Applications to nonorthogonal problems. *Technometrics*, 12(3):69–82, 1970.
16. A. Hoerl and R. Kennard. Ridge regression; biased estimation for nonorthogonal problems. *Technometrics*, 12(3):55–67, 1970.
17. Gert R. G. Lanckriet, Nello Cristianini, Peter L. Bartlett, Laurent El Ghaoui, and Michael I. Jordan. Learning the kernel matrix with semidefinite programming. *Journal of Machine Learning Research*, 5:27–72, 2004.
18. S. Mukherjee, P. Niyogi, T. Poggio, and R. Rifkin. Stability is sufficient for generalization and necessary and sufficient for consistency of empirical risk minimization. Technical Report 024, Massachusetts Institute of Technology, Cambridge, MA, 2002. AI Memo #2002-024.
19. T. Poggio, R. Rifkin, S. Mukherjee, and P. Niyogi. General conditions for predictivity in learning theory. *Nature*, 428:419–422, 2004.
20. T. Poggio, R. Rifkin, S. Mukherjee, and A. Rakhlin. Bagging regularizes. CBCL Paper 214, Massachusetts Institute of Technology, Cambridge, MA, February 2002. AI Memo #2002-003.
21. T. Poggio and S. Smale. The mathematics of learning: Dealing with data. *Notices of the American Mathematical Society (AMS)*, 50(5):537–544, 2003.
22. R. Rifkin. *Everything Old Is New Again: A Fresh Look at Historical Approaches in Machine Learning*. PhD thesis, MIT, 2002.
23. B. Schölkopf and A. Smola. *Learning with Kernels*. MIT Press, 2002.
24. A.N. Tikhonov and V.Y. Arsenin. *Solutions of Ill-posed Problems*. W.H.Wingston, Washington, D.C., 1977.
25. G. Valentini and T. Dietterich. Low bias bagged support vector machines. In *Proc ICML*, pages 752–759, 2003.

Using Advice to Transfer Knowledge Acquired in One Reinforcement Learning Task to Another

Lisa Torrey[1], Trevor Walker[1], Jude Shavlik[1], and Richard Maclin[2]

[1] University of Wisconsin, Madison, WI 53706, USA
{ltorrey, twalker, shavlik}@cs.wisc.edu
[2] University of Minnesota, Duluth, MN 55812, USA
rmaclin@d.umn.edu

Abstract. We present a method for transferring knowledge learned in one task to a related task. Our problem solvers employ reinforcement learning to acquire a model for one task. We then transform that learned model into advice for a new task. A human teacher provides a mapping from the old task to the new task to guide this knowledge transfer. Advice is incorporated into our problem solver using a knowledge-based support vector regression method that we previously developed. This advice-taking approach allows the problem solver to refine or even discard the transferred knowledge based on its subsequent experiences. We empirically demonstrate the effectiveness of our approach with two games from the RoboCup soccer simulator: KeepAway and BreakAway. Our results demonstrate that a problem solver learning to play BreakAway using advice extracted from KeepAway outperforms a problem solver learning without the benefit of such advice.

1 Introduction

We propose a novel method to transfer the knowledge gained in one reinforcement learning (RL) task to a related task. Complex RL domains, such as Robo-Cup soccer [11], can often be divided into several related learnable tasks. *Transfer* is the process of using the knowledge acquired in one task to improve the learning of a related task. For example, the skill of keeping a soccer ball away from opponents can be used to evade players who are defending a goal, making it easier to learn the task of goal scoring.

In this work, we present a method for performing transfer using *advice*. Advice taking is a way to incorporate user guidance into RL and can significantly improve performance in complex domains [6, 7, 9]. In our previous work with advice [9], the user observes the learner performing a task and then provides advice about which actions to prefer in certain situations. In contrast, our method for transfer obtains action preferences automatically from a model learned on a previous task. The user provides a *mapping* that connects the two tasks, allowing this *transfer advice* to be applied in the new task.

We have several reasons for using advice to accomplish this knowledge transfer. It supplies the learner with some prior knowledge of the relative merits of actions in new situations where old skills might apply. It allows a user who is not familiar with the learning algorithm to guide the knowledge transfer simply by specifying the similarities between two tasks. Also, since advice can be refined or discarded by the learner if it is contradicted by experience, transfer advice should not be harmful in the long run even if the user's guidance is imperfect.

In the RoboCup simulated soccer domain [11], we extract transfer advice from a task called *KeepAway* and apply it to another task called *BreakAway*. The KeepAway game was originally introduced by Stone and Sutton [16]. The game we call BreakAway [9] is the subtask of shooting goals. Both of these games are set on a field with two teams of players, and contain actions for controlling the soccer ball. However, the two games use different field layouts and have different objectives. We provide mapping advice that points out the similarities that do exist, and our algorithm produces transfer advice that captures a reinforcement learner's knowledge about KeepAway. We then give this advice to a new problem solver to allow it to use KeepAway skills wherever they also apply in BreakAway.

The next section describes the RoboCup domain from the RL perspective. The following section gives more detail on our RL implementation and the way that it incorporates advice. After that, we introduce our transfer advice algorithm and demonstrate its potential with some initial results.

2 Reinforcement Learning in RoboCup

Reinforcement learning [17] is a continual learning process in which an agent navigates through an environment trying to earn *rewards*. The environment's state is usually represented by a set of *features*, and the agent executes *actions* that cause the state to change. Typically an agent learns a Q-function, which estimates the best long-term sum of rewards it could receive starting with a specific action from the current state. The agent's *policy*, or procedure for choosing actions, is usually to take the action with the highest Q-value in the current state. After taking the action and receiving some reward, the agent updates its estimate of that Q-value to improve its Q-function.

In the learning task of M-on-N KeepAway (see Figure 1), the objective of the M reinforcement learners called *keepers* is to keep the ball away from N (usually $M-1$) hand-coded players called *takers*. The game ends when an opponent takes the ball or when the ball goes out of bounds. A keeper needs to make an action choice only when it has possession of the ball; it may choose to hold the ball, pass to its closest teammate, or pass to its furthest teammate. It does not have movement options.

Our KeepAway state representation is the one designed by Stone and Sutton [16], which consists of features that capture simple geometric properties of the learner's field perspective, such as distances to other players and angles formed by trios of players. They describe relative distances from the learner rather than absolute locations. In our implementation, the three learners share a single Q-function learned from the combination of their experiences, and they all receive a $+1$ reward for each time step their team keeps the ball.

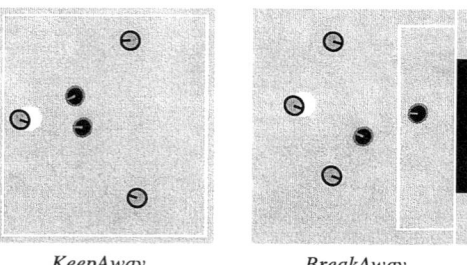

KeepAway *BreakAway*

Fig. 1. Samples of 3-on-2 KeepAway and BreakAway games. The ball is the white circle, and is held by a keeper on the left (a light circle with a dark border) and an attacker on the right. The two opponents (dark circles with light borders) are both takers on the left, but on the right, one is a defender and the other a goalie.

In M-on-N BreakAway (see Figure 1), the objective of the M reinforcement learners called *attackers* is to score a goal against $N-1$ hand-coded *defenders* and a hand-coded *goalie*. The game ends when they succeed, when an opponent takes the ball, when the ball goes out of bounds, or after a time limit of 10 seconds. When an attacker has possession of the ball, it has a learnable action choice: to move with the ball, to pass the ball to its closest or furthest teammate, or to shoot the ball at the goal. We limit movement to four choices: forward towards the center of the goal, away from the goal, and clockwise or counterclockwise along a circle centered at the goal. The shoot action directs the ball at the center, right side, or left side of the goal, whichever is least blocked by the goalie.

Our BreakAway state representation also consists of features measuring important distances and angles, many of which are similar to KeepAway features. The new features include distances and angles involving the goal, and the time left in the game. The learners share a single model, and they all receive a +2 reward for a goal, 0 for a failed shot, and -1 for the other game endings.

In our RL method, the learners approximate the Q-function by solving a linear optimization problem. Following Stone and Sutton's approach [16], we use *tile coding* to include some non-linear features in this problem, which allows the model to express more complex functions. Tile coding discretizes each numeric feature into several overlapping tilings, each containing a set of discrete tiles. Each tile is represented by a Boolean feature that is true when the numeric value falls into the tile interval and false otherwise. Through this process, we add 64 Boolean features to the state space for every numeric feature. We have found, as did Stone and Sutton, that this addition to the state space significantly improves learning for RoboCup.

Neither of these games is trivial, especially since the soccer simulator incorporates noise into players' sensors and actions. BreakAway is the more difficult of the two, because it contains only one positive reward that is rarely received by chance (the goalie can easily block random shots). Learners in BreakAway also have more actions to choose from and a larger state space to navigate.

3 Background: Support Vector Regression

Our learners employ a type of RL called SARSA with a one-step look-ahead to estimate Q-values [17]. Our implementation uses support vector regression (SVR). We use a linear optimization method proposed by Mangasarian et al. [10] and extended in Maclin et al. [8, 9] to compute a model that approximates the Q-function. We train the learner in batches: it uses the most recent model to play 100 games, and then updates the model using these new training examples to get a better Q-function approximation.

The main structure in a learned model is a weight vector w, which has one weight for each feature in the feature vector x. Each action has its own weight vector and offset term b, and the expected Q-value of taking that action from the state described by x is $wx + b$. Our learners take the action that scores the highest with probability $(1 - \epsilon)$, and take a sub-optimal exploratory action with probability ϵ, where ϵ typically is a small number between 0.01 and 0.05.

To compute the weight vector for an action, we find the subset of training examples in which that action was taken and place those feature vectors into rows of a data matrix A. Using the previous model and the actual rewards received during those training steps, we compute new Q-value estimates and place them into an output vector y. The optimal weight vector is then described by

$$Aw + be = y \tag{1}$$

where e denotes a vector of ones (we omit this for simplicity from now on).

In practice, we prefer to have non-zero weights for only a few important features in order to keep the model simple and avoid overfitting the training examples. We therefore introduce *slack* variables s that allow inaccuracies on each example, and a penalty parameter C for trading off these inaccuracies with the complexity of the solution. The resulting minimization problem is

$$\min_{(w,b,s)} ||w||_1 + \nu|b| + C||s||_1 \\ s.t. \quad -s \leq Aw + b - y \leq s. \tag{2}$$

where $|\cdot|$ denotes an absolute value, $||\cdot||_1$ denotes a sum of absolute values, and ν is a penalty on the offset term. By solving this problem, we can produce a weight vector w for each action that compromises between accuracy and simplicity.

In Mangasarian et al.'s [10] Knowledge Based Kernel Regression (KBKR) method, advice can be given in the form of a rule about a single action. This rule creates new constraints on the problem solution, in addition to the constraints from the training data. Recently, we introduced an extension to KBKR called Preference-KBKR [9], which allows advice about pairs of actions in the form

$$Bx \leq d \implies Q_p(x) - Q_n(x) \geq \beta, \tag{3}$$

which can be read as:

> If the current state satisfies ($Bx \leq d$), the Q-value of the preferred action p should exceed that of the non-preferred action n by at least β.

For example, consider giving the advice that shooting is better than moving ahead when the distance to the goal is at most 10. The vector B would have one row with a 1 in the column for the "distance to goal" feature and zeros elsewhere. The vector d would contain only the value 10, and β could be set to any small positive number.

Just as we allowed some inaccuracy on the training examples, we allow advice to be followed only partially. To do so, we introduce slack variables z and ζ and penalty parameters μ_1 and μ_2 for trading off the impact of the advice on the solution with the impact of the training examples.

The new minimization problem addresses all the actions together so that it can apply constraints to their relative values. Multiple pieces of preference advice can be incorporated, each with its own B, d, p, n, and β. We use the CPLEX commercial software program to solve the resulting linear program:

$$\min_{(w_a, b_a, s_a, z_i, \zeta_i \geq 0, u_i \geq 0)} \sum_{a=1}^{m}(||w_a||_1 + \nu|b_a| + C||s_a||_1) + \sum_{i=1}^{k}(\mu_1||z_i||_1 + \mu_2\zeta_i) \quad (4)$$

s.t. for each action $a \in \{1, \ldots, m\}$:
$$-s_a \leq A_a w_a + b_a - y_a \leq s_a$$
for each piece of advice $i \in \{1, \ldots, k\}$:
$$-z_i \leq w_p - w_n + B_i^T u_i \leq z_i$$
$$-d^T u_i + \zeta_i \geq \beta_i - b_p + b_n.$$

4 Transfer Advice

In order to transfer knowledge gained on one task to a related task, we automatically extract advice that tells the learner to prefer some actions over others in new situations based on its experience in the old task. This *transfer advice* is incorporated into the learning procedure for the new task as explained in the previous section. Figure 2 summarizes the overall process.

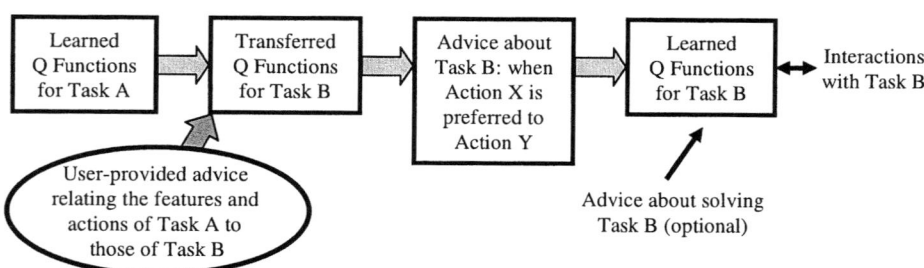

Fig. 2. Transferring knowledge using advice. Advice may also have been given when learning Task A.

As an example, suppose we learned in KeepAway that when a taker was near, passing to the nearest teammate was better than any other action. Our algorithm might transfer this knowledge to BreakAway by generating advice that when a defender is near, passing to the nearest teammate is better than any other action.

This kind of advice is not the only way, or the most obvious way, to transfer knowledge. One alternative would be to translate the actions and features of the old task into actions and features of the new task, and then apply the old Q-function directly to the new task, hoping that it would provide a good starting point for learning. However, if the new task has a different reward structure, these estimates might be uninformative. Simply transferring the Q-function from KeepAway would give a BreakAway learner inaccurate initial estimates.

Instead of transferring Q-values, our method transfers a partial policy that covers some regions of the feature space. By telling the learner to *prefer* some actions over others in those regions, we give *relative* constraints on Q-values instead of specifying them absolutely. This approach is more robust to differences in the tasks' reward structures.

The only input our method requires from a human teacher is a *mapping* that translates features and actions in the old task to features and actions in the new task. For example, we might map KeepAway features involving the nearest taker to BreakAway features involving the nearest defender, and the KeepAway action *HoldBall* to the BreakAway action *MoveAhead*.

Using this mapping, our algorithm evaluates a state from the perspective of the old task. If one old action would have been better than all the others in this situation, it gives transfer advice that recommends taking the corresponding action in the new task. Table 1 gives the general form of the transfer advice algorithm, and Table 2 gives a simple but concrete example. Note that this direct translation of a learned model into advice is possible because we represent both models and advice as linear expressions of features.

There are a few complications to this basic procedure. For example, sometimes an old feature has no logical analogue in the new task. In these cases, the user may map the old feature f to a constant value instead of a new feature f'. For example, the takers in 3-on-2 KeepAway do not have corresponding defenders in 2-on-1 BreakAway, since the goalie behaves differently from a defender. The user could set the features describing distances to takers to their maximum

Table 1. The basic algorithm to create transfer advice. We set the constant Δ to 1 in our experiments. See Table 2 for more details.

GIVEN
    A learned model of Task A AND
    A mapping from Task A to Task B
DO
    for each $a \in Actions(TaskA)$ generate advice:
        IF for each $b \in Actions(TaskA), b \neq a : \quad Q'_a - Q'_b \geq \Delta$
        THEN PREFER a' TO ALL b' in Task B

Table 2. A simple demonstration of extracting transfer advice. The actions in the old task are a, b, and c, and the corresponding actions in the new task are a', b', and c'. The learned model for the old task is a set of linear Q-value expressions with weights w and features f, and these are translated into advice that uses the corresponding new task features f'.

OLD TASK MODEL:	ADVICE FORMAT:
$Q_a = w_{a1} * f_1 + w_{a2} * f_2 + w_{a0}$	IF $Q'_a - Q'_b \geq \Delta$
$Q_b = w_{b1} * f_1 + w_{b0}$	AND $Q'_a - Q'_c \geq \Delta$
$Q_c = w_{c2} * f_2 + w_{c0}$	THEN prefer a' to b' and c'
USER-PROVIDED MAPPING:	FULL ADVICE EXPRESSION:
$(a, b, c) \longrightarrow (a', b', c')$	IF $(w_{a1} - w_{b1}) * f'_1 + w_{a2} * f'_2 + w_{a0} - w_{b0} \geq \Delta$
$(f_1, f_2) \longrightarrow (f'_1, f'_2)$	AND $w_{a1} * f'_1 + (w_{a2} - w_{c2}) * f'_2 + w_{a0} - w_{c0} \geq \Delta$
TRANSLATED EXPRESSIONS:	THEN prefer a' to b' and c'
$Q'_a = w_{a1} * f'_1 + w_{a2} * f'_2 + w_{a0}$	
$Q'_b = w_{b1} * f'_1 + w_{b0}$	
$Q'_c = w_{c2} * f'_2 + w_{c0}$	

value, implying that the nonexistent defenders are too far away to affect the learner's actions. Another example is the feature describing a player's distance to the center of the KeepAway field. The user could set that feature to the average value of its range. We use these constant mappings in the experiments reported later. To handle a feature in the new task that has no logical analogue in the old task, we simply leave the new feature out of the mapping.

We create one advice rule for each old action that has an analogue, indicating when the analogue looks like the best choice based on experience in the old task. The other new actions (such as *MoveLeft* in BreakAway) must be learned independently by the agent. To handle old actions that have no analogues, we also simply leave the old action out of the mapping.

Since we added tile features from the tile encoding of numeric features, we also need to map the tiles of each KeepAway feature to tiles of a BreakAway feature. We automatically map tiles to maximize the amount of the BreakAway feature range that they share. This method does not require mapped features to have identical ranges, since that would severely restrict the mapping.

Remapping is a further capability that allows the learner to apply old knowledge in multiple ways. For example, an attacker can clearly use KeepAway skills to evade defenders on the BreakAway field; with a little cleverness, it might be able to use those same skills to shoot. Suppose the learner imagines a teammate is standing inside the goal. Then, a decision on whether to pass to that teammate corresponds to a decision on whether to shoot. We could do this by mapping all the features involving the teammate to features involving the goal. However, if this were the *only* mapping, it would prevent the learner from considering actually passing to the real teammate. To let the learner consider both actions, we create two sets of advice, using first one mapping and then the other. We included such a remapping in our experiments.

Situation-dependent mappings allow old knowledge to be used differently in different areas of the new feature space. For example, we might only want to map a KeepAway action to the BreakAway action *shoot* when the learner is close to the goal, because we know that soccer players should only shoot over short distances. We could do this by providing one mapping that applies when the learner is near the goal and a different one that applies when the learner is far from the goal. We did not use this situation-dependent mapping in our experiments; we expected that the KeepAway passing skills would already prevent attackers from shooting from too far away.

5 RoboCup Transfer Advice

The two RoboCup tasks we explore have significant differences that make transfer a non-trivial problem. In KeepAway, learners should make the game last as long as possible, but in BreakAway, they should end the game quickly by scoring a goal. Learners in KeepAway cannot choose to move, but learners in BreakAway can. KeepAway takers will always move towards the ball, but the BreakAway goalie will not. There are also different numbers of players.

However, there are also some useful similarities between the tasks. Many of the features map directly, and some of the actions are identical. On a conceptual level, the BreakAway attackers must play KeepAway while trying to score.

We designed the default mappings shown in Table 3 to take advantage of these similarities for transfer from 3-on-2 KeepAway to 2-on-1 BreakAway. The BreakAway features and actions that have no KeepAway analogues do not appear in these tables. The KeepAway features that have no BreakAway analogues are mapped to constants within their ranges.

We then used the remapping capability to apply KeepAway skills to shooting. The two remappings in Table 4 advise the learner to imagine that its nearest teammate is standing first in the left side of the goal, and then in the right side. If a pass to that teammate would have been the best action, the advice will recommend shooting. There was no BreakAway feature to describe the distance from the goalie to a goal section, so we used a constant value in its place.

Using a high-performing 3-on-2 KeepAway model that was trained without any advice [8], we applied these mappings and our transfer advice algorithm to create advice for 2-on-1 BreakAway. The process produced five advice items, each capturing one of the five KeepAway "skills": the three original actions and the two remapped pass actions. For example, this is the form of the advice that shows how to apply the KeepAway "hold ball" skill to BreakAway:

$$
\begin{aligned}
\text{IF} \quad & Q'_{HoldBall} - Q'_{PassFar} \geq \Delta \text{ AND} \\
& Q'_{HoldBall} - Q'_{PassNear\_remap1} \geq \Delta \text{ AND} \\
& Q'_{HoldBall} - Q'_{PassNear} \geq \Delta \text{ AND} \\
& Q'_{HoldBall} - Q'_{PassNear\_remap2} \geq \Delta
\end{aligned}
$$

THEN PREFER *MoveAhead* TO *PassNear* AND *Shoot*

Table 3. Default action and feature mappings from KeepAway to BreakAway. *Near* and *Far* refer to teammates' distances from the learner. The learner is L, the keepers are K's, the takers are T's, and the attackers are A's.

KeepAway	BreakAway
PassNear	PassNear
HoldBall	MoveAhead
dist(L, near K)	distance(L, near A)
other player distances	MAX_RANGE
min angle(near K, L, any T)	MID_RANGE
min angle(near K, L, any T)	MID_RANGE
distances to field center	MID_RANGE

Table 4. Action and feature remappings that apply KeepAway skills to shooting

Remapping 1: *PassNear to Shoot*	
KeepAway	BreakAway
dist(L, near K)	dist(L, goal left)
min dist(near K, any T)	MID_RANGE
min angle(near K, L, any T)	angle(goal left, L, goalie)
Remapping 2: *PassNear to Shoot*	
KeepAway	BreakAway
dist(L, near K)	dist(L, goal right)
min dist(near K, any T)	MID_RANGE
min angle(near K, L, any T)	angle(goal right, L, goalie)

Essentially, this advice says that if holding the ball would be safer than passing towards a teammate or towards the goal, then moving forward with the ball is probably safer than passing or shooting.

6 Empirical Results

The linear program presented in Equation 4 contains parameters ν, C, μ_1, and μ_2. The first two we set by tuning on KeepAway games without using any advice. This led to C being set to $2500*(0.1+0.9(1-e^{\#GamesPlayed/10,000}))/\#features$ and ν to 100. We exponentially increase C because as RL progresses the estimates of Q (which are infinite sums) become more accurate. We next chose μ_1 and μ_2 by running some tuning games using transfer advice, selecting $\mu_1 = 0.01$ and $\mu_2 = 1.0$. We decay these initial μ values by $e^{(-\#GamesPlayed/2,500)}$, since we expect that transfer advice will be less valuable as the amount of experience in the new domain increases. We only tried a small number of possible settings for each parameter, and after choosing our parameter values, we trained on a fresh set of games – we report the results on this final set of games.

Figure 3 shows the results of our transfer experiments. Training runs with and without transfer advice are compared. The curves were generated by batch training after every 100 games and averaging over 10 different runs; each data point shown is smoothed over the previous 1000 games (the results from the first 100 games are not included in these averages except at the first point on the x axis, where Games Played = 100, since no learning took place until after the first 100 games).

The curve on the left shows the average reinforcement per game that learners earn as they train, since that is the quantity that the learners attempt to maximize. The curve on the right shows a more intuitive measure of performance: the probability that the learners will score a goal as a function of the number of games played.

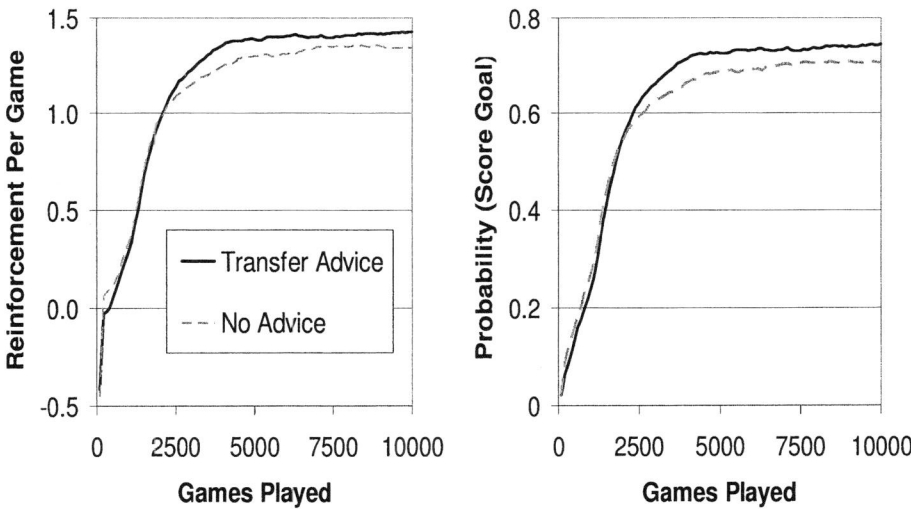

Fig. 3. Performance as a function of BreakAway games played by two different metrics, with a learner using transfer advice compared against a learner using no advice

These results show that the transfer advice gives a reinforcement learner a modest advantage in learning to score goals. Advice was slightly detrimental at first as the learners refined it, but after about 2,500 games it began to improve performance, and in the end it led to a higher asymptotic result. We have obtained qualitatively similar results when transferring to 3-on-2 BreakAway, although in this task the probability of scoring a goal is above 0.5.

7 Related Work

A number of researchers have explored methods for providing advice to learning algorithms. Clouse and Utgoff [2] allow a human observer to step in and advise the learner to take a specific action. Lin [6] "replays" teacher sequences to bias a learner towards a teacher's performance. Gordon and Subramanian [3] accept advice in the form IF *condition* THEN *achieve goals* and then use genetic algorithms to adjust it with respect to the data. Maclin and Shavlik [7] also developed an IF-THEN advice language, but incorporated the rules into a neural network for later adjustment. Price and Boutilier [12] designed a method for reinforcement learners to imitate expert agents in the same domain. Andre and Russell [1] describe a language for creating learning agents whose policies are constrained by user commands. Laud and DeJong [5] use reinforcements to shape the learner. Kuhlmann et al. [4] developed a rule-based advice system that increases Q-values by a fixed amount. In recent work [9], we developed the Preference-KBKR method, which allows advice to be specified in the form of action preferences. Our current work differs from these previous advice-taking methods because it extracts advice from a model learned in another task, instead of employing user-designed advice.

Other related work deals with knowledge transfer in machine learning. Some early research focuses on learning a simpler version of a task and applying that knowledge to a more difficult version of the same task. Selfridge et al. [13] call this "directed training" and use it in robotics. Singh [15] addresses transfer of knowledge between sequential decision tasks, where an agent keeps track of useful action subsequences for use in later tasks. Thrun and Mitchell [19] study transfer between problems in a "lifelong learning" framework of many related Boolean classification tasks. Taylor and Stone [18] have investigated copying Q-functions to transfer between KeepAway games of different team sizes. Sherstov and Stone [14] have investigated "action transfer" in RL, which uses transfer to improve learning on tasks with large action spaces.

8 Conclusions and Future Work

We have presented a novel technique of extracting knowledge gained on one task and automatically transferring it to a related task to improve learning. Our experiments demonstrate that the difficult BreakAway task in RoboCup soccer can be learned more effectively using advice transferred from the related KeepAway task.

Our key idea is that we can view the models learned in an old task as a source of advice for a new task. Since we represent both our learned models and advice as linear expressions of features, all the user needs to do is match the features and actions of the old task to the new one. Since advice-taking systems are robust to imperfections in the advice they receive, the user's guidance need only be approximate.

In future work, we plan to evaluate the sensitivity of our algorithm to errors and omissions in the user's mapping advice. We may also investigate ways to further automate the process by helping the user design a mapping. We have already begun to adapt the transfer advice process to work with non-linear models.

When a new learning task arises in a domain, it is likely that human experts will be able to provide information about how the new task relates to known tasks. Learning algorithms should be able to exploit this information to extract knowledge from these known tasks. Transfer advice shows potential as an effective and intuitive way to do this. It can increase human ability to interact productively with reinforcement learners, and we believe that such interaction will be important for scaling RL to large problems.

Acknowledgements

The research is partially supported by DARPA grant HR0011-04-1-0007 and United States Naval Research Laboratory grant N00173-04-1-G026. The BreakAway code is available at ftp://ftp.cs.wisc.edu/machine-learning/shavlik-group/robocup/breakaway. We would also like to thank Michael Ferris for his assistance in improving the efficiency of our linear programs.

References

1. D. Andre and S. Russell. Programmable reinforcement learning agents. In *NIPS*, 2001.
2. J. Clouse and P. Utgoff. A teaching method for reinforcement learning. In *Proc. ICML '92*, 1992.
3. D. Gordon and D. Subramanian. A multistrategy learning scheme for agent knowledge acquisition. *Informatica*, 17:331–346, 1994.
4. G. Kuhlmann, P. Stone, R. Mooney, and J. Shavlik. Guiding a reinforcement learner with natural language advice: Initial results in RoboCup soccer. In *AAAI Workshop on Supervisory Control of Learning and Adaptive Systems*, 2004.
5. A. Laud and G. DeJong. Reinforcement learning and shaping: Encouraging intended behaviors. In *ICML*, 2002.
6. L. Lin. Self-improving reactive agents based on reinforcement learning, planning, and teaching. *Machine Learning*, 8:293–321, 1992.
7. R. Maclin and J. Shavlik. Creating advice-taking reinforcement learners. *Machine Learning*, 22:251–281, 1996.
8. R. Maclin, J. Shavlik, L. Torrey, and T. Walker. Knowledge-based support vector regression for reinforcement learning. In *IJCAI Workshop on Reasoning, Representation, and Learning in Computer Games*, 2005.
9. R. Maclin, J. Shavlik, L. Torrey, T. Walker, and E. Wild. Giving advice about preferred actions to reinforcement learners via knowledge-based kernel regression. In *AAAI*, 2005.
10. O. Mangasarian, J. Shavlik, and E. Wild. Knowledge-based kernel approximation. *JMLR*, 5:1127–1141, 2004.
11. I. Noda, H. Matsubara, K. Hiraki, and I. Frank. Soccer server: A tool for research on multiagent systems. *Applied Artificial Intelligence*, 12:233–250, 1998.

12. B. Price and C. Boutilier. Implicit imitation in multiagent reinforcement learning. In *ICML*, 1999.
13. O. Selfridge, R. Sutton, and A. Barto. Training and tracking in robotics. In *IJCAI*, 1985.
14. A. Sherstov and P. Stone. Improving action selection in MDP's via knowledge transfer. In *AAAI*, 2005.
15. S. Singh. Transfer of learning by composing solutions of elemental sequential tasks. *Machine Learning*, 8(3-4):323–339, 1992.
16. P. Stone and R. Sutton. Scaling reinforcement learning toward RoboCup soccer. In *ICML*, 2001.
17. R. Sutton and A. Barto. *Reinforcement Learning: An Introduction*. MIT Press, Cambridge, MA, 1998.
18. M. Taylor and P. Stone. Behavior transfer for value-function-based reinforcement learning. In *4th Int. Joint Conf. on Autonomous Agents and Multiagent Sys.*, 2005.
19. S. Thrun and T. Mitchell. Learning one more thing. In *IJCAI*, 1995.

A Distance-Based Approach for Action Recommendation

Ronan Trepos[1,2], Ansaf Salleb[1], Marie-Odile Cordier[1],
Véronique Masson[1], and Chantal Gascuel[2]

[1] IRISA-INRIA, Campus Universitaire de Beaulieu, 35042, Rennes Cedex - France
{rtrepos, asalleb, cordier, masson}@irisa.fr
[2] INRA UMR SAS, Agrocampus rue de Saint Brieuc, 35042, Rennes Cedex - France
Chantal.Gascuel@rennes.inra.fr

Abstract. Rule induction has attracted a great deal of attention in Machine Learning and Data Mining. However, generating rules is not an end in itself because their applicability is not so straightforward. Indeed, the user is often overwhelmed when faced with a large number of rules.
In this paper, we propose an approach to lighten this burden when the user wishes to exploit such rules to decide which actions to do given an unsatisfactory situation . The method consists in comparing a situation to a set of classification rules. This is achieved using a suitable distance thus allowing to suggest action recommendations with minimal changes to improve that situation. We propose the algorithm DAKAR for learning action recommendations and we present an application to an environmental protection issue. Our experiment shows the usefulness of our contribution in decision-making but also raises concerns about the impact of the redundancy of a set of rules in learning action recommendations of quality.

Keywords: Decision support, actionability, rule-based classifier, generalized Minkowski metrics, maximally discriminant descriptions.

1 Introduction

Rule induction has attracted a lot of attention in Machine Learning and Data Mining communities. However, the exploitation of a set of rules induced is usually and merely let to the end-user. Overwhelmed by the number of rules, the user is also often frustrated because the applicability of these rules is not so immediate. This makes the post-analysis of induced rules as a great challenge and a necessary step to assist the user in his work as in decision making. Indeed, rather than simply presenting the rules listing to decision-makers, the ideal is to translate these rules into feasible and concrete actions.

In this paper, we are interested in rule-based classifiers. Although useful in real applications, classifying new instances is not enough; user needs more help when he tries to use the classification model beyond the prediction purpose. It is the case when the user wishes to decide which action to accomplish in order to improve an unsatisfactory situation. For instance, how to cure an ill patient given a set of rules describing ill and not ill patients. This brings us to the notion of actionability, described in [21] as follows : "a pattern is interesting to the user if the user can do something about it; that is the user can react to it to his or her advantage". Although some recent works have addressed the problem of learning actionable knowledge [4, 5, 8, 9, 13, 17, 18, 23], in our point of view, this topic remains under investigation and deserves more attention.

The purpose of this paper is to develop a new method for recommending actions. We propose the algorithm DAKAR (Discovery of Actionable Knowledge And Recommendations) which works as follows: starting from an unsatisfactory situation and relying on a set of classification rules, DAKAR discovers a set of action recommendations that propose minimal changes to the domain-expert in order to improve that situation.

More precisely, we focus on propositional frameworks, where a situation is expressed by a conjunction of attribute-value pairs. In our case, an action is a modification of values of some attributes of the situation. We compute actions involving "little" changes in the initial situation. This is achieved in DAKAR thanks to the generalized Minkowski metric proposed in [7] which allows us to compute the distance between two descriptions. In our approach, a weight is assigned to each feature in order to take into account how flexible it is. The search space of actions is defined as the set of *maximally discriminant descriptions* that differentiates an unsatisfactory situation from a set of classification rules characterizing what is satisfactory, according to a distance threshold δ. This space is explored considering two properties we have defined, which are the *coherence* and the *validity* of actions. DAKAR uses a beam-search strategy to find the best actions, according to a quality criterion, to suggest to the user.

This paper is organized as follows: in section 2, we present the state of the art of the actionability issue. Section 3 is devoted to our approach and to DAKAR algorithm. Experimental tests are described in section 4 and we conclude in section 5 with a summary of our contribution and future directions.

2 Related Work

This section is a survey of the approaches developed in both Machine Learning and Data Mining literature to address the actionability issue. In [21], Silberschatz and Tuzhilin evoked for the first time the term *actionability* in the context of interestingness measures for patterns evaluation. They classify such measures into objective (data-driven) and subjective (user-driven) measures. According to them, from the subjective point of view, a pattern is interesting if it is:

- actionable : the end-user can act on it to his advantage.
- unexpected : the end-user is surprised by such finding.

As pointed out by the authors, actionability is difficult to capture; they propose rather to capture it through unexpectedness, arguing that unexpected patterns are those that lead the expert to make some actions.

While many works have addressed the unexpectedness issue (see for instance [3] for a survey), the actionability remains to be further investigated even if we noticed recently a great interest from researchers in developing new methods for the discovery of actionable knowledge.

We will focus in the following on the methods developed to address actionability issue by using classifiers. Readers interested in actionability in other tasks, such as clustering, can consult the state of the art proposed by He et al. [5].

In [10], the authors propose a method that prune all non actionable rules from a large set of association rules. The idea is to discard the more general rules using their specialized rules (having more conditions in the left-hand side) with higher quality. Although their approach facilitate the hard task of analyzing large sets of rules, strictly speaking, it does not identify truly action rules.

Lavrač et al. [8] used subgroup discovery to generate actionable knowledge. It is interesting to notice how the authors distinguished actionable rules from operational ones. Operational rules are somewhat actionable "ready to use" rules, which, if applied, will affect a target population immediately.

Shapiro and Matheus [13] developed a health-care system named KEFIR dealing with *deviations*. The system embodies a *recommendation generator* that suggests corrective actions in response to some relevant deviations discovered in the data. Here, corrective actions are defined *a priori* by health-care experts.

A decision-theoretic framework evaluating classification systems from an economic point of view is proposed in [4]. Here, the relationship between the quality of a classification system and the expected payoff to the company is formalized. Classification systems are compared, using their confusion matrices, in terms of their *effectiveness* in decision making. Actions suggested are predefined by the user.

Ling et al. [9] consider mining *optimal actions* in CRM (Customer Relationship Management) relying on decision trees models. They aim at finding those actions that change customers from undesired status to a desired one. An action is merely a change in the value of an attribute. These actions are chosen so as to maximize the expected net profit by taking into consideration their costs.

In [17], the authors show how to discover action rules that allow to move from a given class to another one. This is achieved by comparing pairs of rules having different classes in the right-hand side. Features are divided into: stable (features that cannot be changed) and flexible. An action rule involves only flexible features and shows what are the changes to deploy in order to realize the class change. In business applications, action rules are useful to identify customers for whom some changes in their flexible features will bring them from a profit ranking group to a better one.

The two first approaches [10, 8] work directly on rules to address the actionability issue while the others address it via action recommendations. The studies proposed in [13, 4] aim at recommending predefined actions to the user and the systems proposed in [9, 17] discover actions to be recommended. Comparisons between our approach and the closest works [9, 17] are given throughout this paper.

3 Framework Description

3.1 The Learning Task

We propose an approach for mining actionable knowledge. The task we address aims at improving a given situation with regard to a rule-based classifier. It can be defined informally as follows:

"Given a situation for which an unsatisfactory class $\ominus$ corresponds, what are the minimal changes (actions) to do in this situation in order to improve that situation to a satisfactory class $\oplus$?"

For instance, given a situation describing a high level pollution in an area, what are the advices to be suggested to reduce that pollution.

In this paper, we propose to discover actions through a set of classification rules. Before giving the algorithm DAKAR, let us first introduce some basic definitions. Let $X_1, .., X_n$ be features taking their values in the domains $Dom_1, .., Dom_n$ respectively.

Definition 1. (Instance) *An instance is an object described by a conjunction of instantiated features denoted by:* $\bigwedge_{i=1,...,n} (X_i = v_i)$.

Definition 2. (Description) *A description is a conjunction defined on a subset of features as follows:* $D = \bigwedge_{i=1,..,m} (X_{k_i} \in d_{k_i})$
where $d_{k_i} \subseteq Dom_{k_i}$, $\{k_1, ..., k_m\} \subseteq \{1, .., n\}$ *and* $k_i \neq k_j \forall i, j$.

Definition 3. (Extended description) *A description can be extended to all the features as follows:* $\widehat{D} = \bigwedge_{i=1,...,m} (X_{k_i} \in d_{k_i}) \bigwedge_{j \notin \{k_1,...,k_m\}} (X_j \in Dom_j)$.
where $d_{k_i} \subseteq Dom_{k_i}$, $\{k_1, ..., k_m\} \subseteq \{1, .., n\}$.

For the rest of the paper, a description is considered in its extended form and actions and situations are extended descriptions.

Definition 4. (Classification rule) *A classification rule is an implication of the form $Descr \Longrightarrow Class$ where $Descr$ is a description and $Class$ is the corresponding class label ($\ominus$ or $\oplus$).*

Definition 5. (Coverage) *We say that a description* $D = \bigwedge_{i=1,...,n} (X_i \in d_i)$ *covers an instance* $I = \bigwedge_{i=1,...,n} (X_i = v_i)$ *iff* $\forall i, v_i \in d_i$. *The set of instances (among all possible instances) covered by D will be denoted by $cov(D)$.*

Notice that $cov(D) = cov(\widehat{D})$. For a classification rule $R : Descr \Longrightarrow Class$, we define $cov(R) = cov(Descr)$.

A set of classification rules $\mathcal{R}$ is seen as the union of two sets: $\mathcal{R}^\oplus$ and $\mathcal{R}^\ominus$ corresponding respectively to the set of rules characterizing class $\oplus$ and class $\ominus$. This can be extended easily to multi-class problems.

Definition 6. (Outcome situation) *An action applied to a situation leads to another description called an outcome situation.*
Given a situation $S = \bigwedge_{i=1,..,n}(X_i \in s_i)$ *and an action* $A = \bigwedge_{i=1,..,n}(X_i \in a_i)$, *the outcome situation* $outcome(S, A)$ *is computed as follows:*

$$outcome(S, A) = \bigwedge_{i=1,..,n}(X_i \in o_i) \quad \text{where } o_i = \begin{cases} s_i & \text{if } a_i = Dom_i \\ a_i & \text{otherwise} \end{cases}$$

When proposing actions to the user, we have to take into consideration their practical applicability. This can be achieved by considering the *flexibility* of the features involved in the action. This notion is further explained in the following.

3.2 On the Need of a Suitable Distance Metric

In [17], the notion of feature flexibility is used to find action rules. Features are divided into two groups : *stable* (features that cannot be changed) and *flexible*. In their approach, action rules are designed with flexible features.

This division into two groups is interesting but is rather strict and not always sufficient. For example, a physician would prefer, if possible, prescribing medicines to advising a surgical intervention to an ill patient. However, in their work, such two flexible features are identically considered. In our approach, to take into account this differentiation, each feature is assigned with a given *flexibility weight*. Moreover, the notion of feature flexibility is not sufficient. For example, making a diet is in many cases an advice given by physicians but its feasibility depends on the goal we want to achieve. If the weight to loose is about 80 kilograms, this advice is impractical. In the other hand, the advice of loosing 2 kilograms is quite practical. The outcome situation (when action is applied) must be relatively "close" to the initial situation. For these reasons, a metric distance capturing the difficulty of improving a situation thanks to an action seems to be adapted to our problem.

The literature abounds with definitions of metric distances between two descriptions. Relying on an empirical comparative study [11], we have chosen the generalized Minkowski metric proposed by Ichino and Yaguchi [7] which handles both qualitative and quantitative features. It also integrates weights and deals with dissimilarities between two feature values. We rewrite it according to our notations. Let us consider two extended descriptions :

$$D = \bigwedge_{1..n}(X_i \in d_i) \quad d_i \subseteq Dom_i$$
$$D' = \bigwedge_{1..n}(X_i \in d'_i) \quad d'_i \subseteq Dom_i$$

The normalized and weighted dissimilarity measure called the generalized Minkowski distance of order p defined in [7] is given by :

$$d_p(D, D') = \left[\sum_{i=1}^{n}\{w_i \ \psi(d_i, d'_i)\}^p\right]^{1/p}$$

where the flexibility weights $w_i > 0$, $i \in \{1, .., n\}$ are chosen so that $\sum_{i=1}^{n} w_i = 1$ and $\psi(d_i, d'_i)$ is a normalized distance between the sub-domains d_i and d'_i of

Dom_i (see [7] for more details). The generalized Minkowski distance satisfies $0 \leq d_p(D, D') \leq 1$ and it is proved that this distance satisfies all the axioms for a metric.

3.3 The Search Space of Actions

In this subsection, we define the search space of the actions. We are given an initial situation $S = \bigwedge_{i=1,..,n}(A_i \in s_i)$ classified in $\ominus$ and a set of rules $\mathcal{R} = \mathcal{R}^\oplus \cup \mathcal{R}^\ominus$. An obvious approach is to define the search space of actions as the whole space of descriptions. This space is first restricted thanks to the property of *validity* defined as follows.

Definition 7. (The validity of an action relatively to a situation) *An action A is said to be valid relatively to a situation S if*
$$\text{cov}(S) \cap \text{cov}(A) = \{\}$$

Thus, an instance covered by the initial situation is not covered by the outcome situation when a valid action is applied. To consider only valid actions, we use the *maximally discriminant set* denoted by *discr* which is defined for S and a description $D = \bigwedge_{i=1,..,n}(A_i \in d_i)$ by:
$$discr(S, D) = \bigcup_{i=1,..,n}\{A_i \in (d_i - s_i)\}$$
For a rule $R : Descr \implies Class$, we define $discr(S, R) = discr(S, Descr)$. Notice that an element in $discr(S, D)$ is a valid action relatively to S. The notion of maximally discriminant has already been used in [19] in designing a learner inspired by the version spaces framework [12].

In order to consider descriptions that are likely to be "good" actions, we construct the maximally discriminant set between S and the description part of one rule in $\mathcal{R}^\oplus$. Intuitively, this set is composed of the attribute-value pairs that make the difference between the rules of class $\oplus$ and the situation of class $\ominus$.

Example 1. Let {*weight,medicines*} be a set of features taking respectively their values in $Dom_1 = [40, 120]$ and $Dom_2 = \{$no, tablets, syrup$\}$. The quantitative feature *weight* represents the weight of a patient while the qualitative feature *medicines* represents the treatment prescribed to the patient. Let $R_1^\oplus$, $R_2^\oplus$ and $R_3^\ominus$ be three rules:

$R_1^\oplus : weight \in [50, 80] \rightarrow$ not ill
$R_2^\oplus : weight \in [90, 110] \land medicines \in \{syrup\} \rightarrow$ not ill
$R_3^\ominus : weight \in [65, 120] \land medicines \in \{no\} \rightarrow$ ill

We consider an ill patient in the following situation S:
$$weight \in [70] \land medicines \in \{no\}.$$
We compute maximally discriminant sets:
$$discr(S, R_1^\oplus) = \{weight \in [50, 70[, weight \in]70, 80],$$
$$medicines \in \{\text{tablets,syrup}\}\}$$
$$discr(S, R_2^\oplus) = \{weight \in [90, 110], medicines \in \{syrup\}\}$$

In [18], an action rule relies on only one rule. For each rule in $\mathcal{R}^\oplus$ corresponds an action which guarantees to get an outcome situation with a better class (at least one rule of $\mathcal{R}^\oplus$ covers the outcome situation). In our point of view, an action should rely on the entire set of rules. Thus, by combining attribute-value pairs of these rules, new actions can be suggested.

The set of elementary actions $\mathcal{A}$ is given by $\bigcup_{R \in \mathcal{R}^\oplus} discr(S, R)$ and an action is a conjunction of such elements. Our search space of actions is the set:

$$\{\bigwedge_{\text{elem} \in E} \text{elem} | E \subseteq \mathcal{A}\}$$

Actions considered by our method embodies those that would be suggested by the system in [18]. Let us also notice that the search space as defined above embodies some actions that are not to be considered because they do not fulfill the *coherency* property defined as follows:

Definition 8. (The coherency of an action) *An action A is said to be coherent if* $\text{cov}(A) \neq \{\}$.

Example 2. In the Example 1, the set of elementary actions $\mathcal{A}$ is $\{weight \in [50, 70[, weight \in]70, 80], medicines \in \{\text{tablets,syrup}\}, weight \in [90, 110], medicines \in \{\text{syrup}\}\}$. An action is a conjunction composed by elements of a subset of $\mathcal{A}$. We have to discard the action $weight \in [50, 70[\wedge weight \in [90, 110]$ equivalent to $weight \in [\ ]$ which is not coherent.

In practice, an action is not coherent if it involves an empty value for at least one attribute. Let us emphasize that applying an action to a situation does not guarantee to get an outcome situation with a better class than the initial situation. That is why, we need a criterion for assessing the quality of actions. We classify the outcome situation using the set of rules. We rely on the confidence of the rules covering the outcome situation O to evaluate the quality of an action A. We defined the *quality* measure by:

$$\text{quality}(A) = \sum_{R \in \mathcal{R}^\oplus, \text{cov}(O) \subseteq \text{cov}(R)} \text{conf}(R) - \sum_{R \in \mathcal{R}^\ominus, \text{cov}(O) \subseteq \text{cov}(R)} \text{conf}(R)$$

where $O = outcome(S, A)$ and where $\text{conf}(R)$ is the usual confidence[1] of the rule R. Notice that $quality(A) > 0$ means that O is covered by at least one rule in $\mathcal{R}^\oplus$.

Moreover, as pointed out in subsection 3.2, we favor actions that involve a little change in the initial situation. This is achieved by verifying that the distance between the outcome situation (obtained when an action is applied to the initial situation) and the initial situation itself does not exceed a parameter δ given by the user. We term such privileged actions δ-*cost* actions.

All the requirements for explaining DAKAR algorithm are now available.

3.4 DAKAR Algorithm

The aim of DAKAR (Discovery of Actionable Knowledge and Recommendations) algorithm is to find the set of the *best* actions. The algorithm explores the search

---
[1] The confidence of a rule $R : Descr \Longrightarrow C$ in a database is the number of examples of class C covered by $Descr$ divided by the total number of examples covered by $Descr$.

Algorithm 1: Dakar algorithm

Input: - a set of rules $\mathcal{R} = \mathcal{R}^\oplus \cup \mathcal{R}^\ominus$
- a situation $\mathcal{S}$
- a distance threshold δ
- a maximal beam size N

Output: - a set of actions

$\mathcal{A} = \bigcup_{R \in \mathcal{R}^\oplus} discr(\mathcal{S}, R)$
$Beam = \{\}$
$NewBeam = \{true\}$
while $Beam \neq NewBeam$ **do**
    $Beam \leftarrow NewBeam$
    foreach $action \in Beam$ **do**
        foreach $elem \in \mathcal{A}$ **do**
            $newaction \leftarrow (action \wedge elem)$
            if $newaction$ coherent and δ-cost **then**
                $NewBeam \leftarrow NewBeam \cup \{newaction\}$
                while $card(Beam) > N$ **do**
                      $worstaction \leftarrow Argmin_{A \in NewBeam} quality(A)$
                      $NewBeam \leftarrow NewBeam - \{worstaction\}$

return sorted Beam

space of actions using a beam search strategy : it maintains a set (called *Beam*) of the best actions the algorithm has constructed up till now. Initially the beam is set to {true}, which means that no action is constructed. During the exploration of the search space, DAKAR specializes actions of the beam and keeps only the best ones w.r.t. the criterion we defined earlier. DAKAR is given in algorithm 1.

4 Experiments

We implemented DAKAR in Sicstus Prolog and we conducted an experimental evaluation of our algorithm on an environmental application related to streamwater pollution by pesticides. This application is developed in the context of the project SACADEAU [2]. In our experiments, we used a dataset generated by a model which outputs a class of pollution given information about farming works, climate, soil, etc. The set of attributes and their descriptions is given in Table 1. It is a multi-class application where pollution classes are ordered by experts by taking into account legals thresholds (class 4 is the least satisfactory class). The model is an oracle since it provides the function *simulation* : *situation* $\rightarrow$ *class* and we define the *benefit* of an action A applied to a situation S, by $benefit(A) = simulation(S) - simulation(outcome(S, A))$. An action A is said *positive* when its benefit is positive.

Our system was tested on 150 unsatisfactory situations (of class 1, 2, 3 or 4). In presented experiments, the size of the beam was 5 ; thus, DAKAR proposed 5 actions for each situation. The distance threshold δ varied from 0 to 0.5.

Table 1. Some attributes of the SACADEAU application and their descriptions

Name	Domain	Flexibility	Description
strat	{pre,post}	0.001	pesticide application strategy of the farmer
molec	{atrazine,new}	0.003	pesticide used by the farmer
hedge	{0%,90%}	0.006	percentage of river border with a hedge
basin	{concave,convex}	0.33	typology of the catchment area
orga_matter	{2%,5%}	0.33	soil composition in organic matter
climate	[1;5]	0.33	wetness of the climate (1:not wet)
class	{0,1,2,3,4}	-	severity of the pollution (0:no pollution)

A set of rules ,with minimal support 20, was generated by ICL [15] (rules are not ordered).

A first evaluation is to show qualitatively the utility of using a distance for recommending actions. Let us give an example of DAKAR execution on a situation of class 4 :

```
strategy=post, molecules=atrazine, hedge=0%,
basin=convex, orga_matter=5%, climate=4
```

The two best actions recommended by DAKAR, with benefit 2 and 1 respectively, are given below:

```
1 - hedge=90%, molec=new, strat=pre      2 - molec=new, strat=pre
    (quality = 1.50 ; distance=0.005)        (quality = 1.35 ; distance=0.002)
```

Both actions suggest to apply pesticides before plants grow up (pre-emergence strategy) and to use new molecules rather than atrazine. The quality of these two actions are almost the same whereas the distance involved by the first action is more than two times the distance involved by the second. Concretely, experts could decide that in a short term, installing a hedge on 90% of the river border is not a necessary action for improving the situation.

Our algorithm uses the distance to take into account a threshold δ, but we can imagine an algorithm using both quality and distance in the criterion as done in [9] where a function of profit is maximized.

A second qualitative evaluation concerns interest of the quality criterion. There is an example of situation of class 3 :

```
strategy=pre, molecules=new, hedge=0%,
basin=convex, orga_matter=2%, climate=3
```

The two best actions recommended by our system (having a benefit of 1 and -1 respectively) are :

```
1 - hedge=90%                            2 - hedge=90%, strat=post
    (quality = 0.64, distance = 0.005)       (quality = -0.56, distance = 0.005)
```

The first action is the only one, among the five recommended actions, to get a positive quality. Installing a hedge on 90% of the river border seems to be the necessary action for improving the situation.

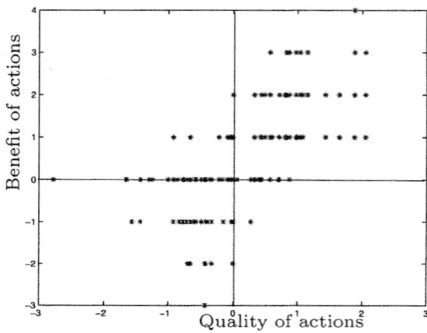 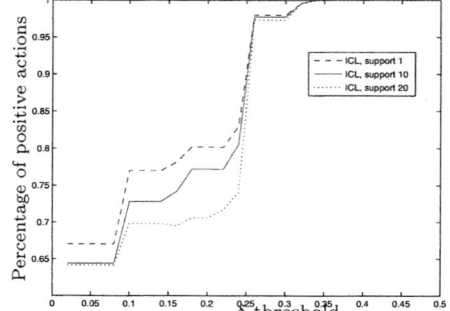

Fig. 1. Actions plotted according to their quality and their effective benefit

Fig. 2. Percentage of positive recommended actions according to the size of the rule set and the distance parameter δ

From this point, only the action maximizing the quality criterion in the beam are considered. We plotted, in Figure 1, recommended actions according to their quality and their effective benefit. Note that the quality of an action A is a good prediction of the efficiency of A if ($quality(A) < 0$ and $benefit(A) \leq 0$) or ($quality(A) > 0$ and $benefit(A) > 0$).

In Figure 2, the experiment raises another concern about the relationship between the redundancy in a set of classification rules and the efficiency of recommended actions. In [22], the author studied the effect of the redundancy of a classification rule set on the task of predicting a class. In his experiments, a redundant classification rule set has better accuracy on classification.

Using ICL, three classification rule sets were learned with support parameter equal to 1, 10 and 20, leading to set of 19, 35 and 63 rules respectively. We evaluated the three sets of rules, by comparing the efficiency of the actions they suggested when used in DAKAR. We plotted in Figure 2 the efficiency of recommended actions in function of the parameter δ for the three sets of rules.

As expected, the efficiency of actions proposed by DAKAR is globally increasing in the parameter δ. Moreover, we notice that the more the classification rule set is redundant, the more the actions are effective. The impact of the redundancy in rules on Sebag's distance between two instances expressed by Horn clauses was also pointed out in [20]. Her distance is based on the coverage of instances by a theory and the more the theory is redundant, the more this distance is of interest.

We repeated the same experiment for three rule sets generated by three systems : C4.5 [14], ICL [15] and Apriori[2] [1]. Supposing that Apriori is more redundant than ICL which is more redundant than C4.5, we compared the efficiency of the actions suggested by the three sets of rules. Once again, the more the set of rules is redundant, the more the actions are effective.

---

[2] Note that we constrained the association rules generated by Apriori to contain only the class in their right hand side.

5 Conclusion

In this paper we have investigated the task of learning actionable knowledge and recommendations to the user. We attempted to answer the following question: how to go beyond the simple use of classification rules in prediction by making them actionable?

Our contribution is as follows: given a situation, the algorithm we propose allows the user to further exploit a set of classification rules in order to decide what are the actions to accomplish in order to improve that situation. The algorithm looks for the best actions involving a little change in the initial situation. This is achieved thanks to an actionability approach relying on a *distance*.

Our framework has been applied to an environmental dataset related to pollution. We have learned some actionable knowledge concerning the possible recommendations one can adopt in order to reduce the pollution. Such recommendations take into account the degree of *flexibility* of each feature. Experiments have shown the feasibility of this task. They also raise some concerns about the impact of the redundancy of rules on the quality of actions recommended by our system. The approach we propose can be improved in the following directions. First, extend the framework to first order learners. In this case, we need other kinds of distance metrics handling literals, such as those proposed in [6, 16]. Second, study the impact of the chosen distance metric on the quality of the recommended actions.

In our point of view, action recommendation is a promising issue with many practical applications such as healthcare, environmental protection and customer analysis. There is clearly much research to be done in the formalization of the task of learning useful and actionable knowledge from both methods and interestingness measures points of view.

Acknowledgments. We thank INRA for the simulator and Christel Vrain for useful comments on an early draft of this paper.

References

1. R. Agrawal, T. Imielinski, and A. N. Swami. Mining association rules between sets of items in large databases. In Peter Buneman and Sushil Jajodia, editors, *Proceedings of the 1993 ACM SIGMOD*, pages 207–216. ACM Press, 1993.
2. M.-O. Cordier. SACADEAU: A decision-aid system to improve stream-water quality. *ERCIM News. Special issue on Environmental Modelling*, (61):35–36, April 2005.
3. B. Duval, A. Salleb, and C. Vrain. Méthodes et mesures d'intérêt pour l'extraction de règles d'exception. *Revue des Nouvelles Technologies de l'Information - Mesures de Qualité pour la Fouille de Données RNTI-E-1*, pages 119–140, 2004.
4. Y. Elovici and D. Braha. A decision-theoretic approach to data mining. *IEEE Transactions on Systems, Man, and Cybernetics, Part A*, 33(1):42–51, 2003.
5. Z. He, X. Xu, and S. Deng. Data Mining for Actionable Knowledge: A Survey. *ArXiv Computer Science e-prints*, January 2005.

6. A. Hutchinson. Metrics on terms and clauses. In *ECML*, pages 138–145, 1997.
7. M. Ichino and H. Yaguchi. Generalized minkowski metrics for mixed feature-type data analysis. *IEEE Transactions on Systems, Man, and Cybernetics*, 24(4):698–708, 1994.
8. N. Lavrač, B. Cestnik, D. Gamberger, and P. Flach. Decision support through subgroup discovery: Three case studies and the lessons learned. *Machine Learning*, 57(1-2):115–143, 2004.
9. C. X. Ling, T. Chen, Q. Yang, and J. Cheng. Mining optimal actions for profitable CRM. In *ICDM*, pages 767–770, 2002.
10. Bing Liu, Wynne Hsu, and Yiming Ma. Identifying non-actionable association rules. In *KDD '01: Proceedings of the seventh ACM SIGKDD international conference on Knowledge discovery and data mining*, pages 329–334, New York, NY, USA, 2001. ACM Press.
11. D. Malerba, F. Esposito, V. Gioviale, and V. Tamma. Comparing dissimilarity measures in symbolic data analysis. In *Joint Conferences on "New Techniques and Technologies for Statistcs" and "Exchange of Technology and Know-how"(ETK-NTTS'01)*, pages 473–481, 2001.
12. T. M. Mitchell. Generalization as search. *Artif. Intell.*, 18(2):203–226, 1982.
13. G. Piatetsky-Shapiro and C. Matheus. The interestingness of deviations. In *AAAI Workshop on Knowledge Discovery in Databases*, pages 25–36, Menlo Park, CA, 1994. AAAI Press.
14. J. R. Quinlan. *C4.5: programs for machine learning*. Morgan Kaufmann Publishers Inc., San Francisco, CA, USA, 1993.
15. L. De Raedt and W. Van Laer. Inductive constraint logic. In *ALT '95: Proceedings of the 6th International Conference on Algorithmic Learning Theory*, pages 80–94, London, UK, 1995. Springer-Verlag.
16. J. Ramon, M. Bruynooghe, and W. Van Laer. Distance measures between atoms. In *CompulogNet Area Meeting on Computational Logic and Machine Learing*, pages 35–41. University of Manchester, UK, May 1998.
17. Z. W. Ras and L.-S. Tsay. Discovering extended action-rules (system dear). In *IIS*, pages 293–300, 2003.
18. Z. W. Ras and A. Wieczorkowska. Action-rules: How to increase profit of a company. In *PKDD*, pages 587–592, 2000.
19. M. Sebag. Delaying the choice of bias: A disjunctive version space approach. In *ICML*, pages 444–452, 1996.
20. M. Sebag. Distance induction in first order logic. In *ILP '97: Proceedings of the 7th International Workshop on Inductive Logic Programming*, pages 264–272. Springer-Verlag, 1997.
21. A. Silberschatz and A. Tuzhilin. What makes patterns interesting in knowledge discovery systems. *IEEE Trans. On Knowledge And Data Engineering*, 8:970–974, 1996.
22. L. Torgo. Controlled redundancy in incremental rule learning. In *ECML*, pages 185–195, 1993.
23. Q. Yang, J. Yin, C. X. Ling, and T. Chen. Postprocessing decision trees to extract actionable knowledge. In *ICDM*, pages 685–688, 2003.

Multi-armed Bandit Algorithms
and Empirical Evaluation

Joannès Vermorel[1] and Mehryar Mohri[2]

[1] École normale supérieure, 45 rue d'Ulm, 75005 Paris, France
joannes.vermorel@ens.fr
[2] Courant Institute of Mathematical Sciences,
719 Broadway, New York, NY 10003, USA
mohri@cs.nyu.edu

Abstract. The multi-armed bandit problem for a gambler is to decide which arm of a K-slot machine to pull to maximize his total reward in a series of trials. Many real-world learning and optimization problems can be modeled in this way. Several strategies or algorithms have been proposed as a solution to this problem in the last two decades, but, to our knowledge, there has been no common evaluation of these algorithms.

This paper provides a preliminary empirical evaluation of several multi-armed bandit algorithms. It also describes and analyzes a new algorithm, POKER (Price Of Knowledge and Estimated Reward) whose performance compares favorably to that of other existing algorithms in several experiments. One remarkable outcome of our experiments is that the most naive approach, the ϵ-greedy strategy, proves to be often hard to beat.

1 Introduction

In many real-world situations, decisions are made in order to maximize some expected numerical reward. But decisions, or the actions they generate, do not just bring in more reward, they can also help discover new knowledge that could be used to improve future decisions. Such situations include clinical trials [11] where different treatments need to be experimented with while minimizing patient losses, or adaptive routing efforts for minimizing delays in a network [4]. The questions that arise in all these cases are related to the problem of balancing reward maximization based on the knowledge already acquired and attempting new actions to further increase knowledge, which is known as the exploitation vs. exploration tradeoff in reinforcement learning.

The multi-armed bandit problem, originally described by Robins [19], is an instance of this general problem. A multi-armed bandit, also called K-armed bandit, is similar to a traditional slot machine (one-armed bandit) but in general has more than one lever. When pulled, each lever provides a reward drawn from a distribution associated to that specific lever. Initially, the gambler has no knowledge about the levers, but through repeated trials, he can focus on the most rewarding levers.

This paper considers the *opaque* bandit problem where a unique reward is observed at each round, in contrast with the *transparent* one where all rewards are observed [14]. To our knowledge, there is no empirical comparison for the transparent bandit problem either. More formally, the opaque stochastic K-armed bandit (*bandit* for short) can be seen as a set of real distributions $\mathcal{B} = \{R_1, \ldots, R_K\}$, each distribution being associated to the rewards brought in by a specific lever.[1] Let $\mu_1, \ldots, \mu_K$ be the mean values associated to these reward distributions. The gambler plays iteratively one lever at each round and observes the associated reward. His objective is to maximize the sum of the collected rewards. The *horizon* H is the number of rounds that remains to be played. The bandit problem is formally equivalent to a one-state Markov Decision Process (MDP), but the general study of MDPs goes beyond the scope of this paper.

A different version of the bandit problem has been studied by [10, 23, 9, 8] where the reward distributions are assumed to be known to the player. This problem is not about balancing exploration and exploitation, it admits an optimal solution based on the so-called Gittins indices. This paper deals with bandit problems found in practice where the assumption about the prior knowledge of the payoffs typically does not hold (see for example section 4).

The *regret* ρ after T rounds is defined as the difference between the reward sum associated to an optimal strategy and the sum of the collected rewards $\rho = T\mu^* - \sum_{t=1}^{T} \widehat{r}_t$ where μ^* is the maximal reward mean, $\mu^* = \max_k \{\mu_k\}$, and $\widehat{r}_t$ the reward at time t. A strategy whose average regret per round tends to zero with probability 1 for any bandit problem when the horizon tends to infinity is a *zero-regret strategy*. Intuitively, zero-regret strategies are guaranteed to converge to an optimal strategy, not necessarily unique, if enough rounds are played.

The problem of determining the best strategy for the gambler is called the multi-armed bandit problem. Many strategies or algorithms have been proposed as a solution to this problem in the last two decades, but, to our knowledge, there has been no common evaluation of these algorithms. This paper provides the first preliminary empirical evaluation of several multi-armed bandit algorithms. It also describes and analyzes a new algorithm, POKER (Price Of Knowledge and Estimated Reward) whose performance compares favorably to that of other existing algorithms in several experiments.

The paper is organized as follows. We first present an overview of several bandit strategies or algorithms (Section 2), then introduce a new algorithm, POKER (Section 3), and describe our experiments with both an artificially generated dataset and a real networking dataset. The results of an empirical evaluation of several bandit algorithms, including POKER are reported in Section 4.

2 Bandit Algorithms Overview

The exploration vs. exploitation tradeoff is often studied under more general models such as MDPs. We have restricted this overview to methods that apply to the stateless case, specific to the bandit problem. There is, however, a significant amount of literature dealing with MDPs, see [17, 6] for a review. Slowly changing worlds have also been considered in [22, 3].

---

[1] Several algorithms have also been designed for the non-stochastic bandit problem [3] where much weaker assumptions are made about the levers' rewards, but this paper will focus on the stochastic bandit problem which has been studied the most so far.

2.1 The ϵ-Greedy Strategy and Semi-uniform Variants

ϵ-greedy is probably the simplest and the most widely used strategy to solve the bandit problem and was first described by Watkins [24]. The **ϵ-greedy strategy** consists of choosing a random lever with ϵ-frequency, and otherwise choosing the lever with the highest estimated mean, the estimation being based on the rewards observed thus far. ϵ must be in the open interval $(0,1)$ and its choice is left to the user. Methods that imply a binary distinction between exploitation (the greedy choice) and exploration (uniform probability over a set of levers) are known as *semi-uniform* methods.

The simplest variant of the ϵ-greedy strategy is what we will refer to as the **ϵ-first strategy**. The ϵ-first strategy consists of doing the exploration all at once at the beginning. For a given number $T \in \mathbb{N}$ of rounds, the levers are randomly pulled during the ϵT first rounds (pure exploration phase). During the remaining $(1-\epsilon)T$ rounds, the lever of highest estimated mean is pulled (pure exploitation phase). Here too, ϵ must be in the open interval $(0,1)$ and its choice is left to the user. The ϵ-first strategy has been analyzed within the PAC framework by [7] and [16]. Even-Dar et al. show in [7] that a total of $\mathcal{O}\left(\frac{K}{\alpha^2} \log\left(\frac{K}{\delta}\right)\right)$ random pulls suffices to find an α-optimal arm with probability at least $1-\delta$. This result could be interpreted as an analysis of the asymptotic behavior of the ϵ-first strategy.

In its simplest form the ϵ-greedy strategy is sub-optimal because asymptotically, the constant factor ϵ prevents the strategy from getting arbitrarily close to the optimal lever. A natural variant of the ϵ-greedy strategy is what we will call here the **ϵ-decreasing strategy**. The ϵ-decreasing strategy consists of using a decreasing ϵ for getting arbitrarily close to the optimal strategy asymptotically (the ϵ-decreasing strategy, with an ϵ function carefully chosen, achieves zero regret). The lever with the highest estimated mean is always pulled except when a random lever is pulled instead with an ϵ_t frequency where t is the index of the current round. The value of the decreasing ϵ_t is given by $\epsilon_t = \min\left\{1, \frac{\epsilon_0}{t}\right\}$ where $\epsilon_0 > 0$. The choice of ϵ_0 is left to the user. The first analysis of the ϵ-decreasing strategy seems to be by Cesa-Bianchi and Fisher [5] for an algorithm called GREEDYMIX. GREEDYMIX slightly differs from the ϵ-decreasing strategy as just presented because it uses a decreasing factor of $\log(t)/t$ instead of $1/t$. Cesa-Bianchi and Fisher prove, for specific families of reward distributions, a $\mathcal{O}(\log(T)^2)$ regret for GREEDYMIX where T is the number of rounds. This result is improved by Auer et al. [1] who achieve a $\mathcal{O}(\log(T))$ regret for the ϵ-decreasing strategy as presented above with some constraint over the choice of the value ϵ_0. Four other strategies are presented in [1] beside ϵ-decreasing. Those strategies are not described here because of the level of detail this would require. We chose the ϵ-decreasing strategy because the experiments by [1] seem to show that, with carefully chosen parameters, ϵ-decreasing is always as good as other strategies.

A variant of the ϵ-decreasing algorithm is introduced in [20]. The lever of highest estimated mean is always pulled except when the *least-taken* lever is pulled with a probability of $4/(4+m^2)$ where m is the number of times the least-taken lever has already been pulled. In the following, we refer to this method as the **LeastTaken** strategy. Used as such, the LEASTTAKEN method is likely to provide very poor results in situations where the number of levers K is significant compared to the horizon H. Therefore, as for the other methods, we introduce an exploration parameter $\epsilon_0 > 0$ such that the probability of selecting the leasttaken lever is $4\epsilon_0/(4+m^2)$. The choice of ϵ_0 is left to the user. The LEASTTAKEN method is only introduced as a heuristic (see [21]), but it is clear that this method, modified or not, is a zero-regret strategy.

2.2 The SoftMax Strategy and Probability Matching Variants

The **SoftMax strategy** consists of a random choice according to a Gibbs distribution. The lever k is chosen with probability $p_k = e^{\hat{\mu}_k/\tau}/\sum_{i=1}^n e^{\hat{\mu}_i/\tau}$ where $\hat{\mu}_i$ is the estimated mean of the rewards brought by the lever i and $\tau \in \mathbb{R}^+$ is a parameter called the *temperature*. The choice of τ's value is left to the user. SOFTMAX appears to have been proposed first in [15]. More generally, all methods that choose levers according to a probability distribution reflecting how likely the levers are to be optimal, are called *probability matching* methods.

The SOFTMAX strategy (also called Boltzmann Exploration) could be modified in the same way as the ϵ-greedy strategy into **decreasing SoftMax** where the temperature decreases with the number of rounds played. The decreasing SOFTMAX is identical to the SOFTMAX but with a temperature $\tau_t = \tau_0/t$ that depends on the index t of the current round. The choice of the value of τ_0 is left to the user. The decreasing SOFTMAX is analyzed by Cesa-Bianchi and Fisher (1998) in [5] with the SOFTMIX algorithm. The SOFTMIX slightly differs from the decreasing SOFTMAX as just presented since it uses a temperature decreasing with a $\log(t)/t$ factor instead of a $1/t$ factor. The SOFTMIX strategy has the same guarantees than the GREEDYMIX strategy (see here above). To our knowledge, no result is known for the $1/t$ decreasing factor, but results similar to the ϵ-decreasing strategy are expected. The experiments in [5] show that GREEDYMIX outperforms SOFTMIX, though not significantly. Therefore, for the sake of simplicity, only the GREEDYMIX equivalent is used in our experiments (Section 4).

A more complicated variant of the SOFTMAX algorithm, the **Exp3** "exponential weight algorithm for exploration and exploitation" is introduced in [2]. The probability of choosing the lever k at the round of index t is defined by

$$p_k(t) = (1-\gamma)\frac{w_k(t)}{\sum_{j=1}^K w_j(t)} + \frac{\gamma}{K}, \qquad (1)$$

where $w_j(t+1) = w_j(t)\exp\left(\gamma\frac{r_j(t)}{p_j(t)K}\right)$ if the lever j has been pulled at time t with $r_j(t)$ being the observed reward, $w_j(t+1) = w_j(t)$ otherwise. The choice of the value of the parameter $\gamma \in (0,1]$ is left to the user. The main idea is to divide the actual gain $r_j(t)$ by the probability $p_j(t)$ that the action was chosen. For a modified version of EXP3, with γ decreasing over time, it is shown by [3], that a regret of $\mathcal{O}(\sqrt{KT\log(K)})$ is achieved. The EXP3 strategy was originally proposed by Auer et al. (2002) in [3] along with five variants for the non-stochastic bandit problem. The other variants are not described here due to the level of detail required. Note also that the non-stochastic bandit is a generalization of the stochastic one with weaker assumptions, thus the theoretical guarantees of EXP3 still apply here.

More specific methods exist in the literature if additional assumptions are made about the reward distributions. We will not cover the case of boolean reward distributions (too specific for this paper, see [25] for such methods). Nevertheless, let us consider the case where Gaussian reward distributions are assumed; [25] describes a method that explicitly estimates $p_i = P[\mu_i = \mu^*]$ under that assumption. This method was also previously introduced in [18] but limited to the two-armed bandit. The explicit formula would require a level of details that goes beyond the scope of this paper and will not be given here. This method will be referred to in the following as the **GaussMatch** method.

2.3 The Interval Estimation Strategy

A totally different approach to the exploration problem is to attribute to each lever an "optimistic reward estimate" within a certain confidence interval and to greedily choose the lever with the highest optimistic mean. Unobserved or infrequently observed levers will have an over-valued reward mean that will lead to further exploration of those levers. The more a lever is pulled and the closer its optimistic reward estimate will be to the true reward mean. This approach called *Interval Estimation* (referred as INTESTIM in the following) is due to Kaelbling (1993) in [12]. To each lever is associated the $100 \cdot (1 - \alpha)\%$ reward mean upper bound where α is a parameter in $(0, 1)$ whose exact value is left to the user. At each round, the lever of highest reward mean upper bound is chosen. Note that smaller α values lead to more exploration.

In [12], the INTESTIM algorithm is applied to boolean rewards. Since we are dealing here with real distributions, we will assume that the rewards are normally distributed and compute the upper bound estimate according based on that assumption. Formally, for a lever observed n times with $\widehat{\mu}$ as empirical mean and $\widehat{\sigma}$ as empirical standard deviation, the α upper bound is defined by $u_\alpha = \widehat{\mu} + \frac{\widehat{\sigma}}{\sqrt{n}} c^{-1}(1 - \alpha)$ where c is the cumulative normal distribution function defined by $c(t) = \frac{1}{\sqrt{2\pi}} \int_{-\infty}^{t} exp(-x^2/2) dx$. Choosing normal distributions is arbitrary but seems reasonable if nothing more is known about the lever reward distributions. In this paper, this choice is also motivated by the fact that part of the experiments have been performed with normally distributed levers (see Section 4).

Many variants of INTESTIM have been proposed in the generalized model of MDPs. 32 different algorithms are discussed in [17] (IEQL+ may be the most well known of the introduced variant). But in the simpler stateless situation, all these variants are equivalent to INTESTIM.

To our knowledge, no theoretical results are known about the INTESTIM algorithm for the real-valued bandit problem (as opposed to the simpler boolean-valued bandit where the rewards could take only the values 0 and 1). In its simplest form, as just presented, INTESTIM is clearly not a zero-regret strategy (it suffices to consider the case where the optimal lever has been initially very poorly estimated), but a proper control of the parameter α could make this strategy achieve zero regret.

3 The POKER Strategy

The "Price of Knowledge and Estimated Reward" (POKER) strategy relies on three main ideas: pricing uncertainty, exploiting the lever distribution, and taking into account the horizon.

The first idea is that a natural way of balancing exploration and exploitation is to assign a price to the knowledge gained while pulling a particular lever. This idea has been already used in the bandit literature. In particular, the notion of "value of information" has been intensively studied in several domains and goes far beyond the scope of this paper. In the bandit literature, it is sometimes referred to as "exploration bonuses" [17, 6]. The objective is to quantify the uncertainty in the same units as the rewards.

The second idea is that the properties of unobserved levers could potentially be estimated, to a certain extent, from the levers already observed. This is particularly useful when there are many more levers than rounds. Most of the work on the bandit problem is centered on an asymptotic viewpoint over the number of rounds, but we believe that in many practical situations, the number of rounds may be significantly smaller than the number of levers (see next section).

The third observation is that the strategy must explicitly take into account the horizon H, i.e., the number of rounds that remains to be played. Indeed, the amount of exploration clearly depends on H, e.g., for $H = 1$, the optimal strategy is reduced to pure exploitation, that is to choosing the lever with the highest estimated reward. In particular, the horizon value can be used to estimate the *price* of the knowledge acquired.

3.1 Algorithm

Let $\mu^* = \max_i \{\mu_i\}$ be the highest reward mean and let j_0 be the index of the best reward mean estimate: $j_0 = \operatorname{argmax}_i \{\widehat{\mu}_i\}$. We denote by $\widehat{\mu}^*$ the reward mean of j_0. By definition of μ^*, $\mu^* \geq \mu_{j_0} = \widehat{\mu}^*$. $\mu^* - \widehat{\mu}^*$ measures the reward mean improvement. We denote the expected reward improvement by $\delta_\mu = \mathrm{E}[\mu^* - \widehat{\mu}^*]$.

At each round, the expected gain when pulling lever i is given by the product of the expected reward mean improvement, δ_μ, and the probability of an improvement $\mathrm{P}[\mu_i - \widehat{\mu}^* \geq \delta_\mu]$. Over a horizon H, the knowledge gained can be exploited H times. Thus, we can view $\mathrm{P}[\mu_i \geq \widehat{\mu}^* + \delta_\mu]\delta_\mu H$ as an estimate of the knowledge acquired if lever i is pulled. This leads us to define the lever pricing formula for the POKER strategy as:

$$p_i = \widehat{\mu}_i + \mathrm{P}[\mu_i \geq \widehat{\mu}^* + \delta_\mu]\delta_\mu H, \qquad (2)$$

where p_i is the price associated to the lever i by the casino (or the value of lever i for the gambler). The first term, $\widehat{\mu}_i$, is simply the estimated reward mean associated to the lever i, the second term an estimate of the knowledge acquired when lever i is pulled.

Let us also examine how the second term is effectively computed. Let $\widehat{\mu}_{i_1} \geq \cdots \geq \widehat{\mu}_{i_q}$ be the ordered estimated means of the levers already observed. We chose to define the estimated reward improvement by $\delta_\mu = (\widehat{\mu}_{i_1} - \widehat{\mu}_{i_{\sqrt{q}}})/\sqrt{q}$. The index choice $f(q) = \sqrt{q}$ is motivated by its simplicity and the fact that it ensures both $f(q) \to \infty$ (variance minimization) and $f(q)/q \to 0$ (bias minimization) when $q \to \infty$. Empirically, it has also been shown to lead to good results (see next section).

Let $\mathcal{N}(x, \mu, \sigma) = \frac{1}{\sqrt{2\pi}\sigma} \exp\left(\frac{(x-\mu)^2}{2\sigma^2}\right)$ be the normal distribution. Let $\widehat{\mu}_i$ be the mean estimate, $\widehat{\sigma}_i$ be the standard deviation estimate and n_i the number of pulls for the lever i, the probability $\mathrm{P}[\mu_i \geq \widehat{\mu}^* + \delta_\mu]$ can be approximated by

$$\Phi_{\widehat{\mu}_i,\frac{\widehat{\sigma}_i}{\sqrt{n_i}}}(\widehat{\mu}^* + \delta_\mu) = \int_{\widehat{\mu}^*+\delta_\mu}^{\infty} \mathcal{N}\left(x, \widehat{\mu}_i, \frac{\widehat{\sigma}_i}{\sqrt{n_i}}\right) dx. \quad (3)$$

This would be the exact probability if $\widehat{\mu}_i$ followed a normal distribution. Note that the central limit theorem guarantees that, in the limit, the mean estimate $\widehat{\mu}_i$ of the reward distribution is normally distributed.

Algorithm 1 shows the pseudocode of the procedure POKER which takes three arguments: the reward function $\mathbf{r} : [1, K] \to \mathbb{R}$, the number of levers $K \in \mathbb{N}^*$ and the number of rounds to be played $T \in \mathbb{N}^*$. In the pseudocode, $n[i]$ represents the number of times lever i has been pulled. $\mu[i]$ (resp. $\sigma[i]$), the reward mean (resp. the estimate of the reward standard deviation) of the lever i, is used as a shortcut for $\frac{r[i]}{n[i]}$ (resp $\sqrt{\frac{r_2[i]}{n[i]} - \frac{r[i]^2}{n[i]^2}}$). $\widehat{\mathbb{E}}_{k,n[k]>0}$ denotes the empirical mean taken over the set of levers previously pulled.

A round is played at each iteration through the loop of lines $2 - 14$. The computation of the price for each lever is done at lines $7 - 12$. The estimates of the mean and standard deviation of each lever are computed in lines $8 - 9$. Note that if the lever has not been observed yet, then the set of levers already observed is used to provide *a priori* estimates. The price is computed at line 10. The *initialization* of the algorithm has been omitted to improve readability. The initialization simply consists of pulling twice two random levers so that i_0 and i_1 are well-defined at line 4.

Algorithm 1. $Poker(r, K, T)$

1: **for** $i = 0$ to K **do** $n[i] \leftarrow r[i] \leftarrow r_2[i] \leftarrow 0$ **end for**
2: **for** $t = 1$ to T **do**
3:    $q \leftarrow |\{i, r[i] > 0\}|$
4:    $i_0 \leftarrow \text{argmax}_i\{\mu[i]\}$; $i_1 \leftarrow j$ such that $|\{i, \mu[i] > \mu[j]\}| = \sqrt{q}$
5:    $\delta_\mu \leftarrow (\mu[i_0] - \mu[i_1])/\sqrt{q}$; $\mu^* \leftarrow \text{argmax}_i\{\mu[i]\}$
6:    $p_{max} \leftarrow -\infty$; $i_{max} \leftarrow$ UNDEFINED
7:    **for** $i = 1$ to K **do**
8:       **if** $n[i] > 0$ **then** $\mu \leftarrow \mu[i]$ **else** $\mu \leftarrow \widehat{\mathbb{E}}_{k,n[k]>0}[\mu[k]]$ **endif**
9:       **if** $n[i] > 1$ **then** $\sigma \leftarrow \sigma[i]$ **else** $\sigma \leftarrow \widehat{\mathbb{E}}_{k,n[k]>1}[\sigma[k]]$ **endif**
10:      $p \leftarrow \mu + \delta_\mu(T-t)\int_{\mu^*+\delta_\mu}^{\infty} \mathcal{N}\left(x, \mu[i], \frac{\sigma[i]}{\sqrt{n[i]}}\right) dx$
11:      **if** $p > p_{max}$ **then** $p_{max} \leftarrow p$, $i_{max} \leftarrow i$ **endif**
12:   **end for**
13:   $r \leftarrow r(i_{max})$; $n[i_{max}] \mathrel{+}= 1$; $r[i_{max}] \mathrel{+}= r$; $r_2[i_{max}] \mathrel{+}= r^2$
14: **end for**

Algorithm 1 gives an *offline* presentation of POKER, but POKER is in fact intrinsically an *online* algorithm. The horizon value $T-t$ (line 10 in Algorithm 1) could simply be set to a constant value. Notice that the amount of exploration has to be controlled in some way. Most of the algorithms presented in section 2 have an exploration tuning parameter. We believe that the horizon is an intuitive and practical exploration control parameter, especially compared to the τ parameter for the SOFTMAX or the α parameter of INTESTIM.

It is easy to see that POKER is a zero-regret strategy. The proof is very technical however and requires more space than we can afford here. The following gives a sketch of the proof.

3.2 POKER is a Zero-Regret Strategy - Sketch of the Proof

Let us consider a game played by POKER where rounds are indexed by t such as $t = 1$ refers to the first round and $t = H$ refers to the last round. The proof has two parts: first, an argument showing that all levers are pulled a significant number of times; then, using the first part, establishing the fact that a "bad" lever cannot be pulled too frequently.

Let $m_i(t)$ be the number of times the lever i has been pulled till round t and assume that all rewards are bounded by $R > 0$. Then, by Hoeffding's inequality, $P[\mu_i \geq \widehat{\mu}_i + \delta_\mu] \leq \exp(-2m_i(t)\frac{\delta_\mu^2}{R^2})$ for $i = 1, \ldots, K$. Since $\widehat{\mu}^* > \widehat{\mu}_i$, this implies that: $P[\mu_i \geq \widehat{\mu}^* + \delta_\mu] \leq \exp(-2m_i(t)\frac{\delta_\mu^2}{R^2})$ for $i = 1, \ldots, K$.

Now, it is clear that $m_i(H)$ tends to infinity on average when H tends to infinity. Just consider that $p_i(t)$ at fixed t tends to infinity when H tends to infinity. The same argument shows also that for any $\epsilon > 0$, $m_i(\epsilon H)$ tends to infinity when H tends to infinity.

Let m_H be such that $\exp(-2m_H \frac{\delta_\mu^2}{R^2})\delta_\mu H < r/2$. Given the asymptotic behavior of m_i just discussed, there exists t_1 such that for all i, $m_i(t_1) > m_H$ with probability q. Let $r > 0$ be a given regret. Assume that for a given lever distribution, playing POKER implies that there exists a lever i and a constant $\alpha > 0$ such that $m_i(H) > \alpha H$ (frequent lever assumption) and $\mu_i < \mu^* - r$ (poor lever assumption) for any H. Let i be such a lever. The existence of i is the negation of the zero-regret property. Choose H large enough such that $\frac{t_1}{H} < \alpha$.

The probability that the lever i is played at least once in the interval is $[t_1, H]$ is expressed by the probability that the price p_i be the highest price, formally $P[\exists t \geq t_1 : p_i(t) \geq p^*(t)]$. The inequality $\exp(-2m_H \frac{\delta_\mu^2}{R^2})\delta_\mu H < r/2$ implies that (the quantifier and argument t are omitted for simplicity):

$$P[p_i \geq p^*] \leq P\left[\widehat{\mu}_i + \frac{r}{2} - \widehat{\mu}^* > 0\right]. \quad (4)$$

Since all levers have already been pulled at least m_H times by definition of t_1, by Hoeffding's inequality (using the fact that $\mu_i + \frac{r}{2} - \mu^* < -\frac{r}{2}$) the probability of that event is bounded as follows:

$$P\left[\widehat{\mu}_i + \frac{r}{2} - \widehat{\mu}^* > 0\right] \leq P\left[\widehat{\mu}_i - \widehat{\mu}^* > \mu_i - \mu^* + \frac{r}{2}\right] \leq \exp[-m_H \frac{r^2}{2R^2}]. \quad (5)$$

Thus, the lever i has a probability greater than q of not verifying $m_i(H) > \alpha H$ for H large enough. Additionally, by choosing H large enough, the probability q can be made arbitrarily close to 1. This conclusion contradicts the uniform existence (for any H) of the lever i. POKER is a zero-regret strategy.

4 Experiments

This section describes our experiments for evaluating several strategies for the bandit problem using two datasets: an artificially generated dataset with known and controlled distributions and a real networking dataset.

Many bandit methods requires all levers to be pulled once (resp. twice) before the method actually begins in order to obtain an initial mean (resp. a variance) estimate. In particular, INTESTIM requires two pulls per lever, see [17]. However this *pull-all-first* initialization is inefficient when a large number of levers is available because it does not exploit the information provided by the known lever distribution (as discussed in the second idea of POKER here above). Therefore, in our experiments, the mean and variance of unknown levers, whenever required, are estimated thanks to the known lever distribution. In order to obtain a fair comparison, the formula in use is always identical to the formula used in POKER.

4.1 Randomly Generated Levers

The first dataset is mainly motivated by its simplicity. Since normal distributions are perhaps the most simple non-trivial real distributions, we have chosen to generate normally distributed rewards. This choice also fits the underlying assumptions for the algorithms INTESTIM and GAUSSMATCH.

The dataset has been generated as follows: all levers are normally distributed, the means and the standard deviations are drawn uniformly from the open interval $(0, 1)$. The objective of the agent is *to maximize the sum of the rewards*. The dataset was generated with 1000 levers and 10 000 rounds. The bandit strategies have been tested in three configurations: 100 rounds, 1000 rounds, 10 000 rounds which correspond to the cases of less rounds than levers, as many rounds as levers, or more rounds than levers. Although we realize that most of the algorithms we presented were designed for the case where the number of rounds is large compared to the number of lever, we believe (see here below or [4]) that the configuration with more levers than rounds is in fact an important case in practice. Table 1 (columns R-100, R-1k and R-10k) shows the results of our experiments obtained with 10 000 simulations. Note that the numbers following the name of the strategies correspond to the tuning parameter values as discussed in section 2.

4.2 URLs Retrieval Latency

The second dataset corresponds to a real-world data retrieval problem where redundant sources are available. This problem is also commonly known as the *Content Distribution Network* problem (CDN) (see [13] for a more extensive introduction). An agent must retrieve data through a network with several redundant sources available. For each retrieval, the agent selects one source and waits until the data is retrieved[2]. The objective of the agent is *to minimize the sum of the delays* for the successive retrievals.

In order to simulate the retrieval latency problem under reproducible conditions, we have used the home pages of more than 700 universities as sources. The home pages have been retrieved roughly every 10 min for about 10 days (~1300 rounds), the retrieval latency being recorded each time in milliseconds[3]. Intuitively each page is associated to a lever, and each latency is associated to a

---

[2] We assume that the agent could try only *one* source at a time, in practice he will only be able to probe simultaneously a very limited number of sources.

[3] The dataset has been published under a public domain license, making it accessible for further experiments in the same conditions. It can be accessed from sourceforge.net/projects/bandit.

Table 1. Experimental results for several bandit algorithms. The strategies are compared in the case of several datasets. The R-x datasets corresponds to a maximization task with random Gaussian levers (the higher the score, the better). The N-x datasets corresponds to a minimization task with levers representing retrieval latencies (the lower the score, the better). The numbers following the strategy names are the tuning parameters used in the experiments.

Strategies	R-100	R-1k	R-10k	N-130	N-1.3k
POKER	0.787	0.885	0.942	203	132
ϵ-greedy, 0.05	0.712	0.855	0.936	733	431
ϵ-greedy, 0.10	0.740	0.858	0.916	731	453
ϵ-greedy, 0.15	0.746	0.842	0.891	715	474
ϵ-first, 0.05	0.732	0.906	0.951	735	414
ϵ-first, 0.10	0.802	0.893	0.926	733	421
ϵ-first, 0.15	0.809	0.869	0.901	725	411
ϵ-decreasing, 1.0	0.755	0.805	0.851	738	411
ϵ-decreasing, 5.0	0.785	0.895	0.934	715	413
ϵ-decreasing, 10.0	0.736	0.901	0.949	733	417
LEASTTAKEN, 0.05	0.750	0.782	0.932	747	420
LEASTTAKEN, 0.1	0.750	0.791	0.912	738	432
LEASTTAKEN, 0.15	0.757	0.784	0.892	734	441
SOFTMAX, 0.05	0.747	0.801	0.855	728	410
SOFTMAX, 0.10	0.791	0.853	0.887	729	409
SOFTMAX, 0.15	0.691	0.761	0.821	727	410
EXP3, 0.2	0.506	0.501	0.566	726	541
EXP3, 0.3	0.506	0.504	0.585	725	570
EXP3, 0.4	0.506	0.506	0.594	728	599
GAUSSMATCH	0.559	0.618	0.750	327	194
INTESTIM, 0.01	0.725	0.806	0.844	305	200
INTESTIM, 0.05	0.736	0.814	0.851	287	189
INTESTIM, 0.10	0.734	0.791	0.814	276	190

(negative) reward. The bandit strategies have been tested in two configurations: 130 rounds and 1300 rounds (corresponding respectively to $1/10^{th}$ of the dataset and to the full dataset). Table 1 (columns N-130 and N-1.3k) shows the results which correspond to the average retrieval latencies per round in milliseconds. The results have been obtained through 10 000 simulations (ensuring that the presented numbers are significant). The order of the latencies was randomized through a random permutation for each simulation.

4.3 Analysis of the Experimental Results

Let us first examine the ϵ-greedy strategy and its variants. Note that all ϵ-greedy variants have similar results for carefully chosen parameters. In particular, making the ϵ decrease does not significantly improve the performance. The ϵ_0 (the real parameter of the ϵ-decreasing strategy) also seems to be less intuitive than the ϵ parameter of the ϵ-greedy strategy. Although very different from the ϵ-greedy, the SOFTMAX strategy leads to very similar results. But its EXP3 variant seems to have a rather poor performance, its results are worse than any other strategy independently of the parameters chosen. The reason probably lies in the fact that the EXP3 has been designed to optimize its asymptotic behavior which does not match the experiments presented here.

The two "pricing" strategies POKER and INTESTIM significantly outperform all of the other strategies on the networking dataset, by a factor of 2 for INTESTIM and a factor of 3 for POKER. Against the random generated dataset, INTESTIM performs significantly worse than the other strategies, a rather unexpected result since the generated dataset perfectly fits the INTESTIM assumptions, while POKER is always as good as the best strategy for any parameter. We do not have yet proofs to justify the "good" behavior of the two pricing methods on the networking dataset, but this seems related to the "shape" of the networking data. The networking data proves to be very peaky with latencies that cover a wide range of values from 10 ms to 1000 ms with peaks to 10000 ms. With that data, exploration needs to be carefully handled because trying a new lever could prove to be both a major improvement or a major cost. It seems that strategies with a dynamic approach for the level of exploration achieve better results than those where the amount of exploration is fixed *a priori*.

5 Conclusion

In the case where the lever reward distributions are normally distributed, simple strategies with no particular theoretical guarantees such as ϵ-greedy tend to be hard to beat and significantly outperform more complicated strategies such as EXP3 or *Interval Estimation*. But, the ranking of the strategies changes significantly when switching to real-world data. Pricing methods such as *Interval Estimation* or POKER significantly outperform naive strategies in the case of the networking data we examined. This empirical behavior was rather unexpected since the strategies with the best asymptotic guarantees do not provide the better results, and could not have been inferred from a simple comparison of the theoretical results known so far. Since this is, to our knowledge, the first attempt to provide a common evaluation of the most studied bandit strategies, the comparison should still be viewed as preliminary. Further experiments with data from different tasks might lead to other interesting observations. We have made the experimental data we used publicly available and hope to collect, with the help of other researchers, other datasets useful for benchmarking the bandit problem that could be made available from the same web site.

References

1. P. Auer, N. Cesa-Bianchi, and P. Fischer. Finite Time Analysis of the Multiarmed Bandit Problem. *Machine Learning*, 47(2/3):235–256, 2002.
2. P. Auer, N. Cesa-Bianchi, Y. Freund, and R. E. Schapire. Gambling in a Rigged Casino: the Adversarial Multi-Armed Bandit Problem. In *Proceedings of the 36th Annual Symposium on Foundations of Computer Science (FOCS '95)*, pages 322–331. IEEE Computer Society Press, Los Alamitos, CA, 1995.
3. P. Auer, N. Cesa-Bianchi, Y. Freund, and R. E. Schapire. The nonstochastic multiarmed bandit problem. *SIAM Journal on Computing*, 32(1):48–77, 2002.
4. B. Awerbuch and R. Kleinberg. Adaptive Routing with End-to-End feedback: Distributed Learning and Geometric Approaches. In *Proceedings of the 36th ACM Symposium on Theory of Computing (STOC 2004)*, pages 45–53, 2004.

5. N. Cesa-Bianchi and P. Fischer. Finite-Time Regret Bounds for the Multiarmed Bandit Problem. In *Proceedings of the 15th International Conference on Machine Learning (ICML 1998)*, pages 100–108. Morgan Kaufmann, San Francisco, CA, 1998.
6. R. W. Dearden. *Learning and Planning in Structured Worlds*. PhD thesis, University of British Columbia, 2000.
7. E. Even-Dar, S. Mannor, and Y. Mansour. PAC Bounds for Multi-Armed Bandit and Markov Decision Processes. In *Fifteenth Annual Conference on Computational Learning Theory (COLT)*, pages 255–270, 2002.
8. E. Frostig and G. Weiss. Four proofs of gittins' multiarmed bandit theorem. *Applied Probability Trust*, 1999.
9. J. C. Gittins. *Multiarmed Bandits Allocation Indices*. Wiley, New York, 1989.
10. J. C. Gittins and D. M. Jones. A dynamic allocation indices for the sequential design of experiments. In *Progress in Statistics, European Meeting of Statisticians*, volume 1, pages 241–266, 1974.
11. J. P. Hardwick and Q. F. Stout. Bandit Strategies for Ethical Sequential Allocation. *Computing Science and Statistics*, 23:421–424, 1991.
12. L. P. Kaelbling. *Learning in Embedded Systems*. MIT Press, 1993.
13. B. Krishnamurthy, C. Wills, and Y. Zhang. On the use and performance of content distribution networks. In *SIGCOMM IMW*, pages 169–182, November 2001.
14. N. Littlestone and M. K. Warmuth. The Weighted Majority Algorithm. In *IEEE Symposium on Foundations of Computer Science*, pages 256–261, 1989.
15. D. Luce. *Individual Choice Behavior*. Wiley, 1959.
16. S. Mannor and J. N. Tsitsiklis. The Sample Complexity of Exploration in the Multi-Armed Bandit Problem. In *Sixteenth Annual Conference on Computational Learning Theory (COLT)*, 2003.
17. N. Meuleau and P. Bourgine. Exploration of Multi-State Environments: Local Measures and Back-Propagation of Uncertainty. *Machine Learning*, 35(2):117–154, 1999.
18. R. L. Rivest and Y. Yin. Simulation Results for a New Two-Armed Bandit Heuristic. Technical report, Laboratory for Computer Science, M.I.T., February 1993.
19. H. Robbins. Some Aspects of the Sequential Design of Experiments. In *Bulletin of the American Mathematical Society*, volume 55, pages 527–535, 1952.
20. M. Strens. *Learning, Cooperation and Feedback in Pattern Recognition*. PhD thesis, Physics Department, King's College London, 1999.
21. M. Strens. A Bayesian Framework for Reinforcement Learning. In *Proceedings of the 7th International Conf. on Machine Learning*, 2000.
22. R. S. Sutton. Integrated Architecture for Learning, Planning, and Reacting Based on Approximating Dynamic Programming. In *Proceedings of the seventh international conference (1990) on Machine learning*, pages 216–224. Morgan Kaufmann Publishers Inc., 1990.
23. P. Varaiya, J. Walrand, and C. Buyukkoc. Extensions of the multiarmed bandit problem: The discounted case. In *IEEE Transactions on Automatic Control*, volume AC-30, pages 426–439, 1985.
24. C. J. C. H. Watkins. *Learning from Delayed Rewards. Ph.D. thesis*. Cambridge University, 1989.
25. J. Wyatt. *Exploration and Inference in Learning from Reinforcement*. PhD thesis, University of Edinburgh, 1997.

Annealed Discriminant Analysis

Gang Wang, Zhihua Zhang, and Frederick H. Lochovsky

Department of Computer Science,
Hong Kong University of Science and Technology,
Clear Water Bay, Kowloon, Hong Kong
{wanggang, zhzhang, fred}@cs.ust.hk

Abstract. Motivated by the analogies to statistical physics, the deterministic annealing (DA) method has successfully been demonstrated in a variety of applications. In this paper, we explore a new methodology to devise the classifier under the DA method. The differential cost function is derived subject to a constraint on the randomness of the solution, which is governed by the temperature T. While gradually lowering the temperature, we can always find a good solution which can both solve the overfitting problem and avoid poor local optima. Our approach is called *annealed discriminant analysis* (ADA). It is a general approach, where we elaborate two classifiers, i.e., distance-based and inner product-based, in this paper. The distance-based classifier is an annealed version of linear discriminant analysis (LDA) while the inner product-based classifier is a generalization of penalized logistic regression (PLR). As such, ADA provides new insights into the workings of these two classification algorithms. The experimental results show substantial performance gains over standard learning methods.

1 Introduction

The deterministic annealing (DA) technique has demonstrated substantial performance improvement over clustering, classification and constrained optimization problems [1, 2, 3, 4, 5]. Since DA is strongly motivated by the analogies to statistical physics [6], it regards the optimization problem in question as a thermal system. The Lagrange multiplier in the problem represents the temperature of the system, which is used to control the level of randomness, and the cost function corresponds to the free energy of the system. The minimum of the free energy determines the state of the system at thermal equilibrium. To achieve the equilibrium state, one tracks the minimum of the free energy while gradually lowering the temperature. At the limit of low temperature, minimum energy is reached. In other words, the DA technique performs annealing as it maintains the cost function at its minimum while gradually lowering the temperature. With careful annealing, this process can avoid many shallow local minima of the specified cost and finally produce a non-random solution. The DA technique is attractive since it possesses two important advantages: (1) the ability to minimize the cost function even when its gradients vanish almost everywhere; (2) the ability to avoid many poor local optima.

Since direct classification error minimization mostly leads to an NP-hard problem [7], the goal of the learning methods is to avoid the computational difficulties of this hard problem. Usually, we transform the learning problem into an optimization problem, where an objective function is proposed. With different criteria, such as maximum likelihood, maximum posterior estimation, least L-norm error, or maximum margin, we can construct different classifiers. Wabha [8] treated these classifiers as performing "soft" or "hard" classifications. Soft classification, such as logistic regression models, assigns an object based on a conditional probability of this object in some class, while hard classification, such as SVMs, does not use the probability. We bridge the gap between these two kinds of classification problems through the DA approach. Instead of treating the "soft" and "hard" separately, we formulate the objective by a "hard" notion, and solve it by a "soft" way.

In this paper, we formulate the classification problem based on the discriminant functions. The optimal hypotheses is hard to find directly, since the problem is both a "hard" classification problem and NP-hard. However, with the introduction of a conditional probability in DA, the classification becomes soft. Hence, the original non-differentiable cost function that results in an NP-hard problem becomes differentiable. Interestingly, this "soft" problem also tends to the original "hard" problem as the temperature approaches zero. In addition, Rose [4] argued that the entropy can play a role in the regularization. Therefore, motivated by these observations, we investigate the application of the DA technique to the classification problem and devise a new kind of method called annealed discriminant analysis (ADA). Since ADA is a general formulation, we present two possible implementations, i.e., distanced-based classifier and inner product-based classifier. The distanced-based classifier is closely related to linear discriminant analysis (LDA), since the parameters of LDA are real means of the categories while the parameters of the distanced-based classifier are the "soft" means, which are estimated from the iterative updating procedure. Thus, the distanced-based classifier can be seen as an annealed version of LDA. The inner product-based classifier is a generalization of penalized logistic regression (PLR) since they become the same when setting the temperature to one. Therefore, ADA provides new insights into the workings of these existing classification algorithms.

The rest of this paper is organized as follows. Section 2 derives the ADA algorithm based on the discriminant functions and the DA approach. Two implementations of ADA are elaborated in section 3. Section 4 reports our experiment setup and results. The last section presents the concluding remarks.

2 Problem Formulation

Let $\mathcal{T} = \{(\mathbf{x}_i, c_i)\}$ be a training set of N labelled vectors, where $\mathbf{x}_i \in \mathbf{R}^d$ is a feature vector and $c_i \in \mathcal{I}$ is its class label from an index set $\mathcal{I} = \{1, 2, \ldots, C\}$. A classifier is a mapping $F : \mathbf{R}^d \to \mathcal{I}$, which assigns a class label in $\mathcal{I}$ to each vector in $\mathbf{R}^d$. A training pair $(\mathbf{x}, c) \in \mathcal{T}$ is correctly classified if $F(\mathbf{x}) = c$.

We code c_i as a binary C-vector $\mathbf{y}_i = (y_{i1}, y_{i2}, \ldots, y_{iC})'$ with values all zero except a 1 in position c if the class is c. We shall interchangeably use c_i and $\mathbf{y}_i$ to indicate the class label of $\mathbf{x}_i$ in this paper.

2.1 Problem Definition

We formulate a classifier in terms of a set of discriminant functions $\{g(\mathbf{x}; \boldsymbol{\theta}_j) \mid j = 1, 2, \ldots, C\}$ such that an input vector $\mathbf{x}$ is assigned to the class c if and only if

$$g(\mathbf{x}; \boldsymbol{\theta}_c) \geq g(\mathbf{x}; \boldsymbol{\theta}_j) \text{ for all } j \neq c, \tag{1}$$

where the parameter $\boldsymbol{\theta} = \{\boldsymbol{\theta}_j\}_{j=i}^{C}$ is a set of vectors for indexing the discriminant functions. Here the discriminant functions are general, which can be directly defined as many function forms such as Gaussian, linear, etc. The above classification rule defines a "hard" classification [8]. Denoting the conditional probability of the class c given $\mathbf{x}_i$ by $p_{ic} = p(c|\mathbf{x}_i)$, this "hard" classification implies that

$$p_{ic} = \begin{cases} 1 & c = \operatorname{argmax}_j g(\mathbf{x}_i; \boldsymbol{\theta}_j) \\ 0 & \text{otherwise.} \end{cases} \tag{2}$$

Let $\mathbf{g}_i = (g(\mathbf{x}_i; \theta_1), g(\mathbf{x}_i; \theta_2), \ldots, g(\mathbf{x}_i; \theta_C))'$ and $\|\mathbf{g}_i\|_\infty = \max\{g(\mathbf{x}_i; \boldsymbol{\theta}_j)\}_{j=1}^{C}$. For a hypotheses indexed by the parameter $\hat{\boldsymbol{\theta}}$, if a case $\mathbf{x}_i$ has correctly been classified according to (1), we have $\|\mathbf{g}_i\|_\infty = \mathbf{y}_i'\mathbf{g}_i$. Otherwise we have $\|\mathbf{g}_i\|_\infty > \mathbf{y}_i'\mathbf{g}_i$. This leads us to define a classification error

$$L(\boldsymbol{\theta}) = \frac{1}{N} \sum_i \left| \|\mathbf{g}_i\|_\infty - \mathbf{y}_i'\mathbf{g}_i \right| = \frac{1}{N} \sum_i \left(\|\mathbf{g}_i\|_\infty - \mathbf{y}_i'\mathbf{g}_i \right). \tag{3}$$

If all training samples have been correctly classified by this classifier, (3) will arrive at its minimum zero. Hence our task is to find a set of parameters $\{\boldsymbol{\theta}_j\}$ minimizing the classification error. Alternatively, with the above definition for p_{ic}, we can rewrite (3) as

$$L(\boldsymbol{\theta}) = \frac{1}{N} \sum_i \left(\sum_j p_{ij} g(\mathbf{x}_i; \boldsymbol{\theta}_j) - \mathbf{y}_i'\mathbf{g}_i \right) \tag{4}$$

due to $\sum_j p_{ij} g(\mathbf{x}_i; \boldsymbol{\theta}_j) = \|\mathbf{g}_i\|_\infty$. Minimizing the classification error (3) or (4) w.r.t. $\boldsymbol{\theta}$ requires searching all possible "hard" conditional probabilities, and therefore results in an NP-hard problem. To find an approximate searching strategy to obtain the best parameter $\boldsymbol{\theta}$ to minimize the classification error (4) is also not straightforward because this error function is non-differentiable. Even if we get a solution, it often suffers from the overfitting problem. Thus, our current problem is how to search in the parameter space to get a good solution. The essence of the DA technique [4] is to cast the optimization problem into a probabilistic framework, considering a "randomness" characterized by a probabilistic assignment of data to classes. The DA approach is a good choice to deal with these problems.

2.2 Deterministic Annealing Approach

Recall that the minimization of $L(\boldsymbol{\theta})$ w.r.t. $\boldsymbol{\theta}$ is intractable since $L(\boldsymbol{\theta})$ is non-differentiable. Our departure is replacing the discrete $\{p_{ij}\}$ with a continuous density function $\{p_{ij}\}^1$ and finding a differential function to approximate $L(\boldsymbol{\theta})$. Since $\{p_{ij}\}$ are now unknown continuous density distribution functions, our problem is how to select $\{p_{ij}\}$. Let

$$E = \sum_i \sum_j p_{ij} g(\mathbf{x}_i; \boldsymbol{\theta}_j) \tag{5}$$

E is a variational function where its parameters $\{p_{ij}\}$ are determined by the discriminant functions. From the definition of the conditional probability in (2), $\{p_{ij}\}$ need to maximize E given a hypotheses. Therefore we are seeking $\{p_{ij}\}$ maximizing E subject to a specified level of randomness measured by the Shannon entropy while assuming the parameters of the discriminant functions are fixed. The entropy is defined as

$$H = -\sum_i \sum_j p_{ij} \log p_{ij}.$$

Maximum entropy is inspired by the well known principle of Occam's razor, which states that the simplest model that accurately represents the data is the most desirable. This criteria tends to induce the parsimony model to fit the data. Conveniently, this optimization is reformulated as maximization of the Lagrangian

$$F = E + TH \tag{6}$$

where T is the Lagrange multiplier. For large value of T, the probabilities mainly attempt to maximize the entropy, and as T approaches zero, it maximizes E.

Maximizing F w.r.t. p_{ij} is straightforward, giving rise to the Gibbs distribution [9]

$$p_{ij} = \frac{\exp(\frac{g(\mathbf{x}_i; \boldsymbol{\theta}_j)}{T})}{\sum_k \exp(\frac{g(\mathbf{x}_i; \boldsymbol{\theta}_k)}{T})}. \tag{7}$$

The corresponding maximum of F is obtained by plugging (7) back into (6)

$$F^* = \max_{\{p_{ij}\}} F = T \sum_i \log \sum_j \exp(\frac{g(\mathbf{x}_i; \boldsymbol{\theta}_j)}{T}). \tag{8}$$

It is easy to see

$$T \log \sum_j \exp(\frac{g(\mathbf{x}_i; \boldsymbol{\theta}_j)}{T}) \geq T \log \exp(\frac{\mathbf{y}'_i \mathbf{g}_i}{T}) = \mathbf{y}'_i \mathbf{g}_i.$$

---
[1] The "hard" conditional probability p_{ij} takes binary values. For notation simplicity, we still denote the soft conditional probability as p_{ij}.

Hence replacing $\|\mathbf{g}_i\|_\infty$ with $T\log\sum_j \exp(\frac{g(\mathbf{x}_i;\boldsymbol{\theta}_j)}{T})$ in $L(\boldsymbol{\theta})$, we obtain a differential cost function:

$$Q(\boldsymbol{\theta}) = \frac{1}{N}\sum_i\left[T\log\sum_j\exp(\frac{g(\mathbf{x}_i;\boldsymbol{\theta}_j)}{T}) - \mathbf{y}'_i\mathbf{g}_i\right] \quad (9)$$

to approximate $L(\boldsymbol{\theta})$. We address the optimization problem on minimization of $Q(\boldsymbol{\theta})$ w.r.t. $\boldsymbol{\theta}$ alternatively.

Theorem 1. *Let p_{ij} and $Q(\boldsymbol{\theta})$ be defined by (7) and (9), respectively. For a fixed parameter $\boldsymbol{\theta}$,*

1. $\lim_{T\to\infty} p_{ij} = \frac{1}{C}$ for $j = 1,\ldots,C$.

2. $\lim_{T\to 0} p_{ic} = \begin{cases} 1 & c = argmax_j g(\mathbf{x};\boldsymbol{\theta}_j) \\ 0 & otherwise; \end{cases}$,
   $\lim_{T\to 0} Q(\boldsymbol{\theta}) = L(\boldsymbol{\theta})$;

3. $Q(\boldsymbol{\theta})$ is monotone decreasing with respect to decreasing T.

We omit the proof due to the space limitations. This theorem states that at infinite temperature T, the conditional probabilities $\{p_{ij}\}$ are soft as they are uniformly distributed for all categories. At the limit of zero temperature, the classification is hard where each case is assigned to the category whose discriminant function value is largest. When the conditional probabilities $\{p_{ij}\}$ become hard, F in (6) tends to E in (5), and consequently the cost function $Q(\boldsymbol{\theta})$ in (9) degenerates to $L(\boldsymbol{\theta})$ in (3). Thus, the original problem is in fact a "zero temperature problem". This motivates a criterion for updating T: start with a high value of temperature T and track the minimum while lowering T. Since $Q(\boldsymbol{\theta})$ is monotone decreasing with respect to the temperature T, the above algorithm will try to converge to a global minimum. The entire algorithm is presented in Table 1.

Table 1. A brief sketch of the ADA algorithm

0. Initialize T with a comparatively large value $T^{(0)}$
1. Initialize $\boldsymbol{\theta}^{(0)}$
2. Repeat
3.   Lower temperature: $T^{(t)} = q(T^{(t-1)})$
4. $\boldsymbol{\theta}^{(t)} = \arg\min_{\boldsymbol{\theta}} Q(\boldsymbol{\theta}^{(t-1)})$
5.   Validate the performance for $(\boldsymbol{\theta}^{(t)}, T^{(t)})$
6. Until the parameters converge
7. Select $(\boldsymbol{\theta}^{(t)}, T^{(t)})$
8. Classify cases based on (7)

The algorithm consists of two-level iterations. In the inner iteration, for a fixed T, we optimize the $Q(\boldsymbol{\theta})$. We can not get the closed form to update the parameters, hence we resort to a numerical optimizer, such as the conjugate gradient algorithm, to find the parameter values.

For the outer iteration, in our experiments, we use an exponential schedule for reducing T, i.e., $q(T) = \alpha T$, where $\alpha < 1$ in our experiments. From the perspective of the learning problem, we start with a very simple model with zero variance. We then gradually increase the complexity of the model. Since the bias would reduce faster than the variance increases, thus the prediction error would decrease also. However, when the variance increases faster than the bias at a certain temperature, overfitting occurs. Therefore, the final converging parameters from "hard" partitions may not reach the best performance due to the overfitting problem. Consequently, we need to select parameters according to their performance on the validation set. Empirically, the optimal parameter can be obtained at the temperature that causes the conditional probabilities to be almost "hard" while still a little "soft". Since the temperature T controls the level of the randomness of the solution, we try the model to fit the data with different complexity from simple to complex as the temperature decreases. Therefore, we are certain to find an optimal classifier based on the ADA algorithm.

[2, 4] also discuss the supervised learning problem using DA methods, but they are different from our ADA method. In their work, they construct the space partitioning functions as two components: a parametric space partition (structured partition) and a parametric local model per partition cell, while in our approach we integrate them by using only the discriminant function. Furthermore, they employ the notion of the regression problem by defining the distortion to derive the learning algorithm, while ADA directly formulates the classification problem by a discriminant function.

3 Annealed Discriminant Analysis

In this section, we will discuss two implementations in ADA, i.e., distance-based classifier and inner product-based classifier. The first one is related to linear discriminant analysis(LDA) and the second is related to penalized logistic regression(PLR).

3.1 Distance-Based Classifier (dADA)

The discriminant functions are defined as

$$g(\mathbf{x}; \boldsymbol{\mu}_j) = -(\mathbf{x} - \boldsymbol{\mu}_j)' \boldsymbol{\Sigma}^{-1} (\mathbf{x} - \boldsymbol{\mu}_j) \quad j = 1, \ldots, C \tag{10}$$

where $\boldsymbol{\Sigma}$ is the covariance matrix which is evaluated in advance from the training data, and the parameter $\boldsymbol{\mu}_j \in \mathbf{R}^d$ indicates the mean of the j-th category. A case $\mathbf{x}$ will be classified to the category c_j when the distance between its mean $\boldsymbol{\mu}_j$ and $\mathbf{x}$ is the least, and correspondingly the j-th discriminant function g_j is the largest. The decision boundary, corresponding to $g(\mathbf{x}; \boldsymbol{\mu}_k) = g(\mathbf{x}; \boldsymbol{\mu}_j)$, forms a hyperplane, i.e.,

$$f(\mathbf{x}) = \mathbf{x} \boldsymbol{\Sigma}^{-1} (\boldsymbol{\mu}_j - \boldsymbol{\mu}_k) + \boldsymbol{\mu}_k' \boldsymbol{\Sigma}^{-1} \boldsymbol{\mu}_k - \boldsymbol{\mu}_j' \boldsymbol{\Sigma}^{-1} \boldsymbol{\mu}_j = 0 \tag{11}$$

If $f(\mathbf{x}) > 0$, the case $\mathbf{x}$ will be classified to the j-th category. Otherwise, $\mathbf{x}$ will be classified to the k-th category.

To find the optimal parameter $\boldsymbol{\mu}^{(t)}$ such that $\boldsymbol{\mu}^{(t)} = \arg\min_{\mu} Q(\boldsymbol{\mu})$ at a certain temperature, the gradient of the cost function Q is

$$\frac{\partial Q}{\partial \boldsymbol{\mu}_j} = \frac{2}{N} \sum_i [(p_{ij} - y_{ij})\boldsymbol{\Sigma}^{-1}(\mathbf{x}_i - \boldsymbol{\mu}_j)] \quad (12)$$

where p_{ij}, with the form in (7), contains the parameter $\boldsymbol{\mu}$ via the discriminant functions. Since we cannot find the closed form for updating the parameters, we use the scaled conjugate gradient (SCG) optimizer [10], which is an extremely efficient algorithm, to get the parameters.

In LDA [11], cases in each category are assumed from a multivariate Gaussian, and all Gaussian distributions have a common covariance matrix $\boldsymbol{\Sigma}$. So the discriminant functions of LDA are defined the same as in (10) where $\boldsymbol{\mu}_j$ is estimated as the mean of the j-th category and the covariance $\boldsymbol{\Sigma}$ is evaluated from the training data. We note that the only difference between dADA and LDA is in how to estimate the parameters. The parameters in LDA are the real means of categories, while the means of dADA are the "soft" means, which are estimated from the iterative updating procedure. Therefore, the distance-based classifier can be seen as an annealed version of LDA. The experiment result in the next section shows that dADA performs much better than LDA.

3.2 Inner Product-Based Classifier (pADA)

The discriminant functions are defined as

$$g(\mathbf{x}; \boldsymbol{\lambda}_j) = \boldsymbol{\lambda}_j' \mathbf{x} \quad j = 1, \ldots, C \quad (13)$$

where $\boldsymbol{\lambda}_j \in \mathbf{R}^d$ is the parameter of the inner product-based classifier. In this case, the decision boundary is also a hyperplane. Plugging (13) back into the cost function Q (9) we get

$$Q(\boldsymbol{\theta}) = \frac{T}{N} \sum_i [\log \sum_j \exp(\frac{\boldsymbol{\lambda}_j' \mathbf{x}_i}{T}) - \sum_j y_{ij} \frac{\boldsymbol{\lambda}_j' \mathbf{x}_i}{T}] \quad (14)$$

The gradient of the cost function Q is

$$\frac{\partial Q}{\partial \boldsymbol{\lambda}_j} = \frac{1}{N} \sum_i [(p_{ij} - y_{ij})\mathbf{x}_i] \quad (15)$$

The parameter estimation in this problem is different from the distance-based classifier. From the gradient in (15), we notice that the conditional probabilities p_{ij} are constrained to be equivalent to the supervised label y_{ij} when minimizing the cost function Q. Since the discriminant functions $\{g(\mathbf{x}; \boldsymbol{\lambda}_j)\}$ can take any value ranging from negative infinity to positive infinity, the temperature in this definition can not control the randomness of the conditional probabilities. When the temperature is extremely high, the parameter λ will also take a large value to make $p_{ij} = y_{ij}$. Therefore, annealing has no effect no matter what is the temperature. The inner product discriminant functions seem to absorb the temperature T into the parameters λ, so the cost function in (14) can be simplified as

$$Q(\boldsymbol{\theta}) = \frac{1}{N} \sum_i [\log \sum_j \exp(\boldsymbol{\lambda}_j' \mathbf{x}_i) - \sum_j y_{ij} (\boldsymbol{\lambda}_j' \mathbf{x}_i)] \qquad (16)$$

This cost function is exactly the same as the cost function of logistic regression [12], which has been widely studied in statistics. However, since the optimal parameters of this cost function (16) try to satisfy $p_{ij} = y_{ij}$ directly, this formulation suffers from the overfitting problem.

To overcome this problem, we need to limit the range of the discriminant functions. We add a penalty term to the cost function such that

$$Q_{new}(\boldsymbol{\theta}) = \frac{1}{N} \sum_i [T \log \sum_j \exp(\frac{\boldsymbol{\lambda}_j' \mathbf{x}_i}{T}) - \sum_j y_{ij} (\boldsymbol{\lambda}_j' \mathbf{x}_i)] + \frac{\varepsilon}{2} \sum_j \boldsymbol{\lambda}_j' \boldsymbol{\lambda}_j \qquad (17)$$

where the regularization parameter ε controls the range of the values of the parameters λ. Consequently, the temperature T again governs the level of the randomness of the solution. The gradient of the cost function Q_{new} (17) becomes

$$\frac{\partial Q_{new}}{\partial \boldsymbol{\lambda}_j} = \frac{1}{N} \sum_i [(p_{ij} - y_{ij}) \mathbf{x}_i] + \varepsilon \sum_j \boldsymbol{\lambda}_j \qquad (18)$$

We also use the SCG optimizer to search for the optimal parameters in this classifier.

Penalized logistic regression (PLR) [13] began to gain attention recently because it not only performs as well as the SVM in two class classification, but can also naturally be generalized to the multi-class case. Furthermore, PLR provides an estimate of the conditional probability. As we can see, the cost function in (17) is the same as the negative log-likelihood of PLR when setting the temperature $T = 1$. Therefore, PLR is a special case of the pADA. Our approach gives a clear physical interpretation for PLR, where the temperature T controls the randomness of the solution, and the regularization parameter ε limits the range of the parameters. It is always laborious to select a good regularization parameter in PLR. We will see in the experiment that our algorithm can always find the optimal solution regardless of the value of the the regularization parameter, thereby, avoiding many attempts to examine it.

4 Experimental Results

4.1 WebKB: Web Pages Collection

The WebKB data set is a medium size collection, containing web pages gathered from several universities' computer science departments. The pages are divided into seven categories: student, faculty, staff, course, project, department and other. In this paper, we use the four most populous entity-representing categories: student, faculty, course, and project, which all together contain 4199 pages. A held-out set with 20% of the data was selected randomly. The other 80% was used as training data. Reserving those terms occurring at least six times in a corpus, we have 3359 training documents with a vocabulary size of 7161. We then use information gain to select 500 of the most predictive features and delete the cases without features.

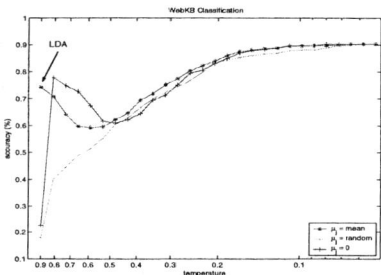

(a).The dADA accuracy with three initial values (1) means (2) random (3) zero are compared. The cooling rate is $T_i = 0.9T_{i-1}$. The final accuracy with different initial values converges when T is nearly zero.

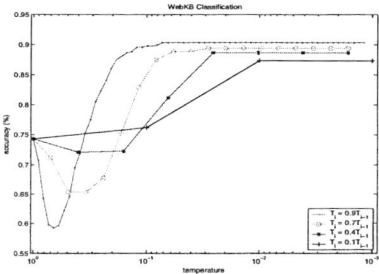

(b).The dADA accuracy with four different cooling rates are compared. The initial values are set to the means of the categories. The slower cooling rate will get better accuracy.

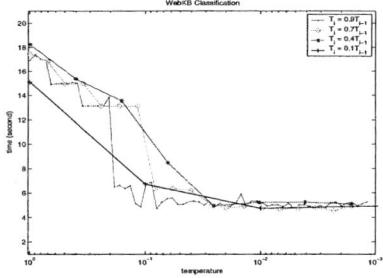

(c).The dADA time complexity with different cooling rates, where the setting is the same as in (b). The cost decreases as temperature is low.

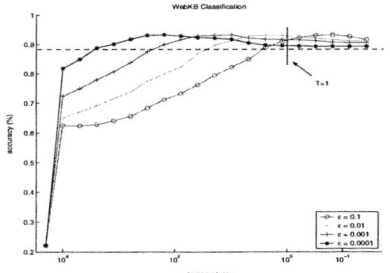

(d).The pADA accuracy based on different regularization parameters. The dashed line is the accuracy of the logistic regression without regularization.

Fig. 1. The experiments on the WebKB dataset. The x-axis is a logarithm scale.

In the distance-based classifier, we use three ways to initialize the parameter values: (1) mean of each category; (2) a random number from all possible feature values; (3) zero. From Figure 1(a), we can see although these three lines have with different start points and different convergence traces, they merge in the end. The final accuracy of the ADA approach in fact is independent of the initial values. However, this is true only when we use a slow temperature cooling rate.

In this experiment, we lower the temperature with a comparatively slow rate, such as $T_i = 0.9T_{i-1}$. When the parameters are initialized to the means of the categories, the classifier becomes LDA, and its classification accuracy is 74.3%, much lower than the accuracy (90.3%) obtained by dADA. The LDA line is concave shaped. It goes down in the beginning since high temperature biases the conditional probability to be uniform. When the temperature is about 0.6, the line begins to go up, and finally finds the optimum.

Temperature cooling rate is also an important factor that impacts the performance in ADA. Different cooling rates are compared in Figure 1(b), where the initial values are set to the means of the corresponding categories. Although all rates can provide comparatively good accuracies, a slower cooling rate will give a better result. When the cooling rate is too quick, such as $T_i = 0.1T_{i-1}$, only three steps of optimization are performed before $T = 0.001$. Therefore, the search for the optimal solution is insufficient before the conditional probabilities become hard, and such an optimization is easily trapped by local optima. In the annealing process, we also measure the time complexity when minimizing the cost at each temperature, as shown in Figure 1(c). We can see the algorithm is more time consuming at a high temperature, and speeds up as temperature decreases. At a given temperature, the SCG optimizer spends similar time when the temperature is low for different cooling rates. Hence, there is a tradeoff between the accuracy and time complexity. We should choose a faster cooling rate if we prefer an efficient algorithm; otherwise, we should select a slower cooling rate to get better solutions. No overfitting occurs in dADA in the WebKB collection.

In the inner product-based classifier, the regularization parameter ε controls the range of the parameter values, and the temperature T governs the level of randomness. The results for different regularization parameters are shown in Figure 1(d), where the starting point of each line is the accuracy of the initial parameter value. The initial parameters $\{\lambda_j\}$ are set to zero, which gives uniform conditional probabilities, an effect equivalent to that of infinite temperature. All the four lines have a similar shape. While gradually lowering the temperature, the accuracy increases until we get the best accuracy at the peak. Then the classifier begins to overfit, and accuracy drops. There is a relationship between the temperature T and the regularization parameter ε. When ε is large, the optimal solution is obtained at a higher temperature, and vice verse. The regularization parameter seems to only determine the temperature at which the maximum accuracy is reached. Therefore, no matter what the value of ε is, we can always find a good solution through annealing, which outperforms the logistic regression algorithm, whose accuracy is shown as the dashed line in the figure. Our model is equivalent to PLR when setting $T = 1$. Therefore, PLR is a special case of pADA. It is clear that the best regularization parameter of PLR is obtained by positioning the peak of the line at $T = 1$., which is always a laborious task.

4.2 Newsgroups: Discussion Articles Collection

The Newsgroups data set is a comparatively large collection containing about 20000 articles evenly divided among 20 UseNet discussion groups. Many of the categories fall into confusable clusters; for example, five of them are comp.* discussion groups and three of them are religion. When tokenizing this collection, we skip the UseNet headers and subject line, and select 1000 features.

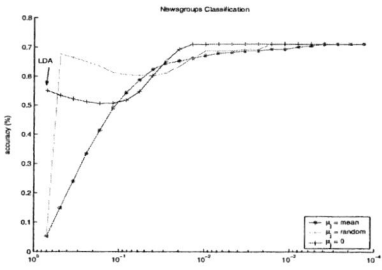

(a).The dADA accuracy with three initial values (1) means (2) random (3) zero are compared. The cooling rate is $T_i = 0.9T_{i-1}$. The final accuracy with different initial values converges when T is nearly zero.

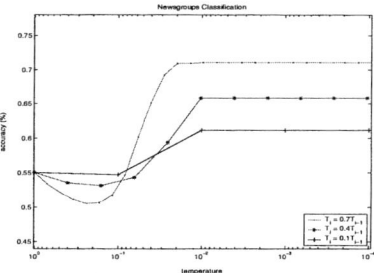

(b).The dADA accuracy with four different cooling rates are compared. The initial values are set to the means of the categories. The slower cooling rate will get better accuracy.

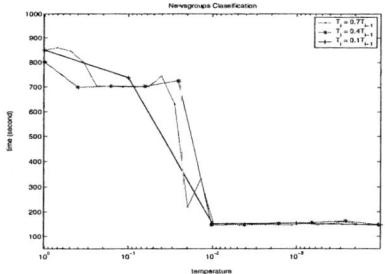

(c).The dADA time complexity with different cooling rates, where the setting is the same as in (b). The cost decreases as temperature is low.

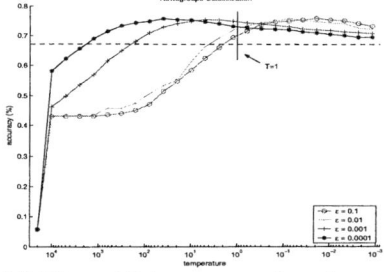

(d).The pADA accuracy based on different regularization parameters. The dashed line is the accuracy of the logistic regression without regularization.

Fig. 2. The experiments on the Newsgroup dataset. The x-axis is a logarithm scale.

For the distance-based classifier, its results are shown in Figure 2(a)-(c). They are similar to the results for WebKB. In Figure 2(a), since there are a total of 20 categories, the accuracy is about 5% for the random and zero initial values. LDA's accuracy is 55%. The distance-based classifier of ADA finally gets a much better result, i.e., 71% regardless of the initial values of the parameters. The conclusion that the optimal solution results from a slower cooling rate is more obvious in this experiment (Figure 2(b)). The accuracy from $T_i = 0.7T_{i-1}$ is nearly 10% higher than from $T_i = 0.1T_{i-1}$. Newsgroups is a dataset much larger than WebKB. Hence optimizer spends more time minimizing the cost function at a given temperature, as shown in Figure 2(c). As temperate lowers, it will spend less time. The time spent at a low temperature is only about one eighth of the time of a high temperature. For the inner product-based classifier, the result is shown in Figure 2(d), which is also very similar to the result for WebKB. The optimal classifier can obtain accuracy 75.5%, while that of logistic regression is 68.8%.

5 Conclusions

In this paper, we propose a novel classification method called annealed discriminant analysis (ADA). A probabilistic framework was constructed by randomization of the conditional probability, which is based on the principle of maximum entropy. The annealing process was introduced by controlling the Lagrange multiplier T based on the deterministic annealing approach, which is interpreted as gradually trading entropy of the associations for reduction of the cost function. While gradually lowering the temperature, the global optimum can be obtained independent of the choice of initial configuration. The distance-based classifier, an annealed version of linear discriminant analysis, outperforms the standard linear discriminant analysis. The inner-product based classifier, which can be seen as a generalized penalized logistic regression, provides the optimal solution, which is insensitive to the regularization parameter. The experiments demonstrate ADA's ability to provide substantial gains over existing methods.

References

1. Hofmann, T., Buhmann, J.: Pairwise data clustering by deterministic annealing. IEEE Transactions on Pattern Analysis and Machine Intelligence **19** (1997) 1–14
2. Miller, D., Rao, A.V., Rose, K., Gersho, A.: A global optimization technique for statistical classifier design. IEEE Transaction on Signal Processing **44** (1996) 3108–3122
3. Rao, A., Miller, D., Rose, K., Gersho, A.: A deterministic annealing approach for parsimonious design of piecewise regression models. IEEE Transactions on Pattern Analysis and Machine Intelligence **21** (1999) 159–173
4. Rose, K.: Deterministic annealing for clustering, compression, classification, regression, and related optimization problem. Proceedings of the IEEE **86** (1998) 2210–2239
5. Yuille, A.L., Stolortz, P., Utans, J.: Statistical physics, mixtures of distributions, and the *em* algorithm. Neural Computation **6** (1994) 334–340
6. Rose, K., Gurewitz, E., Fox, G.C.: Statistical mechanics and phase transitions in clustering. Physics Review Letter **65** (1990) 945–948
7. Zhang, T.: Statistical analysis of some multi-category large margin classification methods. Journal of Machine Learning Research **5** (2004) 1225–1251
8. Wahba, G.: Soft and hard classification by reproducing kernel Hilbert space methods. Proceedings of the National Academy of Sciences **99** (2002) 16524–16530
9. Geman, S., Geman, D.: Stochastic relaxation, Gibbs distributions, and the Bayesian restoration of images. IEEE Transactions Pattern Analysis and Machine Intelligence **6** (1984) 721–741
10. Nabney, I.: Netlab: algorithms for pattern recognition. Springer-Verlag (2001)
11. Hastie, T., Tishiran, R., Friedman, J.: The Elements of Statistical Learning: Data Mining, Inference, and Prediction. Springer-Verlag (2001)
12. McLachlan, G.J.: Discriminant analysis and statistical pattern recognition. John Wiley & Sons (1992)
13. Zhu, J., Hastie, T.: Classification of gene microarrays by penalized logistic regression. Biostatistics **5** (2004) 427–443

Network Game and Boosting

Shijun Wang and Changshui Zhang

State Key Laboratory of Intelligent Technology and Systems,
Department of Automation, Tsinghua University, Beijing 100084, China
wsj02@mails.tsinghua.edu.cn, zcs@mail.tsinghua.edu.cn

Abstract. We propose an ensemble learning method called Network Boosting which combines weak learners together based on a random graph (network). A theoretic analysis based on the game theory shows that the algorithm can learn the target hypothesis asymptotically. The comparison results using several datasets of the UCI machine learning repository and synthetic data are promising and show that Network Boosting has much resistance to the noisy data than AdaBoost through the cooperation of classifiers in the classifier network.

1 Introduction

With the rapid development of various business and scientific research based on information technology, the number and the size of distributed databases increase continuously. For the massiness of the distributed datasets, the conditional data mining techniques based on central process on a single computer are not appropriate for today's need. New technologies are required for distributed applications.

In recent 10 years, the ensemble learning methods become a hot topic in the machine learning community. Two of the most popular techniques for constructing ensembles are bootstrap aggregation ("bagging" [1]) and the Adaboost family of algorithms ("boosting" [2-4]). Both of these methods operate by taking a base learning algorithm and invoking it many times with different training sets.

The Bagging algorithm (Bootstrap aggregating) [1] uses bootstrap samples to build the base classifiers. Each bootstrap sample is formed by uniformly sampling from the training set with replacement. The accuracy can be improved through building multiple versions of base classifier when unstable learning algorithms (e.g. neural networks, decision trees) are used.

The AdaBoost algorithm [3], calls a given base learning algorithm repeatedly and maintains a distribution of weights over the training set in a series of rounds $t = 1, ..., T$. During the training progress, the weights of incorrectly classified examples are increased so that the weak learner is forced to focus on the hard examples in the training set.

While the overall success of AdaBoost, there is increasing evidence that boosting algorithms are not quite as immune from overfitting [5]. Krieger et al. [6] introduced a new ensemble learning strategy called BB algorithm based on the careful application of both bagging and boosting. They demonstrated experimentally that the performance of this algorithm is superior to boosting when the training set is noisy. Other noisy tolerant boosting algorithms include $AdaBoost_{Reg}$ [7], AveBoost2 [8], et al.

To satisfy the requirement of rapid developing distributed applications, Fan [9] and Lazarevic [10][11] proposed the distributed versions of boosting for parallel and distributed data mining. The distributed boosting algorithms put more efforts on the disjoint partitions of the data set (d-sampling) and the mechanism is designed for such purpose.

In this paper, we propose a new ensemble learning method called Network Boosting (NB) which combines classifiers on the basis of a network. Through the communication between classifiers, the misclassified samples' weights increase during the training progress. The final classification decision is made through the majority voting of all the hypotheses learned in the training progress. Under the game theory framework, we prove that the Network Boosting algorithm can learn target hypothesis asymptotically. The difference between distributed boosting algorithm and Network Boosting lies in the cooperation mechanism between distributed sites (classifiers).

In chapter 2 we propose the classifier network and the mechanism of Network Boosting (NB). Chapter 3 gives the proof of the convergence of the NB algorithm. Results of comparisons on UCI data sets and the comparisons on noisy data are shown in chapter 4. Chapter 5 concludes with a short summary.

2 Classifier Network and Network Boosting

The idea of Network Boosting comes from our recent research [13, 14] on complex network [15]. In a complex system, the complexity comes from the self-organization or emergence of structure and function from the interaction between the constituent parts of the system. So we introduce the cooperation of classifiers based on a network and expect high accuracy and noise resistance as emergent functions of the classifier network and network boosting scheme.

From biology over computer science to sociology the world is abundant in networks [15]. In the present work, we use random graph as the topology of our classifier network for it has much resistance to the targeted attack [16] and is more suitable for the distributed applications. A random graph is a collection of points, or vertices, with lines, or edges, connecting pairs of them at random. Starting with the influential work of Erdos and Renyi in the 1950s and 1960s [17], the study of random graphs has a long history.

Based on the communication structure, we construct a classifier network in which the nodes are classifiers and links between nodes represent the relationship between classifier pairs. If there is a link between node i and node j, then classifier i will exchange information with classifier j during the training progress.

The dynamic integration approach contains two phases. Assume there are K nodes (classifiers) in the network and the training round is T. In the learning phase, given training set $Z = \langle (x_1, y_1), (x_2, y_2), ..., (x_l, y_l) \rangle$, each classifier on the classifier network is provided with the same training instances and maintains a weight record $w_{k,t}(i)$ for $k = 1, ..., K$, $t = 1, ..., T$, $i = 1, ..., l$ of the instances respectively. Then the classifier in the classifier network is built by the training set sampled from the training data according to the weights record of the training data it holds. After that, the weights of the instances of every node are updated according to the classification results of the node and its neighbors. The classifier network is trained T rounds in such way.

In the application phase, the final classification of the committee is formed by all the hypotheses the classifier network learned during the training progress so that for a new instance its label is decided by the voting. The algorithm is listed in Fig. 1.

Algorithm Network Boosting

Input: Examples $Z = \langle (x_1, y_1), (x_2, y_2), ..., (x_l, y_l) \rangle$
Network N
Training rounds T
Sampling parameter ρ
Weight update parameter β

Initialize: $w_{k,1}(x_i) = 1$ for all sample $i = 1, ..., l$ and node $k = 1, ..., K$

Do for: 1. Generate a replicate training set $T_{k,t}$ of size $l\rho$, by weighted sub-sampling with replacement from training set Z for $k = 1, 2, ..., K$.
2. Train the classifier (node) C_k in the classifier network with respect to the weighted training set $T_{k,t}$ and obtain hypothesis $h_{k,t} : x \mapsto \{-1, +1\}$ for $k = 1, ..., K$.
3. Update the weight of instance i of node k:

$$w_{k,t+1}(i) = w_{k,t}(i) \beta^{I(h_{k,t}(x_i) = y_i) + \sum_n I(h_{n,t}(x_i) = y_i)} / Z_{k,t}, \quad (1)$$

where node n is neighbor of node i. I is indication function and $Z_{k,t}$ is a normalization constant, such that $\sum_{i=1}^{l} w_{k,t+1}(x_i) = 1$.

Output: Final hypothesis by majority voting using the learned hypotheses $h_{k,t} : x \mapsto \{-1, +1\}$ for $k = 1, ..., K$ and $t = 1, ..., T$.

Fig. 1. Algorithm Network Boosting

For convenience, we use $NB(K, T, \rho, \beta)$ denoting the parameters used by the Network Boosting when the network is given.

3 Network Game and Boosting

Freund and Schapire [18] showed that boosting can be cast in a game-theoretic framework [19][20][21]. They treated the problem of learning as a repeated game and refer to the row player as the learner and the column player as the environment. Let M be the mistake matrix in which entry $M(i, j)$ is the loss suffered by the row player (learner). The game is played from the row player's perspective and leave the column player's (environment) loss or utility unspecified. Mixed strategies are used by the row and column players in each round. That is, the row player chooses a distribution P over the rows of M and the column player chooses a distribution Q over columns. The row player's expected loss in the round t is computed as

$$M(P_t, Q_t) = \sum_{i,j} P_t(i) M(i,j) Q_t(j) = P_t^T M Q_t.$$

If the column player uses a mixed strategy but the row player chooses a single row i (pure strategy), then the (expected loss) is $\sum_j M(i,j) Q_j$ which we denote by $M(i,Q)$. The notation $M(P,j)$ is defined similarly.

Given a weak learning algorithm, the goal of boosting is to run the weak learning algorithm many times in the repeated play with the environment (instances), and to combine the learned hypotheses into a final hypothesis with error rate as small as possible. Von Neumann's well-known minmax theorem states that

$$\max_Q \min_P M(P,Q) = v = \min_P \max_Q M(P,Q), \qquad (2)$$

for every matrix M. The common value v of the two sides of the equality is called the value of the game M. Freund and Schapire [18] proved that by using the LW algorithm, the average loss in the repeated game is not much lager than the game value v. Here we extend the proof of Freund and Schapire for boosting algorithm to the Network Boosting algorithm.

Let X be a finite set of instances and H be finite set of hypotheses $h: X \to \{-1, 1\}$. Let $c: X \to \{-1, 1\}$ be an unknown target concept, not necessarily in H.

The mistake matrix M has rows and columns indexed by instances and hypotheses, respectively.

$$M(x,h) = \begin{cases} 1, & if\ h(x) = c(x) \\ 0, & otherwise \end{cases}. \qquad (3)$$

Assuming (H,c) is γ learnable (so that there exists a γ-weak learning algorithm). On each round t, the learner k in the classifier network computes mixed strategy $P_{k,t}$ by normalizing the weights:

$$P_{k,t}(i) = \frac{w_{k,t}(i)}{\sum_{i=1}^{l} w_{k,t}(i)}.$$

Given $M(i, Q_{k,t})$ for each node k at round t, the environment updates the weights by the simple multiplicative rule:

$$w_{k,t+1}(i) = w_{k,t}(i) \beta^{M(i,Q_{k,t}) + \sum_n M(i,Q_{n,t})} \qquad (4)$$

where node n is neighbor of node k and $\beta \in [0,1)$.

Theorem 1. For any node k in the classifier network, the accumulative loss suffered by the instances with parameter $\beta \in [0,1)$ satisfies:

$$\sum_{t=1}^{T} M(P_{k,t}, Q_{k,t}) \leq c_\beta \ln l + \alpha_\beta \min_P \sum_{t=1}^{T} \{M(P, Q_{k,t})\} +$$

$$\alpha_\beta \left(\min_j \sum_{t=1}^{T} \sum_n M(j, Q_{n,t}) - \sum_{t=1}^{T} \min_i \sum_n M(i, Q_{n,t}) \right) \quad (5)$$

where $\alpha_\beta = \frac{\ln(1/\beta)}{1-\beta}$ and $c_\beta = \frac{1}{1-\beta}$.

The proof of Theorem 1 is given in the appendix.

From Theorem 1 it is clear that when β approaches 1, α_β also approaches 1 and the accumulative loss of row player in the T rounds repeated play will not be much greater than the loss of the best strategy for node k.

Corollary 2. Under the conditions of Theorem 1 and with β set to

$$\frac{1}{1 + \sqrt{\frac{2 \ln l}{T}}}$$

the average per-trial loss suffered by the instances in node k when T is large enough is

$$\frac{1}{T} \sum_{t=1}^{T} M(P_{k,t}, Q_{k,t}) \leq \min_P \frac{1}{T} \sum_{t=1}^{T} \{M(P, Q_{k,t})\} + \Delta_T \quad (6)$$

where

$$\Delta_T = \sqrt{\frac{2 \ln l}{T}} + \frac{\ln l}{T}.$$

Proof: See Section 2.2 in Freund and Shapire [2] and note that

$$\frac{1}{T} \left(\min_j \sum_{t=1}^{T} \sum_n M(j, Q_{n,t}) - \sum_{t=1}^{T} \min_i \sum_n M(i, Q_{n,t}) \right)$$

approaches 0 when T is large enough.

Corollary 3. Under the conditions of corollary 2, the average expected loss of the instances over K nodes in the T trainings when T is large enough is

$$\frac{1}{KT} \sum_{k=1}^{K} \sum_{t=1}^{T} M(P_{k,t}, Q_{k,t}) \leq v + \Delta_T \quad (7)$$

where v is the value of game M.

Proof: Let P^* be a minmax strategy for M so that for all column strategies $Q_{k,t}$, for all $k = 1, ..., K$ and $t = 1, ..., T$, $M(P^*, Q_{k,t}) \le v$. According to Corollary 2,

$$\frac{1}{KT} \sum_{k=1}^{K} \sum_{t=1}^{T} M(P_{k,t}, Q_{k,t}) \le \frac{1}{KT} \sum_{k=1}^{K} \sum_{t=1}^{T} M(P^*, Q_{k,t}) + \Delta_T$$
$$\le v + \Delta_T$$

Proof end.

On each round t at the node k, $Q_{k,t}$ may be a pure strategy $h_{k,t}$ and should be chosen to maximize

$$M(P_{k,t}, h_{k,t}) = \sum_{i=1}^{l} P_{k,t} M(i, h_{k,t}) = \Pr_{x \sim P_{k,t}}[h_{k,t}(x) = c(x)]$$

In other words, $h_{k,t}$ should have maximum accuracy with respect to distribution $P_{k,t}$. It's just the goal of weak learner. According to the minmax theorem:

$$\min_{x} \max_{Q} M(x, Q) = \min_{P} \max_{Q} M(P, Q)$$
$$= v$$
$$= \max_{Q} \min_{P} M(P, Q) = \max_{h} \min_{P} M(P, h)$$

each classifier on the network will learn the target hypothesis asymptotically. So the combined hypotheses learned by the classifier network will compute a final hypothesis h_{fin} identical to target c for sufficiently large T.

4 Experiment Results

4.1 Experiments on UCI Repository

In this section we present experiments of C4.5, Bagging, AdaBoost.M1, BB and Network Boosting on the UCI data sets. We use the implementations of C4.5, Bagging, AdaBoost.M1 and BB provided by Weka in our experiments [22]. The experimental setting is described before the results of the experiments. We employed 16 domains drawn from the UCI Repository [12]. Previously comparisons of AdaBoost, Bagging and other dynamic classifier integration methods were made in [23] [5] [24] [7]. The main characteristics of the 16 data sets are presented in Table 1.

We performed statistical tests to compare the five algorithms. For all the domains we generate 100 random partitions into training and test set with proportion 60 : 40. Then we train a classifier and compute its test set error on each partition. C4.5 is employed as base classifier in all the ensemble methods without the pruning.

In our experiments, we found that sampling parameter 33% achieves better performance. The same conclusion is drawn in BB algorithm [6]. About the size and the connection probability of the classifier network, we found that the accuracy can be improved if the size of the network becomes large (with the expense of more calculation demand); the smaller connection probability often leads to better results for higher connection probability makes the environment more chaostic.

In order to play fairly, 300 C4.5 base classifiers were used in these four ensemble methods. For AdaBoost, we constructed ensembles of at most 300 classifiers. However, if the AdaBoost algorithm terminated early (because a classifier had weighted error greater than 0.5 or unweighted error equal to zero), then a smaller ensemble was necessarily used. For BB algorithm, $BB(30, 10, 1/3)$ was used. That is, the aggregate BB classifier is a combination of 300 base classifiers, resulting from the combination of 30 subsamples of 10 boosting iterations. For Network Boosting, a classifier network contains 30 classifiers and based on a random graph with connection probability 0.07 for each pair of nodes and 10 training steps was built. The sampling parameter $\rho = 1/3$ and $\beta = 0.5$ were used for all the data sets.

Table 1. Description of UCI datasets

Dataset	Instances	Classes	Features	
			Discrete	Continuous
audiology	226	24	69	-
breast-w	699	2	-	9
colic	368	2	15	7
credit-a	690	2	9	6
diabetes	768	2	-	8
glass	214	6	-	9
heart-c	303	2	7	6
heart-h	294	2	7	6
hepatitis	155	2	13	6
iris	150	3	-	4
labor	57	2	8	8
lymph	148	4	15	3
soybean	683	19	35	-
vehicle	846	4	-	18
vote	435	2	16	-
waveform	300	3	-	40

Table 2 shows the average error rate (err) and standard deviation (std) of each data set tested by every algorithm and results of significance tests of Bagging, AdaBoost, BB with NB. "+" and "-" mean that there is significant difference between the results of the two algorithms. From the table we can find that NB can improve the accuracy significantly compared to Bagging, AdaBoost and BB.

Learning curve analysis provides a powerful tool to inspect the dynamics of an ensemble learning method [25]. In Figure 2 we show the performance of NB algorithm on different training steps. Due to lack of space, we do not include the results for all 16 datasets, but present 5 representative datasets. Every point in

Table 2. Comparisons of C4.5 and four ensemble methods on UCI datasets. The columns S1, S2 and S3 show the results of significance tests (at 0.05 the significance level) of Bagging, AdaBoost.M1 and BB with Network Boosting respectively.

Name	C4.5	Bagging	AdaBoost	BB	NB			
	err ± std	err ± std	err ± std	err ± std	S1	S2	S3	err ± std
audiology	.2818 ± .0463	.2332 ± .0489	.2126 ± .0420	.2671 ± .0500	-		+	.2264 ± .0461
breast-w	.0610 ± .0125	.0412 ± .0101	.0319 ± .0074	.0339 ± .0101	+	-		.0356 ± .0082
colic	.1792 ± .0263	.1559 ± .0244	.1955 ± .0348	.1561 ± .0229		+		.1598 ± .0242
credit-a	.1695 ± .0176	.1400 ± .0169	.1391 ± .0158	.1337 ± .0173				.1368 ± .0166
diabetes	.2753 ± .0242	.2427 ± .0186	.2647 ± .0201	.2374 ± .0188	+	-		.2439 ± .0221
glass	.3353 ± .0459	.2852 ± .0443	.2572 ± .0493	.3003 ± .0444	+		+	.2662 ± .0410
heart-c	.2413 ± .0355	.2089 ± .0357	.1984 ± .0285	.1780 ± .0281	+	+		.1793 ± .0309
heart-h	.2155 ± .0338	.2008 ± .0282	.2028 ± .0307	.1906 ± .0315	+	+		.1897 ± .0303
hepatitis	.2200 ± .0479	.1829 ± .0387	.1697 ± .0402	.1700 ± .0383	+	+	+	.1563 ± .0359
iris	.0618 ± .0305	.0582 ± .0271	.0647 ± .0257	.0602 ± .0313				.0583 ± .0229
labor	.2139 ± .0899	.1687 ± .0790	.1430 ± .0733	.1652 ± .0865	+	+	+	.1096 ± .0548
lymph	.2500 ± .0484	.2150 ± .0459	.1790 ± .0372	.1840 ± .0485	+	+	+	.1618 ± .0460
soybean	.1259 ± .0223	.0936 ± .0205	.0843 ± .0171	.0927 ± .0200	+	+	+	.0742 ± .0144
vehicle	.2968 ± .0231	.2622 ± .0205	.2322 ± .0203	.2553 ± .0226	+		+	.2373 ± .0195
vote	.0518 ± .0164	.0403 ± .0136	.0541 ± .0158	.0415 ± .0129		+		.0435 ± .0132
waveform	.3142 ± .0395	.2108 ± .0417	.1758 ± .0337	.1727 ± .0303	+	+	+	.1621 ± .0286
average	.2058	.1712	.1628	.1649				.1526

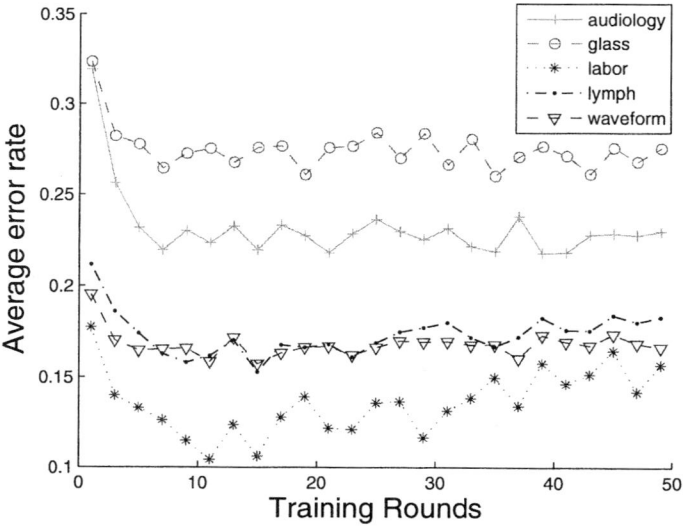

Fig. 2. Learning curves of NB on several UCI data sets

the graph is the average error rate of 50 tests at the given training round on that dataset. From the figure we can find that NB can learn the target hypothesis quickly after only about 10 training rounds.

4.2 Experiments on Synthetical Data Set

First we begin by specifying a simple model used by Krieger [6]. We suppose that there are five dependent feature variables, $X_1, ..., X_5$. We generate each feature i.i.d. from a uniform distribution on the unit interval. The class label Y is binary and determined only by X_1 and X_2 according to the following rule:

$$Y = \begin{cases} 1, X_1 \leq X_2 \\ 0, otherwise. \end{cases} \quad (8)$$

Furthermore, we assume that addition of noise which randomly and independently flips the observed class label with some fixed probability $1-p$. Under this distortion we have that $P(Y=1|X_1 > X_2) = 1 - p$ and $P(Y=0|X_1 \leq X_2) = 1 - p$. The special case where $p = 1$ corresponds to noiseless data. We generate a training set consisting of 1000 pairs (Y, X) from the Unit Square model. To test our classifier we provide a noiseless test data set of 10000 points. For bagging and AdaBoost, 300 base classifiers are used; for BB, BB(30,10,1/3) is used; for Network Boosting, we use NB(30,10,1/3,β) with different β. The connection probability of network is set 0.07.

Table 3. Comparisons on UnitSquare model

	p=1	p=0.9	p=0.8	p=0.7
C4.5	0.0333±0.0037	0.0615±0.0098	0.0881±0.0169	0.1282±0.0291
Bagging	0.0243±0.0035	0.0388±0.0069	0.0576±0.0108	0.0909±0.0232
AdaBoost	0.0236±0.0030	0.0757±0.0171	0.0878±0.0144	0.1278±0.0244
BB(30,10,1/3)	0.0227±0.0039	0.0405±0.0057	0.0596±0.0107	0.0935±0.0231
NB(30,10,1/3,0.5)	0.0204±0.0025	0.0434±0.0070	0.0693±0.0134	0.1286±0.0316
NB(30,10,1/3,0.7)	0.0204±0.0034	0.0379±0.0059	0.0616±0.0113	0.1110±0.0367
NB(30,10,1/3,0.9)	**0.0194±0.0038**	**0.0361±0.0067**	**0.0512±0.0115**	**0.0872±0.0216**

In Table 3 the comparison results of average error rate and standard deviation are shown on 100 tests. Network Boosting shows high resistance to noise than others. The significance test (t-test with significance level 0.05) shows that the results of NB(30,10,1/3,0.9) are significantly better than the results of AdaBoost when data are noisy (p=0.9, p=0.8, p=0.7). With the increasing β, NB algorithm shows higher ability on defeating noise for the weights of noisy data will increase slowly with bigger β. As every thing has two sides, with bigger β, the Network Boosting algorithm needs more training rounds to converge to the target hypothesis.

5 Conclusion

In this paper a technique for dynamic integration of classifiers was experimented. The algorithm is easily run in a distributed system. Under the game theory framework, we prove that the average expected loss suffered by row player (environment) is not much larger than that of the game value which means that as a dual problem the combined hypotheses is an approximate maxmin strategy. Through the cooperation between classifiers, the classifier network shows remarkable resistance to overfitting. For the additional computation requirement introduced by the communication between classifiers (nodes) is small and can be ignored, the efficiency of NB is equal to Bagging, AdaBoost and BB when the same number of base classifiers and sample parameter (when generating training data for each base classifier) are used.

The proposed dynamic integration technique Network Boosting was evaluated with C4.5, AdaBoost, bagging and BB on 16 data sets from the UCI machine learning repository. The results achieved are promising. In order to show the Network Boosting's ability on overfitting, we compared it with others on UnitSquare model.

In addition, under some conditions, Network Boosting can be reduced to AdaBoost and Bagging. If there is just one node in the network and weighted voting is used, then Network Boosting reduces to AdaBoost; if the training steps of Network Boosting is one, it just equates the bagging algorithm.

Through the experiments, random graph performs well and is a good choice for NB. How about the performance of Network Boosting if other topologies introduced? Such topologies include small-world network, scale-free network and grid network. Further researches are need in the future on explore the dynamic mechanism of Network Boosting on different network topologies.

References

1. Breiman, L.: Bagging predictors. Machine Learning, (1996) 24 (2):123-140
2. Freund, Y., Schapire, R.E.: A decision-theoretic generalization of on-line learning and an application to boosting. European Conference on Computational Learning Theory, (1995)
3. Freund, Y., Schapire, R.E.: Experiments with a new boosting algorithm. In Proceedings of the Thirteenth International conference on Machine Learning, (1996)
4. Schapire, R.E.: A brief introduction to boosting. In Proceedings of the Sixteenth International Joint Conference on Artificial Intelligence, (1999)
5. Dietterich, T.G.: An experimental comparison of three methods for constructing ensembles of decision trees: Bagging, boosting, and randomization. Machine Learning, 40. (2000) 139-158
6. Krieger, A., Long, C., Wyner, A.: Boosting noisy data. In Proceedings of the Eighteenth International conference on Machine Learning, (2001)
7. Rätsch, G., Onoda, T., and Muller, K.R.: Soft margins for AdaBoost. Machine Learning, 42 (3). (2001) 287–320
8. Oza N.C.: AveBoost2: Boosting for Noisy Data. 5th International Workshop, Multiple Classifier Systems. (2004)

9. Fan, W., Stolfo, S.J., Zhang, J.: The application of AdaBoost for distributed, scalable and on-line learning. In SIGKDD, (1999)
10. Lazarevic, A., Obradovic, Z.: The distributed boosting algorithm. In SIGKDD, (2001)
11. Lazarevic, A., Obradovic, Z.: Boosting algorithm for parallel and distributed learning. Distributed and Parallel Databases, (2002) 11, 203-229
12. Merz, C.J., Murphy, P.M.: UCI repository of machine learning databases. http://www.ics.uci.edu/ ~mlearn/MLRepository.html. (1996)
13. Wang Shijun and Zhang Changshui: Weighted competition scale-free network. Phys. Rev. E **70**, 066127 (2004) .
14. Wang Shijun and Zhang Changshui: Microscopic model of financial markets based on belief propagation. Physica A **354C**, 496 (2005) .
15. Albert, R. and Barabási, A.: Statistical mechanics of complex networks. Reviews of Modern Physics, 74 (1). (2002) 47–97
16. Albert, R., Jeong, H. and Barabási, A.: Error and attack tolerance of complex networks. Nature, 406 (2000) 378-382
17. Bollobas, B.: Random Graphs. Academic, London, (1985)
18. Freund, Y., Schapire, R.E.: Game theory, on-line prediction and boosting. Proceedings of the Thirteenth International conference on Machine Learning, (1996)
19. Fudenberg, D., and Tirole, J.: Game Theory. MIT Press, (1991)
20. Freund, Y., and Schapire, R.E.: Adaptive game playing using multiplicative weights. Game and Economic Behavior, 29. (1999), 79-103
21. Breiman, L.: Prediction games and arcing algorithms. Neural Computation, 11. (1999) 1493-1517
22. Witten I.H. and Frank E.: *Data Mining: Practical machine learning tools with Java implementations* (Morgan Kaufmann, San Francisco, 2000)
23. Quinlan., J.R.: Bagging, boosting, and C4.5. In Proceedings of the Thirteenth NationalConference on Artificial Intelligence, AAAI Press/MIT Press. (1996) 725-730
24. Bauer, E., and Kohavi, R.: An empirical comparison of voting classification algorithms: Bagging, boosting, and variants. Machine Learning, 36 (1-2). (2000) 105-139
25. Melville P. and Mooney R.: Constructing Diverse Classifier Ensembles Using Artificial Training Examples. Proceedings of the Eighteenth International Joint Conference on Artificial Intelligence. (2003) 505-510

Appendix. Proof of Theorem 1

Proof: For $t = 1, ..., T$, we have that

$$
\begin{aligned}
\sum_{i=1}^{l} w_{k,t+1}(i) &= \sum_{i=1}^{l} w_{k,t}(i) \beta^{M(i,Q_{k,t}) + \sum_{n} M(i,Q_{n,t})} \\
&\leq \sum_{i=1}^{l} w_{k,t}(i)(1-(1-\beta)M(i,Q_{k,t})) \beta^{\sum_{n} M(i,Q_{n,t})} \\
&\leq \sum_{i=1}^{l} w_{k,t}(i)(1-(1-\beta)M(i,Q_{k,t})) \beta^{\min_{i} \sum_{n} M(i,Q_{n,t})} \\
&= \left(\sum_{i=1}^{l} w_{k,t}(i)\right)(1-(1-\beta)M(P_{k,t},Q_{k,t})) \beta^{\min_{i} \sum_{n} M(i,Q_{n,t})}
\end{aligned}
\tag{9}
$$

The first line uses the definition of $w_{k,t+1}(i)$. The second line comes from the fact that $\beta^x \leq 1 - (1-\beta)x$ for $\beta > 0$ and $x \in [0,1]$. The last line uses the definition of $P_{k,t}$. So we can get the following inequation if we unwrap the Eq.(9)

$$\sum_{i=1}^{l} w_{k,t+1}(i) \leq l \prod_{t=1}^{T} (1 - (1-\beta) M(P_{k,t}, Q_{k,t})) \times \prod_{t=1}^{T} \beta^{\min_i \sum_n M(i, Q_{k,t})}$$

$$= l \prod_{t=1}^{T} (1 - (1-\beta) M(P_{k,t}, Q_{k,t})) \times \beta^{\sum_{t=1}^{T} \min_i \sum_n M(i, Q_{k,t})} \quad (10)$$

Next, note that, for any j,

$$\sum_{i=1}^{l} w_{k,T+1}(i) \geq w_{k,T+1}(j) = \beta^{\sum_{t=1}^{T} M(j, Q_{k,t}) + \sum_n M(j, Q_{n,t})}$$

Combining with Eq.(10) and taking logs gives

$$(\ln \beta) \sum_{t=1}^{T} \left\{ M(j, Q_{k,t}) + \sum_n M(j, Q_{n,t}) \right\}$$
$$\leq \ln l + \sum_{t=1}^{T} \ln(1 - (1-\beta) M(P_{k,t}, Q_{k,t})) + \ln \beta \sum_{t=1}^{T} \min_i \sum_n M(i, Q_{n,t}) \quad (11)$$
$$\leq \ln l - (1-\beta) \sum_{t=1}^{T} M(P_{k,t}, Q_{k,t}) + \ln \beta \sum_{t=1}^{T} \min_i \sum_n M(i, Q_{n,t})$$

Since $\ln(1-x) \leq -x$ for $x < 1$. Rearranging terms, and noting that this expression holds for any given j

$$\sum_{t=1}^{T} M(P_{k,t}, Q_{k,t})$$
$$\leq \frac{\ln l}{1-\beta} + \frac{\ln(1/\beta)}{1-\beta} \min_j \sum_{t=1}^{T} \left\{ M(j, Q_{k,t}) + \sum_n M(j, Q_{n,t}) \right\} + \frac{\ln \beta}{1-\beta} \sum_{t=1}^{T} \min_i \sum_n M(i, Q_{n,t})$$
$$= \frac{\ln l}{1-\beta} + \frac{\ln(1/\beta)}{1-\beta} \min_P \sum_{t=1}^{T} \{M(P, Q_{k,t})\} + \frac{\ln(1/\beta)}{1-\beta} \times$$
$$\left(\min_j \sum_{t=1}^{T} \left\{ \sum_n M(j, Q_{n,t}) \right\} - \sum_{t=1}^{T} \min_i \sum_n M(i, Q_{n,t}) \right).$$

Model Selection in Omnivariate Decision Trees

Olcay Taner Yıldız and Ethem Alpaydın

Department of Computer Engineering,
Boğaziçi University TR-34342, Istanbul, Turkey
yildizol@cmpe.boun.edu.tr, alpaydin@boun.edu.tr

Abstract. We propose an omnivariate decision tree architecture which contains univariate, multivariate linear or nonlinear nodes, matching the complexity of the node to the complexity of the data reaching that node. We compare the use of different model selection techniques including AIC, BIC, and CV to choose between the three types of nodes on standard datasets from the UCI repository and see that such omnivariate trees with a small percentage of multivariate nodes close to the root generalize better than pure trees with the same type of node everywhere. CV produces simpler trees than AIC and BIC without sacrificing from expected error. The only disadvantage of CV is its longer training time.

1 Introduction

A decision tree is made up of internal decision nodes and terminal leaves. The input vector is composed of p attributes, $\boldsymbol{x} = [x_1, \ldots, x_p]^T$, and the aim in classification is to assign $\boldsymbol{x}$ to one of K mutually exclusive and exhaustive classes. Each internal node m implements a decision function, $f_m(\boldsymbol{x})$, where each branch of the node corresponds to one outcome of the decision. Each leaf of the tree carries a class label. Geometrically, each $f_m(\boldsymbol{x})$ defines a discriminant in the p-dimensional input space dividing it into as many subspaces as there are branches. As one takes a path from the root to a leaf, these subspaces are further subdivided until we end up with a part of the input space which contains the instances of one class only.

In a *univariate* decision tree, the decision at internal node m uses only one attribute, i.e., one dimension of $\boldsymbol{x}$, x_j. If that attribute is numeric, the decision is of the form

$$f_m(\boldsymbol{x}) : x_j + w_{m0} > 0 \tag{1}$$

where w_{m0} is some constant number. This defines a discriminant which is orthogonal to axis x_j, intersects it at $x_j = -w_{m0}$ and divides the input space into two.

A *linear multivariate* decision tree, each internal node uses a linear combination of all attributes:

$$f_m(\boldsymbol{x}) : \boldsymbol{w}_m^T \boldsymbol{x} + w_{m0} = \sum_{j=1}^{p} w_{mj} x_j + w_{m0} > 0 \tag{2}$$

To be able to apply the weighted sum, all the attributes should be numeric and discrete values need be represented numerically (usually by 1-of-L encoding) beforehand. Note that the univariate numeric node is a special case of the multivariate linear node, where all but one of w_{mj} is 0 and the other, 1. In this linear case, each decision node divides the input space into two with a hyperplane of arbitrary orientation and position where successive decision nodes on a path from the root to a leaf further divide these into two and the leaf nodes define polyhedra in the input space.

In a *nonlinear multivariate* decision tree, the decision takes the form

$$f_m(\mathbf{x}) : \sum_{j=1}^{k} w_j \phi_j(\mathbf{x}) > 0 \tag{3}$$

where $\phi_j(\mathbf{x})$ are the nonlinear basis functions. In this work, we use a polynomial basis function of degree 2 where for example for $\mathbf{x} \in \Re^2$, $\phi(\mathbf{x}) = [\ 1, x_1, x_2, x_1^2, x_2^2, x_1 x_2]$ which gives us a quadratic tree.

Surveys of work on constructing and simplifying decision trees can be found in [1], [2] and [3]. A recent survey comparing different decision tree methods with other classification algorithms is given in [4].

In this paper, we compare model selection techniques AIC, BIC and CV in the context of decision tree induction. In Section 2, we show how to apply model selection techniques in tree induction and we briefly explain the model selection techniques. In Section 3 we give the related work in the literature. We give our experiments and results in Section 4 and conclude in Section 5.

2 Tuning Model Complexity

The model selection problem in decision trees can be defined as choosing the best model at each node of the tree. In our experiments, we use three candidate models, namely, univariate, linear multivariate, and nonlinear multivariate (quadratic). At each node of the tree, we train these three models to separate two class groups from each other and choose the best. While going from the univariate to more complex nodes, the idea is to check if we can have a large decrease in bias with a small increase in variance.

We have previously proposed Omnivariate Decision Tree [5], where we have used CV to decide the best model from three different models including univariate model, linear perceptron and as nonlinear model multilayer perceptron. In this work, we have also included AIC and BIC in model selection and used quadratic model as the nonlinear model because it learns faster than the multilayer perceptron model. The use of PCA to decrease model complexity is another contribution of this work.

For finding the best split at a decision node we use Linear Discriminant Analysis (LDA) [6]. Since we have binary nodes, if we have $K > 2$ classes, these classes must be divided into two class groups and LDA is used to find the best split to separate these two class groups. We use the heuristic of splitting $K > 2$ classes into two groups originally proposed by Guo and Gelfand [7].

For the univariate model, we use univariate LDA and the model complexity is two, one for the index of the used attribute and one for the threshold. For the multivariate linear model, we use multivariate LDA and to avoid a singular covariance matrix, we use PCA with $\epsilon = 0.99$ to get k new dimensions and the model complexity is $k + 1$. For the multivariate quadratic model, we choose a polynomial kernel of degree 2 $((x_1+x_2+\ldots+x_d+1)^2)$ and use multivariate LDA to find the weights. Again to avoid a singular covariance matrix, we use PCA with $\epsilon = 0.99$ to get m new dimensions and the model complexity is $m + 1$. Then, we calculate the generalization error of each candidate model using the corresponding loglikelihood and model complexity. In the last step, we choose the optimal model having the least generalization error.

To calculate the error at a decision node, we must first assign classes to the left and right child nodes. Assume that C_L and C_R are classes assigned to the left and right nodes respectively. N_i^L and N_i^R are the number of instances of class i choosing left and right branches and N_{C_L} and N_{C_R} denote the number of instances of the classes C_L and C_R respectively.

$$N_{C_L} = \arg\max_i N_i^L, N_{C_R} = \arg\max_i N_i^R \tag{4}$$

The error at the decision node will be calculated by subtracting the number of instances of these two classes (which are correctly classified as they will label the leaves) from the total number of instances

$$e = \frac{N - N_{C_L} - N_{C_R}}{N} \tag{5}$$

When N is the total number of instances, N_i is the number of instances of class i, and N^L and N^R are the total number of instances choosing left and right branches respectively, the loglikelihood is given as

$$\mathcal{L} = \sum_{i=1}^{K} N_i^L \log \frac{N_i^L}{N^L} + \sum_{i=1}^{K} N_i^R \log \frac{N_i^R}{N^R} \tag{6}$$

Akaike Information Criterion AIC [8] is calculated as

$$AIC = 2(-\mathcal{L} + d) \tag{7}$$

where $\mathcal{L}$ represents the loglikelihood of the data and d represents the number of free parameters of the model. We choose the model with the smallest AIC over the three models we have.

Bayesian Information Criterion BIC [9] is calculated as

$$BIC = -\mathcal{L} + \frac{d}{2} \log N \tag{8}$$

where N is the number of data points. Like in AIC, we choose the model with the smallest BIC value.

Cross-validation We use 5×2 cross-validation and train all three models and test them on the validation set ten times and then apply the one-sided version of the 5×2 cv t test [10].

When we have two candidate models we choose the simple model, if it has smaller or equal error rate compared to the complex model. Only if the complex model has significantly smaller error rate then it is chosen. When we have three candidate models, univariate U, linear multivariate L, multivariate quadratic Q in increasing order of complexity with population error rates denoted by e_U, e_L, e_Q, we choose one considering both expected error and model complexity. Q is chosen if $H_0 : e_L \leq e_Q$ and $H_0 : e_U \leq e_Q$ are rejected. Otherwise, L is chosen if $H_0 : e_U \leq e_L$ is rejected. Otherwise U is chosen.

Note that AIC and BIC do not require a validation set and training is done once, whereas with CV, in each fold, half of the data is left out for validation and training is done ten times.

3 Related Work

LDA was first used in Friedman[11] for constructing decision trees. The algorithm has binary splits at each node, where a split is like in C4.5, i.e. $x_i < w_0$ but x_i can be an original variable, transgenerated, or adaptive. Linear discriminant analysis is applied to construct an adaptive variable. Kolmogorof-Smirnoff distance is used as the error measure. When there are more than $K > 2$ classes, it converts the problem into K different subproblems, where each subproblem separates one class from others. LTREE [12] is a multivariate decision tree algorithm with binary splits. LTREE uses LDA to construct new features, which are linear combinations of the original features. For all constructed features, the best split is found using C4.5's exhaustive search technique. Best of these is selected to create the two children of the current node. These new constructed features can also be used down the tree in the children of that node. Functional Trees [13] make simultenaous use of functional nodes and functional leaves in prediction problems. Bias-variance decomposition of the error showed that, the variance can be reduced using functional leaves, while bias can be reduced using functional inner nodes.

In CART [14], parameter adaptation is through backfitting: At each step, all the coefficients w_{mj} except one is fixed and that coefficient is tuned for possible improvement in terms of impurity. One cycles through all j until there is no further improvement. In OC1 [15], an extension to CART is made to get out of the local optima. A small random vector is added to w_m once there is convergence through backfitting. Adding a vector perturbs all coefficients together and makes a conjugate jump in the coefficient space. Another extension proposed is to run the method several (20-50) times and choose the best solution in terms of impurity.

In FACT [16], with K classes a node can have K branches. Each branch has its modified linear discriminant function calculated using LDA and an instance is channeled to the ith branch to minimize an estimated expected risk.

QUEST [17] is a revised version of FACT and uses binary splits at each decision node. It solves the problem of dividing K classes into two classes by using unsupervised 2-means clustering on the class means of the data. QUEST also differs from FACT in the way that it does not assume equal variances and uses Quadratic Discriminant Analysis (QDA) to find the two roots for the split point and uses the appropriate one. CRUISE[18] is a multivariate algorithm with K-way nodes. Like FACT, CRUISE finds $K-1$ splits using LDA. The departure from FACT occurs when the split assigns the same class to all its K children. Because such a split is not useful, the best next class is chosen. Another departure occurs while assigning a class to a leaf: When there are two or more classes which have the same number of instances in that leaf, FACT selects randomly one of them but CRUISE selects the class which has not been assigned to any leaf node.

In LMDT [19], with K classes, as in FACT, a node is allowed to have K branches. For each class, i.e., branch, there is a vector of parameters, and the node implements a K-way split. There is an iterative algorithm that adjusts the parameters of classes to minimize the number of misclassifications, rather than an impurity measure as entropy or Gini.

In Logistic model trees [20], logistic classification is used to find the best split at each decision node. They use a stagewise fitting process to construct logistic classification models that can select relevant attributes in the data.

4 Experiments

The proposed omnivariate trees are compared on twenty-two datasets from the UCI machine learning repository [21]. We compare pure univariate, linear and quadratic trees with omnivariate trees based on AIC, BIC, and CV. Our comparison criteria are generalization error (on the validation folds of 5×2 cross-validation), complexity (as measured by the total number of free parameters in the tree) and learning time (seconds on a Pentium Xeon 2.7). The error, model complexity and learning time figures contain boxplots, where the box has lines at the lower quartile, median, and upper quartile values. The whiskers are lines extending from each end of the box to show the extent of the rest of the data. Outliers, shown with '+', are data with values beyond the ends of the whiskers.

In Section 4.1, we give our results in two datasets, *pendigits* and *segment* in detail and in Section 4.2, we give our results on all twenty-two datasets.

4.1 Results on *Pendigits* and *Segment*

Figures 1 and 2 show the expected error, model complexity and learning time plots for *pendigits* (*pen*) and *segment* (*seg*) respectively. On *pendigits*, the pure quadratic tree is more accurate than the pure linear tree which in turn is more accurate than the pure univariate tree. On *segment*, the pure univariate tree is more accurate than the pure linear tree which in turn is more accurate than the pure quadratic tree. On *pendigits*, omnivariate trees have expected error close

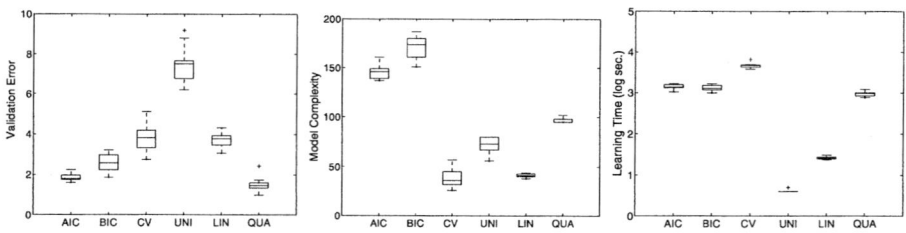

Fig. 1. The expected error, model complexity and learning time plots for *pendigits*

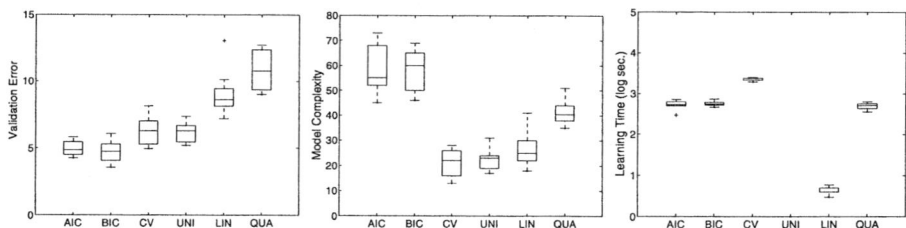

Fig. 2. The expected error, model complexity and learning time plots for *segment*

to the pure quadratic tree and on *segment*, they have expected error close to that of the pure univariate tree showing that they can automatically adapt to the problem. Omnivariate tree with CV produces smaller trees (in terms of the total number of parameters in the tree) than AIC and BIC. AIC and BIC have similar performances with respect to tree complexity even though BIC penalizes the complex models more. Due to this reason, on *pendigits*, AIC selects quadratic nodes more, which makes it better in terms of expected error compared to BIC and CV. Since CV uses 5×2 cross-validation, its learning time is higher than that of AIC and BIC. AIC and BIC trees also have their postpruning stages where the AIC (or BIC) of a subtree is compared to that of a leaf to possibly be replaced by it.

Figures 3 and 4 show the number of times of univariate, multivariate linear and multivariate quadratic nodes are selected at different levels of tree for *pendigits* and *segment* respectively. We see that more complex nodes are selected early in the tree, closer to the root where the problem is more complex and where there is more data. As we go down the tree, we have less data and complex nodes overfit and get rejected. Since pure quadratic tree is the best on *pendigits* and pure univariate tree is the best on *segment*, and since the omnivariate tree follows the best model, it selects the quadratic node on *pendigits* and the univariate node on *segment* more in the upper levels of the tree. AIC selects more complex nodes than BIC, which selects more complex nodes than CV, though in terms of the overall number of nodes, CV has the least because CV-based postpruning prunes more than AIC-based or BIC-based postpruning.

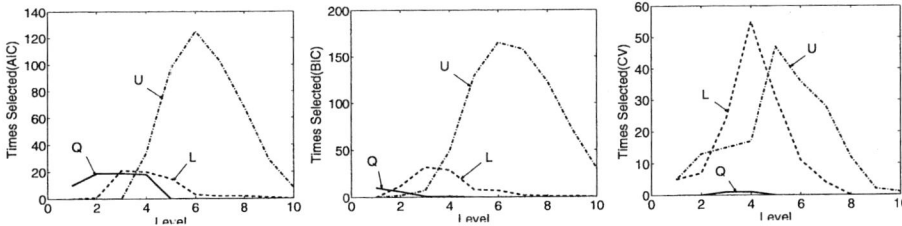

Fig. 3. The number of times univariate, multivariate linear and multivariate quadratic nodes selected at different levels of tree for *pendigits*

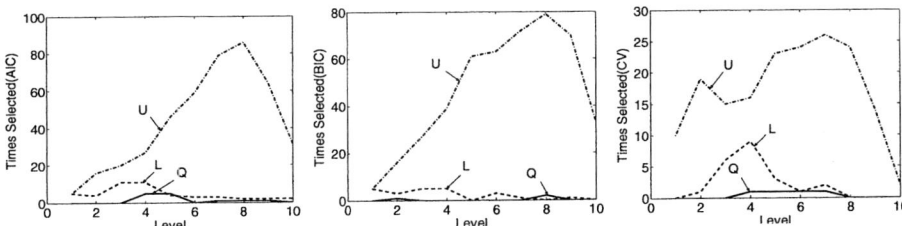

Fig. 4. The number of times univariate, multivariate linear and multivariate quadratic nodes selected at different levels of tree for *segment*

4.2 Results on all Datasets

The average and standard deviations of expected error and model complexity of decision trees produced by different model selection techniques and univariate, multivariate linear and multivariate quadratic decision trees for twenty-two datasets are given in Tables 1, 2, and 3 respectively. Since there are more than two decision tree algorithms to compare, we give two tables where in the first table the raw results are shown. The third table contains pairwise comparisons; the entry (i, j) in this second table gives the number of datasets (out of 22) on which method i is statistically significantly better than method j with at least 95% confidence. In the third table, row and column sums are also given. The row sum gives the number of datasets out of 22 where the algorithm on the row outperforms at least one of the other algorithms. The column sum gives the number of datasets where the algorithm on the column is outperformed by at least one of the other algorithms.

In general, omnivariate trees are more accurate than pure trees in terms of expected error. The number of wins of omnivariate trees against pure trees is more than the number of wins of pure trees against omnivariate ones. We also see that if there is a significant difference between the pure trees, the omnivariate tree follows the better tree. For example, on *balance*, the pure linear tree is the most accurate and omnivariate trees have similar accuracy to the linear tree by including many linear nodes. On *car*, pure univariate and linear trees are the best

Table 1. The average and standard deviations of expected errors of omnivariate decision trees and pure trees

Set	Pure Decision Trees			Omnivariate Decision Trees		
	UNI	LIN	QUA	AIC	BIC	CV
bal	25.89± 4.92	12.00± 1.92	24.10± 2.96	13.22± 1.56	12.70± 2.03	10.62± 1.13
bre	5.69± 1.65	4.41± 0.54	3.72± 0.87	5.06± 1.12	4.92± 0.90	4.63± 1.33
bup	40.17± 6.31	33.86± 4.17	41.22± 1.44	37.80± 4.06	37.44± 4.00	35.94± 4.80
car	7.38± 1.67	8.52± 1.64	21.32± 1.93	5.83± 1.07	6.08± 0.85	7.29± 1.77
der	6.99± 1.88	3.33± 1.01	8.75± 1.99	5.74± 1.69	5.69± 1.48	7.70± 1.75
eco	22.42± 3.78	18.17± 2.37	19.45± 2.62	21.41± 3.13	19.23± 2.30	19.74± 3.21
fla	11.15± 0.54	11.39± 0.75	11.15± 0.54	14.79± 3.28	12.14± 2.49	11.21± 0.63
gla	40.48± 9.06	42.71± 3.02	43.59± 6.21	36.80± 3.72	34.30± 3.12	38.40± 6.20
hab	26.54± 0.21	26.47± 0.16	26.41± 0.97	33.58± 4.08	26.47± 0.16	26.60± 0.39
hep	21.67± 1.95	20.39± 0.87	18.33± 2.88	22.57± 3.85	21.93± 4.26	21.93± 3.22
iri	5.47± 4.10	3.07± 1.41	4.80± 3.51	4.14± 1.93	4.27± 2.07	5.73± 1.99
iro	14.14± 2.80	11.56± 2.25	9.51± 2.62	11.51± 2.24	13.79± 1.65	12.71± 2.10
mon	20.79± 7.39	27.50±10.65	16.90± 2.21	10.42± 3.58	9.21± 3.30	20.65± 6.61
pen	7.50± 0.93	3.70± 0.38	1.52± 0.37	1.86± 0.20	2.57± 0.44	3.83± 0.79
pim	29.77± 3.90	23.10± 1.18	26.69± 3.04	30.70± 1.89	29.61± 2.90	30.78± 5.52
seg	6.19± 0.75	9.05± 1.66	10.92± 1.47	4.96± 0.53	4.72± 0.77	6.27± 1.07
tic	13.69± 4.47	29.42± 2.12	27.94± 4.83	18.89± 3.63	8.39± 1.67	16.41± 4.20
vot	4.83± 1.32	5.34± 2.04	8.69± 1.99	5.98± 1.73	5.98± 1.75	4.32± 0.54
wav	25.86± 1.09	14.77± 0.57	15.52± 0.46	20.47± 0.39	20.64± 1.04	16.25± 1.49
win	15.95± 4.16	3.15± 1.91	7.42± 4.00	5.40± 1.68	7.16± 4.59	6.15± 3.76
yea	48.99± 4.04	45.09± 2.50	47.72± 3.64	51.07± 2.03	50.89± 1.63	49.96± 4.95
zoo	10.70± 4.29	22.61± 5.07	21.50± 5.85	5.32± 2.73	5.32± 2.73	11.22± 4.69

and the omnivariate trees select univariate and linear nodes more. On *wave* and *wine*, pure linear and quadratic trees are more accurate than the pure univariate tree and the omnivariate trees have expected error close to the expected error of those trees. The model complexity table shows that CV constructs simpler trees than AIC and BIC. It has more wins (22 against 10 and 15) and less losses (6 against 20 and 22). We see that, CV chooses smaller trees but with more complex nodes and the trees constructed by CV are as accurate as trees constructed by AIC and BIC. Since omnivariate trees try all possible models, they have learning time more than those of trees and because CV tries all possible models ten times (because of 5×2 cross-validation), it has the longest learning time.

The number of times the univariate, multivariate linear and multivariate quadratic nodes are selected in omnivariate decision trees produced by AIC, BIC and CV are given in Table 4. We see that, as expected, quadratic nodes are selected the least and the univariate nodes are selected the most. Although CV has the smallest tree complexity, it has the highest percentage of multivariate nodes (linear 22 percent, nonlinear 1.74 percent). AIC and BIC trees do not prune as much as the CV tree and therefore their node counts are higher than the CV tree.

Table 2. The average and standard deviations of model complexities of omnivariate decision trees and pure trees

Set	Pure Decision Trees			Omnivariate Decision Trees		
	UNI	LIN	QUA	AIC	BIC	CV
bal	11.7± 4.7	17.9± 1.3	106.9± 0.9	45.5± 5.9	43.2± 10.0	17.0± 0.0
bre	6.0± 3.2	10.2± 0.4	37.1± 1.0	28.0± 10.0	22.4± 5.0	17.1± 12.0
bup	5.3± 4.9	7.3± 2.8	6.1± 9.8	52.3± 5.3	45.1± 16.8	7.9± 4.6
car	28.6± 4.7	19.9± 2.5	110.1± 1.4	67.9± 9.8	63.0± 10.3	27.3± 6.5
der	7.2± 1.2	33.7± 0.5	112.2± 1.5	25.7± 14.7	13.3± 2.1	6.4± 0.7
eco	5.5± 2.9	10.7± 1.3	21.0± 1.4	30.5± 7.8	26.8± 2.8	4.8± 1.2
fla	0.3± 0.9	3.9± 8.2	0.0± 0.0	17.8± 3.4	2.4± 5.1	0.4± 1.3
gla	6.9± 3.7	11.3± 2.4	21.9± 2.6	29.7± 3.7	30.2± 3.9	7.6± 2.3
hab	1.0± 3.2	0.0± 0.0	3.3± 5.3	36.1± 3.7	0.0± 0.0	0.7± 2.2
hep	2.1± 3.2	5.8± 9.3	28.8± 24.9	12.8± 3.2	13.3± 2.2	2.6± 5.9
iri	3.6± 1.0	5.7± 0.5	10.5± 0.5	4.5± 1.4	4.1± 1.7	3.0± 0.0
iro	4.2± 1.9	29.6± 0.7	57.4± 2.9	36.8± 7.9	18.2± 2.5	17.2± 14.5
mon	9.1± 3.6	8.4± 3.6	26.2± 0.4	37.5± 5.4	29.8± 2.2	17.1± 11.8
pen	72.0± 8.2	41.4± 2.0	97.4± 2.2	146.0± 7.7	171.5± 11.5	38.5± 10.0
pim	7.4± 7.6	9.5± 0.8	36.0± 12.7	101.1± 15.6	92.2± 10.5	4.0± 5.3
seg	22.8± 4.1	26.3± 6.7	41.7± 4.9	58.0± 9.8	57.9± 8.0	21.0± 5.4
tic	21.4± 3.5	21.5± 3.0	96.6± 66.7	185.0± 58.1	52.8± 9.6	20.3± 9.2
vot	2.9± 1.5	16.9± 0.7	82.8± 2.4	13.6± 3.0	10.0± 3.9	2.4± 1.3
wav	35.9± 14.3	26.6± 1.7	221.0± 1.2	406.2± 96.4	331.2± 10.4	23.8± 0.9
win	4.0± 0.7	14.0± 0.0	48.0± 1.2	14.3± 0.7	11.4± 4.2	13.1± 3.6
yea	20.0± 10.3	20.2± 4.7	37.6± 3.9	287.9± 13.8	281.3± 13.4	6.9± 3.6
zoo	6.7± 0.8	15.8± 0.9	25.7± 1.6	8.1± 0.9	8.1± 0.9	6.2± 1.1

Table 3. Pairwise comparisons of expected error and model complexities of omnivariate decision trees and pure trees

	Expected Error							Model Complexity						
	AIC	BIC	CV	UNI	LIN	QUA	$\sum$		AIC	BIC	CV	UNI	LIN	QUA	$\sum$
AIC	0	2	5	7	7	10	14	AIC	0	1	0	0	3	9	10
BIC	4	0	5	9	7	10	15	BIC	10	0	0	0	5	11	15
CV	5	3	0	5	4	8	15	CV	21	18	0	3	11	20	22
UNI	4	1	1	0	3	6	8	UNI	21	19	6	0	12	19	21
LIN	9	6	5	10	0	9	17	LIN	17	14	2	3	0	19	21
QUA	7	6	3	6	3	0	11	QUA	12	9	0	0	0	0	12
$\sum$	14	10	12	17	8	13		$\sum$	22	20	7	4	15	20	

The number of times univariate, multivariate linear and multivariate quadratic nodes selected at different levels of tree for AIC, BIC and CV is given in Figure 5. We see that AIC selects quadratic nodes more than BIC. This is in accordance with the literature stating that BIC has a tendency to choose simple models [22]. BIC selects more quadratic nodes than CV in the early levels of the tree. For linear nodes, their percentages are close to each other.

Table 4. The number of times univariate, multivariate linear and multivariate quadratic nodes selected in decision trees produced by AIC, BIC, and CV

Set	AIC			BIC			CV		
	UNI	LIN	QUA	UNI	LIN	QUA	UNI	LIN	QUA
bal	261	34	0	251	21	0	0	10	0
bre	143	18	1	119	14	1	18	8	2
bup	416	44	8	400	26	1	21	9	0
car	452	77	0	433	47	0	101	22	0
der	64	14	0	123	0	0	51	3	0
eco	232	30	4	230	18	0	32	6	0
fla	164	3	1	22	0	0	3	0	0
gla	273	9	5	283	7	2	65	1	0
hab	309	21	13	0	0	0	6	0	0
hep	116	2	0	123	0	0	4	1	0
iri	26	8	1	22	9	0	20	0	0
iro	93	11	6	172	0	0	20	11	0
mon	107	5	13	35	3	10	28	1	7
pen	465	65	66	742	92	18	176	137	2
pim	799	40	9	853	23	1	4	4	0
seg	454	48	13	487	24	3	174	22	4
tic	596	8	11	516	2	0	160	10	7
vot	122	4	0	89	1	0	14	0	0
wav	2792	59	5	3072	30	0	1	27	0
win	8	14	0	31	7	0	10	12	0
yea	2401	157	60	2662	102	18	50	8	1
zoo	71	0	0	71	0	0	52	0	0
$\sum$	10364	671	216	10736	426	54	1010	292	23
%	92.12	5.96	1.92	95.72	3.80	0.48	76.22	22.04	1.74

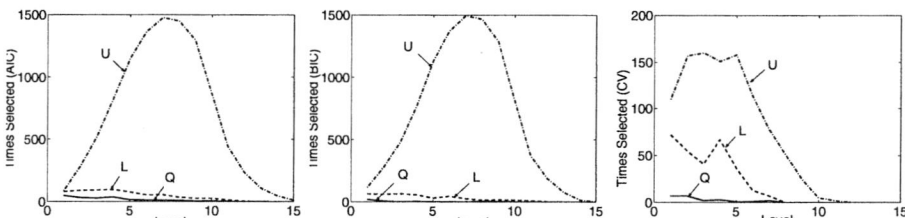

Fig. 5. Number of times univariate, multivariate linear and multivariate quadratic nodes selected at different levels of tree for AIC, BIC and CV

5 Conclusion

We propose a novel decision tree architecture, the omnivariate decision tree, which contains both univariate, multivariate linear, and multivariate quadratic nodes. The ideal node type is determined via model selection using AIC, BIC or CV. Such a tree, instead of assuming the same bias at each node, matches the complexity of a node with the data reaching that node.

Our simulation results indicate that such an omnivariate architecture generalizes better than pure trees with the same type of node everywhere. As expected, the quadratic node, is selected the least, followed by the linear node and the univariate node. More complex nodes are selected early in the tree closer to the root. Since there are more nodes in the lower levels, the percentage of univariate nodes is much higher ($> 90\%$ for AIC and BIC, $> 75\%$ for CV). This shows that having a small percentage of multivariate (linear or quadratic) nodes is effective.

CV finds simpler trees than BIC which in turn finds simpler trees than AIC. Although omnivariate CV trees are simple, they contain complex nodes (multivariate linear and nonlinear) more than AIC and BIC. All three methods have nearly the same error rate. CV produces simpler models without sacrificing from the expected error. But it has the disadvantage that its training time is longer due to multiple cross-validation runs.

In the literature, in choosing between nodes or choosing node parameters, accuracy (information gain or some other measure calculated from fit to data) is used in growing the tree and some other measure (cross-validation error on a pruning set or MDL) has been used to prune the tree; the same is also true for rule learners such as Ripper [23]. Our work proposes to use one criterion (AIC, BIC, CV) in both growing the tree *and* pruning it. We believe this makes more sense than many approaches where separate criteria are used to grow the tree and then to prune it to alleviate overfitting. Because our approach allows choosing among multiple models, it is also possible to have different algorithms for the same node type and choose between them. That is, one can have a palette of univariate nodes (one by LDA, one by information gain, etc) and the best one will then be chosen. The same also holds for linear or nonlinear (quadratic, other kernels, etc) nodes. Our emphasis is on the idea of an omnivariate decision tree and the sound use of model selection in inducing it, rather than the particular type of nodes we use in our example decision tree. The nice thing about LDA is that the same criterion can be used in training univariate, linear and quadratic nodes and we know that any difference is due to node complexity.

The same model selection idea can also be applied in regression trees by creating an omnivariate regression tree where at each node there are three candidate models, namely, univariate model, linear multivariate model and linear quadratic model. Then the candidate models at each node try to minimize the sum of mean square errors of child nodes. For CV based model selection, the same 5×2 paired t test can be used for comparing the mean square errors of the candidate models. One can also include different type of models in the leaf nodes such as linear models and can make model selection for the leaf nodes for both classification and regression trees.

Acknowledgements

This work has been supported by the Turkish Academy of Sciences, in the framework of the Young Scientist Award Program (EA-TÜBA-GEBİP/2001-1-1) and Boğaziçi University Scientific Research Projects 02A104D and 03K120250.

References

1. Breslow, L.A., Aha, D.W.: Simplifying decision trees: A survey. Technical Report AIC-96-014, Navy Center for Applied Research in AI, Naval Research Laboratory, Washington DC, USA (1997)
2. Murthy, S.K.: Automatic construction of decision trees from data: A multidisciplinary survey. Data Mininig and Knowledge Discovery **2** (1998) 345–389
3. Yıldız, O.T., Alpaydın, E.: Linear discriminant trees. International Journal of Pattern Recognition and Artificial Intelligence **19** (2005) 323–353
4. Lim, T.S., Loh, W.Y., Shih, Y.S.: A comparison of prediction accuracy, complexity, and training time of thirty-three old and new classification algorithms. Machine Learning **40** (2000) 203–228
5. Yıldız, O.T., Alpaydın, E.: Omnivariate decision trees. IEEE Transactions on Neural Networks **12** (2001) 1539–1546
6. Alpaydın, E.: Introduction to Machine Learning. The MIT Press (2004)
7. Guo, H., Gelfand, S.B.: Classification trees with neural network feature extraction. IEEE Transactions on Neural Networks **3** (1992) 923–933
8. Akaike, H.: Information theory and an extension of the maximum likelihood principle. In: Second International Symposium on Information Theory. (1973) 267–281
9. Schwarz, G.: Estimating the dimension of a model. Annals of Statistics **6** (1978) 461–464
10. Dietterich, T.G.: Approximate statistical tests for comparing supervised classification learning classifiers. Neural Computation **10** (1998) 1895–1923
11. Friedman, J.H.: A recursive partitioning decision rule for non-parametric classification. IEEE Transactions on Computers (1977) 404–408
12. Gama, J.: Discriminant trees. In: 16th International Conference on Machine Learning, New Brunswick, New Jersey, Morgan Kaufmann (1999) 134–142
13. Gama, J.: Functional trees. Machine Learning **55** (2004) 219–250
14. Breiman, L., Friedman, J.H., Olshen, R.A., Stone, C.J.: Classification and Regression Trees. John Wiley and Sons (1984)
15. Murthy, S.K., Kasif, S., Salzberg, S.: A system for induction of oblique decision trees. Journal of Artificial Intelligence Research **2** (1994) 1–32
16. Loh, W.Y., Vanichsetakul, N.: Tree-structured classification via generalized discriminant analysis. Journal of the American Statistical Association **83** (1988) 715–725
17. Loh, W.Y., Shih, Y.S.: Split selection methods for classification trees. Statistica Sinica **7** (1997) 815–840
18. Kim, H., Loh, W.: Classification trees with unbiased multiway splits. Journal of the American Statistical Association (2001) 589–604
19. Brodley, C.E., Utgoff, P.E.: Multivariate decision trees. Machine Learning **19** (1995) 45–77
20. Landwehr, N., Hall, M., Frank, E.: Logistic model trees. In: Proceedings of the European Conference in Machine Learning. (2003) 241–252
21. Blake, C., Merz, C.: UCI repository of machine learning databases (2000)
22. Hastie, T., Tibshirani, R., Friedman, J.: The Elements of Statistical Learning. Springer Verlag, New York (2001)
23. Cohen, W.W.: Fast effective rule induction. In: The Twelfth International Conference on Machine Learning. (1995) 115–123

Bayesian Network Learning with Abstraction Hierarchies and Context-Specific Independence

Marie desJardins[1], Priyang Rathod[1], and Lise Getoor[2]

[1] Department of Computer Science and Electrical Engineering,
University of Maryland, Baltimore County
[2] Computer Science Department,
University of Maryland, College Park

Abstract. Context-specific independence representations, such as tree-structured conditional probability tables (TCPTs), reduce the number of parameters in Bayesian networks by capturing local independence relationships and improve the quality of learned Bayesian networks. We previously presented Abstraction-Based Search (ABS), a technique for using attribute value hierarchies during Bayesian network learning to remove unimportant distinctions within the CPTs. In this paper, we introduce TCPT ABS (TABS), which integrates ABS with TCPT learning. Since expert-provided hierarchies may not be available, we provide a clustering technique for deriving hierarchies from data. We present empirical results for three real-world domains, finding that (1) combining TCPTs and ABS provides a significant increase in the quality of learned Bayesian networks (2) combining TCPTs and ABS provides a dramatic reduction in the number of parameters in the learned networks, and (3) data-derived hierarchies perform as well or better than expert-provided hierarchies.

1 Introduction

Bayesian networks (BNs) are a widely used representation for capturing probabilistic relationships among variables in a domain of interest [12]. They can be used to provide a compact representation of a joint probability distribution by capturing the dependency structure among the variables, and can be inductively learned from data [5, 8].

The conditional probability distributions associated with discrete variables in a BN are most commonly represented as explicit conditional probability tables (CPTs), which specify a multinomial distribution over the values of a variable for each combination of values of its parents. However, researchers have found that explicitly representing *context-specific independence* (CSI) relationships in the BN can reduce the number of parameters required to describe the BN [2]. In particular, learning methods have been developed that use tree-structured CPTs [7] and graph-structured CPTs [4] to represent the CSI relationships among the variables.

In previous work, we presented Abstraction-Based Search (ABS) [6], which used background knowledge in the form of expert-provided attribute value hierarchies (AVHs) during BN learning. ABS searches the space of possible abstractions at each variable in the BN. The abstraction process effectively collapses the corresponding rows of the CPT, thus reducing the number of parameters needed to represent the BN and improving the quality of the learned BN.

The abstractions provided by AVHs in ABS are complementary to those provided by TCPTs. Therefore, in this paper, we provide a new version of abstraction-based search, TCPT ABS (TABS), which integrates ABS with TCPTs. Our empirical results show that TABS significantly 1) improves the quality of the learned BN and 2) reduces the number of parameters required to represent a learned BN, compared to standard BN learning, ABS, or TCPT learning alone.

A second contribution of this paper is an agglomerative clustering-based method for deriving AVHs from the training data used for learning the BN. Our original motivation for developing this technique was to enable the use of AVHs in domains where expert-provided AVHs are not available. However, in our experiments, we found that in general, the learned AVHs yielded equally accurate BNs (using a log likelihood measure) as expert AVHs — and the learned AVHs resulted in substantially fewer parameters in the BNs than expert AVHs.

The remainder of the paper is organized as follows. We first give background on BNs, TCPTs, and learning methods for BNs with TCPTs. Next, we introduce the ABS and TABS methods for incorporating AVHs into the learning process, and the clustering algorithm for deriving AVHs from training data. We then provide experimental results in three real-world domains, and finally present related work, conclusions, and future work.

2 Bayesian Networks

We assume that the reader has some familiarity with basic concepts of BNs [12] and local search-based methods for learning BNs [8]. In this section, we briefly introduce the notation, learning methods, and scoring functions that are used in the remainder of the paper.

A BN is a directed acyclic graph that represents the joint probability distribution of a set of random variables, $\mathbf{X} = \{x_1, x_2, \ldots, x_n\}$. We assume that these variables are all discrete and finite. The domain of variable x_i is given by the set $\{v_{i1}, v_{i2}, \ldots, v_{ir_i}\}$, where r_i is the number of values that x_i may take. A BN over the set of variables $\mathbf{X}$ is represented as a pair, $B = (G, \Theta)$. G, the BN structure, is a directed acyclic graph over $\mathbf{X}$, where the edges represent dependencies between variables. The BN parameters, Θ, specify the set of conditional probabilities associated with B. A variable x_i is independent of its non-descendents in the network, given its parents π_i. Using this conditional independence assumption, the joint probability distribution can be factored as:

$$P(\mathbf{X}) = \prod_i P(x_i | \pi_i). \tag{1}$$

Given a set of m instances, $D = \{d_1, d_2, \ldots, d_m\}$, where each d_j is an attribute vector $\langle d_{1j}, d_{2j}, \ldots, d_{nj} \rangle$, we would like to learn a BN that best matches the data. Since this problem is NP-hard [3], typically a simple greedy hill-climbing

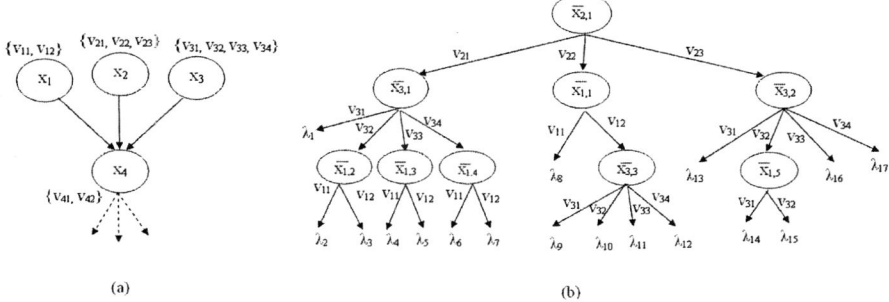

Fig. 1. (a) A partial view of the Bayesian network; (b) TCPT at variable x_4

search is used. The local search operators are $Add(x_i, x_j)$, which adds x_i as a parent of x_j; $Delete(x_i, x_j)$, which removes x_i from the parent set of x_j; and $Reverse(x_i, x_j)$, which reverses the edge between x_i and x_j. At each step, the new graph is evaluated using a scoring function; if the modification leads to a better network, then it is retained. When there are no missing values in the data, the scoring function can be decomposed locally, so that when an edge is added, modified or deleted, only the score of the variable x_i whose parent set π_i changed needs to be re-scored.

In our work, we use the Minimum Description Length (MDL) scoring criteria which attempts to select the hypothesis (i.e., the BN B) that minimizes the description length of the data D encoded using the BN. There are two components of the encoded data: the BN itself and the data encoding using the BN. The description length (DL) of the BN can be further decomposed into the DL of the structure, plus the DL of the (maximum likelihood) parameters. The DL of the data is given by its conditional entropy. The mathematical derivation of the MDL score is given by Bouckaert and others [1, 11].

3 Tree-Structured CPTs

In the TCPT representation, each variable in the BN has an associated tree-structured CPT. These trees specify the conditional probability of the values of a variable x_i, given its parents π_i. The leaves represent different conditional distributions over the values of x_i; the path from the root to a leaf defines the parent context for that distribution. In many cases, given a particular context of a subset of π_i, the value of x_i is independent of the rest of the parents in π_i. TCPTs can capture this local dependency structure.

We use the notation T_{x_i} to refer to the TCPT associated with the BN variable x_i. Each variable x_j that is a parent of x_i in the BN will have one or more corresponding nodes in T_{x_i}. We will refer to these tree nodes as $\bar{X}_j$ (to distinguish them from the variable x_j in the BN). Let $\#(\bar{X}_j)$ be the number of times that $\bar{X}_j$ appears in the tree; we will refer to these tree nodes as $\bar{X}_{j,p}$ ($p = 1, 2, \ldots, \#(\bar{X}_j)$). Each such tree node appears in a different *context* in the tree. The context of a

Procedure RefineTree(λ, $\bar{X}_{new}$)
1. remove λ from $RefCand$
2. replace λ with $\bar{X}_{new}$, and create $|Val(\bar{X}_{new})|$ new leaf nodes below $\bar{X}_{new}$
3. for each child λ' of $\bar{X}_{new}$,
    a. set $Candidates(\lambda') = Candidates(\lambda)$ - $\{\bar{X}_{new}\}$
    b. add λ' to $RefCand$

Procedure ExtendTree(x_i)
1. select a leaf node λ for refinement from $RefCand$ with probability
    $prob \propto |Candidates(\lambda)|$
2. $\bar{X}_{new} = argmin_t\{Score(T_{x_i} \cup \bar{X}_t)\}$
    where $\bar{X}_t$ is an instance of the tth candidate in $Candidates(\lambda)$
3. RefineTree($\lambda, \bar{X}_{new}$)

Fig. 2. TCPT learning algorithm: The RefineTree and ExtendTree procedures

node $\bar{X}_{j,p}$ is defined by the branches (variable/value pairs) along the path from $\bar{X}_{j,p}$ to the root of the TCPT. We use $\Upsilon(\bar{X}_{j,p})$ to denote the context of $\bar{X}_{j,p}$.

For example, Figure 1(b) shows the TCPT at node x_4 of the BN shown in Figure 1(a). T_{x_4} includes three instances of $\bar{X}_3$: (1) $\bar{X}_{3,1}$, whose context is $\Upsilon(\bar{X}_{3,1}) = [(\bar{X}_{2,1} = v_{21})]$, (2) $\bar{X}_{3,2}$, whose context is $\Upsilon(\bar{X}_{3,2}) = [(\bar{X}_{2,1} = v_{23})]$, and (3) $\bar{X}_{3,3}$, with context, $\Upsilon(\bar{X}_{3,3}) = [(\bar{X}_{2,1} = v_{22}), (\bar{X}_{1,1} = v_{12})]$.

We use $Val(\bar{X}_{j,p}) = \{\bar{v}_{j,p1}, \bar{v}_{j,p2}, \ldots\}$ to denote the set of values $\bar{X}_j$ can take in the tree. In the standard TCPT representation, $|Val(\bar{X}_{j,p})| = r_j$, the domain size of x_j, and every non-leaf instance of $\bar{X}_j$ will have r_j outgoing edges. (When using AVHs, the branches can be associated with abstract values, so the branching factor will depend on the context of the node (Section 4.3).) The set of all $(\Upsilon(\lambda), \lambda)$ pairs associated with leaf nodes in T_{x_i} defines the CPT of x_i.

Learning TCPTs. Boutilier et al. [2] present a method for learning TCPTs by applying a recursive tree building algorithm each time a parent is added to a variable x_i in the BN. The TCPTs are generated using an MDL-based scoring function that trades off the complexity of the tree structure with the information gain that it provides. The tree building process is followed by a post-pruning step to remove unnecessary distinctions in the tree. Tree learning is a sub-step of the BN structure learning algorithm: each time a variable x_j is added to the parent set of another variable x_i, the TCPT for x_i is re-learned.

We propose an alternative TCPT learning approach, in which the BN structure learning process is redefined as the process of learning the TCPTs associated with individual variables. Instead of adding or removing edges from the network structure, we use adding and removing nodes in the individual TCPTs as the basic operations in the hill-climbing search. If the TCPT of x_i does not already contain an instance of x_j, then adding such an instance has the effect of adding an edge from x_j to x_i in the network. Similarly, removing the last occurrence of x_j from the TCPT of x_i is equivalent to removing the edge from x_j to x_i.

In our representation, each leaf node λ has an associated set of *Candidates*, which specifies the candidate variables that are available for further splitting the tree at that node. When refining the TCPT, the algorithm tries all possible variables in this set and then selects the refinement that offers the largest improvement in the MDL score.

Initially, the root starts with all $\bar{X}_j$s except itself in its *Candidates* set. As the TCPT is refined, the procedure RefineTree (Figure 2) propagates these candidates to the new leaf nodes after removing the candidate associated with the selected refinement. In Figure 1, the root $\bar{X}_{2,1}$, initially has two candidates for each of its outgoing edge: $Candidates = \{\bar{X}_1, \bar{X}_3\}$. When the candidate $\bar{X}_3$ is selected for refinement at edge v_{21}, the leaf is replaced with $\bar{X}_{3,1}$, and the candidate set of each of $\bar{X}_{3,1}$'s child leaf node is set to $\{\bar{X}_1\}$. On the other hand, when $\bar{X}_1$ is selected for refinement at edge v_{22}, the leaf node at that edge is replaced with $\bar{X}_{1,1}$, and each of its child leaf node's candidate set is set to $\{\bar{X}_3\}$.

The BN structure is learned by recursively splitting leaf nodes in the TCPTs. Each TCPT maintains a list $RefCand$, which lists the candidate nodes in the tree that can be further refined—i.e., leaf nodes whose *Candidates* sets are non-empty. Initially, this set contains only the root of the tree; it is updated as branches are added to the tree during the splitting process.

The optimal single-step refinement can be found by evaluating all possible refinements ($RefCand$s) for all variables in the BN, and choosing the one that most improves the MDL score. However, this is computationally intensive; therefore, we instead randomly choose the next BN variable to refine, and use the procedure ExtendTree (Figure 2) to select a leaf node to refine. The probability of a leaf node being selected for refinement is proportional to the size of the *Candidates* set at that node. The selected node is then refined using the candidate split that leads to the largest improvement in the MDL score of the tree. This process of selecting a variable and then refining its TCPT is performed until a local minimum is reached in the MDL score for the BN.

4 Learning BNs Using Abstraction Value Hierarchies

We next discuss AVHs in more detail, and then describe the ABS and TABS learning algorithms.

4.1 Attribute Value Hierarchies

An attribute value hierarchy (AVH) defines an IS-A hierarchy for a categorical feature value. The leaves of the AVH describe base-level values; these are the values that occur in the training set. The interior nodes describe abstractions of the base-level values. The intent is that the AVH is designed to define useful and meaningful abstractions in a particular domain.

Figure 3 shows an AVH for the Workclass attribute in a U.S. Census domain, which describes an individual's employer type. At the root, all workclass types are grouped together. Below this are three abstract workclass values—Self-employed, Government, and Unpaid—and one base-level value—Private. Each of the abstract values is further subdivided into the lower-level. As shown by

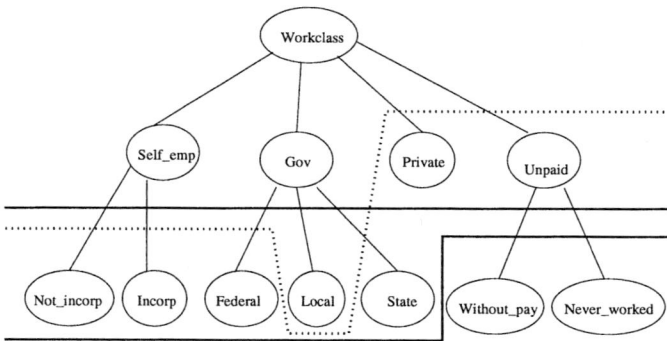

Fig. 3. AVH for the Workclass attribute, with legal (solid) and illegal (dotted) abstraction levels

this example, an AVH need not be balanced (i.e., path length from leaf values to the root can vary), and the branching factor (number of children) can vary within the hierarchy.

A cut through the tree defines an *abstraction level*, which is equivalent to a mutually exclusive and complete set of abstract attribute values. Figure 3 shows three different abstraction levels for the workclass attribute. Each abstraction level contains the set of values immediately above the cut line. The solid lines correspond to *legal* abstraction levels. The upper abstraction level includes the values Self_emp, Gov, Private, and Unpaid. The lower abstraction level includes the values Not_incorp, Incorp, Federal, Local, State, Private, and Unpaid. In this case, the lower abstraction level makes more distinctions than the upper abstraction level. The dotted line corresponds to an *illegal* abstraction level: for example, it includes both Gov and Local, which are not mutually exclusive.

The AVH helps to bias our search over appropriate abstractions for a categorical attribute. Without the hierarchy to guide us, we would need to consider arbitrary subsets of the base-level values for abstractions. Here, the AVH tells us which combinations of the values are meaningful (and, hopefully, useful in density estimation).

4.2 Abstraction-Based Search

There are two key tasks to be performed when learning a probabilistic model: scoring a candidate model and searching the space of possible models. We describe how these are done when CPTs associated with nodes can be represented at different abstraction levels.

The original ABS algorithm [6] extended the standard search over network structures as follows. When an edge is added to the network, the parent is added at its most abstract level (i.e., using the top-level values in the AVH). For example, if Workclass is chosen as a parent of another node, the initial abstraction level would be {Self_emp, Gov, Private, Unpaid}.

ABS extends the standard set of BN search operators—arc addition, arc deletion, and arc reversal—with two new operators: Refine(x_i, x_j, l) and Abstract

(x_i, x_j, l). The search process is a greedy search algorithm that repeatedly applies these five operators to the current network, evaluates the resulting network using the Bayesian score based on the MDL approach, and replaces the current network with the new one if the latter outscores the former.

If x_i is the parent of x_j, and its current abstraction level is $\{v'_{i1}, \ldots, v'_{ik'}\}$, Refine($x_i, x_j, l$) refines the lth value of the abstraction, v'_l by replacing v'_l with the set of values of its children in the AVH. During the search process, ABS attempts to apply Refine to each value of each abstraction in the current network. Refine only succeeds if the value it is applied to is an abstract value (i.e., if the value has children in the AVH).

Similarly, if x_i is the parent of x_j, and its current abstraction level is $\{v'_{i1}, \ldots, v'_{ik'}\}$, Abstract($x_i, x_j, l$) abstracts the lth value of the abstraction, v'_l by replacing v'_l and its siblings with the value of their parent in the AVH. Again, during search, ABS attempts to apply Abstract to each value of each abstraction level. Abstract only succeeds if the parent value is below the root node of the AVH and all of the value's siblings appear in the abstraction level. For example, in the lower abstraction level shown in Figure 3, neither condition is satisfied for the value Unpaid: its parent value is the root node of the hierarchy, and Unpaid's siblings Self_emp and Gov do not appear in the abstraction level.

4.3 The TCPT ABS Learning Algorithm

TCPTs take advantage of the fact that the value of a node can be independent of the values of a subset of its parents, given a local context. By incorporating AVHs into TCPT, we can also take advantage of the fact that certain parent values may have similar influences on the conditional probabilities of the child node. This reduces the branching factor of nodes with AVHs, and allows the decision about whether to make a distinction between certain values to be postponed until it is required. As a result, we are able to reduce the number of parameters that are required to be learned for the BN.

Our TCPT ABS (TABS) learning algorithm (Figure 4) extends the TCPT refining algorithm RefineTree described in Section 3, with some provisions for adding nodes from AVHs into the TCPT.

Procedure RefineTreeAbs($\lambda, \bar{X}_{new}$)
    1. remove λ from $RefCand$
    2. replace λ with $\bar{X}_{new}$, and create $|Val(\bar{X}_{new})|$ new leaf nodes below $\bar{X}_{new}$
    3. for each child λ' of $\bar{X}_{new}$,
        a. set $Candidates(\lambda') = Candidates(\lambda) - \{\bar{X}_{new}\}$
        b. for each child value v_{ij} of λ' in the AVH of $\bar{X}_{new}$,
            (i). if v_{ij} is an abstract value,
                add a new candidate V'_{ij} to $Candidates(\lambda')$
        c. add λ' to $RefCand$

Fig. 4. TABS learning algorithm: The RefineTreeAbs procedure

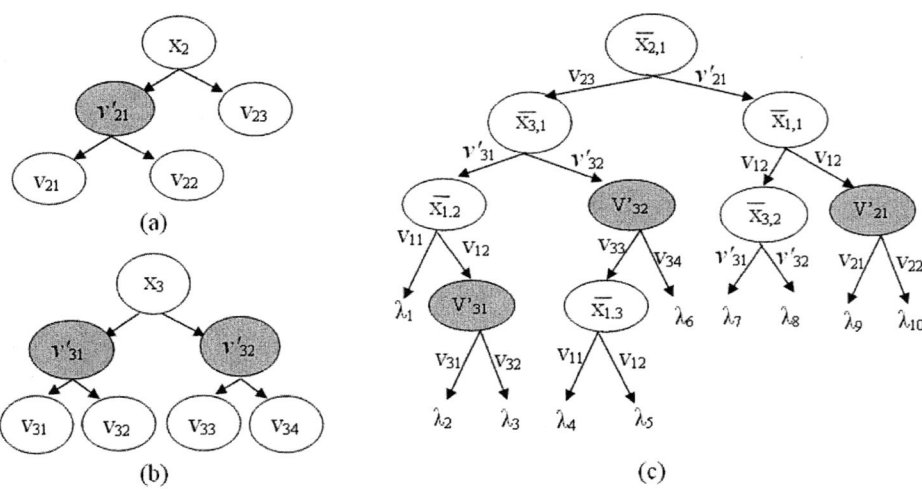

Fig. 5. (a) AVH of x_2; (b) AVH of x_3; (c) TCPT at variable x_4 learned with TABS-E

Suppose we have an AVH for x_i; the leaves of the AVH are the r_i base values of x_i, $\{v_{i1}, v_{i2}, \ldots, v_{ir_i}\}$. The internal, or abstract, values in the AVH are given by $\{v'_{i1}, v'_{i2}, \ldots\}$. Each abstract value corresponds to a set of base values. In TABS, when a new tree node is added to a TCPT, it is added at its most abstract level in the AVH. In other words, when a node $\bar{X}_{j,p}$ is added to a TCPT, its $Val(\bar{X}_{j,p})$ includes the set of values in the AVH of x_j that are the immediate children of the root node.

For example, suppose that the BN variables x_2 and x_3 in the BN of Figure 1(a) have associated AVHs, as shown in Figures 5(a) and (b). When these variables are used to split a TCPT node, the set of new branches will be $Val(\bar{X}_{2,1}) = \{v'_{21}, v_{23}\}$ and $Val(\bar{X}_{3,1}) = \{v'_{31}, v'_{32}\}$, as shown in Figure 5(c). Since the nodes associated with the abstract values can be further refined, we create candidate splits for the abstract values, V'_{jk}, and add these to $Candidates$ set of the leaf node associated with the abstract value v'_{jk}. This candidate refinement can be instantiated later through a refine step to split the tree. $Val(V'_{jk})$ is set to the set of values that are immediate descendants of v'_{jk} in the AVH of x_j.

In essence, this enables us to avoid making unnecessary distinctions among similar values until it is deemed necessary. For example, in Figure 5(c), when we add node $\bar{X}_{3,1}$, making a distinction between values v_{31} and v_{32} does not offer any gain in terms of the MDL score. However, once the tree is further split and node $\bar{X}_{1,2}$ is added, the distinction between v_{31} and v_{32} become more prominent and so we add the split V'_{31} in the next step.

5 Generating AVHs Using Agglomerative Clustering

It is not always possible to have access to sufficient domain knowledge or the services of a domain expert to create hierarchies of attribute values. Therefore,

Procedure BuildAVH(x_i,C)
for c from 1 to $r_i - 1$ do
  1. find the clusters C_p, C_q in C such that $Dist(C_p, C_q)$ is minimized
  2. create a new cluster $C_r = C_p \bigcup C_q$, and make this new cluster the parent of C_p and C_q in the hierarchy
  3. remove C_p and C_q from C for the next iteration

Fig. 6. Agglomerative clustering algorithm for deriving AVHs from training data

we have developed an agglomerative clustering-based method for deriving AVHs from the training data used to build the BN.

Given a set of instances D, our goal is to find a hierarchical clustering of the values for each variable x_i. First, we put all of the instances d_j that have a particular value for x_i into a cluster, resulting in r_i clusters: $C = \{C_1, C_2, \ldots, C_{r_i}\}$, where $C_k = \{d_j | x_{ij} = v_{ik}\}$. These are the initial "leaf clusters."

The BuildAVH procedure shown in Figure 6 uses average-link agglomerative clustering to iteratively merge pairs of clusters. The distance $Dist(C_p, C_q)$ is defined to be the distance between the centroids of the clusters. (Note that variable x_i is ignored in computing the centroids and distances when deriving the AVH for x_i.) For nominal attributes, we use the most frequently occurring value (mode) of the attribute as the centroid. We use the Hamming distance for measuring the distance between two centroids. The above technique is repeated for each attribute x_i, yielding a binary AVH.

6 Experimental Results

In this section, we describe results of experiments on three real-world data sets from the UC Irving Machine Learning Repository [9]: Mushroom, Nursery, and U.S. Census (ADULT).

Data Sets. The nursery data set (12960 instances) has nine nominal variables, six of which have associated expert-provided AVHs. This data set is the shallowest data set that we tested. Most of the AVHs have depth one with a maximum branching factor of three, except for the class variable, which has five values. The Mushroom data set (5644 instances) has 23 variables, 17 of which have associated expert-provided AVHs. This data set also has variables with hierarchies that are very shallow, but some variables have a higher branching factor (up to five). The ADULT data set (45222 instances), which is derived from U.S. Census data, has 14 variables (five continuous and nine nominal). We discretized the continuous variables manually, and created AVHs by hand for nine of the variables.

We also generated data-derived AVHs using the clustering technique described in Section 5. Since these AVHs are binary trees, they are much deeper than the expert-provided AVHs.

Experiments. We compared six different learning algorithms: (1) FLAT: Hill-climbing with "flat" CPTs—i.e., without abstraction or TCPTs; (2) ABS-E:

Table 1. Average log likelihood on the three data sets

| | Log Likelihood Score ||||||
	Nursery		Mushroom		Adult	
FLAT	-21769	±1.57	-8680.2	±5.58	-86740	±105.48
ABS-E	-21770	±3.72	-8683.4	±8.18	-86741	±138.92
ABS-D	-21762	±29.02	-8668.8	±7.95	-84058	±152.18
TCPT	-21736	± 1.55	-8594.5	±22.55	-86180	±21.91
TABS-E	-21735	±2.92	**-8557.0**	±15.58	-86165	±24.40
TABS-D	**-21634**	±24.11	-8610.4	±11.72	**-83670**	±105.24

ABS using expert-provided AVHs; (3) ABS-D: ABS using data-derived AVHs; (4) TCPT: TCPT learning; (5) TABS-E: TABS with expert-provided AVHs; and (6) TABS-D: TABS with data-derived AVHs. Five-fold cross-validation was used to estimate performance. Each algorithm was run five times on each split and the network with the best MDL score from these five was retained. The results reported below are the average results over test sets for the different cross-validation splits.

Discussion. Table 1 shows the average log likelihood and standard deviations for the 18 experiments that we ran. TCPTs consistently improve the log likelihood of learned BNs, relative to FLAT. (Note that log likelihoods of smaller magnitude correspond to a better fit to the data.) The use of AVHs alone improves the score although this is not true in all cases. However, note that the combination of the two, the TABS algorithms, are always the best performers. In two cases, on Nursery and Adult, the TABS-D algorithm gives significant improvement, while for Mushroom, the TABS-E algorithm gives the best improvement. The results on the most complex data set, ADULT, are the most striking.

Table 2 shows the average number of parameters and average number of edges in the learned BNs. The BNs learned by TCPT have more edges on average than those learned by FLAT. Similarly, ABS/TABS result in more edges than FLAT/TCPT (although in some cases, the increase is small). One would expect these more structurally complex BNs to require a larger number of parameters. However, in most cases, the resulting networks have more edges and *fewer* parameters. In particular, TABS-D consistently yields an equal or greater number of edges as TCPT, while significantly decreasing the number of parameters in all three domains. (On average, TABS-D uses 55.6% fewer parameters than TCPT.)

Table 2. Average number of parameters and edges for learned BNs

| | Nursery || Mushroom || Adult ||
	Params	Edges	Params	Edges	Params	Edges
FLAT	272.0	11.91	2280.2	43.33	2991.4	22.26
ABS-E	263.6	12.16	2114.8	45.06	2729.6	23.88
ABS-D	234.6	12.63	2446.2	44.93	2496.6	22.13
TCPT	369.4	29.25	1838.2	75.33	2591.2	44.6
TABS-E	286.6	32	1304.2	89.17	3236.6	52.84
TABS-D	**182.2**	29.4	**915.4**	106.4	**1763.4**	49.9

7 Related Work

Zhang and Honavar have presented methods for using AVHs to learn decision trees [13] and Naïve Bayes models [14]. Their decision tree learning method has some similarities to our TCPT construction process, in that it maintains local contexts at each tree node, and always uses the "most abstract" split available at a given point in the tree. However, their scoring method is based on information gain rather than an MDL score, and is applied to classification problems rather than density estimation. Zhang and Honavar allow the data to be represented with partially specified attribute values—that is, an attribute can take on any value in the AVH, not just leaf values. They impute leaf values probabilistically, based on global frequency counts. Our work could potentially be extended to permit partially specified values using a similar method. Alternatively, one might wish to use local frequency counts instead (i.e., impute values based on context-dependent counts), or to explicitly use "fractional instances" rather than imputing a single value to each partially specified attribute.

Kang et al. [10] give a method for generating AVTs using a hierarchical agglomerative clustering approach. However, since they are focused on pure classification tasks, the similarity measure for merging clusters is based only on the class distributions of the instances associated with a given group of values. (They use Jensen-Shannon divergence on these distributions to measure distance, although they point out that many other divergence measures are possible.) In contrast, we use a measure of distance in attribute space, making our similarity measure appropriate for non-classification (density estimation) tasks.

Previous methods for learning TCPTs typically allow each split in the tree to be either a *full split* (which includes a branch for each of the associated variable's values) or a *binary split* (which includes one branch for a selected value, and groups the remaining values into a second branch). The binary split is a type of naïve abstraction—but this abstraction is purely local (i.e., it does not take into account expert-provided knowledge or global knowledge about the similarity of attribute values), and is costly in terms of the number of possible abstractions that must be tested. Although we have focused on TCPTs in this paper, other variations of CSI representations, such as decision graphs [4] and decision tables [7] could also benefit from AVHs. In effect, AVHs provide additional knowledge—either from an expert in the case of expert-provided AVHs, or from the entire data set in the case of data-derived data—that can be used to identify groups of values that are likely to behave similarly.

8 Conclusions and Future Work

We have presented TABS, an extension to Abstraction-Based Search that integrates attribute value hierarchies (AVHs) with tree-structured conditional probability tables (TCPTs). We also described a clustering-based algorithm for constructing AVHs from the training data used for learning a BN. We showed that the use of AVHs significantly improves the accuracy of the learned BN and reduces the number of parameters required to represent the learned BN. In particular, TABS with the data-derived AVHs consistently yields BNs with the smallest number of parameters.

In future work, we plan to investigate variations to the tree-learning algorithm and to the clustering techniques for deriving AVHs, including non-binary agglomerative clustering. We also plan to extend our learning methods to permit partially specified (abstract) values in the data, and to support a decision graph representation of local structure.

Acknowledgements

Thanks to Jun Zhang of Iowa State University for providing the AVHs for Nursery and Mushroom data sets. This work was partially funded by NSF #0325329 and by UMBC's NSF ADVANCE grant. Lise Getoor was funded by NSF #0423845, with additional support from the National Geospatial Agency and the ITIC KDD program.

References

1. R. R. Bouckaert. Probabilistic network construction using the minimum description length principle. Technical Report RUU-CS-94-27, Utrecht University, 1994.
2. C. Boutilier, N. Friedman, M. Goldszmidt, and D. Koller. Context-specific independence in Bayesian networks. In *Proceedings of UAI-96*, pages 115–123, 1996.
3. D. M. Chickering, D. Geiger, and D. Heckerman. Learning Bayesian Networks is NP-Hard. Technical Report MSR-TR-94-17, Microsoft Research, November 1994.
4. D. M. Chickering, D. Heckerman, and C. Meek. A Bayesian approach to learning Bayesian networks with local structure. In *Proceedings of UAI-97*, pages 80–89, 1997.
5. G. F. Cooper and E. Herskovits. A Bayesian method for the induction of probabilistic networks from data. *Machine Learning*, 9(4):309–347, 1992.
6. M. desJardins, L. Getoor, and D. Koller. Using feature hierarchies in Bayesian network learning. In *Proceedings of SARA-02*, pages 260–270, 2000.
7. N. Friedman and M. Goldszmidt. Learning bayesian networks with local structure. In *Proceedings of UAI-96*, pages 252–262, 1996.
8. D. Heckerman. A Tutorial on Learning Bayesian Networks. Technical Report MSR-TR-95-06, Microsoft Research, March 1995.
9. S. Hettich, C.L. Blake, and C.J. Merz. UCI repository of machine learning databases, 1998.
10. D.K. Kang, A. Silvescu, J. Zhang, and V. Honavar. Generation of attribute value taxonomies from data for data-driven construction of accurate and compact classifiers. In *Proceedings of ICDM-04*, 2004.
11. W. Lam and F. Bacchus. Learning Bayesian belief networks: An approach based on the MDL principle. *Computational Intelligence*, pages 269–293, 1994.
12. J. Pearl. *Probabilistic Reasoning in Intelligent Systems: Networks of Plausible Inference*. Morgan Kaufmann, 1988.
13. J. Zhang and V. Honavar. Learning decision tree classifiers from attribute value taxonomies and partially specified data. In *Proceedings of ICML-03*, 2003.
14. J. Zhang and V. Honavar. AVT-NBL: An algorithm for learning compact and accurate naive Bayes classifiers from attribute value taxonomies and data. In *Proceedings of ICDM-04*, 2004.

Learning to Complete Sentences

Steffen Bickel, Peter Haider, and Tobias Scheffer

Humboldt-Universität zu Berlin, Department of Computer Science,
Unter den Linden 6, 10099 Berlin, Germany
{bickel, haider, scheffer}@informatik.hu-berlin.de

Abstract. We consider the problem of predicting how a user will continue a given initial text fragment. Intuitively, our goal is to develop a "tab-complete" function for natural language, based on a model that is learned from text data. We consider two learning mechanisms that generate predictive models from collections of application-specific document collections: we develop an N-gram based completion method and discuss the application of instance-based learning. After developing evaluation metrics for this task, we empirically compare the model-based to the instance-based method and assess the predictability of call-center emails, personal emails, and weather reports.

1 Introduction

This paper addresses the problem of predicting the succeeding words of an initial fragment of natural language text. This problem setting is motivated by applications that include repetitive tasks such as writing emails in call centers or letters in an administrative environment; many resulting documents are to some degree governed by specific underlying patterns that can be learned. The benefit of an assistance system to the user depends on both the number of helpful suggestions and the number of unnecessary distractions that they experience. Performance metrics for other text learning problems do not match the idiosyncrasies of this problem; we therefore have to discuss an appropriate evaluation scheme.

Generative N-gram language models provide a natural approach to the construction of sentence completion systems; in addition, instance-based learning can easily be applied to this problem. In order to gain insights on the benefit of sentence completion methods in various application areas, we conduct experiments using diverse document collections: a collection of call-center emails with many similar emails, weather reports, cooking recipes, and, on the other extreme, the disclosed Enron corpus of personal email communication of Enron's management staff.

The rest of this paper is organized as follows. We review related work in Section 2. In Section 3, we discuss the problem setting and appropriate performance metrics. We develop the N-gram-based completion method in Section 4. In Section 5, we discuss empirical results. Section 6 concludes.

2 Related Work

Shannon [13] analyzed the predictability of sequences of letters. He found that written English has a high degree of redundancy. Based on this finding, it is natural to ask whether it is possible to support users in the process of writing text by learning and predicting the intended next keystrokes, words, sentences, or even paragraphs. Darragh and Witten [1] have developed an *interactive keyboard* that uses the sequence of past keystrokes to predict the most likely succeeding keystrokes. Clearly, in an unconstrained application context, keystrokes can only be predicted with limited accuracy. In the specific context of entering URLs, completion predictions are commonly provided by web browsers [3].

Motoda and Yoshida [12] and Davison and Hirsh [2] developed a Unix shell which predicts the command stubs that a user is most likely to enter, given the current history of entered commands. Korvemaker and Greiner [9] have developed this idea into a system which predicts entire command lines. The Unix command prediction problem has also been addressed by Jacobs and Blockeel who predict the next command using variable memory Markov models [7].

In the context of *natural language*, several typing assistance tools for apraxic [5, 14] and dyslexic [11] persons have been developed. These tools provide the user with a list of possible word completions to select from. For these particular users, scanning and selecting from lists of proposed words is usually more efficient than typing. By contrast, scanning and selecting from many displayed options can slow down skilled writers [10, 11]. Assistance tools have furthermore been developed for translators. Computer aided translation systems combine a translation model and a language model in order to provide a (human) translator with a list of suggestions [4]. Grabski and Scheffer [6] have previously developed an indexing method that efficiently retrieves the sentence from a collection that is most similar to a given initial fragment.

3 Problem Setting

Given an initial text fragment, a predictor that solves the sentence completion problem has to conjecture *as much of the sentence that the user currently intends to write*, as is possible with high confidence—preferably, but not necessarily, the entire remainder. The corresponding learning problem is to find such a predictor, given a corpus that is governed by the same distribution of sentences.

What is an appropriate performance measure for this problem? The perceived benefit of an assistance system is highly subjective, but it is influenced by quantitative factors that we can measure. We define a system of two conflicting performance indicators: *precision* (the inverse risk of unnecessary distractions) and *recall* (the keystroke savings). Keystroke savings obtained by accepting suggestions and distraction caused by (rejected) suggestions contribute to the overall benefit of a system. However, the exact trade-off between the increased typing speed due to saved keystrokes and the time lost because of distractions is highly user-specific; any measurement of the actual time savings is a projection of these conflicting goals for a particular group of users.

For a given sentence fragment, a completion method may, but need not, cast a completion conjecture. Whether – and how many – words are suggested will typically be controlled by a confidence threshold. Given an individual sentence fragment, we consider the entire conjecture to be falsely positive if at least one word is wrong. This harsh view reflects previous results which indicate that selecting, and then editing, a suggested sentence can take longer than writing that sentence from scratch [10]. In a conjecture that is entirely accepted by the user, the entire string is a true positive. Note that a conjecture may contain only a part of the remaining sentence and therefore the *recall*, which refers to the length of the missing part of the current sentence, may be smaller than 1.

For a given test collection, precision and recall are defined in Equations 1 and 2. *Recall* is the fraction of saved keystrokes (disregarding the interface-dependent single keystroke that is most likely required to accept a suggestion); *precision* is the ratio of characters that the users have to scan for each character they accept. Varying the confidence threshold of a sentence completion method results in a *precision recall curve* that characterizes the system-specific trade-off between *keystroke savings* and *unnecessary distractions*.

$$Precision = \frac{\sum_{\text{accepted completions}} \text{string length}}{\sum_{\text{suggested completions}} \text{string length}} \quad (1)$$

$$Recall = \frac{\sum_{\text{accepted completions}} \text{string length}}{\sum_{\text{all queries}} \text{length of missing part}} \quad (2)$$

4 Algorithms for Sentence Completion

We derive our solution to the sentence completion problem based on a linear interpolation of N-gram models, and briefly discuss an instance-based method that provides an alternative approach and baseline for our experiments.

In order to solve the sentence completion problem with an N-gram model, we need to find the most likely word sequence $w_{t+1}, \ldots, w_{t+T}$ given a word N-gram model and an initial sequence $w_1, \ldots, w_t$; that is, we need to decode $\text{argmax}_{w_{t+1},\ldots,w_{t+T}} P(w_{t+1}, \ldots, w_{t+T} | w_1, \ldots, w_t)$. The N-th order Markov assumption constrains each w_t to be dependent on at most w_{t-N+1} through w_{t-1}. The individual $P(w_t | w_{t-N+1}, \ldots, w_{t-1})$ are the parameters of the model.

Learning Linearly Interpolated N-Gram Models.
Given a fixed Markov order N and a document collection, an N-gram model is learned by estimating the probability of all combinations of N words.

One solution to overcome sparsity problems of higher order N-grams is to use a weighted linear mixture of N-gram models, $1 \leq n \leq N$, Equation 3.

$$P(w_N | w_1, \ldots, w_{N-1}) = \lambda_1 P(w_N) + \sum_{n=2}^{N} \lambda_n P(w_N | w_{N-n+1}, \ldots, w_{N-1}) \quad (3)$$

We learn Models for all n, $1 \leq n \leq N$ on a training fraction, adjust the parameters λ_n such that the likelihood of a hold-out fraction is maximized, and retrain the N-gram models with these fixed λ_n on the entire data collection.

Efficient Decoding.
We have to find the most likely completion, $\text{argmax}_{w_{t+1},\ldots,w_{t+T}}$ $P(w_{t+1},\ldots,w_{t+T}|w_1,\ldots,w_t)$ *efficiently*, even though the size of the *search space* is |vocabulary size|^T. The auxiliary variable $\delta_{t,s}(w'_1,\ldots,w'_N|w_{t-N+2},\ldots,w_t)$ in Equation 4 quantifies the greatest possible probability over all arbitrary word sequences $w_{t+1},\ldots,w_{t+s}$, followed by the word sequence $w_{t+s+1} = w'_1,\ldots,w_{t+s+N} = w'_N$, conditioned on the initial word sequence $w_{t-N+2},\ldots,w_t$. Equation 5 utilizes the N-th order Markov assumption, in Equation 6, we introduce a new random variable w'_0 for w_{t+s}. We can now refer to the definition of δ and see the recursion in Equation 7.

$$\delta_{t,s}(w'_1,\ldots,w'_N|w_{t-N+2},\ldots,w_t) \quad (4)$$

$$= \max_{w_{t+1},\ldots,w_{t+s}} P(w_{t+1},\ldots,w_{t+s},w_{t+s+1}=w'_1,\ldots,w_{t+s+N}=w'_N|w_{t-N+2},\ldots,w_t)$$

$$= \max_{w_{t+1},\ldots,w_{t+s}} P(w'_N|w'_1,\ldots,w'_{N-1}) \quad (5)$$

$$P(w_{t+1},\ldots,w_{t+s},w_{t+s+1}=w'_1,\ldots,w_{t+s+N-1}=w'_{N-1}|w_{t-N+2},\ldots,w_t)$$

$$= \max_{w'_0} \max_{w_{t+1},\ldots,w_{t+s-1}} P(w'_N|w'_1,\ldots,w'_{N-1}) \quad (6)$$

$$P(w_{t+1},\ldots,w_{t+s-1},w_{t+s}=w'_0,\ldots,w_{t+s+N-1}=w'_{N-1}|w_{t-N+2},\ldots,w_t)$$

$$= \max_{w'_0} P(w'_N|w'_1,\ldots,w'_{N-1})\delta_{t,s-1}(w'_0,\ldots,w'_{N-1}|w_{t+N-2},\ldots,w_t) \quad (7)$$

Exploiting the N-th order Markov assumption, we can now express our target probability in terms of δ in Equation 8.

$$\max_{w_{t+1},\ldots,w_{t+T}} P(w_{t+1},\ldots,w_{t+T}|w_{t-N+2},\ldots,w_t) \quad (8)$$

$$= \max_{w'_1,\ldots,w'_N} \delta_{t,T-N}(w'_1,\ldots,w'_N|w_{t-N+2},\ldots,w_t)$$

The last N words in the most likely sequence are $\text{argmax}_{w'_1,\ldots,w'_N} \delta_{t,T-N}(w'_1,\ldots,w'_N|w_{t-N+2},\ldots,w_t)$. Variable Ψ, defined in Equation 9 collects the preceding most likely words; it can be determined in Equation 10. We have now found a Viterbi algorithm that is linear in T.

$$\Psi_{t,s}(w'_1,\ldots,w'_N|w_{t-N+2},\ldots,w_t) \quad (9)$$

$$= \text{argmax}_{w_{t+s}} \max_{w_{t+1},\ldots,w_{t+s-1}} P(w_{t+1},\ldots,w_{t+s},w_{t+s+1}=w'_1,\ldots,w_{t+s+N}=w'_N|w_{t-N+2},\ldots,w_t)$$

$$= \text{argmax}_{w'_0} \delta_{t,s-1}(w'_0,\ldots,w'_{N-1}|w_{t-N+2},\ldots,w_t) P(w'_N|w'_1,\ldots,w'_{N-1}) \quad (10)$$

The Viterbi algorithm starts with the most recently entered word w_t and moves iteratively into the future. The process terminates when the N-th token in the highest scored δ is a period, or when the highest δ score is below a threshold θ. In each step, Viterbi has to store and update |vocabulary size|^N many δ values – unfeasibly many except for very small N. Therefore, in Table 1 we develop a Viterbi beam search algorithm which is linear in T and in the beam width. When the globally most likely sequence $w^*_{t+1},\ldots,w^*_{t+T}$ has an initial subsequence $w^*_{t+1},\ldots,w^*_{t+s}$ which is not among the k most likely sequences of length s, then that optimal sequence is not found.

Table 1. Sentence completion with Viterbi beam search algorithm

Input: N-gram language model, initial sentence fragment $w_1, \ldots, w_t$, beam width k, confidence threshold θ.

1. Viterbi initialization:
   Let $\delta_{t,-N}(w_{t-N+1}, \ldots, w_t | w_{t-N+1}, \ldots, w_t) = 1$;
   Let $s = -N + 1$;
   $beam(s-1) = \{\delta_{t,-N}(w_{t-N+1}, \ldots, w_t | w_{t-N+1}, \ldots, w_t)\}$.
2. **Do** Viterbi recursion **until** break:
   (a) **For all** $\delta_{t,s-1}(w'_0, \ldots, w'_{N-1}|\ldots)$ in $beam(s-1)$, **for all** w_N in vocabulary, store $\delta_{t,s}(w'_1, \ldots, w'_N|\ldots)$ (Equation 7) in $beam(s)$ and calculate $\Psi_{t,s}(w'_1, \ldots, w'_N|\ldots)$ (Equation 10).
   (b) **If** $\operatorname{argmax}_{w_N} \max_{w'_1, \ldots, w'_{N-1}} \delta_{t,s}(w'_1, \ldots, w'_N|\ldots) = period$ **then** break.
   (c) **If** $\max \delta_{t,s}(w'_1, \ldots, w'_N | w_{t-N+1}, \ldots, w_t) < \theta$ **then** decrement s; break.
   (d) Prune all but the best k elements in $beam(s)$.
   (e) Increment s.
3. Let $T = s + N$. Collect words by path backtracking:
   $(w^*_{t+T-N+1}, \ldots, w^*_{t+T}) = \operatorname{argmax} \delta_{t,T-N}(w'_1, \ldots, w'_N|\ldots)$.
   For $s = T - N \ldots 1$: $w^*_{t+s} = \Psi_{t,s}(w^*_{t+s+1}, \ldots, w^*_{t+s+N} | w_{t-N+1}, \ldots, w_t)$.

Return $w^*_{t+1}, \ldots, w^*_{t+T}$.

Instance-based Sentence Completion

An alternative to N-gram models is to retrieve, from the training collection, the sentence that starts most similarly, and use its remainder as a completion hypothesis. The cosine similarity of the tfidf representation of the initial fragment to be completed, and an equally long fragment of each sentence in the training collection gives both a selection criterion for the nearest neighbor and a confidence measure that can be compared against a threshold in order to achieve a desired precision recall balance. Grabski and Scheffer [6] have developed an indexing structure that retrieves the most similar (in terms of cosine similarity) sentence fragment in sub-linear time.

5 Empirical Studies

We investigate (a) how N-gram models compare to the instance-based method in terms of precision/recall; (b) how well N-gram models complete sentences from collections with diverse properties. We use four document collections. The first contains emails sent by the customer center of a large online store [6] (7094 sentences). The second contains 3189 personal emails sent by Enron executive Jeff Dasovich, extracted from the Enron email corpus [8]. The third collection contains textual daily weather reports of five years. The last collection contains about 4000 cooking recipes.

We reserve 1000 sentences of each data set for testing and split the remaining sentences in training (75%) and tuning (25%) set for λ_n. We mix N-gram models up to an order of five. The beam width k is set to 20. We randomly draw 1000 sentences and a position at which we split it into initial fragment and remainder to be predicted. We loop over the number of words to predict, decode the most likely completion of that length, and provide a human evaluator with both, the true sentence as well as the initial fragment plus the current completion conjecture. The judges decide whether they would accept this prediction without any changes, given that they intend to write the actual sentence. For each judged prediction length, we record the threshold that would lead to that prediction; thus, we determine precision and recall for all thresholds.

Figure 1 compares the precision recall curves of the N-gram and instance-based methods. Note that the maximum possible recall is typically much smaller than 1. Recall measures the rate of keystroke savings; a value of 1 indicates that the user saves *all* keystrokes. Some of the precision recall curves have a concave

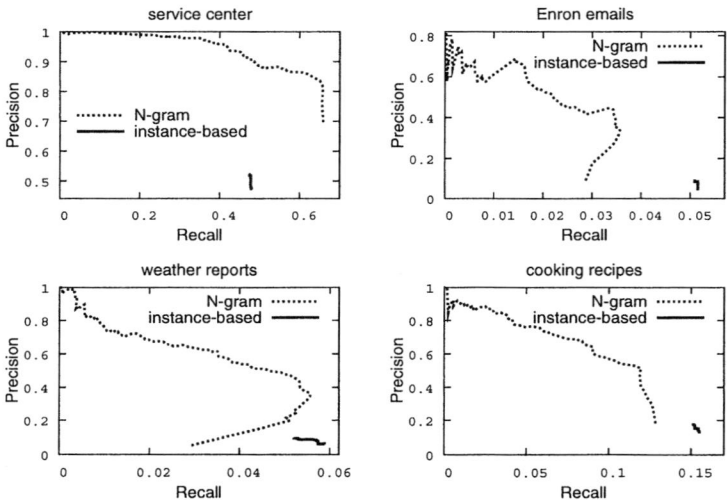

Fig. 1. Precision recall curves for N-gram and instance-based methods

shape. Decreasing the threshold value increases the number of predicted words, but it also increases the risk of at least one word being wrong. In this case, the entire sentence counts as an incorrect prediction, causing a decrease in both, precision and recall. Therefore – unlike in the standard information retrieval setting – recall does not increase monotonically when the threshold is reduced.

For three data collections, the instance-based learning method achieves the highest maximum recall (each conjecture predicts the entire remainder of the sentence—at a low precision), but for nearly all recall levels the N-gram model achieves a much higher precision. For practical applications, a high precision avoids distracting, wrong predictions. The N-gram model can be tuned to a wide range of different precision recall trade-offs (precision can often reach 1), whereas the threshold has little influence on precision and recall of the instance-based method. The standard error of the measurements is below 0.016.

How do precision and recall depend on the string length of the initial fragment? Figure 2 details this relationship. The performance of the instance-based method depends crucially on a long initial fragment. The N-gram model works best when the initial fragment is at least four $(N-1)$, but the model does not benefit from additional tokens.

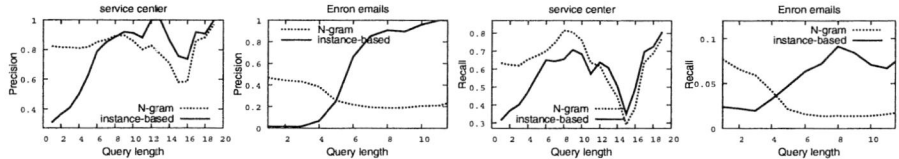

Fig. 2. Precision and recall dependent on string length of initial fragment (words)

The four text collections have diverse properties. The N-gram model performs remarkably on the service center emails. Users can save 60% of their keystrokes with 85% of all suggestions being entirely accepted by the users, or save 40% keystrokes at a precision of over 95%. For cooking recipes, users can save 8% keystrokes at 60% precision or 5% at 80% precision. For weather reports, possible keystroke savings are 2% at 70% correct suggestions or 0.8% at 80%. Finally, Jeff Dasovich of Enron can enjoy only a marginal benefit: below 1% of keystrokes are saved at 60% precision, or 0.2% at 80% precision.

We observe that these performance results correlate with the entropy of the data sets, and with the N-gram mixture weights. The service center data has an entropy of only 1.41 (*i.e.*, 1.41 bits are needed, on average, to encode the next token, given the four preceding tokens); they are excellently predictable. A mixing weight of 40% is assigned to the 3-gram, 30% to the 4-gram and 10% to the 5-gram model. The entropy of the cooking recipes and the weather reports are 4.14 and 4.67, respectively. About 25% probability mass are assigned to the each of the unigram, bigram, and trigram model.

For the Enron data, $\lambda_1 = 50\%$ is assigned to the unigram and $\lambda_2 = 30\%$ to the bigram; hence, the model can often just guess stop words that have a high prior probability. Jeff Dasovich's personal emails have an entropy of 7.17 and are therefore almost as unpredictable as Enron's share price. This argues that the entropy of a text collection is an excellent measure that indicates whether, for a given discourse area, a user will benefit from sentence completion.

6 Conclusion

We find precision (the number of suggested characters that the user has to read for every character that is accepted) and recall (the rate of keystroke savings) to be appropriate performance metrics for the problem of predicting subsequent words in a given initial fragment. We developed an efficient sentence completion method based on N-gram language models.

Our experiments lead to two main conclusions. (a) The N-gram based completion method has a better precision recall profile than the nearest neighbor method. It can be tuned to a wide range of trade-offs, a high precision can be obtained. (b) Whether sentence completion is helpful strongly depends on the diversity of the document collection. For service center emails, a keystroke saving of 60% can be achieved at 85% acceptable suggestions; by contrast, only a marginal keystroke saving of 0.2% can be achieved for Jeff Dasovich's personal emails at 80% acceptable suggestions. The entropy of the text is a strong indicator of the potential benefit of sentence completion that can easily be measured.

Acknowledgment. This work has been supported by the German Science Foundation DFG under grants SCHE540/10-1 and SCHE540/10-2.

References

1. J. Darragh and I. Witten. *The Reactive Keyboard*. Cambridge University Press, 1992.
2. B. Davison and H. Hirsh. Predicting sequences of user actions. In *AAAI/ICML Workshop on Predicting the Future: AI Approaches to Time Series Analysis*, 1998.
3. M. Debevc, B. Meyer, and R. Svecko. An adaptive short list for documents on the world wide web. In *Proceedings of the International Conference on Intelligent User Interfaces*, 1997.
4. G. Foster. *Text Prediction for Translators*. PhD thesis, University of Montreal, 2002.
5. N. Garay-Vitoria and J. Abascal. A comparison of prediction techniques to enhance the communication of people with disabilities. In *Proceedings of the 8th ERCIM Workshop User Interfaces For All*, 2004.
6. K. Grabski and T. Scheffer. Sentence completion. In *Proceedings of the ACM SIGIR Conference on Information Retrieval*, 2004.
7. N. Jacobs and H. Blockeel. User modelling with sequential data. In *Proceedings of the HCI International*, 2003.
8. B. Klimt and Y. Yang. The Enron corpus: A new dataset for email classification research. In *Proceedings of the European Conference on Machine Learning*, 2004.
9. B. Korvemaker and R. Greiner. Predicting Unix command lines: adjusting to user patterns. In *Proceedings of the National Conference on Artificial Intelligence*, 2000.
10. P. Langlais, M. Loranger, and G. Lapalme. Translators at work with transtype: Resource and evaluation. In *Proceedings of the third international Conference on Language Resources and Evaluation*, 2002.
11. T. Magnuson and S. Hunnicutt. Measuring the effectiveness of word prediction: The advantage of long-term use. Technical Report TMH-QPSR Volume 43, Speech, Music and Hearing, KTH, Stockholm, Sweden, 2002.
12. H. Motoda and K. Yoshida. Machine learning techniques to make computers easier to use. In *Proceedings of the Fifteenth International Joint Conference on Artificial Intelligence*, 1997.
13. C. Shannon. Prediction and entropy of printed english. In *Bell Systems Technical Journal, 30, 50-64*, 1951.
14. W. Zagler and C. Beck. FASTY - faster typing for disabled persons. In *Proceedings of the European Conference on Medical and Biological Engineering*, 2002.

The Huller: A Simple and Efficient Online SVM

Antoine Bordes[1,2] and Léon Bottou[2]

[1] Ecole Supérieure de Physique et de Chimie Industrielles, Paris, France
[2] NEC Labs America, Princeton, NJ, USA

Abstract. We propose a novel online kernel classifier algorithm that converges to the Hard Margin SVM solution. The same update rule is used to both add and remove support vectors from the current classifier. Experiments suggest that this algorithm matches the SVM accuracies after a single pass over the training examples. This algorithm is attractive when one seeks a competitive classifier with large datasets and limited computing resources.

1 Introduction

Support Vector Machines (SVMs) [1] are the successful application of the kernel idea [2] to large margin classifiers [3]. Early kernel classifiers [2] were derived from the perceptron [4], a simple and efficient online learning algorithm. Many authors have sought to replicate the SVM success by applying the large margin idea to such simple online algorithms [5, 6, 7, 8, 9, 10].

This paper proposes a simple and efficient online kernel algorithm which combines several desirable properties:

- Continued iterations of the algorithm eventually converge to the exact Hard Margin SVM classifier.
- Like most SVM algorithms, and unlike most online kernel algorithms, it produces classifiers with a bias term. Removing the bias term is a known way to simplify the numerical aspects of SVMs. Unfortunately, this can also damage the classification accuracy [11].
- Experiments on a relatively clean dataset indicate that a single pass over the training set is sufficient to produce classifiers with competitive error rates, using a fraction of the time and memory required by state-of-the-art SVM solvers.

Section 2 reviews the geometric interpretation of SVMs. Section 3 presents a simple update rule for online algorithms that converge to the SVM solution. Section 4 presents a critical refinement and describes its relation with previous online kernel algorithms. Section 5 reports experimental results. Finally section 6 discusses the algorithm capabilities and limitations.

2 Geometrical Formulation of SVMs

Figure 1 illustrates the geometrical formulation of SVMs [12, 13]. Consider a training set composed of patterns x_i and corresponding classes $y_i = \pm 1$. When

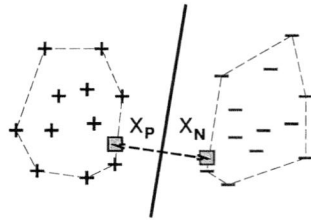 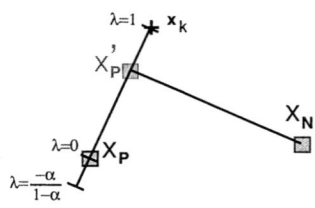

Fig. 1. Geometrical interpretation of Support Vector Machines

Fig. 2. Basic update of the HULLER

the training data is separable, the convex hulls formed by the positive and negative examples are disjoint. Consider two points X_P and X_N belonging to each convex hull. Make them as close as possible without allowing them to leave their respective convex hulls. The median hyperplane of these two points is the maximum margin separating hyperplane.

The points X_P and X_N can be parametrized as

$$\begin{array}{lll} X_P = \sum_{i \in \mathcal{P}} \alpha_i x_i & \sum_{i \in \mathcal{P}} \alpha_i = 1 & \alpha_i \geq 0 \\ X_N = \sum_{j \in \mathcal{N}} \alpha_j x_j & \sum_{j \in \mathcal{N}} \alpha_j = 1 & \alpha_j \geq 0 \end{array} \quad (1)$$

where sets $\mathcal{P}$ and $\mathcal{N}$ respectively contain the indices of the positive and negative examples. The optimal hyperplane is then obtained by solving

$$\min_{\alpha} \|X_P - X_N\|^2 \quad (2)$$

under the constraints of the parametrization (1). The separating hyperplane is then represented by the following linear discriminant function:

$$\hat{y}(x) = (X_P - X_N)\, x + (X_N X_N - X_P X_P)/2 \quad (3)$$

Since X_P and X_N are represented as linear combination of the training patterns, both the optimization criterion (2) and the discriminant function (3) can be expressed using dot products between patterns. Arbitrary non linear classifiers can be derived by replacing these dot products by suitable kernel functions. For simplicity, we discuss the simple linear setup and leave the general kernel framework to the reader.

3 Single Example Update

We now describe a first iterative algorithm that can be viewed as a simplification of the nearest point algorithms discussed in [14, 11]. The algorithm stores the position of points X_P and X_N using the parametrization (1). Each iteration considers a training pattern x_k and updates the position of X_P (when $y_k = +1$) or X_N (when $y_k = -1$.)

Figure 2 illustrates the case where x_k is a positive example (negative examples are treated similarly). The new point X'_P is *a priori* the point of segment

$[X_P, x_k]$ that minimizes the distance $\|X'_P - X_N\|^2$. The new point X'_P can be expressed as $X'_P = (1 - \lambda)X_P + \lambda x_k$ with $0 \leq \lambda \leq 1$.

This first algorithm is flawed: suppose that the current X_P contains a non zero coefficient α_k that in fact should be zero. The algorithm cannot reduce this coefficient by selecting example x_k. It must instead select other positive examples and slowly erode the coefficient α_k by multiplying it by $(1 - \lambda)$. A simple fix was proposed by Haffner [15]. If the coefficient α_k is strictly positive, we can safely let λ become slightly negative without leaving the convex hull. The revised constraints on λ are then $-\alpha_k/(1 - \alpha_k) \leq \lambda \leq 1$.

The optimal value of λ can be computed analytically by first computing the unconstrained optimum λ_u. When x_k is a positive example, solving the orthogonality equation $(X_P - X'_P)(X_N - X'_P) = 0$ for λ yields:

$$\lambda_u = \frac{(X_P - X_N)(X_P - x_k)}{(X_P - x_k)^2} = \frac{X_P^2 - X_N X_P - X_P x_k + X_N x_k}{X_P^2 + x_k^2 - 2X_P x_k} \quad (4)$$

Similarly, when x_k is a negative example, we obtain:

$$\lambda_u = \frac{(X_N - X_P)(X_N - x_k)}{(X_N - x_k)^2} = \frac{X_N^2 - X_N X_P - X_N x_k + X_P x_k}{X_N^2 + x_k^2 - 2X_N x_k} \quad (5)$$

A case by case analysis of the constraints shows that the optimal λ is:

$$\lambda = \min\left(1, \max\left(\frac{-\alpha_k}{1 - \alpha_k}, \lambda_u\right)\right) \quad (6)$$

Both expressions (4) and (5) depend on the quantities $X_P X_P$, $X_N X_P$, and $X_N X_N$ whose computation could be expensive. Fortunately there is a simple way to avoid this calculation: in addition to points X_P and X_N, our algorithm also maintains three scalar variable containing the values of $X_P X_P$, $X_N X_P$, and $X_P X_P$. Their values are recursively updated after each iteration: when x_k is a positive example,

$$\begin{aligned} X'_P X'_P &= (1-\lambda)^2 X_P X_P + 2\lambda(1-\lambda) X_P x_k + \lambda^2 x_k x_k \\ X_N X'_P &= (1-\lambda) X_N X_P + \lambda X_N x_k \\ X_N X_N &= X_N X_N \end{aligned} \quad (7)$$

and similarly, when x_k is a negative example,

$$\begin{aligned} X_P X_P &= X_P X_P \\ X'_N X_P &= (1-\lambda) X_N X_P + \lambda x_k X_P \\ X'_N X'_N &= (1-\lambda)^2 X_N X_N + 2\lambda(1-\lambda) X_N x_k + \lambda^2 x_k x_k \end{aligned} \quad (8)$$

Figure 3 shows the resulting update algorithm. The cost of one update is dominated by the calculation of $X_P x_k$ and $X_N x_k$. This calculation requires the dot products between x_k and all the current support vectors, i.e. the training examples x_i with non zero coefficient α_i in the parametrization (1).

UPDATE(k):
- Compute $X_P x_k$, $X_N x_k$, and $x_k x_k$.
- Compute λ_u using equations (4) or (5).
- Compute λ using equation (6)
- $\alpha_i \leftarrow (1 - \lambda)\alpha_i$ for all i such that $y_i = y_k$.
- $\alpha_k \leftarrow \alpha_k + \lambda$.
- Update $X_P X_P$, $X_N X_P$ and $X_N X_N$ using equation (7) or (8).

Fig. 3. Algorithm for the basic update

HULLER:
- Initialize X_P and X_N by averaging a few points.
  Compute initial $X_P X_P$, $X_N X_P$, and $X_N X_N$.
- Iterate:
  - Pick a random p such that $\alpha_p = 0$
  - **UPDATE(p)**
  - Pick a random r such that $\alpha_r \neq 0$
  - **UPDATE(r)**

Fig. 4. The HULLER algorithm

4 Insertion and Removal

Simply repeating this update for random examples x_k works poorly. Most of the updates do nothing because they involve examples that are not support vectors and have no vocation to become support vectors. A closer analysis reveals that the update operation has two functions:

– Performing an update for an example x_k such that $\alpha_k = 0$ represents an attempt to insert this example into the current set of support vectors. This occurs when the optimal λ is greater than zero, that is, when the point x_k violates the SVM margin conditions.
– Performing an update for an example x_k such that $\alpha_k \neq 0$ will optimize the current solution and possibly remove this example from the current set of support vectors. The removal occurs when the optimal λ reaches its (negative) lower bound.

Recent work on kernel perceptrons [10] also rely on two separate processes to insert and remove support vectors from the expression of the current separating hyperplane. This paper discusses a situation where both functions are implemented by the same update rule (figure 2). Picking the examples x_k randomly gives a disproportionate weight to the insertion function.

The HULLER algorithm, figure 4, corrects this imbalance by allocating an equivalent computing time to both functions. First, it picks a random example that is not a current support vector and attempts to insert it into the current set of support vectors. Second, it picks a random example that is a current support vector and attempts to remove it from the current set of support vectors. This simple modification has a dramatic effect on the convergence speed.

5 Experiments

The HULLER algorithm was implemented in C and benchmarked against the state-of-the-art SVM solver LIBSVM[1] on the well known MNIST[2] handwritten digit dataset. All experiments were run with a RBF kernel width parameter $\gamma = 0.005$. Both LIBSVM and the HULLER implementation use the same code to compute the kernel values and similar strategies to cache the frequently used kernel values. The cache size was initially set to 256MB.

Figure 5 reports the experimental results on the ten problems consisting of classifying each of the ten digit category against all other categories. The HULLER algorithm was run in epochs. Each epoch sequentially scans the randomly permuted MNIST training set and attempts to insert each example into the current set of support vectors (first update operation in figure 4). After each insertion attempt, the algorithm attempts to remove a random support vector (second update operation in figure 4.)

The HULLER×1 results were obtained after a single epoch, that is after processing each example once. The HULLER×2 results were obtained after two epochs. All results are averages over five runs.

The HULLER×2 test errors (top left graph in figure 5) closely match the LIBSVM solution. This is confirmed by counting the number of support vectors (bottom left graph), The HULLER×2 computing times usually are slightly shorter than the already fast LIBSVM computing times (top right graph).

The HULLER×1 test errors (top left graph in figure 5) are very close to both the HULLER×2 and LIBSVM test errors. Standard paired significance tests indicate that these small differences are not significant. This accuracy is achieved after less than half the LIBSVM running time, and, more importantly, after a single sequential pass over the training examples. The HULLER×1 always yields a slightly smaller number of support vectors (bottom left graph). We believe that a single HULLER epoch fails to insert a few examples that appear as support vectors in the SVM solution. A second epoch recaptures most missing examples.

Neither the HULLER×1 or HULLER×2 experiments yield the exact SVM solution. On this dataset, the HULLER typically reaches the SVM solution after five epochs. The corresponding computing times are not competitive with those achieved by LIBSVM.

These results should also be compared with results obtained with a theoretically justified kernel perceptron algorithm. Figure 5 contains results obtained with the AVERAGED PERCEPTRON [5] using the same kernel and cache size. The first epoch runs very quickly but does not produce competitive error rates. The AVERAGED PERCEPTRON approaches[3] the LIBSVM or HULLER×1 accuracies after ten epochs[4]. The corresponding training times stress the importance of the kernel cache size. When the cache can accomodate the dot products of all examples with all support vectors, additional epochs require very little computation. When this is not the case, the AVERAGED PERCEPTRON times are not competitive.

---

[1] http://www.csie.ntu.edu.tw/~cjlin/libsvm
[2] http://yann.lecun.com/exdb/mnist
[3] This is consistent with the empirical results reported in [5] (table 3).
[4] The Averaged Perceptron theoretical guarantees only hold for a single epoch.

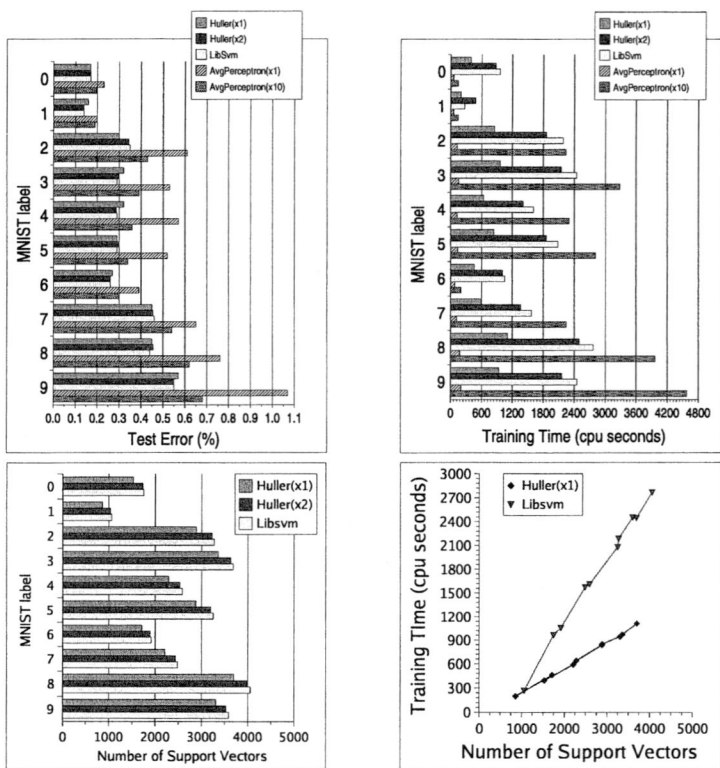

Fig. 5. MNIST results for the HULLER (one and two epochs), for LIBSVM, and for the AVERAGED PERCEPTRON (one and ten epochs). Top left: test error accuracies. Top right: training time. Bottom left: number of support vectors. Bottom right: training time as a function of the number of support vectors.

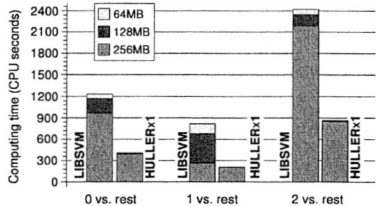

Fig. 6. Computing times with various cache sizes. Each color indicates the additional time required when reducing the cache size. The HULLER times remain virtually unchanged.

Figure 6 shows how reducing the cache size affects the computing time. Whereas LIBSVM experiences significantly increased training times, the HULLER training times are essentially unchanged. The most dramatic case is the separation of digit "1" versus all other categories. The initial 256MB cache size is sufficient for holding all the kernel values required by LIBSVM. Under these condition, LIBSVM runs almost as quickly as the HULLER×1. Reducing the kernel cache size to 128MB doubles the LIBSVM training time and does not change the HULLER training times.

A detailed analysis of the algorithms indicate that LIBSVM runs best when the cache contains all the dot products involving a potential support vector and an arbitrary example: memory requirements grow with both the number of support vectors and the number of training examples. The HULLER runs best when the cache contains all the dot products involving two potential support vectors: the memory requirements grow with the number of support vectors only. This indicates that the HULLER is best suited for problems involving a large separable training set.

6 Discussion

Fast start versus deep optimization. The HULLER processes many more examples during the very first training stages. After processing the first pair of examples, the SMO core of LIBSVM must compute 120000 dot products to update the example gradients and choose the next pair. During the same time, the HULLER processes at least 500 examples. By the time LIBSVM has reached the fifth pair of examples, the HULLER has processed a minimum of 1500 fresh examples. Online kernel classifiers without removal step tend to slow down sharply because the number of support vectors increases quickly. The removal step ensures that the number of current support vectors does not significantly exceed the final number of support vectors.

To attain the exact SVM solution with confidence, the HULLER also must compute all the dot products it did not compute in the early stages. On the other hand, when the kernel cache size is large enough, LIBSVM already knows these values and can use this rich local information to move more judiciously. This is why LIBSVM outperforms the huller in the final stages of the optimization. Nevertheless, the HULLER produces competitive classifiers well before reaching the point where it gets outpaced by state-of-the-art SVM optimization packages such as LIBSVM.

Noisy datasets. The HULLER addresses the hard margin SVM problem and therefore performs poorly on noisy datasets [16]. Most online kernel classifiers share this limitation. However, soft margin support vector machines *with quadratic slacks* [16] can be implemented as hard margin support vector machines with a modified kernel $K_C(\boldsymbol{x}_i, \boldsymbol{x}_j) = K(\boldsymbol{x}_i, \boldsymbol{x}_j) + \frac{1}{C}\delta_{ij}$. However, the resulting classifier is not directly comparable to the standard soft-margin SVM with linear slacks.

7 Conclusion

The HULLER is a novel online kernel classifier algorithm that converges to the Hard Margin SVM solution. Experiments suggest that it matches the SVM accuracies after a single pass over the training examples. Time and memory requirements are then modest in comparison to state-of-the-art SVM solvers.

Acknowledgment. Part of this work was funded by NSF grant CCR-0325463.

References

1. Vapnik, V.N.: The Nature of Statistical Learning Theory. Springer Verlag, New York (1995)
2. Aizerman, M.A., Braverman, É..M., Rozonoér, L.I.: Theoretical foundations of the potential function method in pattern recognition learning. Automation and Remote Control **25** (1964) 821–837
3. Vapnik, V., Lerner, A.: Pattern recognition using generalized portrait method. Automation and Remote Control **24** (1963) 774–780
4. Rosenblatt, F.: The perceptron: A probabilistic model for information storage and organization in the brain. Psychological Review **65** (1958) 386–408
5. Freund, Y., Schapire, R.E.: Large margin classification using the perceptron algorithm. In Shavlik, J., ed.: Machine Learning: Proceedings of the Fifteenth International Conference, San Francisco, CA, Morgan Kaufmann (1998)
6. Frieß, T.T., Cristianini, N., Campbell., C.: The kernel Adatron algorithm: a fast and simple learning procedure for support vector machines. In Shavlik, J., ed.: 15th International Conf. Machine Learning, Morgan Kaufmann Publishers (1998) 188–196
7. Gentile, C.: A new approximate maximal margin classification algorithm. Journal of Machine Learning Research **2** (2001) 213–242
8. Li, Y., Long, P.: The relaxed online maximum margin algorithm. Machine Learning **46** (2002) 361–387
9. Crammer, K., Singer, Y.: Ultraconservative online algorithms for multiclass problems. Journal of Machine Learning Research **3** (2003) 951–991
10. Crammer, K., Kandola, J., Singer, Y.: Online classification on a budget. In Thrun, S., Saul, L., Schölkopf, B., eds.: Advances in Neural Information Processing Systems 16. MIT Press, Cambridge, MA (2004)
11. Keerthi, S.S., Shevade, S.K., Bhattacharyya, C., Murthy, K.R.K.: A fast iterative nearest point algorithm for support vector machine classifier design. Technical Report Technical Report TR-ISL-99-03, Indian Institute of Science, Bangalore (1999) http://guppy.mpe.nus.edu.sg/~mpessk/npa_tr.ps.gz.
12. Bennett, K.P., Bredensteiner, E.J.: Duality and geometry in SVM classifiers. In Langley, P., ed.: Proceedings of the 17th International Conference on Machine Learning, San Francisco, California, Morgan Kaufmann (2000) 57–64
13. Crisp, D.J., Burges, C.J.C.: A geometric interpretation of ν-SVM classifiers. In Solla, S.A., Leen, T.K., Müller, K.R., eds.: Advances in Neural Information Processing Systems 12, MIT Press (2000)
14. Gilbert, E.G.: Minimizing the quadratic form on a convex set. SIAM J. Control **4** (1966) 61–79
15. Haffner, P.: Escaping the convex hull with extrapolated vector machines. In Dietterich, T., Becker, S., Ghahramani, Z., eds.: Advances in Neural Information Processing Systems 14, Cambridge, MA, MIT Press (2002) 753–760
16. Cortes, C., Vapnik, V.: Support vector networks. Machine Learning **20** (1995) 273–297

Inducing Hidden Markov Models to Model Long-Term Dependencies

Jérôme Callut and Pierre Dupont

Department of Computing Science and Engineering,
INGI, Université catholique de Louvain,
Place Sainte-Barbe 2,
B-1348 Louvain-la-Neuve, Belgium
{jcal, pdupont}@info.ucl.ac.be

Abstract. We propose in this paper a novel approach to the induction of the structure of Hidden Markov Models. The induced model is seen as a lumped process of a Markov chain. It is constructed to fit the dynamics of the target machine, that is to best approximate the stationary distribution and the mean first passage times observed in the sample. The induction relies on non-linear optimization and iterative state splitting from an initial order one Markov chain.

Keywords: HMM topology induction, Partially observable Markov models, Mean first passage times, Lumped Markov process, State splitting algorithm.

1 Introduction

Hidden Markov Models (HMMs) are widely used in many pattern recognition areas, including applications to speech recognition [10], biological sequence modeling [4], information extraction [5,6] and optical character recognition [8], to name a few. In most cases, the model structure, also referred to as topology, is defined according to some prior knowledge of the application domain. Automatic techniques for inducing the HMM topology are interesting as the structures are sometimes hard to define *a priori* or need to be tuned after some task adaptation. The work described here presents a new approach towards this objective.

Previous works with HMMs mainly concentrated either on hand-built models (*e.g.* [5]) or heuristics to refine predefined structures combined with EM estimation [6]. More principled approaches are the Bayesian merging technique due to Stolcke [12] and the maximum likelihood state-splitting method of Ostendorf and Singer [9]. The former approach however has not been shown to clearly outperform alternative approaches while the latter is specific to the subclass of left-to-right HMMs modeling speech signals.

The present contribution describes a novel approach to the structural induction of HMMs. The general objective is to induce the structure and to estimate the parameters of a HMM from a sample assumed to have been drawn from an unknown target HMM. The goal however is not the identification of the target model but the induction of a model sharing with the target the main features of the distribution it generates. We restrict here our attention to features that can be deduced from the sample. These features are closely related to fundamental quantities of a Markov process, namely the *stationary distribution* and *mean first passage times* (MFPT). In other words, the induced model is built to fit the dynamics of the target machine observed in the sample, not necessarily to match its structure.

Section 2 reviews some useful definitions coming from the theory of discrete Hidden Markov Models and Markov Chains. We use here a specific representation class for distributions generated by HMMs, called *Partially Observable Markov Models* (POMMs). This class is general enough since any discrete HMM can equivalently be represented by a POMM [2].

HMMs are able to model a class of distributions broader than finite order Markov chains. In particular, section 3 describes why HMMs, with an appropriate topology, are well suited to represent long term probabilistic dependencies in a compact way. We also argue why accurate modeling of these dependencies cannot be achieved through the classical approach of Baum-Welch estimation of a fully connected model. These observations motivate the use of MFPT to guide the search of an appropriate model. The resulting induction algorithm is presented in section 4. Comparative results given in [3] illustrate the superiority of POMM induction over variable order Markov chains (equivalent to back-off smoothed Ngrams) and EM estimation of a fully connected HMM.

2 Partially Observable Markov Models, Markov Chains and Lumped Processes

We introduce here Partially Observable Markov Models and we review some fundamental notions of the Markov chains theory.

Definition 1 (POMM). *A Partially Observable Markov Model (POMM) is a HMM $M = \langle \Sigma, Q, A, B, \iota \rangle$ where Σ is an alphabet, Q is a set of states, $A : Q \times Q \to [0,1]$ is a mapping defining the probability of each transition, $B : Q \times \Sigma \to [0,1]$ is a mapping defining the emission probability of each letter on each state, and $\iota : Q \to [0,1]$ is a mapping defining the initial probability of each state. Moreover, the emission probabilities satisfy: $\forall q \in Q, \exists a \in \Sigma$ such that $B(q,a) = 1$.*

In other words, each state of a POMM only emits a single letter. This model is called *partially* observable since, in general, several distinct states can emit the same letter. As for a HMM, the observation of a string emitted during a random walk does not allow one to identify the states from which each letter was emitted. However, the observations define *state subsets* from which each letter may have been emitted. Any distribution generated by a HMM with $|Q|$ states over an alphabet Σ can be represented by a POMM with $\mathcal{O}(|Q|.|\Sigma|)$ states [2].

The notion of POMM is closely related to a standard Markov Chain (MC). Indeed, in the particular case where all states emit a different letter, the process of a POMM is fully observable. Moreover the Markov property is satisfied as, by definition, the probability of any transition only depends on the current state. Some fundamental properties of a Markov chain are recalled hereafter and the links between a POMM and a MC are further detailed. A MC can be represented by a 3-tuple $T = \langle Q, A, \iota \rangle$ where Q is a finite set of states, A is a $|Q| \times |Q|$ transition probability matrix and ι is a $|Q|$−dimensional vector representing the initial probability distribution. The *stationary distribution* and *mean first passage times* are two fundamental quantities characterizing the dynamics of a Markov chain[1]. The stationary distribution is a $|Q|$−dimensional stochastic vector $\boldsymbol{\pi}$ such that $\boldsymbol{\pi}^T A = \boldsymbol{\pi}^T$. The q-th entry of $\boldsymbol{\pi}$ can be interpreted as the expected proportion of the time the Markov process in steady-state reaches state q. Given two states q and q', the Mean First Passage Time (MFPT) $M_{qq'}$ is the expected number of steps before reaching state q' for the first time while leaving initially from state q.

Given a MC, a partition can be defined on its state set and the resulting process is said to be *lumped*.

Definition 2 (Lumped process). *Given a regular MC, $T = \langle Q, A, \iota \rangle$, let $q^{(t)}$ be the state reached at time t during a random walk in T. The set $\kappa = \{\kappa_1, \kappa_2, \ldots, \kappa_r\}$ denotes a partition of the set of states Q. The function $K_\kappa = Q \to \kappa$ maps the state q to the block of κ that contains q. The lumped process $T/\!/\kappa$ outcomes $K_\kappa(q^{(t)})$ at time t.*

While the states are fully observable during a random walk in a MC, a lumped process is associated with random walks where only state *subsets* are observed. In this sense, the lumped process makes the MC only partially observable as in the case of a POMM. Conversely, a random walk in a POMM can be considered as a lumped process of its underlying MC with respect to an *observable partition* of its state set. Each block of the observable partition corresponds to the state(s) emitting a specific letter. In this case, both models define the same string distribution. The induction algorithm presented in section 4 is based on the MFPT extended to lumped processes.

Definition 3 (MFPT for a lumped process). *Given a regular MC $T = \langle Q, A, \iota \rangle$, κ a partition of Q and κ_i, κ_j two blocks of κ, an absorbing MC T^{κ_j} is created from T by transforming every state of κ_j to be absorbing. Furthermore, let $\boldsymbol{w}^{\kappa_j}$ be the MTA vector of T^{κ_j}. The mean first passage time $M_{ij}/\!/\kappa$ from κ_i to κ_j in the lumped process $T/\!/\kappa$ is defined as follows: $M_{ij}/\!/\kappa = \sum_{q \in \kappa_i} \frac{\pi_q}{\pi_{\kappa_i}} w_q^{\kappa_j}$ if $\kappa_i \neq \kappa_j$ and $M_{ii}/\!/\kappa = \frac{1}{\pi_{\kappa_i}}$, where π_q is the stationary distribution of state q in T, $\pi_{\kappa_i} = \sum_{q \in \kappa_i} \pi_q$ is the stationary distribution of the block κ_i in the lumped process $T/\!/\kappa$ and $\boldsymbol{w}^{\kappa_j}$ is the mean time to absorption vector related to κ_j [3,7].*

---

[1] We focus here on *regular* MCs, which are MCs with strongly connected transition graphs and no periodic states [7].

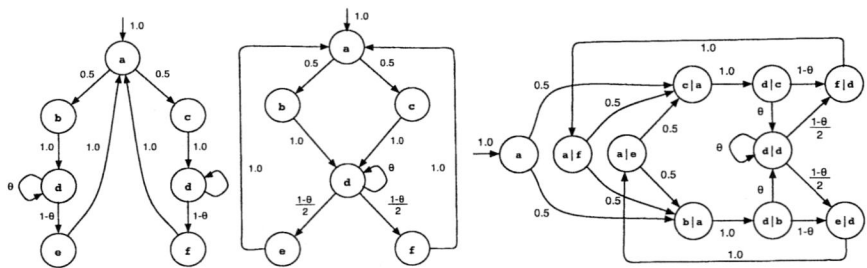

Fig. 1. A parametric POMM T_θ (left) modeled by an order 1 MC (center) or an order 2 MC (right)

3 Modeling Long-Term Probabilistic Dependencies

A stochastic process $\{X_t | t \in \mathbb{N}\}$ contains long-term dependencies if an outcome at time t significantly depends on an outcome that occurred at a much earlier time t': $P(X_t | X_{t-1}, \ldots, X_{t'}) \neq P(X_t | H)$ when $H = \{X_{t-1}, \ldots, X_{t-p}\}$ and $p < t - t'$. Hence, the *relevant history size* for such a process is defined as the minimal size of H such that $P(X_t | X_{t-1}, \ldots, X_{t'}) = P(X_t | H)$, $\forall t, t' \in \mathbb{N}, t' < t$. When the size of the relevant history is bounded, Markov chains of a sufficient order can model the long-term dependencies. On the other hand, if a conditioning event $X_{t'}$ can be arbitrarily far in the past, more powerful models such as HMMs or POMMs are required.

3.1 Modeling Long-Term Dependencies with Finite Order MC

Let us consider the parametric POMM T_θ displayed on the left of Figure 1. Emission of e or f in this model depends on whether b or c was emitted right before the last consecutive d's. Depending on the number of consecutive d's, the b or c outcomes can be arbitrarily far in the past. In other words, the size of the relevant history (*i.e.* the number of consecutive d's + 1) is unbounded. The expected number of consecutive d's is however finite and given by $\sum_{i=0}^{\infty} \theta^i = \frac{1}{1-\theta}$. Consequently, the expected size of the relevant history is $\frac{1}{1-\theta} + 1$. It should be noted that when $\theta = 0$, T_θ can be modeled accurately by an order 2 MC[2] since the relevant history size equals 2.

A model would badly fit the distribution defined by T_θ if it would first emit f rather than e after having emitted b. The probability of such an event is $P_{error} = P(t_f < t_e | X_t = b)$ where t_f and t_e denote the respective times of the first f or e after the outcome b. In the target model T_θ, $P_{error} = 0$. If the same process is modeled by an order 1 MC (center of Figure 1), $P_{error} = 0.5$. Indeed, when the process reaches state d, there is an equal probability to reach states e or f. In particular, these probabilities do not depend on previous emissions of b or c.

---

[2] A state label b|a in an order 2 MC means that the process emits b after having emitted a. The probability of the transition from state b|a to state d|b encodes the second order dependence $P(X_t = d | X_{t-1} = b, X_{t-2} = a)$.

An order 2 MC, as depicted on the right of Figure 1, would have $P_{error} = 0.475$ when $\theta = 0.95$. In general, the error of an order p MC is given by $P_{error} = \frac{\theta^{p-1}}{2}$. For instance, when $\theta = 0.95$, the expected size of the relevant history is 21 and P_{error} for such a model is still 0.17. Bounding the error probability to 0.1 would require to estimate a MC of order $p = \lceil \log_{0.95}(0.2) + 1 \rceil = 33$. An accurate estimate of such a model requires a huge amount of training data, very unlikely to be available in practice. Hence, POMMs and HMMs can better model long-term dependencies when the relevant history size is unbounded.

3.2 Topology Matters to Fit Long-Term Dependencies with HMMs

Bengio has shown that the use of a good HMM topology is crucial in order to model long term dependencies [1]. Indeed, the classical Baum-Welch algorithm applied to a fully connected graph is hindered by a phenomenon of diffusion of credit: the probability of being in a state at time t becomes gradually independent of the states reached at a previous time $t' \ll t$. In other words, the dependencies on the past outcomes of the process ends up vanishing. This phenomenon is related to the powers of the transition matrix A used in the forward and backward recursions of the Baum-Welch algorithm. Let ι_t be a row vector representing the distribution of being in each state at time t. This distribution d steps further is given by $\iota_{t+d} = \iota_t A^d$. If the successive powers of A converge quickly to a rank 1 matrix[3] then ι_{t+d} becomes independent of ι_t. In such a case, the estimation algorithm is likely to be stuck in an inappropriate local minimum of the likelihood function.

For a primitive matrix[4] A, the rate of convergence to rank 1 can be characterized using the Perron-Frobenius theorem [11]. It implies that a primitive stochastic matrix has a unique eigenvalue equal to 1 and that all other eigenvalues are strictly smaller than 1 (in absolute value). If the rank of A is r, then the spectral decomposition of A is given by $A = \lambda_1 U_1 V_1^T + \ldots + \lambda_r U_r V_r^T$, where λ_i is the i-th largest eigenvalue in absolute value and U_i, V_i are respectively the right-hand and left-hand eigenvectors associated with λ_i. Furthermore, the spectral decomposition of A^d is given by $A^d = \lambda_1^d U_1 V_1^T + \ldots + \lambda_r^d U_r V_r^T$ that is, taking A to the power d amounts to take its eigenvalues to the power d. Consequently, while taking the successive powers of A, $\lambda_1 = 1$ remains unchanged and all other eigenvalues are decreasing until cancellation. The rate of convergence to rank 1 follows a geometric progression with a ratio that can be approximated by the second[5] largest eigenvalue λ_2.

Classically, the Baum-Welch algorithm is initialized with a uniform random matrix[6]. Such a matrix typically has a very low λ_2. The Baum-Welch algorithm is thus badly conditioned to learn long-term dependencies when initialized in this way. On the other hand, initializing this algorithm with a matrix having λ_2 close to 1 requires prior knowledge of the model topology.

---
[3] All rows of a rank 1 stochastic matrix are equal.
[4] The transition matrix of a regular MC is primitive.
[5] In the case of the POMM T_θ of Figure 1, $\lambda_2 = \theta$.
[6] Each entry is uniformly drawn in [0, 1] and rows are normalized to sum up to 1.

Table 1. MFPT in $T_{0.95}$ (left), modeled by an order 1 MC (center) or an order 2 MC (right)

$T/\!/\kappa$	e	f
b	21.0	67.0
c	67.0	21.0

MC_1	e	f
b	44.0	44.0
c	44.0	44.0

MC_2	e	f
b	42.85	45.15
c	45.15	42.85

3.3 Long-Term Dependencies and MFPT

The MFPT in a lumped process $T/\!/\kappa$ contains information about the long-term dynamics of the process. Indeed, the MFPT from the block κ_b to the block κ_e is an expectation of the length of random walks starting with b before emitting e for the first time. Let us assume that the emission of e is conditioned by the fact that the process has first emitted b. The MFPT from b to e is equal to the expected length of the relevant history to predict e from b. Table 1 shows some interesting MFPT in the example T_θ of Figure 1 with $\theta = 0.95$. In the target T_θ, $M_{be} = M_{cf}$ is equal to the expected size of the relevant history (21, see section 3.1). Furthermore, there is a rather long expected time between the outcomes b and f (equivalently between c and e). When T_θ is approximated by an order 1 MC, $M_{be} = M_{bf} = M_{ce} = M_{cf} = 44$. This means that independently of whether (b or c) were emitted, the outcomes e and f are expected to occur 44 steps later. An order 2 MC only slightly improves the fit to the correct MFPT with respect to an order 1 model.

4 POMM Induction to Model Long-Term Dependencies

A random walk in a POMM can be seen as its underlying MC lumped with respect to the observable partition, as detailed in section 2. We present here an induction algorithm making use of this relation. Given a data sample, assumed to have been drawn from a target POMM TP, our induction algorithm estimates a model EP fitting the dynamics of the MC related to TP. The estimation relies on the stationary distribution and the mean first passage times which can be derived from the sample.

In the present work, we focus on distributions that can be represented by POMMs without final (or termination) probabilities and with regular underlying MC. Since the target process TP never stops, the sample is assumed to have been observed in steady-state. Furthermore, as the transition graph of TP is strongly connected, it is not restrictive to assume that the data is a unique finite string s resulting from a random walk through TP observed during a finite time[7]. Under these assumptions, all transitions of the target POMM and all letters of its alphabet will tend to be observed in the sample. Such a sample can be called *structurally complete*.

---

[7] The sample statistics could equivalently be computed from repeated finite samples observed in steady-state.

```
Algorithm POMMSTATESPLIT
Input: A string s from a target POMM
       A precision parameter ϵ
Output: A POMM EP_cur
EP  ← initialize(s);
M̂   ← sampleMFPT(s);
Lik ← logLikelihood(EP, s);
repeat
    Lik_cur ← Lik;
    EP_cur  ← EP;
    foreach state q in EP_cur do
        EP_new  ← optimizeMFPT(EP_cur, q, M̂);
        Lik_new ← logLikelihood(EP_new, s);
        if Lik_new > Lik then
            EP  ← EP_new;
            Lik ← Lik_new;
until (Lik − Lik_cur)/Lik_cur < ϵ;
return EP_cur
```

Algorithm 1: POMM Induction by state splitting

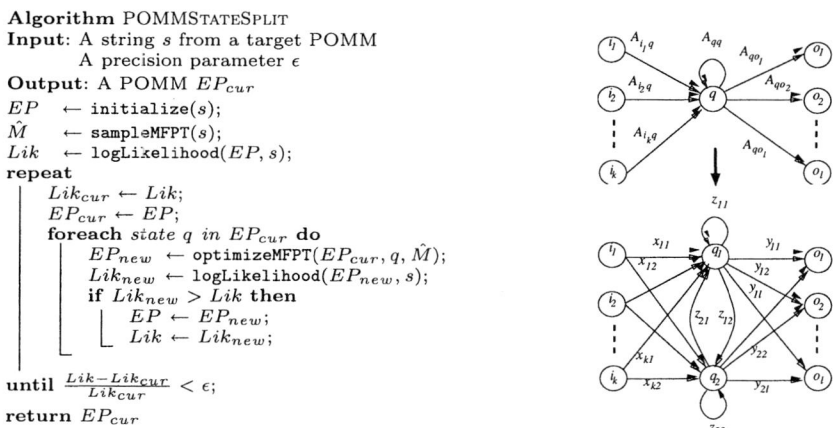

Fig. 2. Splitting of state q

As the target process TP can be considered as a lumped process, each letter of the sample s is associated with a unique state subset of the observable partition κ. All estimates introduced here are related to the state subsets of the target lumped process. The starting point of the induction algorithm is an order 1 MC estimated from the sample. For any pair of letters a, b the transition probability $\hat{A}_{ab}$ is estimated by maximum likelihood by counting how many times a letter a is immediately followed by b in the sample. The stationary distribution of this order 1 MC fits the letter distribution observed in the sample. However, this is not sufficient to reproduce the target dynamics. Hence, the induced model is further required to comply with the MFPT between the blocks of $TP/\!/\kappa$, that is between the letters observed in the sample. Given a string s defined on an alphabet Σ, let $\hat{M}$ denote a $|\Sigma| \times |\Sigma|$ matrix where $\hat{M}_{ab}$ is the average number of symbols after an occurrence of a in s to observe the first occurrence of b.

Algorithm 1 describes the induction algorithm. Iterative state splitting in the current model allows one to increase the fit to the MFPT as well as the likelihood of the model with respect to s, while preserving the stationary distribution. After the construction of the initial order 1 MC, $\hat{M}$ is estimated from s and the log-likelihood of the initial model is computed. At each iteration step, every state q of the current model is considered as a candidate for splitting. During the call to optimizeMFPT, the considered state q is split into two new states q_1 and q_2 as depicted in Fig. 2. The *input states* $i_1, \ldots, i_k$ and *output states* $o_1, \ldots, o_l$ are those directly connected to q in the current model[8], in which all transition probabilities A are known. The topology after splitting provides additional degrees of freedom in the transition probabilities. The new transition probabilities x, y, z form the variables of an optimization problem, which can be represented by the matrices X $(k \times 2), Y$ $(2 \times l)$ and Z (2×2).

---

[8] Input and output states are not necessarily distinct.

The objective function to be minimized measures a least squares error with respect to the target MFPT: $W(X,Y,Z) = \sum_{i,j=1,\ i\neq j}^{|\Sigma|} (\hat{M}_{ij} - M_{ij}/\!/\kappa)^2$, where $M_{ij}/\!/\kappa$ is computed according to definition 3. The best model according to the log-likelihood value is selected and the process is iterated till convergence of the log-likelihood function. The optimization problem is non-linear both in the objective function and the constraints. It can be solved using a Sequential Quadratic Programming (SQP) method [3].

5 Conclusion

We propose in this paper a novel approach to the induction of the structure of Hidden Markov Models. The induced model is constructed to fit the dynamics of the target machine, that is to best approximate the stationary distribution and the mean first passage times (MFPT) observed in the sample. HMMs are able to model a class of distributions broader than finite order Markov chains. They are well suited to represent in a compact way long term probabilistic dependencies. Accurate modeling of these dependencies cannot be achieved however through the classical approach of Baum-Welch estimation of a fully connected model. These observations motivate the use of MFPT to guide the search of an appropriate model topology. The proposed induction algorithm relies on non-linear optimization and iterative state splitting from an initial order one Markov chain. Experimental results illustrate the advantages of the proposed approach as compared to Baum-Welch HMM estimation or back-off smoothed Ngrams.

Our future work will include extension of the proposed approach to other classes of models, such as lumped processes of periodic or absorbing Markov chains. The current implementation of our induction algorithm considers all states of the current model as candidates for splitting. More efficient ways of selecting the best state to split at any given step are under study. Applications of the proposed approach to larger datasets will also be considered, typically in the context of language or biological sequence modeling.

Acknowledgment[9]

The authors wish to thank Philippe Delsarte for many fruitful discussions about this work.

References

1. Y. Bengio and P. Frasconi. Diffusion of context and credit information in markovian models. *Journal of Artificial Intelligence Research*, 3:223–244, 1995.
2. J. Callut and P. Dupont. A Markovian approach to the induction of regular string distributions. In *Grammatical Inference: Algorithms and Applications*, number 3264 in Lecture Notes in Artificial Intelligence, pages 77–90, Athens, Greece, 2004. Springer Verlag.

---

[9] This work is partially supported by the *Fonds pour la formation à la Recherche dans l'Industrie et dans l'Agriculture (F.R.I.A.)* under grant reference F3/5/5-MCF/FC-19271.

3. J. Callut and P. Dupont. Learning hidden markov models to fit long-term dependencies. Technical Report 2005-9, Université catholique de Louvain, July 2005.
4. R. Durbin, S. Eddy, A. Krogh, and G. Mitchison. *Biological sequence analysis.* Cambridge University Press, 1998.
5. D. Freitag and A. McCallum. Information extraction with HMMs and shrinkage. In *Proc. of the AAAI-99 Workshop on Machine Learning for Information Extraction*, 1999.
6. D. Freitag and A. McCallum. Information extraction with HMM structures learned by stochastic optimization. In *Proc. of the Seventeenth National Conference on Artificial Intelligence, AAAI*, pages 584–589, 2000.
7. J.G. Kemeny and J.L. Snell. *Finite Markov Chains.* Springer-Verlag, 1983.
8. E. Levin and R. Pieraccini. Planar Hidden Markov modeling: from speech to optical character recognition. In C.L. Giles, S.J. Hanton, and J.D. Cowan, editors, *Advances in Neural Information Processing Systems*, volume 5, pages 731–738. Morgan Kauffman, 1993.
9. M. Ostendorf and H. Singer. HMM topology design using maximum likelihood successive state splitting. *Computer Speech and Language*, 11:17–41, 1997.
10. L. Rabiner and B.-H. Juang. *Fundamentals of Speech Recognition.* Prentice-Hall, 1993.
11. E. Senata. *Non-negative Matrices and Markov Chains.* Springer-Verlag, 1981.
12. A. Stolcke. *Bayesian Learning of Probabilistic Language Models.* Ph. D. dissertation, University of California, 1994.

A Similar Fragments Merging Approach to Learn Automata on Proteins

François Coste and Goulven Kerbellec*

Symbiose, IRISA, Campus de Beaulieu,
35042 Rennes Cedex, France
{Francois.Coste, Goulven.Kerbellec}@irisa.fr

Abstract. We propose here to learn automata for the characterization of proteins families to overcome the limitations of the position-specific characterizations classically used in Pattern Discovery. We introduce a new heuristic approach learning non-deterministic automata based on selection and ordering of significantly similar fragments to be merged and on physico-chemical properties identification. Quality of the characterization of the major intrinsic protein (MIP) family is assessed by leave-one-out cross-validation for a large range of models specificity.

1 Introduction

Proteins are essential to the structure and function of all living cells and viruses. They are amino acid chains that fold into three-dimensional structures. Most of the times, only the amino acid chain – a sequence over 20 letters each representing one amino acid – is known. Determination of the structure or the function of proteins from their sequences is one of the major challenges in molecular biology. One of the most successful approaches is to define signatures of known *families* of biologically related proteins (typically at the functional or structural level). A representative example of this approach is the well-known Prosite database [1] gathering patterns defined essentially by experts for a large number of protein families. Automatic Pattern Discovery is a dynamic research field [2, 3]. Among the state-of-the-art algorithms, Pratt [4] (chosen to be the default pattern discovery tool proposed on the Prosite web site), Teiresias[5] or Splash[6] have been successfully designed to generate Prosite patterns, i.e. sub-regular expression, while, concerning stochastic models, the corresponding state of the art would be training profile hidden Markov models (which are left-right hidden Markov models focusing on so-called "match" positions and handling deletions or insertions of symbols) as in the commonly used tools HMMER [7] and SAM [8]. An important feature of these approaches is that they are limited to *position-specific* characterizations: neither relations between positions – for instance, if we consider the disulfide bond between cysteines, the fact that when a cysteine amino acid is present at position i there should be necessarily another cysteine at position j – nor alternative paths (disjunction over more than one position) can be

---

* Goulven Kerbellec is supported by a PhD research grant from Région Bretagne.

represented, whereas it could be done in true regular expressions or automata. We address in this paper the task of learning *automata* for the characterization of proteins families to overcome the current position-specific limitation of Pattern Discovery. Learning automata has been widely studied in Grammatical Inference, notably by state merging techniques whose more representative algorithm is certainly RPNI [9,10]. RPNI has been shown to have identification properties and good performances on artificial data. The number of needed data may be reduced with the help of the EDSM heuristic which has won the Abbadingo competition, still on artificial data. In contrast, while the application to genomic sequences seems to be a promising field for Grammatical Inference, not much work has been published on this matter (if we restrict ourselves to methods actually discovering a grammar and not just training its weight parameters, which would for instance exclude the work of Sakakibara on stochastic context free grammars for the prediction of RNA structure [11] but would include the application of Sequitur [12] to infer a hierarchical structure on DNA sequences without generalization capabilities). Concerning the application of such methods for the characterization of proteins, we are only aware of the early work of Yokomori [13] on learning locally testable languages, a subclass of automata which may be linked to *n-grams* and to persistent splicing systems, for the identification of protein α-chain regions.

Our main contribution in this article is the proposition of a new heuristic approach in the state-merging framework allowing a successful inference of automata for the characterization of proteins. The approach, sketched in Algorithm 1, consists of two main stages: first a *characterization* stage, introduced in section 2, detects and orders similar protein fragment pairs, then a *generalization* stage, described in section 3, merges the candidate fragment pairs to identify globally conserved areas and physico-chemical properties. We present a first validation of our approach on a real task of protein characterization in section 4. Technical details are omitted here due to space limitation. We refer interested readers to the associated technical report [14] for more details.

Algorithm 1. Significantly Similar Fragment Merging Approach

---

procedure SFP_MERGING(S: set of sequences, q: quorum, $\mathcal{G}$: set of amino acid groups, $\lambda_G, \lambda_\Sigma$: likelihood tests thresholds)
$\triangleright$ Characterization stage (section 2)

$L \leftarrow$ LIST_OF_SFP(S)
L.SORT_BY_REPRESENTATIVITY_SCORE(S)
$\triangleright$ Generalization stage (section 3)

$A \leftarrow$ MAXIMUM_CANONICAL_AUTOMATA(S)
for each *sfp* $\in L$ **do** $\triangleright$ Merging Fragment Pairs
  A.MERGE_IF_ADMISSIBLE(*sfp*)
A.GAP_GENERALIZATION(q) $\triangleright$ Representative Fragments
A.INFORMATIVE_POSITIONS($\mathcal{G}, \lambda_G, \lambda_\Sigma$) $\triangleright$ Physico-chemical Properties
return A

2 Characterization

Significantly similar fragment pairs. Our method relies on a set of significantly similar fragment pairs (SFP) for the characterization stage. When considering protein sequences, such a set can be extracted from the sequences by DIALIGN2 [15]. DIALIGN2 is a multiple alignment tool whose first step consists in finding all fragment pairs such that their similarity is significantly larger than expected on random sequences. In DIALIGN2, these SFP are then combined to make a multiple alignment optimizing the global sum of weights under consistency constraints. In our approach, this set of SFP is considered as a first selection of interesting fragments such that merging them is potentially interesting.

Ordering Similar Fragment Pairs. The selection of these fragments is based only on sequence-to-sequence comparison. We introduce two scores, detailed in [14], to rank these fragment pairs according to their representativeness of the whole protein family. The first score estimates the support in other sequences of the family, i.e. it counts for each SFP the number of sequences containing a fragment sufficiently similar to it. The second score relies on a set of proteins not belonging to the family to give priority to discriminative characteristic SFP [16]. It evaluates how the support of the SFP in the family implies its proportion to be supported in the family and in the other set of sequences. Each score defines an heuristic ordering of the SFP. We will refer to these ordering as being respectively the *support heuristic* and the *implication heuristic*.

3 Generalization

Merging Fragment Pairs. The first generalization step applies the classical state-merging scheme popularized by RPNI [9] and EDSM [17] to SFP. We consider the more general case allowing to learn non-deterministic automata. Following the definitions of [18], to which we refer the reader for details, the general sketch of this kind of algorithm is to first construct an automaton, named *maximal canonical automaton* (MCA), representing exactly the training set of sequences and, then, to generalize the recognized language by *merging* (unifying) some of its states. State merging algorithms can be distinguished by their choice of states to merge. We propose here to merge iteratively the states corresponding to the SFP identified in the characterization stage, beginning by SFP with higher representativeness. This ordering is taken into account by introducing a preservation constraint over the previously merged fragments. Namely, after each SFP merging, a constraint stating that the resulting states can not be merged together is set. Further SFP mergings that would violate such constraint are discarded.

Representative Fragments. Merging the SFP allows to identify hot spots: sets of contiguous positions where lots of fragments have been merged. Besides, some positions may be involved in none of SFP merges. These latter localizations are clearly not representative of the family. We propose to treat them as "gaps". We introduce classically a quorum parameter. If a state is used by less sequences than specified by the quorum, it is merged with its neighbors. This step allows to keep only the characteristic regions and is an important generalization step for long proteins. Several variations around this scheme could be implemented. Statistical information like the length or the amino acid composition of the gap could also be considered and added to the model. The version presented here is the simple one used in the experiments.

Identification of Physico-chemical Properties. We propose here to recover the important physico-chemical properties of the amino acids at each position of the representative fragments with respect to the function or the structure of the family. The approach takes as input a set $\mathcal{G}$ of eventually overlapping substitution groups representing important physico-chemical properties (typically the groups proposed by Taylor [19]). For each position, likelihood tests are used to decide whether the set of amino-acids should be expanded to the smallest group including the set or else whether it should be expanded to the whole alphabet Σ if the distribution of the amino-acids appears to be random (see [14]). These tests introduce two threshold parameters λ_G and λ_Σ allowing to tune the risk when expanding to a group or else to Σ.

4 Experiments

We evaluated our approach on the major intrinsic protein (MIP) family [20]. The MIP family has functional and structural properties such as transmembrane channels, well-known to be important for water, alcohol and small molecules transport across cell membranes thanks to P. Agre (Nobel Prize in Chemistry "for the discovery of water channels", 2003). UNIPROT, a biological protein sequence database, contains 911 proteins annotated as being members of the MIP family. Of these 911, 159 protein sequences (denoted hereafter by the set T) are present in SWISSPROT which is the reliable annotated public reference database used by Prosite. Of this set, a biologist expert has identified only 79 sequences with a real biological experiment-based annotation (a lot of proteins being annotated "by similarity"). By filtering out the sequences with more than 90% of identity, this set was then reduced to 44 sequences (set M). Of this set, the expert has identified 24 water-specific sequences (set W+) and 16 glycerol or small molecule facilitator sequences (set W-). Let us notice the difficulty of the discrimination task between these MIP, some sequences of W+ being closer to some sequences of W- than to the other sequences of W+. We have established also a control set composed of sequences close to MIP sequences and identified by the expert as being outside the family (set C).

All the experiments were performed with an implementation of our approach named Protomata-L using DIALIGN2 with the following options : `-nta -thr 5 -afc`. The group expansion of Protomata-L has been done with the sets of physico-chemical properties proposed in Fig. 5 of [19] except the "unions" group, and $\lambda_G = 10^{-7}$, $\lambda_\Sigma = 10^{-19}$. Even with our unoptimized code, the execution never exceeded 10 minutes on a 3GHz desktop station.

Table 1. Comparison of 4 MIP signature patterns

Method	Precision	Recall	F-mes.	Pattern
Prosite (reference)	95%	91%	0.93	[HNQA]DNP[STA][LIVMF][ST][LIVMF][GSTAFY]
Pratt	90%	78%	0.83	GX(2)[FILMV]NP[AS]X[DST][FIL][AGP]
Teiresias	23%	89%	0.37	[ILMV]X(10)[ST]X(3)[ILMV]NX[AG]X(3)[AG]
Protomata-L	100%	87%	0.93	[ACGSTV]X[ACFGILMV]N[ACGPV][AGS][ACFGILMV][DNST][ACFGILMV][ACGSTV]X[ACFGHIKLMTVWY]X(12)[FMY]X[ACFGHIKLMTVWY]XQ[ACFGHIKLMTVWY][ACFGILMV][AGS][AGS]

First Common Fragment. For this first set of experiments, in order to compare our fragment merging approach with Pratt[4] and Teiresias[5] methods and Prosite hand-made pattern[1], we restricted Protomata-L to return only the first common fragment shared by all sequences, using support heuristic. Pratt and Teiresias were used with their default parameters, except the parameter W (maximum length) of Teiresias that was set to 50 to allow longer pattern to be discovered. The patterns were learned from the set M and tested on the set T. Even if the set T was used in Prosite for the design of the pattern, a scan of the Prosite's pattern on SWISSPROT database returns false positive as well as false negative sequences with respect to T. Table 1 summarizes the results of such scans for the three patterns. The recall of our approach is close to Prosite's pattern recall while our precision remains at 100%. Let us remark that in our false positives, one was not a full sequence and 16 were annoted as MIP by similarity. When comparing our approach with Pratt and Teiresias, the comparison is clearly in favor of Protomata-L with respect to both the precision and the recall.

Water-Specific MIP subfamily. In this second set of experimentations, we focused on the characterization of the water-specific MIP subfamily set W+, using the set W- as counter-example. This discrimination task is motivated by a better understanding of the transport of these molecules. We used it to study the quality of the characterization on closely related sets of sequences at increasing specificity levels. Due to the small number of available sequences, a leave-one-out cross-validation scheme was used to evaluate our approach. For each couple of positive and negative sequences $(w+, w-)$, the training was achieved using the remaining sequences of W+ and W-. For each leave-one-out datasets, several automata – ranging from short automata (like in the previous paragraph) to larger automata characterizing almost all the length of the MIP topology – were obtained by using an increasing number of SFP. Each automaton was then evaluated according to the distance for acceptation of the positive sequence left out $w+$, the negative sequence left out $w-$, and also of the closest sequence c in the control set C. The *distance for acceptation* refers here to the minimal cost of amino acid substitutions needed in the sequence for its acceptation by

---

[1] Preliminary tests, not reported here, showed that RPNI and EDSM were not able to propose pertinent automata from this kind of data.

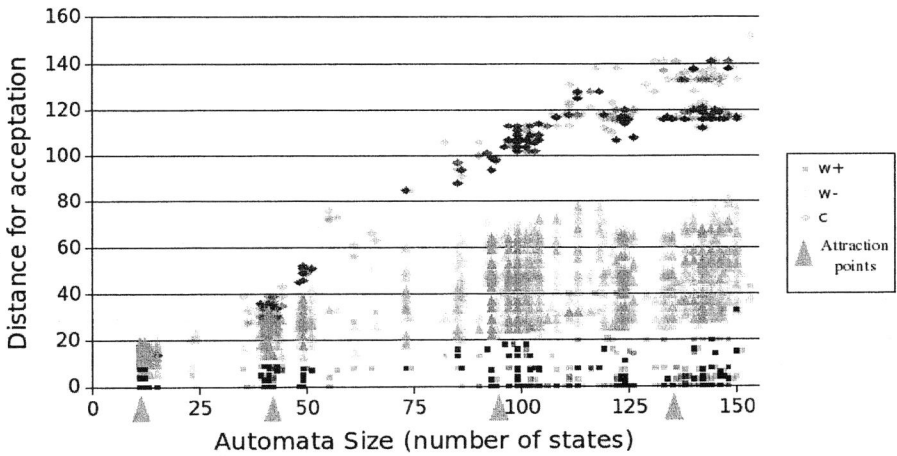

Fig. 1. Characterization of the Water Specific MIP family

the automaton (the cost of each amino acid substitution being given by the classical substitution matrix Blosum62 [21]). Fig. 1 presents the results of all these experiments when using the implication heuristic and a quorum of 100%. On the size axis, we highlighted 4 attraction points which are related to the progressive emergence of common sub-patterns, the first one corresponding to the first common fragment. The separation of the different sets of sequences is manifest and grows along the automata size axis until an inflexion point near 100 states. Behind this inflexion point, the merged SFP do not contribute anymore to the discrimination but only to a more precise characterization of the family without showing over-generalization evidence. Table 2 sums up the results of the automata at the attraction points for the classification task between W+ and W-, with strict acceptance and with a distance threshold acceptance. In the latter case, the closest counter-example distance from the automata was taken as the threshold distance for acceptance. The approach was then able to raise 100% of precision and 100% of recall for automata sizes of 40 or even 100 states.

Table 2. Performance on classification task (W+ vs W-)

Automata Size	Strict			Threshold		
	Precision	Recall	F-mes.	Precision	Recall	F-mes.
10	100%	92%	0.96	100%	96%	0.98
40	100%	71%	0.83	100%	100%	1.00
100	100%	54%	0.70	100%	100%	1.00
130	100%	42%	0.59	100%	96%	0.98

5 Conclusion

This study shows – even if it has to be confirmed on other sets of sequences – that good automata can be learned successfully on proteins. The proposed heuristic approach can be applied to the characterization of a family of proteins from positive examples only. It is also able to benefit from available counter-examples to produce more subtle models performing well in the discrimination of a closely related family of sequences. Depending on the application, the level of precision of the learned models can be chosen, ranging from short characteristic models (for classification tasks) to more detailed and explanatory models (for modeling the family of sequences). As proved by performance in leave-one-out cross-validation, the more specific models have still good prediction accuracy when allowing a small distance for acceptation to compensate the limited number of available examples. An alternative way to handle unpredictable family variation would be to use the learned automata as the underlying structure of probabilistic automata, or hidden Markov models, and estimate their stochastic parameters by the classical well-studied training methods. The advantage of our approach is that these variations are treated outside the model by measuring the distance to it, allowing the models to focus only on an explicit characterization of the important properties of the training sequences. We think that we could even improve the prediction accuracy by using distances taking into account the weights of the amino acids at each position with respect to the training sequences, but this has still to be implemented and tested.

Compared to classical protein Pattern Discovery algorithms, our approach introduces several new ideas. Globally, we think that, besides the ability to learn a more expressive class of model, the fundamental difference of Protomata-L with these Pattern Discovery approaches consists in the introduction of the similarity of fragments (which reflects the conservation of the site and probably the conservation of some structural aspects of it) as an important criterion for the characterization. This allows to consider the characterization of positions according to their context. Protomata-L introduces also the possibility to produce discriminative characterization of a set of sequences with respect to another one. With regard to Grammatical Inference, the confrontation of the classical state-merging techniques with a real application has lead to a new approach based on merging similar fragments. The sole application specific parts are the first and the last step of our approach (the selection of the SFPs step and the physico-chemical properties identification step) and could be replaced by similar modules for other applications. All the remaining of the approach is generic and we expect it to be an inspiration source for new theoretical or algorithmic developments. Among the originalities with respect to the classical approaches, we would like to point out the consideration of the similarity between the symbols of the alphabet, the choice of the non-deterministic representation of automata, the use of fragment-based heuristic to infer this kind of models, the identification of informative positions and the discriminative setting with respect to counter-examples (or unlabeled set of sequences) which replaces the classical compatibility setting and allows to handle some noisy counter-examples.

References

1. Hulo, N., Sigrist, C.J.A., Le Saux, V., Langendijk-Genevaux, P.S., Bordoli, L., Gattiker, A., De Castro, E., Bucher, P., Bairoch, A.: Recent improvements to the PROSITE database. Nucl. Acids Res. **32** (2004) D134–137
2. Rigoutsos, I , Floratos, A., Parida, L., Y.Gao, Platt, D.: The emergence of pattern discovery techniques in computational biology. Metabolic Engineering **2** (2000) 159–177
3. Brejova, B., DiMarco, C., Vinar, T., Hidalgo, S., Holguin, G., Patten, C.: Finding Patterns in Biological Sequences. Unpublished project report for CS798G (2000)
4. Jonassen, I., Collins, J., Higgins, D.: Finding flexible patterns in unaligned protein sequences. Protein Science **4** (1995) 1587–1595
5. Rigoutsos, I , Floratos, A.: Combinatorial pattern discovery in biological sequences: the TEIRESIAS algorithm. Bioinformatics **14** (1998) 55–67
6. Califano, A.: Splash: structural pattern localization analysis by sequential histograms. Bioinformatics **16** (2000) 341–357
7. Eddy, S.: Hmmer user's guide: biological sequence analysis using prole hidden markov models. http://hmmer.wustl.edu/ (1998)
8. Karplus, K.: Hidden markov models for detecting remote protein homologies. Bioinformatics **14** (1998) 846–865
9. Oncina, J., Garcia, P.: Inferring regular languages in polynomial update time. Pattern Recognition and Image Analysis (1992) 49 – 61
10. Lang, K.J.: Random dfa's can be approximately learned from sparse uniform examples. 5th ACM workshop on Computation Learning Theorie (1992) 45 – 52
11. Sakakibara, Brown, Hughey, Mian, Sjolander, Underwood, Haussler: Recent methods for RNA modeling using stochastic context-free grammars. In: CPM: 5th Symposium on Combinatorial Pattern Matching. (1994)
12. Nevill-Manning, C., Witten, I.: Identifying hierarchical structure in sequences: A linear-time algorithm. Journal of Artificial Intelligence Research **7** (1997) 67–82
13. Yokomori, T.: Learning non-deterministic finite automata from queries and counterexamples. Machine Intelligence **13** (1994) 169–189
14. Coste, F., Kerbellec, G.: A similar fragments merging approach to learn automata on proteins. Technical report, IRISA, PI-1735 (2005)
15. Morgenstern, B.: DIALIGN 2: improvement of the segment-to-segment approach to multiple sequence alignment. Bioinformatics **15** (1999) 211–218
16. Lerman, I., Azé, J.: Indice probabiliste discriminant de vraisemblance du lien pour des données volumineuses. RNTI-E-1, numéro spécial Mesures de Qualité pour la Fouille des Données, H. Briand, M. Sebag, R. Gras, F. Guillet, CEPADUES (2004) 69–94
17. Lang, K.J., Pearlmutter, B.A., Price, R.A.: Results of the abbadingo one DFA learning competition and a new evidence-driven state merging algorithm. Lecture Notes in Computer Science **1433** (1998) 1–12
18. Coste, F., Fredouille, D.: What is the search space for the inference of nondeterministic, unambiguous and deterministic automata ? Technical report, IRISA - INRIA, RR-4907 (2003)
19. Taylor, W.R.: The classification of amino acid conservation. Journal of theoretical Biology **119** (1986) 205–218
20. Karkouri, K.E., Gueune, H., Delamarche, C.: Mipdb: a relational database dedicated to mip family proteins. Biol Cell **97** (2005) 535–543
21. Henikoff, S., Henikoff, J.: Amino acid substitution matrices from protein blocks. Proc. Natl. Acad. Sci. USA **89** (1992) 10915–10919

Nonnegative Lagrangian Relaxation of K-Means and Spectral Clustering

Chris Ding, Xiaofeng He, and Horst D. Simon

Lawrence Berkeley National Laboratory Berkeley,
CA 94720, USA.
{chqding, xhe, hdsimon}@lbl.gov

Abstract. We show that K-means and spectral clustering objective functions can be written as a trace of quadratic forms. Instead of relaxation by eigenvectors, we propose a novel relaxation maintaining the nonnegativity of the cluster indicators and thus give the cluster posterior probabilities, therefore resolving cluster assignment difficulty in spectral relaxation. We derive a multiplicative updating algorithm to solve the nonnegative relaxation problem. The method is briefly extended to semi-supervised classification and semi-supervised clustering.

1 Introduction

Data clustering is one of the essential tasks in unsupervised learning. One of the most popular and efficient clustering methods is the K-means method which uses prototypes (centroids) to represent clusters by optimizing the squared error function. Starting from an initial guess of centroids, K-means iteratively improves the clustering in EM style algorithm to local minima.

In recent years spectral clustering emerges as a solid approach for data clustering. Spectral clustering evolves from spectral graph partitioning and have well-motivated clustering objective functions. In the spectral relaxation, the continuous approximations of the discrete cluster indicators can be obtained as eigenvectors of the Laplacian matrix of the similarity graph (edge weights as the pairwise similarity). Because eigenvector entries have both plus and minus signs, spectral clustering is most conveniently applied to 2-way clustering problems using a single eigenvector. When applying to multi-way (K-way) clustering, assigning cluster memberships becomes indirect: (1) the 2-way spectral clustering is recursively applied or (2) an embedding to a space spanned by eigenvectors is first done and some other methods, such as K-means [1] are then used.

In this paper, we propose a novel approach to solve the multi-way spectral clustering problem. Instead of spectral relaxation of clustering indicators we propose nonnegative relaxation of clustering indicators, i.e., maintaining the nonnegativity of them. In this way, the original clustering indicators become class (cluster) posterior probabilities. Besides resolving the cluster assignment problem, this added interpretability is theoretically appealing.

Our approach starts with a reformulation of K-means and kernel K-means clusterings which allows the use of eigenvectors as cluster indicator vectors. Spectral clustering objective function can be also reformulated as the maximization of quadratic forms. From there, instead of eigenvector relaxation, we perform nonnegative relaxation.

Our nonnegative relaxation approach is inspired by the nonnegative matrix factorization(NMF)[3,4,2]. We provide a systematic exposition of this approach with illustrative examples and applications to internet newgroups data.

2 Kernel K-Means and Spectral Clustering

In this section, we show that K-means and Spectral clustering can be written as minimization of a quadratic form.

K-means clustering is one of the most widely used clustering methods, with many current extensions. It uses the centroids of clusters, to characterize the data. The objective function is to minimize the sum of squared errors,

$$J_k = \sum_{k=1}^{K} \sum_{i \in C_k} ||\mathbf{x}_i - \mathbf{m}_k||^2, \qquad (1)$$

where $X = (\mathbf{x}_1, \cdots, \mathbf{x}_n)$ is the data matrix and $\mathbf{m}_k = \sum_{i \in C_k} \mathbf{x}_i / n_k$ is the centroid of cluster C_k of n_k points. Extension to kernel K-means is similarly defined.

There are 3 variants of spectral clustering objective functions. Here we focus on the normalized cut[5]. The multi-way clustering objective function is

$$J = \sum_{1 \leq p < q \leq K} \frac{s(C_p, C_q)}{\rho(C_p)} + \frac{s(C_p, C_q)}{\rho(C_q)} \qquad (2)$$

where $s(C_k, C_\ell) = \sum_{i \in C_k} \sum_{j \in C_\ell} w_{ij}$, and $\rho(C_k) = \sum_{i \in C_k} d_i$, $d_i = \sum_j W_{ij}$.

Here we reformulate the K-means and normalized cut. The solution of clustering is represented by K non-negative cluster membership indicator vectors: $H = (\mathbf{h}_1, \cdots, \mathbf{h}_K)$, where

$$\mathbf{h}_k = (0, \cdots, 0, \overbrace{1, \cdots, 1}^{n_k}, 0, \cdots, 0)^T / n_k^{1/2} \qquad (3)$$

For example, the nonzero entries of $\mathbf{h}_1$ give data points belonging to the first cluster. We have

Theorem 1. For K-means and Kernel K-means the clustering objective function can be written as

$$\max_{H^T H = I, \ H \geq 0} J_k = \text{Tr}(H^T W H), \qquad (4)$$

where $W = (w_{ij}); w_{ij} = \mathbf{x}_i^T \mathbf{x}_j$ for K-means and $w_{ij} = \phi(\mathbf{x}_i)^T \phi(\mathbf{x}_j)$ for Kernel K-means . For spectral clustering, the clustering objective function becomes

$$\max_{H^T D H = I,\ H \geq 0} J_s = \mathrm{Tr}(H^T W H) \tag{5}$$

where $D = \mathrm{diag}(d_1, \cdots, d_n)$. Proofs are outlined in [2].

Theorem 1 shows that spectral clustering is almost identical to Kernel K-means clustering: they maximize the same clustering objective function, the only difference is at the orthogonality constraints of the cluster indicators H: H is orthogonal for K-means, while H is D-orthogonal, i.e., $H^T D H = I$, for spectral clustering.

3 Spectral Relaxation

It is instructive to review the spectral relaxation (eigenvector solution) to K-means and normalized cut, before we turn to the nonnegative relaxation. By "relaxation" we mean that the discrete cluster indicators H are approximated by continuous quantities. Spectral relaxation are obtained by relaxing (ignoring) the nonnegative constraint $H \geq 0$.

For K-means, the solution are given by eigenvectors of W: $W\mathbf{h}_k = \alpha_k \mathbf{h}_k$, $k = 1 \cdots K$. For Normalized Cut, the solution are given by $W\mathbf{h}_k = \alpha_k D\mathbf{h}_k$, which can be rewritten as $(D-W)\mathbf{h}_k = \lambda_k D\mathbf{h}_k$, $\lambda_k = 1 - \alpha_k$, giving the familiar eigenvector equation for normalized cut. $L = D - W$ is the Laplacian matrix of graph with weight matrix W.

A difficulty in eigenvector relaxation is that the original H are nonnegative while the eigenvectors solutions for H have many negative entries. This makes it difficult to identify cluster members. This cluster assignment problem would be much easier if entries of H are nonnegative. In that case, we may interpret the i-th row of H as the posterior probability for the i-th object belonging to each of the K clusters. This motivate us to consider the nonnegative relaxation of the next section.

4 Nonnegative Lagrangian Relaxation (NLR)

We propose nonnegative Lagrangian relaxation of the quadratic form which enforce the nonnegative constraint on H. With this, H can be interpreted as the posterior probability. The cluster assignment problem is resolved trivially: at convergence, we simply assign the i-th object to the cluster with the largest posterior probability, i.e., the large entry of the i-th row of H. This is a major advantage over eigenvector relaxation.

4.1 NLR for Kernel K-Means

We wish to optimize the quadratic form of Eq.(4) with both orthogonality and nonnegative constraints. We follow the standard optimization theory and derive the KKT conditions. To find the maxima, we introduce the Lagrangian function

$$L = \operatorname{Tr} H^T W H - \sum_{ij} \alpha_{ij}(H^T H - I)_{ij} - \sum_{ij} \beta_{ij} H_{ij} \qquad (6)$$

where the Lagrangian multipliers $\alpha_{ij} = \alpha_{ji}$ are to enforce $H^T H = I$, and the Lagrangian multipliers β_{ij} enforce nonnegative constraints, $H_{ij} \geq 0$. The first order KKT condition for local maxima is $0 = \frac{\partial L}{\partial H_{ik}} = 2WH - 2H\alpha - \beta$, and the complementary slackness condition $\beta_{ik} H_{ik} = 0$, which leads to

$$(WH - H\alpha)_{ij} H_{ij} = 0. \qquad (7)$$

This is a fixed point equation that the solution must satisfy at convergence. From this, we obtain $\alpha_{ii} = (H^T W H)_{ii}$; this gives the diagonal elements of α. To obtain the off-diagonal elements of α, we ignore nonnegativity of H and obtain $\alpha = H^T W H$. Thus the diagonal elements of the constraint $H^T W H = I$ are vigorously enforced, while the off-diagonal elements of $H^T W H = I$ are enforced at the level of ignoring nonnegativity of H. This slight relaxation of the orthogonality of H have the benefits of soft clustering interpretation (see §4.3).

We derive an algorithm to compute the nonnegative relaxation and prove its convergence. The algorithm has the style of NMF. Given an existing solution or an inital guess, we iteratively improve the solution by updating the variables with the following rule,

$$H_{ik} \leftarrow H_{ik} \sqrt{\frac{(WH)_{ik}}{(H\alpha)_{ik}}}, \quad \alpha = H^T W H. \qquad (8)$$

Clearly this updating rule satisfies the fixed point equation Eq.(7). The following theorem assures its convergence to local maxima.

Theorem 2. Under the updating rule, the Lagrangian function $L(H) = \operatorname{Tr} H^T W H - \operatorname{Tr} \alpha(H^T H - I)$ is monotonically increasing (non-decreasing), $L(H^{(0)}) \leq L(H^{(1)}) \leq \cdots \leq L(H^{(t)}) \leq \cdots$. Since L is bounded from above, the convergence of this algorithm is thus established.
Proof. Outline of the proof is given in Appendix A.

4.2 NLR for Normalized Cut

Normalized Cut differs from K-means in the different orthogonality condition: $H^T D H = I$. The Lagrangian function becomes $L = \operatorname{Tr} H^T W H - \operatorname{Tr} \alpha(H^T D H - I) - \operatorname{Tr} \beta^T H$. The fixed point equation is $(WH - DH\alpha)_{ik} H_{ik} = 0$. The Lagrangian multipliers are given by $\alpha = H^T W H$. The multiplicative update rule is

$$H_{ik} \leftarrow H_{ik} \sqrt{\frac{(WH)_{ik}}{(DH\alpha)_{ik}}}, \quad \alpha = H^T W H, \qquad (9)$$

under which the Lagrangian function is monotonically increasing (non-decreasing).

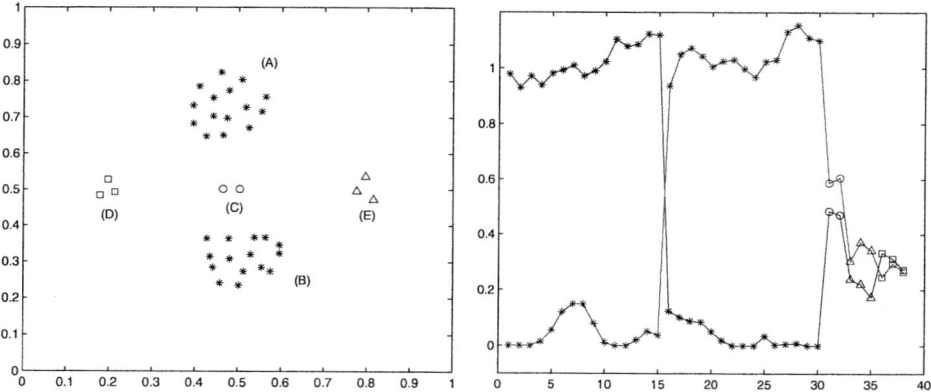

Fig. 1. Left: A 2D dataset of 38 data points. Right: Their $H = (\mathbf{h}_1, \mathbf{h}_2)$ values are shown as blue and red curves. H values for points in regions $\{C, E, D\}$ indicate they are fractionally assigned to clusters.

An illustrative example. We demonstrate NLR by a simple example. Fig.1 (left panel) shows a 2D example of 38 points. The similarity between $\mathbf{x}_i, \mathbf{x}_j$ is computed using Gaussian kernel $W_{ij} = \exp(-\|\mathbf{x}_i - \mathbf{x}_j\|^2/2)$. The data has two dominant clusters. We set $k = 2$ The resulting cluster indicators $\mathbf{h}_1, \mathbf{h}_2$ are shown in Fig.1 (right panel).

If we do a hard clustering by assigning each data point x_i to the cluster $c = \arg\max_k H_{ik}$, we get those points in regions (A, C, E) as one cluster, and the points in regions (B, D) as another cluster. This can be see from the figure (points in C are x_{31}, x_{32}; points in E are x_{33}, x_{34}, x_{35}; points in D are x_{36}, x_{37}, x_{38};) These results are identical to a K-means clustering results.

However, we see that the magnitudes of $\mathbf{h}_1, \mathbf{h}_2$ on points in C are very close to each other. This indicates that a partial (soft) cluster assignment would be more appropriate. Furthermore, the magnitude of $\mathbf{h}_1, \mathbf{h}_2$ on points in E, D are even smaller, indicating they do not belong to either of the dominant clusters. In fact, all points in C, E, D can be considered as outliers. In general, if $\sum_k H_{ik}$ is far below the average value, we may consider $\mathbf{x}_i$ as an outlier. This can be rigorously quantified.

5 Nonnegative Relaxation of Bipartite Graph Clustering

The approach of §2 can be easily extended to bipartite graphs. A bipartite graph is specified by a nonnegative rectangular matrix, its adjacency matrix $B = (b_{ij})$, which can be equivalently viewed as a contingency table in statistics. We call the two types nodes of the bipartite graph as row nodes and column nodes. Bipartite graph clustering is equivalent to simultaneous clustering of rows and columns. Let $F = (\mathbf{f}_1, \cdots, \mathbf{f}_k)$ be the indicator matrix for row clustering, e.g., $\mathbf{f}_k$ is the cluster indicator for the k-th row-cluster. $\mathbf{f}_k$ has the same form of $\mathbf{h}_k$ as in Eq.(3). Analogously, we define the indicator matrix $G = (\mathbf{g}_1, \cdots, \mathbf{g}_k)$ for column clustering. We combine the row and column nodes together as $W = \begin{pmatrix} 0 & B \\ B^T & 0 \end{pmatrix}$, $\mathbf{h}_k = \frac{1}{\sqrt{2}}\begin{pmatrix} \mathbf{f}_k \\ \mathbf{g}_k \end{pmatrix}$, $H = \frac{1}{\sqrt{2}}\begin{pmatrix} F \\ G \end{pmatrix}$ where the factor $1/\sqrt{2}$ allows the simultaneous normalizations $\mathbf{h}_k^T \mathbf{h}_k = 1$, $\mathbf{f}_k^T \mathbf{f}_k = 1$, and $\mathbf{g}_k^T \mathbf{g}_k = 1$. The Kernel K-means clustering objective function becomes

$$\max_{\substack{F^T F = I; \\ G^T G = I; \\ F, G \geq 0}} J_{kb} = \frac{1}{2}\mathrm{Tr}\begin{pmatrix} F \\ G \end{pmatrix}^T \begin{pmatrix} 0 & B \\ B^T & 0 \end{pmatrix} \begin{pmatrix} F \\ G \end{pmatrix} = \mathrm{Tr}(F^T B G). \quad (10)$$

To gain intuition about this objective function, we write $J_{kb} = \sum_k \frac{s(R_k, C_k)}{\sqrt{|R_k| |C_k|}}$ where $s(R_k, C_k) = \sum_{i \in R_k} \sum_{j \in C_k} b_{ij}$. The bipartite graph clustering objective maximizes the within-cluster similarities $s(R_1, C_1), \cdots, s(R_K, C_K)$.

It can be shown that the Normalized Cut clustering objective function for the bipartite graph[7] can be written as

$$\max_{\substack{F^T DF = I; \\ G^T DG = I; \\ F, G \geq 0}} J_{sb} = \mathrm{Tr}\,(F^T B G). \quad (11)$$

5.1 Spectral Relaxation

If we ignore the nonnegativity constraints, the above problem of simultaneous clustering of rows and columns can be solved by spectral relaxation. With the same analysis as in §3, the solution of J_{kb} in Eq.(10) are given by the eigenvalue equation Eq.(3), or explicitly as $\begin{pmatrix} 0 & B \\ B^T & 0 \end{pmatrix}\begin{pmatrix} \mathbf{f}_k \\ \mathbf{g}_k \end{pmatrix} = \lambda_k \begin{pmatrix} \mathbf{f}_k \\ \mathbf{g}_k \end{pmatrix}$ The solutions are given by singular value decomposition of B: $\mathbf{f}_k$ are given by the principal directions (eigenvectors of BB^T) and $\mathbf{g}_k$ are given by the principal components (eigenvectors of $B^T B$).

For Normalized Cut, the solution of J_{sb} in Eq.(11) are given by $\begin{pmatrix} 0 & B \\ B^T & 0 \end{pmatrix}\begin{pmatrix} \mathbf{f}_k \\ \mathbf{g}_k \end{pmatrix}$
$= \lambda_k \begin{pmatrix} D_r & \\ & D_c \end{pmatrix}\begin{pmatrix} \mathbf{f}_k \\ \mathbf{g}_k \end{pmatrix}$, where the diagonal matrix D_r contains row sums of B and D_c contains column sums of B. The solutions are $\mathbf{f}_k = D_r^{-1/2} \mathbf{u}_k$ and $\mathbf{g}_k = D_c^{-1/2} \mathbf{v}_k$, where $\mathbf{u}_k$ and $\mathbf{v}_k$ are given by SVD of $D_r^{-1/2} B D_c^{-1/2}$.

5.2 Nonnegative Relaxation

The nonnegative relaxation for bipartite graph clustering can be easily derived. For example, for kernel K-means type clustering, the update rules are

$$F_{ik} \leftarrow F_{ik}\sqrt{\frac{(BG)_{ik}}{(F\alpha)_{ik}}}, \quad G_{ik} \leftarrow G_{ik}\sqrt{\frac{(B^T F)_{ik}}{(G\alpha)_{ik}}}, \quad \alpha = \frac{F^T BG + GB^T F}{2}. \quad (12)$$

5.3 Equivalence to Nonnegative Matrix Factorization

We demonstrate a close relationship between bipartite graph K-means clustering and nonnegative matrix factorization (NMF). We have the following:

Theorem 3. The simultaneous clustering of rows and columns using the K-means clustering objective function is equivalent to the following NMF optimization problem,

$$\min_{\substack{F^T F = I; \\ G^T G = I; \\ F, G \geq 0}} J_2 = ||B - FG^T||^2. \tag{13}$$

Therefore, NMF provides yet another way to solve the bipartite graph kernel K-means clustering problem. The update rules of NMF are

$$F_{ik} \leftarrow F_{ik} \frac{(BG)_{ik}}{(FG^T G)_{ik}}, \quad G_{ik} \leftarrow G_{ik} \frac{(B^T F)_{ik}}{(GF^T F)_{ik}}. \tag{14}$$

They are quite similar to NLR update rule of Eq.(12).

6 Experiments on Internet Newsgroups

We perform experiments on the well-known 20-newsgroup Internet newsgroups dataset. We use two sets of 5-newsgroup combinations:

	A		B
NG2:	comp.graphics	NG2:	comp.graphics
NG9:	rec.motorcycles	NG3:	comp.os.ms-windows
NG10:	rec.sport.baseball	NG8:	rec.autos
NG15:	sci.space	NG13:	sci.electronics
NG18:	talk.politics.mideast	NG19:	talk.politics.misc

In Dataset A, clusters moderately overlap. In dataset B, clusters strongly overlap. To accumulate sufficient statistics, we generate 5 random datasets for each 5-newsgroup combinations: 100 documents were randomly sampled from each newsgroup. K-means, NLR and NMF are applied to these 5 random sampled datasets. The results for clustering accuracy using the known class labels are listed in Table 1 for dataset A and B. Both NMF and NLR improve over K-means substantially; NLR always gives better results than NMF.

dataset A			dataset B		
K-means	NMF	NLR	K-means	NMF	NLR
0.748	0.864	0.876	0.531	0.612	0.620
0.790	0.904	0.916	0.491	0.590	0.606
0.815	0.886	0.912	0.576	0.608	0.642
0.862	0.886	0.902	0.632	0.652	0.654
0.873	0.883	0.884	0.697	0.711	0.734

We have discussed the importance of the orthogonality of H with regard to clustering. The normalized orthogonality, $(H^T H)_{nm} = D^{-1/2}(H^T H)D^{-1/2}$, where $D = \text{diag}(H^T H)$, are given below:

$$\text{NLR:} \begin{bmatrix} 1 & 0.044 & 0.111 & 0.062 & 0.041 \\ & 1 & 0.069 & 0.065 & 0.044 \\ & & 1 & 0.075 & 0.071 \\ & & & 1 & 0.058 \\ & & & & 1 \end{bmatrix} \quad \text{NMF:} \begin{bmatrix} 1 & 0.107 & 0.189 & 0.130 & 0.126 \\ & 1 & 0.063 & 0.088 & 0.114 \\ & & 1 & 0.078 & 0.097 \\ & & & 1 & 0.095 \\ & & & & 1 \end{bmatrix}$$

One can see that off-diagonal elements are generally small. NLR has better orthogonality than NMF.

7 Extensions to Semi-supervised Learning

The quadratic clustering of Theorem 1 can be extended to semi-supervised learning. (1) Let C contains information on partially labeled data and input paramter $\rho > 0$, $\max \text{Tr}[H^T W H + 2\rho C^T H]$ is identical to the semi-supervised classification of Zhou et al. [8]. (2) In semi-supervised clustering, one performs clustering with constraints[6]: must-link constraints (contained in A) and cannot-link constraints (contained in B). A, B are symmetric matrices containing $\{0,1\}$. Replacing W by $W + \rho A - \rho B$ in Eq.(4) is equivalent to constrained K-means clustering. The advantage of this framework is the consistency of various learning taskes.

References

1. F. R. Bach and M. I. Jordan. Learning spectral clustering. *Neural Info. Processing Systems 16 (NIPS 2003)*, 2003.
2. C. Ding, X. He, and H.D. Simon. On the equivalence of nonnegative matrix factorization and spectral clustering. *Proc. SIAM Data Mining Conf*, 2005.
3. D.D. Lee and H. S. Seung. Algorithms for non-negatvie matrix factorization. In T. G. Dietterich and V. Tresp, editors, *Advances in Neural Information Processing Systems*, volume 13. The MIT Press, 2001.
4. F. Sha, L.K. Saul, and D.D. Lee. Multiplicative updates for nonnegative quadratic programming in support vector machines. In *Advances in Neural Information Processing Systems 15*, pages 1041–1048. 2003.
5. J. Shi and J. Malik. Normalized cuts and image segmentation. *IEEE. Trans. on Pattern Analysis and Machine Intelligence*, 22:888–905, 2000.
6. K. Wagstaff, C. Cardie, S. Rogers, and S. Schroedl. Constrained k-means clustering with background knowledge. *Proc. Int'l Conf. Machine Learning*, 2001.
7. H. Zha, X. He, C. Ding, M. Gu, and H.D. Simon. Bipartite graph partitioning and data clustering. *Proc. Int'l Conf. Information and Knowledge Management (CIKM 2001)*, 2001.
8. D. Zhou, O. Bousquet, T.N. Lal, J. Weston, and B. Schölkopf. Learning with local and global consistency. *Proc. Neural Info. Processing Systems*, 2003.

Appendix A

Outline of proof of Theorem 2. We use the auxilliary function. A function $G(H, \tilde{H})$ is called an auxiliary function of L if it is satisfies $G(H, H) = L(H)$, $G(H, \tilde{H}) \leq L(H) \forall H, \tilde{H}$. Define $H^{(t+1)} = \arg\max_H G(H, H^{(t)})$. By construction, we have $L(H^{(t)}) = G(H^{(t)}, H^{(t)}) \leq G(H^{(t+1)}, H^{(t)}) \leq L(H^{(t+1)})$. Thus $L(H^{(t)})$ is monotonic increasing. We can show that

$$G(H, \tilde{H}) = \sum_{kij} W_{ij} \tilde{H}_{ik} \tilde{H}_{jk} (1 + \log \frac{H_{ik} H_{jk}}{\tilde{H}_{ik} \tilde{H}_{jk}}) - \sum_{ik} \frac{(\tilde{H}\alpha)_{ik} H_{ik}^2}{\tilde{H}_{ik}}$$

is an auxiliary function of L. Setting $\partial G(H, \tilde{H})/\partial H_{ik} = 0$ leads to $H_{ik}^2 = \tilde{H}_{ik}^2 (W\tilde{H})_{ik}/(\tilde{H}\alpha)_{ik}$. Setting $H^{(t+1)} = H$, $H^{(t)} = \tilde{H}$, we obtain Eq.(8). □

Severe Class Imbalance: Why Better Algorithms Aren't the Answer

Chris Drummond[1] and Robert C. Holte[2]

[1] Institute for Information Technology, National Research Council Canada,
Ottawa, Ontario, Canada, K1A 0R6
Chris.Drummond@nrc-cnrc.gc.ca
[2] Department of Computing Science, University of Alberta,
Edmonton, Alberta, Canada, T6G 2E8
holte@cs.ualberta.ca

Abstract. This paper argues that severe class imbalance is not just an interesting technical challenge that improved learning algorithms will address, it is much more serious. To be useful, a classifier must appreciably outperform a trivial solution, such as choosing the majority class. Any application that is inherently noisy limits the error rate, and cost, that is achievable. When data are normally distributed, even a Bayes optimal classifier has a vanishingly small reduction in the majority classifier's error rate, and cost, as imbalance increases. For fat tailed distributions, and when practical classifiers are used, often no reduction is achieved.

1 Introduction

Class imbalance, and the difficulties that result, has been a topic of much interest in recent years in machine learning [1]. When classes are imbalanced, existing learning algorithms often produce classifiers that do little more than predict the most common class. It seems intuitive that a practical classifier must do much better on the minority class, often the one of greatest interest, even if this means sacrificing performance on the majority class. If the overall error rate becomes worse, so the reasoning goes, then it fails to capture what practically matters and alternative measures are needed. Researchers have looked at separate error rates for positive and negative classes [2], the functional relationship between them [3] and the area under the function [4].

Although we use expected cost, we feel it is less a matter that the measure is wrong, it is more that the majority classifier is very hard to beat when classes are severely imbalanced. Differential costs may reduce the problem bur they are by no means guaranteed to eliminate it. We are not simply reiterating a common observation that sometimes the majority classifier's error rate is so small that it seems little can be done to improve on it. We are making the stronger claim that a "relative reduction" in error rate is often unachievable. We use the fraction of the majority classifier's error rate removed because it is important to consider what success means when a trivial classifier gets only say 1% wrong. In this case, a classifier with a 0.4% error rate has an error rate reduction of 0.6, a respectable value. This is equivalent to a 20% error rate when the classes are balanced and the majority classifier gets 50% wrong. This idea is especially intuitive when considering misclassification costs [5,6]. The success of a classifier is how much it reduces the cost when using a trivial classifier. Even a Bayes optimal classifier, at least as good as the majority classifier, often only has a small relative cost reduction. As imbalance increases, this becomes even smaller. For practical algorithms just performing as well as the majority classifier becomes progressively harder. Improved learning algorithms will not eliminate the problem. If the application is inherently noisy, no amount of boosting, bagging or kernelizing can produce performance beyond Bayes optimal.

Our results address applications where all instances of one class have the same misclassification costs. If costs are highly non-linear, say it is enough to classify a small number instances correctly ignoring the rest, our arguments are not relevant. This may be true in some information retrieval tasks, where only a very small fraction of the positive instances are required to satisfy a query. Occasionally, a small performance gain over the majority classifier is the difference between success and failure. We claim that many, if not most, classification applications are not of either type. At the very least, our own experience tells us, the type of application addressed here is common enough that the conclusions we draw should be relevant to many researchers and practitioners.

2 Visualizing the Problem

This section gives a brief introduction to cost curves [7], a way to visualize classifier performance over different misclassification costs and class distributions.

The error rate of a binary classifier is a convex combination of the likelihood functions $P(-|+)$, $P(+|-)$, where $P(L|C)$ is the probability that an instance of class C is labeled L and the coefficients $P(+)$, $P(-)$ are the class priors:

$$E[Error] = \underbrace{P(-|+)}_{FN} P(+) + \underbrace{P(+|-)}_{FP} P(-)$$

Estimates of the likelihoods are the false positive (FP) and false negative (FN) rates. A straight line, such as the one in bold in Figure 1, gives the error rate on the y-axis (ignore the axis labels in parentheses for the moment), for each possible prior probability of an instance belonging to the positive class on the x-axis. If this line is completely below another line, representing a second classifier, it has a lower error rate for every probability. If they cross, each classifier is better for some range of priors. Of particular note are the two trivial classifiers, the dashed lines in the figure. One always predicts that instances are negative, the other that instances are positive. Together they form the majority classifier, the shaded triangle in Figure 1, which predicts the most common class. The figure shows that any single classifier with a non-zero error rate will always be outperformed by the majority classifier if the priors are sufficiently skewed, therefore of little use. Even a good classifier produces too many false positives when negative examples are very common [8].

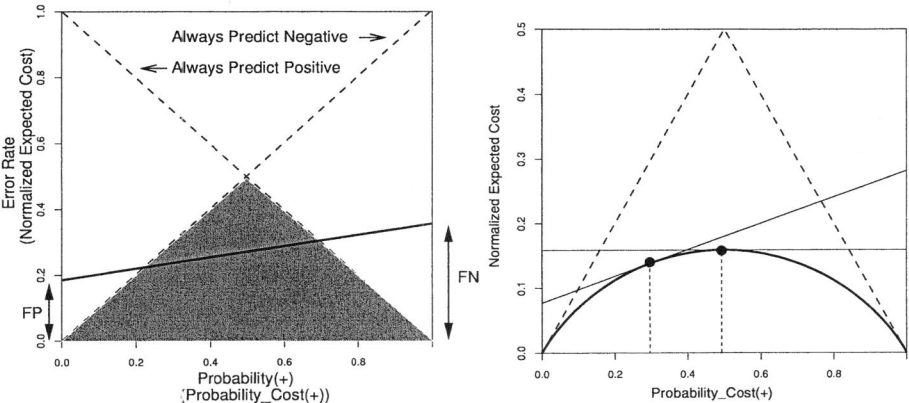

Fig. 1. Visualizing Performance   **Fig. 2.** The Cost Curve

If misclassification costs are taken into account, expected error rate is replaced by expected cost, as defined by Equation 1. The expected cost is also a convex combination of the prior probabilities, but plotting it against the priors would produce a y-axis that no longer ranges from zero to one. The expected cost is normalized by dividing by the maximum value, given by Equation 2. The costs and priors are combined into the Probability_Cost(+) on the x-axis, as in Equation 3. Applying the same normalization factor results in an x-axis that ranges from zero to one, as in Equation 4. The positive and negative Probability_Cost(_)'s now sum to one, as was the case with the probabilities.

$$E[Cost] = FN * C(-|+)P(+) + FP * C(+|-)P(-) \qquad (1)$$
$$max(E[Cost]) = C(-|+)P(+) + C(+|-)P(-) \qquad (2)$$
$$PC(+) = C(-|+)P(+) \qquad (3)$$
$$Norm(E[Cost]) = FN * PC(+) + FP * PC(-) \qquad (4)$$

With this representation, the axes in Figure 1 are simply relabeled, using the text in parentheses, to account for costs. Misclassification costs and class frequencies are more imbalanced the further away from 0.5, the center of the diagram. The lines are still straight. There is still a triangular shaded region, but now representing the classifier predicting the class that has the smaller expected cost. For simplicity we shall continue to refer to it as the majority classifier.

In Figure 2 the straight continuous lines are Bayes optimal classifiers for two different class frequencies or costs, indicated by the vertical dashed lines. The classifier represented by the horizontal line is optimal when the classes and costs are balanced. The second classifier is optimal when there are more negative examples, or they are more costly to misclassify. If the optimal classifier is identified for every probability-cost value and a point put on each line at that value, as indicated by the black dots in Figure 2, the set of such points defines the continuous bold curve. So generally as the balance changes, there is a smooth trade-off between positives that are incorrectly classified and negatives that are incorrectly classified. Most practical learning algorithms also generate different classifiers for different priors and make a principled trade off between the number of errors on the positive and negative classes. They produce similar curves, although their curves will generally be above the curve in Figure 2 because their performance will fall somewhat short of Bayes optimal.

3 Imbalance and Performance

In this section, we show that a Bayes optimal classifier performs only marginally better than a trivial classifier when there is severe imbalance. This difference is even smaller if the likelihood functions have fat tails or the classifier suboptimal.

3.1 Increasing Imbalance

Figure 3 shows cost curves for the Bayes optimal classifier for two, unit variance, normal distributions, representing the likelihood functions for two classes. The continuous curves are for 3 different distances between their means. The distances were chosen to make the relative cost reduction when the classes are balanced 0.2, 0.5 and 0.8. The series of progressively smaller triangles, the dotted lines, we call cost reduction contours. They are triangles because the majority classifier is a triangle. Each contour indicates the reduction in cost achieved by the new classifier as a fraction of the cost of using the majority classifier. For instance, the central contour, marked 0.5, indicates a reduction of one half of the cost. The continuous curves cross multiple contours indicating a decreasing relative cost reduction as imbalance increases.

Zooming in on the lower left hand corner of Figure 3 gives Figure 4. Here negative instances are much more common than the positives, or more costly to

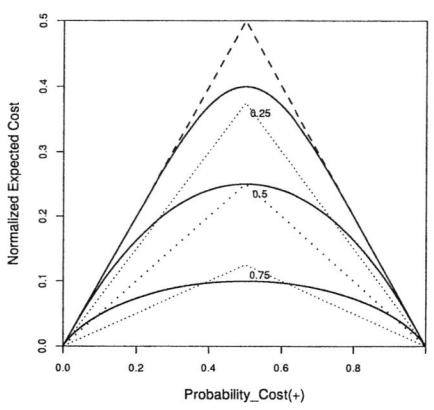

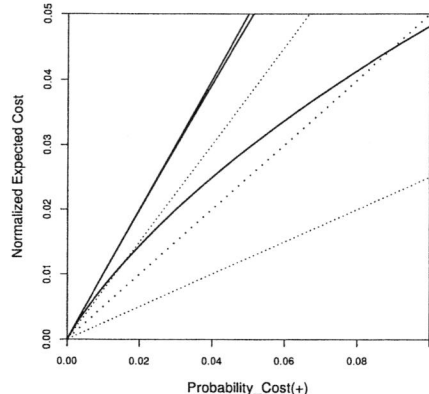

Fig. 3. Different Separations

Fig. 4. Severe Imbalances

misclassify. The upper two curves have become nearly indistinguishable from the majority classifier for ratios about 20:1. The lowest cost curve has crossed the 0.5 cost reduction contour at an imbalance of about 10:1 and crossed the 0.25 cost reduction contour at about 50:1. So even starting with a very good classifier with a 0.8 relative cost reduction when there is no imbalance (i.e. a 10% error rate), the benefit decays rapidly as imbalance increases.

3.2 Different Distributions

In this section we investigate what happens if the data are not drawn from normal distributions. We use the "power exponential" distribution, shown in Figure 5, which has a factor controlling the fatness of the tails. The bold curve is the normal distribution, this acts as the standard for tail fatness. At one extreme is the double exponential, or Laplace, distribution. At the other extreme is the uniform distribution. The double exponential distribution is relatively low in the middle and spreads out widely, giving it the fat-tails. As the factor is increased the center rises and thickens as the tails diminish. Ultimately, as we approach the uniform distribution, the tails thin out and disappear.

Figure 6 shows cost curves when the distributions in Figure 5 are used to define the likelihood functions for both classes. The distances between their means were chosen so that all curves have the same normalized expected cost of 0.2 when balanced. The curve for the normal distribution is the bold continuous line. Curves with fatter tails are even more sensitive to imbalance. The topmost curve is for the double exponential. It has exactly the same cost as the majority classifier when imbalance is about 8:1 or 1:8. The distributions with fatter tails than the normal distribution all have a relative cost reduction of only 0.1 if the imbalance is greater than 10:1. It is true, however, that distributions with thinner tails than the normal distribution reduce the cost proportionally more. In fact, two overlapping uniform distributions (the thinnest possible tails and the lowest continuous curve in Figure 6) have the same relative cost reduction for severe imbalance as for perfect balance.

If uniform distributions give consistent performance perhaps nominal attributes do as well. Uniform distributions are like a single nominal attribute with three values, the middle one is where they overlap. Suppose there are 100 positives with value A, 100 with value B and 100 negatives with value B, 100 with value C, see the top left of the Figure 7. Varying the imbalance produces a triangular cost curve, the same as with uniform distributions. But suppose some of the negative and positive classes are redistributed such that values A and C no longer contain just one class, shown at the top right of Figure 7. This produces the upper bold curve where the classifier has the same performance as the majority classifier for ratios as low as 6:1.

3.3 Practical Algorithms

This section explores what happens when a practical, not a Bayes optimal, classifier is used. We look at the popular one nearest neighbor algorithm. Its error

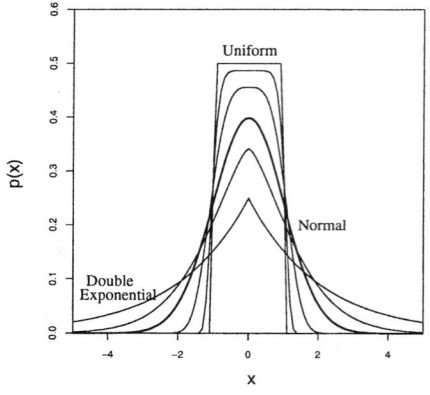

Fig. 5. Changing the Tails

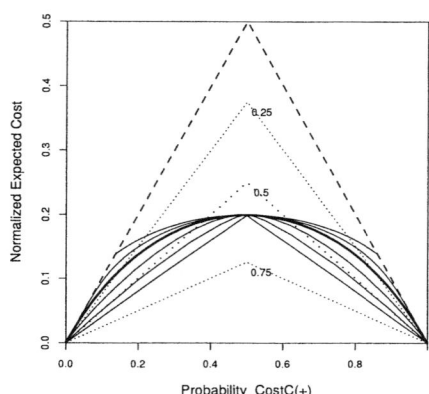

Fig. 6. Different Distributions

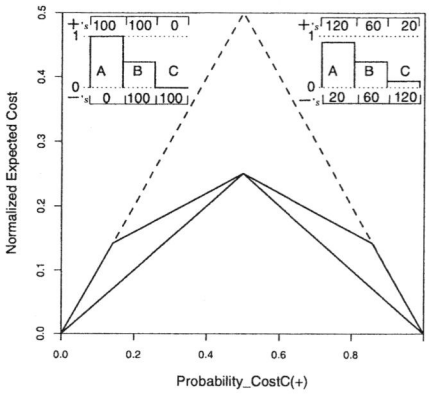

Fig. 7. Discrete Distributions

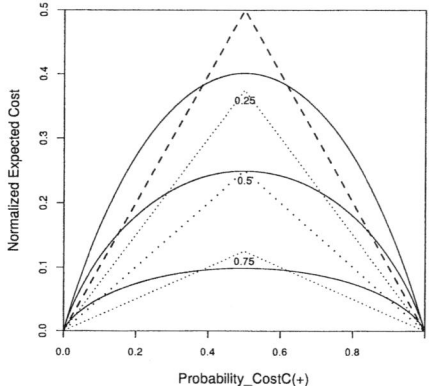

Fig. 8. One Nearest Neighbor

rate is known to be no worse than twice Bayes optimal. In the limit of training set size, the algorithm will classify an instance as positive (negative) in proportion to the probability of its being positive (negative). To generate the cost curves in Figure 8, we again vary the distance between two normal distributions. The topmost curve has the smallest distance and only a small relative cost reduction even when priors and costs are balanced. Even relatively mild imbalances remove this benefit. All classifiers will perform worse than the majority classifier, differing only in the degree of imbalance at which it occurs. The top two curves show a performance worse than the majority classifier for class ratios as low as 10:1. The best classifier performs worse when the ratio is greater than 100:1. But even at 10:1 the cost reduction has fallen from 0.8 to 0.5 and at 50:1 to 0.1.

In summary, for a constant relative cost reduction there must be pure regions containing a large fraction of each class. Otherwise, it becomes vanishingly small as imbalance increases. We experimented informally with C4.5 [9] on 10 UCI data sets [10], with ten or more instances at each leaf. On six data sets (sonar, diabetes, hepatitis, vote, labor and breast cancer) there were very few pure leaves, accounting for a small fraction of the instances. LetterK produced a pure leaf for the majority class representing about a third of the data, but no pure leaf for a significant fraction of the minority class. Hypothyroid and sick produced large leaves that were almost pure but only for the majority class. One dataset, chess (KRvKP7), produced pure leaves across almost the entire instance space. Here C4.5 has a very low error rate that persists even if imbalance is very extreme.

This paper used expected cost to evaluate classifiers. Costs are a very general way of measuring performance, but there are other measures. Probably the most popular is the "area under the curve" of an ROC plot. Although it has advantages over error rate [4], we feel it obscures the severe imbalance problem. All ROC curves have the two trivial classifiers, forming the majority classifier, as their endpoints. If we use the slope of the curve to chose the appropriate classifier [11], these endpoints will be chosen for severe imbalance, unless the slope is zero or inifinity. Although increased "area under the curve" is indicative of better performance it does not guarantee that a classifier is immune to severe imbalance.

4 Reducing the Problem

Our representation emphasizes the close relationship between misclassification costs and class frequencies. Cost imbalance is potentially just as problematic as class imbalance. We might hope that the minority class is the more costly to misclassify, counteracting class imbalance and moving towards the center of our diagram. But if class imbalance is severe, say 100:1, a severe cost imbalance of similar magnitude is needed to solve the problem. This may occur in situations where missing a true alarm has major consequences. Some work by one author involves detecting wheel failures on trains. Failures leading to major accidents, however rare, would incur considerable costs. High costs inevitably produce a high rate of false alarms. Although users may initially find this unacceptable, demonstrating an overall cost reduction should overcome any misgivings.

Another way to reduce the problem is to generalize what it means to belong to the minority class. For trains, we might instead of predicting a wheel failure predict an "axle" failure for either wheel sharing an axle. There are two axles on a truck (4 wheels), two trucks on a car (8 wheels) and many cars on a train (100's wheels). The choice of granularity depends on the costs inherent in the application. Predicting failures at the car level, or even the train level, should reduce costs considerably. Predicting at the wheel level may have only a small additional benefit. Raising the granularity of the prediction task will often keep most, if not all, of the benefits while considerably reducing the imbalance. This may be part of the reason for success of some earlier work with imbalanced classes. Fawcett and Provost [6], rather than classifying individual cellular phone calls as fraudulent, classified days of phone use as indicative of fraudulent behavior. This was primarily intended to reduce noise in the application but had an additional benefit of reducing class imbalance.

So if imbalance is severe, before exploring alternatives algorithms we argue that one should explore alternative class definitions. One should establish a "lower bound" – the most balanced application in terms of costs and class frequencies that might be solved and still be useful. If this is impossible, the task is likely inherently difficult to solve and time may be better spent elsewhere.

5 Conclusions

This paper has shown that there is a fundamental limit on classifier performance (given by the Bayes optimal classifier) that is often little better than that of the majority classifier. Non-normal distributions and practical algorithms often exacerbate the problem. We have argued that there is not an algorithmic solution. Only by redefining the classification task can the problem be addressed. [1]

References

1. Chawla, N.V., Japkowicz, N., Kolcz, A., eds.: Proc. of ICML'2003 Workshop on Learning from Imbalanced Data Sets. (2003)
2. Cardie, C., Howe, N.: Improving minority class prediction using case-specific feature weights. In: Proc. of 14th Int. Conf. on Machine Learning. (1997) 57–65
3. Provost, F., Fawcett, T., Kohavi, R.: The case against accuracy estimation for comparing induction algorithms. In: Proc. of 15th Int. Conf. on Machine Learning. (1998) 43–48
4. Ling, C.X., Huang, J., Zhang, H.: AUC: a statistically consistent and more discriminating measure than accuracy. In: Proc. of 18th Int. Joint Conf. on Artificial Intelligence. (2003) 519–524
5. Pazzani, M., Merz, C., Murphy, P., Ali, K., Hume, T., Brunk, C.: Reducing misclassification costs. In: Proc. of 11th Int. Conf. on Machine Learning. (1994) 217–225
6. Fawcett, T., Provost, F.: Adaptive fraud detection. Data Mining and Knowledge Discovery 1 (1997) 291–316
7. Drummond, C., Holte, R.C.: Explicitly representing expected cost: An alternative to ROC representation. In: Proc. of 6th Int. Conf. on Knowledge Discovery and Data Mining. (2000) 198–207
8. Axelsson, S.: The base-rate fallacy and its implications for the difficulty of intrusion detection. In: Proc. of 6th ACM Conf. on Computer & Communications Security. (1999) 1–7
9. Quinlan, J.R.: C4.5 Programs for Machine Learning. Morgan Kaufmann (1993)
10. Blake, C.L., Merz, C.J.: UCI repository of machine learning databases, University of California, Irvine, CA. www.ics.uci.edu/~mlearn/MLRepository.html (1998)
11. Provost, F., Fawcett, T.: Robust classification systems for imprecise environments. In: Proc. of 15th Nat. Conf. on Artificial Intelligence. (1998) 706–713

---

[1] Partially funded through the Alberta Ingenuity Centre for Machine Learning.

Approximation Algorithms for Minimizing Empirical Error by Axis-Parallel Hyperplanes

Tapio Elomaa[1], Jussi Kujala[1], and Juho Rousu[2]

[1] Institute of Software Systems,
Tampere University of Technology
[2] Department of Computer Science,
Royal Holloway University of London
elomaa@cs.tut.fi, jussi.kujala@tut.fi, juho@cs.rhul.ac.uk

Abstract. Many learning situations involve separation of labeled training instances by hyperplanes. Consistent separation is of theoretical interest, but the real goal is rather to minimize the number of errors using a bounded number of hyperplanes. Exact minimization of empirical error in a high-dimensional grid induced into the feature space by axis-parallel hyperplanes is NP-hard. We develop two approximation schemes with performance guarantees, a greedy set covering scheme for producing a consistently labeled grid, and integer programming rounding scheme for finding the minimum error grid with bounded number of hyperplanes.

1 Introduction

In supervised learning a training sample $S = \{(x_1, y_1), (x_2, y_2), \ldots, (x_n, y_n)\}$ of n labeled instances is given. The instance vectors x_i are composed of the values of d attributes and the class labels y_i usually come from a relatively small set C. The objective of a learning algorithm is to categorize the examples given to reflect the true classification of all instances. However, since it can only be observed through the training sample, a common subtask in learning algorithms is to fit a hypothesis closely to the training examples.

In real-world domains fully consistent separation of instances is mostly impossible due to noise and other inherent complications. Instead, one needs to solve an optimization problem of *empirical (or training) error minimization*, finding the hypothesis that errs in the classification of minimum number of training examples. Indeed, Vapnik's [1] *empirical risk minimization* principle suggests to choose the hypothesis with minimal training error. Fitting the hypothesis too closely to the training sample is, though, seen to lead to *overfitting* and, therefore, some form of *regularization* is required to guide error minimization.

By generalization error bounding techniques the error minimizing hypothesis does not have true error far from optimal. Unfortunately, in many classes finding the minimum error hypothesis is computationally intractable. It is, e.g., NP-hard to solve for the class of monomials, i.e. hyperplanes, in arbitrary dimension [2]. We will develop approximation algorithms for one such intractable problem, separating points by a restricted number of axis-parallel hyperplanes.

This problem is related to practice, e.g., through the problem of naïve Bayesian classification in which the small number of decision boundaries per attribute taken together divides the input space into hyper-rectangular cells each of which gets an assigned class according to the relevant marginal distributions.

The axis-parallel separation problem that we study is, though, not quite the same problem because it does not take marginal distributions into account. However, this is a necessary step on the road to developing an optimal discretization algorithm for Naïve Bayes and general Bayesian networks. Discretization of numerical attributes is a central problem in learning network structure [3].

We consider the d-dimensional Euclidean instance space $\mathbb{R}^d$. For the ease of illustration, we will be mainly dealing with the two-dimensional case, $d = 2$. Sometimes we also set $|C| = 2$ for the sake of clarity.

2 Problem Definition and Prior Work

Axis-parallel hyperplanes arise in classifiers that compose their hypothesis from value tests for single attributes. Denote the value of an attribute A for the instance vector x by $\text{val}_A(x)$. For a numerical attribute A the value test is of the form $\text{val}_A(x) \leq t$, where t is a threshold value. Now, $\text{val}_A(x) = t$ defines an axis-parallel hyperplane that divides the input space in two half-spaces.

We are interested in the situation where the number of hyperplanes is restricted. If we are at liberty to choose the number of hyperplanes at will, we can always guarantee zero error for consistent data by separating each point to its own subset. Minimizing the number of hyperplanes needed to obtain a consistent partitioning is NP-complete, but can be approximated with ratio d in $\mathbb{R}^d$ [4].

At least two natural ways exist to partition a plane using axis-aligned straight lines (Fig. 1): They can define a hierarchy of nested half-spaces or a grid on the whole input space. An archetype example of the former method is top-down induction of decision trees. The root attribute first halves the whole instance space, its children the resulting subspaces, and so forth. The final subspaces (the leaves of a decision tree) are eventually assigned with a class label prediction, e.g., by choosing the majority label of the examples in the subspace. In our example five lines lead to six nested half-spaces. In the alternative division of the input

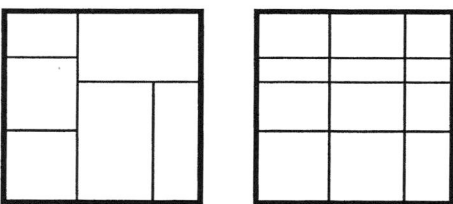

Fig. 1. Two ways of separating the plane by the same set of hyperplanes: nested half-spaces and the grid defined by hyperplanes penetrating each other

space the lines always span through the whole input space and penetrate each other. Using the corresponding five lines leads to a grid of twelve cells.

2.1 Connection to Naïve Bayesian Discretization

The grid defined by hyperplanes penetrating each other is a result of executing several attribute value tests simultaneously. Our interest in this problem comes through Naïve Bayes, which predicts for each instance x the most probable class $\arg\max_{c \in C} \mathbf{P}(c \mid x)$ as determined by the training data. Probability estimation is based on the *Bayes rule* $\mathbf{P}(c \mid x) = \mathbf{P}(x \mid c) \mathbf{P}(c) / \mathbf{P}(x)$.

In determining the most probable class the values of all attributes of the instance are all looked at simultaneously because of the (naïve) assumption that the attributes $A_1, \ldots, A_d$ are independent of each other given the class, which indicates that $\mathbf{P}(x \mid c) = \prod_{i=1}^{d} \mathbf{P}(\mathrm{val}_{A_i}(x) \mid c)$. The probabilities are estimated from the marginal distributions of the training sample S. A common way of handling a numerical attribute A is to discretize its value range into successive half-open intervals $t_{j-1} < \mathrm{val}_A(x_i) \leq t_j$ using threshold values $t_1, t_2, \ldots$ after which the numerical attribute can be handled similarly as a nominal one.

In decision tree learning the value ranges of numerical attributes can often be discretized to a small number of intervals without a loss in training accuracy [5]. The same is true for optimal discretization of Naïve Bayes: its *decision boundaries* for each dimension can be recovered without loss of accuracy after discretization [6]. Together all decision boundaries of the d dimensions divide the input space into a hyper-grid in which each cell gets labeled by the class that is most probable according to the evidence contained in the training set.

Let R be one of the hyper-rectangles induced by the chosen axis-parallel hyperplanes minimizing training error. In other words, R is a convex region defined by the value of each attribute A_i restricted to some interval R_i contained in R. As empirical error is minimized in R, it must be that $\mathbf{P}(R, c)$ is maximized within R for (one of) the majority class(es) c. When the instances come from a product distribution, we can apply the naïve Bayesian assumption to get

$$\mathbf{P}(R, c) = \mathbf{P}(R \mid c) \mathbf{P}(c) = \mathbf{P}(c) \prod_{i=1}^{d} \mathbf{P}(R_i \mid c).$$

This product is the numerator in the equation determining the prediction of Naïve Bayes and actually chooses the same class as Naïve Bayes. Since c has maximum probability within R, it must also be the choice of Naïve Bayes within this bin in a discretization. Hence, the Naïve Bayes optimal discretization is attained on the axis-parallel hyperplanes that minimize empirical error. However, this does not hold for all possible data distributions.

2.2 Related Work

The simplest linear separator class, single unrestricted hyperplanes, is usually considered to be a too restricted class of hypotheses for practical purposes because of the restrictions of the *perceptron* algorithm. There have, though, been many successful applications of even such simple hypotheses and *kernel methods* can take advantage of linear machines combined with other techniques [7].

Minimizing empirical error has been studied extensively in connection of decision trees. Optimal decision tree construction is NP-complete in general settings [8] and in arbitrary dimensions [9, 10]. Furthermore, optimal decision tree learning is highly inapproximable [11]. In fixed dimensions Das and Goodrich [12] have shown that it is NP-complete to decide whether points of $\mathbb{R}^3$ that come from two classes have a consistent linear decision tree of at most k nodes.

The problem of separating two point sets with k unconstrained hyperplanes is NP complete in general dimension and solvable in polynomial time in fixed dimension [2, 9]. Grigni et al. [11] have shown that, unless NP=ZPP, the number of nodes containing linear decision functions (hyperplanes) in a decision tree cannot be approximated within any fixed polynomial. Moreover, the depth of such a classifier cannot be approximated within any fixed constant.

Auer et al. [13] devised an algorithm that minimizes empirical error in the class of two-level decision trees. Dobkin and Gunopulos [14] further consider learning restricted decision trees and studied the learnability of piecewise linear and convex concepts in low dimensions defined as the intersection of a constant number of half-spaces [15]. Dobkin et al. [16] also show that minimizing empirical error (in binary classification) is equivalent to computing the maximum bi-chromatic discrepancy. They are thus able to devise algorithms for minimizing error for axis-aligned boxes and hyperplanes.

Chlebus and Nguyen [17] showed the NP-completeness of consistent partitioning of the real plane using minimum number of axis-parallel lines that penetrate each other by reducing the minimum set cover problem in polynomial time to it. Hence, we cannot expect to find an efficient algorithm to solve the problem of our interest exactly (unless P=NP). Based on this result one can also prove Naïve Bayes optimal discretization to be NP-hard [6].

Călinescu et al. [4] dealt also with the problem that we consider here. However, they were interested in the case of consistent partitioning and used as many hyperplanes as needed to obtain complete separation of different colored points. We, on the other hand, are interested in the more realistic problem of restricted number of hyperplanes and inconsistent data. Nevertheless, we are able to take advantage of the proof techniques of Călinescu et al. [4].

3 Minimum Set Cover Approximation

As a reduction from minimum set cover to the consistent partitioning of the real plane has been used [17], it seems natural also to try to approximate empirical error minimization through that problem. Given a set U of n items, a collection $\mathcal{S}$ of m subsets of U, and a natural number k, the set covering problem is [18]:

> SET COVER$(U, \mathcal{S}, k)$: Does there exist a collection of at most k subsets $\{S_{r_1}, \ldots, S_{r_k}\} \subset \mathcal{S}$ such that every item of U is contained in at least one of the sets in the collection?

SET COVER is approximable within $\ln n + 1$, but not within $(1-\varepsilon)\log n$ for any $\varepsilon > 0$. The algorithm attaining the logarithmic approximation ratio is the straightforward greedy covering method, which chooses to the evolving cover the subset that contains the largest number of yet uncovered elements [18].

The problem of consistent partitioning of $\mathbb{R}^d$ with axis-parallel hyperplanes is:

> CONSAXIS(S, n): Given a set S of n points $\{x_1, \ldots, x_n\} \subset \mathbb{R}^d$ each labeled either positive or negative, find a consistent partitioning of S with axis-parallel hyperplanes using as few hyperplanes as possible.

We reduce CONSAXIS to SET COVER, which allows us to use the greedy set covering algorithm to solve the CONSAXIS problem. Given an instance S of the CONSAXIS problem, we generate a new element $u_{x,x'}$ corresponding to each conflicting pair of labeled points (x, y) and (x', y'), where $y \neq y'$, in S. Let U be the set of all such generated elements. In the worst case $|U| = \Omega(n^2)$.

It is sufficient to restrict the axis-parallel hyperplanes to a set $\mathcal{H}$ of at most $n - 1$ *canonical hyperplanes* per dimension. There is a canonical hyperplane per consecutive points with respect to a dimension (say, at the average coordinate between the two). In terms of cut point analysis [5], they correspond to the *bin borders* of the axes. In empirical error minimization one can further reduce the number of intervals [5]. For each $h \in \mathcal{H}$ we create a set that has a representative for each pair of conflicting examples that can be separated by h ($\equiv \text{val}_{A_i}(x) = t$):

$$H(X, t) = \{ u_{x,x'} \in U \mid \text{val}_{A_i}(x) \leq t \leq \text{val}_{A_i}(x') \lor \text{val}_{A_i}(x') \leq t \leq \text{val}_{A_i}(x) \}$$

Let H denote the collection of all such sets. Now, H is an instance of the SET COVER problem such that its solution defines a set of hyperplanes which, by construction, separate all conflicting example pairs from each other.

Applying the greedy set covering algorithm to the collection of sets H constructed above, gives an approximation algorithm for CONSAXIS with approximation quality $O(k^*(1 + \ln n^2)) = O(k^*(1 + 2\ln n))$, where k^* is the minimum number of axis-parallel hyperplanes needed to consistently partition the set S.

Inconsistent data is also easy to handle. Determine the majority class within a set of all examples with the same instance vector and delete all members of the minority classes before converting the problem.

In practice one is often allowed or wants to use only k hyperplanes for the partition. The bounded number of hyperplanes now at our disposal does not necessarily suffice to reach the lowest error, and the goal becomes to attain as low error as possible using them.

When the number of hyperplanes is not restricted, no polynomial-time algorithm has approximation guarantee $1 + c$, where $c > 0$ is a constant [4]. I.e., by using a constant factor c more hyperplanes than in the optimal solution, one cannot guarantee to attain zero error. This result also implies a limitation to the situation where the number of hyperplanes is restricted: Assume that there were a polynomial-time algorithm with a constant approximation guarantee (to the number of erroneously labeled instances). More specifically, assume that

$$\text{APP}_{(1+c)k} \leq \delta \,\text{OPT}_k,$$

where APP_k denotes the error of the approximate solution using k hyperplanes and OPT_k stands for the minimum error using k hyperplanes. Now, setting $\text{OPT}_k = 0$ yields an exact polynomial-time algorithm for the unrestricted case, which contradicts the fact that no such algorithm exists. Thus, no polynomial-time algorithm can guarantee an error at most a constant δ times that of the optimal algorithm using only a constant factor c more hyperplanes.

Set covering of conflicting pairs does not give an approximation algorithm in this case, because even though the evolving set cover (partition) reduces the number of conflicts of the sample, it does not guarantee diminishing error. Consider, e.g., four examples divided by one hyperplane into two subsets both containing one positive and one negative example; two classification conflicts have been removed by the hyperplane, but the error of this partition has not reduced.

4   Linear Programming Approximation

We will first formulate the axis-parallel separation problem as a zero-one integer program, and then give its linear program (LP) relaxation. The general problem of zero-one integer programming is NP-hard. However, for the LP relaxation, in which the integral constraints are replaced by ones that allow the variables to assume real values in $[0, 1]$, many efficient methods for solving are known.

We use two sets of binary variables. A variable w_i, $1 \leq i \leq n$, has value 1 if point p_i is not separated by the chosen hyperplanes from all points of different class, otherwise $w_i = 0$. The second set of variables z_j represents the axis-parallel hyperplanes. There are at most $d(n-1)$ of them. If a hyperplane $h_j \in \mathcal{H}$ is included in the set of solution lines, then $z_j = 1$ and otherwise $z_j = 0$.

Because each point that is not separated by the chosen lines from all points of different class will unavoidably lead to a misclassification, our objective is to minimize the number of such points. I.e., we want to optimize:

$$\min \sum_{i=1}^{n} w_i$$

with constraints

$$\sum_{j=1}^{d(n-1)} z_j \leq k \text{ and } w_u + w_v + \sum z_j \geq 1.$$

The first constraint ensures that at most k hyperplanes are chosen. The second one is called the *separation condition*, and there is one for each pair of points p_u and p_v that have different class. The sum is taken over all those lines that separate the two points. The separation condition is sufficient because in each such pair at least one of the following holds:

- Either p_u or p_v, or both, is destined to be an error (in conflict with the label of the cell). In this case the separation condition is fulfilled by $w_u + w_v \geq 1$.
- A hyperplane h_j has been chosen that separates p_u and p_v. In this case the separation condition is fulfilled by $z_j = 1$.

Note that any value assignment for the w_i and z_j variables that satisfies the separation condition corresponds to a grid, where a point p_u that is labeled correct ($w_u = 0$) will only share its cell with points with the same label and points destined to be errors ($w_v = 1$).

Let us now turn to the LP relaxation, where the variables $\hat{w}_i$ and $\hat{z}_j$ take real values in $[0, 1]$. Obviously, the value of the solution to the relaxed problem using k lines, LP_k, is at most that of the integer program, OPT_k; $LP_k \leq \text{OPT}_k$. Let us consider all pairs of points p_u and p_v for which it holds $\hat{w}_u + \hat{w}_v \geq C$ for some constant C, $0 < C \leq 1$. We now round the values $\hat{w}$ so that in each such pair at least one variable gets value 1. A straightforward way is to round up all those variables that have $\hat{w}_i \geq C/2$. The remaining $\hat{w}$ variables are rounded down to 0. In the worst case we have to round up $n-1$ variables. The number of these variables determines an approximation to the solution of the optimization problem. Hence, this approach can guarantee an approximation ratio of

$$(2/C)\sum_{i=1}^{n} \hat{w}_i = (2/C)LP_k \leq 2\,\text{OPT}_k/C.$$

It remains to round the values $\hat{z}_j$. Here we adapt the counting based rounding procedure of Călinescu et al. [4]. Any two points p_u and p_v that need to be separated by a hyperplane after rounding of $\hat{w}$ values have $\hat{w}_u + \hat{w}_v < C$. By the separation condition, in the solution of the LP relaxation the sum of variables corresponding to hyperplanes in between the points is $\sum \hat{z}_j > 1 - C$. In order to include one of those to our rounded solution, we systematically go through the hyperplanes by dimensions and cumulate the sum of their $\hat{z}$ values. In the plane as long as the sum is below $(1-C)/2$ we round the $\hat{z}_j$ variables down to 0. We choose all those lines that make the total sum reach or exceed $(1-C)/2$. The sum is then reset to 0 and we continue to go through the lines.

Consider a conflicting pair of points which need to be separated by a line. If no vertical line was chosen to separate them, their cumulative sum must have been strictly below $(1-C)/2$, and one of the horizontal lines in between the two is guaranteed to make the sum reach and exceed the threshold. As the sum of the fractional variables still obeys the upper bound of k by the first constraint, this way we may end up picking at most $2k/(1-C)$ lines to our approximation.

Let APP_k denote the value of the above described rounding procedure and line selection using k lines. By the above computation, we have that

$$\text{APP}_{2k/(1-C)} \leq 2\,\text{OPT}_k/C.$$

Thus, we have demonstrated an approximation algorithm for the separation problem. As necessitated, the algorithm uses more lines and makes more false classifications than the optimal solution. For example, when $C = 1/2$, we have $\text{APP}_{4k} \leq 4\,\text{OPT}_k$. The general form of the above performance guarantee in d dimensions is $\text{APP}_{dk/(1-C)} \leq d \cdot \text{OPT}_k/C$.

5 Conclusion and Future Work

In this paper we studied two approaches for developing an approximation algorithm for separating classified points by axis-parallel hyperplanes. The first approach using the minimum set covering only works when the number of hyperplanes is not restricted, but a LP relaxation of an integer programming formulation of the problem yields an approximation algorithm also using only a bounded number of hyperplanes.

The LP approach can easily be extended to situations where the hyperplanes are not perpendicular to each other or are higher dimensional polynomials. The practicality of the approximation schemes remains to be studied. Even though, LP solvers are in principle efficient and sparse matrix techniques can in our case be used to further speed them up, the space complexity of the proposed approach defies the most straightforward implementation.

References

1. Vapnik, V.N.: Estimation of Dependencies Based on Empirical Data. Springer, New York (1982)
2. Kearns, M.J., Schapire, R.E., Sellie, L.M.: Toward efficient agnostic learning. Machine Learn. **17** (1994) 115–141
3. Friedman, N., Geiger, D., Goldszmidt, M.: Bayesian network classifiers. Machine Learn. **29** (1997) 131–163
4. Călinescu, G., Dumitrescu, A., Wan, P.J.: Separating points by axis-parallel lines. In: Proc. Sixteenth Canadian Conference on Computational Geometry. (2004) 7–10
5. Elomaa, T., Rousu, J.: Efficient multisplitting revisited: Optima-preserving elimination of partition candidates. Data Mining and Knowl. Discovery **8** (2004) 97–126
6. Elomaa, T., Rousu, J.: On decision boundaries of naïve Bayes in continuous domains. In: Knowledge Discovery in Databases: PKDD 2003, Proc. Seventh European Conference. Volume 2838 of LNAI., Heidelberg, Springer (2003) 144–155
7. Shawe-Taylor, J., Cristianini, N.: Kernel Methods for Pattern Analysis. Cambridge University Press, Cambridge (2004)
8. Hyafil, L., Rivest, R.R.: Constructing optimal binary decision trees is NP-complete. Inf. Process. Lett. **5** (1976) 15–17
9. Megiddo, N.: On the complexity of polyhedral separability. Discrete Comput. Geom. **3** (1988) 325–337
10. Blum, A., Rivest, R.R.: Training a 3-node neural net is NP-complete. Neural Networks **5** (1992) 117–127
11. Grigni, M., Mirelli, V., Papadimitriou, C.H.: On the difficulty of designing good classifiers. SIAM J. Comput. **30** (2000) 318–323
12. Das, G., Goodrich, M.: On the complexity of optimization problems for 3-dimensional convex polyhedra and decision trees. Comput. Geom. **8** (1997) 123–137
13. Auer, P., Holte, R.C., Maass, W.: Theory and application of agnostic PAC-learning with small decision trees. In: Proc. Twelfth International Conference on Machine Learning, San Francisco, CA, Morgan Kaufmann (1995) 21–29
14. Dobkin, D., Gunopulos, D.: Geometric problems in machine learning. In: Applied Computational Geometry. Volume 1148 of LNCS., Heidelberg, Springer (1996) 121–132
15. Dobkin, D., Gunopulos, D.: Concept learning with geometric hypotheses. In: Proc. Eighth Annual Conference on Computational Learning Theory, New York, NY, ACM Press (1995) 329–336

16. Dobkin, D., Gunopulos, D., Maass, W.: Computing the maximum bichromatic discrepancy, with applications in computer graphics and machine learning. J. Comput. Syst. Sci. **52** (1996) 453–470
17. Chlebus, B.S., Nguyen, S.H.: On finding optimal discretizations for two attributes. In: Rough Sets and Current Trends in Computing, Proc. First International Conference. Volume 1424 of LNAI., Heidelberg, Springer (1998) 537–544
18. Vazirani, V.V.: Approximation Algorithms. Springer, Heidelberg (2001)

A Comparison of Approaches for Learning Probability Trees

Daan Fierens, Jan Ramon, Hendrik Blockeel, and Maurice Bruynooghe

Department of Computer Science, Katholieke Universiteit Leuven,
Celestijnenlaan 200A, 3001 Leuven, Belgium
{daanf, janr, hendrik, maurice}@cs.kuleuven.be

Abstract. Probability trees (or Probability Estimation Trees, PET's) are decision trees with probability distributions in the leaves. Several alternative approaches for learning probability trees have been proposed but no thorough comparison of these approaches exists.

In this paper we experimentally compare the main approaches using the relational decision tree learner Tilde (both on non-relational and on relational datasets). Next to the main existing approaches, we also consider a novel variant of an existing approach based on the Bayesian Information Criterion (BIC). Our main conclusion is that overall trees built using the C4.5-approach or the C4.4-approach (C4.5 without post-pruning) have the best predictive performance. If the number of classes is low, however, BIC performs equally well. An additional advantage of BIC is that its trees are considerably smaller than trees for the C4.5- or C4.4-approach.

Keywords: (Relational) Decision trees, probability estimation.

1 Introduction

Probability trees (or Probability Estimation Trees, PET's) are decision trees with in the leaves probability distributions on a set of classes [11]. They are useful in a number of ways, e.g. for ranking instances according to the probability of belonging to a certain class [11] or as a compact way of specifying conditional probability distributions (for instance in Bayesian networks) [5].

Several alternative approaches for learning probability trees have been proposed in the literature but currently no thorough comparison of these approaches exists. Hence, it is unclear which approaches are preferable under which circumstances. The goal of this paper is to compare the main existing approaches and a novel variant. We incorporated them in the relational decision tree learner Tilde [2] and evaluate them by performing experiments on benchmark datasets and on manipulated datasets. We use both non-relational and relational datasets.

In Section 2 we give a high-level algorithm for learning probability trees, of which the main existing approaches are instantiations. In Section 3 we experimentally compare these approaches. In Section 4 we conclude.

2 Learning Probability Trees

Probability trees are learned from a dataset D of instances labelled with their true class. Tilde [2], the *relational* decision tree learner we use, represents instances as first-order logic interpretations and tests in internal nodes as Prolog queries (since such tests either succeed or fail, trees are binary). We use Tilde because it can handle relational datasets in addition to non-relational ones.

Probability trees are typically learned in two steps. In the first step we top-down induce a tree $\mathcal{T}$ as follows. We start from the empty tree and for each candidate-test T compute the heuristic value $h(T)$. Call T_{best} the best of all candidate-tests, i.e. $T_{best} = argmax_T(h(T))$. If $h(T_{best}) < Thr$ with Thr a certain threshold we return a leaf (so Thr determines a kind of stopping-criterion). Otherwise we make T_{best} the root of the tree and apply the same procedure recursively to learn the left- and right-subtrees. In the second step we can apply bottom-up *post-pruning* (to avoid overfitting): we first prune the left- and right-subtrees giving $\mathcal{T}_{pruned}$ and then check whether $\mathcal{T}_{pruned}$ is 'better' than a single leaf according to some pruning-criterion.

The main approaches all fit into this generic two-step approach and correspond to different choices of the heuristic function $h(.)$, Thr and the pruning-criterion (if post-pruning is used). We now briefly discuss these approaches. Some more details are given in [4].

C4.5 (error-based post-pruning) Provost and Domingos [11] discuss learning probability trees using C4.5. This means that $h(T)$ is information-gain of T ($gain(T)$), Thr is 0 (any information-gain is acceptable) and error-based post-pruning is applied[1]. We refer to Tilde applied with these parameters as **C4.5**.

C4.4 (no pruning) Provost and Domingos [11] argue that pruning is harmful for probability trees. The idea is that probability estimation is conceptually different from majority-classification (the focus of C4.5). Hence they propose to use C4.4, i.e. C4.5 without any post-pruning. We refer to Tilde applied with these parameters as **C4.4**. Obviously, **C4.4** builds extremely large trees.

Minimum Description Length (MDL) Friedman and Goldszmidt [5] define an MDL-score for probability trees and use it to derive a *stopping-criterion* for the tree-building. Concretely this means that $h(T)$ is $N_{node}.gain(T)$ and Thr is 0.5 $(NbClasses - 1) \ log_2 N + log_2 NbTests + 2$, where N is the total number of examples, N_{node} is the number of examples in the current node and $NbTests$ is the number of candidate-tests considered. In terms of MDL, $h(T)$ is the decrease in description length of the data and Thr is the increase in description length of the tree due to adding T to the tree [5]. We refer to this approach as **MDLs**.

Using MDL as a stopping-criterion (using the above Thr) we easily get stuck in local optima of the MDL-score. As an alternative we can use $Thr = 0$ and

---
[1] Like Provost and Domingos, we do not apply 'collapsing' [11] since it harms probability estimates too much.

apply *post-pruning* based on MDL-reasoning [5]. We refer to this approach as **MDLp**. **MDLp** builds trees at least as large as those for **MDLs**.

Bayesian Information Criterion (BIC) Inspired on the above MDL-score, we can define a BIC-score for probability trees (as far as we know, we are the first to apply BIC to probability trees). BIC [12] is a general approach equivalent to a form of MDL where the the description length of the model only depends on its number of independent parameters. In the context of probability trees this means that $h(T)$ is the same as for **MDLs** but Thr now is $0.5 \, (NbClasses - 1) \, log_2 N$. We refer to this approach as **BICs**. **BICs** builds trees at least as large as those for **MDLs** (since Thr is strictly lower for **BICs**).

As an alternative we can again use $Thr = 0$ and apply post-pruning based on BIC-reasoning. We refer to this approach as **BICp**. **BICp** builds trees at least as large as those for **BICs**.

Chi-square score Neville et al. [10] discuss learning probability trees using the chi-square (χ^2) statistic. Concretely, $h(T)$ is the χ^2-score of T and Thr is determined by the sampling distribution of χ^2 for significance level $p = \frac{0.1}{NbTests}$ and degrees of freedom $df = NbClasses - 1$. No post-pruning is used. We refer to this approach as **Chi**.

The above list is not complete. Some other existing approaches and the reasons for not considering them in our work are given in [4].

3 Experimental Comparison

To the best of our knowledge, **C4.5** and **C4.4** are the only of the above approaches that have already been compared (Provost and Domingos [11] conclude that neither of the two is significantly better than the other). In this section we make a thorough comparison of all approaches mentioned above.

3.1 Experiments on Benchmark Datasets: Setup and Results

Table 1 gives an overview of the datasets used. All non-relational datasets are from the UCI-repository [8], except *asm* [6]. All relational datasets are standard ILP-benchmarks [1, 7, 13] (*trains* was artificially generated [9]; for *hiv* the classes 'inactive' and 'moderately active' were taken together).

To evaluate predictive performance of probability trees we use the *Area Under the ROC-curve (AUC)*, or *Expected AUC* for multi-class problems [11]. As noted in [11], AUC can be used as a quality measure for probability estimates since a high AUC indicates that, with proper re-calibration of probabilities, probability estimates will be good. To evaluate the size of the trees we use the *number of leaf nodes* (this is the number of internal nodes plus one since trees are binary). We perform 10-fold cross-validation (except for datasets smaller than 500 examples where we perform five times 3-fold cross-validation to keep test-sets large enough) and report averages and standard deviations of results over the test-sets.

Table 2 shows the experimental results (the upper half of each table shows two-class problems, the lower half shows multi-class problems). We compared

Table 1. Characteristics of the non-relational (left) and relational (right) datasets: number of examples, number of classes and number of candidate-tests for the root

	N	NbClasses	NbTests		N	NbClasses	NbTests
asm	999	2	170	biodegradability	328	2	47
audiology	226	24	125	carcinogenesis	330	2	305
pen digits	7494	10	160	diterpenes	1504	23	210
primary tumor	339	22	29	hiv	41768	2	49
voting	435	2	16	mutagenesis	230	2	139
yeast	1484	10	45	trains	25000	2	73

Table 2. Experimental results: AUC (upper table, in %) and tree size (lower table)

	C4.4	C4.5	MDLs	MDLp	BICs	BICp	Chi
asm	58.7±4.7	**62.8±3.7**	**69.6±4.4**	**69.6±4.4**	**67.4±3.8**	**66.0±3.5**	**69.5±4.3**
biodegr.	74.9±6.7	75.4±4.8	63.9±4.0	64.1±2.9	73.0±4.7	71.6±5.3	64.5±4.0
carcinog.	59.1±5.8	59.3±6.7	50.0±0.0	50.0±0.0	54.0±2.7	57.2±3.2	50.0±0.0
hiv	74.8±3.3	53.9±1.1	64.1±2.1	70.5±3.1	66.8±3.3	72.4±3.3	67.0±3.2
mutagenesis	77.0±5.0	71.7±4.9	71.6±7.0	74.5±4.4	72.8±8.2	75.8±6.6	71.9±6.0
trains	86.3±0.5	**89.2±0.6**	**89.0±0.6**	**89.2±0.5**	**89.2±0.6**	**89.4±0.5**	**89.3±0.5**
voting	98.6±0.7	96.5±2.1	97.4±1.1	97.7±1.4	98.3±1.5	98.4±0.9	98.5±1.2
audiology	98.8±0.8	98.7±0.7	75.3±2.7	75.6±2.4	80.9±5.5	81.2±5.0	97.4±1.1
diterpenes	85.4±2.5	85.8±1.8	70.4±3.7	71.2±2.6	71.5±3.8	72.0±2.9	82.0±2.5
pen digits	99.5±0.1	99.4±0.1	98.7±0.2	98.7±0.2	98.9±0.3	98.9±0.3	99.4±0.1
pr. tumor	71.5±3.1	73.3±4.3	65.8±5.3	67.7±1.8	67.9±1.9	67.5±1.9	72.7±4.0
yeast	75.8±3.2	**79.6±3.5**	**78.3±2.5**	**78.3±2.5**	**78.3±2.5**	**78.3±2.5**	**79.1±4.0**

	C4.4	C4.5	MDLs	MDLp	BICs	BICp	Chi
asm	352±14	64±11	3±0	3±0	6±2	7±3	3±0
biodegradability	72±5	30±5	2±1	2±1	10±2	12±4	4±2
carcinogenesis	95±8	35±7	1±0	1±0	5±2	8±3	1±0
hiv	1391±76	15±2	8±3	32±4	26±3	55±4	33±3
mutagenesis	42±4	9±5	2±0	2±0	5±2	5±2	2±0
trains	4664±55	484±29	38±2	49±4	68±6	92±6	64±3
voting	21±3	6±3	3±1	3±1	6±1	6±1	6±1
audiology	24±1	24±2	2±0	2±0	3±1	3±1	18±3
diterpenes	127±11	64±5	3±1	4±1	4±1	4±1	14±2
pen digits	254±8	214±7	36±2	36±2	42±3	42±3	126±4
primary tumor	129±5	79±7	2±0	2±0	2±0	2±0	5±1
yeast	447±34	123±13	6±0	6±0	6±0	6±0	23±3

AUC's for each of the approaches to AUC's for **C4.4** (which performs best) by means of two-tailed paired t-tests ($p=0.05$). An AUC in boldface (resp. underlined) indicates that this AUC is significantly higher (resp. lower) than that for **C4.4**. A more detailed statistical analysis is given in [4].

As for running times, the approaches using an explicit stopping criterion (**MDLs**, **BICs** and **Chi**) are a factor 8 to 52 faster than the others [4].

3.2 Discussion and Further Experiments

As mentioned we used **C4.4** as the reference method for performing significance tests on the AUC's in Table 2. Hence, when reporting wins/ties/losses for a certain method we always mean wins/ties/losses of that method versus **C4.4**.

Overall Observations. From Table 2 we see that overall **C4.4** performs best although there are some datasets where it is outperformed (most notably *asm*). **C4.5** performs almost as well (the number of wins/ties/losses for **C4.5** is 3/5/4). This confirms the conclusions of Provost and Domingos [11]. Trees for **C4.5**, however, are always significantly smaller than trees for **C4.4**, except on *audiology* (see [4] for a statistical analysis). Note that the dramatic performance of **C4.5** on *hiv* is probably due to the strongly skewed class-distribution (only 3.6% of positive examples). In [3] we discuss a controlled experiment showing that **C4.5** indeed performs badly on strongly skewed datasets.

MDL and **Chi** overall perform clearly worse than **C4.4** (wins/ties/losses for **MDLs** are 3/0/9, for **MDLp** 3/2/7, for **Chi** 3/3/6). Trees for MDL and **Chi** are always significantly smaller than trees for **C4.4** or **C4.5**, except on *voting* and *hiv* [4]. Results for BIC are discussed in the next section.

Influence of the Number of Classes. An interesting observation from Table 2 is that BIC performs well for two-class problems but not for the multi-class problems we considered (that all have $NbClasses \geq 10$). On the two-class problems, wins/ties/losses for **BICs** are 2/3/2, for **BICp** 2/4/1. This means that on two-class problems, BIC performs at least as well as **C4.4** (or any other approach), while BIC has the additional advantage of building much smaller trees.

On the multi-class problems, the picture looks rather different, however. Wins/ties/losses for **BICs** and **BICp** are both 1/0/4: **C4.4** clearly outperforms BIC here. One explanation for this is the fact that Thr for **BICs** is $0.5\ (NbClasses - 1)\ log_2 N$. So if $NbClasses$ is high, then Thr is high as well and only tests T with a very high heuristic value $h(T)$ (larger than Thr) are accepted and hence very small trees are built. This suggests that **BICs** could be improved by making the dependency of Thr on $NbClasses$ less strong (i.e. less than linear) since then trees built for a high $NbClasses$ will be larger (although such a modification would deviate from the original theoretical foundations of BIC [12]). Similar remarks apply to **BICp**. Note that these observations (and their explanation) also hold for MDL but to a smaller extent, e.g. for **MDLp** wins/ties/losses on two-class problems are 2/2/3, on multi-class problems 1/0/4.

We performed an additional controlled experiment to investigate the influence of the number of classes. We started from *diterpenes*, a dataset having 23 classes on which **BICs** and **BICp** performed badly. In each step we merged the two least frequent classes, until only three classes were left. Figure 1 shows the results obtained from 10-fold cross-validation. In the top panels we show AUC, in the bottom panels tree size (on a logarithmic axis). We show **MDLs**, **MDLp**, **BICs** and **BICp** in the left panels and **BICp** (the best of the previous four), **C4.5**,

C4.4 and **Chi** in the right panels. We see that results for **MDLs**, **MDLp**, **BICs** and **BICp** are always very close to each other. For these approaches both tree size and AUC quickly decrease as the number of classes increases. Interestingly, there is almost no such decrease for **C4.5**, **C4.4** and **Chi**. Figure 1 shows that as a consequence **MDLs**, **MDLp**, **BICs** and **BICp** can compete with the other approaches when *NbClasses* is 3 or 5, but are outperformed when *NbClasses* goes higher. This confirms the above observation that MDL and BIC do not work well for multi-class problems, and its explanation.

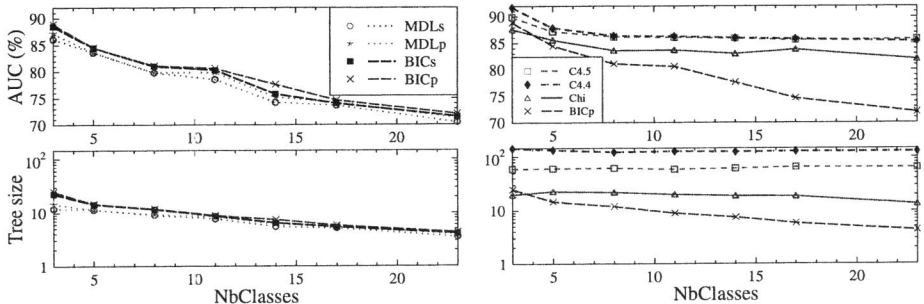

Fig. 1. Influence of the number of classes for *diterpenes*

Influence of the Number of Examples We also investigated the influence of the number of examples in the dataset. We learned trees from subsets of *hiv* containing a variable number of examples (we evaluate them on a separate test-set of 6768 examples). Figure 2 shows the results. We see that results (both AUC and tree size) for **MDLs**, **MDLp**, **BICs** and **Chi** are very close to each other for all sizes of the dataset. For small datasets ($N<15000$) also **BICp** is very close to the previous four. Interestingly however, for larger datasets **BICp** learns larger trees than the others, resulting in higher AUC's. This suggests that for larger datasets BIC for post-pruning (**BICp**) is more useful as compared to BIC as a stopping-criterion (**BICs**).

We performed the same experiment for *trains* (using a test-set of 5000 examples), see Figure 3. Again results for **MDLs**, **MDLp**, **BICs** and **Chi** are close to each other for all sizes of the dataset (except the very low ones, $N \leq 3000$). Unlike for *hiv*, however, **BICp** is very close to the previous four for all sizes of the dataset and does not become better than these four for larger datasets. Also we see that **C4.4** seems to overfit for all sizes of the dataset (it builds the largest trees but has the lowest AUC). The degree of overfitting is not heavily influenced by the size of the datasets. This is probably due to two competing effects [11]. On the one hand: if the dataset grows, trees grow as well (Figure 3), increasing the probability of overfitting. On the other hand, if the dataset grows, the number of examples in the leaves would increase, making probability estimates more reliable, thus decreasing the probability of overfitting. Why **C4.4** overfits on some datasets but not on others is currently an open question.

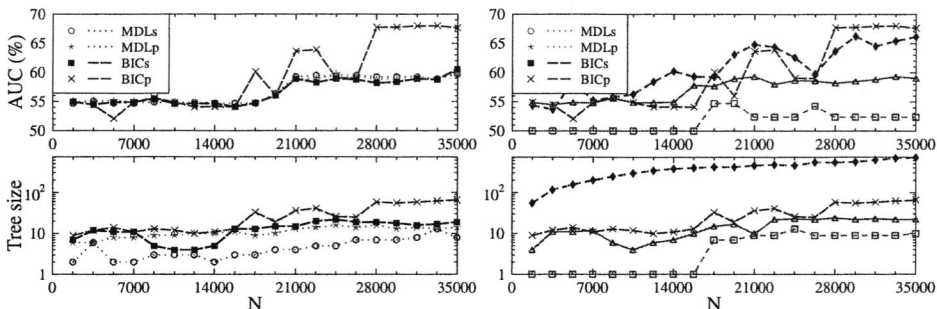

Fig. 2. Influence of the number of examples N for *hiv*

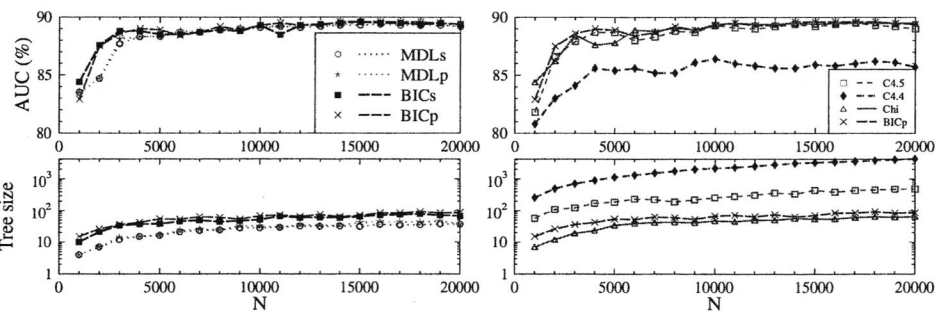

Fig. 3. Influence of the number of examples N for *trains*

Influence of the Number of Tests. We also investigated the influence of the number of candidate-tests. This seemed interesting since this parameter occurs in the definition of Thr for MDL and **Chi** but no interesting trends were found [4].

4 Conclusions

We reviewed and experimentally compared the main approaches for learning probability trees including a novel variant based on the Bayesian Information Criterion (BIC). We conclude that overall the C4.4-approach performs best, and the C4.5-approach second best. However, trees are much smaller for the latter than for the former. Interestingly, if the number of classes is low, BIC performs equally well. An additional advantage of BIC is that its trees are considerably smaller than trees for the C4.5- or C4.4-approaches. If the number of classes is too high (≥ 8 in our experiments), BIC fails because trees are too small.

An interesting idea for future research is to try to improve performance of BIC on multi-class problems by decreasing the influence of the number of classes on the stopping- or post-pruning-criterion.

Acknowledgements

DF is supported by the Institute for the Promotion of Innovation through Science and Technology in Flanders (IWT Vlaanderen). JR and HB are post-doctoral fellows of the Fund for Scientific Research (FWO) of Flanders. The authors thank Kristian Kersting and the reviewers for useful comments.

References

[1] ILPnet2 applications descriptions. http://www-ai.ijs.si/~ilpnet2/apps/.
[2] H. Blockeel and L. De Raedt. Top-down induction of first order logical decision trees. *Artificial Intelligence*, 101(1-2):285–297, June 1998.
[3] D. Fierens, J. Ramon, H. Blockeel, and M. Bruynooghe. A comparison of approaches for learning first-order logical Probability Estimation Trees. In *Inductive Logic Pogramming, 15th Int. Conference (ILP05), Late-breaking Papers*, 2005.
[4] D. Fierens, J. Ramon, H. Blockeel, and M. Bruynooghe. A comparison of approaches for learning probability trees. Technical Report CW 418, Department of Computer Science, Katholieke Universiteit Leuven, 2005.
[5] N. Friedman and M. Goldszmidt. Learning Bayesian networks with local structure. In *Learning and Inference in Graphical Models*. Cambridge: MIT Press, 1998.
[6] A. J. Knobbe. Data mining for adaptive system management. In *Proceedings of the 1st International Conference and exhibition on the Practical Application of Knowledge Discovery and Data Mining (PADD97)*, 1997.
[7] S. Kramer, L. De Raedt, and C. Helma. Molecular feature mining in HIV data. In *Proceedings of the 7th ACM SIGKDD International Conference on Knowledge Discovery and Data Mining (KDD01)*, pages 136–143, 2001.
[8] C. Merz and P. Murphy. UCI repository of machine learning databases http://www.ics.uci.edu/~mlearn/mlrepository.html, 1996. Irvine, CA: University of California, Department of Information and Computer Science.
[9] D. Michie, S. Muggleton, D. Page, and A. Srinivasan. To the international computing community: A new east-west challenge. Technical report, Oxford University Computing Laboratory, Oxford, UK, 1994. Available at ftp.comlab.ox.ac.uk.
[10] J. Neville, D. Jensen, L. Friedland, and M. Hay. Learning relational probability trees. In *Proceedings of the 9th ACM SIGKDD International Conference on Knowledge Discovery and Data Mining (KDD03)*, 2003.
[11] F. Provost and P. Domingos. Tree induction for probability-based ranking. *Machine Learning*, 52:199–216, 2003.
[12] G. Schwarz. Estimating the dimension of a model. *Annals of Statistics*, 6:461–464, 1978.
[13] A. Srinivasan, R. King, and D. Bristol. An assessment of ILP-assisted models for toxicology and the PTE-3 experiment. In *Proceedings of the seventh international conference on Inductive Logic Programming (ILP99)*, 1999.

Counting Positives Accurately Despite Inaccurate Classification

George Forman

Hewlett-Packard Labs,
Palo Alto, CA 94304 USA
ghforman@hpl.hp.com

Abstract. Most supervised machine learning research assumes the training set is a random sample from the target population, thus the class distribution is invariant. In real world situations, however, the class distribution changes, and is known to erode the effectiveness of classifiers and calibrated probability estimators. This paper focuses on the problem of accurately estimating the number of positives in the test set—*quantification*—as opposed to classifying individual cases accuratel y. It compares three methods: classify & count, an adjusted variant, and a mixture model. An empirical evaluation on a text classification benchmark reveals that the simple method is consistently biased, and that the mixture model is surprisingly effective even when positives are very scarce in the training set—a common case in information retrieval.

1 Motivation and Scope

We address the problem of estimating the number of positives in a target population, given a training set from which to learn to distinguish positives from negatives. This could be used, for example, to estimate the number of news articles about terrorism each month, or the volume of advertising by a competitor over time. Unlike previous literature in machine learning, our end goal is not to determine a classification for each item, but only to estimate the number of positives—*quantification* as opposed to *classification*. This is an important problem in real-world situations where the class distribution may shift over time in the target population. It is then needed to track, detect and report noteworthy shifts in the class distribution, to calibrate probability-estimation classifiers, and to select a binary classification threshold to optimize F-measure or misclassification costs on an ROC curve [2,5]. It is also needed to calibrate classifiers that are used on different target populations, such as in medical settings where the training set does not represent a random sample of each target population.

The obvious solution is to train a binary classifier from the training data, and count its positive predictions on the test set. For example, Fig. 1 shows the result of this method as we vary the proportion of positives in a particular test set. The classifier consistently overestimates/underestimates the positives when the test set deviates from the balanced class distribution used in training, even though this classifier achieves nearly 90% F-measure in cross-validation testing. Unfortunately, as we demonstrate later, this method consistently leads to poor results—unless the classifier is extremely accurate, which can require substantial cost to get enough training data and may never be feasible for some tasks.

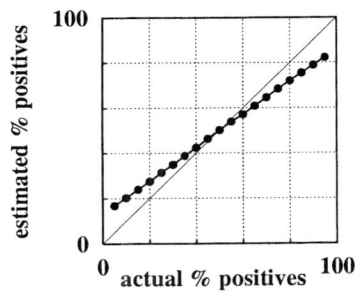

Fig. 1. Counting positives via a classifier trained with 100 positives and 100 negatives yields a poor estimate of the count as we vary the test class distribution, even though the classifier achieves nearly 90% F-measure in cross-validation.

Table 1. Summary of parameters considered in the empirical comparison

P = 10...200	Positives in training set	\multicolumn{2}{l}{Counting Methods:}
N = 100...1000	Negatives in training set	CC	Classify & Count
p = 5...95%	Percent positives in test set	AC	Adjusted CC
\multicolumn{2}{l}{Benchmark: 21 binary text classification tasks}	MM	Mixture Model
\multicolumn{2}{l}{Learning Algorithms:}	\multicolumn{2}{l}{Performance Metrics:}
SVM	Support Vector Machine	Err	estimated p − actual p
NB	Naive Bayes	AbsErr	|Err|
NBM	Multinomial Naive Bayes	CE	Normalized Cross-Entropy

Although accurate classification is *sufficient* for estimating the count accurately, it is not *necessary*. Even with a mediocre classifier, the count can be accurate if the false positives are canceled out by a balanced number of false negatives. This raises the question of whether estimating the count alone can be accomplished more accurately and/or with less training data.

We describe and evaluate two such superior methods: one based on adjusting the binary classifier's count, the other based on a mixture model of the distribution of classifier scores, as described in section 3. We empirically compare their ability to accurately track varying test class distributions under a variety of training set compositions. In such a study it is important to vary the training and testing class distributions as independent parameters, in contrast with most classification research practice, which assures the class distribution is the same in training and testing via random sampling or cross-validation. We are especially interested in the situation where there are a small number of positives to train from—a common case in information retrieval and bioinformatics where positives are rare and obtaining labels costs human effort. Table 1 provides an overview of the range of parameters we studied. The experiment protocol and its results are described in sections 4 and 5, respectively. Next, we complement this introduction with a discussion of related work to help scope this work.

2 Related Work

The great majority of the machine learning literature assumes the class distribution is invariant between training and testing. Some work focuses on improving classification accuracy when the target class distribution is imbalanced, usually by over-sampling the minority class or under-sampling the majority class to balance the training set, where induction algorithms are more effective. The work of Weiss & Provost [5], for example, carefully studies the effect of varying the training distribution to optimize classification accuracy for a given test set.

Many works mention the need to adjust the class priors to match the test distribution. This is usually assumed to be done via foreknowledge or a manual inspection of a random sample. Even in such papers, their performance goal is only to improve binary classification accuracy or probability estimation [1], and not to accurately count positives in test sets as here. Some works specifically seek to factor out the effect of class distribution by, for example, evaluating classification performance via *balanced accuracy* or the area under the ROC curve (AUC).

Finally, some work attempts to detect class drift—when the character of a class with respect to its feature space changes over time, suddenly or gradually. Class drift falls outside the scope of this paper. We only consider shifts in the relative populations of positives and negatives.

3 Theoretical Framework of Counting Methods

In this section, we describe the theoretical framework of three methods for estimating the count of positives. We also list two intuitive methods that do not work.

3.1 CC: Classify & Count

This is the obvious method. First, we learn a binary classifier from the training data, such as a Support Vector Machine (SVM) or Naïve Bayes model. We then apply it to each item of the test set, and count the number of times it predicts positive. If the predictions are nearly perfect, then the count will be nearly accurate, no matter what the test class distribution. This should be successful where the two classes are very well separated, e.g. distinguishing news articles written in German vs. English.

If the classes are not well separated, then there will be some number of false positives and false negatives, and it is unlikely that these would be closely balanced. Moreover, any induction algorithm that is designed to maximize its accuracy on the training set will prefer the negative class if positives are the minority, a common case. It leads to systematically underestimating the count. (This suggests artificially balancing the training set to achieve a balance between false positives and false negatives. This is ineffective and even ill-conceived, as discussed in section 3.4.)

3.2 AC: Adjusted Count

This method is an extension to the straightforward *classify & count* method. Although the class labels are not available on the test set, consider the counts that would appear in the 2x2 confusion matrix below:

	Prediction:	
Actual Class:	Positive	Negative
Positive	TP	FN
Negative	FP	TN

The observed count is the sum of true positives TP and false positives FP. We can model each of these counts separately as:

$$observed\_count = TP + FP$$
$$TP = TPR * actual\_positives \qquad (1)$$
$$FP = FPR * actual\_negatives = FPR * (total - actual\_positives)$$

where TPR is the true positive rate of the classifier, P(predict +|actual +), and FPR is its false positive rate, P(predict -|actual -). These are estimated from the training set, as discussed below. Solving this system of equations, we obtain:

$$actual\_positives = (observed\_count - FPR * total) / (TPR - FPR) \qquad (2)$$

This adjustment to the count is the essence of this method, but there are a few additional points. First, observe that the denominator could go to zero. This would only happen with a worthless classifier that is equally likely to predict positive for either class. Normally TPR >> FPR, so the denominator is positive and somewhat less than 1.0. But if TPR < FPR, then the classifier is more likely to predict positive for negative items than for positive items. In this situation, one could reverse the outputs of the classifier. Re-deriving for this case ends up with the exact same equation, so it may be used without special casing for a negative denominator. In these situations, FPR*total is likely to exceed the observed count of positives, so the numerator will also be negative. Finally, the adjusted count may under some situations predict a negative number of positives or more positives than the total test cases. Thus, we limit its output to the range [0, total].

To estimate TPR and FPR for a given classifier, standard techniques may be used, such as stratified 10-fold cross-validation on the training set (divide the training set into 10 subsets, testing each one with a classifier trained on the other 9; stratification ensures that the minority class is evenly distributed among the folds). It yields a 2x2 confusion matrix, and we compute TPR = TP/(TP+FN), and FPR = FP/(FP+TN).

3.3 MM: Mixture Model

Many binary classifier models consist of a scoring mechanism and a threshold on the score to choose between predicting positive or negative. The induction algorithm has to learn both how to score positives higher than negatives and how to pick the threshold well. In the MM method, we eliminate this second step, and only use the scoring portion. We then consider the *distribution* of scores generated by the

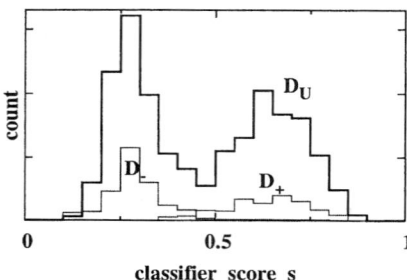 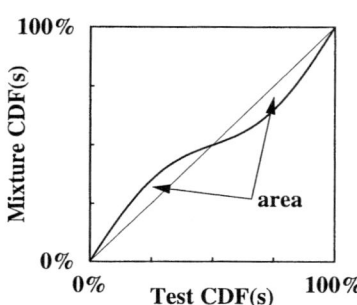

Fig. 2. Histograms of classifier scores   **Fig. 3.** P-P plot comparing two CDFs

classifier. After training the classifier, we determine the empirical probability distribution D_+ of scores that it generates on the positive training examples, and separately D_- for the negative training examples. Then, during testing, we model the observed distribution D_U of scores on the unlabeled data as the mixture (see Fig. 2):

$$\text{total} * D_U = \text{actual\_positives} * D_+ + \text{actual\_negatives} * D_- \qquad (3)$$

Finally, to estimate the positive count, we determine which mixture of positives and negatives would yield the closest fit to D_U. This is the essence of the method, but there remain several design choices:

1. *How to obtain the distributions D_+ and D_- from the training set*: If we train on all the training data, and then observe the classifier scores on the training data, the separation between positive and negative scores will be overly optimistic compared with the actual test distribution. Instead we use stratified f-fold cross-validation, and gather the scores from each fold into one distribution. Strictly speaking, these scores were generated from f different classifiers, but if f is large, then these classifiers share most of their training data in common.
2. *Whether the empirical distributions found during training should be reduced to a parametric model of a distribution*: Based on the range of variation, we decided not to try to fit the distributions to parametric models, which also avoids adding parameters to the algorithm that may need to be optimized.
3. *Whether to characterize the distributions by their empirical probability density function (PDF) or their cumulative distribution function (CDF)*: Using the PDF requires discretizing the counts into artificial bins. If the bin size is too small, then the estimates in each bin become noisy. This would create additional parameters for tuning. We selected CDF.
4. *Whether to give special treatment to test scores that fall outside the range of scores observed during training*: Optionally, test items that score higher than any score observed during training could be treated separately, i.e. surely included in the final positive count, and excluded from the mixture model fitting. Likewise scores smaller than any observed score in training could be treated separately as a negative. We include this refinement.
5. *How to measure the goodness of fit between D_U and the mixture model*: Given two CDFs, the standard way to measure their difference is the Kolmogorov-Smirnov statistic, which measures the maximum difference between the two for all scores.

While common, this coarse metric does not consider finer differences in the shape of the fit. For this reason, we developed another difference metric we call PP-Area, described below. Another choice would be the standard Anderson-Darling statistic, but it is known to emphasize the tails of the distribution, which is not what we need for this application. (The well-known Chi-Squared statistic is appropriate only for discrete PDFs.)

6. *How to determine the mixture that optimizes the fit*: For research purposes, we compute the goodness of fit for each value from 0% to 100% positives stepping by 0.5% returning the best, but in practice one could use hill-climbing methods.

We name this particular collection of design choices the "Countess" method.

PP-Area: a difference metric for two CDFs.

Given two CDFs, a well-known method for visually comparing them is to plot one vs. the other while varying their input threshold, yielding a Probability-Probability plot, or P-P plot (see Fig. 3.). If the two CDFs yield the same probability at each input, then they generate a perfect 45° line. By sighting down this line, one can get an intuitive feel for the level of agreement between two CDFs, commonly to decide whether an empirical distribution matches a parametric distribution. To reduce this linearity test to computation, it would be natural to measure the mean-squared-error (MSE) of the points on the PP curve to the 45° line. But MSE is highly sensitive to the maximal difference, as is Kolmogorov-Smirnov.

Our solution is to measure the difference between two CDFs as the area where the PP curve deviates from the 45° line. This has well defined behavior partly because the curve always begins at (0,0), ends at (1.0,1.0), and is monotonic in both x and y. It also has the intuitive property of being commutative, unlike MSE or mean-error.

3.4 Non-solutions

If the classes are not well separated by a classifier, then a tradeoff must be made between precision vs. recall (false negatives vs. false positives). This tradeoff is manifested in the threshold used by a binary classifier. During training it is optimized for accuracy in risk minimization methods, such as SVM. One ill-conceived idea is to try to adjust this threshold at training time so as to balance false positives and false negatives. This is not possible because balancing these two depends explicitly on the class distribution, which may vary in testing.

Another ill-conceived idea is the following: Rather than have the classifier output a hard binary decision despite its uncertainty, use a classifier that outputs a probability estimate for each item. Then, estimate the positive count as the sum of probabilities over the test set. Again, this cannot work because the probability estimates depend explicitly on the class distribution; the calibrated probabilities would become uncalibrated whenever the test class distribution varies.

4 Experiment Protocol

To compare these methods, we conducted an empirical evaluation. The standard methodology of cross-validation to obtain training and testing sets is not appropriate. Instead, we must independently vary the class distribution in the training set and the

Table 2. Benchmark data sets, the specific classes used as positive, and their sizes

Dataset	Source	Cases	Classes	# Positives in Each Class
fbis	TREC	2463	3,7,10	387, 506, 358
la1	LA Times	3204	0,1,3,5	354, 555, 943, 738
la2	LA Times	3075	0,1,3,5	375, 487, 905, 759
ohscal	OHSUMED	11162	0...9	1159, 709, 764, 1001, 864, 1621, 1037, 1297, 1450, 1260

test set to determine how well various methods can track the test distribution, despite variations in the training set they are given. To this end, we randomly drew 200 positives and 1000 negatives from each benchmark classification task as the maximum training set. We then trained with various subsets of this data, reducing the number of positives and negatives independently. Likewise, from the remaining data, we randomly removed positives or negatives to achieve various desired testing class distributions. We varied the test distribution from 5% positive to 95%, stepping by 5% increments.

Datasets: We used publicly available text classification datasets and used 21 "one vs. all other classes" classification tasks that had sufficient positives and negatives to cover the variety of experimental conditions (see Table 2) [3]. These datasets contain from 2000 to 31,000 binary word features.

Learning algorithms: The bulk of our experiments were conducted with linear Support Vector Machines (SVM), which is considered state of the art for text classification. We later replicated the experiments for Naïve Bayes and Multinomial Naïve Bayes [4]. Given that feature selection has shown to improve SVM results, we also replicated the experiments with feature selection via Bi-Normal Separation [3].

Error metrics: In order to be able to average across tasks with different numbers of positives, a natural error metric is the estimated percent positive minus the actual percent positive. By averaging across conditions, we can determine whether a method has a positive or negative bias. But suppose a method guesses 0% or 100% randomly; it would also have a zero bias on average. Thus, it is also important to consider an unsigned measure of error. Absolute error is one candidate, but estimating 41% when the ground truth is 45% is not nearly as 'bad' as estimating 1% when the ground truth is 5%. For this reason, cross-entropy is often used as an error measure. To be able to average across different test class distributions, however, it needs to be normalized so that a perfect estimate always yields zero error. Hence, the normalized cross-entropy is defined as follows:

$$\text{normCE}(p,x) = \text{CE}(p,x) - \text{CE}(p,p)$$
$$\text{CE}(p,x) = -p \log_2(x) - (1-p) \log_2(1-x) \tag{4}$$

where x is the estimate of the actual percent positives p in testing. Since cross-entropy goes to infinity as x goes to 0% or 100%, if a method estimates zero positives, we adjust its estimate to half a count out of the entire test set for purposes of evaluating its normalize cross-entropy error. Likewise, if a method estimates that all the test items are positive, we back it off by half a count. (Note that this error metric will increasingly penalize a method for estimating zero positives as the test set size grows. Intuitively it is worse to estimate zero positives among thousands of test cases than among ten.)

for each of 21 benchmark tasks—distinguishing positive class c in dataset d:
| set aside 200 positives and 1000 negatives for training, the rest for testing
| for P = 10,20,50,100,200 training positives:
| for N = 100,200,500,1000 training negatives:
| | for each classifier C: SVM, NB, NBM; with and without feature selection
| | train C on training set (size P+N)
| | perform 50-fold cross-validation to estimate TPR, FPR, D_+ and D_-
| | for p = 5% to 95% by 5%:
| | | select maximal test set such that p% are positive
| | | apply C to test set
| | | for each of the methods:
|_ |_ |_   estimate x% positives, and record result & error.

Fig. 4. Overall experiment procedure in pseudo-code

Cross-validation folds for calibration: The adjustment method and the mixture model both require cross-validation to generate calibrated values during training. We chose f=50 folds for this study. (Note that if there are fewer than f positives in the training set, some of the test folds will contain no positives. We experimented with using only min(f,P,N) folds, but generally found no improvement.)

Experiment Procedure: The overall experiment procedure is shown in Fig. 4. In total there were over 20,000 experiment jobs consuming over a hundred CPU days. These ran in parallel on the HP Utility Data Center in a few days. We used the WEKA software in Java to provide the base classifiers [6].

5 Experiment Results

We begin by evaluating how the estimates of each method are biased by the composition of the training set, holding the test set fixed. Fig. 5 shows each method's estimate, averaged over all benchmark tasks, as we vary the training set. The test set for each task is fixed with p=20% positives. (Except where stated otherwise, hereafter the classifier is a linear SVM with all features, calibrated via 50-fold cross-validation on the training set.) Though MM tends to overestimate by a small amount, it is striking that it is so close to the target p=20% when there are only P=10 training positives. CC and AC are not competitive with P=10, and they underestimate more

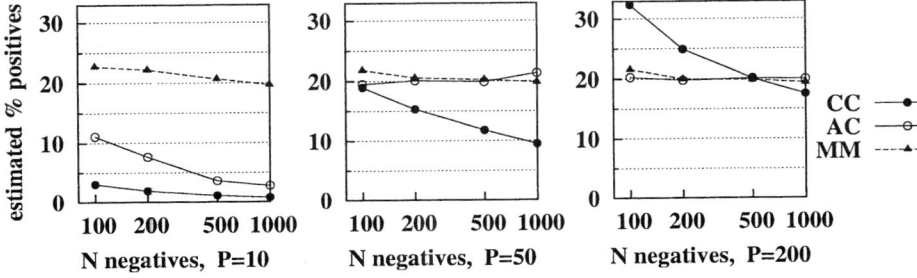

Fig. 5. Sensitivity to training set composition, with actual test positives p=20%

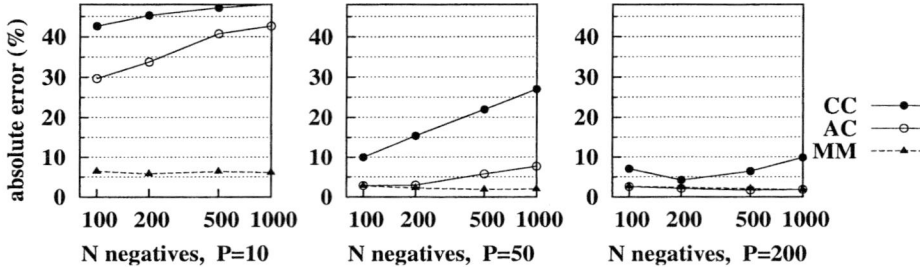

Fig. 6. Absolute error averaged over all test conditions p=5–95% and all tasks

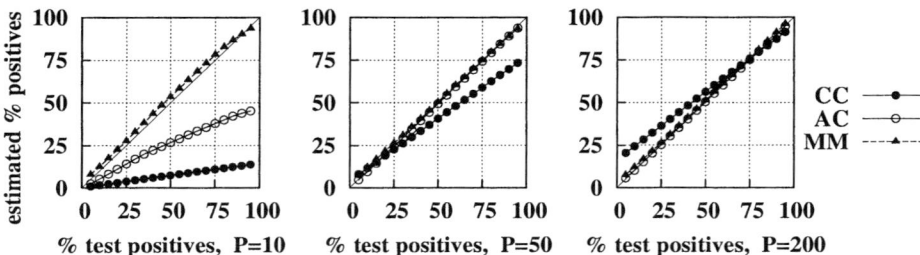

Fig. 7. Ability to track % testing positives, training with N=100 negatives

strongly as the imbalance of training negatives N increases. In contrast, additional training negatives help MM converge for each value of P.

With more positives, we see AC also converge to 20%. But more training data do not make CC converge—it is always tuned for a specific percentage of positives. Popular wisdom suggests the best classification performance for this test set should be when the training distribution matches 20%; however, CC performed best with ~30% training positives (P:N = 50:100, 200:500, and, not shown, 100:200). Hence, were it magically possible to always match the training class distribution to that of testing, it would still not make CC an effective method of counting positives.

The results presented so far were for a single fixed percentage of test positives. Next we average over all tasks and all testing situations: p=5%–95% positives. Instead of averaging the error, which reveals positive or negative bias, we average the absolute error to determine how far the estimate lies from the true answer on average. Fig. 6. shows this as we vary the training set as before. Again, MM performs surprisingly well given only P=10 training positives, achieving ~6% absolute error on average, regardless of the number of training negatives N. With P=50 or 200 training positives, MM achieves ~2% absolute error on average. With P=200 training positives, AC is competitive. Recall the ideal method should be as insensitive as possible to the training set size and class distribution: strongly recommending MM.

Next we hold the *training* set fixed and measure the ability of each method to track various percentages of positives in the test set. Fig. 7 shows for each method the estimate, averaged across all benchmark tasks, as we vary the percentage of positives in the test set p=5% to 95%. We use N=100, which was least favorable to MM in Fig. 5. For P=10 we see that MM is alone effective and AC becomes competitive with enough positives. MM shows a slight positive bias.

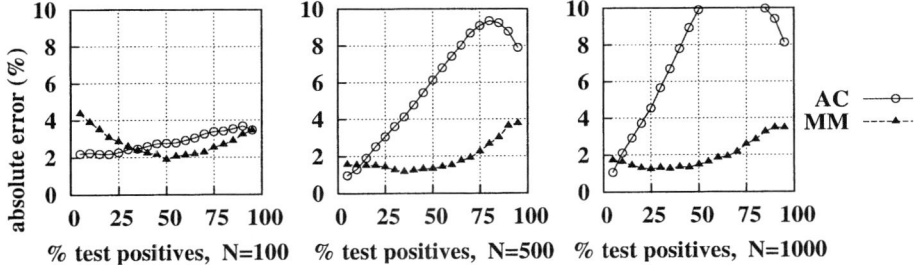

Fig. 8. Absolute error averaged over all tasks, comparing AC and MM at P=50

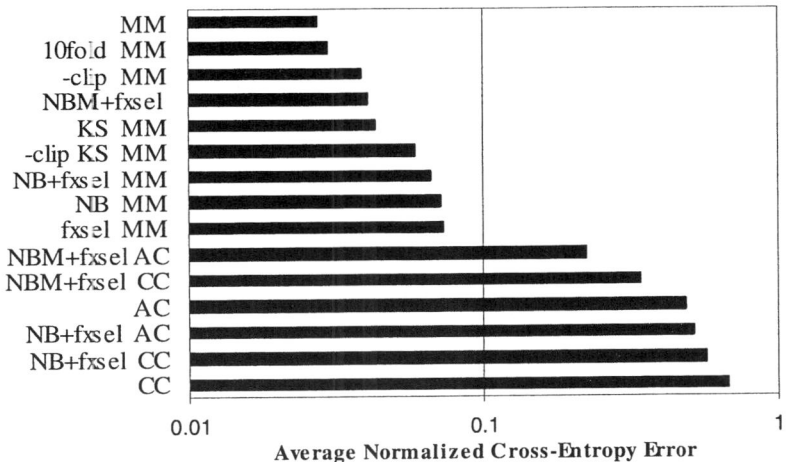

Fig. 9. Lesion study results, averaged over tasks, training, and testing situations

While the view in Fig. 7 gives a good overview of the biases, next we zoom in to examine the differences in absolute error between MM and AC. We show this only for P=50, as the results are uninteresting at P=10 and undifferentiated at P=200. We see a consistent picture in Fig. 8. When the testing set contains a high percentage of positives, MM estimates better than AC, especially as the number of negative training examples grows for a fixed number of training positives. However, when testing with a small percentage of positives, the MM estimates worse than AC, especially with few training negatives. Recall that MM exhibits a small but consistent positive bias; this systematically hurts its estimate when there is a small percentage of testing positives.

Lesion Study: The MM method includes a number of design choices. We performed a lesion study to evaluate other choices. Fig. 9 summarizes the effect of each of these independent changes by showing the normalized cross-entropy averaged over all benchmark tasks, all training set compositions, and all test situations. In every case, the changes resulted in worse estimation (our choices were made prior to the study, with the exception of range clipping, which was suggested by preliminary results). We describe these lesions in ranked order: 10fold MM uses 10-fold cross-validation, rather than 50-fold—a small loss in performance for one fifth the training time, *if* that one-time computational cost is significant in one's application. -clip MM does not use range clipping—clipping benefits substantially when there are few training positives. NBM+fxsel MM uses the Multinomial Naïve Bayes model with feature selection, in place of SVM; without feature selection NBM failed sometimes. KS MM uses the standard Kolmogorov-Smirnov statistic in place of our PP-Area metric; -clip KS MM is similar, but without clipping as well. NB+fxsel MM uses Naïve Bayes with feature selection, instead of SVM; NB MM uses Naïve Bayes with all features. fxsel MM adds feature selection to SVM. (Whenever feature selection was applied, the 200 best features were selected via Bi-Normal Separation.)

For comparison, we also include the other major methods **AC** and **CC**. These are also shown with alternate learning methods that generated a somewhat better balance between false positives and false negatives. Although they improve the estimates, they are not competitive with MM or any of its variants.

6 Discussion

In most machine learning research, where the objective is accurate classifications, each item in the test set provides an additional test result, which may contribute to an average. In contrast, a single test item by itself is not sufficient for evaluating a method for quantification. This must be done on an entire *batch* of test items at a time, and yields only a single scalar estimate. For this reason, evaluation requires concocting many different test situations over many benchmark tasks. In this way, research on counting requires more experimental design. We hope that the test conditions we designed provide useful guidance for others. In our framework, we varied the percentage of test positives from p=5%–95% as a reasonable experimental gamut. However, we recognize that in many situations the estimator will not be called on to span this entire gamut well. For the common situation of rare positives, it may be that other methods will excel. But obtaining statistical significance in this realm may prove difficult, as it requires a much larger benchmark to evaluate the tails properly.

Stepping outside the box of machine learning, another way to estimate the positives in a population is to have a person—an expensive, slow, but presumably perfect classifier—manually count in a random sample. Let us sketch the labor required for comparison. Supposing you wish to have the width of the 95% confidence interval be half of the estimate. For example, if the estimate were 40%, then the person would need to classify 100 items to get the confidence interval down to 40%±10%. Alternately, for a confidence interval of 4%±1% one would need to examine 1500 items—the labor increases greatly and non-linearly for rarer classes of positives. For obtaining a single count, certainly the labor may be dwarfed by the effort to set up a machine learning solution. But if a count or many such counts must be performed every day, the complexity of a computerized solution may be quickly amortized. Likewise, if hundreds or thousands of different classes need to be counted just once, again the machine learning solution can greatly reduce the effort spent by the person to classify items. Indeed, the manual classification can serve both as a rough estimate, and as a training set for a machine learning quantifier that can examine the complete dataset or can be applied to next month's dataset.

7 Conclusion

This paper highlights the problem of assessing the number of positives in a population via machine learning—quantification. It is a valuable real-world task, but is commonly overlooked for the natural goal of improving classification accuracy. The issue is made invisible by common machine learning research methodology, which selects the training set and testing set so the class distribution is the same. We laid out an evaluation framework, which varies the training and testing distributions independently to determine which method minimizes error measured as normalized cross-entropy. We described and evaluated three methods. The straightforward and probably most common method of classifying and counting positives should only be used when an extremely accurate classifier can be learned with available training data.

Opportunities for future work include: evaluating non-text benchmark domains, extending to multi-class classification tasks, and inventing superior methods. We identified two avenues for future work which are ill-conceived and cannot succeed: calibrating the threshold at training time and calibrated probability estimation. Finally, the most successful methods can be folded back in to calibrate classifiers at testing time to improve their accuracy or probability estimation.

References

1. Bennett, P.: Using Asymmetric Distributions to Improve Text Classifier Probability Estimates. Proc. ACM SIGIR Conference on Research and Development in Information Retrieval, July-August (2003)
2. Fawcett, T.: ROC graphs: Notes and practical considerations for data mining researchers. Tech report HPL-2003-4. Hewlett-Packard Laboratories, Palo Alto, CA, USA (2003)
3. Forman, G.: An Extensive Empirical Study of Feature Selection Metrics for Text Classification. Journal of Machine Learning Research 3 (2003) 1289-1305
4. McCallum, A., Nigam, K.: A Comparison of Event Models for Naive Bayes Text Classification. AAAI/ICML Workshop on Learning for Text Categorization (1998) 41-48
5. Weiss, G., Provost, F.: Learning when Training Data are Costly: The Effect of Class Distribution on Tree Induction. J. of Artificial Intelligence Research 19 (2003) 315-354
6. Witten, I.H., Eibe Frank, E.: Data Mining: Practical machine learning tools with Java implementations. Morgan Kaufmann, San Francisco (2000)

Optimal Stopping and Constraints for Diffusion Models of Signals with Discontinuities

Ramūnas Girdziušas and Jorma Laaksonen

Helsinki University of Technology, Laboratory of Computer and
Information Science, P.O. Box 5400, FI-02015 HUT, Espoo, Finland
{Ramunas.Girdziusas, Jorma.Laaksonen}@hut.fi

Abstract. Gaussian process regression models can be utilized in recovery of discontinuous signals. Their computational complexity is linear in the number of observations if applied with the covariance functions of nonlinear diffusion. However, such processes often result in hard-to-control jumps of the signal value. Synthetic examples presented in this work indicate that Bayesian evidence-maximizing stopping and knowledge whether signal values are discrete help to outperform the steady state solutions of nonlinear diffusion filtering.

1 Introduction

Discontinuous signals can be efficiently recovered from noisy observations by employing Gaussian processes (GPs) whose mean function conditioned on the data solves nonlinear diffusion equations. Computations scale linearly with the number of data points and the increasing input dimensionality if one utilizes the additive operator splitting [12] or probabilistic simulation [3].

Nonlinear diffusion models operate upon iterative application of the principle 'smooth less where the spatial gradient of the signal is larger'. Paradoxically, such a filtering results in discontinuous jumps of signal values yielding better preserved edges and the possibility to restore signals hidden in a large-variance noise.

This work investigates nonlinear diffusion priors for Gaussian process regression. We show that diffusion can be optimally stopped long before it approaches the steady state by employing the Bayesian evidence criterion. In addition, the signal can be constrained to take either binary or any set of values in $O(n)$ number of multiplications per iteration. This is obtained by reformulating the matrix inversion of the Thomas algorithm as a dynamic programming problem.

Section 2 states Bayesian evidence-maximizing Gaussian process regression as means to solve the smoothing problem. Section 3 discusses efficient linear diffusion prior and its smoothing characteristics from the stochastic process viewpoint. Its variational interpretation and nonlinear extension is introduced in Section 4. An example of optimal stopping is given in Section 5 whereas a general approach to impose the discrete constraints on the values of the diffusion outcome is presented in Section 6. Concluding remarks are stated in Section 7.

2 Gaussian Process Regression

Let us consider a grid of n spatial locations and gather the observations into vector $\mathbf{y} \in \mathbb{R}^n$. Let us denote the model output as $\mathbf{u} \in \mathbb{R}^n$. If we assume that the joint predictive density of the model outcome and the hyperparameter vector $\boldsymbol{\theta}$ is unimodal, then in the absence of any specific knowledge about optimal hyperparameters $\boldsymbol{\theta}^*$, the location of the posterior mode can be determined by employing the Bayesian Evidence framework [7]. At the optimal point $(\mathbf{u}^*, \boldsymbol{\theta}^*)$ the following equations should hold:

$$\mathbf{u}^* = \arg\max_{\mathbf{u}} \; p(\mathbf{y}|\mathbf{u}, \boldsymbol{\theta}^*) p(\mathbf{u}|\boldsymbol{\theta}^*), \tag{1}$$

$$\boldsymbol{\theta}^* = \arg\max_{\boldsymbol{\theta}} \; p(\mathbf{y}|\mathbf{u}^*, \boldsymbol{\theta}) \frac{p(\mathbf{u}^*|\boldsymbol{\theta})}{p(\mathbf{u}^*|\mathbf{y}, \boldsymbol{\theta})}. \tag{2}$$

Eqs. (1) and (2) indicate that the parameters and hyperparameters are solved by balancing their likelihood and prior solutions. In spite of the absence of any *a priori* information about the possible hyperparameter values, the Bayesian Evidence framework determines the model hyperparameters $\boldsymbol{\theta}^*$ that maximize the data likelihood and the ratio between the prior and posterior modes.

Let us further assume that the joint vector of the observations $\mathbf{y}$ and the model outcome $\mathbf{u}$ comes from the probability density

$$\begin{pmatrix} \mathbf{u} \\ \mathbf{y} \end{pmatrix} | \boldsymbol{\theta} \sim \mathcal{N}\left(\begin{pmatrix} 0 \\ 0 \end{pmatrix}, \begin{pmatrix} \mathbf{K}_\theta & \mathbf{K}_\theta \\ \mathbf{K}_\theta & \mathbf{K}_\theta + \theta_0 \mathbf{I} \end{pmatrix} \right). \tag{3}$$

Eq. (3) assumes that each value of the measurement vector $\mathbf{y}$ is contaminated by additive Gaussian noise, whose variance is denoted by θ_0. The marginal distribution $p(\mathbf{u})$ represents a sample of a zero-mean Gaussian process U with the covariance matrix $\mathbf{K}_\theta \in \mathbb{R}^{n \times n}$ which depends on a small number of hyperparameters $\boldsymbol{\theta}$ [10]. Under Eq. (3), Eqs. (1) and (2) reduce to

$$\mathbf{u}^* = \arg\min_{\mathbf{u}} \left(\frac{1}{\theta_0^*} \|\mathbf{y} - \mathbf{u}\|^2 + \mathbf{u}^T \mathbf{K}_{\theta^*}^{-1} \mathbf{u} \right) = (\mathbf{I} + \theta_0^* \mathbf{K}_{\theta^*}^{-1})^{-1} \mathbf{y}, \tag{4}$$

$$\boldsymbol{\theta}^* = \arg\min_{\boldsymbol{\theta}} \left(\frac{1}{\theta_0} [\|\mathbf{y} - \mathbf{u}^*\|^2 + (\mathbf{u}^*)^T (\mathbf{y} - \mathbf{u}^*)] \right.$$
$$\left. + \ln[(2\pi\theta_0)^n \det(\mathbf{K}_\theta + \theta_0 \mathbf{I})] \right). \tag{5}$$

Therefore, the GP regression minimizes the Euclidean $\|\cdot\|^2$ norm between the data and the model output while maintaining certain regularity properties of the model outputs via their quadratic form determined by the inverse kernel matrix $\mathbf{K}_\theta^{-1}$. Probabilistic Eqs. (1)–(3) complete the regression problem by providing the model selection criterion. The upper part of Eq. (5) is the best-fit likelihood $p(\mathbf{y}|\mathbf{u}^*, \boldsymbol{\theta})$ whereas the second term represents the ratio in Eq. (2) known as the Occam's factor [7].

Whenever the true signal is discontinuous and $n > 10^3$, well-known covariance functions such as Gaussian kernel can not be applied to construct the matrix $\mathbf{K}_\theta$ because Eq. (4) would blur the edges whereas Eq. (5) would be hard to interpret, evaluate and minimize.

3 Linear Diffusion Prior

Consider univariate smoothing of the observations on the discrete grid $x_0 = 0, x_1 = h, x_2 = 2h, \ldots, x_{n+1} = 1$ by employing the GP model Eq. (4) with the covariance matrix whose elements $[\mathbf{K}_\theta]_{ij}$ are given by the function

$$k(x_i, x_j) = \min[f(x_i), f(x_j)], \quad x \mapsto f(x) = \int_0^x g^{-1}(x) dx, \qquad (6)$$

where $g^{-1}(x)$ is any density function on the interval $x \in [0, 1]$. In the case of $g^{-1}(x) \equiv 1$, this GP model corresponds to *a priori* assumption that the process $U \equiv W$ is Wiener-Levý, also known as Brownian motion (BM). It can be considered as the simplest smoothing assumption embodied in the notion of 'integrated white noise' whose paths can be simulated according to:

$$w_i = w_{i-1} + \sqrt{h}z, \quad z \sim \mathcal{N}(0,1), \quad w_0 = 0. \qquad (7)$$

Regression with the covariance function of Brownian motion is an important smoothing device. A great variety of GP models, including neural networks with infinite number of hidden sigmoidal or radial basis units, are unlikely to outperform this simple model. Moreover, the BM covariance matrix yields a tridiagonal inverse, which requires only $O(n)$ number of multiplications to solve Eq. (4).

Surprisingly, an extension $g^{-1}(x) \neq const$ also yields a tridiagonal inverse covariance matrix, which makes Eq. (6) applicable to spatially selective smoothing. One can derive the corresponding Ito stochastic differential equation [9]:

$$dU_x = \frac{1}{2} g(U_x) g'(U_x) dx + g(U_x) dW_x, \quad U_0 = 0. \qquad (8)$$

Such an equation indicates that by postulating the model Eq. (6), we assume that the univariate data represents noisy observations of a deterministic drift perturbed with a *diffusion* term $g(U_x)dW_x$. GP regression with covariance as in Eq. (6) already represents *a hidden diffusion*. This comes in contrast to Bayesian evidence maximizing determination of the drift and diffusion terms in the case when $\theta_0 = 0$ [11].

The BM covariance function Eq. (6) can be modified for the BM process which is constrained on the other end, e.g. $u_1 = 0$:

$$k(x_i, x_j) = \min[f(x_i), f(x_j)] - f(x_i)f(x_j). \qquad (9)$$

Such a function also yields a tridiagonal inverse covariance matrix. A very general consideration of such matrices in light of Markov processes can be found in [5].

Smoothing properties of Eqs. (6) and (9) can also be explained by a deterministic argument based on variational calculus. This view, which is discussed in the next section, is especially helpful in choosing the function g, clarifying the effect of the boundary conditions on the regression outcome and further extending Eqs. (6) and (9).

4 Nonlinear Diffusion Prior

The presence of discontinuities demands a careful choice of the function $g(x)$, whose effect can be seen by considering the variational nature of the conditional expectation operator in the GP regression. A continuous counterpart of Eq. (4) in the case of the deformed BM covariance function, given by Eq. (6), is

$$u^* = \arg\inf_u \int_0^1 \left(\theta_0 g(x)(\partial_x u)^2 + (u-y)^2\right)dx, \quad s.t. \quad u(0) = 0, \quad \partial_x u(1) = 0, \quad (10)$$

where $y \equiv y(x)$ and $u \equiv u(x)$. In the case of the GP model Eq. (9) the last condition changes to $u(1) = 0$. Boundary conditions ensure that iterative regularization produces a unique solution.

Variational calculus such as Eq. (10) is useful in deriving explicit expressions for the inverse of the covariance matrix. Summary of the results in the case of general boundary conditions can be found in Section A.

Clearly, the function $g(x)$ acts as a spatially-dependent penalty term for the squared derivative of the model output. It can be chosen in such a way that the smoothing depends on a rough estimate of the spatial derivative of the observations [12, 4]:

$$g(x) \mapsto g[y(x)] \equiv 1 - e^{-c\left(\frac{\partial_x y_\sigma}{\lambda}\right)^{-s}}. \quad (11)$$

Here the time-dependent observations y are passed through a Gaussian filter of variance σ^2 resulting in the signal y_σ, whose spatial derivative's value is denoted by $\partial_x u_\sigma$. The constant c can always be chosen beforehand so that the diffusion of the original noisy signal y takes place only in the low derivative regions where $|\partial_x u_\sigma| < \lambda$ [4]. The even number $s \geq 2$ denotes the sharpness of the nonlinearity. Eq. (10) used with Eq. (11) comprises the basic step in the iterative edge-preserving filtering [12, 6]. Similar models can be found in physics, e.g. two-dimensional shear band formation in granular medium [13].

In order to reveal discontinuities, it is not sufficient to introduce Eq. (11). However, an iterative re-application of Eq. (4) with the covariance matrix defined by Eqs. (6) and (11) helps. While all the functions involved are continuous, paradoxically, the iteration eventually develops discontinuities.

If we now consider the discrete grid $x_1 = h, x_2 = 2h, \ldots, x_n = 1 - h$ and organize the observations into a single vector $\mathbf{u}_0 = \mathbf{y} \in \mathbb{R}^n$, then the iterative application of Eq. (4) corresponds to a GP regression with the matrix $\mathbf{K}_\theta$:

$$\mathbf{I} + \theta_0 \mathbf{K}_\theta^{-1} = (\mathbf{I} + \tau \mathbf{K}_1^{-1})(\mathbf{I} + \tau \mathbf{K}_2^{-1}) \cdots (\mathbf{I} + \tau \mathbf{K}_m^{-1}), \quad (12)$$

where the matrices $\mathbf{K}_t^{-1}$ are given by Eq. (17). The variance θ_0 of a single regularization step in Eq. (10) becomes the time step size if the iterated Eq. (10) is viewed as an implicit Euler stepping of classical diffusion equations with nonlinear diffusion coefficient $g(u)$. Eq. (12) presents a way to smooth the observations in $O(nm)$ multiplications. Needless to state, the iterated composition of the inverse tridiagonal matrices comprises an efficient GP model with a non-sparse covariance matrix and its inverse.

5 Evidence-Maximizing Stopping

Eq. (12), when used together with Eq. (5), gives a formal approach towards determination of numerous diffusion parameters, including a finite optimal stopping time m which usually outperforms solutions that approach the steady state $m \to \infty$. In the case of a small variance θ_0 of the additive noise, Eq. (5) reduces to 'decorrelation' between the estimated noise and the model output' [8].

Fig. 1 indicates the results obtained by filtering a synthetic signal with linear and nonlinear diffusion algorithms. The simulation was performed with $n = 1000$ observations and the noise level was set to $\theta_0 = 0.44$.

Comparison of Fig. 1(a) vs. (b) and (c) vs. (d) reveals that the optimally stopped diffusion would clearly outperform the steady state in both cases. Logevidence criterion exhibits features that are similar to the mean squared error criterion between the filtering outcome and the true signal. Linear diffusion filtering blurs the edges of the signal whereas the nonlinear case preserves them.

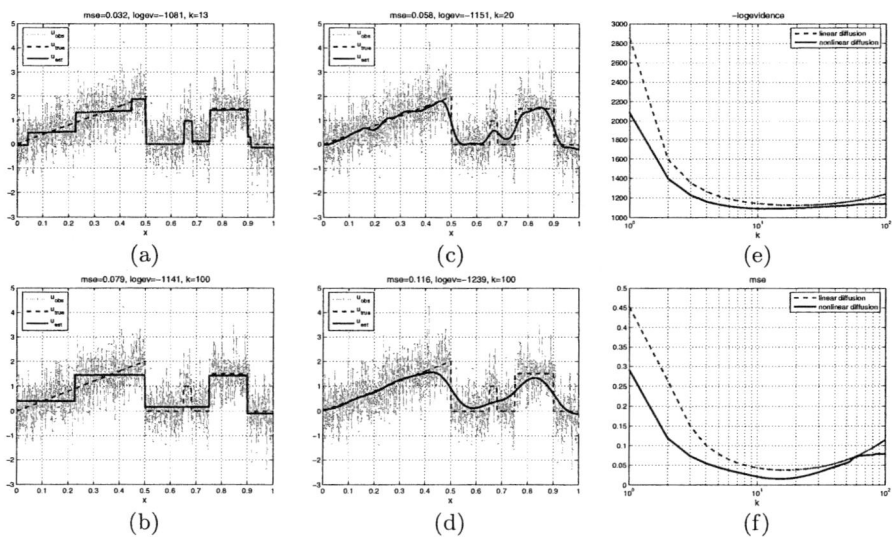

Fig. 1. Linear and nonlinear diffusion filtering from the GP regression viewpoint: (a) the outcome of nonlinear diffusion filtering at the optimal stopping time $k^* = 13$, (b) the result approaching the steady state at $k = 100$, (c) optimally stopped linear diffusion filtering at $k = 20$, (d) linear diffusion at $k = 100$, (e) negative logevidence as a function of the iteration counter k, (f) time evolution of the mean squared errors between the true and estimated signal. The stopping is performed according to negative logevidence values, which closely matches the mean squared error criterion which could be considered as a true (unknown) stopping criterion. The steady state of the linear diffusion with reflecting boundary conditions is a constant signal, i.e. the average of the observations.

6 Extension to Non-Gaussian Diffusion

A computational bottleneck of the diffusion filtering lies in the evaluation of the matrix-vector product $\mathbf{u}_t = (\mathbf{I} + \tau \mathbf{K}_t^{-1})^{-1}\mathbf{u}_{t-1}$, clf. Eq. (12). It is a common practice to implement such a procedure by applying the Thomas algorithm [12]. It splits the matrix $(\mathbf{I} + \tau \mathbf{K}_t^{-1})$ into a product of lower and upper-bidiagonal matrices, followed by an inversion-free forward substitution $\mathbf{L}\tilde{\mathbf{u}}_k = \mathbf{u}_{k-1}$ and a backward pass $\mathbf{U}\mathbf{u}_k = \tilde{\mathbf{u}}_k$. The procedure requires about $O(n)$ number of multiplications.

This computation can be viewed as a particular case of the dynamic programming approach applied to solve the variational problem in Eq. (10). Such an observation allows to introduce any discrete constraints $u \in \mathcal{U}$ into a single diffusion step with only the cost of $O(card(\mathcal{U}) \cdot n)$ multiplications. In order to see this, one can define the state variable $\lambda \equiv u_{s-1}$ and introduce the value function

$$v_s(\lambda) = \min_{u_s,\ldots,u_n \in \mathcal{U}} \sum_{j=s}^{n} [\tau g_j(u_j - \lambda)^2 + (u_j - y_j)^2]. \tag{13}$$

Solution to Eq. (10) when $u \in \mathcal{U}$ can then be solved recursively in two stages. During the backward pass, one solves n one-dimensional minimization problems

$$v_s(\lambda) = \min_{u_s \in \mathcal{U}} [v_{s+1}(u_s) + \tau g_s(u_s - \lambda)^2 + (u_s - y_s)^2], \quad v_{n+1} = 0 \tag{14}$$

for $s = n, n-1, \ldots, 1$ and tracks the optimal solutions $\varphi_s(\lambda) = \arg\min_{u_s \in \mathcal{U}}[\cdot]$. A solution to the constrained Eq. (10) can then be found by using the initial condition $u_1^* = 0$ and tracing forward $u_s^* = \varphi_s(u_{s-1}^*)$, $s = 2, \ldots, n$. Whenever $\mathcal{U} \equiv \mathbb{R}$, an analytic solution of Eq. (14) would further reduce the computational complexity, but this formulae turns out to be just a variant of the Thomas algorithm.

The procedure based on Eqs. (13) and (14) can be derived by writing the Hamilton-Bellman-Jacobi equation for the variational problem Eq. (10) and applying the Euler algorithm to obtain its discrete counterpart [2]. Alternatively, this recursive formulae can be viewed as the Viterbi algorithm used to determined the optimal state sequence of the backward hidden Markov model (HMM). Such an HMM at the location $x_{s=n} = nh$ emits the observation y_n with the Gaussian density of mean u_n and variance τ and jumps to the next state $s-1$ with a probability whose logarithm up to an additive constant is $\ln a_{n,s-1} = g_n(u_n - u_{s-1})^2$. The case of the boundary conditions in Eq. (10) corresponds to *a priori* unspecified initial probability of the state $u_{s=n}$. In this manner, the process then generates all n observations finally ending in the state $u_{s=1} = 0$.

This generalization of the Thomas algorithm is examined in Fig. 2. A standard single step of the nonlinear diffusion performs rather poorly as in Fig. 2a, especially when the noise is non-Gaussian, clf. Fig. 2b,c. In these last two cases the nonlinear diffusion would not converge to the true signal if more iterations followed. However, if we specify the knowledge that the signal values can only become binary, the whole problem can be solved in just one iteration.

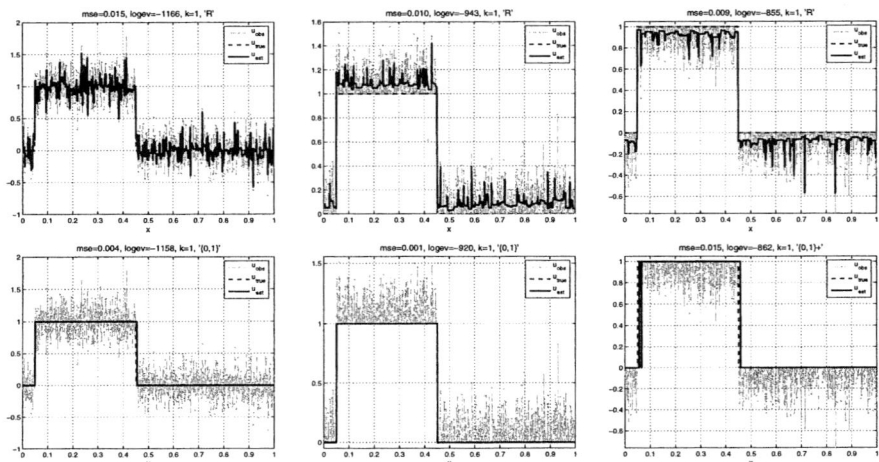

Fig. 2. Filtering a level change in additive noise. The first row illustrates the outcome of nonlinear diffusion filtering, whereas the second row shows the solutions obtained with just one iteration of diffusion whose outcome is constrained to take binary values of either 0 or 1. The first column displays the experiment with Gaussian noise whose variance is $\theta_0 = 0.04$. The second and third columns correspond to the experiments with non-Gaussian noise, obtained by setting either positive or negative values of the noise to zero.

7 Conclusions

The principle of nonlinear diffusion filtering needs systematic control mechanisms to cope with discontinuities. By performing computer simulations with synthetic data, we have examined two particular solutions to such a problem: (i) optimal diffusion stopping and (ii) constraining of the diffusion outcome to take only discrete values. The first principle was implemented by viewing the diffusion filtering as Gaussian process regression. The second approach was examined by viewing the Thomas algorithm as a dynamic programming procedure. Both methods provide efficient implementations.

References

1. I. Babuška, M. Práger, E. Vitásek, and R. Radok. *Numerical Processes in Differential Equations*. John Wiley and Sons, Ltd., 1966.
2. R. E. Bellman and S. E. Dreyfus. *Applied Dynamic Programming*. Princeton University Press, 1962.
3. F.M. Buchmann and W.P. Petersen. Solving Dirichlet problems numerically using the Feynman-Kac representation. *Bit Numerical Mathematics*, 43(3):519–540, 2003.
4. Frederico D'Almeida. Nonlinear diffusion toolbox. MATLAB Central.
5. A. Kavčić and J.M.F. Moura. Matrices with banded inverses: inversion algorithms and factorization of Gauss–Markov processes. *IEEE Trans. on Information Theory*, 46(4):1495–1509, July 2000.

6. M. Lassas and S. Siltanen. Can one use total variation prior for edge-preserving Bayesian inversion? *Inverse Problems*, 20:1537–1563, October 2004.
7. D.J.C. MacKay. Bayesian Interpolation. *Neural Computation*, 4(3):415–447, 1992.
8. P. Mrázek and M. Navara. Selection of optimal stopping time for nonlinear diffusion filtering. *Int. Journal of Computer Vision*, 52(2):189–203, 2003.
9. J. Nicolau. A method for simulating non-linear stochastic differential equations in $\mathbb{R}^1$. Technical report, Universidade Técnica de Lisboa, 2004.
10. A. O'Hagan and J. F. C. Kingman. Curve fitting and optimal design for prediction. *J. R. Statist. Soc. B*, 40(1):1–42, 1978.
11. N. G. Polson and G. O. Roberts. Bayes factors for discrete observations from diffusion processes. *Biometrika*, 8(1):11–26, March 1994.
12. J. Weickert, B. M. ter Haar Romeny, and M. A.Viergever. Efficient and reliable schemes for nonlinear diffusion filtering. *IEEE Trans. on Image Processing*, 7(3):398–410, March 1998.
13. T. P. Witelski. A discrete model for an ill-posed nonlinear parabolic PDE. *Physica D*, 160:189–221, 2001.
14. T. Yamamoto. Inversion formulas for tridiagonal matrices with applications to boundary value problems. *Numer. Funct. Anal. and Optimiz.*, 22(4):357–385, 2001.

A Inverse BM Covariance Matrix

This summary derives the covariance matrix of GP regression with deformed BM covariance functions in the case of general boundary conditions. We use discrete approximation [1] and extend several existing results which can be found in [14].

Consider a discrete grid $x_0 = 0, x_1 = h, x_2 = 2h, \ldots, x_{n+1} = 1$. Then a single iteration of Eq. (10) with boundary conditions

$$\alpha_1 u(0) + \beta_1 \partial_x u(0) = \gamma_1, \tag{15}$$

$$\alpha_2 u(1) + \beta_2 \partial_x u(1) = \gamma_2 \tag{16}$$

reduces to solving a linear system of equations, which corresponds to an optimal solution of Eq. (4) with $\mathbf{y} = (y_1 - \delta_1, y_2, \cdots, y_{n-1}, y_n - \delta_2)^T \in \mathbb{R}^n$ and the tridiagonal inverse covariance matrix

$$\mathbf{K}_t^{-1} = \frac{\tau}{h^2} \begin{pmatrix} g_1 + g_2 & -g_2 & & & \\ -g_2 & g_2 + g_3 & -g_3 & & \\ & \ddots & \ddots & \ddots & \\ & & -g_{n-1} & g_{n-1} + g_n & -g_n \\ & & & -g_n & g_n + g_{n+1} \end{pmatrix}. \tag{17}$$

Here $\delta_1 = g_1 \gamma_1/(\alpha_1 + h\beta_1)$, $\delta_2 = g_{n+1}\gamma_2/(\alpha_2 + h\beta_2)$ and the elements are

$$g_1 = [g(u_{k-1}(x_1)) + g(u_{k-1}(x_0))]h\beta_1/(\alpha_1 + h\beta_1), \tag{18}$$

$$g_i = g(u_{k-1}(x_i)) + g(u_{k-1}(x_{i-1})), \quad i = 2, \ldots, n, \tag{19}$$

$$g_{n+1} = g(u_{k-1}(x_{n+1})) + g(u_{k-1}(x_n))h\beta_2/(\alpha_2 + h\beta_2). \tag{20}$$

The boundary conditions are preserved with $o(h^2)$ accuracy whereas $o(h^4)$ holds elsewhere. However, this is valid only if $y(x)$ is sufficiently continuous [1]. In the case of a single iteration $m = 1$, the constant $\tau = \theta_0$. When Eq. (4) is iterated, Eqs. (18)–(20) are estimated at the time instant $t - 1$ according to Eq. (11) by replacing $y(x)$ with the estimate $u_{t-1}(x)$.

An Evolutionary Function Approximation Approach to Compute Prediction in XCSF

Ali Hamzeh and Adel Rahmani

Department of Computer Engineering,
Iran University of Science and Technology, Narmak, Tehran, Iran
{hamzeh, rahmani}@iust.ac.ir

Abstract. XCSF is a new extension to XCS that is developed to extend XCS's reward calculation capability via computing. This new feature is called *computable prediction*. The first version of XCSF tries to find the most appropriate equation to compute each *classifier's* reward using a weight update mechanism. In this paper, we try to propose a new evolutionary mechanism to compute these equations using genetic algorithms.

1 Introduction

XCSF [1] is a new extension to XCS [2] which extends ability of learning classifier systems to enable them to compute environmental rewards instead of memorizing them in all situations. In [1], author proposed XCSF and designed it to compute a linear piece-wise approximation for payoff function. This function is approximated using linear equations, which consist of two real coefficients that are called *weights*. These *weights* are updated using Widrow-Hoff update rule [3]. With respect to described issues in [4] to update these *weights*, we try to employ Genetic Algorithms [5] to approximate desired payoff functions. The rest of this paper is organized as follows: in the next section, we describe XCSF in brief, and then some relevant works on XCSF are presented. Then we describe our proposed method and our benchmark problems. At last, new method's results are presented and discussed.

2 XCSF in Brief

XCSF [1] is a model of learning classifier system that extends the typical concept of classifiers through the introduction of a computed classifier prediction. To develop XCSF, XCS has to be modified in three respects: (i) classifier conditions are extended for numerical inputs, as done in XCSI [6]; (ii) classifiers are extended with a vector of weights $\vec{w}$, that are used to compute the classifier prediction; (iii) The original update of the classifier prediction must be modified so that the weights are updated instead of the classifier prediction. These three modifications result in a version of XCS, XCSF [1] that maps numerical inputs into actions [7] with an associated calculated prediction.

Classifiers: In XCSF, classifiers consist of a condition, an action, and four main parameters. The condition specifies which input states the classifier matches; as in

XCSI[6], it is represented by a concatenation of interval predicates, $int_i = (l_i; u_i)$, where l_i ("*lower*") and u_i ("*upper*") are integers, though they might be also real. The action specifies the action for which the payoff is predicted. The four parameters are: (i) The weight vector $\vec{w}$, used to compute the classifier prediction as a function of the current input; (ii) The prediction error ε, that estimates the error affecting the classifier prediction; (iii) The fitness F that estimates the accuracy of the classifier prediction; (iv) The numerosity *num*, a counter used to represent different copies of the same classifier.

Performance Component: XCSF works as XCS. At each time step t, XCSF builds a match set [M] containing the classifiers in the population [P] whose condition matches the current sensory input s_t; if [M] contains less than θ_{mna} actions, covering takes place and creates a new classifier that matches the current inputs and has a random action. Each interval predicate $int_i = (l_i; u_i)$ in the condition of a covering classifier is generated as $l_i = s_t(i) - rand_i(r_0)$, and $u_i = s_t(i) + rand_i(r_0)$, where $s_t(i)$ is the input value of state s_t matched by the interval predicated in_i, and the function $rand_i(r_0)$ generates a random integer in the interval $[0; r_0]$ with r_0 fixed integer. The weight vector $\vec{w}$ of covering classifiers is initialized with zero values; all the other parameters are initialized as in XCS [8]. For each action a_i in [M], XCSF computes the system prediction which estimates the payoff that XCSF expects when action a_i is performed. As in XCS, in XCSF the system prediction of action a is computed by the fitness-weighted average of all matching classifiers that specify action a. However, in contrast with XCS, in XCSF the classifier prediction is computed as a function of the current state s_t and the classifier vector weight $\vec{w}$. Following a notation similar to [8], the system prediction for action a in state s_t, $P(s_t; a)$, is defined as:

$$P(s_t, a) = \frac{\sum_{cl \in [M]_a} cl.p(s_t) \times cl.F}{\sum_{cl \in [M]_a} cl.F} \quad (1)$$

Where cl is a classifier, $[M]_a^i$ represents the subset of classifiers in [M] with action a, $cl.F$ is the fitness of cl ; $cl.p(s_t)$ is the prediction of cl computed in the state s_t. In particular, $cl.p(s_t)$ is computed as:

$$cl.p(s_t) = cl.w_0 \times x_0 + \sum_{i>0} cl.w_i \times s_t(i) \quad (2)$$

Where $cl.w_i$ is the weight w_i of cl and x_0 is a constant input. The values of $P(s_t; a)$ form the prediction array. Next, XCSF selects an action to perform. The classifiers in [M] that advocate the selected action are put in the current action set [A]; the selected action is sent to the environment and a reward r is returned to the system together with the next input state s_{t+1}. Note that when XCSF is applied to function approximation problems, as in this paper, there is only one dummy action that the system can perform which has not actual effect on the environment [6].

Reinforcement Component: XCSF uses the incoming reward r to update the parameters of classifiers in action set [A]. First, the reward r is used to update the weight vector $\vec{w}$ using a modified delta rule [3] as follows For each classifier $cl \in [A]$, each weight $cl.w_i$ is adjusted by a quantity Δw_i computed as:

$$\Delta w_i = \frac{\eta}{|\vec{x}_{t-1}|^2}(r - cl.p(s_{t-1}))x_{t-1}(i) \qquad (3)$$

Where η is the correction rate and $\vec{x}_{t-1}$ is defined as the input state vector s_{t-1} augmented by a constant x_0 (i.e. $x_{t-1} = \langle x_0, s_{t-1}(1), \vec{s}_{t-1}(2),..., s_{t-1}(n) \rangle$) and is the norm of vector $\vec{x}_{t-1}$ for further details refer to [1] The values Δw_i are used to update the weights of classifier cl as:

$$cl.w_i \leftarrow cl.w_i + \Delta w_i \qquad (4)$$

A classifier in XCSF basically represents a perceptron with a linear activation function [9] which is applied only on the inputs that match the classifier condition. Then the prediction error ε is updated as:

$$cl.\varepsilon \leftarrow cl.\varepsilon + \beta(|r - cl.p(s_{t-1})| - cl.\varepsilon) \qquad (5)$$

Classifier fitness is updated as in XCS. First, the raw accuracy κ of the classifiers in [A] is computed as follows.

$$\kappa = \begin{cases} 1 & \text{if } \varepsilon \leq \varepsilon_0 \\ \alpha(\varepsilon/\varepsilon_0)^{-\nu} & \text{otherwise.} \end{cases} \qquad (6)$$

The raw accuracy is used to calculate the relative accuracy ε_0 as

$$\kappa' = \frac{\kappa \times num}{\sum_{cl \in [A]}(cl.\kappa \times cl.num)} \qquad (7)$$

Where $cl.\kappa$ is the raw accuracy of classifier cl; $cl.num$ is the numerosity of classifier cl. Finally, the relative accuracy κ' is used to update the classifier fitness as: $F \leftarrow F + \beta(\kappa' - F)$.

Discovery Component: The genetic algorithm in XCSF works as in XCSI [6]. The genetic algorithm is applied to classifiers in [A]. It selects two classifiers with probability proportional to their fitness, copies them, and with probability χ performs crossover on the copies; then, with probability μ it mutates each allele. Crossover and mutation work as in XCSI.

3 Relevant Works on XCSF

In [4], the authors study generalization in XCSF and introduce several different approaches to improve the generalization capabilities of XCSF. At first, they present experimental evidence showing that while XCSF always evolves accurate approximations, the types of generalizations evolved can be influenced by the input range. The presented results show that when the inputs are limited to small values,

XCSF evolves (accurate) piecewise linear approximations, as expected. But when the input range includes large values, XCSF does not fully exploit its learning capabilities and tends to evolve (accurate) piecewise constant approximations.

In [11] authors take XCSF one step further and apply it to typical reinforcement learning problems involving delayed rewards. In essence, they use XCSF as a method of generalized (linear) reinforcement learning to evolve piecewise linear approximations of the payoff surfaces of typical multistep problems. Achieved results show that XCSF can easily evolve optimal and near optimal solutions for problems introduced in the literature to test linear reinforcement learning methods.

Authors show in [12] that how XCSF can be easily extended to allow polynomial approximations. They test the extended version of XCSF on various approximation problems and shows that quadratic/cubic approximations can be used to significantly improve XCSF's generalization capabilities.

Moreover, in [13] authors apply XCSF to the learning of Boolean functions. The presented results show that XCS with computable linear prediction performs optimally in typical Boolean domains and it allows more compact solutions evolving classifiers that are more general compared with XCS.

4 XCSF with Evolutionary Function Approximation Approach

In this section, we describe overall architecture and implementation details of the proposed extension to XCSF. As we described in previous section, Widrow-Hoff update rule encounter some difficulties in certain range of input variables. In [4], some solutions to solve these problems are proposed. We are trying to propose a new solution which has no need to any weight update process to approximate desired payoff functions. This new system is called XCSF-G. XCSF-G's overall architecture is the same as XCSF with some minor modifications. However, the major difference between XCSF-G and traditional XCSF is classifier's structure. Classifier's structure is XCSF-G is modified to support GA function approximation capability.

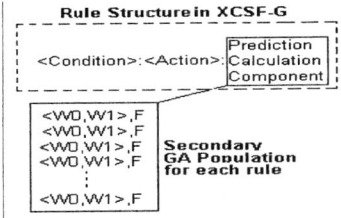

Fig. 1. Structure of XCSF-G's rule

In this type of rule, prediction is calculated by a secondary population of chromosomes which is allocated for each rule separately.

4.1 Evolutionary Prediction Calculation Procedure

In this section we describe important points to understand genetic algorithm-based prediction calculation method:

4.1.1 Calculate Prediction

To illustrate this, we describe structure of secondary population's chromosomes.

These chromosomes contain two real numbers. These numbers are imagined as w_0 and w_1 in XCSF for each rule. To calculate prediction for each rule, we follow this procedure: At first, we choose best chromosome in the secondary population with respect to fitness and calculate the prediction using equation 7:

$$w_0 + w_1 x_1 \tag{7}$$

where w_0 and w_1 are evolved genes in the best chromosome of the population and x_1 is environmental input for the current state.

4.1.2 Secondary Population's Architecture

As we mentioned in previous section, to calculate prediction for each rule, we must choose best chromosome of its secondary population with respect to its fitness. So fitness calculation of the secondary population is one of the most important parts of XCSF-G. In fitness calculation routine, the most important goal is to select the individual with lowest error rate in previous prediction estimation epochs. So, in XCSF-G fitness calculation is done using rule's *prediction error*. In every trial of XCSF-G's life cycle, a tuple is made of environmental input and reward; we call this tuple an *Estimation Twin (ET)*. *ET*s are listed and memorized for each fired rule which was involved in reward gathering procedure. When number of stored ET's of a specified rule reaches a predefined threshold n_{ET}, then fitness calculation of secondary populations of this rule begins as follows:

- For each chromosome, estimated output for given input is calculated using equation 7 separately and overall error is calculated using equation:

$$E_j = \frac{\sum_{i=1}^{n}[G_j(x_i) - P(x_i)]^2}{n_{ET}} \tag{8}$$

Where $G_j(x_i)$ is estimated value of $j'Th$ chromosome for x_i and $P(x_i)$ is environmental reward for the same input. Then fitness for $j'Th$ chromosome is calculated using:

$$F_j = e^{-E_j} \tag{9}$$

- After calculating fitness for all chromosomes, mating pool for secondary population is constructed using tournament selection [10] with tour size of two.
- After selecting parents from mating pool randomly, one offspring is generated using parent's genes with respect to their calculated fitness.

$$w_0^c = \frac{f^{p1} w_0^{p1} + f^{p2} w_0^{p2}}{f^{p1} + f^{p2}}, \quad w_1^c = \frac{f^{p1} w_1^{p1} + f^{p2} w_1^{p2}}{f^{p1} + f^{p2}} \tag{10}$$

- Above procedure is repeated until next generation of secondary population is constructed completely.

4.1.3 Initial Population Initialization

After producing new rule in XCSF-G, secondary population for this rule must be initialized. This population is initialized randomly and their fitness's are set to a random number in [0; 0.1) interval.

5 Design of Experiments

All the experiments discussed in this paper involve single step problems and are performed following the standard design used in the literature [4, 5]. In each experiment XCSF has to learn to approximate a target function $f(x)$; each experiment consists of a number of problems that XCSF(-G) must solve. For each problem, an example $\langle x, f(x) \rangle$ of the target function $f(x)$ is randomly selected; x is input to XCSF(-G) whom computes the approximated value $\hat{f}(x)$ has the expected payoff of the only available dummy action; the action is virtually performed (the action has no actual effect), and XCSF(-G) receives a reward equal to $f(x)$. Each problem is either a learning problem or a test problem. In learning problems, the genetic algorithm is enabled while it is turned off during test problems. The covering operator is always enabled, but operates only if needed. XCSF performance is measured as the accuracy of the evolved approximation $\hat{f}(x)$ with respect to the target function $f(x)$. To evaluate the evolved approximation $\hat{f}(x)$ we measure the mean absolute error, MAE:

$$MAE = \frac{1}{n}\sum_{x}\left|f(x) - \hat{f}(x)\right| \qquad (11)$$

Where n is the number of points for which $f(x)$ is defined. In particular we use the average MAE over the performed experiments, dubbed MAE.

6 Experimental Results

We now compare XCSF with XCSF-G. For this purpose, we have considered problems from *sin* family. This family is very flexible. It means that we can change range of input variable and function slope with very simple parameter setting. This feature helps us to analyze our solution's weaknesses and advantages with respect to discussed issues in [4]. This family of problems is represented using equation 13:

$$f(x) = \sin(Slp * \pi(Up - x)/50) \qquad (12)$$

where *Slp* determines function's slope and *Up* determines range of input variable. In this paper, *Slp* and *Up* are chosen from table 1:

Table 1. Experienced values for *Up* and *Slp*

Up	Slp		
	1	2	5
50	PR1	PR2	PR3
1050	PR4	PR5	PR6

This table is interpreted as follows: the problem number determines *Slp* and *Up*, for example *PR1* is presented using equation 13 and *PR5* is determined with equation 14.

$$PR1(x) = \sin(\pi(50 - x)/50) \qquad (13)$$

$$PR5(x) = \sin(2\pi(1050 - x)/50) \qquad (14)$$

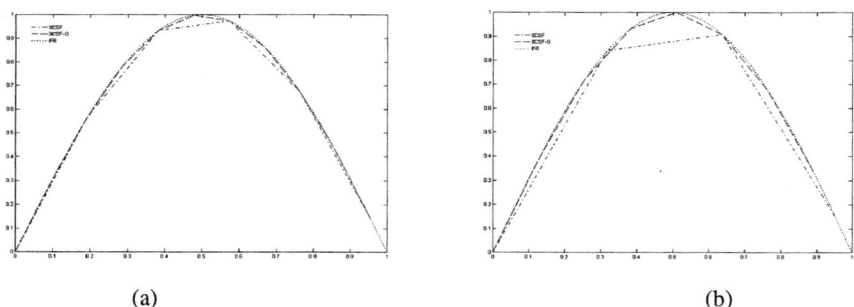

Fig. 2. XCSF (dashed-dot), XCSFG (dashed) in PR1 (a) and PR4 (b), PRs are dotted lines.

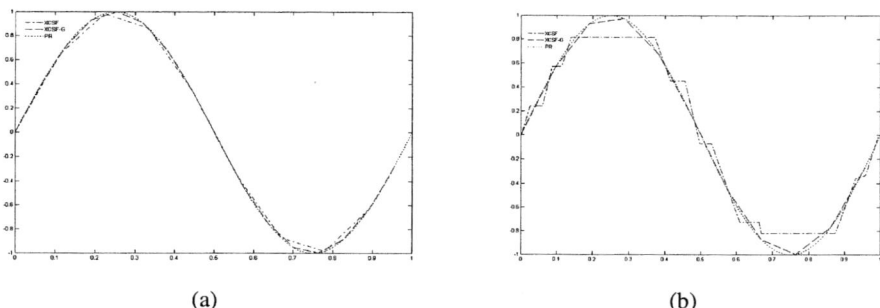

Fig. 3. XCSF (dashed- dot), XCSFG (dashed) in PR2 (a) and PR5 (b), PRs are dotted lines

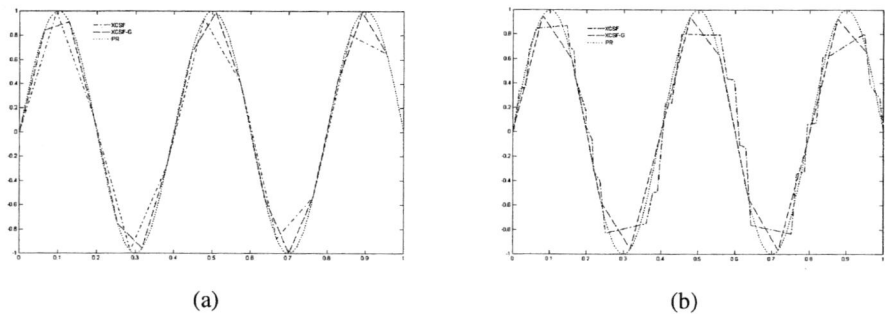

Fig. 4. XCSF (dashed line), XCSFG (dashed) in PR3 (a) and PR6 (b), PRs are dotted lines

It is notable that input variable x is chosen from the interval $[Up\text{-}50, Up]$ for all problems. For the experiments discussed here we always use the same parameter settings: $N = 1000$; $\beta = 0.2$; $\alpha = 0.1$; $\nu = 5$; $\chi = 0.8$, $\mu = 0.04$, $\theta_{nma} = 1$, $\theta_{del} = 50$; $\theta_{GA} = 50$; $\delta = 0{:}1$; GA-subsumption is on with $\theta_{sub} = 50$; while action-set subsumption is off. Secondary genetic population in XCSF-G's size is equal to 50 and $n_{ET}=10$. Below

XCSF and XCSF-G are compared in described problems and their approximated functions are shown in figure 2 to 4. These figures are drawn using the following procedure. Both XCSF and XCSF-G are allowed to run for 1500 learning trials then all of the 300 selected values which are uniformly distributed in the learning interval (e.g. [0,50]) are fed to both of them and this procedure is repeated 50 times and average values for this 50 runs are plotted in figures 2 to 4.

7 Discussion

As it was mentioned in previous sections, the numerical parameter to evaluate XCSF and XCSF-G is *MAE* that is calculated using equation 12. This value is calculated using 300 uniformly distributed points between $[Up-50, Up]$. These values are shown in table 2.

Table 2. *MAE* values for XCSF and XCSF-G

Problem Number	XCSF's MAE	XCSF-G's MAE
PR1	0.015	0.009
PR2	0.019	0.014
PR3	0.02	0.04
PR4	0.05	0.01
PR5	0.15	0.025
PR6	0.4	0.06

It is clear that XCSF and XCSF-G both can solve the set of problems with small input values (such as *PR1*, *PR2* and *PR3*). But an interesting issue is that when the desired function to approximate becomes more complex, XCSF-G seems to be less accurate than XCSF and becomes slightly weaker to approximate complex functions such as *PR3*. However, the most interesting issue arises when input range changes from small real numbers to big ones (e.g *Up* is set to 1050 instead of 50). In this set of problems XCSF's performance decreases dramatically as described in [4]. This issue is obvious by only looking to proposed approximation of XCSF for *PR4* to *PR6*. it is clear that XCSF proposed a piece-wise constant approximation for these problems as discussed in [4] and table 2 confirms this idea. XCSF's *MAE* becomes larger in *PR4-6* than their similar problems in *PR1-3*, but XCSF-G's performance just slightly changes and is significantly better than XCSF's performance.

References

1. Wilson, S. W. (2002). *Classifiers that approximate functions*. Journal of Natural Computating 1 (2-3), 211-234.
2. Wilson, S. W. (1995). *Classifier Fitness Based on Accuracy*. Evolutionary Computation 3.
3. Widrow, B. and M. E. Hoff (1988). Adaptive *Switching Circuits*, Chapter *Neurocomputing: Foundation of Research*, pp. 126-134. Cambridge: The MIT Press.
4. Lanzi, P. L., D. Loiacono, S. W. Wilson, and D. E. Goldberg (2005). *Generalization in the XCSF Classifier System: Analysis, Improvement, and Extension*. Technical Report 2005012, Illinois Genetic Algorithms Laboratory.

5. Holland, J. H. (1975). *Adaptation in Natural and Artificial Systems*. Ann Arbor: University of Michigan Press. Republished by the MIT press, 1992.
6. Wilson, S. W. (2001). *Function approximation with a classifier system*. In proceedings of the Genetic and Evolutionary Computation Conference (GECCO-2001), San Francisco, California, USA, pp. 974-981. Morgan Kaufmann.
7. Wilson, S. W. (2004). *Classifier systems for continuous payoff environments*. In Genetic and Evolutionary Computation -GECCO-2004, Part II, Volume 3103 of Lecture Notes in Computer Science, Seattle, WA, USA, pp. 824-835. Springer-Verlag.
8. Butz, M. V. and S. W. Wilson (2002). *An algorithmic description of XCS*. Journal of Soft Computing 6 (3-4), 144-153.
9. Haykin, S. (1998). *Neural Networks: A Comprehensive Foundation*. Prentice Hall PTR.
10. Butz, M. V., K. Sastry, and D. E. Goldberg (2003). *Tournament selection: Stable fitness pressure in XCS*. In Genetic and Evolutionary Computation - GECCO-2003, Volume 2724 of LNCS, Chicago, pp. 1857-1869. Springer-Verlag.
11. Lanzi, P. L., D. Loiacono, S. W. Wilson, and D. E. Goldberg (2005). *XCS with Computable Prediction in Multistep Environments*. Technical Report 2005008, Illinois Genetic Algorithms Laboratory.
12. Lanzi, P. L., D. Loiacono, S. W. Wilson, and D. E. Goldberg (2005). Extending *XCSF Beyond Linear Approximation*. Illinois Genetic Algorithms Laboratory University of Illinois at Urbana-Champaign.
13. Lanzi, P. L., D. Loiacono, S. W. Wilson, and D. E. Goldberg (2005). *XCS with Computable Prediction for the Learning of Boolean Functions*. Technical Report 2005007, Illinois Genetic Algorithms Laboratory.

Using Rewards for Belief State Updates in Partially Observable Markov Decision Processes

Masoumeh T. Izadi and Doina Precup

McGill University, School of Computer Science,
3480 University St., Montreal, QC, Canada, H3A2A7

Abstract. Partially Observable Markov Decision Processes (POMDP) provide a standard framework for sequential decision making in stochastic environments. In this setting, an agent takes actions and receives observations and rewards from the environment. Many POMDP solution methods are based on computing a *belief state*, which is a probability distribution over possible states in which the agent could be. The action choice of the agent is then based on the belief state. The belief state is computed based on a model of the environment, and the history of actions and observations seen by the agent. However, reward information is not taken into account in updating the belief state. In this paper, we argue that rewards can carry useful information that can help disambiguate the hidden state. We present a method for updating the belief state which takes rewards into account. We present experiments with exact and approximate planning methods on several standard POMDP domains, using this belief update method, and show that it can provide advantages, both in terms of speed and in terms of the quality of the solution obtained.

1 Introduction

Sequential decision making and control problems in dynamic environments with incomplete and uncertain information have been the focus of many researchers in different disciplines. Designing agents that can act under uncertainty is mostly done by modelling the environment as a Partially Observable Markov Decision Process (POMDP) [2]. In POMDPs, an agent interacts with a stochastic environment at discrete time steps. The agent takes actions, and as a result, receives observations and rewards. The agent then has to find a way of choosing actions, or policy, which maximizes the total reward received over time. Most POMDP planning methods try to construct a Markovian state signal using a model of the environment and the history of actions and observations experienced by the agent. This signal is called a belief state. Planning methods then use reward information in order to associate an (optimal) action to each belief state.

The fact that rewards are only used in the computation of the optimal policy, but not in updating the belief state, is due to the fact that POMDPs have roots in Markov Decision Processes (MDPs). In an MDP, the agent is provided with Markovian state information directly, and uses the rewards in order to obtain an optimal policy. The same scenario has been carried out to POMDP planning methods as well, except now the Markovian belief state has to be recovered from the history. However, rewards are still used only in policy computation, and not in updating the belief state. Intuitively, it seems that rewards can carry useful information, which can help the agent guess the hidden state more precisely. Indeed, in related work, James et al. [7] used rewards to update information about the state of an agent, in the context of predictive state representations (PSRs). They noted that for some of the domains used in their experiments, using the reward information seemed to help in finding better policies. Our goal in this paper is to investigate whether rewards can be used to produce a similar effect using traditional POMDP planning methods. Intuitively, in some tasks, rewards can provide additional information, not captured by observations. In this case, we expect that using rewards could result in a better estimate of the belief state, and perhaps, in belief states that can identify more precisely the hidden state of the system. If the hidden state were known with better precision, the action choices of the agent could be better as well.

In this paper we describe how rewards can be used for updating belief states. We evaluate empirically the merit of this method, compared with usual belief updates, on several POMDP benchmarks, using both exact and approximate planning, and find that using rewards can be beneficial, if they contained additional information that is not captured in the observations. We find that using rewards can help decrease the entropy of the belief states.

2 Partially Observable Markov Decision Processes

Formally, a POMDP is defined by the following components: a finite set of hidden states S; a finite set of actions A; a finite set of observations Z; a transition function $T : S \times A \times S \to [0,1]$, such that $T(s,a,s')$ is the probability that the agent will end up in state s' after taking action a in state s; an observation function $O : A \times S \times Z \to [0,1]$, such that $O(a,s',z)$ gives the probability that the agent receives observation z after taking action a and getting to state s'; an initial belief state b_0, which is a probability distribution over the set of hidden states S; and a reward function $R : S \times A \times S \to \Re$, such that $R(s,a,s')$ is the immediate reward received when the agent takes action a in hidden state s and ends up in state s'. Additionally, there can be a discount factor, $\gamma \in (0,1)$, which is used to weigh less rewards received farther into the future.

The goal of planning in a POMDP environment is to find a way of choosing actions, or policy, which maximizes the expected sum of future rewards $E[\sum_{t=0}^{T} \gamma^t r_{t+1}]$ where T is the number of time steps left to go in a finite horizon problem, or ∞ in an infinite horizon problem. The agent in a POMDP does not have knowledge of the hidden states, it only perceives the world through noisy observations as defined by the observation function O. Hence, the agent must keep a complete history of its actions and observations, or a sufficient statistic of this history, in order to act optimally. The sufficient statistic in a POMDP is the belief state b, which is a vector of length $|S|$ specifying a probability distribution over hidden states. The elements of this vector, $b(i)$, specify the conditional probability of the agent being in state s_i, given the initial belief b_0 and the history (sequence of actions and observations) experienced so far. After taking action a and receiving observation z, the agent updates its belief state using Bayes' Rule:

$$b'(s') = P(s'|b,a,z) = \frac{O(a,s',z)\sum_{s \in S}b(s)T(s,a,s')}{P(z|a,b)} \quad (1)$$

The denominator is a normalizing constant and is given by the sum of the numerator over all values of $s' \in S$:

$$P(z|a,b) = \sum_{s \in S} b(s) \sum_{s' \in S} T(s,a,s')O(a,s',z)$$

We can transform a POMDP into a "belief state MDP" [2]. Under this transformation, the belief state b becomes the (continuous) state of the MDP. The actions of the belief MDP are the same as in the original POMDP, but the transition and reward functions are transformed appropriately, yielding the following form of Bellman optimality equation for computing the optimal value function, V^*:

$$V^*(b) = \max_{a \in A} \sum_{z \in Z} P(z|a,b) \left[\sum_{s \in S} b(s) \left(\sum_{s'} b'(s') R(s,a,s') \right) + \gamma V^*(b') \right]$$

where b' is the unique belief state computed based on b, a and z, as in equation (1). As in MDPs, the optimal policy that the agent is trying to learn is greedy with respect to this optimal value function. The problem here is that there are infinite number of belief states b, so solving this equation exactly is very difficult.

Exact solution methods for POMDPs take advantage of the fact that value functions for belief MDPs are piecewise-linear and convex functions, and thus can be represented by a finite number of hyperplanes in the space of beliefs. Value iteration updates can be performed directly on these hyperplanes. Unfortunately, exact value iteration is intractable for most POMDP problems with more than a few states, because the size of the set of hyperplanes defining the value function can grow exponentially with each step. Approximate solution methods usually rely on maintaining hyperplanes only for a subset of the belief simplex. Different methods use different heuristics in order to define which belief points are of interest (e.g. [1],[5], [9], [11]).

3 Using Rewards in the Computation of Belief States

Reward signals may provide useful information about the true state of a POMDP system. Although many of the POMDP benchmarks used to evaluate POMDP planning algorithms (e.g., from Tony Cassandra's repository [3]) have been designed in such a way that rewards do not carry any additional information that is not contained in the observations, extra information could potentially be present. In this section, we describe a straightforward way of using rewards in the process of updating belief states.

As described in the previous section, rewards in POMDPs are given as a function $R(s,a,s')$, which depends on the current state, the next state and the action taken. Hence, we can treat rewards as random variables, with a conditional probability distribution $P(r|s,a,s')$, where $P(r|s,a,s') = 1$ if and only if $r = R(s,a,s')$, and 0 otherwise. Note that if we had additional information about the distribution of immediate rewards, instead of just knowing the expected values, this could be naturally incorporated in this framework.

If there is only a discrete, finite set of reward values possible in the MDP, $\{r_1, r_2, ...r_k\}$, where each r_i represents the immediate reward for taking some action a from some hidden state s, this probability distribution can be easily specified using a table. We note that in most POMDP examples, the number of possible immediate rewards satisfies this assumption, and is often very small. However, if this assumption is not satisfied, e.g. if reward are continuous, a conditional probability distribution over rewards can still be specified in some parametric form, based on the given model of the POMDP.

We note that rewards and observations are conditionally independent given the current state s, the next state s' and the action a. From now on we will treat rewards in the same way as observations in predictions about the future. The definition of a history will be extended to include the rewards: $h = a_1 z_1 r_1 .... a_n z_n r_n$.

We define belief state updates based on rewards and observations, by analogy with equation (1), as follows:

$$b'(s') = P(s'|r,z,a,b) = \frac{P(b,a,s',r,z)}{P(b,a,r,z)}$$

$$= \frac{\sum_{s \in S} b(s) T(s,a,s') O(a,s',z) P(r|s,a,s')}{\sum_{s' \in S} \sum_{s \in S} b(s) T(s,a,s') O(a,s',z) P(r|s,a,s')}$$

Value functions are computed in this case analogously to the case of regular beliefs. We will call this model Reward-based POMDP (RPOMDP).

Rewards have been used by Poupart and Boutilier [10] in designing a compression method for POMDPs. The value-directed POMDP compression algorithm of Poupart and Boutilier is close to RPOMDP model. This algorithm computes a low dimensional representation of a POMDP directly from the model parameters R, T, O by finding Krylov subspaces for the reward function under belief propagation. The Krylov subspace for a vector and a matrix is the smallest subspace that contains the vector and is closed under multiplication by the matrix. The authors use the smallest subspace that contains the immediate reward vector and is closed under a set of linear functions defined by the dynamics of the POMDP model. James et al's variation of PSRs in [7] also represents reward as a part of observation. It is interesting to note that this definition of PSRs makes it very similar to value-directed compression [10] for POMDPs.

4 Empirical Evaluations

In this section we focus on studying the effect of using rewards in belief state updates. We selected five standard domains from the POMDP repository [3] and from [10]. Table 1 lists these problems with their characteristics. We chose three domains in which the rewards provide additional information compared to observations. These domains are: Network, line4-2goals and coffee. The other two domains are ones in which rewards possess the same information as the observations (4x4 grid world) or rewards have more information than observations only for special actions (shuttle).

We performed a set of experiments to test the effect of rewards in reducing the uncertainty about the hidden states on selected domains. The entropy of the agent's beliefs have been measured for both the POMDP and RPOMDP model on 100 time steps running the same random policy. Figure 1 shows the result of this experiment in the five domains. The graphs are averages taken over 5 independent runs. For the network,

Table 1. Domains used in the experiments

Domain	$|S|$	$|\mathcal{A}|$	$|O|$	$|\mathcal{R}|$
line4-2goals	4	2	1	2
network	7	4	2	6
4x4 grid	16	4	2	2
shuttle	8	3	5	3
coffee	32	2	3	12

Table 2. Performance comparison of exact solutions for POMDP original model and RPOMDP model

Domain	infinite horizon POMDP	infinite horizon RPOMDP	finite horizon POMDP	finite horizon RPOMDP
line4-2goals				
time	0.01	0.01	0.00	0.00
α-vectors	2	2	2	2
reward	0.466	0.466	0.465	0.465
network				
time	4539.15	5783.02	2.89	3.24
α-vectors	487	549	197	216
reward	293.185	340.15	121.27	173.94
coffee				
time	-	6.35	103	0.23
α-vectors	N/A	5	263	5
reward	N/A	0.00	0.00	0.00
4x4 grid				
time	5578.5	6459.3	231	316
α-vectors	243	243	245	248
reward	1.209	1.209	1.073	1.073
shuttle				
time	-	-	1270	81.4
α-vectors	N/A	N/A	2011	1152
reward	N/A	N/A	11.974	11.237

line4-2goals and coffee domains, the uncertainty of RPOMDP beliefs decreases considerably and it stays always lower than the entropy of POMDP beliefs. Shuttle and 4x4 grid do not show noticeable difference for POMDP and RPOMDP running a random policy. This is expected since the rewards carry little more or no more information than the observations for some of the actions.

In a second set of experiments, we used exact and approximate POMDP solution techniques to evaluate the performance of the RPOMDP model in terms of time to reach an optimal solution, the reached optimal value functions, and the complexity of the optimal value function with respect to the number of alpha vectors used to represent it.

The fastest exact solution method for POMDPs is the *Witness* algorithm [2]. We ran this algorithm on all of the domains, but an optimal solution could not be found in a rea-

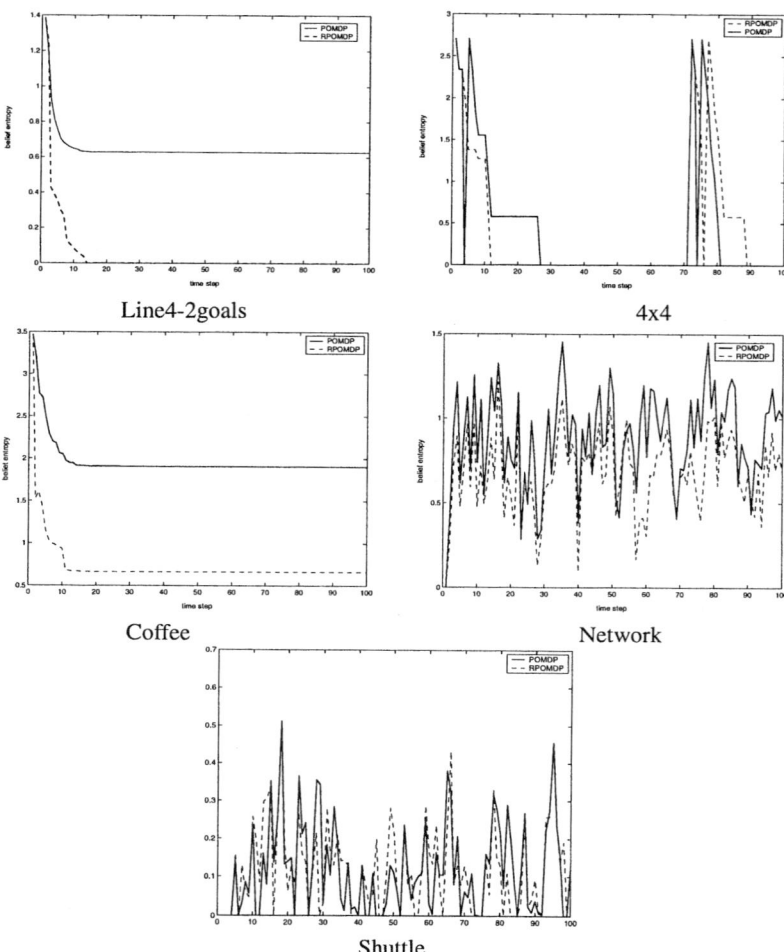

Fig. 1. Comparison of the uncertainty in the agent's state of the world, using standard POMDP belief update vs. RPOMDP belief update, for 5 different tasks

sonable time for the shuttle and coffee domains. Table 2 shows a comparison between POMDP and RPOMDP for updating the belief states, when the Witness algorithm is used to finnd an optimal policy for a finite horizon 10 as well as for an infinite horizon. The reward reported in this table corresponds to the value of an initial belief state drawn uniformly. The dashes in the table show the cases where the algorithm has not been able to solve the problem in 5 hours. The results for the coffee domain are quite interesting interesting. The Witness algorithm cannot perform more than 14 iterations in the time allowed with the usual belief state update, but can solve the problem very quickly when the belief update includes rewards as well. It turns out that the true beliefs for this problem occur on a very low dimensional manifold as it has been stated in [10] and it seems that RPOMDP can take advantage of this problem structure.

One of the most promising approaches for finding approximate POMDP value functions are point-based methods. In this case, instead of optimizing the value function over the entire belief space, only specific beliefs are considered. In our experiments we used the PBVI algorithm [9] together with regular and reward-based belief state updates. In PBVI, a finite set of reachable belief points is selected heuristically, and values are computed only for these points. The algorithm has an anytime flavor, adding more points over time to increase the accuracy of the value function representation. The results of the evaluation are shown in Table 3. We have ran the PBVI algorithm for 10 iterations for each domain and the results are averages over 5 independent runs. The results are obtained when starting with a specified initial belief. In all cases, we performed 10 belief set expansion of PBVI to obtain a value function. Then, we ran 250 trials of the standard PBVI algorithm. Each trial runs for 250 steps. We averaged the results obtained over these trials, and over 5 independent runs. The results in Table 3 confirm that for the problems in which rewards possess information about states more than observations, a significant improvement can be achieved with respect to time, quality of the solution obtained, or both. For the cases in which rewards do not help reduce the belief state entropy, there is no gain. Although RPOMDP in these cases might not sacrifice the solution quality, it can increase the computation time.

Table 3. Performance comparison of approximate solutions for POMDP original model and RPOMDP model

Domain	POMDP	RPOMDP
line4-2goals		
time	0.00	0.00
α-vectors	2	2
beliefs	232	157
discounted reward	1.24	0.48
network		
time	2	62
α-vectors	23	208
beliefs	714	500
discounted reward	240.63	352.9
coffee		
time	4	6
α-vectors	24	6
beliefs	323	169
discounted reward	-1.92	-0.97
shuttle		
time	0.8	0.01
α-vectors	17	18
beliefs	122	125
discounted reward	329.56	32.96
4x4 grid		
time	2.4	8.2
α-vectors	24	24
beliefs	460	468
discounted reward	3.73	3.75

5 Conclusions and Future Work

In this paper we studied the probabilistic reformulation of the POMDP model, focusing on the assumption that rewards carry information about the states of the world independent of observations. Following this assumption we represent and update belief states taking into account the reward signal as part of the feedback that the agent receives from the environment in order to reduce the uncertainty about the state of the world. We presented the results of an empirical study confirming that the RPOMDP model is very useful in reducing the entropy of beliefs for some domains. In this case, better solutions can be obtained as well, and computation time is typically reduced.

This research can be extended in several directions. This model can be used to study from a different perspective the space of reachable beliefs. Belief state entropy can be used in order to guide more intelligent exploration strategies. In practical problems, often the evolution of beliefs following a trajectory is embedded in a low dimensional space. In the case of RPOMDP, linear dimensionality reduction involves no information loss. We plan to study further how this way of updating beliefs affect non-linear compression algorithms.

References

1. Bonet, B. (2002) An epsilon-optimal grid-based algorithm for partially observable Markov decision processes. *Proceedings of ICML*, 51-58.
2. Cassandra,A., T., Littman, M., and Kaelbling L., P.(1997) A simple, fast, exact methods for partially observable Markov decision processes.*Proceedings of UAI*.
3. Cassandra,A. T. Tony's POMDP page (1999). http://www.cs.brown.edu/research/ai/pomdp/code/index.html
4. Givan,R., Dean,T., and Greig, M.(2003) Equivalence notions and model minimization in Markov Decision Processes. *Journal of Artificial Intelligence*, 147:163-223(61).
5. Hauskrecht, M.(2000) Value-function approximation for partially observable Markov decision process. *Journal of Artificial Intelligence Research* 13:33-94.
6. Izadi, M. T., Rajwade,A., and Precup, D.(2005) Using core beliefs for point-based value iteration. *Proceedings of IJCAI*.
7. James, M., R., Singh, S., and Littman, M., L.(2004) Planning with Predictive State Representations.In *Proceedings of ICML*, 304–311.
8. Littman,M. L., Sutton, R., and Singh, S.(2002) Predictive representations of state. In *Proceedings of NIPS*, 1555–1561.
9. Pineau,J., Gordon, G., and Thrun,S .(2003) Point-based value iteration: An anytime algorithms for POMDPs. *Proceedings of IJCAI*, 1025–1032.
10. Poupart, P., and Boutilier, C.(2002) Value-directed Compression of POMDPs. *Proceedings of NIPS*,1547-1554.
11. Smith, T., and Simmons, R. (2004) Heuristic search value iteration for POMDPs. *Proceedings of UAI*.

Active Learning in Partially Observable Markov Decision Processes

Robin Jaulmes, Joelle Pineau, and Doina Precup

McGill University, School of Computer Science,
3480 University St., Montreal, QC, H3A2A7

Abstract. This paper examines the problem of finding an optimal policy for a Partially Observable Markov Decision Process (POMDP) when the model is not known or is only poorly specified. We propose two approaches to this problem. The first relies on a model of the uncertainty that is added directly into the POMDP planning problem. This has theoretical guarantees, but is impractical when many of the parameters are uncertain. The second, called MEDUSA, incrementally improves the POMDP model using selected queries, while still optimizing reward. Results show good performance of the algorithm even in large problems: the most useful parameters of the model are learned quickly and the agent still accumulates high reward throughout the process.

1 Introduction

Partially Observable Markov Decision Processes (POMDPs) are a popular framework for sequential decision-making in partially observable domains (Littman et al, 1995). Many recent algorithms for efficient planning in POMDPs have been proposed (e.g., Pineau et al. 2003; Poupart & Boutilier 2005).

However most of these rely crucially on having a known model of the environment. On the other hand, experience-based approaches have been proposed which rely strictly on experimentation with the system to learn a model which can then be used for planning (e.g., McCallum, 1996; Brafman and Shani, 2005; Singh et al. 2004). Yet these typically require very large amounts of data, and are therefore impractical (to date) for large problems. In practice, we would often prefer a more flexible trade-off between these two extremes.

In particular, in many applications it is relatively easy to provide a rough model, though much harder to provide an exact one, and so we would like to use some experimentation to improve our initial model. The overall goal of this work is to investigate POMDP approaches which can combine a partial model of the environment with direct experimentation, in order to produce solutions that are robust to model uncertainty, while scaling to large domains.

We based our work on the idea of *active learning* (Cohn et al. 1996), a well-known machine learning technique for classification tasks with sparsely labeled data. The goal is to select which examples should be labeled by considering the expected information gain. These ideas extend nicely to dynamical systems such as HMMs (Anderson & Moore 2005). Applying these ideas to POMDPs, we assume the availability of an oracle that can provide the agent with exact information about the current state, upon request.

This is a reasonable assumption in a number of real-world POMDP domains. Our work is motivated especially by applications in robotics and dialogue management, where a human is routinely involved in the initial calibration of the robot. However, we assume that using the oracle is expensive and reserved for the learning phase, where we will use it as little as possible.

Our first technique is conceptually simple, though not scalable. In essence, given a problem with model uncertainty, we extend the original problem formulation to include one additional state feature for each uncertain model parameter. The extended model is used for planning, thereby allowing us to obtain a better way of choosing actions, which is also robust to the uncertainty in the model. As discussed in Section 3, this is a straightforward extension of the standard POMDP formulation, which performs well when there are few uncertain parameters but scales poorly.

Our second technique, presented in Section 4, uses oracle queries while the agent interacts optimally with the environment. The query result is used only to improve the model, not in the action selection process. In this framework the uncertainty is represented using a Dirichlet distribution over all possible models, and its parameters are updated whenever new experience is acquired.

2 Partially Observable Markov Decision Processes

We assume the standard POMDP formulation (Kaelbling et al., 1998). A POMDP consists of a finite set of states S, actions A and observations Z. The model is defined by transition probabilities $\{P^a_{s,s'}\} = \{p(s_{t+1} = s'|s_t = s, a_t = a)\}$ and observation probabilities $\{O^a_{s,z}\} = \{p(z_t = z|s_t = s, a_{t-1} = a)\}, \forall z \in Z, \forall s, s' \in S, \forall a \in A$. It also has a discount factor $\gamma \in (0,1]$ and a reward function $R : S \times A \times S \times Z \to \mathbb{R}$, such that $R(s_t, a_t, s_{t+1}, z_{t+1})$ is the immediate reward for the corresponding transition.

At each time step, the agent is in an unknown state $s_t \in S$. It executes action $a_t \in A$, arriving in unknown state $s_{t+1} \in S$ and getting observation $z_{t+1} \in Z$. Agents using POMDP planning algorithms typically keep track of the belief state $b \in \mathbb{R}^{|S|}$, which is a probability distribution over all states given the history experienced so far. A policy is a function that associates an action to each possible belief state. Solving a POMDP means finding the policy that maximizes the expected return $E(\sum_{t=1}^{T} \gamma^t R(s_t, a_t, s_{t+1}, z_{t+1}))$. While finding an exact solution to a POMDP is computationally intractable, many methods exist for finding approximate solutions. In this paper, we use a point-based algorithm (Pineau et al. 2003), in order to compute POMDP solutions. However, other approximations could be used.

We assume the reward function is known, since it is directly linked to the task that the agent should execute, and we focus on learning $\{P^a_{s,s'}\}$ and $\{O^a_{s,z}\}$. These probability distributions are typically harder to specify correctly by hand, especially in real applications. For instance in robotics, the sensor noise and motion error are often unknown. We focus on a model-based approach because in many applications the model of the dynamics and observations are re-usable.

To learn the transition and observation models, we assume the agent has the ability to ask a query that will correctly identify the current state (we discuss later how the correctness assumption can be relaxed). This is a strong assumption, but not entirely unrealistic. In fact, in many tasks it is possible (but very costly) to have access to the full state information; it usually requires asking a human to label the state. As a result, clearly we want the agent to make as few queries as possible.

3 Decision-Theoretic Model Learning in POMDPs

The first algorithm we propose assumes that (1) the parameters of the POMDP model are not known exactly (2) the agent can perform query actions, and (3) these queries are expensive, so they should not be used too much. Based on these three assumptions, we modify the original POMDP model in order to reflect model uncertainty explicitly. First, we increase the number of states: for each uncertain model parameter, we add a new state feature. This feature is typically discretized into n levels. For instance, suppose that for some pair of states $s, s' \in S$ and action $a \in A$ we know that $P^a_{ss'} \in [0.5, 1.0]$. We will discretize this interval in n bins and then the state space will receive a new feature, which can take n possible values. We thereby obtain n groups of states; the transitions are such that they always occur between states in the same group. Second, we need to add a "query" action to the set of actions. Finally, we have to set the reward function such that it penalizes query actions adequately.

We analyze the performance of this algorithm on the standard Tiger problem (Littman et al., 1995). We assume that we do not know the probability of the sensor providing the correct state information and consider three possible levels of this probability: 0.7, 0.8 and 0.9.

Even with such a simple setting, no exact POMDP solution can be found, but the approximate planning algorithm with a finite horizon finds solutions.

Figure 1 depicts the policies found and the expected reward, as a function of the query penalty. The policies found either alternate between query and the optimal action, or never do any query at all, if the query penalty is too high. Even when no query is done, the agent still manages to learn the observation probabilities. However, we think this is an artifact of having a Listen action, which is in effect a noisy version of a Query action. The fact that some policies use the Listen action but not the Query action suggests that noisy queries may be sufficient to learn the parameters of the system.

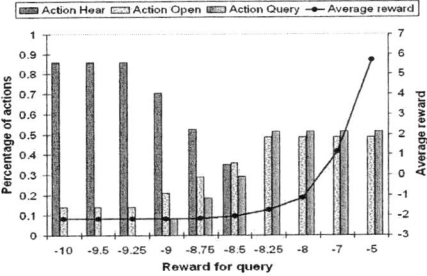

Fig. 1. Experimental results on the Tiger problem using decision-theoretic model learning. The bars indicate the % of time each action is chosen (during both learning and testing). The line indicates performance of the optimal solution obtained with each reward parameter.

This approach will not scale well for large POMDPs, because the number of states is multiplied by n^k where n is the number of possible values for a given parameter and k is the number of uncertain parameters. This greatly increases the complexity of the belief state and the complexity of the policy. Furthermore, the cost of the query can be very difficult to establish. The results above show that if the cost is too low, the query action is used as part of permanent policies instead of being used only in the beginning to gather information about the model. On the other hand, if the cost is too high, it is likely that the query action will never be picked.

4 Active Learning in POMDPs

In the context of POMDPs, transition and observation probabilities are typically specified according to multinomial distributions. Therefore, we now investigate using a Dirichlet distribution to represent the uncertainty over these model parameters (for each state-action pair).

Consider an N-dimensional multinomial distribution with parameters $(\theta_1, \ldots \theta_N)$. A Dirichlet distribution is a probabilistic distribution over the θs, parameterized by hyper-parameters $(\alpha_1, \ldots \alpha_N)$. The likelihood of the multinomial parameters is defined by:

$$p(\theta_1 \ldots \theta_N | D) = \frac{\Pi_{i=1}^N \theta_i^{\alpha_i - 1}}{Z(D)}, \text{ where } Z(D) = \frac{\Pi_{i=1}^N \Gamma(\alpha_i)}{\Gamma(\Sigma_{i=1}^N \alpha_i)}$$

The maximum likelihood multinomial parameters $\theta_1^* \ldots \theta_N^*$ can be computed as:
$\theta_i^* = \frac{\alpha_i}{\Sigma_{k=1}^N \alpha_k}, \forall i = 1, \ldots N$

The Dirichlet distribution is convenient because its hyper-parameters can be updated directly from data, and we can sample from it using Gamma distributions.

Our algorithm, called MEDUSA for "Markovian Exploration with Decision based on the Use of Sampled models Algorithm" is an active learning approach that follows a familiar scenario. First, the agent samples a number of POMDP models according to the current Dirichlet distribution. The agent takes an action in the environment, and as a result, obtains an observation. At this point, the agent can decide to query the oracle for the true identity of the hidden state. If it does so, it updates the Dirichlet parameters according to the result of the query. This process is repeated until the distribution over models is sufficiently well-known. Table 1 provides a detailed description of these steps, including the implementation details.

A few aspects of this approach are worth discussing further. First, every time a new model is sampled, the agent finds the corresponding (near-)optimal policy, which is then used to select actions. This allows reasonable performance throughout the active learning process: as the sampled models improve, so will the quality of the actions chosen. This also allows the agent to focus the active learning in regions of the state space most often visited by good policies.

We also note that our active learning approach assumes a learning rate, λ. This is used to update the parameters of the Dirichlet distribution over models following each query. In the experiments, we used a fixed learning rate throughout; however this could be varied (e.g., decreasing over time, as is often done in reinforcement learning). Another important characteristic of our approach is that we need not specify a separate

Table 1. The MEDUSA algorithm

1. Let $|S|$, $|Z|$ be the number of states and observations, and $\lambda \in (0,1)$ be the learning rate.
2. Initialize the necessary Dirichlet distributions.
   For any unknown transition probability, $T^a_{s,\cdot}$, define $Dir \sim \{\alpha_1, \ldots \alpha_{|S|}\}$.
   For any unknown observation $O^a_{s,\cdot}$, define $Dir \sim \{\alpha_1, \ldots \alpha_{|Z|}\}$.
3. Sample n POMDPs $P_1, \ldots P_n$ from these distributions. (We typically use $n=20$).
4. Compute the (normalized) probability of each model: $\{w_1, \ldots w_n\}$.
5. Solve each model $P_i \to \pi_i, i = 1, \ldots n$. (We use a finite point-based approximation.)
6. Initialize the history $h = \{\}$
7. Initialize a belief for each model $b_1 = \ldots = b_n = b_0$ (We assume a known initial belief b_0).
8. Repeat:
   (a) Compute the optimal actions for each model: $a_1 = \pi_1(b_1), \ldots a_n = \pi_n(b_n)$.
   (b) Pick and apply an action to execute: $a_i = \pi_i(b_i)$ is chosen with probability w_i.
   (c) Receive an observation z and update the history $h = \{h, a, z\}$
   (d) Update the belief state for each model: $b'_i = b_i^{a,z}, i = 1..n$.
   (e) If desired, query the current state, which reveals s, s'.
   (f) Update the Dirichlet parameters according to the query outcome:
   $\alpha(s, a, s') \leftarrow \alpha(s, a, s') + \lambda$
   $\alpha(s', a, z) \leftarrow \alpha(s', a, z) + \lambda$
   (g) Recompute the POMDP weights: $\{w'_1, \ldots w'_n\}$.
   (h) At regular intervals, remove the model P_i with the lowest weight and redraw another model P'_i according to the current Dirichlet distribution. Solve the new model: $P'_i \to \pi'_i$ and update its belief $b'_i = b^h_0$, where b^h_0 is the belief resulting when starting in b_0 and seeing history h.

Dirichlet parameter for *each* unknown POMDP parameter. It is often the case that a small number of hyper-parameters suffice to characterize the model uncertainty.

For example, noise in the sensors may be highly correlated over all states and therefore we could use a single set of hyper-parameters for all states. In this setup, the corresponding hyper-parameter would be updated whenever action a is taken and observation z is received, regardless of the state.

Finally, while Table 1 assumes that a query for the state is performed at every time step, this need not be the case. The decision of when to query could be addressed in a decision-theoretic way (as in section 3), but this is intractable when there are many unknown parameters. In the experimental section below, we investigate various heuristics for deciding when to query. Another approach (which we have not investigated yet) could be to use queries which do not directly reveal the state, but provide related information, since it is possible to update the parameters of the Dirichlet distribution even without explicit state identification.

5 Experimental Results

We evaluate MEDUSA first on the standard Tiger problem from Tony Cassandra's repository, considering two cases: (1) The observation probabilities when the *Listen* action is performed are unknown. (2) All parameters are unknown.

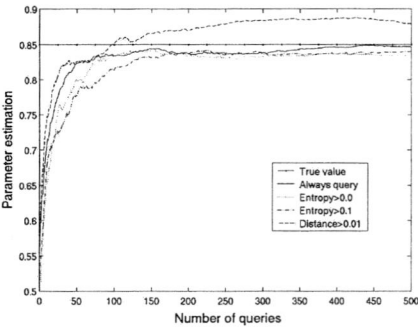 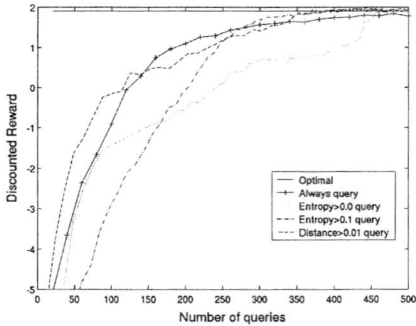

Fig. 2. Experiment 1: Convergence of the estimated parameter $O^{Listen}_{TL,HL}$ (left). Discounted reward as a function of the number of queries (right).

In the first experiment, we assume that all parameters are set to their correct value, except the $O^{Listen}_{\cdot,\cdot}$ parameters. (Note that in this experiment the Dirichlet distribution implicitly enforces $O^{Listen}_{s,HL} = 1.0 - O^{Listen}_{s,HR}, \forall s \in S$.) We test the following heuristics for deciding when to query the state:

- Always query: perform a query at every step.
- Entropy>0.0: query when models disagree on which action to select.
- Entropy>0.1: query when the entropy of the probability distribution over actions, as suggested by the different models, is larger than 0.1.
- Distance>0.01: query when the distance between the belief states corresponding to the different models is too large. This distance is defined by: $\sum_{k=1}^{n} w_k \sum_{i \in S} (b_k(i) - \hat{b}(i))^2$, where $\forall i, \hat{b}(i) = \sum_{k=1}^{n} w_k b_k(i)$

Otherwise, the algorithm is applied exactly as described in Table 1. We also show the return corresponding to the optimal solution obtained when solving the problem with the known parameters.

As shown in Figure 2, the algorithm allows the agent to learn the correct parameters, and performance quickly improves with additional queries. There is no significant difference between the various heuristics for choosing when to perform queries. This suggests that most queries are useful for learning the model.

In the second experiment, all transition and observation probabilities are learned simultaneously. As shown in Figure 3, all correct parameters are learned accurately with few queries (200-300), and about 2000 queries are needed to reach the optimal reward. In comparison, recent results for learning models use on the order of $10^6 - 10^7$ steps to learn this problem and others of similar size(Singh et al. 2004). We note, however, that these algorithms are not allowed to query an oracle for additional information, and therefore face a harder problem.

We also tested the scaling of the algorithm on a larger domain called *Tiger-Grid* (Littman et al. 1995). It has 36 states, 5 actions, 17 observations, for a total of 9000+ parameters. It also features probability distributions that are more characteristic of real robots, including noisy motion and sensors. In a domain of this size, it is unlikely that all parameters will be uncorrelated. More likely, there are a few effects (e.g., sensor noise)

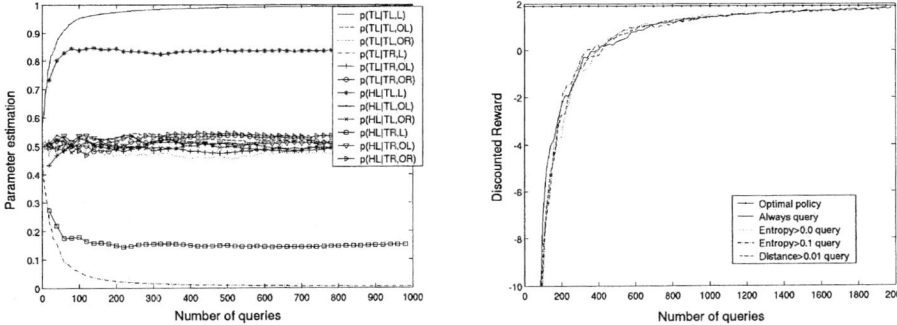

Fig. 3. Experiment 2: Convergence of the parameters for the "always-query" case (left). Discounted reward as a function of the number of queries (right).

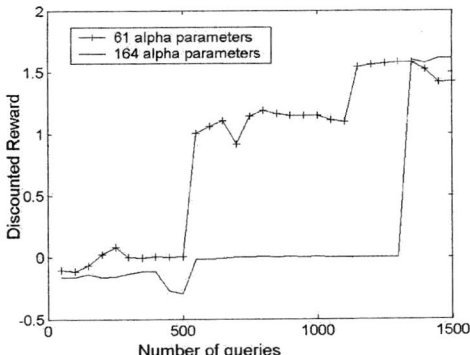

Fig. 4. Experiment 3: Discounted reward as a function of the number of queries for Tiger-grid domain for different numbers of alpha parameters.

that are similar over a number of states. Therefore, the uncertainty in these parameters can be correlated through a single hyper-parameter, rather than learning all parameters independently. In the experiments, we apply the algorithm described in Table 1 and vary the number of α parameters used. The results in Figure 4 confirm that with the appropriate number of parameters, the algorithm can effectively improve the model using queries. As expected, the speed of learning depends on the number of hyper-parameters. Thus, our approach can effectively trade-off learning speed versus model accuracy.

6 Discussion

Chrisman (1992) was among the first to propose a method for acquiring a POMDP model from data. Shatkay & Kaelbling (1997) used a version of the Baum-Welch algorithm to learn POMDP models for robot navigation. Bayesian exploration was proposed by Dearden et al.(1999) to learn the parameters of an MDP. Their idea was to reason about model uncertainty using Dirichlet distributions over uncertain model parameters. The initial Dirichlet parameters can capture the rough model, and they can also be easily updated to reflect experience. The algorithm we present in Section 4 can be viewed as an extension of this work to the POMDP framework, though it is different in many respects, including the handling of exploration vs exploitation.

Recent work by Anderson and Moore (2005) examines the question of active learning in HMMs. In particular, their framework for model learning addresses a very similar problem (albeit without the complication of actions). The solution they propose selects queries to minimize error loss (i.e., loss of reward). However, their work is not directly applicable since they are concerned with picking the best query for a large set of possible queries. In our framework, there is only one query to consider, which reveals the current state.

Finally, our work resembles some of the recent approaches for handling model-free POMDPs (McCallum, 1996; Brafman & Shani, 2005; Singh et al. 2004). Unlike these approaches, we make here strong assumptions about the existence of an underlying state which allows us to partly specify a model whenever possible, thereby making the learning problem much more tractable (e.g., orders of magnitude fewer examples). The other key assumption we make, which is not used in model-free approaches, regards the existence of an oracle (or human) for correctly identifying the state following each query. We are currently studying how this assumption can be relaxed.

The question of when to do queries, and whether to consider a more varied set of queries is of interest. Clearly the decision-theoretic approach of Section 3 can contribute to this decision. However, using this approach calls for POMDP algorithms that can handle very large (possibly continuous) state spaces, and these are currently lacking. MEDUSA has a very good performance and scales nicely, but a theoretical analysis of its convergence properties remains to be done. Our next goal is to apply MEDUSA to the control of a mobile interactive robot.

References

Anderson, B. and Moore, A. "Active Learning in HMMs". ICML 2005.
Brafman, R. I. and Shani, G. "Resolving perceptual asliasing with noisy sensors". NIPS 2005.
Cohn, D. A., Ghahramani, Z. and Jordan, M. I. "Active Learning with Statistical Models". NIPS 1996.
Dearden, R.,Friedman, N.,Andre, N., "Model Based Bayesian Exploration". UAI 1999.
Kaelbling, L., Littman, M. and Cassandra, A. "Planning and Acting in Partially Observable Stochastic Domains" Artificial Intelligence. vol.101. 1998.
Littman, M., Cassandra, A., and Kaelbling,L. "Learning policies for partially observable environments: Scaling up", Technical Report. Brown University, 1995.
McCallum, A. K. Reinforcement Learning with Selective Perception and Hidden State. Ph.D. Thesis. University of Rochester. 1996.
Pineau, J., Gordon, G. and Thrun, S. "Point-based value iteration: An anytime algorithm for POMDPs". IJCAI. 2003.
Poupart, P. and Boutilier, C. "VDCBPI: an Approximate Scalable Algorithm for Large Scale POMDPs". NIPS 2005.
Singh, S., Littman, M., Jong, N. K., Pardoe, D., and Stone, P. "Learning Predictive State Representations". ICML 2003.

Machine Learning of Plan Robustness Knowledge About Instances

Sergio Jiménez, Fernando Fernández*, and Daniel Borrajo

Departamento de Informática, Universidad Carlos III de Madrid,
Avda. de la Universidad, 30. Leganés (Madrid), Spain
sjimenez@inf.uc3m.es, fernando@cs.cmu.edu, dborrajo@ia.uc3m.es

Abstract. Classical planning domain representations assume all the objects from one type are exactly the same. But when solving problems in the real world systems, the execution of a plan that theoretically solves a problem, can fail because of not properly capturing the special features of an object in the initial representation. We propose to capture this uncertainty about the world with an architecture that integrates planning, execution and learning. In this paper, we describe the PELA system (Planning-Execution-Learning Architecture). This system generates plans, executes those plans in the real world, and automatically acquires knowledge about the behaviour of the objects to strengthen the execution processes in the future.

1 Introduction

Suppose you have just been engaged as a project manager in an organization. The organization staff consists of two programmers, **A** and **B**. Theoretically **A** and **B** can do the same work, but probably they will have different skills. So it would be common sense to evaluate their work in order to assign them tasks according to their worthy.

In this example, it seems that the success of fulfilling a task depends on which worker performs which task, that is how actions are instantiated, rather than depending on what state the action is executed. The latter would be, basically, what reinforcement learning does in the case of MDP models (fully instantiated states and actions). It does not depend either on the initial characteristics of a given instance, because the values of these characteristics might not be known "a priori". Otherwise, they could be modelled in the initial state. For instance, one could represent the level of expertise of programmers, as a predicate expertise-level(programmer,task,prob) where prob could be a number, reflecting the uncertainty of the task to be carried out successfully by the programmer. Then, the robustness of each plan could be computed by cost-based planners. So, we would like to acquire knowledge only about the uncertainty associated to instantiated actions, without knowing "a priori" the facts from the

---

* Fernando Fernández is currently with the Computer Science Department Carnegie Mellon University, funded by a MEC-Fulbright grant.

state that should be true in order to influence the execution of an action. Examples of this type of situations arise in many real world domains, such as project management, workflow domains, robotics, etc. We are currently working in the domain of planning tourist visits. In this domain, we want to propose plans that please the tourist as much as possible, and we have to deal with the uncertainty about which is the best day to visit a place.

With an architecture that integrates planning, execution and learning we want to achieve a system that is able to learn some knowledge about the effects of actions execution, but managing a rich representation of the action model. Thus, the architecture can be used for flexible kinds of goals as in deliberative planning, together with knowledge about the expected future reward, as in Reinforcement Learning [1]. A similar approach is followed in [2], but they learn the operators (actions models), while our goal is to acquire heuristics (as control knowledge) to guide the planner search towards more robust solutions. In a classical AI setting, our approach tries to separate the domain model that might be common to many different problems within the domain, from the control knowledge that can vary over time. And we propose to gradually and automatically acquire this type of control knowledge through repeated cycles of planning, execution and learning, as it is commonly done in most real world planning situations by humans.

2   The Planning-Execution-Learning Architecture

The aim of the architecture is to automatically acquire knowledge about the objects behaviour in the real world to generate plans whose execution will be more robust. Figure 1 shows a high level view of the proposed architecture.

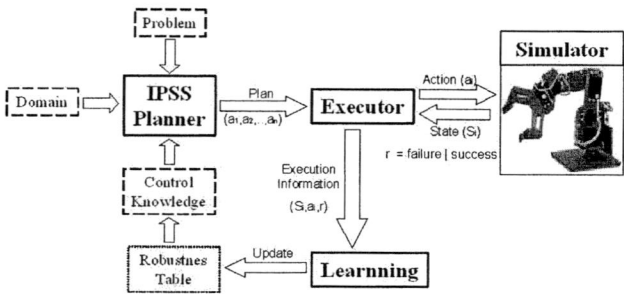

Fig. 1. High level view of the planning-execution-learning architecture

To acquire this knowledge, the system begins with a deterministic knowledge of the world dynamics and observes the effects that the execution of its actions causes in the real world. The system registers whether an action execution is successful or not in the real world. So it has information about the possibility of succeed on executing an action in the real world. This is what we call the *robustness* of an action. To use this information, the system defines control knowledge that decides the instantiation of the actions. So, the planner will choose the best bindings for the actions according to the acquired robustness information. We have developed a preliminary prototype of such architecture, that we call PELA (Planning-Execution-Learning Architecture). To make this prototype come true, we have made the following assumptions (we describe how we plan to relax them in the future work section).

1. A domain consists of a set of operators or actions, and a set of specific instances that will be used as parameters of the actions. This is something relatively different from the way in which planning domains are handled, since they usually do not include specific instances, which appear in the planning problems. This assumption is only needed for learning and it is not really needed for deterministic planning purposes.
2. As we are working in a preliminary prototype, the robustness of the execution of plan actions only depends on the instantiation of the actions parameters, and it does not depend on the states before applying the actions.

2.1 Planning

For the planning task we have used the nonlinear backward chaining planner IPSS [3]. The inputs to the planner are the usual ones (domain theory and problem definition), plus declarative control knowledge, described as a set of control rules. These control rules act as domain dependent heuristics. They are the main reason we have used this planner, given that they provide an easy method for declarative representation of automatically acquired knowledge [4]. IPSS planning-reasoning cycle involves as decision points: select a goal from the set of pending goals and subgoals; choose an operator to achieve a particular goal; choose the bindings to instantiate the chosen operator and apply an instantiated operator whose preconditions are satisfied or continue subgoaling on another unsolved goal. The output of the planner, as we have used it in this paper, is a total-ordered plan.

2.2 Execution

The system executes step by step the sequence of actions proposed by the planner to solve a problem. When the execution of a plan step is a failure the execution process is aborted. To test the architecture, we have developed a module that simulates the execution of actions in the real world. This simulator module receives an action and returns whether the execution succeeded or failed. It is very simple for the time being as it doesn't take care of the current state of the world. The simulator keeps a probability distribution function as a model of execution for each possible action. When the execution of an action has to be simulated, the simulator generates a random value following its corresponding distribution probability. If the generated random value satisfies the model, the action is considered successfully executed.

2.3 Learning

The process of acquiring the knowledge can be seen as a process of updating the robustness table. This table registers the estimation of success of an instantiated action in the real world. It is composed of tuples of the form `<op-name, op-params, r-value>` op-name is the action name, op-params is the list of the instantiated parameters and r-value is the robustness value. In the planning tourist visits domain, as we want to capture the uncertainty about which is the best day for a tourist to visit a fixed place we register the robustness of the operator `PREPARE-VISIT` with the parameters `PLACE` and `DAY`. An example of the robustness-table for this domain is Table 1.

Table 1. An example of a Robustness-Table for the planning tourist visits domain

Action	Parameters	Robustness
prepare-visit	(PRADO MONDAY)	5.0
prepare-visit	(PRADO TUESDAY)	6.0
prepare-visit	(PRADO WEDNESDAY)	8.0
prepare-visit	(PRADO THURSDAY)	4.0
prepare-visit	(PRADO FRIDAY)	2.0
prepare-visit	(PRADO SATURDAY)	1.0
prepare-visit	(PRADO SUNDAY)	1.0
prepare-visit	(ROYAL-PALACE MONDAY)	2.0
prepare-visit	(ROYAL-PALACE TUESDAY)	2.0
...		

We update the robustness value of the actions using the learning algorithm shown in Figure 2. According to this algorithm [5], when the action execution is successful, we increase the robustness of the action, but if the action execution is a failure, the new robustness value is the square root of the old robustness value.

```
Function Learning (ai, r,Rob-Table):Rob-Table
```
ai: executed action
r: execution outcome (failure or success)
Rob-Table: Table with the robustness of the actions

if r=success
    Then
        robustness(ai,Rob-Table) = robustness(ai,Rob-Table) +1
    Else
        robustness(ai,Rob-Table) = $\sqrt{robustness(ai, Rob-Table)}$
Return Rob-Table;

Fig. 2. Algorithm that updates the robustness of one action

2.4 Exploitation of Acquired Knowledge

Control rules guide the planner among all the possible actions, choosing the action bindings with the greatest robustness value in the Robustness Table. In the planning tourist visits domain, these control rules will make the planner prefer the most 'robust' day to prepare the visit of the tourist `<user-1>` to the place <place-1>. An example of these control rules is shown in Figure 3. Suppose that a tourist called Mike wants to visit the Prado museum, the system will decides to prepare the visit to the Prado museum on Wednesday, among all the possible instantiations, because PREPARE-VISIT PRADO WEDNESDAY 8.0 is the tuple with the greatest robustness value in the Robustness-Table for the PRADO. To achieve a balance between exploration and exploitation the system only use the control rules in 80% of the times.

```
(control-rule prefer-bindings-prepare-visit
  (IF
    (and
            (current-goal (prepared-visit <user-1> <place-1>))
            (current-operator prepare-visit)
            (true-in-state (current-time <user-1> <day-1> <time-1>))
            (true-in-state (current-time <user-1> <day-2> <time-2>))
            (diff <day-1> <day-2>)
            (more-robustness-than
                  (list 'prepare-visit <place-1> <day-1>)
                  (list 'prepare-visit <place-1> <day-2>))))
(THEN prefer bindings ((<day> . <day-1>))((<day> . <day-2>))))
```

Fig. 3. Control rule for preferring the best day to visit a museum

3 Experiments and Results

The experiments carried out to evaluate the proposed architecture have been performed in the planning tourist visits domain. The used domain is a simplification of the SAMAP project domain [6], but given that this is preliminary work, we have left out the part of path planning. We assume a tourist is always able to move from any zone in the city to another. The operators in this domain are MOVE, VISIT-PLACE and PREPARE-VISIT. In order to test the system we have developed a simulator that emulates the execution of the planned actions in the real world. The simulator decides whether visiting a place is a failure or not. It decides with probability 0.1 that the visit was successfully in Mondays, Tuesdays, Wednesdays or Thursdays. And with probability 0.5 when the visit happens on Fridays, Saturdays or Sunday.

We have used a test problem set with 100 random generated problems with different complexity. The state of the random problems represents the free time of the tourist for each day in the week, its available money and its initial location. The problem goals describe the places the tourist wants to visit. We measure the complexity of the problems in terms of the available time the user has to visit all the goals. For that purpose we have defined the following ratio:

```
                  complexity = goals-time / available-time
```
Where goals-time represents the time needed to visit all the goals and available-time represents the sum of the tourist free time. So, when a problem have a complexity ratio over 1.0 the planner will not be able to find a solution.

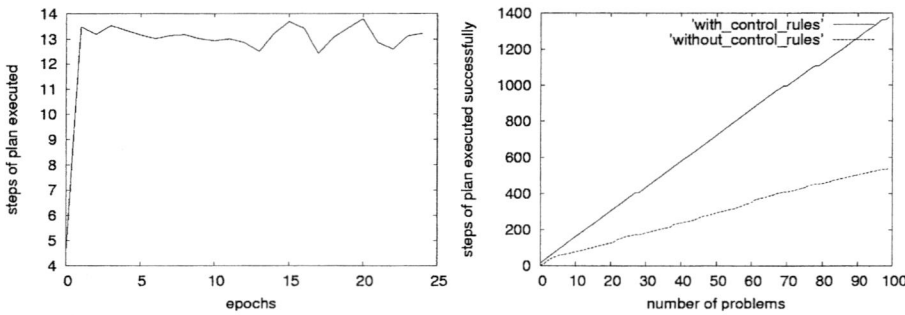

Fig. 4. Steps of plan successfully executed in the planning tourist visits domain

The first graph in figure 4 shows the evolution of the learning process. This graph presents the number of successfully executed actions for 25 epochs. This number converges quickly to approximately 13-14 steps. The average length of the plans that solve the problems from the test set is 19,5. So, in terms of percentage, 13-14 steps executed succesfully represents approximately 66-72% percentage of plan executed succesfully. The fast convergence is because of failure and success probabilities for an action don't change with time. The second graph in figure 4 compares the behaviour of our system to the behaviour of a system that does not use the learned knowledge in the planning process. The number of successful actions is computed after 25 epochs of learning with a ten random problems train set.

4 Related Work

Learning to plan and act in uncertain domains is an important kind of machine learning task. Most of literature in the field separates this task in two different phases: A first phase to capture the uncertainty and a second phase to plan dealing with it.

1. A first phase when the uncertainty is captured, [2] propose to obtain the world dynamics by learning from examples representing action models as probabilistic relational rules. A similar approach was previously used in propositional logic in [7]. [8] proposes using Adaptive Dynamic Programming, this technique allows reinforcement learning agents to build the transition model of an unknown environment whereas the agent is solving the Markov Decission Process through exploring the transitions.
2. A second phase when problems are solved using planners able to handle actions with probabilistic effects. This kind of Planning is a well studied problem [9]. We can also include in this second phase the systems that solve Markov Decission Processes. The standard Markov Decission Process algorithms seek a policy (a function to choose an action for every possible state)

that guarantees the maximum expected utility. So, once the optimal policy is found planning under uncertainty can be considered as following the policy starting from the initial state [10].

So, as our system propose the integration of these two phases, it presents several differences with the previous systems:

- Our system does not learn a probabilistic action model, the system starts with a deterministic description of the actions. Then it explores the environment not to learn the whole world dynamics but to complete the domain theory.
- We don't assume completely the object abstraction as we are interested in domains where the execution of an action depends on the identity of the instances rather than on their type.
- Our system uses the learnt information about instances as control knowledge so it keeps separately the domain model from the control knowledge.

We have also found another architecture that integrates planning, executing and learning to in a similar way. [11] interleaves high-level task planning with real world robot execution and learns situation-dependent control rules from selecting goals to allow the planner to predict and avoid failures. The main differences between this architecture and ours, are that: we don't learn control rules, control rules are part of the initial domain representation, what we learn is the robustness of the actions. And we don't guide the planner choosing the goals but choosing the instantiations of the actions.

5 Future Work

We plan to remove, when possible, the initial assumptions, mentioned in the introduction section. Relaxing the first assumption requires generating robustness knowledge with generalized instances and then mapping new problems instances to those used in the acquired knowledge. As we described in the introduction section, we believe this is not really needed in many domains, since one always has the same instances in all problems of the same domain. In that case, we have to assure that there is a unique mapping between real world instances and instance names in all problems. When new instances appear, their robustness values can be initialized to a specific value, and then gradually be updated with the proposed learning mechanism. To relax the second assumption, we will use a more complex simulator that considers not only the instantiated action, but also the state before applying each action. We are planning to test the system with the simulator and the domains of the probabilistic track of the International Planning Competition[1]. Thus, during learning, the reinforcement formula should also consider the state where it was executed.

---

[1] http://ipc.icaps-conference.org/

One could use standard reinforcement learning techniques [12] for that purpose, but states in deliberative planning are represented as predicate logic formulae. One solution would consist on using relational reinforcement learning techniques [13].

And finally, for the time being the learning algorithm and the exploration-exploitation strategy we use are very simple, both of them must be studied deeper [14] in order to obtain better results in more realistic domains.

References

1. Kaelbling, L.P., Littman, M.L., Moore, A.W.: Reinforcement learning: A survey. Journal of Artificial Intelligence Research **4** (1996) 237–285
2. Pasula, H., Zettlemoyer, L., Kaelbling, L.: Learning probabilistic relational planning rules. In: Proceedings of the Fourteenth International Conference on Automated Planning and Scheduling. (2004)
3. Rodrguez-Moreno, M.D., Borrajo, D., Oddi, A., Cesta, A., Meziat, D.: Ipss: A problem solver that integrates planning and scheduling. Third Italian Workshop on Planning and Scheduling (2004)
4. Veloso, M., Carbonell, J., Pérez, A., Borrajo, D., Fink, E., Blythe, J.: Integrating planning and learning: The PRODIGY architecture. Journal of Experimental and Theoretical AI **7** (1995) 81–120
5. Nareyek, A.: Choosing search heuristics by non-stationary reinforcement learning (2003)
6. Fernández, S., Sebastiá, L., Fdez-Olivares, J.: Planning tourist visits adapted to user preferences. Workshop on Planning and Scheduling. ECAI (2004)
7. Garca-Martnez, R., Borrajo, D.: An integrated approach of learning, planning, and execution. Journal of Intelligent and Robotic Systems **29** (2000) 47–78
8. Barto, A., Bradtke, S., Singh, S.: Real-time learning and control using asynchronous dynamic programming. Technical Report, Department of Computer Science, University of Massachusetts, Amherst (1991) 91–57
9. Blythe, J.: Decision-theoretic planning. AI Magazine, Summer (1999)
10. Koening, S.: Optimal probabilistic and decision-theoretic planning using markovian decision theory. Master's Report, Computer Science Division University of California, Berkeley (1991)
11. Haigh, K.Z., Veloso, M.M.: Planning, execution and learning in a robotic agent. In: AIPS. (1998) 120–127
12. Watkins, C.J.C.H., Dayan, P.: Technical note: Q-learning. Machine Learning **8** (1992) 279–292
13. Dzeroski, S., Raedt, L.D., Driessens, K.: Relational reinforcement learning. Machine Learning **43** (2001) 7–52
14. Thrun, S.: Efficient exploration in reinforcement learning. Technical Report C,I-CS-92-102, Carnegie Mellon University (1992)

Two Contributions of Constraint Programming to Machine Learning

Arnaud Lallouet and Andreï Legtchenko

Université d'Orléans — LIFO,
BP6759, F-45067 Orléans
lallouet, legtchen@lifo.univ-orleans.fr

Abstract. A constraint is a relation with an active behavior. For a given relation, we propose to learn a representation adapted to this active behavior. It yields two contributions. The first is a generic meta-technique for classifier improvement showing performances comparable to boosting. The second lies in the ability of using the learned concept in constraint-based decision or optimization problems. It opens a new way of integrating Machine Learning in Decision Support Systems.

1 Introduction

A constraint is a relation with an active behavior. In Constraint Programming, relations are used to model decision or optimization problems. Its success relies on two aspects: first the model is high level, declarative and easy to understand and second, there exists a range of powerful techniques to find and optimize solutions. The key concept of Constraint Programming is that relations are actively used during search for enforcing a *consistency*. In the context of finite domains constraints, consistencies are used to reduce variable domains in order to limit the search effort. The more the domains get reduced, the less branches are explored in the search tree. It works so well that, while theoretically intractable, many problems are practically solvable.

But the model is usually limited to relations which are completely known. In this paper, we propose to learn concepts as constraints. We call them *open constraints* because they are only partially known by a set of positive and negative examples. While the acquisition of such an object has been extensively studied in Machine Learning, no other work, to the authors' best knowledge, has considered to acquire the relation in such a way that consistency inference could be performed. This paper deals with the induction of a relation using a representation suitable for constraint propagation.

The first contribution is a generic meta-technique for classifier improvement. The constraint-based representation involves a decomposition of the relation in multiple parts according to some projections. Each part is learnable with classical techniques and the relation is reconstituted by a vote mechanism. By reference to Constraint Programming and because they represent a kind of internal consistency of the relation, we call the resulting representation a *Consistency Checking*

Classifier. It happens that classical techniques are improved by this decomposition and the resulting combination of decisions. The improvement provided by this technique is different and orthogonal to boosting [5]. Actually, both can be combined and the best results are obtained by using both techniques at the same time.

The second contribution is the transformation of a classifier into a propagator. We show that if the relation is acquired with the suggested constraint representation, the relation can be turned into a constraint. In order to do this, the classifiers are transformed into propagators which ensure the active behavior of the constraint. This allows Machine Learning to be used in new applications when included in constraint-based decision support systems. Basically, this kind of system routinely considers millions of alternatives and tries to find a satisfactory solution. Using a relation represented by a classifier inside such a system imposes to first generate an alternative and evaluate it with the classifier. This technique, known as "generate and test", is computationally very expensive. The purpose of an active constraint is to filter wrong alternatives much earlier in the search process.

We first present a short introduction to constraint solving useful to understand the idea of consistency checking classifier and the transformation of a classifier into propagator. Section 3 is devoted to the presentation of the learning technique and its experimental evaluation. In section 4, we present shortly how to turn a classifier into propagator.

2 Open Constraints

First, let us set the notations we use. Let V be a set of variables and $D = (D_X)_{X \in V}$ be the family of their finite domains. For $W \subseteq V$, we denote the Cartesian product $\Pi_{X \in W} D_X$ by D^W. For a set E, we denote by $\mathcal{P}(E)$ its powerset, by $\overline{E}$ its complementary and by $|E|$ its cardinal. Projection of a tuple (or a set of tuples) on a set of variables is denoted by $|$. For $X \in W$, we denote by W_{-X} the set $W \setminus \{X\}$.

A *constraint* $c = (W, T)$ is composed of a subset $W \subseteq V$ of variables and a relation $T \subseteq D^W$. A *Constraint Satisfaction Problem* (or CSP) is a set of constraints. A *solution* of a CSP is an assignment of the variables which satisfy all constraints. *Solving* a CSP means finding a solution but in some cases it is also required to find the best solution according to an external optimization criterion. Instead of searching in a space of possible assignments, a *search state s* is composed of a set of currently possible values for each variable. Formally, $s = (s_X)_{X \in V}$ where $s_X \subseteq D_X$. It represents the set $\Pi_{X \in V} s_X$. This representation is economic in term of space but the counterpart is that only Cartesian products are representable. Thus an assignment is represented by a search state in which all variable domains are singletons.

Domains are reduced by the application of *propagators*. A propagator for a constraint $c = (W, T)$ and a variable $X \in W$ is a function f_X which reduces the domain s_X of variable X in such a way that no solution of c included in the search state s is lost [2]. In other words, a propagator suppresses values which do not occur in any solution: these values have no *support* in the constraint. The most reducing propagator is the one associated with the well-known *arc-consistency*. It only keeps in the domain of a variable the values which can be extended to a solution of the constraint. Propagators for all constraints are iterated up to reach their greatest fixpoint, and this defines the expected consistency. A possible way to implement a propagator is to associate a boolean function $f_{X=a}$ to every value $a \in D_X$. We call such a function an *Elementary Reduction Function* (or ERF). This function takes as input the current domain of all variables but X, i.e. $s|_{W_{-X}}$, and answers *true* if there is a support for $X = a$ in c according to the current search state s and *false* otherwise. By applying ERFs associated to each value of the domain, we are able to reconstitute a propagator: $f_X(s|_W) = s_X \cap \{a \in D_X \mid f_{X=a}(s|_{W_{-X}}) = true\}$. An ERF must be correct, which means that it does not suppress a value which has a support. But it can be incomplete, i.e. that an unsupported value may remain undetected if the condition verified by the ERF is too weak.

In classical Constraint Programming, all relations are completely known. If we want to use a concept known by positive and negative examples as a constraint, we have to switch to a broader setting:

Definition 1 (Open Constraint).
An open constraint *is a triple* $c = (W, c^+, c^-)$ *where* $c^+ \subseteq D^W, c^- \subseteq D^W$ *and* $c^+ \cap c^- = \emptyset$.

In an open constraint $c = (W, c^+, c^-)$, c^+ represents the set of known allowed tuples (positive examples) and c^- the forbidden ones (negative examples). The remaining tuples are unknown. For an open constraint $c = (W, c^+, c^-)$, the learning task is to find a complete relation compatible with the open one, i.e. a constraint $c' = (W, T)$ such that $c^+ \subseteq T$ and $c^- \subseteq \overline{T}$. We call such a constraint c' an *extension* of the open constraint c.

3 Consistency Checking Classifiers

A classical learning technique for a relation consists in finding a classifier which answers *true* for a tuple which belongs to the relation and *false* otherwise. Inspired by the way constraints check their satisfiability, we propose instead to learn the projections of the relation on the hyperplane orthogonal to a value of a variable. For an open constraint $c = (W, c^+, c^-)$, a variable $X \in W$ and a value $a \in D_X$, this projection is defined by:

$$c_{<X=a>} = (W_{-X}, \{t|_{W_{-X}} \mid t \in c^+ \wedge t|_X = a\}, \{t|_{W_{-X}} \mid t \in c^- \wedge t|_X = a\})$$

Since the projection defines a new relation, we can use an arbitrary classifier to learn it. We call it an *elementary classifier* by analogy with ERFs. We build an elementary classifier for all values in the domain of all variables and we call this set an *consistency checking classifier*.

Definition 2 (Consistency Checking Classifier).
Let $c = (W, c^+, c^-)$ be an open constraint, $X \in W$, $a \in D_X$ and let $cl_{<X=a>}$ be a classifier for the relation $c_{<X=a>}$. A consistency checking classifier (or CCC) for c is the set of elementary classifiers $\{cl_{<X=a>} \mid X \in W, a \in D_X\}$.

Following the intuition of ERFs for solving, we can use these elementary classifiers to decide if a tuple belongs to the extension of the open constraint or not. It can be done by checking if the tuple gets rejected by the classifiers. Let $t \in D^W$ be a candidate tuple and let $(cl_{<X=t|_X>}(t|_{W-X}))_{X\in W}$ be the family of 0/1 answers of the elementary classifiers which are concerned by the tuple. We can interpret the answers according two points of view: (a) *vote with veto*: the tuple is accepted if and only if accepted by all classifiers, (b) *majority vote*: the tuple is accepted if accepted by a majority of elementary classifiers. Many other combinations could be envisaged [13] but our aim in this article is only to prove the validity of the method, not to find the best combination of votes. In the rest of this section, we only consider majority vote.

In order to learn the projection relations, we used two types of classifiers in our experiments: a multi-layer perceptron (MLP) and the C5.0 decision tree learning algorithm. For $W \subseteq V$, a *neuron* is a function $n : \mathbb{R}^{|W|} \to \mathbb{R}$ computing the weighted sum of its inputs followed by a threshold sigmoid unit. A dummy input set at 1 is added to tune the threshold. Let $(\omega_X)_{X\in W}$ be the weights associated with each input variable and ω_0 be the adjustment weight for the dummy input. Here is the function computed by a neuron taking as input $t = (t_X)_{X\in W}$:

$$\eta(t) = \frac{1}{1 + e^{\omega_0 - \sum_{X\in W} \omega_X . t_X}}$$

For a constraint $c = (W, c^+, c^-)$, the classifier we build for $X = a$ is a tree of neurons with one hidden layer as depicted in figure 1. Let $(\eta_i)_{i\in I}$ be the intermediary nodes and *out* be the output node. All neurons of the hidden layer have as input a value for each variable in W_{-X} and are connected to the output node. Let us call $n_{<X=a>}$ the network which concerns $X = a$. Since neurons are continuous, we use an analog coding of the domains: D is mapped on $[0..1]$ by coding $a_i \in D$ by i/n. The output is in the interval $[0..1]$ and we choose as convention that the value a should be removed from the domain of X if $out \leq 0.5$. This threshold is the last level of the network depicted in figure 1. The networks are trained by the classical backpropagation algorithm [12]. For decision trees, we use the See5.0 system [11]. This system implements the C5.0 algorithm, which is an evolution of C4.5 [9] and also the technique of boosting [5].

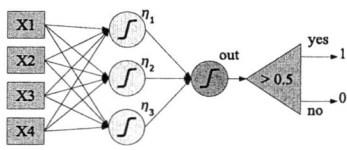

Fig. 1. Structure of the ANN

The classification technique has been run on a database called **salad** defining the concept of recipe for good salads and the following training sets from the

UCI Machine Learning repository[1]: **mush**: mushroom, **cancer**: breast-cancer-wisconsin, **votes**: house-votes-84, **spam**: spambase, **hepat**: hepatitis, **cr-scr**: credit screening. Continuous data are discretized such that roughly the same number of examples is put in each interval. As for boosting, the learning time is proportional to the learning time of the underlying technique (typically less than a minute for decision trees in our benchmarks). To evaluate and compare

Table 1. Learning results

Database	salad	mush	cancer	votes	spam	hepat	cr-scr
Arity	22	22	9	16	58	20	16
Size of DB	334	8124	699	435	4601	155	690
Type	symb	symb	symb	symb	cont	mixed	mixed
Domain sz	2-4	2-12	10	2	2-29	2-4	2-14
# neurons in HL	3	3	5	5	10	5	5
MLP err	3.89	1.75	4.49	5.78	10.80	22.07	16.12
C5.0 err	9.86	1.39	5.46	3.71	8.65	20.63	14.35
C5.0b err	4.83	0.31	3.67	4.37	5.85	17.23	12.89
# classifiers	64	115	89	32	487	49	90
CCC (MLP) err	**3.64**	0.81	3.48	3.77	7.30	17.30	15.95
CCC (C5.0) err	4.58	0.81	**2.61**	3.68	6.90	19.53	13.87
CCC (C5.0b) err	3.88	**0.27**	2.90	**3.62**	**4.90**	**16.83**	**12.73**

the technique, we used a classical 10-fold cross-validation repeated 3 times. Results are shown in Table 1: the database arity (*Arity*); *Size of DB* in number of tuples (only 500 are actually considered for mushroom); *Type* between *symb*olic, *cont*inuous or *mixed*; the range of domain sizes of the variables (*Domain sz*); number of neurons in the hidden layer of the MLP (*# neurons in HL*); average error ratio of the underlying techniques we used, i.e. multi-layer perceptron (*MLP*), C5.0 and C5.0 with boosting (*C5.0b*); the number of classifiers we learn for each relation with the CCC technique; error rate for the consistency checking classifier on top of an underlying technique. The best result in classification is depicted in bold face. The first remark is that the CCC technique always improves its underlying technique. It also provides an improvement in classification comparable in performance to boosting, boosting being slightly better in average. But since both are usable at the same time, it appears that using CCC on top of one of the classifiers is able to outperform its underlying technique.

4 From Classifiers to Solvers

The second contribution consists in extending learning technique to problem solving. In order to do this, we propose to transform a consistency-checking classifier into a propagator. Then, a learned concept can be used for problem

---
[1] http://www.ics.uci.edu/~mlearn

solving. While a classifier gives an answer for a single tuple, a propagator gives an answer for a Cartesian product. Since a propagator should never reject a solution, its answer should be *false* only if the absence of solution in the search space is proven. If there is a solution or if the absence of solution cannot be ensured because a full computation would be too expensive, then the answer has to be *true*. Because of the independent schedule of propagators [2], the learned relation is the one obtained in *veto mode*. It yields that the concept is more centered on positive examples, which is an advantage in optimization problems.

The simplest way to know if there is a solution in such a search space is to apply the elementary classifier on each tuple and combine all results with a disjunction. Unfortunately, this solution is computationally intractable for reasonable constraint arity or domain size. Another idea could be to first generate off-line the solutions of the extension of the constraint and use them for solving with a standard but efficient arc-consistency propagation algorithm like GAC-schema [4]. Unfortunately again, the generation time and representation size are prohibitive. Since actually covering the whole Cartesian product is impossible, the intuition of the method is to cover it *virtually*. In order to do this, we have to find a cheap sufficient condition to ensure that a sub-space does not contain any solution. We expose on two examples the cases of decision trees and multi-layer perceptrons.

Example 1 (Decision tree). Consider the decision tree depicted in figure 2 and assume that it is associated with the value $X = 1$. The domain of the other variables are $(Y \mapsto \{0, 1, 2, 3\}, Z \mapsto \{0, 1\}, T \mapsto \{2, 3\})$. In order to know if

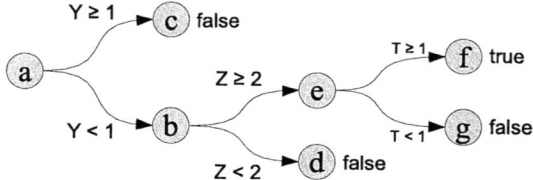

Fig. 2. A decision tree

there is a solution in this space, we define an output value $eval(n)$ for a node n of the tree. We start from node a and evaluate the conditions to get to the children nodes b and c. Both conditions are satisfied by some element of the search space, so the result will be the disjunction of the evaluation of both nodes: $eval(a) = eval(b) \vee eval(c)$. In order to evaluate b, we test the conditions of the children nodes d and e. Since the condition for node e is not met, we can stop here the evaluation of the subtree and return $eval(e) = false$. Since $eval(d) = false$, we can complete the evaluation of node b with $eval(b) = eval(d) \vee eval(e) = false \vee false = false$. Back to a, we output $eval(a) = false \vee false = false$. The answer of the classifier is the answer of the root of the decision tree. It yields that value 1 should be suppressed from X's domain.

This transformation of a function from set to powerset is known as *extension to sets* [14]. The case of decision trees is particularly interesting since it allows a fast computation of this extension. This is not the case for arithmetic functions, but they can be given a less precise extension called *extension to intervals* [8]. We call $Int_{\mathbb{R}}$ the interval lattice built on the set $\mathbb{R}$ of real numbers. First, all functions have extensions to intervals. Let $f : \mathbb{R} \to \mathbb{R}$ be a function. A function $F : Int_{\mathbb{R}} \to Int_{\mathbb{R}}$ is an extension to intervals of f if $\forall I \in Int_{\mathbb{R}}, \forall x \in I, f(x) \in F(I)$. An extension F is monotonic if $A \subseteq B \Rightarrow F(A) \subseteq F(B)$. Between all extensions to intervals of f, there is a smallest one, called *canonical extension to intervals*: $\widehat{f}(I) = [\{f(x) \mid x \in I\}]$. The canonical extension is monotonic. Here are the canonical extensions to intervals of the operators used in perceptrons:

$$[a,b] + [c,d] = [a+c, b+d]$$
$$[a,b] \times [c,d] = [\min(P), \max(P)] \text{ where } P = \{ac, ad, bc, bd\}$$
$$\exp([a,b]) = [\exp(a), \exp(b)]$$

Division is not a problem in our setting since no interval contains 0 (see the sigmoid denominator). If e is an expression using these operators and E the same expression obtained by replacing each operator by a monotonic extension, then $\forall I \in Int_{\mathbb{R}}, \forall x \in I, e(x) \in E(I)$. This property of monotonic extensions is called "The Fundamental Theorem of Interval Arithmetic" [8]. It also holds when domains are replaced by cartesian products of intervals. By taking the canonical extension of all basic operators in an expression e, we do not always obtain an extension E which is canonical. We instead call it the *natural* extension.

Example 2 (Multi-layer perceptron). The multi-layer perceptron $n_{<X=a>}$ defines naturally a boolean function of its input variables. Let $N_{<X=a>}$ be its natural interval extension, defined by taking the canonical extension of each basic operator $+, -, \times, /, \exp$. Then, by using as input the current domain of the variables, we can obtain a range for its output. In order to do this, we compute the interval range of every neuron of the hidden layer and we use these results to feed the output neuron and compute its domain. Since we put a 0.5 threshold after the output neuron, we can reject the value a for X if the maximum of the output range is less than 0.5, which means that all tuples are rejected in the current domain intervals. Otherwise, the value remains in the domain.

The extension (to sets or to intervals) $CL_{<X=a>}$ of the classifier $cl_{<X=a>}$ is an ERF. The resulting propagator defines a consistency for the constraint. We have also experimented the resulting consistencies. Decision trees and multi-layer perceptrons provide a consistency weaker than arc-consistency but faster to evaluate. While arc-consistency could theoretically be obtained for some decision trees, it is not generally the case. Related work in constraint acquisition does not provide any technique for learning a constraint and building its propagator at the same time [3, 1, 6, 10]. The same holds for the work in Inductive Logic Programming [7] since Prolog evaluation implements generate and test. On the other hand the logic program representation is even more concise than ours.

5 Conclusion

In this paper, we propose a generic meta-technique for learning a relation and a way to use Machine Learning techniques in decision or optimization problems. The first involves a decomposition of the relation in projections and improves the performances in classification. The second consists in the transformation of the classifier into a constraint propagator, which allows to use the classifier on sub-spaces instead of only tuples. We hope this work will foster cross-fertilization between these two fields.

References

1. Slim Abdennadher and Christophe Rigotti. Automatic generation of rule-based constraint solvers over finite domains. *ACM TOCL*, 5(2), 2004.
2. K.R. Apt. *Principles of Constraint Programming*. Cambridge University Press, 2003.
3. K.R. Apt and E. Monfroy. Automatic generation of constraint propagation algorithms for small finite domains. In *Int. Conf. on Constraint Programming*, volume 1713 of *LNCS*, pages 58–72. Springer, 1999.
4. Christian Bessière and Jean-Charles Régin. Arc-consistency for general constraint networks: preliminary results. In *IJCAI*, pages 398–404, Nagoya, Japan, 1997. Morgan Kaufmann.
5. Y. Freund and R. Shapire. A short introduction to boosting. *Journal of Japanese Society for Artificial Intelligence*, 14(5):771–780, 1999.
6. Arnaud Lallouet, Thi-Bich-Hanh Dao, Andreï Legtchenko, and AbdelAli Ed-Dbali. Finite domain constraint solver learning. In Georg Gottlob, editor, *International Joint Conference on Artificial Intelligence*, pages 1379–1380, Acapulco, Mexico, 2003. AAAI Press.
7. Nada Lavrac and Saso Dzeroski. *Inductive Logic Programming: Techniques and Applications*. Ellis Horwood, 1994.
8. Ramon E. Moore. *Interval Analysis*. Prentice Hall, 1966.
9. J. Quinlan. *C4.5: Programs for Machine Learning*. Morgan Kaufmann, 1993.
10. F. Rossi and A. Sperduti. Acquiring both constraint and solution preferences in interactive constraint system. *Constraints*, 9(4), 2004.
11. RuleQuest Research. See5: An informal tutorial, 2004. http://www.rulequest.com/see5-win.html.
12. D.E. Rumelhart, G.E. Hinton, and R.J. Williams. Learning internal representations by error propagation. *Parallel Distributed Processing*, vol 1:318–362, 1986.
13. Grigorios Tsoumakas, Ioannis Katakis, and Ioannis P. Vlahavas. Effective voting of heterogeneous classifiers. In J.-F. Boulicaut, F. Esposito, F. Giannotti, and D. Pedreschi, editors, *ECML*, volume 3201 of *LNCS*, pages 465–476, Pisa, Italy, September 20-24 2004. Springer.
14. R. C. Young. The algebra of multi-valued quantities. *Mathematische Annalen*, 104:260–290, 1931.

A Clustering Model Based on Matrix Approximation with Applications to Cluster System Log Files

Tao Li and Wei Peng

School of Computer Science, Florida International University,
11200, SW 8th street, Miami, FL, 33199
{taoli, wpeng002}@cs.fiu.edu

Abstract. In system management applications, to perform automated analysis of the historical data across multiple components when problems occur, we need to cluster the log messages with disparate formats to automatically infer the common set of semantic situations and obtain a brief description for each situation. In this paper, we propose a clustering model where the problem of clustering is formulated as matrix approximations and the clustering objective is minimizing the approximation error between the original data matrix and the reconstructed matrix based on the cluster structures. The model explicitly characterizes the data and feature memberships and thus enables the descriptions of each cluster. We present a two-side spectral relaxation optimization procedure for the clustering model. We also establish the connections between our clustering model with existing approaches. Experimental results show the effectiveness of the proposed approach.

1 Introduction

1.1 Background on System Log Files

With advancement in science and technology, computing systems are becoming increasingly more complex with an increasing variety of heterogeneous software and hardware components. They are thus becoming increasingly more difficult to monitor, manage and maintain. A popular approach to system management is based on analyzing system log files. The data in the log files describe the status of each component and record system operational changes.

The heterogeneous nature of the system makes the data more complex and complicated. As we know, a typical computing system contains different devices (e.g., routers, processors, and adapters) with different software components (e.g., operating systems, middleware, and user applications), possibly from different providers (e.g., Cisco, IBM, and Microsoft). These various components have multiple ways to report events, conditions, errors and alerts. The heterogeneity and inconsistency of log formats make it difficult to automate problem determination [5]. For example, there are many different ways for the components to report the start up process. Some might log "the component has started", while others might say that "the component has changed the state from starting to running". Imagine that we would like to automatically perform the following rule: if any component has started, notify the system operators. Given the inconsistent content and sometimes subtle differences in the way components report the "started" process, writing a program to automate this simple task is difficult, if not impossible [10]. One would need to know all the messages that reflect the "started" status, for all the components involved in the solution. Every time a new component is installed, the program has to be updated by adding the new component's specific terminology for reporting "started" situations. This makes it difficult to perform automated analysis of the historical event data across multiple components when problems occur.

To perform automated analysis of the historical event data across multiple components when problems occur, we need to categorize the text messages with disparate formats into common situations [10]. Clustering techniques are then needed to automatically *infer the common set of situations* from historical data and *obtain a brief description for each situation*. This would create consistency across similar fields and improve the ability to correlate across multiple component logs.

1.2 Clustering

As a fundamental and effective tool for efficient organization, summarization, navigation and retrieval of large amount of documents, clustering has been very active and enjoying a growing amount of attention with the ever-increasing growth of the on-line information. The clustering problem can be intuitively described as the problem of finding, given a set W of some n data points in a multi-dimensional space, a partition of W into classes such that the points within each class are *similar* to each other. The clustering problem has been studied extensively in machine learning [11], databases [7, 13], and statistics [2] from various perspectives and with various approaches and focuses.

Despite significant research on various clustering methods, few attempts have been made to obtain the descriptions for each cluster. In this paper, we present a clustering model [1] where the problem of clustering is formulated as matrix approximations. The model explicitly characterizes the data and feature memberships and thus enables the descriptions of each cluster. The goal of clustering is then transformed to minimizing the approximation error between the original data matrix and the reconstructed matrix based on the cluster structures. We provide an optimization procedure based on two-side spectral relaxation. In addition, we show the connections between our model with other clustering algorithms.

The rest of the paper is organized as follows: Section 2 introduces the notations and describes the general clustering model, Section 3 presents the optimization procedures based on two-side spectral relaxations, Section 4 presents the experimental results on system log data, finally, our discussions and conclusions are presented in Section 5.

2 The Clustering Model

We first present the clustering model for clustering problem. The notations used in the paper are introduced in Table 1.

---

[1] In this paper, we use model and framework interchangeably.

Table 1. Notations used throughout the paper

$W = (w_{ij})_{n \times m}$	The Data set
$D = (d_1, d_2, \cdots, d_n)$	Set of data points
$F = (f_1, f_2, \cdots, f_m)$	Set of features
K	Number of clusters for data points
C	Number of clusters for features
$P = \{P_1, P_2, \cdots, P_K\}$	Partition of D into K clusters
$i \in P_k, 1 \leq k \leq K$	i-th data point in cluster P_k
$p_1, p_2, \cdots, p_K$	Sizes for the K data clusters
$Q = \{Q_1, Q_2, \cdots, Q_C\}$	Partition of F into C clusters
$q_1, q_2, \cdots, q_C$	Sizes for the C feature clusters
$j \in Q_c, 1 \leq c \leq C$	j-th feature in cluster Q_c
$A = (a_{ik})_{n \times K}$	Matrix designating the data membership
$B = (b_{jc})_{m \times C}$	Matrix designating the feature membership
$X = (x_{kc})_{K \times C}$	Matrix specifies/indicates the association between data and features or the cluster representation
Trace(M)	Trace of the Matrix M

The model is formally specified as follows:

$$W = AXB^T + E \quad (1)$$

where matrix E denotes the error component. The first term AXB^T characterizes the information of W that can be described by the cluster structures. A and B designate the cluster memberships for data points and features, respectively. X specifies cluster representation. Let $\hat{W}$ denote the approximation AXB^T and the goal of clustering is to minimize the approximation error (or *sum-of-squared-error*)

$$\begin{aligned} O(A, X, B) &= \| W - \hat{W} \|_F^2 \\ &= \text{Trace}[(W - \hat{W})(W - \hat{W})^T] \\ &= \sum_{i=1}^{n} \sum_{j=1}^{m} (w_{ij} - \hat{w}_{ij})^2 \quad (2) \\ &= \sum_{i=1}^{n} \sum_{j=1}^{m} (w_{ij} - \sum_{k=1}^{K} \sum_{c=1}^{C} a_{ik} b_{jc} x_{kc})^2 \quad (3) \end{aligned}$$

Note that the Frobenius norm, $\| M \|_F$, of a matrix $M = (M_{ij})$ is given by $\| M \|_F = \sqrt{\Sigma_{i,j} M_{ij}^2}$.

3 The Optimization Procedure

Without loss of generality, we assume that the rows belong to a particular cluster are contiguous, so that all data points belonging to the first cluster appear first and the second cluster next, etc [2]. Then A can be represented as $A = \begin{bmatrix} 1 & 0 & \cdots & 0 \\ 1 & 0 & \cdots & 0 \\ \vdots & 0 & \cdots & 0 \\ 0 & 1 & \cdots & 0 \\ 0 & 1 & \cdots & 0 \\ \vdots & \vdots & \cdots & \vdots \\ 0 & 0 & \cdots & 1 \\ \vdots & \vdots & \cdots & \vdots \\ 0 & 0 & \cdots & 1 \end{bmatrix}$. Note that

$A^T A = \begin{bmatrix} p_1 & 0 & \cdots & 0 \\ 0 & p_2 & \cdots & 0 \\ \cdots & \cdots & \cdots & \cdots \\ 0 & 0 & \cdots & p_K \end{bmatrix}$ is a diagonal matrix with the cluster size on the diagonal. The inverse of $A^T A$ serves as a weight matrix to compute the centroids. Hence, in general, if A and B denote the cluster membership, then we have $A^T A = diag(p_1, \cdots, p_K)$ and $B^T B = diag(q_1, \cdots, q_C)$ are two diagonal matrices.

Double K-Means. Suppose $A = (a_{ik}), a_{ik} \in \{0, 1\}, \sum_{k=1}^{K} a_{ik} = 1, B = (b_{jc}), b_{jc} \in \{0, 1\}$, $\sum_{c=1}^{C} b_{jc} = 1$. Thus, based on Equation 3, we obtain

$$O(A, X, B) = \| W - \hat{W} \|_F^2 = \sum_{i=1}^{n} \sum_{j=1}^{m} (w_{ij} - \sum_{k=1}^{K} \sum_{c=1}^{C} a_{ik} b_{jc} x_{kc})^2$$

$$= \sum_{k=1}^{K} \sum_{c=1}^{C} \sum_{i \in P_k} \sum_{j \in Q_c} (w_{ij} - x_{kc})^2 \qquad (4)$$

For fixed P_k and Q_c, it is easy to check that the optimum X is obtained by $x_{kc} = \frac{1}{p_k q_c} \sum_{i \in P_k} \sum_{j \in Q_c} w_{ij}$. In other words, X can be thought as the matrix of centroids for the two-side clustering problem and it represents the associations between the data clusters and the feature clusters [3]. $O(A, X, B)$ can then be minimized via a two-side iterative procedure (i.e., the natural extensions of the K-means type algorithm for two-side cases [1, 3, 8].

Spectral Relaxation. If we relax the conditions on A and B, requiring $A^T A = I_K$ and $B^T B = I_C$, we would obtain an optimzation procedure based on a two-side spectral relaxation. Similar ideas have been explored in for gene expression data in [4]. Here we illustrated in our clustering model. Note that

$$O(A, X, B) = \| W - AXB^T \|_F^2$$
$$= \text{Trace}((W - AXB^T)(W - AXB^T)^T)$$
$$= \text{Trace}(WW^T) + \text{Trace}(XX^T) - 2\text{Trace}(AXB^T W^T)$$

Since $\text{Trace}(WW^T)$ is constant, hence minimizing $O(A, X, B)$ is equivalent to minimizing

$$O'(A, X, B) = \text{Trace}(XX^T) - 2\text{Trace}(AXB^T W^T). \qquad (5)$$

---
[2] This can also be applied to column clusters.

The minimum of Equation 5 is achieved where $X = A^T W B$ as $\frac{\partial O'}{\partial X} = X - A^T W B$. Plugging $X = A^T W B$ into Equation 5, we have

$$O'(A, X, B) = \text{Trace}(XX^T) - 2\text{Trace}(AXB^T W^T)$$
$$= \text{Trace}(A^T W BB^T W^T A) - 2\text{Trace}(AA^T W BB^T W^T)$$
$$= \text{Trace}(WW^T) - 2\text{Trace}(A^T W BB^T W^T A)$$

Since the first term $\text{Trace}(WW^T)$ is constant, minimizing $O'(A, X, B)$ is thus equivalent to maximizing $Trace(A^T W BB^T W^T A)$.

Let $G = WB$, then $Trace(A^T W BB^T W^T A) = Trace(A^T GG^T A)$.

Proposition 1. *Given B, $Trace(A^T GG^T A)$ can be maximized by constructing A with the eigenvectors of GG^T corresponding to the K largest eigenvalues.*

Note that $\text{Trace}(A^T W BB^T W^T A) = \text{Trace}(B^T W^T AA^T W B)$. Denote $H = W^T A$. Similarly, we have

Proposition 2. *Given A, $Trace(B^T HH^T B)$ can be maximized by constructing B with the eigenvectors of HH^T corresponding to the C largest eigenvalues.*

Proposition 1 and Proposition 2 can be proved via matrix computations [6] and they lead to an alternating optimization procedure to maximize $Trace(A^T W BB^T W^T A)$, i.e., update B to maximize $Trace(A^T W B W^T B^T A)$ and update A to maximize $Trace(B^T W^T AA^T W B)$. The alternative optimization procedure can be thought as a two-side generalization of the spectral relaxation [12]. After obtaining the relaxed A and B, the final cluster assignments of the data points and features are obtained by applying ordinary K-means clustering in the reduced spaces. A short description of the clustering procedure is presented as *Algorithm 1*.

Algorithm 1. Two-Side Spectral Relaxation

Input: ($W_{n \times m}$, K and C)
Output: P, Q: set of clusters;
begin
1   Initialize A;
2.   **Iteration:** Do while the stop criterion is not met
       begin
2.1   Update B to maximize $Trace(A^T W B W^T B^T A)$
2.2   Compute $X = A^T W B$
2.3   Update A to maximize $Trace(B^T W^T AA^T W B)$
       end
3.   Get the final clusterings P and Q
end

4 Experiments

We performed experimental studies to 1) show that the clustering model can identify the inherent structure in real application studies on system log files, and 2) verify that our proposed clustering method can improve the clustering performance. Due to space limit, we only present a case study on clustering system log files, showing that the cluster model can identify the inherent structures of the datasets.

4.1 Log Data Generation

The log files used in our experiments are collected from several different machines with different operating systems using logdump2td (NT data collection tool) developed at IBM T.J. Watson Research Center. The raw log files contains a free-format ASCII description of the event. In our experiment, we apply clustering algorithms to group the messages into different situations. To pre-process text messages, we remove stop words and skip HTML labels.

4.2 Experimental Results on Log Data

The general cluster framework introduced in Section 2 explicitly models both data and feature assignments. With the feature assignments, we can get the distinguishing words for each cluster and consequently obtain a description for the cluster. We use *Algorithm 1* described in Section 3 in our experiments.

Figure 1 shows the original word-document matrix of the log file and the reordered matrix obtained by arranging rows and columns based on the cluster assignments. The figure reveals the hidden sparse structure of both the document message and word clusters.

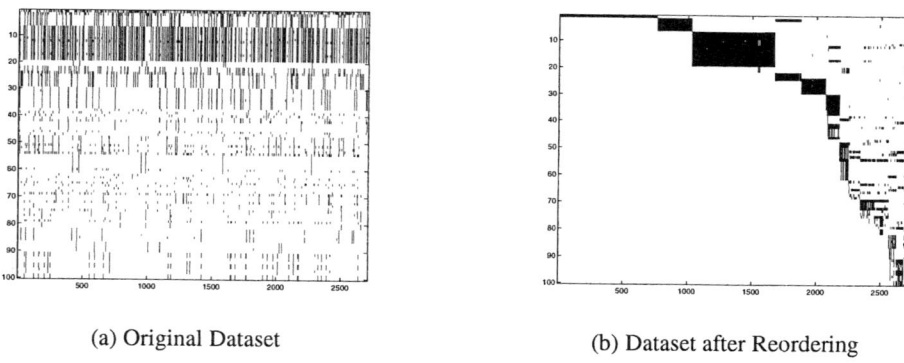

(a) Original Dataset   (b) Dataset after Reordering

Fig. 1. Visualization of the original message-data matrix and the reordered document-data matrix

Table 2 lists the discriminating words for several clusters. We can derive meaningful common situations from the cluster results. For example, cluster 1 mainly concerns product configuration, Cluster 2 is about aspects related to a connection to another component, Cluster 3 describes the problem of creating temporary files etc.

Table 2. Keywords and their clusters

Cluster Number	Words
1	product, configuration, completed
2	inventory, server, respond, network, connection, party, root
3	create, temporary, file
4	exist, directory, domain, contacted, contact, failed, certificate, enrollment
5	profile, service, version, faulting, application, module, fault, address
6	completed, update, installation
7	service, started, application, starting
8	stopped, restarted, completed, failed, shell, explorer

The case study on clustering log message files for computing system management provides a successful story of applying the cluster model in real applications. The log messages are relatively short with a large vocabulary size [9]. Hence they are usually represented as sparse high-dimensional vectors. In addition, the log generation mechanisms implicitly create some associations between the terminologies and the situations. Our clustering model explicitly models the data and feature assignments and is also able to exploit the association between data and features. The synergy of these factors leads to the good application on system management.

5 Discussions and Conclusions

Based on different constraints on the matrices A, B and X, our cluster model encompasses different clustering algorithms. The relationships between our clustering model and other well-known clustering approaches can be briefly summarized in Figure 2.

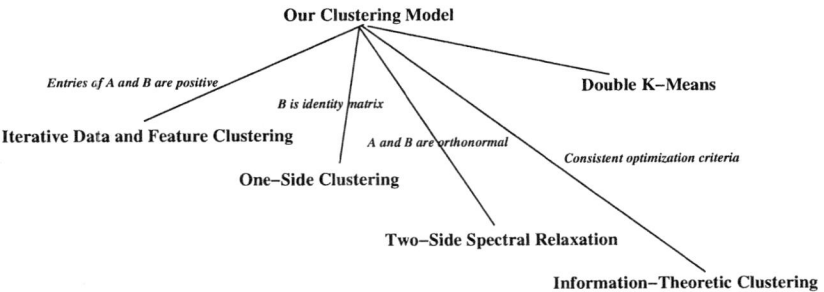

Fig. 2. Relations of Our Clustering Models and Other Approaches

In this paper, we present a clustering model and investigates its applications to cluster system log data. The model explicitly characterizes the data and feature memberships and thus enables the descriptions of each cluster. A two-side spectral relaxation method is presented as the optimization procedure for clustering. In addition, we also establish the connections between our clustering model with existing approaches. Experimental results show the effectiveness of the proposed approach.

Acknowledgment

This project is supported by an IBM Shared University Research(SUR) award and an IBM Faculty Award. Wei Peng is supported by a Florida International University Presidential Graduate Fellowship.

References

1. D. Baier, W. Gaul, and M. Schader. Two-mode overlapping clustering with applications to simultaneous benefit segmentation and market structuring. In R. Klar and O. Opitz, editors, *Classification and Knowledge Organization*, pages 577–566. Springer, 1997.
2. Marsha Berger and Isidore Rigoutsos. An algorithm for point clustering and grid generation. *IEEE Trans. on Systems, Man and Cybernetics*, 21(5):1278–1286, 1991.
3. William Castillo and Javier Trejos. Two-mode partitioning: Review of methods and application and tabu search. In K. Jajuga, A. Sokolowski, and H.-H. Bock, editors, *Classification, Clustering and Data Analysis*, pages 43–51. Springer, 2002.
4. Hyuk Cho, Inderjit S. Dhillon, Yuqiang Guan, and Suvrit Sra. Minimum sum-squared residue co-clustering of gene experssion data. In *Proceedings of the SIAM Data Mining Conference*, 2004.
5. Gary Dudley, Neeraj Joshi, David M. Ogle, Balan Subramanian, and Brad B. Topol. Autonomic self-healing systems in a cross-product it environment. *International Conference on Autonomic Computing*, pages 312–313, 2004.
6. Gene H. Golub and Cahrles F. Van Loan. *Matrix Computations*. The Johns Hopkins University Press, 1996.
7. Sudipto Guha, Rajeev Rastogi, and Kyuseok Shim. CURE: an efficient clustering algorithm for large databases. In *Proceedings of the 1998 ACM SIGMOD International Conference on Management of Data*, pages 73–84. ACM Press, 1998.
8. Vichi Maurizio. Double k-means clustering for simultaneous classification of objects and variables. In S. Borra, R. Rocci, M. Vichi, and M. Schader, editors, *Advances in Classification and Data Analysis*, pages 43–52. Springer, 2001.
9. Jon Stearley. Towards informatic analysis of syslogs. In *Proceedings of IEEE International Conference on Cluster Computing*, Sept. 2004.
10. Brad Topol, David Ogle, Donna Pierson, Jim Thoensen, John Sweitzer, Marie Chow, Mary Ann Hoffmann, Pamela Durham, Ric Telford, Sulabha Sheth, and Thomas Studwell. Automating problem determination: A first step toward self-healing computing systems. IBM White Paper, October 2003. http://www-106.ibm.com/developerworks/autonomic/library/ac-summary/ac-prob.html.
11. Andrew Webb. *Statistical Pattern Recognition*. Wiley, 2002.
12. Hongyuan Zha, Xiaofeng He, Chris Ding, and Horst Simon. Spectral relaxation for k-means clustering. In *Proceedings of Neural Information Processing Systems*, 2001.
13. Tian Zhang, Raghu Ramakrishnan, and Miron Livny. BIRCH: an efficient data clustering method for very large databases. In *Proceedings of ACM SIGMOD International Conference on Management of Data*, pages 103–114. ACM Press, 1996.

Detecting Fraud in Health Insurance Data: Learning to Model Incomplete Benford's Law Distributions

Fletcher Lu[1] and J. Efrim Boritz[2]

[1] School of Computer Science, University of Waterloo & Canadian Institute of Chartered Accountants,
66 Grace Street, Scarborough, Ontario, Canada, M1J 3K9
f2lu@cs.uwaterloo.ca

[2] School of Accountancy, University of Waterloo,
200 University Avenue West, Waterloo, Ontario, Canada, N2L 3G1
jeboritz@watarts.uwaterloo.ca

Abstract. Benford's Law [1] specifies the probabilistic distribution of digits for many commonly occurring phenomena, ideally when we have complete data of the phenomena. We enhance this digital analysis technique with an unsupervised learning method to handle situations where data is incomplete. We apply this method to the detection of fraud and abuse in health insurance claims using real health insurance data. We demonstrate improved precision over the traditional Benford approach in detecting anomalous data indicative of fraud and illustrate some of the challenges to the analysis of healthcare claims fraud.

1 Introduction

In this paper we explore a new approach to detecting fraud and abuse by using a digital analysis technique that utilizes an unsupervised learning approach to handle incomplete data. We apply the technique to the application area of healthcare insurance claims. We utilize real health insurance claims data, provided by Manulife Financial, to test our new technique and demonstrate improved precision for detecting possible fraudulent insurance claims.

A variety of techniques for detecting fraud have been developed. The most common are supervised learning methods, which train systems on known instances of fraud patterns to then detect these patterns in test data. A less common approach is to have a pattern for *non-fraudulent* data and then compare the test data to this pattern. Any data that deviates significantly from the *non-fraudulent* pattern could be indicative of possible fraud [2]. The difficulty with the latter approach for fraud detection is in obtaining a pattern that one is confident is free of fraud. Digital analysis is an approach which addresses this difficulty. Benford's Law [1] is one digital analysis technique that specifies a model of non-fraudulent data that test data may be compared against.

In 1938 Frank Benford demonstrated that for many naturally occurring phenomena, the frequency of occurrences of digits within recorded data follows a certain logarithmic probability distribution (a Benford distribution). This Benford's Law can only be applied to complete recorded data. However, incomplete records are very common. We introduce an algorithm to detect and adjust the distribution to take into account missing data. By doing so, we allow for true anomalies such as those due to fraud and abuse to be more accurately detected.

In this paper, we consider the situation where data is contiguously recorded so that the only missing data are due to cutoffs below and/or above some thresholds. Our algorithm, which we will call Adaptive Benford, adjusts its distribution of digit frequencies to account for any missing data cutoffs and produces a threshold cutoff for various ranges of digits. Our algorithm then uses those learned values to analyse test data. We return any digits exceeding a learned set of threshold bounds.

We apply our Adaptive Benford algorithm to the analysis of real healthcare insurance claims data provided by Manulife Financial. The data is a list of health, dental and drug insurance reimbursement claims for a three year period covering a single company's group benefits plan with all personal information removed.

2 Background

2.1 Benford's Law and Fraud Detection

As Benford's Law is a probability distribution with strong relevance to accounting fraud, much of the research on Benford's Law has been in areas of statistics [3, 4] as well as auditing [5, 2]. The first machine learning related implementation was done by Bruce Busta & Randy Weinberg [6].

The significant advantage of using the digital analysis approach over previous supervised learning methods for fraud detection is that we are not restricted to already known instances of fraud [7, 8]. By looking for anomalies that deviate from the expected Benford distribution that a data set should follow, we may discover possible *new* fraud cases.

2.2 Digit Probabilities

Benford's Law is a mathematical formula that specifies the probability of leading digit sequences appearing in a set of data. What we mean by *leading digit sequences* is best illustrated through an example. Consider the set of data

$$S = \{231, 432, 1, 23, 634, 23, 1, 634, 2, 23, 34, 1232\}.$$

There are twelve data entries in set S. The digit sequence '23' appears as a leading digit sequence (i.e. in the first and second position) 4 times. Therefore, the probability of the first two digits being '23' is $\frac{4}{9} \approx 0.44$. The probability is computed out of 9 because only 9 entries have at least 2 digit positions. Entries with less than the number of digits being analysed are not included in the probability computation.

The actual mathematical formula of Benford's law is:

$$P(D = d) = \log_{10}(1 + \frac{1}{d}), \tag{1}$$

where $P(D = d)$ is the probability of observing the digit sequence d in the first 'y' digits and where d is a sequence of 'y' digits. For instance, Benford's Law would state that the probability that the first digit in a data set is '3' would be $\log_{10}(1+\frac{1}{3})$. Similarly, the probability that the first 3 digits of the data set are '238', would be $\log_{10}(1 + \frac{1}{238})$. The numbers '238' and '23885' would be instances of the first three digits being '238'. However this probability would not include the occurrence '3238', as '238' is not the *first* three digits in this instance.

2.3 Benford's Law Requirements

In order to apply equation 1 as a test for a data set's digit frequencies, Benford's Law requires that:

1. The entries in a data set should record values of similar phenomena. In other words, the recorded data cannot include entries from two different phenomena such as both census population records and dental measurements.
2. There should be no built-in minimum or maximum values in the data set. In other words, the records for the phenomena must be complete, with no artificial start value or ending cutoff value.
3. The data set should not be made up of assigned numbers, such as phone numbers.
4. The data set should have more small value entries than large value entries.

Further details on these rules may be found in [9]. Under these conditions, Benford noted that the data for such sets, when placed in ascending order, often follows a geometric growth pattern.[1] Under such a situation, equation 1 specifies the probability of observing specific leading digit sequences for such a data set.

The intuitive reasoning behind the geometric growth of Benford's Law is based on the notion that for low values it takes more time for some event to increase by 100% from '1' to '2' than it does to increase by 50% from '2' to '3'. Thus, when recording numerical information at regular intervals, one often observes low digits much more frequently than higher digits, usually decreasing geometrically.

3 Adaptive Benford

As section 2.3 specifies, one of the requirements to be able to apply Benford's law is that there are 'no built-in minimum or maximum values.' However, often data is only partially observed, such as when only a single month of expenses are reported. Adaptive Benford's Law has been designed to handle such missing data situations.

3.1 Missing Data Inflating

The problem with traditional Benford's Law and incomplete data is that the frequency of the digits that are observed become inflated when computed as a probability. For instance, Benford's Law states that in a data set, a first digit of '4' should occur with probability $\log_{10}(1 + \frac{1}{4}) \approx 0.0969$. Suppose with complete data, out of 100 observations, 4

---
[1] Note: The actual data does *not* have to be recorded in ascending order. This ordering is merely an illustrative tool to understand the intuitive reasoning for Benford's law.

appeared as a first digit 10 times, which closely approximates the Benford probability. However if the data set is incomplete with only 50 observations recorded, but all 10 occurrences of first digit 4 are still recorded, then we get a probability of $10/50 = 0.20$, essentially inflating the probability of digits that are observed higher due to the missing digits not being included in the total count for the probability computation.

3.2 Algorithm

Under the condition that we are aware that the observed data follows a Benford distribution and is contiguous, if we are missing data only above or below an observed cutoff, we can use this knowledge to artificially build the missing data. First, let

- d be a leading digit sequence of length i.
- $f_{d,\text{observed}}$ be the frequency that the leading digit sequence d occurs in the data set, and
- $P(D_i)$ be the Benford probability for digit sequence D_i, where D_i is any digit sequence of length i.

Now, consider that to compare the actual frequency of occurrence of a leading digit sequence 'd' to the actual Benford probability we would compute the ratio:

$$\frac{f_{d,\text{observed}}}{\sum_{D_i} f_{D_i,\text{observed}}} \simeq P(D_i = d), \qquad (2)$$

where the denominator is summed over all digit sequences of the same length as digit sequence 'd', in other words over all digits of length i. Let

$$C_i = \sum_{D_i} f_{D_i,\text{observed}}. \qquad (3)$$

Then equation 2 can be rearranged to

$$\frac{f_{d,\text{observed}}}{P(D_i = d)} \simeq \sum_{D_i} f_{D_i,\text{observed}} = C_i, \qquad (4)$$

C_i is essentially a constant scaling factor for *all* digit sequences of the same length i. If there are missing digit sequences in our observed data due to cutoff thresholds, we can compute C_i using the observed digit sequences, since those sequences that do still appear should still follow the Benford's Law probabilities.

In order to produce a best fit for the missing data, we average over all possible C_i values for a given digit sequence length i. Therefore, let

$$C_i = \frac{f_{d,\text{observed}}/P(D_i = d)}{|\text{digit sequences of length i}|}. \qquad (5)$$

This scaling factor C_i will be used to 'fill-in' the missing data of our Benford distribution.

As an example, C_2 would be the averaged constant scaling factor over all first two digit frequencies. We use C_i to multiply our Benford probabilities for the digit sequences of length i and use that as a benchmark to compare the frequencies of the actual observed data against.

Appendix A illustrates the Adaptive Benford algorithm. The major steps of the Adaptive Benford algorithm are:

1. Compute the C_i constant values for various leading digit sequence lengths.
2. Compute artificial Benford frequencies for the digit sequence lengths.
3. Compute a standard deviation for each of the sequence lengths.
4. Flag any digit sequences in the recorded data that deviate more than an upper bound number of standard deviations from the artificial Benford frequencies.

We compute the artificial Benford frequencies as follows:

$$f_{d, expected} = C_i \times \log_{10}(1 + \frac{1}{d}). \tag{6}$$

We scale up to actual frequencies in contrast to dividing by a sum total of observed instances that would produce probabilities. By doing so, we avoid the inflating effect we noted in section 3.1. We may compute a variance against observed data by:

$$\sigma^2_{expected, i} = \frac{1}{n_i} \sum_{D_i} (f_{D_i, observed} - f_{D_i, expected})^2, \tag{7}$$

where n_i is the number of different digit sequences of size i. We compute an upper bound U_i based on a number of standard deviations from the artificial Benford frequencies. We use this upper bound to determine if the observed data deviates enough to be considered anomalous and potentially indicative of fraud or abuse.

4 Experiments

For the purposes of our experiments, we will analyse up to the first 3 leading digit sequences. The choice of digit sequence lengths to be analysed is dependent on the data set's entries (the digit lengths of the data set's elements as well as the number of elements in the data set). For a further discussion on choice of digit sequence length see [10].

4.1 Census Data Tests

As an initial test of our system we use as a test database the year 1990 population census data for municipalities in the United States, which has been analysed previously by Nigrini [9] and been verified to follow a Benford Law distribution.

Table 1 records the amount of conformity for complete and incomplete census data whereby we measure conformity as the percentage of digit sequences that fall within ±2 standard deviations of the Benford estimate value out of the total number of digit

Table 1. Census Data: Percentage of Digits within ± two standard deviations of Benford and Adaptive Benford distributions.

Range of Values x 10^4	Data Size	Classic Benford	Adaptive Benford
Complete Census	3141	96.2%	94.9%
100,000 - 1,100,000	431	85.0%	89.4%
200,000 - 1,200,000	220	85.6%	96.9%
300,000 - 1,300,000	144	49.5%	94.4%
400,000 - 1,400,000	106	30.8%	91.7%
500,000 - 1,500,000	84	32.0%	87.2%
600,000 - 1,600,000	65	34.0%	84.0%
700,000 - 1,700,000	48	33.8%	82.4%
800,000 - 1,800,000	36	19.2%	82.7%
900,000 - 1,900,000	24	11.8%	73.5%

sequences that had non-zero frequency.[2] We modified the 1990 census data to include sets of various population ranges of municipalities. Notice that for the range 100,000-1,100,000 all leading digit sequences may start with any of 1,2,...,9. However, for the range 900,000-1,900,000, the only possible leading digits start with 9 or 1. With fewer possible leading digit sequences, the inflating effect mentioned in section 3.1 becomes more likely, resulting in lower conformity as the population range shifts higher. The Adaptive Benford, which compensates for the cutoff data, produces higher conformity values, ranging from 73.5% to 96.9%.

4.2 Health Insurance Data Tests

We now analyse health insurance claims data covering general health, dental and drug claims for financial reimbursement to Manulife Financial covering a single company's group benefits plan for its employees from 2003 to 2005. With recorded data before 2003 cutoff, we expect 'inflated' percentages of *anomalous* digits with traditional Benford compared with our Adaptive Benford method.

Our goal is to detect anomalies in our data sets that may be indicative of fraud activity. Table 2 reports the percentage of anomalous digit sequences for the insurance database for various data sets. As expected, by handling missing data ranges due to cutoff levels, Adaptive Benford can be more precise, reporting fewer actual anomalous digit sequences then traditional Benford. We used a 95% upper bound confidence interval as our anomaly threshold.

The main advantage of our Adaptive Benford algorithm over traditional Benford for fraud detection is its improved precision for detecting anomalies. The goal, once anomalous digit sequences have been identified, is then to determine the data entries that are causing the high amounts of anomalous digit sequences. A forensic auditor may then,

---

[2] The two standard deviations should cover approximately 95% of the digit sequences if the data conforms to Benford's distributions. The standard deviation used for all tests of table 1 are computed using the complete 1990 census data.

Table 2. Health Insurance Fraud Detection: Comparing Traditional and Adaptive Benford against percentage of anomalous digit sequences.

Data Set	Description	Data Size	Classic Benford	Adaptive Benford
1	Misc. Dental Charges	589	21.05%	11.48%
2	Expenses Submitted by Provided	31,693	3.77%	3.44%
3	Submitted Drug Costs	6,149	16.80%	10.40%
4	Submitted Dispensing Fee	7,644	18.18%	9.09%
5	Excluded Expenses	1,167	10.39%	5.19%
6	Expenses after deductibles	29,215	3.65%	3.13%
7	Coinsurance reductions	3,871	8.85%	6.19%
8	Benefit Coordination Reductions	286	29.29%	6.06%
9	Net Amount Reimbursed	28,132	4.40%	3.70%

for instance, decide whether these entries are likely cases of fraud or abuse. Making such decisions is often a qualitative judgement call dependent often on factors related to the specific application area. Anomalies, in some cases, may be due to odd accounting or data entry practices that are not actual instances of fraud. We therefore have avoided here labeling our reported anomalies as actual fraud. Instead, we emphasize that these digit sequence anomalies are to be used as a tool to indicate possible fraud.

5 Discussion and Conclusions

In contrast to typical supervised learning methods which will train on known fraud instances, our Adaptive Benford algorithm models the data to an expected non-fraudulent Benford data pattern and any large anomalies are reported as possible fraud.[3] Our Adaptive Benford algorithm allows us to analyse data even when the data is partially incomplete. We made such an analysis with incomplete health insurance data, which only included data for a three year period. Our Adaptive Benford algorithm reports fewer anomalous digit sequences, avoiding the transient effect due to artificial cutoff start and end points for recorded data. This produces a more precise set of anomalous leading digit sequences than traditional Benford for forensic auditors to analyse for fraud. In effect, our Adaptive Benford algorithm removes requirement 2 of the rules specified in section 2.3 needed for Benford's Law to be applied. Our Adaptive Benford algorithm therefore expands the areas where Benford's Law may be applied.

Acknowledgments

We would like to thank Manulife Financial for providing the insurance data and Mark Nigrini for providing the census data. We would also like to thank the Canadian Institute of Chartered Accountants and the Natural Sciences and Engineer Research Council (NSERC) for providing funding.

---

[3] This modeling is under the pre-condition that, if we had a complete data set without fraud activity, it should follow a Benford distribution. (i.e. The complete, non-fraudulent, data set satisfies the requirements of section 2.3.

A Adaptive Benford Algorithm

Let S be the observed testing data
  Let U_i be an upper bound on the number of standard deviations
  For digit sequences $d = 1,2,3,...,$Upperbound:
    $f_{d,observed}$ = number of times digit sequence d appears as a leading digit sequence in S
  For i = 1...Upperbound on digit length:
    Let n_i be number of digits of length i that appeared at least once in S
    Compute over all digit sequences D_i of length i:
      $\hat{C}_i = \frac{1}{n_i} \sum_{D_i} \frac{f_{D_i,observed}}{\log_{10}(1+\frac{1}{D_i})}$
    Compute for each digit sequence d of length i:
      $f_{d,expected} = \hat{C}_i \times \log_{10}(1 + \frac{1}{d})$
    Compute over all digit sequences D_i of length i:
      $\hat{\sigma}_i^2 = \frac{1}{n_i} \sum_{D_i} (f_{D_i,observed} - f_{D_i,expected})^2$
    Compute for each digit sequence d of length i:
      if $U_i < \frac{f_{d,observed} - f_{d,expected}}{\sigma_i}$ then store d as anomalous

References

1. Benford, F.: The Law of Anomalous Numbers. In: Proceedings of the American Philosophical Society. (1938) 551–571
2. Crowder, N.: Fraud Detection Techniques. Internal Auditor **April** (1997) 17–20
3. Pinkham, R.S.: On the Distribution of First Significant Digits. Annals of Mathematical Statistics **32** (1961) 1223–1230
4. Hill, T.P.: A Statistical Derivation of the Significant-Digit Law. Statistical Science **4** (1996) 354–363
5. Carslaw, C.A.: Anomalies in Income Numbers: Evidence of Goal Oriented Behaviour. The Accounting Review **63** (1988) 321–327
6. Busta, B., Weinberg, R.: Using Benford's Law and neural networks as a review procedure. In: Managerial Auditing Journal. (1998) 356–266
7. Fawcett, T.: AI Approaches to Fraud Detection & Risk Management. Technical Report WS-97-07, AAAI Workshop: Technical Report (1997)
8. Bolton, R.J., Hand, D.J.: Statistical Fraud Detection: A Review. Statistical Science **17(3)** (1999) 235–255
9. Nigrini, M.J.: Digital Analysis Using Benford's Law. Global Audit Publications, Vancouver, B.C., Canada (2000)
10. Nigrini, M.J., Mittermaier, L.J.: The Use of Benford's Law as an Aid in Analytical Procedures. In: Auditing: A Journal of Practice and Theory. Volume 16(2). (1997) 52–67

Efficient Case Based Feature Construction

Ingo Mierswa and Michael Wurst

Artificial Intelligence Unit, Department of Computer Science,
University of Dortmund, Germany
{mierswa, wurst}@ls8.cs.uni-dortmund.de

Abstract. Feature construction is essential for solving many complex learning problems. Unfortunately, the construction of features usually implies searching a very large space of possibilities and is often computationally demanding. In this work, we propose a case based approach to feature construction. Learning tasks are stored together with a corresponding set of constructed features in a case base and can be retrieved to speed up feature construction for new tasks. The essential part of our method is a new representation model for learning tasks and a corresponding distance measure. Learning tasks are compared using relevance weights on a common set of base features only. Therefore, the case base can be built and queried very efficiently. In this respect, our approach is unique and enables us to apply case based feature construction not only on a large scale, but also in distributed learning scenarios in which communication costs play an important role. We derive a distance measure for heterogeneous learning tasks by stating a set of necessary conditions. Although the conditions are quite basic, they constraint the set of applicable methods to a surprisingly small number.

1 Introduction

Many inductive learning problems cannot be solved accurately by using the original feature space. This is due to the fact that standard learning algorithms cannot represent complex relationships as induced for example by trigonometric functions. For example, if only base features X_1 and X_2 are given but the target function depends highly on $X_c = \sin(X_1 \cdot X_2)$, the construction of the feature X_c would ease learning – or is necessary to enable any reasonable predictions at all [1, 2, 3]. Unfortunately, feature construction is a computationally very demanding task often requiring to search a very large space of possibilities [4, 5]. In this work we consider a scenario in which several learners face the problem of feature construction on different learning problems. The idea is to transfer constructed features between similar learning tasks to speed up the generation in such cases in which a successful feature has already been generated by another feature constructor. Such approaches are usually referred to as Meta Learning [6].

Meta Learning was applied to a large variety of problems and on different conceptual levels. The importance of the representation bias, which is closely related to feature construction, was recognized since the early days of Meta

Learning research [7, 8]. The key to many Meta Learning methods is the definition of similarity between different learning tasks [9, 10]. In this work we propose a Meta Learning scheme that compares two learning tasks using only relevance weights assigned to a set of base features by the individual learners.

This is motivated by a set of constraints found in many distributed Meta Learning scenarios. Firstly, the retrieval of similar learning tasks and relevant features usually has to be very efficient, especially for interactive applications. This also means that methods should enable a best effort strategy, such that the user can stop the retrieval process at any point and get the current best result. Secondly, the system should scale well with an increasing number of learning tasks. Also, it has to deal with a large variety of heterogeneous learning tasks, as we cannot make any strict assumptions on the individual problems. Finally, as many Meta Learning systems are distributed, communication cost should be as low as possible. As a consequence, methods that are based on exchanging examples or many feature vectors are not applicable.

2 Basic Concepts

Before we state the conditions which must be met by any method comparing learning tasks using feature weights only, we first introduce some basic definitions. Let T be the set of all learning tasks, a single task is denoted by t_i. Let X_i be a vector of numerical random variables for task t_i and Y_i another random variable, the target variable. These obey a fixed but unknown probability distribution $Pr(X_i, Y_i)$. The components of X_i are called *features* X_{ik}. The objective of every *learning task* t_i is to find a function $h_i(X_i)$ which predicts the value of Y_i. We assume that each set of features X_i is partitioned in a set of *base features* X_B which are common for all learning tasks $t_i \in T$ and a set of *constructed features* $X_i \setminus X_B$.

We now introduce a very simple model of feature relevance and interaction. The feature X_{ik} is assumed to be irrelevant for a learning task t_i if it does not improve the classification accuracy:

Definition 1. *A feature X_{ik} is called* IRRELEVANT *for a learning task t_i iff X_{ik} is not correlated to the target feature Y_i, i.e. if $Pr(Y_i|X_{ik}) = Pr(Y_i)$.*

The set of all irrelevant features for a learning task t_i is denoted by IF_i.

Two features X_{ik} and X_{il} are alternative for a learning task t_i, denoted by $X_{ik} \sim X_{il}$ if they can be replaced by each other without affecting the classification accuracy. For linear learning schemes this leads to the linear correlation of two features:

Definition 2. *Two features X_{ik} and X_{il} are called* ALTERNATIVE *for a learning task t_i (written as $X_{ik} \sim X_{il}$) iff $X_{il} = a + b \cdot X_{ik}$ with $b > 0$.*

This is a very limited definition of alternative features. However, we will show that most weighting algorithms are already ruled out by conditions based on this simple definition.

3   Comparing Learning Tasks Efficiently

The objective of our work is to speed up feature construction and improve prediction accuracy by building a case base containing pairs of learning tasks and corresponding sets of constructed features. We assume that a learning task t_i is completely represented by a feature weight vector w_i. The vector w_i is calculated from the base features X_B only. This representation of learning tasks is motivated by the idea that a given learning scheme approximate similar constructed features by a set of base features in a similar way, e.g. if the constructed feature "$\sin(X_{ik} \cdot X_{il})$" is highly relevant the features X_{ik} and X_{il} are relevant as well.

Our approach works as follows: for a given learning task t_i we first calculate the relevance of all base features X_B. We then use a distance function $d(t_i, t_j)$ to find the k most similar learning tasks. Finally, we create a set of constructed features as union of the constructed features associated with these tasks.

This set is then evaluated on the learning task t_i. If the performance gain is sufficiently high (above a given fixed threshold) we store task t_i in the case base as additional case. Otherwise, the constructed features are only used as initialization for a classical feature construction that is performed locally. If this leads to a sufficiently high increase in performance, the task t_i is also stored to the case base along with the locally generated features.

While feature weighting and feature construction are well studied tasks, the core of our algorithm is the calculation of d using only the relevance values of the base features X_B. In a first step, we define a set of conditions which must be met by feature weighting schemes. In a second step, a set of conditions for learning task distance is defined which makes use of the weighting conditions.

Weighting Conditions. *Let w be a* WEIGHTING FUNCTION $w : X_B \to \mathbb{R}$. *Then the following must hold:*

(W1) $w(X_{ik}) = 0$ if $X_{ik} \in X_B$ is irrelevant
(W2) $F_i \subseteq X_B$ is a set of alternative features. Then

$$\forall S \subset F_i, S \neq \emptyset : \sum_{X_{ik} \in S} w(X_{ik}) = \sum_{X_{ik} \in F_i} w(X_{ik}) = \hat{w}$$

(W3) $w(X_{ik}) = w(X_{il})$ if $X_{ik} \sim X_{il}$
(W4) Let AF be a set of features where

$$\forall X_{ik} \in AF : (X_{ik} \in IF_i \lor \exists X_{il} \in X_B : X_{ik} \sim X_{il}).$$

Then

$$\forall X_{il} \in X_B : \nexists X_{ik} \in AF : X_{il} \sim X_{ik} \land w'(X_{il}) = w(X_{il})$$

where w' is a weighting function for $X'_B = X_B \cup AF$.

These conditions state that irrelevant features have weight 0 and that the sum of weights of alternative features must be constant independently of the actual number of alternative features used. Together with the last conditions this guarantees that a set of alternative features is not more important than a single feature of this set. Obviously, this is a desired property of a weighting function used for the comparison of learning tasks. In the following we assume that for a modified space of base features X'_B the function w' denotes the weighting function for X'_B according to the definition in (W4).

Additionally, we can define a set of conditions which must be met by distance measures for learning tasks which are based on feature weights only:

Distance Conditions. *A* DISTANCE MEASURE *d for learning tasks is a mapping* $d : T \times T \to \mathbb{R}^+$ *which should fulfill at least the following conditions:*

(D1) $d(t_1, t_2) = 0 \Leftrightarrow t_1 = t_2$
(D2) $d(t_1, t_2) = d(t_2, t_1)$
(D3) $d(t_1, t_3) \leq d(t_1, t_2) + d(t_2, t_3)$
(D4) $d(t_1, t_2) = d(t'_1, t'_2)$ *if* $X'_B = X_B \cup IF$ *and* $IF \subseteq IF_1 \cap IF_2$
(D5) $d(t_1, t_2) = d(t'_1, t'_2)$ *if* $X'_B = X_B \cup AF$ *and* $\forall X_k \in AF : \exists X_l \in X_B :$ $X_k \sim X_l$

(D1)–(D3) represent the conditions for a metric. These conditions are required for efficient case retrieval and indexing. (D4) states that irrelevant features should not have an influence on the distance. Finally, (D5) states that adding alternative features should not have an influence on distance.

4 Negative Results

In this section we will show that many feature weighting approaches do not fulfill the conditions (W1)–(W4). Furthermore, one of the most popular distance measures, the euclidian distance, cannot be used as a learning task distance measure introduced above.

Lemma 1. *Any feature selection method does not fulfill the conditions (W1)–(W4).*

Proof. For a feature selection method, weights are always binary, i.e. $w(X_{ik}) \in \{0, 1\}$. We assume a learning task t_i with no alternative features and $X'_B = X_B \cup \{X_{ik}\}$ with $\exists X_{il} \in X_B : X_{il} \sim X_{ik}$, then either $w'(X_{il}) = w'(X_{ik}) = w(X_{il}) = 1$, leading to a contradiction with (W2), or $w'(X_{il}) \neq w'(X_{ik})$ leading to a contradiction with (W3). □

Lemma 2. *Any feature weighting method for which $w(X_{ik})$ is calculated independently of $X_B \setminus X_{ik}$ does not fulfill the conditions (W1)–(W4).*

Proof. We assume a learning task t_i with no alternative features and $X'_B = X_B \cup \{X_{ik}\}$ with $\exists X_{il} \in X_B : X_{il} \sim X_{ik}$. If w is independent of $X_B \setminus X_{ik}$ adding X_{ik} would not change the weight $w'(X_{il})$ in the new feature space X'_B. From (W3) follows that $w'(X_{ik}) = w'(X_{il}) = w(X_{il})$ which is a violation of (W2). □

Lemma 2 essentially covers all feature weighting methods that treat features independently such as information gain [11] or Relief [12]. The next theorem states that the euclidian distance cannot be used as a distance measure based on feature weights.

Theorem 3. *Euclidean distance does not fulfill the conditions (D1)–(D5).*

Proof. We give a counterexample. We assume that a weighting function w is given which fulfills the conditions (W1)–(W4). Further assume that learning tasks t_i, t_j are given with no alternative features. We add an alternative feature X_{ik} to X_B and get $X'_B = X_B \cup \{X_{ik}\}$ with $\exists X_{il} \in X_B : X_{il} \sim X_{ik}$. We infer from conditions (W2) and (W3) that

$$w'(X_{ik}) = w'(X_{il}) = \frac{w(X_{il})}{2} \quad \text{and} \quad w'(X_{jk}) = w'(X_{jl}) = \frac{w(X_{jl})}{2}$$

and from condition (W4) that

$$\forall p \neq k : w'(X_{ip}) = w(X_{ip}) \quad \text{and} \quad \forall p \neq k : w'(X_{jp}) = w(X_{jp}).$$

In this case the following holds for the euclidian distance

$$d(t'_i, t'_j) = \sqrt{S + 2\left(w'(X_{ik}) - w'(X_{jk})\right)^2} = \sqrt{S + 2\left(\frac{w(X_{ik})}{2} - \frac{w(X_{jk})}{2}\right)^2}$$

$$= \sqrt{S + \frac{1}{2}\left(w(X_{ik}) - w(X_{jk})\right)^2} \neq \sqrt{S + \left(w(X_{ik}) - w(X_{jk})\right)^2} = d(t_i, t_j)$$

with

$$S = \sum_{p=1, p\neq k}^{|X_B|} \left(w'(X_{ip}) - w'(X_{jp})\right)^2 = \sum_{p=1, p\neq k}^{|X_B|} \left(w(X_{ip}) - w(X_{jp})\right)^2. \qquad \square$$

5 Positive Results

In this section we will prove that a combination of feature weights delivered by a linear Support Vector Machine (SVM) with the Manhattan distance obeys the proposed conditions. Support Vector Machines are based on the work of Vapnik in statistical learning theory [13]. They aim to minimize the regularized risk $R_{reg}[f]$ of a learned function f which is the weighted sum of the empirical risk $R_{emp}[f]$ and a complexity term $||w||^2$:

$$R_{reg}[f] = R_{emp}[f] + \lambda ||w||^2.$$

The result is a linear decision function $y = \text{sgn}(w \cdot x + b)$ with a minimal length of w. The vector w is the normal vector of an optimal hyperplane with a maximal margin to both classes. One of the strengths of SVMs is the use of kernel functions to extend the feature space and allow linear decision boundaries after efficient nonlinear transformations of the input [14]. Since our goal is the construction of (nonlinear) features during preprocessing we can just use the most simple kernel function which is the dot product. In this case the components of the vector w can be interpreted as weights for all features.

Theorem 4. *The feature weight calculation of SVMs with linear kernel function meets the conditions (W1)–(W4).*

Proof. Since these conditions can be proved for a single learning task t_i we write X_k and w_k as a shortcut for X_{ik} and $w(X_{ik})$.

(W1) Sketch We assume that the SVM finds an optimal hyperplane. The algorithm tries to minimize both the length of w and the empirical error. This naturally corresponds to a maximum margin hyperplane where the weights of irrelevant features are 0 if enough data points are given.

(W2) SVMs find the optimal hyperplane by minimizing the weight vector w. Using the optimal classification hyperplane with weight vector w can be written as $y = \text{sgn}(w_1 x_1 + \ldots + w_i x_i + \ldots + w_m x_m + b)$. We will show that this vector cannot be changed by adding the same feature more than one time. We assume that all alternative features can be transformed into identical features by normalizing the data. Adding $k-1$ alternative features will result in

$$y = \text{sgn}\left(\ldots + \underbrace{(w_i^1 + \ldots + w_i^k)}_{\text{alternative features}} x_i + \ldots + b\right).$$

However, the optimal hyperplane will remain the same and does not depend on the number of alternative attributes. This means that the other values w_j will not be changed. This leads to $w_i = \sum_{l=1}^{k} w_i^l$ which proofs condition (W2).

(W3) The SVM optimization minimizes the length of the weight vector w. This can be written as

$$w_1^2 + \ldots + w_i^2 + \ldots + w_m^2 \stackrel{!}{=} \min.$$

We replace w_i using condition (W2):

$$w_1^2 + \ldots + \left(\hat{w} - \sum_{j \neq i} w_j\right)^2 + \ldots + w_m^2 \stackrel{!}{=} \min.$$

In order to find the minimum we have to partially differentiate the last equation for all weights w_k:

$$\frac{\partial}{\partial w_k}\left(\ldots + \left(\hat{w} - \sum_{j \neq i} w_j\right)^2 + w_k^2 + \ldots\right) = 0$$

$$\Leftrightarrow \quad 2w_k - 2\left(\hat{w} - \sum_{j \neq i} w_j\right) = 0 \quad \Leftrightarrow \quad w_k + \sum_{j \neq i} w_j = \hat{w}$$

The sum on the left side contains another w_k. This leads to a system of linear equations of the form $\ldots + 0 \cdot w_i + \ldots + 2 \cdot w_k + \ldots = \hat{w}$. Solving this system of equations leads to $w_p = w_q$ (condition (W3)).

(W4) Sketch We again assume that a SVM finds an optimal hyperplane given enough data points. Since condition (W1) holds adding an irrelevant feature would not change the hyperplane and thus the weighting vector w for the base features will remain. The proofs of conditions (W2) and (W3) state that the optimal hyperplane is not affected by alternative features as well. □

In order to calculate the distance of learning tasks based only on a set of base feature weights we still need a distance measure that met the conditions (D1)–(D5).

Theorem 5. *Manhattan distance does fulfill the conditions (D1)–(D5).*

Proof. The conditions (D1)–(D3) are fulfilled due to basic properties of the manhattan distance. Therefore, we only give proofs for conditions (D4) and (D5).

(D4) We follow from the definition of the manhattan distance that

$$d(t'_i, t'_j) = \sum_{X_{ip}, X_{jp} \in X_B} |w'_i(X_{ip}) - w'_j(X_{jp})| + \underbrace{\sum_{X_{iq}, X_{jq} \in IF} |w'_i(X_{iq}) - w'_j(X_{jq})|}_{0}$$

$$= d(t_i, t_j)$$

from (W4).

(D5) Sketch We show the case for adding k features with $\forall X_{ik} : X_{ik} \sim X_{il}$ for a fixed $X_{il} \in X_B$:

$$d(t'_i, t'_i) = \sum_{p=1, p \neq k}^{|X_B|} |w'_i(X_{ip}) - w'_j(X_{jp})| + (k+1) \cdot |w'_i(X_{ik}) - w'_j(X_{jk})|$$

$$= \sum_{p=1, p \neq k}^{|X_B|} |w_i(X_{ip}) - w_j(X_{jp})| + |w_i(X_{ik}) - w_j(X_{jk})| = d(t_i, t_j)$$

from (W4) and (W2). □

Therefore, we conclude that SVM feature weights in combination with manhattan distance fulfill the necessary constraints for an efficient learning task distance measure based on feature weights.

6 Conclusion and Outlook

We presented a Meta Learning approach to feature construction that compares tasks using relevance weights on a common set of base features only. After stating some very basic conditions for such a distance measure, we have shown that a SVM as base feature weighting algorithm and the manhattan distance fulfill these conditions, while several other popular feature weighting methods and distance measures do not. In [15] we have presented experimental results indicating that our method can speed up feature construction considerably. Our approach is therefore highly relevant for practical problems involving feature construction. Some limitations of the work presented here are the following. Firstly, our definition for alternative or exchangeable features is rather simple and should be generalized to a weaker concept as e. g. highly correlated features. Also, complex interactions between features are not covered by our conditions. However, it is very interesting that the conditions stated in this work are already sufficient to rule out large sets of feature weighting methods and distance measures. Finally, the assumption of estimating the distance of constructed features by the distance of base features is well motivated, though it would be interesting to analyze this relationship analytically to get a better estimation in which cases our approach can be successfully applied.

References

1. Blum, A.L., Langley, P.: Selection of relevant features and examples in machine learning. Artificial Intelligence (1997) 245–271
2. Dash, M., Liu, H.: Feature selection for classification. International Journal of Intelligent Data Analysis **1** (1997) 131–156
3. Koller, D., Sahami, M.: Toward optimal feature selection. In: Proc. of the ICML. (1996) 129–134
4. Mierswa, I., Morik, K.: Automatic feature extraction for classifying audio data. Machine Learning Journal **58** (2005) 127–149
5. Wolpert, D., Macready, W.: No free lunch theorems for optimisation. IEEE Trans. on Evolutionary Computation **1** (1997) 67–82
6. Vilalta, R., Drissi, Y.: A perspective view and survey of meta-learning. Artificial Intelligence Review **18** (2002) 77–95
7. Baxter, J.: Learning internal representations. In: Proc. of the eighth annual conference on Computational learning theory '95, ACM Press (1995) 311–320
8. Baxter, J.: A model of inductive bias learning. Journal of Artificial Intelligence Research **12** (2000) 149–198
9. Ben-David, S., Schuller, R.: Exploiting task relatedness for multiple task learning. In: Proc. of the Sixteenth Annual Conference on Learning Theory 2003. (2003)
10. Thrun, S., O'Sullivan, J.: Discovering structure in multiple learning tasks: The TC algorithm. In Saitta, L., ed.: Proc. of the ICML, San Mateo, CA, Morgen Kaufmann (1996)
11. Quinlan, R.: Induction of decision trees. Machine Learning **1** (1986) 81–106
12. Kira, K., Rendell, I.A.: The feature selection problem: Traditional methods and a new algoirthm. In: 10th National Conference on Artificial Intelligence, MIT Press (1992) 129–134
13. Vapnik, V.N.: The Nature of Statistical Learning Theory. Springer, New York (1995)
14. Schölkopf, B., Smola, A.J.: Learning with Kernels – Support Vector Machines, Regularization, Optimization, and Beyond. MIT Press (2002)
15. Mierswa, I., Wurst, M.: Efficient feature construction by meta learning – guiding the search in meta hypothesis space. In: Proc. of the ICML Workshop on Meta Learning. (2005)

Fitting the Smallest Enclosing Bregman Ball

Richard Nock[1] and Frank Nielsen[2]

[1] Université Antilles-Guyane
rnock@martinique.univ-ag.fr
[2] Sony Computer Science Laboratories, Inc.
Frank.Nielsen@acm.org

Abstract. Finding a point which minimizes the maximal distortion with respect to a dataset is an important estimation problem that has recently received growing attentions in machine learning, with the advent of one class classification. We propose two theoretically founded generalizations to arbitrary Bregman divergences, of a recent popular smallest enclosing ball approximation algorithm for Euclidean spaces coined by Bădoiu and Clarkson in 2002.

1 Introduction

Consider the following problem: given a set of observed data $\mathcal{S}$, compute some accurate set of parameters, or simplified descriptions, that *summarize* ("fit well") $\mathcal{S}$ according to some criteria. This problem is well known in various fields of statistics and computer science. In many cases, it admits two different formulations:

(1.) Find a point $\mathbf{c}^*$ which minimizes an *average distortion* with respect to $\mathcal{S}$.
(2.) Find a point $\mathbf{c}^*$ which minimizes a *maximal distortion* with respect to $\mathcal{S}$.

These two problems are cornerstones of different subfields of applied mathematics and computer science, such as (i) parametric estimation and the computation of *exhaustive* statistics for broad classes of distributions in statistics, (ii) one class classification and clustering in machine learning, (iii) the one center problem and its generalizations in computational geometry, among others [1, 2, 5, 7]. The main unknown in both problems is what we mean by *distortion*.

In fact, many examples of distortion measures found in domains concerned by the problems above (computational geometry, machine learning, signal processing, probabilities and statistics, among others) fall into a *single* family of distortion measures known as Bregman divergences [3]. Informally, each of them is the tail of the Taylor expansion of a strictly convex function. Using a neat result in [2], it can be shown that the solution to problem (1.) above is always the average member of $\mathcal{S}$, *regardless of the Bregman divergence*. This means that problem (1.) can be solved in optimal linear time / space in the size of $\mathcal{S}$: since $\mathcal{S}$ may be huge, this property is crucial. Unfortunately, the solution of (2.) does not seem to be as affordable; tackling the problem with quadratic programming buys an expensive time complexity cubic in the worst case, and the space complexity is quadratic [8]. Notice also that it is mostly used with L_2^2. Instead of

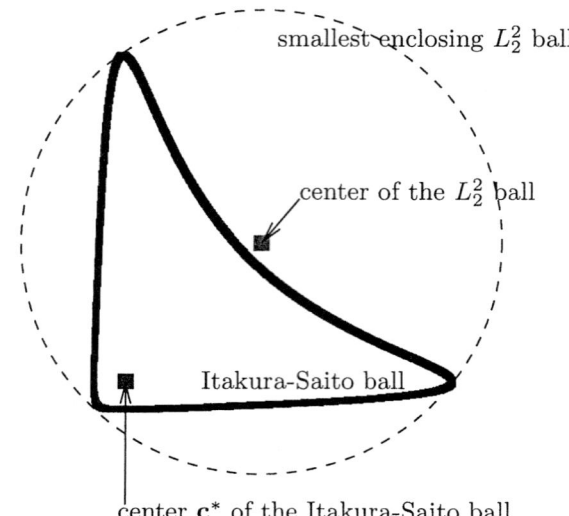

Fig. 1. An optimal Itakura-Saito ball and its smallest enclosing L_2^2 ball, for $d = 2$. Notice the poor quality of this *optimal* approximation: the center of the L_2^2 ball does not even lie inside the Itakura-Saito ball.

finding an exact solution, a recent approach due to [1] *approximates* the solution of the problem for L_2^2: the user specifies some $\varepsilon > 0$, and the algorithm returns, in time *linear* in the size of $\mathcal{S}$ (quadratic in $1/\varepsilon$) and in space *linear* in the size of $\mathcal{S}$, the center **c** of a ball which is at L_2^2 divergence no more than $\varepsilon^2 r^*$ from $\mathbf{c}^*$. Here, r^* is the squared radius of the so-called *smallest enclosing ball* of $\mathcal{S}$, whose center $\mathbf{c}^*$ is obviously the solution to problem (2.). Let us name this algorithm the Bădoiu-Clarkson algorithm, and abbreviate it BC. The key point of the algorithm is its simplicity, which deeply contrasts with quadratic programming approaches: basically, after having initialized **c** to a random point of $\mathcal{S}$, we iterate through finding the farthest point away from the current center, and then move along the line between these two points. The popularity of the algorithm, initially focused in computational geometry, has begun to spread to machine learning as well, with its adaptation to fast approximations of SVM training [8].

The applications of BC have remained so far focused on L_2^2, yet the fact that the algorithm gives a clean and simple approach to problem (2.) for *one* Bregman divergence naturally raises the question of whether it can be tailored to approximating problem (2.) *for any* Bregman divergence as well. Figure 1 highlights the importance of this issue.

In this paper, we propose two theoretically founded generalizations of BC to arbitrary Bregman divergences, along with a bijection property that has a flavor similar to a Theorem of [2]: we show a bijection between the set of Bregman divergences and the set of the most commonly used functional averages, which yields that each element of the latter set encodes the minimax distortion solution for a Bregman divergence. This property is the cornerstone of our modifications to BC. The next Section presents some definitions. Section 3 gives the theoretical foundations and Section 4 the experiments regarding our generalization of BC.

2 Definitions

Our notations mostly follow those of [1,2]. Bold faced variables such as **x** and $\boldsymbol{\alpha}$, represent column vectors. Sets are represented by calligraphic upper-case alphabets, e.g. $\mathcal{S}$, and enumerated as $\{\mathbf{s}_i : i \geq 1\}$ for vector sets, and $\{s_i : i \geq 1\}$ otherwise. The jth component of vector **s** is noted s_j, for $j \leq 1$. Vectors are supposed d-dimensional. We write $\mathbf{x} \geq \mathbf{y}$ as a shorthand for $x_i \geq y_i, \forall i$. The cardinal of a set $\mathcal{S}$ is written $|\mathcal{S}|$, and $\langle .,. \rangle$ defines the inner product for real valued vectors, i.e. the dot product. Norms are L_2 for a vector, and Frobenius for a matrix. Bregman divergences are a parameterized family of distortion measures: let $F : \mathcal{X} \rightarrow I\!R$ be strictly convex and differentiable on the interior $int(\mathcal{X})$ of some convex set $\mathcal{X} \subseteq I\!R^d$. Its corresponding Bregman divergence is:

$$D_F(\mathbf{x'},\mathbf{x}) = F(\mathbf{x'}) - F(\mathbf{x}) - \langle \mathbf{x'}-\mathbf{x}, \boldsymbol{\nabla}_F(\mathbf{x}) \rangle \ . \tag{1}$$

Here, $\boldsymbol{\nabla}_F$ is the gradient operator of F. A Bregman divergence has the following properties: it is convex in **x'**, always non negative, and zero iff $\mathbf{x} = \mathbf{x'}$. Whenever $F(\mathbf{x}) = \sum_{i=1}^d x_i^2 = \|\mathbf{x}\|_2^2$, the corresponding divergence is the squared Euclidean distance (L_2^2): $D_F(\mathbf{x'},\mathbf{x}) = \|\mathbf{x} - \mathbf{x'}\|_2^2$, with which is associated the common definition of a ball in an Euclidean metric space:

$$\mathcal{B}_{\mathbf{c},r} = \{\mathbf{x} \in \mathcal{X} : \|\mathbf{x}-\mathbf{c}\|_2^2 \leq r\} \ , \tag{2}$$

with $\mathbf{c} \in \mathcal{S}$ the center of the ball, and $r \geq 0$ its (squared) radius. Eq. (2) suggests a natural generalization to the definition of balls for arbitrary Bregman divergences. However, since a Bregman divergence is usually not symmetric, any $\mathbf{c} \in \mathcal{S}$ and any $r \geq 0$ define actually two dual *Bregman balls*:

$$\mathcal{B}_{\mathbf{c},r} = \{\mathbf{x} \in \mathcal{X} : D_F(\mathbf{c},\mathbf{x}) \leq r\} \ , \tag{3}$$
$$\mathcal{B}'_{\mathbf{c},r} = \{\mathbf{x} \in \mathcal{X} : D_F(\mathbf{x},\mathbf{c}) \leq r\} \ . \tag{4}$$

Remark that $D_F(\mathbf{c},\mathbf{x})$ is always convex in **c** while $D_F(\mathbf{x},\mathbf{c})$ is not always, but the *boundary* $\partial \mathcal{B}_{\mathbf{c},r}$ is not always convex (it depends on **x**, given **c**), while $\partial \mathcal{B}'_{\mathbf{c},r}$ is always convex. In this paper, we are mainly interested in $\mathcal{B}_{\mathbf{c},r}$ because of the convexity of D_F in **c**. The conclusion of the paper extends some results to build $\mathcal{B}'_{\mathbf{c},r}$ as well. Let $\mathcal{S} \subseteq \mathcal{X}$ be a set of m points that were sampled from $\mathcal{X}$. A *smallest enclosing Bregman ball* (SEBB) for $\mathcal{S}$ is a Bregman ball $\mathcal{B}_{\mathbf{c}^*,r^*}$ with r^* the minimal real such that $\mathcal{S} \subseteq \mathcal{B}_{\mathbf{c}^*,r^*}$. With a slight abuse of language, we will refer to r^* as the *radius* of the ball. Our objective is to approximate as best as possible the SEBB of $\mathcal{S}$, which amounts to minimizing the radius of the enclosing ball we build. As a simple matter of fact indeed, the SEBB is unique.

Lemma 1. *The smallest enclosing Bregman ball $\mathcal{B}_{\mathbf{c}^*,r^*}$ of $\mathcal{S}$ is unique.*

(proof omitted due to the lack of space) Algorithm 1 presents Bădoiu-Clarkson's algorithm for the SEBB approximation problem with the L_2^2 divergence [1].

Algorithm 1: BC($\mathcal{S}, T$)

Input: Data $\mathcal{S} = \{\mathbf{s}_1, \mathbf{s}_2, ..., \mathbf{s}_m\}$;
Output: Center **c**;
Choose at random $\mathbf{c} \in \mathcal{S}$;
for $t = 1, 2, ..., T-1$ do
$\quad\quad \mathbf{s} \leftarrow \arg\max_{\mathbf{s}' \in \mathcal{S}} \|\mathbf{c} - \mathbf{s}'\|_2^2$;
$\quad\quad \mathbf{c} \leftarrow \frac{t}{t+1}\mathbf{c} + \frac{1}{t+1}\mathbf{s}$;

3 Extending BC

The primal SEBB problem is to find:

$$\arg\min_{\mathbf{c}^*, r^*} r^* \text{ s.t. } D_F(\mathbf{c}^*, \mathbf{s}_i) \leq r^*, \forall 1 \leq i \leq m . \tag{5}$$

Its Lagrangian is $L(\mathcal{S}, \boldsymbol{\alpha}) = r^* - \sum_{i=1}^m \alpha_i(r^* - D_F(\mathbf{c}^*, \mathbf{s}_i))$, with the additional Karush-Kuhn-Tucker condition $\boldsymbol{\alpha} \geq \mathbf{0}$. The solution to (5) is obtained by minimizing $L(\mathcal{S}, \boldsymbol{\alpha})$ for the parameters $\mathbf{c}^*$ and r^*, and then maximize the resulting dual for the Lagrange multipliers. We obtain $\partial L(\mathcal{S}, \boldsymbol{\alpha})/\partial \mathbf{c}^* = \boldsymbol{\nabla}_F(\mathbf{c}^*) \sum_{i=1}^m \alpha_i - \sum_{i=1}^m \alpha_i \boldsymbol{\nabla}_F(\mathbf{s}_i)$ and $\partial L(\mathcal{S}, \boldsymbol{\alpha})/\partial r^* = 1 - \sum_{i=1}^m \alpha_i$. Setting $\partial L(\mathcal{S}, \boldsymbol{\alpha})/\partial \mathbf{c}^* = \mathbf{0}$ and $\partial L(\mathcal{S}, \boldsymbol{\alpha})/\partial r^* = 0$ yields $\sum_{i=1}^m \alpha_i = 1$ and:

$$\mathbf{c}^* = \boldsymbol{\nabla}_F^{-1}\left(\sum_{i=1}^m \alpha_i \boldsymbol{\nabla}_F(\mathbf{s}_i)\right) . \tag{6}$$

Table 1. Some common Bregman divergences and their associated functional averages. The second row depicts the general I (information) divergence, also known as Kullbach-Leibler (KL) divergence on the d-dimensional probability simplex. On the fourth row, A is the inverse of the covariance matrix [2].

domain	$F(\mathbf{s})$	$D_F(\mathbf{c}, \mathbf{s})$	c_j ($1 \leq j \leq d$)
		L_2^2 norm	arithmetic mean
$\mathbb{R}^d$	$\sum_{j=1}^d s_j^2$	$\sum_{j=1}^d (c_j - s_j)^2$	$\sum_{i=1}^m \alpha_i s_{i,j}$
$(\mathbb{R}^{+,*})^d$		(I/KL)-divergence	geometric mean
/ d-simplex	$\sum_{j=1}^d s_j \log s_j - s_j$	$\sum_{j=1}^d c_j \log(c_j/s_j) - c_j + s_j$	$\prod_{i=1}^m s_{i,j}^{\alpha_i}$
		Itakura-Saito distance	harmonic mean
$(\mathbb{R}^{+,*})^d$	$-\sum_{j=1}^d \log s_j$	$\sum_{j=1}^d (c_j/s_j) - \log(c_j/s_j) - 1$	$1/\sum_{i=1}^m (\alpha_i/s_{i,j})$
		Mahalanobis distance	arithmetic mean
$\mathbb{R}^d$	$\mathbf{s}^T A \mathbf{s}$	$(\mathbf{c} - \mathbf{s})^T A(\mathbf{c} - \mathbf{s})$	$\sum_{i=1}^m \alpha_i s_{i,j}$
	$p \in \mathbb{N}\setminus\{0,1\}$		weighted power mean
$\mathbb{R}^d/\mathbb{R}^{+d}$	$(1/p)\sum_{j=1}^d s_j^p$	$\sum_{j=1}^d \frac{c_j^p}{p} + \frac{(p-1)s_j^p}{p} - c_j s_j^{p-1}$	$\left(\sum_{i=1}^m \alpha_i s_{i,j}^{p-1}\right)^{1/(p-1)}$

Because F is strictly convex, ∇_F is bijective, and $\mathbf{c}^*$ lies in the convex closure of $\mathcal{S}$. Finally, we are left with finding:

$$\arg\max_{\boldsymbol{\alpha}} \sum_{i=1}^{m} \alpha_i D_F\left(\nabla_F^{-1}\left(\sum_{j=1}^{m} \alpha_j \nabla_F(\mathbf{s}_j)\right), \mathbf{s}_i\right) \text{ s.t. } \boldsymbol{\alpha} \geq \mathbf{0}, \sum_{i=1}^{m} \alpha_i = 1 \ . \quad (7)$$

This problem generalizes the dual of support vector machines: whenever $F(\mathbf{s}) = \sum_{i=1}^{d} s_i^2 = \langle \mathbf{s}, \mathbf{s} \rangle$ (Table 1), we return to their kernel-based formulation [4]. There are essentially two categories of Lagrange multipliers in vector $\boldsymbol{\alpha}$. Those corresponding to points of $\mathcal{S}$ lying on the interior of $\mathcal{B}_{\mathbf{c}^*, r^*}$ are zero, since these points satisfy their respective constraints. The others, corresponding to the *support points* of the ball, are strictly positive. Each $\alpha_i > 0$ represents the contribution of its support point to the computation of the circumcenter of the ball. Eq. (6) is thus some *functional average* of the support points of the ball, to compute $\mathbf{c}^*$.

3.1 The Modified Bădoiu-Clarkson Algorithm, MBC

There is more on eq. (6). A Bregman divergence is not affected by linear terms: $D_{F+q} = D_F$ for any constant q [6]. Thus, the partial derivatives of F in $\nabla_F(.)$ determine entirely the Bregman divergence. The following Lemma is then immediate.

Lemma 2. *The set of functional averages (6) is in bijection with the set of Bregman divergences (1).*

The connection between the functional averages and divergences is much interesting because the classical means commonly used in many domains, such as convex analysis, parametric estimation, signal processing, are valid examples of functional averages. A nontrivial consequence of Lemma 2 is that each of them encodes the SEBB solution for an associated Bregman divergence. Apart from the SEBB problem, this is interesting because means are popular statistics, and we give a way to favor the choice of a mean against another one depending on the *domain* of the data and its "natural" distortion measure. Table 1 presents some Bregman divergences and their associated functional averages, for the most commonly encountered.

Speaking of bijections, previous results showed the existence of a bijection between Bregman divergences and the family of exponential distributions [2]. This has helped the authors to devise a generalization of the k-means algorithm. In our case, Lemma 2 is also of some help to generalize BC. Clearly, the dual problem in eq. (7) does not admit the convenient representation of SVMs, and it seems somehow hard to use a kernel trick replacing the elements of $\mathcal{S}$ by local transformations involving F prior to solving problem (7). However, the dual suggests a very simple algorithm to approximate $\mathbf{c}^*$, which consists in making the parallel between $\nabla(\mathbf{c}^*) = \sum_{i=1}^{m} \alpha_i \nabla_F(\mathbf{s}_i)$ (6) and the arithmetic mean in Table 1, and consider (6) as the solution to a minimum distortion problem involving gradients into a L_2^2 space. We can thus seek:

$$\arg\min_{\mathbf{g}^*, r'^*} r'^* \text{ s.t. } \|\mathbf{g}^* - \nabla_F(\mathbf{s}_i)\|_2^2 \leq r'^*, \forall 1 \leq i \leq m \ . \quad (8)$$

Finally, approximating (5) amounts to running the so-called Modified Bădoiu-Clarkson algorithm in the gradient space, MBC. Because ∇_F is bijective, this is guaranteed to yield a solution. The remaining question is whether $\nabla_F^{-1}(\mathbf{g}) = \mathbf{c}$ is close enough from the solution $\mathbf{c}^*$ of (5). The following Lemma upperbounds the sum of the two divergences between $\mathbf{c}$ and any point of $\mathcal{S}$, as a function of r'^*. It shows that the two centers can be very close to each other; in fact, they can be *much* closer than with a naive application of Bădoiu-Clarkson directly in $\mathcal{S}$. The Lemma makes the hypothesis that the Hessian of F, H_F, is non singular. As a matter of fact, it is diagonal (without zero in the diagonal) for all classical examples of Bregman divergences, see Table 1, so this is not a restriction either. In the Lemma, we let f denote the minimal non zero value of the Hessian norm inside the convex closure of $\mathcal{S}$: $f = \min_{\mathbf{x} \in \mathrm{co}(\mathcal{S}): \|H_F(\mathbf{x})\|_2 > 0} \|H_F(\mathbf{x})\|_2$.

Lemma 3. $\forall s \in \mathcal{S}$, we have:

$$D_F(s, \nabla_F^{-1}(g)) + D_F(\nabla_F^{-1}(g), s) \leq (1+\varepsilon)^2 r'^* / f \;, \tag{9}$$

where $g = \mathrm{BC}(\{\nabla_F(\mathbf{s}_i) : \mathbf{s}_i \in \mathcal{S}\}, T)$, r'^* is defined in eq. (8), and ε is the error parameter of BC.

(proof omitted due to the lack of space) Remark that Lemma 3 is optimal, in the sense that if we consider $D_F = L_2^2$, then each point $\mathbf{s}_i \in \mathcal{S}$ becomes $2\mathbf{s}_i$ in $\mathcal{S}'$. The optimal radii in (5) and (8) satisfy $r'^* = 4r^*$, and we have $f = 2$. Plugging this altogether in eq. (9) yields $2\|\mathbf{c}-\mathbf{s}\|_2^2 \leq (1+\varepsilon)^2 \times 4r^*/2$, i.e. $\|\mathbf{c}-\mathbf{s}\|_2 \leq (1+\varepsilon)\sqrt{r^*}$, which is exactly Bădiou-Clarkson's bound [1] (here, we have fixed $\mathbf{c} = \nabla_F^{-1}(\mathbf{g})$, like in Lemma 3). Remark also that Lemma 3 upperbounds the sum of both possible divergences, which is very convenient given the possible asymmetry of D_F.

3.2 The Bregman-Bădoiu-Clarkson Algorithm, BBC

It is straightforward to check that at the end of BC (algorithm 1), the following holds true:

$$\begin{cases} \mathbf{c} = \sum_{i=1}^m \hat{\alpha}_i \mathbf{s}_i \;, \sum_{i=1}^m \hat{\alpha}_i = 1 \;, \hat{\boldsymbol{\alpha}} \geq \mathbf{0} \;, \\ \forall 1 \leq i \leq m, \hat{\alpha}_i \neq 0 \text{ iff } \mathbf{s}_i \text{ is chosen at least once in BC }. \end{cases}$$

Since the furthest points chosen by BC ideally belong to $\partial \mathcal{B}_{\mathbf{c}^*, r^*}$, and the final expression of $\mathbf{c}$ matches the arithmetic average of Table 1, it comes that BC *directly* tackles an iterative approximation of eq. (6) for the L_2^2 Bregman divergence. If we replace L_2^2 by an arbitrary Bregman divergence, then BC can be generalized in a quite natural way to algorithm BBC (for Bregman-Bădoiu-Clarkson) below. Again, it is straightforward to check that at the end of BBC, we have generalized the iterative approximation of BC to eq. (6) for any Bregman divergence, as we have:

$$\begin{cases} \mathbf{c} = \nabla_F^{-1}\left(\sum_{i=1}^m \hat{\alpha}_i \nabla_F(\mathbf{s}_i)\right) \;, \sum_{i=1}^m \hat{\alpha}_i = 1 \;, \hat{\boldsymbol{\alpha}} \geq \mathbf{0} \;, \\ \forall 1 \leq i \leq m, \hat{\alpha}_i \neq 0 \text{ iff } \mathbf{s}_i \text{ is chosen at least once in BC }. \end{cases}$$

Algorithm 2: BBC($\mathcal{S}$)

Input: Data $\mathcal{S} = \{\mathbf{s}_1, \mathbf{s}_2, ..., \mathbf{s}_m\}$;
Output: Center $\mathbf{c}$;
Choose at random $\mathbf{c} \in \mathcal{S}$;
for $t = 1, 2, ..., T-1$ do
$\quad \mathbf{s} \leftarrow \arg\max_{\mathbf{s}' \in \mathcal{S}} D_F(\mathbf{c}, \mathbf{s}')$;
$\quad \mathbf{c} \leftarrow \nabla_F^{-1}\left(\frac{t}{t+1}\nabla_F(\mathbf{c}) + \frac{1}{t+1}\nabla_F(\mathbf{s})\right)$;

The main point is whether $\hat{\boldsymbol{\alpha}}$ is a good approximation to the true vector of Lagrange multipliers $\boldsymbol{\alpha}$. From the theoretical standpoint, the proof of BC's approximation ratio becomes tricky when lifted from L_2^2 to an arbitrary Bregman divergence, but it can be shown that many of the key properties of the initial proof remain true in this more general setting. An experimental hint that speaks for itself for the existence of such a good approximation ratio is given in the next Section.

4 Experimental Results

Due to the lack of space, we only present results on BBC. To evaluate the quality of the approximation of BBC for the SEBB, we have ran the algorithm for three popular representative Bregman divergences. For each of them, averages over a hundred runs were performed for $T = 200$ center updates (see algorithm 2). In each run, a random Bregman ball is generated, and $\mathcal{S}$ is sampled uniformly at random in the ball. Since we know the SEBB, we have a precise idea of the quality of the approximation found by BBC on the SEBB. Figure 2 gives a synthesis of the results for $d = 2$. [1]'s bound is plotted for each divergence,

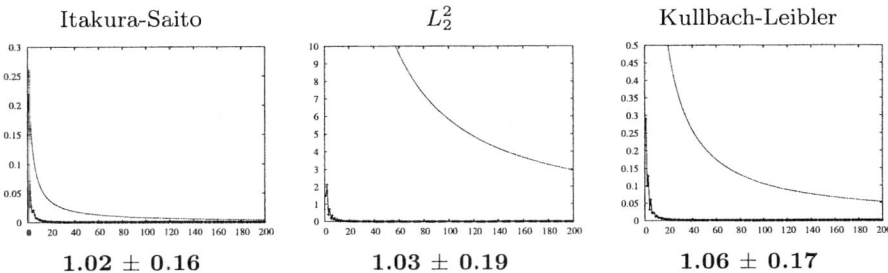

Fig. 2. Average approximation curves for 100 runs of BBC algorithm for three Bregman divergences: Itakura-Saito, L_2^2 and KL ($d = 2, m = 1000, T = 200$). The dashed curves are Bădoiu-Clarkson's error bound as a function of the iteration number t, and the bottom, plain curves, depict $(D_F(\mathbf{c}^*, \mathbf{c}) + D_F(\mathbf{c}, \mathbf{c}^*))/2$ as a function of t for each divergence, where $\mathbf{c}$ is the output of BBC and $\mathbf{c}^*$ is the optimal center. The bottom number depict the estimated error (%) ± standard deviation.

Table 2. Estimated errors for the SEBB problem for data generated using a mixture of u gaussians, for $u = 1, 3, 5, 10, 20$. Conventions and parameters follow Figure 2.

u	Itakura-Saito	L_2^2	Kullbach-Leibler
1	0.37 ± 0.06	0.43 ± 0.09	0.39 ± 0.08
3	0.40 ± 0.04	0.41 ± 0.10	0.41 ± 0.06
5	0.41 ± 0.04	0.43 ± 0.10	0.41 ± 0.04
10	0.40 ± 0.02	0.44 ± 0.09	0.42 ± 0.05
20	0.41 ± 0.02	0.43 ± 0.08	0.41 ± 0.04

even when it holds formally only for L_2^2. The other two curves give an indication of the way this bound behaves with respect to the experimental results. It is easy to see that for each divergence, there is a very fast convergence of the center found, **c**, to the optimal center **c***. Furthermore, the experimental divergences are always much smaller than [1]'s bound, *for each divergence* (very often by a factor 100 or more). We have checked this phenomenon for higher dimensions, up to $d = 20$. Following [7], the errors given are the ratio of the number of support points over the whole number of points. A good method would typically select a very small number of points, regardless of the domain. While this is clearly displayed in Figure 2, Table 2 goes deeper in this phenomenon, as it displays the errors when the points are drawn from random mixtures of Gaussians. Even in this case, where the Gaussians may be very distant from each other, MBC with the three Bregman divergences of Figure 2 still displays a very low error.

References

1. M. Bădoiu and K.-L. Clarkson. Optimal core-sets for balls, 2002. Manuscript.
2. A. Banerjee, S. Merugu, I. Dhillon, and J. Ghosh. Clustering with bregman divergences. In *Proc. of the 4th SIAM International Conference on Data Mining*, pages 234–245, 2004.
3. L. M. Bregman. The relaxation method of finding the common point of convex sets and its application to the solution of problems in convex programming. *USSR Comp. Math. and Math. Phys.*, 7:200–217, 1967.
4. C. J. C. Burges. A tutorial on support vector machines for pattern recognition. *Data Mining and Knowledge Discovery*, 2:121–167, 1998.
5. K. Crammer and G. Chechik. A needle in a haystack: local one-class optimization. In *Proc. of the 21th International Conference on Machine Learning*, 2004.
6. C. Gentile and M. Warmuth. Proving relative loss bounds for on-line learning algorithms using Bregman divergences. In *Tutorials of the 13th International Conference on Computational Learning Theory*, 2000.
7. D. Tax and R. Duin. Support Vector Domain Description. *Pattern Recognition Letters*, 20:1191–1199, 1999.
8. I. W. Tsang, J. T. Kwok, and P.-M. Cheung. Core Vector Machines: fast SVM training on very large datasets. *Journal of Machine Learning Research*, 6:363–392, 2005.

Similarity-Based Alignment and Generalization

Daniel Oblinger, Vittorio Castelli, Tessa Lau, and Lawrence D. Bergman

IBM T.J. Watson Research, New York
{oblio, vittorio, tessalau, bergmanl}@us.ibm.com

Abstract. We present a novel approach to learning predictive sequential models, called *similarity-based alignment and generalization*, which incorporates in the induction process a specific form of domain knowledge derived from a similarity function between the points in the input space. When applied to Hidden Markov Models, our framework yields a new class of learning algorithms called *SimAlignGen*. We discuss the application of our approach to the problem of programming by demonstration– the problem of learning a procedural model of user behavior by observing the interaction an application Graphical User Interface (GUI). We describe in detail the SimIOHMM, a specific instance of *SimAlignGen* that extends the known Input-Output Hidden Markov Model (IOHMM). Empirical evaluations of the SimIOHMM show the dependence of the prediction accuracy on the introduced similarity bias, and the computational gains over the IOHMM.

1 Introduction

Many domains require building predictive models from multiple observed data sequences. Examples from the biological domain include protein and DNA sequence alignment or prediction, and from the financial domain include market performance prediction and risk analysis. In the computer networking domain, models of network performance or detection of illegal intrusions have also been learned from observed data sequences. Learning approaches for these domains (like Hidden Markov Model induction [1]) rely primarily on the sequence data itself and utilize little (if any) additional domain knowledge. In this paper we investigate a particular form of domain knowledge that we call similarity knowledge. We show how this knowledge can be employed in learning predictive models from sequential data, and empirically measure the impact of utilizing this additional source of knowledge.

A second thrust of this paper is to present a novel approach for using sequence modeling techniques like HMM learning for the problem of PBD [2, 3] described in Section 2. We will show that, in the PBD domain, similarity knowledge is readily available and that its use improves learning performance

Contributions of this paper include:

- A novel application of traditional sequence alignment algorithms to PBD for learning procedures with complex structure.

- The *SimAlignGen* class of algorithms, an extension of traditional HMMs that that adds a similarity function over the input as a new source of bias.
- An instance of an *SimAlignGen*algorithm, the SimIOHMM, implemented as part of a PBD system on the Microsoft Windows platform.
- An empirical evaluation of the SimIOHMM's ability to learn a real-world procedure from demonstrations and of its significant performance improvement over the IOHMM.

2 An HMM Approach to PBD

For the purposes of this paper, we define *programming by demonstration* as the problem of generating a procedure model consistent with a set of demonstrations. Each demonstration is a sequence of events, such as user actions and changes to the application GUIs. A procedure model is consistent with a demonstration if it correctly predicts the actions in the sequence given the prior events in that sequence. Existing PBD systems work well when there is a fixed number of steps in the procedure [4] or when the procedure author can identify the specific step to be generalized [5]. These assumptions are violated when a procedure contains a large number of steps and has complex structure, such as conditional branches. Known sequence learning algorithms like HMMs seem appropriate in these cases since they focus on the problem of identifying optimal sequence alignment.

In this section we briefly outline the primary components necessary for applying these sequence alignment algorithms in the PBD context. A user demonstrates procedures by performing actions, such as clicking the mouse or pressing keyboard keys, on an application's GUI. In response, the application updates the GUI contents. An *instrumentation component* captures both user and application actions. An *abstraction component* converts the stream of events recorded by the instrumentation into a sequence of *snapshot-action pairs*, called a *trace*. Logically, a snapshot-action pair represents the complete content of the GUI at a point in time, coupled with the action performed by the user. Using the snapshot-action representation we can reduce the problem of learning a procedure to that of predicting the user action from the content of the GUI (and perhaps its history).

The *learning algorithm* combines multiple traces into a procedure model, that can be automatically executed by an *execution component*. The ability of simultaneously combining multiple traces into a procedure model is a feature of our approach that differentiates it from other work in PBD.

3 The *SimAlignGen* Family of Algorithms

In the PBD domain the visual cues prevalent on GUIs provide a source of knowledge which can be explicitly used to augment the sequence data employed by traditional HMM learning. Typically, an expert can determine how far along a user is in performing a task by observing the content of the visible windows. We provide this visual similarity knowledge to our family of algorithms as a similarity function, which returns a real-valued score measuring "similarity" between two captured GUI snapshot action pairs (S,A). Formally: **Similarity** : $((S \times A) \times (S \times A)) \rightarrow \Re^+$. Thus, instances of the *SimAlignGen* family of algorithms accept an input set of traces, namely, of snapshot-action pairs, and a real-valued similarity function over the snapshot-action pairs. *SimAlignGen* algorithms first align the snapshot-action pairs by simultaneously employing three sources of constraint described blow, and then generate an executable procedure model based on the partitioning result. Here, the *alignment* of a set of traces is formally defined as a partition of the snapshot-action pairs. A useful alignment for our purposes is one that groups similar snapshot-action pairs, such that each set of the partition corresponds to what a human would think of as a step in the procedure model. The three sources of constraint are:

1. The alignment should preserve transitions between successive steps. For example, let trace 1 consist of step A followed by step B and trace 2 consist of step A' followed by B'; then aligning A with A' and B with B' is a good alignment, since it preserves the ordering of transitions within the traces.
2. The alignment should yield sets that can be *generalized*: for each partition set, we should be able to induce a predictive map from snapshot to action.
3. The snapshots in a partition set should be *similar* according to the provided similarity function.

Constructing a learner with the first two biases—transition preservation and generalization—is a difficult problem for which no optimal algorithm exists. One solution consists of iteratively alternating two steps: finding the best alignment of the training data consistent with a given transition and generalization structure, and finding the best transition and generalization structure consistent with a given alignment of the training data. If we represent the alignment by associating with each snapshot-action pair a probability distribution over the partition sets, we can immediately reduce the iterative algorithm to the Baum-Welch algorithm,an expectation-maximization (E-M) algorithm used to induce discrete Hidden Markov Models from sequences of symbols [1]. We interpret the E-step as a way of determining the best alignment of the sequences relative to a given HMM, and the M-step as a way of inducing the best procedure model given an alignment. For PBD applications, where user actions are often dependent on the current "place" within the procedure and on the content of the screen, it is additionally necessary to induce predictive mappings from inputs (snapshots) to outputs (actions) and next states. Bengio and Frasconi [6] introduced an extension to HMMs, called the Input-Output Hidden Markov Model, or IOHMM, that satisfies this assumption. IOHMMs predict the next state and the next output symbol as a function of the current state and of the current input symbol.

The third source of constraint above cannot be employed by either HMM or IOHMM algorithms, yet as we discussed it is a natural form of knowledge in the PBD domain. These algorithms do not take any form of explicit knowledge about the domain, rather they rely entirely on the dataset provided.

SimAlignGen algorithms extend Hidden Markov Model induction by incorporating this similarity domain knowledge as a bias on the alignments which the algorithm considers in its search for a predictive model of the observed data.

We now formally define the SimIOHMM by describing how it differs from the standard IOHMM as described in [6]. We use standard notational convention.

Bengio and Frasconi's IOHMM

The goal of a IOHMM is to model the *conditional* distribution of an output sequence $\mathbf{Y}$ given an input sequence $\mathbf{U}$ as an HMM, i.e., by postulating the existence of a hidden variable, the *state* X, belonging to a finite set $\mathcal{X}$, such that
$$\mathbb{P}\left[(\mathbf{U}_t, \mathbf{Y}_t, X_t) \mid \{(\mathbf{U}_j, \mathbf{Y}_j, X_j)\}_{j=1}^{t-1}\right] = \mathbb{P}\left[(\mathbf{U}_t, \mathbf{Y}_t, X_t) \mid X_{t-1}\right].$$
The same structure is inherited by the conditional distribution of the outputs given the inputs (i.e., $\mathbb{P}\left[(\mathbf{Y}_t, X_t) \mid \mathbf{U}_t, \{(\mathbf{U}_j, \mathbf{Y}_j, X_j)\}_{j=1}^{t-1}\right]$) that can now be written as $\mathbb{P}\left[(\mathbf{Y}_t, X_t) \mid \mathbf{U}_t, X_{t-1}\right]$. Note that this probability can be further decomposed as $\mathbb{P}\left[X_t \mid \mathbf{U}_t, X_{t-1}\right] \mathbb{P}\left[Y_t \mid X_t, \mathbf{U}_t, X_{t-1}\right] = \mathbb{P}\left[X_t \mid \mathbf{U}_t, X_{t-1}\right] \mathbb{P}\left[Y_t \mid X_t, \mathbf{U}_t\right]$, namely, as a conditional transition probability to state X_t given the previous state and the input at time t, and a conditional probability of the output at time t given the state and input at time t. Hence, inducing a IOHMM is equivalent to estimating the initial probability distribution over the states, $\mathbb{P}\left[X_0\right]$ (note that the first input is observed at $t = 1$), the transition probabilities $\mathbb{P}\left[X_t \mid \mathbf{U}_t, X_{t-1}\right]$, and the conditional output probabilities $\mathbb{P}\left[Y_t \mid X_t, \mathbf{U}_t\right]$. The transition an output probabilities are assumed to be time-independent, namely, for every s and t,
$$\mathbb{P}\left[X_t = a \mid \mathbf{U}_t = u, X_{t-1} = b\right] = \mathbb{P}\left[X_s = a \mid \mathbf{U}_s = u, X_{s-1} = b\right] \text{ and}$$
$$\mathbb{P}\left[Y_t = y \mid X_t = x, \mathbf{U}_t = u\right] = \mathbb{P}\left[Y_s = y \mid X_s = x, \mathbf{U}_s = u\right].$$
These assumptions make the IOHMM very flexible and yet computationally manageable. The IOHMM allows arbitrarily long time-dependence between the input-output pairs, and is therefore more powerful than a fixed-order Markov model. At the same time, the IOHMM can be efficiently induced from training data using the Baum-Welch algorithm, consisting of two steps: an Expectation step, where the training sequences are aligned to an existing model, and a Maximization step, there the model is updated given the alignment.

The IOHMM E-step efficiently computes a probability distribution over the state space for each input-output pair by means of two steps: the forward recursion computes, for each time t the joint probability of the state at time t and all outputs up to time t given the inputs up to time t; the backward recursion computes the probability of the outputs after time t, given the state at time t and the inputs from time t on. The results of the forward and backward recursions are then appropriately combined, for each t, to estimate the probability distribution over the states as well as the posterior transition probabilities.

The M-step efficiently recomputes the initial probability distribution over the states, the conditional transition probabilities given the current input, and the conditional distributions of the output given the current state and input either by maximum likelihood or with a generic likelihood estimation method. Bengio and Frasconi followed the latter approach, and used neural networks in the M-step. The efficiency of the M-step stems from the fact that the *global* maximization of the likelihood is performed by *separately* maximizing the likelihoods at each individual state, namely, by finding the parameters that maximize the transition and output probabilities for each state given the results of the expectation step.

The SimIOHMM

The SimIOHMM extends the IOHMM by further incorporating the bias described earlier in this Section. To this end, each hidden Markov state is associated with one or more representative inputs, as well as with a transition and output distribution. The representative inputs come into play during the E-step and are updated during the M-step, as follows.
The E-Step. The forward recursion is

$$\alpha_{i,t} = \mathbb{P}\left[\mathbf{y}_t \mid X_t = i, \mathbf{u}_t\right] \mathbb{S}\left(\mathbf{u}_t, \mathbf{v}_i\right) \sum_{\ell \in \mathcal{X}} \phi_{i,\ell}(\mathbf{u}_t) \alpha_{\ell, t-1}, \tag{1}$$

which adds to [6–Equation(20)] the additional term $\mathbb{S}(\mathbf{u}_t, \mathbf{v}_i)$, the similarly score between the input $\mathbf{u}_t$ and the representative sample $\mathbf{v}_i$ of state i, that provides the required bias. Similarity, the backward recursion is

$$\beta_{i,t} = \sum_{\ell \in \mathcal{X}} \mathbb{S}\left(\mathbf{u}_{t+1}, \mathbf{v}_\ell\right) \mathbb{P}\left[\mathbf{y}_{t+1} \mid X_{t+1} = \ell, \mathbf{u}_{t+1}\right] \phi_{\ell,i}(\mathbf{u}_{t+1}) \beta_{\ell, t+1}, \tag{2}$$

which again adds a bias term to [6–Equation(22)].[1]

The bias term $\mathbb{S}(\mathbf{u}_t, \mathbf{v}_i)$, a similarity score, is designed to concentrate the distribution over the states at time t onto those states having representative samples similar to $\mathbf{u}_t$. For sake of simplicity, assume that each state has a unique representative sample. Then $\mathbb{S}(\mathbf{u}_t, \mathbf{v}_i)$ is computed as follows: first, the distances $\{d(\mathbf{u}_t, \mathbf{v}_i)\}_{i=1}^{|\mathcal{X}|}$ between $\mathbf{u}_t$ and the representatives of the states are computed; then these distances are converted into a similarity score by means of a kernel $K(\cdot)$ (for example, a finite-support decreasing function or a Gaussian):

$$\mathbb{S}(\mathbf{u}_t, \mathbf{v}_i) = K\left(d(\mathbf{u}_t, \mathbf{v}_i)\right).$$

The definition of $\mathbb{S}(\cdot, \cdot)$ can be obviously extended to capture the similarities between input-output pairs, rather than between inputs. Adding the bias term substantially improves the training time and can improve the classification accuracy, as illustrated in the experiments section.
The M-step. The M-step of the SimIOHMM consists of the M-Step of the IOHMM, plus the recomputation of representative samples. For each HMM state, the sample with highest alignment probability becomes the new representative.

4 Experimental Results

We evaluate our *SimAlignGen* in two ways. We evaluate the utility of using a similarity bias for learning HMM models in a general setting using synthetic data where we can vary the "correctness" of similarity data presented. We then evaluate the predictive performance of this approach in a practical PBD setting implemented on the Microsoft Windows GUI where we measure the effectiveness of the *SimAlignGen* approach as well as the utility of the similarity bias.

---

[1] The small discrepancies with the actual Equation [6–Equation(22)] are due to typographical errors in the original paper.

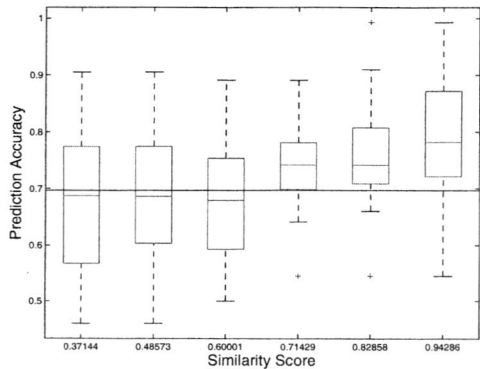

Fig. 1. Accuracy as a function of similarity score

Experiment 1: Effectiveness of similarity knowledge

We measure the accuracy of the SimIOHMM as a function of the correctness of the similarity information presented, and compare it to the accuracy of the IOHMM. We expect the performance of *SimAlignGen* algorithms to vary as a function of how well the similarity knowledge matches the process underlying the generated data. We quantify this degree of match by introducing a *similarity correctness* score. Given dataset generated by an HMM and a similarity function, we compute the similarities between each sample and the other samples in the dataset, and find its nearest neighbor. We then define the similarity correctness as the fraction of samples that were generated by the same HMM state as their nearest neighbor. Thus a score of 100% would imply that is possible to partition the dataset points into sets corresponding to the generating Markov nodes using the similarity function alone. Lesser scores are associated with increasing levels of "noise", or misinformation regarding the underlying generating process.

The data for the experiments is constructed as follows. We start with an HMM template with 10 hidden states. We instantiate an HMM from the template by randomly generating, for each node, a probability distribution on input (binary) feature vectors, a conditional probability distribution on the (binary) outputs given the inputs, and a conditional transition distribution given the inputs. The additional feature used to compute the similarity score is the index number for the state generating each data point to which a zero-mean Gaussian perturbation of chosen variance is added. Figure 1 shows the accuracy of SimIOHMM as a function of the correctness of the provided similarity knowledge. The graph is generated from 180 runs of the SimIOHMM obtained from three-fold cross validation of 60 data sets from different randomly generated HMM models. Each dataset is composed of 400 data-points (20 traces with 20 snapshot-action pairs in each) along with a varying Gaussian noise added to the similarity feature. A similarity correctness score and an accuracy were computed for each run. The resulting points are binned according to similarity score and then averaged to produce the predictive accuracies reported in the box plot.

The box plot shows the median, upper and lower quartile as well as the maximum and minimum accuracies obtained at each level.

The horizontal line just below 70% represents the average comparative IOHMM performance (which does not take into account similarity knowledge). As expected *SimAlignGen* outperforms IOHMMs when the similarity bias provides an accurate model of the underlying HMM. Conversely, learning performance is degraded by a similarity bias that does not represent well the model generating the data. In this experiment the cross-over point between the performance of the two algorithms is between 60% and 70% similarity correctness.

This result raises the question of what kind of correctness scores can we expect in practical applications to programming by demonstration. To investigate this question we used our system to observe eleven Microsoft Window®'s users whose task was to modify the DNS settings of the machine according to written instruction. We then annotated each snapshot-action pair with a label that specifies the corresponding documentation step, and computed the similarity correctness score for the Windows®-specific similarity function implemented in our system (This similarity functions combines several factors, including the previous action taken by the user, and the text on the title bar of the window with focus, etc). We finally obtained a similarity correctness of 88%, much above the 60-70% cross over point for the two algorithms. This is not unsurprising: different parts of an underlying application will intentionally have many redundantly distinguishing GUI features as cues to the user. *SimAlignGen* is a novel approach to leveraging those redundant cues towards inducing a procedure model.

Experiment 2: SimIOHMM training time

In our second set of experiments we measure the performance of the SimIOHMM as part of a PBD system for capturing procedures on the Microsoft Windows GUI. In addition to the gains in accuracy demonstrated above, we show that SimIOHMM can result in substantial reductions in training time and better scalability as a function of training set size when compared with IOHMMs. Figure 2(a) shows the average training time verses number of training traces.

In the figure, it is apparent that the from the viewpoint of training time, the SimIOHMM scales much better than the IOHMM, and that the ratio of the IOHMM training time to the SimIOHMM training time is superlinear in the number of training traces. The faster training time of the SimIOHMM is due to the fact that the training sets used to train the classifiers tend to be smaller. The main reason is that a snapshot-action pair can be aligned only with states having similar representative samples. A way of measuring this effect is by analyzing the dispersion of the alignment distributions $\gamma_n(t)$ for the training traces once convergence is reached. A measure of dispersion of a probability distribution is its entropy. Figure 2 (b) shows the average entropy (in bits) of the alignment at convergence as a function of the number of training traces. The experiments are the same used for Figure 2 (a). Due to the similarity bias, the SimIOHMM yields substantially more concentrated alignment probabilities than the IOHMM, and the difference between these entropies is an increasing function of the number of traces. These findings are also confirmed by the analysis of simulated data.

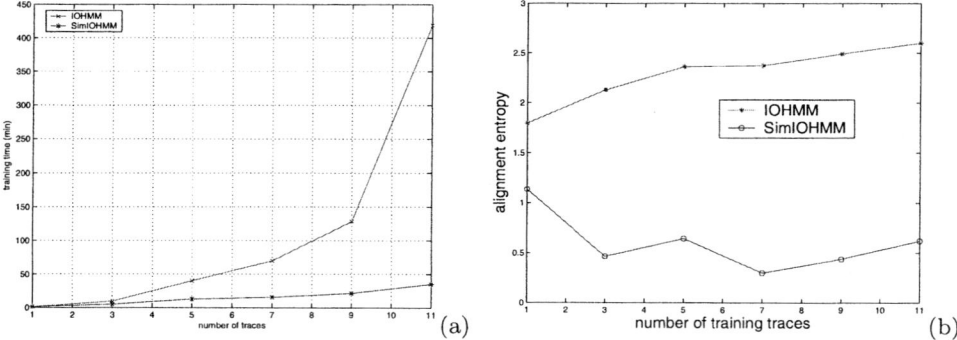

Fig. 2. (a) Training time for IOHMM and SimIOHMM as a function of the number of training traces. (b) Alignment entropy (in bits) for IOHMM and SimIOHMM as a function of the number of training traces.

5 Conclusions

This paper presents an approach to procedure model induction based on the idea of similarity-based alignment and generalization, and makes the following contributions: (i) a novel approach to PBD based on similarity-based alignment and generalization; (ii) the *SimAlignGen* class of algorithms that extend traditional sequence alignment algorithms by the addition of a third bias based on a *similarity metric*; (iii) an instance of an *SimAlignGen* algorithm, called SimIOHMM, which has been implemented as part of a programming by demonstration system on the Windows platform; and (iv) an empirical evaluation showing accuracy improvements as a function of synthetic similarity data, and large efficiency improvements over traces collected from a real-world procedure.

References

1. Rabiner, L.R., Juang, B.H.: An introduction to Hidden Markov Models. IEEE ASSP Magazine (1986) 4–15
2. Cypher, A., ed.: Watch what I do: Programming by demonstration. MIT Press, Cambridge, MA (1993)
3. Lieberman, H., ed.: Your Wish is My Command: Giving Users the Power to Instruct their Software. Morgan Kaufmann (2001)
4. Lau, T., Domingos, P., Weld, D.S.: Version space algebra and its application to programming by demonstration. In: Proc. Sevententh Int. Conf. on Machine Learning. (2000) 527–534
5. Maulsby, D., Witten, I.H.: Cima: an interactive concept learning system for end-user applications. Applied Artificial Intelligence **11** (1997) 653–671
6. Bengio, Y., Frasconi, P.: Input-Output HMM's for sequence processing. IEEE Trans. Neural Networks **7** (1996) 1231–1249

Fast Non-negative Dimensionality Reduction for Protein Fold Recognition

Oleg Okun[1], Helen Priisalu, and Alexessander Alves[2]

[1] Infotech Oulu, 4500, 90014 Oulu, Finland
[2] LIACC, Rua do Campo Alegre, 823, 4150 Porto, Portugal
FEUP, Rua Dr Roberto Frias, 4200-465 Porto, Portugal

Abstract. In this paper, dimensionality reduction via matrix factorization with nonnegativity constraints is studied. Because of these constraints, it stands apart from other linear dimensionality reduction methods. Here we explore nonnegative matrix factorization in combination with a classifier for protein fold recognition. Since typically matrix factorization is iteratively done, convergence can be slow. To alleviate this problem, a significantly faster (more than 11 times) algorithm is proposed.

1 Introduction

It is not uncommon that for certain data sets the number of attributes m is greater than the number of examples n. In such cases, the effect referred to as curse of dimensionality occurs, which negatively influences on clustering and classification of a given data set. Dimensionality reduction is typically used to mitigate this effect. The simplest way to reduce dimensionality is to linearly transform the original data. Given the original, high-dimensional data gathered in an $n \times m$ matrix $\mathbf{V}$, a transformed matrix $\mathbf{H}$, composed of m r-dimensional vectors ($r < n$ and often $r \ll n$), is obtained from $\mathbf{V}$ according to the following linear transformation $\mathbf{W}: \mathbf{V} \approx \mathbf{WH}$, where $\mathbf{W}$ is an $n \times r$ (basis) matrix. It is said that $\mathbf{W}$ and $\mathbf{H}$ are the factorized matrices and $\mathbf{WH}$ is a factorization of $\mathbf{V}$. PCA and ICA are well-known techniques performing this operation.

Nonnegative matrix factorization (NMF) also belongs to this class of methods. Unlike the others, it is based on nonnegativity constraints on all matrices involved. Thanks to this fact, it can generate a part-based representation, since no subtractions are allowed. Due that, it is claimed that NMF is capable of decomposing the whole object into meaningful parts, and having such a decomposition can make object recognition easier and often more accurate.

Lee and Seung [1] proposed a simple iterative algorithm for NMF and proved its convergence. The factorized matrices are initialized with positive random numbers before starting matrix updates. It is well known that initialization is of importance for any iterative algorithm: properly initialized, an algorithm converges faster. However, this issue was not yet investigated in case of NMF. In this paper, our contribution is *two modifications accelerating algorithm convergence*: 1) feature scaling prior to NMF and 2) combination of two techniques for mapping unseen data with theoretical proof of faster convergence.

Because of its straightforward implementation, NMF has been applied to pattern classification (faces, handwritten digits, documents) [2,3,4]. Here we extend the application of NMF to bioinformatics: NMF coupled with a classifier is applied to protein fold recognition. Our results show a dramatic acceleration of NMF convergence (greater than 11 times on average), compared to the conventional algorithm. Moreover, statistical analysis of the error rates demonstrates that dimensionality reduction done by NMF prior to the classification in reduced space does not cause significant accuracy degradations.

2 Nonnegative Matrix Factorization

Given the nonnegative matrices $\mathbf{V}$, $\mathbf{W}$ and $\mathbf{H}$ whose sizes are $n \times m$, $n \times r$ and $r \times m$, respectively, we aim at such factorization that $\mathbf{V} \approx \mathbf{WH}$. The value of r is selected according to the rule $r < \frac{nm}{n+m}$ in order to obtain dimensionality reduction. NMF provides the following simple learning rule guaranteeing monotonical convergence to a local maximum [1]:

$$W_{ia} \leftarrow W_{ia} \sum_{\mu} \frac{V_{i\mu}}{(WH)_{i\mu}} H_{a\mu} , \qquad (1)$$

$$W_{ia} \leftarrow \frac{W_{ia}}{\sum_j W_{ja}} , \qquad (2)$$

$$H_{a\mu} \leftarrow H_{a\mu} \sum_{i} W_{ia} \frac{V_{i\mu}}{(WH)_{i\mu}} . \qquad (3)$$

The matrices $\mathbf{W}$ and $\mathbf{H}$ are initialized with positive random values. Eqs. (1-3) iterate until convergence to a local maximum of the following objective function:

$$F = \sum_{i=1}^{n} \sum_{\mu=1}^{m} (V_{i\mu} \log(WH)_{i\mu} - (WH)_{i\mu}) . \qquad (4)$$

After learning the NMF basis functions, i.e. the matrix $\mathbf{W}$, unseen data in the matrix $\mathbf{H}_{new}$ are mapped to r-dimensional space by fixing $\mathbf{W}$ and using one of the following techniques:

1. randomly initializing $\mathbf{H}$ and iterating Eq. 3 until convergence,
2. initializing $\mathbf{H}_{new} = (\mathbf{W}^T\mathbf{W})^{-1}\mathbf{W}^T\mathbf{V}_{new}$, since $\mathbf{V}_{new} = \mathbf{WH}_{new}$, where $\mathbf{V}_{new}$ contains the new data.

Further we will call the first technique *iterative* while the second - *direct*, because the latter provides a straightforward non-iterative solution.

3 Our Contribution

We propose two modifications in order to accelerate convergence of the iterative NMF algorithm.

The first modification concerns feature scaling (normalization) linked to the initialization of the factorized matrices. Typically, these matrices are initialized with positive random numbers, say uniformly distributed between 0 and 1, in order to satisfy the nonnegativity constraints. Hence, elements of **V** (matrix of the original data) also need to be within the same range. Given that V_j is an n-dimensional feature vector, where $j = 1,\ldots,m$, its components V_{ij} are normalized as follows: V_{ij}/V_{kj}, where $k = \arg\max_l V_{lj}$. In other words, components of each feature vector are divided by the maximal value among them. As a result, feature vectors are composed of components whose nonnegative values do not exceed 1. Since all three matrices (**V**, **W**, **H**) have now entries between 0 and 1, it takes much less time to perform matrix factorization $\mathbf{V} \approx \mathbf{WH}$ (values of the entries in the factorized matrices do not have to grow/decrease much in magnitude in order to satisfy the stopping criterion for the objective function F in Eq. 4) than if **V** had the original (unnormalized) values. Given that the same iterative algorithm is used in both cases (unnormalized and normalized features), it takes less time to change from 0.5 to 0.7 (normalized feature) than to change from 0.5 to 10 (unnormalized feature), because on each step the convergence rate is the same. As additional benefit, MSE becomes much smaller, too, because a difference of the original (V_{ij}) and approximated $((WH)_{ij})$ values becomes smaller, given that mn is fixed. Though this modification is simple, it brings significant speed of convergence as will be shown below.

The second modification concerns initialization of NMF iterations for mapping unseen data (aka generalization), i.e. after the basis matrix **W** has been learned. Since such a mapping in NMF involves only the matrix **H** (**W** is kept fixed), its initialization is to be done. We propose to initially set **H** to $(\mathbf{W}^T\mathbf{W})^{-1}\mathbf{W}^T\mathbf{V}_{new}$, i.e. to the solution provided by the direct mapping technique with zeroing negative values as in Section 2, because 1) it provides a better initial approximation for $\mathbf{H}_{new}$ than a random guess, and 2) it moves the start of iterations closer toward the final point, since the objective function F in Eq. 4 is increasing [1], and the inequality $F^{direct} > F^{iter}$ always holds *at initialization* (theorem below proves this fact), where F^{direct} and F^{iter} stand for the values of F when using the direct and iterative techniques, respectively.

Theorem 1. *Given F^{direct} and F^{iter} are values of the objective function when mapping unseen data with the direct and iterative techniques, respectively. Then $F^{direct} - F^{iter} > 0$ always holds at the start of iterations when using Eq. 3.*

Proof. By definition,

$$F^{iter} = \sum_{i=1}^{n}\sum_{j=1}^{m}(V_{ij}\log(WH)_{ij} - (WH)_{ij}) ,$$

$$F^{direct} = \sum_{i=1}^{n}\sum_{j=1}^{m}(V_{ij}\log V_{ij} - V_{ij}) \ .$$

The difference $F^{direct} - F^{iter}$ is equal to

$$\sum_{i=1}^{n}\sum_{j=1}^{m}(V_{ij}\log V_{ij} - V_{ij} - V_{ij}\log(WH)_{ij} + (WH)_{ij}) =$$

$$\sum_{i=1}^{n}\sum_{j=1}^{m}\left(V_{ij}(\log\frac{V_{ij}}{(WH)_{ij}} - 1) + (WH)_{ij}\right) =$$

$$\sum_{i=1}^{n}\sum_{j=1}^{m}\left(V_{ij}\log\frac{V_{ij}}{10(WH)_{ij}} + (WH)_{ij}\right) \ .$$

Given all three matrices involved are nonnegative, the last expression is positive if either condition is satisfied:

1. $\log\frac{V_{ij}}{10(WH)_{ij}} > 0$,
2. $(WH)_{ij} > V_{ij}\log\frac{10(WH)_{ij}}{V_{ij}}$.

Let us introduce a new variable, t: $t = \frac{V_{ij}}{(WH)_{ij}}$. Then the above conditions can be written as

1. $\log\frac{t}{10} > 0$ or $\log t > 1$,
2. $1 > t\log\frac{t}{10}$ or $\log t < \frac{t+1}{t}$.

The first condition is satisfied if $t > 10$ whereas the second if $t < t_0$ ($t_0 \approx 12$). Therefore either $t > 10$ or $t < 12$ should be satisfied for $F^{direct} > F^{iter}$. Since the union of both conditions covers the whole interval $[0, +\infty[$, it means that $F^{direct} > F^{iter}$, independently of t, i.e. of whether $V_{ij} > (WH)_{ij}$ or not. Q.E.D. □

Because our approach combines both direct and iterative techniques for mapping unseen data, we will call it *iterative2*.

4 Summary of Our Algorithm

1. Scale both training and test data and randomly initialize the factorized matrices as described in Section 3. Choose r.
2. Iterate Eqs. 1-3 until convergence to obtain the NMF basis matrix $\mathbf{W}$ and to map training data to NMF (reduced) space.
3. Given $\mathbf{W}$, map test data by using the direct technique. Set to zero negative values in the resulting matrix $\mathbf{H}_{new}^{direct}$.
4. Fix the basis matrix and iterate Eq. 3 until convergence by using $\mathbf{H}_{new}^{direct}$ at initialization of iterations.

5 Experiments

Experiments with NMF involve estimation of the error rate when combining NMF and a classifier. Three techniques for generalization are used: direct, iterative, and iterative2. The training data are mapped into reduced space according to Eqs. 1-3 with simultaneous learning of the matrix **W**. Tests were repeated 10 times to collect statistics necessary for comparison of three generalization techniques. Each time, a different random initialization for learning the basis matrix **W** was used, but the same learned basis matrix was utilized in each run for all generalization techniques in order to create as fair comparison of three generalization techniques as possible.

Values of r (dimensionality of reduced space) were set to 25, 50, 75, and 88 (max), which constitutes 20%, 40%, 60%, and 71.2% of the original dimensionality, respectively. In all reported statistical tests $\alpha = 0.05$. All algorithms were implemented in MATLAB running on a Pentium 4 (3 GHz CPU, 1GB RAM).

5.1 Data

In bioinformatics, it is rather common to use a single data set in experiments, since many tasks in this field are much more difficult than those in general machine learning. A challenging data set [5] was used in experiments. The data set contains the 27 most populated folds represented by seven or more proteins. Ding and Dubchak already split it into the training and test sets, which we will use as other authors did. Feature vectors have 125 dimensions. The training set consists of 313 protein folds having no more than 35% of the sequence identity for aligned subsequences longer than 80 residues. The test set of 385 folds is composed of protein sequences of less than 40% identity with each other and less than 35% identity with the proteins of the first set. This, as well as multiple classes, many of which sparsely represented, render this task extremely difficult.

5.2 Classification Results

The K-Local Hyperplane Distance Nearest Neighbor (HKNN) [6] was selected as a classifier, since it demonstrated a competitive performance. Table 1 shows the error rates obtained with HKNN, SVM, and various neural networks when classifying protein folds in the original, 125-dimensional space.

The *normalized* features were used since feature normalization prior to HKNN increases classification accuracy. The optimal values for two parameters of HKNN, K and λ, determined via cross-validation, are 7 and 8, respectively.

Let us now turn to the error rates in dimensionally reduced space. For each value of r, NMF followed by HKNN were repeated 10 times. As a results, a 40x6 matrix containing the error rates was generated. This matrix is then subjected to the one-way analysis of variance (ANOVA) and multiple comparison tests in order to make statistically driven conclusions. Table 5.2 shows identifiers associated with the generalization techniques. Error bars for all generalization techniques are given in Fig. 1.

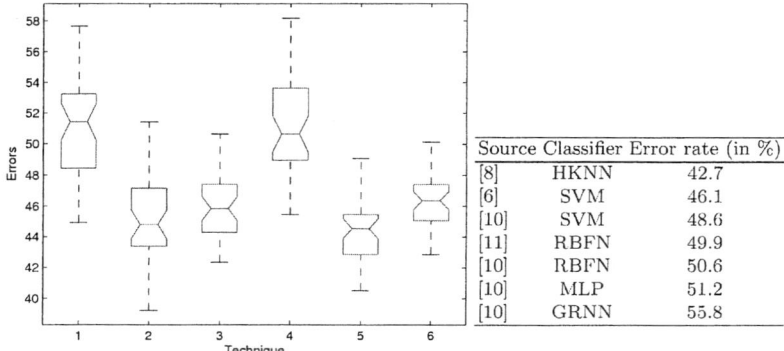

Fig. 1. (a) Error bars resulting from NMF using six generalization techniques; (b) Classification errors on the original space of the protein folds dataset

The one-way ANOVA test is first utilized in order to find out whether the mean error rates of all six techniques are the same (null hypothesis $H_0 : \mu_1 = \mu_2 = \cdots = \mu_6$) or not. If the returned p-value is smaller than $\alpha = 0.05$, the null hypothesis is rejected, which implies that the mean error rates are not the same. The next step is to determine which pairs of means are significantly different, and which are not by means of the multiple comparison test.

Table 5.2 contains results of the multiple comparison test and it is seen that these results confirm that the direct technique stands apart from both iterative techniques. The main conclusions from Table 5.2 are $\mu_1 = \mu_4$ and $\mu_2 = \mu_3 = \mu_5 = \mu_6$, i.e. there are two groups of techniques, and the mean of the first group is larger than that of the second group.

The last column in Table 5.2 points to the very interesting result: whether feature normalization prior to NMF is applied or not, the standard deviation of the error rate of our technique is lower than that for the conventional one, which, in turn, is lower than the standard deviation for the direct technique. It implies that our modifications of NMF led to a *visible reduction in the deviation of classification error*! This reduction is caused by shrinking the search space of possible factorizations, and it is larger if normalization prior to NMF is used.

Table 1. Mean error for each generalization technique (standard error 0.4)

Identifier	Technique	Scaling prior to NMF	Mean error	Std. deviation
1	Direct	No	50.93	3.08
2	Iterative	No	44.94	2.52
3	Iterative2	No	45.98	2.11
4	Direct	Yes	51.38	3.31
5	Iterative	Yes	44.52	2.13
6	Iterative2	Yes	46.32	1.72

Fast Non-negative Dimensionality Reduction 671

Table 2. Results of the multiple comparison test

Identifier	Identifier 2	Lower bound	Difference	Upper bound	Outcome
4	5	5.25	6.87	8.48	Reject $H_0 : \mu_4 \neq \mu_5$
4	2	4.83	6.45	8.07	Reject $H_0 : \mu_4 \neq \mu_2$
4	3	3.79	5.41	7.03	Reject $H_0 : \mu_4 \neq \mu_3$
4	6	3.45	5.07	6.69	Reject $H_0 : \mu_4 \neq \mu_6$
4	1	-1.16	0.46	2.07	Accept $H_0 : \mu_4 = \mu_1$
1	5	4.79	6.41	8.03	Reject $H_0 : \mu_1 \neq \mu_5$
1	2	4.38	5.99	7.61	Reject $H_0 : \mu_1 \neq \mu_2$
1	3	3.34	4.96	6.57	Reject $H_0 : \mu_1 \neq \mu_3$
1	6	3.00	4.61	6.23	Reject $H_0 : \mu_1 \neq \mu_6$
6	5	0.18	1.80	3.42	Reject $H_0 : \mu_6 \neq \mu_5$
6	2	-0.24	1.38	3.00	Accept $H_0 : \mu_6 = \mu_2$
3	5	-0.16	1.46	3.07	Accept $H_0 : \mu_3 = \mu_5$

Table 3. Gains in time resulted from modifications of the conventional NMF algorithm

	Gain due to scaling prior to NMF for learning generalization learning+generalization					Gain due to initialization for generalization	
r	R_1	R_2	R_3	R_4	R_5	R_6	R_7
88	11.9	11.4	10.4	11.7	11.5	1.5	1.4
75	13.8	12.9	13.1	13.6	13.7	1.6	1.6
50	13.2	11.1	12.5	12.6	13.1	1.6	1.7
25	9.5	6.4	8.8	8.7	9.5	1.6	2.2
Average	12.1	10.4	11.2	11.6	11.9	1.6	1.8

That is, our initialization eliminates some potentially erroneous solutions before iterations even start and leads to more stable classification error.

One can say that the error rates in reduced space are larger than the error rate (42.7%) achieved in the original space. However, it is not, in general, uncommon to observe similar effects when doing classification after dimensionality reduction (see, e.g. [7]). Nevertheless, we observed that sometimes error in reduced space can be lower than 42.7: for example, the minimal error when applying the iterative technique with no scaling before NMF and $r = 50$ is 39.22, while the minimal error when using the iterative2 technique under the same conditions is 42.34. Varying errors can be attributed to the fact that NMF factorization of a given matrix may not be unique. Finally, even though NMF+HKNN led to the higher error rates than HKNN alone, the former was nevertheless superior (see Tables 1 and 5.2) to neural networks and comparable to SVMs, applied without NMF.

5.3 Time Results

Table 3 presents speed gains resulted from our modifications for different dimensionalities of reduced space. R1 stands for the speed gains due to scaling on the task of learning and mapping training data. R2 and R3 are the speed gains obtained due to scalling on the generalization task using iterative and iterative2. R4 and R5 are the same gains obtained on the task of training followed by generalization. R6 and R7 are the speed gains obtained due to applying iterative2 instead of iterative versus scaling. As a result, the average gain in time obtained with our modifications is more than 11 times.

6 Conclusion

The main contribution of this work is two modifications of the basic NMF algorithm and its practical application to a challenging real-world task, namely protein fold recognition. The first modification concerns feature scaling before NMF while the second modification combines two known generalization techniques, which we called direct and iterative; the former is used as a starting point for updates of the latter, thus leading to a new generalization technique. We proved (both theoretically and experimentally) that our technique converges faster than the ordinary iterative technique. On the data set studied, the average gain in convergence speed exceeds 11 times.

When combining the modified NMF with a classification algorithm, statistical analysis of the obtained results indicates that the mean error associated with the direct technique is higher than that related to either iterative technique while both iterative techniques lead to the statistically similar error rates. Since our technique provides a faster mapping of unseen data, it is advantageous to apply it instead of the ordinary one. In addition, our technique results in a smaller deviation of classification error, thus making classification more stable.

References

1. Lee, D., Seung, H.: Learning the parts of objects by non-negative matrix factorization. Nature 401 (1999) 788-791
2. Buciu, I.,Pitas, I.: Application of non-negative and local non-negative matrix factorization to facial expression recognition. In: Proceedings of the Seventeenth International Conference on Pattern Recognition, Cambridge, UK. (2004) 288-291
3. Chen, X., Gu, L., Li, S., Zhang, H.J.: Learning representative local features for face detection. In: Proceedings of the 2001 IEEE Conference on Computer Vision and Pattern Recognition, Kauai, HW. (2001) 1126-1131
4. Guillamet, D.e.a.: Introducing a weighted non-negative matrix factorization for image classification. Pattern Recognition Letters 24 (2003) 2447-2454
5. Ding, C.,Dubchak, I.: Multi-class protein fold recognition using support vector machines and neural networks. Bioinformatics 17 (2001) 349-358
6. Vincent, P., Bengio, Y.: K-local hyperplane and convex distance nearest neighbor algorithms. In Dietterich, T., Becker, S., Ghahramani, Z., eds.: Advances in Neural Information Processing Systems 14. MIT Press, Cambridge, MA (2002) 985-992
7. Pal, N., Chakraborty, D.: Some new features for protein fold recognition. In: LNCS - ICANN/ICONIP 2003. Volume 2714. Springer (2003) 1176-1183

Mode Directed Path Finding

Irene M. Ong[1], Inês de Castro Dutra[2], David Page[1], and Vítor Santos Costa[2]

[1] Department of Biostatistics and Medical Informatics,
University of Wisconsin – Madison, WI 53706 USA
[2] COPPE/Sistemas, UFRJ
Centro de Tecnologia, Block H-319, Cx. Postal 68511
Rio de Janeiro, Brasil

Abstract. Learning from multi-relational domains has gained increasing attention over the past few years. Inductive logic programming (ILP) systems, which often rely on hill-climbing heuristics in learning first-order concepts, have been a dominating force in the area of multi-relational concept learning. However, hill-climbing heuristics are susceptible to local maxima and plateaus. In this paper, we show how we can exploit the links between objects in multi-relational data to help a first-order rule learning system direct the search by explicitly traversing these links to find paths between variables of interest. Our contributions are twofold: (i) we extend the *pathfinding* algorithm by Richards and Mooney [12] to make use of *mode declarations*, which specify the mode of call (input or output) for predicate variables, and (ii) we apply our extended path finding algorithm to *saturated bottom clauses*, which anchor one end of the search space, allowing us to make use of background knowledge used to build the saturated clause to further direct search. Experimental results on a medium-sized dataset show that path finding allows one to consider interesting clauses that would not easily be found by Aleph.

1 Introduction

Over the past few years there has been a surge of interest in learning from multi-relational domains. Applications have ranged from bioinformatics [9], to web mining [2], and security [7]. Typically, learning from multi-relational domains has involved learning rules about distinct entities so that they can be classified into one category or another. However, there are also interesting applications that are concerned with the problem of learning whether a number of entities are connected. Examples of these include determining whether two proteins interact in a cell, whether two identifiers are aliases, or whether a web page refers to another web page; these are examples of link mining [6]. A number of approaches for exploiting link structure have been proposed; most of these approaches are graph based, including SUBDUE [3], and ANF [10].

Our focus is on first-order learning systems such as ILP. Most of the approaches in ILP rely on hill-climbing heuristics in order to avoid the combinatorial explosion of hypotheses that can be generated in learning first-order concepts. However, hill-climbing is susceptible to local maxima and local plateaus, which is an important factor for large datasets where the branching factor per node can be very large [4, 5]. Ideally, saturation-based search and a good scoring method should eventually lead us to interesting clauses, however, the search space can grow so quickly that we risk never reaching an interesting path in a reasonable amount of time (see Figure 1). This prompted us to consider alternative ways, such as *pathfinding* [12], to constrain the search space.

Richards and Mooney [12] realized that the problem of learning first-order concepts could be represented using graphs. Thus, using the intuition that if two nodes interact there must exist an explanation of the interaction, they proposed that the explanation should be a connected path linking the two nodes. However, pathfinding was originally proposed in the context of the FOIL ILP system, which does not rely on creating a *saturated clause*. A seminal work in directing the search in ILP systems was the use of *saturation* [14], which generalizes literals in the seed example to build a *bottom clause* [8], which anchors one end of the search space. Hence, we propose to find paths in the saturated clause.

The original pathfinding algorithm assumes the background knowledge forms an undirected graph. In contrast, the saturated clause is obtained by using *mode declarations*: in a nutshell, a literal can only be added to a clause if the literal's *input* variables are known to be bound. Mode declarations thus embed directionality in the graph formed by literals. Our major insight is that a saturated clause for a moded program can be described as a directed *hypergraph*, which consists of nodes and hyperarcs that connect a nonempty set of nodes to one target node. Given this, we show that path finding can be reduced to reachability in the hypergraph, whereby each *hyperpath* will correspond to a hypothesis. However, we may be interested in non-minimal paths and in the composition of paths. We thus propose and evaluate an algorithm that can enumerate all such hyperpaths according to some heuristic.

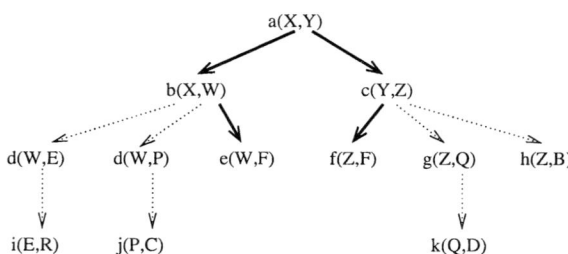

Fig. 1. Search space induced by a saturated clause. The literal at the root of the graph represents the head of the saturated clause. All the other literals in the graph are literals from the body of the saturated clause. Bold arcs indicate a possibly interesting path linking X to Y. Dotted arcs indicate parts of the search space that will not lead to determining connectivity of X and Y.

2 The Saturated Clause and Hypergraph

The similarities between the properties of a saturated clause and a hypergraph provide a natural mapping from one to the other. A directed hypergraph $\mathcal{H}$ is defined by a set of nodes N and a set of hyperarcs H. A hyperarc has a nonempty set of source nodes $S \subseteq N$ linked to a single target node $i \in N$ [1].

A saturated clause can be mapped to a hypergraph in the following way. First, as a saturated clause is formed by a set of literals, it is thus natural to say that each literal L_i is a node in the hypergraph. Second, we observe that each literal or node L_i may need several input arguments, and that each input argument may be provided from a number of other literals or nodes. Thus, if a node L_i has a set of input variables, I_i, each hyperarc is given by a set of literals generating I_i and L_i. Specifically, a mapping can be generated as follows:

1. Each node corresponds to a literal, L_i.
2. Each hyperarc with $N' \subseteq N$ nodes is generated by a set $\mathcal{V}$ of $i-1$ variables $V_1, \ldots, V_{i-1}$ appearing in literals $L_1, \ldots, L_{i-1}$. The mapping is such that
   (i) every variable $V_k \in I_i$ appears as an output variable of node L_k
   (ii) every variable V_k appears as argument k in the input variables, I_i, of L_i.

Intuitively, the definition says that nodes in $L_1, \ldots, L_{N'-1}$ with output variables that generates input variables for node $L_{N'}$, will be connected by hyperarcs. Note that if node $L_{N'}$ has a single input argument, the hyperarc will reduce to a single arc. Note also that the same variable may appear as different input arguments, or that the same literal may provide different output variables.

Figure 2a shows an example saturated clause and resulting hypergraph. The literal at the root of the graph, $a(X, Y)$, is the head of the saturated clause. Other literals in the graph appear in the body of the saturated clause. All literals of arity 2 have mode $+, -$, that is, input and output. Literal $e(F, B, D)$, has arity 3 and mode $+, +, -$. Arcs in the figure correspond to dependencies induced by variables, thus there is an arc between $c(X, W)$ and $d(W, F)$ because $d(W, F)$ requires input variable W. On the other hand, there is no arc between $c(X, B)$ and $f(C, B)$ since variable B is an output variable in both cases. All of the literals except $e(F, B, D)$ has a single input variable, hence those hyperarcs consists of a single arc. However, there are four hyperarcs for node $e(F, B, D)$; they are $d(W, F), c(X, B), g(A, F)$ and $f(C, B)$.

Before we present the path finding algorithm, we need to perform a simple transformation. The graph for a saturated clause is generated from the seed example, L_0. If the seed example has M arguments, it generates M variables, which we transform as follows:

1. Generate M new nodes L'_j, where $j = 1, ..., M$, such that each node will have one of the variables in L_0. Each such node will have an output variable V_j.
2. Replace the edge between L_0 and some other node induced by the variable V_j by an edge from the new node L'_j.

Figure 2b shows this transformation for the hypergraph in Figure 2a. Path generation thus reduces to finding all hyperpaths that start from nodes $L'_1, \ldots, L'_M$.

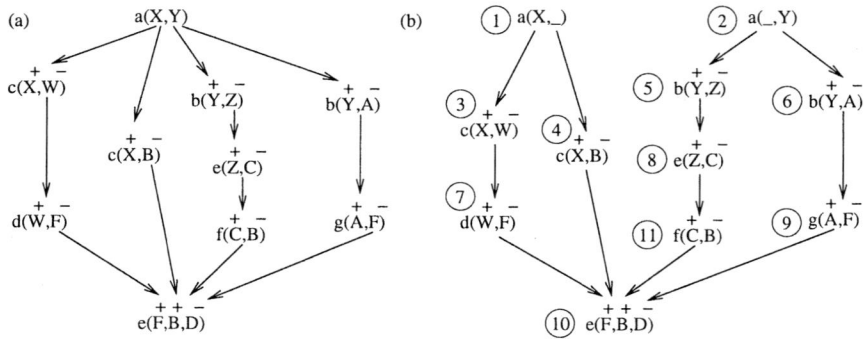

Fig. 2. (a) Hypergraph of our example saturated clause where $a(X,Y)$ is the head of the clause and '+' indicates input variable, '−' indicates output variable: $a(X,Y) \leftarrow c(X,W), c(X,B), b(Y,Z), b(Y,A), d(W,F), e(Z,C), g(A,F), e(F,B,D), f(C,B)$. (b) Transformation of hypergraph (a) splits the head literal into its component arguments, which then serve as different sources for the path finding algorithm. The number preceeding each literal indicates the label that will be used for that literal in Figure 3.

3 Algorithm

In directed graphs, a path π is a sequence of edges $e_1, e_2, \ldots, e_k$ and nodes $n_1, n_2, \ldots, n_k$, such that $e_i = (n_{i-1}, n_i), 1 \leq i \leq k$. The shortest hyperpath problem is the extension of the classic shortest path problem to hypergraphs. The problem of finding shortest hyperpaths is well known [1, 11]. We do not require optimal hyperpaths; rather, we want to be able to enumerate all possible paths, and we want to do it in the most flexible way, so that we can experiment with different search strategies and heuristics.

We present our path finding algorithm through the transformed hypergraph shown in Figure 2b. First, we want to emphasize that our goal is to generate paths in the 'path finding' sense, which is slightly different from the graph theoretical sense. More precisely, a hyperpath will lead from a node to a set of other nodes in the hypergraph (i.e. a *path* is a set of hyperpaths), each starting from different source nodes, such that the two hyperpaths have a variable in common. For example, in Figure 2b, nodes $\{1,4\}$ form a hyperpath, and nodes $\{2,5,8,11\}$ form another hyperpath. Since nodes 4 and 11 share variable B, $\{1,2,4,5,8,11\}$ form a *path*. Our algorithm generates paths as *combinations* of hyperpaths.

Given hypergraph $\mathcal{H}$, which includes information for input and output variables for each node or literal, *source* nodes and desired $maxdepth$ (a function of clause length), we describe an algorithm that returns a list of paths connecting all input variables. Figure 3 illustrates our path finding algorithm on the example hypergraph in Figure 2b. The numbered nodes in Figure 3 correspond to the labels of literals in Figure 2b. The depth of the graph is indicated on the left hand side. Current paths are expanded at each depth if the node to be expanded has its input variables bound. Otherwise, they are crossed out (e.g., $P(2,2)$ and $P(3,3)$). $VariableSet(s,d)$ represents the set of variables reachable

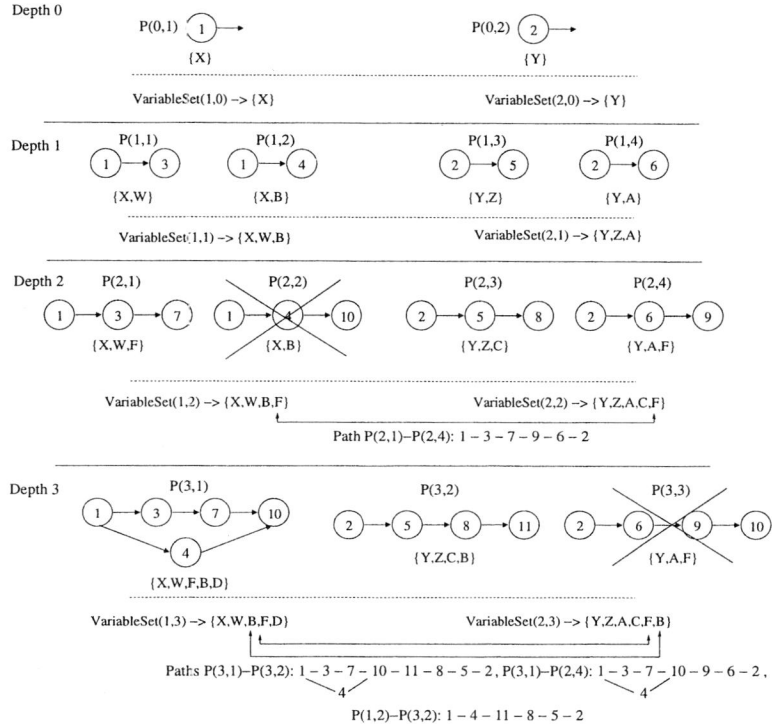

Fig. 3. Illustration of path finding algorithm using mode declarations. The numbered nodes in the graphs are the labels of literals in Figure 3.

from s at depth d. They are used to find common variables between variable sets of different sources at a particular depth. Hyperpaths found so far are indicated by $P(d, n)$, where d indicates the depth and n is the node index at that depth. Paths found are denoted $P(d, n_1) - P(d, n_2)$.

For each source and each depth, starting at depth 1, the algorithm proceeds:

1. Expand paths from previous depth, $d - 1$, only if **input** variables for the newly expanded node, n, exist in $VariableSet(s, d-1)$ of the previous depth and are bound by parents reachable at the current depth (i.e., all n's **input** variables are bound by parent nodes which contain n's **input** variables).
2. Place all variables reachable from s at current depth d in $VariableSet(s, d)$.
3. Check $VariableSet$ of each source at the current depth for an intersection of variables; for each variable in the intersection create paths from permutations of all nodes containing the variable, including those from previous depths.

Depth 0 corresponds to the initial configuration with our 2 source nodes, 1 and 2, which we represent as hyperpaths $P(0, 1)$ and $P(0, 2)$ respectively. The variables of source nodes 1 and 2, X and Y are placed into their respective variable sets ($VariableSet(1, 0)$ and $VariableSet(2, 0)$). We begin at Depth 1. Node 1 has two hyperpaths of size 2; one to node 3 (shown by hyperpath $P(1, 1)$)

and the other to node 4 ($P(1,2)$). Node 2 can reach nodes 5 and 6 giving hyperpaths $P(1,3)$ and $P(1,4)$. At this depth we can reach variables W and B from X, and variables Z and A from Y, indicated by $VariableSet(1,1)$ and $VariableSet(2,1)$. Since we do not have an intersection of the variable sets, we cannot build a path.

Depth 2 corresponds to expanding the hyperpaths of nodes 3, 4, 5 and 6. Hyperpath $P(1,1)$ can reach node 7 allowing X to reach variable F. Hyperpath $P(1,2)$ tries to expand to node 10, but this hyperpath only contains variable B, whereas node 10 requires both F and B as input, hence $P(2,2)$ is not expanded (crossed out). Hyperpath $P(1,3)$ can be expanded with 8, and hyperpath $P(1,4)$ can be extended with node 9. At this point we have hyperpaths from the first argument reaching variables W, B, F, and from the second argument reaching Z, A, C, F. Variable F can be reached with hyperpaths starting at the nodes that define variables X and Y, so we have a path. We thus find that if we combine hyperpaths $P(2,1)$ and $P(2,4)$ we have our first path: 1, 3, 7, 9, 6, 2 ($P(d, n_1) - P(d, n_2)$).

At Depth 3, hyperpath $P(2,1)$ can reach node 10 by merging with hyperpath $P(1,2)$. This creates the hyperpath $P(3,1)$ which reaches variables X, W, F, B, D. Hyperpath $P(2,3)$ is expanded to include node 11 but hyperpath $P(2,4)$ cannot be expanded to include node 10 as it does not contain variable B required as an input variable for node 10. Hence $P(3,3)$ is omitted. Now we have two new hyperpaths that can be combined between themselves and with older hyperpaths to generate new paths. Hyperpath $P(3,1)$ reaches variables X, W, F, B, D. We can build a new path by connecting $P(3,1)$ with hyperpath $P(3,2)$, as they both share variable B. $P(3,2)$ can also be connected to $P(2,4)$, as they both share F. Hyperpaths $P(3,2)$ and $P(1,2)$ share variable B, so we can generate the new path $P(3,2) - P(1,2)$. For hyperpaths that are already a path, as they touch X and Y, we can further extend them by merging them with other hyperpaths, obtaining non-minimal paths.

4 Experimental Evaluation

Paths found can be used in a number of ways. One way is to use Richards and Mooney's method to perform search by generating a number of paths, and then refining them [12, 15]. Alternatively, one can consider the paths found as a source of extra information that can be used to extend the background knowledge (i.e., add paths as background knowledge). In this case, paths can be seen as intensional definitions for new predicates in the background knowledge.

We used the UW-CSE dataset by Richardson and Domingos [13] for a first study of path finding on a heavily relational dataset. The dataset concerns learning whether one entity is advised by other entity based on real data from the University of Washington CS Department. The example distribution are skewed as we have 113 positive examples versus 2711 negative examples. Following the

Table 1. Theory Comparison

Folds	Aleph		Path Finding	
	# Clauses	Avg Clause Length	# Clauses	Avg Clause Length
Theory	2	4.5	2	5
AI	3	3.7	2	5.5
Graphics	3	4	2	6
Languages	1	3	3	7
Systems	1	4	3	5.7

Table 2. Test Set Performance (results given as percentage)

Folds	Aleph			Path Finding		
	Recall	Precision	F1 measure	Recall	Precision	F1 measure
Theory	38	27	32	81	11	19
AI	63	9	16	75	12	21
Graphics	85	46	60	95	20	33
Languages	22	100	36	33	100	50
Systems	87	8	15	82	9	16

original authors, we divided the data into 5 folds, each one corresponding to a different group in the CS Department. We perform learning in two ways for our control and experiment. In the first approach, we used Aleph to generate a set of clauses. In the second approach, we used path finding to find paths, which are treated as clauses. Further, we allow Aleph to decorate paths with attributes by trying to refine each literal on each path.

We were interested in maximizing performance in the precision recall space. Thus, we extended Aleph to support scoring using the f-measure. The search space for this experiment is relatively small, so we would expect standard Aleph search to find most paths. The two systems do find different best clauses, as shown in Table 1 which show both number of clauses and average clause length, including the head literal. Although most of the clauses found by Aleph are paths, the path finding implementation does find longer paths that are not considered by Aleph and also performs better on the training set.

Table 2 summarizes performance on the test set. This dataset is particularly hard as each fold is very different from the other [13], thus performance on the training set may not carry to the testing set. Both approaches perform similarly on the Systems fold. The AI fold is an example where both approaches learn a common rule, but path finding further finds an extra clause which performs very well on the training set, but badly on the test data. On the other hand, for the Languages fold both approaches initially found the same clause, but path finding goes on to find two other clauses, which in this case resulted in better performance. We were surprised that for both Graphics and Systems, path finding found good relatively small clauses that were not found by Aleph.

5 Conclusions and Future Work

We have presented a novel algorithm for path finding in moded programs. Our approach takes advantage of mode information to reduce the number of possible paths and generate only legal combinations of literals. Our algorithm is based on the idea that the saturated clause can be represented as a hypergraph, and the use of hyperpaths within the hypergraph to compose the final paths. Muggleton used a similar intuition in *seed* based search, using a heuristic to classify clauses: a clause's score depends on coverage and the distance the literals have to each entity [8]. In contrast, our approach is independent of scoring function.

Preliminary results on a medium sized dataset showed that path finding allows one to consider a number of interesting clauses that would not easily be considered by Aleph. On the other hand, path finding does seem to generate longer clauses, which might be more vulnerable to overfitting. In future work we plan to combine paths using the approach in Davis *et al.* [4] as well as apply this algorithm to larger datasets, where path finding is necessary to direct search.

Acknowledgments

Support for this work was partially funded by U.S. Air Force grant F30602-01-2-0571. The first author acknowledges support from NLM training grant 5T15LM005359. This work was done while Inês and Vítor were visiting UW-Madison. Finally, we thank Ian Alderman for helpful discussions and Rich Maclin for comments on the paper.

References

1. G. Ausiello, R. Giaccio, G. Italiano, and U. Nanni. Optimal traversal of directed hypergraphs. Technical report, Dipartimento di Informatica e Sistemistica, Universit di Roma La Sapienza, 1997.
2. S. Chakrabarti. *Mining the Web*. Morgan Kaufman, 2002.
3. D. Cook and L. Holder. Graph-based data mining. *IEEE Intelligent Systems*, 15:32–41, 2000.
4. J. Davis, I. Dutra, D. Page, and V. S. Costa. Establishing identity equivalence in multi-relational domains. In *Proc. of Intelligence Analysis*, 2005.
5. J. Davis, V. Santos Costa, I. Ong, D. Page, and I. Dutra. Using bayesian classifiers to combine rules. In *3rd Workshop on MRDM at KDD*, 2004.
6. L. Getoor. Link mining: A new data mining challenge. *SIGKDD Explorations*, 5:84–89, 2003.
7. D. Jensen. Prospective assessment of AI technologies for fraud detection: A case study. In *Working Papers of the AAAI-97 Workshop on Artificial Intelligence Approaches to Fraud Detection and Risk Management*, 1997.
8. S. Muggleton. Inverse entailment and Progol. *New Generation Computing*, 13:245–286, 1995.
9. D. Page and M. Craven. Biological applications of multi-relational data mining. *SIGKDD Explorations*, 5:69–79, 2003.
10. C. Palmer, P. Gibbons, and C. Faloutsos. Anf: A fast and scalable tool for data mining in massive graphs. In *Proc. of ACM SIGKDD on Knowledge Discovery and Data Mining*, 2002.

11. G. Ramalingam and T. W. Reps. An incremental algorithm for a generalization of the shortest-path problem. *Journal of Algorithms*, 21:267–305, 1996.
12. B. Richards and R. Mooney. Learning relations by pathfinding. In *National Conference on AI*, pages 50–55, 1992.
13. M. Richardson and P. Domingos. Markov logic networks. Technical report, Dept. of Computer Science and Engineering, University of Washington, Seattle, WA, 2004.
14. C. Rouveirol. Flattening and saturation: Two representation changes for generalization. *Machine Learning*, 14:219–232, 1994.
15. S. Slattery and M. Craven. Combining statistical and relational methods for learning in hypertext domains. In *Proc. of ILP*, pages 38–52, 1998.

Classification with Maximum Entropy Modeling of Predictive Association Rules

Hieu X. Phan[1], Minh L. Nguyen[1], S. Horiguchi[2], Bao T. Ho[1], and Y. Inoguchi[1]

[1] Japan Advanced Institute of Science and Technology,
1-1, Asahidai, Tatsunokuchi, Ishikawa, 923-1211, Japan
{hieuxuan, nguyenml, inoguchi, bao}@jaist.ac.jp
[2] Tohoku University, Aoba 6-3-09 Sendai,
980-8579, Japan
susumu@ecei.tohoku.ac.jp

Abstract. This paper presents a new classification model in which a classifier is built upon predictive association rules (PARs) and the maximum entropy principle (maxent). In this model, PARs can be seen as confident statistical patterns discovered from training data with strong dependencies and correlations among data items. Maxent, on the other hand, is an approach to build an estimated distribution having maximum entropy while obeying a potentially large number of useful features observed in empirical data. The underlying idea of our model is that PARs have suitable characteristics to serve as features for maxent. As a result, our classifier can take advantage of both the useful correlation and confidence of PARs as well as the strong statistical modeling capability of maxent. The experimental results show that our model can achieve significantly higher accuracy in comparison with the previous methods.

1 Introduction

Building efficient classifiers is a major task of machine learning research. Given a training set of data instances together with their class labels, the classification task is to induce a classifier that can predict labels for unseen instances. Traditional methods for this task have followed various approaches like rule learning [5] [6], decision trees [21], and statistical models (e.g., Naive Bayes [10]).

With the emergence of high–performance data mining techniques for large–scale databases, recent studies have shown that associative classification, using confident PARs discovered from training data, is competitive with the traditional methods in terms of both accuracy and scalability. The associative classification methods, such as CBA [16], CAEP [9], CMAR [17], and ART [3], build classifiers based on confident PARs whose consequent is a class label. Since the number of PARs is usually large, these methods attempt to select a subset by pruning the original set according to some heuristic assumption. The selected rules are then used to predict labels for new instances in a number of ways: ranking and searching for the most appropriate rule (CBA), computing an aggregated differentiating score based on emerging patterns to determine the most suitable class

(CAEP), analyzing to select a small subset of the most related rules and making a collective classification decision on that subset (CMAR), and classifying with a decision list of PARs which is built by using Occam's razor as an inductive bias (ART), i.e., giving a higher priority to simpler hypotheses.

This presents a new strategy to build a classifier upon PARs and maxent. In our approach, those PARs are treated as features/constraints of the maxent distribution, and each of them is associated with a learnable weight. Training the classifier is to find the weight values that maximize the entropy of the above distribution. Once trained, the classifier can predict a label for each new data instance by summing over the learned weights of PARs belonging to different class labels in order to determine the most appropriate one. The main motivation of our approach can be summarized as follows.

- PARs are confident facts with highly correlated conjunctions of data items at their antecedent. And they, in a sense, can be viewed as complex statistic patterns hidden in empirical data. Thus, incorporating those PARs into a statistical model means that we can project the original feature space into a richer one where PARs can cover and control various classifying situations.
- Maxent is a powerful statistical model that can include millions of overlapping, non–independent features/constraints, and thus provides enough room for a potentially large number of PARs. Further, the maxent distribution is totally consistent with the maximum likelihood distribution [2]. Thus, our classifier relies not only on confident implications, but also on a solid statistical principle. Also, this principle can be seen as an inductive bias for inducing our classifier because maxent follows Occam's razor to choose the least complex distribution among the others that satisfy empirical constraints.
- Unlike other rule-based classifiers, our method predicts class labels for new instances based on multiple PARs w.r.t the global interaction among them and the aggregation of their weights. Obviously, this helps avoid prediction based on a single PAR, which sometimes leads to biased decisions. This is very important because predicting based on a high-ranked rule is not always optimal for hard instances that may exist in ambiguous or unbalanced data.

The remainder of the paper is organized as follows. Section 2 mainly presents our classification model. Section 3 gives the experimental results and some discussion. Finally, conclusions are given in Section 4.

2 The Proposed Classification Model

2.1 Conditional Maximum Entropy

Although maxent has a long history and a wide range of applications, this paper confines this principle to the problem of building a model that can best describe empirical data. Intuitively, maxent models all that is known and assume nothing about what is unknown [2]. In other words, given a collection of facts, choose a model consistent with all the facts, but otherwise as uniform as possible. Maxent has been successfully applied to many natural language processing tasks, e.g. machine translation [2], named entity recognition [4], and POS tagging [22].

Given a training dataset $D = \{(o^i, l^i)\}_{i=1}^{n}$ in which o^i is the ith data instance and $l^i (\in \mathcal{L})$ is its class label. Conditional maxent is a conditional distribution $P(l|o)$ – the conditional probability of having the class label l given the instance o. To train maxent model, experimenters have to determine significant features in the training data and integrate them into the model in terms of constraints. Maxent features have the form of two–argument function $f : (o, l) \to R$ below:

$$f_{<cp,\, l'>}(o, l) = \begin{cases} 1 \text{ if } l = l' \text{ and } cp(o) = \text{TRUE} \\ 0 \text{ otherwise} \end{cases} \quad (1)$$

where l' is a particular label and cp is a particular context predicate indicating a useful property of o. The maxent model is consistent with D w.r.t every feature f_i by satisfying constraints like $E(f_i) = F(f_i)$: the expected value of f_i w.r.t D is equal to the expected value of f_i w.r.t $P(l|o)$. The maxent model is the distribution having the highest entropy while satisfying those constraints. Using the Lagrange multipliers method and theory of constrained optimization, Pietra et al. [20] proved that maxent model is unique and has the exponential form.

$$P_\lambda(l|o) = \frac{1}{Z_\lambda(o)} \exp\left(\sum_{i=1} \lambda_i f_i(o, l)\right), \quad (2)$$

where λ_i is the weight associated with f_i, and $Z_\lambda(o)$ is the normalizing factor. Maxent is trained by setting the weight set $\{\lambda_1, \ldots\}$ to maximize the entropy $H(P_\lambda)$. The maxent model was often trained using GIS [7]. Recent studies [19] have shown that quasi–Newton methods like L–BFGS [18] are more efficient than the others. Once trained, the model will be used to predict labels for unseen data. Given a new instance o, the predicted label of o is $l_o = \text{argmax}_{l \in \mathcal{L}} P_\lambda(l|o)$.

2.2 Mining Predictive Association Rules from Training Data

Let $\mathcal{A} = (A_1, \ldots, A_m)$ be a data schema of m attributes in which A_i is either discrete or continuous. For any continuous attribute, its domain can be divided into non–overlapping intervals by using discretization methods [11], [12] so that all attributes can be treated uniformly as discrete. Let $\mathcal{L} = \{l_1, \ldots, l_q\}$ be the class attribute having q class labels. Given a training data $D = \{(o^i, l^i)\}_{i=1}^{n}$ of n data instances in which each $o^i = (a_1^i, \ldots, a_m^i)$ follows the above schema and l^i is a label associated with o_i. PAR, discovered from D, is a special type of association rule [1] and has the form:

$$\{[A_{i_1} = a_{i_1}] \wedge [A_{i_2} = a_{i_2}] \wedge \ldots \wedge [A_{i_k} = a_{i_k}]\} \Rightarrow l, \quad (3)$$

where the PAR antecedent is a conjunction of k attribute-value pairs and the consequent is a class label. The support of a PAR is the number of instances in D that match both its antecedent and its consequent. The confidence of a PAR is the conditional probability that an instance matches the consequent given that it matches the antecedent. Confident PARs are those whose support and confidence are greater than or equal to given minimum support (*minsup*) and minimum confidence (*minconf*), respectively.

We use the FP–growth algorithm [14], a very efficient frequent pattern mining technique, to mine association rules [1]. Then, we filter confident PARs from outputs of FP–growth. Unlike the previous methods, we apply different *minconf* thresholds ($minconf_1, \ldots, minconf_k$) corresponding to different antecedent lengths. This is because of an important observation that short rules usually have smaller confidence but are very useful for generalization while long rules have higher confidence but often are too specific.

2.3 MEPAR: Maximum Entropy Modeling of PARs

This section describes how to incorporate confident PARs into the maxent model to build our classifier – MEPAR. As mentioned earlier, maxent features are two–argument functions $f_{<cp, l'>}(o, l)$. For example, in the problem of determining part–of–speech (POS) labels (e.g., noun, verb, adjective, etc.) for English words using a maxent model, we should include the useful fact that "if a word o ends with a suffix *tive*, it is very likely that the word o is an adjective". We interpret this fact as a maxent feature $f_{<\text{suffix\_tive, adj}>}(o, l)$. Obviously, this feature is useful for predicting POS labels for new words because it relies on a confident statistic from empirical data. Interestingly, confident PARs are also confident facts in training data, and thus can naturally be incorporated into the maxent model as normal maxent features. Given a confident PAR $r : \{[A_{i_1}=a_{i_1}] \land \ldots \land [A_{i_k}=a_{i_k}]\} \Rightarrow l^r$, its corresponding maxent feature can be written as,

$$f_{<\text{match\_}\{\ldots\}, l^r>}(o, l) = \begin{cases} 1+\text{conf}(r) & \text{if } l = l^r \text{ and "}o\text{ matches} \\ & \{[A_{i_1}=a_{i_1}] \land \ldots \land [A_{i_k}=a_{i_k}]\}\text{"} \\ 0 & \text{otherwise} \end{cases} \quad (4)$$

In (4), a feature is active (= 1 + conf(r)) if the label l of o is matching with l^r and o holds the antecedent of r. Training maxent is very complicated in such a way that features interact with each other to yield an optimal estimated distribution over the training data. Thus, the learned weight of a PAR not only reflects how important the PAR is but also w.r.t the global optimum. One important observation is that the maxent model relies mainly on the occurrence frequency of its features and ignores feature confidence. In our model, we provide a priori for PARs by adding their confidence (conf(r)) to their corresponding feature values. After being trained, MPEAR can be used to predict class labels for unseen instances: given a new instance o^j, its predicted label l^j will be:

$$l^j = \text{argmax}_{l \in \mathcal{L}} \ P_\lambda(l|o^j)$$

$$= \text{argmax}_{l \in \mathcal{L}} \ \frac{1}{Z_\lambda(o^j)} \exp\left(\sum_{r=1}^{N} \lambda_{<\text{match\_}\{\ldots\}, l^r>} \ f_{<\text{match\_}\{\ldots\}, l^r>}(o^j, l)\right)$$

$$= \text{argmax}_{l \in \mathcal{L}} \ \sum_{r=1}^{N} \lambda_{<\text{match\_}\{\ldots\}, l^r>} \ f_{<\text{match\_}\{\ldots\}, l^r>}(o^j, l), \quad (5)$$

3 Experiments

3.1 Experimental Environments, Parameters, and Evaluation

The experiments were performed using our C/C++ implementation of maxent (FlexME: www.jaist.ac.jp/~hieuxuan/flexcrfs/flexcrfs.html#FlexME). PARs were discovered by using an efficient implementation of FP–growth by B. Goethals.

We used two groups of datasets from UCI ML Repository [15] as the experimental data. The first group includes 26 datasets which were tested with CBA [16] and CMAR [17] and the second group contains 13 datasets which were tested with ART [3]. Data discretization was done by using the entropy–based discretization method in [11]. The code is taken from MLC++ library [13].

All experimental parameters and results of learning methods for the first data group were derived from CMAR [17]; and those of the learning methods for the second data group were taken from ART [3].

We discovered all PARs with the antecedent length $k = 1, \ldots, 5$ with $minconf_1 = 40\%, minconf_2 = 70\%, minconf_3 = 80\%, minconf_4 = 90\%, minconf_5 = 95\%$, respectively. The $minsup$ is 1%. All the experimental results, including ours, were obtained from 10–CV (ten fold cross–validation) tests.

3.2 Experimental Results

For each dataset, we performed 10–CV test, and in each CV–fold we trained MEPAR for 50 L–BFGS iterations and then chose the highest accuracy to calculate the 10–CV accuracy. We observed that MEPAR models for UCI datasets converged around the first 20 L–BFGS iterations.

Table 1 shows the results of five methods (C4.5 [21], CBA [16], CAEP [9], CMAR [17], and ours – MEPAR) for the first data group. The first column is the list of 26 datasets; the second is the number of records; the third is the number of attributes; and the fourth is the number of class labels. The results for C4.5, CBA, and CMAR were taken from [17]; the results for CAEP were taken from [9] in which the results of several datasets are ignored because of their omission from the original paper. The ninth is the accuracy of our model, MEPAR, and the last column is the accuracy of normal maxent (i.e., without PARs). For each row, the highest accuracy is printed using italics.

In the first data group, MEPAR outperformed the other methods on 24 of 26 datasets including both the largest dataset (Waveform, 5,000 records) and the smallest one (Labor, 57 records). MEPAR performs well on datasets with a large number of attributes. This is because these datasets usually generate a large number of PARs with rich dependencies among data items, very useful for the MEPAR model. For those with small number of attributes, MEPAR obtains accuracies similar to the others. The average accuracy of MEPAR is 88.39%, significantly higher than those of CMAR, CBA, C4.5, and normal maxent.

Table 2 shows the results of six methods (ART [3], C4.5 [21], RIPPER$_{k=2}$ [6], CN2 [5], Naive Bayes [10], and ours – MEPAR) for the second data group. The experimental results of ART, C4.5, RIPPER, CN2, and Naive Bayes were

Table 1. Accuracy comparison: C4.5, CBA, CAEP, CMAR, and MEPAR

Datasets	#Rec	#Attr	#Cls	C4.5	CBA	CAEP	CMAR	MEPAR	N.Maxent
Anneal	898	38	6	94.8	97.9	N/A	97.3	*98.9*	97.5
Austra	690	14	2	84.7	84.9	86.2	86.1	*88.4*	88.0
Auto	205	25	7	80.1	78.3	N/A	78.1	*83.5*	*83.5*
Breast	699	10	2	95	96.3	97.3	96.4	*97.8*	97.2
Cleve	303	13	2	78.2	82.8	83.3	82.2	*85.3*	82.2
Crx	690	15	2	*84.9*	84.7	N/A	*84.9*	84.6	83.0
Diabetes	768	8	2	74.2	74.5	N/A	75.8	*77.6*	*77.6*
German	1000	20	2	72.3	73.4	72.5	74.9	*76.6*	73.5
Glass	214	9	7	68.7	73.9	N/A	70.1	*81.9*	81.7
Heart	270	13	2	80.8	81.9	83.7	82.2	*84.8*	*84.8*
Hepatitis	155	19	2	80.6	81.8	83.0	80.5	*84.8*	82.6
Horse	368	22	2	82.6	82.1	N/A	82.6	*86.7*	86.0
Hypo	3163	25	2	99.2	98.9	N/A	98.4	*99.4*	*99.4*
Iono	351	34	2	90.0	92.3	90.0	91.5	*94.3*	92.5
Iris	150	4	3	*95.3*	94.7	94.7	94.0	94.7	94.7
Labor	57	16	2	79.3	86.3	N/A	89.7	*90.0*	86.3
Led7	3200	7	10	73.5	71.9	N/A	72.5	*74.3*	73.8
Lymph	148	18	4	73.5	77.8	N/A	83.1	*90.0*	*90.0*
Pima	768	8	2	75.5	72.9	75.0	75.1	*78.4*	76.2
Sick	2800	29	2	*98.5*	97.0	N/A	97.5	97.9	97.3
Sonar	208	60	2	70.2	77.5	N/A	79.4	*90.0*	88.6
Tic-tac-toe	958	9	2	99.4	*99.6*	99.1	99.2	99.2	99.1
Vehicle	846	18	4	72.6	68.7	66.3	68.8	*76.3*	74.9
Waveform	5000	21	3	78.1	80.0	84.7	83.2	*87.3*	85.5
Wine	178	13	3	92.7	95.0	97.1	95.0	*98.3*	*98.3*
Zoo	101	16	7	92.2	96.8	N/A	*97.1*	*97.1*	*97.1*
Average				83.34%	84.69%	N/A	85.22%	**88.39%**	87.36%

taken from [3]. The last column is the accuracy of MEPAR. In this data group, MEPAR performed better than the others on 7 of 13 datasets. It also performed well on both large (Nursery, Mushroom, Splice) and small ones (Lenses, Lung–cancer). The average accuracy of MEPAR is significantly higher than those of the others.

we also analyzed the stability of MEPAR. Figure 1 shows a comparison of the log–likelihood and the accuracy between two cases: normal maxent (without PARs) and MEPAR (with PARs). The left graph shows that the log–likelihood of MEPAR increases more strongly than that of the normal maxent. This means that MEPAR can describe the empirical data better. The right graph depicts the accuracy values of MEPAR and the normal maxent as functions of the number of training iterations. As we can see, the accuracy of MEPAR is significantly higher than that of the normal maxent. Further, the accuracy of MEPAR increases smoothly, without large fluctuations of the normal maxent.

Table 2. Accuracy comparison: ART, C4.5, RIPPER, CN2, N. Bayes, and MEPAR

Datasets	#Rec	#Attr	#Cls	ART	C4.5	RIPPER	CN2	N.Bayes	MEPAR
Audiology	226	69	24	65.2	81.4	73.9	75.6	23.4	*84.1*
Car	1728	6	4	*98.6*	92.9	78.4	93.9	70.0	97.0
Chess	3198	35	2	97.7	99.2	99.2	*99.4*	62.5	96.3
Hayes–roth	160	4	3	84.4	73.8	78.1	76.2	61.9	*87.5*
Lenses	24	5	3	70.0	*81.7*	65.0	76.7	63.3	80.0
Lung–cancer	32	56	3	40.8	43.3	45.0	39.2	43.3	*53.3*
Mushrooms	8124	22	2	98.5	*100.*	*100.*	*100.*	94.3	*100.*
Nursery	12960	8	5	*99.1*	96.2	96.7	98.1	88.0	98.5
Soybean	683	35	19	91.5	*93.7*	91.1	92.1	58.7	92.8
Splice	3190	60	3	89.3	94.1	93.1	92.3	51.9	*96.1*
Tic-tac-toe	958	9	2	81.6	83.8	97.5	98.0	65.3	*99.2*
Titanic	2201	3	2	78.6	*79.1*	78.3	75.8	68.0	78.1
Vote	435	16	2	95.9	95.9	94.9	94.7	89.2	*97.2*
Average				83.94%	85.76%	83.94%	85.54%	64.61%	**89.24%**

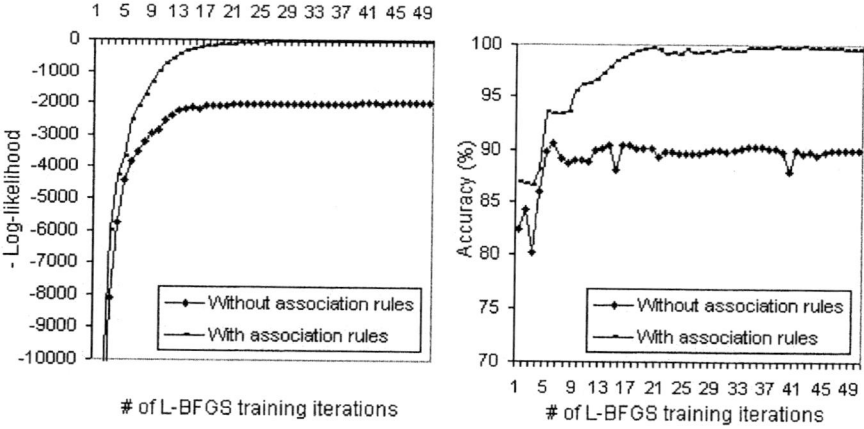

Fig. 1. Log–likelihood and accuracy as functions of # of L–BFGS training iterations (with and without PARs) – measured on the Nursery dataset at the 1st fold of 10–CV

4 Conclusions

This paper presented the hybrid classification model, MEPAR, that is based on PARs discovered from training data and maxent. Unlike other rule–based methods, our model predicts labels for new data instances based on multiple PARs whose weights are trained using maxent. This ensures that weights of PARs not only precisely measure how important the PARs are, but are also consistent with the empirical data. Also, a prediction based on multiple PARs should avoid biased decisions. Our future work will focus on how to tune parameters automatically in order to obtain higher performance. Also, the theoretical aspect will be further investigated to clarify why MEPAR can achieve such high accuracy.

References

1. Agrawal, R. and Srikant, R. (1994). Fast algorithms for mining association rules. In Proceedings of VLDB, 487–499.
2. Berger, A., Della Pietra, S., and Della Pietra V. (1996). A maximum entropy approach to natural language processing. Computational Linguistics, 22(1):39–71.
3. Berzal, F., Cubero, J., Sanchez, D., and Serrano, J. (2004). ART: A hybrid classification model. Machine Learning, 54:67–92.
4. Borthwick, A. (1999). A maximum entropy approach to named entity recognition. PhD dissertation, Dept. of CS, New York University.
5. Clark, P. and Nibblett, T. (1989). The CN2 induction algorithm. Machine Learning, 3(4):261–283.
6. Cohen, W. (1995). Fast effective rule induction. In Proceedings of ICML, 115–123.
7. Darroch, N. and Ratcliff, D. (1972). Generalized iterative scaling for log–linear models. The Annals of Mathematical Statistics, 43:1470–1480.
8. Dong, G. and Li, J. (1999). Efficient mining of emerging patterns: discovering trends and differences. In Proceedings of ACM SIGKDD.
9. Dong, G., Zhang, X., Wong, L., and Li, J. (1999). CAEP: Classification by aggregating emerging patterns. In Proceedings of Discovery Science.
10. Duda, R., Hart, P., and Stork, D. (2000). Pattern Classification. Wiley Interscience.
11. Fayyad, M. and Irani, B. (1993). Multi–interval discretization of continuous–valued attributes for classification learning. In Proceedings of IJCAI, 1022–1027.
12. Kohavi, R. and Sahami, M. (1996). Error–based and entropy–based discretization of continuous features. In Proceedings of ACM SIGKDD.
13. Kohavi, R., John, G., Long, R., Manley, D., and Pfleger, K. (1994). MLC++: a machine learning library in C++. In Tools with artificial intelligence, 740–743.
14. Han, J., Pei, J., Yin, Y. (2000). Mining frequent patterns without candidate generation. In Proceedings of ACM SIGMOD, 1–12.
15. Hettich, S., Blake, L., and Merz, J. (1998). UCI Repository of machine learning databases. http://www.ics.uci.edu/~mlearn/MLRepository.html. Irvine, CA: University of California, Department of Information and Computer Science.
16. Liu, B., Hsu, W., and Ma, Y. (1998). Integrating classification and association rule mining. In Proceedings of ACM SIGKDD.
17. Li, W., Han, J., and Pei, J. (2001). CMAR: Accurate and efficient classification based on multiple class–association rules. In Proceedings of IEEE ICDM.
18. Liu, D. and Nocedal, J. (1989). On the limited memory BFGS method for large–scale optimization. Mathematical Programming, 45:502–528.
19. Malouf, R. (2002). A comparison of algorithms for maximum entropy parameter estimation. In Proceedings of CoNLL.
20. Pietra, S., Pietra, V., and Lafferty, J. (1997). Inducing features of random fields. IEEE Transactions on Pattern Analysis and Machine Intelligence, 19(4):380–393.
21. Quinland, J. (1993). C4.5: Programs for machine learning. Morgan Kaufmann.
22. Ratnapharkhi, A. (1996). A maximum entropy model for part–of–speech tagging. In Proceedings of EMNLP.

Classification of Ordinal Data Using Neural Networks

Joaquim Pinto da Costa[1] and Jaime S. Cardoso[2]

[1] Faculdade Ciências Universidade Porto,
Porto, Portugal
jpcosta@fc.up.pt
[2] Faculdade Engenharia Universidade Porto / INESC Porto,
Porto, Portugal
jaime.cardoso@inescporto.pt

Abstract. Many real life problems require the classification of items in naturally ordered classes. These problems are traditionally handled by conventional methods for nominal classes, ignoring the order. This paper introduces a new training model for feedforward neural networks, for multiclass classification problems, where the classes are ordered. The proposed model has just one output unit which takes values in the interval [0,1]; this interval is then subdivided into K subintervals (one for each class), according to a specific probabilistic model. A comparison is made with conventional approaches, as well as with other architectures specific for ordinal data proposed in the literature. The new model compares favourably with the other methods under study, in the synthetic dataset used for evaluation.

1 Introduction

Many pattern recognition problems involve classifying examples into classes which have a natural ordering. Settings in which it is natural to rank instances arise in many fields, such as information retrieval [1], collaborative filtering [2] and econometric modelling [3].

Suppose that examples in a classification problem belong to one of K classes, numbered from 1 to K, corresponding to their natural order if one exists, and arbitrarily otherwise. The learning task is to select a prediction function $f(\mathbf{x})$ from a family of possible functions that minimizes the expected *loss*.

Although conventional methods for nominal classes could be employed, the use of techniques designed specifically for ordered classes results in simpler classifiers, making it easier to interpret the factors that are being used to discriminate among classes [3]. We propose a classifier for ordered classes based on neural networks by imposing that the output layer with K units has just one mode, corresponding to the predicted class. In fact the model is equivalent to a network with just one output unit, as the final layer serves only to compute the error and has no weights associated with its input values (see figure 1).

The novel proposed algorithm attains the best generalization capability for the group of methods evaluated.

2   A Neural Network Architecture for Ordinal Data

To use a neural network for classification, we need to construct an equivalent function approximation problem by assigning a target value for each class. For a two-class problem we can use a network with a single output, and binary target values: 1 for one class, and 0 for the other. The training of the network is commonly performed using the popular mean square error. For multiclass classification problems (1-of-K, where $K > 2$) we use a network with K outputs, one corresponding to each class, and target values of 1 for the correct class, and 0 otherwise. Since these targets are not independent of each other, however, it is no longer appropriate to use the same error measure. The correct generalization is through a special activation function (the softmax) designed so as to satisfy the normalization constraint on the total probability.

However this approach does not retain the ordinality or rank order of the classes and is not, therefore, appropriate for ordinal multistate classification problems.

Let us formulate the problem of separating K ordered classes $C_1, \cdots, C_K$. Consider the training set $\{\mathbf{x}_i^{(k)}\}$, where $k = 1, \cdots, K$, denotes the class number, $i = 1, \cdots, \ell_k$ is the index within each class, and $\mathbf{x}_i^{(k)} \in \mathbb{R}^p$. Let $\ell = \sum_{k=1}^{K} \ell_k$ be the total number of training examples.

Given a new query point $\mathbf{x}$, Bayes decision theory suggests to classify $\mathbf{x}$ in the class which maximizes the *a posteriori* probability $P(C_k|\mathbf{x})$. To do so, one usually has to estimate these probabilities, either implicitly or explicitly. Suppose for instance that we have 7 classes and, for a given point $\mathbf{x}_0$, the highest probability is $P(C_5|\mathbf{x}_0)$; we then attribute class C_5 to the given point. If there is not an order relation between the classes, it is perfectly natural that the second highest *a posteriori* probability is, for instance, $P(C_2|\mathbf{x})$. However, if the classes are ordered, $C_1 < C_2 <, \ldots, < C_7$, classes C_4 and C_6 are closer to class C_5 and therefore the second and third highest *a posteriori* probabilities should be attained in these classes. This argument extends easily to the classes, C_3 and C_7, and so on. This is the main idea behind the method proposed here, which we now detail.

Our method assumes that in a supervised classification problem with ordered classes, the random variable class associated with a given query $\mathbf{x}$ should be unimodal. That is to say that if we plot the *a posteriori* probabilities $P(C_k|\mathbf{x})$, from the first C_1 to the last C_K, there should be only one mode in this graphic. Here, we apply this idea in the context of neural networks. Usually in neural networks, the output layer has as many units as there are classes, K. We will use the same order for these units and the classes. In order to force the output values (which represent the *a posteriori* probabilities) to have just one mode, we will use a parametric model for these output units. This model consists in assuming that the output values come from a binomial distribution, $B(K-1, p)$. This distribution is unimodal in most cases and when it has two modes, these are for contiguous values, which makes sense in our case, since we can have exactly the same probability for two classes. This binomial distribution takes integer values in the set $\{0, 1, \ldots, K-1\}$; value 0 corresponds to class C_1, value

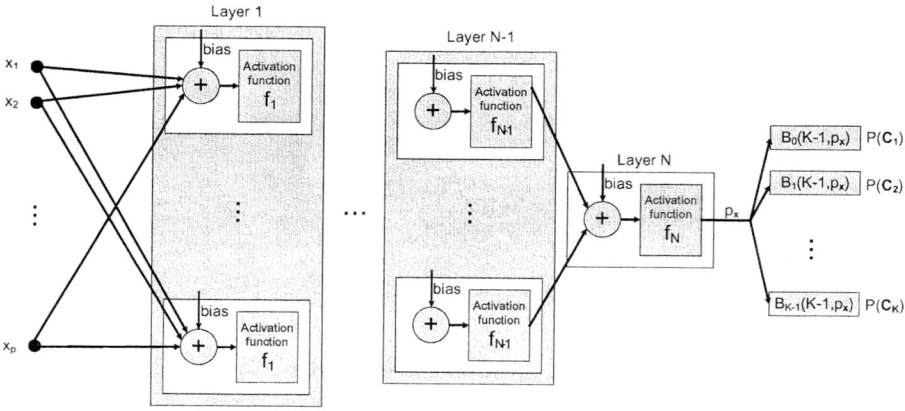

Fig. 1. unimodal neural network architecture

1 to class $\mathcal{C}_2$ and so on until value $K-1$ to class $\mathcal{C}_K$. As K is known, the only parameter left to be estimated from this model is the probability p. We will therefore use a different architecture for the neural network; that is, the output layer will have just one output unit, corresponding to the value of p – figure 1. For a given query $\mathbf{x}$, the output of the network will be a single numerical value in the range [0,1], which we call $p_\mathbf{x}$. Then, the probabilities $P(\mathcal{C}_k|\mathbf{x})$ are calculated from the binomial model:

$$P(\mathcal{C}_k|\mathbf{x}) = \frac{(K-1)! p_\mathbf{x}^{k-1}(1-p_\mathbf{x})^{K-k}}{(k-1)!(K-k)!}, \quad k=1,2,\ldots,K$$

In fact these probabilities are calculated recursively, to save computing time:

$$\frac{P(\mathcal{C}_k|\mathbf{x})}{P(\mathcal{C}_{k-1}|\mathbf{x})} = \frac{p_\mathbf{x}(K-k+1)}{(k-1)(1-p_\mathbf{x})}, \text{ and so } P(\mathcal{C}_k|\mathbf{x}) = P(\mathcal{C}_{k-1}|\mathbf{x})\frac{p_\mathbf{x}(K-k+1)}{(k-1)(1-p_\mathbf{x})}.$$

We start with $P(\mathcal{C}_1|\mathbf{x}) = (1-p_\mathbf{x})^{K-1}$ and compute the other probabilities, $P(\mathcal{C}_k|\mathbf{x})$, $k=2,3,\ldots,K$, using the above formula.

When the training case $\mathbf{x}$ is presented, the error is defined as

$$\sum_{k=1}^{K}(P(\mathcal{C}_k|\mathbf{x}) - \delta(k - \mathcal{C}_\mathbf{x}))^2$$

where $\delta(n) = \begin{cases} 1 \text{ if } n=0 \\ 0 \text{ otherwise} \end{cases}$ and $\mathcal{C}_\mathbf{x}$ the true class of $\mathbf{x}$. The network is trained to minimize the average value over all training cases of such error. Finally, in the test phase, we choose the class k which maximizes the probability $P(\mathcal{C}_k)$.

3 Experimental Results

In this section we present experimental results for several models based on neural networks, when applied to a synthetic dataset.

3.1 Implementation Details

We compared the following algorithms:

- Conventional neural network (cNN). To test the hypothesis that methods specifically targeted for ordinal data improve the performance of a standard classifier, we tested a conventional feed forward network, fully connected, with a single hidden layer, trained with the traditional least square approach.
- Pairwise NN (pNN): Frank [4] introduced a simple algorithm that enables standard classification algorithms to exploit the ordering information in ordinal prediction problems. First, the data is transformed from a K-class ordinal problem to $K-1$ binary class problems. To predict the class value of an unseen instance the probabilities of the K original classes are estimated using the outputs from the $K-1$ binary classifiers.
- Costa [5], following a probabilistic approach, proposes a neural network architecture (itNN) that exploits the ordinal nature of the data, by defining the classification task on a suitable space through a "partitive approach". It is proposed a feedforward neural network with $K-1$ outputs to solve a K-class ordinal problem. The probabilistic meaning assigned to the network outputs is exploited to rank the elements of the dataset.
- proposed unimodal model (uNN), as previously introduced.

Experiments were carried out in Matlab 7.0 (R14), making use of the Neural Network Toolbox[1].

The first three models were configured with a single hidden layer and trained with Levenberg-Marquardt back propagation method, over 2000 epochs. The uNN model was also configured with a single hidden layer and trained with the lsqnonlin Matlab function over 1000 iterations.

The number of neurons in the hidden layer was experimentally set for the best performance.

3.2 Measuring Classifier Performance

Having built a classifier, the obvious question is "how good is it?". This begs the question of what we mean by good. The obvious answer is to treat every misclassification as equally likely. This translates to adopting the non-metric indicator function $l_{0-1}(f(\mathbf{x}), y) = 0$ if $f(\mathbf{x}) = y$ and $l_{0-1}(f(\mathbf{x}), y) = 1$ if $f(\mathbf{x}) \neq y$, where $f(\mathbf{x})$ and y are the predicted and true classes, respectively. Measuring the performance of a classifier using the l_{0-1} loss function is equivalent to simply

---
[1] The code is available upon request to the authors.

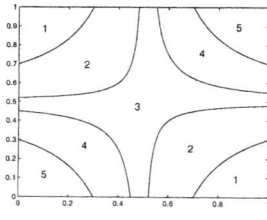 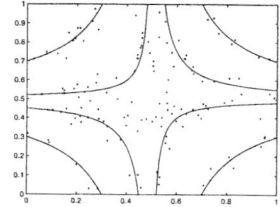

(a) Classes' boundaries.   (b) Scatter plot of the data points wrongly ranked. Number of wrong points: 14.2%.

Fig. 2. Test setup for 5 classes in $\mathbb{R}^2$

considering the misclassification error rate (MER). However, for ordered classes, losses that increase with the absolute difference between the class numbers are more natural choices in the absence of better information [3].

The mean absolute error (MAE) criterion takes into account the degree of misclassification and is thus a richer criterion than MER. The loss function corresponding to this criterion is $l(f(\mathbf{x}), y) = |f(\mathbf{x}) - y|$.

A variant of the above MAE measure is the root mean square error (RMSE), where the absolute difference is replaced with the square of the difference, $l(f(\mathbf{x}), y) = (f(\mathbf{x}) - y)^2$.

Finally, the performance of the classifiers was also assessed with the Spearman coefficient (r_s), a nonparametric rank-order correlation coefficient, well established in the literature.

3.3 Experimental Methodology and Results

To check the adequacy of the proposed model we generated a synthetic dataset in a similar way to Herbrich [1].

We generated 1000 example points $\mathbf{x} = [x_1 \ x_2]^t$ uniformly at random in the unit square $[0, 1] \times [0, 1] \subset \mathbb{R}^2$. Each point was assigned a rank y from the set $\{1, 2, 3, 4, 5\}$, according to

$$y = \min_{r \in \{1,2,3,4,5\}} \{r : b_{r-1} < 10(x_1 - 0.5)(x_2 - 0.5) + \varepsilon < b_r\}$$

$$(b_0, b_1, b_2, b_3, b_4, b_5) = (-\infty, -1, -0.1, 0.25, 1, +\infty)$$

where ε is a random value, normally distributed with zero mean and standard deviation $\sigma = 0.125$. Figure 2(a) shows the five regions and figure 2(b) the points which were assigned to a different rank after the corruption with the normally distributed noise.

In order to compare the different algorithms, and similarly to [1], we randomly selected training sequences of point-rank pairs of length ℓ ranging from 20 to 100. The remaining points were used to estimate the classification error, which were

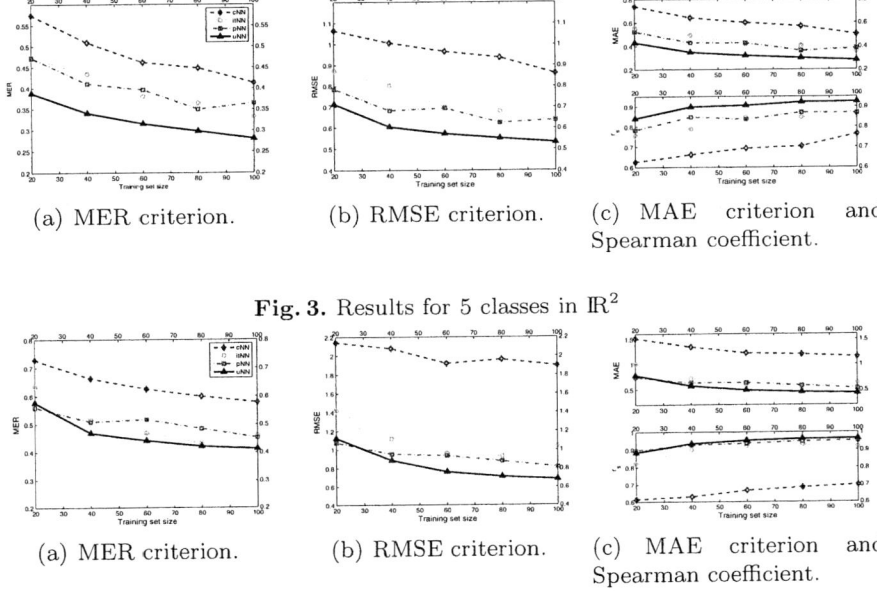

(a) MER criterion. (b) RMSE criterion. (c) MAE criterion and Spearman coefficient.

Fig. 3. Results for 5 classes in $\mathbb{R}^2$

(a) MER criterion. (b) RMSE criterion. (c) MAE criterion and Spearman coefficient.

Fig. 4. Results for 10 classes in $\mathbb{R}^2$

averaged over 10 runs of the algorithms for each size of the training sequence. Thus we obtained the learning curves shown in figure 3, for 5 neurons in the hidden layer.

Accuracy dependence on the number of classes. To investigate the relation between the number of classes and the performance of the evaluated algorithms, we also ran the four models on the same dataset but with 10 classes.

This time each point was assigned a rank y from the set $\{1,2,3,4,5,6,7,8,9,10\}$, according to

$$y = \min_{r \in \{1,2,3,4,5,6,7,8,9,10\}} \{r : b_{r-1} < 10(x_1 - 0.5)(x_2 - 0.5) + \varepsilon < b_r\}$$

$$(b_0, b_1, b_2, b_3, b_4, b_5, b_6, b_7, b_8, b_9, b_{10}) = \\ (-\infty, -1.75, -1, -0.5, -0.1, 0.1, 0.25, 0.75, 1, 1.75, +\infty)$$

where ε is a random value, normally distributed with zero mean and standard deviation $\sigma = 0.125/2$.

The learning curves obtained for this arrangement are shown in figure 4 (again, for 5 neurons in the hidden layer).

Accuracy dependence on the data dimension. The described experiments in $\mathbb{R}^2$ were repeated for data points in $\mathbb{R}^4$, to evaluate the influence of data dimension on the models' relative performance.

Table 1. Results for 5 classes in $\mathbb{R}^4$ (MER;RMSE;MAE;r_s)

Set size	cNN	pNN	itNN	uNN
100	(0.64;1.60;1.12;0.28)	(0.59;1.14;0.81;0.58)	(0.61;1.39;0.96;0.42)	(0.63;1.58;1.12;0.48)
200	(0.61;1.53;1.05;0.36)	(0.53;0.97;0.66;0.70)	(0.53;1.13;0.75;0.63)	(0.47;1.03;0.64;0.75)
300	(0.57;1.44;0.94;0.44)	(0.51;0.91;0.61;0.75)	(0.45;0.97;0.60;0.73)	(0.39;0.80;0.46;0.84)
400	(0.52;1.36;0.85;0.52)	(0.48;0.86;0.57;0.77)	(0.35;0.76;0.42;0.84)	(0.33;0.68;0.37;0.89)
500	(0.51;1.27;0.80;0.57)	(0.44;0.79;0.50;0.82)	(0.29;0.65;0.32;0.88)	(0.31;0.67;0.35;0.89)

We generated 2000 example points $\mathbf{x} = [x_1\ x_2\ x_3\ x_4]^t$ uniformly at random in the unit square in $\mathbb{R}^4$.

For 5 classes each point was assigned a rank y from the set $\{1, 2, 3, 4, 5\}$, according to

$$y = \min_{r \in \{1,2,3,4,5\}} \{r : b_{r-1} < 1000 \prod_{i=1}^{4}(x_i - 0.5) + \varepsilon\ < b_r\}$$

$$(b_0, b_1, b_2, b_3, b_4) = (-\infty, -2.5, -0.5, 0.5, 3, +\infty)$$

where ε is a random value, normally distributed with zero mean and standard deviation $\sigma = 0.25$.

Finally, for 10 classes the rank was assigned according to the rule

$$y = \min_{r \in \{1,2,3,4,5,6,7,8,9,10\}} \{r : b_{r-1} < 1000 \prod_{i=1}^{4}(x_i - 0.5) + \varepsilon\ < b_r\}$$

$$(b_0, b_1, b_2, b_3, b_4, b_5, b_6, b_7, b_8, b_9, b_{10}) = (-\infty, -5, -2.5, -1, -0.4, 0.1, 0.5, 1.1, 3, 6, +\infty)$$

where ε is a random value, normally distributed with zero mean and $\sigma = 0.125$. The results are presented in a tabular form, tables 1 and 2.

Network complexity One final point to make in any comparison of methods regards complexity. The number of learnable parameters for each model is presented in table 3.

Table 2. Results for 10 classes in $\mathbb{R}^4$ (MER;RMSE;MAE;r_s)

Set size	cNN	pNN	itNN	uNN
100	(0.81;3.42;2.54;0.25)	(0.79;2.10;1.60;0.66)	(0.76;2.83;1.99;0.49)	(0.79;3.25;2.36;0.34)
200	(0.78;3.24;2.32;0.33)	(0.74;1.73;1.31;0.80)	(0.68;2.28;1.50;0.66)	(0.65;2.16;1.41;0.72)
300	(0.74;3.04;2.14;0.42)	(0.70;1.55;1.14;0.84)	(0.54;1.37;0.84;0.88)	(0.58;1.74;1.07;0.80)
400	(0.74;3.08;2.11;0.44)	(0.67;1.42;1.03;0.87)	(0.47;1.13;0.66;0.92)	(0.51;1.15;0.71;0.91)
500	(0.70;2.88;1.95;0.49)	(0.63;1.29;0.92;0.89)	(0.42;0.96;0.55;0.94)	(0.47;1.01;0.61;0.93)

4 Conclusion

This study presents a new approach to neural networks training for ordinal data. The main idea is to retain the ordinality of the classes by imposing a parametric model for the output probabilities.

Table 3. Number of parameters for each neural network model

Model	cNN	pNN	itNN	uNN
$\mathbb{R}^2, K=5$	45	21×4	39	21
$\mathbb{R}^2, K=10$	75	21×9	69	21

Model	cNN	pNN	itNN	uNN
$\mathbb{R}^4, K=5$	165	97×4	148	97
$\mathbb{R}^4, K=10$	250	97×9	233	97

The study compares the results of the proposed model with conventional neural network for nominal classes, and two models proposed in the literature specifically for ordinal data.

Simple misclassification, mean absolute error, root mean square error and spearman coefficient are used as measures of performance for all models and used for model comparison. This new method is likely to produce a simpler and more robust classifier, and compares favourably with state-of-the-art methods.

Other directions in future work include the use of similar networks with two or more output units and more flexible models other than the binomial. We think this increased flexibility might improve further the results for more complicated problems, like when we increase the number of classes and of dimensions in our experiments. Another idea which we will consider consists in using these type of models in conjunction with other learning algorithms, like for instance SVMs. We plan also to investigate the performance of this type of models for non ordinal classes.

References

1. Herbrich, R., Graepel, T., Obermayer, K.: Regression models for ordinal data: a machine learning approach. Technical Report TR-99/03, TU Berlin (1999)
2. Shashua, A., Levin, A.: Ranking with large margin principle: Two approaches. In: Neural Information and Processing Systems (NIPS). (2002)
3. Mathieson, M.J.: Ordinal models for neural networks. In Refenes, A., Abu-Mostafa, Y., Moody, J., eds.: Neural Networks in Financial Engineering, World Scientific, Singapore (1995)
4. Frank, E., Hall, M.: A simple approach to ordinal classification. In: Proceedings of the 12th European Conference on Machine Learning. Volume 1. (2001) 145–156
5. Costa, M.: Probabilistic interpretation of feedforward network outputs, with relationships to statistical prediction of ordinal quantities. International Journal Neural Systems **7** (1996) 627–638

Independent Subspace Analysis on Innovations

Barnabás Póczos, Bálint Takács, and András Lőrincz*

Eötvös Loránd University, Pázmány P. sétány 1/C,
Budapest, Hungary 1117
barn@ludens.elte.hu,
{takbal, andras.lorincz}@elte.hu,
http://nipg.inf.elte.hu/

Abstract. Independent subspace analysis (ISA) that deals with multi-dimensional independent sources, is a generalization of independent component analysis (ICA). However, all known ISA algorithms may become ineffective when the sources possess temporal structure. The innovation process instead of the original mixtures has been proposed to solve ICA problems with temporal dependencies. Here we show that this strategy can be applied to ISA as well. We demonstrate the idea on a mixture of 3D processes and also on a mixture of facial pictures used as two-dimensional deterministic sources. ISA on innovations was able to find the original subspaces, while plain ISA was not.

1 Introduction

Independent Component Analysis (ICA) [1, 2] aims to recover linearly or non-linearly mixed independent and hidden sources. There is a broad range of applications for ICA, such as blind source separation and blind source deconvolution [3], feature extraction [4], denoising [5]. Particular applications include, e.g., the analysis of financial data [6], data from neurobiology, fMRI, EEG, and MEG (see, e.g., [7, 8] and references therein). For a recent review on ICA see [9].

Original ICA algorithms are 1-dimensional: all sources are assumed to be independent real valued stochastic variables. However, applications where not all, but only certain groups of the sources are independent may have high relevance in practice. In this case, independent sources can be multi-dimensional. Consider, e.g., the generalization of the cocktail-party problem, where independent groups of musicians are playing at the party. This is the subject of Independent Subspace Analysis (ISA), an extension of ICA, also called Multi-dimensional Independent Component Analysis [10, 11]. Efforts have been made to develop ISA algorithms [10, 11, 12, 13, 14, 15, 16]. Certain approaches use 2-dimensional Edgeworth expansion [12] leading to sophisticated equations. They have not been extended to 3 or higher dimensions. Another suggestion is to start with ICA and then permute the columns of the mixing matrix to find the best ISA estimation [10]. This case has not been worked out and permutations may not be general

---

* Corresponding author.

enough. Another recent approach searches for independent subspaces via kernel methods [14].

These ISA algorithms all have a serious drawback: they require independently and identically distributed (i.i.d.) sources. For the ICA problem several authors [17, 18, 19] suggested that the innovation process, instead of the original mixtures, could be used if input had a temporal structure. The innovation process can be calculated relatively easily, if one assumes that the sources are AR processes. Here we propose to compute the innovation process of the mixed signal by assuming an underlying autoregressive (AR) process first, and then to apply our new, efficient ISA algorithms [15, 16].

The paper is built as follows: Section 2 is an overview of the ISA problem. Section 3 presents the motivation for using the innovation process. This section describes the corresponding ISA algorithm. Numerical simulations are presented in Section 4. Short discussion and conclusions are provided in Section 5.

2 The ISA Model

Assume we have d of m-dimensional independent sources denoted by $\boldsymbol{y}^1, \ldots, \boldsymbol{y}^d$, respectively, where $\boldsymbol{y}^i \in \mathbb{R}^m$. Let $\boldsymbol{y} = [(\boldsymbol{y}^1)^T, \ldots, (\boldsymbol{y}^d)^T]^T \in \mathbb{R}^{dm}$, where superscript T stands for transposition. We assume that these sources are hidden and we can only observe the following signal

$$\boldsymbol{x} = \boldsymbol{A}\boldsymbol{y} \tag{1}$$

where $\boldsymbol{A} \in \mathbb{R}^{dm \times dm}$. The task is to recover hidden source $\boldsymbol{y}$ and mixing matrix $\boldsymbol{A}$ given the observed signal $\boldsymbol{x} \in \mathbb{R}^{dm}$. In the ISA model we assume that $\boldsymbol{y}^i \in \mathbb{R}^m$ is independent of $\boldsymbol{y}^j \in \mathbb{R}^m$ for $i \neq j$. For the special case of m=1, the ICA problem is recovered.

In the ICA problem, given the signals, sources $\boldsymbol{y}^i$ ($i = 1, \ldots, d$) can be recovered only up to sign, up to arbitrary scaling factors, and up to an arbitrary permutation. The ISA task has more freedom; signals $\boldsymbol{y}^i$ can be recovered up to an arbitrary permutation and an m-dimensional linear, invertible transformation. It is easy to see this by considering matrix $\boldsymbol{C} \in \mathbb{R}^{dm \times dm}$ made of a permutation matrix of size $d \times d$, where each element is made of an $m \times m$ block-matrix having invertible $\boldsymbol{C}_i$ blocks replacing the non-zero elements of the permutation matrix. Then, $\boldsymbol{x} = \boldsymbol{A}\boldsymbol{y} = \boldsymbol{A}\boldsymbol{C}^{-1}\boldsymbol{C}\boldsymbol{y}$, and because $\boldsymbol{y}^i$ is independent of $\boldsymbol{y}^j$, thus $\boldsymbol{C}_i\boldsymbol{y}^i$ is independent of $\boldsymbol{C}_j\boldsymbol{y}^j$ $\forall i \neq j$. That is, in the ISA model, matrices $\boldsymbol{A}$ and $\boldsymbol{A}\boldsymbol{C}^{-1}$ and sources $\boldsymbol{y}^i$ and $\boldsymbol{C}_i\boldsymbol{y}^i$ are indistinguishable. This ambiguity of the ISA task can be lowered by assuming $E\{\boldsymbol{y}\} = \boldsymbol{0}$, and $E\{\boldsymbol{y}\boldsymbol{y}^T\} = \boldsymbol{I}_{md}$, where E is the expected value operator, $\boldsymbol{I}_n$ is the n-dimensional identity matrix. Similarly, by scaling observed signal $\boldsymbol{x}$, one can assure that $E\{\boldsymbol{x}\} = \boldsymbol{0}$, and $E\{\boldsymbol{x}\boldsymbol{x}^T\} = \boldsymbol{I}_{md}$, which is called the whitening of the inputs. Then, Eq. (1) ensures that $E\{\boldsymbol{x}\boldsymbol{x}^T\} = \boldsymbol{A}E\{\boldsymbol{y}\boldsymbol{y}^T\}\boldsymbol{A}^T$ and $\boldsymbol{I}_{md} = \boldsymbol{A}\boldsymbol{A}^T$. It then follows that under our assumptions, signals $\boldsymbol{y}^i$ can be recovered up to permutation and up to m-dimensional orthogonal transformation in the ISA problem. In other words, if $\boldsymbol{C}_i \in \mathbb{R}^{m \times m}$

is an arbitrary orthogonal matrix, then signals x will not provide information whether the original sources correspond to y^i or, instead, to $C_i y^i$. For the 1D case this is equivalent to the uncertainty that $C_i = 1$ or $C_i = -1$. That is, in 1D, the sign of y^i is not determined. Thus, without any loss of generality, it is satisfactory to restrict the search for mixing matrix A (or, for its inverse, i.e., for separation matrix W) to the set of orthogonal matrices.

2.1 The ISA Objective

We introduce the ISA objective subject to the constraint of $W^T W = I_{md}$. The separation matrix W is amongst the global minima of this ISA objective function. Let $I(y^1, \ldots, y^d)$ denote the mutual information between vectors $y^1, \ldots, y^d \in \mathbb{R}^m$. Further, let $H(y)$ denote the joint Shannon-entropy of vector-valued stochastic variable y. Let $y = Wx$. Then

$$I(y^1, y^2, \ldots, y^d) = -H(x) + \log|W| + H(y^1) + \ldots + H(y^d) \tag{2}$$

Our task is to minimize (2). However, $H(x)$ is constant and $W^T W = I$. Thus $\log|W| = 0$ and the minimization of (2) is equivalent to the minimization of

$$J(W) \doteq H(y^1) + \ldots + H(y^d). \tag{3}$$

2.2 Multi-dimensional Entropy Estimation

Recently, we have developed efficient solutions to the ISA problem [15, 16], which are based on efficient multi-dimensional estimations of the entropy $H(y^i)$. Under mild assumptions, the Beadword-Halton-Hammersley theorem [20, 21] approximates Rényi's α-entropy, which in turn can be used for approximation of the Shannon entropy. This estimation is asymptotically unbiased and strongly consistent [20]. We modify the result of this theorem by a monotone increasing transformation and propose the following estimation [15]: Let $\{y^i(1), \ldots, y^i(n)\}$ be an i.i.d. sample set from distribution y^i. Let $\mathcal{N}_{k,j}^i$ be the k nearest neighbors of $y^i(j)$ in this sample set. Then a possible estimation of $H(y^i)$ up to an irrelevant additive and multiplicative constant is the following:

$$\hat{H}^1(y^i) \doteq \lim_{\gamma \to 0} \sum_{j=1}^{n} \sum_{z \in \mathcal{N}_{k,j}^i} \|z - y^i(j)\|^\gamma \tag{4}$$

In [15] we also derived another estimation for the entropy:

$$\hat{H}^2(y^i) \doteq \sum_{j=1}^{n} \sum_{z \in \mathcal{N}_{k,j}^i} \log(\|z - y^i(j)\|) \tag{5}$$

2.3 Optimization and Error Measurement

We have used ICA as a preprocessing step, because (3) can be written as

$$J(\boldsymbol{W}) = \sum_{j=1}^{d}\sum_{i=1}^{m} H(y_i^j) - \sum_{j=1}^{d} I(y_1^j,\ldots,y_m^j), \qquad (6)$$

Then, the minimization of (3) is equivalent to the maximization of the mutual information ($I(y_1^j,\ldots,y_m^j)$ for all j) *within* the subspaces. To this end, 1-dimensional (1D) D Jacobi-rotations can be applied between the components. Details can be found in [15, 16]. 1D global search is executed in each 1D optimization. An iteration cycle is made of $m^2 d(d-1)/2$ steps of 1D optimization tasks, which is much less demanding than the exhaustive search for optimal rotation in $\mathbb{R}^{md \times md}$. According to [10] in some cases, only 90 degree rotations (i.e., permutations of the components between subspaces) were allowed. Cycles are repeated until convergence.

Note also that if the ISA algorithm works properly, then the product of the estimated separation matrix $\boldsymbol{W}$ and the original mixing matrix $\boldsymbol{A}$ produces a permutation matrix made of $m \times m$ blocks. We measure the distance of $\boldsymbol{WA}$ and the permutation matrix by using a generalization of the Amari-distance [22]. Let b_{ij} denote the sum of the absolute values of elements at the intersection of the $i(m-1)+1,\ldots,im$ rows and the $j(m-1)+1,\ldots,jm$ columns of matrix $\boldsymbol{WA}$. Then the generalized Amari-distance $\rho(\boldsymbol{A},\boldsymbol{W})$ is defined as follows:

$$\rho(\boldsymbol{A},\boldsymbol{W}) \doteq \frac{1}{2d}\sum_{i=1}^{d}\left(\frac{\sum_{j=1}^{d}|b_{ij}|}{\max_j |b_{ij}|} - 1\right) + \frac{1}{2d}\sum_{j=1}^{d}\left(\frac{\sum_{i=1}^{d}|b_{ij}|}{\max_i |b_{ij}|} - 1\right) \geq 0 \qquad (7)$$

Clearly, $\rho(\boldsymbol{A},\boldsymbol{W}) = 0$ iff $\boldsymbol{WA}$ is a permutation matrix made of $m \times m$ blocks. Amari distance is a non-monotonic function of our objective, but low Amari distance is a good sign of the success of the optimization.

3 ISA Using Innovations

The innovation process $\hat{\boldsymbol{s}}(t)$ of a stochastic process $\boldsymbol{s}(t)$ can be written as

$$\hat{\boldsymbol{s}}(t) = \boldsymbol{s}(t) - \boldsymbol{E}(\boldsymbol{s}(t)|t,\boldsymbol{s}(t-1),\boldsymbol{s}(t-2),\ldots), \qquad (8)$$

see e.g., [17] and the cited references. In other words, the innovation process is the error of the best prediction. Estimation of the innovation process can be performed by approximating the conditional expectation of Eq. (8), which is the best prediction of $\boldsymbol{s}(t)$ given its past in the least mean-square sense. This regression problem can be approximated by ordinary linear AR or by more sophisticated nonlinear predictions.

A special group of time-dependent stochastic processes are formed by m-dimensional τ-order AR processes:

$$\boldsymbol{y}(t) = \boldsymbol{F}_1 \boldsymbol{y}(t-1) + \ldots + \boldsymbol{F}_\tau \boldsymbol{y}(t-\tau) + \boldsymbol{\epsilon} \qquad (9)$$

where $\boldsymbol{F}_p$ are $m \times m$ matrices and $\boldsymbol{\epsilon}$ is an m-dimensional i.i.d. noise. Note that for AR processes the innovation is equivalent to the $\boldsymbol{\epsilon}$ noise. If such processes are mixed in the ISA problem, then the task is to identify and 'subtract' the deterministic part of the temporal process and to recover the mixed, but i.i.d. noises. Mixed noise components then enable the ISA procedure.

In the ISA problem, the innovation process of the mixed input is the same as the mixture of the innovations of the original processes

$$\boldsymbol{A}\hat{\boldsymbol{y}}(t) = \boldsymbol{x}(t) - \boldsymbol{E}(\boldsymbol{x}(t)|t, \boldsymbol{x}(t-1), \boldsymbol{x}(t-2), \dots) = \hat{\boldsymbol{x}}(t) \qquad (10)$$

because of the linearity of the expectation operator. Mixing matrix $\boldsymbol{A}$ is the same for both the original and for the innovation processes. Therefore an ISA estimation which operates on the innovation process identifies the desired model.

3.1 Algorithm

We extended the ISA algorithm of [15]: We preprocessed the mixed data by the autoregressive model of [23]. The order of the AR model was also estimated. In the next step, traditional ICA processing was used on the gained innovation process, i.e., on the error of the prediction. This step was followed by a series of Jacobi-rotations. For all rotations the global minimum of cost function J was computed, where entropy was estimated through Eq. (4) or Eq. (5). For all Jacobi-rotations, 1D global optimizations using exhaustive search for each single rotational angle $\theta \in [-\frac{\pi}{2}, \frac{\pi}{2}]$, or, only simple permutations were made.

4 Computational Experiments

First, we tested ISA on an artificial problem of mixed processes with known innovation processes. 2nd-order AR process were generated; the coefficient matrices of the AR process were selected randomly. Each subspace had 3 dimensions (there were 6 subspaces in total). Independent noise was added from six different 3D wireframe shapes used as sampling distributions (Fig. 1). The data, which consisted of 6×3 dimensional vectors, were mixed with random matrix $\boldsymbol{A} \in \mathbb{R}^{18 \times 18}$.

Here we ensured that an AR model *is sufficient* for the estimation of the innovations. Plain ISA was not able to separate the independent sources from the data (Fig. 1(e)). The combination of the autoregressive model and the ISA algorithm could, however, recover the original distributions (Figs. 1(d) and 1(f)).

In another experiment, we used 6 different facial images with 50×50 pixels (Fig. 2(a)). The pixel values were linearly scaled and truncated to integers such that their sum was 100,000 for each image. Then we scanned the images from left-to-right and from top-to-bottom and took the 2D coordinate samples of the pixels as many times as directed by the value of each pixel. This is referred to as the 'pixelwise' procedure in the caption of Fig. 2. In this case, ISA could not find the proper subspaces because the sampling is very far from being temporally independent (Figs. 2(c) and 2(e)). The problem *is not* an AR problem, there are

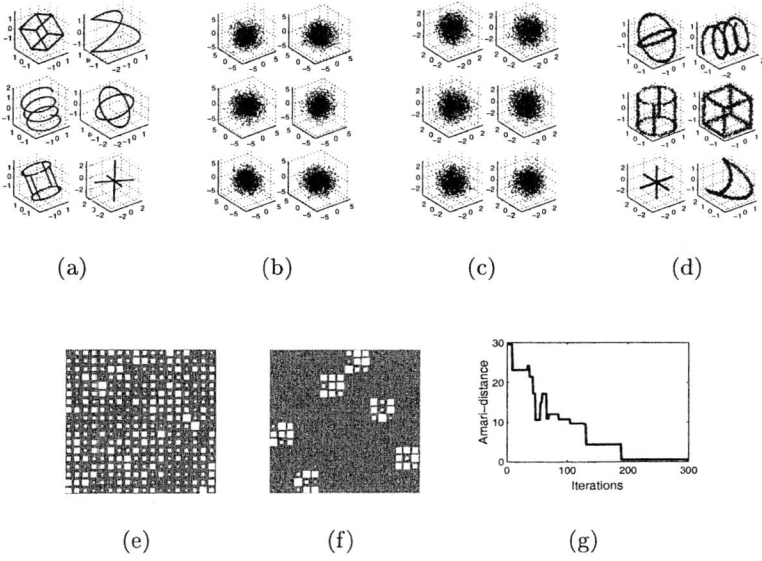

Fig. 1. ISA results for the 3D illustrative example
(a): noise of AR processes, (b): AR processes before mixing, (c): innovations, (d): estimated sources of innovations, (e): Performance without using innovations, (f): Performance with innovations, (g): Amari distance. Performance is shown in the form of Hinton-diagrams on the product of mixing and estimated separation matrices.

strong echoes in these 'processes' from one line to another one. Arguably, the 'processes' are deterministic. Nevertheless, when we used the innovation, ISA estimated the subspaces properly as shown in Figs. 2(d) and 2(f). Figures were produced using Eq. (5), but both Eqs. (4) and (5) gave similar results.

5 Discussion and Conclusions

We have introduced the innovation process into independent subspace analysis. This step is useful if the sources have a temporal structure, but the noises in the processes are independent. A 2D problem using 'processes' generated from mixtures of facial pictures was also demixed by the innovationX process.

The concept of innovation in blind source separation techniques and the fact that it extends the range of addressable problems for ICA is not new. Autoregressive processes were used in [17, 18, 19, 24, 25] for modelling the independent sources. Some ICA algorithms assume that independent sources have different autocorrelation structures and use temporal second-order correlations. If this restriction is not fulfilled, e.g., if the sources have approximately the same distributions, then separation may fail. Generalization to the multi-dimensional case is not trivial.

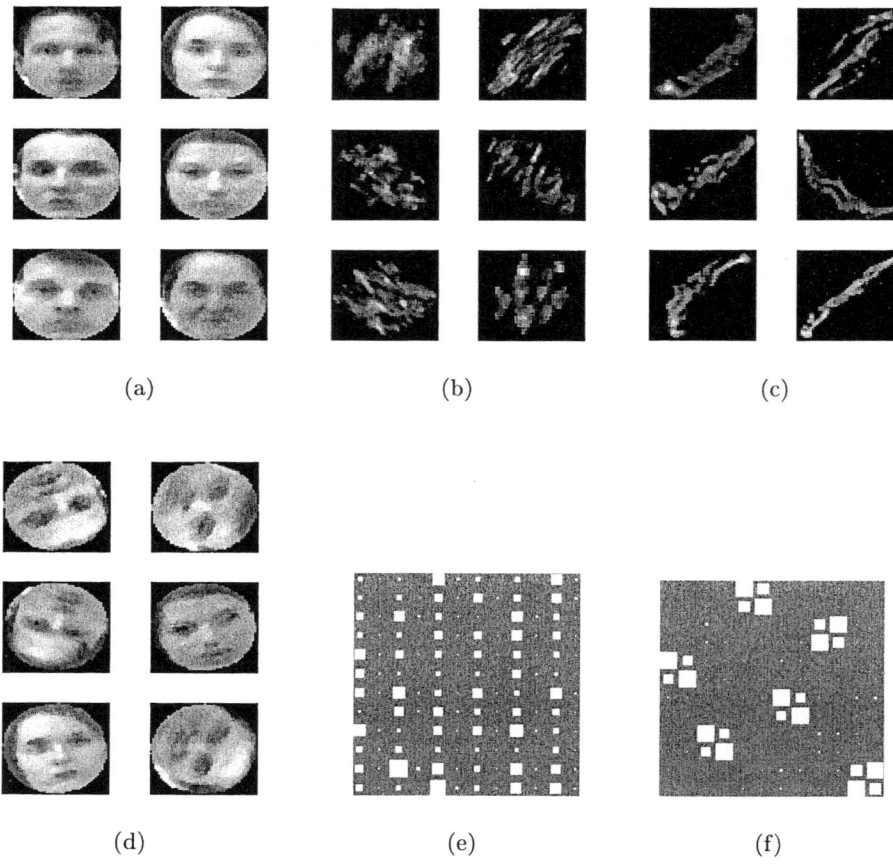

Fig. 2. Example when multi-dimensional samples drawn pixelwise (a): original facial images, (b): mixed sources, pixelwise sampling, (c): ISA estimations, (d): estimations with ISA on innovations, (e): performance of ISA, (f): performance of ISA on innovations. Image quality is enhanced by median-filter.

Processes which are not stationary, are hard to manage with ISA, because the estimation of some quantities, e.g., the entropy and the expectations are hard. However, for AR ISA problems, the innovation is i.i.d. and our algorithm works properly. Hyvärinen [17] also argues that the innovation process has other valuable properties: Innovations are usually *more independent* from each other than the original processes, because the independence of the innovations does not imply that the original processes were independent - only the opposite is true. In summary, switching to the innovation process before processing the data can lead to more accurate estimations of the mixing matrix.

Our numerical simulations demonstrate that ISA alike to ICA may benefit from innovations. For AR processes, the underlying model remains unchanged when the original data are replaced by the innovations. We note that for the pixelwise case, the AR assumption is not valid, the problem is deterministic. Still, ISA on the 'innovations' produced good results. Thus, the robustness of the ISA makes the AR assumption *the trick of demixing*.

References

1. Jutten, C., Herault, J.: Blind separation of sources: An adaptive algorithm based on neuromimetic architecture. Signal Proc. **24** (1991) 1–10
2. Comon, P.: Independent component analysis, a new concept? Signal Proc. **36** (1994) 287–314
3. Bell, A.J., Sejnowski, T.J.: An information maximisation approach to blind separation and blind deconvolution. Neural Comp. **7** (1995) 1129–1159
4. Bell, A.J., Sejnowski, T.J.: The 'independent components' of natural scenes are edge filters. Vision Research **37** (1997) 3327–3338
5. Hyvärinen, A.: Sparse code shrinkage: Denoising of nongaussian data by maximum likelihood estimation. Neural Comp. **11** (1999) 1739–1768
6. Kiviluoto, K., Oja, E.: Independent component analysis for parallel financial time series. In: Proc. of ICONIP'98. Volume 2. (1998) 895–898
7. Makeig, S., Bell, A.J., Jung, T.P., Sejnowski, T.J.: Independent component analysis of electroencephalographic data. In: Proc. of NIPS. Volume 8. (1996) 145–151
8. Vigário, R., Jousmaki, V., Hamalainen, M., Hari, R., Oja, E.: Independent component analysis for identification of artifacts in magnetoencephalographic recordings. In: Proc. of NIPS. Volume 10. (1997) 229–235
9. Hyvärinen, A., Karhunen, J., Oja, E.: Independent Component Analysis. John Wiley, New York (2001)
10. Cardoso, J.: Multidimensional independent component analysis. In: Proc. of ICASSP'98, Seattle, WA. (1998) 1941
11. Hyvärinen, A., Hoyer, P.: Emergence of phase and shift invariant features by decomposition of natural images into independent feature subspaces. Neural Comp. **12** (2000) 1705–1720
12. Akaho, S., Kiuchi, Y., Umeyama, S.: MICA: Multimodal independent component analysis. In: Proc. of IJCNN. (1999) 927–932
13. Vollgraf, R., Obermayer, K.: Multi-dimensional ICA to separate correlated sources. In: Proc. of NIPS. Volume 14. (2001) 993–1000
14. Bach, F.R., Jordan, M.I.: Finding clusters in independent component analysis. In: Proc. of ICA2003. (2003) 891–896
15. Póczos, B., Lőrincz, A.: Independent subspace analysis using k-nearest neighborhood distances. In: Proc. of ICANN, Warsaw, Poland. (2005) (accepted).
16. Póczos, B., Lőrincz, A.: Independent subspace analysis using geodesic spanning trees. In: Proc. of ICML, Bonn, Germany. (2005) (accepted).
17. Hyvärinen, A.: Independent component analysis for time-dependent stochastic processes. In: Proc. of ICANN, Skövde, Sweden. (1998) 541–546
18. Choi, S.: Acoustic source separation: Fundamental issues. In: Proc of. ICSP, Seoul, Korea. (1999) 505–510
19. Cheung, Y., Xu, L.: Dual multivariate auto-regressive modeling in state space for temporal signal separation. IEEE Trans. on Sys. Man. and Cyb. (**33**) 386–398
20. Yukich, J.E.: Probability Theory of Classical Euclidean Optimization Problems. Volume 1675 of Lecture Notes in Math. Springer-Verlag, Berlin (1998)

21. Costa, J.A., Hero, A.O.: Manifold learning using k-nearest neighbor graphs. In: Proc. of ICASSP, Montreal, Canada. (2004)
22. Amari, S., Cichocki, A., Yang, H.: A new learning algorithm for blind source separation. In: Proc. of NIPS. Volume 8. (1996) 757–763
23. Schneider, T., Neumaier, A.: Algorithm 808: ARfit - A Matlab package for the estimation of parameters and eigenmodes of multivariate autoregressive models. ACM Trans. Math. Softw. **27** (2001) 58–65
24. Penny, W.D., Everson, R., Roberts, S.J.: Hidden Markov independent component analysis. In Giroliami, M., ed.: Advances in Independent Component Analysis. Springer (2000) 3–22
25. Pearlmutter, B.A., Parra, L.C.: A context-sensitive generalization of ICA. In: Proc. of ICONIP'96, Hong Kong. (1996) 151–157

On Applying Tabling to Inductive Logic Programming*

Ricardo Rocha[1], Nuno Fonseca[1], and Vítor Santos Costa[2]

[1] DCC-FC & LIACC,
University of Porto, Portugal
{ricroc, nf}@ncc.up.pt
[2] Department of Biostatistics and Medical Informatics,
University of Wisconsin-Madison, USA
vitor@biostat.wisc.edu

Abstract. Inductive Logic Programming (ILP) is an established subfield of Machine Learning. Nevertheless, it is recognized that efficiency and scalability is a major obstacle to an increased usage of ILP systems in complex applications with large hypotheses spaces. In this work, we focus on improving the efficiency and scalability of ILP systems by exploring tabling mechanisms available in the underlying Logic Programming systems. Tabling is an implementation technique that improves the declarativeness and performance of Prolog systems by reusing answers to subgoals. To validate our approach, we ran the April ILP system in the YapTab Prolog tabling system using two well-known datasets. The results obtained show quite impressive gains without changing the accuracy and quality of the theories generated.

1 Introduction

Inductive Logic Programming (ILP) has been successfully applied to problems in several application domains [1]. Nevertheless, the flexibility of ILP comes at a price: for complex applications with large hypotheses spaces, ILP systems can take several hours, if not days, to return a theory. Past research on improving the efficiency of ILP systems has mainly focused in reducing their sequential execution time, either by reducing the number of hypotheses generated [2,3], or by efficiently testing candidate hypotheses [4,5]. One key observation in this research is that ILP search space is highly redundant: we repeatedly test similar, and sometimes even the same, hypotheses. This argues for using techniques such as *memoing* or *tabling* [6], that have been developed for this very purpose.

On the other hand, ILP systems are often developed on top of logic programming systems, such as Prolog systems. One reason is that ILP systems can

---

* This work has been partially supported by APRIL (POSI/SRI/40749/2001), Myddas (POSC/EIA/59154/2004), U.S. Air Force (grant F30602-01-2-0571), and by funds granted to LIACC through the Programa de Financiamento Plurianual, Fundação para a Ciência e Tecnologia (FCT) and Programa POSC. Nuno Fonseca is funded by the FCT grant SFRH/BD/7045/2001.

benefit from the extensive work done in improving the performance of Prolog systems. An emerging technology is *tabling*, that showed to be very effective for a variety of applications. Tabling based models can reduce the search space, avoid looping, and have better termination properties than traditional Prolog based models. The question thus arises if the tabling mechanisms being developed for efficient execution of logic programs can be useful in improving ILP performance.

In this work, we show that tabling can indeed significantly reduce the execution time of ILP applications. We present two different approaches to achieve this goal. Our first approach is a direct application of tabling to query execution. The second approach is designed to take advantage of the redundancy in ILP search. We validate our approach by experimenting the April ILP system [7] on two well known ILP datasets. One advantage of using April in our study is that it includes a strong caching mechanism, thus giving us a good baseline for our studies. Tabling is implemented through the YapTab Prolog tabling system [8].

The remainder of the paper is organized as follows. First, we introduce the motivation for our work. Then, we briefly describe tabling for logic programs. Next, we discuss how tabling can be used to speedup ILP applications. We then present initial experimental results and conclude by outlining some conclusions.

2 Background and Motivation

The fundamental goal of an ILP system is to find a consistent and complete *theory*, from a set of examples and prior knowledge, the *background knowledge*, that explains all given positive examples, while being consistent with the given negative examples. In general, the background knowledge and the set of examples can be arbitrary logic programs.

Since it is not usually obvious which set of hypotheses should be selected as the theory, an ILP system must traverse the *hypotheses space* searching for a set with the desired properties. A general ILP system thus spends most of its time evaluating hypotheses, either because the number of examples is large or because testing each example is computationally hard.

An important characteristic of ILP systems is that they generate candidate hypotheses (clauses) which have many similarities among them. Usually, these similarities tend to correspond to common prefixes (subgoals) among the candidate hypotheses.

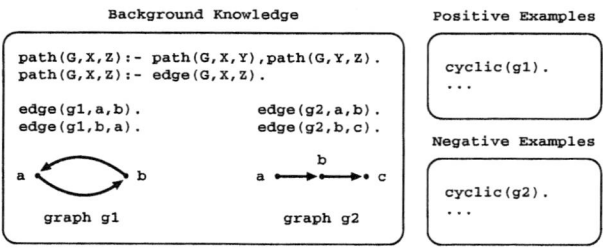

Fig. 1. Representing cyclic graphs in a ILP dataset

Consider, for example, a background knowledge containing a set of directed graphs, represented by `edge/3` facts, with a relation of reachability, given by a `path/3` predicate (see Fig. 1 for details). Consider also that we are interested in learning the concept of being a cyclic graph.

Now assume that, during the search process, the ILP system generates an hypothesis 'cyclic(G):- path(G,X,Y).' which obtains *good coverage*, that is, the number of positive examples covered by it is high and the number of negative example is low. Then, it is quite possible that the system will use it to generate more specific hypotheses such as 'cyclic(G):- path(G,X,Y),edge(G,Y,Z).'.

Computing the coverage of an hypothesis requires, in general, running all positives and negatives examples against the clause. For example, to evaluate if the example cyclic(g1) is covered by the hypothesis 'cyclic(G):-path(G,X,Y).', the system executes the goal once(path(g1,X,Y)). The once/1 predicate is a primitive that prunes over the search space preventing the unnecessary search for further answers. It can be defined in Prolog as 'once(Goal):- call(Goal),!.'.

If the same example, cyclic(g1), is later evaluated against the other hypothesis, goal once(path(g1,X,Y),edge(g1,Y,Z)), part of the computation of path(g1,X,Y) will be repeated. This suggests two approaches to avoid recomputation. First, if the computation of path(g1,X,Y) is computationally expensive, we can table this query. Second, the subgoal path(g1,X,Y) forms a prefix of the new clause. We can *table prefixes*, in the hope that they will be called repeatedly.

Notice that both approaches have problems. The first approach will only work if the computation for a subgoal is expensive. It will bring no benefit if, say, the subgoal reduces to a database access. The second approach is only useful if we repeatedly generate the same prefix. If we have a large number of prefixes which are only called a few times, we may need large amounts of space to store the tables, and gain little time-wise. To best implement these approaches requires some understanding of the basic tabling mechanisms, that we discuss next.

3 Tabling for Inductive Logic Programming

The basic idea behind tabling is straightforward: programs are evaluated by storing newly found answers for current subgoals in an appropriate data space, called the *table space*. The method then uses this table to verify whether calls to subgoals are repeated. Whenever such a repeated call is found, the subgoal's answers are recalled from the table instead of being re-evaluated against the program clauses. One of the major characteristics of this execution model is that it reduces the search space by avoiding the recomputation of tabled subgoals. This is the most significant contribution that tabling can offer to ILP. Moreover, because tabling based models are also able to avoid infinite loops, they can ensure termination for a wider class of programs. The latter can be useful when dealing with datasets with recursive definitions in the background knowledge.

3.1 Tabled Evaluation

Figure 2 uses the example from the background knowledge in Fig. 1 to illustrate how tabling works. At the top, the figure shows the program code (the left box), and the final state of the table space (the right box). Declaration ':-table path/3.' indicates that calls to predicate path/3 should be tabled. The main sub-figure below shows the evaluation sequence for the query goal

'?- path(g1,b,Z).'. Note that traditional Prolog would immediately enter an infinite loop because the first clause of path/3 leads to a repeated call to path(g1,b,Z). In contrast, if tabling is applied then termination is ensured.

Whenever a tabled subgoal is first called, a new entry is added to the table space. We name these calls *generator nodes* (nodes depicted by white oval boxes). In this example, the execution begins with a generator. The first step is to resolve path(g1,b,Z) against the first clause for path/3, creating node 1. Node 1 is a variant call to path(g1,b,Z). We do not resolve the subgoal against the program at these nodes, instead we consume answers from the table. Such nodes are thus called *consumer nodes* (nodes depicted by black oval boxes). At this point, the table does not have answers for this call, and thus, the current evaluation is *suspended*. We then backtrack to node 0, thus calling edge(g1,b,Z). The edge/3 predicate is not tabled, hence it must be resolved against the program, as Prolog would. The first clause for edge/3 fails, but the second succeeds obtaining an answer for path(g1,b,Z) (step 4).

In the continuation, we backtrack again to node 0, but now it has no more clauses left to try. So, we check whether it has *completed*. It has not, as node 1 has now one unconsumed answer. We thus forward the answer to it, and path(g1,a,Z) is then called. As this is the first call to path(g1,a,Z), we add a new entry for it in the table, and proceed as shown in the bottommost tree.

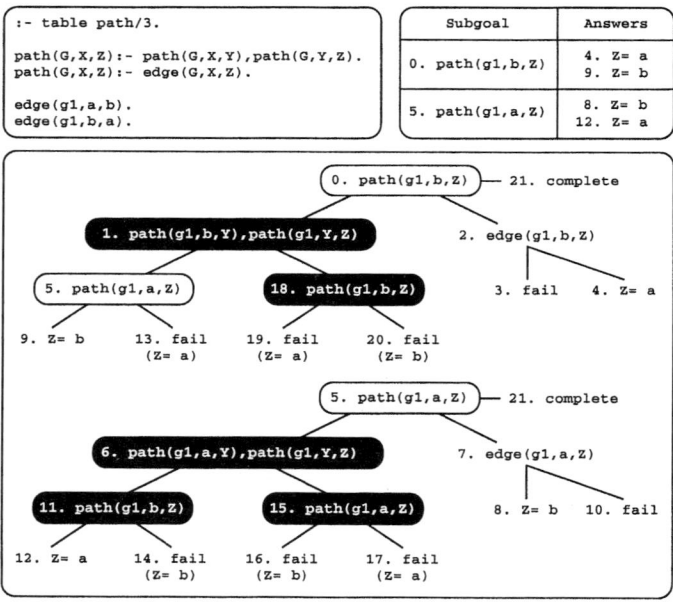

Fig. 2. A tabled evaluation

Again, path(g1,a,Z) calls itself recursively, suspends at node 6, backtracks, and succeeds with Z=b (step 8). We then follow a Prolog-like strategy and continue forward execution. The binding Z=b is thus returned to path(g1,b,Z) and stored in its table entry (step 9). This will be the last answer to path(g1,b,Z), but we can only prove so after fully exploiting the tree.

We then fail in step 10, backtrack to node 5, and resume node 6 with answer Z=b. This leads to a new consumer for path(g1,b,Z) (node 11). The table has two answers for it, so we can continue immediately. This gives new answers to path(g1,a,Z) (step 12) and to path(g1,b,Z) (step 13). However, this last answer repeats what we found in step 4. Tabled resolution do not stores duplicate answers in the table. Instead, repeated answers *fail*. This is how we avoid unnecessary computations, and even looping in some cases.

Backtracking sends us back to consumer node 11. We then consume the second answer for it, which generates a repeated answer, so we fail again (step 14). We then try the second answer for node 6, again leading to a repeated subgoal (node 15) and two repeated answers (steps 16 and 17). We then fail back to node 5, but at this point, all answers to the consumers below (nodes 6, 11, and 15) have been tried. However, unfortunately, node 5 cannot complete, because it depends on subgoal path(g1,b,Z) (node 11). Completing path(g1,a,Z) earlier is not safe because we can loose answers. Note that, new answers can still be found for subgoal path(g1,b,Z). If new answers are found, node 11 should be resumed with the newly found answers, which in turn can lead to new answers for subgoal path(g1,a,Z). If we complete sooner, we can loose such answers.

Execution thus backtracks and we try the answer left for node 1. Steps 19 to 20 show that again we only get repeated answers. We fail and return to node 0. All nodes in the trees for node 0 and node 5 have been exploited. As these trees do not depend on any other tree, we are sure no more answers are forthcoming, so at last step 21 declares the two trees to be complete.

3.2 Tabling Subgoals and Conjunction of Subgoals

The first application of tabling in ILP is simply to table subgoals. The main advantage of this approach is that we need to perform minimal changes to the ILP system. A drawback is that this technique will not help if the subgoal generates a very small computation, say, if the subgoal is defined extensionally in the database as Prolog facts. A second approach is to take advantage of the tabling paradigm and replace the conjunction of predicates in the hypotheses with proper tabled predicates inferred during execution. Consider, for example, the following set of hypotheses:

```
cyclic(G):- edge(G,X,Y), path(G,Y,Z), edge(G,Z,X).
cyclic(G):- edge(G,X,Y), path(G,Y,Z), edge(G,X,Z).
cyclic(G):- edge(G,X,Y), path(G,Y,Z), path(G,Z,X).
```

Note that the two first subgoals, edge(G,X,Y) and path(G,Y,Z), are common to all the hypotheses. Thus, if we are able to table the conjunction of both, we only need to compute it once. This idea can be recursively applied as the system generates more specific hypothesis. This idea is similar to the *query packs* technique proposed by Blockeel *et al.* [4].

To implement this approach, we designed the following solution. First, we use a single predicate, t_all/2, to table all the conjunctions. The first argument for t_all/2 is an atom that defines the name given to the conjunction. The second is the set of variables involved. This predicate then calls a t_conj/2 predicate (with the same arguments) where the conjunctions are defined. The clauses for the t_conj/2 predicate are dynamically asserted by the ILP system as new conjunctions are generated. A conjunction of N subgoals is defined as the conjunction of the $N-1$ previous subgoals followed by the Nth subgoal. For example, we would have the following clauses for the set of hypotheses above:

```
% the tabled predicate for all the conjunctions
:- table t_all/2.
t_all(ConjunctionName,VarsList):- t_conj(ConjunctionName,VarsList).

% level 1 conjunctions
t_conj(edge,[V1,V2,V3]):- edge(V1,V2,V3).
t_conj(path,[V1,V2,V3]):- path(V1,V2,V3).

% level 2 conjunctions
t_conj(edge_path,[V1,V2,V3,V4,V5,V6]):- t_all(edge,[V1,V2,V3]),
                                        t_all(path,[V4,V5,V6]).
```

Finally, we need to transform the clauses for the hypotheses. We thus replace the conjunctions of subgoals in the hypotheses to calls to the t_all/2 predicate. For example, the previous set of hypotheses will be transformed to:

```
cyclic(G):- t_all(edge_path,[G,X,Y,G,Y,Z]), t_all(edge,[G,Z,X]).
cyclic(G):- t_all(edge_path,[G,X,Y,G,Y,Z]), t_all(edge,[G,X,Z]).
cyclic(G):- t_all(edge_path,[G,X,Y,G,Y,Z]), t_all(path,[G,Z,X]).
```

Note that this may cause the same variables to appear at several positions in the second argument for the t_all/2 predicate (e.g., both G and Y appear twice for edge_path). In practice, the tabling engine only stores the answers once for each different variable, so this only has a small cost. A major problem with our approach is the amount of memory that is needed to represent the answers for the different conjunctions. A simple solution is to abolish the full set of tables from the table space when we run out of memory. An alternative would be to abolish the tables potentially useless when we backtrack in the hypotheses space. This later approach requires further study to avoid incorrect deletions.

At that point, we should reinforce the differences between tabling and between the approach of tabling conjunction of subgoals. Tabling is an implementation technique that comes for free if using a Prolog engine with such support. The tabling of conjunctions is an alternative evaluation strategy that can be explored by ILP systems. Like in query packs, this is done automatically in the innards of the ILP system, and can be parameter controlled. Thus, the final user of the system only needs to declare the strategy to be used: no tabling, subgoal tabling, or subgoal and conjunction tabling.

4 Initial Experimental Results

To evaluate the impact of using tabling in real application problems, we ran the April ILP system [7] with the YapTab Prolog tabling system [8] using two ILP datasets: *mutagenesis* and *carcinogenesis*. April was configured to find hypotheses using breadth-first search, and to evaluate hypotheses using a heuristic that relies on the number of positive and negative examples. YapTab is based on the current development version of Yap, version 4.5.7. The environment for our experiments was an AMD Athlon MP 2600+ processor with 2 GBytes of main memory and running the Linux kernel 2.6.11.

To evaluate hypotheses we experimented with three different approaches: **(i)** without tabling; **(ii)** subgoals being evaluated using tabling; and **(iii)** subgoals and conjunction of subgoals being evaluated using tabling.

Table 1 shows the running times, in seconds, and the table memory usage, in Mbytes, for the three approaches. We use **na** to mark the experiments not ran and **mo** to mark the runs where a memory overflow occurred. Note that we are not considering any strategy to avoid memory overflows. The value **nodes** is the upper bound on the number of hypotheses, and **hypotheses** is the number of hypotheses effectively generated during the search.

Table 1. Running times and table usage with one example as seed

Datasets	Running Time (s)			Table Usage (Mb)	
nodes/hypotheses	without	subgs	conjs	subgs	conjs
mutagenesis					
1,000/981	> 4 hours	94	92	2	6
10,000/6,514	na	162	140	5	205
20,000/14,020	na	169	146	6	281
30,000/20,299	na	197	mo	6	mo
40,000/26,484	na	219	mo	6	mo
50,000/32,852	na	236	mo	6	mo
carcinogenesis					
1,000/998	1	1	1	3	11
10,000/9,998	7	9	13	11	259
20,000/19,998	81	91	mo	11	mo
30,000/29,932	121	124	mo	11	mo
40,000/39,932	161	154	mo	11	mo
50,000/49,869	225	209	mo	12	mo

The results obtained for *mutagenesis* show that tabled evaluation can significantly reduce the execution time for these kind of problems. In particular, for the subgoal approach the gains are quite impressive. The theorem proving effort involved to evaluate a single example against an hypothesis is quite high for this dataset. The conjunction approach also achieved the goal of reducing the execution time (however, we were not able to use more than 20,000 nodes). Regarding memory usage, the results show an insignificant increase in memory consumption when tabling subgoals and a more considerable increase when tabling conjunctions of subgoals.

In the *carcinogenesis* dataset, the results where not so good. The main reason for this relies on the type of predicates that compose its background knowledge. In this dataset most of the predicates are defined extensionally in the database as Prolog facts, and thus, it is quite difficult for the tabling engine reduce the execution time. Even so, when we increase the size of the search space for the *carcinogenesis* dataset (for more than 40,000 nodes), the tabling subgoal approach slightly reduces the execution time when compared with the execution without tabling. Regarding the conjunction approach we were not able to see its impact in this dataset.

The results obtained suggest that tabling is particular suited for ILP applications with a background knowledge non-deterministic, as the *mutaganesis* dataset. The results also confirm that tabling is not suitable for datasets with a background knowledge defined extensionally. However, apart the small extra memory consumption in the case of tabling subgoals, the execution with tabling do not introduces significant overheads.

5 Conclusions and Further Work

In this work, we proposed the ability of using tabling mechanisms available in the underlying Logic Programming systems to minimize recomputation in ILP systems. The results obtained showed that tabling based models are indeed able to improve the performance of ILP applications. In particular, for some applications, they show quite impressive gains. As tabled evaluation does not influences the accuracy and quality of the models found, we believe that our proposals would apply to several ILP systems.

A major problem with our current implementation, is that we can increase the table memory usage arbitrarily when tabling conjunction of subgoals. We plan to study how we can abolish potentially useless tables when we backtrack in the hypotheses space. We also plan to further investigate the impact of applying our proposals to a larger set of ILP applications.

References

1. Network of Excellence in Inductive Logic Programming ILPnet2: (ILP Applications) Available from http://www.cs.bris.ac.uk/~ILPnet2/Applications.
2. Nédellec, C., Rouveirol, C., Adé, H., Bergadano, F., Tausend, B.: Declarative Bias in ILP. In Raedt, L.D., ed.: Advances in Inductive Logic Programming. IOS Press (1996) 82–103
3. Sebag, M., Rouveirol, C.: Tractable Induction and Classification in First-Order Logic via Stochastic Matching. In: International Joint Conference on Artificial Intelligence, Morgan Kaufmann (1997) 888–893
4. Blockeel, H., Dehaspe, L., Demoen, B., Janssens, G., Ramon, J., Vandecasteele, H.: Improving the Efficiency of Inductive Logic Programming Through the Use of Query Packs. Journal of Artificial Intelligence Research **16** (2002) 135–166
5. Santos Costa, V., Srinivasan, A., Camacho, R., Blockeel, H., Demoen, B., Janssens, G., Struyf, J., Vandecasteele, H., Laer, W.V.: Query Transformations for Improving the Efficiency of ILP Systems. Journal of Machine Learning Research **4** (2002) 465–491
6. Michie, D.: Memo Functions and Machine Learning. Nature **218** (1968) 19–22
7. Fonseca, N., Camacho, R., Silva, F., Santos Costa, V.: Induction with April: A Preliminary Report. Technical Report DCC-2003-02, Department of Computer Science, University of Porto (2003)
8. Rocha, R., Silva, F., Santos Costa, V.: YapTab: A Tabling Engine Designed to Support Parallelism. In: Conference on Tabulation in Parsing and Deduction. (2000) 77–87

Learning Models of Relational Stochastic Processes

Sumit Sanghai, Pedro Domingos, and Daniel Weld

University of Washington, Seattle WA 98195, USA
{sanghai, pedrod, weld}@cs.washington.edu

Abstract. Processes involving change over time, uncertainty, and rich relational structure are common in the real world, but no general algorithms exist for learning models of them. In this paper we show how Markov logic networks (MLNs), a recently developed approach to combining logic and probability, can be applied to time-changing domains. We then show how existing algorithms for parameter and structure learning in MLNs can be extended to this setting. We apply this approach in two domains: modeling the spread of research topics in scientific communities, and modeling faults in factory assembly processes. Our experiments show that it greatly outperforms purely logical (ILP) and purely probabilistic (DBN) learners.

1 Introduction

Stochastic processes involving the creation and modification of objects and relations over time are widespread, but relatively poorly studied. Examples of such systems include social networks, manufacturing processes, bioinformatics, natural language, etc. Until recently, graphical models like DBNs and HMMs were the most powerful representations for reasoning about stochastic sequential phenomena. However, modeling relational domains using these graphical models requires exhaustively representing all possible objects and the relations among them. Such a model is both hard to learn and difficult to understand. For example, consider a social network such as an evolving scientific community. One might wish to model the spread of topics across the various groups of researchers. This might mean discovering rules such as "An author's interest in topics in the future is influenced by the interests of his main collaborators and the communities in which he has recently participated." Such rules, being probabilistic, cannot be encoded using pure first-order logic. But a DBN or an HMM would require a model for each individual researcher, and would not generalize from one author to another.

In recent years, researchers have proposed many approaches to combining aspects of first-order logic with probabilistic representations [6]. The most powerful of these is Markov logic networks (MLNs), which combine Markov networks and (for the first time) the full power of first-order logic [14]. However, these models lack the dynamic nature of DBNs and HMMs. Previously, we introduced dynamic probabilistic relational models (DPRMs) [15] and relational dynamic Bayesian networks (RDBNs) [17] for modeling relational stochastic processes, but no learning methods have been proposed for these models, limiting their applicability.

In this paper we extend MLNs to model time-changing relational data. We term this extension DMLNs. Learning DMLNs is relatively easy, requiring only straightforward modifications to an MLN learner. We apply DMLN learning in two domains: the evolution of research topics in high-energy physics and fault modeling of mechanical assembly plans. Our experiments show that DMLNs greatly outperform a purely probabilistic approach (DBN learning) and a purely logical approach (ILP).

In the next section, we cover MLNs. Then, we introduce DMLNs and describe the learning methods for them (see [16] for more details). Finally, we report our experimental results and conclude with a discussion of related and future work.

2 Markov Logic Networks

A *Markov network* (also known as Markov random field) is a model for the joint distribution of a set of variables $X = (X_1, X_2, \ldots, X_n)$ [5]. It is composed of an undirected graph G on the variables and a set of non-negative potential functions ϕ_k for the state of each clique in the graph. The joint distribution represented by a Markov network is given by $P(X = x) = \frac{1}{Z} \prod_k \phi_k(x_{\{k\}})$ where $x_{\{k\}}$ is the state of the kth clique (i.e., the state of the variables that appear in that clique). Z, known as the *partition function*, is given by $Z = \sum_{x \in X} \prod_k \phi_k(x_{\{k\}})$. Markov networks are often conveniently represented as *log-linear models*, with each clique potential replaced by an exponentiated weighted sum of features of the state: $P(X = x) = \frac{1}{Z} \exp(\sum_j w_j f_j(x))$. This paper will focus on binary features, $f_j(x) \in \{0, 1\}$. In the presence of large cliques, logical functions of the state of the cliques can be used as features leading to a more compact representation than the potential-function form. MLNs take advantage of this.

A first-order knowledge base (KB) can be seen as a set of hard constraints on the set of possible worlds: if a world violates even one formula, it has zero probability. The basic idea in MLNs is to soften these constraints: when a world violates one formula in the KB it is less probable, but not impossible. The fewer formulas a world violates, the more probable it is. Each formula has an associated weight that reflects how strong a constraint it is: the higher the weight, the greater the difference in log probability between a world that satisfies the formula and one that does not, other things being equal.

Definition 1. *[14] A Markov logic network L is a set of pairs (F_i, w_i), where F_i is a formula in first-order logic and w_i is a real number. Together with a finite set of constants $C = \{c_1, c_2, \ldots, c_{|C|}\}$, it defines a Markov network $M_{L,C}$ as follows:*

1. *$M_{L,C}$ contains one binary node for each possible grounding of each predicate appearing in L. The value of the node is 1 if the ground predicate is true, and 0 otherwise.*
2. *$M_{L,C}$ contains one feature for each possible grounding of each formula F_i in L. The value of this feature is 1 if the ground formula is true, and 0 otherwise. The weight of the feature is the w_i associated with F_i in L.*

Thus there is an edge between two nodes of $M_{L,C}$ iff the corresponding ground predicates appear together in at least one grounding of one formula in L. An MLN can be viewed as a *template* for constructing Markov networks. The probability distribution over possible worlds x specified by the ground Markov network $M_{L,C}$ is given by

$$P(X=x) = \frac{1}{Z} \exp\left(\sum_{i=1}^{F} w_i n_i(x)\right) \quad (1)$$

where F is the number formulas in the MLN and $n_i(x)$ is the number of true groundings of F_i in x. As formula weights increase, an MLN increasingly resembles a purely logical KB, becoming equivalent to one in the limit of all infinite weights. In this paper we focus on MLNs whose formulas are largely function-free clauses and assume domain closure, ensuring that the Markov networks generated are finite [14]. In this case the groundings of a formula are obtained simply by replacing its variables with constants in all possible ways.

3 Modeling Relational Stochastic Processes

Traditionally, graphical models like dynamic Bayesian networks (DBNs), hidden Markov models (HMMs), etc., have been used to model the joint distribution of variables involved in complex stochastic processes. They have been quite successful in practice (e.g., [12]), but they cannot be used to compactly model complex domains with multiple classes, objects and relationships. Modeling such domains requires the representational power of first-order logic. DPRMs [15] and RDBNs [17] provide some of it, and could in principle be learned using ILP and PRM learning techniques, but to date this has not been attempted. In this paper, we instead extend MLNs and their learning algorithms [14,11] to dynamic domains. This extension turns out to be quite straightforward, and gives us the full power of MLNs in dynamic domains. We experimentally demonstrate the effectiveness of this approach.

3.1 Dynamic Markov Logic Networks

In a relational stochastic process, the *world* is not static. A ground predicate can be *true* or *false* depending on the time step t. To model a dynamic relational domain we use the following approach:

1. Instead of standard first-order predicates, we use *fluents*, a special form of predicate having an additional time argument. Time is modeled as a non-negative integer variable. Each predicate in the network is now of the form $R(x_1, \ldots, x_n, t)$, where t denotes time.
2. Our model includes a successor function $succ(t)$, which maps the integer t, representing time, to $t + 1$, i.e., $succ(0) = 1$, $succ(1) = 2$, and so on.
3. We define a *dynamic Markov logic network* (DMLN) to be a set of weighted formulas defined on the fluents.
4. Each formula in the DMLN contains exactly one variable denoting a time slice, and constants may not be used as a fluent's time argument. For example, we disallow formulae such as:
  $\forall$Auth, Topic, t, t' : Writes(Auth, Topic, t) => Writes(Auth, Topic, t').
  The only exception to this is that we allow formulas where all time arguments are the constant 0; these represent the initial distribution.

5. To enforce the first-order Markov assumption, each term in each formula in the DMLN is restricted to at most one application of the *succ* function, i.e., a term such as $succ(succ(t))$ is disallowed. This precludes a ground predicate at time t from depending on ground predicates at time $t-2$ or before.

Given the domain of constants, i.e., the objects at each time slice and the time range of interest, the DMLN will give rise to a ground Markov network whose nodes correspond to the grounding of the predicates (fluents) for each time slice.

3.2 Learning DMLNs

As is common in graphical models, we divide learning DMLNs into two separate problems: parameter learning and structure learning.

The weights of a DMLN can be learned in the same manner as in MLNs, by maximizing the likelihood of a relational database [14]. (A closed-world assumption is made, whereby all ground atoms not in the database are assumed false.) However, as in Markov networks, this requires computing the expected number of true groundings of each formula, which can take exponential time. Although this computation can be done approximately using Markov chain Monte Carlo (MCMC) inference [5], Richardson and Domingos found this to be too slow. Instead, they maximized the pseudo-likelihood of the data, a widely used alternative measure [3]. If x is a possible world (relational database) and x_l is the lth ground atom's truth value, the pseudo-log-likelihood of x given weights w is

$$\log P_w^*(X=x) = \sum_{l=1}^{n} \log P_w(X_l=x_l|MB_x(X_l)) \qquad (2)$$

where $MB_x(X_l)$ is the state of X_l's *Markov blanket* in the data (*i.e.*, the truth values of the ground atoms co-occuring with it in some ground formula). Computing the pseudo-likelihood and its gradient does not require inference, and is therefore much faster.

3.3 Structure Learning in DMLNs

In theory one can learn a fully general DMLN for any relational stochastic process. In other words, one could use a single large example to store a history of the entire relational process and learn a DMLN which does not obey the first-order Markovian restrictions. However, this might lead to an unintuitive model and costly inference. In addition, if the number of time slices is large, formulas involving the time variable may become complex and difficult to learn.

However, we can make certain restrictions on the formulas learned and also equip the learner with background knowledge, making the task easier. We divide the structure learning problem into distinct classes depending on the information provided to the learner:

Learning DMLNs with a Markovian assumption: Like learning in a DBN, we can split the domain into multiple examples. Each example, corresponding to a time step t, is a pair of states at time t and $t+1$. When learning, one can avoid formulas which only involve predicates at time t. A model learned in this way is automatically first-order Markovian and stationary.

Learning in presence of background knowledge: The learner is provided with a set of formulas as background knowledge and allowed to modify existing formulas and add a small number of additional formulas so as to maximize the likelihood of the data.

Learning with templates: In ILP systems learning becomes practical only when combined with a *declarative bias*. For example, when learning a relational stochastic process involving actions, one might want to make sure that each formula contains at least one action. This restriction can be specified using templates. Other forms of bias include restricting the number of predicates in a formula, defining an order on the predicates to be considered during search, creating new predicates and formulas for them, etc.

All of these cases can be handled by appropriately extending the MLN learning techniques [11], as we now show.

The structure learned is the one that maximizes the pseudo-likelihood of the database [11]. The algorithm starts with a set of unit clauses and greedily adds or modifies clauses that give the best pseudo-likelihood. At every iteration, weights for all candidate structures are learned. To do this, the weights are initialized to their values from the previous iteration and they quickly converge to the optimum. Each new candidate clause is obtained by adding or removing predicates from already present clauses, or flipping the signs of the predicates. One of two search techniques is used: (i) a beam search where a set of b best clauses is selected and modified until the pseudo-likelihood ceases to improve, and finally the clause which gives the best pseudo-likelihood is added, or (ii) shortest-first search where all good clauses of a smaller length l are added before adding any of a higher length.

The above algorithm may be combined with the first-order Markovian assumption and templates to learn DMLNs. As we will see in the experiments below, no other techniques are needed.

In this paper, we apply our learned model to infer a distribution over the immediately succeeding time step. Additionally, in our examples, all the state variables are observed. So, we use a standard Gibbs sampler for inference.

4 Experiments

In this section we learn DMLNs for two domains in an effort to answer the following questions about methods for learning models of relational stochastic processes.

Q1 Do DMLNs outperform purely logical approaches such as ILP?
Q2 Do DMLNs outperform purely probabilistic methods such as DBN learning?
Q3 Can formulas that model the dynamics of a relational world be learned, and do such formulas outperform pure parameter learning?
Q4 Does enforcing the Markovian assumption improve the accuracy of a learned DMLN?
Q5 Do templates help in learning better DMLNs?

We investigate these questions by applying our algorithms to problems in two domains: (a) modeling the spread of research topics in the theoretical high-energy physics community, and (b) modeling faults in factory assembly processes.

4.1 Evolution of Topics in High-Energy Physics

For our first domain we used the dataset from the KDDCup 2003 [8] which is a collection of papers from the theoretical high energy physics (hep-th) area of arXiv.org. This dataset consists of 30,000 papers authored by 9,000 scientists over 10 years. We restricted the author set to scientists who have published at least 10 papers. To identify the topics of the papers we ran Kleinberg's burst-detection algorithm [10] on the words appearing in the titles and abstracts of the papers. We intersected the top "bursty" words with words appearing in highly-cited papers and chose the top fifty. Thus, each paper may be associated with multiple topics. In addition, we clustered both authors and journals using K-means, and added a relation connecting them to their clusters. We organized this dataset into constants of different types, e.g., Author, Paper, Journal, etc., and predicates, e.g., AuthorOf, HasTopic, Cites, etc.

Our task was modeling the evolution of topic popularity over time. Specifically, we wished to predict the distribution of each author's paper topics for one year, given the distribution over previous years along with citation patterns, and the interests of scientific communities in which she publishes. The test predicate was set to Authored(A, Topic, Year).

We compared DMLNs with five alternative methods: a purely logical approach (the CLAUDIEN ILP engine [4]), a purely probabilistic method (DBN learning), and three approaches that use only statistics concerning the author's topic distribution in previous years. These latter approaches include predicting the most recent topic distribution (*LYr*), predicting the average of distributions across the last three years (*Avg*), and extrapolating the average gradient of the topic distributions over the last three years (*Gdnt*). To compute probabilities using CLAUDIEN, we associate a very high weight (of 20) with each formula. We used three test sets, the topic distributions for years 2000, 2001 and 2002, always using a training set consisting of the data up to the test year. Our results were similar for all three years, so we report results only for 2002.

We compared structure learning with and without background knowledge. The knowledge consisted of formulas such as: authors' future interests are influenced by their past interests, collaborators' interests, and the interests of highly cited authors from the same author cluster; authors are more likely to publish on "bursting" topics than on "dead" ones; authors publish on topics that are "hot" in their favorite journals or other journals in the same journal cluster; etc. We used these formulas first as the complete structure (i.e., we only performed parameter learning) and then as

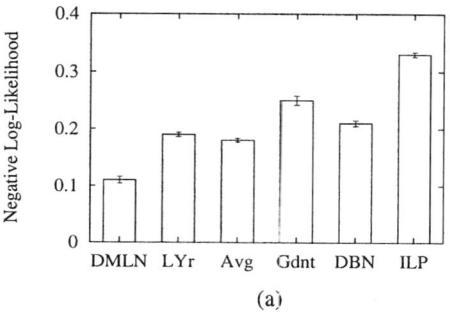
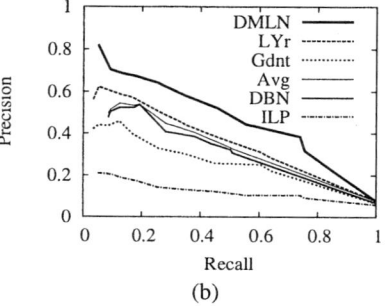

Fig. 1. DMLNs outperform the other methods at predicting author-topic distributions

background knowledge (here we learned additional formulas). Learning DMLNs without background knowledge does better than CLAUDIEN, DBN learning and the other methods, but the difference is insignificant. Both knowledge-based approaches did well, and we report on the latter approach, which was marginally better.

We present our results by plotting the negative log-likelihood (Figure 1(a)) and the precision-recall curves (Figure 1(b)). Each measure has its own advantages: the negative log-likelihood directly measures the quality of the probability estimates, while the precision-recall curves are insensitive to the large number of true negatives (i.e., ground predicates that are false and predicted to be false). The figures show clearly that DMLNs learned with background knowledge surpass all other approaches in this domain.

4.2 Faults in Manufacturing Assembly Plans

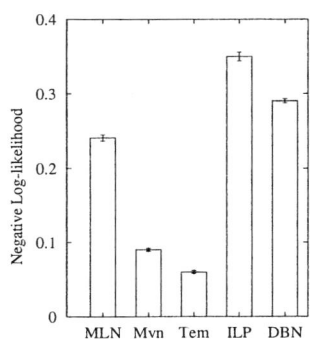

Fig. 2. DMLNs with templates/Markovian assumption outperform other algorithms when learning action models

For our second test, we used a completely-observable version of Sanghai et al.'s [15,17] manufacturing domain. An example in this domain is an execution trace of an assembly plan comprised of actions such as Paint, Polish, Bolt, etc. There are three classes of objects: Plate, Bracket and Bolt, with propositional attributes such as weight, shape, color, surface type, hole size and hole type, and relations for the parts to which they are attached. Actions are performed at every time step and are fault-prone; for example, a Weld action may fail or may weld two incorrect objects based on their similarity to the original objects. This gives rise to uncertainty in the domain and the corresponding dependence model for the various attributes. Given the simulated execution trace of a plan in this domain, we wished to use learning to recover each action's exact fault model.

Since it is clear that DMLN parameter learning would excel in this domain if given a good set of formulas, we compared DMLN learning (with *no* background knowledge) to CLAUDIEN and DBN learning. Our goal was to answer questions Q3, Q4 and Q5 by learning structure in various settings, i.e., without any help, splitting the examples into time slice pairs, and using templates. We considered a template that made the following restrictions: 1) at most one action predicate per clause, 2) only negated action predicates in clauses, 3) at most five predicates per clause, and 4) biasing to shorter clauses.

Figure 2 shows the negative log-likelihood of unbiased DMLN learning, DMLNs with a Markovian assumption, and DMLNs with templates, compared with ILP and DBN learning, when applied to a 1000-step assembly plan with 100 objects. These results illustrate the ability of DMLNs to learn both the relational structure and the probabilistic parameters of a time-changing process. DBNs have the disadvantage that they separately learn formulas for each ground predicate, while CLAUDIEN has the disadvantage that it gives inaccurate probability predictions. DMLNs combine the capabilities of each. We also note that templates and formulas obeying the first-order Markovian assumption lead to improved learning.

We also tested our algorithms on plans of varying length. As expected, every algorithm improves with an increasing number of time slices.

The DMLN structure learning algorithm took around 7 hours on the hep-th data and 5 hours on the assembly data. CLAUDIEN was allowed to run for a maximum of 15 hours on both the datasets.

5 Discussion

Several researchers have worked on temporal prediction in relational domains like social networks. Successful models include preferential attachment [2] and its extensions. But, many of these models are domain specific and do not explicitly represent uncertainty. DMLNs allow easy specification of complex models using first-order formulae. Learning probabilistic relational planning rules has also received some attention [13]. These application-specific techniques may be viewed in terms of DMLN learning.

In recent years, much research has focused on combining uncertainty with first-order logic (or some subset of it) [6]. Relational Markov models (RMMs) [1] and logical hidden Markov models (LOHMMs) [9] can be viewed as special cases of DMLNs. Dynamic object-oriented Bayesian networks (DOOBNs) [7] combine DBNs with OOBNs, but no learning algorithms for them have been proposed.

In conclusion, we have shown that MLNs can be successfully extended to learning models of relational stochastic process. Experimental results show that DMLNs are more accurate than previous approaches, such as DBN learning and ILP. Some directions for future work include handling continuous variables, learning in the presence of missing data and hidden state, modeling object creation and deletion, and applying DMLNs to other complex real-world problems.

Acknowledgements

This work was partly funded by NSF grant IIS-0307906, ONR grants N00014-02-1-0408 and N00014-02-1-0932, DARPA project CALO through SRI grant number 03-000225, a Sloan Fellowship to the second author, and an NSF CAREER Award to the second author.

References

1. C. Anderson, P. Domingos, and D. Weld. Relational Markov models and their application to adaptive Web navigation. In *KDD'02*, pages 143–152, 2002.
2. A. Barabasi and R. Albert. Emergence of scaling in random networks. *Science*, 286, 1999.
3. J. Besag. Statistical analysis of non-lattice data. *The Statistician*, 24:179–195, 1975.
4. L. De Raedt and L. Dehaspe. Clausal discovery. *Machine Learning*, 26(2-3):99–146, 1997.
5. S. Della Pietra, V. Della Pietra, and J.. Lafferty. Inducing features of random fields. *IEEE Transactions on Pattern Analysis and Machine Intelligence*, 19(4), 1997.
6. T. Dietterich, L. Getoor, and K. Murphy, editors. *Proceedings of the ICML-2004 Workshop on Statistical Relational Learning and its Connections to Other Fields.* ACM press, Banff, Canada, 2004.
7. N. Friedman, D. Koller, and A. Pfeffer. Structured representation of complex stochastic systems. In *Proceedings of Fifteenth National Conference on Artificial Intelligence*, 1998.

8. Johannes Gehrke, Paul Ginsparg, and Jon M. Kleinberg. Overview of the 2003 KDD Cup. *SIGKDD Explorations*, 2003.
9. K. Kersting and T. Raiko. 'Say EM' for selecting probabilistic models of logical sequences. In *UAI-05*, Edinburgh, Scotland, 2005. Morgan Kaufmann.
10. Jon Kleinberg. Bursty and hierarchical structure in streams. In *KDD '02*, 2002.
11. S. Kok and P. Domingos. Learning the structure of Markov logic networks. In *ICML'05*, Bonn, Germany, 2005. ACM Press.
12. K. Murphy. *Dynamic Bayesian networks: representation, inference and learning*. PhD thesis, University of California Berkeley, 2002.
13. Hanna Pasula, Luke S. Zettlemoyer, and Leslie Pack Kaelbling. Learning probabilistic relational planning rules. In *ICAPS'04*, pages 683–691, Whistler, Canada, 2004.
14. M. Richardson and P. Domingos. Markov logic networks. *Machine Learning*, 2005. To appear.
15. S. Sanghai, P. Domingos, and D. Weld. Dynamic probabilistic relational models. In *IJCAI'03*, pages 992–1002, Acapulco, Mexico, 2003. Morgan Kaufmann.
16. S. Sanghai, P. Domingos, and D. Weld. Learning models of relational stochastic processes, 2005. http://www.cs.washington.edu/homes/sanghai/lmrsp.pdf.
17. S. Sanghai, P. Domingos, and D. Weld. Relational dynamic Bayesian networks. *Journal of Artificial Intelligence Research*, 2005. To appear.

Error-Sensitive Grading for Model Combination

Surendra K. Singhi and Huan Liu

Department of Computer Science and Engineering,
Arizona State University, Tempe, AZ 85287-8809, USA
surendra@asu.edu, hliu@asu.edu

Abstract. Ensemble learning is a powerful learning approach that combines multiple classifiers to improve prediction accuracy. An important decision while using an ensemble of classifiers is to decide upon a way of combining the prediction of its base classifiers. In this paper, we introduce a novel grading-based algorithm for model combination, which uses cost-sensitive learning in building a meta-learner. This method distinguishes between the grading error of classifying an incorrect prediction as correct, and the other-way-round, and tries to assign appropriate costs to the two types of error in order to improve performance. We study issues in error-sensitive grading, and then with extensive experiments show the empirically effectiveness of this new method in comparison with representative meta-classification techniques.

1 Introduction

The accessibility and abundance of data in today's information age and the advent of multimedia and Internet have made machine learning an indispensable tool for knowledge discovery. Ensemble learning is a powerful and widely used technique which combine the decision of a set of classifiers to make the final prediction, this not only help in reducing the variance of learning, but also facilitates learning concepts (or hypothesis) from training data which are difficult for a single classifier. In large datasets, where there may be multiple functions defining the relationship between the predictor and response variables, ensemble methods allow different classifiers to represent each function individually instead of using one single overly complex function to approximate all the functions.

Building a good quality ensemble is a two steps process. During the first step (model generation phase), the constituent (or base level) classifiers should be selected such that they make independent or uncorrelated errors, or in other words, ensemble should be as diverse as possible. One way of introducing diversity is by varying the bias of learning, i.e., by employing different learning algorithms (results in heterogeneous ensemble); another technique is to keep the learning algorithm same, but manipulate the training data, so that the classifiers learn different functions in the hypothesis space (results in homogeneous ensemble). After an ensemble of classifiers is obtained, the next important step is to construct a meta classifier, which combines the predictions of the base classifiers (or model combination phase). This is the main focus of this paper.

Different model combination techniques, depending upon the methods used by them can be partitioned into three categories i.e., voting, stacking and grading. The nomenclature for these categories was decided based on the most basic methods which represent the underlying principle of the methods falling under that category.

Voting. The techniques in this category are very simple, and widely used with homogeneous ensembles. *Majority voting* is a naive voting technique, in which a simple summation of the output probabilities (or 0, 1 values) of base classifiers is done, and a normalized probability distribution is returned. *Weighted Voting*, is a variation in which, a reliability weight or confidence value inversely proportional to the validation-set error rate, is assigned to each classifier. The meta-classifier then does a weighted sum to arrive at the final class probabilities. In one possible variation, instead of assigning a single reliability weight to the base classifier, for each class a separate reliability weight can be assigned.

Stacking. The stacking techniques are based on the idea of stacked generalization [1]. The distinguishing feature of the stacking techniques is that, the meta-classifier tries to learn the pattern or relationship between the predictions of the base classifiers and the actual class. Stacking with *Multi-response Linear Regression (MLR)* [2], is a stacking technique in which the MLR algorithm is used as the meta-classifier algorithm. Based on probability estimates given by the base-classifiers, meta-training datasets are constructed for **each** class. Then from these meta-training datasets linear regression models are built, the number of linear regression models is same as the number of classes. Dzeroski [3] shows that using Model Tree instead of Multi-response Linear Regression may yield better result. *StackingC* [4] is a variation, in which while building the meta-training datasets, instead of using class probabilities given by the base classifiers for all the different classes; only class probabilities corresponding to the particular class for which regression model is being built, are used. This results in faster model building time for the meta-classifier and also has the added benefit of the giving more diverse models for each classifier.

Grading. The defining feature of methods in this category (also known as referee method [5, 6]) is that, instead of directly finding the relationship between the predictions of the base classifier and the actual class (as in stacking); the meta-classifier grades the base-classifiers, and selects either a single or subset of base-classifier(s) which are likely to be correct for the given test instance. The intuition behind grading is that in large datasets where there may be multiple functions defining the relationship between predictor and response variables, it is important to choose the correct

Table 1. Grading meta-training dataset, for a dataset with m features and n instances

Attributes		Graded
A_1 |....|	A_m	Class
$x_{1,1}$	... $x_{1,m}$	1
$x_{2,1}$	... $x_{2,m}$	1
...	...	...
$x_{n,1}$	... $x_{n,m}$	0

function for any given test instance. In stacking the meta-classifier uses the predictions of the base classifier to decide the way they (predictions) should be combined to make the final decision; but in grading the test instance is used to decide which all base-classifiers, and with what reliability weight should they be used to make the final prediction.

In Grading, the meta-classifier itself is an ensemble of grader classifiers. Corresponding to each base level classifier there is a grader classifier which tries to learn its area of expertise or high predictive accuracies. For training the grader, as shown in Table 1 the original attributes are also used as the attributes for the grading dataset, but instead of using the original class attribute, a new graded class attribute with two possible values 1 (correct prediction) or 0 (incorrect prediction) is used. While making predictions the grader classifier assigns a weight to the base classifier's likelihood of being correct. This weight can be either absolute 1 or 0 score or it can also be a probability values. Only predictions from base classifiers, with reliability weight above a certain threshold or which are more likely to be correct than incorrect are taken; and then these predictions are combined using weighted voting to make the final prediction.

2 Error Sensitive Grading

We propose a new approach to doing Grading which combines cost-sensitive learning in assigning different costs to meta-training instances, and tries to make the graders conservative in assigning prediction tasks to the base classifiers. The intuition behind this method is to increase the prediction accuracy of each base classifier by using it only for instances for which it is very likely to be correct, but an immediate side-effect of this is that the number of instances for which the base classifier is used to make prediction decreases. In this work we study various research issues related to error-sensitive grading, including a new tie-breaking scheme designed for grading.

2.1 Cost-Sensitive Learning

In many machine learning domains, different misclassification incur different penalties and hence misclassification costs are different, given a test instance, cost-sensitive learning aims to predict the class that will lead to the lowest expected cost, where the expectation is computed using the conditional probability of each class and the misclassification cost. The most common method of achieving this objective is by re-balancing the training set given to the learning algorithm, i.e., to change the proportion of positive and negative training examples in the training set by over-sampling or under-sampling. An alternative, if the learning algorithm can use weights on training examples, is to set the weight of each example depending upon the cost.

2.2 Type A vs. Type B Errors

While grading the base classifiers, there could be two types of mistakes: when a base classifier predicts correctly, the grader says it is wrong (**Type A**); or when a base classifier predicts wrongly, the grader considers it right (**Type B**). The issue is that if there are enough good classifiers then it doesn't hurt to leave one out. Yet, including a classifier when it is bad can really hurt performance. So, it is important to differentiate the two types of errors: the cost of Type B errors should be far higher than that of Type A errors. In other words, the cost of classifying an incorrect prediction as a correct prediction should be higher than the cost of classifying a correct prediction as incorrect. A base classifier generally predicts a high percentage of validation instances as correct, and so the majority of instances in the meta-training dataset for the graders are correct, and as a result the grader assigns a lower cost to Type A errors compared to the Type B error. This can lead to poor performance by graders, and hence by the meta-classifier and the ensemble.

2.3 Error Sensitive Grading Algorithm

The balance between the different misclassification costs can be readjusted by explicitly using cost-sensitivity. We call this modified version of grading as Error Sensitive Grading (ESGrading). Assigning higher cost to wrong grading makes the graders conservative in their decision making, i.e., the grader will predict a base classifier to be correct only when it is extremely sure. But one immediate drawback of making the graders conservative is that none of the base classifiers may be selected to predict on a test instance, to avoid this limitation the ensemble should have a large pool of diverse classifiers, so that the graders choose at least one base classifier to make the prediction. While using error-sensitive grading an important parameter which has to be chosen is, the different misclassification costs, because it is this cost which determines how conservative the grader should be. As graders have to deal with binary classification problem, i.e., predict whether the base classifier is correct or incorrect, the misclassification cost of two types can be combined into a single cost-ratio, which we define below.

Definition 1 (Cost-ratio). *It is the ratio of cost of Type A error over cost of Type B error.*

A lower value of the cost-ratio means that there is a heavy penalty for predicting an incorrect base classifier as correct. A value of cost-ratio equal to 1 means that the cost of grader misclassifying a base-classifier, whether the base-classifier is correct or incorrect is equal (the method is then equivalent to normal Grading). A value of cost-ratio equal to 0 on the other hand, indicates that the base classifier should never misclassify an incorrect base-classifier as correct, that is the base-classifier should never be trusted. To prove our hypothesis we did an experiment of varying the cost-ratio and observing the error rate of Grading method (Figure 1). In this experiment we used 10 bagged decision trees (Weka J4.8, a JAVA port to C4.5 Release 8 [7]) classifiers at the base level and decision trees again as the grader. The figure confirms to intuition and shows how when

Algorithm 1. Error-Sensitive Grading algorithm

procedure ESGRADING(baseClassifiers,validSet)
  $costRatio \leftarrow FindCostRatio(baseClassifiers, validSet)$
  for all $classifier \in baseClassifiers$ **do**
    $Grader \leftarrow BuildGrader(classifier, costRatio, validSet)$
    Add $Grader$ to the meta-classifiers
  end for
end procedure

procedure FINDCOST(baseClassifiers,validSet)
  for $costRatio \leftarrow 0.0$ to 1.0 Step δ **do**
    Find cross validation error on validation set using $costRatio$ and the base classifiers
  end for
  return $costRatio$ with minimum cross validation error
end procedure

the cost is close to 0, the graders will be conservative and none of the base-classifiers will be predicted to be correct, and this results in a higher error, as the default majority-voting tie-breaking will be used. As the cost is increased the error rate decreases till it reaches a low-point after which it again begins to increase as the graders becomes lax in their grading and more base-classifiers are predicted to be correct.

One way to determine this cost-ratio is using cross-validation. It helps dynamically adjust the cost depending upon the number and diversity of base classifiers in an ensemble. When there are a large number of diverse base classifiers, then the graders can afford to be more conservative in picking base classifiers for making prediction, as the probability that at least one correct base classifier will be picked is high. On the other hand, when the number of base classifiers is small, the graders should be comparatively lenient to avoid the possible scenarios in which no base classifiers is picked for model combination. Using cross validation to determine the cost helps in striking the balance between making the graders conservative or lenient.

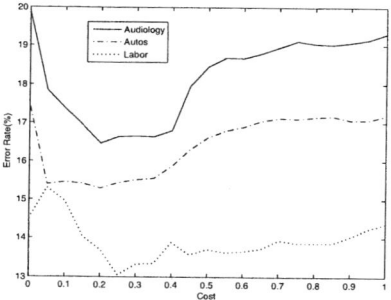

Fig. 1. Error rate of Error Sensitive Grading vs. the cost ratio

Algorithm 1 shows how to create an Error Sensitive Grading meta-classifier. The first step is to call the procedure $FindCostRatio$ to decide the cost-ratio which should be used. The variable $validSet$ is used to denote the validation set for building the meta-learner. The procedure $FindCostRatio$ evaluates various cost-ratios and then uses cross validation to build graders via cost-sensitive learning and finally determines the error rate. The cost-ratio associated with the least error rate is returned and then used to build the final graders with the entire validation dataset.

2.4 Tie Breaking for Grading

In the Grading method as proposed by [6], when there is a tie in the likelihood of an instance belonging to different classes, the meta-classifier checks which of the class has higher prior probability and accordingly makes a decision. We suggest an alternative scheme in which instead of completely ignoring the predictions of some of the base classifiers (the classifiers with higher probability of being wrong than correct), the grader should assign a delta (close to zero) probability to all such classifiers being correct. This will ensure that under normal circumstances the meta-classifier only uses the prediction of the graders which are correct, but when there is a tie, majority voting is used.

In our experiments (not shown here due to space limitation), we observed that in general the ties are so rare that this tie-breaking scheme does not make any difference for the normal Grading algorithm. But in Error Sensitive Grading when the number of base classifiers is small, and the cost-ratio is close to 0, the graders may assign higher probability to all the base classifiers of being wrong than correct, and then none of the base classifiers will be selected to make the final prediction. In such, a scenario the above tie-breaking scheme is a better alternative (than the current prior probability method of breaking ties), because it makes use of majority voting to break the ties.

2.5 Time Complexity of Error-Sensitive Grading

The time complexity of Error-Sensitive Grading algorithm depends upon the method used for setting the cost-ratio. When c-fold cross-validation is used to determine cost-ratio, and t different cost-ratios are tried, then the time complexity is $O(c * t * G)$ where G is the time complexity of the Grading method. Grading is a time-consuming algorithm, but because learning is done offline, generally time is not a big issue for building classifiers.

3 Experiments and Discussion

For empirical evaluation we chose nineteen datasets from the UCI Machine Learning Repository [8]. Following the research done in [9], for all the experiments the reported results are obtained by ten ten-fold stratified cross-validations and t-test is done with calibrated degrees of freedom equal to 10. The reported estimates are the average of the 100 runs and the values after the ± sign is the average standard deviation. Superscripts denote significance levels for the difference in accuracy between the Error Sensitive Grading and the corresponding algorithm, using a one-tailed paired t test: 1 is 0.01, 2 is 0.025, 3 is 0.05, 4 is 0.1 and 5 is above 0.1.

We decided to use bagging [10] to study the effect of error sensitive grading as it is a widely used ensemble method and easily allows us to adjust the number of base classifiers. We implemented the Error Sensitive Grading method within WEKA [11]. All other algorithms are available within WEKA, but we

Table 2. Error rate for Bagging with different model combination techniques

Dataset	Maj. Voting	Stacking MT	StackingC	Grading	E. S. Grading
AUDIOLOGY	19.59 ± 6.73[1]	20.40 ± 6.91[1]	17.53 ± 5.92[4]	19.36 ± 6.66[2]	18.36 ± 6.26
AUTOS	16.97 ± 5.81[2]	17.17±6.03[4]	15.95±5.68[5]	17.41±5.90[1]	16.14±5.51
CREDIT-A	13.78± 4.62[5]	14.85 ± 5.10 [3]	14.75 ± 5.00[2]	13.69 ± 4.59[2]	13.91 ± 4.66
CREDIT-G	26.73 ± 8.95[5]	28.86 ± 9.65[1]	28.06 ±9.41[1]	26.84 ± 8.99[5]	26.74±8.93
GLASS	26.32 ± 8.94[3]	28.23 ±9.84[4]	27.08 ± 9.23[5]	26.61 ± 9.09[4]	26.88 ± 9.22
HEART-C	21.22 ± 7.17[2]	22.58 ± 7.79[5]	22.42±7.61[5]	21.76 ± 7.40[3]	22.08 ± 7.51
HEPATITIS	18.25 ±6.13[5]	21.02 ±7.15[1]	18.80±6.38[5]	19.43±6.67[5]	18.97±6.63
HYPO	0.45 ± 0.16[5]	7.64 ±2.56 [1]	0.43 ± 0.15[5]	0.46 ±0.16[2]	0.43 ± 0.15
KR	0.63±0.22[5]	0.56 ± 0.22[5]	0.57 ± 0.23[5]	0.64 ± 0.23[4]	0.60 ± 0.22
LABOR	16.03 ± 5.95 [3]	15.77± 6.00[4]	14.23 ± 5.11[5]	13.8 ± 4.99[5]	14.2 ± 5.26
PRIMARY-TUMOR	56.49 ± 18.90[1]	58.59 ± 19.57[2]	58.94 ± 19.68[1]	57.58 ± 19.24 [5]	57.55 ± 19.24
SEGMENT	2.55± 0.88[3]	2.80±0.99[1]	2.44±0.87[5]	2.51±0.84[4]	2.45±0.83
SICK	1.16 ±0.39[1]	1.07±0.39[5]	1.07±0.38[5]	1.11 ± 0.38[2]	1.09 ±0.38
SONAR	21.78 ± 7.50[5]	25.76 ± 9.09[1]	22.43 ±7.92[2]	21.30 ± 7.37[5]	21.24 ± 7.33
SOYBEAN	7.44 ± 2.56[5]	7.01 ±2.43[5]	6.87±2.45[5]	7.61±2.64[2]	7.19±2.48
SPLICE	5.68 ±1.90[5]	6.27 ±2.10[1]	5.79±1.93[3]	5.87 ±1.96[1]	5.69 ±1.90
VEHICLE	25.59± 8.57 [5]	25.48 ± 8.58[5]	25.30 ± 8.47 [5]	25.48±8.55 [5]	25.36±8.50
VOTE	3.56±1.22[4]	3.67±1.51[5]	3.81±1.37[5]	3.63 ± 1.2[5]	3.67 ±1.29
VOWEL	10.06 ± 3.39[1]	13.90 ± 4.72[1]	10.15±3.43[1]	10.47 ± 3.60[1]	9.25,± 3.17
Loss/Tie/Win	3/10/6	0/10/9	0/13/6	2/10/7	-

adapted them to be used with bagging. During the experiments, it was ensured that the meta-classifiers, do not rebuild the base level decision trees built during model generation phase, as it goes against the spirit of meta-classifier as a model-combination method. Moreover, this ensures that the comparison of strengths of different model combination techniques can be done with a lower Type I error, as all the techniques are being used to combine the same set of classifiers.

3.1 Against Different Model Combination Methods

In this experiment we compared Error-Sensitive Grading against different model-combination techniques such as Majority Voting, Stacking with Model Trees, StackingC with MLR, and Grading on the chosen datasets. We used 10 bagged decision trees as the base-classifiers, and for the two grading methods we used decision tree as the grader too. Table 2 shows the results of the experiment. The loss/tie/win row in the table summarizes the number of datasets in which error sensitive grading performed worse, at par, or better than other methods. This loss, tie and win was determined using significance levels of 1, 2, and 3. We can clearly observe from this comparison that Error-Sensitive Grading performs well in comparison with representative methods of model combination.

The reason for the robustness of Error-Sensitive Grading is that it uses cross validation to determine the cost such that in the worst case it will perform similar to Grading or Majority Voting. Depending upon the base classifiers cross validation attempts to adjust the cost such that the graders are selective in picking the base classifiers for predicting the class for a new instance. The reader might observe that Error Sensitive Grading has two losses compared to Grading, the reason for this is that as the same data is used during model generation and then during the meta-classifier creation process, the resultant model sometimes over fits the data and hence does worse.

3.2 Performance with Different Base Classifiers

In this experiment (Table 3) we decided to observe the benefit of Error Sensitive Grading against traditional Grading and Majority Voting when different algorithms (decision tree, naive bayes and support vector machines) are used for building the base classifiers. The Grading meta-learner used for all these experiments was the same i.e., decision tree. Again, the loss/tie/win was determined by using significance levels of 1, 2, and 3 with t-test using the method described earlier. The results for decision tree are from the Table 2. From the table it is quite clear that Error-Sensitive Grading outperforms both Majority Voting, and Grading, across all kinds of base learners. This table shows the robustness and stability of the Error Sensitive Grading method when different types of base classifiers are used.

Table 3. Loss/Tie/Win for ES-Grading vs. Maj. Voting and normal Grading when different algorithms used for base learner.

Algorithm	Maj. Voting	Grading
DECISION TREE	3/10/6	2/10/7
NAIVE BAYES	0/8/11	0/16/3
SUPPORT VECTOR	1/10/8	0/15/4

4 Conclusion and Further Work

In this paper, we proposed a new grading-based method for model combination called Error-Sensitive Grading which applies cost-sensitive learning to grading base classifiers, such that the grader classifiers are made conservative in selective base classifiers for making predictions. We also studied issues about Error-Sensitive Grading such as cost assignment via cross validation, and introduced a new tie-breaking scheme for grading. The experimental results show that Error-Sensitive Grading is very competitive against all types of model combination methods. Using cross-validation to determine the cost is just one possible way, in our future research we plan to study other alternatives to determine the cost.

References

1. Wolpert, D.H.: Stacked generalization. Neural Networks **5** (1992) 241–259
2. Ting, K.M., Witten, I.H.: Issues in stacked generalization. Journal of Artificial Intelligence Research **10** (1999) 271–289
3. Dzeroski, S., Zenko, B.: Is combining classifiers better than selecting the best one? Machine Learning **54** (2004) 255–273
4. Seewald, A.K.: How to make stacking better and faster while taking care of an unknown weakness. In: Ninteenth International Conference on Machine Learning. (2002) 554–561
5. Ortega, J., Koppel, M., Argamon, S.: Arbitrating among competing classifiers using learned refrees. In: Knowledge and Information Systems. Volume 3. (2001)

6. Seewald, A.K., Furnkranz, J.: An evaluation of grading classifiers. In: Advances in Intelligent Data Analysis: 4th International Symposium, Springer-Verlag (2001)
7. Quinlan, J.: C4.5: Programs for machine learning. Morgan Kaufmann (1993)
8. Merz, C.J., Murphy, P.M.: UCI repository of machine learning databases (1998) http://www.ics.uci.edu/m̃learn/MLRepository.html.
9. Bouckaert, R.R.: Choosing between two learning algorithms based on calibrated tests. In: Twentieth International Conference on Machine Learning. (2003)
10. Breiman, L.: Bagging predictors. Machine Learning **24** (1996) 123–140
11. Witten, I., Frank, E.: Data Mining: Practical Machine Learning tools and techniques. 2nd edn. Morgan Kauffmann (2005)

Strategy Learning for Reasoning Agents

Hendrik Skubch and Michael Thielscher

Department of Computer Science,
Technische Universität Dresden,
Germany
{hendrik.skubch, mit}@inf.tu-dresden.de

Abstract. We present a method for knowledge-based agents to learn strategies. Using techniques of inductive logic programming, strategies are learned in two steps: A given example set is first generalized into an overly general theory, which then gets refined. We show how a learning agent can exploit background knowledge of its actions and environment in order to restrict the hypothesis space, which enables the learning of complex logic program clauses. This is a first step toward the long term goal of adaptive, reasoning agents capable of changing their behavior when appropriate.

1 Introduction

Endowing agents with the cognitive capability of reasoning is a major research topic of Artificial Intelligence [1]. The high-level control of a reasoning agent comprises two parts: a background theory which contains knowledge about actions and their effects, and a goal-oriented strategy according to which the agent reasons and acts. Existing programming methods, such as GOLOG [2] or FLUX [3], require the programmer to provide both the background theory for the underlying domain and strategies in view of specific goals. Learning techniques have recently been applied to let agents find out the effects of their actions from experiments [4,5], but the learning of goal directed strategies on top of this has not yet been considered.

In this paper, we present a method to learn strategy programs from examples using Inductive Logic Programming (ILP). As the underlying action formalism we use FLUX, a logic programming method for the design of intelligent agents based on the action formalism of the fluent calculus [6]. One of the key advantages of combining reasoning about actions with learning is that agents can use their background knowledge to considerably restrict the hypothesis space. Thus it becomes possible to learn rather complex clauses including negated conjunctions. Strategies are learned in two steps: First, the given examples are generalized based on the notion of Least General Generalization of [7]. The resulting, overly general theory is then refined to obtain a strategy program that is sound and complete wrt. the given example set.

In the next section, we briefly recapitulate the basics and notations of the agent programming method FLUX. In Section 3, we define the general hypothesis space for FLUX strategies and show how the background theory of a reasoning agent can be used to restrict the search space. In Section 4, we present a method for constructing overly general strategies from examples, and in Section 5 we then explain how these theories are corrected by specialization. In Section 6, we present and discuss experimental results. We conclude in Section 7.

2 FLUX

The fluent calculus [6] is an axiomatic approach for representing and reasoning about actions and change. The basic notion is that of a state and its atomic components, the so-called fluents. The fundamental predicate $holds(F, Z)$ is used to express that fluent F is true in state Z. Actions are specified in the fluent calculus by precondition and effect axioms.

Based on logic programming, FLUX is a method for the design of agents that reason logically about their actions. The background theory BK of a FLUX agent consists of a kernel program encoding the foundational axioms of the fluent calculus, along with domain-dependent knowledge in form of domain constraints, precondition axioms, and state update axioms. Here, we focus on a simplified variant of FLUX in which agents have complete state knowledge, called *Special FLUX* in the remainder of this paper.

On top of the background theory BK, the behavior of FLUX agents is given by logic programs that describe acting strategies. The agents use a state as their mental model of the world, on the basis of which they decide which action to take. As they move along, the agents constantly update their world model to reflect changes they have effected and sensor information they have acquired.

As an example, Figure 1 depicts a FLUX control program for a simple elevator originally formulated in GOLOG [2]. The states in this domain are composed of the three fluents cur_floor(N), on(M) and opened meaning, respectively, that the elevator is at floor N, the button for floor M has been activated, and the door is open. The elevator can perform the actions up(N), down(N) of going up (respectively, down) to floor N; turnoff(N) of turning off the button at floor N; and open, close of opening and closing the door.

3 Hypothesis Space

The hypothesis space is the space of all programs the Inductive Inference Machine (IIM) might consider as a solution to a learning problem. A strategy for a Special FLUX agent is a logic program selecting in each state an action to be executed. Thereby the strategy relates states to actions. We use a single, recursive predicate to express strategies:

```
loop(Z):- strategy(Z,A) ->
          (A \= stop, execute(A,Z,Z2), loop(Z2); true).
```

Here, the predicate strategy/2 selects the action to be executed. For Special FLUX programs, this is the only predicate to be learned.

```
main(Z) :- serve_a_floor(Z,Z1) -> main(Z1) ; park(Z).

serve_a_floor(Z,Z1) :- holds(cur_floor(N),Z), holds(on(M),Z),
                       \+ (holds(on(M1),Z), closer(M1,M,N)),
                       serve(M,Z,Z1).

serve(M,Z,Z4) :- go_floor(M,Z,Z1), execute(open,Z1,Z2),
                 execute(turn_off(M),Z2,Z3), execute(close,Z3,Z4).

go_floor(M,Z,Z1) :- poss(up(M),Z)    -> execute(up(M),Z,Z1) ;
                    poss(down(M),Z)  -> execute(down(M),Z,Z1) ;
                    Z1=Z.

park(Z) :- execute(down(1),Z,Z1), execute(open,Z1,_).

closer(M1,M2,N) :- abs(M1-N)<abs(M2-N).
```

Fig. 1. A simple FLUX strategy for elevator control

The elements of hypothesized programs are called *strategy-clauses*. A strategy-clause is a non-recursive Prolog clause having an instance of *strategy*(Z, A) as head and a body containing atoms and negated conjunctions of atoms. These atoms are defined in BK. With this definition, we assume that the relation between states and actions is functional, i.e., the action to be executed can be uniquely identified by the current state. Moreover, the absence of state update axioms and recursive definitions of strategy-clauses prohibits learned programs from planning.

The set of all examples E provided for the IIM contains pairs (z,a) of a state z and an action a, meaning the agent has to execute action a in state z. In this way, every example is positive. However, given the functional nature of the mapping from states to actions, an example (z,a) implicitly entails negative examples for every action other than a. This treatment of positive-only examples has already been applied in the system FILP [8].

In order to restrict the hypothesis space by expressing additional knowledge about specific domains, we use sorts, modes and occurrence restrictions, described subsequently. Moreover, we restrict the hypotheses space by a maximum *newsize* [9] to achieve finiteness.

Sorts Since the fluent calculus uses a sort signature to categorize terms, it is quite natural to use this information in a corresponding learning algorithm, too. We developed constraint handling rules to restrict variables to be of a certain sort. A relation $\succ_{sort}$ spans a tree in the set of sorts having the universal sort ANY as root. This relation enables us to compute a least general sort roughly following [10].

Modes have been employed with success in a variety of ILP systems [11]. They are used to reflect the computational behavior of predicates. Arguments of predicates are either of input or output mode. Hypothesized clauses are required to obey mode declarations. Put simply, a variable occurrence in an input argument has to be preceded by an occurrence of the same variable in an output argument.

Occurrence restrictions are used to rule out certain combinations of literals in the body of hypothesized clauses. These restrictions can be drawn from domain specific knowledge. For instance, we can express that the arguments of a predicate encoding a binary, irreflexive relation should always differ.

4 Generalization

Examples, understood as pairs (z, a) of a state z and an action a, can trivially be transformed into strategy-clauses: An example $([f_1, \ldots, f_n], a_e)$ corresponds to the clause $strategy(Z, a_e) \leftarrow holds(f_1, Z), \ldots, holds(f_n, Z)$. This transformation can be understood as adding background knowledge to unit clauses, in order to compute a *relative least generalization*. The clauses serve as the input of a generalization procedure based on a sorted version of Plotkin's Least General Generalization [7], where a generalized term $lggs(t_1: s_1, t_2: s_2)$ is of the smallest sort s wrt. $\succ_{sort}$ such that $s \succ_{sort} s_1 \wedge s \succ_{sort} s_2$.

Since the $lggs$ of a set of clauses grows exponentially with the size of the set, we define a generalization operator gs on top of the $lggs$ producing generalizations of constant size. Literals in bodies of strategy-clauses directly or indirectly express properties of the state. In FLUX, a state is represented by a list. Our generalization operator is motivated by the idea that the quality of a generalization of two lists representing states depends on the order of the fluents inside the lists. This order, however, has no semantical meaning[1] and thus ordering can be seen as a task of the generalization algorithm.

Definition 1. *A generalization of two strategy-clauses using sorts:*
Let $c_1 = p_1 \leftarrow l_1 \wedge \ldots \wedge l_n$ and $c_2 = p_2 \leftarrow k_1 \wedge \ldots \wedge k_m$ be two strategy-clauses without negations such that $n \leq m$ then a generalization is given by:

$$gs(c_1, c_2) \stackrel{def}{=} lggs(p_1, p_2) \leftarrow \bigwedge W$$

where W satisfies

- $W \subseteq \{lggs(l_i, k_j) | 1 \leq i \leq n \wedge 1 \leq j \leq m \wedge lggs(l_i, k_j) \text{ is defined}\}$
- $|W| \leq n$
- $(\forall l_i, 1 \leq i \leq n) \, lggs(l_i, x) \in W \wedge lggs(l_i, y) \in W \supset x = y$
- $(\forall k_i, 1 \leq i \leq m) \, lggs(x, k_i) \in W \wedge lggs(y, k_i) \in W \supset x = y$

The choice of W is determined by a heuristic function $g(W, a)$, with a being the action occurring in the head of the clause $gs(c_1, c_2)$. W is chosen to maximize g.

$$g(W, a) \stackrel{def}{=} \sum_{l \in W} \left(\sum_{k \in W \setminus \{l\}} \frac{1}{2} \sigma_{link}(l, k) \right) + \sigma_{link}(l, a) + \frac{1}{1000} \sigma_{comp}(l)$$

---

[1] State composition is commutative and associative in the fluent calculus.

Here,

$\sigma_{link}(x, y) \stackrel{def}{=}$ Number of variables not of sort $STATE$ shared between x and y

$\sigma_{comp}(x) \stackrel{def}{=}$ Number of subexpressions of x − Number of variables in x

In this way, we maximize the number of variable occurrences in multiple literals, while constraining the generalized clause to the size of the smallest clause involved. Variables of sort $STATE$ are ignored, since the variable Z, denoting the current state, occurs in the head of every strategy-clause and in every literal of the form $holds(F, Z)$.

Because maximizing the number of links does not necessarily lead to a unique solution, we incorporate other syntactic information into the heuristic function as well. Intuitively, from two literals which yield the same amount of links, we want to choose the more specific one. Function σ_{comp} allows comparison of literals not comparable by θ-subsumption, but if t_1 θ-subsumes t_2 then $\sigma_{comp}(t_1) \leq \sigma_{comp}(t_2)$. To search for the optimal W efficiently, we use A* [12]. Note that this approach is not limited to strategy-clauses and can be applied to arbitrary horn clauses. In particular, it is designed to deal with clauses built from extensive background knowledge which usually contain many redundant literals.

The Generalization Loop

Initially, for every function symbol a into sort $ACTION$ the corresponding set of examples $\{(z, a(\boldsymbol{x}))|(z, a(\boldsymbol{x})) \in E\}$ is generalized. If a heuristic quality threshold finds the result too general, the corresponding set of examples is split into disjoint subsets. Splitting is done by either instantiating a variable in the corresponding action or by using a fluent as classificator. The first possibility yields a subset for every possible substitution of the chosen variable. The second one yields two sets of examples, one with all examples in whose state the fluent holds and one with all examples in whose state the fluent does not hold. Thus, splitting is a heuristic way of specializing the initial clauses, before the actual top-down search takes place. Generalization, evaluation and splitting are repeated until the quality threshold is reached or no further splitting is possible. The conditions under which splitting is possible also ensure that this process terminates.

5 Specialization

The specialization process searches for a correct program consisting of clauses which are each subsumed by one of the computed generalizations. To be able to introduce negations inside bodies of clauses while still maintaining top-down behavior of the search, we need a way to group multiple literals in a meaningful way. We therefore introduce *computation chains*.

Definition 2. *A computation chain is a conjunction $l_1, \ldots, l_n$ of at least one positive literal, such that for every l_i with $i < n$ at least one output argument of l_i also occurs as input argument in a literal l_j with $j > i$.*

The notion of computation chains, together with sort constraints, allows to add multiple literals to a clause at once in a meaningful manner. This reduces the effects of the plateau problem and enables the use of negated conjunctions as an expressive part of our language. The employed refinement operator $\rho\colon \mathcal{H} \mapsto \mathcal{P}(\mathcal{H})$ computes specializations by either

- unifying two variables of the same sort
- substituting a variable with a function of distinct new variables into the right sort
- adding a computation chain to the body of the clause
- adding the negation of a computation chain to the body of the clause

Note that after addition of a computation chain, the refined clause is still subject to mode restrictions. Therefore, if a variable occurs in an input argument in the chain and not in an output argument, it is bound to a variable occurring in the body of the clause. To maintain the top-down manner of the search, when refining clauses containing negations it is neither allowed to instantiate a variable occurring only negated nor to unify it with any other variable.

The Specialization Loop

Each of the initial schemes becomes the root node of a search tree. The search trees are searched in parallel in a greedy manner, similar to the covering algorithm, which was first used in the AQ system [9].

In each search iteration, the clause with the highest heuristic evaluation in each search tree is refined and replaced by its specializations. A subsequent goal test identifies correct clauses. If a correct clause is found, it is asserted and the corresponding examples are removed.

A post-processing step is applied to both asserted clauses and the final program to remove redundant literals and clauses. A top level loop over generalization and specialization ensures completeness, if a finite hypotheses space is specified.

6 Experimental Results

We first applied the learning algorithm to the elevator control program, originally written in GOLOG [2]. Examples were generated by the strategy depicted in Fig. 1. We provided predicates encoding the binary relations *unequal* and *less-than*, and the ternary relation *closer* in BK. To restrict the hypothesis space, we only used knowledge automatically derivable from a domain axiomatization.

If at least one example indicated that the elevator sometimes has to leave the first floor, a program was learned which is semantically equivalent to the one which generated the examples, otherwise the learned programs always terminate once they reached the first floor. This result was stable throughout all tests.

As a more complex scenario, we chose the mailbot example, described in [13]. The main difference to the elevator scenario lies in the action related to movement. In the elevator scenario, this action has a destination as argument, while

Example Set	Solved (%)	Completeness (%)
Large Search Space		
Optimal	23	0
Good	23	0
Naive	47	25
Medium Search Space		
Optimal	24	2
Good	31	2
Naive	61	44
Small Search Space		
Optimal	18	0
Good	64	37
Naive	92	84

Fig. 2. Results in the Mailbot Scenario

the mailbot can only choose to go up or down, without initially knowing a relation between destinations and directions. Moreover, the mailbot's movement is motivated by two state properties, namely packages to be picked up and packages to be delivered.

Figure 2 shows the results of nine different experiments in the mailbot scenario. We conducted tests using different example sets and hypothesis spaces. "Optimal" denotes example sets generated by an optimal strategy which minimizes the number of actions to solve the problem. "Good" denotes example sets generated by a suboptimal, but sophisticated program, described in [13], while "naive" refers to example sets generated by a very simple strategy.

Each test was repeated using different hypothesis spaces. "Large Search Space" refers to a hypothesis space restricted only by domain dependent knowledge, i.e., sorts, modes and occurrence restrictions are direct consequences of the scenario. We provided the same predicates as we did in the elevator scenario. In the "medium search space", we removed the inequality relation and prohibited instantiations of bags and rooms in the top-down search. The "small search space" is very artificial, as we used additional restrictions not corresponding to any domain property.

Each row in Fig. 2 corresponds to the evaluation of hundred learned programs. The learned programs were tested against 200 instances of the problem. A program solved the problem instance if it delivered all initial packages and terminated, otherwise the test was considered a failure. "Solved" refers to the ratio of solved problem instances by the learned programs. "Completeness" indicates the ratio of learned programs solving all test cases confronted with.

7 Summary

In this paper, we have shown a way to apply ILP techniques to learn simple Special FLUX strategies. The learning algorithm makes strong use of background knowledge to learn programs complete and consistent with the given examples. The approach benefits from the combination of top-down and bottom-up techniques, as the top-down search does not start from unit clauses, but from a set of rather specific clauses, situated nearer potential solutions in the subsumption lattice. The techniques presented here do not depend on specific FLUX characteristics and it should be easy to adopt it to other action formalisms such as GOLOG.

This work is a first attempt to learn strategies for FLUX agents. It is strongly affected by local optima due to the rather wide search trees, i.e., the size of $\rho(C)$. This size leads to comparatively large programs incomplete wrt. the corresponding problems and is the main reason for the bad results in the mailbot scenario (see Figure 2). Reducing the influence of local optima will therefore be one of the main aspects of continuative work.

References

1. McCarthy, J.: Programs with Common Sense. In: Proc. of the Symposium on the Mechanization of Thought Processes. Volume 1., London (1958) 77–84
2. Levesque, H., Reiter, R., Lespérance, Y., Lin, F., Scherl, R.: GOLOG: A logic programming language for dynamic domains. Journal of Logic Programming **31** (1997) 59–83
3. Thielscher, M.: FLUX: A logic programming method for reasoning agents. Theory and Practice of Logic Programming (2005) Available at: www.fluxagent.org.
4. Hume, D., Sammut, C.: Applying inductive logic programming in reactive environments. In Muggleton, S., ed.: Inductive Logic Programming. Academic Press (1992) 539–549
5. Moyle, S., Muggleton, S.: Learning programs in the event calculus. In: ILP '97: Proc. of the 7th Int. Workshop on Inductive Logic Programming, Springer-Verlag (1997) 205–212
6. Thielscher, M.: From situation calculus to fluent calculus: State update axioms as a solution to the inferential frame problem. Artificial Intelligence **111** (1999) 277–299
7. Plotkin, G.: Automatic Methods of Inductive Inference. PhD thesis, Edinburgh University (1971)
8. Bergadano, F., Gunetti, D.: An interactive system to learn functional logic programs. In Bajcsy, R., ed.: Proc. of the 13th Int. Joint Conference on Artificial Intelligence. (1993) 1044–1045
9. Nienhuys-Cheng, S.H., de Wolf, R.: Foundations of Inductive Logic Programming. Springer (1997)
10. Jr., C.D.P., Frisch, A.M.: Generalization and learnability: A study of constrained atoms (1992)
11. Lavrač, N., Džeroski, S.: Inductive Logic Programming - Techniques and Application. Ellis Horwood (1996)
12. Hart, P., Nilsson, N., Raphael, B.: A formal basis for the heuristic determination of minimum cost paths. IEEE Transactions on Systems Science and Cybernetics **4** (1968) 100–107
13. Thielscher, M.: Reasoning Robots The Art and Science of Programming Robotic Agents. Kluwer Academic Publishers (2005)

Combining Bias and Variance Reduction Techniques for Regression Trees

Yuk Lai Suen[1], Prem Melville[2], and Raymond J. Mooney[3]

[1] Dept. of Electrical and Computer Engr., Univ. of Texas at Austin
    suen@ece.utexas.edu
[2] Dept. of Computer Sciences, Univ. of Texas at Austin
    melville@cs.utexas.edu
[3] mooney@cs.utexas.edu

Abstract. Gradient Boosting and bagging applied to regressors can reduce the error due to bias and variance respectively. Alternatively, Stochastic Gradient Boosting (SGB) and Iterated Bagging (IB) attempt to simultaneously reduce the contribution of both bias and variance to error. We provide an extensive empirical analysis of these methods, along with two alternate bias-variance reduction approaches — bagging Gradient Boosting (BagGB) and bagging Stochastic Gradient Boosting (BagSGB). Experimental results demonstrate that SGB does not perform as well as IB or the alternate approaches. Furthermore, results show that, while BagGB and BagSGB perform competitively for low-bias learners, in general, Iterated Bagging is the most effective of these methods.

1 Introduction

The decomposition of a learner's error into *bias* and *variance* terms provides a way of analyzing the behavior of different learning algorithms [1]. Various methods have been devised to reduce either the bias or variance of a learner. Some methods, such as Gradient Boosting [2], can reduce bias by increasing the expressive power of the base learner. While other methods, such as bagging [3], mainly reduce variance by subsampling the training data. There have been some attempts of combining techniques for bias and variance reduction, both for classification [4, 5] and for regression [6, 7]. For regression, Friedman [7] introduced Stochastic Gradient Boosting (SGB) as a method that reduces the variance of Gradient Boosting (GB) by incorporating randomization in the process. Breiman [6] presented a related method, Iterated Bagging (IB) that attempts to reduce the bias of bagging predictors. Despite their similarities, to our knowledge, there has been no direct experimental comparison of these two methods. In this paper, we present a detailed empirical analysis of SGB and IB. We show that IB significantly outperforms SGB when applied to both pruned and unpruned regression trees. We also explored two alternate methods for combining bias and variance reduction techniques for regression — bagging Gradient Boosting (BagGB) and bagging Stochastic Gradient Boosting (BagSGB). Our experiments show that these methods also significantly outperform SGB. In comparison to IB, BagGB and BagSGB are equally effective when applied to unpruned regression trees. However, for pruned regression trees, which have a higher bias, we observe that IB is the most effective at error reduction. This paper also presents a bias-variance analysis of the different algorithms, which provides a better understanding of the relative effectiveness of these methods.

Section 2 provides a brief background on the bias-variance decomposition of error. In section 3, we describe all the algorithms discussed in this paper, and our main experimental results are presented in section 4. In section 5, we discuss the results of our bias-variance analysis; and section 6 presents our future work and conclusions.

2 Bias-Variance Decomposition of Error

The following formulation of the bias-variance (BV) decomposition is based on [8]. Let us assume our data arose from a model $y = F(x) + \epsilon$, where the random error ϵ has $E(\epsilon) = 0$ and $Var(\epsilon) = \sigma_\epsilon^2$. Then the expected prediction error of a regression model $\hat{F}(x)$ for a point $x = x_i$ using squared-error loss can be expressed as:

$$\begin{aligned} \Psi(y, \hat{F}(x_i)) &= E[(y - \hat{F}(x_i))^2 | x = x_i] \\ &= \sigma_\epsilon^2 + [E(\hat{F}(x_i)) - F(x_i)]^2 + E[\hat{F}(x_i) - E(\hat{F}(x_i))]^2 \\ &= \sigma_\epsilon^2 + bias^2(\hat{F}(x_i)) + variance(\hat{F}(x_i)) \end{aligned} \quad (1)$$

The first term is the *irreducible error*, which is the variance of the target function around its true mean $F(x)$. This error cannot be avoided no matter how well we model $F(x)$. The second term is the contribution of squared bias to error, which is the amount by which the average of our estimates differs from the true mean. The last term is the contribution of variance to error, which is the expected squared deviation of $\hat{F}(x_i)$ around its mean. For brevity, we will refer to the contribution of squared bias and variance to error as $bias^2$ and *variance* respectively. In general, more complex models have lower bias and higher variance; e.g., unpruned decision trees tend to have low bias and high variance, while decision stumps have a very high bias but low variance.

3 Algorithms

3.1 Gradient Boosting and Stochastic Gradient Boosting

Gradient Boosting (GB) [2] is an iterative algorithm which constructs additive models by fitting a base learner to the current *residue* at each iteration; where the residue is the gradient of the loss function being minimized with respect to the model values at each data point. In [9], Friedman introduced Stochastic Gradient Boosting (SGB) which improves the accuracy of GB by reducing its error due to variance. In SGB, at each iteration a subsample of data is drawn uniformly at random, without replacement, from the full training set. This random subsample is used to train the base learner to produce a model for the current stage. Friedman [7] states that the idea of using a random subset of the training set at each stages originates from bootstrap sampling in bagging, and has a similar variance-reducing effect on the combined model. The SGB method (for squared-error loss) is presented in Algorithm 1. GB can be viewed as a special case of this algorithm in which the entire training set is used at each iteration, i.e., $f = 1.0$. In our experiments, the shrinkage parameter ν for GB and SGB was set to 1.

Algorithm 1. Stochastic Gradient Boosting

Given: M – maximum number of stages; $\{x_n, y_n\}_{n=1}^N$ – training set of size N; $f = \frac{\tilde{N}}{N}, 0 < \tilde{N} \leq N$ – fraction parameter that determines the size of subsample; ν – shrinkage parameter; $\mathcal{L}$ – base learner

1. For $m = 1$ to M do:
2.   Select random subset $\{x_{\tilde{n}}, y_{(\tilde{n},m)}\}_{\tilde{n}=1}^{\tilde{N}}$ from $\{x_n, y_{(n,m)}\}_{n=1}^N$
3.   Apply learner $\mathcal{L}$ to sample set $\{x_{\tilde{n}}, y_{(\tilde{n},m)}\}_{\tilde{n}=1}^{\tilde{N}}$ to produce predictor $\hat{F}_m$
4.   Replace residues of training set $\{x_n, y_{(n,m)}\}_{n=1}^N$ to form $\{x_n, y_{(n,m+1)}\}_{n=1}^N$, where $y_{(n,m+1)} = y_{(n,m)} - \nu \cdot \hat{F}_m(x_n)$

Output: $y = \sum_{m=1}^M \nu \cdot \hat{F}_m(x)$

3.2 Iterated Bagging

Bagging has been shown to reduce the variance of predictors, while leaving the bias largely unchanged [3]. Iterated Bagging (IB) [6], also known as Adaptive Bagging [10], is an effort to reduce the bias error of the low-variance bagging predictors. Similar to SGB, it is a stage-wise algorithm that attempts to minimize the residue in each stage. IB addresses bias and variance reduction in two ways: (1) it uses low-variance bagging predictors to compute residues and (2) it computes unbiased estimates of residues using out-of-bag calculations [10]. The outline of IB is presented in Algorithm 2. In our experiments, the threshold parameter τ for IB was set to 1.1, as done in [6].

Algorithm 2. Iterated Bagging

Given: M – maximum number of stages; K – number of bagging predictors in each stage; τ – threshold of mean sum-of-squares of residues; $\{x_n, y_n\}_{n=1}^N$ – training set of size N; $\mathcal{L}$ – base learner

1. Initialize minimum residue, $\epsilon_{M^*} = \infty, M^* = 0$
2. For $m = 1$ to M do:
3.   Learn a set of K bagging predictors $\{\beta_{(k,m)}\}_{k=1}^K$ with learner $\mathcal{L}$ applied to bootstrap samples selected from $\{x_n, y_{(n,m)}\}_{n=1}^N$
4.   Calculate the residue $y_{(n,m+1)} = y_{n,m} - \sum_{k=1}^{\hat{K}} \beta_{(\hat{k},m)}(x_n)/\hat{K}$, where $\beta_{(\hat{k},m)}$ is one of the $\hat{K}$ bagging predictors not trained on x_n
5.   Replace residues of the training set to form $\{x_n, y_{(n,m+1)}\}_{n=1}^N$
6.   Calculate the mean sum-of-squares of residues, $\epsilon_m = \sum_{n=1}^N (y_{(n,m+1)})^2/N$
7.   If $\epsilon_m < \epsilon_{M^*}$ then $M^* = m, \epsilon_{M^*} = \epsilon_m$
8.   Exit the loop if $\epsilon_m > \tau \cdot \epsilon_{M^*}$

Output: $y = \sum_{m=1}^{M^*} \sum_{k=1}^K \beta_{(k,m)}(x)/K$

3.3 Bagging GB and Bagging SGB

We explored two alternative approaches to bias-variance reduction — bagging Gradient Boosting (BagGB) and bagging Stochastic Gradient Boosting (BagSGB). BagGB and

BagSGB use GB and SGB, respectively, as the base learners in each stage of building a bagging predictor. A total of K bootstrap sets of training instances are randomly selected to train K GB (or SGB) predictors. The output y of a test input x is predicted by averaging the predictions of the K base predictors.

BagGB should reduce the variance error of predictions by stabilizing the predictions of the GB base learners. BagGB and IB are similar as they both possess two components: (1) a bagging predictor to stabilize the predictions of the base learners by averaging the results of the predictors each trained with a different bootstrap sample and (2) a greedy stage-wise training of base predictors to minimize the residues. The difference between IB and BagGB is that IB performs greedy stage-wise training with a set of bagging predictors to stabilize the predictions of their base learners, while BagGB stabilizes the predictions of a set of base-predictors, each of which performs greedy stage-wise training. Although SGB already attempts to reduce the variance of GB through randomization, we believe that bagging SGB may further enhance its variance reduction.

4 Experimental Evaluation

4.1 Methodology

We ran all our experiments on 25 datasets, with continuous class (target) values, from the UCI repository [11]. Details on the datasets can found in the extended version of this paper [12]. We compared 7 different regression methods, which are listed in Table 1 along with their setup parameters. The performance of most meta-learners (additive models) varies with the number of base models used. In order to make the comparison fair, we chose parameters such that each method produces 100 base models. In the case of IB, this is an upper bound since it can choose to use fewer models. As a base learner for all the meta-learners we used M5' [13], which is regression tree induction modified based on [14] and [15]. We ran separate sets of experiments on pruned M5' and unpruned M5'. In pruned M5', the regression tree is pruned back from the leaves, so long as the expected estimated error decreases. All our results were averaged over 10 runs of 10-fold stratified cross-validation. The difference in performance between two systems was compared using a two-tailed paired t-test ($p < 0.05$).

The performance of SGB and BagSGB is dependent on the fraction parameter f chosen for the experiment. Some values for f perform significantly better than others on the same dataset. In order to compare with the best instances of SGB and BagSGB,

Table 1. Experimental setup of each method

Algorithm	Description
IB	10 stages of IB with 10 stages of bagging each ($M = 10, K = 10$).
BagSGB/BagGB	10 stages of bagging × 10 SGB/GB iterations each ($M = 10$).
SGB/GB	100 iterations ($M = 100$).
Bagging	100 stages of bagging M5' trees.
M5'	pruned or unpruned M5' tree induction

Table 2. Summary of results comparing the different methods

	IB	BagSGB	BagGB	SGB	GB	Bag	M5'	%ErrRed
IB	-	13/1/11	10/6/9	10/12/3	18/4/3	16/1/8	17/1/7	16.44
BagSGB	11/1/13	-	10/8/7	16/5/4	15/5/5	18/4/3	21/2/2	16.35
BagGB	9/6/10	7/8/10	-	10/11/4	15/5/5	16/2/7	18/2/5	15.61
SGB	3/12/10	4/5/16	4/11/10	-	12/10/3	13/1/11	14/5/6	14.39
GB	3/4/18	5/5/15	5/5/15	3/10/12	-	13/0/12	13/1/11	7.45
Bag	8/1/16	3/4/18	7/2/16	11/1/13	12/0/13	-	17/5/3	1.98
M5'	7/1/17	2/2/21	5/2/18	6/5/14	11/1/13	3/5/17	-	-

(a) Base learner: unpruned M5'

	IB	BagSGB	BagGB	SGB	GB	Bag	M5'	%ErrRed
IB	-	18/4/3	20/3/2	23/1/1	24/0/1	19/3/3	22/1/2	16.89
BagSGB	3/4/18	-	9/9/7	19/6/0	18/6/1	19/4/2	22/3/0	11.82
BagGB	2/3/20	7/9/9	-	18/7/0	17/7/1	21/2/2	22/2/1	11.85
SGB	1/1/23	0/6/19	0/7/18	-	2/18/5	13/5/7	16/8/1	8.14
GB	1/0/24	1/6/18	1/7/17	5/18/2	-	13/4/8	16/7/2	8.55
Bag	3/3/19	2/4/19	2/2/21	7/5/13	8/4/13	-	16/7/2	2.59
M5'	2/1/22	0/3/22	1/2/22	1/8/16	2/7/16	2/7/16	-	-

(b) Base learner: pruned M5'

we performed 10 runs of 10-fold cross-validation on SGB and BagSGB with different values of f from $\{0.4, 0.5, 0.6, 0.7, 0.8, 0.9\}$ and selected the f that produced the lowest error for each dataset.

4.2 Results

Tables 2(a) and 2(b) summarize the results of our experiments using unpruned and pruned M5' base learners respectively. Each cell in the tables reports a win/draw/loss comparison between the algorithm in the row versus the algorithm in the column. The win/draw/loss record presents three values, the number of data sets for which algorithm A obtained better, equal, or worse performance than algorithm B with respect to root-mean-squared (RMS) error. A win or loss is only counted if the difference in values is determined to be significant at the 0.05 level by a paired t-test. The last column of each table presents the percentage reduction of the RMS error using different algorithms compared with using M5'. This value is averaged over all the 25 datasets, and provides an indication of the magnitude of improvements one can expect on average. In the following subsections we summarize the key comparisons from Table 2.

IB vs. SGB: Our results show that IB significantly outperforms SGB, both in terms of win/draw/loss records and error reduction. The differences in performance are more dramatic on pruned M5', where IB performs better than SGB on 23 of the 25 datasets, and produces twice the error reduction on average. The marked performance difference on pruned M5' can be attributed to IB's superior bias-reduction.

SGB, BagGB and BagSGB: BagGB performs significantly better than SGB, both for pruned and unpruned M5'. Similarly to IB, the differences are more pronounced on pruned M5′, where BagGB wins over SGB on 18 of the datasets, with no significant losses. The results suggest that applying bootstrap sampling to GB has a better variance-reducing effect than the randomization incorporated in SGB. In fact, applying bagging to SGB (BagSGB), can significantly drive down the error of SGB, as can be seen for both M5′ settings. BagSGB performs marginally better than BagGB in terms of win/draw/loss records, though their error reductions are quite comparable.

IB vs. BagGB/BagSGB: On unpruned M5′, BagGB and BagSGB perform comparably to IB both in terms of win/draw/loss records and error reduction — all methods producing approximately a 16% reduction in RMS error. However, for pruned M5′ trees, which have higher bias, IB exhibits a significant advantage over BagGB and BagSGB. It wins over BagGB and BagSGB on 20 and 18 datasets respectively. We also observe approximately a 5% difference in error reduction between IB and the other methods. IB's effectiveness at debiasing learners makes it a clear winner in higher bias settings.

SGB vs GB: Our results on high-variance unpruned M5′ support the claim in [7] that SGB has a better variance-reducing effect than GB. SGB on average reduced 14.39% of the error of unpruned M5′, while GB reduced only 7.45%. However, SGB has significant wins in only 12 datasets and ties with GB in 10. Although, the error reduction of SGB is quite good, the win/draw/loss results do not suggest as significant an advantage of SGB over GB as in [9]. In fact, on pruned M5′, the performance of SGB and GB are tied on 18 datasets, with SGB performing slightly worse on the other datasets.

Bias-variance reduction vs. bias or variance reduction: GB and bagging focus solely on reducing the bias or the variance of learners. On the other hand, IB, SGB, BagGB and BagSGB attempt to reduce both the contribution of bias and variance to error. For brevity, we will refer to these four methods as BV-methods. Our results show that generally the BV-methods have a significant advantage over GB and bagging, even when using the same number of base models. When compared to GB, BV-methods perform significantly better on at least 12 datasets and lose on at most 5 datasets. The only exception is SGB using pruned M5′, which loses to GB by a margin of 3 datasets. Even when compared to bagging, SGB is less effective than the other BV-methods. It wins by a margin of 2 (13 wins vs. 11 losses) and 6 (13 wins vs. 7 losses) when using unpruned M5′ and pruned M5′ respectively. The other BV-methods win by at least 16 datasets and lose on at most 8 when compared to bagging. The results clearly indicate that combining techniques for bias and variance reduction is more effective than focusing on either component alone.

5 Bias-Variance Analysis

We explain most of our results based on how the different learners effect the bias and variance components of the error. To support our conjectures, we ran additional experiments to explicitly measure the bias and variance reducing effects of the methods presented. As in [6], we performed BV decompositions on three synthetic datasets — *Friedman1, 2* and *3* [1]. We do not introduce noise in these datasets, so that the evalua-

---
[1] Details of the datasets can be found in [12].

Table 3. Methods in order of increasing bias, variance and overall error

Friedman1			Friedman2			Friedman3		
Bias²	Var.	Err.	Bias²	Var.	Err.	Bias²	Var.	Err.
IB	Bag	IB	IB	IB	IB	IB	Bag	IB
GB	BagSGB	BagSGB	GB	Bag	BagSGB	GB	BagSGB	BagGB
SGB	BagGB	BagGB	BagGB	BagSGB	BagGB	SGB	IB	GB
BagGB	IB	GB	SGB	BagGB	GB	BagGB	BagGB	BagSGB
BagSGB	M5′	SGB	BagSGB	GB	SGB	BagSGB	M5′	SGB
M5′	GB	Bag	M5′	M5′	Bag	M5′	SGB	Bag
Bag	SGB	M5′	Bag	SGB	M5′	Bag	GB	M5′

tion of the bias and variance reduction capability of a learner is not confounded with its ability to handle noise. We use synthetic datasets, so that we can control for noise and get better estimates of bias and variance.

To estimate bias and variance we used the method proposed by Kohavi and Wolpert [16], appropriately modified for regression (as opposed to classification). Each dataset was divided into two halves, D and E. D was used to draw our sample of training sets from, and E was used to estimate the terms in the BV decomposition. We generated 50 training sets from D sampled uniformly at random without replacement. Each training set of size 200 was selected from the pool of 400 examples in D. Each learning algorithm was run on each of the training sets and the squared bias and variance terms were calculated on set E based on equation 1. These values were averaged over all 50 train-test cycles. For SGB and BagSGB, we used a fraction $f = 0.6$; which is roughly equivalent to drawing bootstrap samples at each iteration.

Table 3 presents the different algorithms applied to unpruned M5′, in the order of increasing bias, variance and overall error on each dataset. The results for pruned trees were qualitatively similar, though in general the errors were higher for all methods. For detailed results see [12]. We observe that GB performs very well at reducing bias, but does not perform well at variance reduction. In fact, on *Friedman1* and *Friedman3*, GB actually increases the variance of the base learner. Analogously, bagging can increase the bias of the learner, but performs very well in terms of variance reduction. By combining the power of bagging and GB, BagGB produces a lower overall error than each of its components. Similarly, BagSGB improves on the bias reduction of bagging and the variance reduction of SGB, and as a result produces a lower overall error than both component algorithms. IB shows the best performance on overall error, and it appears to be quite effective in reducing both bias and variance. In fact, IB also performs the best in terms of bias reduction on all three datasets.

6 Future Work and Conclusion

We compared four approaches to combining bias and variance reduction techniques — Stochastic Gradient Boosting, Iterated Bagging, bagging Gradient Boosting and bagging Stochastic Gradient Boosting. Our results demonstrate that methods for combining bias and variance reduction (BV-methods) are more effective than methods that focus either on bias or variance in isolation. We also showed that while SGB often improves on GB, it is not very consistent and is easily outperformed by the other BV-methods. Experimental results show that for unpruned trees, which are low-bias learners, BagGB and BagSGB perform somewhat comparably to IB. However, IB, being a more effective bias-reduction method, performs much better compared to other algorithms when applied to pruned trees.

In our study, we restricted our methods to building at most 100 models each. Typically, the performance of these ensemble methods (or additive models) improve with ensemble size. In future work, we would like to explore the relationship between the number of models used and the effectiveness of each method. All our experiments were run on UCI datasets, commonly used in previous studies. However, these datasets are not very large — the largest has 625 instances. It would be good to see how results vary for much larger datasets. Experimenting with base learners other than decision trees, such as neural networks and support vector machines would also be very useful.

Acknowledgments

We like to thank Horris Tse for assistance with running some of the experiments. Prem Melville and Raymond Mooney were supported by DARPA grant HR0011-04-1-007.

References

[1] Geman, S., Bienenstock, E., Dorsat, R.: Neural networks and the bias/variance dilemma. Neural Computation **4** (1992) 1–58
[2] Friedman, J.: Greedy function approximation: a gradient boosting machine. Technical report, Stanford University Statistics Department (1999)
[3] Breiman, L.: Bagging predictors. Machine Learning **24** (1996) 123–140
[4] Valentini, G., Dietterich, T.G.: Low bias bagged support vector machines. In: Proc. of 20th Intl. Conf. on Machine Learning (ICML-2003), Washington, DC (2003) 752–759
[5] Webb, G.: Multiboosting: A technique for combining boosting and wagging. Machine Learning **40** (2000) 159–196
[6] Breiman, L.: Using iterated bagging to debias regressions. Machine Learning **45** (2001) 261–277
[7] Friedman, J.: Stochastic gradient boosting. Technical report, Stanford University Statistics Department (1999)
[8] Hastie, T., Tibshirani, R., Friedman, J.: The Elements of Statistical Learning. Springer Verlag, New York (2001)
[9] Friedman, J., Hastie, T., Tibshirani, R.: Additive logistic regression: a statistical view of boosting. Technical report, Stanford University Statistics Department (2000)
[10] Breiman, L.: Using adaptive bagging to debias regressions. Technical report, UC Berkeley Statistics Department (1999)
[11] Blake, C.L., Merz, C.J.: UCI repository of machine learning databases. http://www.ics.uci.edu/~mlearn/MLRepository.html (1998)
[12] Suen, Y.L., Melville, P., Mooney, R.J.: Combining bias and variance reduction techniques for regression. Technical Report UT-AI-TR-05-321, University of Texas at Austin (2005) www.cs.utexas.edu/ ml/publication.

[13] Wang, Y., Witten, I.: Inducing model trees for continuous classes. ECML Poster Papers (1997) 128–137
[14] Quinlan, J.: Learning with continuous classes. In: Proceedings of 5th Australian Joint Conference on Artificial Intelligience. (1992) 343–348
[15] Breiman, L., Friedman, J.H., Olshen, R., Stone, C.: Classification and Regression Trees. Wadsworth and Brooks, Monterey, CA (1984)
[16] Kohavi, R., Wolpert, D.H.: Bias plus variance decomposition for zero-one loss functions. In Saitta, L., ed.: Proc. of 13th Intl. Conf. on Machine Learning (ICML-96), Morgan Kaufmann (1996)

Analysis of Generic Perceptron-Like Large Margin Classifiers

Petroula Tsampouka and John Shawe-Taylor

School of Electronics and Computer Science,
University of Southampton, UK

Abstract. We analyse perceptron-like algorithms with margin considering both the standard classification condition and a modified one which demands a specific value of the margin in the augmented space. The new algorithms are shown to converge in a finite number of steps and used to approximately locate the optimal weight vector in the augmented space. As the data are embedded in the augmented space at a larger distance from the origin the maximum margin in that space approaches the maximum geometric one in the original space. Thus, our procedures exploiting the new algorithms can be regarded as approximate maximal margin classifiers.

1 Introduction

Rosenblatt's perceptron algorithm [6] is the simplest on-line learning algorithm for binary linear classification [3]. A variant of the perceptron also exists which unlike the original algorithm aims at a solution hyperplane with respect to which the data possess a non-zero margin. The problem, however, of finding the optimal hyperplane has been successfully addressed only with the advent of the Adatron algorithm [1] and later by the Support Vector Machines (SVMs) [7, 2].

Our purpose here is to address the problem of maximal margin classification using the less time consuming, compared to SVMs, perceptron-like algorithms. We work in a space augmented by one additional dimension [3] in which we embed the data by placing them at a distance ρ in the extra dimension and replace the perceptron classification condition with a new one insisting on a specific value of the margin in this augmented space. We show that the algorithms with the modified condition converge in a finite number of steps and use them to approximately locate the solution with maximum margin in the augmented space. As $\rho \to \infty$ the maximum margin in the augmented space approaches the maximum geometric one in the original space. Thus, our algorithmic procedures can be considered as approximate maximal margin classifiers.

Whilst proving convergence of the new algorithms we found it useful to introduce the notion of stepwise convergence, the property of the algorithms that approach the optimal solution vector at each step. Through a formulation involving stepwise convergence we provide a unified approach in establishing convergence for a large class of algorithms with additive perceptron-like update rules.

J. Gama et al. (Eds.): ECML 2005, LNAI 3720, pp. 750–758, 2005.
© Springer-Verlag Berlin Heidelberg 2005

Section 2 contains our theoretical analysis. In Sect. 3 we describe algorithmic implementations aiming at an approximate determination of the maximum margin. Finally, Sect. 4 contains our conclusions.

2 Theoretical Analysis

In what follows we make the assumption that we are given a training set which, even if not initially linearly separable can, by an appropriate feature mapping into a space of a higher dimension, be classified into two categories by a linear classifier. This higher dimensional space in which the patterns are linearly separable will be the considered space. By adding one additional dimension and placing all patterns in the same position $\rho_0 = \rho > 0$ in that dimension we construct an embedding of our data into the so-called augmented space. The advantage of this embedding is that the linear hypothesis in the augmented space becomes homogeneous.

We concentrate on algorithms that update the augmented weight vector $\boldsymbol{a}_t$ by adding a suitable positive amount in the direction of the misclassified (according to an appropriate condition) training pattern $\boldsymbol{y}_k$. The general form of such an update rule is

$$\boldsymbol{a}_{t+1} = \boldsymbol{a}_t + \eta f_t \boldsymbol{y}_k \;, \tag{1}$$

where η is the (constant) learning rate and f_t a function of the current step (time) t which we require to be positive and bounded, i.e.

$$0 < f_{\min} \leq f_t \leq f_{\max} \;. \tag{2}$$

For the special case of the perceptron algorithm $f_t = 1$. Each time the predefined misclassification condition is satisfied by a training pattern the algorithm proceeds to the update of the weight vector. Throughout our discussion a reflection with respect to the origin in the augmented space of the negatively labelled patterns is assumed in order to allow for a common classification condition for both categories of patterns [3]. Also, we use the notation $R = \max_k \|\boldsymbol{y}_k\|$ and $r = \min_k \|\boldsymbol{y}_k\|$.

The relation characterising optimally correct classification of the training patterns by a weight vector $\boldsymbol{u}$ of unit norm in the augmented space is

$$\boldsymbol{u} \cdot \boldsymbol{y}_k \geq \gamma_d \quad \forall k \;. \tag{3}$$

The quantity γ_d, which we call the optimal directional margin, is defined as

$$\gamma_d = \max_{\boldsymbol{u}:\|\boldsymbol{u}\|=1} \min_k \{\boldsymbol{u} \cdot \boldsymbol{y}_k\} \tag{4}$$

and is obviously bounded from above by r. The optimal directional margin determines the maximum distance from the origin in the augmented space of the hyperplane normal to $\boldsymbol{u}$ placing all training patterns on the positive side. In the determination of this hyperplane only the direction of $\boldsymbol{u}$ is exploited with no reference to its projection onto the original space. As a consequence the above maximum margin in the augmented space is not necessarily realised with the same weight vector that gives rise to the optimal geometric margin in the original space. Notice, however, that the existence of a directional margin means that there exists a geometric margin at least as large as the directional one.

First, in Sect. 2.1, we examine algorithms in which the misclassification condition takes the form

$$a_t \cdot y_k \leq b , \qquad (5)$$

where b is a positive parameter. A slight transformation of (5) to

$$u_t \cdot y_k \leq \frac{b}{\|a_t\|} , \qquad (6)$$

where u_t is the weight vector a_t normalised to unity, reveals that the minimum directional margin required by the standard margin condition is lowered as the length of the weight vector grows.

Subsequently, in Sect. 2.2, we examine algorithms with a misclassification condition of the form

$$u_t \cdot y_k \leq \beta , \qquad (7)$$

where β is a positive parameter. Notice that the above condition amounts to requiring a minimum directional margin which is not lowered with the number of steps. Therefore, successful termination of the algorithm leads to a solution with a guaranteed geometric margin at least as large as the directional margin β found. This is an important difference from the misclassification condition of (5) which, as (6) illustrates, cannot by itself guarantee a minimum margin. Obviously, convergence of the algorithm is not possible unless

$$\beta < \gamma_d . \qquad (8)$$

The condition (7) involving only the direction of the weight vector motivates new positive and bounded functions f_t like the function $f_t = (\beta_u - u_t \cdot y_k)/\|y_k\|$ with $\beta_u > \beta$. We consider two cases depending on whether the length of the augmented weight vector is free to grow or is kept constant throughout the algorithm. In the last category of algorithms a fixed-length weight vector is achieved by a renormalisation of the newly produced weight vector to the target margin value β each time an update according to (1) takes place.

A very desirable property of an algorithm is certainly progressive convergence at each step meaning that at each update u_t moves closer to the optimal direction u. Let us assume that

$$u_t \cdot u > 0 . \qquad (9)$$

Because of (9) the criterion for stepwise angle convergence, namely

$$\Delta \equiv u_{t+1} \cdot u - u_t \cdot u > 0 , \qquad (10)$$

can be equivalently expressed as a demand for positivity of D

$$D \equiv (u_{t+1} \cdot u)^2 - (u_t \cdot u)^2 = 2\frac{\eta f_t}{\|a_t\|}(u_t \cdot u)\left\|u_t + \frac{\eta f_t}{\|a_t\|}y_k\right\|^{-2} A , \qquad (11)$$

where use has been made of the update rule (1) and A is defined by

$$A \equiv \boldsymbol{y}_k \cdot \boldsymbol{u} - (\boldsymbol{u}_t \cdot \boldsymbol{u})(\boldsymbol{y}_k \cdot \boldsymbol{u}_t) - \frac{1}{2}\frac{\eta f_t}{\|\boldsymbol{a}_t\|}\left(\|\boldsymbol{y}_k\|^2(\boldsymbol{u}_t \cdot \boldsymbol{u}) - \frac{(\boldsymbol{y}_k \cdot \boldsymbol{u})^2}{(\boldsymbol{u}_t \cdot \boldsymbol{u})}\right). \quad (12)$$

Positivity of A leads to positivity of D on account of (2) and (9) and consequently to stepwise convergence. Actually, convergence occurs in a finite number of steps provided that after some time $\|\boldsymbol{a}_t\|$ and A become bounded from below by a positive constant and $\|\boldsymbol{a}_t\|$ increases at most linearly with t. Following this rather unified approach one can show that sooner or later the algorithms under consideration enter the stage of stepwise convergence and terminate successfully in a finite number of steps. Better time bounds are, however, obtainable by alternative methods.

Finally, Sect. 2.3 contains our derivations which place an upper bound on the optimal geometric margin of a training set in terms of the optimal directional one, thereby leading to an estimate of the optimal geometric margin.

2.1 Algorithms with the Standard Margin Condition

We first analyse the algorithms with the general update rule (1) by calculating an upper bound on the number of updates until a solution is found, thereby extending Novikoff's theorem [5,4]. From the difference $\boldsymbol{a}_{t+1} \cdot \boldsymbol{u} - \boldsymbol{a}_t \cdot \boldsymbol{u}$ we obtain a relation whose repeated application, assuming $\boldsymbol{a}_0 = \boldsymbol{0}$, implies

$$\|\boldsymbol{a}_t\| \geq \boldsymbol{a}_t \cdot \boldsymbol{u} \geq \eta f_{\min}\gamma_{\mathrm{d}} t . \quad (13)$$

Also the difference $\|\boldsymbol{a}_{t+1}\|^2 - \|\boldsymbol{a}_t\|^2$ gives a relation whose repeated application leads to

$$\|\boldsymbol{a}_t\| \leq \sqrt{(\eta^2 f_{\max}^2 R^2 + 2\eta f_{\max} b)t} . \quad (14)$$

Combining (13) and (14) we get Novikoff's time bound

$$t \leq t_{\mathrm{N}} \equiv \frac{f_{\max}^2}{f_{\min}^2}\frac{R^2}{\gamma_{\mathrm{d}}^2}\left(1 + \frac{2}{\eta f_{\max}}\frac{b}{R^2}\right) . \quad (15)$$

We next turn to a discussion of stepwise convergence. From (13) it is clear that for $t > 0$ (9) holds. Also, $\boldsymbol{y}_k \cdot \boldsymbol{u}$ appearing in A is definitely positive due to (3) whereas $\|\boldsymbol{a}_t\|$ increases with time because of (13), thereby making the term of A linear in η negligible. Moreover, (6) shows that the term $(\boldsymbol{u}_t \cdot \boldsymbol{u})(\boldsymbol{y}_k \cdot \boldsymbol{u}_t)$ is suppressed with time. Thus, for time t larger than a critical time t_c positivity of A and consequently of D is accomplished. By using (3), (5) and (13) we obtain

$$A \geq \gamma_{\mathrm{d}} - \frac{1}{2\eta f_{\min}\gamma_{\mathrm{d}} t}\left(2b + \eta f_{\max}(R^2 - \gamma_{\mathrm{d}}^2)\right) . \quad (16)$$

From the above inequality the time sufficient for stepwise convergence to begin is

$$t_c \equiv \frac{1}{2}\frac{f_{\max}}{f_{\min}}\frac{R^2}{\gamma_{\mathrm{d}}^2}\left(1 + \frac{2}{\eta f_{\max}}\frac{b}{R^2} - \frac{\gamma_{\mathrm{d}}^2}{R^2}\right) < \frac{1}{2}\frac{f_{\min}}{f_{\max}}t_{\mathrm{N}} . \quad (17)$$

Therefore, unless the algorithm terminates much before Novikoff's time t_N is exhausted, it will definitely enter the phase of stepwise convergence. Actually, because of (13), (14) and (16) an alternative proof of convergence in a finite number of steps is obtained.

It would be interesting to estimate the margin that the algorithm is able to achieve [4]. For $t = t_N$ (13) and (14) hold as equalities leading to the largest possible value of $\|a_t\|$, namely $\|a_{t_N}\| = \eta f_{\min} \gamma_d t_N$, which provides a lower bound $\beta_{\min} = b/\|a_{t_N}\|$ on the directional margin $\beta = b/\|a_t\|$ appearing in (6)

$$\beta_{\min} = \frac{f_{\min}}{f_{\max}} \frac{\gamma_d}{(2 + f_{\max}(\eta R^2/b))} = \frac{1}{2} \frac{f_{\min}}{f_{\max}} \gamma_d \left(1 - \frac{f_{\max}^2}{f_{\min}^2} \frac{R^2}{\gamma_d^2} t_N^{-1}\right) . \quad (18)$$

The above guaranteed value of the directional margin acquires a maximum of $\frac{1}{2} \frac{f_{\min}}{f_{\max}} \gamma_d \leq \frac{1}{2} \gamma_d$ for $b \gg \eta R^2$ or $t_N \gg R^2/\gamma_d^2$.

2.2 Algorithms with Fixed Directional Margin Condition

Algorithms with Free-Length Weight Vector. In the case that a_t is free to grow indefinitely and $a_0 = 0$ (13) is again obtained and as a consequence for $t > 0$ (9) is once more recovered. Therefore, positivity of D is equivalent to stepwise convergence. By using (3) and (7) we get a lower bound on the η-independent part of A

$$y_k \cdot u - (u_t \cdot u)(y_k \cdot u_t) \geq \gamma_d - \beta , \quad (19)$$

which is definitely positive on account of (8). Furthermore, because of (13) the terms of A linear in η, which are not necessarily positive, become less important with time leading to positivity of A and consequently of D for t larger than a critical time t_c. More formally, employing (3), (7) and (13) we can place a lower bound on A

$$A \geq \gamma_d - \beta - \frac{1}{2} \frac{f_{\max}}{f_{\min}} \frac{1}{\gamma_d t}(R^2 - \gamma_d^2) \quad (20)$$

and demanding positivity estimate the time t_c sufficient for the onset of stepwise convergence

$$t_c \equiv \frac{1}{2} \frac{f_{\max}}{f_{\min}} \frac{R^2}{\gamma_d^2} \left(1 - \frac{\gamma_d^2}{R^2}\right) \left(1 - \frac{\beta}{\gamma_d}\right)^{-1} . \quad (21)$$

Notice the crucial dependence of t_c on $\gamma_d - \beta$. Since we initially set the weight vector to zero, a_t is entirely generated by the first t updates and its norm satisfies the obvious bound

$$\|a_t\| \leq \eta f_{\max} R t . \quad (22)$$

Then, stepwise convergence along with (13), (20) and (22) lead to convergence in a finite number of steps.

Following a Novikoff-like procedure and provided $f_{\min} \gamma_d - f_{\max} \beta > 0$ (which always holds if $f_t = 1$) we can obtain for every positive integer N a relation

$$\frac{t - N}{C_N + \ln \sqrt{t - 1}} \leq \left(\frac{f_{\max}}{f_{\min}} \frac{R}{\gamma_d}\right)^2 \left(1 - \frac{f_{\max}}{f_{\min}} \frac{\beta}{\gamma_d}\right)^{-1} \quad (23)$$

constraining the growth of t. Here

$$C_N = N \frac{f_{\min}}{f_{\max}} \frac{\gamma_d}{R} \left(1 - \frac{f_{\min}}{f_{\max}} \frac{\gamma_d}{R}\right) - \frac{1}{2}\left(\ln N - \frac{1}{N}\right) . \tag{24}$$

If $[x]$ denotes the integer part of x the optimal value of N is given by

$$N_{\text{opt}} = \left[\frac{1}{2} \frac{f_{\max}}{f_{\min}} \frac{R}{\gamma_d} \left(1 - \frac{\beta}{R}\right)^{-1}\right] + 1 . \tag{25}$$

Notice that both (21) and (23) are independent of η. This is an interesting property of all algorithms of this class with $\boldsymbol{a}_0 = \boldsymbol{0}$ under the additional assumption that f_t depends on $\boldsymbol{a}_t$ only through $\boldsymbol{u}_t$. This may be understood by observing that a rescaling of η results in a rescaling of $\boldsymbol{a}_t$ by the same factor which does not affect either the hyperplane normal to $\boldsymbol{a}_t$ or the classification condition.

Algorithms with Fixed-Length Weight Vector. We demand that $\boldsymbol{u}_t \cdot \boldsymbol{u} > 0$ for all t which requires an appropriate choice of the initial condition. Notice that in this particular class of algorithms $\boldsymbol{a}_t$ cannot be set initially to zero since $\|\boldsymbol{a}_t\| = \beta$. We propose that $\boldsymbol{u}_0$ be chosen in the direction of one of the $\boldsymbol{y}_k$'s. Then, due to the form of the update rule and the positivity of f_t, it is obvious that $\boldsymbol{a}_t$ is a linear combination with positive coefficients of the training patterns. Therefore, since according to (3) $\boldsymbol{y}_k$ satisfies $\boldsymbol{y}_k \cdot \boldsymbol{u} > 0$ the same is true for $\boldsymbol{a}_t$ and consequently for $\boldsymbol{u}_t$. Positivity of $\boldsymbol{u}_t \cdot \boldsymbol{u}$ allows us to use positivity of D as a criterion for stepwise convergence. Taking a closer look at A reveals that according to (8) and (19) the η-independent term remains positive throughout the algorithm. For the term linear in η which has no definite sign we conclude that an appropriate choice of η can render it smaller than the η-independent one, thereby leading to stepwise convergence from the first step of the algorithm. More specifically, using (3), (7) and the fact that $\|\boldsymbol{a}_t\| = \beta$ we have

$$A \geq \gamma_d - \beta - \frac{\eta f_{\max}}{2\beta}(R^2 - \gamma_d^2) . \tag{26}$$

Positivity of A and D is achieved for η smaller than the critical value

$$\eta_c \equiv \frac{2}{f_{\max}} \frac{(\gamma_d - \beta)\beta}{R^2}\left(1 - \frac{\gamma_d^2}{R^2}\right)^{-1} . \tag{27}$$

Taking into account (9) and (26) and given that $\|\boldsymbol{a}_t\| = \beta$ stepwise convergence from the first step implies convergence in a finite number of steps.

By placing a t-independent lower bound on Δ defined in (10) and repeatedly applying the resulting inequality it is possible to derive an upper bound on t. For the optimal value of the learning rate

$$\eta_{\text{opt}} \simeq \frac{1}{f_{\max}} \frac{(\gamma_d - \beta)\beta}{R^2}\left(1 + \frac{2\beta}{R}\right)^{-1} \tag{28}$$

we have
$$t < 2\frac{f_{\max}}{f_{\min}}\frac{R^2}{(\gamma_d - \beta)^2}\left(1 + \frac{2\beta}{R}\right)\left(1 - \frac{(\gamma_d - \beta)R}{(R + 2\beta)^2}\right)^{-1}. \quad (29)$$

This bound is rather analogous to the one of the perceptron without margin. The main differences are a factor of 2 and the replacement of γ_d^2 by $(\gamma_d - \beta)^2$.

2.3 Estimating the Optimal Geometric Margin

If we denote by $\boldsymbol{a} = [\boldsymbol{w}\ w_0]$ a weight vector in the augmented space that classifies the patterns correctly the geometric margin $\gamma(\boldsymbol{a})$ of the set is

$$\gamma(\boldsymbol{a}) = \frac{\|\boldsymbol{a}\|}{\|\boldsymbol{w}\|}\gamma_d(\boldsymbol{a}) = \frac{1}{\|\boldsymbol{w}\|}\min_k \{\boldsymbol{a}\cdot\boldsymbol{y}_k\} = \frac{1}{\|\boldsymbol{w}\|}\min_k \{\boldsymbol{w}\cdot\boldsymbol{x}_k + w_0\rho_0\}, \quad (30)$$

where $\gamma_d(\boldsymbol{a})$ is the corresponding directional margin and $\boldsymbol{y}_k = [\boldsymbol{x}_k\ \rho_0]$. Notice that $|w_0|\rho/\|\boldsymbol{w}\|$ (with $\rho = |\rho_0|$) is the distance from the origin of the hyperplane normal to $\boldsymbol{w}$ which cannot exceed $R_x = \max_k \|\boldsymbol{x}_k\|$. Hence, $|w_0|/\|\boldsymbol{w}\| \leq R_x/\rho$. As a consequence, $\|\boldsymbol{w}\| \leq \|\boldsymbol{a}\| = \sqrt{\|\boldsymbol{w}\|^2 + w_0^2} \leq \|\boldsymbol{w}\|\sqrt{1 + R_x^2/\rho^2} = \|\boldsymbol{w}\| R/\rho$ given that $R^2 = \rho^2 + R_x^2$. Then, (30) leads to $\gamma_d(\boldsymbol{a}) \leq \gamma(\boldsymbol{a})$ but also to

$$\gamma(\boldsymbol{a}) \leq \frac{R}{\rho}\gamma_d(\boldsymbol{a}). \quad (31)$$

In the case that the weight vector $\boldsymbol{a}$ is the optimal one $\boldsymbol{a}_{\text{opt}}$ maximising the geometric margin and taking into account that $\gamma_d = \max_{\boldsymbol{a}} \gamma_d(\boldsymbol{a}) \geq \gamma_d(\boldsymbol{a}_{\text{opt}})$ and $\gamma \equiv \gamma(\boldsymbol{a}_{\text{opt}}) = \max_{\boldsymbol{a}} \gamma(\boldsymbol{a}) \geq \max_{\boldsymbol{a}} \gamma_d(\boldsymbol{a}) = \gamma_d$ the inequality (31) leads to

$$1 \leq \frac{\gamma}{\gamma_d} \leq \frac{R}{\rho}. \quad (32)$$

In the limit $\rho \to \infty$, $R/\rho \to 1$ and from (32) $\gamma_d \to \gamma$. Thus, with ρ increasing the optimal directional margin γ_d approaches the optimal geometric one γ.

3 Algorithmic Implementation

In this section we present algorithms seeking the optimal directional margin which, however, due to the analysis of Sect. 2.3 could be used to approximately obtain the optimal geometric margin.

A first implementation makes repeated use of the algorithms of Sect. 2.2. In each round of its application the algorithm looks for a fixed directional margin β according to the condition $\boldsymbol{u}_t \cdot \boldsymbol{y}_k > \beta$. Each round lasts until the condition is satisfied by all $\boldsymbol{y}_k$'s or until an upper bound on the number of checks is reached. The range of feasible β values and therefore the interval that the algorithm should search extends from 0 to r. The search can be performed efficiently by a Bolzano-like bisection method with an initial target margin $\beta = \frac{r}{2}$ and a step parameter set initially to $\frac{r}{2}$. If the algorithm comes up with a solution without exhausting the upper number of checks the round is considered successful. The weight vector is stored as the best solution found so far and is exploited as the initial condition of the next trial, thereby speeding up the procedure substantially. One could also envisage using the final weight vector of an unsuccessful previous round as the initial weight vector of a subsequent one until the first successful trial is reached. At the end of each trial the step is divided by 2. A successful (unsuccessful) trial is followed by an increase (decrease) of the target margin β by the current step value. Therefore, for a sufficiently large upper number of checks, the procedure guarantees that the deviation of β from the maximum margin is halved in each round. Termination occurs when the step reaches a certain predefined value.

A second possibility is to first use the standard perceptron algorithm with margin of Sect. 2.1 in order to obtain a solution with a guaranteed fraction of the existing directional margin given by (18) and then attempt to incrementally boost the margin obtained by repeatedly employing the algorithms of Sect. 2.2. The initial condition of each round of boosting will be the final weight vector of the previous round and the step by which the target margin increases will be determined as a fraction of the margin found in the first stage. The algorithm ends with the first unsuccessful trial. An analogous boosting procedure could follow a first stage of successful employment of the Bolzano-like method.

The above procedures were tested on artificial as well as real-life data with encouraging preliminary results.

4 Conclusions

We examined perceptron-like algorithms with margin and developed a criterion for the stronger requirement of stepwise convergence which allowed us to adopt a unified approach in the analysis. We also proposed a new class of such algorithms in which the standard classification condition is replaced by a more stringent one insisting on a fixed value of the directional margin and proved that they converge in a finite number of steps. Two implementations made possible a fast search for the optimal directional margin. We finally showed that as the data are placed increasingly far in the augmented space the optimal directional margin approaches the optimal geometric one. This observation transforms our procedures into fast and simple approximate maximal margin classifiers.

References

1. Anlauf, J. K., Biehl, M.: The adatron: an adaptive perceptron algorithm. Europhysics Letters **10** (1989) 687–692
2. Cristianini, N., Shawe-Taylor, J.: An Introduction to Support Vector Machines (2000) Cambridge, UK: Cambridge University Press
3. Duda, R. O., Hart, P. E., Stork, D. G.: Pattern Classssification (2000) Wiley-Interscience, 2nd edition

4. Li, Y., Zaragoza, H., Herbrich, R., Shawe-Taylor, J., Kandola, J.: The perceptron algorithm with uneven margins. In ICML'02 379–386
5. Novikoff, A. B. J.: On convergence proofs on perceptrons. In Proceedings of the Symposium on the Mathematical Theory of Automata Volume 12 (1962) 615–622
6. Rosenblatt, F.: The perceptron: A probabilistic model for information storage and organization in the brain. Psychological Review **65**(6) (1958) 386–408
7. Vapnik, V. N.: The Nature of Statistical Learning Theory (1995) Springer Verlag

Multimodal Function Optimizing by a New Hybrid Nonlinear Simplex Search and Particle Swarm Algorithm

Fang Wang and Yuhui Qiu

Intelligent Software and Software Engineering Laboratory,
Southwest China Normal University, Chongqing, 400715, China
{teresa78, yhqiu}@swnu.edu.cn

Abstract. A new hybrid Particle Swarm Optimization (PSO) algorithm is proposed in this paper based on the Nonlinear Simplex Search (NSS) method for multimodal function optimizing tasks. At late stage of PSO process, when the most promising regions of solutions are fixed, the algorithm isolates particles that fly very close to the extrema and applies the NSS method to them to enhance local exploitation searching. Explicit experimental results on famous benchmark functions indicate that this approach is reliable and efficient, especially on multimodal function optimizations. It yields better solution qualities and success rates compared to other three published methods.

1 Introduction

A new research field called Swarm Intelligence (SI) arose [1], [2] in the beginning of 90's, which focuses on analogies of swarm behavior of natural creatures. These optimization techniques suggest that the main ideas of intelligent individuals' socio-cognition can be effectively introduced to develop efficient optimization algorithms. Among all SI algorithms, the Ant Colony Optimization (ACO) proposed by Dorigo [3] is the most well known technique and is mainly used for combinatorial optimization tasks. The Particle Swarm Optimization (PSO) is another SI method, which is mostly used for continuous function optimizing and has been originally proposed by R.C. Eberhart and J. Kennedy [4]. PSO exhibits good performance in solving hard optimization problems and engineering applications, and compares favorably to other optimization algorithms [5], [6].

Numerous variations of the basic PSO algorithm have been projected by researchers in this field [7] to improve its overall performance since its introduction in 1995. Hybrid PSO algorithms with determinate methods, such as the Nonlinear Simplex Search method, are proved to be superior to the original two techniques and have many advantages over other techniques, such as Genetic Algorithms (GAs) and Tabu Search (TS), because these hybrid methods can perform exploration search with PSO and exploitation search with determinate methods [8]. Generating initial swarm by the NSS might improve, but is not satisfying for multimodal function optimizing tasks [9]. Developing the NSS as an operator to the swarm during the optimization may increase the computational complex considerably.

In this paper, the Nonlinear Simplex Search method is adopted at late stage of PSO algorithm when particles fly quite near to the extrema. Experimental results on several famous test functions show that this is a very promising way to increase both the convergence speed and the success rate significantly. We briefly introduce the PSO algorithm and the nonlinear simplex search method in section 2. In section 3, the proposed algorithm and experimental design is described, correlative results of experiments are exhibited in section 4. The paper comes to the end with terse conclusions and some ideas for further work.

2 Background Knowledge

2.1 The Particle Swarm Algorithm

As mentioned in previous section, the particle swarm algorithm is proposed mainly for continuous optimization tasks based on the analogy of swarm of bird and fish school. In PSO algorithm, the population of potential solutions is called swarm, which is usually initialized by a uniform distribution over the search space and then iteratively explores the search space, simulating the movement of a "birds' flock" while searching for food. During the search process, global exchange of information among all individuals, which are called particles, takes place so that each particle can benefit from the current search results of other particles.

In the original PSO formulae, particle i is denoted as $X_i=(x_{i1},x_{i2},...,x_{iD})$, which represents a potential solution to a problem in D-dimensional space. Each particle maintains a memory of its previous best position, $P_i=(p_{i1},p_{i2},...,p_{iD})$, and a velocity along each dimension, represented as $V_i=(v_{i1},v_{i2},...,v_{iD})$. At each iteration, the P vector of the particle with the best fitness in the swarm, designated g, and the P vector of the current particle are combined to adjust the velocity along each dimension, and that velocity is then used to compute a new position for the particle.

The velocity and position of particle i at (t+1)th iteration are updated by [5]:

$$v_{id}^{t+1} = w * v_{id}^t + c_1 * r_1^t * (p_{id}^t - x_{id}^t) + c_2 * r_2^t (p_{gd}^t - x_{id}^t) \qquad (1)$$

$$x_{id}^{t+1} = x_{id}^t + v_{id}^{t+1} \qquad (2)$$

Constants c_1 and c_2 determine the relative influence of the social and cognition components (learning rates), which often both are set to the same value to give each component equal weight; r_1 and r_2 are random numbers uniformly distributed in the interval [0,1]. A constant, Vmax, was used to limit the velocities of the particles. The parameter w, which was introduced as an inertia factor, can dynamically adjust the velocity over time, gradually focusing the PSO into a local search [6].

Maurice Clerc has derived a constriction coefficient K, a modification of the PSO that runs without Vmax, reducing some undesirable explosive feedback effects [10], [11]. The constriction factor is computed as:

$$K = \frac{2}{\left|2-\varphi-\sqrt{\varphi^2-4\varphi}\right|}, \quad \varphi=c_1+c_2, \quad \varphi>4 \qquad (3)$$

With the constriction factor K, the PSO formula for computing the new velocity is:

$$v_{id}^{t+1} = k*(v_{id}^{t} + c_1 * r_1^t *(p_{id}^t - x_{id}^t) + c_2 * r_2^t (p_{gd}^t - x_{id}^t)) \qquad (4)$$

Carlisle and Dozier investigated the influence of different parameters in PSO, selected c_1=2.8, c_2=1.3, population size as 30, and proposed the Canonical PSO [12].

To speed up the convergence process and avoid premature problem, Shi YH [13] proposed a method to linearly decrease the inertia weight (LDW) by:

$$w = w_{max} - (w_{max} - w_{min}) * \frac{iter}{iter_{max}} \qquad (5)$$

Where w_{max} and w_{min} is the maximum and minimum of inertia weight, iter is the current iteration number, $iter_{max}$ is the maximum iteration times.

2.2 The Nonlinear Simplex Search Method

Spendley et al presented the basic simplex method in 1962, which is an efficient sequential optimization method for function minimization tasks, and then improved by Nelder and Mead, to what is called the Nonlinear Simplex Search method [14]. It needs only values and not derivatives of the objective function. In general, the NSS is considered as the best method if the figure of merit is "get something to work quickly".

A *D*-dimensional simplex is a geometrical figure consisting of D+1 vertices (*D*-dimensional points) and all their interconnecting segments, polygonal faces etc. We consider only simplexes that are non-degenerated, i.e., that enclose a finite inner *D*-dimensional volume.

The NSS starts with an initial simplex generated using the found minimum as one of its vertices and generating the rest D points randomly. Then it takes a series of steps as follows to rescale the simplex: first, it finds the points where the objective function is highest (the least favorable trial W) and lowest (the most favorable trial B); then it reflects the simplex around the high point to point R. If the solution is better, it tries an expansion in that direction to point E; else if the solution is worse than the second-highest (next-to-the worst) point Nw, it tries an intermediate point. When the method reaches a "valley floor", the simplex is contracted in the transverse direction in order to ooze down the valley or it can be contracted in all directions, pulling itself in around its lowest point, and started again.

The different moves of a two-dimensional simplex are shown in Figure 1.

At each step, the rejected trial W is replaced by one of the following trials on conditions that:

$$R = \overline{C} + \alpha(\overline{C} - W), \;\; if \;\; f_B < f_R < f_{Nw}$$
$$E = \overline{C} + \gamma(\overline{C} - W), \;\; if \;\; f_R < f_B$$
$$C+ = \overline{C} + \beta^+(\overline{C} - W), \;\; if \;\; f_{Nw} < f_R < f_M$$
$$C- = \overline{C} - \beta^-(\overline{C} - W), \;\; if \;\; f_R > f_M$$

Where $\bar{c}$ is the centroid of the remaining vertices; α, γ, β^+ and β^- is coefficients of reflection, expansion, positive contraction and negative contraction; f_B, f_{Nw}, f_W and f_R is the values of object function on point B, Nw, W and R respectively.

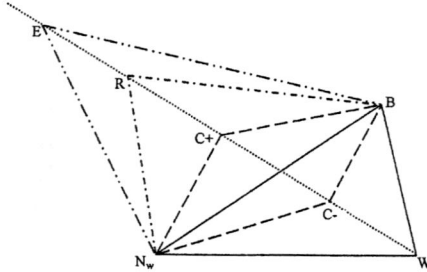

Fig. 1. Different simplex moves from the rejected trial condition, W= the rejected trial, R = reflection, E = expansion, C+ = positive contraction, C- = negative contraction.

3 The Proposed Algorithm and Experimental Design

At late stage of PSO running, promising regions of solutions have been located. Applying the NSS to enhance exploitation search at this stage is capable of improving the solution quality and convergence rate.

We propose a hybrid Nonlinear Simplex Search PSO (NSSPSO) based on the Canonical PSO algorithm, which isolates a particle and apply the NSS to it when it reaches quite close to the extrema (within the diversion radius). If the particle "lands" within a specified precision of a goal solution (error goal) during the NSS running, a PSO process is considered to be successful, otherwise it may be laid back to the swarm and start the next PSO iteration.

The diversion radius is computed as:

$$DRadius = ErrorGoal + \delta \qquad (6)$$

$$\delta = \begin{cases} 100 * ErrorGoal, & \text{if } ErrorGoal <= 10^{-4} \\ 0.01 * ErrorGoal, & \text{otherwise} \end{cases} \qquad (7)$$

In a NSS process, an initial simplex is consists of the isolated particle i and other D vertices randomly generated with the mean of X_i and standard deviation of DRadius.

The stopping criterion is defined as:

$$|f(X_g) - GM| < ErrorGoal \qquad (8)$$

In order to get quicker convergence, we set maximums of iterations in all experiments as a second stopping criterion. In the later case, we consider the search process to be failed.

The benchmark functions [15] on which the proposed algorithm has been tested and compared to other methods in the literature, and the corresponding parameters are listed in Table 1.

Table 1. Benchmark functions used in our experiments

Function	Xmax	GM	Error Goal	Dimension
			10^{-7}	2
Sp: Sphere	100	0	10^{-7}	10
			10^{-4}	30
			10^{-7}	2
Ro: Rosenbrock	30	0	10	10
			100	30
			10^{-7}	2
Ra: Rastrigin	5.12	0	10	10
			100	30
			10^{-7}	2
Gr: Griewank	600	Dimension-1	10^{-1}	10
			10^{-1}	30
Sc: Schaffer	5.12	-1	10^{-4}	2
L3: Levy No.3	10	-176.5418	10^{-4}	2
L8: Levy No.8	10	0	10^{-7}	3
Co: Corana	5.12	0	10^{-7}	4
Fr: Freudenstein	10	0	10^{-7}	2
Go: Goldstern	5.12	3	10^{-7}	2

*Note: for function Sphere, Rosenbrock, Rastrigin and Griewank, three Error Goals are given for separate dimension of three tests. GM is the known theoretic extremum of each test function.

To eliminate the influence of different initial swarms, we implement 200 experiments for each test and the maximum number of PSO iterations is set to be 500, swarm size is 60 for 30-dimension functions and 30 for others. We use symmetric search spaces as [-Xmax...Xmax], and set Vmax=Xmax. In LDW PSO algorithm, $c_1=c_2=2.0$, and the inertia weight w was initially set to 0.9 and gradually decreased toward 0.4. Parameters used in the NSS are: $\alpha =1.0$, $\gamma =2.0$, $\beta^+ = \beta^- =0.5$. We re-implemented all the algorithms mentioned in Section 4 and executed them under the same environment: Matlab 7.0 [16], Pentium IV 2.8GHz CPU, 512M RAM, Windows2000 Professional OS.

4 Experimental Results

The rate of success, mean function evaluations, average optima and total CPU time for each test are listed in Table 2~4. The subscripts of test functions denote different dimensions. The proposed algorithm is denoted as NSSPSO, NS-PSO is another NSS hybrid PSO proposed by Parsopoulos and Vrahatis [9], LDW represents Linearly Decreasing Weight method by Shi YH [5], [6], and CPSO is the Canonical PSO by Carlisle A [12]. From the tables we can see that the overall performance of NSSPSO algorithm is apparently superior to the other 3 algorithms in terms of success rate, solution quality and convergence speed as well, especially on multimodal functions such as Levy No.3, Schaffer, Rosenbrock and Griewank. As to high dimension function optimizing, NSSPSO operates appreciably inferior to NS-PSO due to its computational expense, but is still equal to the Canonical PSO algorithm in most cases. LDW PSO yields poorest performance in nearly all tests.

Table 2. Rate of success, mean function evaluations for each test function

	Rate of success				Mean function evaluations			
	NSSPSO	NS-PSO	CPSO	LDW	NSSPSO	NS-PSO	CPSO	LDW
Ro_2	0.99	0.845	0.97	0.075	7589.6	9421.8	8450.3	14876
Ra_2	1	0.84	1	0.94	2970.6	5573.3	3181.8	9627.1
Gr_2	0.8	0.685	0.735	0.335	8383.9	9397.6	8985.9	13752
Sc	0.7	0.57	0.645	0.2	8662.6	9906.8	9119.7	14194
L3	1	0.83	1	0.155	2595.7	4827	2853.3	14194
L8	1	0.995	1	1	2259.9	2045	2327.6	8526.6
Co	1	0.99	1	1	6493.7	4877.4	5524.5	12159
Fr	0.98	0.52	0.975	0.05	4466.6	9321.1	4349.6	10629
Go	1	0.94	1	1	2844.5	3601.2	2955.4	8510.9
Sp_{10}	1	1	1	0.35	9677.9	5723.4	6306.8	14948
Ro_{10}	0.83	0.945	0.84	0.62	5365.1	3552	5461.6	13600
Ra_{10}	0.963	0.83	0.96	0.71	5390.7	5929.5	5094.3	13471
Gr_{10}	0.845	0.8	0.845	0.515	8997.5	7084.1	7332.3	14124
Sp_{30}	1	1	1	0	11716	13789	15448	30060
Ro_{30}	0.825	0.94	0.795	0	14945	10697	16576	30060
Ra_{30}	0.995	1	1	0.295	8987.1	3475.5	8511.3	29604
Gr_{30}	0.99	1	0.995	0	11019	8999.1	10801	30060

5 Conclusions and Future Work

In this paper, we propose a new hybrid Particle Swarm Optimization algorithm, which applies the Nonlinear Simplex Search method at late stage of PSO running when the most promising regions of solutions have been located. We implement wide variety of experiments on well-known benchmark functions to test the proposed algorithm. The results compared to other 3 published methods demonstrate that this method is very effective and efficient, especially for continuous multimodal function optimization tasks.

Table 3. Average optima for each test function

Test Function	GM	Average optima			
		NSSPSO	NS-PSO	CPSO	LDW
Ro_2	0	7.8299e-8	0.76162	0.002373	1.3522
Ra_2	0	4.7472e-9	0.42783	4.9856e-9	0.059704
Gr_2	1	1.0012	1.003	1.0016	1.0057
Sc	-1	-0.99716	-0.99334	-0.99664	-0.99269
L3	-176.5418	-176.54	-163.17	-176.54	-175.04
L8	0	5.9397e-9	5.8974e-9	6.0348e-9	6.4366e-9
Co	0	7.7393e-9	5.0382e-6	6.7979e-9	6.67e6e-9
Fr	0	0.97969	80.237	1.2246	7.3476
Go	3	3	104.1	3	3
Sp_{10}	0	8.9723e-9	8.2146e-9	8.2073e-9	1.0912e-7
Ro_{10}	0	298.01	461.95	20.688	372.75
Ra_{10}	0	9.6195	10.14	9.7158	10.585
Gr_{10}	9	9.0979	9.1038	9.1003	9.1272
Sp_{30}	0	9.2039e-5	9.3474e-5	9.2407e-5	47.088
Ro_{30}	0	2009.3	100.63	2856.7	79609
Ra_{30}	0	97.418	95.818	97.752	122.48
Gr_{30}	29	29.098	29.094	29.094	30.487

Table 4. Total CPU time for each test function

Test Function	Total CPU time				
	NSSPSO	NS-PSO	CPSO	LDW	Improved
Ro_2	31.031	36.422	31.781	59.984	2.4~48.3%
Ra_2	14.875	27.156	14.906	48.156	0.2~69.1%
Gr_2	42.469	49.141	44.813	72.656	5.2~41.5%
Sc	30.609	35.484	31.047	52.031	1.4~74.5%
L3	13.063	22.688	12.813	69.578	-1.9~81.2%
L8	11.953	10.891	11.188	43.234	-9.7~72.3%
Co	36.719	26.219	28.75	65.922	-29.6~44.3%
Fr	16.672	31.875	14.516	38.094	-4.8~56.2%
Go	10.5	12.859	9.8125	30.438	-7.0~65.6%
Sp_{10}	40.453	23.125	24.656	65.016	-34.9~39.8%
Ro_{10}	22.172	15.266	22.547	60.672	-45.2~63.5%
Ra_{10}	29.359	32.625	27.641	78.469	-6.2~62.6%
Gr_{10}	102.311	42.25	43.156	89.313	-102.1~-14.5%
Sp_{30}	241.98	67.594	68.609	151.52	-187.9~-59.7%
Ro_{30}	79.952	56.281	80.047	162.58	-22.6~50.8%
Ra_{30}	64.094	47.574	60.75	323.47	-19.7~80.2%
Gr_{30}	83.063	71.609	81.547	269.13	-11.9~69.1%

Future work may focus on accelerating the convergence for high dimension problems, extending the approach to constrained multi-objective optimization, and applying the proposed technique in real hybrid intelligent systems.

References

1. Bonabeau, E., Dorigo, M., Theraulaz, G.: Swarm Intelligence: From Natural to Artificial Systems, Oxford Press (1999)
2. Kennedy, J., Eberhart, R. C.: Swarm Intelligence, Kaufmann Publishers, Morgan (2001)
3. Dorigo, M.: Optimization, Learning and Natural Algorithms. Ph.D.Thesis, Politecnico di Milano, Italy (1992) (in Italian)
4. Kennedy, J., Eberhart, R. C.: Particle swarm optimization. Proceedings of IEEE International Conference on Neural Networks, Piscataway, NJ (1995) 1942-1948
5. Shi, Y. H., Eberhart, R. C.: A modified particle swarm optimizer. Proceedings of the IEEE Congress on Evolutionary Computation (CEC 1998), Piscataway, NJ (1998) 69-73
6. Shi, Y. H., Eberhart, R. C.: Parameter selection in particle swarm optimization. Evolutionary Programming VII: Proceedings of the Seventh Annual Conference on Evolutionary Programming, New York (1998) 591-600
7. Parsopoulos, K. E., Vrahatis, M. N.: Recent approaches to global optimization problems through particle swarm optimization, Natural Computing, Vol. 1 (2002) 235-306
8. Shu-Kai S. Fan, Yun-Chia Liang, Erwie Zahara: Hybrid Simplex Search and Particle Swarm Optimization for the Global Optimization of Multimodal Functions, Engineering Optimization, Vol. 36, No. 4 (2004) 401-418
9. Parsopoulos, K. E., Vrahatis, M. N.: Initializing the particle swarm optimizer using the nonlinear simplex Method, in Grmela, A. and Mastorakis, N. E. (eds.) Advances in Intelligent Systems, Fuzzy Systems, Evolutionary Computation, WSEAS Press (2002) 216-221
10. Clerc, M.: The swarm and the queen: towards a deterministic and adaptive particle swarm optimization. Proceedings of the IEEE Congress on Evolutionary Computation (1999) 1951-1957
11. Clerc, M., Kennedy, J.: The particle swarm-explosion, stability, and convergence in a multidimensional complex space, IEEE Transactions on Evolutionary Computation, Vol. 6, No. 1, (2002) 58-73
12. Carlisle, A., Dozier, G.: An off-the-shelf PSO. Proceedings of the Workshop on Particle Swarm Optimization, Indianapolis (2001)
13. Shi, Y. H., Eberhart, R. C.: Empirical study of particle swarm optimization. Proceedings of the IEEE Congress on Evolutionary Computation (CEC 1999), Piscataway, NJ (1999) 1945-1950
14. Nelder, J., Mead, R.: A simplex method for function minimization. Computer Journal, Vol. 7 (1965) 308-313
15. Levy, A., Montalvo, A., Gomez, S., et al.: Topics in Global Optimization, Springer-Verlag, New York (1981)
16. Birge, B.: PSOt: a particle swarm optimization toolbox for use with MATLAB. Proceedings of the IEEE Swarm Intelligence Symposium 2003 (SIS 2003), Indianapolis, Indiana, USA (2003) 182-186

Author Index

Alpaydın, Ethem 473
Alves, Alexessander 665

Badea, Liviu 10
Bang, Sung-Yang 377
Basile, Teresa M.A. 120
Bergman, Lawrence D. 657
Berthold, Michael R. 1
Bessiere, Christian 23
Bickel, Steffen 35, 497
Blockeel, Hendrik 556
Bordes, Antoine 505
Boritz, J. Efrim 633
Borrajo, Daniel 609
Bottou, Léon 505
Brafman, Ronen I. 353
Brand, Matthew 47
Brefeld, Ulf 60
Bruynooghe, Maurice 305, 556
Burnside, Elizabeth 84
Büscher, Christoph 60

Callut, Jérôme 513
Canu, Stéphane 146
Cardie, Claire 2
Cardoso, Jaime S. 690
Castelli, Vittorio 657
Cerquides, Jesús 72
Charpillet, François 389
Choi, Seungjin 377
Cohen, Ira 133
Coletta, Remi 23
Cordier, Marie-Odile 425
Coste, François 522

Davis, Jesse 84
DeJong, Gerald 108, 230
desJardins, Marie 485
Di Mauro, Nicola 120
Ding, Chris 530
Domingos, Pedro 715
Drost, Isabel 96
Drummond, Chris 539

Dupont, Pierre 513
Dutra, Inês de Castro 84, 673

Elomaa, Tapio 547
Epshteyn, Arkady 108
Esposito, Floriana 120

Ferilli, Stefano 120
Fernández, Fernando 609
Fierens, Daan 556
Fonseca, Nuno 707
Forman, George 133, 564

Gascuel, Chantal 425
Getoor, Lise 485
Ghahramani, Zoubin 377
Girdziušas, Ramūnas 576
Greiner, Russell 170
Guigue, Vincent 146

Haider, Peter 497
Hamzeh, Ali 584
He, Xiaofeng 530
Hendrickx, Iris 158
Ho, Bao T. 682
Holte, Robert C. 539
Horiguchi, S. 682

Inoguchi, Y. 682
Izadi, Masoumeh T. 593

Jaulmes, Robin 601
Jiménez, Sergio 609

Kapoor, Aloak 170
Kaski, Samuel 341
Keogh, Eamonn 6
Kerbellec, Goulven 522
Kienzle, Wolf 182
Kohavi, Ron 7
Koriche, Frédéric 23
Kujala, Jussi 547

Laaksonen, Jorma 576
Lallouet, Arnaud 617

Lau, Tessa 657
Laviolette, François 206
Legtchenko, Andreï 617
Li, Ling 242
Li, Tao 625
Li, Xiao-Li 218
Lim, Shiau Hong 230
Lin, Hsuan-Tien 242
Ling, Charles X. 365
Liu, Bing 218
Liu, Huan 724
Lochovsky, Frederick H. 449
López de Màntaras, Ramon 72
Lőrincz, András 698
Lu, Fletcher 633
Lyu, Siwei 255

Maclin, Richard 412
Marchand, Mario 206
Masson, Véronique 425
Matias, Yossi 8
Melville, Prem 268, 741
Mierswa, Ingo 641
Mohri, Mehryar 437
Mooney, Raymond J. 268, 741

Nguyen, Minh L. 682
Nielsen, Frank 649
Nock, Richard 649

Oblinger, Daniel 657
Okun, Oleg 665
Ong, Irene M. 673
O'Sullivan, Barry 23

Page, David 84, 673
Peng, Wei 625
Peters, Jan 280
Phan, Hieu X. 682
Pineau, Joelle 601
Pinto da Costa, Joaquim 690
Póczos, Barnabás 698
Precup, Doina 593, 601
Prescher, Detlef 292
Priisalu, Helen 665
Puolamäki, Kai 341

Qiu, Yuhui 759

Raedt, Luc De 3
Raeymaekers, Stefan 305
Rahmani, Adel 584
Rakotomamonjy, Alain 146
Ramon, Jan 556
Rathod, Priyang 485
Riedmiller, Martin 317
Riggelsen, Carsten 329
Rocha, Ricardo 707
Rousu, Juho 547

Saar-Tsechansky, Maytal 268
Salleb, Ansaf 425
Salojärvi, Jarkko 341
Sanghai, Sumit 715
Santos Costa, Vítor 84, 673, 707
Schaal, Stefan 280
Scheffer, Tobias 35, 60, 96, 497
Schölkopf, Bernhard 182
Shah, Mohak 206
Shani, Guy 353
Shavlik, Jude 412
Shawe-Taylor, John 750
Sheng, Shengli 365
Shimony, Solomon E. 353
Simon, Horst D. 530
Singhi, Surendra K. 724
Skubch, Hendrik 733
Suen, Yuk Lai 741
Sung, Jaemo 377
Szer, Daniel 389

Takács, Bálint 698
Thielscher, Michael 733
Torkkola, Kari 400
Torrey, Lisa 412
Trepos, Ronan 425
Tsampouka, Petroula 750
Tuv, Eugene 400

Uyl, Marten den 194

van den Bosch, Antal 158
Van den Bussche, Jan 305
van Kuilenburg, Hans 194
Vermorel, Joannès 437
Vijayakumar, Sethu 280

Walker, Trevor 412
Wang, Fang 759

Wang, Gang   449
Wang, Shijun   461
Weld, Daniel   715
Wiering, Marco   194
Wurst, Michael   641

Yang, Qiang   365
Yang, Stewart M.   268
Yıldız, Olcay Taner   473

Zhang, Changshui   461
Zhang, Zhihua   449